PSYCHOLOGY
AP* Edition with Discovery Psychology

Philip G. Zimbardo
Stanford University

Robert L. Johnson
Umpqua Community College

Ann L. Weber
University of North Carolina at Asheville

Craig W. Gruber
Belmont High School, Belmont, MA

Allyn & Bacon

Boston New York San Francisco
Mexico City Montreal Toronto London Madrid Munich Paris
Hong Kong Singapore Tokyo Cape Town Sydney

Editor-in-Chief:	Susan Hartman
Series Editor:	Stephen Frail
Senior Development Editor:	Sharon Geary
Editorial Assistant:	Kerri Hart-Morris
Executive Marketing Manager:	Jeanette Koskinas
Production Supervisor:	Roberta Sherman
Manufacturing Buyer:	JoAnne Sweeney
Electronic Composition:	Publishers' Design and Production Services, Inc.
Interior Designer:	John Walker and Publishers' Design and Production Services, Inc.
Photo Researcher:	Sarah Evertson
Cover Administrator:	Joel Gendron

Between the time website information is gathered and then published, it is not unusual for some sites to have closed. Also, the transcription of URLs can result in typographical errors. The publisher would appreciate notification where these errors occur so that they may be corrected in subsequent editions.

Cataloging-in-Publication data unavailable at press time.

Credits

Chapter 1: page 1, © R. Lord/The Image Works; page 2, Public Domain; page 45, © Kelly-Mooney Photography/CORBIS; page 5, © Alan Carey/The Image Works; page 9, © Davis Barber/PhotoEdit; page 11, Archives of the History of American Psychology, University of Akron; page 13, © Bettmann/CORBIS; page 15, © AGStockUSA, Inc./Alamy; page 17, AP/Wide World Photos; page 18, © R. Lord/The Image Works.

Chapter 2: page 27, Courtesy of Craig Gruber; page 29 © V. Richard Haro/Fort Collins Coloradoan; page 31, from "The Cartoon Guide to Statistics" by Larry Gonick & Wollcott Smith; page 35, Hugo Van Lawick/National Geographic Image Collection; page 38, © P. Gontier/Explorer/PhotoResearchers, Inc.; page 39, Courtesy of Philip G. Zimbardo.

Chapter 3: page 61, Courtesy of Philip G. Zimbardo; page 62, Courtesy of Robert Lee Johnson; page 75, Vince Bucci/Getty Images; page 84, Courtesy of Philip G. Zimbardo; page 86 (top), © Dr. Robert Friedland/Science Photo Library/Photo Researchers, Inc.; page 86 (bottom), © SPL/Photo Researchers, Inc.; page 86 (middle), Courtesy of Scott K. Holland, Ph.D.; page 90 (left), © Dana White/PhotoEdit; page 90 (right), © Jeff Greenberg/PhotoEdit; page 90 (bottom), © Esbin-Anderson/The Image Works; page 92 (top) Ralph T. Hutchings; page 92 (bottom), © Stockbyte; page 99, Keystone/Hulton Archive/Getty Images, Inc.

Chapter 4: page 109, © Al Bello/Getty Images; page 110, © Stephen Dalton/Animals, Animals; page 113, © Al Bello/Getty Images; page 116, © Chuck Fishman/Woodfin Camp & Associates; page 123, © Fitz Goro/Time-Life Pictures/Getty Images; page 134, © Superstock, Inc.; page 136, AP/Wide World Photos; page 137 (left and right), © John Neubauer/PhotoEdit; page 138, Public Domain; page 141 (right), M. C. Escher's "Sky and Water 1" © Cordon Art B.V.-Baarn-Holland. All rights reserved; page 141 (left), Victor Vasarely's "Gestalt Bleue" © 2006 Artists Rights Society (ARS), New York/ADAGP, Paris; page 143, Tate Gallery, London/Art Resource, NY 1999 © 2006 Estate of Pablo Picasso/Artists Rights Society (ARS), New York; page 145, © Mark Richards/PhotoEdit; page 146, © Bill Aron/PhotoEdit; page 147, "The Moment Before Death," Russell Sorgi, from Life: The First Fifty Years, 1936–1986 (Little Brown); page 148 (left and right), © Steve Azzara/CORBIS SYGMA; page 150, © Cary Wolinsky/Stock Boston, LLC.

Credits continue on page C-1 following reference section.

WGBH

"Discovering Psychology" is a production of WGBH Boston

Annenberg Media

Funded by Annenberg Media

Printed in the United States of America

10 9 8 7 6 5 4 3 2 1 Q-WC-V 13 12 11 10 09

Allyn & Bacon is an imprint of

PEARSON

www.pearsonhighered.com

ISBN: 0-13-246280-X
ISBN: 978-0-13-246280-8

Brief Contents

Contents

Chapter 1

Chapter 2

Research Methods 26

Biopsychology and the Foundations of Neuroscience 60

Chapter 3

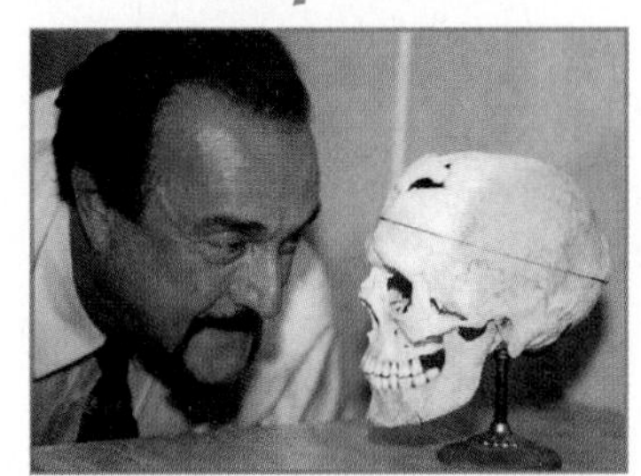

Sensation and Perception 108

Chapter 4

Chapter 5

Learning 194

Chapter 6

Cognition 232

Chapter 7

Emotion and Motivation 296

Chapter 8

Chapter 9

Psychological Development 358

Chapter 13

"You are a very sick rabbit."

Chapter 14

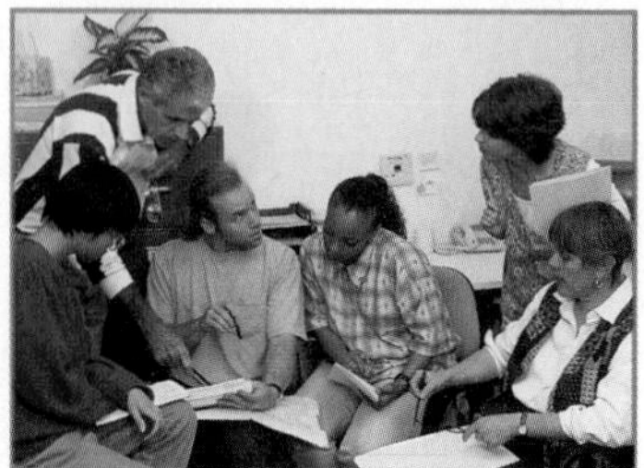

Social Psychology 564

Appendix

To the AP* Student . . .

Psychology: AP Edition with Discovering Pyschology* has been specifically designed to prepare you for the AP* Exam. No one study method or text can be all-inclusive, yet this book was especially written to help you prepare for the exam in May. The chapter organization, outlines, and content coverage closely match not only the content outlines set out by the College Board, but also reflect the current research of the discipline of psychology. The College Board outline for AP* Psychology can be found on p. xxxii.

There is one simple formula for academic success, and the following demonstration will show you what it is. Study this array of letters for a few seconds:

I B M U F O F B I C I A

Now, without peeking, write down as many of the letters as you can (in the correct order).

Most people remember about five to seven letters correctly. A few people get them all. How do these exceptional few do it? They find a pattern. (You may have noticed some familiar initials in the array above: IBM, UFO, FBI, CIA.) Finding the pattern greatly eases the task because you can draw on material that is already stored in memory. In this case, all that needs to be remembered are four "chunks" of information instead of 12 unrelated letters.

The same principle applies to material you study for your psychology class. If you try to remember each piece of information as a separate item, you will have a difficult time. But if instead you look for patterns, you will find your task greatly simplified—and much more enjoyable. So, how can you identify the patterns? With a little help from your friendly authors, who have developed several learning features that will make meaningful patterns what you are reading in this text stand out clearly:

- ***Core Concepts:*** We have organized each major section of every chapter around a single, clear idea called a Core Concept. For example, one of the four Core Concepts in the "Memory" chapter says:

CORE CONCEPT

Human memory is an information processing system that works constructively to encode, store, and retrieve information.

The Core Concept, then, becomes the central idea around which several pages of material—including new terms—are organized. As you read the chapter, then, keeping the Core Concept in mind will help you encode the new terms and ideas related to that concept, store them in your memory, and later retrieve them when you are being tested.

- ***Key Questions:*** Each Core Concept is introduced by a Key Question that also serves as a main heading in the chapter. Here, for example, is a Key Question from the Memory chapter:

WHY DOES MEMORY SOMETIMES FAIL US?

KEY QUESTION

Key Questions such as this will help you anticipate the most important point, or the Core Concept, in the section. In fact, the Core Concept always provides a brief answer to the Key Question. Think of the Key Question as the high beams on your car, helping you focus on what lies ahead. Our key questions should also serve as guides for you to be posing questions of your own about what your are reading.

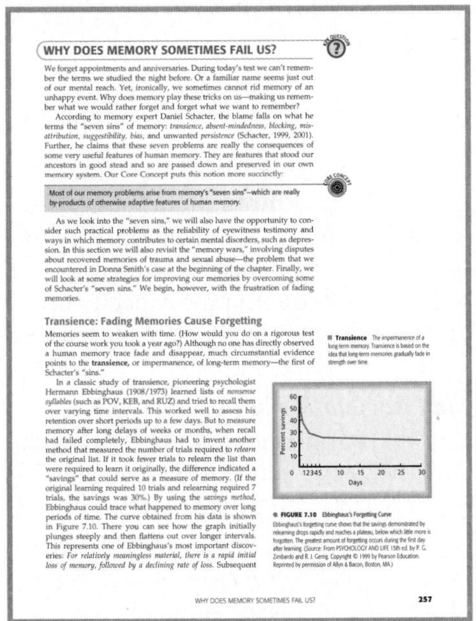

WHY DOES MEMORY SOMETIMES FAIL US?

We forget appointments and anniversaries. During today's test we can't remember the terms we studied the night before. Or a familiar name seems just out of our mental reach. Yet, ironically, we sometimes cannot rid memory of an unhappy event. Why does memory play these tricks on us—making us remember what we would rather forget and forget what we want to remember?

According to memory expert Daniel Schacter, the blame falls on what he terms the "seven sins" of memory: *transience, absent-mindedness, blocking, misattribution, suggestibility, bias,* and unwanted *persistence* (Schacter, 1999, 2001). Further, he claims that these seven problems are really the consequences of some very useful features of human memory. They are features that stood our ancestors in good stead and so are passed down and preserved in our own memory system. Our Core Concept puts this notion more succinctly:

Most of our memory problems arise from memory's "seven sins"—which are really by-products of otherwise adaptive features of human memory.

As we look into the "seven sins," we will also have the opportunity to consider such practical problems as the reliability of eyewitness testimony and ways in which memory contributes to certain mental disorders, such as depression. In this section we will also revisit the "memory wars," involving disputes about recovered memories of trauma and sexual abuse—the problem that we encountered in Donna Smith's case at the beginning of the chapter. Finally, we will look at some strategies for improving our memories by overcoming some of Schacter's "seven sins." We begin, however, with the frustration of fading memories.

Transience: Fading Memories Cause Forgetting

Memories seem to weaken with time. (How would you do on a rigorous test of the course work you took a year ago?) Although no one has directly observed a human memory trace fade and disappear, much circumstantial evidence points to the **transience,** or impermanence, of long-term memory—the first of Schacter's "sins."

Transience The impermanence of a long-term memory. Transience is based on the idea that long-term memories gradually fade in strength over time.

In a classic study of transience, pioneering psychologist Hermann Ebbinghaus (1908/1973) learned lists of *nonsense syllables* (such as POV, KEB, and RUZ) and tried to recall them over varying time intervals. This worked well to assess his retention over short periods up to a few days. But to measure memory after long delays of weeks or months, when recall had failed completely, Ebbinghaus had to invent another method that measured the number of trials required to *relearn* the original list. If it took fewer trials to relearn the list than were required to learn it originally, the difference indicated a "savings" that could serve as a measure of memory. (If the original learning required 10 trials and relearning required 7 trials, the savings was 30%.) By using the *savings method,* Ebbinghaus could trace what happened to memory over long periods of time. The curve obtained from his data is shown in Figure 7.10. There you can see how the graph initially plunges steeply and then flattens out over longer intervals. This represents one of Ebbinghaus's most important discoveries: *For relatively meaningless material, there is a rapid initial loss of memory, followed by a declining rate of loss.* Subsequent

Percent savings
60
50
40
30
20
10
0
12345
10
15
20
25
30
Days

FIGURE 7.10 Ebbinghaus's Forgetting Curve
Ebbinghaus's forgetting curve shows that the savings demonstrated by relearning drops rapidly and reaches a plateau, below which little more is forgotten. The greatest amount of forgetting occurs during the first day after learning. (Source: From PSYCHOLOGY AND LIFE 15th ed. by P. G. Zimbardo and R. J. Gerrig. Copyright © 1999 by Pearson Education. Reprinted by permission of Allyn & Bacon, Boston, MA.)

WHY DOES MEMORY SOMETIMES FAIL US? 257

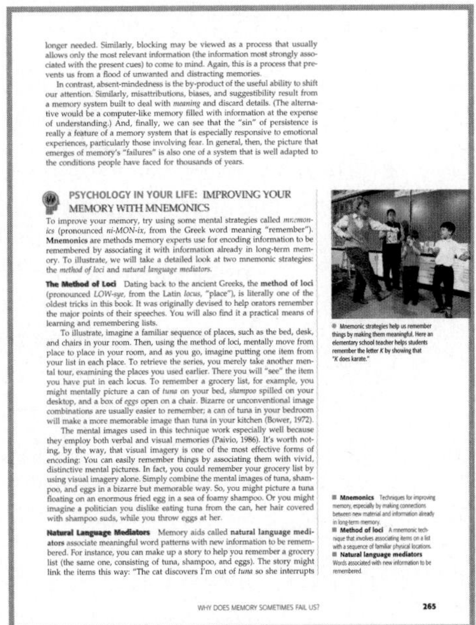

longer needed. Similarly, blocking may be viewed as a process that usually allows only the most relevant information (the information most strongly associated with the present cues) to come to mind. Again, this is a process that prevents us from a flood of unwanted and distracting memories.

In contrast, absent-mindedness is the by-product of the useful ability to shift our attention. Similarly, misattributions, biases, and suggestibility result from a memory system built to deal with *meaning* and discard details. (The alternative would be a computer-like memory filled with information at the expense of understanding.) And, finally, we can see that the "sin" of persistence is really a feature of a memory system that is especially responsive to emotional experiences, particularly those involving fear. In general, then, the picture that emerges of memory's "failures" is also one of a system that is well adapted to the conditions people have faced for thousands of years.

PSYCHOLOGY IN YOUR LIFE: IMPROVING YOUR MEMORY WITH MNEMONICS

To improve your memory, try using some mental strategies called *mnemonics* (pronounced *ni-MON-ix,* from the Greek word meaning "remember"). **Mnemonics** are methods memory experts use for encoding information to be remembered by associating it with information already in long-term memory. To illustrate, we will take a detailed look at two mnemonic strategies: the *method of loci* and *natural language mediators.*

The Method of Loci Dating back to the ancient Greeks, the **method of loci** (pronounced *LOW-sye,* from the Latin *locus,* "place"), is literally one of the oldest tricks in this book. It was originally devised to help orators remember the major points of their speeches. You will also find it a practical means of learning and remembering lists.

To illustrate, imagine a familiar sequence of places, such as the bed, desk, and chairs in your room. Then, using the method of loci, mentally move from place to place in your room, and as you go, imagine putting one item from your list in each place. To retrieve the series, you merely take another mental tour, examining the places you used earlier. There you will "see" the item you have put in each locus. To remember a grocery list, for example, you might mentally picture a can of *tuna* on your bed, *shampoo* spilled on your desktop, and a box of *eggs* open on a chair. Bizarre or unconventional image combinations are usually easier to remember; a can of tuna in your bedroom will make a more memorable image than tuna in your kitchen (Bower, 1972).

The mental images used in this technique work especially well because they employ both verbal and visual memories (Paivio, 1986). It's worth noting, by the way, that visual imagery is one of the most effective forms of encoding: You can easily remember things by associating them with vivid, distinctive mental pictures. In fact, you could remember your grocery list by using visual imagery alone. Simply combine the mental images of tuna, shampoo, and eggs in a bizarre but memorable way. So, you might picture a tuna floating on an enormous fried egg in a sea of foamy shampoo. Or you might imagine a politician you dislike eating tuna from the can, her hair covered with shampoo suds, while you throw eggs at her.

Natural Language Mediators Memory aids called **natural language mediators** associate meaningful word patterns with new information to be remembered. For instance, you can make up a story to help you remember a grocery list (the same one, consisting of tuna, shampoo, and eggs). The story might link the items this way: "The cat discovers I'm out of *tuna* so she interrupts

Mnemonic strategies help us remember things by making them meaningful. Here an elementary school teacher helps students remember the letter *K* by showing that "*K* does karate."

Mnemonics Techniques for improving memory, especially by making connections between new material and information already in long-term memory.

Method of loci A mnemonic technique that involves associating items on a list with a sequence of familiar physical locations.

Natural language mediators Words associated with new information to be remembered.

WHY DOES MEMORY SOMETIMES FAIL US? 265

- ***Psychology in Your Life:*** Psychology has many connections with events in the news and in everyday life, and we have explored one of these connections at the end of each major section in every chapter. What make psychology so fascinating to us and to our students are all the ways in which things learned in this course directly apply to events and experiences in the real world. To illustrate, here are some examples from the "Cognition" chapter:
  - Would You Want a "Photographic" Memory?
  - "Flashbulb" Memories: Where Were You When . . . ?
  - On the Tip of Your Tongue
  - Learning a New Language

  Such connections—practical, down to earth, and interesting—link your reading about psychology with your real-life experiences. They also help you critically evaluate many of the psychological ideas you encounter in the popular press. Also begin to notice how often you read stories about "research shows that . . ." By the end of this course, you will become a much wiser consumer of such information—some of which is often false or misleading.

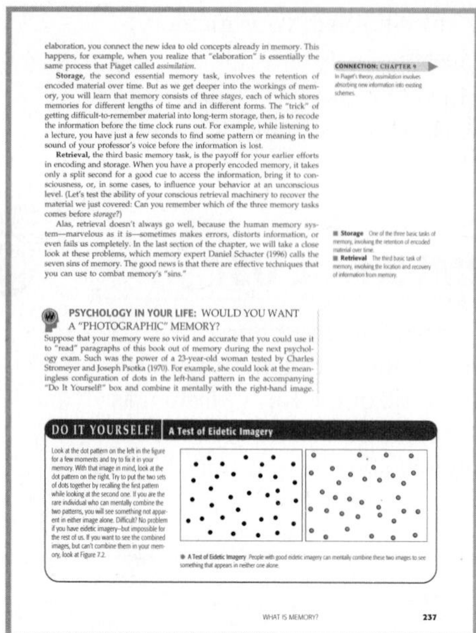

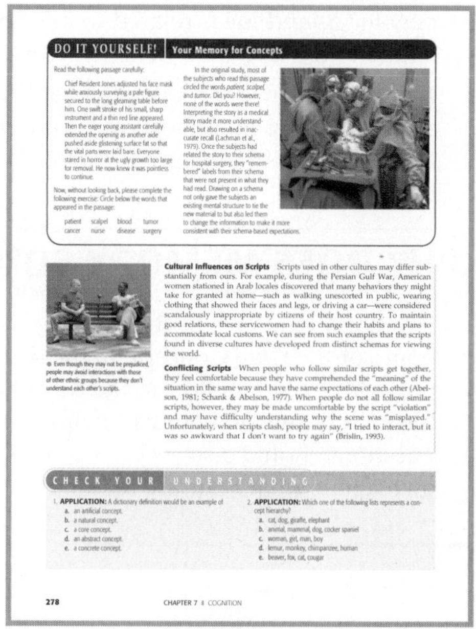

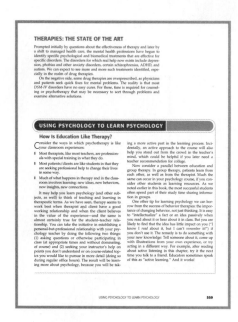

- ***Do It Yourself!*** We have scattered active-learning demonstrations (such as the one at the beginning of this student preface) throughout the book. Besides being fun, these activities have the serious purpose of illustrating principles discussed in the text. In the "Cognition" chapter, for example, one Do It Yourself! box helps you find the capacity of your short-term memory; another lets you test your "photographic memory" ability.
- ***Check Your Understanding and Review Tests:*** Whether you're learning psychology, soccer, or the saxophone, you need feedback on your progress, and that's exactly what you will get from the Check Your Understanding quizzes and the Review Tests. These exercises will let you determine how well you have mastered the material.
- ***Using Psychology to Learn Psychology:*** In a section near the end of every chapter, we explain how you can apply your new knowledge of psychology to make your studying more effective. For example, in Chapter 3, "Biopsychology," we tell you how to put your understanding of the brain to work for more efficient learning. Similarly, at the end of the chapter on "Emotion and Motivation," we explain how to use a new psychological concept of "flow" to boost your own academic motivation. Thus, Using Psychology to Learn Psychology not only reinforces points that you have studied, it brings the material home with immediate and practical applications to your life.

CONNECTION: CHAPTER 12

Retrograde amnesia involves loss of memory for information acquired in the past.

- ***Connection Arrows:*** Important topics in other chapters are often cross-referenced with an arrow in the margin, as you can see in the sample here. The accompanying reference gives you either a preview or reminder of concepts covered in other chapters. This feature helps you see the interrelatedness of ideas in psychology.
- ***Chapter Summaries:*** We have made our summaries rather brief—intended to provide you with an overview of main points in each chapter. They remind you of the patterns instead of loading you with the details. One caution: They are not a substitute for reading the chapters! One helpful hint: Read the summary before you read the rest of the chapter to get a flavor of what's

ahead, then reread the summary after you finish the chapter. Reading the summary before will help you organize the material so that it can be more easily encoded and stored in your memory. And, naturally, reviewing the summary after reading the chapter will reinforce what you have just learned so that you can retrieve more of it in the future.

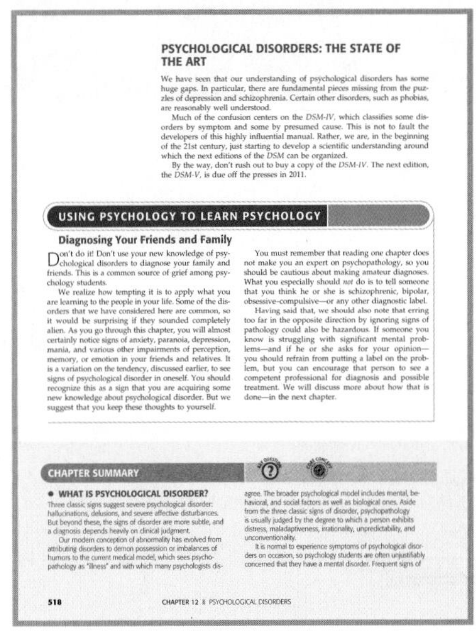

PSYCHOLOGICAL DISORDERS: THE STATE OF THE ART

We have seen that our understanding of psychological disorders has some huge gaps. In particular, there are fundamental pieces missing from the puzzles of depression and schizophrenia. Certain other disorders, such as phobias, are reasonably well understood.

Much of the confusion centers on the *DSM-IV*, which classifies some disorders by symptom and some by presumed cause. This is not to fault the developers of this highly influential manual. Rather, we are, in the beginning of the 21st century, just starting to develop a scientific understanding around which the next editions of the *DSM* can be organized.

By the way, don't rush out to buy a copy of the *DSM-IV*. The next edition, the *DSM-V*, is due off the presses in 2011.

USING PSYCHOLOGY TO LEARN PSYCHOLOGY

Diagnosing Your Friends and Family

Don't do it! Don't use your new knowledge of psychological disorders to diagnose your family and friends. This is a common source of grief among psychology students.

We realize how tempting it is to apply what you are learning to the people in your life. Some of the disorders that we have considered here are common, so it would be surprising if they sounded completely alien. As you go through this chapter, you will almost certainly notice signs of anxiety, paranoia, depression, mania, and various other impairments of perception, memory, or emotion in your friends and relatives. It is a variation on the tendency, discussed earlier, to see signs of psychological disorder in oneself. You should recognize this as a sign that you are acquiring some new knowledge about psychological disorder. But we suggest that you keep these thoughts to yourself.

You must remember that reading one chapter does not make you an expert on psychopathology, so you should be cautious about making amateur diagnoses. What you especially should *not* do is to tell someone that you think he or she is schizophrenic, bipolar, obsessive-compulsive—or any other diagnostic label.

Having said that, we should also note that erring too far in the opposite direction by ignoring signs of pathology could also be hazardous. If someone you know is struggling with significant mental problems—and if he or she asks for your opinion—you should refrain from putting a label on the problem, but you can encourage that person to see a competent professional for diagnosis and possible treatment. We will discuss more about how that is done—in the next chapter.

CHAPTER SUMMARY

• WHAT IS PSYCHOLOGICAL DISORDER?

Three classic signs suggest severe psychological disorder: hallucinations, delusions, and severe affective disturbances. But beyond these, the signs of disorder are more subtle, and a diagnosis depends heavily on clinical judgment.

Our modern conception of abnormality has evolved from attributing disorders to demon possession or imbalances of humors to the current medical model, which sees psychopathology as "illness" and with which many psychologists disagree. The broader psychological model includes mental, behavioral, and social factors as well as biological ones. Aside from the three classic signs of disorder, psychopathology is usually judged by the degree to which a person exhibits distress, maladaptiveness, irrationality, unpredictability, and unconventionality.

It is normal to experience symptoms of psychological disorders on occasion, so psychology students are often unjustifiably concerned that they have a mental disorder. Frequent signs of

518 CHAPTER 12 ■ PSYCHOLOGICAL DISORDERS

- ***Our Recommended Books and Videos:*** Your authors hope that your interest in psychology will give you new lenses with which to look at the world beyond this book. When you do, you will discover something related to behavior and mental processes nearly everywhere. To pique this interest, every chapter offers a list of relevant, stimulating books and videos that will extend the scope of your learning.
- ***AP* Review:*** To further your preparation for the exam, your authors have included an AP* Review section at the end of each chapter. Consisting of two parts, the review provides a brief vocabulary review as well as a sample essay question. Similar in style and content to what you will experience on the AP* Exam, this section will help you assess your comprehension of the chapter concepts. Answers to the vocabulary review can be found at the end of the text.
- ***Discovering Psychology Viewing Guides:*** At the back of this textbook, you will find Viewing Guides that will guide your viewing of the *Discovering Psychology: Updated Edition* videos, produced by WGBH Boston with funding by Annenberg Media. Your instructor may have access to these videos, or you may view them online within MyPsychLab™ or at www.learner.org. The Viewing Guides include a list of key terms and people, review questions, and some essay questions and activities to help you master the important concepts introduced in the videos.

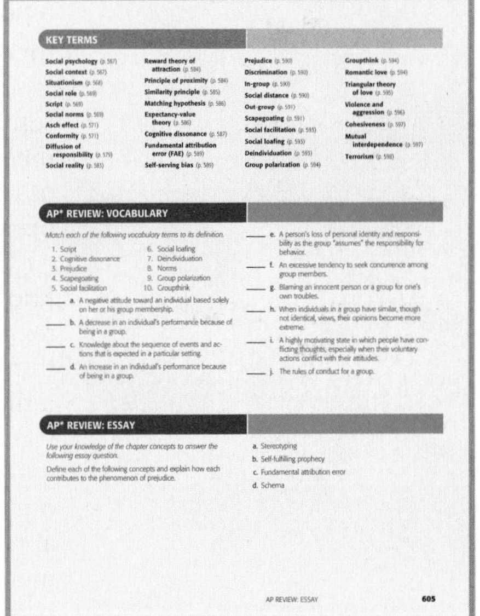

KEY TERMS

Social psychology (p. 567)
Social context (p. 567)
Situationism (p. 568)
Social role (p. 569)
Script (p. 569)
Social norms (p. 569)
Asch effect (p. 571)
Conformity (p. 571)
Diffusion of responsibility (p. 579)
Social reality (p. 583)
Reward theory of attraction (p. 584)
Principle of proximity (p. 584)
Similarity principle (p. 585)
Matching hypothesis (p. 586)
Expectancy-value theory (p. 586)
Cognitive dissonance (p. 587)
Fundamental attribution error (FAE) (p. 589)
Self-serving bias (p. 589)
Prejudice (p. 590)
Discrimination (p. 590)
In-group (p. 590)
Social distance (p. 590)
Out-group (p. 591)
Scapegoating (p. 591)
Social facilitation (p. 593)
Social loafing (p. 593)
Deindividuation (p. 593)
Group polarization (p. 594)
Groupthink (p. 594)
Romantic love (p. 594)
Triangular theory of love (p. 595)
Violence and aggression (p. 596)
Cohesiveness (p. 597)
Mutual interdependence (p. 597)
Terrorism (p. 598)

AP* REVIEW: VOCABULARY

Match each of the following vocabulary terms to its definition.

1. Script
2. Cognitive dissonance
3. Prejudice
4. Scapegoating
5. Social facilitation
6. Social loafing
7. Deindividuation
8. Norms
9. Group polarization
10. Groupthink

____ **a.** A negative attitude toward an individual based solely on her or his group membership.
____ **b.** A decrease in an individual's performance because of being in a group.
____ **c.** Knowledge about the sequence of events and actions that is expected in a particular setting.
____ **d.** An increase in an individual's performance because of being in a group.
____ **e.** A person's loss of personal identity and responsibility as the group "assumes" the responsibility for behavior.
____ **f.** An excessive tendency to seek concurrence among group members.
____ **g.** Blaming an innocent person or a group for one's own troubles.
____ **h.** When individuals in a group have similar, though not identical, views, their opinions become more extreme.
____ **i.** A highly motivating state in which people have conflicting thoughts, especially when their voluntary actions conflict with their attitudes.
____ **j.** The rules of conduct for a group.

AP* REVIEW: ESSAY

Use your knowledge of the chapter concepts to answer the following essay question.

Define each of the following concepts and explain how each contributes to the phenomenon of prejudice.

a. Stereotyping
b. Self-fulfilling prophecy
c. Fundamental attribution error
d. Schema

AP REVIEW: ESSAY 605

We have built into this text many other learning features, such as the marginal glossary, and the extensive references list (which can be a good resource for term papers). You will learn more about these as you use the book; but if you want a bit more information on our purposes for including these features, please read the Teacher's Preface.

We have one final suggestion to help you succeed in psychology. While this book is filled with examples to illustrate the most important ideas, you will remember these ideas longer if you generate your own examples as you study. This habit will make the information yours, as well as ours. And so, while we wish you luck on the AP* Exam, we also hope you have a wonderful time journeying through the topic which we love so much.

Phil Zimbardo
Bob Johnson
Ann Weber
Craig Gruber

SUPPLEMENTS FOR STUDENTS

- ***AP* Test Prep Workbook:*** Further preparation for the exam is offered in the AP* Test Prep Workbook. Utilizing review, comprehension, and testing materials—including actual AP* materials from previous exams—this guide is aimed at improving student success. Available for purchase (ISBN: 0-13-173077-0).

To the AP* Teacher . . .

We teachers of psychology have a little secret that we usually don't talk about, even among ourselves: Every introductory text contains more material than a student can possibly learn while taking the first course in psychology. We have tried to include the latest information for the AP* Exam, while not losing the depth and breadth of what we have to "cover" in order for students to be successful.

There is much our students have to know for the exam. In recent years, research findings in the field of neuroscience have revealed many more brain mechanisms underlying development, thinking, learning, perception and every other subfield of psychology than we had previously thought. The test development committee strives to remain current on these trends, and so have we.

Cognitive psychologists, too, have been busy expanding the frontiers of knowledge about implicit memory, concept learning, and cognitive development as well as research to recognize the role of emotion in memory and thinking. Meanwhile, on the clinical front, psychologists have been accumulating evidence for psychological therapies of demonstrable effectiveness—some of which challenge the hegemony of Prozac and Valium.

And, of course, the terrorist attacks of September 11, 2001, have refocused our attention on the origins of aggression and violence. The revelations of the abuses of Iraqi prisoners by American Army reservist MPs raise the fundamental questions of situational versus dispositional explanations for such pathological behavior. Are there just a few bad apples, or was that behavior the product of a systematic corruption of good soldiers in the bad barrel of a war prison?

Obviously, we, as writers of an introductory psychology text, must wrestle with several problems. How can we include the exciting new developments in the field and still acquaint students with all the classic studies, historical trends, and multiple perspectives in the field? How can we add what is new and clearly valuable to understanding the human condition without cutting out a lot of what has been traditional—and, at the same time, keep the book within manageable proportions? How can we make psychology meaningful to students without overwhelming them with information?

For this AP* edition, we authors have had to make some difficult choices. We have had to balance the basic requirements of the AP* outline and enhance and expand sections which we believe will take on ever-increasing roles in the future of AP* Psychology. Accordingly, we hope that you will feel that this text provides a strong foundation of coverage for your class, while presenting what can seem to be an overwhelming amount of information in an informative and enjoyable format.

In order to help you prepare for and deliver your class, each chapter matches closely the content outline for AP* Psychology as set out by the College Board. In addition, we have tried to match chapter length with the same emphasis of coverage reflected in the content outline. For example, chapter 1, "History of Psychology," is brief, as it comprises only 2–4% of the exam, while "Cognition," representing 8–10% of the exam, is longer. While we would prefer to have more information regarding every topic, we have sought to match as best we can the information with the expectations of the College Board for an AP* Psychology course.

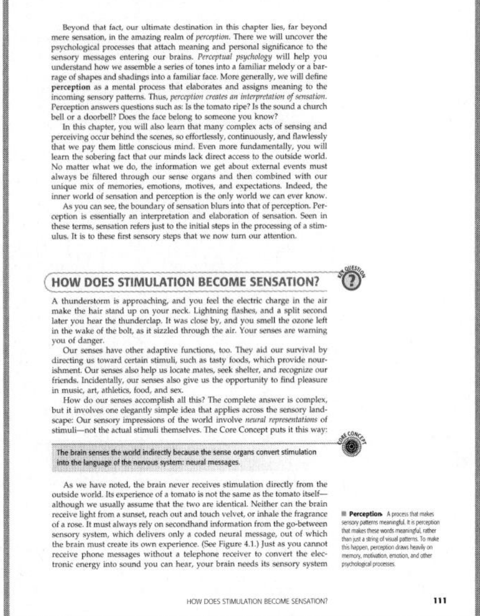

Beyond that fact, our ultimate destination in this chapter lies, far beyond mere sensation, in the amazing realm of *perception*. There we will uncover the psychological processes that attach meaning and personal significance to the sensory messages entering our brains. *Perceptual psychology* will help you understand how we assemble a series of tones into a familiar melody or a barrage of shapes and shadings into a familiar face. More generally, we will define **perception** as a mental process that elaborates and assigns meaning to the incoming sensory patterns. Thus, *perception creates an interpretation of sensation*. Perception answers questions such as: Is the tomato ripe? Is the sound a church bell or a doorbell? Does the face belong to someone you know?

In this chapter, you will also learn that many complex acts of sensing and perceiving occur behind the scenes, so effortlessly, continuously, and flawlessly that we pay them little conscious mind. Even more fundamentally, you will learn the sobering fact that our minds lack direct access to the outside world. No matter what we do, the information we get about external events must always be filtered through our sense organs and then combined with our unique mix of memories, emotions, motives, and expectations. Indeed, the inner world of sensation and perception is the only world we can ever know.

As you can see, the boundary of sensation blurs into that of perception. Perception is essentially an interpretation and elaboration of sensation. Seen in these terms, sensation refers just to the initial steps in the processing of a stimulus. It is to these first sensory steps that we now turn our attention.

KEY QUESTION

HOW DOES STIMULATION BECOME SENSATION?

A thunderstorm is approaching, and you feel the electric charge in the air make the hair stand up on your neck. Lightning flashes, and a split second later you hear the thunderclap. It was close by, and you smell the ozone left in the wake of the bolt, as it sizzled through the air. Your senses are warning you of danger.

Our senses have other adaptive functions, too. They aid our survival by directing us toward certain stimuli, such as tasty foods, which provide nourishment. Our senses also help us locate mates, seek shelter, and recognize our friends. Incidentally, our senses also give us the opportunity to find pleasure in music, art, athletics, food, and sex.

How do our senses accomplish all this? The complete answer is complex, but it involves one elegantly simple idea that applies across the sensory landscape: Our sensory impressions of the world involve *neural representations* of stimuli—not the actual stimuli themselves. The Core Concept puts it this way:

CORE CONCEPT

The brain senses the world indirectly because the sense organs convert stimulation into the language of the nervous system: neural messages.

As we have noted, the brain never receives stimulation directly from the outside world. Its experience of a tomato is not the same as the tomato itself—although we usually assume that the two are identical. Neither can the brain receive light from a sunset, reach out and touch velvet, or inhale the fragrance of a rose. It must always rely on secondhand information from the go-between sensory system, which delivers only a coded neural message, out of which the brain must create its own experience. (See Figure 4.1.) Just as you cannot receive phone messages without a telephone receiver to convert the electronic energy into sound you can hear, your brain needs its sensory system

■ **Perception** A process that makes sensory patterns meaningful. It is perception that makes these words meaningful, rather than just a string of visual patterns. To make this happen, perception draws heavily on memory, motivation, emotion, and other psychological processes.

HOW DOES STIMULATION BECOME SENSATION? 111

As with every AP* course, the benchmark is to provide a college-level experience for our students in the high school setting. This goes beyond simply "covering" the subject matter. In every chapter, we have tried to make the information and the opportunities for learning more meaningful, so that instead of "leasing the information" (studying and cramming just for the exam), students truly retain what they learn in your class and read in the text.

In order to help you accomplish these goals, our mission has been to help students take the first steps toward becoming "owners" and experts of psychology by revealing to them meaningful patterns that occur throughout the field of psychology. We have developed a number of special pedagogical features in our text that help us achieve that goal:

- ***Core Concepts:*** We have organized the major sections of every chapter around a single, clear idea that we call a Core Concept. Here is an example from the chapter on "Sensation and Perception":

CORE CONCEPT

The brain senses the world indirectly because the sense organs convert stimulation into the language of the nervous system: neural impulses.

  To borrow an old saying, the Core Concepts become the "forest," while the details of the chapter become the "trees."

- ***Key Questions:*** The main headings in each chapter appear in question form, as in this example, which introduces the Core Concept shown above:

KEY QUESTION

HOW DOES STIMULATION BECOME SENSATION?

Fundamental questions such as these help students anticipate and focus on the most important idea, the Core Concept, which serves as a brief answer to the Key Question. Both the Key Questions and the Core Concepts later reappear as organizing features of the Chapter Summary.

- ***Psychology in Your Life:*** One reason that psychology continues to fascinate and involve so many students stems from its obvious relevance to the events in their lives. We explore one of these links between psychology and life at the end of each main division of every chapter. Here are some examples:
  - Emotional Differences between Men and Women Depend on Culture
  - The Origins of Sexual Orientation

stage," such as the "terrible twos," when children are becoming more mobile and independent. But for psychologists who subscribe to the discontinuity view, stages are not simply difficult times. These psychologists define **developmental stages** as periods of life initiated by distinct transitions (changes) in physical or psychological functioning. From a stage perspective, specific abilities, such as walking, talking, or abstract reasoning, appear at specific ages or life periods because different developmental processes come into play. In general, developmental psychologists who take the discontinuity view find that people go through the same stages in the same order—but not necessarily at the same rate.

Developmental stages Periods of life initiated by significant transitions or changes in physical or psychological functioning.

PSYCHOLOGY IN YOUR LIFE: PSYCHOLOGICAL TRAITS IN YOUR GENES

Eye color and the shape of your earlobes are purely genetic traits. Even some food aversions, such as a distaste for broccoli, can be anchored in the genes. But as far as we know, heredity by itself determines none of our more complex psychological characteristics (Horgan, 1993). Where personality traits, temperament, interests, and abilities are concerned, heredity always acts in combination with environment. Outgoing people, for example, aren't just born that way; they have also been encouraged to let their tendencies to extraversion show. Still, it's fair for developmental psychologists and biopsychologists to ask which psychological characteristics have strong genetic links.

A genetic contribution to general intelligence, for example, is well established—although psychologists disagree over the magnitude of heredity's role (Plomin et al., 1994). There is also a good possibility that genes contribute to your sexual orientation (Hamer et al., 1993). And it just may be that an interest in skydiving, rock climbing, or other risky behavior has a substantial genetic component (Hamer, 1997). The evidence suggests that genes also contribute to your basic temperament and personality, including all of the "Big Five" personality factors (Bouchard, 1994; Plomin, 1997).

Likewise, some clinical disorders are associated with genetic abnormalities (Eley, 1997; Gibbs, 1995; Mann, 1994; Plomin et al., 1994). One of the first to be discovered was Huntington's disease, a rare problem that causes aggressive behavior and mental deterioration beginning in midlife (Cattaneo et al., 2002). Depression, a far more common problem, can also have genetic roots (although this doesn't mean that everyone who gets depressed has a genetic problem). Similarly, twin studies have revealed a strong genetic contribution to schizophrenia, a major mental disorder. Fear, too, can have a hereditary basis, especially in those who suffer from a condition known as panic disorder. So can anxiety, the basis for repetitive "neurotic" rituals, such as compulsively checking and rechecking the alarm clock setting, seen in obsessive–compulsive disorder. There's also evidence that the violence that may occur in an antisocial personality and the uncontrollable outbursts of Tourette's syndrome stem ultimately from the genes. And, if you are older, you may worry that every instance of forgetting is a sign of Alzheimer's disease, which (in some forms) arises from a genetic flaw that takes first the memory and then the rest of the mind.

Thus we see that many psychological traits, both desirable and undesirable, have a connection to our genes, as well as in our experience. But, at the risk of playing the same tune too often, we must emphasize: Genetics is not everything. While heredity is involved in nearly all we do, human behaviors also are shaped by environment. And by "environment" we mean not only the influence of learning (including the impact of all our experiences) but also physical factors such as nutrition and physical stress (Brown, 1999).

CONNECTION: CHAPTER 10

The *Big Five* are fundamental traits that reliably distinguish different personality patterns among people in all cultures.

The genetic code, written in DNA, contains our complete hereditary blueprint, grouped into genes and chromosomes.

HOW DO PSYCHOLOGISTS EXPLAIN DEVELOPMENT? 365

DO IT YOURSELF! **Finding Your Locus of Control**

Julian Rotter (1966) has developed a test that assesses a person's sense of internal or external control over events. The test items consist of pairs of contrasting statements, and subjects must choose one statement with which they most agree from each pair. This format is called a forced-choice test. Unlike many other personality tests, the scoring for each item on Rotter's Internal–External Scale is transparent: The test-taker can easily tell in which direction most items are scored. Here are some items from a preliminary version of the test (Rotter, 1971).

You can see which direction you lean by counting the number of statements with which you agreed in each column. Agreement with those in the left column suggests an internal locus of control.

1a. Promotions are earned through hard work and persistence.	1b. Making a lot of money is largely a matter of getting the right breaks.
2a. In my experience I have noticed that there is usually a direct connection between how hard I study and the grades I get.	2b. Many times the reactions of teachers seem haphazard to me.
3a. If one knows how to deal with people they are really quite easily led.	3b. I have little influence over the way other people behave.
4a. People like me can change the course of world affairs if we make ourselves heard.	4b. It is only wishful thinking to believe that one can really influence what happens in society at large.
5a. I am the master of my fate.	5b. A great deal that happens to me is probably a matter of chance.

those with an internal locus of control are not only more likely to get good grades, but they also are more likely to exercise and watch their diets than are externals (Balch & Ross, 1975; Findley & Cooper, 1983). As you might expect, externals are more likely to be depressed (Benassi et al., 1988).

While we may feel more in control of certain situations than others, many studies suggest that locus of control is an important characteristic of our personalities. That is, people tend to approach different situations with assumptions about their ability to control their fate. Therefore, an internal or external disposition seems to be a reliable personality characteristic—although Rotter resists calling this a *trait* because he believes the term conveys the erroneous idea that internality–externality is fixed and unchangeable. You can evaluate your own locus of control by following the instructions in the "Do It Yourself!" box above.

Evaluating the Social-Cognitive Approach to Personality Critics argue that the cognitive theories generally overemphasize rational information processing and overlook both emotion and unconscious processes as important components of personality. So, for those who feel that emotions and motives are central to the functioning of human personality, the cognitive approaches to personality have a blind spot. However, because emotion and associated unconscious processes have assumed a greater role in cognitive psychology recently, we can anticipate a new generation of cognitive theories of personality that do take these aspects of personality into account (Mischel & Shoda, 1995).

A real strength of the social-cognitive theories is their foundation of solid psychological research—unlike most of the ideas proposed by the Freudians, neo-Freudians, and humanists. You will recall, for example, Bandura's famous Bobo doll experiment, which we discussed in Chapter 6. The price paid for the social-cognitive theories, however, is that they are much less comprehensive than the old and grand theories of personality proposed by Freud and his followers. The payoff, however, has come in the form of both explanations and treatments for a number of mental disorders that often seem to involve observational learning, particularly anxiety-based disorders, such as phobias, and behavior disorders in children.

CONNECTION: CHAPTER 12

Other anxiety disorders include *panic disorder* and *obsessive–compulsive disorder*.

WHAT FORCES SHAPE OUR PERSONALITIES? 427

- A Critical Look at "Learning Styles"
- How Psychoactive Drugs Affect the Nervous System
- Explaining Unusual People and Unusual Behavior

Such real-life explorations not only make psychology come alive, but they also promote critical thinking by helping students evaluate some of the pop psychology they encounter in the media. We believe that learning how psychologists think about real-life issues can help your students become wiser consumers of information in the public media pertaining to mind, brain, and behavior.

Remember that the goal of this and other self-review exercises is to change behavior in order to become healthier and more resilient—not to change things about yourself that you believe in and value. By learning about other resilient people—reading about them or listening to people you probably already know—you will identify the most realistic goals for this effort and the best ways to meet those goals.

EMOTION AND MOTIVATION: THE STATE OF THE ART

Recent advances in neuroscience have produced deep insights into our emotions. Long neglected by behaviorists and purely cognitive psychologists, emotions can now be seen as vital components of our thought processes—even those we once thought of as purely rational. Yet, many details of emotion remain unclear, particularly the details of the brain's emotional circuitry. Another major area that cries out for new research involves ways of treating emotional disorders, such as depression and various anxiety-related disorders, which represent major health problems all over the world. And, while we're at it, we also need effective ways of helping people develop the "emotional intelligence" needed to control anger and other impulsive behavior.

As for motivation, the basic neural processes have received relatively little attention—compared to the explosion in research in emotion in the past decade. The state of the art is a somewhat detailed understanding of individual motives, but only a fragmentary "big picture" of how diverse motives, such as hunger, sexuality, and achievement, go together. Thus, motivation is a field of psychology that is ripe for a revolution.

USING PSYCHOLOGY TO LEARN PSYCHOLOGY

Motivating Yourself

The world's greatest achievements in music, art, science, business, and countless other pursuits often stem from the intrinsic motivation of people pursuing ideas in which they are deeply interested. You achieve this state of mind when focusing intently on some problem or activity that makes you lose track of time and become oblivious to events around you. Psychologist Mihaly Csikszentmihalyi calls this **flow** (1990, 1998).

Although some people turn to drugs or alcohol to experience an artificial feeling of flow, meaningful work produces more satisfying and more sustained flow experiences. In fact, one type of flow experience identified by Csikszentmihalyi (1990) is very similar to the goal of *n Ach* as identified by McClelland (1987b), namely the pleasure of mastering a challenging task.

Flow In Csikszentmihalyi's theory, an intense focus on an activity, accompanied by increased creativity and near-ecstatic feelings. Flow involves intrinsic motivation.

What is the link with studying and learning? If you find yourself lacking in motivation to learn the material for some class, the extrinsic promise of grades may not be enough to prod you to study. You may, however, be able to trick yourself into developing intrinsic motivation and flow by posing this question: What do people who are specialists in this field find interesting? Among other things, the experts are fascinated by an unsolved mystery, a theoretical dispute, or the possibility of an exciting practical application. A psychologist, for example, might wonder: "What motivates violent behavior?" Or, "How can we increase people's motivation to achieve?" Once you find such an issue, try to find out what solutions have been proposed. In this way, you will share the mind set of those who are leaders in the field. And—who knows?—perhaps you will become fascinated with the field, too.

USING PSYCHOLOGY TO LEARN PSYCHOLOGY 353

- ***Do It Yourself!*** These active-learning boxes offer simple and effective demonstrations of principles discussed in the text. Many are borrowed from demonstrations we have used successfully in our own classrooms. They include, among other topics, locating one's blind spot, demonstrating the concept of mental set, finding the capacity of working memory, checking one's locus of control, wrestling with IQ test items, and second-guessing a surprising social psychology experiment.
- ***Using Psychology to Learn Psychology:*** In a special section at the end of every chapter, we consider how some aspect of the chapter applies to studying and learning. For example, in the context of biopsychology, we show students how to put their knowledge of the brain to work for more efficient learning. Similarly, in the discussion of thinking, students learn how the psychology of expertise (as in de Groot's studies of chess masters) applies to their mastery of the concepts in psychology. Thus, "Using Psychology to Learn Psychology" not only reinforces points that students have learned, it brings the material home with immediate and practical applications to their lives.
- ***Connection Arrows:*** Uniquely in this book, important topics in other chapters are often cross-referenced with an arrow in the margin. These icons are used in place of the phrase, "as we will see in Chapter X." A brief explanatory note accompanies these arrows, giving students a headline preview of the discussion to be found

CONNECTION: CHAPTER 5

The "biological clock," located in the hypothalamus, regulates our *circadian rhythms*.

in the referenced chapter. We intend this feature to convey the sense of psychology as a web of interconnecting ideas.

- ***Our Recommended Books and Videos:*** At the end of each chapter in the AP* edition, you'll find a short section in which we list our top picks of worthwhile books and videos, both classics and contemporary. Each has been selected as illustrative of some concept in the chapter.
- ***AP* Review:*** To further prepare students for the exam, we have included an AP* Review section at the end of each chapter. Consisting of two parts, the review provides a brief vocabulary review as well as a sample essay question. Similar in style and content to what students will experience on the AP* Exam, this section will help them assess their comprehension of the chapter concepts. Answers to the vocabulary review can be found at the end of the text. The essay questions that can be assigned to students as rubrics for answering the essay questions can be found in the AP* Edition Teacher's Resource Manual.
- ***The Discovering Psychology Video Programs:*** We are thrilled to be able to fuse the widely successful *Discovering Psychology* video series, hosted by Phil Zimbardo, with our textbook. The two mediums complement each other in a way that will benefit both instructors and students. Each chapter of the textbook is correlated with one or more of the *Discovering Psychology: Updated Edition* videos, produced by WGBH Boston with funding by Annenberg Media. At the end of this textbook, we have included Viewing Guides with key terms lists, program review questions, as well as essay questions and activities you may wish to assign to your students.

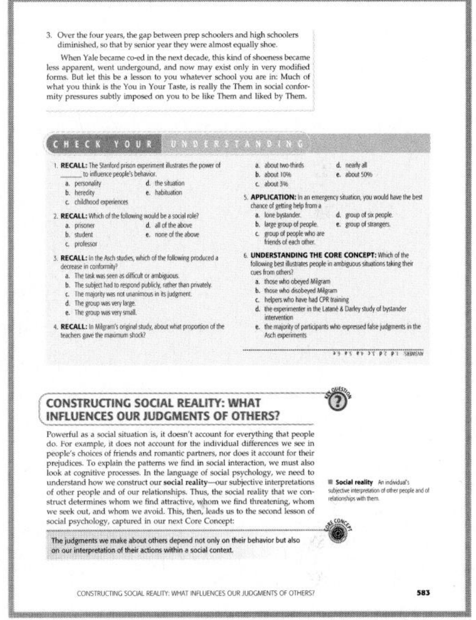

3. Over the four years, the gap between prep schoolers and high schoolers diminished, so that by senior year they were almost equally shoe.

When Yale became co-ed in the next decade, this kind of shoeness became less apparent, went undergound, and now may exist only in very modified forms. But let this be a lesson to you whatever school you are in: Much of what you think is the You in Your Taste, is really the Them in social conformity pressures subtly imposed on you to be like Them and liked by Them.

CHECK YOUR UNDERSTANDING

1. **RECALL:** The Stanford prison experiment illustrates the power of _______ to influence people's behavior.
   a. personality
   b. heredity
   c. childhood experiences
   d. the situation
   e. habituation
2. **RECALL:** Which of the following would be a social role?
   a. prisoner
   b. student
   c. professor
   d. all of the above
   e. none of the above
3. **RECALL:** In the Asch studies, which of the following produced a decrease in conformity?
   a. The task was seen as difficult or ambiguous.
   b. The subject had to respond publicly, rather than privately.
   c. The majority was not unanimous in its judgment.
   d. The group was very large.
   e. The group was very small.
4. **RECALL:** In Milgram's original study, about what proportion of the teachers gave the maximum shock?
   a. about two-thirds
   b. about 10%
   c. about 3%
   d. nearly all
   e. about 50%
5. **APPLICATION:** In an emergency situation, you would have the best chance of getting help from a
   a. lone bystander.
   b. large group of people.
   c. group of people who are friends of each other.
   d. group of six people.
   e. group of strangers.
6. **UNDERSTANDING THE CORE CONCEPT:** Which of the following best illustrates people in ambiguous situations taking their cues from others?
   a. those who obeyed Milgram
   b. those who disobeyed Milgram
   c. helpers who have had CPR training
   d. the experimenter in the Latané & Darley study of bystander intervention
   e. the majority of participants who expressed false judgments in the Asch experiments

ANSWERS: 1 d 2 d 3 c 4 a 5 a 6 e

KEY QUESTION

CONSTRUCTING SOCIAL REALITY: WHAT INFLUENCES OUR JUDGMENTS OF OTHERS?

Powerful as a social situation is, it doesn't account for everything that people do. For example, it does not account for the individual differences we see in people's choices of friends and romantic partners, nor does it account for their prejudices. To explain the patterns we find in social interaction, we must also look at cognitive processes. In the language of social psychology, we need to understand how we construct our **social reality**—our subjective interpretations of other people and of our relationships. Thus, the social reality that we construct determines whom we find attractive, whom we find threatening, whom we seek out, and whom we avoid. This, then, leads us to the second lesson of social psychology, captured in our next Core Concept:

Social reality An individual's subjective interpretation of other people and of relationships with them.

CORE CONCEPT

The judgments we make about others depend not only on their behavior but also on our interpretation of their actions within a social context.

CONSTRUCTING SOCIAL REALITY: WHAT INFLUENCES OUR JUDGMENTS OF OTHERS? 583

Along with these unique features, this edition of *Psychology: AP* Edition with Discovering Psychology* offers the breadth and depth of content plus the tried-and-true pedagogical devices that are standard for any modern introductory psychology text:

- ***Marginal glossaries:*** In *Psychology: AP* Edition with Discovering Psychology,* the most important terms appear in **boldface,** with their glossary definitions readily accessible in the margin. Then, at the end of the book, a comprehensive Glossary section gathers together all the terms and definitions from each chapter.
- ***Check Your Understanding and Chapter Review Tests:*** Reviewers have told us that they want a book that promotes active reader involvement. *Psychology: AP* Edition with Discovering Psychology* does this in many ways. One of the most important for student learning is the Check Your Understanding feature, which offers a brief quiz at the end of each main chapter section. This is a quick checkup for the student to determine if she or he has gotten the main points from what was just read. We have written these quizzes so that they reinforce specific information from the chapters as well as some of the more abstract concepts. Accordingly, some questions call for simple recall, while others call for deeper analysis or application of material. In addition, at least one question in each Check Your Understanding quiz is aimed squarely at the Core Concept of the section. Similarly, the Review Test and AP* Review section at the end of each chapter helps students assess their overall retention and understanding of the material in that chapter before going on to start the next one.

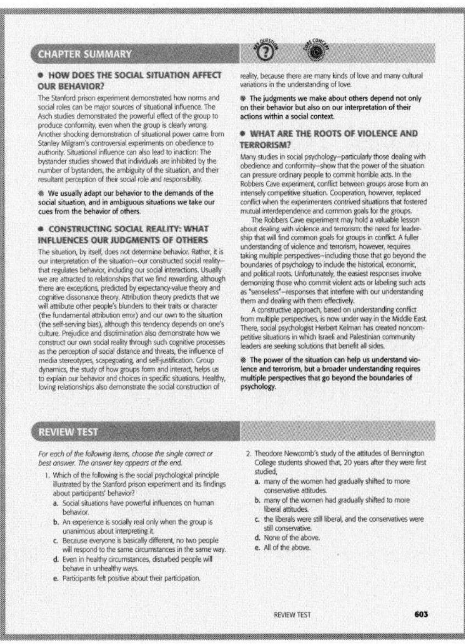

CHAPTER SUMMARY

KEY QUESTION CORE CONCEPT

HOW DOES THE SOCIAL SITUATION AFFECT OUR BEHAVIOR?

The Stanford prison experiment demonstrated how norms and social roles can be major sources of situational influence. The Asch studies demonstrated the powerful effect of the group to produce conformity, even when the group is clearly wrong. Another shocking demonstration of situational power came from Stanley Milgram's controversial experiments on obedience to authority. Situational influence can also lead to inaction: The bystander studies showed that individuals are inhibited by the number of bystanders, the ambiguity of the situation, and their resultant perception of their social role and responsibility.

We usually adapt our behavior to the demands of the social situation, and in ambiguous situations we take our cues from the behavior of others.

CONSTRUCTING SOCIAL REALITY: WHAT INFLUENCES OUR JUDGMENTS OF OTHERS

The situation, by itself, does not determine behavior. Rather, it is our interpretation of the situation—our constructed social reality—that regulates behavior, including our social interactions. Usually we are attracted to relationships that we find rewarding, although there are exceptions, predicted by expectancy-value theory and cognitive dissonance theory. Attribution theory predicts that we will attribute other people's blunders to their traits or character (the fundamental attribution error) and our own to the situation (the self-serving bias), although this tendency depends on one's culture. Prejudice and discrimination also demonstrate how we construct our own social reality through such cognitive processes as the perception of social distance and threats, the influence of media stereotypes, scapegoating, and self-justification. Group dynamics, the study of how groups form and interact, helps us to explain our behavior and choices in specific situations. Healthy, loving relationships also demonstrate the social construction of reality, because there are many kinds of love and many cultural variations in the understanding of love.

The judgments we make about others depend not only on their behavior but also on our interpretation of their actions within a social context.

WHAT ARE THE ROOTS OF VIOLENCE AND TERRORISM?

Many studies in social psychology—particularly those dealing with obedience and conformity—show that the power of the situation can pressure ordinary people to commit horrible acts. In the Robbers Cave experiment, conflict between groups arose from an intensely competitive situation. Cooperation, however, replaced conflict when the experimenters contrived situations that fostered mutual interdependence and common goals for the groups.

The Robbers Cave experiment may hold a valuable lesson about dealing with violence and terrorism: the need for leadership that will find common goals for groups in conflict. A fuller understanding of violence and terrorism, however, requires taking multiple perspectives—including those that go beyond the boundaries of psychology to include the historical, economic, and political roots. Unfortunately, the easiest responses involve demonizing those who commit violent acts or labeling such acts as "senseless"—responses that interfere with our understanding them and dealing with them effectively.

A constructive approach, based on understanding conflict from multiple perspectives, is now under way in the Middle East. There, social psychologist Herbert Kelman has created noncompetitive situations in which Israeli and Palestinian community leaders are seeking solutions that benefit all sides.

The power of the situation can help us understand violence and terrorism, but a broader understanding requires multiple perspectives that go beyond the boundaries of psychology.

REVIEW TEST

For each of the following items, choose the single correct or best answer. The answer key appears at the end.

1. Which of the following is the social psychological principle illustrated by the Stanford prison experiment and its findings about participants' behavior?
   a. Social situations have powerful influences on human behavior.
   b. An experience is socially real only when the group is unanimous about interpreting it.
   c. Because everyone is basically different, no two people will respond to the same circumstances in the same way.
   d. Even in healthy circumstances, disturbed people will behave in unhealthy ways.
   e. Participants felt positive about their participation.
2. Theodore Newcomb's study of the attitudes of Bennington College students showed that, 20 years after they were first studied,
   a. many of the women had gradually shifted to more conservative attitudes.
   b. many of the women had gradually shifted to more liberal attitudes.
   c. the liberals were still liberal, and the conservatives were still conservative.
   d. None of the above.
   e. All of the above.

REVIEW TEST 603

- ***Chapter Summaries:*** The goal of each Chapter Summary is to provide students with a brief overview of the main points in that chapter, organized around the Key Questions and Core Concepts. We hope that you will advise your students to review these chapter summaries *before* reading the chapter, to get a preview of the chapter content and organization, and then again *after* having read the chapter, to reinforce their learning.

- ***Culture and Gender:*** Nearly every chapter brings in a culture- or gender-related concept. We have not trivialized this material by setting it aside in special boxes. Rather, culture and gender have been fully integrated with whatever psychological topic is being presented in the running text.
- ***State of the Art:*** Chapters end with a "State of the Art" section, which briefly characterizes and reviews what's known in that particular field of psychology, and also points to the unknowns that are ripe for research. One of the things we're trying to do here is to get budding young researchers thinking about what the unsolved problems and big mysteries are in psychology.
- ***Making the Abstract Concrete:*** You will find a new emphasis on providing concrete examples of abstract concepts, along with an increased use of metaphors and similes, where appropriate—all designed to help students assimilate unfamiliar and abstract ideas. We think your students will find this especially helpful in mastering difficult concepts in biopsychology.

This text has been developed with a close eye on content coverage and accuracy. While no book can be altogether free of slipups, we think you'll agree that this text does an extraordinarily good job of getting psychology right.

We think you will enjoy the introduction to psychology presented in this book—both the content coverage and it's match to the expectations of the College Board, as well as the pedagogical features designed to enhance student interest and learning. After all, this text relies consistently on well-grounded principles of psychology to teach psychology, as well as the expertise of one of the best known and well-spoken psychologists today, Philip G. Zimbardo.

TEACHER SUPPLEMENTS

The following supplements will also enhance teaching and learning for you and your students and are available to qualified adopters.

Most of the teacher supplements and resources for this book are available electronically on the Instructor Resource Center. Upon adoption, or to preview, please go to PearsonSchool.com/Advanced and click "Online Teacher Supplements". You will be required to complete a one-time registration subject to verification before being emailed access information to download materials.

- ***AP* Edition Teacher's Resource Manual:*** Created by Craig Gruber, Belmont High School, this helpful teaching companion features at-a-glance grids, handouts, lecture enhancements, detailed chapter outlines, activities for the classroom, and other valuable course organization material for new and experienced instructors. In addition, rubrics for grading the AP* Review Essay questions are included in the Teacher's Resource Manual (ISBN: 0-13-173183-1).
- ***AP* Test Bank* (ISBN: 0-13-173184-X):** Laura Brandt has created a test bank containing over 2000 questions, including multiple choice, true/false, short answer, and essay (each with an answer justification). All questions are labeled with a page reference, difficulty ranking, and a type designation. This product is also available in an AP* TestGen computerized version for use in creating tests in the classroom (ISBN: 0-13-173181-5).
- ***AP* Edition PowerPoint Presentation:*** This useful package contains detailed outlines of key points for each chapter supported by charts, graphs,

diagrams, and other visuals from the textbook. The presentation also contains links to the companion website for corresponding activities (ISBN: 0-13-173180-7).

- *MyPsychLab*™ is a web-based interactive and instructive multimedia resource for students and teachers. Features include an online e-book with integrated icons highlighting and linking to relevant video, animations, simulations, and quizzes. In addition, pre- and post-tests results generate a customized study plan to help students identify their weaknesses and focus their time and energies most effectively. In addition, **MyPsychLab™** offers access to Research Navigator, an online research tool containing four exclusive databases of credible and reliable source material—the EBSCO Academic Journal and Abstract Database, *New York Times* Search by Subject Archive, "Best of the Web" Link Library, and *Financial Times* Article Archive and Company Financials.
- ***Discovering Psychology Videos:*** Written, designed, and hosted by Phil Zimbardo, this set of 26 half-hour videos is produced by WGBH Boston and funded by Annenberg Media. The videos can be purchased from WGBH, or they can be viewed in streaming format within MyPsychLab™ or at www.learner.org. The perfect complement to *Psychology: AP* Edition with Discovering Psychology*, this course supplement is a landmark educational resource that reveals psychology's contribution not only to understanding the puzzles of behavior but also to identifying solutions and treatments to ease the problems of mental disorders. It has won numerous prizes and is widely used in the United States and throughout the world.
- ***Faculty Guide for the Discovering Psychology Telecourse:*** The Faculty Guide provides additional support material for each of the *Discovering Psychology: Updated Edition* videos, including a Program Summary, Test Questions, and Answer Keys to the Program Review and Questions to Consider sections of the Viewing Guides (ISBN: 0-205-69929-4).

MyPsychLab™ System Requirements

- Windows 2000, Windows XP, and Windows Vista
- Web browser (Internet Explorer 6.0/7.0 or later for optimum performance)
- Required plug-ins from the MyPsychLab™ Installation Wizard (found on the Announcements page in your course)

Plug-Ins (Available Through Installation Wizard)

- TestGen Plugin
- RealOne Player
- Adobe Flash Player
- Macromedia Shockwave Player
- Adobe Reader

High school teachers can obtain teacher and student preview or adoption access in one or two ways:

- By registering online at www.PearsonSchool.com/Access_Request
- Through the use of a physical pincode card. High school adopters will receive an adopter access pincode card (ISBN: 0-13-034391-9) with their textbook order. Preview access pincode cards may be requested using ISBN: 0-13-111598-9.

Both adopter and preview pincode cards include follow-on directions and provide teacher and student access.

A NOTE OF THANKS

This project would never have become a reality without the help of others who have been relentlessly supportive and helpful throughout the textbook process. Susan Hartman, Editor-in-Chief, has been wonderful at guiding us through this process. Sharon Geary, Senior Development Editor, has been nurturing, prodding, and demanding (when the times call for it), and impressed upon us to do even more, even better than we had thought we were capable. She is a fabulous editor. Stephen Frail came up with the idea of integrating the *Discovering Psychology* Viewing Guides into this textbook.

The job of making the manuscript into a book fell to Roberta Sherman, Production Editor, and Connie Day, copyeditor. We think they did an outstanding job.

We are sure that none of the above would be offended if we reserve our deepest thanks for our spouses and closest colleagues. Phil thanks his wonderful wife, Christina Maslach, for her endless inspiration and for modeling what is best in academic psychology.

Ann thanks her long-suffering spouse, John Quigley, for always and readily encouraging her efforts and assuring her that she's "the best." It will surprise no one who knows her that Ann also thanks her six cats and one perfect dog for their abiding, accepting love and for providing perspective and acceptance, no matter what. She also would like to thank her students and colleagues in the Department of Psychology, UNC at Asheville, for providing feedback, input, and inspiration of the teaching profession as well as the minutia of composing a book—lessons, examples, gimmicks, and especially ideas and images that don't work and so have to be deleted before the manuscript ever sees the light of publication!

Bob is grateful to his spouse and friend, Michelle, who put up with long conversations on topics psychological, Bob's undone household chores, and much gratification delayed—mostly without complaint. She has been a wellspring of understanding and loving support. His thanks, too, go to Rebecca, their daughter, who has taught him the practical side of developmental psychology—and now, much to her own astonishment, possesses a graduate degree in psychology. In addition, he thanks his friends and colleagues Mike Vasey, Suzy Horton, and Kandis Mutter, who read and commented on the previous edition and on portions of the text. It would be impossible to thank them enough.

Craig thanks his wonderful wife Heather for putting up with undone unpacking and painting, and for relentlessly assuring him that this text would "turn out great." In addition, Craig would like to acknowledge James Brady, his cousin, and author of chemistry books, for providing expert advice, as well as Tony Riley at American University, who has been a fabulous mentor. Of course he is always thankful for the support of Stephen, Peter, and Karen Gruber and their spouses for their support and tolerance for discussing psychology topics at every family event in the recent past. Lastly thanks to Jack and Joan Gruber who have done more and supported him more than one would think possible for parents to do.

We would like to thank the many experts and teachers of introductory psychology who also shared their constructive criticism with us on every chapter and feature of the AP* edition of this text:

Suzanne Allen, Creekview High School, TX

Samuel Goldsmith Becker, Worthington High School, MN

Hugh Cantebury, South Forsyth High School, GA

James K. Denson, Kempsville High School, VA
Lenny Eagleman, Liberty High School, MO
William Elmhorst, Marshfield High School, WI
Audrey Erickson, Moorhead High School, MN
Louis Farrar, Charter Oak High School, CA
John Harrington, Belton High School, MO
Tami Hendrix, Mansfield Summit High School, TX
Eileen E. Hermansen, Rancho Buena Vista High School, CA
Ruthie R. Hiett, Parkview Arts and Sciences Magnet High School, AR
Travis Hodge, Perris High School, CA
Nina L. Kearns, Highlands High School, KY
Mary M. Kelsay, Addison Trail High School, IL
Amy Jones, Bountiful High School, UT
Jeanie Lamreaux, Clarkston High School, MI
Kathleen Manz, Voorhees High School, NJ
David Mark, DRS HALB Yeshiva High School, NY
Jim Matiya, Carl Sandburg High School, IL
Linell McCormick, Governor Mifflin Schools, PA
Kay S. Miller, Sheldon ISD, TX
Susan Morton, Teaneck High School, NJ
Bob Nelson, Pearce High School, TX
Daniel E. Parent, South Aiken High School, SC
Kevin Rippe, Lincoln East High School, NE
Richard Roberts, AC Reynolds High School, NC
Daniel Sanecki, Holmdel High School, NJ
David Schleh, New Richmond High School, NJ
Clay Sisman, Laguna Hills High School, CA
John Sopko, Springville Griffith Institute High School, NY
Mary Spilis, Sylvania Northview High School, OH
Sylvia Turner, Aiken High School, SC
Deborah L. Wood, Centennial High School, TN

If you have any recommendations of your own that we should consider for the next edition, please write to us! Address your comments to:

Craig Gruber
P.O. Box 712
Lincoln, MA 01773

or send e-mail to:

cgruber@american.edu

Thanks to all of our colleagues whose feedback has improved our text. Thanks also to all instructors of this most-difficult-to-teach course for taking on the pedagogical challenge and conveying to students their passion about the joys and relevance of psychological science and practice.

ABOUT THE AUTHORS

Phil Zimbardo

Philip Zimbardo, Ph.D., Stanford University professor, has been teaching the Introductory Psychology course for nearly 50 years and has been writing the basic text for this course, as well as the Faculty Guides and Student Workbooks, for the past 35 years. In addition, he has helped to develop and update the PBS-TV series, *Discovering Psychology,* that is used in many high school and university courses both nationally and internationally. He has been called the "Face and Voice of Psychology" because of this popular series and his other media presentations. Zimbardo also loves to conduct and publish research on a wide variety of subjects, as well as teaching and engaging in public and social service activities. He has published more than 300 professional and popular articles and chapters and 50 books of all kinds. He is currently engaged in writing a trade book on the psychology of evil that relates his classic Stanford Prison Experiment to the abuses at Iraq's Abu Ghraib Prison. Please see these websites for more information: www.zimbardo.com, www.prisonexperiment.org, www.psychologyMatters.org.

Robert Johnson

Robert Johnson, Ph.D, taught introductory psychology for 28 years at Umpqua Community College. He is especially interested in applying psychological principles to the teaching of psychology and in encouraging linkages between psychology and other disciplines. In keeping with those interests, Bob founded the Pacific Northwest Great Teachers Seminar, of which he was the director for 20 years. He was also one of the founders of PT@CC (Psychology Teachers at Community Colleges), serving as its executive committee chair during 2004. That same year he also received the Two-Year College Teaching Award given by the Society for the Teaching of Psychology. Bob has long been active in APA, APS, the Western Psychological Association, and the Council of Teachers of Undergraduate Psychology.

Bob loves to write about psychology almost as much as he loves to teach. Aside from his contributions as a coauthor of *Psychology: Core Concepts,* he is particularly proud of his articles in *Teaching of Psychology.* Recently he began a term as the editor of *The General Psychologist,* the newsletter of the Society for General Psychology (Division 1 of APA). He is working on a book that brings to light what Shakespeare had to say about psychology.

Bob and his wife live on the North Umpqua River in southern Oregon, where they can go kayaking in their front yard or bicycling in the valleys of the Cascade Mountains. In his spare time he likes making pottery and Thai curries.

Ann L. Weber

Ann L. Weber, Ph.D., is professor of psychology at the University of North Carolina at Asheville, where for almost three decades she has taught General Psychology, Social Psychology, and the Psychology of Close Relationships, among other courses. She came to UNCA after completing her undergraduate work at The Catholic University of America and graduate work at The Johns Hopkins University. *Psychology: Core Concepts* is one of her many student-oriented texts and study guides, in addition to scores of books and other writings on close relationships, loss, and grief. As a consultant, she conducts workshops on subjects from managing stress and surviving breakups to learning humor and perspective from relationships with pets. Her many recognitions for teaching include UNCA's Distinguished Teacher Award and the Outstanding Teacher Award from the International Association for Relationship Research. Currently she is writing and developing courses on psychology in film and the relationships between people and animals. She and her husband live in the mountains of western North Carolina with five cats, two dogs, and a steady stream of fostered companion animals.

Craig W. Gruber

Craig W. Gruber is an Assistant Principal at Belmont High School, in Belmont, Massachusetts. In addition to his administrative role, he is an active and involved teacher with over 16 years of classroom work at both the high school and college level. Craig also serves as an active AP* College Board consultant, a role he has held since 1993. He completed his undergraduate psychology work at American University followed by a Masters of Science degree in Gifted and Talented Education studies from Johns Hopkins University. Craig established one of the only high school psychology laboratories, and is the founding editor of the *Whitman Journal of Psychology.* Craig's role as teacher, mentor, and researcher as well as his love of psychology have all come together in this text. Craig and his wife Heather live in Sudbury, Massachusetts.

AP* Psychology Exam Content Outline

Here are the major content areas covered by the AP* Psychology Exam, as well as the approximate percentages of the multiple-choice section that are devoted to each area. *Psychology: AP* Edition with Discovering Psychology* has been developed to reflect this organization, coverage, and emphasis.

Content Area	*Percentage Goals for Exam (multiple-choice section)*
I. History and Approaches	**2–4%**
A. Logic, Philosophy, and History of Science	
B. Approaches	
1. Biological	
2. Behavioral	
3. Cognitive	
4. Humanistic	
5. Psychodynamic	
6. Sociocultural	
7. Evolutionary/sociobiological	
II. Research Methods	**6–8%**
A. Experimental, Correlational, and Clinical Research	
1. Correlational (e.g., observational, survey, clinical)	
2. Experimental	
B. Statistics	
1. Descriptive	
2. Inferential	
C. Ethics in Research	
III. Biological Bases of Behavior	**8–10%**
A. Physiological Techniques (e.g., imaging, surgical)	
B. Neuroanatomy	
C. Functional Organization of the Nervous System	
D. Neural Transmission	
E. Endocrine System	
F. Genetics	
IV. Sensation and Perception	**7–9%**
A. Thresholds	
B. Sensory Mechanisms	
C. Sensory Adaptation	
D. Attention	
E. Perceptual Processes	
V. States of Consciousness	**2–4%**
A. Sleep and Dreaming	
B. Hypnosis	
C. Psychoactive Drug Effects	
VI. Learning	**7–9%**
A. Classical Conditioning	
B. Operant Conditioning	
C. Cognitive Processes in Learning	
D. Biological Factors	
E. Social Learning	
VII. Cognition	**8–10%**
A. Memory	
B. Language	
C. Thinking	
D. Problem Solving and Creativity	
VIII. Motivation and Emotion	**7–9%**
A. Biological Bases	
B. Theories of Motivation	
C. Hunger, Thirst, Sex, and Pain	
D. Social Motives	
E. Theories of Emotion	
F. Stress	

Content Area	*Percentage Goals for Exam (multiple-choice section)*
IX. Developmental Psychology	**7–9%**
A. Life-Span Approach	
B. Research Methods (e.g., longitudinal, cross-sectional)	
C. Heredity–Environment Issues	
D. Developmental Theories	
E. Dimensions of Development	
1. Physical	
2. Cognitive	
3. Social	
4. Moral	
F. Sex Roles, Sex Differences	
X. Personality	**6–8%**
A. Personality Theories and Approaches	
B. Assessment Techniques	
C. Self-concept, Self-esteem	
D. Growth and Adjustment	
XI. Testing and Individual Differences	**5–7%**
A. Standardization and Norms	
B. Reliability and Validity	
C. Types of Tests	
D. Ethics and Standards in Testing	
E. Intelligence	
F. Heredity/Environment and Intelligence	
G. Human Diversity	

Content Area	*Percentage Goals for Exam (multiple-choice section)*
XII. Abnormal Psychology	**7–9%**
A. Definitions of Abnormality	
B. Theories of Psychopathology	
C. Diagnosis of Psychopathology	
D. Anxiety Disorders	
E. Somatoform Disorders	
F. Mood Disorders	
G. Schizophrenic Disorders	
H. Organic Disorders	
I. Personality Disorders	
J. Dissociative Disorders	
XIII. Treatment of Psychological Disorders	**5–7%**
A. Treatment Approaches	
1. Insight therapies: psychodynamic/humanistic approaches	
2. Behavioral approaches	
3. Cognitive approaches	
4. Biological approaches (psychopharmacology/psychosurgery)	
B. Modes of Therapy (e.g., individual, group)	
C. Community and Preventive Approaches	
XIV. Social Psychology	**7–9%**
A. Group Dynamics	
B. Attribution Processes	
C. Interpersonal Perception	
D. Conformity, Compliance, Obedience	
E. Attitudes and Attitude Change	
F. Organizational Behavior	
G. Aggression/Antisocial Behavior	

DISCOVERING PSYCHOLOGY CHAPTER-PROGRAM PREVIEW GUIDE

Core Concepts Chapter Number	Core Concepts Chapter Title	Discovering Psychology Video Program	Discovering Psychology Video Program Description
Chapter 1	Introduction and History of Psychology	**Program 1:** Past, Present, and Promise	**Program 1** introduces psychology as the scientific study of behavior and mental processes. It looks at how psychologists work from a variety of theoretical models and traditions, record and analyze their observations, and attempt to unravel the mysteries of the mind.
Chapter 2	Research Methods	**Program 2:** Understanding Research	**Program 2** demonstrates the how's and why's of psychological research. By showing how psychologists rely on systematic observation, data collection, and analysis to find out the answers to their questions, this program reveals why the scientific method is used in all areas of empirical investigation.
Chapter 3	Biopsychology and the Foundations of Neuroscience	**Program 3:** The Behaving Brain	Psychologists who study the structure and composition of the brain believe that all our thoughts, feelings, and actions have a biological and chemical basis. **Program 3** explains the nervous system and the methods scientists use to explore the link between physiological processes in the brain and psychological experience and behavior.
		Program 4: The Responsive Brain	**Program 4** takes a closer look at the dynamic relationship between the brain and behavior. We'll see how the brain controls behavior and, conversely, how behavior and environment can cause changes in the structure and the functioning of the brain.
Chapter 4	Sensation and Perception	**Program 7:** Sensation and Perception	**Program 7** explores how we make contact with the world outside our brain and body. We'll see how biological, cognitive, social, and environmental influences shape our personal sense of reality, and we'll gain an understanding of how psychologists use our perceptual errors to study how the constructive process of perception works.
Chapter 5	States of Consciousness	**Program 13:** The Mind Awake and Asleep	**Program 13** describes how psychologists investigate the nature of sleeping, dreaming, and altered states of conscious awareness. It also explores the ways we use consciousness to interpret, analyze, and even change our behavior.
		Program 14: The Mind Hidden and Divided	**Program 14** considers the evidence that our moods, behavior, and even our health are largely the result of multiple mental processes, many of which are out of conscious awareness. It also looks at some of the most dramatic phenomena in psychology, such as hypnosis and the division of human consciousness into "two minds" when the brain is split in half by surgical intervention.
Chapter 6	Learning	**Program 8:** Learning	Learning is the process that enables humans and other animals to profit from experience, anticipate events, and adapt to changing conditions. **Program 8** explains the basic learning principles and the methods psychologists use to study and modify behavior. It also demonstrates how cognitive processes, such as insight and observation, influence learning.
Chapter 7	Cognition	**Program 9:** Remembering and Forgetting	**Program 9** explores memory, the complex mental process that allows us to store and recall our previous experiences. It looks at the ways cognitive psychologists investigate memory as an information-processing task and at the ways neuroscientists study how the structure and functioning of the brain affect how we remember and why we forget.
		Program 10: Cognitive Processes	The study of mental processes and structures–perceiving, reasoning, imagining, anticipating, and problem solving–is known as cognition. **Program 10** explores these higher mental processes, offering insight into how the field has evolved and why more psychologists than ever are investigating the way we absorb, transform, and manipulate knowledge.
		Program 11: Judgment and Decision Making	**Program 11** explores the decision-making process and the psychology of risk taking, revealing how people arrive at good and bad decisions. It also looks at the reasons people lapse into irrationality and how personal biases can affect judgment.

Core Concepts Chapter Number	Core Concepts Chapter Title	Discovering Psychology Video Program	Discovering Psychology Video Program Description
Chapter 8	Emotion and Motivation	**Program 12:** Motivation and Emotion	What moves us to act? Why do we feel the way we do? **Program 12** shows how psychologists study the continuous interactions of mind and body in an effort to explain the enormous variety and complexities of human behavior.
Chapter 9	Psychological Development	**Program 5:** The Developing Child	**Program 5** looks at how advances in technology and methodology have revealed the abilities of newborn infants, giving researchers a better understanding of the role infants play in shaping their environment. In contrast to the nature-versus-nurture debates of the past, today's researchers concentrate on how heredity and environment interact to contribute to the developmental process.
		Program 17: Sex and Gender	**Program 17** looks at the similarities and differences between the sexes resulting from the complex interaction of biological and social factors. It contrasts the universal differences in anatomy and physiology with those learned and culturally acquired, and it reveals how roles are changing to reflect new values and psychological knowledge.
		Program 18: Maturing and Aging	Thanks to growing scientific interest in the elderly, research on aging has replaced many myths and fears with facts. **Program 18** focuses on what scientists are learning about life cycle development as they look at how aging is affected by biology, environment, and lifestyle.
Chapter 10	Personality	**Program 15:** The Self	What makes each of us unique? What traits and experiences make you? **Program 15** describes how psychologists systematically study the origins and development of self-identity, self-esteem, and other aspects of our thoughts, feelings, and behaviors that make up our personalities.
Chapter 11	Testing and Individual Differences	**Program 16:** Testing and Intelligence	Just as no two fingerprints are alike, no two people have the same set of abilities, aptitudes, interests, and talents. **Program 16** explains the tools psychologists use to measure these differences. It also describes the long-standing controversy over how to define intelligence and how IQ tests have been misused and misapplied. Is it wise, accurate, or fair to reduce intelligence to a number? Researchers are currently debating the value of intelligence and personality tests.
Chapter 12	Psychological Disorders	**Program 21:** Psychopathology	**Program 21** describes the major types of mental illnesses and some of the factors that influence them—both biological and psychological. It also reports on several approaches to classifying and treating mental illness and explains the difficulties of defining abnormal behavior.
Chapter 13	Therapies for Psychological Disorders	**Program 22:** Psychotherapy	**Program 22** looks at psychotherapy and therapists, the professionals trained to help us solve some of our most critical problems. You will learn about different approaches to the treatment of mental, emotional, and behavioral disorders and the kind of helping relationships that therapists provide.
Chapter 14	Social Psychology	**Program 19:** The Power of the Situation	**Program 19** investigates the social and situational forces that influence our individual and group behavior and how our beliefs can be manipulated by other people.
		Program 20: Constructing Social Reality	**Program 20** explores our subjective view of reality and how it influences social behavior. It reveals how your perceptions and reasoning ability can be influenced in positive and negative ways, and it increases our understanding of how psychological processes govern interpretation of reality.

Key Question Chapter Outline

What Is Psychology—and What Is It *Not*?

Psychology and Critical Thinking
What Do Psychologists Do?

What Are Psychology's Historical Roots?

Structuralism: Focus on Structure—and the Founding of Scientific Psychology
Functionalism: Focus on Function
Gestalt Psychology: Focus on the Whole Instead of the Parts
Behaviorism: Eliminate the Mind and Focus on Behavior
Psychoanalysis: Focus on the Unconscious Mind

What Are the Perspectives Psychologists Use Today?

Biological View
Developmental View
Cognitive View
Psychodynamic View
Humanistic View
Behavioral View
Sociocultural View
Evolutionary/Sociobiological View
Trait View

CORE CONCEPTS

▼ Psychology is a broad field with many specialties, but fundamentally, psychology is the scientific study of behavior and mental processes.

▼ Modern psychology developed from several conflicting traditions, including structuralism, functionalism, Gestalt psychology, behaviorism, and psychoanalysis.

▼ Nine main perspectives characterize modern psychology: the biological, developmental, cognitive, psychodynamic, humanistic, behavioral, sociocultural, evolutionary/sociobiological and trait views.

Psychology in Your Life

Knowing the Difference between a Psychologist and a Psychiatrist

Psychologists are not always therapists—nor are they physicians.

An Introspective Look at the Necker Cube

This famous figure changes only in your mind.

Psychology as a Major

To call yourself a psychologist, you'll need graduate training.

USING PSYCHOLOGY TO LEARN PSYCHOLOGY:
Studying with Key Questions and Core Concepts

Chapter 1

Introduction and History of Psychology

PEOPLE REFERRED TO HIM as Clever Hans because, to all appearances, he was exceptionally smart. But another characteristic made his case truly remarkable: Hans was a horse. His celebrity grew from public demonstrations in which he apparently solved math problems. "What is 12 plus 7?" a bystander might ask, and Hans would tap 19 times with his hoof. He wasn't *always* right, mind you, but most of the time Hans gave correct answers to problems involving simple addition, subtraction, multiplication, and division—even square roots. Nor were his presumed talents limited to math: When presented with questions written on large cards, Hans would spell out answers by tapping the ground to indicate letters on an alphabet board.

As Hans's fame spread throughout Europe and America, he became the world's most famous animal. But the scientific community, as you might expect, had its skeptics. Could a horse think and reason? Surely not. But then, how could they explain Hans's apparent talents?

One fall day in 1904, a committee of scientists, assembled by Carl Stumpf, director of the Berlin Psychological Institute, paid a visit to Hans's owner, Wilhelm von Osten, to investigate the matter. The group brought a variety of backgrounds to the task, including psychology, zoology, and veterinary medicine. For good measure, Stumpf also brought along a circus animal trainer and a prominent politician. For his part, Mr. Von Osten obligingly put Hans through his intellectual paces, while the committee observed. Their initial skepticism soon gave way to fascination at the horse's performance. More

Clever Hans

important for the committee's mission, they found no hint that von Osten was cheating.

Nevertheless, one of the committee members, psychologist Oskar Pfungst, remained suspicious. He wondered whether the horse might be responding to cues unconsciously given by von Osten. Dr. Pfungst, therefore, proposed a more controlled test of Hans's abilities. Could the horse correctly answer questions when its owner Osten did not know the answer or was out of sight? Sure enough, when von Osten was not allowed to see the written questions, Hans failed the test. Likewise, when von Osten could see the questions but was required to stand behind a curtain or otherwise outside the horse's field of vision, Hans could not answer.

Von Osten was deeply disappointed with the results. But, to his credit, he cooperated with Pfungst to find out exactly what sorts of cues the horse had been sensing. A slight lean forward served as the signal for Hans to start tapping. The "stop" sign could be a subtle straightening of von Osten's posture, a rise of his eyebrows, or even a flaring of his nostrils. Hans, it turned out, was a clever horse, indeed–clever at reading almost imperceptible physical cues. When it came to verbal and math skills, however, his abilities were just average . . . for a horse.

KEY QUESTION

WHAT IS PSYCHOLOGY—AND WHAT IS IT *NOT*?

In a generic sense, everyone is a psychologist. We all study people, analyze their behavior, try to understand what they are thinking and feeling, and attempt to predict what they will do next. But there is a real difference between the commonsense psychology your Uncle Felix or Aunt Ethel uses in everyday life and the psychology you will learn about in the following pages. We have already glimpsed the latter in Dr. Pfungst's skeptical "show-me-the-evidence" approach. More specifically, the working definition of psychology that we will use throughout this book is a part of our Core Concept for this section of the chapter:

CORE CONCEPT

Psychology is a broad field with many specialties, but fundamentally, psychology is the scientific study of behavior and mental processes.

We can find the original meaning of **psychology** in the Greek roots of the word. *Psyche* means "mind"—which the ancient Greeks believed to be separate and distinct from the physical body—and the suffix *-ology* means "a field of study." Therefore, *psychology* literally means "the study of the mind." Psychologists today, however, use the broader definition that we included in our Core Concept: Psychology includes not only *mental processes* but also *behaviors*. That is to say, psychology's domain extends across both directly observable behaviors (talking, smiling, and crying, for example) and the internal mental processes that can be only indirectly observed (such as thinking, feeling, and desiring). Psychologists have not always agreed on these boundaries for their field—particularly on whether subjective mental processes could be explored by a discipline that claims to be a science.

The other important part of our definition, then, involves this scientific aspect of psychology. In brief, the *science* of psychology is based on objective, verifiable evidence obtained with the same care used by Pfungst in his study of Clever Hans.

Psychology The scientific study of behavior and mental processes.

Psychologists have set the standard for the methodology and scientific study of behaviors and mental processes. By making the **empirical approach** the standard for all psychological research, psychologists have been able to conduct studies that have changed the way we think. Giving you a more complete explanation of what we mean by the science of psychology will occupy much of the rest of the chapter.

For the moment, we want to focus on a point that is only implied in our definition of psychology: the notion that psychology is *not* mere speculation about human nature, nor is it a body of folk wisdom about people that "everybody knows" to be true. Throughout this book you will find many examples of such "commonsense" ideas that psychological science has shown to be false.

■ **Empirical approach** A study conducted via careful observations and scientifically based research.

DO IT YOURSELF! Is It Psychological Science or Psychobabble?

"Show me the evidence!" is the rallying cry of critical thinking. This rule has not penetrated our popular culture, where books tell us that men are from Mars and women are from Venus and that some people think with the "left brain" and others with the "right brain." In fact, much that is called psychology by the popular press and on TV is not based on science at all. Likewise, it is a good bet that you will find many volumes in the "Psychology and Self-Help" section of your local bookstore that are based on nothing more than speculation, exaggeration, or misunderstanding–what we call *pseudopsychology* and psychologist Carol Tavris (2000) more scathingly labels *psychobabble.* Whichever term you prefer, your authors hope that this book will help you spot bogus psychology for what it is.

Now, let's put a sampling of your psychological beliefs to the test. Some of the following statements are true, and some are false. Don't worry if you get a few–or all–of the items wrong: You will have lots of company. The point is that what so-called common sense teaches us about psychological processes may not withstand the scrutiny of a scientific test. Mark each of the following statements as "true" or "false." (The answers are given at the end.)

____ 1. It is a myth that most people use only about 10% of their brains.

____ 2. During your most vivid dreams, your body may be paralyzed.

____ 3. Psychological stress can cause physical illness.

____ 4. The color red exists only as a sensation in the brain. There is no "red" in the world outside the brain.

____ 5. Bipolar (manic-depressive) disorder is caused by a conflict in the unconscious mind.

____ 6. The newborn child's mind is essentially a "blank slate" on which everything he or she will know is "written" (learned) by experience.

____ 7. Everything that happens to us leaves a permanent record in memory.

____ 8. You were born with all the brain cells that you will ever have.

____ 9. Intelligence is a nearly pure genetic trait that is fixed at the same level throughout a person's life.

____ 10. Polygraph ("lie detector") devices are remarkably accurate in detecting physical responses that, in the eye of a trained examiner, reliably indicate when a suspect is lying.

Answers: The first four items are true; the rest are false. Below you will find some brief explanations for each item; you will find more detail in the chapters indicated in parentheses.

1. *True:* This *is* a myth. We use all parts of our brains every day. (See Chapter 2, "Biopsychology and the Foundations of Neuroscience.")
2. *True:* During our most vivid dreams, which occur during rapid eye movement sleep (REM), the voluntary muscles in our body are paralyzed, with the exception of those controlling our eyes. (See Chapter 3, "States of Consciousness.")
3. *True:* The link between mind and body can make you sick when you are under chronic stress. (See Chapter 10, "Stress, Health, and Well-Being.")
4. *True:* Strange as it may seem, all sensations of color are created in the brain itself. Light waves do have different frequencies, but they have no color. The brain interprets the various frequencies of light as different colors. (See Chapter 4, "Sensation and Perception.")
5. *False:* There is no evidence at all that unconscious conflicts play a role in bipolar disorder. Instead, the evidence suggests a strong biochemical component. The disorder usually responds well to certain drugs, hinting that it involves faulty brain chemistry. Research also suggests that this faulty chemistry may have a genetic basis. (See Chapter 12, "Mental Disorders," and Chapter 13, "Therapies for Mental Disorders.")
6. *False:* Far from being a "blank slate," the newborn child has a large repertoire of built-in abilities and protective reflexes. The "blank slate" myth also ignores the child's genetic potential. (See Chapter 9, "Psychological Development.")
7. *False:* Although many details of our lives are remembered, there is no evidence that memory records all the details of our lives. In fact, we have good reason to believe that most of the information around us never reaches memory and that what does reach memory often becomes distorted. (See Chapter 7, "Cognition.")
8. *False:* Contrary to what scientists thought just a few years ago, some parts of the brain continue to create new cells throughout life. (See Chapter 2, "Biopsychology and the Foundations of Neuroscience.")
9. *False:* Intelligence is the result of both heredity and environment. Because it depends, in part, on environment, your level of intelligence (as measured by an IQ test) can change throughout your life. (See Chapter 7, " Cognition.")
10. *False:* Even the most expert polygrapher can incorrectly classify a truth-teller as a liar or fail to identify someone who is lying. Objective evidence supporting the accuracy of lie detectors is meager. (See Chapter 8, "Emotion and Motivation.")

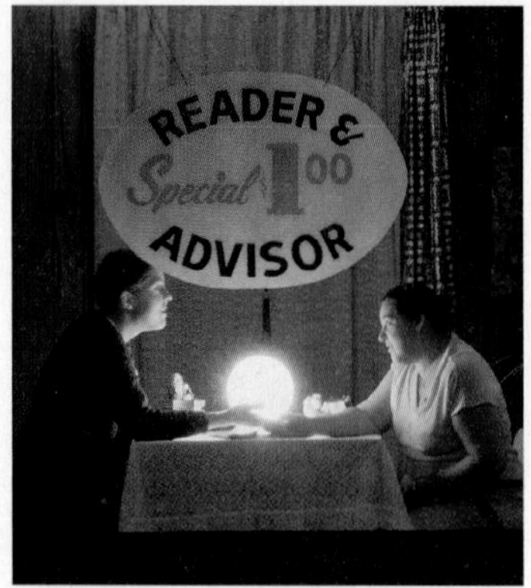
READER &
Special 1.00
ADVISOR

● Fortune tellers, astrologers, and other practitioners of pseudopsychology don't bother to verify their claims with the same care that Pfungst used to test Clever Hans.

Could some of your own beliefs be among them? We challenge you to find out by taking the quiz in the box, "Do It Yourself! Is it Psychological Science or Psychobabble?"

Psychology and Critical Thinking

The Clever Hans incident occurred over one hundred years ago. Yet people today seem as eager as ever to embrace fantastic claims—especially those of mysterious powers of the mind and supernatural influences on our personalities. For evidence, we have to look no further than the horoscope in the daily newspaper. Never mind that astrology has been thoroughly debunked (Schick & Vaughn, 2001).[1] And the same goes for graphology (the bogus science of handwriting analysis), fortune telling, and the purported power of subliminal messages in the movies or on TV to persuade us to buy certain products or vote for certain politicians. All fall under the heading of **pseudopsychology:** phony, unscientific psychology masquerading as the real thing.

One of the goals your authors have for this book is to help you differentiate between psychology and pseudopsychology—that is, to *think critically* about claims made under the name of psychology. Most people, of course, think of themselves as good thinkers—just using common sense—but, as we will see over and over again in this book, what masquerades as psychological common sense has often turned out to be wrong. "Common sense," after all, has led many people to accept uncritically the polygraph (the so-called lie detector), the superiority of certain racial groups, demonic possession as a cause of mental illness, the primative brain operation sometimes called the "lobotomy," and the notion that horrific deeds (such as the recent torture of prisoners in Iraq) are perpetrated by just a few "bad apples."

Harmful Effects of Pseudopsychology So, what's the big deal if people want to believe such things? We—your authors, Phil, Bob, Ann, and Craig—suggest that there are two sets of problems.

First, those who uncritically accept the claims of pseudoscientific psychology risk depriving themselves of some *real* psychological insights that are even more interesting and useful. To give one example, few people realize that we humans are highly susceptible to **confirmation bias.** That is, we pay attention to events that confirm our beliefs and ignore evidence that contradicts them (Halpern, 2002). Knowledge of the confirmation bias helps us understand why, for example, astrology fans usually remember those days when the horoscope seems accurate and forget the days when it misses the mark.

The second set of problems with pseudopsychology involves the potential for more serious harm. For example, unfounded psychological beliefs (*pseudopsychology*) can waste time, money, and talent—even lives—as you will see when we discuss false "recovered memories" of sexual abuse (in Chapter 7) or when the presumption of female intellectual inferiority keeps women out of "men's jobs." Some people still don't know that psychological science long ago demonstrated that memory is not always accurate and that neither sex is intellectually inferior to the other (Neisser et al., 1996).

Pseudopsychology can also provide a fertile field for fraud. This happens when people are bilked by fortune tellers, handwriting analysts (grapholo-

■ **Pseudopsychology** Erroneous assertions or practices set forth as being scientific psychology.

■ **Confirmation bias** The tendency to attend to evidence that complements and confirms our beliefs or expectations, while ignoring evidence that does not.

[1]Throughout this book you will find that we use brief citations in parentheses calling your attention to a complete bibliographic reference found in the "References" section, beginning on p. R-1, near the end of this book. These brief in-text citations give the authors' last names and the publication date. With the complete reference in hand, your library can help you find the original source.

gists), or astrologists, who claim to have special knowledge of personality. Still another form of harm (of special concern to psychologists) involves diminished public support for legitimate psychological science.

Merely raising questions about accepted pseudoscientific beliefs can sometimes be dangerous. For example, in some parts of the United States only a few decades ago, those who dared to question the presumed mental and moral inferiority of African Americans were sometimes beaten, jailed, or lynched. Even today, in many regions of the world, posing critical questions about the status of women or particular racial groups still carries dire consequences.

When skeptical psychologists tested the claims for facilitated communication, they found that it wasn't the autistic children who were responsible for the messages.

Dangerous Therapies: The Facilitated Communication Fiasco Yet another potential harmful consequence of pseudoscientific psychology lurks in unvalidated therapies for psychological disorders. Let's consider an example involving *facilitated communication,* a widely acclaimed treatment for *autism* (a developmental disorder that can severely impair attention, language, and social functioning) that was popular in the 1990s. The treatment (which we will explain in a moment) is based on the erroneous belief that autism sufferers can have impressive verbal abilities that lie hidden by their disorder.

In brief, facilitated communication is a method by which a helper (or *facilitator*) attempts to communicate with an autistic person by asking questions and then assisting the person to respond by typing or pointing to letters on a letter board. (You can see how this is done in the accompanying photo.) You may have already identified the problem with this method: making sure that it is the autistic person who is really responding, rather than the facilitator.

Initially, the reports on facilitated communication were promising—even enthusiastic. But some psychologists were skeptical. They pointed out that the glowing reports were simply anecdotes, lacking in strict scientific controls. They also expressed concern that the helper might be consciously or unconsciously guiding the child's hand to produce the messages. (You have probably noticed the parallels with the case of Clever Hans.)

Sure enough, when studies of facilitated communication were done under controlled conditions, the results showed the skeptics' concerns to be well founded (Cabay, 1994; Wheeler et al., 1993). When the facilitator knew the questions being asked, the autistic child would seem to give sensible answers. But when "blinders" were applied—by hiding the questions from the facilitator—the answers were inaccurate or nonsensical. In fact, the experiments that demonstrated the flaws in facilitated communication employed essentially the same design that Dr. Pfungst used almost a century before to test Clever Hans.

Sadly, even though facilitated communication had extended hope to beleaguered parents and teachers, psychological research dashed those hopes. Moreover, the consequences of an uncritical belief in facilitated communication proved worse than false hopes. Not only did the use of facilitated communication mean that more effective treatments were delayed, but many parents blamed themselves when their children did not respond as expected to the treatment (Levine et al., 1994). Worst of all may have been the false accusations of sexual abuse derived from facilitated messages thought to have come from the autistic children (Bicklen, 1990; Heckler, 1994). The controlled studies left little doubt that the messages describing abuse originated wholly in the minds of the facilitators. In the wake of these findings, the American Psychological Association (2003b) denounced facilitated communication as a failure and relegated it to the junk pile of ineffective therapies.

The Skeptical Psychologist What lesson can you, as a student of psychology, draw from the facilitated communication fiasco and from the case of Clever

Hans? After all, you won't be able to run your own scientific test on every fantastic-sounding claim that comes along. We hope that you will develop a skeptical, critical attitude about reports of amazing new treatments, dramatic psychological "breakthroughs," and products that claim to help you develop "untapped potential." And we hope you will always pause to ask: Is there a simpler explanation? Has someone done a controlled test? Could the claims be merely the result of people's *expectations*—that is, could *confirmation bias* be at work? By doing so, you will have adopted the skeptical, show-me-the-evidence attitude of a good psychologist. This is exactly the approach that we will take on the journey through psychology that we begin in this chapter.

What Do Psychologists Do?

In the next few pages you will discover that psychology is a more diverse field than most people realize. Many students enroll in their first psychology course expecting that it will deal mainly with mental disorders and psychological therapies. But they soon find that psychology is also about learning, memory, perception, intelligence, personality, social interaction, thinking, emotion, and many more concepts that we will explore throughout this book. In the remainder of this section, we will first confront a stereotype about psychologists, and then we will show you three main ways to be a psychologist. After that, you will learn about some of the field's principal areas of specialization and, finally, about the difference between psychologists and psychiatrists.

Not All Psychologists Are Therapists Contrary to the popular stereotype, not all psychologists are therapists. You will find them at work almost everywhere: in education, industry, sports, prisons, government, churches, and temples, in private practice, and in the psychology departments of colleges and universities (see Figure 1.1). Psychologists also work for athletic teams, engineering firms, consulting firms, and the courts (both the judicial and the NBA variety). In these diverse settings, they perform a wide range of tasks, including teaching, research, assessment, and equipment design, as well as psychotherapy. Psychology's specialties are too numerous to cover them all here, but we can give you the flavor of the field by first dividing psychology into three broad categories.

Three Ways Of Doing Psychology Broadly speaking, we can divide psychology into three main branches or categories: *experimental psychology, teaching of psychology,* and *applied psychology.* **Experimental psychologists** are the workhorses who do the basic research in psychology. Most are faculty members at a college or university. This group, also called *research psychologists,* is the smallest of the three major branches of psychology (Fríncke & Pate, 2004).

■ **Experimental psychologists** Psychologists who do research on basic psychological processes—as contrasted with applied psychologists; also called *research psychologists.*

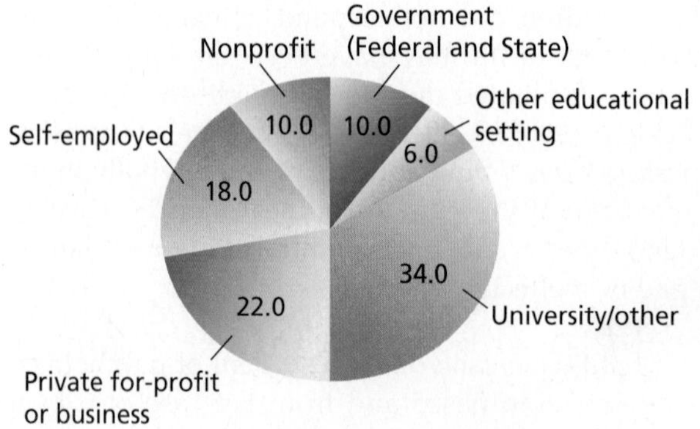

Government (Federal and State)
Nonprofit
Other educational setting
Self-employed
10.0
10.0
6.0
18.0
34.0
22.0
University/other
Private for-profit or business

● **FIGURE 1.1** Work Settings of Psychologists

(Updated information from *Employed Doctoral Scientists and Engineers, by Sector of Employment, Broad Field of Doctorate and Sex: 2001,* National Science Foundation.)

The second category, **teachers of psychology,** overlaps with the experimentalists, because most researchers also teach classes at the colleges or universities where they do their experimental work. Increasingly, however, large numbers of psychologists are hired by high schools, colleges, and universities primarily to teach. Community colleges alone employ some 9000 psychologists in teaching positions across the United States (Johnson & Rudmann, 2004).

Applied psychologists use the knowledge developed by experimental psychologists to tackle human problems, such as training, equipment design, and psychological treatment. Applied psychologists work in a wide variety of places such as schools, clinics, factories, social service agencies, airports, hospitals, and casinos. All told, some 64% of the doctoral-level psychologists in the United States work primarily as applied psychologists, and that percentage has been steadily increasing since the 1950s (Kohout & Wicherski, 2000; Rosenzweig, 1992; Stapp et al., 1985).

Applied Psychological Specialties What, exactly, do applied psychologists do? Here are profiles of some of the most popular applied specialties:

- *Industrial and organizational psychologists* (often called *I/O psychologists*) specialize in modifying the work environment to maximize productivity and morale. Some I/O psychologists develop interview and testing procedures to help organizations select new employees; some develop programs to train and retain employees; and others specialize in market research.
- *Sports psychologists,* as you might expect, work with athletes to help them maximize their performance. They deal with enhancing motivation, controlling emotions under pressure, and planning practice sessions. Many major sports franchises have sports psychologists on staff.
- *Engineering psychologists* work at the interface between people and equipment. Some design devices, such as control panels or airplane instrument displays, for easy and reliable human use. Some do psychological detective work to discover what went wrong in accidents attributed to "human error." Engineering psychologists are usually employed by private industry or the government and often work on a team with other scientists.
- *School psychologists* have expertise in the problems of teaching and learning. Typically, they work for a school district, where they diagnose learning and behavior problems and consult with teachers, students, and parents. School psychologists may spend a good deal of time administering, scoring, and interpreting psychological tests.
- *Rehabilitation psychologists* serve with physicians, nurses, counselors, and social workers on teams that may treat patients with both physical and mental disorders, such as stroke, spinal cord injury, alcoholism, drug abuse, or amputation. Some work in a hospital setting. Others work for social service agencies and for sheltered workshops that provide job training for people with disabilities.
- *Clinical psychologists* and *counseling psychologists* work with people who have problems with social and emotional adjustment or those who face difficult choices in relationships, careers, or education. About half of all doctoral-level psychologists list clinical or counseling psychology as their specialty (American Psychological Association, 2003c). The clinician is more likely to have a private practice involving psychological testing and long-term therapy, while the counselor is more likely to work for an agency or school and to spend fewer sessions with each client.

More information on the career possibilities in psychology can be found in *Careers in Psychology for the Twenty-First Century,* published by the American Psychological Association (2003a).

■ **Teachers of psychology**
Psychologists whose primary job is teaching, typically in high schools, colleges, and universities.

■ **Applied psychologists**
Psychologists who use the knowledge developed by experimental psychologists to solve human problems.

PSYCHOLOGY IN YOUR LIFE: KNOWING THE DIFFERENCE BETWEEN A PSYCHOLOGIST AND A PSYCHIATRIST

Students sometimes worry that their psychology professors are going to "psychoanalyze" them. Apparently, they believe that psychologists stand ever vigilant—just waiting for signs of mental disorder to appear. To put your mind at rest, this is only a stereotype: People commonly think that all psychologists are *clinical* psychologists—but you have already learned that isn't true. In fact, many psychologists have no training at all in the diagnosis and treatment of mental disorders.

One other point of confusion blurs the public image of psychology: the distinction between *psychology* and *psychiatry*. **Psychiatry** is a medical specialty, not a part of psychology. Psychiatrists hold MD (Doctor of Medicine) degrees and have also had specialized training in the treatment of mental and behavioral problems. Therefore, psychiatrists are licensed to prescribe medicines and to perform other medical procedures. Consequently, psychiatrists tend to view patients from a *medical* perspective. In the public mind, however, psychiatry often gets confused with clinical psychology because both professions treat people suffering from mental disorders. Psychologists like to point out that, while psychiatric training emphasizes mental illness, it gives short shrift to basic *psychological* topics, such as perception, learning, psychological testing, and developmental issues.

In contrast with psychiatry, psychology is a much broader field, encompassing many different specialties. Each specialty—such as experimental, engineering, teaching, and I/O psychology—has its own focus. As we have seen, most have nothing to do with the diagnosis and treatment of mental disorders. Moreover, while psychologists typically hold doctoral degrees, their training is not in medicine. (Only a few psychologists have taken the necessary medical coursework that qualifies them to prescribe drugs for psychological problems.) Instead, graduate training in psychology focuses on training in research methods, along with advanced study in a particular psychological specialty.

So, now you can sound smarter than most people when you talk about psychology and psychiatry. But what about the difference between a psychologist and a *psychoanalyst*? We'll look into that in the next section.

■ **Psychiatry** A medical specialty dealing with the diagnosis and treatment of mental disorders.

CHECK YOUR UNDERSTANDING

1. **RECALL:** Experiments showing facilitated communication to be ineffective were similar to the experiment that exposed Clever Hans. Specifically, what did both experimental procedures have in common?
   a. Neither the horse nor the autistic children could see the questions.
   b. Neither Von Osten nor the facilitators could see the questions.
   c. Both Hans and the autistic children were given incentives for producing correct answers.
   d. In both situations, correct answers were given about half the time.
   e. Intentional deceit was the goal of both experiments.
2. **APPLICATION:** The *confirmation bias* refers to a mental process that explains, among other things, why people
   a. engage in risky behavior.
   b. seek help from psychiatrists.
   c. believe in astrology.
   d. become autistic.
   e. study psychology.
3. **RECALL:** Which one would be considered an applied psychologist?
   a. an I/O psychologist
   b. a social worker
   c. a psychologist doing basic research
   d. a professor of psychology at the university
   e. a psychiatrist

4. **APPLICATION:** Which one of the following would be most likely to do research on learning or memory?
   a. an applied psychologist
   b. a psychiatrist
   c. an I/O psychologist
   d. a professor of psychology at the university
   e. an experimental psychologist

5. **UNDERSTANDING THE CORE CONCEPT:** Psychology is different from other disciplines, such as psychiatry, that deal with people because
   a. psychology focuses on mental disorder.
   b. psychology is a broader field, covering all aspects of behavior and mental processes.
   c. psychologists must have doctoral degrees.
   d. psychologists do research.
   e. psychology focuses only on animal research.

ANSWERS: 1. b 2. c 3. a 4. e 5. b

KEY QUESTION
?

WHAT ARE PSYCHOLOGY'S HISTORICAL ROOTS?

People have probably always speculated about human behavior and mental processes. Written records, dating back some 25 centuries to the Greek philosophers Socrates, Plato, and Aristotle, include ideas about consciousness and madness. They observed that emotions can distort thinking and that our perceptions are merely interpretations of the external world. Most people today would probably agree with many of these ancient ideas—and so would modern psychology.

Throughout history, people have been interested in the causes of behavior. Psychology's roots can be traced back to the work and ideas of the ancient Greek philosophers. Having a strong background in the origin of these ideas will make the study of psychology much easier to understand.

● The ancient Greeks believed that anger, such as we see in this enraged driver, comes from the spleen, but it never occurred to them to put their theories to a controlled test.

There is endless debate about the beginnings of the study of human behavior. Oftentimes the approaches of the ancient Greeks have been oversimplified and accorded only a passing mention. However, the basis for the development of Western thought has its beginnings in ancient Greece. And although there was no formal study of psychology during this time, the issues and ideas raised by the Greeks are quite similar to theories we still discuss today.

The first real glimpse of how classical philosophy became a precursor to modern psychology can be seen in the study of the philosopher Plato. Some have described Plato's quest for knowledge and understanding as the quest for perfect knowledge. Delving into areas like cognition, he was the first philosopher credited with the study of gaining knowledge (Plato, 380 B.C.)!

After Plato, the philosopher Aristotle developed theories of sensation, perception, cognition, memory, problem solving, and ethics. His approach to learning defined science until the advent of empiricism (Aristotle).

On the other hand, the Greeks also came up with some psychological notions that now seem quaint or amusing. They believed, for example, that emotions flow from the heart, the liver, and the spleen and that mental disorder could be caused by excessive bile. Following their lead, we still use the metaphor of "heartfelt" emotions, and we may "vent the spleen" when we are angry.

But we can give the Greeks only partial credit for laying the historical foundations for psychology. At roughly the same time, Asian and African societies were developing their own psychological ideas. In Asia, Yoga and Buddhism were exploring consciousness, which they attempted to control with meditation. Meanwhile, in Africa, other explanations for personality and mental disorder were emerging from traditional spiritual beliefs (Berry et al., 1992). Based on these *folk psychologies*, shamans (healers) developed therapies rivaling in effectiveness the treatments used in Western psychology and psychiatry today (Lambo, 1978). It was, however, the Greek tradition and, later, the Roman Catholic Church that most influenced the development of Western psychology as a science.

Oddly—and significantly—it never occurred to any of the ancient thinkers to put their speculations to a test, in the same way that Pfungst tested his suspicions about Clever Hans. In the Greek mind, truth came from casual observation, logic, and the authority of experts. Then, a few hundred years later, when the medieval Church gained control of Europe, clerics sought to minimize inquiry into human nature because they had little interest in the "world of the flesh." In fact, the Church taught that the mind and soul operate completely outside the natural laws that govern worldly objects and events. For medieval Christians, the human mind—like the mind of God—presented an unsolvable mystery.

This view prevailed until the 17th century, when French philosopher René Descartes (*Day-CART*) dared to assert that human sensations and behaviors are based on activity in the nervous system. His idea fit well with exciting new discoveries about the biology of nerve circuits in animals. For example, science had just shown how the sense organs convert stimulation into the nerve impulses and muscular responses. This discovery allowed scientists, for the first time, to see that there were biological processes (rather than mysterious spiritual forces) behind sensation and simple reflexive behaviors. Yet despite these major advances, psychology itself would not become a distinct scientific discipline for another two centuries after Descartes. As we will see, it took two revolutionary ideas to make a science of psychology possible.

Before we get to that, however, let's take a moment to state our Core Concept for this section, which emphasizes five of the competing viewpoints that emerged in the early days of psychology, as the field struggled to become a science:

CORE CONCEPT

Modern psychology developed from several conflicting traditions, including structuralism, functionalism, Gestalt psychology, behaviorism, and psychoanalysis.

After you have studied this section, you should be able to explain the basic assumptions of each tradition and the issues on which they were in conflict.

Why Study the History of Psychology? The history of psychology, although it may seem like not much happened before Wundt in 1879, is rich. Knowing the philosophy that shaped the early psychologists helps us understand why they thought the way they did. In addition, it enables all of us who are students of psychology to understand how and why psychology grew into the field that it is today. Before this text, you may not have considered how Plato and Aristotle are connected to modern thought. Studying the history of psychology is important, because knowing where psychology came from gives us a better idea of where it is going.

Structuralism: Focus on Structure—and the Founding of Scientific Psychology

One of the two revolutionary ideas to shape the early development of psychology emerged in the mid-1800s. In his book *On the Origin of Species* (1859), Charles Darwin suggested a biological kinship between humans and animals.

For psychologists this would mean that discoveries about animal biology and behavior could be applied (with caution, of course) to people. So, for example, Helmholtz's pioneering research on nerve impulses in frogs helped psychologists understand human reflexes. Likewise, Darwin's insight meant that Pavlov's later work on learning in dogs could also throw light on human learning—as we shall see in Chapter 6.

The second big idea that shaped the early science of psychology arose in chemistry, where scientists had noticed patterns in properties of the chemical elements that led them to develop the *periodic table.* At one stroke, the periodic table made the processes underlying chemical reactions clear. This achievement particularly intrigued one Wilhelm Wundt, a German scientist (who, incidentally, became the first person to call himself a "psychologist"). Wundt wondered: Could a similar approach simplify our understanding of the mind? Could he discover "the elements of conscious experience"? Wundt's quest for the elements of consciousness became known as **structuralism,** because it focused on revealing the most basic "structures" or components of the mind (Fancher, 1979), rather than what consciousness (of the mind) could do.

To pursue his dream of establishing a science of consciousness, in 1879 Wundt established an institute for psychological research at the University of Leipzig. There, in a new laboratory, Wundt and his students began to conduct studies on what they supposed to be the "elements" of consciousness: sensation and perception, memory, attention, emotion, cognition, learning, and language. All our mental activity, they asserted, consisted of combinations of such basic processes. In their experiments, they presented trained volunteers with a variety of simple stimuli and asked them to respond with the press of a lever or a description of their sensations—a technique called **introspection.**

● In 1879, Wilhelm Wundt (1832–1920) founded the first formal laboratory devoted to experimental psychology. He's shown here (center) in his laboratory in Leipzig in 1912.

From the outset, structuralism was a magnet for critics, who attacked and ridiculed Wundt from all sides. In particular, many objected to his introspective method as being too subjective. After all, they said, how can we judge the accuracy of people's description of their thoughts and feelings?

But Wundt has had the last laugh—even though structuralism no longer exists as a recognized "school" of psychology. Psychologists still rely on his introspective method for obtaining dream reports and evidence of perceptual changes, such as those you will experience in the Necker cube demonstration in the upcoming "Psychology in Your Life" section. And there is one more reason why Wundt, if he were alive today, would still be laughing: The topics that he and his students first identified and explored can be found as chapter headings in every introductory psychology text, including this one.

Functionalism: Focus on Function

One of the most vocal of Wundt's critics, the American psychologist William James, argued that structuralism's approach was far too narrow. (He also said that it was boring—which didn't help his already strained relationship with Wundt [Fancher, 1979].) James argued that psychology should include the *function* of consciousness, not just its *structure.* In a famous metaphor, he pictured

■ **Structuralism** A historical school of psychology devoted to uncovering the basic structures that make up mind and thought. Structuralists sought the "elements" of conscious experience.

■ **Introspection** The process of reporting on one's own conscious mental experiences.

■ **Functionalism** A historical school of psychology that believed mental processes could best be understood in terms of their adaptive purpose and function.

■ **Gestalt psychology** A historical school of psychology that sought to understand how the brain works by studying perception and perceptual learning. Gestalt psychologists believed that percepts consist of meaningful wholes (in German, *Gestalts*).

■ **Behaviorism** A historical school (as well as a modern perspective) that has sought to make psychology an objective science focused only on behavior–to the exclusion of mental processes.

a "stream of consciousness" as a mental process that had no static structure but was continually flowing, changing, and interacting with the environment. Appropriately, James's brand of psychology became known as **functionalism.**

James found Charles Darwin's ideas much more interesting than Wundt's. In particular, he liked Darwin's emphasis on organisms *adapting* to their environments. James therefore proposed that psychology should explain how people adapt—or fail to adapt—to the everyday world outside the laboratory. Recurring bouts of depression probably added to his concern with problems of everyday living (Ross, 1991).

Where did this approach lead the functionalists? Much of their work had a practical bent: They were the first *applied* psychologists. James wrote extensively on the development of learned "habits," emotions, the psychology of religion, and teaching. Appropriately, one of his followers, John Dewey, founded the "progressive education" movement, which emphasized learning by *doing,* rather than by merely listening to lectures and memorizing facts.

Gestalt Psychology: Focus on the Whole Instead of the Parts

Another challenge to Wundt's structuralism came from a rebellious group in his native Germany. In some respects, their approach, known as **Gestalt psychology,** was exactly the opposite of the structuralists': The Gestalt psychologists were interested in how we construct "perceptual wholes" (or *Gestalts,* in German), such as our perception of a face, rather than just a conglomeration of lines, colors, and textures. (The structuralists, you will remember, focused on the parts, or elements of consciousness, not on the whole.) But for Gestalt psychology, understanding perception was merely the means to the even more important end of understanding how the brain works. Like both the structuralists and the functionalists, psychologists of the Gestalt "school" (or philosophical approach) relied on introspection.

Prominent Gestalt psychologists include Max Wertheimer, who studied visual illusions and ambiguous figures, such as the Necker cube, which you will see in a moment (page 14). Another psychologist, Wolfgang Köhler, extended the reach of Gestalt psychology to *insight learning,* an overlooked form of learning marked by sudden "Aha!" experiences. We will see much more of the Gestaltists in our study of perception (Chapter 4).

Behaviorism: Eliminate the Mind and Focus on Behavior

CONNECTION: CHAPTER 6

John Watson and his colleague Rosalie Rayner performed a notorious study in which they taught a young boy, Albert, to fear furry objects.

A particularly feisty group, known as the *behaviorists,* disagreed with nearly everyone. Most notably, they proposed the novel idea that consciousness should not be a part of psychology at all! John B. Watson, the leader of the behavioral movement, argued that a true and objective science of psychology should deal solely with observable events: *stimuli* from the environment and the organism's *responses.* **Behaviorism,** said Watson, should be the science of *behavior*—not of the mind.

In general, behaviorism rejected any psychology of subjective mental processes. But, in particular, behaviorists objected to *introspection,* the practice of asking people to report on their mental experiences—a technique that the structuralists, functionalists, and Gestalt psychologists all used. Watson and his behaviorist followers cared nothing about what people were *thinking.* Instead, they wanted to know how people would *act* (for example, whether a child would respond with fear to a rabbit that, on an earlier presentation, had been accompanied by a sudden loud noise).

● Sigmund Freud (1856–1939), shown here in the office of his Vienna home, developed the psychodynamic approach to behavior.

We will encounter behaviorism again in the next section of the chapter because it is one of the ancestral lines of psychology that continues to live on in the present day.

Psychoanalysis: Focus on the Unconscious Mind

Yet another objection to Wundt's approach to psychology came from medicine—specifically from the Viennese physician Sigmund Freud and his disciples, who were pioneering the *psychoanalytic method* of treating mental disorders. Their conceptual approach, called **psychoanalysis,** asserted that mental disorders arise from conflicts in the *un*conscious mind. Accordingly, they maintained that the definition of psychology should be expanded to include the unconscious.

Because psychoanalytic theory remains a force in modern psychology, we will talk more about Freud and his ideas later in the chapter. But for now, you should know that psychoanalysis and behaviorism outlasted structuralism, functionalism, and Gestalt psychology. Today, few would call themselves structuralists, functionalists, or Gestaltists. Yet—and this is the important point—the legacies of these early approaches, along with those of behaviorism and psychoanalytic theory, can be found woven through the fabric of modern psychology. We will return for a big-picture overview of modern psychology, a field still marked by multiple viewpoints, right after we show you how a famous image makes two profound points.

■ **Psychoanalysis** An approach to psychology based on Sigmund Freud's assertions, which emphasize unconscious processes. The term is used to refer broadly both to Freud's psychoanalytic theory and to his psychoanalytic treatment method.

PSYCHOLOGY IN YOUR LIFE: AN INTROSPECTIVE LOOK AT THE NECKER CUBE

The cube in Figure 1.2A will trick your eye—or, more accurately, it will trick your brain. If you look at it for a few moments, it will suddenly seem to change perspectives. For a time you may see it as if from the upper right (Figure 1.2B), and then it will abruptly shift and appear as though you were seeing it from the lower left (Figure 1.2C).

It may take a few moments to see the shift. But once you see it change, you won't be able to prevent it from alternating back and forth, seemingly at random. Try showing the cube to a few friends and asking them what they see.

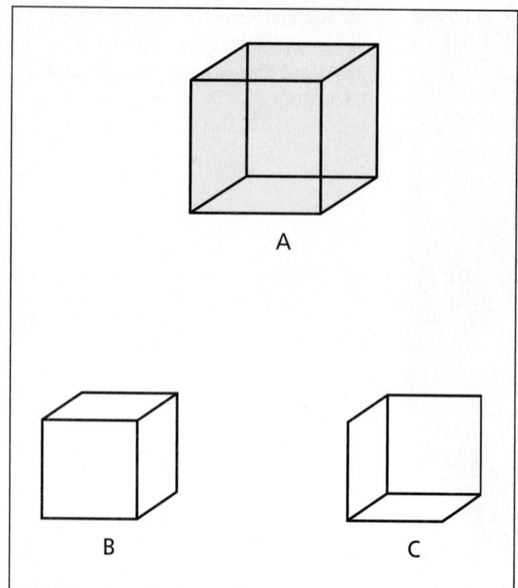
A
B
C

● **FIGURE 1.2** The Necker Cube Perspective

We feel compelled to confess that the alternating-cube phenomenon was not discovered by a psychologist. Rather, it was first noticed by Swiss geologist Louis Necker in 1832, while he was looking at cube-shaped crystals under a microscope. Since that time, it has been known in his honor as the Necker cube. For our purposes, Necker's amazing cube illustrates two important points.

First, it illustrates the much-maligned process of *introspection*, pioneered by Wundt and his students. Please note that the only way we can demonstrate that the Necker cube changes perspectives in our minds is by having people look at it and report what they see. And why is this important to psychology? Only the hardest of the hard-core behaviorists would deny that something happens mentally within a person looking at the cube. Moreover, whatever it is involves more than simply seeing lines on a page. In fact, the Necker cube demonstrates that we add *meaning* to our sensations—a process called *perception*, which will be a main focus of a later chapter. *The take-away message is that we don't simply* sense *the world as it "really" is, but we* perceive *it by adding our own interpretations.*

The second important point is this: The Necker cube can serve as a metaphor for the multiple perspectives in psychology. Just as there is no single right way to see the cube, there is no single perspective in psychology that gives us one right understanding of behavior and mental processes. Put another way, to understand psychology fully, we must alternately shift our viewpoints among multiple perspectives. And what are those perspectives? We will explore seven of the most important ones in the next section.

CONNECTION: CHAPTER 4

Gestalt psychologists intensely studied how individuals perceive ambiguous objects.

CHECK YOUR UNDERSTANDING

1. **RECALL:** The ancient Greeks' approach to psychology was not scientific because they
   a. failed to check their opinions against controlled observations.
   b. were more interested in art and music than in truth.
   c. believed that all truth was revealed in sacred texts given by their gods.
   d. lived in an age before precise measuring instruments had been developed.
   e. did not publish their results.

2. **RECALL:** René Descartes made a science of psychology possible when he suggested that
   a. science should be based entirely on common sense rather than on religion.
   b. replicability of results was essential.
   c. the elements of conscious experience could be arranged into a periodic table.
   d. psychology should be a branch of philosophy.
   e. sensations and perceptions are the result of activity in the nervous system.

3. **RECALL:** One of the roots of cognitive psychology sought to identify the "elements of conscious experience." Adherents to this viewpoint were called
   a. structuralists.
   b. functionalists.
   c. Gestalt psychologists.
   d. behaviorists.
   e. psychoanalysts.

4. **APPLICATION:** Which of the following is a method you would use to tell whether a friend had experienced a perceptual shift while viewing the Necker cube?
   a. behaviorism
   b. introspection
   c. structuralism
   d. sensation
   e. perception

5. **UNDERSTANDING THE CORE CONCEPT:** Modern psychology has strong roots in all of the following traditions except
   a. Greek philosophy.
   b. biology.
   c. astrology.
   d. functionalism.
   e. structuralism.

ANSWERS: 1. a 2. e 3. a 4. b 5. c

KEY QUESTION

WHAT ARE THE PERSPECTIVES PSYCHOLOGISTS USE TODAY?

During the past century, the picture of psychology was both enriched and complicated by ideas borrowed from many sources. The result is a field that resembles a slightly dysfunctional family, with a few common interests and lots of family squabbles. In our Core Concept we simplify this family portrait by focusing on nine especially important viewpoints:

CORE CONCEPT

> Nine main perspectives characterize modern psychology: the biological, developmental, cognitive, psychodynamic, humanistic, behavioral, sociocultural, evolutionary/sociobiological, and trait views.

The champions of each view see behavior and mental processes in a slightly different way—much like nine artists portraying the same scene from different vantage points. You are likely to find experimental psychologists and teachers of psychology holding any of these viewpoints. Among applied psychologists who do counseling, therapy, and personnel selection work, however, the trait and clinical views predominate. As you read the following pages, you should focus on the important ideas that distinguish each view from the others.

The Biological View

The **biological view** emphasizes how our physical makeup and the operation of our brains influence our personality, preferences, behavior patterns, and abilities. More specifically, psychologists taking the biological approach search for the causes of behavior in heredity, in the nervous system and the endocrine (hormone) system, and in the effects of environmental insults such as disease (*not* insults of the other kind). As you might imagine, the biological view has strong roots in medicine and biological science. Often, the enterprise of biological psychology, along with biology, neurology, and other disciplines interested in brain processes, is referred to as **neuroscience.**

● The biological view led to the discovery that certain patterns of brain waves are associated with the hidden world of dreams.

Neuroscience is a "hot" area at the moment. Thanks to spectacular advances in computers and brain-imaging techniques, neuroscientists have made amazing strides in understanding the brain during the past decade. Among their achievements, they have begun to unravel the mystery of how our eyes and brain convert light waves into vision. They have also learned how damage to certain parts of the brain can destroy specific abilities, such as speech, social skills, or memory. And they have discovered brain wave patterns associated with the hidden world of sleep and dreams.

One important variation on the biological view again draws on the ideas originally proposed by the famous British scholar and naturalist Charles Darwin. **Evolutionary psychology** suggests that many human traits arise from hereditary characteristics established in our remote ancestral past. In this view, our genetic makeup—including our most deeply ingrained behaviors—were shaped by the conditions our ancestors faced thousands of years ago.

All through the history of the species, environmental forces have pruned the human family tree, favoring the survival and reproduction of those individuals with the most adaptive mental and physical characteristics. Charles Darwin called this *natural selection.* Through this process, the physical characteristics of a species evolve (change) in the direction of characteristics that give the fittest organisms a competitive advantage.

■ **Biological view** The psychological perspective that searches for the causes of behavior in the functioning of genes, the brain and nervous system, and the endocrine (hormone) system.

■ **Neuroscience** The field devoted to understanding how the brain creates thoughts, feelings, motives, consciousness, memories, and other mental processes.

■ **Evolutionary psychology** A relatively new specialty in psychology that sees behavior and mental processes in terms of their genetic adaptations for survival and reproduction.

Proponents of evolutionary psychology say that virtually all human behavior—even the most destructive behavior, such as warfare, homicide, and racial discrimination—has grown out of genetic tendencies that once may have helped humans adapt and survive. This approach has also suggested some highly controversial explanations for certain gender differences—why, for instance, men typically have more sexual partners than do women.

The Developmental View

Change may be the only constant in our lives. In the **developmental view,** psychological change results from an interaction between the *heredity* programmed in our genes and the experiences presented by our *environment.* A big question, however, involves the relative contributions made by our genes and by our surroundings in shaping who we become: Which counts more heavily, heredity or environment, *nature* or *nurture*?

Developmental psychologists also study how we change as we grow older and how we change by developing social skills, learning language, and assimilating the expectations of our culture. Much of their research has focused on *child* development. Increasingly, however, developmental psychologists have begun to look at how development unfolds in teens and adults. In the developmental chapter of this book, we will explore the sweeping patterns of psychological change seen across the lifespan, from before birth to old age.

The Cognitive View

The next of psychology's multiple modern perspectives suggests that our thoughts and actions arise from the way we *interpret* our experiences. From this viewpoint, understanding ourselves requires that we look in our minds, as well as at our biology.

In the **cognitive view,** our actions are profoundly influenced by the way we process information streaming in from our environment. Cognitive psychologists study all sorts of mental processes, or **cognitions**—thoughts, expectations, perceptions, and memories, as well as states of consciousness. You might think of them as the heirs to the best of the structuralist, functionalist, and Gestalt traditions.

Modern cognitive psychologists have also borrowed from linguistics the idea that our most basic language abilities are wired into our brains at birth (Pinker, 2002). From computer science they have borrowed the metaphor of the brain as a biological computer—designed as a processor of information (Gardner, 1985; Gazzaniga, 1998a; Sperry, 1988). And from medicine they have borrowed the technology that now allows visualizing the activity of the brain and connecting it to mental processes. Cognitive psychologists who are especially interested in the connections among mind, brain, and behavior have pioneered a hybrid field called **cognitive neuroscience.**

A special interest in mental health and mental disorder characterizes the **clinical view.** Most commonly, you will find its adherents practicing counseling or psychotherapy. But the two main groups that this perspective includes—*psychodynamic psychology* and *humanistic psychology*—have taken that interest in different directions.

The Psychodynamic View

The term *psychodynamic* comes from the belief that the mind (psyche) is a reservoir of energy (dynamics). Accordingly, **psychodynamic psychology** says that we are motivated primarily by the energy of irrational desires generated in our unconscious minds (Murray et al., 2000). This approach has been especially

■ **Developmental view** The psychological perspective emphasizing changes that occur across the lifespan.

■ **Cognitive view** The psychological perspective emphasizing mental processes, such as learning, memory, perception, and thinking, as forms of information processing.

■ **Cognitions** Mental processes, such as thinking, memory, sensation, and perception.

■ **Cognitive neuroscience** An interdisciplinary field emphasizing brain activity as information processing; involves cognitive psychology, neurology, biology, computer science, linguistics, and specialists from other fields who are interested in the connection between mental processes and the brain.

■ **Clinical view** The psychological perspective emphasizing mental health and mental illness. Psychodynamic and humanistic psychology are variations on the clinical view.

■ **Psychodynamic psychology** A clinical viewpoint emphasizing the understanding of mental disorders in terms of unconscious needs, desires, memories, and conflicts.

attractive to practitioners who specialize in psychotherapy. As a result, the psychodynamic perspective has emphasized the treatment of mental disorders over scientific research.

The best-known representative of the psychodynamic approach was Sigmund Freud, who founded *psychoanalysis* (and whom we met earlier in our tour of psychology's historical "schools"). Originally a medical technique devised to treat mental disorders, psychoanalysis portrays the mind as a sort of mental boiler that holds the rising pressure of unconscious sexual and destructive desires, along with memories of traumatic events. Even today, most psychoanalysts are medical doctors with a specialty in psychiatry and advanced training in Freudian methods. (And now you know the difference between a *psychologist* and a *psychoanalyst.*)

CONNECTION: CHAPTER 10

Freud's *theory of personality* emphasized the unconscious causes of everyday behavior, as well as mental disorder.

The Humanistic View

The other main variation on the clinical view is called **humanistic psychology.** According to this perspective, our actions are hugely influenced by our self-concept and by our need for personal growth and fulfillment. Far more than the psychoanalysts, humanistic therapists emphasize the positive side of our nature: human ability, growth, and potential.

Led by the likes of Abraham Maslow (1968, 1970, 1971) and Carl Rogers (1951, 1961, 1977), humanistic psychologists have also rejected what they saw as the cold, mechanical approach of scientific psychology. In its place, they have offered a model of human nature emphasizing the free will people have to make choices affecting their lives. They have also pressed psychology to take a greater interest in feelings and the self-concept (Cushman, 1990). As you might have suspected, humanistic psychologists have not produced a great deal of scientific research, although their voluminous writings have had a major impact on the practice of counseling and psychotherapy.

● Humanistic psychologists are interested in discovering how self-actualizing individuals, such as Martin Luther King, Jr., are able to unleash their potential for leadership and creativity.

The Behavioral View

A wholly different approach harks back to John Watson and the early days of psychology. *Behaviorism* says we should look for the causes of behavior in our environment rather than in our biology or our minds (Murray et al., 2000). This **behavioral view,** then, calls attention to the ways rewards and punishments shape how we act.

As we saw a few pages ago, in our discussion of psychology's historical roots, behaviorism first emerged as a revolution against the subjective methods used by Wundt, James, and others in the structuralist and functionalist traditions. In brief, the behaviorists totally reject a science of inner experience. Instead, they choose to study the person entirely from the outside, focusing only on what they can observe directly: the effects of people, objects, and events on behavior. And this is still the approach taken by hard-core behaviorists (although we will see in Chapter 6 that some renegades, calling themselves *cognitive behaviorists,* have opened behaviorism's door to mental processes). The behaviorists have made their greatest contribution by giving us a detailed understanding of how the environment affects learning—especially through rewards and punishments.

B. F. Skinner, the most influential American behaviorist, argued that the concept of "mind" has led psychology in circles, chasing something so subjective that it cannot even be proved to exist (Skinner, 1987, 1989, 1990). (Think about it: Can you prove that you have a mind?) As Skinner noted wryly, "The crucial age-old mistake is the belief that . . . what we feel as we behave is the cause of our behaving" (Skinner, 1989, p. 17).

■ **Humanistic psychology** A clinical viewpoint emphasizing human ability, growth, potential, and free will.

■ **Behavioral view** A psychological perspective that finds the source of our actions in environmental stimuli, rather than in inner mental processes.

Sociocultural view A psychological perspective emphasizing the importance of social interaction, social learning, and a cultural perspective.

Culture A complex blend of language, beliefs, customs, values, and traditions developed by a group of people and shared with others in the same environment.

The Sociocultural View

Who could deny that people exert powerful influences on each other? The **sociocultural view** makes this idea of *social influence* the focus of psychology. Social psychologists have used this perspective to probe the mysteries of liking, loving, prejudice, aggression, obedience, and conformity.

And speaking of culture (as we were a moment ago), even social psychologists overlooked the effects of the larger social context called **culture** until recently. As a complex blend of human language, beliefs, customs, values, and traditions, culture exerts profound influences on all of us—as we can readily see by comparing people in, say, the California-Mexican culture of San Diego with the Scandinavian-based culture of Minnesota. Psychology's blindness to culture was due, in part, to the beginnings of scientific psychology in Europe and North America, where most psychologists lived and worked under similar cultural conditions (Lonner & Malpass, 1994; Segall et al., 1998).

Now the perspective has begun to broaden. Although nearly half of the world's half-million psychologists still live and work in the United States, it is encouraging to note that interest in psychology is also growing in countries outside of Europe and North America (Pawlik & d'Ydewalle, 1996; Rosenzweig, 1992, 1999). Even so, most of our psychological knowledge still has a North American/European flavor (Cushman, 1990). Recognizing this bias, cross-cultural psychologists have begun the long task of reexamining the "laws" of psychology across cultural and ethnic boundaries (Fowers & Richardson, 1996; Gergen et al., 1996; Segall et al., 1998; Triandis, 1994, 1995).

The Evolutionary/Sociobiological View

Do you think your ancestors 150 years ago behaved similarly to the way you and your family behave today? Did they face the same survival challenges we face in the modern world? The evolutionary/sociobiological approach to psychology examines individual behavior through the lens of natural selection. This method looks at behavior as both adaptive and hereditary. At its most basic level, this approach applies the evolutionary theories of Charles Darwin to individual behavior. In this way psychologists can trace the development of behaviors unique to specific animals, or even species-specific behavior patterns, and show how they have adaptively evolved over time. Studying the species-specific behavior patterns of animals helps us understand human behavior patterns. One key component of the evolutionary approach is that these theorists look at genetics not as the key to what makes people different, but as the means by which we have evolved, and continue to evolve, into the thinking beings we are today. Indeed, it is possible to think of evolutionary psychology as an approach, rather than a specific field of study, such as behavioral genetics.

● Cross-cultural psychologists, such as this researcher in Kenya, furnish important data for checking the validity of psychological knowledge.

The Trait View

The Greeks, who seem to have had their hands in almost everything, proclaimed that our personalities are ruled by four body *humors* (fluids): blood, phlegm, melancholer, and yellow bile. Depending on which fluid is most abundant, the individual's personality might be sanguine (dominated by blood), slow and deliberate (phlegm), melancholy (melancholer), or angry and aggressive (yellow bile).

We no longer buy into the ancient Greeks' typology, of course, but their idea of personality traits lives on in modern psychology, especially among psychologists interested in personality and personality testing. *Traits,* to a psychologist, are long-lasting personality characteristics, such as introversion or extraversion—as contrasted with temporary mood states. This **trait view** is common among psychologists who do mental testing, including clinical, counseling, and I/O psychologists.

CONNECTION: CHAPTER 10
People's personalities differ on five major trait dimensions, cleverly called the *Big Five.*

The trait view is widely embraced by experimentalists and teachers of psychology, especially among those who are interested in the field of personality. We will see later in the book that proponents of this trait perspective have identified five major personality dimensions, cleverly named the *Big Five.* Significantly, these dimensions have proved to be valid for classifying people living in virtually any culture around the world.

■ **Trait view** A psychological perspective that views behavior and personality as the products of enduring psychological characteristics.

To summarize the perspectives we have just covered, please have a look at Table 1.1. There you will find an overview of the main viewpoints that make

TABLE 1.1 Nine Major Perspectives in Modern Psychology

Perspective	Overview	What Determines Behavior?	Problems and Questions for Study
Biological	We are essentially complex biological systems that respond to both hereditary and environmental influences. This view includes *evolutionary psychology.*	Behavior is determined by brain structure and chemicals, and by inborn responses to external cues for survival and reproduction.	How do heredity, the nervous system, and the endocrine system produce behavior and mental processes? Evolutionary psychologists seek to learn how behaviors may be linked to evolutionary changes that conferred a survival or reproductive advantage on our ancestors.
Developmental	People undergo predictable patterns of change throughout their lives.	Behavior is determined by the interaction of nature and nurture (heredity and environment).	What are the patterns that characterize developmental change? What are the genetic and environmental influences underlying these patterns?
Cognitive	People are information-processing systems.	Behavior is the result of our mental interpretations of our experience.	How do mental processes, including sensation, perception, learning, memory, and language, influence behavior?
Psychodynamic	*Psychodynamic psychology* emphasizes dark forces in the unconscious.	Psychodynamic theory sees behavior as arising from unconscious needs, conflicts, repressed memories, and childhood experiences.	How does the energy generated in the unconscious mind motivate our actions and account for mental disorders?
Humanistic	*Humanistic psychology* emphasizes human growth and potential.	Humanistic theory focuses on the influence of self-concept, perceptions, and interpersonal relationships, and on need for personal growth.	How can humanistic theory be applied to enhance mental health through counseling and therapy?
Behavioral	Our behavior is primarily shaped by learning.	In accordance with the laws of behavioral learning, we respond to stimulus cues and to our history of rewards and punishments.	What are the "laws" that associate our responses with stimulus conditions? How can they be applied to improve the human condition?
Sociocultural	People are social animals, so human behavior must be interpreted in its social context.	Behavior is heavily influenced by culture, by social norms and expectations, and by social learning.	Under what conditions is the social and cultural situation predictive of behavior? How are social influences different across cultures?
Evolutionary/ Sociobiological	Behavior has developed and adapted over time.	Behavior is determined by natural selection.	How do behavior and individual differences develop and change?
Trait	Individual differences result from differences in our underlying patterns of stable characteristics (traits).	Behavior results from each person's unique combination of traits.	How many fundamental traits are there? How can we use trait patterns to predict behavior?

up the spectrum of modern psychology. A few moments taken to fix these perspectives in your mind will pay big dividends in your understanding of the chapters that follow, where we will refer to them often.

The Changing Face of Psychology

Modern psychology is a field in flux. Over the last several decades, the biological, cognitive, and developmental perspectives have become dominant. And among psychologists espousing a sociocultural perspective, those who put the emphasis on culture are gaining ascendancy. Meanwhile, the behavioral camp seems to be losing ground, as are the Freudian folk, among those holding the clinical perspective. We also call your attention to an especially noteworthy trend among psychologists who are women and members of minority groups.

Ethnic minorities—especially Asians, African Americans, and Latinos—are becoming psychologists in increasing numbers (Kohout, 2001). Even more striking is the new majority status of women in psychology. In 1906, only 12% of American psychologists were women, according to a listing in *American Men of Science* (named with no irony intended). By 1921 the proportion had risen above 20%. And now, women receive approximately two-thirds of the new doctorates awarded in psychology each year (Kohout, 2001).

Although psychology has always included a higher proportion of women than any of the other sciences, women have too often found gender-related biases in their psychological career paths (Furumoto & Scarborough, 1986). For example, G. Stanley Hall, one of the pioneers of American psychology, maintained that academic work would ruin a woman's health and cause deterioration of her reproductive organs. Nevertheless, as early as 1905 the American Psychological Association elected its first female president, Mary Whiton Calkins (Furumoto, 1991). Calkins had earlier been denied a doctorate by Harvard University because of her gender, even though she had completed all the requirements. In these early days of psychology, as in all fields of science, women were pressured to choose between marriage and career. Amazingly, even those who managed a career were usually limited to teaching at women's colleges, positions with less prestige. Still, they made important contributions to their developing field, as you can see in a sampling presented in Table 1.2.

TABLE 1.2 Early Contributions Made by Women in Psychology

	Research Area	Institutional Affiliation
Christine Ladd Franklin	logic and color vision	Johns Hopkins University
Kate Gordon	memory and attention	Mt. Holyoke, Carnegie Tech.
Julia Gulliver	dreams and the subconscious self	Rockford University
Alice Hinman	attention and distraction	University of Nebraska
Lillien Martin	psychophysics	Wellesley College
Anna McKeag	pain	Bardwell School
Naomi Norsworthy	abilities of the child	Columbia Teachers College
Millicent Shinn	child development	unaffiliated
Helen Thompson	mental traits	Mt. Holyoke College
Margaret Washburn	perception	Vassar College
Mabel Williams	visual illusions	unaffiliated

Source: The 1906 edition of *American Men of Science.*

PSYCHOLOGY IN YOUR LIFE: PSYCHOLOGY AS A MAJOR

Becoming a full-fledged psychologist requires substantial training beyond the bachelor's degree. The psychology graduate student takes advanced classes in one or more specialized areas and develops skills as a scholar, researcher, or even practitioner. Upon completion of the program, the student receives a master's or doctor's degree, typically a PhD (Doctor of Philosophy), an EdD (Doctor of Education), or a PsyD (Doctor of Psychology).

Satisfying careers are available, however, at various levels of education in psychology. In most states, a license to practice psychology requires a graduate degree (usually a doctorate) and a supervised internship. Most college and university teaching or research jobs in psychology also require a doctorate.

A master's degree, typically requiring two years of study beyond the bachelor's level, may qualify you for employment as a psychology instructor at the high school level or as an applied psychologist in certain specialties, such as counseling. Master's-level psychologists are common in human service agencies, as well as in private practice (although many states do not allow them to advertise themselves as "psychologists"). In addition, many practitioners with master's degrees in the related field of social work offer therapy for emotional problems.

Holders of associate degrees and bachelor's degrees in psychology or related human services fields may find jobs as psychological aides and technicians in agencies, hospitals, nursing homes, and rehabilitation centers. If this is your goal, however, you should know that salaries at this level are relatively low (Kohout, 2000). A bachelor's degree in psychology, coupled with training in business or education, can also lead to interesting careers in personnel management or education.

Aside from studying to be a psychologist, some students aspire to be psychiatrists. To become a psychiatrist, a student must graduate from college, go to medical school for an MD (Doctor of Medicine), and then complete an extensive residency and training program. It takes about the same amount of time to become a psychiatrist as to become a psychologist, but psychiatrists and psychologists serve different purposes. Only psychiatrists can engage in "true" psychoanalysis or prescribe medication.

If you would like further information about job prospects and salary levels for psychologists, the U.S. Department of Labor's *Occupational Outlook Handbook* is a good place to start. Your high school's career or counseling center probably has a copy.

CHECK YOUR UNDERSTANDING

1. **APPLICATION:** Which of the following approaches to psychology would say that the differences between the behavior of males and females are the result of different survival and reproduction issues faced by the two sexes?
   a. psychoanalytic theory
   b. evolutionary/sociobiological psychology
   c. the trait view
   d. the sociocultural perspective
   e. the biological view

2. **RECALL:** Mental processes such as perception, thinking, and remembering are sometimes called
   a. social cues.
   b. affective events.
   c. neural nets.
   d. dependent variables.
   e. cognition.

(*continues*)

3. **APPLICATION:** If you were a teacher trying to understand how students learn, which of the following viewpoints would be most helpful?
   a. the cognitive view
   b. psychoanalytic theory
   c. evolutionary psychology
   d. the trait view
   e. the developmental view

4. **UNDERSTANDING THE CORE CONCEPT:** In which one of the following sets are *all* factors associated with the perspective indicated?
   a. memory, personality, environment: the behavioral perspective
   b. changes through the lifespan, changes as the result of mental disorders, changes a result of social pressure: the developmental perspective
   c. mental health, mental disorder, mental imagery: the trait perspective
   d. neuroscience, evolutionary psychology, genetics: the biological perspective
   e. sensation, perception, memory: the psychoanalytic perspective

ANSWERS: 1. b 2. e 3. a 4. d

USING PSYCHOLOGY TO LEARN PSYCHOLOGY

Studying with Key Questions and Core Concepts

In this book, your authors have attempted to help you find meaningful patterns that will aid you in making a mental map (sometimes called a *cognitive map*) of every chapter. To do so, we have built in many learning devices. Among the most important are the Key Questions and the Core Concepts. Let us show you how using these features can make your study of psychology easier.

The Key Questions, which take the place of the familiar section headings in each chapter, give you a "heads up" by signaling what to watch for as you read. For example, one of the Key Questions from this chapter asked, "What are the perspectives psychologists use today?" It alerted you to the idea that psychologists have some special ways of looking at mind and behavior that are different from those used in the past. You are much more likely to remember these new concepts if you approach them with an appropriate question in mind (Bransford et al., 1986; Brown & Campione, 1986; Glaser, 1984). You can also use the Key Question as a review-check of your understanding of each section before the next test. If you have a study partner, try asking each other to give detailed answers to the key questions.

You can think of Core Concepts as brief responses to the Key Questions. They also highlight the central idea in each chapter section—as previews of coming attractions. It is important to realize that a Core Concept is not a complete answer but a capsule summary of ideas to be fleshed out. As you come to understand the meaning of a Core Concept, you will see that the details of the section—the terms, names, and important research—will fall easily into place. And to reinforce your understanding, it is a good idea to revisit the Core Concept after you have finished reading the section. In fact, this is precisely what the brief end-of-section quizzes (Check Your Understanding) are designed to do.

Another good way to use the Core Concepts is to see if you can explain how the terms in boldface link to the Core Concepts. Let's take the second Core Concept in this chapter, which says;

> Modern psychology developed from several conflicting traditions, including structuralism, functionalism, Gestalt psychology, behaviorism, and psychoanalysis.

Can you explain, for example, how the term *introspection* is related to this Core Concept? (Sample answer: Only the behaviorists, among the historical schools in psychology, refused to use introspection because it was subjective.)

Together, then, the Key Questions and Core Concepts are designed to pose important questions that lead you to the big ideas in the chapter. They will help you step back from the details to see meaningful patterns.

CHAPTER SUMMARY

KEY QUESTION

CORE CONCEPT

• WHAT IS PSYCHOLOGY—AND WHAT IS IT *NOT*?

All psychologists are concerned with some aspect of behavior and mental processes. Unlike the pseudosciences, scientific psychology demands solid evidence to back up its claims. Within psychology there are many specialties that fall in three broad areas. Experimental psychologists primarily do research, but they often teach, as well. Those who are primarily teachers of psychology work in a variety of settings, including colleges, universities, and high schools. Applied psychologists practice many specialties, such as engineering, school, rehabilitation, and clinical psychology, and counseling. In contrast with psychology, psychiatry is a medical specialty that deals with mental disorder.

● **Psychology is a broad field with many specialties, but fundamentally, psychology is the scientific study of behavior and mental processes.**

• WHAT ARE PSYCHOLOGY'S HISTORICAL ROOTS?

Psychology has its roots in several often-conflicting traditions stretching back to the ancient Greeks. René Descartes helped the study of the mind to become scientific, through his insight that sensations and behaviors are linked to activity in the nervous system. The formal beginning of psychology as a science is traced to the establishment by Wundt of the first psychological laboratory in 1879. Wundt's structuralism advocated understanding mental processes such as consciousness by investigating their contents and structure. Another early school of psychology, known as functionalism, argued that mental processes are best understood in terms of their adaptive purposes and functions. Also in opposition to structuralism, Gestalt psychology focused on perceptual "wholes," rather than on parts of consciousness. Psychoanalysis differed from the other schools of psychology by emphasizing the unconscious, while behaviorism staked its uniqueness on a rejection of introspection.

● **Modern psychology developed from several conflicting traditions, including structuralism, functionalism, Gestalt psychology, behaviorism, and psychoanalysis.**

• WHAT ARE THE PERSPECTIVES PSYCHOLOGISTS USE TODAY?

Modern psychology encompasses nine main viewpoints. The biological view looks for the causes of behavior in physical processes such as brain function and genetics. Using cutting-edge technology, neuroscientists using this perspective have made many discoveries about brain function. Many biological psychologists take an evolutionary approach, assuming that human behavior and mental processes are based on genetic adaptations for survival and reproductive advantage. This approach has generated influential theories that explain gender differences and aggressive behavior. The developmental view calls attention to mental and behavioral changes that occur throughout the lifespan. Such changes result from the interaction of heredity and environment. The cognitive view emphasizes information processing; it has made many discoveries about learning, memory, sensation, perception, language, and thinking. Cognitive neuroscientists are especially interested in the link between the brain and mental processes. The psychodynamic view, pioneered by Sigmund Freud, proposes that behavior and thought are influenced by inner, often unconscious psychological forces and conflicts. Its impact has been greatest in therapy. The humanistic view, characterizes human functioning as motivated by a desire to grow, be productive, and fulfill one's human potential. Both have influenced our understanding of personality and the practice of psychotherapy. The behavioral view rejects mentalistic explanations and explains behavior in terms of observable stimuli and responses. It has given us powerful insights into the nature of learning. The sociocultural view recognizes the power of society and cultural context on individual thought, feeling, and action, notably through social learning. Cross-cultural psychologists, who take a sociocultural perspective, are working to incorporate information about other cultures into a field that has historically been dominated by psychologists from Europe and the United States. The evolutionary/sociobiological view takes the approach that changes in behavior have an evolutionary or adaptive cause. The trait view emphasizes enduring personality characteristics, and it is popular among applied psychologists involved in mental testing and clinical work.

● **Nine main perspectives characterize modern psychology: the biological, developmental, cognitive, psychdynamic, humanistic, behavioral, sociocultural, evolutionary/sociobiological, and trait views.**

REVIEW TEST

For each of the following items, choose the single best answer. The answer key appears at the end.

1. Psychology's scientific origins are usually traced to the late 19th century, when ______ established the first psychological laboratory.

   a. Sigmund Freud
   b. William James
   c. John B. Watson
   d. Max Wertheimer
   e. Wilhelm Wundt

2. "To understand consciousness or behavior, you must focus on the probable purpose of an action or process." This statement reflects the arguments of
   a. humanism.
   b. functionalism.
   c. Gestalt psychology.
   d. structuralism.
   e. behaviorism.

3. According to the ______ approach, which is a variation of the ______ view, a person's behavior and personality develop as a result of unconscious inner tensions and conflicts.
   a. behaviorist/trait
   b. evolutionary/biological
   c. introspective/cognitive
   d. psychodynamic/clinical
   e. structuralist/behavioral

4. Which of psychology's nine perspectives says that psychology should *not* study mental processes, such as sensation, perception, memory, thinking, motivation, and emotion?
   a. behavioral
   b. biological
   c. cognitive
   d. evolutionary/sociobiological
   e. trait

5. According to the evolutionary approach in modern psychology, human behavior is the result of the natural selection of behaviors that promote
   a. cultural conformity.
   b. ability to process information.
   c. survival and reproduction.
   d. conflict between individual goals and societal limits.
   e. appropriate responses to novel situations.

6. All of the following areas are applied psychology specialties, *except*
   a. cognitive psychology.
   b. counseling psychology.
   c. clinical psychology.
   d. school psychology.
   e. industrial/organizational psychology.

7. The cognitive view of psychology:
   a. subscribes to the idea that changes as we grow affect our personality.
   b. has a special interest in mental health and mental disorders.
   c. has a special interest in how the operation of your brain influences personality.
   d. subscribes to the idea that human traits arise from hereditary characteristics.
   e. subscribes to the idea that thoughts and actions arise from the way we interpret experiences.

8. Which researcher is most closely associated with the founding of humanistic psychology?
   a. Sigmund Freud
   b. Max Wertheimer
   c. William James
   d. Carl Rogers
   e. John Watson

9. The tendency to attend to evidence that confirms our expectations is known as:
   a. confirmational bias.
   b. empirical investigation.
   c. functionalism.
   d. introspection.
   e. Gestalt perspective.

10. The statement "Behavior has developed over eons of time" most directly reflects the perspective of
   a. developmental psychology.
   b. clinical psychology.
   c. behavioral psychology.
   d. trait psychology.
   e. evolutionary psychology.

ANSWERS: 1. e 2. b 3. d 4. a 5. c 6. a 7. e 8. d 9. a 10. e

AP* REVIEW: VOCABULARY

Match each of the following vocabulary terms to its definition.

1. Psychology
2. Structuralism
3. Functionalism
4. Cognitive view
5. Trait view
6. Developmental view
7. Behavioral view
8. Evolutionary/sociobiological view
9. Biological view
10. Humanistic view

_____ a. People are information-processing systems.

_____ b. Behavior is shaped by learning.

_____ c. The scientific study of behavior and mental processes.

_____ d. Emphasized human growth and potential.

_____ e. Behavior has developed and adapted over time.

_____ f. People are complex systems that respond to both environmental and hereditary influences.

_____ g. School of psychology devoted to uncovering the basic structures that make up mind and thought.

_____ h. People undergo predictable patterns of change throughout their lives.

_____ i. School of psychology that believed that mental processes should be understood in terms of their adaptive purpose.

_____ j. Individual differences result in our underlying patterns of stable characteristics.

AP* REVIEW: ESSAY

Use your knowledge of the chapter concepts to answer the following essay question.

There are many differing approaches to psychology. Two of them are diametrically opposed, namely the psychodynamic and behavioral approaches. Describe how these views of psychology differ, being sure to address the following:

a. founders

b. main areas of interest

c. typical research topics

KEY TERMS

Psychology (p. 2)
Empirical approach (p. 3)
Pseudopsychology (p. 4)
Confirmation bias (p. 4)
Experimental psychologists (p. 6)
Teachers of psychology (p. 7)
Applied psychologists (p. 7)
Psychiatry (p. 8)
Structuralism (p. 11)
Introspection (p. 11)
Functionalism (p. 12)
Gestalt psychology (p. 12)
Behaviorism (p. 12)
Psychoanalysis (p. 13)
Biological view (p. 15)
Neuroscience (p. 15)
Evolutionary psychology (p. 15)
Developmental view (p. 16)
Cognitive view (p. 16)
Cognitions (p. 16)
Cognitive neuroscience (p. 16)
Clinical view (p. 16)
Psychodynamic psychology (p. 16)
Humanistic psychology (p. 17)
Behavioral view (p. 17)
Sociocultural view (p. 18)
Evolutionary/sociobiological view (p. 18)
Trait view (p. 19)

OUR RECOMMENDED BOOKS AND VIDEOS

ARTICLE

Morgeson, F. P., Seligman, M. E. P., Sternberg, R. J., Taylor, S. E., & Manning, C. M. (1999). Lessons learned from a life in psychological science: Implications for young scientists. *American Psychologist, 54,* 106–115. Interested in becoming a psychologist? Read this article in which a panel of well-known psychologists discuss their early careers and reveal what they know now that they wish they had known then.

BOOKS

Burr, C. (2004). *The emperor of scent: A true story of perfume and obsession.* New York: Random House. We know least about our most ancient sense. Yet in this true story, when a likable scientist claims he has discovered the true inner workings of the sense of smell, he is dismissed by peers, must struggle to publish his findings in *Nature,* and next meets with resistance from the fragrance industry. This book is an exposé of scientific publication as well as an exploration of the olfactory sense.

Hunt, M. (1993). *The story of psychology.* New York: Doubleday. The fascinating anecdotes, summaries, and documentation in this book cover the lives and times of what Morton Hunt calls "the Magellans of the mind," from ancient philosophy to modern research.

Pinker, S. (2003). *The blank slate: The modern denial of human nature.* New York: Viking. Steven Pinker, MIT psychology professor and author of *How the Mind Works* and *The Language Instinct,* uses wit, poetry, and comedy to argue against the notion that the human infant's brain is a "blank slate" at birth, insisting that evolution provides strong, inherited, survival-oriented skills—with ample room for shaping by culture and experience.

VIDEO

Fast, cheap, and out of control. (1997, color, 82 min). Directed by Errol Morris; starring Dave Hoover, George Mendonca, Ray Mendez, and Rodney Books. This documentary has interviews with four eccentric "geniuses"—a lion tamer, a topiary gardener, an expert on the African naked mole rat, and an MIT robotics scientist—mixed with B-movie footage and running commentary on life and human nature. (*Rating PG*)

Key Question Chapter Outline

CORE CONCEPTS

Psychology in Your Life

How Do Psychologists Develop New Knowledge?

- The Five Steps of the Scientific Method
- Types of Psychological Research
- Sources of Bias in Research (or Anywhere Else)
- Ethics in Research
- Questions Science Cannot Answer

Psychologists, like researchers in all other sciences, use the scientific method to test their ideas empirically.

Getting in Deeper

Whatever your major, consider getting a student membership in a professional organization and reading some of the journals.

How Do We Make Sense of the Data?

- Developing Your Own Survey
- Organizing the Data
- Describing the Data with Descriptive Statistics
- Correlation: A Relationship Between Two Variables
- Making Inferences with Inferential Statistics

▼

Researchers use statistics for two major purposes: (1) descriptively to characterize measurements made on groups or individuals and (2) inferentially to judge whether those measurements are the result of chance.

Statistics in Politics

Politicians rely on statistics to measure the responses to their platform, ideas, and job performance.

USING PSYCHOLOGY TO LEARN PSYCHOLOGY
Research in Practice

Chapter

2

Research Methods

Japan versus America: Differences in Health and Body Image
10

YUMI AND MARIA WERE TWO teenage girls from similar suburban backgrounds who grew up together and attended the same schools. Intrigued by their psychology class discussions, Yumi, of Japanese descent, and Maria, of European/American descent, began contemplating whether the differences in their heritage affected their views on personal issues.

The teens were determined to find out if Japanese and American teenagers viewed body image and health issues differently. Specifically, they wanted to know if either group perceived themselves as heavier or thinner; whether or not there were differences in the perceptions of body image between the two groups; and whether there were any differences between body image and health among the groups.

Admittedly a complicated quest, the teens first looked around for existing information to answer these questions. Finding none, the girls decided to conduct their own research. So, how did two teenagers from Washington, D.C. go about finding answers to their questions? They used a scientific approach. Beginning with their initial discussions, the identification of their questions, the review of available research, and on through the creation of a survey, analysis of the results, and a review of their methodology, Yumi and Maria employed the basic methods of science—the same principles and processes psychologists use everyday to answer their own questions, test their own theories, and gain knowledge. The scientific method, whether conducted by teenagers to answer personal questions about their peers, or conducted by psychologists, is our focus in this chapter.

HOW DO PSYCHOLOGISTS DEVELOP NEW KNOWLEDGE?

As early as 1880, psychologists were challenging the claims of spiritualists and psychics (Coon, 1992). But even today, psychology continues to dispute the unfounded claims of *pseudoscience,* which seem to blossom faster than they can be nipped in the bud. Modern sources of questionable psychology include practitioners of astrology, palmistry, graphology, biorhythm analysis, and any number of psychics, seers, and prophets who claim to have special insights into people's personalities and to be able to predict their futures.

But what makes psychology different from the pseudoscientific approaches to understanding people? Answer: None of the pseudosciences has survived trial by the *scientific method,* which is a way of rigorously testing ideas against objective observations. Instead, pseudoscience is based on mere speculation and anecdote—and on human gullibility.

You might think this a snobbish view for psychologists to take. Why can't we make room for many different approaches to the understanding of people? In fact, we do. Psychologists have no problem with sociology, anthropology, and psychiatry, for example, as partners in the enterprise of understanding people. Psychologists reject only those approaches that claim to have "evidence" but offer only anecdotes and testimonials.

What, then, makes psychology a real science? Again, it's the *method.* As our Core Concept for this section says:

Psychologists, like researchers in all other sciences, use the scientific method to test their ideas empirically.

What is this marvelous method? Simply put, the **scientific method** is a process for putting ideas to an objective pass–fail test. At the heart of this testing procedure is **empirical investigation,** the collecting of objective information firsthand by making careful measurements based on direct experience. Literally, *empirical* means "experience based"—as contrasted with speculation based solely on faith, hope, authority, or common sense. To investigate a question empirically is to collect evidence yourself, rather than relying solely on a logical argument or appealing to the opinion of "experts." Ultimately, a main goal of psychological science is to develop explanations for behavior and mental processes—explanations based on solid empirical studies. We call these explanations *theories.*

CONNECTION: CHAPTER 6

Social learning is acquiring a new behavior by watching others and seeing how they are rewarded and punished for their behavior.

In brief, a **theory** is a testable explanation for a set of facts or observations (Kerlinger, 1985; Kukla, 1989). Please note that this definition may be quite different from the way you customarily use the term. In everyday language, "theory" can mean "wild speculation" or a mere "hunch"—an idea that has no evidence to support it. "It's only a theory," people may say. But *theory* means something quite different to a scientist. The essence of a scientific theory is its power to explain the facts and its ability to be tested objectively. Some theories have a great deal of evidence to support them, while others are highly speculative. Examples of well-supported theories include Einstein's theory of relativity, the germ theory of disease, Darwin's theory of natural selection, and, in psychology, social learning theory (which we will discuss in Chapter 6).

■ **Scientific method** A five-step process for empirical investigation of a hypothesis under conditions designed to control biases and subjective judgments.
■ **Empirical investigation** An approach to research that relies on sensory experience and observation as research data.
■ **Theory** A testable explanation for a set of facts or observations. In science, a theory is *not* just speculation or a guess.

To illustrate the scientific method in action, we would remind you how Dr. Pfungst put Clever Hans to the test. But to take a more recent example, let's look at a simple and elegant psychological experiment published in the *Journal of the American Medical Association* by . . . a fourth grader (Rosa et al., 1998)! Meet Emily Rosa of Loveland, Colorado. Emily's school science project, it turned out, challenged a widely held belief in the power of *therapeutic touch* (TT).

In the early 1990s, TT was touted as a medical therapy, and Emily's mother, a nurse, had explained to her how TT practitioners attempted to promote healing by moving their hands over the patient's body without directly touching it. In doing so, they believed that they were detecting and manipulating an energy field radiating from the body. These practitioners claimed they could use TT to treat a wide range of medical and psychological problems—from colic to cancer and arthritis to depression (Gorman, 1999). So effective was it believed to be that the technique was being taught in more than 100 colleges and universities in 75 countries and used by nurses in at least 80 U.S. hospitals.

But did it really work, or was it just another example of flawed common sense? Emily Rosa suspected that TT practitioners were really detecting their own beliefs and expectations, rather than a "human energy field." So she put their claims to a simple experimental test, the details of which we will use to illustrate the scientific method.

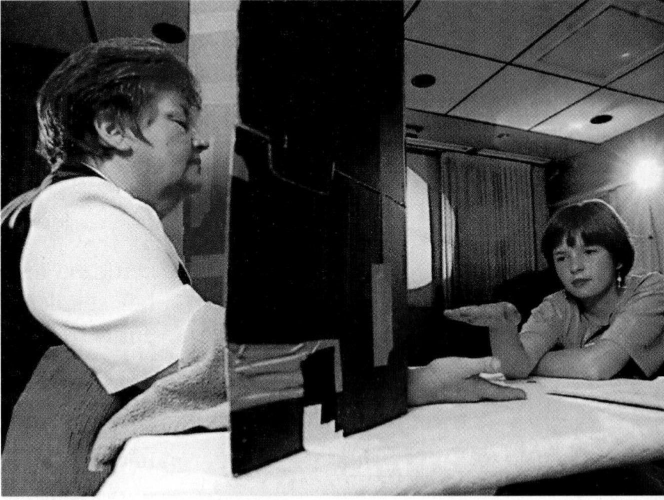

Emily Rosa's experiment

The Five Steps of the Scientific Method

Testing any scientific assertion requires five steps. (See Figure 2.1.) These steps are essentially the same whether the study involves psychology, biology, chemistry, astronomy, or any other scientific discipline. Thus it is the *method* that makes these fields scientific, not their subject matter. Ideally, a researcher (such as Emily Rosa) who follows the scientific method will proceed as follows.

Developing a Hypothesis The first step calls for coming up with a testable idea, or prediction. Scientists call this prediction a **hypothesis.** The term literally means "little theory" because it often represents only one piece of a larger

Hypothesis A statement predicting the outcome of a scientific study; a statement describing the relationship among variables in a study.

1. Developing a hypothesis

2. Performing a controlled test

?

3. Gathering objective data

Trial	Correct	Incorrect
1	✓	
2		✓
3	✓	✓
4		

4. Analyzing the results

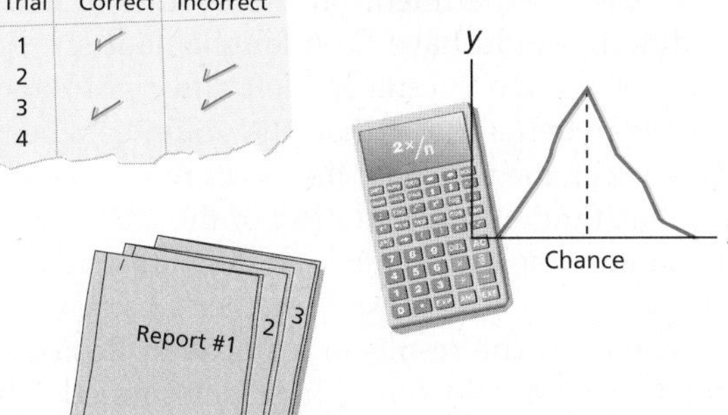
y
x
Chance
Report #1
2
3

5. Publishing, criticizing, and replicating the results

FIGURE 2.1 Five Steps of the Scientific Method

theoretical puzzle. For example, a hypothesis stating that introverted people are attracted to extraverted people might be part of a larger, more complex theory tying together all the factors that affect romantic attraction. Sometimes, however, a hypothesis can be just an interesting idea that piques the scientist's curiosity—as was the case in Emily Rosa's experiment. Her hypothesis came simply from questioning the value of a treatment (therapeutic touch) that everyone "knew" to be effective.

Like any good scientist, Emily stated her hypothesis in such a way that it could be tested and *falsified* (shown to be either correct or incorrect). To make her suspicion testable, Rosa had to follow an ironclad requirement of all scientific research: She had to give **operational definitions** for all the terms in her hypothesis. That is, she had to specify the exact procedures (operations) she would use in setting up the experimental conditions and measuring the results.

Emily wondered: Could TT practitioners accurately sense the presence of her hand when it was placed above one of their hands but out of sight? She hypothesized that they could not. In our earlier example, the study of Clever Hans, Dr. Pfungst also operationalized his hypothesis by stating that the horse could not give the right number of taps with its hoof when it couldn't see its owner or when the owner couldn't see the written questions. Here again, the hypothesis was stated *operationally*—in terms of the procedures that would be used to test it.

So far, so good. But, of course, a scientific study must not stop with a hypothesis. The great failing of pseudosciences like astrology is that they never take the other steps necessary to verify or reject their assertions. Among scientists, however, a hypothesis will be taken seriously only after it has been subjected to rigorous testing.

Performing a Controlled Test A hypothesis must undergo an "ordeal of proof"—a test that it will either pass or fail. Here's how Emily Rosa conducted her test: She invited each of 21 TT practitioners (varying in experience from 1 to 27 years) to determine which of their two hands (thrust, palms up, through holes in a screen) was closest to one of her own hands (held palm down, a few inches from either of the practitioner's hands).

In order to control the conditions of her experiment, Rosa varied only one part of the situation on each trial: whether her hand was above the subject's left or right hand. We call this variable condition the **independent variable (IV).** Think of the independent variable as a condition that the experimenter changes *independently* of all the other carefully controlled experimental conditions. The independent variable always involves a systematic variation on the conditions that the experimenter is evaluating in a study. In Pfungst's study of Clever Hans, the independent variable involved systematically changing the conditions so that (a) Hans could not see his owner or (b) the owner could not see the questions being asked.

In Rosa's experiment on therapeutic touch, control over the experimental conditions would have been laughable if she had simply held her hand alternately above the volunteers' left and right hands or followed some other predictable pattern. That is, had the volunteers been able to guess which response was correct, the results of the experiment would have meant nothing. The solution was **random presentation** of the stimulus, which meant that chance alone determined the order in which the stimulus was presented. Random presentation is one tool in the experimenter's bag of tricks for controlling expectations that can skew the results of a study. In Rosa's experiment, randomization was achieved by a coin flip, which determined whether she presented her hand above the practitioner's left or right hand. And in Pfungst's study, randomization meant that there was no predictable pattern (such as 2, 4, 6, 8 . . .) in the correct answers to the problems presented to Hans and his trainer.

■ **Operational definitions** Specific descriptions of concepts involving the conditions of a scientific study. Operational definitions are stated in terms of how the concepts are to be measured or what operations are being employed to produce them.

■ **Independent variable (IV)** A stimulus condition so named because the experimenter changes it independently of all the other carefully controlled experimental conditions.

■ **Random presentation** A process by which chance alone determines the order in which the stimulus is presented.

Gathering Objective Data In the third step of the scientific method, the scientist collects objective **data**: information gathered by direct observation. Such data depend only on the manipulations of the experimental conditions (the independent variable). The data must *not* depend on the experimenter's hopes, expectations, or personal impressions. In Emily Rosa's experiment, the data consisted of the number of correct and incorrect responses during the test—whether the practitioners responded correctly to the placement of her hand. Such responses are referred to as the **dependent variable (DV).** The term comes from the assumption that the responses of participants in an experiment *depend* directly on the conditions to which they have been exposed. As a result, the data will depend on how the independent variable has been manipulated. (You might think of the independent variable as the *stimuli* you are studying and of the dependent variable as the *responses* made by the participants in your experiment.)

In designing an experiment, the dependent variable must also be given an operational definition. That is, the researcher must specify the procedures (operations) that were used in measuring the responses being observed. This is exactly what Emily Rosa did when she described how she required her participants to respond with guesses of "left" or "right." The dependent variable in Pfungst's study consisted of the horse's hoof-tapping response to each question presented.

Analyzing the Results and Accepting or Rejecting the Hypothesis In the fourth step of the scientific method, the researcher examines the results (the data) to see whether the hypothesis survived the test. Based on that analysis, the hypothesis is accepted or rejected. Making this determination usually necessitates some special mathematical tools, particularly if the data require a close call. Statistical analysis can tell the researcher whether the observed results rise to the level of *significance*—that is, whether the results are likely due to the independent variable or merely due to chance.

A detailed explanation of statistics is beyond the scope of this book. In fact, it's a subject for a whole course in itself. But to give you a glimpse of this world, the second part of this chapter offers a brief introduction to statistics.

■ **Data** Pieces of information, especially information gathered by a researcher to be used in testing a hypothesis. (Singular: *datum.*)

■ **Dependent variable (DV)** The measured outcome of a study; the responses of the subjects in a study.

WHAT MAKES STATISTICS UNIQUE IS ITS ABILITY TO QUANTIFY UNCERTAINTY, TO MAKE IT PRECISE. THIS ALLOWS STATISTICIANS TO MAKE CATEGORICAL STATEMENTS, WITH COMPLETE ASSURANCE—ABOUT THEIR LEVEL OF UNCERTAINTY!
GOOD CHOICE! I'M 95% CONFIDENT THAT TONIGHT'S SOUP HAS PROBABILITY BETWEEN 73% AND 77% OF BEING REALLY DELICIOUS!

from "The Cartoon Guide to Statistics" by Larry Gonick & Wollcott Smith

There you will find a summary of key points and examples of how psychological concepts are *quantified* (measured and expressed as numbers) and how those quantities can provide meaning and understanding.

In Rosa's experiment, the statistical analysis was remarkably simple. The chances of getting a correct answer merely by guessing were 50%. That is, half the time the TT practitioners could be expected to give the right answer, even if they had no ability to sense the "human energy field." Accordingly, Rosa set this standard: Her subjects would have to perform significantly above the chance level to support the claim that they can detect a "human energy field." They did not, so she concluded that practitioners of therapeutic touch were not sensing human energy fields.

Much the same analysis applied to Pfungst's study, where the chance level of correct responses would be near zero, and *any* consistent level of correct responses would have supported the hypothesis that Clever Hans could read and calculate. That hypothesis, however, was rejected, because Hans's responses were incorrect when cues from his owner were controlled.

Publishing, Criticizing, and Replicating the Results In the fifth step of the scientific method, researchers must find out whether their work can withstand the scrutiny and criticism of the scientific community. To do so, they might communicate their results to colleagues by publishing them in a professional journal, presenting a paper at a professional meeting, or writing a book. (You may recall that Emily Rosa published her results in the *Journal of the American Medical Association.*) Then they wait for the critics to respond.

If colleagues find the study interesting and important—and especially if it challenges a widely held theory—they may look for flaws in the research design: Did the experimenter choose the participants properly? Were the statistical analyses done correctly? Could other factors account for the results?

Some critics complained that Rosa's experiment was not an accurate representation of the conditions under which therapeutic touch is done: They claimed that TT depends on the transfer of emotional energy during a medical crisis, and because Emily was not sick she didn't have disturbances in her energy field that could be detected by TT practitioners.

Critics could have checked Rosa's work by *replicating* it. To **replicate** her experiment they would redo it, perhaps under slightly different control conditions, to see whether they would get the same results. But as far as we know, Rosa's experiment was never replicated. (Nor was Pfungst's.) At this point, then, we can say that Rosa's experimental results have withstood the scientific test. We should also note that Emily's research earned her a check for $1000 from the Skeptics Society. She also received a plaque from the *Guinness Book of Records* for being the youngest researcher to have a paper published in a major medical journal.

Criticism and replication of research are a part of a thorough, and sometimes intimidating, screening process that goes on behind the scientific scenes to filter out poorly conceived and executed research. As a result, fewer than 2% of the papers submitted to psychological journals get into print without major revisions. In fact, the majority never see print at all (Eichorn & VandenBos, 1985). Journal editors and book publishers (including the publishers of this book) routinely seek the opinion of several expert reviewers for each submission before agreeing to publish it. Different reviewers often focus their criticism on different facets of the study (Fiske & Fogg, 1990). As a result, the author usually receives helpful, if sometimes painful, suggestions for revision. Only when a hypothesis has survived all these tests will editors put it in print and scholars tentatively accept it as scientific "truth." We should emphasize, however, that scientific findings are always tentative—forever in

■ **Replicate** In research, this refers to doing a study over to see whether the same results are obtained. As a control for bias, replication is often done by someone other than the researcher who performed the original study.

jeopardy from a new study that might require a new interpretation and relegate previous work to the scientific scrap heap. Granted, it is an imperfect system, but it is the best method ever developed for testing ideas about the natural world.

Types of Psychological Research

Everything we have ever learned is because of an experiment. Whether we conducted it ourselves or learned it from someone else, it came from an experiment. Some experiments are intentional, such as Newton's experiment to determine the force of gravity or Franklin's discovery of electricity, and some are accidental, such as the discovery of penicillin or how we learned that the stove was hot.

Clearly, research is an essential component of our everyday lives. To be fair, however, not all research is created equal. We look at two methodologies: the experiment, and a variety of quasi-experimental methods. The experiment is probably what first comes to mind when we think of research methodology.

Experimental Method There are many ways to approach the experimental method. Perhaps the best way is to examine the steps in designing an experiment. Table 2.1 lists the components of the research process for an experiment.

The first step in the research process begins with basic inquiry—that is, getting a research idea. What makes you curious? Is there a particular phenomenon that you wonder about, such as learning or remembering? Developing a research question involves generating an hypothesis that is testable, verifiable, and refutable. To determine these things you have to read the literature on your research idea. Some of it can be hard to find, and sometimes it is necessary to narrow down your topic.

After you have developed your hypothesis, you will need to establish your variables. In an experiment we look at three types of variables: independent, dependent, and extraneous (confounding). The independent variable (IV) is the one that the experimenter controls. For example, if you were to conduct an experiment on the effect of light on plant growth, the amount of light provided would be the IV. The dependent variable (DV) is what we measure. In that plant experiment, the amount of growth of the plant is the DV. **Confounding** or **extraneous variables** are other things that can affect the outcome of the experiment. In our example, you would have to ensure that no extra light reached your plants (other than what you specified in your design).

■ **Experiment** A kind of research in which the researcher controls all the conditions and directly manipulates the conditions, including the independent variable.
■ **Confounding** or **extraneous variables** Variables that have an unwanted influence on the outcome of an experiment.
■ **Controls** Constraints that the experimenter places on the experiment to ensure that each subject has the exact same conditions.

The next task is to ensure that you have **controls**—that is, to ensure that all groups in the experiment are treated exactly the same, except for the IV. In the plant experiment, you would have to ensure that all the plants received the same amount of water, were the same species and age, were exposed to the same temperature, and so on. All of these precautions are necessary so that we can be certain that the data we get at the end of the experiment can be replicated and that our conclusions are valid.

Following the development of your procedures, variables, and controls, you will need to select your subjects. Subjects are drawn from a population, which consists of everyone who fits the description of your test group. For example, if we wanted to test how high school students learn, our population would be all high school students. It would be impossible to test every single high school student, so to compensate for that, we would take a representative sample of the population. (See Figure 2.2.)

TABLE 2.1 Components of the Research Process

Components of the Research Process
Developing a research question
Surveying the literature
Hypothesis
Independent variable (IV)
Dependent variable (DV)
Extraneous variables
Controls
Sampling/Subjects (random assignment to groups)
Procedure
Results/Statistics
Discussion

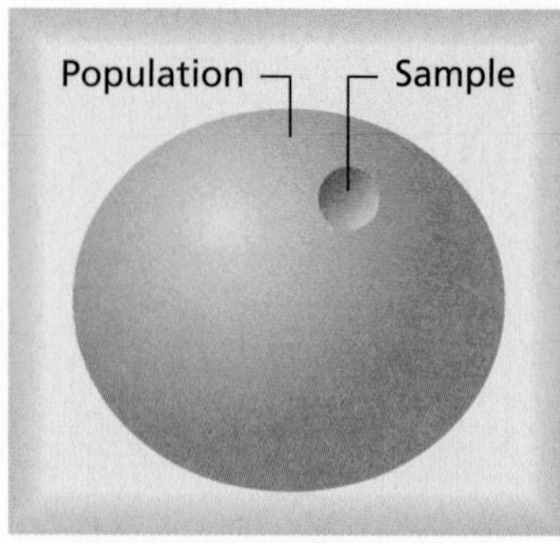
Population
Sample

● **FIGURE 2.2** A representative sample consists of randomly selected individuals who accurately represent the targeted population.

To do that we would randomly select individuals who accurately represent the population of high school students. This is a time-consuming and costly process, but it ensures that that our data will reflect the results we would get if we tested everyone. The ability to choose anyone from the population is referred to as random selection.

Another key thing to keep in mind is that every subject of an experiment must have an equal chance of being in the experimental group (which receives the IV) or the control group (which receives either a placebo or nothing). This is called **random assignment.** Each member of the sample has an equal likelihood of being chosen for the experimental group.

Once the subjects have been selected and assigned, the experiment can begin. Carefully following the procedures laid out in the research design, experimenters conduct their experiment. In their design, they must account for, and try to control, as many aspects of the experiment as possible. The reason for this is to try to remove the influence of outside influences on the experiment. As we have seen, these influences are called *extraneous variables*. The use of controls limits the influence of these so that the results of the experiment accurately reflect what is being tested.

At the conclusion of the experiment, data is collected and subjected to statistical analysis.

Non-Experimental Methods Given that experiments—painstakingly applied—can yield true cause-and-effect statements about a situation, why wouldn't we always do experiments? There are times when we cannot do so for ethical or practical reasons. Take, for example, research on cancer. To conduct a true experiment on a possible cure for lung cancer, we would have to give people lung cancer and then try to cure it. This, of course, would be morally indefensible. Instead, we would choose subjects based on the preexisting condition of having lung cancer, and try to cure them. This design is a *non-experimental* design.

Non-experimental methods can yield useful data. But, they are just not true experiments because they are missing a component of the experiment, usually in the area of controls. Of the seven non-experimental methods listed in Table 2.2, none should be disregarded; rather, all of them need to be applied carefully and with a great deal of planning.

Take the cancer experiment mentioned above. This design, in which we choose subjects on the basis of a preexisting condition, is called **ex post facto** research. We chose this method mainly in response to ethical considerations. Because our treatment for lung cancer is not guaranteed (it is being tested), the treatment might not work. In addition, ethical considerations arise in *not* giving someone the best possible treatment!

■ **Random assignment** Each subject of the sample has an equal likelihood of being chosen for the experimental group of an experiment.

■ **Ex post facto** Research in which we choose subjects based on a pre-existing condition.

■ **Correlational study** A type of research that is mainly statistical in nature. Correlational studies determine the relationship (or correlation) between two variables.

TABLE 2.2 Seven Non-Experimental Methodoligies

- Ex-post facto design
- Correlation study
- Survey
- Naturalistic observation
- Longitudinal study
- Cross-sectional study
- Cohort-sequential study

Correlational Studies An alternative "quasi" design is called a **correlational study.** What we are doing here is seeing the relationship (or correlation) between two variables. For example, when the surgeon general first began telling people that smoking and lung cancer were related, that statement was based on the correlation between people who smoke and the incidence of lung cancer among those people. Not everyone who smokes gets lung cancer, and not everyone who gets lung cancer smokes, but there is a very high correlation between smoking and lung cancer. As scientists often put it, *correlation does not necessarily mean causation.*

Scientists usually express the degree of correlation as a number. This requires calculating a statistic known as the *correlation coefficient*, often symbolized in formulas as the letter *r*. The correlation coefficient summarizes the relationship between the two variables. It can range from a negative number as low as –1.0 to a positive number as high as +1.0.

We won't go into the details of calculating the correlation coefficient here. The important idea is to develop a feeling for what *positive correlation, negative correlation,* and *zero correlation* mean. If the variables have no relationship at all, their correlation is 0. You would expect a zero correlation between shoe size and GPA, for example. If, however, the two variables show a relationship in which they vary in the same direction (as the values of one variable increase, so do those of the other), then we say they have a positive correlation. An example of a positive correlation is the moderate relationship (approximately + 0.4) between SAT scores and college grades.

It is important to understand that *a correlation can show a strong relationship even when it is negative.* Let us suppose that a measure of anxiety (such as a checklist of anxiety-related symptoms) shows a correlation of – 0.7 between anxiety and time spent studying. In other words, more study is associated with less anxiety. Even though this is a negative correlation, it shows a *stronger* relationship than, for example, the positive correlation between SAT scores and grades (+ 0.4).

Another research method is the **survey.** Again, a survey is not a true experiment, but if conducted correctly, it can yield useful data. When designing a survey, the researcher must take great care to make sure the questions are not skewed or biased toward a particular answer. Also, when comparing survey results, one needs to go back and look at both surveys to make sure that the questions and answer scales are parallel. You need to be certain that questions were being asked the same way in order to be able to compare the results and draw conclusions. We will give a detailed example of the survey method later in the chapter.

In **naturalistic observation,** subjects are observed in their natural environment. This method is a good choice for studying, say, child-rearing practices, people's shopping habits, or public courting behaviors. In order to remove demand characteristics, which are cues the experimenter inadvertently gives that tell the subject what "good" results are, the subjects in a naturalistic observation should not know they are being observed. This ensures that the behavior being observed is the actual behavior in its natural state. This approach is also used extensively to study animal behavior in the wild. (Jane Goodall used it in her classic studies of chimpanzee culture.) Because a researcher merely observes, rather than controlling the conditions or manipulating the independent variable, naturalistic observations are made under far less controlled conditions than experiments.

What if you wanted to investigate the long-range effects of something? The type of research you might be most interested in is called a **longitudinal study.** In this type of study, one group of subjects is followed and observed (or examined, surveyed, etc.) for an extended period of time, such as 20 years. The benefit of this research is that you have the same subject group throughout. The drawbacks are time and expense.

The next two methodologies were developed to avoid the time and expense of the longitudinal study. The **cross-sectional study** examines a representative cross section of the population and tests/surveys these subjects at one specific time. This will yield data similar to longitudinal data but not so accurate. The **cohort-sequential study** yields better data. Here the investigators take a cross section of the population and then follow each *cohort* or group for a short

■ **Survey** A quasi-experimental method in which questions are asked to subjects. When designing a survey, the researcher has to be careful that the questions are not skewed or biased toward a particular answer.

■ **Naturalistic observation** A research method in which subjects are observed in their natural environment.

■ **Longitudinal study** A type of study in which one group of subjects is followed and observed (or examined, surveyed, etc.) for an extended period of time (years).

■ **Cross-sectional study** A study in which a representative cross section of the population is tested or surveyed at one specific time.

■ **Cohort-sequential study** A research method in which a cross section of the population is chosen and then each cohort is followed for a short period of time.

● Jane Goodall used the method of naturalistic observation to study chimpanzee behavior.

period of time. This study can take less time than the longitudinal design, is much less susceptible to bias, and therefore yields more accurate data than a cross-sectional study.

Sources of Bias in Research (or Anywhere Else)

Think of an issue on which you have strong feelings and opinions—perhaps abortion, euthanasia, or capital punishment. On such topics, our emotions make it difficult to reason objectively. Likewise, emotionally loaded topics can bring out biases that affect the ways an experimenter designs a study, collects the data, or interprets the results. Fortunately, the scientific method, with its public procedures and openness to replication, provides a powerful means to check on an experimenter's bias. Still, scientists would rather save themselves embarrassment by identifying and controlling their biases before they hit print. Here are some forms of bias to which they must be alert.

Personal bias involves an individual's beliefs, preferences, assumptions, or prejudices. Often these are not obvious to the individual holding such biases. For example, in his book *Even the Rat Was White,* psychologist Robert Guthrie (1998) points out the personal bias in the long tradition of using mainly white subjects in psychological research. Whatever form it takes, personal bias can cause scientists to notice only the evidence confirming their hypotheses and to ignore contrary data.

Expectancy bias also affects observations when observers expect—and look for—certain outcomes. We can see expectancy bias at work in a classic study in which psychology students timed groups of rats running through a maze (Rosenthal & Jacobson, 1968a). The experimenters told some students that their rats were especially bright; other students heard that their rats were slow learners. (In fact, the experimenters had randomly selected both groups of rats from the same litters.) Amazingly, the students' data showed that rats believed to be bright outperformed their supposedly duller littermates.

These sources of bias not only can lead to erroneous conclusions but also can be expensive. Imagine that you are a psychologist working for a pharmaceutical company that wants you to design a test for a new drug. With millions of dollars riding on the outcome, you will want to do it right. But what about the doctors who are going to be prescribing the drug to patients in your study? Surely those doctors will have high hopes for the drug, as will their patients. And so the stage is set for bias to creep into your study along with people's expectations.

We have seen that a common strategy for controlling expectancy bias in a drug study is to keep participants in the research experimentally "blind," or uninformed, about whether they are getting the real drug or a placebo. An even better strategy is to keep *both* the participants and the experimenter clueless about which group receives what treatment. In a drug study, this would mean that neither the researchers nor the participants would know (until the end of the study) which individuals were getting the new drug and which were getting the placebo. Such a research strategy is called a **double-blind study.** This strategy ensures that the experimenters will not inadvertently treat the experimental group differently from the control group, so that neither group will have any idea about the expected response to the pills they are taking.

Aside from these forms of observer bias, researchers must also try to identify other possible influences on the behavior being studied—influences other than the independent variable. Such *confounding variables* are factors that could be confused with the independent variable and thus distort the results. Consider, for example, a study of a stimulant drug (such as Ritalin) used to control hyperactive behavior among schoolchildren. What might be some confound-

■ **Personal bias** The researcher allowing personal beliefs to affect the outcome of a study.

■ **Expectancy bias** The researcher allowing his or her expectations to affect the outcome of a study.

■ **Double-blind study** An experimental procedure in which both researchers and participants are uninformed about the nature of the independent variable being administered.

ing variables? The drug's effect might differ because of different body weights, eating schedules, or time, method, or setting of administration. Unless arrangements are made to control all such possible confounding variables—that is, to expose all the subjects to identical conditions—the researcher has no way of knowing which factors really produced the results.

CONNECTION: CHAPTERS 5 AND 13

Paradoxically, stimulants seem to calm hyperactive behavior in children with ADHD.

Ethics in Research

Ethical considerations are an overarching component of all research. These issues range from the basic question "Should the research be conducted?" (as is being argued today regarding the use of stem cells) to questions such as "Should research be approved even if there is no direct application for it?" (in essence, the issue of basic versus applied research). Dess and Foltin (2005) pose seven questions involving what they call the "Ethics Cascade" (see Table 2.3).

The questions posed here are not simple, nor are their answers. Ethical guidelines such as the APA's "Ethical Principles of Psychologists and Code of Conduct" (2002) must be followed in the conduct of *all* research. Each research institution must have an **Institutional Review Board (IRB)** that reviews and approves all research. In addition, animal research must also be approved by an **Institutional Animal Care and Use Committee (IACUC).** Gruber (2005) also points out that all animal research must comply with the *ABCs of laboratory animal research* (Appropriate, Beneficial, and Caring).

IACUCs and IRBs are put in place to ensure not only that researchers and institutions comply with federal, state, and local laws and regulations, but also that all research is conducted ethically and humanely. No researcher takes his or her work lightly, and the ethics involving all research—be it human or animal—is serious indeed.

Deception The use of *deception* poses an especially knotty problem. The APA's "Ethical Principles" states that under most circumstances, participation in research should be voluntary and informed. That is, we should advise volunteers of what challenges they will face and give them a real opportunity to drop out of the study if they want to. But what if you are interested in the "good Samaritan" problem—the conditions under which people will help a stranger in distress? If you tell people that you have contrived a phony emergency situation and ask them whether they are willing to help, you will spoil the very effect you are trying to study. Consequently, the guidelines do allow for deception under some conditions, provided that no substantial risks are likely to accrue to the participants.

■ **Institutional Review Board (IRB)** A committee at each institution where research is conducted to review every experiment for ethics and methodology.

■ **Institutional Animal Care and Use Committee (IACUC)** A committee at each institution where research is conducted to review every experiment *involving animals* for ethics and methodology.

TABLE 2.3 Summary of Steps in the Ethics Cascade

I. Who should decide what is morally justifiable in the conduct of research?
II. Are controlled research studies ever necessary or appropriate?
III. Should all research have a foreseeable practical benefit?
IV. At whom should research be directed?
V. What specific topics are worthy of research?
VI. What particular research methodologies are scientifically valid, as well as ethically appropriate?
VII. Of the valid methods, which should be used?

Source: From LABORATORY ANIMALS IN RESEARCH AND TEACHING, Ethics, Care, and Methods edited by Chana K. Akins, Sangeeta Panicker, Christopher L. Cunningham. Chapter 2, The Ethics Cascade, Nancy K. Dess and Richard W. Foltin. APA Press, Washington, DC, 2004, reprinted with permission.

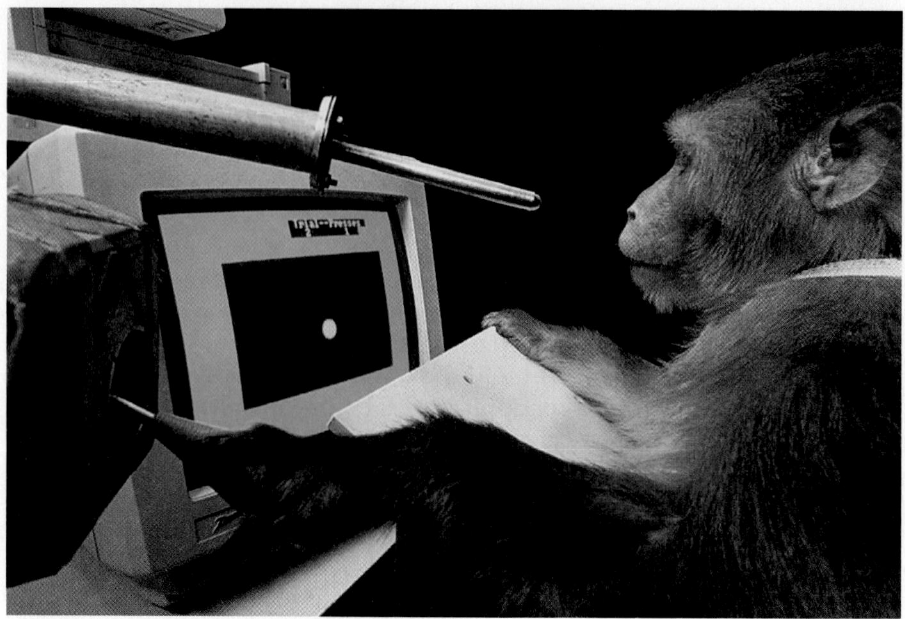

● People are sharply divided on the use of laboratory animals in research.

When deception is used, the APA guidelines require that participants be informed of the deception as soon as is possible without compromising the study's research goals. Individuals used in deceptive research must also be *debriefed* after the study to make sure that they suffer no lasting ill effects. Despite these precautions, some psychologists remain opposed to the use of deception in any form of psychological research (Baumrind, 1985; Bower, 1998d).

Animal Studies Another long-standing ethical issue surrounds the use of laboratory animals, such as rats, pigeons, and monkeys. As far back as the mid-1800s, scientists used animals in their research for a variety of reasons. These included the relative simplicity of animals' nervous systems and the relative ease with which a large number of individuals could be maintained under controlled conditions. Animals have also served as alternatives to human subjects when a procedure was deemed risky or outright harmful. Concerned about the issue as long ago as 1925, the American Psychological Association established a Committee on Precautions in Animal Experimentation, which adopted guidelines for animal research (Dewsbury, 1990). The American Psychological Association's "Ethical Principles of Psychologists" (2002) directs researchers to provide decent living conditions for animal subjects and to weigh any discomfort caused them against the value of the information sought in the research. A 1985 federal law also imposes legal restrictions on animal research (Novak & Suomi, 1988).

Recent years have seen a renewal of concern, both inside and outside of psychology, about the use of animals as subjects, particularly when the research involves painful or damaging procedures, such as brain surgery, electrode implants, and pain studies. Some people feel that the limitations should be more stringent on studies using humanlike animals, such as chimpanzees. Others believe that limitations or outright bans should apply to all animal research, including studies of simple animals such as sea slugs (which are often used in neurological studies). Many psychologists, however, support animal research under the APA guidelines (Blum, 1994). Heated debate about this issue continues.

TABLE 2.4 What Questions Can the Scientific Method *Not* Answer?

The scientific method is not appropriate for answering questions that cannot be put to an objective, empirical test. Here are some examples of such issues:

Topic	Question
Ethics	What are the ethical issues involved in animal research?
Values	Which culture has the best attitude toward work and leisure?
Morality	When is it morally acceptable to go to war?
Preferences	Is rap music better than blues?
Aesthetics	Was Picasso more creative than Van Gogh?
Existential issues	What is the meaning of life?
Religion	How do people of faith explain natural disasters?
Law	What should be the speed limit on interstate highways?

Although science can help us understand such issues, the answers ultimately must be settled by logic, faith, legislation, consensus, or other means that lie beyond the scope of the scientific method.

Questions Science Cannot Answer

It is important to understand that science is not the best approach for finding answers to every important question in our lives. Even scientists don't take a scientific approach to everything. The scientific method is merely the best way to find answers to testable questions about the natural world—the world of atoms and animals, of stones and stars, and of behavior and mental processes. On the other hand, science is *not* appropriate for answering questions that cannot be empirically tested—such as questions of ethics, morality, religious beliefs, or preferences. To see what we mean, please look at Table 2.4, which shows some of the questions that science can never answer.

PSYCHOLOGY IN YOUR LIFE: GETTING IN DEEPER

Whatever your intended major field of study, you will want to learn more about the professional role your chosen field will expect you to play. You can do this in several ways: by attending events sponsored by your major department, by getting to know your professors personally, and by taking out student memberships in professional organizations. You should also develop a habit of scanning the field's main magazines, journals, and newsletters. For those readers who are considering a major in psychology, we suggest that you investigate the following resources.

● Dr. Phil Zimbardo, one of your authors, served as president of the American Psychological Association in 2002.

Professional Organizations in Psychology The largest and oldest professional association for psychologists, the American Psychological Association (APA), has well over 150,000 members and affiliates (American Psychological Association, 2004). The American Psychological Society (APS) was formed just a few years ago to give a stronger voice to academic and research psychologists. Although the APS is a much smaller organization, it has won wide respect; many psychologists belong both to the APA and to the APS.

These groups have student memberships that include nearly all privileges at a fraction of full membership costs. If you are thinking of majoring in psychology, ask your instructor for information about student membership in a professional psychology association. Also consider attending a state, regional, or national convention to get a better sense of what psychologists are really like. These conventions also offer an opportunity for students to present their own research. You could do so, too.

Consider, also, joining a student psychology group, if your school has one. If none is available, you may be able to organize a psychology club or a chapter of a national honorary society, such as Psi Beta (at a two-year college) or Psi Chi (at a four-year college or university).

Psychology-Related Journals and Magazines Professional groups sponsor newsletters or journals that help keep their members abreast of new developments in the field. Psychology majors should begin looking over a few of the main ones every month. Some publish general-interest articles; others contain highly technical reports tailored for those with specialized advanced training. We suggest taking your first plunge into the psychological literature with one or more of these:

- *Monitor on Psychology*—the monthly news magazine of the APA
- *Current Directions in Psychological Science*—a semimonthly APS journal that provides short reviews on trends and controversies in all areas of psychology
- *American Psychologist*—the flagship journal of the APA
- *Psychological Science*—the premiere journal of the APS
- *Whitman Journal of Psychology*—a biannual journal of high school research

In addition, there are several popular magazines in which you may find psychological articles of interest:

- *Discover*—a science magazine written for the general public
- *Scientific American*—another general-interest science magazine
- *Science News*—a weekly magazine consisting of brief blurbs on breaking news in all areas of science, including psychology
- *The Skeptical Inquirer*—a take-no-prisoners, pseudoscience-bashing magazine published by CSICOP, the Committee for the Scientific Investigation of Claims of the Paranormal

Don't feel that you must keep up on the entire psychological literature. Nobody can. Read what interests you in these publications.

Electronic Resources in Psychology The printed psychological literature is vast and growing quickly. As a result, anyone wanting to find out what is known on a special topic must know how to access the information on the Internet and in an electronic database. There are several general databases available, such as Expanded Academic Index and Ebsco Academic Search Elite. The best electronic resource specifically for psychology is PsychInfo, an online computer database offered by the American Psychological Association. Most such resources require a paid subscription, although they may be available through your campus library.

In addition, a huge amount of free information about psychology is available on the Internet. A good place to start looking would be the American Psychological Association's home page on the World Wide Web at http://www.apa.org or the American Psychological Society's home page at http://www.psychologicalscience.org. Remember that Web addresses often change. Remember, also, that anyone can put anything on the Internet, so be skeptical!

CHECK YOUR UNDERSTANDING

1. **RECALL:** A theory is
   a. an unsupported opinion.
   b. a testable explanation for what has been observed.
   c. the opposite of a fact.
   d. a statement that has not yet been supported with facts.
   e. an experimental supposition.

2. **RECALL:** A scientific study should begin with
   a. a controlled test.
   b. a hypothesis.
   c. data collection.
   d. risk/gain assessment.
   e. background reading.

3. **APPLICATION:** Which of the following could be an operational definition of "fear"?
   a. an intense feeling of terror and dread when thinking about some threatening situation
   b. panic
   c. a desire to avoid something
   d. moving away from a stimulus
   e. moving toward a stimulus

4. **ANALYSIS:** The conditions involving the independent variable could also be thought of as
   a. cognitions.
   b. experimenter biases.
   c. responses.
   d. results.
   e. stimuli.

5. **RECALL:** Which is the only form of research that can determine cause and effect?
   a. a case study
   b. a correlational study
   c. an experimental study
   d. a naturalistic observation
   e. a survey

6. **ANALYSIS:** Random assignment of subjects to different experimental conditions is a method for controlling differences between
   a. the dependent variable and the independent variable.
   b. the experimental group and the control group.
   c. empirical data and subjective data.
   d. heredity and environment.
   e. controls and extraneous variables.

7. **RECALL:** In which kind of research does the scientist have the most control over variables that might affect the outcome of the study?
   a. a case study
   b. cohort-sequential study
   c. a correlational study
   d. an experimental study
   e. a naturalistic observation

8. **ANALYSIS:** Which one of the following correlations shows the strongest relationship between two variables?
   a. +0.4
   b. +0.38
   c. −0.7
   d. 0.05
   e. −0.9

9. **ANALYSIS:** Which one of the following is a good method for controlling expectancy bias?
   a. performing a case study
   b. joining a professional organization
   c. consulting the APA's "Ethical Principles of Psychologists and Code of Conduct"
   d. doing a double-blind study
   e. clearly describing the intended results to the subjects

ANSWERS: 1. b 2. b 3. d 4. e 5. c 6. b 7. d 8. e 9. d

HOW DO WE MAKE SENSE OF THE DATA?

KEY QUESTION
?

A longitudinal study was conducted at Bennington College examining political views of students and how they are influenced by campus culture. This longitudinal study was begun in the 1930's, and continued through 1984. The authors of the study, Alwin, Newcomb, and Cohen, found that students' political views can be profoundly influenced by their campus culture—which should make it interesting for you to think about the climate of political opinion of your current school, and of your future college. Do the students and faculty at your school lean toward the liberal or the conservative end of the spectrum? And are the students at your school typical of their counterparts elsewhere in the country? In the following pages we will use these questions as a starting point for an exploration of the statistical methods psychologists use to make sense of the data they gather in their research.

Every fall, the *Chronicle of Higher Education* publishes its "Almanac Issue," which reports the results of a survey of first-year students at colleges and universities across the country. Table 2.5 shows how a national sample stood on a number of political issues (*Chronicle of Higher Education*, 2004). We will use this survey as the basis for assessing the political attitudes of your classmates and comparing them with those of other students across the United States.

We will begin by converting the items in the national survey into a scale that measures liberal and conservative attitudes. The second step will be to determine how you might use that scale to assess your psychology class or some other sample of students at your college or university. Next, we will show you how the resulting data might be organized and analyzed so that you could compare your own survey results with the national student survey data. In addition, we will discuss how your data could be linked, or *correlated*, with other measures, such as income, gender, or grade-point average. Then, in the final part of this section, we will point out some of the statistical pitfalls into which the unwary researcher may fall.

CORE CONCEPT

Researchers use statistics for two major purposes: (1) descriptively to characterize measurements made on groups or individuals and (2) inferentially to judge whether those measurements are the result of chance.

Statistics can be used in a myriad of ways. Perhaps the most obvious one is through the use of surveys.

Developing Your Own Survey

A look at Table 2.5 reveals that the items on the national survey are written in two different ways. Some questions are worded so that agreement is a "conservative" response. (Item 1 is an example of conservative wording: "There is

TABLE 2.5 National Student Survey Data

Agree strongly or somewhat that:	Conservative/ liberal wording	Agree	Majority response	Liberal response[a]
1. There is too much concern in the courts for the rights of criminals.	Conservative	61.1%	Conservative	38.9%
2. Abortion should be legal.	Liberal	54.5%	Liberal	54.5%
3. The death penalty should be abolished.	Liberal	32.6%	Conservative	32.6%
4. Marijuana should be legalized.	Liberal	38.8%	Conservative	38.8%
5. It is important to have laws prohibiting homosexual relationships.	Conservative	26.1%	Liberal	73.9%
6. The federal government should do more to control the sale of handguns.	Liberal	76.5%	Liberal	76.5%
7. Racial discrimination is no longer a problem in America.	Conservative	22.4%	Liberal	77.6%
8. Wealthy people should pay a larger share of taxes than they do now.	Liberal	53.1%	Liberal	53.1%
9. Same-sex couples should have the right to legal marital status.	Liberal	59.4%	Liberal	59.4%
10. Affirmative action in college admissions should be abolished.	Conservative	52.8%	Conservative	52.8%
11. The activities of married women are best confined to the home and family.	Conservative	21.7 %	Liberal	78.3%
12. Federal military spending should be increased.	Conservative	38.4%	Liberal	61.6%

[a]The score in this column has been converted to the same terms as the Liberal–Conservative Scale (LCS) scoring system. So when the question has been worded conservatively, the LCS score is calculated by subtracting the percentage who agree from 100.

too much concern in the courts for the rights of criminals.") Other items are worded so that agreement is a "liberal" response. (Item 3, for example, is worded in the liberal direction: "The death penalty should be abolished.") Good surveys are constructed in this way to be neutral and to control for the tendency some people have of simply agreeing or disagreeing with each statement.

In Table 2.5 we have indicated on each item whether agreement with the statement indicates a liberal or a conservative attitude. While you may disagree with our judgment about the liberalness or conservativeness of a particular item, it is important to note that you can clearly see what we mean by "liberal" and "conservative" by the way we have designated each item. By doing so, we have given *operational definitions* of the terms *liberal* and *conservative.* Together these items comprise what we will call our Liberal–Conservative Scale (LCS). By administering the LCS to your class, you can not only obtain political attitude scores for students in your class but also compare the class's responses with the national survey data.

To score the responses obtained on the LCS, we will give one point for each of the following "liberal" items with which a respondent *agrees:* 2, 3, 4, 6, 8, and 9. Further, we will give another point for each of the following "conservative" items with which a respondent *disagrees:* 1, 5, 7, 10, 11, and 12. Accordingly, high scores will indicate a liberal tendency, and low scores will indicate a conservative tendency. (There is no value judgment here: Neither a high nor a low score is judged as being better.)

To illustrate how we might use the LCS in a study of students' political attitudes, let's suppose that we have administered the LCS to a class of 50 students. The resulting data (which we have contrived) appear in Table 2.6. By merely counting the questions on which the majority gave a liberal response, we find that our class was more conservative (with conservative majorities on six items) than the national sample (which had liberal majorities on eight items).

Although this is an interesting result, there is much more that can be learned by organizing the data obtained from our survey. Let's first take a look, in the next section, at the *raw data.*

Organizing the Data

In addition to the data showing how students responded on each question, we obtained the following set of LCS scores for the class:

4	4	8	3
3	3	7	9
6	7	8	9
6	6	1	4
3	6	11	8
7	1	8	5
8	7	5	7
1	1	6	5
4	6	10	7
9	8	5	8
2	4	8	4
5	6	2	3
10	2		

TABLE 2.6	Distribution of LCS Responses from a Class of 50 College Students			
Agree strongly or somewhat that:	**Number of respondents who agree**	**Agree**	**Majority response**	**Liberal response**
1. There is too much concern in the courts for the rights of criminals.	36	72%	Conservative	28%
2. Abortion should be legal.	28	56%	Liberal	56%
3. The death penalty should be abolished.	19	38%	Conservative	38%
4. Marijuana should be legalized.	24	48%	Conservative	48%
5. It is important to have laws prohibiting homosexual relationships.	16	32%	Liberal	68%
6. The federal government should do more to control the sale of handguns.	24	48%	Conservative	48%
7. Racial discrimination is no longer a problem in America.	14	28%	Liberal	72%
8. Wealthy people should pay a larger share of taxes than they do now.	24	48%	Conservative	48%
9. Same-sex couples should have the right to legal marital status.	32	64%	Liberal	64%
10. Affirmative action in college admissions should be abolished.	31	62%	Conservative	38%
11. The activities of married women are best confined to the home and family.	13	26%	Liberal	74%
12. Federal military spending should be increased.	19	38%	Liberal	62%

As you can see immediately, a set of raw data in this form is nearly impossible to interpret. Accordingly, our first task is to arrange the LCS scores into a **frequency distribution,** as shown in Table 2.7. In the "Frequency" column of the table, you will see, for example, that four students received a score of 1, three scored 2, and so on. Grouping of the data in this way makes much more sense than did the array of raw data above. Going one step further, we can convert the data into a bar graph called a **histogram,** which we have drawn in Figure 2.3. In this diagram, you can more readily see that the students' scores are not evenly distributed across the scale. The histogram also makes it obvious that the scores are more clustered near the middle of the distribution than they are at the ends.

■ **Frequency distribution** A summary chart, showing how frequently each of the various scores in a set of data occurs.
■ **Histogram** A bar graph depicting a frequency distribution. The height of the bars indicates the frequency of a group of scores.
■ **Descriptive statistics** Statistical procedures used to describe characteristics and responses of groups of subjects.

Describing the Data with Descriptive Statistics

We can bring our data into even sharper focus by calculating some simple **descriptive statistics,** which are numbers that describe the main characteristics of the data. In particular, psychologists often find it useful to find a number that represents the middle of a distribution—the central point around which the scores seem to cluster. This is called a *measure of central tendency.* Additionally, researchers usually want a statistic that indicates the spread of the dis-

TABLE 2.7 Frequency Distribution of LCS Scores for a Class

LCS score	Frequency	LCS score × frequency
1	4	4
2	3	6
3	5	15
4	6	24
5	5	25
6	7	42
7	6	42
8	8	64
9	3	27
10	2	20
11	1	11
12	0	0
	Σ = 50	Σ = 280

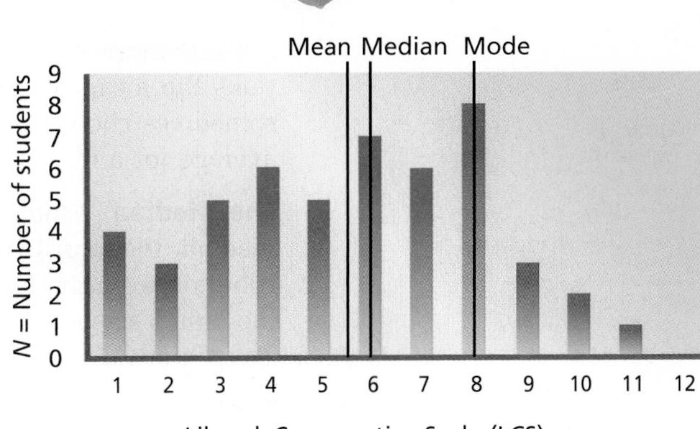
Mean Median Mode
N = Number of students
0
1
2
3
4
5
6
7
8
9
1 2 3 4 5 6 7 8 9 10 11 12
Liberal–Conservative Scale (LCS) score

● **FIGURE 2.3** Distribution of Liberal–Conservative Scale (LCS) Scores for a Hypothetical Class

The height of each bar indicates how many respondents obtained exactly that score on the LCS. Note that the three averages, the *mean,* the *median,* and the *mode,* are in different locations with the distribution not perfectly symmetrical. The mean is heavily influenced by extreme outlying scores, such as the four students who scored 1 on the LCS.

tribution—how closely the scores bunch up around the central point. This is called a *measure of variability.*

Measures of Central Tendency: Finding the Center of the Distribution You are undoubtedly more familiar with the everyday name for measures of central tendency: *averages.* As their more formal name suggests, measures of central tendency help us locate the center of a set of measurements, such as we have from the responses we obtained on the Liberal–Conservative Scale. Three forms of central tendency are most commonly used: the *mean,* the *median,* and the *mode.* Let's look briefly at each in turn.

The Mean Most people think only of the **mean** when they hear the word *average.* The mean is, no doubt, familiar to you as the statistic used to calculate your grade-point average. And it is the statistic that psychologists most often use to describe sets of data. To find the mean, you simply add up all the scores in a distribution and divide by the total number of scores. The calculation is summarized by the following formula:

$$M = \Sigma X \div N$$

Here M is the mean, Σ (the Greek capital letter *sigma*) is the summation of what immediately follows it, X represents each individual score, and N represents the total number of scores. In our example, to calculate the mean we would first add up all the Liberal–Conservative Scale scores (ΣX). The resulting sum is 280. Then we would divide that sum by the total number of scores ($N = 50$). Thus our mean (M) of the LCS scores for the class would be

$$M = 280 \div 50 = 5.6$$

Usually the mean is a good indicator of the center of the distribution, as you will note in Figure 2.3. Unfortunately, it has one potential flaw: Under some circumstances the mean can be unduly influenced by extreme scores. When the distribution is relatively symmetrical, this is not a problem. But when the scores bunch up toward one end of a distribution (in a *skewed* distribution),

■ **Mean** The measure of central tendency most often used to describe a set of data—calculated by adding all the scores and dividing by the number of scores.

a few extreme scores at the other end can have a disproportionate effect that pulls the mean toward the extreme score. Because of this effect, researchers sometimes choose one of the other measures of central tendency to find an average for a highly skewed distribution.

The Median One of the alternative measures of central tendency is the **median,** the middle score—the score that separates the upper half of the distribution from the lower half. In our example, the median is 6. That is, half of the scores are 6 or higher, and the other half are 6 or lower. (See Figure 2.3.) The big advantage of the median is that it is not distorted by extreme scores.

The Mode The third and simplest of the averages, or measures of central tendency, is called the **mode.** It is merely the score that occurs more often than any other. In our data, more students received a score of 8 than any other number, as shown in Figure 2.3. The modal response for this class on our conservative–liberal scale, therefore, is 8. Although the mode is the easiest index of central tendency to determine, it is often the least useful, especially when the sample is relatively small.

Take a look again at the distribution of scores in Table 2.7 and Figure 2.3. Which of the averages seems to fit the distribution best? Is it the mean of 5.6, the median of 6, or the mode of 8?

Using Averages How can we use averages to compare the class we tested with student responses on the national survey? As shown in the last two columns of Table 2.4, it is easy to convert the national survey percentages to indicate liberal responses—much as we did for the LCS scores. The mean of these national percentages is 58.2. That figure is higher than the mean of our own data set, which is 53.7. These two scores jibe with our earlier comparison of the two groups and further confirm that our class gave, on the average, more conservative responses than the national sample.

Measures of Variability: Finding the Spread of the Distribution In addition to knowing which score best represents the distribution's center, it is often useful to know how well the average represents the distribution as a whole. That is, we may want to know whether most of the scores cluster closely near the average or whether they are spread widely. We use statistics called *measures of variability* to describe the "spread-outness," of scores around some measure of central tendency.

To illustrate why variability is important, suppose that you are a third-grade teacher, and it is the beginning of the school year. Knowing that the average child in your class can read a third-grade-level book will help you to plan your lessons. You could plan more effectively, however, if you knew how similar or how divergent the reading abilities of the 30 children are. Do they all read at about the same level—that is, do they have *low variability?* If so, then you can develop a fairly standard third-grade lesson. But what if the group has *high variability,* with several who can read fourth-grade material and others who can barely read at all? In the latter case, the average reading level is not so representative of the entire class, and you will have to plan a variety of lessons to meet the children's varied needs.

The simplest measure of variability is the **range,** the difference between the highest and the lowest values in a frequency distribution. Returning to the scores produced by our hypothetical class on the Liberal–Conservative Scale, you can see in Figure 2.4 that the scores range from 1 to 11. Thus, to compute the range, you need know only two scores, the highest and the lowest.

While the range is simple to determine, psychologists usually prefer measures of variability that take into account all the scores in a distribution, not just the extremes. The most widely used alternative is the **standard deviation (SD),**

■ **Median** A measure of central tendency for a distribution, represented by the score that separates the upper half of the scores in a distribution from the lower half.

■ **Mode** A measure of central tendency for a distribution, represented by the score that occurs more often than any other.

■ **Range** The simplest measure of variability, represented by the difference between the highest and the lowest values in a frequency distribution.

■ **Standard deviation (SD)** A measure of variability that indicates the average difference between the scores and their mean.

a measure of variability that shows an average difference between each score and the mean. To calculate the standard deviation of a distribution, you need to know the mean of the distribution, along with the individual scores. Although the arithmetic involved in calculating the standard deviation is easy, the formula is a bit more complicated than the one used to calculate the mean and will not be presented here. The general procedure, however, involves subtracting the value of each individual score from the mean and then determining an average of those mean deviations. (Many calculators have a button for computing the standard deviation of a set of scores.)

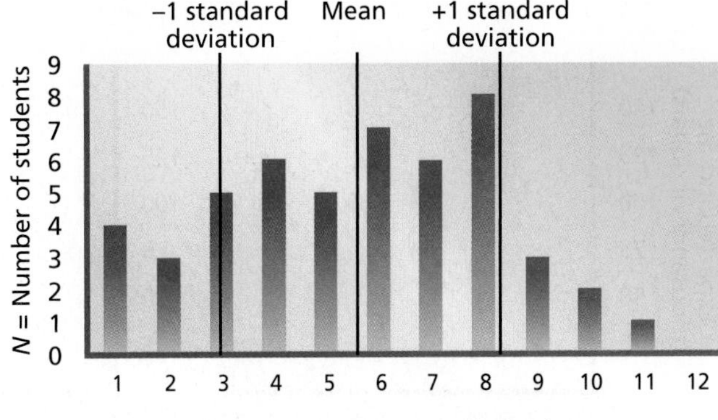

–1 standard deviation
Mean
+1 standard deviation
N = Number of students
0
1
2
3
4
5
6
7
8
9
1 2 3 4 5 6 7 8 9 10 11 12
Liberal–Conservative Scale (LCS) score

● **FIGURE 2.4** The Range and Standard Deviation: Distribution of Liberal–Conservative Scale (LCS) Scores for a Hypothetical Class

The range and standard deviation are both measures of the variability or spread of a distribution. Note that most of the scores lie within one standard deviation of the mean.

Happily, the standard deviation is easy to interpret. The larger the standard deviation, the more spread out the scores are; the smaller the standard deviation, the more the scores bunch together around the mean. In our example, the standard deviation of the LCS scores is approximately 2.6. This indicates that approximately two-thirds of the group's scores can be found within 2.6 points of the mean (which is 5.6). To say the same thing in different words, about two-thirds of the scores in our distribution lie between 3 and 8.2.

Together, the mean and the standard deviation tell us much about a distribution of scores. In particular, they indicate where the center of the distribution is and how closely the scores cluster around the center. It's a fact worth remembering that a span of one standard deviation on either side of the mean covers approximately 68% of the scores in a **normal distribution.**

Earlier we determined that the hypothetical data we obtained with our Liberal–Conservative Scale revealed that students in the class we surveyed were, on the average, more conservative than students who took the national survey. The standard deviation shows, however, that there is considerable variation in opinion. In fact, several students (eight, to be exact) in our sample were *more* liberal than the national average. The resulting study is a correlational study.

Correlation: A Relationship Between Two Variables

Now let's take our research a step further by asking whether a person's tendency toward liberalism or conservatism is related to other personal characteristics. Do conservatives come from more affluent families? Are liberals more introverted? Do conservatives get better grades? Are liberals more likely to major in the social sciences and humanities, while conservatives major in business or the natural sciences? Such questions deal with **correlation,** which is a relationship between *variables*. The resulting study is a correlational study.

To illustrate, suppose we have a hypothesis stating that the conservative students at your school are more money-oriented than the liberal students. (This hypothesis may be true—or it may *not* be true. Only a scientific test can tell.) We can put our hypothesis to a test by first defining "money-orientation" as "expected earnings five years after graduation." Next, we would obtain a sample of students from your school and request two items of information from each of them: (a) how much money they expect to be making five years after graduation and (b) their score on our Liberal–Conservative Scale. Our hypothesis, then, would predict that scores on the LCS would be associated—or *correlated*—with expected income. Specifically, we would predict that lower income estimates would be associated with higher LCS scores, while higher expected incomes would come from respondents with lower LCS scores. An analysis of the data should reveal whether or not the hypothesis is true.

■ **Normal distribution** A bell-shaped curve, describing the spread of a characteristic throughout a population.

■ **Correlation** A relationship between variables, in which changes in one variable are reflected in changes in the other variable–as in the correlation between a child's age and height.

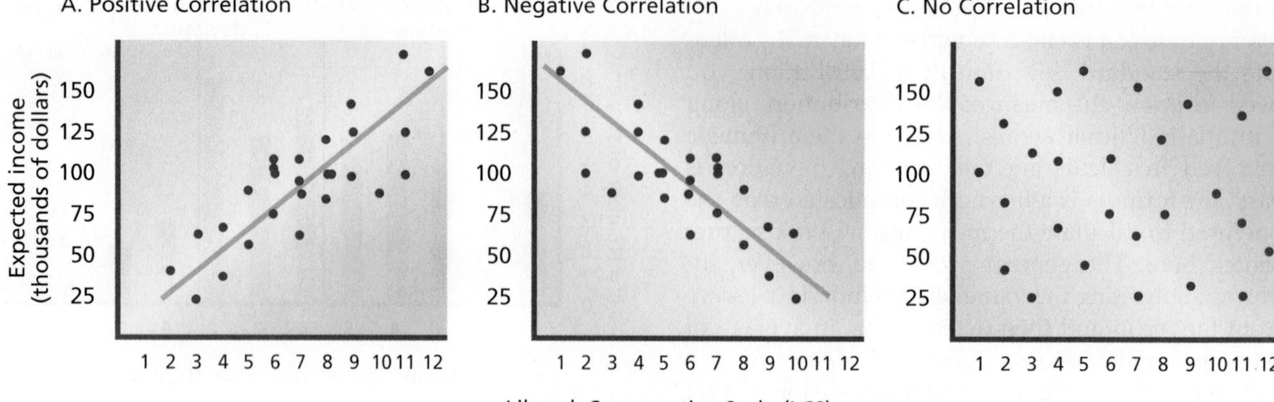
A. Positive Correlation
B. Negative Correlation
C. No Correlation
Expected income (thousands of dollars)
150
125
100
75
50
25
1 2 3 4 5 6 7 8 9 10 11 12
Liberal–Conservative Scale (LCS) score

● **FIGURE 2.5** Three Types of Correlation
A. Positive Correlation; B. Negative Correlation; C. No Correlation

For certain, we will get one of three possible outcomes: a *positive correlation*, a *negative correlation*, or *no correlation* between expected income and LCS scores. Each of these possibilities is shown graphically for a class of 26 students in Figure 2.5. Note that if we find a positive correlation, then increasing LCS scores will be associated with increasing expected incomes. In this case, the points on the graph would cluster near an upward-sloping line, as in Figure 2.5A. If, however, the two variables turn out to have a negative correlation, then increasing LCS scores will be associated with decreasing income expectations—and the points on the graph will cluster near a downward-sloping line, as in Figure 2.5B. (A negative-correlation pattern was predicted by our hypothesis.) If there is no correlation (or a near-zero correlation), the dots will fall randomly all over the graph, as in Figure 2.5C.

We can tell most precisely which one of these relationships we have by looking at the **correlation coefficient,** a number that falls between –1.0 and +1.0. (You will also learn how to calculate this number in your introductory statistics class.) If people with high scores on one variable tend to have high scores on the other variable, the correlation is positive, and the correlation coefficient will also be positive (greater than 0). If, however, people with high scores on one variable tend to have low scores on the other variable, the correlation is negative, and the coefficient will also be negative (less than 0). If there is no consistent relationship between the scores, the correlation will be close to 0.

Making Inferences with Inferential Statistics

Now that we have seen how to use descriptive statistics to describe a set of data, let's turn to **inferential statistics,** which are used to determine (infer) whether the scores from two or more groups are essentially the same or different. For example, if you hypothesized that time spent studying is associated with the grades students receive, you could use inferential statistics to compare the average amount of study time in a sample of students with high grades to that of a sample with low grades. The details of the statistical tests we could use in this example are beyond the scope of this brief introduction to statistics. Suffice it to say that most inferential statistics take into account the differences between mean scores of each group, along with their standard deviations.

■ **Correlation coefficient** A number between –1 and +1 expressing the degree of relationship between two variables.

■ **Inferential statistics** Statistical techniques (based on probability theory) used to assess whether the results of a study are reliable or whether they might be simply the result of chance. Inferential statistics are often used to determine whether two or more groups are essentially the same or different.

To be sure that any differences you find are real, you must also factor in the size of the sample you used. As you might expect, with a small sample, a relatively large difference in grades between the two sample groups is required before you can conclude that the samples represent truly different populations. In addition, you must consider the distribution of scores in both groups. Do the sample scores approximate a normal distribution? If not, you may have to use alternative statistical tests—which you will learn about in a course on statistics.

Sampling To have confidence in your results you must, of course, make sure that your sample was selected in an unbiased manner. The safest way is to select participants at random, by a method such as drawing names from a hat. Sometimes obtaining a **random sample** is not practicable: Just imagine trying to get a random sample of all college students in the country! A good alternative is to take a **representative sample.** (This is what the Gallup Poll and other major polling services do.) A representative sample reflects the important variables in the larger population in which you are interested—variables such as age, income level, ethnicity, and geographic distribution. Remarkably, a carefully selected representative sample of only a few hundred persons is often sufficient for public-opinion pollsters to obtain a highly accurate reflection of the political opinions of the entire population of a country.

Statistical Significance A researcher who finds a difference between the mean scores for two sample groups must ask whether it occurred simply because of chance or whether it represents a real difference between the two populations from which the samples were drawn. To illustrate, suppose that we compare the mean scores on the Liberal–Conservative Scale for the men and women we surveyed. If gender has no influence on liberal–conservative attitudes, then we would expect the two means to be fairly similar, and any slight difference between the samples would be due to chance. This would most likely be the case, say, if we sampled 25 men and 25 women and their mean LCS scores differed by only .1 point.

But what if the difference between the scores for the two groups is somewhat larger—say, 3 points? As you learned earlier, less than a third of the scores in a normal distribution should be greater than one standard deviation above or below the mean. So, if there is no real difference between the men's group and the women's group, the chances of getting a male sample with a mean score that is more than, say, two standard deviations above or below the mean for the female sample would be very small. Thus, a researcher who does get a difference that great would feel fairly confident that the difference is a real one and is somehow related to gender. The actual computation required to demonstrate this takes the sample size, the size of the difference, and the spread of the scores into consideration. Again, the details of this computation are beyond the scope of this book, but they are not difficult.

By common agreement, psychologists accept a difference between the groups as "real" or "significant" when the probability that it might be due to chance is less than 5 in 100 (indicated by the notation $p < .05$). A **significant difference,** then, is one that meets this criterion. However, in some cases, even stricter probability levels are used, such as $p < .01$ (less than 1 in 100) and $p < .001$ (less than 1 in 1000).

As you can see, any conclusion drawn from inferential statistics is only a statement of the probability that the results reflect a real difference in the world, rather than a chance difference in the samples selected. Science is never about absolute certainty. Truth in science is always open to revision by later data from better studies, developed from better hypotheses and better samples.

■ **Random sample** A sample group of subjects selected by chance (without biased selection techniques).

■ **Representative sample** A sample obtained in such a way that it reflects the distribution of important variables in the larger population in which the researchers are interested–variables such as age, income level, ethnicity, and geographic distribution.

■ **Significant difference** Psychologists accept a difference between the groups as "real," or significant, when the probability that it might be due to an atypical sample drawn by chance is less than 5 in 100 (indicated by the notation $p < .05$)

PSYCHOLOGY IN YOUR LIFE: STATISTICS IN POLITICS

It is statistics that tell us what numbers mean. Each consumer product survey or opinion poll ends with a statement on how significant the data are and what they mean. In politics, surveys and statistics dictate how campaigns spend their money, where candidates spend their time, and (to some extent) what candidates say. By conducting surveys, candidates can find out the best way to phrase a message and learn to whom they should say it. By surveying a representative sample of her or his (potential) constituents, a candidate can test ideas and advertisements, and then modify them based on the results, before "going public" with platforms or ads.

The numbers that candidates get from the surveys are the key components here. Survey questions that demonstrate little or no significance (statistically) let the candidate know that the issue a question addresses is not important to constituents, and in a campaign this information is very important. A candidate talking about issues that are not relevant or important to their constituents is not a candidate who is going to win election! Candidates (and campaigns) often employ psychologists to write surveys and analyze their results to help tailor the message so that the candidates can spend their time and money talking about the issues that they—as well as the people they would like to represent—care about.

CHECK YOUR UNDERSTANDING

1. **ANALYSIS:** Which of the following correlation coefficients would a statistician know, at first glance, is a mistake?
   a. 0.0
   b. +1.1
   c. +1.0
   d. −0.7
   e. −0.2

2. **RECALL:** Which of the following is a measure of central tendency?
   a. mean
   b. correlation
   c. random sample
   d. frequency distribution
   e. histogram

3. **RECALL:** The simplest measure of variability is
   a. mean.
   b. median.
   c. mode.
   d. standard deviation.
   e. range.

4. **ANALYSIS:** Most psychologists accept a difference between groups as "real," or significant, under which of the following conditions?
   a. $p < .5$
   b. $p < .3$
   c. $p < .1$
   d. $p < .05$
   e. $p = 0$

ANSWERS: 1. b 2. a 3. e 4. d

USING PSYCHOLOGY TO LEARN PSYCHOLOGY

Research in Practice

Yumi and Maria learned all about the different research methods we have considered in this chapter. As we look at their study, we can see all of the essential aspects of research. They began with an abstract that summarizes the research and its findings. Following is their actual introduction. They conducted a lengthy discussion of the available research on the topic, culling their information from a variety of authors and current and relevant sources.

In the course of their literature review, Yumi and Maria discovered the best method to use (the survey) and developed their instrument, which was translated into Japanese for student use overseas. The report also describes their data collection and analysis methodologies; clearly identifies the items in their survey that they would change; and indicates how they would change them. Finally, the conclusion explains their reactions to what they discovered: "Surprisingly, both genders of the Japanese are less happy with their bodies although their BMI's are generally lower than [those of] Americans" (Kallman & Rydlun, 2002).

This study below shows all the hallmarks of good research. It is through conscientious investigation such as this that we have learned virtually everything we know about the natural world.

Japan vs. America: Differences in Health and Body Image

Maria Kallman and Yumi Rydlun

Walt Whitman High School

ABSTRACT

It has been shown that Japanese and American teenagers' lifestyles differ significantly in their level of physical activity and eating habits. In comparing Japanese and American teenagers' health habits and body image, conclusions can be drawn regarding the implications of lifestyle habits on body image. A multi-faceted survey was developed to assess lifestyle health habits and body image in a culturally non-biased way. Two hundred surveys were distributed to Japanese and American teenagers in their native languages. It was hypothesized that due to the different cultural factors in Japan such as a more balanced diet and more physical exercise, Japanese teenagers would be happier with their bodies. Data found that overall, the subjects' lifestyles did not differ significantly in health between the two countries, and, to further nullify the hypothesis, showed that the Japanese teenagers were less happy with their bodies.

INTRODUCTION/LIT REVIEW

Body image, or the way we perceive our physical selves, is generally at an all-time low during the teenage years (Sneddon, 1999). The transitional teenage years make teens especially susceptible to outside influences on their self-perception. In the United States, recent studies have shown that at least 50% of adolescent girls read fashion magazines such as *Seventeen* or *Vogue* regularly, and therefore are exposed to the media's projection of what is ideal (Sneddon, 1999). This ideal is becoming harder and harder to achieve. For example, in 1920 the popular film star and owner of the 'perfect body,' Anette Kellerman, was 5 feet 3 inches tall and weighed 130 pounds, with a healthy body mass index of 23. Today, renowned supermodel Kate Moss is 5 feet 7 inches and weighs 100 pounds, with a BMI of about 16 (Sneddon, 1999). In addition, a generation ago, the average model weighed 8% less than the average woman, whereas now, she weighs 23% less (Sneddon, 1999).

The unachievable nature of these body types causes teens to revert to dieting, their self-esteem drops, and they become prone to eating disorders. In addition to promoting an impossibly, often unhealthy body weight, magazines, television, and the numerous diet products available "can give girls the message that dieting is a necessary part of growing up as a woman" (Sneddon, 1999). Similarly, television and magazines favor muscular men with washboard stomachs. As boys hit puberty, they become aware of their stature. "In contrast to the girls, boys want to put on more weight than take it off" (Sneddon, 1999). Males can easily be embarrassed in the locker rooms, and may turn to steroid use to increase muscle mass. Dr. Gary Wadler, winner of a 1993 International Olympic Committee prize for his work on drugs and sports, related steroid takers to victims of eating disorders like anorexia and bulimia. "One is the relentless pursuit of bigness, the other is the relentless pursuit of thinness." (Sneddon, 1999). However, it has been found that western societies' excessive valuation of thinness does not generalize to other cultures, although focus on women's beauty is just as apparent. Another study suggests that white British females had more concern about appearance than black or Asian groups (Ramachandran, 1994).

One of the major differences between Japan and America's health is diet-related. Until recently, the Japanese were mostly free of heart disease, breast, and lung cancer, and still live longer than Americans (Brody, 1999). Fourteen or fifteen percent of Japanese daily calories are from fat, whereas groups such as the National Academy of Sciences and the American Heart Association have recommended that Americans reduce their consumption of fat so that it makes up a maximum of 30% of their daily caloric intake (Brody, 1997). In addition, a traditional Japanese diet, which includes many soybeans and vegetables, has been proven to raise levels of a compound called genistein which blocks angiogenesis, the growth of new blood vessels. Among other benefits, a diet with many vegetables like that of the Japanese lessens the risk of developing large tumors because tumors require angiogenesis in order to be fed (Brody, 1997). Furthermore, in addition, American's diets have been found to be much higher in red meat, while Japanese prefer fish. Red meat is higher in saturated fat than fish, and has many long-term negative effects on health, including detrimental effects on blood pressure and cholesterol. Yet although Japanese traditionally have eaten a healthier diet with more vegetables and fish, and less red meat and fast food, in the recent years the country has begun to adopt American fast food and eating habits.

A healthy lifestyle requires not only a smart diet but physical activity as well. Despite the national obsession with dieting, the *Los Angeles Times* writes that 50% of thirteen- to nineteen-year-olds in the U.S. do not engage in strenuous physical activity (Sneddon, 1999). A major difference in the activity levels of American teens and those throughout much of the rest of the world lies in their mode of transportation. Most American cities and suburbs are relatively spread out and roads are designed mainly for car travel, as opposed to Europe and Asia, where suburbs are less common and most parts of cities are walking or bike-riding distance from a person's residence. In addition, American teens can easily obtain a driver's license around age 16, whereas in Japan, a large fee is required and the minimum age is 18. Japanese city streets are also much more crowded with pedestrians and bikes and therefore it is difficult to navigate a car.

A sedentary lifestyle has been cited as responsible for as many as 250,000 deaths per year in the U.S. (Brody, 1999). Exercise has many benefits, such as boosting the immune system by increasing numbers of white blood cells, strengthening bones to ward off osteoporosis, increasing basal metabolic rate, and, perhaps most importantly, lowering the risk of heart disease. Low physical activity in high school students has been associated with negative behaviors, and adolescents who are overweight are at a greater risk of being overweight as adults (Risk, 2000). According to a recent study by the National Center for Health Statistics in the Centers for Disease Control and Prevention, the number of overweight American adults, which was stable until 1980, abruptly jumped to one-third of adults by 1991, and then to one-half by 1996 (Brody, 1997).

It is mostly in the psychological benefits of exercise, however, that lies the link between body image and health. Numerous studies have shown a positive correlation between a healthy lifestyle and positive self-worth. Correlational research has suggested that physical activity strongly improves the development of a positive self-concept, which encompasses many aspects of an individual's self-esteem including body image (Kazdin, 2000). Exercise also has a positive impact on a variety of psychological outcomes such as mood, symptoms of depression and anxiety, perceived stress, and psychological well-being, which are factors that have been linked to improvement in health-related quality of life (Kazdin, 2000).

Other factors of a healthy lifestyle include low amounts of stress, restricted use of alcohol and drugs, adequate amounts of sleep, and limited consumption of caffeine. Caffeine has a negative effect on calcium metabolism, which suppresses bone growth in adolescents (Brody, 1997).

Based on these findings, it can be inferred that a healthy lifestyle, including exercise and a well-balanced diet, is highly correlated with a positive body image. This study will investigate possible correlations between health and body image and how they may differ among Japanese and American teenagers. We hypothesize that Japanese teenagers eat a healthier diet, get more exercise, and lead a generally healthier lifestyle, and are therefore happier with their bodies.

METHODS

Participants

Surveys were randomly distributed to students in Japan and America. In Japan, two co-ed private high schools, one all-female private high school, and one university in the Tokyo and Odawara areas were surveyed. In the U.S., one co-ed private high-school and one co-ed public high school in the metropolitan Washington area were surveyed. All of the schools were composed of students of similar socioeconomic background. Approximately 50 surveys were distributed in Japanese to the Japanese schools, and about 70 English versions of the survey were distributed to the U.S. schools. Of the 129 U.S. surveys that were returned, 70 subjects were male and 59 were female. Of the 173 Japanese surveys returned, 57 were male and 116 were female.

Survey

We formulated a 26-question survey to address four main areas: eating habits, exercise and physical health, health and lifestyle habits, and body image (see survey on page 54).

Procedure

We converted the Japanese metric measurements of weight and height into inches and pounds, and then calculated each subject's BMI by using the following formula:

$$\frac{\text{weight in pounds}}{\text{height (inches squared)}} \times 703$$

We then calculated each subject's Ideal Variance Index, a measurement of the difference between subjects' actual ten-pound weight range and their ideal weight. For the questions answered with words, we assigned numerical values to each word choice. To calculate participation in sports, we assigned a 1 to each 'no' and a 2 for each 'yes' for both questions 15 and 17 (Do you play sports in school? Outside of school?). We deleted any subjects who left fields blank in analyzing each question.

Results

While our study collected data that examined a number of health and body image issues, significant data was found that pertain to the following areas. Overall, the BMIs of the Japanese were significantly lower than those of the Americans ($p < .05$), yet more U.S. teens are content with their weight than the Japanese ($p < .05$) (fig. 2). There is a negative correlation among all groups between BMI and ideal weight, which shows that heavier people want to lose more weight (correl. –0.602 for females; –0.44 for males) (fig. 3). Japanese females weigh themselves significantly more often than the U.S. females ($p < .05$) while the difference between males was insignificant. Overall, the Japanese are less satisfied with their bodies than the Americans ($p < .05$) (fig 11).

Other data suggest that Japanese eat more candy as snacks, whereas Americans eat more grains (fig. 4), yet American teenagers prefer water and soda while the Japanese drink more fruit juice and milk. Also, teenagers in the United States use more drugs and alcohol (fig. 5,6). The Japanese sleep an average of 42 minutes less than the U.S. teens ($p < .05$) (fig. 8). Altogether, males eat more red meat; Japanese males eat less than the U.S. males, but Japanese females eat more than the U.S. females (fig. 7). Japanese males are significantly more stressed than the U.S. males, while the Japanese females are significantly less stressed than the U.S. females ($p < .05$) (fig. 9). American teenagers participate in significantly more sports than Japanese teenagers ($p < .05$) (fig. 10).

Dieting practices were insignificant between Japan and America, and there was no significant difference of weighing frequency between males of Japan and the U.S.

ANALYSIS

Through our surveys, we were able to show that Japanese teenagers are smaller in general by using height and weight to calculate BMI. We were also able to find many significant differences between Japan and America in a variety of different areas as well as areas in which the two countries were similar. For example, despite previous data that suggested that Japan had a healthier diet, our data showed that our Japanese subjects' diets were similar to those of the U.S. teens surveyed.

Perhaps the most significant flaw in the experiment was making the weight ranges too large so that calculating BMI became somewhat inaccurate. Also, there was no range for a weight over 190 pounds, and no height range over seventy six, consequently there was no way of calculating the BMI of some subjects. Seventeen percent of U.S. males were labeled as 'undefined' and not included in the graphs and calculations. The final BMI for each subject is based on the mean of the subject's minimum possible BMI and the maximum possible BMI, calculated using the smallest weight and the largest height, and the largest weight and the smallest height of the range, respectively. This range of BMI was about 2 units. This also made the ideal variance index somewhat of a loose estimate of subjects' satisfaction with their weight.

Similarly, the range for question 6 (how many times per week do you eat fast food) was 1–3, while it should have been 1, 2, 3, etc. to be more accurate. To make a better comparison of stress and body image, a scale from 0 to 5 would have been more helpful on question 10 (are you stressed?) rather than a response of always, sometimes, or never.

In addition, in order to get a better understanding of physical activity levels in each country, the survey could have included a question pertaining to the subject's daily mode of transportation.

The study would have been more accurate with more surveys, especially because many subjects left answers blank, but limited time and resources prevented surveying more subjects. The Japanese left many more fields blank than the U.S. subjects. Fifteen percent of Japanese males and 34 percent of Japanese females were omitted from the BMI calculations because one or more necessary fields were left blank. In addition, 9.5% of Japanese females excluded question 20 (are you unhappy with your body?) and 8% of the Japanese females left question 21 blank (Do you diet?). The survey could have included a few more questions relevant to body image, and excluded some irrelevant ones.

DISCUSSION

Surprisingly, both genders of the Japanese high schoolers are less happy with their bodies although their BMIs are generally lower than the Americans. In addition, the Japanese females weigh themselves more often than their U.S. counterparts. Although it was hypothesized that Japanese would have a healthier diet and lifestyle, in fact, the two countries' diets were similar and seemed to have no correlation to body image. However, Americans indicate that they play more sports than the Japanese, which could be a reason why they have a better body image overall. However, the survey questions related to diet and exercise could have been written more clearly to get a more accurate perception of health. These results lead us to the conclusion that the cultures of Japan and America, as they pertain to health habits, do not differ very much in the teen years, but that the societal ideals in Japan might be thinner than in the U.S.

REFERENCES

Brody, J. (1999). *Book of Health.* New York: The New York Times Company.

Kazdin, A. (Ed). (2000). Exercise and Physical Activity. In *The encyclopedia of psychology* (Vol. 2, pp. 285–287). Oxford: Oxford University Press.

Kazdin, A (Ed). (2000). Sport Psychology. In *The encyclopedia of psychology* (Vol. 7, pp. 456–458). Oxford: Oxford University Press.

Ramachandran, V. (Ed). (1994). Body Image Disturbance. In *The encyclopedia of human behavior* (Vol. 1). San Diego: Academic Press.

Sneddon, P. (1999). *Body Image: A Reality Check.* New Jersey: Enslow Publishers.

U.S. Department of Health and Human Services. (2000). Risk Behaviors: Adolescent Health. Hyattsville, MD: MacKay, A., Fingerhut, L., and Duran, C.

SURVEY

Please circle one:

Are you: MALE FEMALE

How old are you? 13 14 15 16 17 18 19

How much do you weigh? (in pounds)

<91 91–100 101–110 111–120 121–130 131–140

141–150 151–160 161–170 171–180 181–190 >190

What is your height? (in inches)

<60 61–63 64–66 67–69 70–72 73–75 >76

Do you usually eat breakfast, lunch, and dinner? YES NO

Do you usually eat between 9 PM and 5 AM? YES NO

In which category is your most typical snack food?

__ Candy

__ Fruits/vegetables

__ Grains (bread, cereal, rice, crackers)

__ Protein (peanut butter, tofu, meat, fish)

__ Dairy (yogurt, cheese, milk)

Do you prefer: Soda Fruit Juice Water Milk

Do you drink caffeinated beverages regularly? (coffee, tea, soda)

YES NO

About how many times do you eat fast food per week?

0 1–3 4–6 7–10 10+

About how long does it take you to eat dinner? (in minutes)

<10 11–20 21–30 31–40 41–50 51–60 61+

About how often do you eat red meat per week?

0 1 2 3 4 5 6 7+

Do you play on a school sports team? YES NO

If yes, how many hours per week do you practice?

6–8 9–11 12–14 15–17 18–20 20+

Do you participate in sports not affiliated with school? YES NO

If yes, what? ____

How many hours per week do you practice? ______________________

How many hours of sleep do you get on school nights?

3 4 5 6 7 8 9+

Do you feel stressed? always sometimes never

Do you smoke cigarettes daily? YES NO

If yes, how many packs? .5 1 1.5 2+

Do you consume alcohol? often sometimes never

Do you do other drugs recreationally? often sometimes never

Are you UNhappy with your body? often sometimes never

Do you diet to change your body? often sometimes never

What is your ideal weight? _______________

How often do you weigh yourself?

___ Everyday

___ More than once a week

___ Once a week

___ Once every two weeks

___ More than once a month

___ Hardly ever

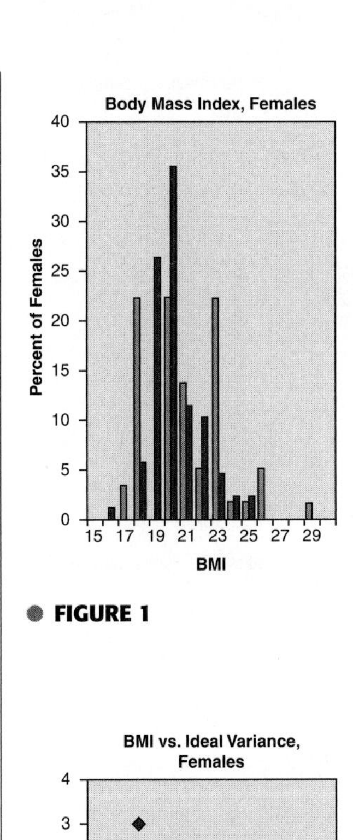
Body Mass Index, Females
Percent of Females
BMI

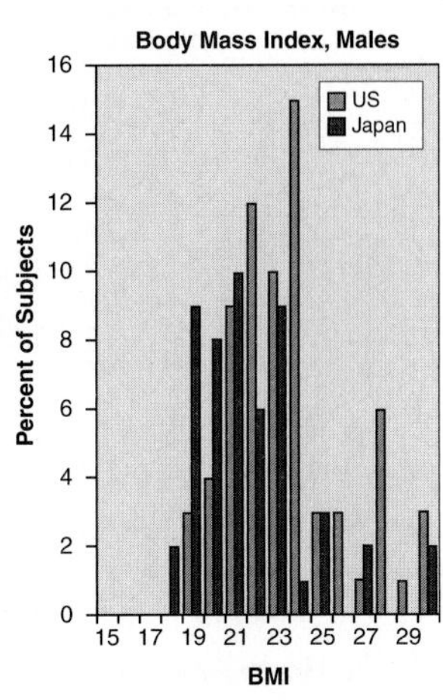
Body Mass Index, Males
US
Japan
Percent of Subjects
BMI

● **FIGURE 1**

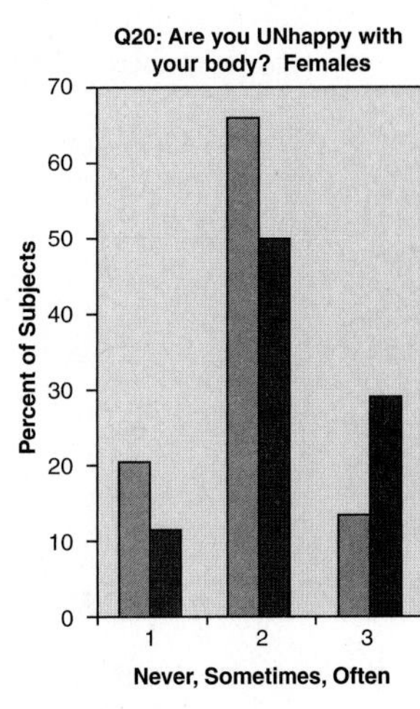
Q20: Are you UNhappy with your body? Females
Percent of Subjects
Never, Sometimes, Often

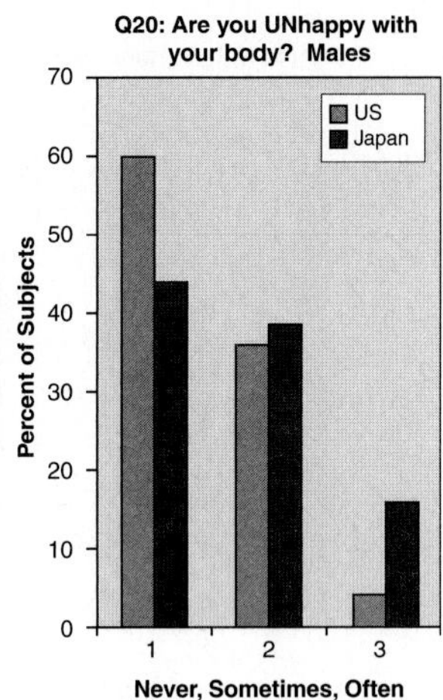
Q20: Are you UNhappy with your body? Males
US
Japan
Percent of Subjects
Never, Sometimes, Often

● **FIGURE 2**

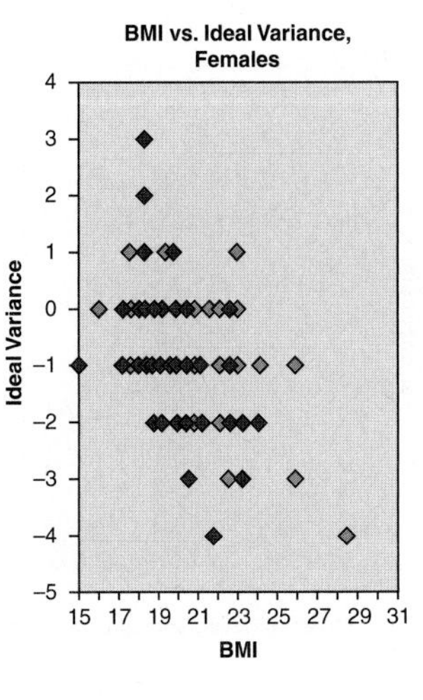
BMI vs. Ideal Variance, Females
Ideal Variance
BMI

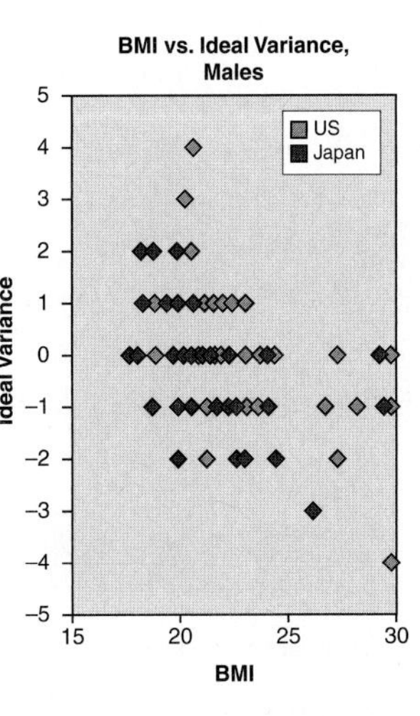
BMI vs. Ideal Variance, Males
US
Japan
Ideal Variance
BMI

● **FIGURE 3**

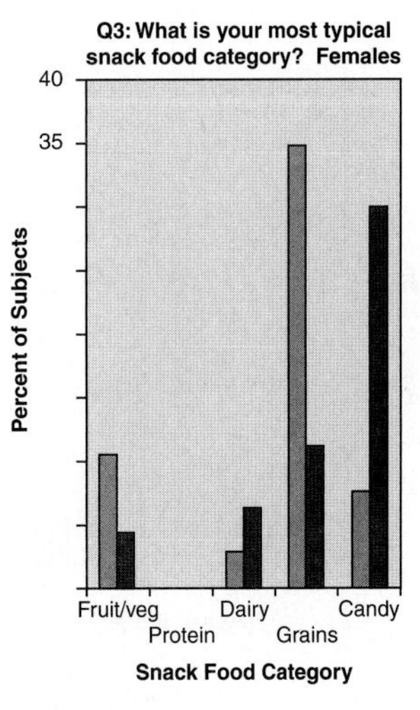
Q3: What is your most typical snack food category? Females
Percent of Subjects
Fruit/veg
Protein
Dairy
Grains
Candy
Snack Food Category

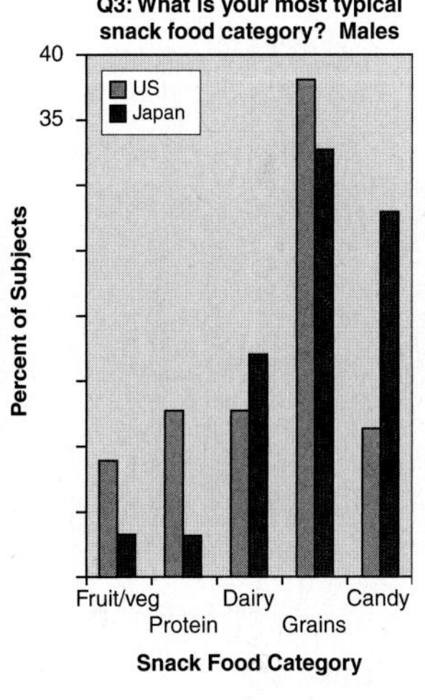
Q3: What is your most typical snack food category? Males
US
Japan
Percent of Subjects
Fruit/veg
Protein
Dairy
Grains
Candy
Snack Food Category

● **FIGURE 4**

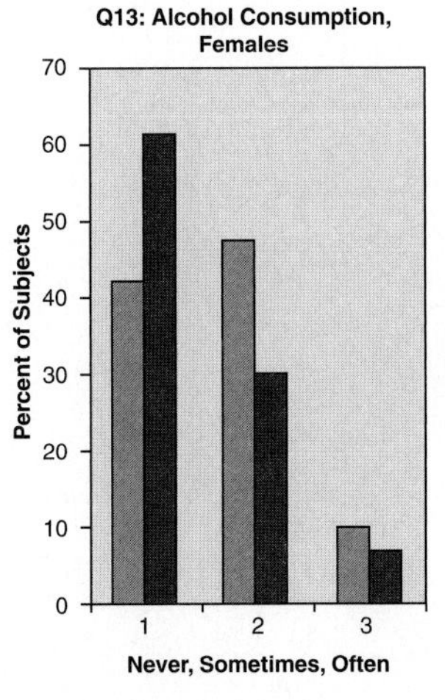
Q13: Alcohol Consumption, Females
Percent of Subjects
Never, Sometimes, Often

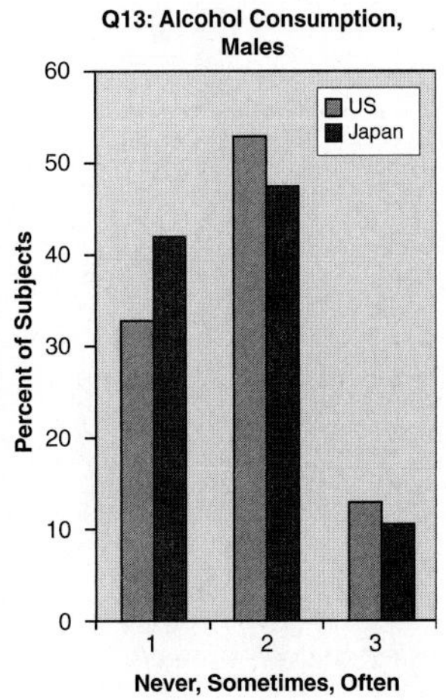
Q13: Alcohol Consumption, Males
US
Japan
Percent of Subjects
Never, Sometimes, Often

● **FIGURE 5**

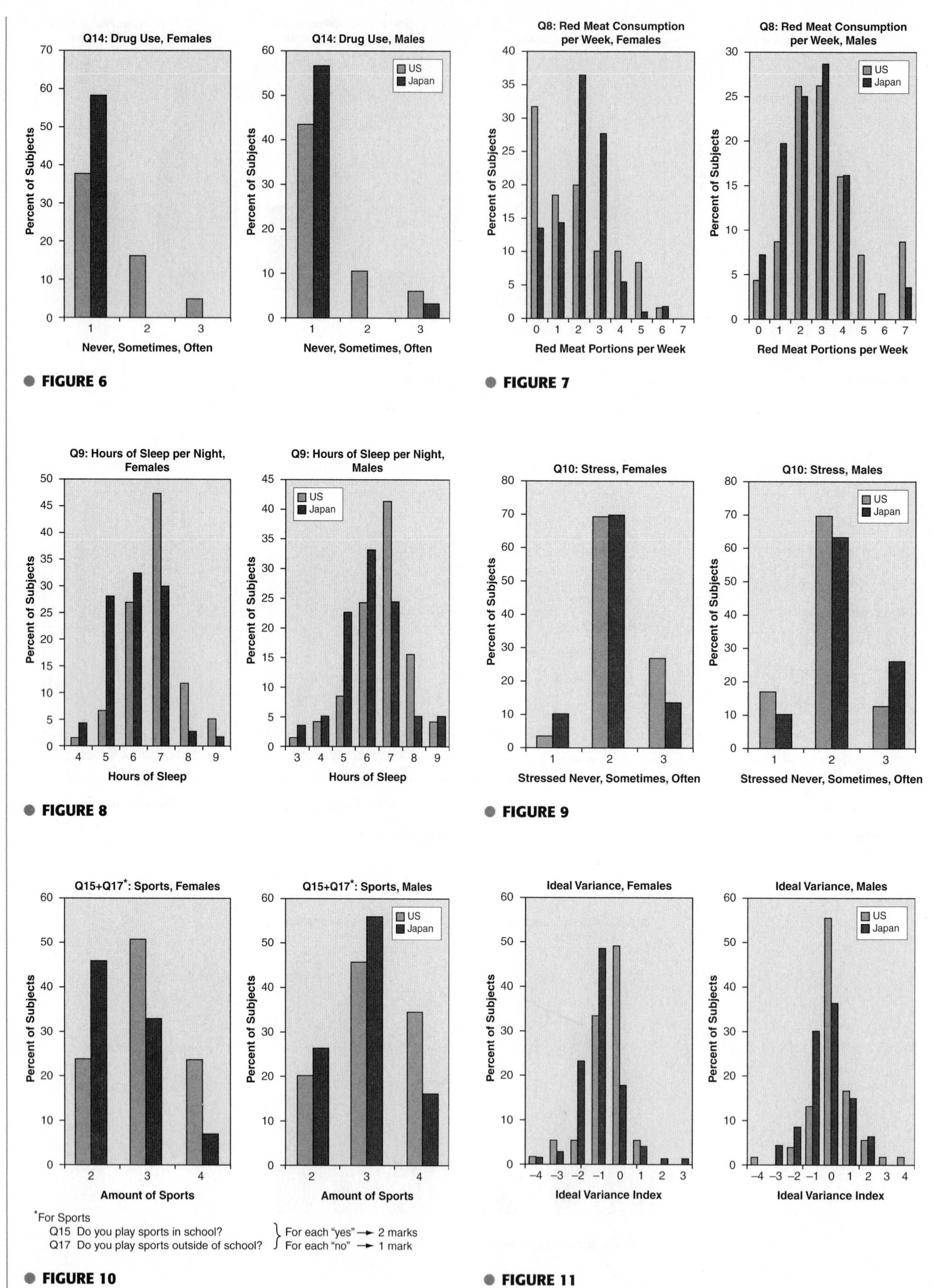

Q14: Drug Use, Females
Percent of Subjects
Never, Sometimes, Often
Q14: Drug Use, Males
US
Japan
Q8: Red Meat Consumption per Week, Females
Red Meat Portions per Week
Q8: Red Meat Consumption per Week, Males
Q9: Hours of Sleep per Night, Females
Hours of Sleep
Q9: Hours of Sleep per Night, Males
Q10: Stress, Females
Stressed Never, Sometimes, Often
Q10: Stress, Males
Q15+Q17*: Sports, Females
Amount of Sports
Q15+Q17*: Sports, Males
Ideal Variance, Females
Ideal Variance Index
Ideal Variance, Males

FIGURE 6

FIGURE 7

FIGURE 8

FIGURE 9

*For Sports
Q15 Do you play sports in school?
Q17 Do you play sports outside of school?
For each "yes" → 2 marks
For each "no" → 1 mark

FIGURE 10

FIGURE 11

CHAPTER SUMMARY

KEY QUESTION
?

CORE CONCEPT

● HOW DO PSYCHOLOGISTS DEVELOP NEW KNOWLEDGE?

Psychologists use many different methods to conduct research and gain new knowledge. In an experiment, the steps in performing an experiment are designed to produce results that are replicable. Although they may seem laborious, they are followed so that any result can be either proven or refuted. In contrast to the experiment, the seven quasi-experimental methods do not demonstrate cause and effect, but rather, demonstrate how certain phenomena are related.

All research is conducted in such a way to eliminate any sources of bias be they confounding or extraneous variables. Even though it was discussed last, ethical considerations are the cornerstone of all research. No experiment or study can be conducted without the approval of a research panel such as an IRB or an IACUC.

● **Psychologists, like researchers in all other sciences, use the scientific method to test their ideas empirically.**

● HOW DO WE MAKE SENSE OF THE DATA?

By organizing and analyzing data, psychologists (and all researchers) can draw conclusions about the data they collect. Descriptive statistics help us describe the main characteristics of the data such as mean, median, and mode, as well as finding the spread of the data and the relationship between variables, as in a correlation.

Inferential statistics let us know what the data mean, and allow us to make decisions based on the data and its significance. Data is considered to be significant when the probability that it might be due to chance is less that 5 in 100 ($p < .05$). Some studies may have stricter criteria.

● **Researchers use statistics for two major purposes: (1) descriptively to characterize measurements made on groups or individuals and (2) inferentially to judge whether those measurements are the result of chance.**

REVIEW TEST

For each of the following items, choose the single best answer. The correct answers appear at the end.

1. Which of the following is an aspect of an experiment that the experimenter *cannot* control?
   a. controls
   b. dependent variable
   c. extraneous variables
   d. hypothesis
   e. independent variable
2. Which experimental method establishes cause and effect?
   a. cohort-sequential study
   b. correlational study
   c. experiment
   d. ex post facto design
   e. survey
3. Which of the following is *not* a step in the "ethics cascade"?
   a. *Who should decide* what is morally justifiable in the conduct of research?
   b. Are controlled research studies *ever* necessary or appropriate?
   c. Should all research have a *foreseeable practical benefit?*
   d. Who should conduct research?
   e. What *specific topics* are worthy of research?
4. The mean is the
   a. average.
   b. range.
   c. middle score.
   d. most frequently occurring score.
   e. standard deviation.
5. Which type of study is the "next best thing" to a longitudinal study?
   a. cross-sectional study
   b. cohort-sequential study
   c. ex post facto design
   d. naturalistic observation
   e. survey
6. What do researchers use to summarize, describe, and analyze the results of their research?
   a. case studies
   b. experiments
   c. naturalistic observations
   d. statistics
   e. surveys
7. The primary purpose of a survey is to
   a. describe an entire population.
   b. determine cause-and-effect relationships.
   c. discover attitudes and beliefs.
   d. find correlations between variables.
   e. test hypotheses.
8. A survey would be most useful in determining
   a. how common alcohol abuse is among high school students.
   b. how people develop over time.
   c. whether praise leads to more long-lasting changes in behavior than punishment.
   d. the effect of laughter on illness.
   e. whether rats run mazes faster in darkness or in light.

9. Sample is to population as
   a. child is to adult.
   b. large is to small.
   c. not representative is to representative.
   d. part is to whole.
   e. valid is to invalid.

10. Which of the following correlation coefficients indicates the strongest link between two variables?
   a. +0.4
   b. 0.0
   c. −0.4
   d. 0.8
   e. −0.9

ANSWERS: 1. c 2. c 3. d 4. a 5. b 6. d 7. c 8. a 9. d 10. e

KEY TERMS

Scientific method (p. 28)
Empirical investigation (p. 28)
Theory (p. 28)
Hypothesis (p. 29)
Operational definition (p. 30)
Independent variable (IV) (p. 30)
Random presentation (p. 30)
Data (p. 31)
Dependent variable (DV) (p. 31)
Replicate (p. 32)
Experiment (p. 33)
Confounding or **extraneous variables** (p. 33)
Controls (p. 33)
Random assignment (p. 34)
Ex post facto (p. 34)
Correlational study (p. 34)
Survey (p. 35)
Naturalistic observation (p. 35)
Longitudinal study (p. 35)
Cross-sectional study (p. 35)
Cohort-sequential study (p. 35)
Personal bias (p. 36)
Expectancy bias (p. 36)
Double-blind study (p. 36)
Institutional Review Board (IRB) (p. 37)
Institutional Animal Care and Use Committee (IACUC) (p. 37)
ABCs of laboratory animal research (p. 37)
Frequency distribution (p. 44)
Histogram (p. 44)
Descriptive statistics (p. 44)
Mean (p. 45)
Median (p. 46)
Mode (p. 46)
Range (p. 46)
Standard deviation (SD) (p. 46)
Correlation (p. 47)
Normal distribution (p. 47)
Correlation coefficient (p. 48)
Inferential statistics (p. 48)
Random sample (p. 49)
Representative sample (p. 49)
Significant difference (p. 49)

AP* REVIEW: VOCABULARY

Match each of the following vocabulary terms to its definition.

1. Cohort-sequential study
2. Dependent variable
3. Double-blind study
4. Empirical investigation
5. Hypothesis
6. Independent variable
7. Operational definitions
8. Random assignment
9. Replication
10. Standard deviation (SD)

_____ **a.** A stimulus condition so named because the experimenter changes it independently of all the other carefully controlled experimental conditions.

_____ **b.** This type of study takes a cross section of the population and then follows each cohort for a short period of time.

_____ **c.** An approach to research that relies on sensory experience and observation for research data.

_____ **d.** An explanation of how concepts are to be measured or what operations are being employed to produce them.

_____ **e.** A measure of variability that indicates the average difference between the scores and their mean.

_____ **f.** Doing a study over to see whether the same results are obtained.

_____ **g.** Ensures that each subject in an experiment must have an equal chance of being in the experimental group or the control group.

_____ **h.** A statement predicting the outcome of a scientific study; a statement describing the relationship among variables in a study.

_____ **i.** An experimental procedure in which neither the participants nor the experimenters working directly with them know what effects the independent variable may have or to which participants it is being administered.

_____ **j.** The measured outcome of a study; the responses of the subjects in a study.

AP* REVIEW: ESSAY

Use your knowledge of the chapter concepts to answer the following essay question.

Design an experiment to see how development changes over time. Your response should include two experimental methods and should enumerate the pros and cons of each. Be sure that your response includes

a. Two methods, with pros and cons of each
b. Subject selection
c. Methodology
d. Means for analyzing data
e. Drawing a conclusion
f. Discussion of any relevant ethical issues

OUR RECOMMENDED BOOKS AND VIDEOS

BOOKS

Abramson, Charles I. (1990). *Invertebrate learning: A source book*. Washington, D.C.: APA. This spiral-bound book provides a plethora of experiments and information on learning in invertebrates. It discusses methods as well as ethics and specific experiments.

Akins, Chana K., Panicker, S. and Cunningham, C. (eds.) (2004). *Laboratory animals in research and teaching: Ethics, care, and methods*. Washington, D.C.: APA. This book by a collection of authors discusses animals in teaching and research in universities, colleges and high schools. There is an excellent section on ethics.

Blatner, David (1999). *The joy of pi*. New York: Walker & Co. Kids love it because it is loaded with neat graphics, histories, and fun facts about the world's favorite number.

Jacobs, Harold R. (1994). *Mathematics—a human endeavor*. New York: W.H. Freeman & Co. A great book that connects math to the world around us.

Guide for the Care and Use of Laboratory Animals, National Research Council (1994), National Academy Press. This book describes the humane care and use of animals for institutions of all sizes and resources. An absolute must for anyone considering research.

VIDEOS

Stand and Deliver. A great film about teaching mathematics (calculus) in inner city Los Angeles, and the trials and tribulations of the students and an extraordinary teacher (Jaime Escalante). (*Rating PG*)

The Andromeda Strain. Film about a virus that lands in Arizona, and researchers from labs across the United States rush to fight and destroy it before millions die. (*Rating G*)

Mon Oncle d'Amérique. The behavioral theories of Henri Laborit are discussed in this comedy/drama set as a pseudo-documentary. Well acted. The film is in French with English subtitles. Winner of six French Caesar Awards. (*Rating PG*)

Key Question Chapter Outline

CORE CONCEPTS

Psychology in Your Life

How Are Genes and Behavior Linked?

Evolution and Natural Selection
Genetics and Inheritance

▼ Evolution has fundamentally shaped psychological processes because it favors genetic variations that produce adaptive behavior.

Choosing Your Children's Genes

Within your lifetime, parents may be able to select genetic traits for their children. What price will we pay for these choices?

How Does the Body Communicate Internally?

The Neuron: Building Block of the Nervous System
Divisions of the Nervous System
The Endocrine System

▼ The brain coordinates the body's two communications systems, the nervous system and the endocrine system, which use similar chemical processes to communicate with targets throughout the body.

How Psychoactive Drugs Affect the Nervous System

Chemicals used to alter thoughts and feelings usually affect the actions of hormones or neurotransmitters. In so doing, they may also stimulate unintended targets, where they produce unwanted side effects.

How Does the Brain Produce Behavior and Mental Processes?

Windows on the Brain
Three Layers of the Brain
Lobes of the Cerebral Cortex
The Cooperative Brain
Cerebral Dominance
The Split Brain: "I've Half a Mind to . . ."

▼ The brain is composed of many specialized modules that work together to create mind and behavior.

Brain Damage and Behavior

Everyone knows somebody who has suffered brain damage from an accident, a tumor, or a stroke. The symptoms suggest which part of the brain was damaged.

Biopsychology: The State of the Art

USING PSYCHOLOGY TO LEARN PSYCHOLOGY
Putting Your Knowledge of the Brain to Work

Chapter

3

Biopsychology and the Foundations of Neuroscience

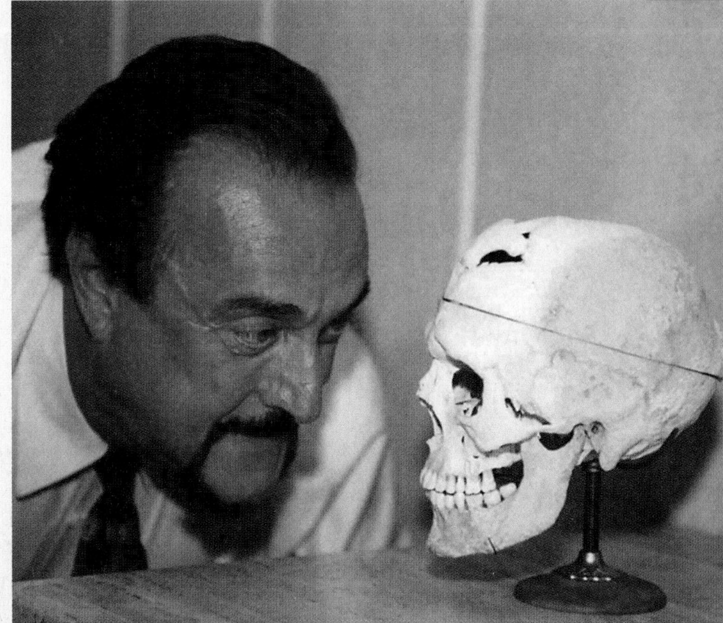

I HADN'T NOTICED DAD dragging the toe of his right foot ever so slightly as he walked. But my mother noticed it on their nightly tour of the neighborhood, when he wasn't keeping up with her brisk pace. I just figured that he was slowing down a bit in his later years.

Dad, too, casually dismissed his symptom, but Mom was persistent. She scheduled an appointment with the doctor. In turn, the doctor scheduled a brain scan that showed a remarkably large mass—a tumor—on the left side of Dad's brain. You can see what the neurologist saw in Figure 3.1—an image taken ear-to-ear through the head.

When I saw the pictures, I knew immediately what was happening. The tumor was located in an area that would interfere with tracking the position of the foot. As I remembered learning in my introductory psychology class, each side of the brain communicates with the opposite side of the body—so it made sense that the tumor showing so clearly on the left side of Dad's brain (right side of the image) was affecting communications with his right foot.

The neurologist also told us that the diseased tissue was not in the brain itself. Rather, it was in the saclike layers surrounding the brain and spinal cord. That was good news, in an otherwise bleak report. Still, the mass was growing and putting pressure on the brain. The recommendation was surgery—which occurred after an anxious wait of a few weeks.

During this difficult time, I remember feeling grateful for my professional training. As a psychologist, I knew something about the brain, its disorders, and treatments.

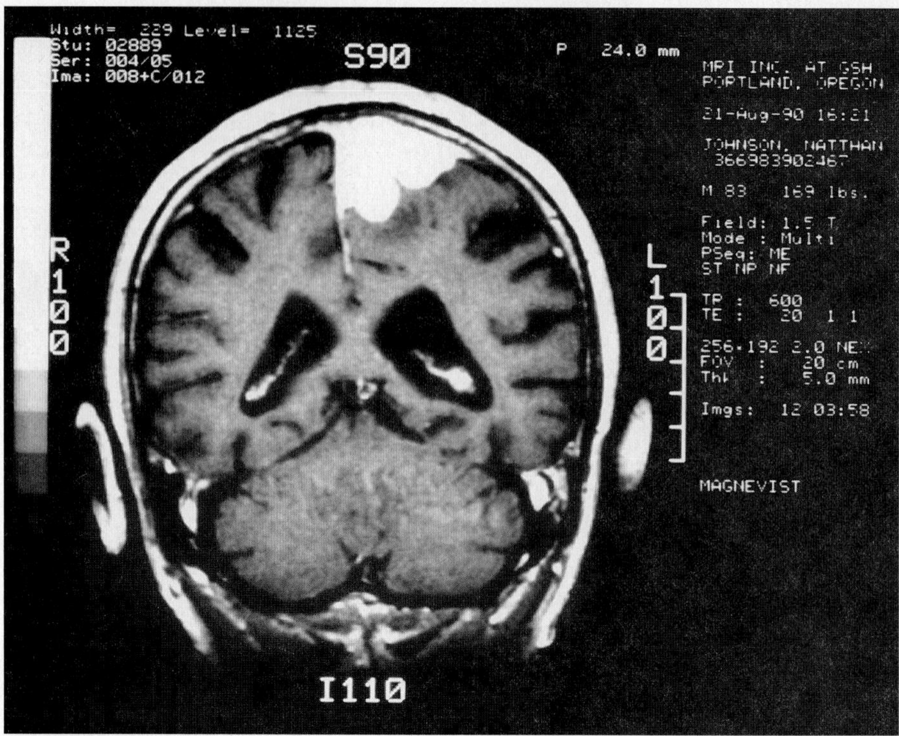
Stu: 02889
Ser: 004/05
Ima: 008+C/012
S90
P 24.0 mm
R
1
0
0
L
1
0
0
Imgs: 12 03:58
MAGNEVIST
I110

● **FIGURE 3.1** MRI Image of a Brain Tumor

This image, showing a side-to-side section toward the back of the head, reveals a large mass on the left side of the brain, in a region involved with tracking the position of the right foot. Visible at the bottom is a cross section of the cerebellum. Also visible are the folds in the cerebral cortex covering the brain. Near the center, you can see two of the brain's ventricles (hollow spaces filled with cerebrospinal fluid), which are often enlarged, as they are here, in Alzheimer's disease. The scan is of the father of one of your authors.

This allowed me to shift perspectives—from son to psychologist and back again. It helped me deal with the emotions that rose to the surface when I thought about the struggle for the organ of my father's mind.

Sadly, the operation did not produce the miraculous cure for which we had hoped. Although brain surgery is performed safely on thousands of patients each year—many of whom receive immense benefits in the quality and lengths of their lives—one has to remember that it is a procedure that is usually done on very sick people. In fact, the operation did give Dad some time with us that he may otherwise not have had.

—RJ

You, too, probably know someone—a relative or a friend—who has suffered a brain injury. It might have involved a tumor, an auto accident, a combat wound, encephalitis (inflammation of the brain), a stroke, or some other trauma, including a difficult birth. This chapter is a tribute to the scores of thousands who have incurred such injuries and allowed themselves to be studied by scientists trying to understand how the brain works. In the following pages, you will learn about the resulting discoveries, as we explore the physical basis of mind and behavior.

What do we know about the brain? In the simplest terms, it is about the size of a grapefruit, it weighs about 3 pounds, and it has a pinkish-gray and wrinkled surface. But such bland facts give us no hint of the brain's amazing structure and capabilities. The home of some 100 billion nerve cells, each making connections with up to 10 thousand other nerve cells, the human brain is the most complex structure known. Its intricate circuitry makes our largest computers seem primitive by comparison. Indeed, its cells outnumber all the stars in the galaxy.

At birth, the brain has an extra supply of nerve cells, and many surplus ones die in the first few years of our lives. By adolescence the number stabilizes. Although our brains generate some new nerve cells throughout our lives, the total remains essentially constant once we reach adulthood (Barinaga, 2003a; Gage, 2003; Kempermann & Gage, 1999). This neural stability may be essential for the continuity of learning and memory over a long lifetime (Rakic, 1985). Even so, the nerve cells in our brains do continue to expire at a low rate: A mere 200,000 will die every day of your adult life (Dowling, 1992). Fortunately, because we start out with so many and generate some new ones along the way, we end up with more than 98% of our supply after 70 years.

As for its capabilities, the brain uses its vast nerve circuitry to regulate all our body functions, control our behavior, generate our emotions and desires, and process the experiences of a lifetime. In addition—and unlike any ordinary computer—the brain has circuits capable of producing emotions, motives, and insights. This dazzling array of abilities may seem to involve something far more than a mere knot of nervous tissue lying inside our heads—and it does! Yet when disease, drugs, or accidents destroy brain cells, the biological basis of the human mind becomes apparent. We are then forced to recognize that biology underlies all human sensation and perception, learning and memory, passion and pain, reason—and even madness.

Most remarkable of all, the human brain has the ability to think about itself. This is one of the fascinations for researchers in **biopsychology,** a rapidly growing specialty that lies at the intersection of biology, behavior, and mental processes. Increasingly, biopsychologists are collaborating with cognitive psychologists, biologists, computer scientists, chemists, neurologists, linguists and others interested in the connection between brain and mind—how the circuitry of the brain produces mental processes and behavior. The result is a vibrant interdisciplinary field known as **neuroscience** (Kandel & Squire, 2000).

In this chapter, you will see that biopsychologists and other neuroscientists have made many discoveries that have practical applications in everyday life. For example, we now know that sleep patterns are controlled by specific parts of the brain—with the result that we now have effective treatments for a variety of sleep disorders. Likewise, the attraction of certain psychoactive drugs, such as cocaine, heroin, and methamphetamine, makes sense only when we understand how these drugs interact with chemicals made in the brain. And, as we pointed out earlier, a little knowledge of biopsychology will be helpful when someone you know sustains brain damage as the result of an accident, stroke, or Alzheimer's disease.

CONNECTION: CHAPTER 5
Neuroscientists have discovered the causes and treatments for many *sleep disorders.*

We will begin our exploration of biopsychology and neuroscience at the most basic level—by considering the twin domains of *genetics* and *evolution,* both of which have shaped our bodies and minds. Then we will examine the *endocrine system* and the *nervous system,* the two communication channels carrying messages throughout the body. Finally, we will focus on the brain itself. As we follow this path, please keep in mind that we are not asking you to undertake a mere academic exercise: You will be learning how biological processes shape your every thought, feeling, and action.

■ **Biopsychology** The specialty in psychology that studies the interaction of biology, behavior, and mental processes.

■ **Neuroscience** A relatively new interdisciplinary field that focuses on the brain and its role in psychological processes.

KEY QUESTION

HOW ARE GENES AND BEHAVIOR LINKED?

Just as fish have an inborn knack for swimming and most birds are built for flight, we humans also have *innate* (inborn) abilities. At birth, the human brain is already "programmed" for language, social interaction, self-preservation, and many other functions, as we can see in the interaction between babies and their caregivers. Babies "know," for example, how to search for the breast and how to communicate through coos and cries. We'll look more closely at the menu of innate human behaviors in our discussion of human development (Chapter 4), but for now, this is the question: How did such potential come to be woven into the brain's fabric?

The scientific answer rests on the concept of **evolution,** the process by which succeeding generations of organisms change as they adapt to changing environments. We can observe evolution in action on a microscopic level, when an antibiotic doesn't work because a strain of bacteria has evolved a resistance. Over much longer time spans, generations of larger and more complex organisms also change, as they adapt to changing climates, competitors, diseases, and food supplies. In our species, for example, change has favored large brains suited to language, complex problem solving, and social interaction.

Our Core Concept for this section makes this evolutionary process the link between genetics and behavior.

CORE CONCEPT

Evolution has fundamentally shaped psychological processes because it favors genetic variations that produce adaptive behavior.

The idea of evolution is both simple and powerful. In this section we begin our explanation of evolution with the story of Charles Darwin, who gave the idea of evolutionary change to the world. Then we will consider an idea Darwin never knew: how *genetics* produces the molecular machinery that makes evolution work—and ultimately influences all our psychological processes.

Evolution and Natural Selection

Although he had trained for both medicine and the ministry, Charles Darwin decided that biology was his calling. So, in 1831, he signed on as a naturalist aboard HMS *Beagle,* a British research vessel commissioned to survey the coastline of South America. Returning five years later with numerous specimens and detailed records of the many unusual life-forms and fossils he had found, Darwin also brought home the radical idea of a relationship among species. Struck by the similarities among the various animals and plants he studied, Darwin concluded that all creatures, including humans, share a common ancestry.

He knew this notion flew in the face of accepted scholarship, as well as the religious doctrine of creationism. Thus, in his famous book, *On the Origin of Species* (1859), Darwin carefully made the case for the evolution of life. And controversial it was. The essential features of his argument, however, withstood withering attacks, and eventually the theory of evolution created a fundamental change in the way people saw their relationship to other living things (Keynes, 2002; Mayr, 2000).

What was the evidence that led Darwin to his radical conclusion about the evolution of organisms? Again and again on the voyage, he had observed organisms that were exquisitely adapted to their environments: flowers that attracted certain insects, birds with beaks perfectly suited to cracking certain

■ **Evolution** The gradual process of biological change that occurs in a species as it adapts to its environment.

seeds. He had also observed *variation* among individuals within a species: Some finches, for example, had bigger, stronger beaks than others, just as some humans are taller than others or have better eyesight (Weiner, 1994). Such variations gave some individuals an advantage over others in the struggle for survival and reproduction. This, then, suggested a mechanism for evolution: a "weeding out" process that he called **natural selection.** By means of natural selection, those individuals best adapted to the environment are more likely to flourish and reproduce; those that are poorly adapted will tend to leave fewer progeny, and their line may die out. (You may have heard this described as "survival of the fittest," a term Darwin disliked.) For the fortunate individuals whose ancestors had accumulated new traits that allowed them to adapt and survive, the result "would be the formation of a new species," claimed Darwin (1859).

Applied to psychology, evolution makes sense of many things that would otherwise seem arbitrary. For example, evolutionary psychologists have pointed out that human *phobias* (extreme and incapacitating fears) almost always involve stimulation that signaled danger to our ancestors (snakes, lightning, blood), rather than dangerous conditions of more recent origin (radiation, electricity, automobiles). In the same way, the fact that we spend about a third of our lives asleep makes much more sense in an evolutionary context (sleep kept our ancestors out of trouble in the dark) than it does as an adaptive behavior in a modern world with artificial lights. Evolution also explains certain innate preferences and distastes, such as the attractiveness of sweets and fatty foods (good sources of valuable calories for our ancestors) and a dislike for bitter-tasting substances (often a sign of poisons).

"Evolution" is, of course, an emotionally loaded term, and many people misunderstand its real meaning. For example, some believe that Darwin's theory says humans "come from monkeys." But neither Darwin nor any other evolutionary scientist has ever said that. Rather, they say we had a common ancestor millions of years ago—a big difference. Another evolutionary misconception holds that behavior can alter hereditary traits. But giraffes didn't get long necks from stretching to reach leaves high in the trees. Instead, the doctrine of natural selection says that the ancestors of modern giraffes were variants that had a survival advantage over their shorter-necked cousins. Over time, then, the longer-necked trait came to dominate the population. In the same way, evolving human traits, such as a big brain adapted for language, gave our ancestors an advantage in the competitive struggle for survival and reproduction (Buss et al., 1998).

We should be clear that the basic principles of evolution, while still controversial in some quarters, have been accepted by virtually all scientists for more than a century. That said, we should note that evolutionary theory is a controversial newcomer to psychology. It is not that psychologists dispute Darwin—most do not. Rather, the controversy centers on whether an evolutionary approach places too much emphasis on *nature,* the biological basis of psychology, and not enough emphasis on *nurture,* the role of learning. This *nature–nurture controversy* is a long-standing issue in psychology that we will meet again and again throughout this book. Sometimes it is also called the *heredity vs. environment* issue.

In later chapters we will discuss specific evolutionary explanations that have been advanced to explain aggression, jealousy, sexual orientation, physical attraction and mate selection, parenting, cooperation, temperament, morality, and (always a psychological hot potato) gender differences. But for now, let us turn our attention to the biological underpinnings of evolutionary change.

CONNECTION: CHAPTERS 7 AND 9

The *nature–nurture controversy* is a prominent issue in developmental psychology and in intelligence testing.

■ **Natural selection** The driving force behind evolution, by which the environment "selects" the fittest organisms.

Genetics and Inheritance

Remarkably, Darwin knew nothing of genetics. Although he correctly described how natural selection works, he lived long before scientists understood the biology behind evolutionary change. From our perspective, some 150 years after Darwin, we know that the individual variations that caught his attention arise from random genetic differences among individuals.

In principle, the genetic code is quite simple. Much as the microscopic pits in a CD encode information that can become pictures or music, your *genes* encode information that can become your inherited traits. Consider your own unique combination of traits. Your height, weight, facial features, and hair color, for example, all originate in the encoded genetic "blueprint" inherited from your parents and inscribed in every cell nucleus in your body. Psychologists have shown that many of our psychological characteristics, too, are influenced by genetics, including basic temperament, tendency to fears, and certain behavior patterns (Pinker, 2002).

Yet, despite your genetic heritage, you are a unique individual—different from either of your parents. One source of difference lies in your experience, in the environment in which you grew up—distinct in time and, perhaps, in place from that of your parents. The other main source of difference between you and your parents comes from heredity—the random combination of traits that each parent passed on to you from past generations in their own family lines. These include the color of your hair, eyes, and skin, as well as aspects of your personality. This hybrid inheritance produced your unique **genotype,** the genetic pattern that makes you different from anyone else on earth.

If the genotype is the "blueprint," then the resulting physical structure is the **phenotype.** All your physical characteristics make up your phenotype, including not only your visible traits but also the chemistry and "wiring" of your brain. We should hasten to point out that although the phenotype is based in biology, it is not completely determined by heredity. Heredity never acts alone but always in partnership with the environment, which includes such biological influences as nutrition, disease, and stress. For example, poor medical care that results in a birth defect counts as an environmental influence on the phenotype.

Now, with these ideas about heredity, environment, genotypes, and phenotypes fresh in mind, let's turn to the details of heredity and individual variation that Darwin never knew.

Chromosomes, Genes, and DNA In the film *Jurassic Park,* scientists recovered the genetic code for dinosaurs and created an island full of reptilian problems. The story, of course, was science fiction, yet the film rested on an important scientific fact: Every cell nucleus in the body carries a complete set of biological instructions for building the organism. For humans, these instructions are contained in 23 pairs of chromosomes, which, under a high-powered microscope, look like tiny twisted threads. Zooming in for a close look, we find that each chromosome consists of a long and tightly coiled chain of **DNA** (deoxyribonucleic acid), a molecule that just happens to be especially well suited to storing this biological information.

Genes are the "words" that make up the organism's instruction manual. Encoded in discrete segments of DNA, each gene contributes to the operation of the organism by specifying a single protein. Thousands of such proteins, in turn, serve as the building blocks for the organism's physical characteristics (the phenotype) and the regulation of the body's internal operations. Genes, because they are not precisely the same in each individual, are also the biological source of the variation that caught Darwin's attention.

■ **Genotype** An organism's genetic makeup.

■ **Phenotype** An organism's observable physical characteristics.

■ **DNA** A long, complex molecule that encodes genetic characteristics. DNA is an abbreviation for *deoxyribonucleic acid.*

■ **Gene** Segment of a chromosome that encodes the directions for the inherited physical and mental characteristics of an organism. Genes are the functional units of a chromosome.

The genes occur in sequence on the **chromosomes,** like a string of words in a coded sentence. But the chromosomes are much more than mere genetic paragraphs. They also contain "punctuation" that indicates where each gene begins and ends, along with instructions specifying how and when the genes are to be expressed (Gibbs, 2003). Although these instructions are not yet well understood, genetic scientists have shown that the instructions for gene expression are crucial to the proper functioning of every cell in our bodies. Errors in gene expression can lead to physical and developmental problems, including mental retardation. At the extreme, flawed gene expression can produce fatal diseases.

■ **Chromosome** Tightly coiled threadlike structure along which the genes are organized, like beads on a necklace. Chromosomes consist primarily of DNA.

On a still smaller scale (now we're getting beyond the power of microscopes to resolve), genes are composed of even smaller molecular units called *nucleotides* that serve as individual "letters" in the genetic "words." But instead of a 26-letter alphabet, the genetic code uses just four nucleotides, even though a particular gene may require hundreds of nucleotides to specify a particular protein.

Physically, the nucleotides fit together in pairs, rather like the opposing teeth in a zipper. Then, when a protein is needed, the nucleotides in the appropriate segment of DNA "unzip," forming a jagged pattern, or template, from which the protein is built. (See Figure 3.2.)

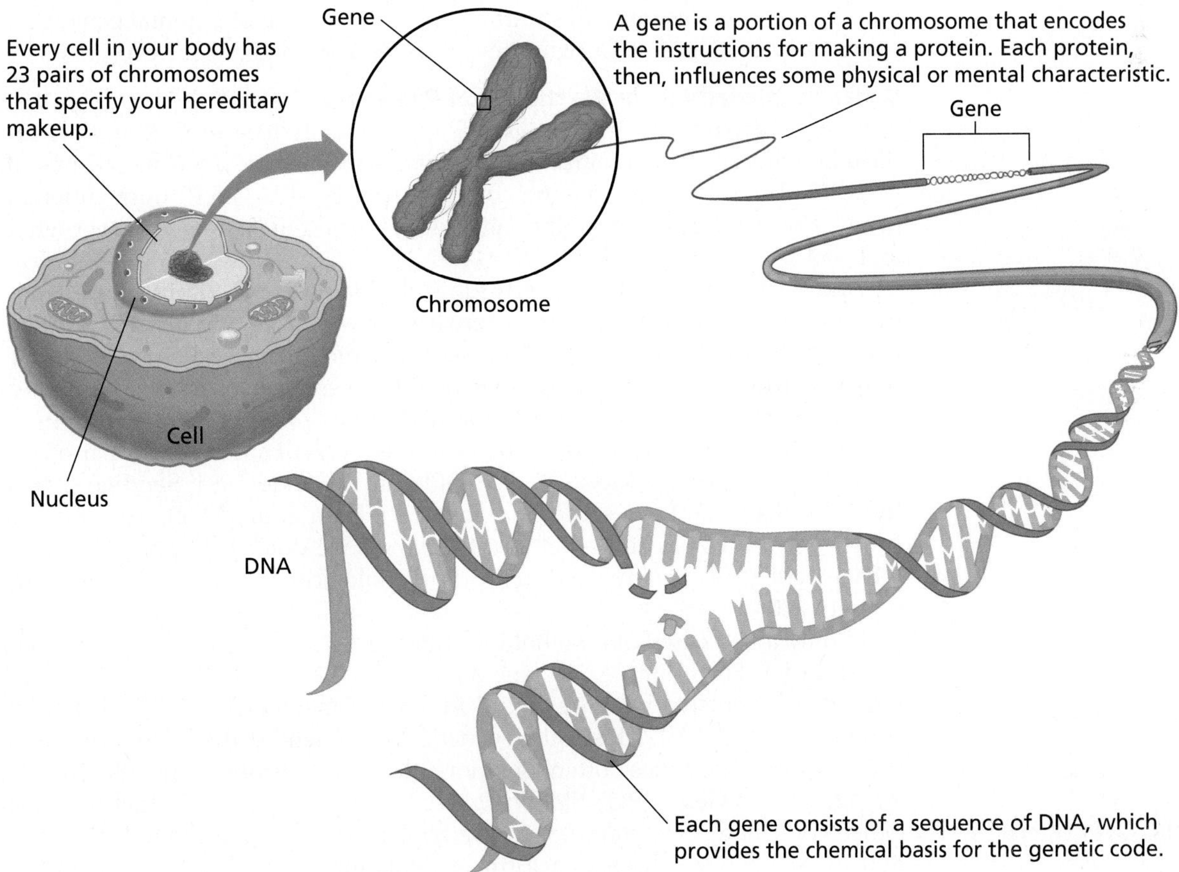
Every cell in your body has 23 pairs of chromosomes that specify your hereditary makeup.
Gene
A gene is a portion of a chromosome that encodes the instructions for making a protein. Each protein, then, influences some physical or mental characteristic.
Gene
Chromosome
Cell
Nucleus
DNA
Each gene consists of a sequence of DNA, which provides the chemical basis for the genetic code.

● **FIGURE 3.2** DNA, Genes, and Chromosomes

A chromosome is composed mainly of a tightly coiled strand of DNA, an incredibly long molecule. Each chromosome contains thousands of genes, along with instructions for the "when" and "how" of gene expression. Genes themselves are segments of DNA. Each gene contains instructions, coded in the four-nucleotide alphabet, for making a protein. The Human Genome Project recently identified the sequence of nucleotides in all 23 pairs of our chromosomes.

How many genes does it take to make a human? According to current estimates, the complete package of human DNA contains approximately 30,000 genes—surprisingly few, in view of the human organism's complexity (Netting & Wang, 2001; Pennisi, 2003). Together with their supplemental instructions, your genes reside on 46 chromosomes, arranged in 23 pairs. One in each pair came from your mother, with the remaining 23 being your father's genetic contribution. As if that weren't complicated enough, duplicate copies of all this genetic information are crammed inside the billions of cell nuclei throughout your body. It's much the same as a large corporation that relies on many individual computers, each of which requires its own copy of the operating system software.

Two of the 46 chromosomes warrant special mention: the **sex chromosomes.** Named X and Y for their shape, these chromosomes carry genes encoding for a male or a female phenotype. We all inherit one X chromosome from our biological mothers. In addition, we receive either an X (for females) or a much smaller Y (for males) from our biological fathers. When they pair up, two X chromosomes (XX) contain the code for femaleness, while an XY pair codes for maleness. In this sense, then, the chromosomes we get from our fathers determine our biological sex.

It is important to note that you do not inherit copies of *all* your father's and mother's genes. Rather you get half of each, randomly shuffled—which explains why siblings all have slightly different genotypes (unless they are identical twins). This random shuffling and recombining of parental genes produces the variation that Darwin viewed as the raw material for evolution.

Genetic Explanations for Psychological Processes Most of the foregoing discussion of heredity and genetics could apply equally to fruit flies and butterflies, hollyhocks and humans. All organisms follow the same basic laws of heredity. The differences among different species arise, then, from different genetic "words" spelled with the same four letters of life's universal four-letter alphabet.

And what does all this have to do with psychology? Simply put, genes influence our psychological characteristics as well as our physical traits. In later chapters we will explore the extent to which genes affect such diverse human attributes as intelligence, personality, mental disorders, reading and language disabilities, and (perhaps) sexual orientation. (See Bouchard, 1994; Caspi et al., 2002; DeAngelis, 1997; Gelernter, 1994; Hamer, 1997; Lai et al., 2001; Plomin, Owen, & McGuffin, 1994; Plomin & Rende, 1991; Saudino, 1997.) Even our fears can have some genetic basis (Hariri et al., 2002). But, because genetic psychology is still a field in its infancy, we don't yet know how or to what extent genes are involved in most psychological processes (Hamer, 2002; Plomin, 2003.)

In only a few cases can we hold a single gene responsible for a psychological disorder. For example, just one abnormal gene has been linked to a rare pattern of impulsive violence found in several members of a Dutch family (Brunner et al., 1993). Most other genetically influenced disorders appear to involve multiple genes, often on more than one chromosome (Boomsma, Anokhin, & de Geus, 1997; Plomin, 2000). Experts think it likely that multiple genes contribute, for example, to schizophrenia, a severe mental disorder, and to Alzheimer's disease, a form of dementia. (See Morrison-Bogorad & Phelps, 1997; Plomin, Owen, & McGuffin, 1994; Skoog et al., 1993; St. George-Hyslop, 2000.)

CONNECTION: CHAPTER 12

Schizophrenia is a psychotic disorder that affects about one out of 100 persons.

■ **Sex chromosomes** The X and Y chromosomes that determine our physical sex characteristics.

So, does this mean that heredity determines our psychological destiny? Will you grow up to be like your Uncle Henry? Not to worry. To reiterate: Heredity never acts alone. *Both* heredity and environment always work together to influence our behavior and mental processes (Pinker, 2002). Even identical twins, who share the same genotype, display individual differences in appearance and personality that result from their distinct experiences, such as exposure to different people, places, chemicals, and diseases. Moreover, studies show that when one identical twin acquires a psychological disorder known to have a genetic basis (schizophrenia, for example), the other twin does not necessarily develop the same disorder. This is the takeaway message: *Never attribute psychological characteristic to genetics alone* (Ehrlich, 2000a, b; Mauron, 2001).

An example of the interaction between heredity and environment—and one of the rays of hope that emanate from biopsychology—can be seen in a condition called *Down syndrome.* Associated with an extra chromosome 21, this disorder includes markedly impaired physical development, as well as mental retardation. Only a few years ago, people with Down syndrome faced bleak and unproductive lives, shut away in institutions, where they depended almost wholly on others to fulfill their basic needs. Now, a better understanding of the disorder, along with a deeper appreciation for the interaction between genetics and environment, has changed that outlook. Although no cure has been found, today we know that people with Down syndrome are capable of considerable learning, despite their genetic impairment. With special programs that teach life skills, those with Down syndrome now learn to care for themselves, work, and establish some personal independence.

PSYCHOLOGY IN YOUR LIFE: CHOOSING YOUR CHILDREN'S GENES

Scientists already have the ability to control and alter the genetics of animals, like Dolly, the late and famous fatherless sheep that was cloned from one of her mother's cells. But what are the prospects for genetic manipulation in people? Scientists working on the Human Genome Project have recently completed a "first draft" of the human genetic code (Pennisi, 2001). The rest of the 21st century will see us mining this data for insight into the genetic basis for many physical and mental disorders. High on the list will be disorders that affect millions: cancer, heart disease, schizophrenia, and Alzheimer's disease. But not all the promise of human genetics lies in the future. We can already sample fetal cells and search for certain genetic disorders, such as Down syndrome. Data drawn from the Human Genome Project will greatly expand this ability. Psychologists also expect it to teach us something about the genetic basis for human differences in abilities, emotions, and resistance to stress (Kosslyn et al., 2002).

Right now, with a little clinical help, parents can select the sex of a child with a fair degree of certainty. And, within your lifetime, parents may be able to select specific genes for their children, much as you select the components of a deli sandwich. It is likely that we will learn to alter the DNA in a developing fetus in order to add or delete certain physical and mental traits (Henig, 1998). This might be done by infecting the fetus with a harmless virus containing desirable genes that will alter or replace the genetic blueprint in every cell of the body. Another approach might involve injecting *stem cells* ("generic" cells that have not fully committed themselves to becoming a particular type of tissue) that have desirable genetic characteristics (Doetsch, 2002). But what will be the price of this technology?

This developing genetic knowledge will surely create some new problems, as well as promises. Take *cloning,* for example. While most people do not favor the cloning of entire humans, the possibility exists of cloning specific organs or tissues—again from stem cells, a procedure currently under severe restrictions by the U.S. government. Proponents point out that cloned organs could potentially cure heart, liver, and kidney failure, as well as diabetes and arthritis (Pool, 1998). But one difficulty arises from the source of cells for such research. Because donor embryos most often come from extras produced during *in vitro* fertilization procedures, many people oppose this work (Wheeler, 1999). Eventually, perhaps, we will learn to build a new organ out of the recipient's own cells.

There will be psychological issues, as well. Undoubtedly, parents in this brave new genetic world will want their children to be smart and good looking—but, we might wonder, by what standards will intelligence and looks be judged? And what will be the costs? Will everyone be able to place an order for their children's genes—or only the very wealthy? You can be certain that the problems we face will be simultaneously biological, psychological, political, and ethical (Fackelmann, 1998; Patenaude, Guttmacher, & Collins, 2002).

In general, the more we learn about behavior genetics, the more clearly we can see the powerful biological forces that shape human potential and life experience. We can also glimpse the problems to be faced when we learn to manipulate these genetic forces. Already, psychologists are called on to provide guidance about how genetic knowledge can best be applied (Bronheim, 2000; Plomin, 1997; Plomin & McClearn, 1993), particularly in helping people assess genetic risks in connection with family planning. We invite you to grapple with these issues by answering the following questions:

- If you could select three genetic traits for your children, which ones would you select?
- How would you feel about raising children you have adopted or fostered but to whom you are not genetically related?
- If a biological child of yours might be born disabled or fatally ill because of your genetic heritage, would you have children anyway? What circumstances or conditions would affect your decision?
- If you knew you might carry a gene responsible for a serious medical or behavioral disorder, would you want to be tested before having children? And would it be fair for a prospective spouse to require you to be tested before conceiving children? Or would it be fair for the state to make such a requirement?

These questions, of course, have no "right" answers; but the answers you give will help you define your stand on some of the most important issues we will face in the 21st century.

CHECK YOUR UNDERSTANDING

1. **RECALL:** Which of the following processes are involved in natural selection, the driving force behind evolution? (More than one may be correct.)
   a. Individuals best adapted to the environment have a survival advantage.
   b. Some individuals reproduce more successfully than others.
   c. The offspring of some individuals survive in greater numbers than do those of others.
   d. Individuals that are poorly adapted tend to have fewer offspring.
   e. All are correct.

2. **RECALL:** Which of the following is a characteristic that might be a part of your phenotype?
   a. your height and eye color
   b. the members of your family
   c. what you have learned in school
   d. the childhood diseases you have had
   e. your genetic makeup

3. **RECALL:** Which of the following statements expresses the correct relationship?
   a. Genes are made of chromosomes.
   b. DNA is made of chromosomes.
   c. Nucleotides are made of genes.
   d. Genes are made of DNA.
   e. Phenotype dictates genotype.
4. **ANALYSIS:** In purely evolutionary terms, which one would be a measure of your own success as an organism?
   a. your intellectual accomplishments
   b. the length of your life
   c. the number of children you have
   d. the contributions that you make to the happiness of humanity
   e. your ability to find food and water
5. **UNDERSTANDING THE CORE CONCEPT:** Behavior consistently found in a species is likely to have a genetic basis that evolved because the behavior has been adaptive. Which of the following human behaviors illustrates this concept?
   a. driving a car
   b. sending astronauts to the moon
   c. Down syndrome
   d. language
   e. thinking

ANSWERS: 1. e 2. a 3. d 4. c 5. d

KEY QUESTION
?

HOW DOES THE BODY COMMUNICATE INTERNALLY?

You are driving on a winding mountain road, and suddenly a car is coming directly at you. At the last instant, you and the other driver swerve in opposite directions. Your heart pounds—and it keeps pounding for several minutes after the danger has passed. Externally, you have avoided a potentially fatal accident. Internally, your body has responded to two kinds of messages from its two communication systems.

One of these is the fast-acting *nervous system,* with its extensive network of nerve cells that carries messages in pulses of electrical and chemical energy throughout the body. It is this network that first comes to your rescue in an emergency, carrying the orders that accelerate your heart and tense your muscles for action. The other communication network, the slower-acting *endocrine system,* sends follow-up messages that support and sustain the emergency response initiated by the nervous system. To do this, the endocrine glands, including the pituitary, thyroid, adrenals, and gonads, use the chemical messengers we call *hormones.* Coincidentally, communication between nerve cells also relies on chemicals that are suspiciously similar to hormones, as we shall see.

It is important to understand that the two internal message systems cooperate to arouse us not only in stressful situations, such as the narrowly avoided auto accident, but in happier emotional circumstances, such as when you receive an unexpected "A" on a test or fall in love. They also work together when we are in states of low arousal, to keep the vital body functions operating smoothly. This cooperation between the endocrine system and the nervous system is coordinated by the nervous system's chief executive, the brain—which brings us to our Core Concept:

CORE CONCEPT

The brain coordinates the body's two communications systems, the nervous system and the endocrine system, which use similar chemical processes to communicate with targets throughout the body.

Why is this notion important for your understanding of psychology? For one thing, these two communication systems are the biological bedrock for all our thoughts, emotions, and behaviors. For another, when the biology goes awry, the result can be a variety of unfortunate effects on the brain and mental functions, such as stroke, Alzheimer's disease, and schizophrenia. Still another reason for studying the biology behind the body's internal communications is that it helps us understand how drugs, such as caffeine, alcohol, and Prozac, can change the chemistry of the mind.

We will begin our tour of these vital communication systems with a close look at the building block of the nervous system: the *neuron.* Next, we will see how networks of neurons, each having similar functions, work together as components of the *nervous system.* Then we will consider the *endocrine system,* a network of glands that operates in parallel with the nervous system to send information throughout the body. Finally, in the last section of the chapter, we will probe the mysteries of that "great raveled knot" of neurons: the *brain* itself.

The Neuron: Building Block of the Nervous System

On the most basic level, every part of the nervous system is made of the same components, called *nerve cells* or neurons. In simplest terms, a **neuron** is merely a cell specialized to receive, process, and transmit information to other cells. And neurons do that very efficiently. A typical neuron may receive information from a thousand other neurons and, within a fraction of a second, "decide" to pass it along at speeds up to 100 meters per second to a thousand more neurons—sometimes as many as 10,000 (Pinel, 2003).

■ **Neuron** Cell specialized to receive and transmit information to other cells in the body—also called a *nerve cell.* Bundles of many neurons are called *nerves.*

■ **Sensory neuron** Nerve cell that carries messages from sense receptors toward the central nervous system. Also called an *afferent neuron.*

Types of Neurons While neurons vary in shape and size, they all have essentially the same structure, and they all send messages in essentially the same way. Still, biopsychologists distinguish three major classes of neurons according to their location and function: *sensory neurons, motor neurons,* or *interneurons.* (See Figure 3.3.) **Sensory neurons,** or *afferent neurons,* act like one-way

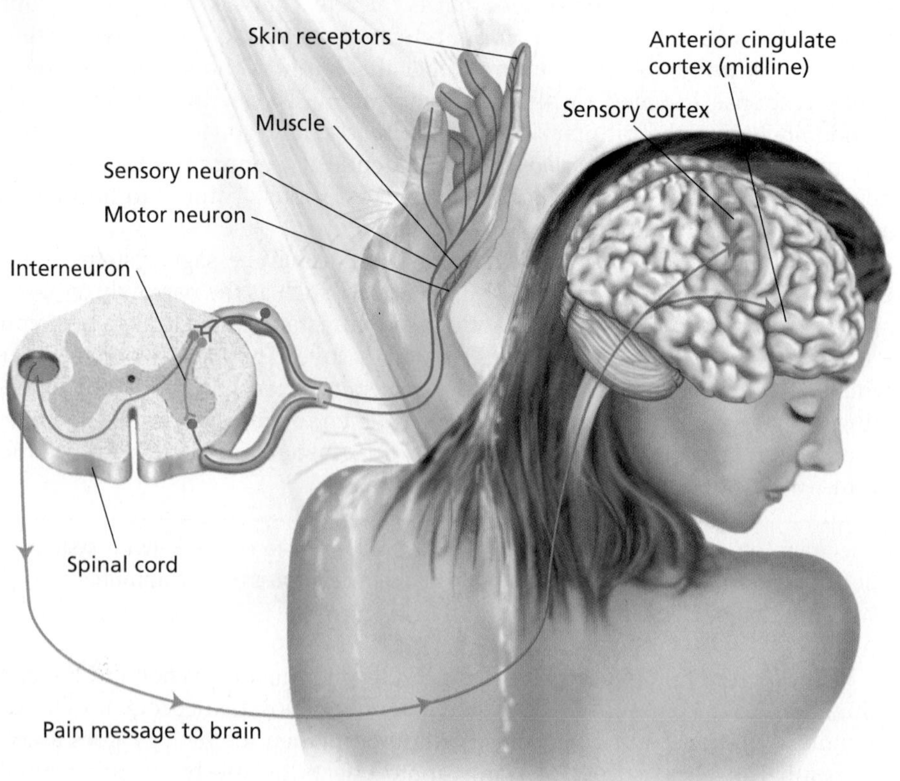
Skin receptors
Anterior cingulate cortex (midline)
Sensory cortex
Muscle
Sensory neuron
Motor neuron
Interneuron
Spinal cord
Pain message to brain

● **FIGURE 3.3** Sensory Neurons, Motor Neurons, and Interneurons

Information about the water temperature in the shower is carried by thousands of *sensory neurons* (afferent neurons) from the sense organs to the central nervous system. In this case, the message enters the spinal cord and is relayed, by *interneurons,* to the brain. There, the information is assessed and a response is initiated (turn the water temperature down!). These instructions are sent to the muscles by means of *motor neurons* (efferent neurons). Large bundles of the message-carrying fibers from these neurons are called *nerves.*

streets that carry traffic from the sense organs *toward* the brain. Accordingly, afferent neurons treat the brain to all your sensory experience, including vision, hearing, taste, touch, smell, pain, and balance. For example, when you test the water temperature in the shower with your hand, afferent neurons carry the message toward the brain. By contrast, **motor neurons,** or *efferent neurons,* form the one-way routes that transport messages *away* from the brain to the muscles, organs, and glands. So, in our shower example, the motor neurons deliver the message from the brain that tells your hand just how much to move the shower control knob.

Sensory and motor neurons rarely communicate directly with each other, except in the simplest of reflexive circuits. Instead, they usually rely on the go-between **interneurons** (also shown in Figure 3.3), which make up most of the billions of cells in the brain and spinal cord. Interneurons relay messages from sensory neurons to other interneurons or to motor neurons, sometimes in complex pathways. In fact, the brain itself is mostly a network of billions of intricately connected interneurons.

■ **Motor neuron** Nerve cell that carries messages away from the central nervous system toward the muscles and glands. Also called an *efferent neuron.*

■ **Interneuron** A nerve cell that relays messages between nerve cells, especially in the brain and spinal cord.

■ **Dendrite** A branched fiber that extends outward from the main cell body and carries information into the neuron.

How Neurons Work A look at Figure 3.4 will help you visualize the parts of a neuron. The "receiver" parts, which accept most of the incoming messages, consist of finely branched fibers called **dendrites.** These dendritic fibers extend outward from the cell body, where they act like a net, collecting messages received by direct stimulation (such as pressure, light, and sound) or from the activity of neighboring neurons.

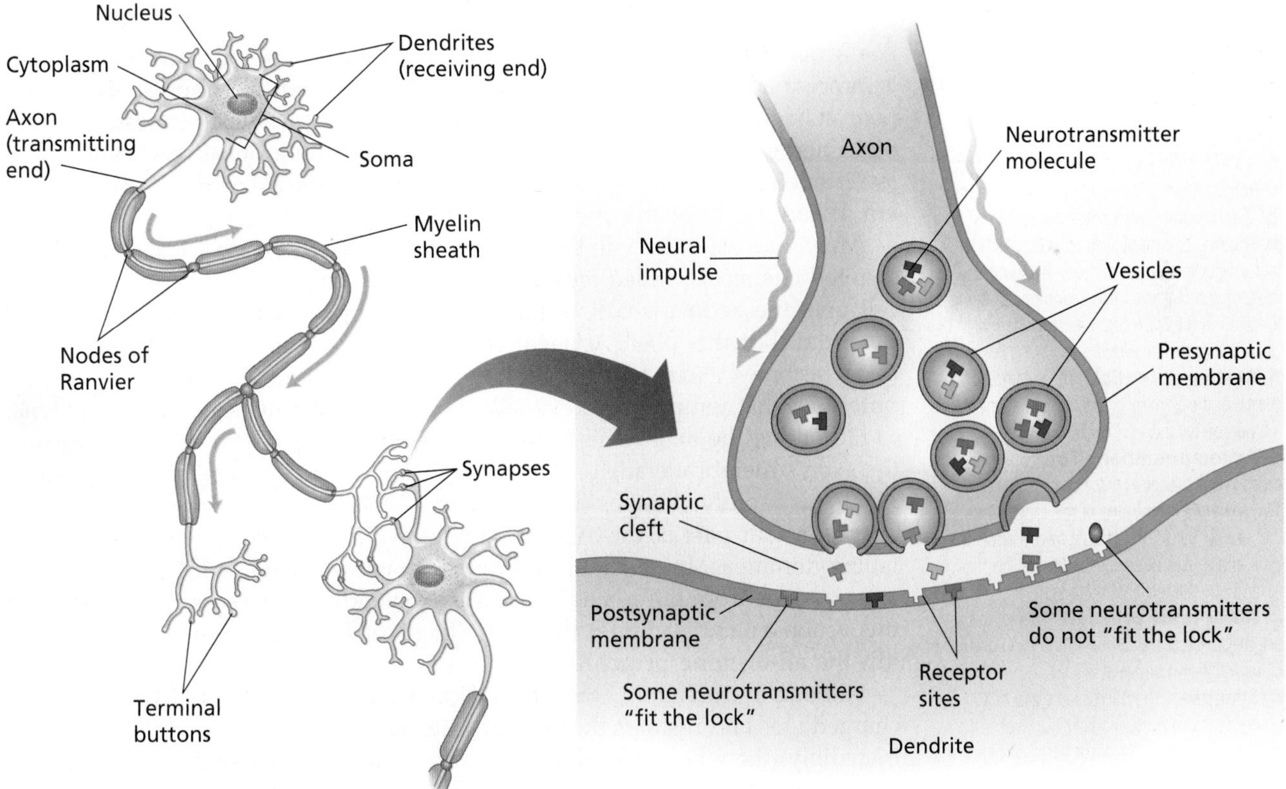
Nucleus
Cytoplasm
Dendrites (receiving end)
Axon (transmitting end)
Soma
Myelin sheath
Nodes of Ranvier
Synapses
Terminal buttons
Axon
Neurotransmitter molecule
Neural impulse
Vesicles
Presynaptic membrane
Synaptic cleft
Postsynaptic membrane
Some neurotransmitters do not "fit the lock"
Receptor sites
Some neurotransmitters "fit the lock"
Dendrite

● **FIGURE 3.4** Structure and Function of the Neuron

A typical neuron receives thousands of messages at a time through its *dendrites* and *soma* (cell body). When the soma becomes sufficiently aroused, its own message is then passed to the *axon,* which transmits it by means of an *action potential* to the cell's *terminal buttons.* There tiny *vesicles* containing *neurotransmitters* rupture and release their contents into the *synapse* (synaptic cleft). Appropriately shaped transmitter molecules arriving at the postsynaptic membrane can dock at *receptors,* where they stimulate the receiving cell. Excessive transmitter is taken back into the "sending" neuron by means of *reuptake.*

Significantly, neuroscientists have discovered that dendrites can undergo subtle modifications when we learn (Barinaga, 2000; Kennedy, 2000; Matus, 2000). This discovery has launched a search for drugs that might encourage the changes in dendrites associated with learning. While students will probably never be able to take a pill instead of a psychology class, they may one day be able to ingest harmless chemicals that will help them remember what they have read or heard in class. For the moment, the best we have to offer is coffee—which actually acts as a mild, but temporary, stimulus to the dendrites (Julien, 2001). (The evidence that caffeine promotes learning is controversial.)

Dendrites complete their job by passing incoming messages to the central part of the neuron, the *cell body* or **soma.** Not only does the soma contain the cell's nucleus and life-support machinery, it also has the executive job of assessing all the messages the cell receives from the dendrites (and also directly from other neurons). In this process, the input from a single synapse carries little weight, because a typical neuron may receive messages from hundreds or even thousands of other neurons. And, to make the situation more complex, some of these messages can be *excitatory* (saying, in effect, "Fire!") or *inhibitory* ("Don't fire!"). Just how aroused the cell body becomes depends on the sum total of all the incoming messages.

When excitation triumphs over inhibition, the aroused neuron may generate a message of its own, sent through a single "transmitter" fiber, the **axon,** which can extend over considerable distances. In a college basketball player, the axons connecting the spinal cord with the toes can be more than a meter in length. At the other end of the scale, the axons of interneurons in the brain may span only a tiny fraction of an inch.

The Action Potential Nerve cells employ both electrical and chemical signals to process and transmit information. As we have seen, an impulse in a single neuron begins when a stimulus, such as a sound, a pinprick, or messages from other nerve cells, make the soma excited. When the arousal reaches a critical level, an electrical impulse occurs in the axon, like the electronic flash of a camera. When this happens, the cell is said to "fire."

Much like the battery in that camera, the axon gets its electrical energy from charged chemicals, called *ions.* In its normal, resting state, the ions within the cell give the axon a small negative charge, appropriately called the **resting potential.** But this positive/negative imbalance is easily upset. When the cell body becomes excited, it triggers a cascade of events, known as the **action potential,** that temporarily reverses the charge and causes an electrical signal to race along the axon. This happens when tiny pores open in a small area of the axon's membrane adjacent to the soma, allowing a rapid influx of positive ions. This rapidly changes (we're talking 1/1000 of a second here) the internal charge in that part of the axon from negative to positive. Then, like a row of falling dominoes, these changes progress down the axon, causing an electrical signal to race from the soma toward the axon ending. There's no halfway about this action potential: Either the axon "fires" or it doesn't. Neuroscientists call this the **all-or-none principle.**

Almost immediately, the cell's "ion pump" flushes out the positively charged ions and restores the neuron to its resting potential, ready to fire again. Incredibly, the whole complex cycle may take place in less than a hundredth of a second. It is a mind-boggling performance—but this is not the end of the matter. The information carried by the action potential still must traverse a tiny gap before reaching another cell.

Synaptic Transmission The gap between nerve cells, called the **synapse,** acts as an electrical insulator, preventing the charge speeding down the axon from jumping to the next cell (see Figure 3.4). To pass the message across the *synap-*

■ **Soma** The part of a cell (such as a neuron) containing the nucleus, which includes the chromosomes. Also called the *cell body.*

■ **Axon** In a nerve cell, an extended fiber that conducts information from the *soma* to the *terminal buttons.* Information travels along the axon in the form of an electric charge called the *action potential.*

■ **Resting potential** The electrical charge of the axon in its inactive state, when the neuron is ready to "fire."

■ **Action potential** The nerve impulse caused by a change in the electrical charge across the cell membrane of the axon. When the neuron "fires," this charge travels down the axon and causes neurotransmitters to be released by the terminal buttons.

■ **All-or-none principle** Refers to the fact that the action potential in the axon occurs either full-blown or not at all.

■ **Synapse** The microscopic gap that serves as a communications link between neurons. Synapses also occur between neurons and the muscles or glands they serve.

■ **Terminal buttons** Tiny bulblike structures at the end of the axon, which contain neurotransmitters that carry the neuron's message into the synapse.

■ **Synaptic transmission** The relaying of information across the synapse by means of chemical neurotransmitters.

DO IT YOURSELF! Neural Messages and Reaction

For only a dollar you can find out how long it takes for the brain to process information and initiate a response.

Hold a crisp dollar bill by the middle of the short side, so that it dangles downward. Have a friend put his or her thumb and index fingers on opposite sides and about an inch away from the center of the bill, as shown in the illustration. Instruct your friend to pinch the thumb and fingers together and attempt to catch the bill when you drop it.

If you drop the bill without warning (being careful not to signal your intentions), your friend's brain will not be able to process the information rapidly enough to get a response to the hand before the dollar bill has dropped safely away.

What does this demonstrate? The time it takes to respond reflects the time it takes for the sensory nervous system to take in the information, for the brain to process it, and for the motor system to produce a response. All this involves millions of neurons; and, even though they respond quickly, their responses do take time.

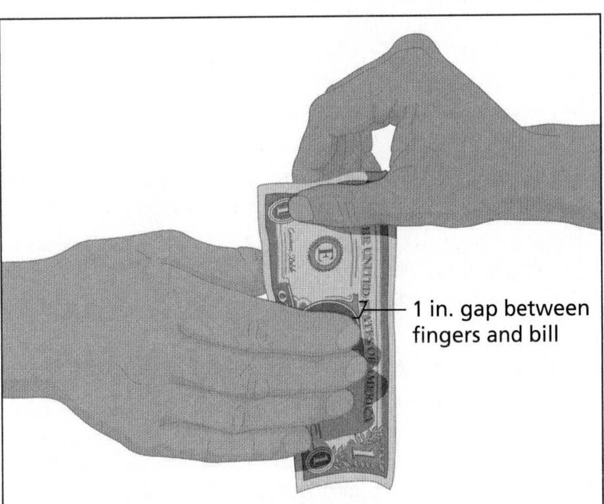
1 in. gap between fingers and bill

tic gap (or *synaptic cleft*), a neuron must initiate a process in tiny bulblike structures called **terminal buttons,** found at the ends of the axon. There, in a remarkable sequence of events known as **synaptic transmission,** the electrical message morphs into a chemical message that easily flows across the synaptic cleft between neurons. This occurs in the following way.

Neurotransmitters At the terminal buttons, the electrical impulse causes a rupture in the small bubble-shaped **synaptic vesicles** (sacs) containing **neurotransmitters,** which are chemicals used in neural communication. (Again, see Figure 3.4.) The vesicles quickly spill their contents—about 5000 transmitter molecules each—into the synaptic cleft (Kandel & Squire, 2000). There, the transmitter molecules diffuse across the gap. If they have the right shape (that is, a shape that complements that of special *receptors* in the membrane of the target cell), the neurotransmitters fit into the receptors, like a key fitting into a lock. This lock-and-key process stimulates the receiving neuron and carries the message forward.

After the transmitter molecules have done their work, they are broken down by other chemicals and recycled back to the terminal buttons, where they are reassembled and reused. In addition, many of the transmitter molecules get recycled before docking at a receptor site. Through a process called *reuptake,* these transmitters are intercepted as they are floating within the synapse and drawn back intact into vesicles. Reuptake, then, has the effect of "turning the volume down" on the message being transmitted between neurons. When we later discuss drug therapy for mental disorders (in Chapter 13), reuptake will be an important term because some important drugs—such as the well-known Prozac—interfere with the reuptake process.

Neuroscientists have identified dozens of different neurotransmitters. Table 3.1 distinguishes several that have proved especially important in psychological functioning. Imbalances in these neurotransmitters are also thought to underlie certain disorders, such as schizophrenia and Alzheimer's disease,

● Michael J. Fox suffers from Parkinson disease, caused by a deficiency of dopamine in his brain.

■ **Synaptic vesicle** A small "container" holding neurotransmitter molecules that then connects to the presynaptic membrane, releasing the neurotransmitter into the synapse.

■ **Neurotransmitters** Chemical messengers that relay neural messages across the synapse. Many neurotransmitters are also hormones.

TABLE 3.1	Seven Important Neurotransmitters		
Neurotransmitter	**Normal function**	**Problems associated with imbalance**	**Substances that affect the action of this neurotransmitter**
Dopamine	Produces sensations of pleasure and reward Used by CNS neurons involved in voluntary movement	Schizophrenia Parkinson's disease	Cocaine Amphetamine Methylphenidate (Ritalin) Alcohol
Serotonin	Regulates sleep and dreaming, mood, pain, aggression, appetite, and sexual behavior	Depression Certain anxiety disorders Obsessive–compulsive disorder	Fluoxetine (Prozac) Hallucinogenics (e.g., LSD)
Norepinephrine	Used by neurons in autonomic nervous system and by neurons in almost every region of the brain Controls heart rate, sleep, stress, sexual responsiveness, vigilance, and appetite	High blood pressure Depression	Tricyclic antidepressants Beta-blockers
Acetylcholine	The primary neurotransmitter used by efferent neurons carrying messages from the CNS Also involved in some kinds of learning and memory	Certain muscular disorders Alzheimer's disease	Nicotine Black widow spider venom Botulism toxin Curare Atropine
GABA	The most prevalent inhibitory neurotransmitter in neurons of the CNS	Anxiety Epilepsy	Barbiturates "Minor" tranquilizers (e.g., Valium, Librium) Alcohol
Glutamate	The primary excitatory neurotransmitter in the CNS Involved in learning and memory	Release of excessive glutamate apparently causes brain damage after stroke	PCP ("angel dust")
Endorphins	Pleasurable sensations and control of pain	Lowered levels resulting from opiate addiction	Opiates: opium, heroin, morphine, methadone

as well as poisoning by black widow spider venom and botulism toxin. It shouldn't surprise us, then, that many drugs used to treat mental disorders employ chemicals that act like neurotransmitters or otherwise affect the action of neurotransmitters on nerve cells. Likewise, drugs of abuse (heroin, cocaine, methamphetamine, for example) either mimic, enhance, or inhibit our brains' natural neurotransmitters. We will talk more about neurotransmitters and their relation to drug action in the upcoming "Psychology in Your Life" section.

Plasticity Neurons have the ability to send messages that produce simple reflexes, as when you automatically withdraw your hand from a painfully hot plate. But neurons also have the ability to *change*—to make new connections or to strengthen old ones. This is a hugely important process known as **plasticity.** It means that the nervous system, and especially the brain, has the ability to adapt or modify itself as the result of experience (M. Holloway, 2003; Kandel & Squire, 2000). Earlier we discussed one form of plasticity that involves the changes within dendrites that are associated with learning. Another form involves making new connections among neurons—as when neurons sprout new dendrites, for example. This process is also believed to be associated with learning. Plasticity may also account for the brain's ability to compensate for injury, as in a stroke or head trauma—a controversial concept (Pinel, 2003). In all these ways, then, plasticity is a property that allows the brain to be restructured and "reprogrammed" by experience.

■ **Plasticity** The nervous system's ability to adapt or change as the result of experience. Plasticity may also help the nervous system adapt to physical damage.

Here is a more subtle point: Because of its neural plasticity, the physical structure of the brain can be changed by its interactions with the outside world (Barinaga, 1996; LeDoux, 2002; Singer, 1995). For example, as a violin player gains expertise, the motor area linked to the fingers of the left hand becomes larger (Juliano, 1998). Increased brain area also develops for the index finger used by a blind reader who learns to use Braille (Elbert et al., 1995; LeDoux, 1996). Usually these changes are beneficial. Occasionally, however, intensely traumatic experiences can alter the brain's emotional responsiveness in detrimental ways (Arnsten, 1998; Caldwell, 1995; Mukerjee, 1995). Thus the brain cells of soldiers who experience combat or people who have been sexually assaulted may undergo physical changes that can produce a permanent hair-trigger responsiveness. This can cause them overreact to mild stressors and even to merely unexpected surprises. Taken together, such findings indicate that neural plasticity can produce changes both in the brain's function and in its physical structure in response to experience (Sapolsky, 1990).

CONNECTION: CHAPTER 8
Extremely threatening experiences can cause posttraumatic stress disorder, which can produce physical changes in the brain.

Glial Cells: A Support Group for Neurons Interwoven among the brain's vast network of neurons is an even greater number of *glial cells* that were once thought to "glue" the neurons together. (The name comes from the Greek word for "glue.") In fact, glial cells do provide structural support for neurons, as well as help in forming new synapses (Gallo & Chittajallu, 2001). New evidence suggests that they may also be a crucial part of the process we call *learning* (Fields, 2004). In addition, the multitalented **glial cells** form a *myelin sheath,* a fatty insulation around many axons in the brain and spinal cord. Like the covering on an electrical cable, the myelin sheath insulates and protects the cell and helps speed the conduction of impulses along the axon (see Figure 3.4). Unfortunately, certain diseases, such as multiple sclerosis (MS), attack the myelin sheath, especially in the motor pathways. The result is poor conduction of nerve impulses, which accounts for the increasing difficulty MS patients have in controlling movement.

So there you have the two main building blocks of the nervous system: neurons, with their amazing plasticity, and their supportive glial cells, which protect the neurons and help to propagate neural messages. But, wondrous as these individual components are, we should point out that in the big picture of behavior and mental processes, a single cell doesn't do very much. It takes thousands upon millions of neurons flashing their electrochemical signals in synchronized waves back and forth through the incredibly complex neural networks in your brain to produce thoughts, sensations, and feelings. Similarly, all your actions arise from waves of nerve impulses delivered to your muscles, glands, and organs through the nervous system. Yet, as we will see in the next "Psychology in Your Life" section, the effects of psychoactive drugs, such as tranquilizers, antidepressants, and painkillers, rely on altering the chemistry underlying these waves at the level of individual cells and their synapses (Deadwyler & Hampson, 1995; Ferster & Spruston, 1995). For the moment, however, let's turn our attention to the neural networks themselves—networks that together make up the *nervous system.*

Divisions of the Nervous System

If you could observe a neural message as it moves from stimulus to response, you would see the signal make a seamless transition from one part of the nervous system to another. It might begin, for example, as a signal in the eyes, then travel to the brain for extensive processing, and finally reemerge from the brain as a message instructing the muscles to respond. In fact, the **nervous system,** made up of all the nerve cells in the body, functions as a single, complex,

■ **Glial cells** Cells that bind the neurons together. Glial cells also provide an insulating covering (the myelin sheath) of the axon for some neurons, which facilitates the electrical impulse.

■ **Nervous system** The entire network of neurons in the body, including the central nervous system, the peripheral nervous system, and their subdivisions.

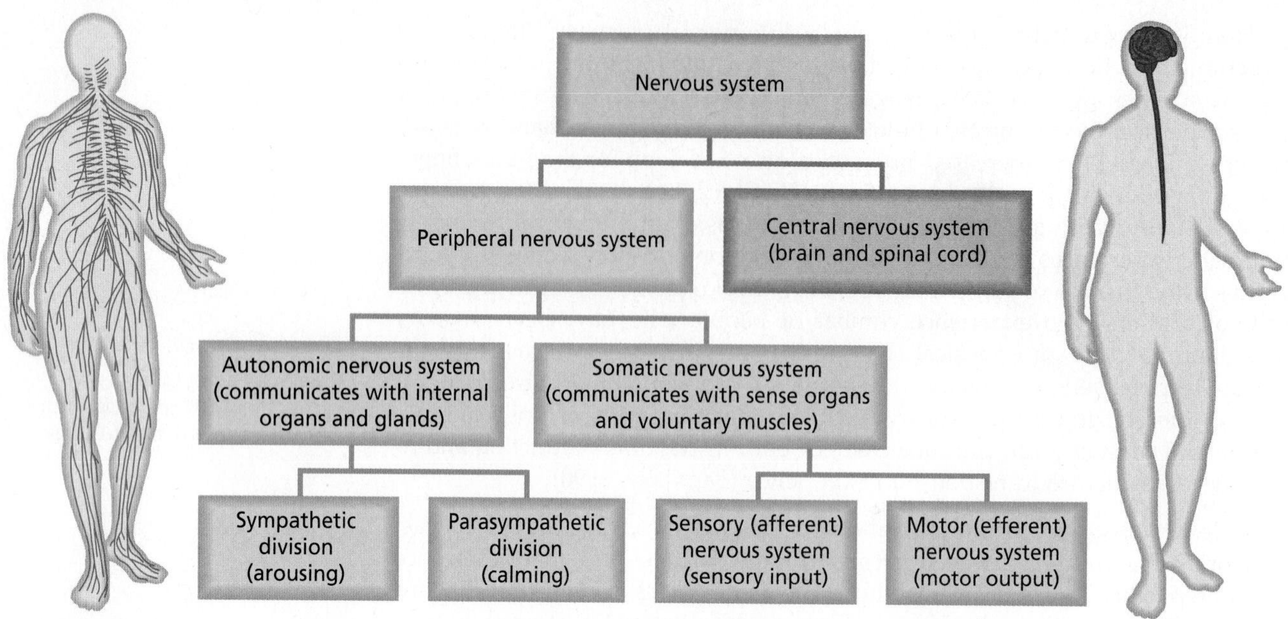
Nervous system
Peripheral nervous system
Central nervous system
(brain and spinal cord)
Autonomic nervous system
(communicates with internal
organs and glands)
Somatic nervous system
(communicates with sense organs
and voluntary muscles)
Sympathetic
division
(arousing)
Parasympathetic
division
(calming)
Sensory (afferent)
nervous system
(sensory input)
Motor (efferent)
nervous system
(motor output)

● **FIGURE 3.5** Organization of the Nervous System
This figure shows the major divisions of the nervous system. (Note: It does *not* show the flow of information in the nervous system!)

and interconnected unit. Nevertheless, we find it convenient to distinguish among divisions of the nervous system, based on their location and on the type of processing they do. The most basic distinction recognizes two major divisions: the *central nervous system* and the *peripheral nervous system.* (See Figure 3.5.)

The Central Nervous System Comprised of the *brain* and *spinal cord,* the **central nervous system** (CNS) serves as the body's "command central." The brain, filling roughly a third of the skull, makes complex decisions, coordinates our body functions, and initiates our behaviors. The spinal cord, playing a supportive role, serves as a sort of neural cable, connecting the brain with parts of the peripheral nervous system extending into the trunk and limbs. (The nerve pathways connecting the brain with the eyes, ears, nose, tongue, skin and muscles of the head, and internal organs do not pass through the spinal cord.)

The spinal cord has another job, too. It takes charge of simple, swift **reflexes** that do not require brain power, such as the knee-jerk reflex your physician elicits with a tap on the knee. We know that the brain does not get involved in these simple reflexes, because a person whose spinal cord has been severed may still be able to withdraw a limb reflexively from a painful stimulus—even though the brain doesn't sense the pain. The brain is required, however, for *voluntary* movements. That's why damage to the nerves of the spinal cord can produce paralysis of the limbs or trunk. As you might expect, the extent of paralysis depends on the location of the damage. In general, the higher the site of damage, the greater the extent of the paralysis. This fact helps explain why an injury high in the spinal cord paralyzed the late actor Christopher Reeve from his neck down.

The Peripheral Nervous System The **peripheral nervous system** (PNS) also plays a supportive role, connecting the central nervous system with the rest of the body through bundles of sensory and motor axons, called *nerves.* Its many branches carry messages between the brain and the sense organs, the internal organs, and the muscles. In this role, the peripheral nervous system carries the incoming messages that tell your brain about the sights, sounds, tastes, smells,

■ **Central nervous system** The brain and the spinal cord.

■ **Reflex** A simple, unlearned response triggered by stimuli—such as the knee-jerk reflex set off by tapping the tendon just below your kneecap.

■ **Peripheral nervous system** All parts of the nervous system lying outside the central nervous system. The peripheral nervous system includes the autonomic and somatic nervous systems.

and textures of the world. Likewise, it carries the outgoing signals that tell your body's muscles and glands how to respond.

You might think of the PNS, therefore, as operating a pick-up-and-delivery service for the central nervous system. If, for example, an aggressive dog approaches you, your PNS picks up the auditory information (barking, growling, snarling) and visual information (bared teeth, hair standing up on the neck) and delivers it to the brain. Quickly, brain circuits assess the situation (Danger!) and communicate with other circuits that give orders for a hasty retreat. The PNS then delivers those orders to mobilize your heart, lungs, legs, and other body parts needed in response to the emergency. It does this through its two major divisions: the *somatic nervous system* and the *autonomic nervous system.* One deals with our external world, the other with our internal responses. (A few moments spent studying Figure 3.5 will help you understand these divisions and subdivisions.)

The Somatic Division of the PNS Think of the **somatic nervous system** as the brain's communications link with the outside world. Its sensory component connects the sense organs to the brain, and its motor component links the CNS with the body's skeletal muscles, the muscles that control voluntary movements. (We met these two divisions earlier in our discussion of sensory and motor neurons.) So, for example, when you see a slice of pizza, the visual image is carried by the somatic division's *afferent* system. Then, if all goes well, the *efferent* system sends instructions to muscles that propel the slice of pizza in just the right direction, into your open mouth.

The Autonomic Division of the PNS The other major division of the PNS takes charge of the pizza once it heads down your throat. It is now in the province of the **autonomic nervous system** (*autonomic* means self-regulating or independent). This network carries signals that control our internal organs to perform such jobs as regulating digestion, respiration, heart rate, and arousal. Amazingly, it does so without our having to think about it—all unconsciously. The autonomic system also works when you are asleep. Even during anesthesia, it can sustain the most basic vital functions.

And—wouldn't you know?—biopsychologists further divide the autonomic nervous system into two major parts: the *sympathetic* and *parasympathetic divisions* (as shown in Figure 3.6). The **sympathetic division** arouses the heart, lungs, and other organs in stressful or emergency situations, when our responses must be quick and powerfully energized. Often called the "fight-or-flight" system, the sympathetic division carries messages that help us respond quickly to a threat either by attacking or fleeing. The sympathetic system also creates the tension and arousal you feel during an exciting movie, a first date, or an oral presentation. Perhaps you can bring to mind what the sympathetic division of your autonomic nervous system was doing during your last public-speaking effort. Was it hard to breathe? Were your palms sweaty? Did your stomach feel queasy?

In contrast, the **parasympathetic division** applies the neural brakes, returning our internal responses to a calm and collected state. But even though it has an opposing action, the parasympathetic division works cooperatively with the sympathetic system, like two children on a teeter-totter. Figure 3.6 shows the most important connections made by these two autonomic divisions.

Now, having completed our whirlwind tour of the nervous system, we return our attention briefly to its partner in internal communication, the *endocrine system.* Again, we will remind you that this system makes use of many of the same chemicals employed in neural communication. In the nervous system we called them *neurotransmitters,* but in the endocrine system, we call these chemical messengers *hormones.*

■ **Somatic nervous system** A division of the peripheral nervous system that carries sensory information to the central nervous system and also sends voluntary messages to the body's skeletal muscles.

■ **Autonomic nervous system** The portion of the peripheral nervous system that sends communications between the central nervous system and the internal organs and glands.

■ **Sympathetic division** The part of the autonomic nervous system that sends messages to internal organs and glands that help us respond to stressful and emergency situations.

■ **Parasympathetic division** The part of the autonomic nervous system that monitors the routine operations of the internal organs and returns the body to calmer functioning after arousal by the sympathetic division.

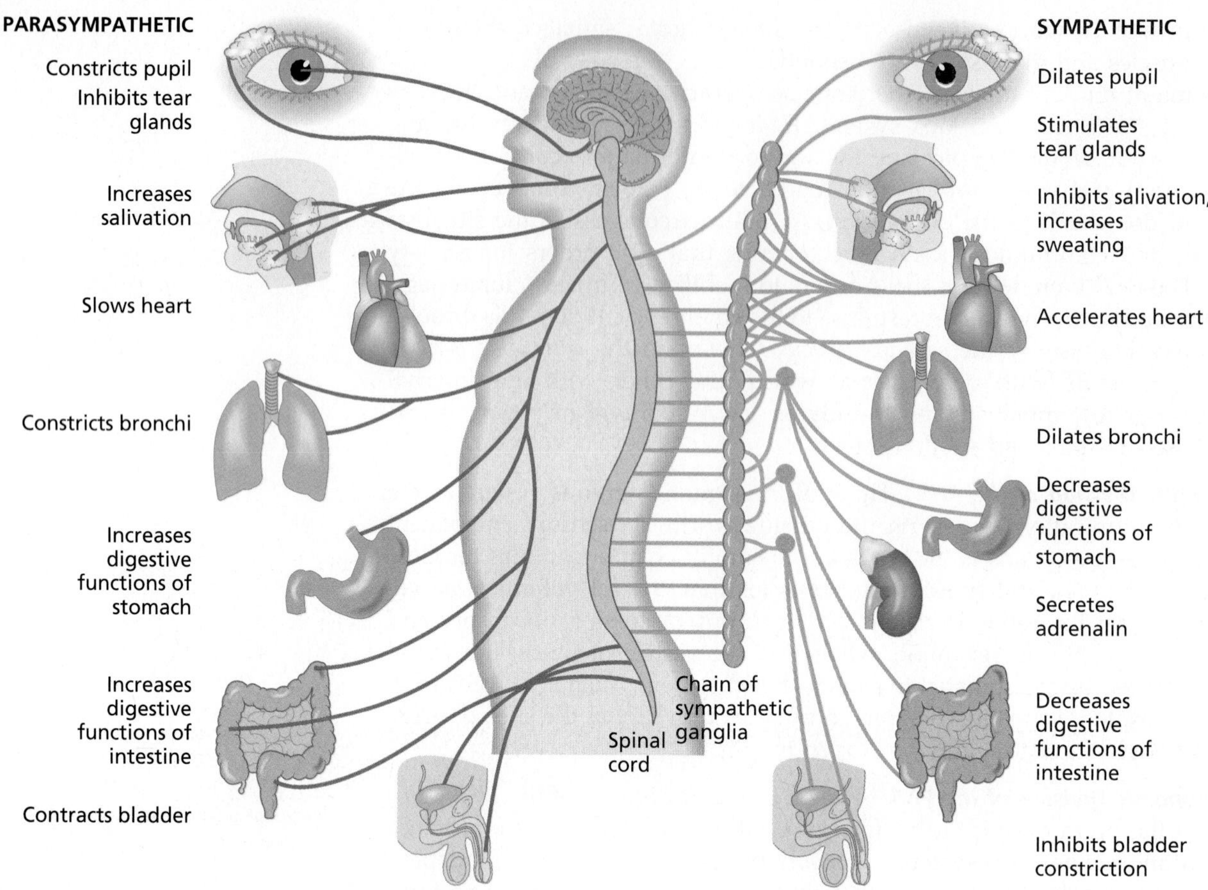
PARASYMPATHETIC
Constricts pupil
Inhibits tear glands
Increases salivation
Slows heart
Constricts bronchi
Increases digestive functions of stomach
Increases digestive functions of intestine
Contracts bladder
SYMPATHETIC
Dilates pupil
Stimulates tear glands
Inhibits salivation, increases sweating
Accelerates heart
Dilates bronchi
Decreases digestive functions of stomach
Secretes adrenalin
Decreases digestive functions of intestine
Inhibits bladder constriction
Chain of sympathetic ganglia
Spinal cord

● **FIGURE 3.6** Divisions of the Autonomic Nervous System

The *parasympathetic nervous system* (at left) regulates day-to-day internal processes and behavior. The *sympathetic nervous system* (at right) regulates internal processes and behavior in stressful situations. On their way to and from the spinal cord, sympathetic nerve fibers make connections with specialized neural clusters called *ganglia.*

The Endocrine System

Consider this little-known fact: Your bloodstream carries *information,* along with oxygen and nutrients. It does so by serving as the communication pathway for the **endocrine system,** shown in Figure 3.7. The glands that make up the endocrine system (which takes its name from the Greek *endo* for "within" and *krinein* for "secrete") transmit information by releasing **hormones** into the bloodstream. Much like neurotransmitters in the nervous system, hormones are chemical messengers that influence not only body functions but behaviors and emotions as well (Damasio, 2003; LeDoux, 2002). For example, hormones from the pituitary stimulate body growth. Hormones from the ovaries and testes influence sexual development and sexual responses. Hormones from the adrenals produce the arousal accompanying fear. And hormones from the thyroid control metabolism (the body's rate of energy use). Once secreted into the blood, hormones circulate throughout the body until delivered to their target muscles, glands, and organs. Table 3.2 outlines the major endocrine glands and the body systems they regulate.

Under normal (unaroused) conditions, the endocrine system works in parallel with the parasympathetic nervous system to sustain our basic body processes. But in a crisis, the endocrine system shifts into a new mode, supporting the actions of the sympathetic nervous system. So, when you encounter a stressor or an emergency (such as the speeding car headed at you), the

■ **Endocrine system** The hormone system–the body's chemical messenger system, including the endocrine glands: pituitary, thyroid, parathyroid, adrenals, pancreas, ovaries, and testes.

■ **Hormone** A chemical messenger used by the endocrine system. Many hormones also serve as neurotransmitters.

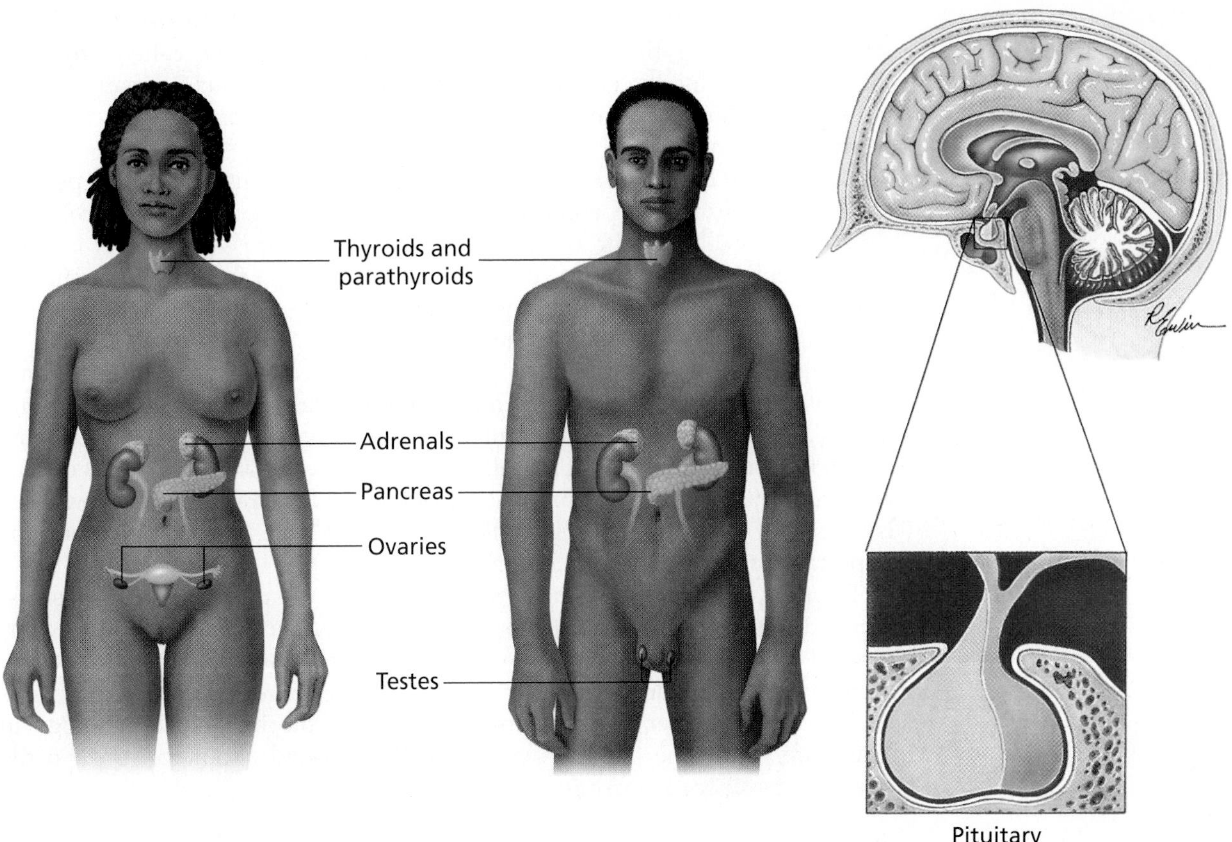
Thyroids and
parathyroids
Adrenals
Pancreas
Ovaries
Testes
Pituitary

● **FIGURE 3.7** Endocrine Glands in Females and Males

The pituitary gland (shown at right) is the "master gland" regulating the endocrine glands, whose locations are illustrated at left. The pituitary gland is under the control of the hypothalamus, an important structure in the limbic system.

TABLE 3.2 Hormonal Functions of Major Endocrine Glands

These Endocrine Glands . . .	Produce Hormones That Regulate . . .
Anterior pituitary	Ovaries and testes Breast milk production Metabolism Reactions to stress
Posterior pituitary	Conservation of water in the body Breast milk secretion Uterus contractions
Thyroid	Metabolism Physical growth and development
Parathyroid	Calcium levels in the body
Pancreas	Glucose (sugar) metabolism
Adrenal glands	Fight-or-flight response Metabolism Sexual desire (especially in women)
Ovaries	Development of female sexual characteristics Production of ova (eggs)
Testes	Development of male sexual characteristics Sperm production Sexual desire (in men)

hormone *epinephrine* (sometimes called *adrenalin*) is released into the bloodstream, sustaining the body's defensive reaction that we called "fight or flight." In this way, the endocrine system finishes what your sympathetic nervous system started, by keeping your heart pounding and your muscles tense, ready for action.

CONNECTION: CHAPTER 8

Prolonged stress messages can produce physical and mental disorders by means of the *general adaptation syndrome*.

Later in the book we will see what happens when this stress state persists too long. For example, people who have stressful jobs or unhappy relationships may develop a chronically elevated level of stress hormones in their blood, keeping them in a state of perpetual arousal. But the price of continued arousal is high. The body may not withstand such long-term stress without suffering some physical consequences.

At the base of your brain, a "master gland," called the **pituitary gland,** attempts to keep all these endocrine responses under tight control. (See Figure 3.7.) It does so by sending out hormone signals of its own through the blood. But the pituitary itself is really only a midlevel manager. It takes orders, in turn, from the brain—in particular from a small neural nucleus to which it is physically appended: the *hypothalamus.* We will have more to say about this important brain structure in a moment.

For now, we want to emphasize the idea that the peripheral nervous system and the endocrine system provide parallel means of communication, coordinated by their link in the brain. Ultimately, the brain decides which messages will be sent through both networks. We will turn our attention to this master "nerve center"—the brain—right after exploring, in "Psychology in Your Life," how the concepts you have just learned about can explain the effects of psychoactive drugs.

PSYCHOLOGY IN YOUR LIFE: HOW PSYCHOACTIVE DRUGS AFFECT THE NERVOUS SYSTEM

The mind-altering effects of marijuana, LSD, cocaine, narcotics, tranquilizers, and sedatives entice millions of users. Millions more jolt their brains awake with the caffeine of their morning coffee, tea, or cola and the nicotine in an accompanying cigarette. Then at night they may reverse the cycle with alcohol and sleeping pills. But how do these substances achieve their effects? The answer to that question involves the ability of *psychoactive drugs* to enhance or inhibit natural chemical processes in our neural circuits.

The ecstasy and the agony of these drugs come mainly from their effects on brain synapses. Some drugs impersonate neurotransmitters by mimicking their effects in the brain. Others act less directly by enhancing or dampening the effects of neurotransmitters. We call those that enhance or mimic neurotransmitters **agonists.** Nicotine, for example, is an agonist because it acts like the neurotransmitter acetylcholine. This has the effect of "turning up the volume" in the acetylcholine pathways (the acetylcholine-using bundles innervating the muscles and connecting certain parts of the brain). By contrast, we call chemicals that dampen or inhibit the effects of neurotransmitters **antagonists.** Curare and botulism toxin are antagonists because they interfere with the neurotransmitter acetylcholine—effectively "turning the volume down." In general, agonists facilitate and antagonists inhibit messages in parts of the nervous system using that transmitter.

The well-known antidepressant Prozac (fluoxetine) does its work as an agonist in the brain's serotonin pathways, where it makes more serotonin available (see Figure 3.8). But, because serotonin's effects are complex, fluoxetine can cause not only changes in mood but, occasionally, undesirable changes in sleep patterns, appetite, and thinking (*Physician's Desk Reference*, 2004).

■ **Pituitary gland** The "master gland" that produces hormones influencing the secretions of all other endocrine glands, as well as a hormone that influences growth. The pituitary is attached to the brain's hypothalamus, from which it takes its orders.

■ **Agonist** Drug or other chemical that enhances or mimics the effects of neurotransmitters.

■ **Antagonist** Drug or other chemical that inhibits the effects of neurotransmitters.

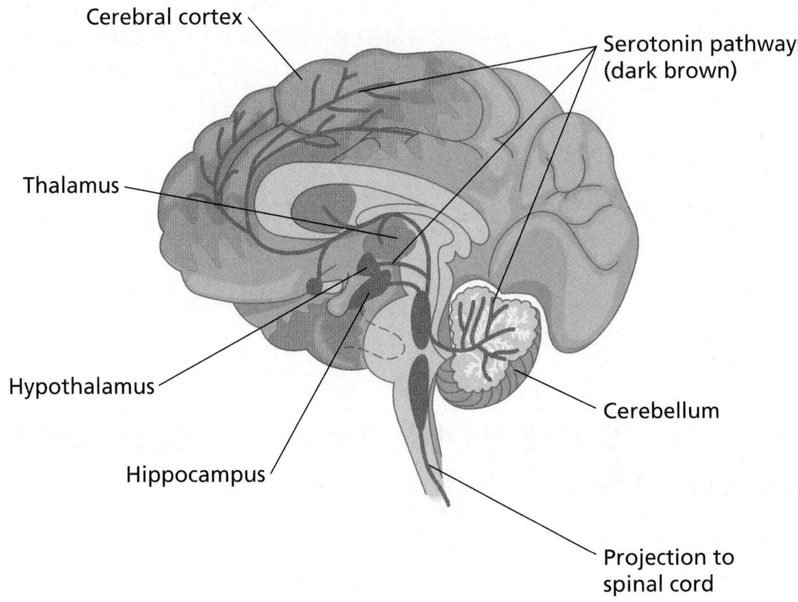
Cerebral cortex
Serotonin pathways
(dark brown)
Thalamus
Hypothalamus
Cerebellum
Hippocampus
Projection to
spinal cord

● **FIGURE 3.8** Serotonin Pathways in the Brain

Each neurotransmitter is associated with certain neural pathways in the brain. In this cross section of the brain, you see the main pathways for serotonin. Drugs that stimulate or inhibit serotonin will selectively affect the brain regions shown in this diagram.

Why the unwanted side effects? The answer to that question involves an important principle about the brain's design. Within the brain are many bundles of neurons—**neural pathways**—that connect different components of the brain. Moreover, each pathway employs only certain neurotransmitters. This fact allows a drug affecting a particular transmitter to target specific parts of the brain. Unfortunately for the drug-takers, different pathways may employ the same neurotransmitter for widely different functions. Thus, serotonin pathways, for example, affect not only mood but sleep, appetite, and cognition. So, taking Prozac (or one of its chemical cousins with other brand names) may treat depression but, at the same time, have side effects on other psychological processes—which explains why the drug ads must list the major possible side effects.

In fact, no psychoactive drug exists that acts like a "magic bullet" that can strike only one precise target in the brain, to work its wonders without causing collateral effects.

■ **Neural pathway** Bundle of nerve cells that follow generally the same route and employ the same neurotransmitter.

CHECK YOUR UNDERSTANDING

1. **RECALL:** Of the body's two main communication systems, the ______ is faster, while the ______ sends longer-lasting messages.
2. **RECALL:** The ______ division of the autonomic nervous system increases the heart rate during an emergency, while the ______ division slows the heart rate after an emergency is over.
3. **RECALL:** Which of the following might carry a neural impulse across the synapse?
   - **a.** an axon
   - **b.** the blood
   - **c.** the cerebrospinal fluid
   - **d.** dopamine
   - **e.** an electrical charge
4. **RECALL:** Which part of the brain communicates directly with the "master gland" of the endocrine system?
   - **a.** the brain stem
   - **b.** the cerebellum
   - **c.** the cortex
   - **d.** the hypothalamus
   - **e.** the pituitary
5. **RECALL:** Make a sketch of two connecting neurons. Describe the location and function of the dendrites, soma, axon, myelin sheath, terminal buttons, synapse.

(continues)

6. **APPLICATION:** Some people seem to have high blood pressure because they have an anxiety response while having their blood pressure taken at the doctor's office. Which part of the nervous system produces this anxiety response?
   a. the cortex
   b. the parasympathetic nervous system
   c. the somatic nervous system
   d. the spinal cord
   e. the sympathetic nervous system

7. **UNDERSTANDING THE CORE CONCEPT:** The chemical messengers in the brain are called ______, while in the endocrine system they are called ______.

ANSWERS: 1. nervous system/endocrine system 2. sympathetic/parasympathetic 3. d 4. d 5. See Figure 3.4 6. e 7. neurotransmitters/hormones

KEY QUESTION

HOW DOES THE BRAIN PRODUCE BEHAVIOR AND MENTAL PROCESSES?

In September 1848, a 25-year-old American railroad worker named Phineas Gage sustained a horrible head injury when a charge of blasting powder drove an iron rod into his face, up through the front of his brain, and out through the top of his head. (See the accompanying photo.) Amazingly, he recovered from this injury and lived another 12 years—but as a psychologically changed man (Fleischman, 2002; Macmillan, 2000). Those who knew him remarked that Gage, once a dependable and likeable crew boss, had become an irresponsible and rowdy ruffian. In essence, he was no longer himself. "Gage was no longer Gage" (Damasio, 1994, p. 8). We cannot help but wonder: Had the site of Gage's injury—the front of his brain—been the home of his "old self"?

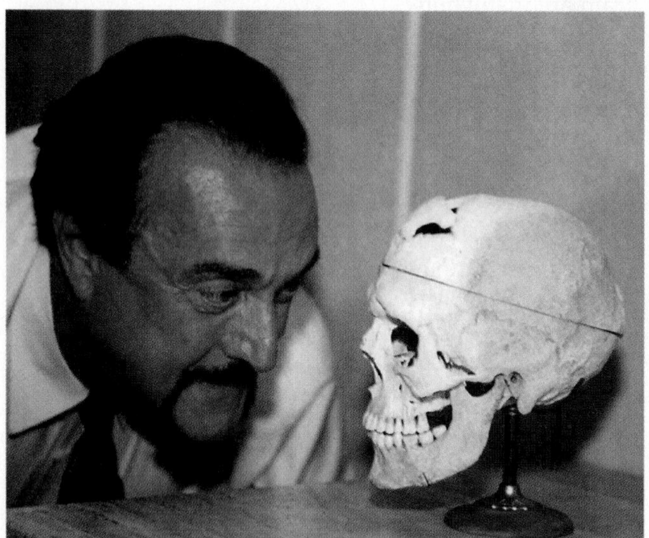

● Author Phil Zimbardo (left) with the skull of Phineas Gage.

Phineas Gage's accident also raises another question: What is the connection between mind and body? Humans have, of course, long recognized the existence of such a link—although they didn't always know the brain to be the organ of the mind. Even today we might speak, as they did in Shakespeare's time, of "giving one's heart" to another or of "not having the stomach" for something when describing disgust. Today we know that love doesn't flow from the heart, nor courage from the digestive system. We now know that emotions, desires, and thoughts originate in the brain. (The news hasn't reached songwriters, who have yet to pen a lyric proclaiming, "I love you with all my brain.") At last, neuroscientists are unraveling the mysteries of this complex organ, revealing it—perhaps a little less romantically than the songwriters do—as a collection of distinct modules that work together like the components of a computer. This new understanding of the brain becomes the Core Concept for this final section of the chapter:

CORE CONCEPT

The brain is composed of many specialized modules that work together to create mind and behavior.

As you study the brain in the following pages, you will find that the brain's modular components have specialized functions (Cohen & Tong, 2001). Some take responsibility for sensations, such as vision and hearing. Some have a part in regulating our emotional lives. Some contribute to memory. Some generate speech and other behaviors. This is the point: The specialized parts of the brain, like an efficient committee, usually manage to work together. Fortunately, from the perspective of a brain owner, many of these brain modules do so automatically and without conscious direction, as when an infant "knows" to look at a person's eyes. But, when something goes wrong with one or more of the brain's components, as in a stroke or Alzheimer's disease—or as happened to Phineas Gage—the biological basis of thought or behavior captures our attention.

Let's begin the story of the brain by seeing how neuroscientists go about opening their windows on its inner workings. As you will see, much of what we know about the brain's inner workings comes from observations of people with brain disease and head injuries—people like Gage.

Windows on the Brain

The brain can never actually touch velvet, taste chocolate, have sex, or see the blue of the sky. It only knows the outside world secondhand, through changing patterns of electrochemical activity in the peripheral nervous system, the neural network that shuttles messages in and out. The brain, the undisputed master of the body and seat of our personality, has no power to act on its own. To do its bidding, the brain must rely on the neural and endocrine communications networks that carry its messages to the muscles, organs, and glands throughout the body.

And what would you see if you could peer beneath the bony skull and behold the brain? The wrinkled appearance of its surface, rather like a giant walnut, offers no hint of the brain's internal structure or function. For that, we need the *EEG, CT scans, MRIs,* and *f*MRIs.

Sensing Brain Waves with the EEG Neuroscientists have learned a great deal about the brain by studying its electrical activity. Using a sensitive device called the **electroencephalograph** (or **EEG**), they can—without opening the skull—record the extremely weak voltage patterns called *brain waves,* sensed by electrodes pasted on the scalp. Much as the lights can tell you which parts of a city are most "alive" at night, the EEG senses which parts of the brain are most active. It can identify, for example, electrical patterns involved in moving the hand or processing a visual image. The EEG can also reveal abnormal waves caused by brain malfunctions, such as occurs in *epilepsy* (a seizure disorder that arises from an electrical "storm" in the brain).

That said, however, the EEG is not a very precise instrument. Within the limits of its sensitivity, it indiscriminately records the brain's electrical activity in the region of the electrode. And because there may be fewer than a dozen electrodes used, the electrical picture of the brain is not detailed. Moreover, the EEG electrodes sample not only the "flash" discharges of the action potential, they also sense other, more subtle electrical charges, such as those in the soma. The result is a coarse, moment-to-moment summary of the electrical activity in millions and millions of neurons lying near the surface of the brain—making it all the more amazing that we can sometimes read the traces of mental processes in the EEG signature, as we will see in more detail in the next chapter.

Mapping the Brain with Electric Probes Half a century ago, the great Canadian neurologist Wilder Penfield opened another window on the brain by "mapping" its pinkish-gray surface with a pen-shaped electric probe. During brain surgery, Penfield stimulated patients' exposed brains with an electrode (a thin wire that conducts a mild electric current, on the order of a flashlight battery) and recorded their responses. (His patients were kept awake, but under local anesthesia, so they felt no pain.)

■ **Electroencephalograph** or **EEG** A device for recording brain waves, typically by electrodes placed on the scalp. The record produced is known as an electroencephalogram (also called an EEG).

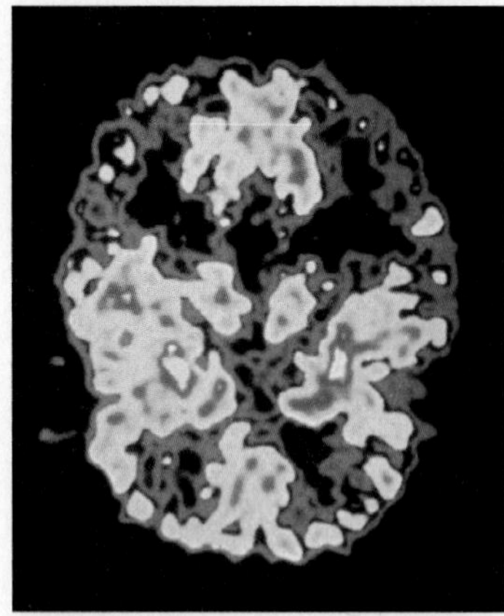

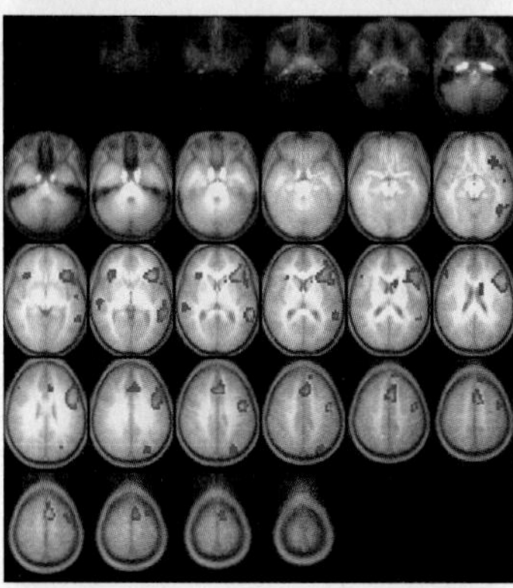

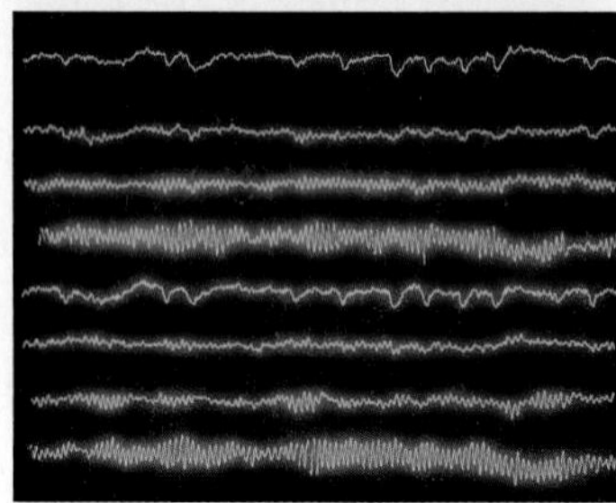

● **FIGURE 3.9** Windows on the Mind

Images from brain-scanning devices. From top: PET, *f*MRI, EEG. Each scanning and recording device has strengths and weaknesses.

This was not just an experiment. As a surgeon, Penfield needed to identify the exact boundaries of the diseased brain areas, to avoid removing healthy tissue. But, as he did so, Penfield was able to demonstrate that the brain's surface is divided into distinct regions, each with different functions. Stimulating a certain spot might cause the left hand to move; another site might produce a sensation, such as a flash of light. Stimulating still other sites might provoke a memory from childhood (Penfield, 1959; Penfield & Baldwin, 1952). Later, other scientists followed Penfield's lead and probed structures deeper in the brain. There they found that electrical stimulation could set off elaborate sequences of behavior and emotions. The overall conclusion from such work is unmistakable: Each region of the brain has its own specific functions.

Computerized Brain Scans Advances in brain science during the last couple of decades have opened new windows on the brain by employing sophisticated procedures collectively known as *brain scans.* Some make images with X rays, others use radioactive tracers, and still others use magnetic fields (Pinel, 2003). Thanks to such scanning methods, scientists can now make vivid pictures of brain tissue without opening the skull and physically invading the brain. Medically, these methods also help neurosurgeons locate brain abnormalities such as tumors or stroke-related damage. Psychologically, the images they obtain from brain scans can show where our thoughts and feelings are processed because specific regions of the brain seem to "light up" when a person reads, speaks, solves problems, or feels certain emotions (Raichle, 1994).

The most common brain-scanning methods currently used are CT scanning, PET scanning, MRI, and *f*MRI. (Barinaga, 1997a; Mogilner et al., 1993):

- **CT scanning,** or **computerized tomography,** creates a computerized image of the brain from X rays passed through the brain at various angles. Tomography (from the Greek *tomos,* "section") detects the soft-tissue structures of the brain that X rays normally do not reveal (see Figure 3.9). CT scanning creates a static image of brain structure.
- **PET scanning,** or **positron emission tomography,** produces an image showing brain activity (rather than brain structure). One common PET technique does so by sensing the concentration of low-level radioactive glucose (sugar), which concentrates in the most active brain circuits. Areas of high concentration show up as brightly colored on the image.
- **MRI,** or **magnetic resonance imaging,** makes highly detailed pictures from tissue responses to powerful pulses of magnetic energy. (Another example of an MRI image can be seen in Figure 3.1, at the beginning of the chapter.) While standard MRI images show brain structure, a newer technique called **functional magnetic resonance imaging (*f*MRI)** can distinguish more active brain cells from less active ones (Alper, 1993; Collins, 2001). Thus, *f*MRI allows neuroscientists to determine which parts of the brain are most active during various mental activities. The *f*MRI technique also produces more detailed images than does PET, as you can see in Figure 3.9. *f*MRI enables us to see the brain actually working, or in vivo (Parry & Matthews, 2002).

Each scanning method has its particular strengths and weaknesses. For example, PET is good at tracking the brain's activity, but not as good as MRI for distinguishing the fine details of brain structure. And neither PET nor MRI work well in studying processes that occur at rates faster than a few seconds, such as a startle response. To capture such short-lived "conversations" among brain cells requires the EEG—which, unfortunately, is limited in its detail (Raichle, 1994). Currently, no single scanning technique gives biopsychologists a perfectly clear "window" on the brain.

■ **CT scanning** or **computerized tomography** A computerized imaging technique that uses X rays passed through the brain at various angles and then combined into an image.

■ **PET scanning** or **positron emission tomography** An imaging technique that relies on the detection of radioactive sugar consumed by active brain cells.

■ **MRI** or **magnetic resonance imaging** An imaging technique that relies on cells' responses in a high-intensity magnetic field.

■ ***f*MRI** or **functional magnetic resonance imaging** A type of MRI that reveals which parts of the brain are most active during various mental activities.

Three Layers of the Brain

What is seen through these windows on the brain depends, of course, on what brain one is examining. Birds and reptiles manage to make a living with a brain that consists of little more than a stalk that regulates the most basic life processes. Creatures with more complex brains—we humans, for example—have essentially the same stalk, the **brain stem.** From an evolutionary perspective, then, this is the part of the brain with the longest ancestry. On top of that stalk, we and our mammalian cousins have evolved two more layers, known as the *limbic system* and the *cerebrum.* (See Figure 3.10.)

Where in the brain do we really live? Is there a module that houses the "self," the real *you*? That question has no easy answer. There are certain parts of the brain stem that you couldn't do without—modules that govern your most vital functions, such as heart rate, breathing, and blood pressure. If something goes radically wrong here, the *you* could vanish. Yet, these are brain-stem functions that are essentially the same as those of any other person, or even a rat or a lizard. For the most part, they operate outside consciousness. Surely, the *you* resides somewhere else.

Perhaps we can find *you* in the brain's middle layer, especially in the limbic system's circuits that generate emotions, memories, and desires. And, although these certainly sound more like the characteristics that make us human, we also should think back to the lesson of Phineas Gage. The iron rod that blasted through his skull and made him a different person didn't touch his brain stem or limbic region. Rather, it tore through the parts of the brain's

■ **Brain stem** The most primitive of the brain's three major layers. It includes the medulla, pons, and reticular formation.

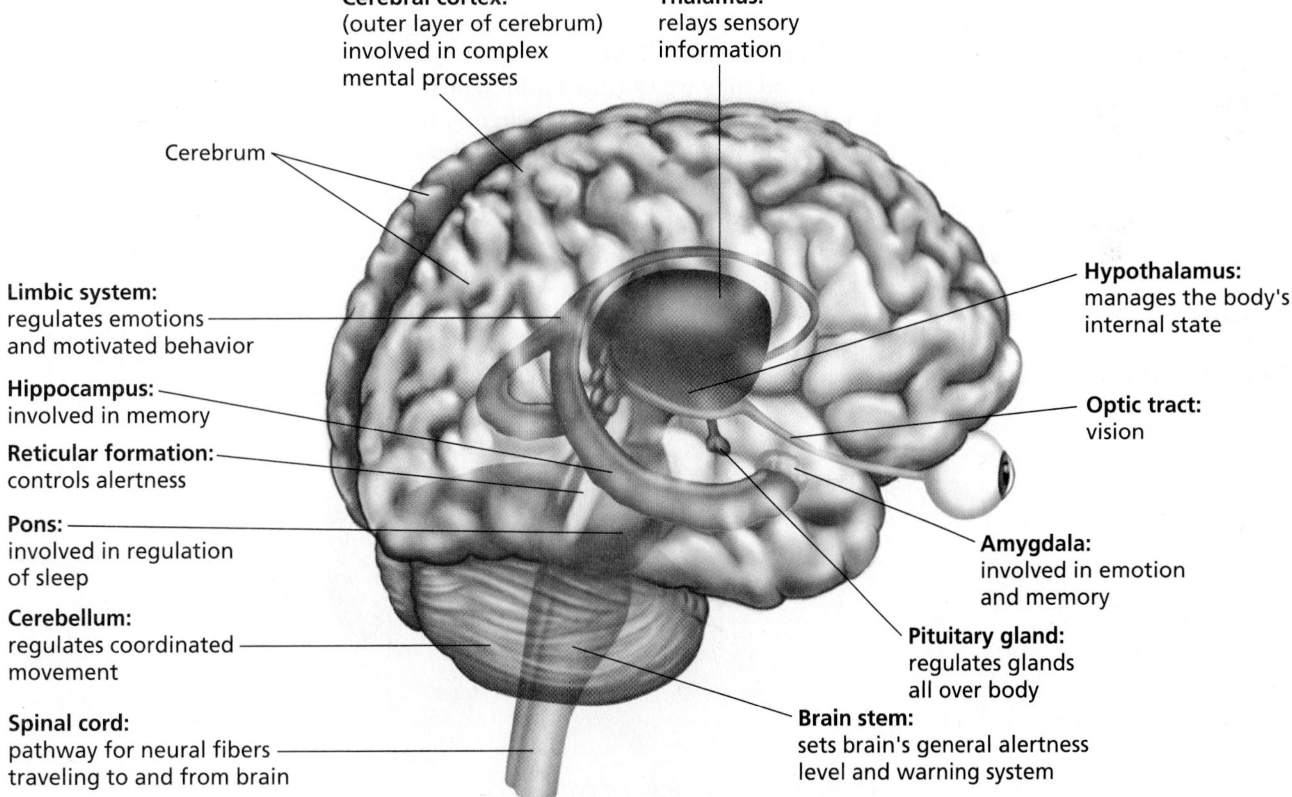
Cerebral cortex:
(outer layer of cerebrum) involved in complex mental processes
Thalamus:
relays sensory information
Cerebrum
Limbic system:
regulates emotions and motivated behavior
Hippocampus:
involved in memory
Reticular formation:
controls alertness
Pons:
involved in regulation of sleep
Cerebellum:
regulates coordinated movement
Spinal cord:
pathway for neural fibers traveling to and from brain
Hypothalamus:
manages the body's internal state
Optic tract:
vision
Amygdala:
involved in emotion and memory
Pituitary gland:
regulates glands all over body
Brain stem:
sets brain's general alertness level and warning system

● **FIGURE 3.10** Major Structures of the Brain

From an evolutionary perspective, the brain stem and cerebellum represent the oldest part of the brain; the limbic system evolved next; and the cerebral cortex is the most recent achievement in brain evolution.

topmost layer, destroying circuits that help us "put it all together"—circuits that combine and integrate our emotions, memories, and desires with thoughts, sensations, and perceptions. Is that where you really live? Again, the answer is not simple, but we will pursue it by examining each of these three layers in more detail.

The Brain Stem and Its Neighbors If you have ever fought to stay awake in class, you have struggled with your brain stem. Most of the time, however, it does its many jobs less obtrusively and less obnoxiously. We can infer one of its jobs from the brain stem's location, linking the spinal cord with the rest of the brain. In this position, the brain stem serves as a conduit for nerve pathways that carry messages traveling up and down the spinal pathway between body and brain. Significantly, these pathways cross as they traverse this region. Therefore, *the crossover of the sensory and motor pathways means that each side of the brain connects to the opposite side of the body.* The left side of the brain controls the right side of the body, and the left side of the body sends sensory signals to the right side of the brain. This is an important idea to remember later, when we try to understand the symptoms seen in brain-injured patients.

Components of the Brain Stem More than just a go-between, the brain stem also connects several important information-processing regions, four of which we will mention here: the *medulla,* the *pons,* the *reticular formation,* and the *thalamus.* (See Figure 3.11.) From an evolutionary standpoint, they are all ancient structures, which can be found in the brains of creatures as diverse as penguins, pigs, pandas, pythons, porcupines, and people.

■ **Medulla** A brain-stem structure that controls breathing and heart rate. The sensory and motor pathways connecting the brain to the body cross in the medulla.

■ **Pons** A brain-stem structure that regulates brain activity during sleep and dreaming. The name *pons* derives from the Latin word for "bridge."

The **medulla,** appearing as a bulge low in the brain stem, regulates basic body functions, including breathing, blood pressure, and heart rate. It operates on "automatic pilot"—without our conscious awareness—to keep our internal organs operating without our having to think about them. An even bigger bulge called the **pons** (the Latin word for *bridge*) appears just above the medulla, where it houses nerve circuits that regulate the sleep and dreaming cycle. True to its name, the pons also acts as a "bridge" that connects the brain stem to the *cerebellum.*

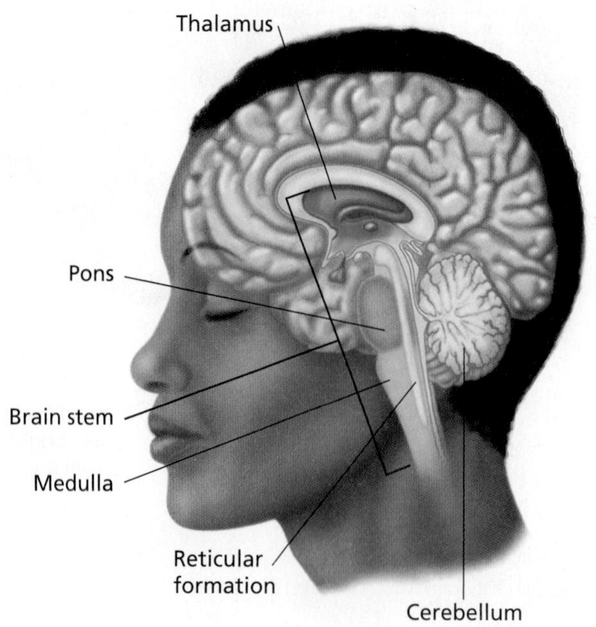
Thalamus
Pons
Brain stem
Medulla
Reticular formation
Cerebellum

● **FIGURE 3.11** The Brain Stem and Cerebellum

These structures in the central core of the brain are primarily involved with basic life processes: breathing, pulse, arousal, movement, balance, and early processing of sensory information.

Running through the center of everything, the **reticular formation** consists of a pencil-shaped bundle of nerve cells that forms the brain stem's core. One of the reticular formation's jobs is keeping the brain awake and alert. Others include monitoring the incoming stream of sensory information and directing attention to novel or important messages. It was the reticular formation against which you were struggling when you became drowsy in class.

From the reticular formation, nerve fibers run, like phone lines, in many directions, but especially down to the spinal cord and up to a small pair of football-shaped structures called the **thalamus.** Perched atop the brain stem, the thalamus lies near the geographic center of the brain. It is also central to the brain in another way: Like the central processing chip in a computer, the thalamus directs nearly all the brain's incoming and outgoing sensory and motor traffic. Accordingly, it receives information from all the senses (except smell) and distributes it to appropriate processing circuits throughout the brain. Incoming visual information, for example, enters the thalamus by way of the optic nerve and is then relayed on to the "gray matter" areas at the back of the brain that specialize in visual perception. Likewise, motor functions use routes between the brain's movement-control areas and the thalamus, which distributes instructions to the neural pathways serving muscles in all parts of the body. And, if that were not enough, the thalamus also seems to have a role in focusing attention—which seems appropriate enough for a structure with its connections to almost everything.

The Cerebellum Lying at the back of the brain stem, the **cerebellum** looks very much like a miniature add-on brain (its name literally means "little brain"), as you can see in Figure 3.11. Although seemingly separate—not actually a part of the brain stem—it works cooperatively with the brain stem and higher brain centers to control those complex movements that we perform without consciously thinking about the details—such as walking, dancing, or drinking from a cup (Spencer et al., 2003; Wickelgren, 1998b). Research also implicates the cerebellum in helping us keep a series of events in order—as we do when listening to the sequence of notes in a melody (Bower & Parsons, 2003). It also gets involved in producing habitual responses on cue—as when you learn to salivate at the sound of the lunch bell (Hazeltine & Ivry, 2002; Raymond et al., 1996; Seidler et al., 2002).

Taken together, the brain stem and cerebellum control the most basic functions of movement and of life itself. Note, again, that much of their work is automatic, functioning largely outside our awareness. The next two layers, however, assert themselves more obviously in consciousness.

The Limbic System: Emotions, Memories, and More We're sorry about your pet canary or goldfish. Only mammals come equipped with a fully developed **limbic system,** a diverse collection of structures that wrap around the thalamus, vaguely in the shape of a pair of ram's horns. (See Figures 3.10 and 3.12.) Together, these structures give mammals greatly enhanced capacity for emotions and memory. These characteristics, it turns out, offer the huge advantage of mental flexibility—so the organism doesn't have to rely solely on the instincts and reflexes that dominate the behavior of simpler creatures.

This layer houses not only modules that process memories, regulate complex motives and emotions, but it is involved in feelings of pleasure and pain. It is also the limbic system that produces fear, rage, and ecstasy. In general, the limbic system elaborates on the simpler urges arising lower in the brain to make mammalian behavior more complex than the behavior of organisms, such as fish or birds, with less complex brains.

Two important limbic structures take their names from their shapes. One, the **hippocampus,** is shaped (vaguely) like a sea horse. Hence, its name—again

■ **Reticular formation** A pencil-shaped structure forming the core of the brain stem. The reticular formation arouses the cortex to keep the brain alert and attentive to new stimulation.

■ **Thalamus** The brain's central "relay station," situated just atop the brain stem. Nearly all the messages going into or out of the brain go through the thalamus.

■ **Cerebellum** The "little brain" attached to the brain stem. The cerebellum is responsible for coordinated movements.

■ **Limbic system** The middle layer of the brain, involved in emotion and memory. The limbic system includes the hippocampus, amygdala, hypothalamus, and other structures.

■ **Hippocampus** A component of the limbic system, involved in establishing long-term memories.

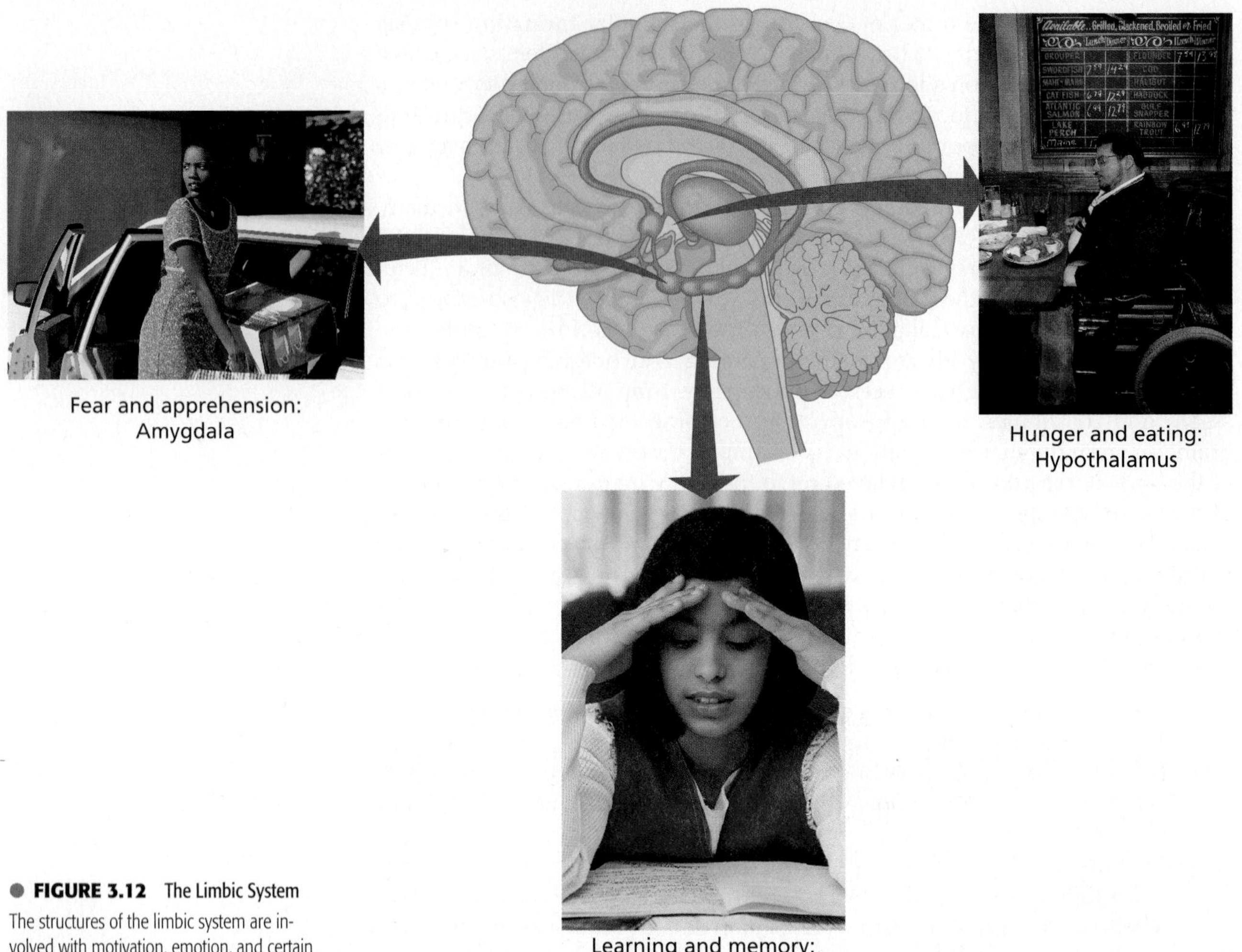
Fear and apprehension:
Amygdala
Hunger and eating:
Hypothalamus
Learning and memory:
Hippocampus

● **FIGURE 3.12** The Limbic System
The structures of the limbic system are involved with motivation, emotion, and certain memory processes.

from Greek. (Actually, there is one hippocampus on each side of the brain, making two *hippocampi.* See Figure 3.12.) The hippocampus's job is to connect your present with your past and to help you remember locations of things in space (Bilkey, 2004; Fyhn et al., 2004; Leutgeb et al., 2004). We can best see how this pair of brain structures works by pondering the regrettable case of H. M., a man who lost his hippocampi.

In 1953, when H. M. was in his early 20s, he underwent a radical and experimental brain operation, intended to reduce the frequency of the seizures that threatened his life (Hilts, 1995). The surgery, which removed most of the hippocampus on both sides of H. M.'s brain, was successful in reducing the frequency of his seizures and may have saved his life. But in another sense, it was a total failure: Ever since the operation, new experiences disappear from his memory almost as soon as they happen. Like the legendary Rip Van Winkle, H. M. draws a blank for the intervening years. He continues to believe he is living in 1953. Later in the book, we will see that H. M. has much to teach us about the structure of memory. Suffice it for now to note that his case illustrates that the hippocampus is a vital part of the brain's memory system. (We hope you will remember H. M. when we revisit him a few chapters hence.)

■ **Amygdala** A limbic system structure involved in memory and emotion, particularly fear and aggression. Pronounced *a-MIG-da-la.*

Another limbic structure, the **amygdala,** also takes its name from its shape: *amygdala* (again in Greek) means "almond." (See Figure 3.12.) Its function was first revealed by Heinrich Klüver and Paul Bucy (1939), who suspected that the amygdala had a role in emotion. To test this idea, they surgically snipped the connections to the amygdala on both sides of the brain in rhesus monkeys. After surgery, these normally foul-tempered beasts became docile and easy to handle, a change so dramatic that it surprised even Klüver and Bucy. Many studies since then have shown conclusively that the amygdala is involved not only in aggression but also in fear—and probably in other emotional responses (Damasio, 2003; LeDoux, 1996; Whalen, 1998). With this in mind, you shouldn't be surprised to hear that the amygdala also seems to have a role in helping us remember emotionally charged events, such as the September 11 attacks or the explosions of the space shuttles *Columbia* and *Challenger.*

The limbic system also contains several "pleasure centers" that give us the good feelings that accompany eating, sex, and other rewarding activities (Olds & Fobes, 1981; Pinel, 2003). On the street, drugs like cocaine, methamphetamine, and heroin generate wild rushes of pleasure and stimulate limbic "pleasure centers," which all seem to involve the neurotransmitter dopamine. But you don't have to take drugs or undergo brain surgery to stimulate the limbic system. The stimulation of food, drink, or sex will indirectly activate limbic pathways, too (Carlson, 2004), as will exciting activities, such as riding a roller-coaster. Studies also show that the rewarding effects from a dose of rich chocolate stimulate the same brain circuits (Small, 2001).

In the laboratory, studies have shown that rats seem to like mild stimulation in these regions. They like it very much, indeed. In fact, if left on their own to press a lever that delivers a mild electric current to one of these sites, they may stimulate themselves up to 10,000 time an hour! Rats will also pay a high price to get this pleasurable stimulation, including crossing a grid that gives painful shocks to their feet, to reach a lever that can send the obviously pleasurable stimulation to their brains. In a few cases, humans too have been given stimulation in the "pleasure centers" (for medical reasons during brain surgery). And what do they say it feels like? The feeling depends on which "pleasure center" is being stimulated, but the sensation at some locations has been likened to an orgasm. Happily, people who have had this experience do not become so obsessed by it as do rats (Valenstein, 1973).

We have already met another limbic structure, the **hypothalamus,** that has many tasks to perform. Rich with blood vessels, as well as with neurons, it primarily serves as your brain's blood-analysis laboratory. By constantly monitoring the blood, it detects small changes in body temperature, fluid levels, and nutrients. When it detects an imbalance (too much or too little water, for example), the hypothalamus immediately responds with orders that regulate appetite, thirst, and body temperature control, among other responses. Because of these functions, the hypothalamus has a major role in motivation.

CONNECTION: CHAPTER 8

The hypothalamus contains important control circuits for the basic *motives* and *drives.*

The hypothalamus makes its influence felt in other ways, as well. It sends neural messages to "higher" processing areas in the brain—making us aware of the needs it senses (hunger, for example). It also exerts its control through the pituitary gland, the body's master gland, which lies attached to the underside of the hypothalamus. As we saw earlier, the hypothalamus links the nervous system with the endocrine system. Thus, messages from the hypothalamus may tell the pituitary gland (the C.E.O. of the endocrine system) to release certain hormones, which then flow through the bloodstream to regulate such responses as heart rate, blushing, sweating, and goose pimples.

Does the hypothalamus have any role in our emotions? It hosts some of the brain's reward circuits, or "pleasure centers," which generate the feeling-good emotions associated with gratifying the hunger, thirst, and sex drives. A second link with emotion involves the hypothalamus's job of regulating the body's responses during emotional arousal. It does so by sending messages to

■ **Hypothalamus** A limbic structure that serves as the brain's blood-testing laboratory, constantly monitoring the blood to determine the condition of the body.

Cerebral cortex The thin gray-matter covering of the cerebral hemispheres, consisting of a ¼-inch layer dense with cell bodies of neurons. The cerebral cortex carries on the major portion of our "higher" mental processing, including thinking and perceiving.

the internal organs via the autonomic nervous system and, as we have noted, to the pituitary gland. In turn, the pituitary regulates the endocrine (hormone) response to emotional arousal and stress.

The Cerebral Cortex: The Brain's Thinking Cap When you look at a whole human brain, you mostly see the bulging *cerebral hemispheres*—a little bigger than your two fists held together. The nearly symmetrical hemispheres form a thick cap that hides most of the limbic system and the brain's central core. Its thin outer layer forms the **cerebral cortex** (cortex comes from Latin for "bark" or "shell"), with its distinctive wrinkled appearance. The seat of our most awesome mental powers, the cortex and its supporting structures account for two-thirds of the brain's total mass. Flattened out, the cortical surface would cover an area roughly the size of a newspaper page, but the wrinkling and folding enable its billions of cells to squeeze into the tight quarters inside your skull. As a result, only about a third of the cortex is visible on the brain's surface.

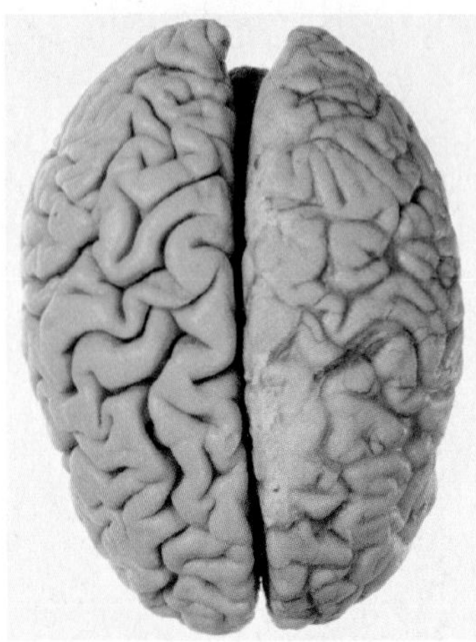

The cerebral hemispheres of the human brain.

Although we humans take pride in our large brains, it turns out that ours are not the largest. All large animals have large brains—a fact more closely related to body size than to intelligence (Pinel, 2003). Nor is the wrinkled cortex a distinctively human trait. Again, all large animals have highly convoluted cortexes. We do have more massive cortexes for our body weight than do other big-brained creatures (Carlson, 2004). Yet, human uniqueness lies more in the function of our brains than in their size. Although no one is sure exactly how or why our species evolved such a large cortex (Buss, 2004), we know that it hosts an amazing array of abilities.

Lobes of the Cerebral Cortex

In the late 1700s, the famous Austrian physician Franz Joseph Gall threw his considerable scientific weight behind the idea that specific regions of the brain control specific mental faculties, such as hearing, speech, movement, vision, and memory. Unfortunately, he carried this otherwise sensible idea to muddle-headed extremes. In his theory of *phrenology,* Gall claimed that the brain had specific regions devoted to such traits as spirituality, hope, benevolence, friendship, destructiveness, and cautiousness. Moreover, he asserted that these traits could be detected as bumps on the skull.

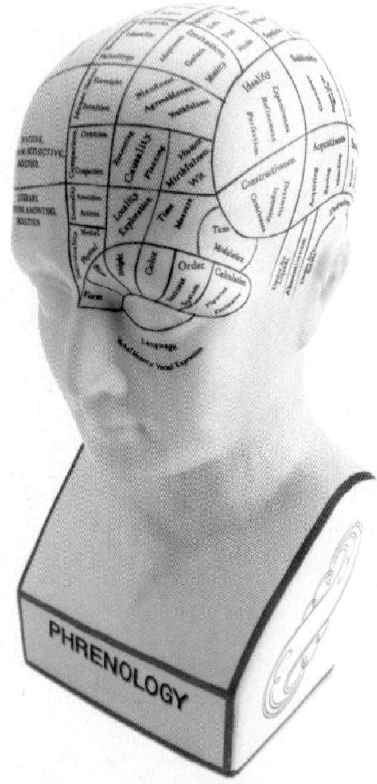
PHRENOLOGY

A phrenology bust showing the supposed locations of mental faculties, such as intuition, morality, friendship, and dignity. Although phrenologists correctly proposed that the brain is organized in modules, the specifics of their theory turned out to be completely wrong.

These ideas captured the public's attention and became enormously popular, even though Gall was mostly wrong about the details of his theory. But he was absolutely right on one small but important point—which is the reason we mention phrenology in this book: his doctrine of *localization of function,* which stated that *different regions of the brain perform different tasks.* Gall merely got the tasks and the locations wrong. We can forgive him, perhaps, because no one in those days had discovered a scientific method for determining exactly which functions were performed by which parts of the brain.

The technology Gall needed was invented about a century later by two German surgeons. In 1870, on a battlefield of the Franco-Prussian War, Gustav Fritsch and Eduard Hitzig seized an unusual opportunity to study living human brains. Their technique (which seems extreme by modern standards) involved a jolt of electricity to the exposed cortex of unfortunate soldiers who had had parts of their skulls blown away in battle. Not surprisingly, most of the cortical regions they tested gave no response: These were the so-called silent areas. But sometimes the stimulation would cause an arm or leg or some other body part to move, notably when a certain strip of tissue in the *frontal lobes* received the electric current (see Figure 3.13). Thus, Fritsch and Hitzig discovered a region, now called the *motor cortex,* that controls a specific function: voluntary movement of body parts. Later research, of course, has expanded on

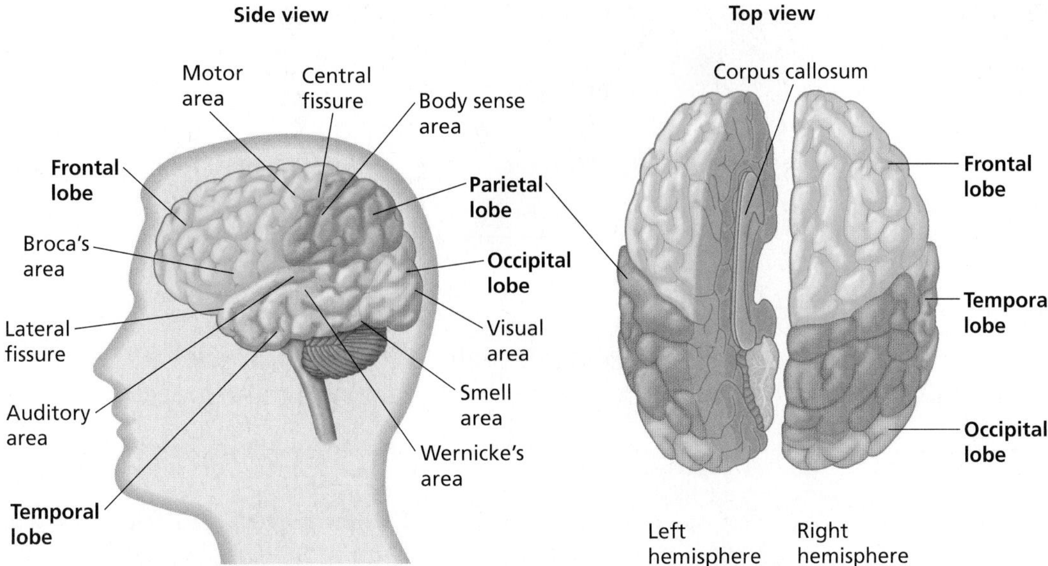
Side view
Motor area
Central fissure
Body sense area
Frontal lobe
Parietal lobe
Broca's area
Occipital lobe
Lateral fissure
Visual area
Smell area
Auditory area
Wernicke's area
Temporal lobe
Top view
Corpus callosum
Frontal lobe
Temporal lobe
Occipital lobe
Left hemisphere
Right hemisphere

● **FIGURE 3.13** The Cerebral Cortex

Each of the two hemispheres of the cerebral cortex has four lobes. Different sensory and motor functions have been associated with specific parts of each lobe. The two hemispheres are connected by a thick bundle of fibers called the corpus callosum.

this work by finding functions for the silent areas all over the cortex. In fact, investigations have extended Gall's doctrine of localization of function to deeper regions beneath the cortex. As a result, the entire brain has now been mapped. Let's see what this map looks like.

The Frontal Lobes Your choice of major, your plans for the summer, and your ability to answer test questions all depend on the cortical regions at the front of your brain, aptly named the **frontal lobes.** Here we find modules working together to perform our higher mental functions, such as planning, deciding, and perceiving (Helmuth, 2003a; Koechlin et al., 2003; Shimamura, 1996). The biological substrates of personality and temperament have important components here, too. We know this from accidents that damage the frontal lobes and produce devastating effects, such as we saw earlier in the case of Phineas Gage.

At the back of the frontal lobe lies a special strip of cortex capable of taking action on our thoughts. Known as the **motor cortex,** this area takes its name from its function: controlling the body's motor movement by sending messages via the motor nerves to the voluntary muscles. As you can see in Figure 3.14, the motor cortex contains an upside-down map of the body. We have represented its functions by the *homunculus* (the cartoonish "little man" in the figure). A look at the motor homunculus reveals that certain parts of the body are disproportionately represented, with the lips, tongue, and hands being particularly exaggerated. One of its largest areas is devoted to the fingers (especially the thumb), reflecting the importance of manipulating objects. (Could this also reflect our human fondness for using "rules of thumb"? Perhaps not.) Another major area sends messages exclusively to the muscles of the face, used in expressions of emotion. Please remember, however, that commands from the motor cortex on one side of the brain control muscles on the opposite side of the body, as we saw in our opening vignette.

■ **Frontal lobes** Cortical regions at the front of the brain that are especially involved in movement and in thinking.

■ **Motor cortex** A narrow vertical strip of cortex in the frontal lobes, lying just in front of the central fissure; controls voluntary movement.

The Parietal Lobes Behind each frontal lobe and running along the top of the brain lie two large patches of cortex that specialize in sensation (see Figure

● **FIGURE 3.14** The Motor Cortex and the Somatosensory Cortex

Actions of the body's voluntary muscles are controlled by the motor cortex in the frontal lobe. The somatosensory cortex in the parietal lobe processes information about temperature, touch, body position, and pain. The diagram shows the proportion of tissue devoted to various activities or sensitivities in each cortex.

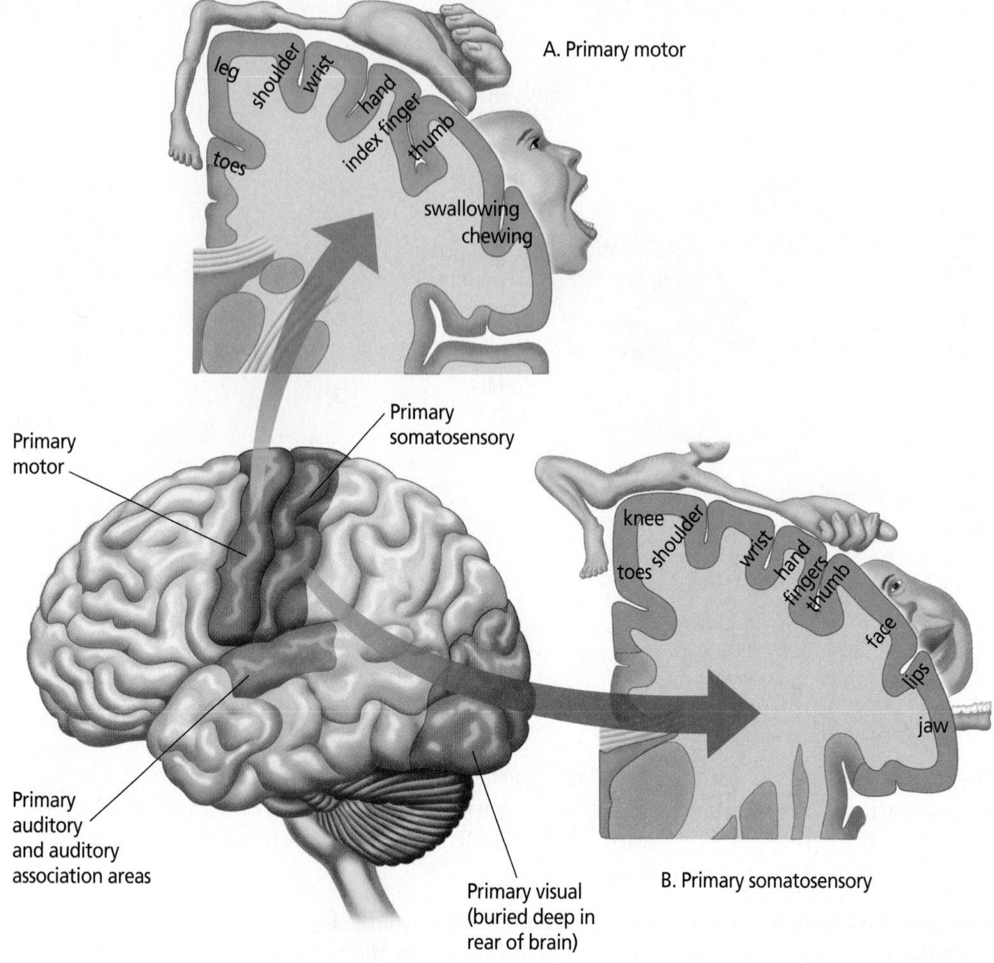
A. Primary motor
leg
shoulder
wrist
hand
index finger
thumb
toes
swallowing
chewing
Primary motor
Primary somatosensory
knee
shoulder
toes
wrist
hand
fingers
thumb
face
lips
jaw
Primary auditory and auditory association areas
Primary visual (buried deep in rear of brain)
B. Primary somatosensory

3.13). These **parietal lobes** allow us to sense the warmth of a hot bath, the smoothness of silk, the pressure and movement of a rude elbow, and the gentleness of a caress. A special parietal strip, known as the **somatosensory cortex,** mirrors the adjacent strip of motor cortex that we found in the frontal lobe. This somatosensory cortex has two main functions. First, it serves as the primary processing area for the sensations of touch, temperature, pain and pressure from all over your body (Graziano et al., 2000; Helmuth, 2000). Second, it relates this information to a mental map of the body to help you locate the source of these sensations.

Other maps in the parietal lobes keep track of the position of body parts, so they prevent you from biting your tongue or stepping on your own toes. And, when your leg "goes to sleep" and you can't feel anything but a tingling sensation, your body position has temporarily disabled the nerve cells that carry sensory information to body maps in the parietal lobe. (It was such a parietal body map that was affected by the tumor described in our opening vignette.)

Besides processing sensation and keeping track of body parts, the parietal lobes—especially the one in the right hemisphere—allow us to locate, in three-dimensional space, the positions of external objects detected by our senses. Meanwhile, the left hemisphere's parietal lobe has its own special talents. It specializes in locating the source of speech sounds, as when someone calls your name. It also works with the temporal lobe to extract meaning from speech and writing.

■ **Parietal lobes** Cortical areas lying toward the back and top of the brain; involved in touch sensation and in perceiving spatial relationships (the relationships of objects in space).

■ **Somatosensory cortex** A strip of the parietal lobe lying just behind the central fissure. The somatosensory cortex is involved with sensations of touch.

The Occipital Lobes During the Apollo 11 mission to the moon, lunar module pilot Edwin Aldrin reported back to Earth that he was experiencing mysterious flashes of light. This celestial display apparently resulted from cosmic rays stimulating his **occipital lobes,** at the back of the brain (see Figure 3.13). Similarly—if less pleasantly—you, too, will "see stars" when a sharp blow to your head bounces your brain around and stimulates its occipital lobes. Under more normal circumstances, the occipital lobes receive stimulation relayed from the eyes to the **visual cortex,** which constructs our moving picture of the outside world.

To create this picture, the brain divides up the incoming visual input and sends it to separate cortical areas for the processing of color, movement, shape, and shading—as we will see in more detail in Chapter 4. There is even a distinct patch of cortex dedicated to the recognition of human faces and another for perception of the human body (Downing et al., 2001; Holden, 1997; Turk et al., 2002). But the occipital lobes do not do all this work alone. As we have noted, they rely on adjacent association areas in the parietal lobes to locate objects in space. They also work with temporal regions to produce visual memories (Ishai & Sagi, 1995; Miyashita, 1995).

The Temporal Lobes When the phone rings or a horn honks, the sound registers in your **temporal lobes,** on the lower side of each cerebral hemisphere (see Figure 3.13). There lies the *auditory cortex,* which helps you make sense of the sounds. In most people, a specialized section of auditory cortex on the brain's left side is dedicated to processing speech sounds. Other parts of the temporal lobes assume the task of storing long-term memories. This is not surprising, because the hippocampus lies directly beneath the temporal lobe—and, if you remember H. M., you will remember that the hippocampus is involved in forming memories.

The first detailed description of temporal lobe function was written at neurosurgeon Wilder Penfield's operating table over 50 years ago.* As his electrical probe touched the temporal lobe's auditory cortex of patients under local anesthesia, they often reported hearing sounds, such as buzzing noises. More surprising, when the probe strayed into nearby temporal regions, it occasionally touched a memory. One patient abruptly exclaimed, "I can see Seven-Up Bottling Company—Harrison Bakery," two of Montreal's large illuminated advertisements. Another patient reported, "There was a piano over there and someone playing. I could hear the song, you know." Still another cried out, "Now I hear people laughing—my friends in South Africa." He was surprised because he seemed to be laughing with his cousins on a South African farm, although he knew he was in surgery in Montreal (Penfield, 1975; Penfield & Jasper, 1954; Penfield & Rasmussen, 1950; Penfield & Roberts, 1959). Such reports leave little doubt that the temporal lobes are involved in both hearing and memory.

■ **Occipital lobes** The cortical regions at the back of the brain, housing the visual cortex.

■ **Visual cortex** The visual processing areas of cortex in the occipital and temporal lobes.

■ **Temporal lobes** Cortical lobes that process sounds, including speech. The temporal lobes are probably involved in storing long-term memories.

TABLE 3.3 Major Functions of the Cortical Lobes

Lobe	Functions
Frontal	Movement, speech, abstract thought
Parietal	Sensations of touch, body position, hearing
Temporal	Hearing, smell, vision
Occipital	Vision

*An overview of the functions of the cortical lobes is shown in Table 3.3.

The Cooperative Brain

Like a championship team, no individual part of the brain takes sole responsibility for emotion, memory, personality, or any other complex psychological characteristic—contrary to the beliefs of Gall and his phrenologists. There are no single "brain centers" for any of the major functions of the mind—attention, consciousness, learning, memory, thinking, language, emotion, or motivation. Rather, every mental and behavioral process involves the coordination and cooperation of many brain networks (Damasio, 2003; LeDoux, 2002). For example, when you do something as simple as answering a ringing telephone, you hear it in your temporal lobes, interpret its meaning with the help of the frontal lobes, visually locate it with your occipital lobes, initiate grasping the phone on the orders of your frontal and parietal lobes, and engage in thoughtful conversation, again using frontal-lobe circuitry. Nor are we talking just about the cortex. Even the cortex cannot do its work without communicating with circuits lying deep beneath the surface: the limbic system, thalamus, brain stem, cerebellum, and other structures.

With the brain's democratic division of labor in mind, it shouldn't surprise you to learn that the largest proportion of the human cortex is devoted to integrating and interpreting information gathered from the sensory parts of the brain. Collectively, these regions are known as the **association cortex.** Diverse parts of the association cortex, then, interpret sensations, lay plans, make decisions, and prepare us for action—precisely the mental powers in which we humans excel and which distinguish us from other animals. We have these capabilities because we have more cortical area committed to making associations than does any nonhuman species.

And now that we have seen how the four lobes in each hemisphere have specialized functions and that we depend on the cooperation of each of the parts, let's turn to some evidence that the two cerebral hemispheres are also specialists at different tasks. These differences fall under the heading of *cerebral dominance*—a commonly misunderstood concept.

Cerebral Dominance

In the mid-1800s, at about the same time that Phineas Gage was recovering from his accident, a French neurologist named Paul Broca was studying patients who had speech impairments that resulted from brain injuries. An especially important case involved a man known in the medical books as "Tan"—a name derived from the only word he was able to speak. After Tan's death, an autopsy revealed severe damage in the left front portion of his brain. This clue prompted Broca to study other patients who had developed *aphasia*—the loss of speech caused by brain damage. Again and again, Broca found damage to the same spot, later named *Broca's area,* that had been damaged in Tan's brain. (See Figure 3.13.) This pattern was one of the early suggestions that the two sides of the brain specialize in different tasks. Subsequent work has confirmed and extended Broca's findings:

- Brain-damaged patients suffering paralysis on the right side of their bodies often develop speech disturbances, suggesting that speech production involves the frontal lobe, usually in the left hemisphere. (Again, please recall that the left hemisphere controls the right side of the body.)
- Damage to other areas in the left parietal and left temporal lobes commonly produces problems in understanding language.

People with right-sided brain injuries less often have speech problems, but they are more likely to have difficulties with *spatial orientation* (locating them-

■ **Association cortex** Cortical regions throughout the brain that combine information from various other parts of the brain.

selves or external objects in three-dimensional space). They may, for example, feel lost in a previously familiar place or be unable to assemble a simple jigsaw puzzle. Musical ability is also associated with the right hemisphere, particularly with Broca's area (Holden, 2001a; Janata et al., 2002; Zatorre & Krumhansl, 2002).

While the two hemispheres appear to be near mirror images of each other, they assume different functions. This tendency for the hemispheres to take charge of different tasks is called **cerebral dominance.** But what many people don't understand about cerebral dominance is this: While some processes are more under the control of the left hemisphere, and others are predominantly right-hemisphere tasks, *both hemispheres work together to produce our thoughts, feelings, and behaviors.*

That's the broad-brush picture of cerebral dominance. Now, let's look at some details, beginning with some new research showing that the dominance pattern is not always the same from one person to another. This work uses a technique called *transcranial magnetic stimulation* (TMS), involving powerful magnetic pulses that can disable parts of the brain temporarily and without causing damage. When TMS is applied to the language areas of the brain, the results show that some people—about 1 in 10 individuals, and mostly left-handers—process language primarily on the *right* side of the brain. Another 1 in 10—again, mostly left-handers—have language functions distributed equally on both sides of the brain (Knecht et al., 2002).

Other studies have shown that, while one hemisphere usually dominates language functions, both sides of the brain get involved. The left side is usually more dominant in processing the "what," or *content,* of speech. The right hemisphere, by contrast, assumes the role of processing the *emotional tone* of speech (Vingerhoets et al., 2003). In fact, the right hemisphere is usually more involved than the left in interpreting the emotional responses of others. The control of one's own negative emotions, such as fear and anger, stems from the right frontal lobe, while the left frontal lobe regulates the positive emotions, such as joy. (For more information, see Beeman & Chiarello, 1998; Davidson, 1992a, b; Heller et al., 1998; McIntosh & Lobaugh, 2003; Posner & Raichle, 1994; Springer & Deutsch, 1993).

Different though they may be, the two hemispheres don't compete with each other (except under the most unusual conditions, which we will describe in a moment). Rather, they make different contributions to the same task. In the lingo of neuroscience, they have different *processing styles.* For example, on matching tasks performed in the psychology lab, the left hemisphere matches objects analytically and verbally—by similarity in function, as in matching eating utensils (*knife* with *spoon*). By contrast, the right hemisphere matches things that look alike or fit together to form a visual pattern—such as matching *coin* to *clock,* which are both round objects (Gazzaniga, 1970; Sperry, 1968, 1982). In general, we can describe the left hemisphere's processing style as more *analytic* and *sequential,* while the right hemisphere interprets experience more *holistically* and *spatially* (Reuter-Lorenz & Miller, 1998).

The differences between the two sides of the brain have captured the public's interest in recent years. Knowing a fad when they see it, smarmy pseudoscientists have proclaimed that people can be typed as "right-brained" or "left-brained." But we want to emphasize that this distinction is simplistic and misleading. The evidence by no means warrants categorizing people in this way. In reality, the differences between the two hemispheres do not outweigh their similarities (Banich, 1998; Trope et al., 1992). Further, as we have seen, the two hemispheres normally don't work either in isolation from each other or at cross-purposes. Rather, they cooperate, each by making its own complementary contribution to our mental lives (see Figure 3.15).

■ **Cerebral dominance** The tendency of each brain hemisphere to exert control over different functions, such as language or perception of spatial relationships.

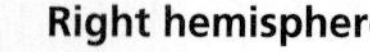
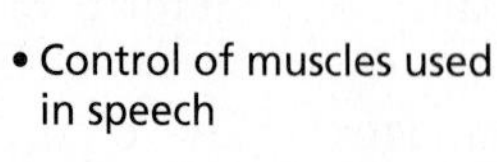
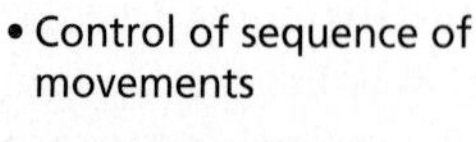
Left hemisphere
• Regulation of positive emotions
• Control of muscles used in speech
• Control of sequence of movements
• Spontaneous speaking and writing
• Memory for words and numbers
• Understanding speech and writing
Right hemisphere
• Regulation of negative emotions
• Responses to simple commands
• Memory for shapes and music
• Interpreting spatial relationships and visual images
• Recognition of faces

● **FIGURE 3.15** Specialization Commonly Found in the Cerebral Hemispheres

There are, however, some exceptions that have actually proved the rule. In a few rare cases, the cerebral hemispheres cannot work together—because they have been disconnected. We are referring to individuals whose brains have been surgically "split." Their story has much to teach us about cerebral dominance in the normal human brain.

The Split Brain: "I've Half a Mind to . . ."

Imagine what your world might be like if the halves of your brain could not communicate. Would you be, literally, "of two minds"? (Or feel "beside yourself"?) A rare surgical procedure, used to treat severe epilepsy, has given us some answers to such questions. The procedure requires that surgeons cut the **corpus callosum,** the bundle of nerve fibers responsible for transferring information between the two hemispheres (Figure 3.16).

The purpose of the surgery is to prevent abnormal electrical rhythms from "echoing" back and forth between the hemispheres and developing into a full-blown seizure (Trope et al., 1992; Wilson et al., 1977). Indeed, after the operation, most patients' seizures diminish in severity. More remarkably (to psychologists), these *split-brain patients* appear mentally and behaviorally unaffected under all but the most unusual conditions. But what really grabbed psychologists' attention were certain odd responses that these individuals made on cleverly contrived tests conducted by Nobel Prize winner Roger Sperry (1968) and his colleague Michael Gazzaniga (1970).

■ **Corpus callosum** The band of nerve cells that connects the two cerebral hemispheres.

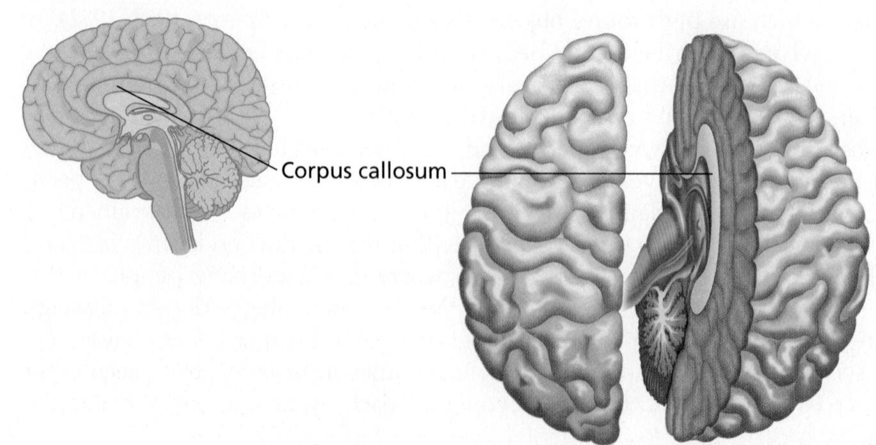
Corpus callosum

● **FIGURE 3.16** The Corpus Callosum
Only the corpus callosum is severed when the brain is "split." This medical procedure prevents communication between the cerebral hemispheres. Strangely, split-brain patients act like people with normal brains under most conditions. Special laboratory tests, however, reveal a duality of consciousness in the split brain.

Roger Sperry won the Nobel Prize in 1981 for his discoveries concerning "the functional specialization of the cerebral hemispheres" (Nobel, 1981). As the Nobel Committee wrote,

> The cerebrum is made up of two halves, the hemispheres, which are structurally identical. These hemispheres are united to one another through a system consisting of millions of nerve fibers. Therefore, each hemisphere is continually informed about what is happening in the other. For more than a century we have known that, despite their similarities and close linking, the two hemispheres generally perform different functions. The left hemisphere is the center for speech and, accordingly, has been described as the dominant one and has been considered to be superior to the right hemisphere. Outside of this, little was known about where in the brain the higher functions were centered until the beginning of the 1960s when Sperry began his investigations. *Sperry has brilliantly succeeded in extracting the secrets from both hemispheres and in demonstrating that they are highly specialized and also that many higher functions are centered in the right hemisphere.*

Sperry truly "opened up" the brain for study and understanding.

● **Roger Sperry**

Research found that split-brain patients could not identify an unseen object, such as a ball, when it was placed in the left hand—although they had no trouble naming the object when it was shifted to the right hand. Or, in another test, most split-brain patients said they saw nothing when an image of a spoon was flashed briefly on the left side of the visual field. Yet, at the same time, the patient's right hand could reach under a visual barrier and pick the spoon out of an array of other objects.

To understand these strange results, you will need some insider information about the pathways used to get visual information from the eyes to the occipital cortex. This is the tricky part: Visual information coming *from each eye* divides into two streams that flow to the opposite sides of the brain. (Figure 3.17 can help you visualize the sensory pathways involved.) For people with intact brains, this fork in the visual road poses no problem. Thanks to the connecting pathways through the corpus callosum, information from both sides of the visual field is accessible to both hemispheres.

In split-brain patients, however, information sharing across the corpus callosum can't happen. Yet, under everyday conditions outside the laboratory, they get along surprisingly well. They simply scan a scene with their eyes, which sends essentially the same visual information to both sides of the brain. Only when the two hemispheres of split-brain patients get entirely different messages does the bizarre psychological reality of the split brain show itself—as it did in the Sperry and Gazzaniga experiments.

Now, put yourself in an experimenter's shoes, and see if you can explain why the split-brain patient responds as shown in Figure 3.18, on page 101. Why is he able to match, using the left hand, the image seen on the left side of the screen? And, why does he fail the same test when he uses the right hand? (Remember, from our discussion of the brain stem, that each hemisphere communicates with the *opposite* side of the body.)

The patient in the figure has been asked to identify an object that had been visualized only by the brain's right hemisphere (because the image had been flashed only on the left side of the screen). The identification task was easily performed by the left hand, which is connected to the right hemisphere, but impossible for the right hand, which communicates with the left hemisphere. So, before reading the caption for Figure 3.18, would you predict that the patient could, or could not, name the object seen on the screen?

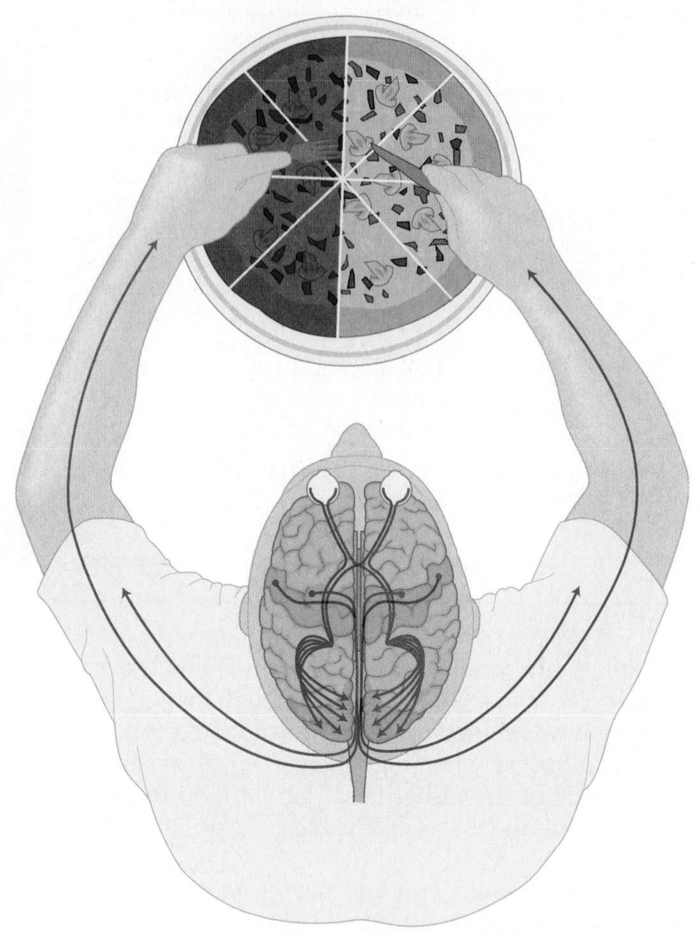

● **FIGURE 3.17** The Neural Pathways from the Eyes to the Visual Cortex

There are two things to notice in this illustration, in which the person is looking at the center of the pizza. First, the information from the left side of the retina in each eye corresponds to the right side of the pizza. Conversely, the right visual field senses the left side of the pizza. (This happens because the lens of the eye reverses the image.) Second, please notice that the left sides of both retinas in the eyes send images to the brain's left visual cortex, while the right sides of the retinas send images to the right visual cortex. As a result, when the eyes are fixated in the center, each side of the brain "sees" the opposite side of the pizza.

Some altogether unexpected effects of having a split brain also showed up in patient reports of their everyday experiences. For example, one patient told how his left hand would unzip his pants or unbutton his shirt at inappropriate times, especially when he was under stress. In fact, it was usually the left hand that would play such tricks. But why? The researchers theorize that the right hemisphere—which has little language ability but controls the left hand—was merely trying to find a way to communicate (Sperry, 1964). It's almost as if the right hemisphere were saying, "Look at me!"

Such cerebral antics point up the most interesting finding in Sperry and Gazzaniga's work: the *duality of consciousness* observed in split-brain patients. It was as if each patient were two separate individuals. When different stimuli were presented to opposite sides of the brain (as in Figure 3.18), the two hemispheres could respond independently. For example, the right hemisphere might direct the left hand to select a pear, and the left hemisphere might tell the right hand to select a glass. In other tests, they found that right-hemisphere responses tended to respond more emotionally, while the left hemisphere was more analytic. As expected, the left hemisphere typically had much more language fluency than did the right.

We must be cautious about generalizing such findings from split-brain patients to individuals with normal brains, says Gazzaniga (1998a, b). He suggests that we think of the human mind as neither a single nor a dual entity but rather as a *confederation of minds,* each specialized to process a specific kind of information. If so, the input from these many separate "miniminds" must be synthesized and coordinated for action by still other (poorly understood)

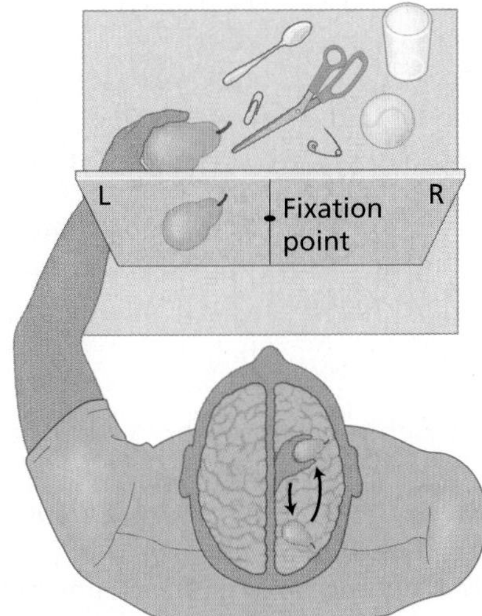
Match
L
R
Fixation point

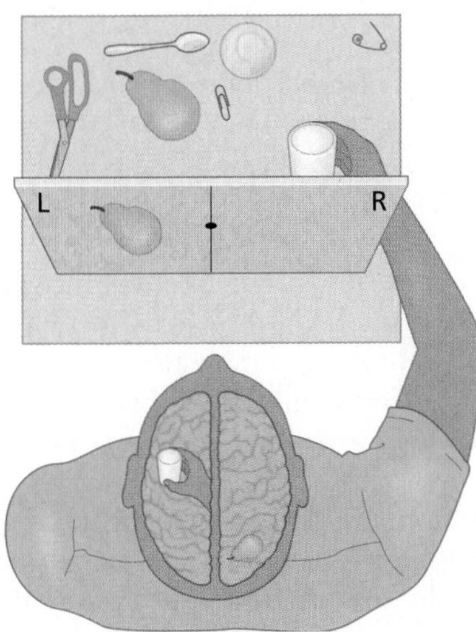
Mismatch
L
R

FIGURE 3.18 Testing a Split-Brain Patient

When a split-brain patient uses the left hand to find a match to a hidden object flashed briefly in the left visual field, eye–hand coordination is normal, because both are registered in the right hemisphere. (The patient, however, cannot name the object because speech is mainly a left-hemisphere function.) Alternatively, when asked to use the right hand to match an object seen in the left visual field, the patient cannot perform the task and mismatches a pear with some other object, such as a glass—although the patient can now name the object in his hand!

executive processors in the brain. The corpus callosum, then, is a connecting pathway that helps our confederation of minds share information. And so, we come full circle to a Core Concept that we encountered at the beginning of this section: The brain is composed of many specialized modules that work together to create mind and behavior (Baynes et al., 1998; Strauss, 1998).

PSYCHOLOGY IN YOUR LIFE: BRAIN DAMAGE AND BEHAVIOR

Nearly everybody knows someone who has suffered brain damage from an accident, a stroke, or a tumor—such as we described in the chapter-opening vignette. Your new knowledge of the brain and behavior will help you understand the problems such people must face. And if you know what abilities have been lost or altered, you can usually make a good guess as to which part of the brain sustained the damage—especially if you bear in mind two simple principles:

1. Each side of the brain communicates with the opposite side of the body. Thus, if symptoms appear on one side of the body, it is likely that the other side of the brain was damaged. (See Figure 3.19.)
2. For most people, speech is mainly a left-hemisphere function.

Now we invite you to use your knowledge of the brain to guess where the damage probably occurred in the brains of the following individuals:

- Edna had a *stroke* (an interruption of blood supply to a part of the brain) and lost her ability to speak, although she could still understand speech. Where did the stroke most likely affect her brain?
- Theo was in an auto accident, which left him with jerky, uncoordinated movements. Brain scans revealed no damage to his cerebral cortex. Where did the accident have its effect in the brain?
- Just prior to her seizures, Lydia has a strange sensation (an "aura") that feels like pinpricks on her left leg. What part of her brain generates this sensation?

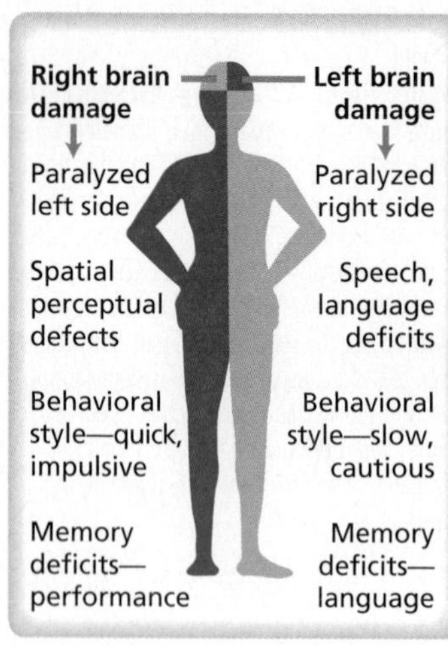
Right brain damage
Left brain damage
Paralyzed left side
Paralyzed right side
Spatial perceptual defects
Speech, language deficits
Behavioral style—quick, impulsive
Behavioral style—slow, cautious
Memory deficits—performance
Memory deficits—language

● **FIGURE 3.19** Effects of Damage to the Cerebral Hemispheres

Edna's case could have a happy ending. Depending on her age, physical condition, the extent of the stroke, and how quickly she received medical attention, she may get some or all of her speech back. Even if Broca's area in her left frontal lobe has been permanently damaged, other parts of Edna's brain may be able to take over some of the lost function. As we have noted, neuroscientists call this the *plasticity* of the brain. Long-term therapy for Edna will emphasize speech therapy.

Theo may also regain some or all his abilities, especially if the affected neural cells in his cerebellum were merely bruised but not destroyed in the accident. Long-term treatment for him will involve physical therapy. Both Edna and Theo may also need psychological therapy to help them cope with any permanent loss of function.

Lydia has epilepsy, originating in her right somatosensory cortex. Like most people with epilepsy, she will probably receive significant help from antiseizure medications. The chances are good that she will be completely symptom-free when the drugs are properly adjusted.

A lesson from all these cases is that people who suffer from brain damage can often receive significant help. Note, too, that help may come in many forms, both physical and mental. Perhaps the most important long-term therapy, however, is social support—a good thing to remember if you know someone who has suffered brain damage. (For more information on social support under stress, see Chapter 8, "Stress, Health, and Well-Being.")

CHECK YOUR UNDERSTANDING

1. **RECALL:** Which technique for studying the brain relies on the brain's electrical activity?
   a. CT
   b. EEG
   c. *f*MRI
   d. MRI
   e. PET

2. **RECALL:** Name the three main layers of the human brain discussed in the text: _______, _______, and _______.

3. **APPLICATION:** A brain tumor in the limbic system is most likely to produce changes in a person's
   a. coordination.
   b. emotions.
   c. hearing.
   d. sleep patterns.
   e. vision.

4. **RECALL:** Make a sketch showing the four lobes of the cerebral cortex. Indicate the main functions of each lobe. Which hemisphere of the brain controls language in most people? Which hemisphere of your brain controls your left hand?

5. **RECALL:** In the split-brain operation, what part of the brain is severed?
   a. the cerebrum
   b. the corpus callosum
   c. the left hemisphere
   d. the occipital lobe
   e. the right hemisphere

6. **ANALYSIS:** The split-brain patient in Figure 3.18 has trouble using the _______ hand to select the object flashed on the left side of the screen.
   a. right
   b. left

   (*Hints:* Which hemisphere controls each hand? Which hemisphere processes information from the left side of the visual field?)

7. **UNDERSTANDING THE CORE CONCEPT:** The brain is composed of many specialized and interconnected modules that work together to create mind and behavior. Can you name at least two specialized parts of the brain that are known to work together? What is the result of the collaboration of the structures you have named?

ANSWERS: 1. **b** 2. the brain stem and cerebellum, the limbic system, the cerebrum 3. **b** 4. See the location of the four lobes in Figure 3.13. The left hemisphere controls language, and the right hemisphere controls your left hand. 5. **b** 6. **a** 7. Examples include the interaction of regions in the four lobes of the cerebral cortex when a person is answering the phone. There are many other examples mentioned in this section.

BIOPSYCHOLOGY: THE STATE OF THE ART

Now that we have had a look at the biology behind psychology, you must be wondering how to put together all the details we have covered. For example, how do all the separate modules in the brain cooperate in processing information, making decisions, and initiating action? The frank answer: No one knows precisely how the components of the brain manage to work together (Horgan, 1993). Do we need a more detailed map of the brain's interconnections? Perhaps. But even if we knew every connection for every nerve cell in the brain, we still wouldn't understand how it senses, thinks, and feels. We would be long on detail and short on insight. What we really need is a good *model,* or theory, of the brain that tells us how the parts work in synchrony. The lack of such a theory represents one of the two biggest mysteries in biopsychology.

The other mystery involves genes and psychological processes. During the last decade, scientists have made great strides in deciphering the human genome, but we still have only the sketchiest understanding of how genes regulate our thoughts, feelings, desires, and actions. How, for example, does a genetic tendency for depression become activated? Does it require some sort of "trigger" from the environment? And, how do the genes communicate with the brain?

So, at the beginning of the 21st century, these are the two burning issues that lie at the cutting edge of theory and research in biopsychology. Students just now entering the field will have an opportunity to find the answers.

USING PSYCHOLOGY TO LEARN PSYCHOLOGY

Putting Your Knowledge of the Brain to Work

The old idea that we use only 10% of our brains is bunk. We hope this chapter has shown you that every part of the brain has a known function, and it gets used every day—but not necessarily for intellectual purposes. We now know that much of the brain merely controls basic biological functions. This tells us that simply engaging more of our brains is not the royal road to increased brain power.

So, have neuroscientists found anything that you can use to improve your memory, especially for the concepts you are learning in your classes? Among their most important discoveries is the revelation that many different regions of the cerebral cortex are involved in learning and memory (Kandel & Squire, 2000). Accordingly, if you can bring more of this cerebral circuitry to bear on your studies (about biopsychology, for example), your brain will lay down a wider web of memories.

To be more specific, reading the material in this book will help you form verbal (language) memories, parts of which involve circuits in the temporal cortex. Taking notes brings the motor cortex of the frontal lobes into play, adding a "motor memory" component to your study. Scanning the accompanying photos, charts, and drawings adds visual and spatial memory components in the occipital and parietal lobes. Listening actively to your professor's lectures and discussing the material with a study partner will engage the auditory regions of the temporal cortex and lay down still other memory traces. Finally, study time spent anticipating what questions will appear on the exam will involve regions of the frontal lobes in your learning process.

In general, the more ways that you can deal with the material—the more sensory and motor channels you can employ—the more memory components you will build in your brain's circuitry. As a result, when you need to remember the material, you will have more possible ways of accessing what you have learned. So, put your knowledge of your brain to work in your studying!

CHAPTER SUMMARY

KEY QUESTION

CORE CONCEPT

• HOW ARE GENES AND BEHAVIOR LINKED?

Charles Darwin's theory of evolution explains behavior as the result of natural selection. Variation among individuals and competition for resources lead to survival of the most adaptive behavior and features. This principle underlies human behavior, as well as that of other animals. Research in genetics has clarified the biological basis for natural selection and inheritance. Our chromosomes contain thousands of genes, carrying traits inherited from our parents. Each gene consists of a DNA segment that encodes for a protein. Proteins, in turn, serve as the building blocks for the organism's structure and function, including the functioning of the brain. While a draft of the human genome was recently completed, we do not yet know precisely how specific genes influence behavior and mental processes.

● **Evolution has fundamentally shaped psychological processes because it favors genetic variations that produce adaptive behavior.**

• HOW DOES THE BODY COMMUNICATE INTERNALLY?

The body's two communication systems are the nervous system and the endocrine system. The neuron, the basic unit of the nervous system, is specialized for processing information. It receives messages by means of stimulation on the dendrites and soma and, when sufficiently aroused, generates an action potential along the axon. Neurotransmitter chemicals relay the message to receptors on cells across the synapse.

The nervous system, composed of billions of interconnected neurons, has two main divisions: the central nervous system (the brain and the spinal cord) and the peripheral nervous system. The peripheral nervous system, in turn, can be divided into the somatic nervous system (further divided into sensory and motor pathways) and the autonomic nervous system, which communicates with internal organs and glands. The somatic division of the autonomic NS is most active under stress, while the parasympathetic division attempts to maintain the body in a more calm state.

The glands of the slower endocrine system also communicate with cells around the body by secreting hormones into the bloodstream. Its activity is controlled by the pituitary gland attached to the base of the brain, where it receives orders from the hypothalamus.

Psychoactive drugs affect the nervous system by influencing the effects of neurotransmitters. Moreover, they may act as agonists or antagonists. Unfortunately for drug users, many neural pathways in the brain may employ the same neurotransmitter, causing unwanted side effects.

● **The brain coordinates the body's two communications systems, the nervous system and the endocrine system, which use similar chemical messengers to communicate with targets throughout the body.**

• HOW DOES THE BRAIN PRODUCE BEHAVIOR AND MENTAL PROCESSES?

Early medicine learned about the brain from the study of brain-injured persons, such as Phineas Gage. In modern times, researchers have opened windows on the brain, using the EEG to sense the brain's electrical activity, along with electric probes sometimes used to stimulate the brain during surgery. In recent years, computer technology has led to brain-scanning techniques, such as CT, PET, MRI, and *f*MRI—each having its advantages and disadvantages.

We can conceive of the brain as being organized in three integrated layers. The brain stem and associated structures (including the medulla, reticular formation, pons, thalamus, and cerebellum) control many vital body functions, along with influencing alertness and motor movement. The limbic system (including the hippocampus, amygdala, and hypothalamus) plays vital roles in motivation, emotion, and memory. The cerebral cortex contains highly specialized modules—each with distinct functions. Its frontal lobes involve both motor functions and higher mental functions. The parietal lobes specialize in sensation, especially the senses of touch and body position. The occipital lobes deal exclusively with vision, while the temporal lobes have multiple roles involved in vision, hearing, and smell. Even though the functions of the brain are highly localized within specific modules, they normally work seamlessly together.

The two cerebral hemispheres are also differently specialized. Language, analytical thinking, and positive emotions are regulated by specific parts of the left hemisphere, while circuits in the right hemisphere control spatial interpretation, visual and musical memory, and negative emotions. If the hemispheres are surgically severed, as when the corpus callosum is cut in split-brain patients, a duality of consciousness emerges. In such cases, each hemisphere functions independently and has no direct awareness of stimulation or cognitive activities affecting the other. In people with intact brains, however, the two hemispheres communicate and cooperate with each other.

● **The brain is composed of many specialized modules that work together to create mind and behavior.**

REVIEW TEST

For each of the following items, choose the single best answer. The correct answers appear at the end.

1. According to Darwin's theory of natural selection,
   a. the environment "selects" organisms that are more complex and more advanced.
   b. the members of a species that are best adapted to their environment are more likely to survive and produce more offspring.
   c. giraffes evolved longer necks because they were constantly reaching for the tender, higher leaves in the tall trees in their environment.
   d. evolution is a process whereby experience modifies an organism's genes.
   e. evolution is the sole factor affecting the behavior of current species.

2. Although Darwin never knew it, evolution takes advantage of genetic ______ that enhance survival and reproduction of the individual.
   a. variations
   b. environments
   c. thoughts
   d. diseases
   e. theories

3. During a neural impulse, a neuron "fires" when
   a. it is physically contacted by another cell that is transmitting the signal.
   b. an electric charge travels down the axon.
   c. it contracts and releases powerful chemicals directly into the bloodstream.
   d. signals entering at the axon travel the length of the cell and exit through the dendrites.
   e. neurotransmitters attach to the dendritic receptors.

4. Neurotransmitters are released by the terminal buttons into the ______, and hormones are released by the endocrine system into the ______.
   a. sympathetic nervous system/parasympathetic nervous system
   b. cortex/brain stem
   c. left hemisphere/right hemisphere
   d. receptor sites/glands
   e. synaptic cleft/bloodstream

5. Which one of the following is an example of behavior controlled primarily by the autonomic nervous system?
   a. typing a sentence accurately on a keyboard
   b. solving a mathematical problem
   c. reading this textbook
   d. feeling hungry
   e. breathing and swallowing while asleep

6. Which form of brain scanning employs radioactive tracers to reveal the most active regions of the brain?
   a. EEG
   b. CT
   c. PET
   d. MRI
   e. *f*MRI

7. Which of the following statements identifying the locations of important brain structures is true?
   a. The hypothalamus is part of the brain stem.
   b. The medulla is part of the limbic system.
   c. The occipital lobe is part of the cerebral cortex.
   d. The limbic system regulates breathing.
   e. The pons is responsible for processing of memory.

8. Which of the three brain layers is often thought of as the "emotional brain"?
   a. the brain stem
   b. the cerebellum
   c. the limbic system
   d. the medulla
   e. the cerebrum

9. What part of the cerebral cortex is most involved with initiating and controlling body movements?
   a. the frontal lobes
   b. the hippocampus
   c. the temporal lobes
   d. the occipital lobes
   e. the parietal lobes

10. The left hemisphere of the cerebral cortex is usually more involved than the right hemisphere in activities such as
    a. recognizing and appreciating visual stimuli.
    b. enjoying and appreciating music.
    c. using spoken and written language.
    d. understanding spatial relationships.
    e. processing emotions.

ANSWERS: 1. b 2. a 3. b 4. e 5. e 6. c 7. c 8. b 9. a 10. c

KEY TERMS

Biopsychology (p. 63)
Neuroscience (p. 63)
Evolution (p. 64)
Natural selection (p. 65)
Genotype (p. 66)
Phenotype (p. 66)
DNA (p. 66)
Gene (p. 66)
Chromosome (p. 67)
Sex chromosomes (p. 68)
Neuron (p. 72)
Sensory neuron (p. 72)
Motor neuron (p. 73)
Interneuron (p. 73)
Dendrite (p. 73)
Soma (p. 74)
Axon (p. 74)
Resting potential (p. 74)
Action potential (p. 74)
All-or-none principle (p. 74)
Synapse (p. 74)
Terminal buttons (p. 74)
Synaptic transmission (p. 74)
Synaptic vesicle (p. 75)
Neurotransmitters (p. 75)
Plasticity (p. 76)
Glial cells (p. 77)
Nervous system (p. 77)
Central nervous system (p. 78)
Reflex (p. 78)
Peripheral nervous system (p. 78)
Somatic nervous system (p. 79)
Autonomic nervous system (p. 79)
Sympathetic division (p. 79)
Parasympathetic division (p. 79)
Endocrine system (p. 80)
Hormone (p. 80)
Pituitary gland (p. 82)
Agonist (p. 82)
Antagonist (p. 82)
Neural pathway (p. 83)
Electroencephalograph or **EEG** (p. 85)
CT scanning or **computerized tomography** (p. 86)
PET scanning or **positron emission tomography** (p. 86)
MRI or **magnetic resonance imaging** (p. 86)
***f*MRI** or **functional magnetic resonance imaging** (p. 86)
Brain stem (p. 87)
Medulla (p. 88)
Pons (p. 88)
Reticular formation (p. 89)
Thalamus (p. 89)
Cerebellum (p. 89)
Limbic system (p. 89)
Hippocampus (p. 89)
Amygdala (p. 90)
Hypothalamus (p. 91)
Cerebral cortex (p. 92)
Frontal lobes (p. 93)
Motor cortex (p. 93)
Parietal lobes (p. 94)
Somatosensory cortex (p. 94)
Occipital lobes (p. 95)
Visual cortex (p. 95)
Temporal lobes (p. 95)
Association cortex (p. 96)
Cerebral dominance (p. 97)
Corpus callosum (p. 98)

AP* REVIEW: VOCABULARY

Match each of the following vocabulary terms to its definition.

1. Genotype
2. Phenotype
3. Gene
4. Chromosome
5. Plasticity
6. Agonist
7. Antagonist
8. Thalamus
9. Motor cortex
10. Association cortex

_____ **a.** Encodes directions for inherited characteristics of an organism.

_____ **b.** The nervous system's ability to adapt or change as a result of experience.

_____ **c.** Cortical regions that combine information from various other parts of the brain.

_____ **d.** An organism's genetic makeup.

_____ **e.** Drug or other chemical that inhibits the effects of neurotransmitters.

_____ **f.** Narrow vertical strip of cortex in the frontal lobes.

_____ **g.** The brain's central "relay station."

_____ **h.** Drug or other chemical that enhances or minics the effects of neurotransmitters.

_____ **i.** Consist primarily of DNA.

_____ **f.** An organism's observable physical characteristics.

AP* REVIEW: ESSAY

Use your knowledge of the chapter concepts to answer the following essay question.

One of the most basic functions of the brain relies on neurons. Describe the function of a neuron/neuron chain, being sure to address each of the following in context and in an appropriate manner.

a. Depolarization

b. Excitation

c. Inhibition

d. Neurotransmitter release/binding to next neuron

e. Reuptake

OUR RECOMMENDED BOOKS AND VIDEOS

ARTICLE

Nash, M. R. (2001, July). The truth and the hype of hypnosis. *Scientific American, 285,* 46–49, 52–55. Everyone has ideas and images of hypnosis: glittering watches, drowsy subjects commanded to feel "verrry sleepy . . ." Modern cognitive science now illuminates how and why hypnosis works in pain relief, memory retrieval, and other applications.

BOOKS

Ackerman, D. (2004). *An alchemy of mind: The marvel and mystery of the brain.* New York: Scribner. Poet and naturalist Diane Ackerman investigates the "crowded chemistry lab" of the human nervous system, discovering how identity emerges within the "three-pound blob" that is the brain.

Finger, S. (1999). *Minds behind the brain.* New York: Oxford University Press. Historian Stanley Finger uses biographical sketches to study the development of brain science from ancient times to the present.

Johnson, S. (2004). *Mind wide open: Your brain and the neuroscience of everyday life.* Writer Steven Johnson describes his own experience undergoing brain scans, empathy tests, and neurofeedback, presenting the results and discussing the processes revealed. If you want to know what such tests feel like and mean, here are clear explanations and inviting glimpses into brain science.

LeDoux, J. (2003). *The synaptic self: How our brains become who we are.* New York: Penguin Books. Descartes asserted that "I think, therefore I am." Neuroscientist Joseph LeDoux once spotted a T-shirt that countered, "I don't know—so maybe I'm not." For LeDoux, getting the joke shows that the brain's hardwired pathways interact with one's unique experiences, producing not only conscious experience, but the unique self. His book is as absorbing as a mystery, with instructive humor.

MacMillan, M. (2002). *An odd kind of fame: Stories of Phineas Gage.* Cambridge, MA: MIT Press. In the mid-19th century, a railway worker in Vermont suffered and survived a horrendous brain injury after an accidental explosion. One hundred and fifty years later, Phineas Gage remains famous in neuropsychology because the injury, mainly to his frontal lobe, altered his personality more than any bodily function—thus pinpointing the brain site of individuality. This is a well-researched, poignant history.

VIDEOS

Awakenings. (1990, color, 121 min.). Directed by Penny Marshall; starring Robin Williams, Robert DeNiro, Julie Kavner. Based on Oliver Sacks's collection of the same title, this is the true story of "sleeping sickness" patients who, after decades in a vegetative state, were briefly "awakened" by one doctor's synthetic dopamine therapy. Does medicine have the right to treat patients if the experimental "cure" might offer only temporary hope? (*Rating PG-13*)

Inherit the Wind. (1960, B&W, 127 min.). Directed by Stanley Kramer; starring Spencer Tracy, Fredric March, Gene Kelly, Dick York. This wonderful adaptation of the stage play is based on the 1925 "monkey trial" of John Scopes, a Tennessee man prosecuted for teaching evolution in his public school class. Watch the movie—then research the facts about the real people behind the characters. (*Rating PG*)

Key Question Chapter Outline

CORE CONCEPTS

Psychology in Your Life

How Does Stimulation Become Sensation?

Transduction: Changing Stimulation to Sensation
Sensory Adaptation
Thresholds
Signal Detection Theory

The brain senses the world indirectly because the sense organs convert stimulation into the language of the nervous system: neural messages.

A Critical Look at Subliminal Persuasion

Subliminal perception occurs, but individual differences in perceptual thresholds make widespread use of subliminal persuasion unworkable.

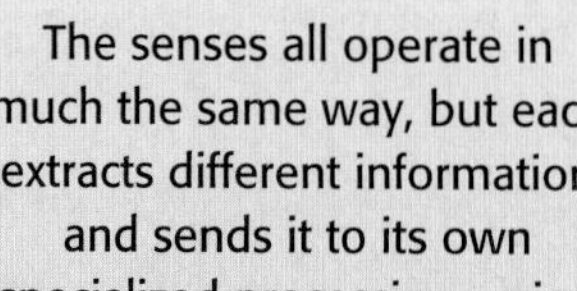

How Are the Senses Alike? And How Are They Different?

Vision: How the Nervous System Processes Light
Hearing: If a Tree Falls in the Forest . . .
How the Other Senses Are Like Vision and Hearing

The senses all operate in much the same way, but each extracts different information and sends it to its own specialized processing region in the brain.

The Experience of Pain

Pain is more than just a stimulus; it is an experience that varies from person to person. Pain control methods include drugs, hypnosis, and—for some—placebos.

What Is the Relationship Between Sensation and Perception?

Perceptual Processing: Finding Meaning in Sensation
Perceptual Ambiguity and Distortion
Theoretical Explanations for Perception

Perception brings *meaning* to sensation, so perception produces an interpretation of the world, not a perfect representation of it.

Seeing and Believing

Magicians and politicians rely on the fact that we don't merely sense the world, we perceive it.

Sensation and Perception: The State of the Art

USING PSYCHOLOGY TO LEARN PSYCHOLOGY:
Studying for the Gestalt

Chapter 4

Sensation and Perception

CAN YOU IMAGINE WHAT your world would be like if you could no longer see colors—but merely black, white, and gray? Such a bizarre sensory loss actually befell Jonathan I., a 65-year-old New Yorker, following an automobile accident (Sacks, 1995). Apparently the trauma of the crash caused damage to a region in his brain that processes color information. At first, Jonathan also had some amnesia for reading letters of the alphabet, which all seemed like nonsensical markings to him. But, after five days, his inability to read disappeared. His loss of color vision, however, persisted as a permanent condition known as *cerebral achromatopsia* (pronounced *ay-kroma-TOP-see-a*).

As you might expect, Jonathan became depressed by this turn of events in his life. The problem was aggravated by the fact that he was a painter whose profession was based on representing his visual images of the world in vivid colors. Now this world of colors was all gone, all drab, all "molded in lead." When he looked at his own paintings, which had seemed bursting with special meaning and emotional associations, all he now saw were unfamiliar and meaningless objects on canvas.

Curiously, Jonathan also lost his memory of color and eventually the names for colors. He could no longer even imagine, for instance, what "red" once looked like. What Jonathan's experience dramatically demonstrated to the researchers and clinicians who studied him and tried to help him was the nonobvious neurological truth that colors do not really exist "out there." Rather, the world of color is constructed by the sensory and perceptual processes in the brain.

Jonathan's story has a more or less happy ending, one that reveals much about the resilience of the human spirit. First, Jonathan became a "night person," traveling and working at night and socializing with other night people. (As we will see in this chapter, good color vision depends on bright illumination such as daylight; most people's color vision is not as acute in the dark of night.) He also became aware that what remained of his vision was remarkably good, enabling him to read license plates from four blocks away at night. Jonathan began to reinterpret his "loss" as a gift in the sense that he was no longer distracted by color and could now focus his work more intently on shape, form, and content. Finally, he switched to painting only in black and white, and critics acclaimed his "new phase" as a success. He has also become good at sculpting, which he had never attempted before his accident. So, as Jonathan's world of color died, a new world of "pure forms" was born in his perception of the people, objects, and events in his environment.

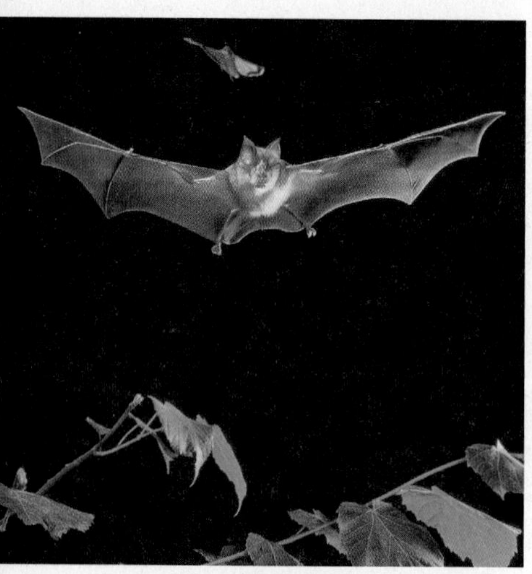

● To hunt small flying objects at night, bats rely on the sensory system of echolocation, a kind of sonar. Bats emit high-frequency sounds that bounce off insects, revealing their locations so the bats can find and eat them.

What are the lessons we can learn from Jonathan's experience? His unusual sensory loss tells us that our picture of the world around us depends on an elaborate sensory system that processes incoming information. In other words, we don't experience the world directly, but instead through a series of "filters" that we call our *senses.* By examining such cases of sensory loss, psychologists have learned much about how the sensory processing system works. And, on a more personal level, case studies like Jonathan allow us momentarily to slip outside our own experience to see more clearly how resilient humans can be in the face of catastrophic loss.

Although the very private processes that connect us with the outside world extend deep into the brain, we will begin our chapter at the surface—at the sense organs. This is the territory of *sensory psychology.* We will define **sensation** simply as the process by which a stimulated receptor (such as the eyes or ears) creates a pattern of neural messages that represent the stimulus in the brain, giving rise to our initial experience of the stimulus. An important idea to remember is that sensation involves changing stimulation (such as a pinprick, a sound, or a flash of light) into a form the brain can understand (neural signals)—much as a cell phone converts an electronic signal into sound waves you can hear.

In this chapter you will see how all our sense organs, in some fundamental ways, are much alike. They all transform physical stimulation (such as light waves) into the neural impulses that give us sensations (such as light and dark). Along the way, you will learn about the psychological basis for color, odor, sound, texture, and taste. When you have finished the chapter, you will know why tomatoes and limes seem to have different hues, why a pinprick feels different from a caress, and why seeing doesn't always give us an accurate basis for believing.

Happily, under most conditions our sensory experience is highly reliable. So, when you catch sight of a friend, the sensation usually registers clearly, immediately, and accurately. Yet we humans do have our sensory limitations—just as other creatures do. In fact, we lack the acute senses so remarkable in many other species: the vision of hawks, the hearing of bats, the sense of smell of rodents, and the sensitivity to magnetic fields found in migratory birds. So, is there a human specialty? In a way, there is: Our species has evolved the sensory equipment that enables us to process a wider range and variety of sensory input than any other creature.

■ **Sensation** The process by which stimulation of a sensory receptor produces neural impulses that the brain interprets as a sound, a visual image, an odor, a taste, a pain, or other sensory image. Sensation represents the first series of steps in processing of incoming information.

Beyond that fact, our ultimate destination in this chapter lies, far beyond mere sensation, in the amazing realm of *perception*. There we will uncover the psychological processes that attach meaning and personal significance to the sensory messages entering our brains. *Perceptual psychology* will help you understand how we assemble a series of tones into a familiar melody or a barrage of shapes and shadings into a familiar face. More generally, we will define **perception** as a mental process that elaborates and assigns meaning to the incoming sensory patterns. Thus, *perception creates an interpretation of sensation.* Perception answers questions such as: Is the tomato ripe? Is the sound a church bell or a doorbell? Does the face belong to someone you know?

In this chapter, you will also learn that many complex acts of sensing and perceiving occur behind the scenes, so effortlessly, continuously, and flawlessly that we pay them little conscious mind. Even more fundamentally, you will learn the sobering fact that our minds lack direct access to the outside world. No matter what we do, the information we get about external events must always be filtered through our sense organs and then combined with our unique mix of memories, emotions, motives, and expectations. Indeed, the inner world of sensation and perception is the only world we can ever know.

As you can see, the boundary of sensation blurs into that of perception. Perception is essentially an interpretation and elaboration of sensation. Seen in these terms, sensation refers just to the initial steps in the processing of a stimulus. It is to these first sensory steps that we now turn our attention.

HOW DOES STIMULATION BECOME SENSATION?

KEY QUESTION
?

A thunderstorm is approaching, and you feel the electric charge in the air make the hair stand up on your neck. Lightning flashes, and a split second later you hear the thunderclap. It was close by, and you smell the ozone left in the wake of the bolt, as it sizzled through the air. Your senses are warning you of danger.

Our senses have other adaptive functions, too. They aid our survival by directing us toward certain stimuli, such as tasty foods, which provide nourishment. Our senses also help us locate mates, seek shelter, and recognize our friends. Incidentally, our senses also give us the opportunity to find pleasure in music, art, athletics, food, and sex.

How do our senses accomplish all this? The complete answer is complex, but it involves one elegantly simple idea that applies across the sensory landscape: Our sensory impressions of the world involve *neural representations* of stimuli—not the actual stimuli themselves. The Core Concept puts it this way:

CORE CONCEPT

The brain senses the world indirectly because the sense organs convert stimulation into the language of the nervous system: neural messages.

As we have noted, the brain never receives stimulation directly from the outside world. Its experience of a tomato is not the same as the tomato itself—although we usually assume that the two are identical. Neither can the brain receive light from a sunset, reach out and touch velvet, or inhale the fragrance of a rose. It must always rely on secondhand information from the go-between sensory system, which delivers only a coded neural message, out of which the brain must create its own experience. (See Figure 4.1.) Just as you cannot receive phone messages without a telephone receiver to convert the electronic energy into sound you can hear, your brain needs its sensory system

■ **Perception** A process that makes sensory patterns meaningful. It is perception that makes these words meaningful, rather than just a string of visual patterns. To make this happen, perception draws heavily on memory, motivation, emotion, and other psychological processes.

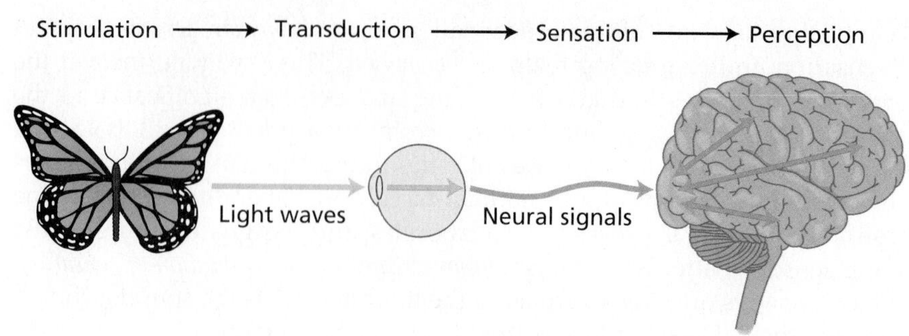
Stimulation
Transduction
Sensation
Perception
Light waves
Neural signals

● **FIGURE 4.1** Stimulation Becomes Perception

For visual stimulation to become meaningful perception, it must undergo several transformations. First, physical stimulation (light waves from the butterfly) are transduced by the eye, where information about the wavelength and intensity of the light is coded into neural signals. Second, the neural messages travel to the sensory cortex of the brain, where they become sensations of color, brightness, form, and movement. Finally, the process of perception interprets these sensations by making connections with memories, expectations, emotions, and motives in other parts of the brain. Similar processes operate on information taken in by the other senses.

to convert the stimuli from the outside world into neural signals that it can comprehend.

To understand more deeply how the world's stimulation becomes the brain's sensation, we need to think about three attributes common to all the senses: *transduction, sensory adaptation,* and *thresholds.* They determine which stimuli will actually become sensation, what the quality and impact of that sensation will be, and whether it grabs our interest. These attributes determine, for example, whether a tomato actually registers in the sensory system strongly enough to enter our awareness, what its color and form appear to be, and how strongly it bids for our attention.

Transduction: Changing Stimulation to Sensation

The idea that basic sensations, such as the redness and flavor of our tomato, are entirely creations of the sense organs and brain may seem incredible to you. But remember that all sensory communication with the brain flows through neurons in the form of neural signals: Neurons cannot transmit light or sound waves or any other external stimulus. Accordingly, none of the light bouncing off the tomato ever actually reaches the brain. In fact, light gets only as far as the back of the eyes, where the information it contains is converted to neural messages. Likewise, the chemicals that signal taste make their way only as far as the tongue, not all the way to the brain.

In all the sense organs, it is the job of the *sensory receptors* to convert incoming stimulus information into electrochemical signals—neural activity—the only language the brain understands. As Jonathan I.'s case suggests, sensations, such as "red" or "sweet" or "cold," occur only when the neural signal reaches the cerebral cortex. The whole process seems so immediate and direct that it fools us into assuming that the sensation of redness is characteristic of a tomato or the sensation of cold is a characteristic of ice cream. But they are not! (You can demonstrate to yourself how light is not necessary for sensations of light with the demonstration in the "Do It Yourself!" box, "Phosphenes Show That Your Brain Creates Sensations.")

Psychologists use the term **transduction** for the sensory process that converts physical energy, such as light or sound waves, into the form of neural messages. Transduction begins with the detection by a sensory neuron of the physical stimulus (such as the sound wave made by a vibrating guitar string). When the appropriate stimulus reaches a sense organ, it activates specialized neurons, called *receptors,* which respond by converting their excitation into a nerve signal. This happens in much the same way that a bar-code reader (which is, after all, merely an electronic receptor) converts the series of lines on a frozen pizza box into an electronic signal that a computer can match with a price. In our own sensory system, it is the neural impulse that carries a code

■ **Transduction** Transformation of one form of energy into another—especially the transformation of stimulus information into nerve signals by the sense organs. Without transduction, ripe tomatoes would not appear red (or pinkish-gray, in the case of tomatoes purchased in many grocery stores).

DO IT YOURSELF! Phosphenes Show That Your Brain Creates Sensations

One of the simplest concepts in perceptual psychology is among the most difficult for most people to understand: The brain and its sensory systems create the colors, sounds, tastes, odors, textures, and pains that you sense. You can demonstrate this to yourself in the following way.

Close your eyes and press gently with your finger on the inside corner of one eye. On the opposite side of your visual field you will "see" a pattern caused by the pressure of your finger—not by light. These light sensations are *phosphenes,* visual images caused by fooling your visual system with pressure, which stimulates the optic nerve in much the same way light does. Direct electrical stimulation of the occipital lobe, sometimes done during brain surgery, can have the same effect. This shows that light waves are not absolutely necessary for the sensation of light. The sensory experience of light, therefore, must be a creation of the brain, rather than a property of objects in the external world.

Phosphenes may have some practical value, too. Several laboratories are working on ways to use phosphenes, created by stimulation sent from a TV camera to the occipital cortex, to create visual sensations for people who have lost their sight (Dobelle, 1977; Leutwyler, 1994; Service, 1999). Another promising approach under development involves replacing a section of the retina with an electronic microchip (Liu et al., 2000). We hasten to add, however, that this technology is in its infancy (Cohen, 2002).

sensation of light

of the sensory event in a form that can be further processed by the brain. To get to its destination, this information-carrying signal travels from the receptor cells along a *sensory pathway* by way of the thalamus to specialized sensory processing areas in the brain. From neural impulses arriving from these pathways, the brain then extracts information about the basic qualities of the stimulus, such as its intensity, pitch, and direction. Please keep in mind, however, that the stimulus itself terminates in the receptor: The only thing that continues on into the nervous system is *information* carried by the neural impulse.

● A swimmer must undergo sensory adaptation when jumping into cool water.

Sensory Adaptation

If you have ever jumped into a cool pool on a hot day, you know that sensation is critically influenced by *change.* In fact, a main role of our stimulus detectors is to announce changes in the external world such as a flash of light, a splash of water, a clap of thunder, the prick of a pin, or the burst of flavor from a dollop of salsa. Thus, our sense organs are change detectors. Their receptors specialize in gathering information about new and changing events.

The great quantity of incoming sensation would quickly overwhelm us, if not for the ability of our sensory systems to adapt. **Sensory adaptation** is the diminishing responsiveness of sensory systems to prolonged stimulation, as when you adapted to the feel of swimming in cool water. Unless it is quite intense or painful, stimulation that persists without changing in intensity or some other quality usually shifts into the background of our awareness. To give another example, you probably did not realize, until we called your attention to it, that your sense of touch had adapted to the press of furniture against

■ **Sensory adaptation** Loss of responsiveness in receptor cells after stimulation has remained unchanged for a while, as when a swimmer becomes adapted to the temperature of the water.

your body. On the other hand, any change in the stimulation you are receiving (if an air conditioner suddenly becomes louder or higher-pitched, for example) will draw your attention. Incidentally, sensory adaptation is why the background music often played in stores is so unmemorable: It has been deliberately selected and filtered to remove any large changes in volume or pitch that might distract attention from the merchandise. (Do you see why it's not a good idea to listen to interesting music while you are studying?)

Thresholds

What is the weakest stimulus that an organism can detect? How dim can a light be and still be visible? How soft can music be and still be heard? These questions refer to the **absolute threshold** for different types of stimulation, which is the minimum amount of physical energy needed to produce a sensory experience. In the laboratory, a psychologist would define this operationally as the intensity at which the stimulus is detected accurately 50% of the time over many trials. Obviously, this threshold will vary from one person to another. So, if you point out a faint star to a friend who says he cannot see it, the star's light is above your absolute threshold (you can see it) but below that of your friend (who cannot).

CONNECTION: CHAPTER 1

An *operational definition* describes a concept in terms of the operations required to produce, observe, or measure it.

A faint stimulus does not abruptly become detectable as its intensity increases. Because of the fuzzy boundary between detection and nondetection, a person's absolute threshold is not absolute! In fact, it varies continually with our mental alertness and physical condition. Experiments designed to determine thresholds for various types of stimulation were among the earliest studies done by psychologists—who called this line of inquiry *psychophysics.* Table 4.1 shows some typical absolute threshold levels for several familiar natural stimuli.

We can illustrate another kind of threshold with the following imaginary experiment. Suppose you are relaxing by watching television on the one night you don't need to study, while your sister busily prepares for an early morning exam. Your sibling asks you to "turn it down a little" to eliminate the distraction. You feel that you should make some effort to comply but really wish to leave the volume as it is. What is the least amount you can lower the volume to prove your good intentions to your sibling while still keeping the volume clearly audible? Your ability to make judgments like this one depends on your **difference threshold,** the smallest physical difference between two stimuli that can still be recognized as a difference.

■ **Absolute threshold** The amount of stimulation necessary for a stimulus to be detected. In practice, this means that the presence or absence of a stimulus is detected correctly half the time over many trials.

■ **Difference threshold** The smallest amount by which a stimulus can be changed and the difference be detected half the time.

TABLE 4.1 Approximate Perceptual Thresholds of Five Senses

Sense Modality	Detection Threshold
Light	A candle flame at 30 miles on a dark, clear night
Sound	The tick of a mechanical watch under quiet conditions at 20 feet
Taste	One teaspoon of sugar in two gallons of water
Smell	One drop of perfume diffused into the entire volume of a three-bedroom apartment
Touch	The wing of a bee falling on your cheek from a distance of one centimeter

Source: From ENCYCLOPEDIC DICTIONARY OF PSYCHOLOGY, 3rd ed. Copyright © 1986 by Dushkin/McGraw-Hill, a division of The McGraw-Hill Companies. Adapted and reprinted by permission of the publisher.

DO IT YOURSELF! An Enlightening Demonstration of Sensory Relationships

In this simple demonstration, you will see how detection of change depends on the intensity of the background stimulation. Find a three-way lamp equipped with a bulb having equal wattage increments, such as a 50–100–150 watt bulb. (Wattage is closely related to brightness.) Then, in a dark room, switch the light on to 50 watts. This will unmistakably increase brightness. Changing from 50 to 100 watts will also seem like a large increase. But why does the last 50-watt increase (from 100 to 150 watts) appear only slightly brighter? Your sensory system does not give you a sensation of the exact brightness. Rather, it compares the stimulus change to the background stimulation, translating the jump from 100 to 150 watts as a mere 50% increase (50 watts added to 100) compared to the earlier 100% increase (50 watts added to 50). This illustrates how your brain computes sensory relationships, rather than absolutes.

If you turn the volume knob as little as possible, your sister might complain, "I don't hear any difference" or "You haven't turned it down enough." By "enough," your sister probably means her difference threshold. Even if you have adjusted the volume downward slightly, the difference might not be large enough to detect. If you hear the difference, it exceeds your own difference threshold; if your sister can hear the difference, it exceeds hers. Suppose you start adjusting the volume and ask your sister to "say when"—to stop you when the adjustment is sufficient to be detected. This minimal amount of change in the signal that is still recognizable is the **just noticeable difference (JND).** The terms *difference threshold, just noticeable difference,* and *JND* are used interchangeably by psychologists.

Investigation of the JND for different senses has yielded some interesting insights into how human stimulus detection works. It turns out that *the JND is always large when the stimulus intensity is high, and small when the stimulus intensity is low.* Psychologists refer to this idea—that the size of the JND is proportional to the intensity of the stimulus—as **Weber's law.** Weber's law is represented by the formula $\Delta I/I = k$, where I is the intensity of the stimulus and k is a constant (there is a different constant for each sense).

And what does Weber's law tell us about adjusting the TV volume? If you have the volume turned up very high, you will have to turn the volume down a lot to make the difference noticeable. On the other hand, if you already have the volume set to a very low level, so that you can barely hear it if you listen carefully, a small adjustment will probably be noticeable enough for your sibling. The same principle operates across all our senses. Knowing this, you might guess that a weight lifter would notice the difference when small amounts were added to light weights, but it would take a much larger addition to be noticeable with heavy weights.

In addition to Weber's law, two other principles affect stimulus detection. **Fechner's law** expresses the relationship between the actual magnitude of the stimulus and its perceived magnitude. An increase in the physical magnitude of a stimulus progressively produces smaller increases in perceived magnitude. The formula for this is $S = k \log R$ (S = sensation, R = stimulus, and k = a constant that differs for each sensory modality). The third principle of stimulus detection is known as **Steven's power law.** This "law" addresses some issues with Fechner's law and why it cannot account for some changes in stimulus detection, and works for a variety of additional stimuli, namely pain and temperature. Steven's power law is written as $S = kI^a$, where S = sensation, k = a constant, I = stimulus intensity, and a = a power exponent that depends on the sense we are measuring. It is through Weber's law, Fechner's law, and Steven's power law that we know and can distinguish among different intensities of stimuli.

■ **Just noticeable difference (JND)** Same as the difference threshold.

■ **Weber's law** This concept says that the size of a JND is proportional to the intensity of the stimulus; the JND is large when the stimulus intensity is high and is small when the stimulus intensity is low. (This concept has *no* connection with Ann Weber, one of your authors.)

■ **Fechner's law** The magnitude of a stimulus can be estimated by the formula $S = k \log R$, where S = sensation, R = stimulus, and k = a constant that differs for each sensory modality (sight, touch, temperature, etc.).

■ **Steven's power law** A law of magnitude estimation that is more accurate than Fechner's law and covers a wider variety of stimuli. It is represented by the formula $S = kI^a$, where S = sensation, k = a constant, I = stimulus intensity, and a = a power exponent that depends on the sense being measured.

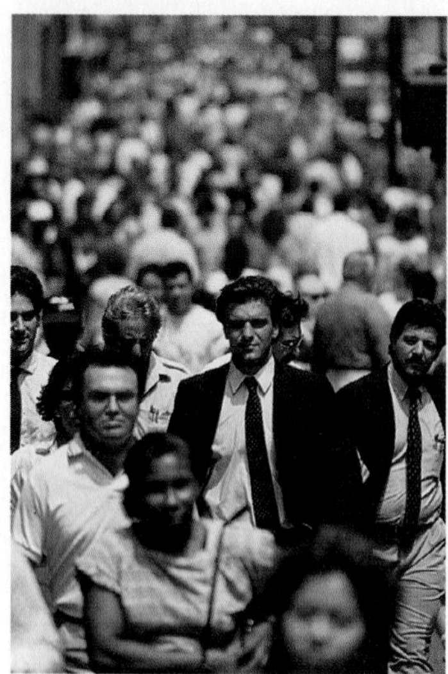

● Signal detection theory says that the background stimulation would make it less likely for you to hear someone calling your name on a busy downtown street than in a quiet park.

What does all this mean for our understanding of human sensation? The general principle is this: We are built to detect *changes* in stimulation and *relationships* among stimuli. You can see how this works in the box, "Do It Yourself! An Enlightening Demonstration of Sensory Relationships."

Signal Detection Theory

A deeper understanding of absolute and difference thresholds comes from *signal detection theory* (Green & Swets, 1966). Originally developed for engineering electronic sensors, signal detection theory uses the same concepts to explain both the electronic sensing of stimuli by devices, such as your TV set, and by the human senses, such as vision and hearing.

According to **signal detection theory,** sensation depends on the characteristics of the stimulus, the background stimulation, and the detector. You may have noticed, for example, that you get more out of an 8 o'clock class if your nervous system has been aroused by a strong cup of coffee. Similarly, a person's interests and biases can affect the "signals" he or she gets from the evening news.

Signal detection theory also helps us understand why thresholds are variable—why, for example, you might notice a certain sound one time and not the next. The classical theory of thresholds ignored the effects of the perceiver's physical condition, judgments, or biases. Thus, in classical psychophysics (the study of stimulation, thresholds, and sensory experience), if a signal were intense enough to exceed one's absolute threshold, it would be sensed; if below threshold, it would be missed. In the view of modern signal detection theory, sensation is not a simple present/absent, yes/no experience.

So, what does signal detection theory offer psychology that was missing in classical psychophysics? One factor is the variability in human judgment. Signal detection theory recognizes that the observer, whose physical and mental status is always in flux, must compare a sensory experience with ever-changing expectations and biological conditions. For example, when something "goes bump in the night" after you have gone to bed, you must decide whether it is the cat, an intruder, or just your imagination. What you decide depends on the keenness of your hearing and what you expect to hear, as well as other noises in the background. By taking into account the variable conditions that affect detection of a stimulus, signal detection theory provides a more accurate portrayal of sensation than did classical psychophysics.

PSYCHOLOGY IN YOUR LIFE: A CRITICAL LOOK AT SUBLIMINAL PERSUASION

Can extremely weak stimulation—stimulation that you don't even notice—affect your mind or behavior? The alluring promise that signals can be processed in your sensory system without awareness lies at the basis of the industry that sells "subliminal" tapes and CDs touted as remedies for obesity, shoplifting, smoking, and low self-esteem. But before you put your money in the mail, let's look at a bit of history and some fundamentals of sensory psychology.

■ **Signal detection theory** Explains how we detect "signals," consisting of stimulation affecting our eyes, ears, nose, skin, and other sense organs. Signal detection theory says that sensation is a judgment the sensory system makes about incoming stimulation. Often, it occurs outside of consciousness. In contrast to older theories from psychophysics, signal detection theory takes observer characteristics into account.

Some years ago, advertising executive James Vicary dramatically announced to the press that he had discovered an irresistible sales technique now known as "subliminal advertising." Vicary said that his method consisted of projecting very brief messages on the screen of a movie theater, urging the audience to "Drink Coke" and "Buy popcorn." He claimed that the ads presented ideas so fleetingly that the conscious mind could not perceive them—yet, he said, the messages would still lodge in the unconscious mind, where they would work on the viewer's desires unnoticed. Vicary also boasted that sales of Coca Cola and popcorn had soared at a New Jersey theater where he tested the technique.

The public was both fascinated and outraged. Subliminal advertising became the subject of intense debate. People worried that they were being manipulated by powerful psychological forces without their consent. As a result, laws were proposed to quash the practice. But aside from the hysteria, was there any real cause for concern? For answers to that question we must return to the concept of *threshold,* the minimum amount of stimulation necessary to trigger a response. The word *subliminal* means "below the threshold" (*limen* = threshold). In the language of perceptual psychology, *subliminal* more specifically refers to stimuli lying near the absolute threshold. Such stimuli may, in fact, be strong enough to affect the sense organs and to enter the sensory system, without causing conscious awareness of the stimulus. But the real question is this: Can subliminal stimuli in this range influence our thoughts and behavior?

Several studies have found that subliminal words flashed briefly on a screen (for less than 1/100 second) can "prime" a person's later responses (Merikle & Reingold, 1990). For example, can you fill in the following blanks to make a word?

S N _ _ _ E L

If you had been subliminally primed by a brief presentation of the appropriate word, it would be more likely that you would have found the right answer, even though you were not aware of the priming stimulus.

Apparently people do respond to stimuli below the absolute threshold, under some circumstances (Greenwald et al., 1996; Reber, 1993). But here is the problem for would-be subliminal advertisers who would attempt to influence us in the uncontrolled world outside the laboratory: Different people have thresholds at different levels. So, what might be *sub*liminal for me could well be *supra*liminal (above the threshold) for you. Consequently, the subliminal advertiser runs the risk that some in the audience will notice—and be angry about—a stimulus aimed slightly below the average person's threshold. In fact, *no controlled research has ever shown that subliminal messages delivered to a mass audience can influence people's buying habits.*

But what about those subliminal recordings that some stores play to prevent shoplifting? Again, no reputable study has ever demonstrated their effectiveness. A more likely explanation for any decrease in shoplifting "associated with" these tapes lies in increased vigilance from employees who know that management is worried about shoplifting. The same goes for the tapes that claim to help you quit smoking, lose weight, become wildly creative, or achieve other dozens of elusive dreams. In a comprehensive study of subliminal self-help techniques, the U.S. Army found all to be without foundation (Druckman & Bjork, 1991). The simplest explanation for reports of success lies in the purchasers' expectations and in the need to prove that they did not spend their money foolishly. And finally, to take the rest of the worry out of subliminal persuasion, you should know that James Vicary eventually admitted that his claims for subliminal advertising were a hoax (Druckman & Bjork, 1991).

The answer to the fill-in-the-blanks problem, by the way, is "snorkel."

CHECK YOUR UNDERSTANDING

1. **RECALL:** The sensory pathways carry information
   a. from the brain to the muscles.
   b. from the brain to the sense organs.
   c. from the central nervous system to the autonomic nervous system.
   d. from the muscles to the brain.
   e. from the sense organs to the brain.

2. **RECALL:** Which one refers to the least amount of stimulation that your perceptual system can detect about half the time?
   a. Fechner's law
   b. the absolute threshold
   c. the action threshold
   d. the difference threshold
   e. the stimulus threshold

3. **APPLICATION:** Which one would involve sensory adaptation?
   a. You no longer pay attention to the feel of the clothes on your body.
   b. The flavor of a spicy salsa on your taco seems hot by comparison with the blandness of the sour cream.
   c. The water in a swimming pool seems warmer after you have been in it for a while than it did when you first jumped in.
   d. You are unaware of a priming stimulus flashed on the screen at 1/100 of a second.
   e. You prefer the feel of silk to the feel of velvet.

4. **RECALL:** Which of the following is a process that adds meaning to incoming information obtained by the sensory systems?
   a. detection
   b. perception
   c. sensation
   d. sensory adaptation
   e. stimulation

5. **UNDERSTANDING THE CORE CONCEPT:** When you hear the sound of a tree falling in the forest, the brain has received nothing but
   a. sound waves from the air.
   b. the vibration of the eardrums.
   c. the sense of the air rushing by you.
   d. sound waves traveling through the sensory pathways.
   e. neural activity in the sensory pathways.

ANSWERS: 1. e 2. b 3. c 4. b 5. e

KEY QUESTION

HOW ARE THE SENSES ALIKE? AND HOW ARE THEY DIFFERENT?

Vision, hearing, smell, taste, touch, pain, body position: In certain ways, all these senses are the same. They all transduce stimulus energy into neural impulses. They are all more sensitive to change than to constant stimulation. And they all provide us information about the world—information that has survival value. But how are they different? With the exception of pain, each sense taps a different form of stimulus energy, and each sends the information it extracts to a different part of the brain. These contrasting ideas lead us to the Core Concept of this section:

CORE CONCEPT

The senses all operate in much the same way, but each extracts different information and sends it to its own specialized processing region in the brain.

Each sense organ has a different design, and each sends neural messages to its own specialized region in the brain. So, in the end, *different sensations occur because different areas of the brain become activated.* Whether you hear a bell or see a bell depends ultimately on which part of the brain receives stimulation. We will explore how this all works by looking at each of the senses in turn. First, we will explore the visual system—the best understood of the senses—to discover how it transduces light waves into visual sensations of color and brightness.

Vision: How the Nervous System Processes Light

Animals with good vision have an enormous biological advantage. This fact has exerted evolutionary pressure to make vision the most complex, best developed, and important sense for humans and most other highly mobile creatures. Good vision helps us detect desired targets, threats, and changes in our physical environment and to adapt our behavior accordingly. So, how does the visual system accomplish this?

The Anatomy of Visual Sensation You might think of the eye as a camera the brain uses to make motion pictures of the world (see Figure 4.2). Like a camera, the eye gathers light, focuses it, converts it to neural signals, and sends these signals on their way for subsequent processing into a visual image. The unique characteristic of the eye—what makes the eye different from other sense organs—lies in its ability to extract the information from light waves, which are simply a form of electromagnetic energy. (Visible light is not fundamentally different from radio waves or X rays, as we shall find.) The eye, then, *transduces* the characteristics of light into neural signals that the brain can process. This transduction happens in the **retina,** the light-sensitive layer of cells at the back of the eye that acts much like the light-sensitive chip in a digital camera.

The real work in the retina is performed by light-sensitive cells known as **photoreceptors,** which operate much like the tiny pixel receptors in a digital camera. These photoreceptors consist of two different types of specialized neurons—the rods and cones that absorb light energy and respond by creating neural impulses (see Figure 4.3). But why two types of photoreceptors?

■ **Retina** The thin, light-sensitive layer at the back of the eyeball. The retina contains millions of photoreceptors and other nerve cells.

■ **Photoreceptors** Light-sensitive cells (neurons) in the retina that convert light energy to neural impulses. The photoreceptors are as far as light gets into the visual system.

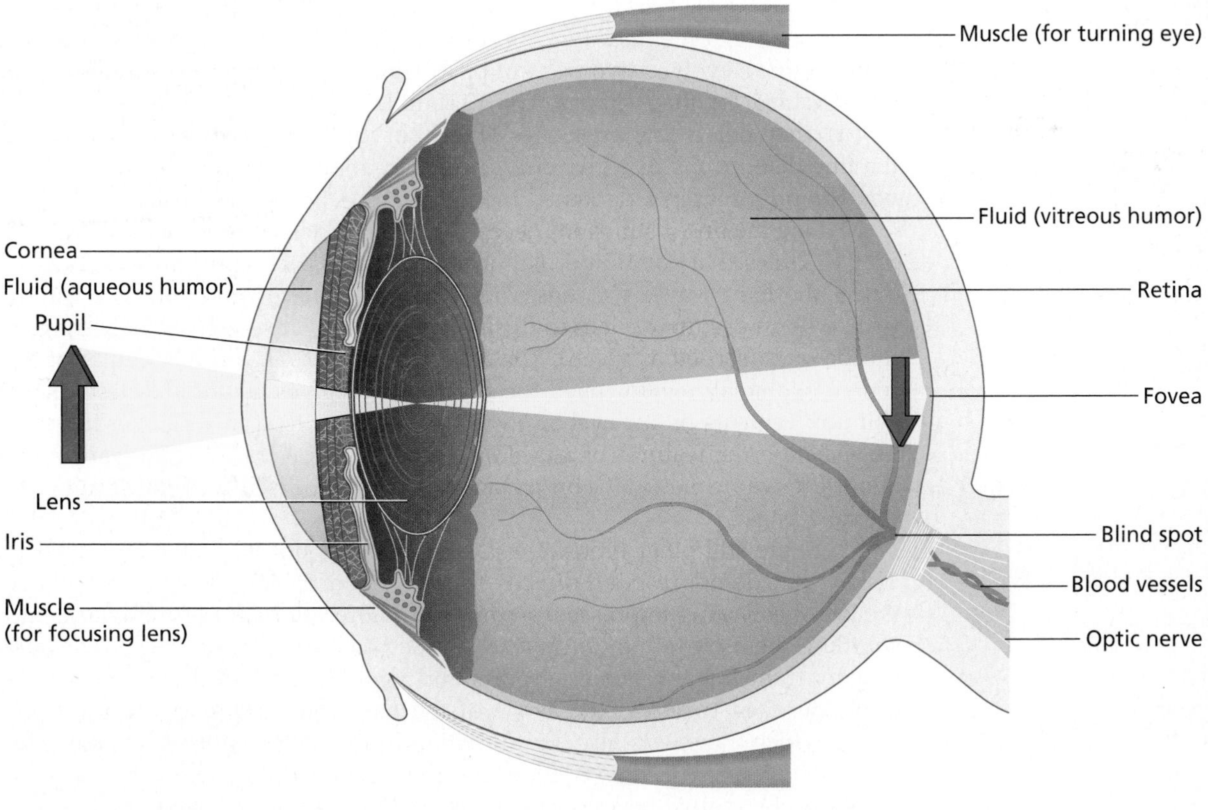

Muscle (for turning eye)
Fluid (vitreous humor)
Retina
Fovea
Cornea
Fluid (aqueous humor)
Pupil
Lens
Iris
Muscle
(for focusing lens)
Blind spot
Blood vessels
Optic nerve

● **FIGURE 4.2** Structures of the Human Eye

● **FIGURE 4.3** Transduction of Light in the Retina

This simplified diagram shows the pathways that connect three layers of nerve cells in the retina. Incoming light passes through the ganglion cells and bipolar cells first before striking the photoreceptors at the back of the eyeball. Once stimulated, the rods and cones transmit information to the bipolar cells (note that one bipolar cell combines information from several receptor cells). The bipolar cells then transmit neural impulses to the ganglion cells. Impulses travel from the ganglia to the brain via axons that make up the optic nerve.

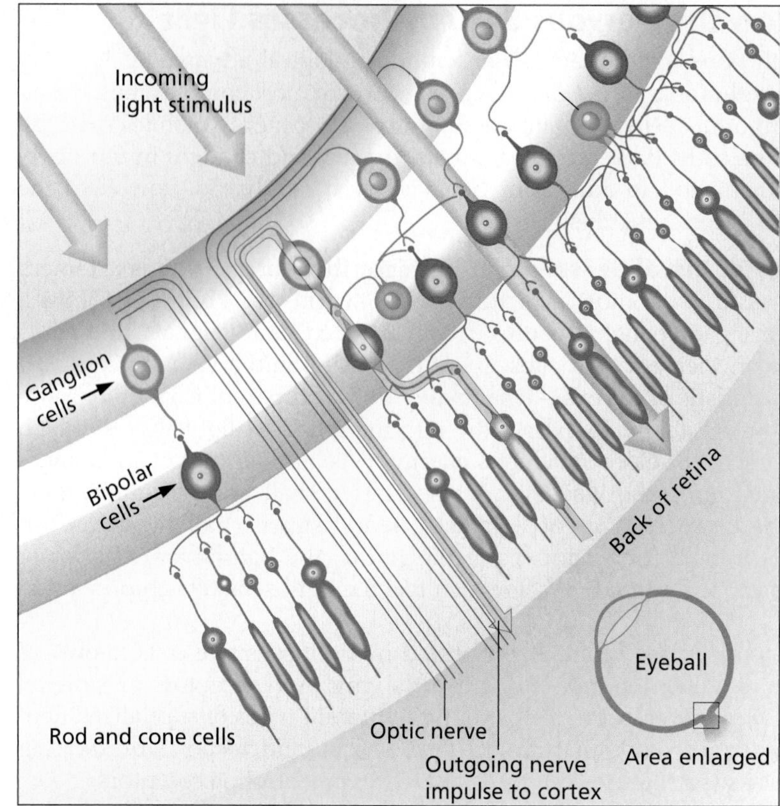
Incoming
light stimulus
Ganglion
cells
Bipolar
cells
Back of retina
Eyeball
Rod and cone cells
Optic nerve
Outgoing nerve
impulse to cortex
Area enlarged

Because we sometimes function in near-darkness and sometimes in bright light, we have evolved two ways of processing, using two distinct receptor cell types named for their shapes. The 125 million tiny **rods** "see in the dark"—that is, they detect low intensities of light at night, though they cannot make the fine distinctions that give rise to our sensations of color. Rod cells enable you to find a seat in a darkened movie theatre.

Making the fine distinctions necessary for color vision is the job of the seven million **cones** that come into play in bright light. Each cone is specialized to detect the light waves we sense either as blue, red, or green. In good light, then, we can use these cones to distinguish ripe tomatoes (sensed as red) from unripe ones (sensed as green). The cones concentrate in the very center of the retina, in a small region called the **fovea,** which gives us our sharpest vision. With movements of our eyeballs, we use the fovea to scan whatever interests us visually—the features of a face or, perhaps, a flower. (You can learn more about the way cones work by trying the "Do It Yourself!" demonstration on the next page.)

There are still other types of cells in the retina, but while they are vital to vision, they do not respond directly to light. In particular, the *bipolar cells* have the job of collecting impulses from many photoreceptors (rods and cones) and shuttling them on to the *ganglion cells,* much as an airline "hub" collects passengers from many regional airports and shuttles them on to other destinations. Bundled together, the axons of the ganglion cells make up the **optic nerve,** which transports visual information from the eye to the brain. (See Figures 4.2 and 4.3.) Again, it is important to understand that your visual system carries no light at all beyond the retina—only patterns of nerve impulses conveying *information* derived from the incoming light.

■ **Rods** Photoreceptors in the retina that are especially sensitive to dim light but not to colors. Strange as it may seem, they are rod-shaped.

■ **Cones** Photoreceptors in the retina that are especially sensitive to colors but not to dim light. You may have guessed that the cones are cone-shaped.

■ **Fovea** The tiny area of sharpest vision in the retina.

■ **Optic nerve** The bundle of neurons that carries visual information from the retina to the brain.

DO IT YOURSELF! The Amazing Afterimage

After you stare at a colored object for a while, cells in your retina will become fatigued, causing an interesting visual effect. When you shift your gaze to a blank surface, you can "see" the object in complementary colors—as a visual afterimage. The "phantom flag" demonstration will show you how this works.

Stare at the dot in the center of the green, black, and orange flag for at least 30 seconds. Take care to hold your eyes steady and not to let them scan over the image during this time. Then quickly shift your gaze to the center of a sheet of white paper or to a light-colored blank wall. What do you see? Have your friends try this, too. Do they see the same afterimage? (The effect may not work for people who are color-blind.)

Afterimages may be negative or positive. Positive afterimages are caused by a continuation of the receptor and neural processes following stimulation. They are brief. An example of positive afterimages occurs when you see the trail of a sparkler twirled by a Fourth of July reveler. Negative afterimages are the opposite or the reverse of the original experience, as in the flag example. They last longer. Negative afterimages operate according to the *opponent-process theory* of color vision, which involves ganglion cells in the retina and the optic nerve. Apparently, in a negative afterimage, the fatigue in these cells produces sensations of a complementary color when they are exposed to white light.

Just as strangely, there is a small area of the retina in each eye where everyone is blind, because that part of the retina has no photoreceptors. This **blind spot** is located at the point where the optic nerve exits each eye, and the result is a gap in the visual field. If your vision is normal, you do not experience blindness there because what one eye misses is registered by the other eye, and the brain "fills in" the spot with information that matches the background. You can find your own blind spot by following the instructions in the "Do It Yourself!" box on the next page.

Processing Visual Sensation in the Brain We *look* with our eyes but we *see* with the brain. To do so, we use a special processing area in the brain to create visual images from the information imported through the optic nerve (see Figure 4.4). In the *visual cortex,* the brain begins working its magic by transforming the incoming neural impulses into visual sensations of color, form, boundary, and movement. Amazingly, the visual cortex also manages to take the two-dimensional patterns from each eye and assemble them into a three-dimensional world of depth (Barinaga, 1998a; Dobbins et al., 1998). With further processing, the cortex ultimately combines these visual sensations with memories, motives, emotions, and sensations of body position and touch to create a representation of the visual world that fits our current concerns and interests (Barinaga, 1999; Batista et al., 1999; de Gelder, 2000; Maunsell, 1995). Now you know why you can be strongly attracted by the visual appeal of appetizing foods if you go grocery shopping when you are hungry.

CONNECTION: CHAPTER 3
The *visual cortex* lies in the brain's occipital lobe.

How the Visual System Creates Brightness Sensations of **brightness** come from the intensity or *amplitude* of light, determined by how much light reaches the

■ **Blind spot** The point where the optic nerve exits the eye and where there are no photoreceptors. Any stimulus that falls on this area cannot be seen.

■ **Brightness** A psychological sensation caused by the intensity of light waves.

DO IT YOURSELF! Find Your Blind Spot

The "blind spot" occurs at the place on the retina where the neurons from the retina bunch together to exit the eyeball and form the optic nerve. There are no light-sensitive cells at this point on the retina. Consequently, you are "blind" in this small region of your visual field. The following demonstrations will help you determine where this blind spot occurs in your visual field.

DEMONSTRATION 1

Hold the book at arm's length, close your right eye, and fix your left eye on the "bank" figure. Keep your right eye closed and bring the book slowly closer. When it is about 10 to 12 inches away and the dollar sign is in your blind spot, the dollar sign will disappear–but you will not see a "hole" in your visual field. Instead, your visual system "fills in" the missing area with information from the white background. You have "lost" your money!

DEMONSTRATION 2

To convince yourself that the brain fills in the missing part of the visual field with appropriate background, close your right eye again and focus on the cross in the lower part of the figure. Once again, keeping the right eye closed, bring the book closer to you as you focus your left eye on the cross. This time, the gap in the line will disappear and will be filled in with a continuation of the line on either side. This shows that what you see in your blind spot may not really exist!

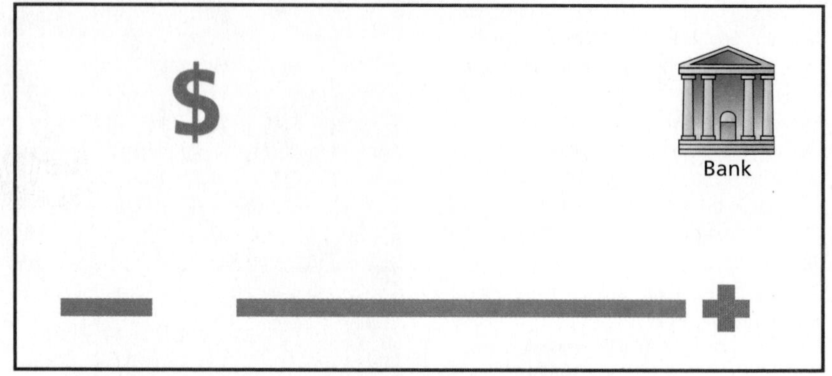
$
Bank

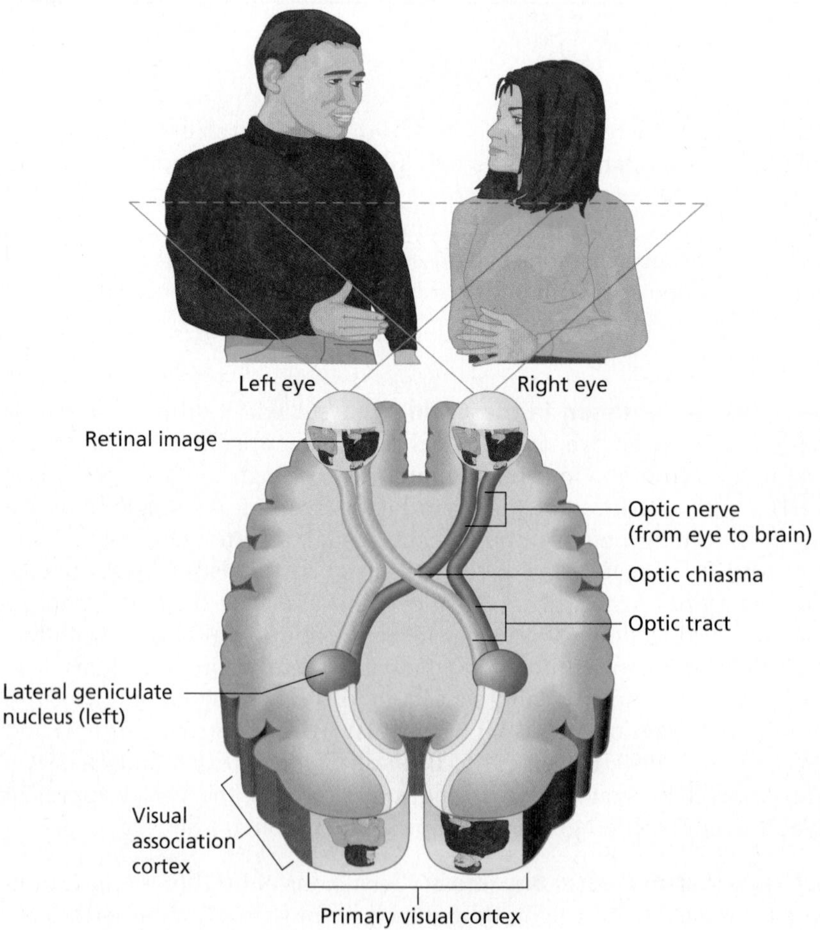
Left eye
Right eye
Retinal image
Optic nerve
(from eye to brain)
Optic chiasma
Optic tract
Lateral geniculate
nucleus (left)
Visual
association
cortex
Primary visual cortex

● **FIGURE 4.4** How Visual Stimulation Goes from the Eyes to the Brain

Light from objects in the visual field projects images on the retinas of the eyes. Please note two important things. First, the lens of the eye reverses the image on the retina–so the image of the man falls on the right side of the retina and the image of the woman falls on the left. Second, the visual system splits the retinal image coming from each eye, so that part of the image coming from each eye crosses over to the opposite side of the brain. (Note how branches of the optic pathway cross at the *optic chiasma.*) As a result, objects appearing in the *left* part of the visual field *of both eyes* (the man, in this diagram) are sent to the *right* hemisphere's visual cortex for processing, while objects in the *right* side of the visual field *of both eyes* (the woman, in this diagram) are sent to the *left* visual cortex. In general, the right hemisphere "sees" the left visual field, while the left hemisphere "sees" the right visual field. (*Source:* From SEEING: Illusion, Brain and Mind by J. P. Frisby. Copyright © 1979. Reprinted by permission of J. P. Frisby.)

TABLE 4.2	Visual Stimulation Becomes Sensation	
Physical Stimulation		**Psychological Sensation**
Wavelength	⟶	color
Intensity (amplitude)	⟶	brightness

Color and brightness are the psychological counterparts of the wavelength and intensity of a lightwave. Wavelength and intensity are physical characteristics of light waves, while color and brightness are psychological characteristics that exist only in the brain.

retina (see Table 4.2). Bright light, as from approaching headlights, involves a more intense light wave, which creates much neural activity in the retina, whereas relatively dim light, from your car's instrument panel, does not. Ultimately, the brain senses brightness by the level of neural activity produced in the retina and passed along through the optic pathways.

How the Visual System Creates Color You may have been surprised to learn that a flower or a ripe tomato, itself, has no **color** or *hue.* Physical objects seen in bright light seem to have the marvelous property of being awash with color; but, as we have noted, the red tomatoes, yellow flowers, green trees, blue oceans, and multihued rainbows are, in themselves, actually quite colorless. Nor does the light reflected from these objects have color. Despite the way the world appears to us, color does not exist outside the brain because color is a *sensation* that the brain creates based on the wavelength of light striking our eyes. Thus, color exists only in the mind of the viewer—a *psychological* property of our sensory experience. Color is created when the wavelength in a beam of light is recoded by the photoreceptors in the form of neural impulses and sent to specialized areas of the brain for sensory processing. To understand more fully how this happens, you must first know something of the nature of light.

■ **Color** Also called *hue.* Color is *not* a property of things in the external world. Rather, it is a *psychological sensation* created in the brain from information obtained by the eyes from the wavelengths of visible light.

■ **Electromagnetic spectrum** The entire range of electromagnetic energy, including radio waves, X rays, microwaves, and visible light.

■ **Visible spectrum** The tiny part of the electromagnetic spectrum to which our eyes are sensitive. The visible spectrum of other creatures may be slightly different from our own.

The eyes detect the special form of energy that we call *visible light.* Physicists tell us that this light is pure energy—fundamentally the same as radio waves, microwaves, infrared light, ultraviolet light, X rays, and cosmic rays. All are forms of *electromagnetic energy,* consisting of waves that move at light's speed limit of nearly 670 million MPH. These waves differ in their *wavelength,* the distance they travel in making one wave cycle, as they vibrate in space, like ripples on a pond (see Figure 4.5). The light we can see occupies but a tiny segment of the vast **electromagnetic spectrum.** Our only access to this electromagnetic spectrum lies through a small visual "window" called the **visible spectrum.** Because we have no biological receptors sensitive to the other portions of the electromagnetic spectrum, we must employ special detection instruments, such as radios and TVs, to help us convert energy in the range outside our vision into signals we can use.

Within the visible spectrum light waves of different wavelengths give rise to different colors. Longer waves make us see a tomato as red, and medium-length waves give rise to the sensations of yellow and green we see in lemons and limes. The shorter waves from a clear sky stimulate sensations of blue. Thus, it is the wavelength of light from which the eye extracts the information used by the brain to construct colors (see Table 4.2).

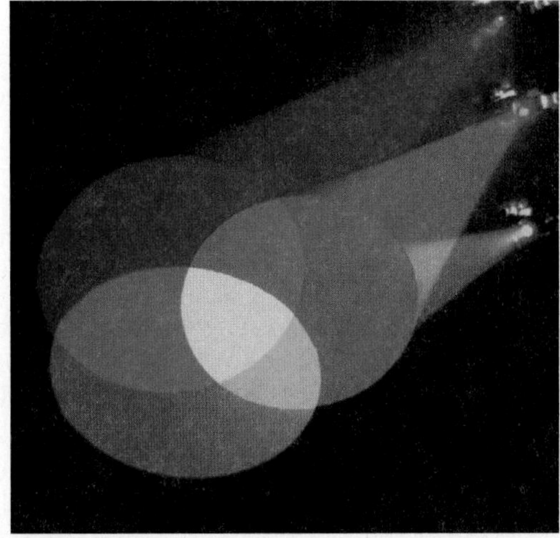

● The combination of any two unique hues yields the complement of a third color. The combination of all three wavelengths produces white light, as does the combination of two complementary colors.

Remarkably, our visual experiences of color, form, position, and depth are all based on processing the same stream of sensory information in different parts of the visual cortex. Colors

● **FIGURE 4.5** The Electromagnetic Spectrum

The only difference between visible light and other forms of electromagnetic energy is *wavelength*. (*Source:* Fig. 2.1, p. 27, "The Electromagnetic Spectrum," from PERCEPTION 3rd ed. by Sekuler & Blake. Copyright © 1994. Reprinted by permission of The McGraw-Hill Companies.)

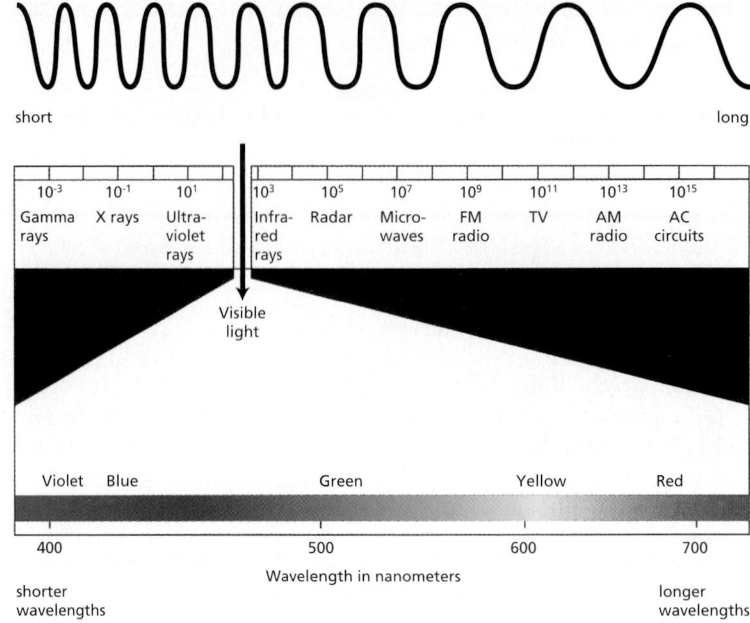

short
long
10^{-3}
10^{-1}
10^{1}
10^{3}
10^{5}
10^{7}
10^{9}
10^{11}
10^{13}
10^{15}
Gamma rays
X rays
Ultra-violet rays
Infra-red rays
Radar
Micro-waves
FM radio
TV
AM radio
AC circuits
Visible light
Violet
Blue
Green
Yellow
Red
400
500
600
700
Wavelength in nanometers
shorter wavelengths
longer wavelengths

themselves are realized in a specialized area, where humans are capable of discriminating among about five million different hues. Other nearby cortical areas take responsibility for processing information about boundaries, shapes, and movements.

Two Ways of Sensing Colors Even though color is realized in the cortex, color processing begins in the retina. There, three different types of cones sense different parts of the visible spectrum—light that we sense as red, green, and blue. This three-receptor explanation for color vision is known as the **trichromatic theory,** and for a time it was considered to account for color vision completely. We now know that the trichromatic theory best explains the initial stages of color vision in the cone cells.

Another explanation, called the **opponent–process theory,** better explains some cases of color blindness, as well as negative **afterimages** (see the "Do It Yourself!" box on p. 121)—both of which involve *opponent*, or complementary, colors. According to the opponent-process theory, from the bipolar cells onward the visual system processes colors in either-or complementary pairs, such as red or green or as yellow or blue. In all subsequent layers of the visual system, then, the sensation of a certain color, such as red, inhibits the sensation of its complement, green. Taken together, the two theories explain color vision: The trichromatic theory explains color processing in the cones, while the opponent-process theory explains what happens in the bipolar cells and beyond.

■ **Trichromatic theory** The idea that colors are sensed by three different types of cones sensitive to light in the red, blue, and green wavelengths. The trichromatic theory explains the earliest stage of color sensation.

■ **Opponent-process theory** The idea that cells in the visual system process colors in complementary pairs, such as red or green or as yellow or blue. The opponent-process theory explains color sensation from the bipolar cells onward in the visual system.

■ **Afterimages** Sensations that linger after the stimulus is removed. Most visual afterimages are *negative afterimages,* which appear in reversed colors.

■ **Color blindness** Typically a genetic disorder (although sometimes the result of trauma, as in the case of Jonathan) that prevents an individual from discriminating certain colors. The most common form is red–green color blindness.

Color Blindness Not everyone sees colors in the same way, because some people are born with a color deficiency. At the extreme, complete **color blindness** is the total inability to distinguish colors. More commonly people merely have a color weakness that causes minor problems in distinguishing colors, especially under low-light conditions. People with one form of color weakness can't distinguish pale colors, such as pink or tan. Most color weakness or blindness, however, involves a problem in distinguishing red from green, especially at weak saturations. Those who confuse yellows and blues are rare, about one or two people per thousand. Rarest of all are those who see no color at all and see only variations in brightness. In fact, only about 500 cases of this total color blindness have ever been reported—including Jonathan I., whom we met at the beginning of this chapter. To see whether you have a major color deficiency, look at Figure 4.6 and note what you see. If you see the number 15 in the dot pattern, your color vision is probably normal. If you see something else, you are probably at least partially color blind.

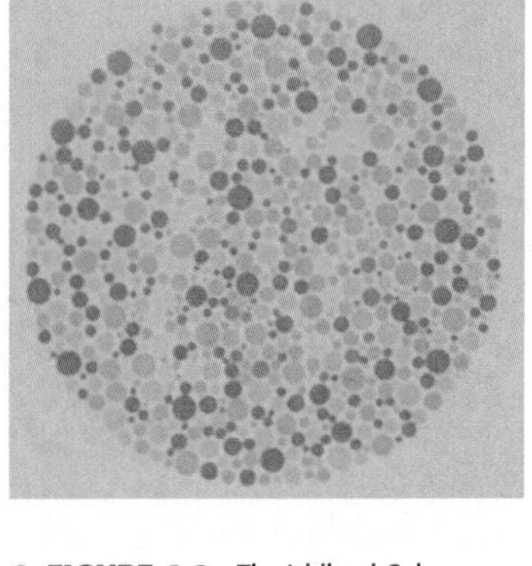

● **FIGURE 4.6** The Ishihani Color Blindness Test

Someone who cannot discriminate between red and green hues will not be able to identify the number hidden in the figure. What do you see? If you see the number 15 in the dot pattern, your color vision is probably normal.

Hearing: If a Tree Falls in the Forest . . .

Imagine how your world would change if your ability to hear were suddenly diminished. You would quickly realize that hearing, like vision, provides you with the ability to locate objects in space, such as the source of a voice calling your name. In fact, hearing may be even more important than vision in orienting us toward distant events. We often hear things, such as footsteps coming up behind us, before we see the source of the sounds. Hearing may also tell us of events that we cannot see, including speech, music, or a car approaching from behind.

But there is more to hearing than its *function.* Accordingly, we will look a little deeper to learn *how* we hear. Specifically, in the next few pages we will review what sensory psychologists have discovered about how sound waves are produced, how they are sensed, and how these sensations of sound are interpreted.

The Physics of Sound: How Sound Waves Are Produced Those Hollywood explosions of spaceships or planets should be absolutely silent! On Earth, the vibrational energy of vibrating objects, such as guitar strings, bells, and vocal cords, transfers to the surrounding medium—usually air—as the vibrating objects push the molecules of the medium back and forth. The resulting changes in pressure spread outward in the form of sound waves that can travel 1100 feet per second in air. In space, however, there is no air or other medium to carry the sound wave, so if you were a witness to a planetary disaster, the experience would be eerily without sound.

Back here on Earth, the purest tones are made by a tuning fork (see Figure 4.7). When struck, a tuning fork produces an extremely simple sound wave that has only two characteristics: *frequency* and *amplitude.* These are the two physical properties of any sound wave that determine how it will be sensed

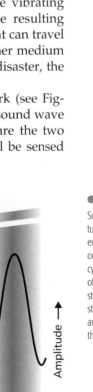

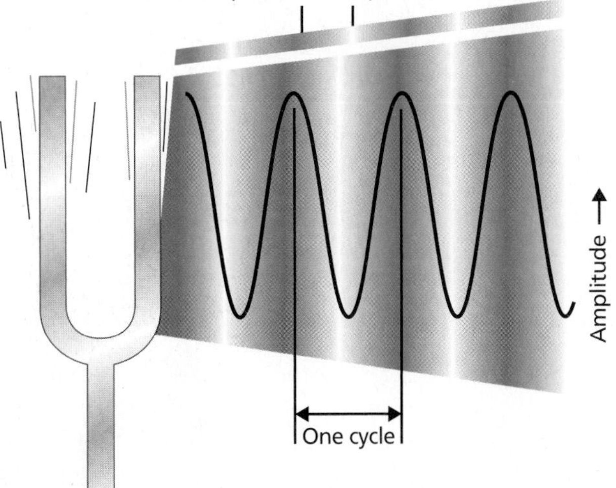
Air: Compression
Expansion
Amplitude
One cycle
Time

● **FIGURE 4.7** Sound Waves

Sound waves produced by the vibration of a tuning fork create waves of compressed and expanded air. The pitch that we hear depends on the *frequency* of the wave (the number of cycles per second). High pitches are the result of high-frequency waves. The *amplitude,* or strength, of a sound wave depends on how strongly the air is affected. In this diagram, amplitude is represented by the height of the graph.

by the brain. **Frequency** refers to the number of vibrations or cycles the wave completes in a given amount of time; it is usually expressed in *cycles per second (cps)* or *hertz (Hz)*. **Amplitude** is a measure of the physical strength of the sound wave (shown in its peak-to-valley height); it is defined in units of sound pressure or energy. When you turn down the volume on your stereo, you are decreasing the amplitude of the sound waves.

Sensing Sounds: How We Hear Sound Waves Much like vision, the psychological sensation of sound requires that waves be transduced into neural impulses and sent to the brain. This happens in four steps:

1. *Airborne sound waves must be relayed to the inner ear.* In this initial transformation, vibrating waves of air enter the outer ear (also called the *pinna*) and strike the *eardrum*, or **tympanic membrane** (see Figure 4.8). This tightly stretched sheet of tissue transmits the vibrations to three tiny bones: the *hammer, anvil,* and *stirrup*, named for their shapes. These bones immediately pass the vibrations on to the primary organ of hearing, the **cochlea,** located in the inner ear.
2. *The cochlea focuses the vibrations on the basilar membrane.* Here in the cochlea, the formerly airborne sound wave becomes "seaborne," because the coiled tube of the cochlea is filled with fluid. As the bony stirrup vibrates against the oval window at the base of the cochlea, the vibrations set the fluid into wave motion, working on the same principle as a submarine sending a sonar "ping" through the water. In turn, the fluid wave spreads through the cochlea, causing a sympathetic vibration in the **basilar membrane,** a thin strip of tissue running through the cochlea.
3. *The basilar membrane converts the vibrations into neural messages.* The swaying of tiny hair cells on the vibrating basilar membrane (much like the swaying of buildings during an earthquake) stimulates sensory nerve endings

■ **Frequency** The number of cycles completed by a wave in a given amount of time, usually a second.
■ **Amplitude** The physical strength of a wave. This is usually measured from peak (top) to valley (bottom) on a graph of the wave.
■ **Tympanic membrane** The eardrum.
■ **Cochlea** The primary organ of hearing; a coiled tube in the inner ear, where sound waves are transduced into nerve messages.
■ **Basilar membrane** A thin strip of tissue sensitive to vibrations in the cochlea. The basilar membrane contains hair cells connected to neurons. When a sound wave causes the hair cells to vibrate, the associated neurons become excited. As a result, the sound waves are converted (transduced) into nerve activity.

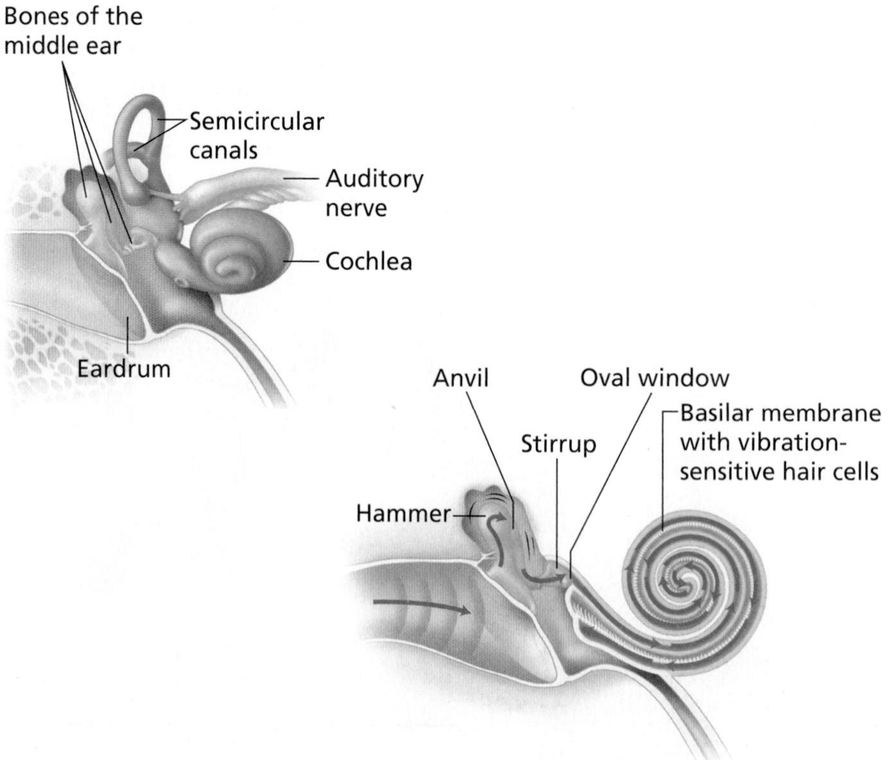
Bones of the middle ear
Semicircular canals
Auditory nerve
Cochlea
Eardrum
Anvil
Oval window
Basilar membrane with vibration-sensitive hair cells
Stirrup
Hammer

● **FIGURE 4.8** Structures of the Human Ear

Sound waves are channeled by the outer ear (*pinna*) through the external canal, causing the tympanic membrane to vibrate. The vibration activates the tiny bones in the middle ear (*hammer, anvil,* and *stirrup*). These mechanical vibrations pass from the oval window to the cochlea, where they set internal fluid in motion. The fluid movement stimulates tiny hair cells along the basilar membrane, inside the cochlea, to transmit neural impulses from the ear to the brain along the auditory nerve.

connected to the hair cells. The excited neurons, then, transform the mechanical vibrations of the basilar membrane into neural activity.

4. *Finally, the neural messages travel to the auditory cortex in the brain.* Neural signals leave the cochlea in a bundle of neurons called the *auditory nerve.* The neurons from the two ears meet in the brain stem, which passes the auditory information to both sides of the brain. Ultimately, the signals arrive in the *auditory cortex* for higher-order processing.

CONNECTION: CHAPTER 3
The auditory cortex lies in the brain's *temporal lobes.*

If the auditory system seems complicated, you might think of it as a sensory "relay team." Sound waves are first funneled in by the outer ear, then handed off from the tissue of the eardrum to bones in the middle ear. Mechanical vibrations of these bones are then passed to the cochlea and basilar membrane, where they finally become neural signals, which are, in turn, passed along to the brain. This series of steps transforms commonplace vibrations into experiences as exquisite and varied as music, doorbells, whispers, shouts, and psychology lectures.

Psychological Qualities of Sound: How We Distinguish One Sound from Another No matter where they come from, sounds have only three sensory qualities: *pitch, loudness,* and *timbre.* In the following discussion, we will show you how the two *physical* characteristics of a sound wave (frequency and amplitude) manage to produce these three *psychological sensations.*

Sensations of Pitch A sound wave's *frequency* determines the highness or lowness of a sound—a quality known as **pitch.** High frequencies produce high pitch, and low frequencies produce low pitch, as you see in Table 4.3. As with light, our sensitivity to sound spans only a limited range of the sound waves that occur in nature. The range of human auditory sensitivity extends from frequencies as low as 20 cps (the lowest range of a subwoofer in a good sound system) to frequencies as high as 20,000 cps (produced by the high-frequency

■ **Pitch** A sensory characteristic of sound produced by the *frequency* of the sound wave.

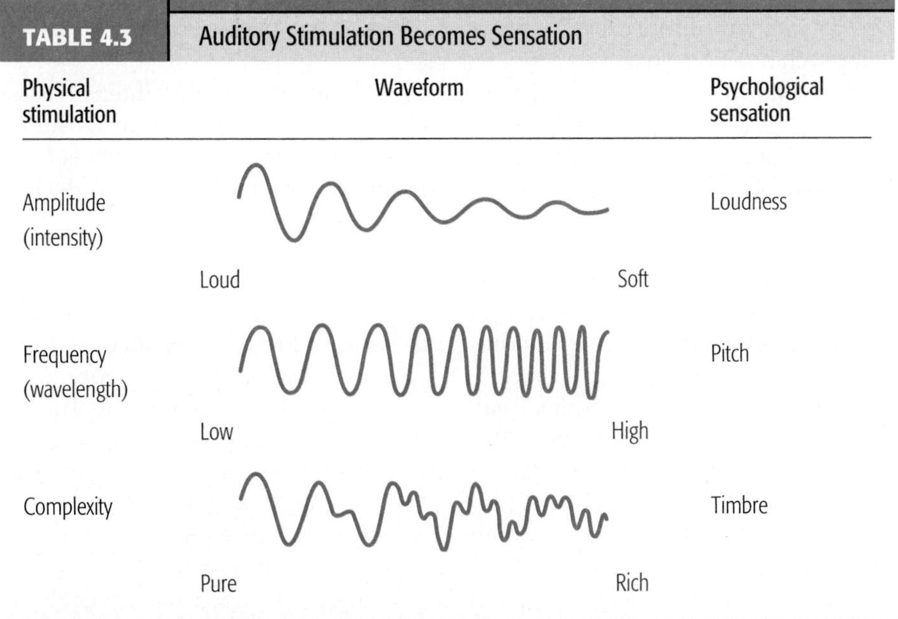

TABLE 4.3 Auditory Stimulation Becomes Sensation

Physical stimulation	Waveform	Psychological sensation
Amplitude (intensity)	Loud — Soft	Loudness
Frequency (wavelength)	Low — High	Pitch
Complexity	Pure — Rich	Timbre

Pitch and loudness are the psychological counterparts of the frequency and amplitude (intensity) of a sound wave. Frequency and amplitude are characteristics of the physical sound wave, while sensations of pitch and loudness exist only in the brain. In addition, sound waves can be complex combinations of simpler waves. Psychologically, we experience this complexity as *timbre.* Compare this table with Table 4.2 for vision.

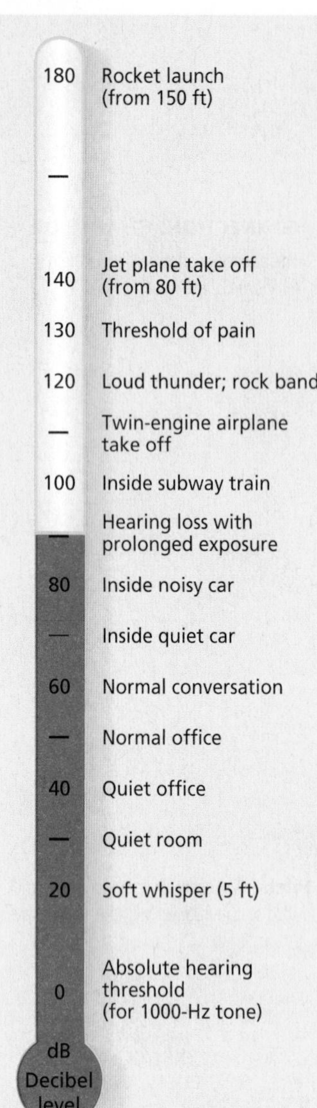
180 Rocket launch (from 150 ft)
140 Jet plane take off (from 80 ft)
130 Threshold of pain
120 Loud thunder; rock band
Twin-engine airplane take off
100 Inside subway train
Hearing loss with prolonged exposure
80 Inside noisy car
Inside quiet car
60 Normal conversation
Normal office
40 Quiet office
Quiet room
20 Soft whisper (5 ft)
0 Absolute hearing threshold (for 1000-Hz tone)
dB Decibel level

● **FIGURE 4.9** Intensities of Familiar Sounds

■ **Loudness** A sensory characteristic of sound produced by the *amplitude* (intensity) of the sound wave.

■ **Timbre** The quality of a sound wave that derives from the wave's complexity (combination of pure tones). *Timbre* comes from the Greek word for "drum," as does the term *tympanic membrane,* or eardrum.

■ **Conduction deafness** An inability to hear resulting from damage to structures of the middle or inner ear.

■ **Nerve deafness (Sensorineural Deafness)** An inability to hear, linked to a deficit in the body's ability to transmit impulses from the cochlea to the brain, usually involving the auditory nerve or higher auditory processing centers.

tweeter in your sound system). Other creatures can hear sounds both higher (in dogs, for example) and lower (in elephants) than we can.

How does the auditory apparatus produce sensations of pitch? Two distinct auditory processes share the task, affording us much greater sensory precision than either could provide alone. Here's what happens:

- When sound waves pass through the inner ear, the basilar membrane vibrates (see Figure 4.8). Different frequencies activate different locations on the membrane. Thus, the pitch one hears depends, in part, on which region of the basilar membrane receives the greatest stimulation. This explanation of pitch perception, known as the *place theory,* says that different *places* on the basilar membrane send neural codes for different pitches to the auditory cortex of the brain—much as keys on different places on a piano keyboard can produce different notes. It turns out that the place theory accounts for our ability to hear high tones—above about 1000 Hz (cycles per second).
- Neurons on the basilar membrane respond with different firing rates for different sound wave frequencies, much as guitar strings vibrating at different frequencies produce different notes. And so, the rate of firing provides another code for pitch perception in the brain. This *frequency theory* explains how the basilar membrane deals with frequencies below about 5000 Hz. (Between 1000 and 5000 Hz, hearing is based on both place and frequency.)

Why is there overlap in the processes described by these two theories—specifically for sounds within the range of 1000 to 5000 Hz? Simple. This is the range of human speech, and our hearing has evolved two different ways of making sure that we are especially sensitive to sounds in this range. And, just to make sure, the auditory canal is shaped to amplify sounds within this speech range.

Sensations of Loudness The **loudness** of a sound is determined by its physical strength or *amplitude* (much as brightness is determined by the intensity of light). More intense sound waves (a shout) produce louder sounds (see Table 4.3), whereas we experience sound waves with small amplitudes (a whisper) as soft. Amplitude, then, refers to the physical sound wave, and loudness is a psychological sensation.

Because we can hear sound waves across a great range of intensity, the loudness of a sound is usually expressed as a ratio rather than an absolute amount. Specifically, sound intensity is measured in units called decibels (dB). Figure 4.9 shows the levels of some representative natural sounds in decibel units.

Sensations of Timbre The bark of a dog, a train whistle, the wail of an oboe, the clink of a spoon in a cup—all sound distinctively different, not just because they have different pitches or loudness but because they are peculiar mixtures of tones. In fact, most natural sound waves are mixtures rather than pure tones (see Figure 4.10). This complex quality of a sound wave is known as **timbre** (pronounced *TAM-b'r*). Timbre is the property that enables you to recognize a friend's voice on the phone or distinguish between the same song sung by different artists.

Now, with all this information about sound in mind, we are in a position to answer an ancient puzzle: If a tree falls in the forest and there is no ear there to hear it, is there a sound? Based on our knowledge of sensory psychology, we can emphatically say, "No." Even though a falling tree makes strong vibrations in the air, we now know that it produces no physical sound because *sound is not a physical phenomenon.* Rather, sound is a purely *psychological sensation* that requires an ear (and the rest of the auditory system) to produce it.

Deafness Deafness is usually one of two types. The first type is called conduction deafness. In **conduction deafness,** the ways in which sound waves are converted to nerve energy have been interfered with or interrupted. Specifically, it is the conduction of the vibrations that has been affected. In most cases, damage has occurred to any of the structures of the middle ear either by sound that has been too loud (see Figure 4.9) or by some sort of trauma. The second type of deafness is called nerve deafness or sensorineural deafness. In **nerve deafness,** there is a problem with how the impulses from the oval window are sent to the brain; in other words, damage has occurred to the auditory nerve or one of the higher auditory processing centers. Most people who are born deaf have this type.

How Are Auditory and Visual Sensations Alike? Earlier we discussed how visual information is carried to the brain by the optic nerve in the form of neural impulses. Now, we find that, in a similar fashion, auditory information is also conveyed to the brain as neural signals—but by a different pathway. So, why do we "see" visual information and "hear" auditory information? As our Core Concept suggested, the answer lies in the region of the cortex receiving the neural message—not on some unique quality of the message itself. In brief, different regions of the brain, when activated, produce different sensations.

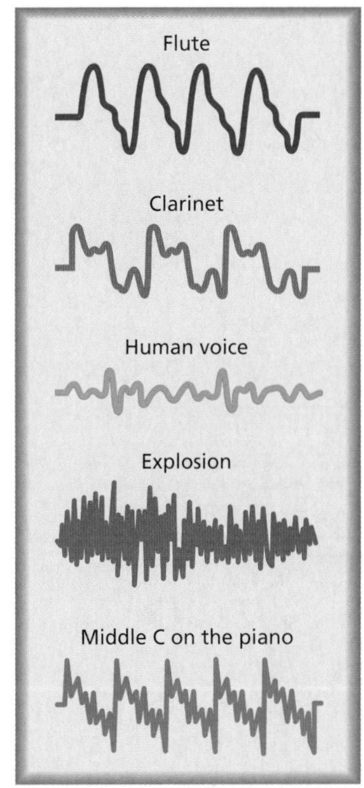
Flute
Clarinet
Human voice
Explosion
Middle C on the piano

● **FIGURE 4.10** Waveforms of Familiar Sounds

Each sound is a distinctive combination of several pure tones. (*Source:* From THE SCIENCE OF MUSICAL SOUNDS by D. C. Miller. Reprinted by permission of Case Western Reserve University.)

How the Other Senses Are Like Vision and Hearing

Of all our senses, vision and hearing have been studied the most. However, our survival and well-being depend on other senses, too. So, to conclude this discussion of sensation, we will briefly review the processes involved in our sense of body position and movement, smell, taste, the skin senses, and pain. (See Table 4.4.) You will note that each gives us information about a different aspect of our internal or external environment. Yet each operates on similar principles. Each transduces physical stimuli into neural activity, and each is more sensitive to change than to constant stimulation. And, as was the case with vision and hearing, each of these senses is distinguished by the type of information it extracts and by the specialized regions of the brain devoted to it.

TABLE 4.4 Fundamental Features of the Human Senses

Sense	Stimulus	Sense organ	Receptor	Sensation
Vision	Light waves	Eye	Rods and cones of retina	Colors, brightness, patterns, motion, textures
Hearing	Sound waves	Ear	Hair cells of the basilar membrane	Pitch, loudness, timbre
Skin senses	External contact	Skin	Nerve endings in skin	Touch, warmth, cold
Smell	Volatile substances	Nose	Hair cells of olfactory epithelium	Odors (musky, flowery, burnt, minty, etc.)
Taste	Soluble substances	Tongue	Taste buds of tongue	Flavors (sweet, sour, salty, bitter)
Pain	Many intense or extreme stimuli: temperature, chemicals, mechanical stimuli, etc.	Net of pain fibers all over the body	Specialized pain receptors, overactive or abnormal neurons	Acute pain, chronic pain
Kinesthetic and vestibular senses	Body position, movement, and balance	Semicircular canals, skeletal muscles, joints, tendons	Hair cells in semicircular canals; neurons connected to skeletal muscles, joints, and tendons	Position of body parts in space

Finally, you will see two patterns emerging in the way the senses process information. First, as was the case with vision and hearing, the other senses also make use of only a fraction of the available stimulation. Second, you will find that the senses are built to be especially sensitive to *changes* in stimulation.

Position and Movement To act purposefully and gracefully, we need constant information about where our limbs and other body parts are in relation to each other and to objects in the environment. Without this knowledge, even our simplest actions would be hopelessly uncoordinated. (You have probably had just this experience when you tried to walk on a leg that had "gone to sleep.") The physical mechanisms that keep track of body position, movement, and balance actually consist of two different systems.

The **vestibular sense** is the body position sense that orients us with respect to gravity. It tells us how our bodies—especially our heads—are postured, whether straight, leaning, reclining, or upside down. The vestibular sense also tells us when we are moving or how our motion is changing. The receptors for this information are tiny hairs (much like those we found in the basilar membrane) in the *semicircular canals* of the inner ear (refer again to Figure 4.8). These hairs respond to our movements by detecting corresponding movements in the fluid of the semicircular canals. Disorders of this sense can cause extreme dizziness and disorientation.

The **kinesthetic sense,** the other sense of body position and movement, keeps track of body parts relative to each other. Your kinesthetic sense makes you aware of crossing your legs, for example, and tells you which hand is closer to the telephone when it rings. Kinesthesis provides constant sensory feedback about what the muscles in your body are doing during motor activities, such as whether to continue reaching for your cup of coffee or to stop before you knock it over (Turvey, 1996).

Receptors for kinesthesis reside in the joints, muscles, and tendons. These receptors, as well as those for the vestibular sense, connect to processing regions in the brain's parietal lobes—which help us make a sensory "map" of the spatial relationship among objects and events. This processing usually happens automatically and effortlessly, outside of conscious awareness, except when we are deliberately learning the movements for a new physical skill, such as swinging a golf club or playing an instrument.

Smell The sense of smell, or **olfaction,** involves a chain of biochemical events. First, odors (in the form of airborne chemical molecules) interact with receptor proteins associated with specialized hairs in the nose (Axel, 1995; Buck & Axel, 1991; Mombaerts, 1999). The stimulated nerve cells associated with these hairs (much like the sensitive hairs we found in the inner ear) convey information about the stimulus to the brain's *olfactory bulbs,* where sensations of smell are realized. These olfactory bulbs can be found on the underside of the brain just below the frontal lobes (Mori et al., 1999). (See Figure 4.11.) Unlike all the other senses, smell signals are not relayed through the thalamus, suggesting that smell evolved earlier than the other senses.

In humans, olfaction has an intimate connection with memory: Certain smells, such as a favorite perfume, can evoke emotion-laden memories (Azar, 1998a; Holloway, 1999). Originally, however, smell was probably a system in primitive organisms for detecting and locating food (Moncrieff, 1951). Even today, smell remains a major factor in survival because it helps us detect and avoid potential sources of danger, such as decaying food.

In many animals, the sense of smell is used for communication. For example, insects such as ants and termites and vertebrates such as dogs and cats communicate with each other by secreting and detecting odorous signals called **pheromones**—especially to signal sexual receptivity, danger, territorial bound-

■ **Vestibular sense** The sense of body orientation with respect to gravity. The vestibular sense is closely associated with the inner ear and, in fact, is carried to the brain on a branch of the auditory nerve.

■ **Kinesthetic sense** The sense of body position and movement of body parts relative to each other (also called *kinesthesis*).

■ **Olfaction** The sense of smell.

■ **Pheromones** Chemical signals released by organisms to communicate with other members of their species. Pheromones are often used by animals as sexual attractants. It is unclear whether or not humans employ pheromones.

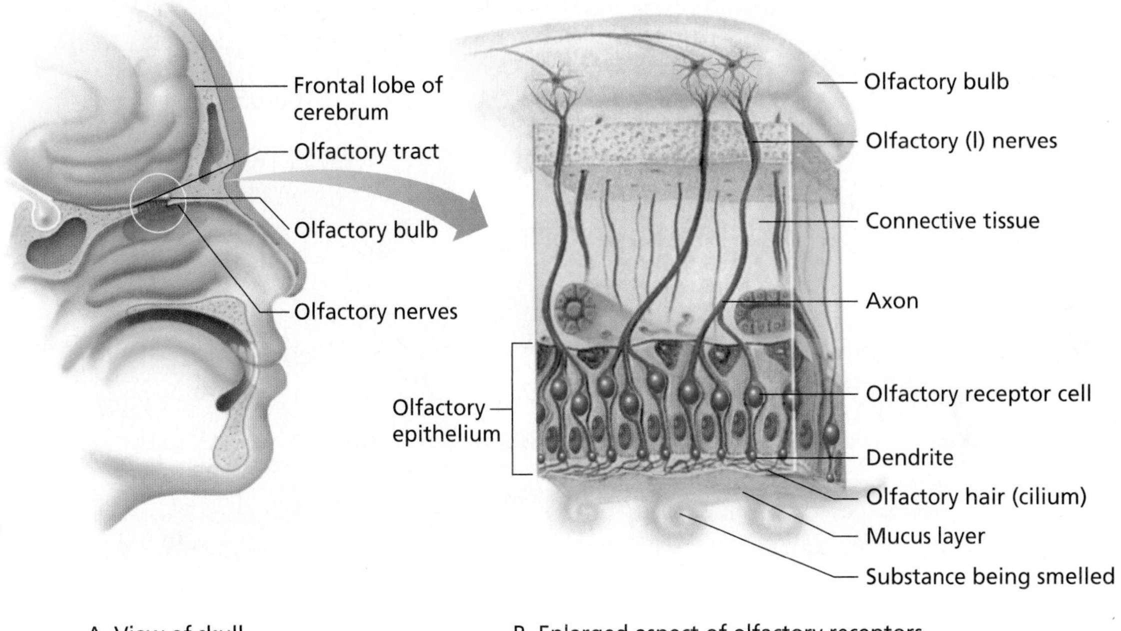
Frontal lobe of cerebrum
Olfactory tract
Olfactory bulb
Olfactory nerves
Olfactory bulb
Olfactory (I) nerves
Connective tissue
Axon
Olfactory epithelium
Olfactory receptor cell
Dendrite
Olfactory hair (cilium)
Mucus layer
Substance being smelled
A. View of skull
B. Enlarged aspect of olfactory receptors

● **FIGURE 4.11** Receptors for Smell

(*Source:* From PSYCHOLOGY AND LIFE 15th ed. by P. G. Zimbardo and R. J. Gerrig. Copyright © 1999 by Pearson Education. Reprinted by permission of Allyn & Bacon, Boston, MA.)

aries, and food sources. We humans seem to use the sense of smell primarily in conjunction with taste to seek and sample food, but some evidence exists to suggest that people may also use sexual pheromones as well as pheromones that help us identify family members by smell (Azar, 1998b; Filsinger & Fabes, 1985; Holden, 1996b).

Taste Like smell, taste is a sense based on chemistry. But the similarity doesn't end there: The senses of taste and smell have a cooperative working relationship. Many of the subtle distinctions you may think of as flavors really come from odors. (Much of the "taste" of an onion is odor, not flavor.) You will also notice this when you have a cold, which makes food seem tasteless because your nasal passages are blocked and you can't smell the food.

Isolated in the laboratory, the sense of taste, or **gustation,** has long been known to have four main qualities: sweet, sour, bitter, and salty. Recently, however, researchers have identified a fifth taste quality called *umami* (Chaudhari et al., 2000). Umami is the flavor associated with monosodium glutamate (MSG), often used in Asian cuisine. It also occurs naturally in protein-rich foods, such as meat, seafood, and cheese.

The taste receptor cells are gathered in *taste buds,* located on the top and side of the tongue, where they can easily sample the molecules in our food and drink. These receptors cluster in small mucous-membrane projections called *papillae,* shown in Figure 4.12. Individuals vary in their sensitivity to taste sensations, a function of the density of these papillae on the tongue (Bartoshuk et al., 1994). Those with more taste buds for bitter flavors are "supertasters," who are more sensitive than regular tasters or extreme "nontasters," which accounts for supertasters' distaste for certain foods, such as broccoli or "diet" drinks. Supertasters also have a survival advantage, because most poisons are bitter (Bartoshuk, 1993).

■ **Gustation** The sense of taste—from the same word root as "gusto"—also called the *gustatory sense.*

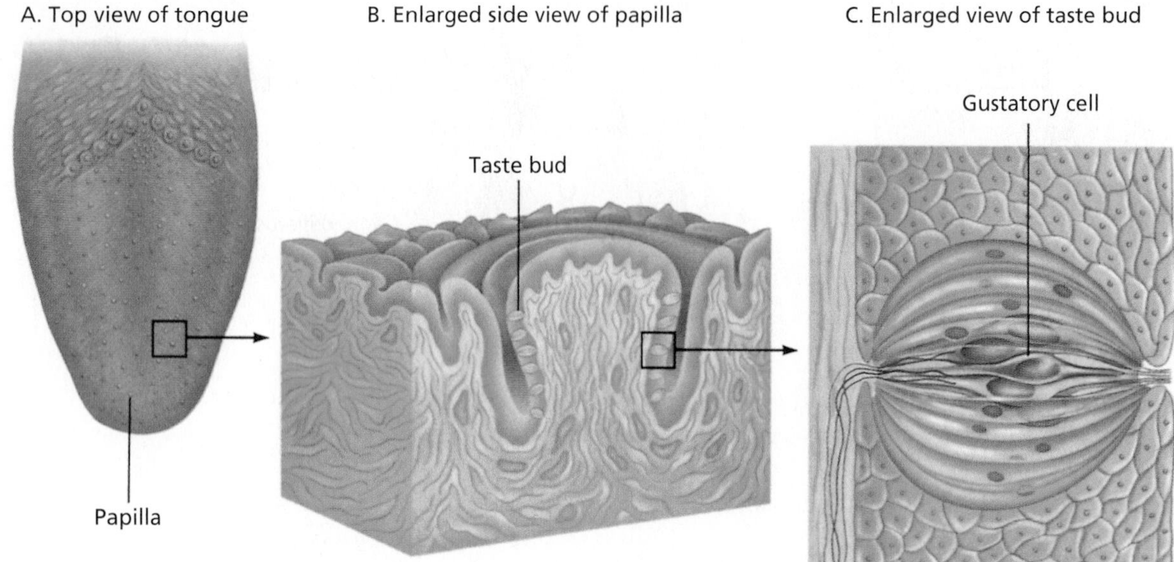
A. Top view of tongue
B. Enlarged side view of papilla
C. Enlarged view of taste bud
Gustatory cell
Taste bud
Papilla

FIGURE 4.12 Receptors for Taste

(A) Distribution of the papillae on the upper side of the tongue; (B) an enlarged view with individual papillae and taste buds visible; (C) one of the taste buds enlarged.

A specialized nerve "hotline" carries nothing but taste messages to the brain. There taste is realized in a specialized region of the parietal lobe's somatosensory cortex. Conveniently for the brain, this area lies next to the patch of cortex that receives touch stimulation from the face (Gadsby, 2000).

Infants have heightened taste sensitivity, which is why you have probably never met a baby who wouldn't cringe at the bitter taste of lemon. This supersensitivity, however, decreases with age. As a result, many elderly people complain that food has lost its taste—which really means that they have lost much of their sensory ability to detect differences in the taste and smell of food. Compounding this effect, taste receptors can be easily damaged by alcohol, smoke, acids, or hot foods. Fortunately, gustatory receptors are frequently replaced (as are the smell receptors). Because of this constant renewal, the taste system is the most resistant to permanent damage of all your senses, and a total loss of taste is extremely rare (Bartoshuk, 1990).

The Skin Senses Consider the skin's remarkable versatility: It protects us against surface injury, holds in body fluids, and helps regulate body temperature. The skin also contains nerve endings that, when stimulated by contact with external objects, produce sensations of touch, warmth, and cold. Like several other senses, these **skin senses** are connected to the somatosensory cortex located in the brain's parietal lobes.

The skin's sensitivity to stimulation varies tremendously over the body, depending in part on the number of receptors in each area. For example, we are ten times more accurate in sensing stimulation on our fingertips than stimulation on our backs. In general, our sensitivity is greatest where we need it most—on our faces, tongues, and hands. Precise sensory feedback from these parts of the body permits effective eating, speaking, and grasping.

One aspect of skin sensitivity—touch—plays a central role in human relationships. Through touch we communicate our desire to give or receive comfort, support, love, and passion (Fisher, 1992; Harlow, 1965; Masters & Johnson, 1966). Touch also serves as a primary stimulus for sexual arousal in humans. And it is essential for healthy mental and physical development; the

■ **Skin senses** Sensory systems for processing touch, warmth, cold, texture, and pain.

lack of touch stimulation can stunt mental and motor development (Anand & Scalzo, 2000; Field & Schanberg, 1990; Spitz, 1946).

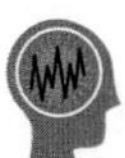

PSYCHOLOGY IN YOUR LIFE: THE EXPERIENCE OF PAIN

If you are in severe pain, nothing else matters. A wound or a toothache can dominate all other sensations. And if you are among the one-third of Americans who suffer from persistent or recurring pain, the experience can be debilitating and can sometimes even lead to suicide (Wallis, 1984). Yet pain is also part of your body's adaptive mechanism that makes you respond to conditions that threaten damage to your body.

Unlike other sensations, pain can arise from intense stimulation of various kinds, such as a very loud sound, heavy pressure, a pinprick, or an extremely bright light. But pain is not merely the result of stimulation. Many people who were born without a limb or have had a limb amputated feel painful sensations that seem to come from the missing part, often called a *phantom limb* (Ramachandran & Blakeslee, 1998). Neurological studies show that the painful phantom sensations do not originate in damaged nerves in the sensory pathways. Rather, the sensations arise in the brain itself. To understand pain, then, we must understand not only painful sensations but mechanisms in the brain that both process and inhibit pain.

The Gate-Control Theory No one has yet developed a theory that explains everything about pain, but Melzack and Wall's **gate-control theory** (1965, 1983) explains a lot. In particular it explains why pain can sometimes be blocked by analgesic drugs, competing stimuli, as in acupuncture, and even by the mere expectation of treatment effects. Their proposal asserts that pain depends on the relative amount of traffic in two different sensory pathways which carry information from the sense organs to the brain.

One route, consisting of neurons with a fatty myelin covering on their axons, handles messages quickly; these *fast fibers* deliver most sensory information to the brain. The smaller *slow fibers,* without the fatty sheaths on their axons, send messages more slowly. Very intense stimuli, such as that caused by tissue injury, send strong signals on the slow fibers.

Melzack and Wall hypothesize that competing messages from the fast fibers can block pain messages in the slow fibers. That is, the fast fibers can close a sort of "spinal gate," preventing the slow fibers' messages from reaching the brain. Consequently, the level of pain you experience from a wound results from the combination of information coming through these two pathways. When you hit your finger with a hammer, you automatically try to close the "gate" by vigorously shaking your hand to generate fast-fiber signals that block the pain.

The "gate," itself, probably operates in a brain stem region called the *periaqueductal gray (PAG).* The exact mechanism is unclear, but we do know that pain-blocking opiates and endorphins act on the PAG. There they cause inhibitory neurons to nullify pain messages ascending in the spinal cord (Basbaum et al., 1976; Basbaum & Fields, 1984; Pinel, 2003). Ultimately, pain signals that pass through the gate are routed to the *anterior cingulate cortex,* located along the fissure separating the frontal lobes, where we believe pain to be sensed (Craig & Reiman, 1996; Vogel, 1996).

The spinal gate can be operated top-down by psychological factors, as well. As noted above, we have long known that people's interpretations of events affect whether or not stimuli are perceived as painful (Turk, 1994). For example, soldiers and athletes often suffer severe injuries that cause little pain

■ **Gate-control theory** An explanation for pain control that proposes we have a neural "gate" that can, under some circumstances, block incoming pain signals.

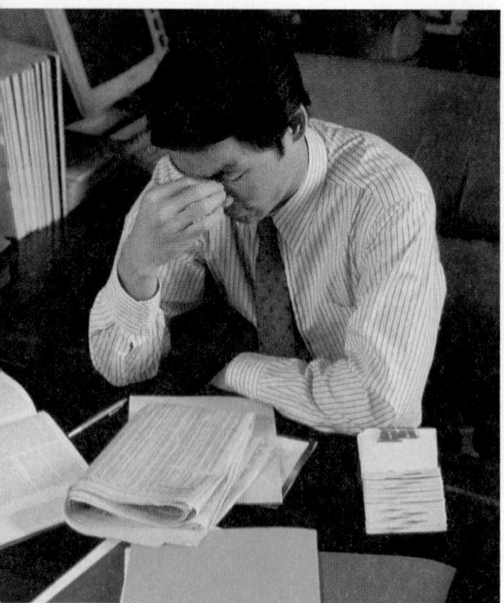

Pain is affected by experience and circumstance. A person who is unhappy may find the pain of a headache unbearable, while another individual, in a more satisfactory job, considers a headache merely annoying.

until the excitement of the battle or contest is over. As we will see in a moment, this mind–body effect on pain is also evident in the action of *placebos* or other sham treatments.

Dealing with Pain Wouldn't it be nice to banish the experience of pain altogether? In reality, such a condition can be deadly. People with congenital insensitivity to pain do not feel what is hurting them, and their bodies often become scarred and their limbs deformed from injuries they could have avoided if their brains were able to warn them of danger. Because of their failure to notice and respond to tissue-damaging stimuli, these people tend to die young (Manfredi et al., 1981). In general, pain serves as an essential defense signal: It warns us of potential harm, and it helps us to survive in hostile environments and to get treatment for sickness and injury.

What can you do if you are in pain? Analgesic drugs, ranging from over-the-counter remedies, such as aspirin and ibuprofen, to prescription narcotics, such as morphine, are widely used and effective. These act in a variety of ways. We have seen that morphine, for example, mimics your body's own pain control substances, the endorphins.

All such drugs—especially the narcotics—can have unwanted side effects. These include addiction or damage to the digestive tract. But, to dispel an old concern, studies have shown that if you must use narcotics to control severe pain, the possibility of your becoming addicted is far less than it would be if you were using narcotics recreationally (Melzack, 1990).

Many people can learn to control pain by psychological techniques, such as hypnosis, deep relaxation, and thought-distraction procedures (Brown, 1998). You may be among those for whom pain can also be modified by *placebos,* mock drugs made to appear as real drugs. For example, a placebo may be an injection of mild saline solution (salt water) or a pill made of sugar. Such fake drugs are routinely given to a control group in tests of new pain drugs. Their effectiveness, of course, involves the people's *belief* that they are getting real medicine. It is important to note, however, that the brain's response to a placebo seems to be essentially the same as that of pain-relieving drugs. Because this **placebo effect** is common, any drug deemed effective must prove itself stronger than a placebo.

Placebo effect A response to a placebo (a fake drug), caused by subjects' belief that they are taking real drugs.

But how do placebos produce their effects? Apparently the expectation of pain relief is enough to cause the brain to release painkilling endorphins. We believe this is so because brain scans show essentially the same pain-suppression areas "light up" when patients take placebos or analgesic drugs (Petrovic et al., 2002). Further, we find that individuals who respond to placebos report that their pain increases when they take the endorphin-blocking drug *naltrexone* (Fields, 1978; Fields & Levine, 1984). It is likely that endorphins are responsible for the pain-relieving effects of acupuncture (Price et al., 1984; Watkins & Mayer, 1982).

Pain Tolerance The threshold of pain varies enormously from person to person. One study, for example, found that electric shocks had to be eight times more powerful to produce painful sensations in their least-sensitive subjects as compared with their most-sensitive subjects (Rollman & Harris, 1987). Another experiment found that brain scans of people who are highly sensitive to pain show greater activation of the thalamus and the anterior cingulate cortex than scans of those with greater pain tolerance (Coghill et al., 2003). These findings may explain why some people always demand Novocain at the dentist, while others may prefer dental work without the added hassle of an injection.

CHECK YOUR UNDERSTANDING

1. **RECALL:** The eyes have two distinct types of photoreceptors: the *rods,* which detect ______, and the *cones,* which detect ______.
   a. color/brightness
   b. low-intensity light/wavelengths corresponding to colors
   c. stimuli in consciousness/stimuli outside of consciousness
   d. bright light/dim light
   e. motion/shape

2. **RECALL:** The *wavelength* of light causes sensations of ______, while the *intensity* of light causes sensations of ______.
   a. depth/color
   b. primary colors/secondary colors
   c. color/brightness
   d. bright light/dim light
   e. motion/shape

3. **RECALL:** The *frequency theory* best explains ______ sounds, while the place theory best explains ______ sounds.
   a. tonal/atonal
   b. simple/complex
   c. low-pitched/high-pitched
   d. loud/soft
   e. pitch/timbre

4. **RECALL:** Which sense makes use of electromagnetic energy?
   a. hearing
   b. olfaction
   c. pain
   d. taste
   e. vision

5. **SYNTHESIS:** What do all of these forms of sensation have in common: vision, hearing, taste, smell, hearing, pain, equilibrium, and body position?
   a. They all involve waves having frequency and amplitude.
   b. They all arise from stimulation that comes only from outside the body.
   c. They all involve higher-order perception.
   d. They all are conveyed to the brain in the form of nerve signals.
   e. They all involve location of stimulation in three-dimensional space.

6. **UNDERSTANDING THE CORE CONCEPT:** Different senses give us different sensations mainly because
   a. they activate different sensory regions of the brain.
   b. they have different intensities.
   c. they travel on different neural pathways.
   d. they involve different stimuli.
   e. we have different memories associated with them.

ANSWERS: 1.b 2.c 3.c 4.e 5.d 6.a

WHAT IS THE RELATIONSHIP BETWEEN SENSATION AND PERCEPTION?

KEY QUESTION
?

So, we have described how sensory signals have been transduced and transmitted to specific regions of your brain for further processing as visual images, pain, odors, and other sensations. What happens then? To understand what that sensory information means, you must enlist your brain's perceptual machinery. Does a bitter taste mean poison? Does a red flag mean danger? Does a smile signify a friendly overture? The Core Concept of this section emphasizes this perceptual elaboration of sensory information:

CORE CONCEPT

Perception brings *meaning* to sensation, so perception produces an interpretation of the world, not a perfect representation of it.

In brief, we might say that the task of perception is to extract sensory input from the environment and organize it into stable, meaningful *percepts.* A **percept,** then, is what we perceive: It is not just a sensation but the associated meaning, as well. Not a simple task, perception must identify features of the world that are invariant (fixed and unchanging) by sorting through a continual flood of information. For example, as you move about the room, the sights in the environment create a rapidly changing, blurred sequence of images—yet you remain sure that it is you who are moving, while the objects around you remain stationary. As we study this complex process, we will first discuss how our perceptual apparatus usually manages to give us an accurate image

■ **Percept** The meaningful product of perception—often an image that has been associated with concepts, memories of events, emotions, and motives.

● **FIGURE 4.13** Who Is This?
Perceptual processes help us recognize Tom Cruise by matching the stimulus to images in memory.

of the world. Then we will look at some illusions and other instances in which perception apparently fails. Finally, we will examine some theories that attempt to identify the most fundamental principles at work behind the scenes in our perceptual processes.

Perceptual Processing: Finding Meaning in Sensation

How does the sensory image of a person (such as the individual pictured in Figure 4.13) become the meaningful percept of someone you recognize? That is, how does mere sensation become an elaborate perception? In the following paragraphs, we will explore some of the physical and mental processes involved in forming perceptions. Let's begin with *feature detectors*—brain cells that operate on the front lines of perceptual processing.

Feature Detectors To help us make perceptual judgments, our brains have specialized groups of cells dedicated to the detection of specific stimulus features, such as length, slant, color, and boundary (Heeger, 1994; Hubel & Wiesel, 1979; Kandel & Squire, 2000; Lettvin et al., 1959; Maunsell, 1995; Zeki, 1992). There is even a part of the occipital lobe containing cells that are especially sensitive to features of the human face (Carpenter, 1999). Perceptual psychologists call such cells **feature detectors.**

Despite our extensive knowledge of feature detectors, we still don't know exactly how the brain manages to combine (or "bind") the multiple features it detects into a single percept of, say, a face. Psychologists call this puzzle the **binding problem,** and it may be the deepest mystery of perceptual psychology (Kandel & Squire, 2000). Yet, a few pieces of this perceptual puzzle may already be in hand: In order to assemble (bind) these pieces into a meaningful percept, the brain apparently synchronizes the firing patterns in different groups of neurons that have each detected different features of an object—much as an orchestra conductor determines the tempo at which all members of the ensemble will play a musical piece (Barinaga, 1998b; Bower, 1998a; Schechter, 1996).

Bottom-Up and Top-Down Processing Perception always involves taking sensory data into the system through receptors and sending it "upward" to the cortex, where a basic analysis, involving the feature detectors, is first performed to determine the characteristics of the stimulus: Is it moving? What color is it? Is it loud, sweet, painful, pleasant smelling, wet, hot . . . ? Often it is these characteristics that determine how we finally perceive an object or event, as when deciding which salsa we want at a Mexican restaurant. Psychologists refer to this as **bottom-up processing.** It is also known as *stimulus-driven processing* because the resulting percept is determined, or "driven," by stimulus features. Other examples include following the motion of a ball, identifying the colors of a flag, and recognizing the sound of a bell. But bottom-up processing is not the only process at work.

A complementary process occurs simultaneously at the "top"—at the highest levels of the cerebral cortex. **Top-down processing** invokes a perceiver's goals, past experience, knowledge, expectations, memory, motivations, or cultural background in the interpretation of an object or event (see Nelson, 1993). You are doing top-down processing when you form a percept based on questions such as these: Will it satisfy my hunger? Is she liberal or conservative? Will that help me get my degree? Because this sort of thinking relies heavily on concepts in the perceiver's own mind, it is also known as *conceptually driven processing.* One more example may clarify what we mean: If you go grocery shopping when you are hungry, top-down processing will probably make you notice ready-to-eat snack foods much more than you would if you had just eaten.

■ **Feature detectors** Cells in the cortex that specialize in extracting certain features of a stimulus.

■ **Binding problem** Refers to the process used by the brain to combine (or "bind") the results of many sensory operations into a single percept. This occurs, for example, when sensations of color, shape, boundary, and texture are combined to produce the percept of a person's face. No one knows exactly how the brain does this. Thus the binding problem is one of the major unsolved mysteries in psychology.

■ **Bottom-up processing** Perceptual analysis that emphasizes characteristics of the stimulus, rather than our concepts and expectations. "Bottom" refers to the stimulus, which occurs at step one of perceptual processing.

■ **Top-down processing** Perceptual analysis that emphasizes the perceiver's expectations, concept memories, and other cognitive factors, rather than being driven by the characteristics of the stimulus. "Top" refers to a mental set in the brain–which stands at the "top" of the perceptual processing system.

(A)

(B)

● **FIGURE 4.14** A Door by Any Other Shape Is Still a Door

(A) A door seen from an angle presents the eye with a distorted rectangle image. (B) The brain perceives the door as rectangular.

Perceptual Constancies We can illustrate another aspect of perception with yet another example of top-down processing. Suppose that you are looking at a door, such as the one pictured in Figure 4.14A. You "know" that the door is rectangular, even though your sensory image of it is distorted when you are not looking at it straight-on. Your brain automatically corrects the sensory distortion, so that you perceive the door as being rectangular, as in Figure 4.14B.

This ability to see an object as being the same shape from different angles or distances is just one example of a **perceptual constancy.** In fact, there are many kinds of perceptual constancies. These include *color constancy,* which enables us to see a flower as being the same color in the reddish light of sunset as in the white glare of midday. *Size constancy* allows us to perceive a person as the same size at different distances and also serves as a strong cue for depth perception. *Shape constancy* is responsible for our ability to see the door in Figure 4.14 as remaining rectangular from different angles. Together these constancies help us identify and track objects in a changing world.

Perceptual Ambiguity and Distortion

A primary goal of perception is to get an accurate "fix" on the world—to recognize friends, foes, opportunities, and dangers. Survival sometimes depends on accurately perceiving the environment, but the environment is not always easy to "read." We can illustrate this difficulty with the photo of black and white splotches in Figure 4.15. What is it? When you eventually extract the stimulus figure from the background, you will see it as a Dalmatian dog walking to the left with its head down. The dog is hard to find because it blends so easily with the background. The same problem occurs when you try to single out a voice against the background of a noisy party.

But it is not just the inability to find an image that causes perceptual problems. Sometimes our perceptions can be wildly inaccurate because we misinterpret an image. This is a common response to stimulus patterns known as *illusions.*

■ **Perceptual constancy** The ability to recognize the same object as remaining "constant" under different conditions, such as changes in illumination, distance, or location.

● **FIGURE 4.15** An Ambiguous Picture
What is depicted here? The difficulty in seeing the figure lies in its similarity to the background.

What Illusions Tell Us about Sensation and Perception When your mind deceives you by interpreting a stimulus pattern in a manner that is demonstrably incorrect, you are experiencing an **illusion.** Typically, illusions become more likely when the stimulus is unclear, when information is missing, when elements are combined in unusual ways, or when familiar patterns are not apparent. Such illusions can help us understand some fundamental properties of sensation and perception—particularly the discrepancy between our percepts and external reality (Coren & Girgus, 1978).

■ **Illusion** You have experienced an illusion when you have a demonstrably incorrect perception of a stimulus pattern, especially one that also fools others who are observing the same stimulus. (If no one else sees it the way you do, you could be having a *delusion* or a *hallucination.* We'll take those terms up in a later chapter on mental disorder.)

Let's first examine a remarkable illusion that works at the level of sensation: the black-and-white Hermann grid (Figure 4.16). As you stare at the center of the grid, note how dark, fuzzy spots appear at the intersections of the white bars. But when you focus on an intersection, the spot vanishes. Why? The answer lies in the way receptor cells in your visual pathways interact with

● **FIGURE 4.16** The Hermann Grid
Why do faint gray dots appear at the intersections of the grid? The illusion, which operates at the sensory level, is explained in the text. (*Source:* "The Hermann Grid" from FUNDAMENTALS OF SENSATION & PERCEPTION by M. W. Levine & J. Shefner. Reprinted by permission of Michael W. Levine.)

each other. The firing of certain cells that are sensitive to light–dark boundaries inhibits the activity of adjacent cells that would otherwise detect the white grid lines. This inhibiting process makes you sense darker regions—the grayish areas—at the white intersections just outside your focus. Even though you know the squares in the Hermann grid are black and the lines are white, this knowledge cannot overcome the illusion, which operates at a more basic, sensory level.

To study illusions at the level of perception, psychologists may employ **ambiguous figures**—stimulus patterns that can be interpreted (top-down) in two or more distinct ways, as in Figures 4.17A and B. Both the vase/faces figure and the Necker cube are designed to confound your interpretations, not just your sensations. Each suggests two conflicting meanings: Once you have seen both, your perception will cycle back and forth between them as you look at the figure. Studies suggest that these alternating interpretations involve the shifting of perceptual control between the left and right hemispheres of the brain (Gibbs, 2001).

Figure 4.18 shows several other illusions thought to operate primarily at the level of perception. All are compelling, and all are controversial—particularly the Müller–Lyer illusion, which has intrigued psychologists for more than 100 years. Disregarding the arrowheads, which of the two horizontal lines in this figure appears longer? If you measure them, you will see that the horizontal lines are exactly the same length. What is the explanation? Answers to that question have been offered in well over a thousand published studies, and psychologists still don't know for sure.

One popular theory, combining both top-down and bottom-up factors, has gathered some support. It suggests that we unconsciously interpret the Müller–Lyer figures as three-dimensional objects. So, instead of arrow heads, we see the ends as angles that project toward or away from us like the inside and outside corners of a building or a room, as in Figure 4.19. The inside corner seems to recede in the distance, while the outside corner appears to extend toward us. Therefore, we judge the outside corner to be closer—and shorter. Why? When two objects make the same size image on the retina and we judge one to be farther away than the other, then we assume that the more distant one is larger.

But what if you had grown up in a culture with no square-cornered buildings? Would you still see one line as longer than the other? In other words, do you have to *learn* to see the Müller–Lyer illusion, or is it "hard-wired" into your brain? The only way to answer such questions is through cross-cultural research. With this in mind, Richard Gregory (1977) went to South Africa to study a group of Zulus who live in what he called a "circular culture." Aesthetically, these people prefer curves to lines and square corners: Their round huts have round doors and windows; they till their fields along curved lines, using curved plows; the children's toys lack straight lines. And, when confronted with the Müller–Lyer, the Zulus saw the lines as nearly the same length. This suggests that the Müller–Lyer illusion is learned. A number of other studies support the conclusion that people who live in "carpentered" environments—where buildings are built with straight sides and 90-degree angles—are more susceptible to the illusion than those who (like the Zulus) live in "noncarpentered" worlds (Segall et al., 1966; Segall et al., 1990; Stewart, 1973).

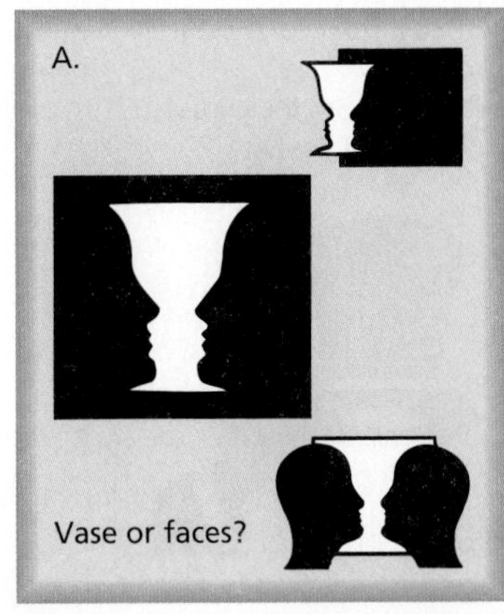
A.
Vase or faces?

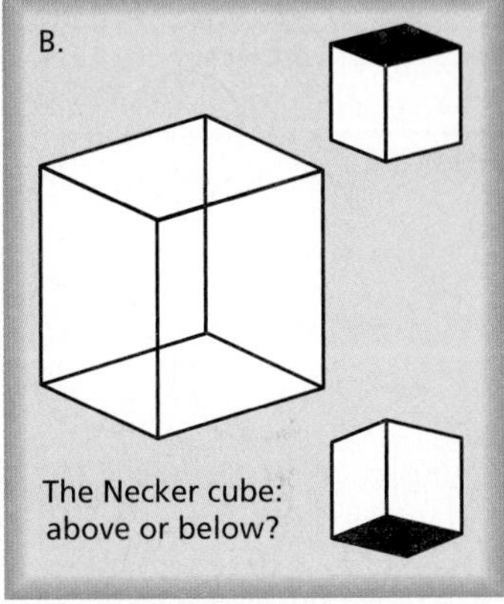
B.
The Necker cube:
above or below?

FIGURE 4.17 Perceptual Illusions
These *ambiguous figures* are illusions of perceptual interpretation.

Applying the Lessons of Illusions Several prominent modern artists, fascinated with the visual experiences created by ambiguity, have used perceptual illusion as a central artistic feature of their work. Consider the two examples of art shown here. *Gestalt Bleue* by Victor Vasarely (see Figure 4.20) produces

Ambiguous figures Images that are capable of more than one interpretation. There is no "right" way to see an ambiguous figure.

A. Use a ruler to answer each question.

Which is larger: the brim or the top of the hat?

Top hat illusion

Is the diagonal line broken?

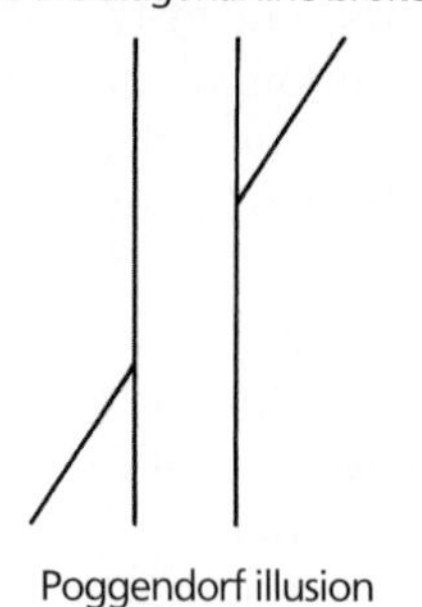

Poggendorf illusion

Which central circle is bigger?

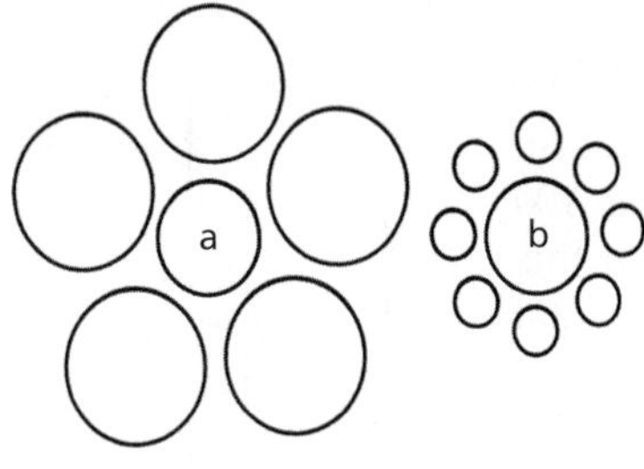
a
b

Ebbinghaus illusion

Which horizontal line is longer?

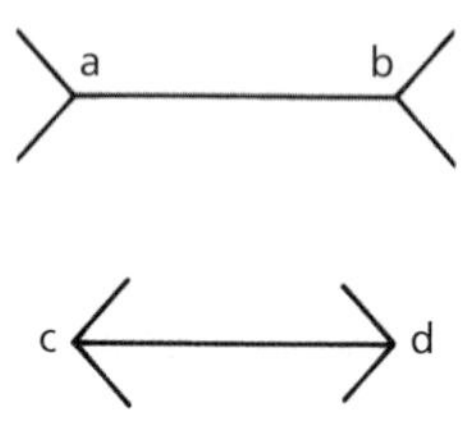
a
b
c
d

Müller–Lyer illusion

Are the vertical lines parallel?

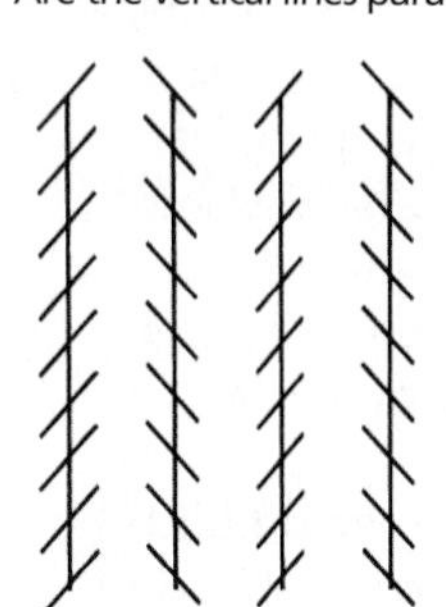

Zöllner illusion

B. Which of the boxes are the same size as the standard box? Which are definitely smaller or larger? Measure them to discover a powerful illusory effect.

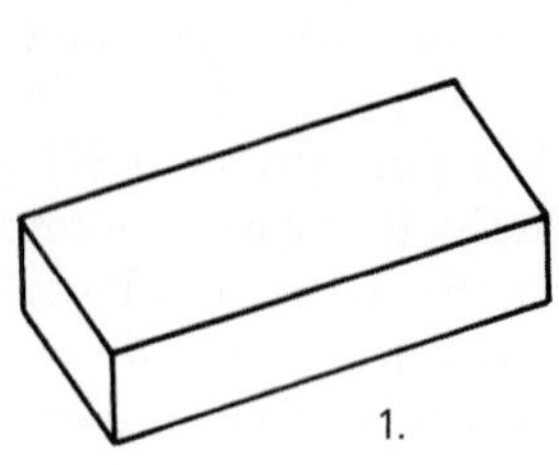

1.

2.

Standard

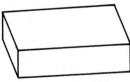

3.

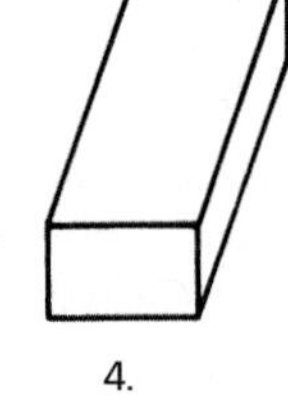

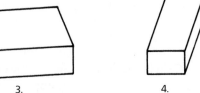

4.

● **FIGURE 4.18** Five Illusions to Tease Your Brain

Each of these illusions involves a bad "bet" made by your brain. What explanations can you give for the distortion of reality that each of these illusions produces? Are they caused by nature or nurture?

depth reversals like those in the Necker cube, with corners that alternately project and recede. In *Sky and Water* by M. C. Escher (see Figure 4.21), you can see birds and fishes only through the process of figure–ground reversal, much like the vase/faces illusion we encountered earlier (in Figure 4.17). The effect of these paintings on us underscores the function of human perception to make sense of the world and to fix on the best interpretation we can make.

To make sense of such illusions, we draw on our personal experiences, learning, and motivation. Knowing this, those who understand the principles of perception often can control illusions to achieve desired effects far beyond the world of painting. Architects and interior designers, for example, create illusions that make spaces seem larger or smaller than they really are. They

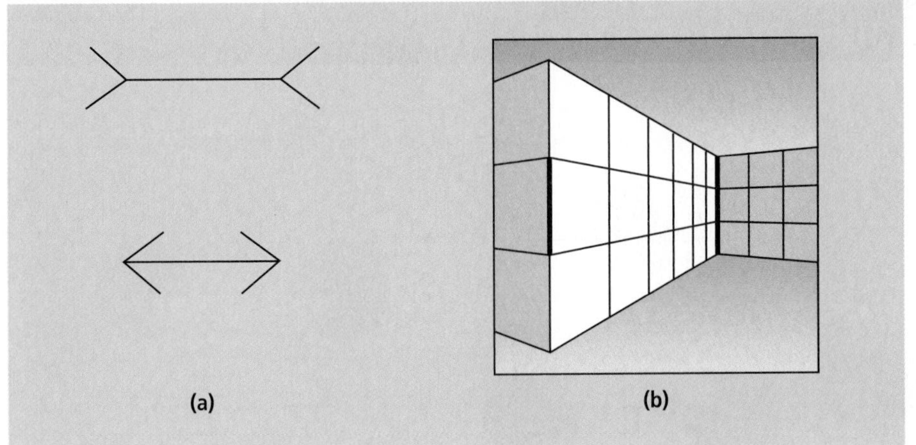
(a)
(b)

● **FIGURE 4.19** The Müller–Lyer Illusion
One explanation for the Müller–Lyer illusion says that your brain thinks it is seeing the inside and outside corners of a building in perspective.

● **FIGURE 4.20** Victor Vasarely's *Gestalt Bleue*

● **FIGURE 4.21** M. C. Escher's *Sky and Water*

may, for example, make a small apartment appear more spacious when it is painted in light colors and sparsely furnished. Similarly, set and lighting designers in movies and theatrical productions purposely create visual illusions on film and on stage. So, too, do many of us make everyday use of illusion in our choices of cosmetics and clothing (Dackman, 1986). For example, light-colored clothing and horizontal stripes can make our bodies seem larger, while dark-colored clothing and vertical stripes can make our bodies seem slimmer. In these ways, we use illusions to distort "reality" and make our lives more pleasant.

Theoretical Explanations for Perception

The fact that perception is an interpretation and the fact that most people perceive illusions in essentially the same ways suggest that some fundamental psychological principles must be involved. Psychologists looking for these fundamental principles have formulated theories that explain how perception works. Below we will examine two of the classic explanations: the *Gestalt theory* of perception and *learning-based inference.* Although these two approaches may seem contradictory at first, they really emphasize complementary influences on perception. The Gestalt theory emphasizes how we organize incoming stimulation into meaningful perceptual patterns—because of the way our

DO IT YOURSELF! Figure Obscures Ground

The tendency to perceive a figure as being in front of a ground is strong. It is so strong, in fact, that you can even get this effect when the perceived figure doesn't actually exist! You can demonstrate this with an examination of the accompanying figure. You probably perceive a fir-tree shape against a ground of red circles on a white surface. But, of course, there is no fir-tree figure printed on the page; the figure consists only of three solid red shapes and a black-line base. You perceive the illusory white triangle in front because the wedge-shaped cuts in the red circles seem to be the corners of a solid white triangle. To see an illusory six-pointed star, look at part B. Here, the nonexistent "top" triangle appears to blot out parts of red circles and a black-lined triangle, when in fact none of these is depicted as such complete figures. Again, this demonstrates that we prefer to see the figure as an object that obscures the ground behind it. (That's why we often call the ground a "*back*ground.")

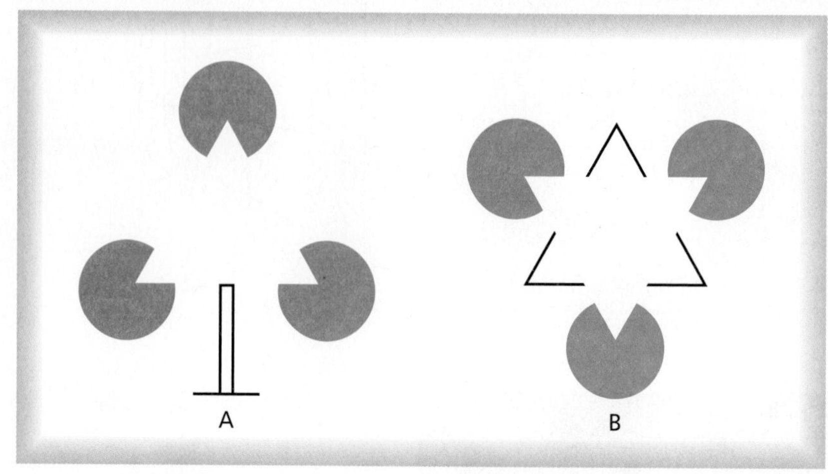
A
B

● **Subjective Contours**

(A) A subjective fir tree; (B) a subjective 6-pointed star.

brains are innately structured. On the other hand, learning-based inference emphasizes learned influences on perception, including the power of expectations, context, and culture. In other words, Gestalt theory emphasizes nature, and learning-based inference emphasizes nurture. As you will see, we need both perspectives to understand the complexities of perception. Let's begin with Gestalt theory's view of the *nature* of perception.

CONNECTION: CHAPTER 9

The *nature–nurture* issue centers on the relative importance of heredity and environment.

Perceptual Organization: The Gestalt Theory You may have noticed that a series of blinking lights, perhaps on a theater marquee, can create the illusion of motion, where there really is no motion. Similarly, there appears to be a white triangle in the "Do It Yourself!" box below—but there *is* no white triangle. And, as we have seen, the Necker cube seems to flip back and forth between two alternative perspectives—but, of course, the flipping is all in your mind.

About 100 years ago, such perceptual tricks captured the interest of a group of German psychologists, who argued that the brain is innately wired to perceive not just stimuli by *patterns* in stimulation (Sharps & Wertheimer, 2000). They called such a pattern a *Gestalt,* the German word for "perceptual pattern" or "configuration." Thus, from the raw material of stimulation, the brain forms a perceptual whole that is more than the mere sum of its sensory parts (Prinzmetal, 1995; Rock & Palmer, 1990). This perspective became known as **Gestalt psychology.**

CONNECTION: CHAPTER 1

Gestalt psychology was one of the historical schools that competed with behaviorism and structuralism.

The Gestaltists pointed out that we perceive a square as a single figure, rather than merely four individual lines. Similarly, when you hear a familiar song, you do not focus on the individual notes. Rather, your brain extracts the melody, which is your perception of the overall *pattern* of notes. Such examples, the Gestalt psychologists argued, show that we always organize sensory information into meaningful patterns, the most basic of which are already present in our brains at birth. Because this approach has been so influential, we will examine some of the Gestalt discoveries in more detail.

■ **Gestalt psychology** From a German word (pronounced *gush-TAWLT*) that means "whole" or "form" or "configuration." (A Gestalt is also a *percept.*) The Gestalt psychologists believed that much of perception is shaped by innate factors built into the brain.

Figure and Ground One of the most basic of perceptual processes identified by Gestalt psychology divides our perceptual experience into *figure* and *ground*. A **figure** is simply a pattern, or Gestalt, that grabs our attention. Everything else becomes **ground,** the backdrop against which we perceive the figure. A melody becomes a figure heard against a background of complex harmonies, and a spicy pepperoni slice becomes a figure against the ground of cheese, sauce, and bread that make up a pizza. Visually, a figure could be a bright flashing sign or a word on the background of a page. And in the ambiguous faces/vase seen in Figure 4.17A, figure and ground reverse when the faces and vase alternately "pop out" as figure.

● In *Weeping Woman,* Picasso challenges our perceptual assumptions by portraying a figure simultaneously from multiple perspectives.

Closure: Filling in the Blanks Our minds seem built to abhor a gap, as you saw in the "Do It Yourself!" box on page 142. Note especially the illusory white triangle—superimposed on red circles and black lines. Moreover, you will note that you have mentally divided the white area into two regions: the triangle and the background. Where this division occurs you perceive *subjective contours:* boundaries that exist not in the stimulus but only in the subjective experience of your mind.

Your perception of these illusory triangles demonstrates a second powerful organizing process identified by the Gestalt psychologists. **Closure** makes you see incomplete figures as wholes by supplying the missing segments, filling in gaps, and making inferences about potentially hidden objects. So, when you see a face peeking around a corner, your mind automatically fills in the hidden parts of the face and body. In general, humans have a natural tendency to perceive stimuli as complete and balanced even when pieces are missing. (Does this ring a ______ with you?) Closure is also responsible for filling in your "blind spot," as you saw on page 122 (Ramachandran, 1992).

In the foregoing demonstrations we have seen how the perception of subjective contours and closure derives from the brain's ability to create percepts out of incomplete stimulation. Now let us turn to the Gestalt laws that explain how we group the stimulus elements that are actually present into Gestalts.

The Gestalt Laws of Perceptual Grouping It's easy to see a school of fish as a single unit—as a Gestalt. But how do we mentally combine hundreds of notes together and perceive them as a single melody? How do we combine the elements of color, shadow, form, texture, and boundary into the percept of a friend's face? And why have thousands of people reported seeing "flying saucers" or the face of Jesus in the scorch marks on a tortilla? That is, how do we pull together in our minds the separate stimulus elements that seem to "belong" together? This is one of the most fundamental problems that the Gestalt psychologists addressed. As we will see, the Gestaltists made great strides in this area, but the basic processes by which perceptual organization works are still debated today (Palmer, 2002). (This problem is closely related to the *binding problem* that we discussed earlier.)

In the heyday of Gestalt psychology, of course, neuroscience was in its infancy, and there were no MRIs or PET scans. Hence, Gestalt psychologists, like Max Wertheimer (1923), had to focus on the problem of perceptual organization in a different way—with arrays of simple figures, such as you see in Figure 4.22. By varying a single factor and observing how it affected the way people perceived the structure of the array, he was able to formulate a set of **laws of perceptual grouping,** which he inferred were built into the neural fabric of the brain.

■ **Figure** The part of a pattern that commands attention. The figure stands out against the ground.

■ **Ground** The part of a pattern that does not command attention; the background.

■ **Closure** The Gestalt principle that identifies the tendency to fill in gaps in figures and to see incomplete figures as complete.

■ **Laws of perceptual grouping** The Gestalt principles of similarity, proximity, continuity, and common fate. These "laws" suggest how our brains prefer to group stimulus elements together to form a percept (Gestalt).

FIGURE 4.22 Gestalt Laws of Perceptual Grouping

(A) Similarity, (B) proximity (nearness), and (C) continuity. In (A) you most easily see the Xs grouped together, while Os form a separate Gestalt. So columns group together more easily than rows. The rows, made up of dissimilar elements, do not form patterns so easily. In (B) dissimilar elements easily group together when they are near each other. In (C), even though the lines cut each other into many discontinuous segments, it is easier to see just two lines—each of which appears to be continuous as a single line cutting through the figure.

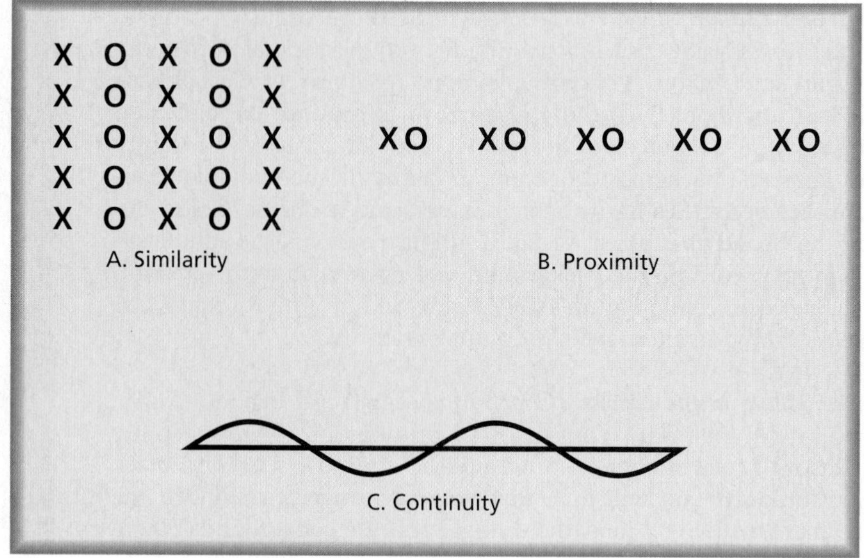
X O X O X
X O X O X
X O X O X
X O X O X
X O X O X
A. Similarity
XO XO XO XO XO
B. Proximity
C. Continuity

According to the **law of similarity,** we group together things that have a similar look (or sound, or feel, and so on). So, when you watch a football game, you use the colors of the uniforms to group the players into two teams because of their similarity, even when they are mixed together during a play. Likewise, in Figure 4.22A you see that the Xs and Os form distinct columns, rather than rows, because of similarity. Any such tendency to perceive things as belonging together because they share common features reflects the law of similarity. You can also hear the law of similarity echoed in the old proverb, "Birds of a feather flock together," which is a commentary not only on human and avian behavior but also on the assumptions we make about perceptual grouping.

Now, suppose that, on one drowsy morning, you mistakenly put on two different-colored socks because they were together in the drawer and you assumed that they were a pair. Your mistake was merely Wertheimer's **law of proximity** (nearness) at work. The proximity principle says that we group things together that are near each other, as you can see in the pairings of the Xs with the Os in Figure 4.22B. On the level of person perception, your parents were invoking the law of proximity when they cautioned you, "You're known by the company you keep."

The Gestalt **law of continuity** can be seen in Figure 4.22C, where the straight line is seen as a single, continuous line, even though it is cut repeatedly by the curved line. In general, the law of continuity says that we prefer smoothly connected and continuous figures to disjointed ones. Continuity also operates in the realm of person perception, where we commonly make the assumption of continuity in the personality of an individual whom we haven't seen for some time. So, despite interruptions in our contact with that person, we will expect to find him or her to be essentially the same person we knew earlier.

There is yet another form of perceptual grouping that we cannot easily illustrate in the pages of a book because it involves motion. But you can easily conjure up your own image that exemplifies the **law of common fate:** Imagine a school of fish, a gaggle of geese, a clowder of cats, or a simply a marching band. When visual elements (the individual fish, geese, cats, or band members) are moving together, you perceive them as a single Gestalt.

According to the Gestalt perspective, each of these examples of perceptual grouping illustrates the profound idea that our perceptions are influenced by

Law of similarity The Gestalt principle that we tend to group similar objects together in our perceptions.

Law of proximity The Gestalt principle that we tend to group objects together when they are near each other. *Proximity* means "nearness."

Law of continuity The Gestalt principle that we prefer perceptions of connected and continuous figures to disconnected and disjointed ones.

Law of common fate The Gestalt principle that we tend to group similar objects together that share a common motion or destination.

innate patterns in the brain. These inborn mental processes, in a top-down fashion, determine the organization of the individual parts of the percept, just as mountains and valleys determine the course of a river. Moreover, the Gestalt psychologists suggested, the laws of perceptual grouping exemplify a more general principle known as the **law of Prägnanz** ("meaningfulness"). This principle states that we perceive the simplest pattern possible—the percept requiring the least mental effort. The most general of all the Gestalt principles, Prägnanz (pronounced *PRAYG-nonce*) has also been called the *minimum principle of perception.* The law of Prägnanz is what makes proofreading so hard to do, as you will find when you examine Figure 4.23. On the other hand, computers are not very good a perceiving patterns, a fact that is exploited by e-mail advertisers to get terms like *C*A*S*H* or *v.i.a.g.r.a* through your computer's "spam" filter undetected.

A
BIRD
IN THE
THE HAND

● **FIGURE 4.23** A Bird in the . . .
We usually see what we expect to see–not what is really there. Look again.

The Nature of Depth Perception Are we born with the ability to perceive depth, or must we learn it? As we will see in our discussion of development in Chapter 11, depth perception appears early, although the idea of being cautious when there is danger of falling seems to develop later in infancy. In a famous demonstration, psychologists Eleanor Gibson and Richard Walk placed infants on a Plexiglas-topped table that appeared to drop off sharply on one end. (See the accompanying photo.) Reactions to the *visual cliff* occurred mainly in infants older than 6 months—old enough to crawl. Most readily crawled across the "shallow" side of the table, but they were reluctant to go over the "edge" of the visual cliff—indicating not only that they could perceive depth but that they associated the drop-off with danger (Gibson & Walk, 1960). Developmental psychologists believe that crawling and depth perception are linked in that crawling helps infants develop their understanding of the three-dimensional world.

● Apprehension about the "visual cliff" develops at about the same time an infant is learning to crawl.

Using another technique, Bower (1971) found evidence of depth perception in infants only 2 weeks old. By fitting his subjects with 3-D goggles, Bower produced powerful "virtual reality" images of a ball moving about in space. When the ball image suddenly appeared to move directly toward the infant's face, the reaction was increased heart rate and obvious anxiety. This suggests that some ability for depth perception is probably inborn or heavily influenced by genetic programming that unfolds in the course of early development. Other depth cues must be learned, as we will see. The result is that everyday depth perception in older children and adults involves a combination of cues. Some of these are *binocular cues,* whereas others are *monocular cues.*

Binocular Cues Certain depth cues, the **binocular cues,** depend on the use of two eyes. You can demonstrate this to yourself: Hold one finger about 6 inches from your eyes and look at it. Now move it about a foot farther away. Do you feel the change in your eye muscles as you focus at different distances? This feeling serves as one of the main cues for depth perception when looking at objects that are relatively close. The term for this, *binocular convergence,* suggests how the lines of vision from each eye converge at different angles on objects at different distances.

Another binocular depth cue, *retinal disparity,* arises from the difference in perspectives of the two eyes. To see how this works, hold a finger about 12 inches from your face and look at it alternately with one eye and then with the other. Notice how you see a different view of your finger with each eye. Because we see greater disparity when looking at nearby objects than we do

■ **Law of Prägnanz** The most general Gestalt principle, which states that the simplest organization, requiring the least cognitive effort, will emerge as the figure. *Prägnanz* shares a common root with *pregnant,* and so it carries the idea of a "fully developed figure." That is, our perceptual system prefers to see a fully developed Gestalt, such as a complete circle–as opposed to a broken circle.

■ **Binocular cues** Information taken in by both eyes that aids in depth perception, including binocular convergence and retinal disparity.

● Air pollution has one useful feature: It provides atmospheric perspective, which helps dwellers in cities such as Los Angeles to judge distance. If you can see it clearly, it must be close!

when viewing distant objects, these image differences coming from each eye provide us with depth information.

Monocular Cues for Depth Perception Not all cues for depth perception require both eyes. A one-eyed pilot we know, who manages to perceive depth well enough to maneuver the airplane safely during takeoffs and landings, lives as proof that one-eye cues convey a great deal of depth information. Here are some of the **monocular cues** that a one-eyed pilot (or a two-eyed pilot, for that matter) could learn to use while flying:

- If two objects that are assumed to be the same size cast different-sized images on the retina, observers usually judge them to lie at different distances. So, a pilot flying low can learn to use the *relative size* of familiar objects on the ground as a cue for depth and distance. Because of this cue, automakers who install wide-angle rear-view mirrors always inscribe the warning on them: "Objects in the mirror are closer than they appear."
- Lighter-colored objects seem closer to us, and darker objects seem farther away. Thus, *light and shadow* work together as a distance cue. You will notice this the next time you drive your car at night, with the headlights on: Objects that reflect the most light appear to be nearer than more dimly lit objects in the distance.
- We assume that closer objects will cut off our vision of more distant objects behind them, a distance cue known as *interposition*. So, we know that partially hidden objects are more distant than the objects that hide them. You can see this effect right in front of you now, as your book partially obscures the background, which you judge to be farther away.
- As you move, objects at different distances appear to move through your field of vision at a different rate or with a different *relative motion*. Look for this one from your car window. Notice how the power poles or fence posts along the roadside appear to move by at great speed, while more distant objects stay in your field of view longer, appearing to move by more slowly. With this cue, pilots learn to set up a perfect glide path to landing by adjusting their descent so that the end of the runway appears to stay at a fixed spot on the windshield: More distant points appear to move upward, and everything nearer seems to move downward.
- Haze or fog makes objects in the distance look fuzzy, less distinct, or invisible, creating another learned distance cue called *atmospheric perspective*. In the accompanying photo you can see that more distant buildings lack clarity through the Los Angeles smog. At familiar airports, most pilots have identified a landmark three miles away. If they cannot see the landmark, they know that they must fly on instruments.

Learning-Based Inference: The *Nurture* of Perception In 1866, Hermann von Helmholtz pointed out the important role of learning (or nurture) in perception. His theory of **learning-based inference** emphasized how people use prior learning to interpret new sensory information. Based on this learning, the observer makes *inferences*—guesses or predictions—about what the sensations mean. This theory explains, for example, why you infer a birthday party when you see lighted candles on a cake.

Ordinarily, such perceptual inferences are fairly accurate. On the other hand, we have seen that confusing sensations and ambiguous arrangements

■ **Monocular cues** Information about depth that relies on the input of just one eye—includes relative size, light and shadow, interposition, relative motion, and atmospheric perspective.

■ **Learning-based inference** The view that perception is primarily shaped by learning (or experience), rather than by innate factors.

can create perceptual illusions and erroneous conclusions. Our perceptual interpretations are, in effect, hypotheses about our sensations. For example, babies learn to expect faces to have certain features in fixed arrangements (pair of eyes above nose, mouth below nose) and that expressions are most easily perceived in the right-side-up arrangement. In fact, we so thoroughly learn about faces in their usual orientation that we fail to "see" facial patterns that violate our expectations. When you look at the two inverted portraits of Britney Spears (Figure 4.24), do you detect any important differences between them? Turn the book upside down for a surprise.

What determines how successful we will be in forming an accurate percept? The most important factors include the *context*, our *expectations*, and our *perceptual set*. We will see that each of these involves a way of narrowing our search of the vast store of concepts in long-term memory.

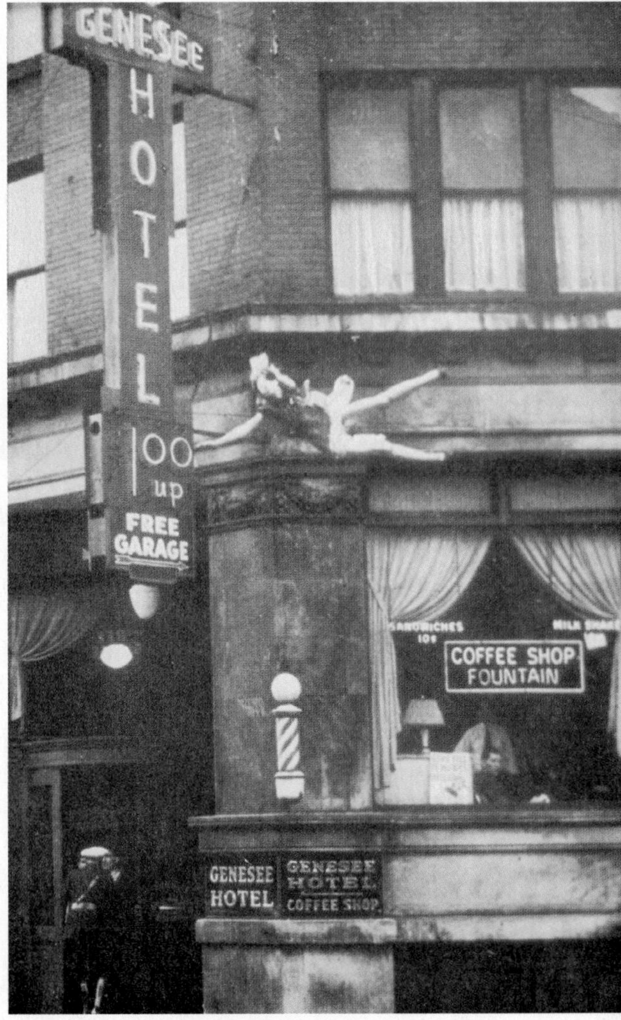
GENESEE
HOTEL
100 up
FREE GARAGE
COFFEE SHOP FOUNTAIN
GENESEE HOTEL
GENESEE HOTEL COFFEE SHOP

● Quickly scan this photo. Then look away and describe as much as you recall. Turn to page 150 to learn what you, or other perceivers, might not have seen.

Context and Expectations Once you identify a context, you form expectations about what persons, objects, and events you are likely to experience (Biederman, 1989). For example, you have probably had difficulty recognizing people you know in situations where you didn't expect to see them, such as in a different city or a new social group. This experience undoubtedly made you realize that it is much harder to recognize people outside their usual setting. The problem, of course, is not that they looked different but that the context was unusual: You didn't expect them to be there. Thus, perceptual identification depends on context and expectations as well as on an object's physical properties. To give a more immediate illustration of our expectations being influenced by the context, take a look at the following:

THE CAT

It says THE CAT, right? Now look again at the middle letter of each word. Physically, these two letters are exactly the same, yet you perceived the first as an H and the second as an A. Why? Clearly, your perception was affected by what you know about words in English. The context provided by T_E makes an H highly likely and an A unlikely, whereas the reverse is true of the context of C_T (Selfridge, 1955).

Although context can fool you into misperceiving some stimuli, as in this demonstration, context is an enormously useful cue to identify ambiguous stimuli, such as in recognizing objects in a dimly lit room or deciphering hard-to-read handwriting. So, if you receive a scenic postcard from a friend whose scrawled note describes "having a wonderful time on v____," you rely on context cues to guess that the V-word is probably vacation, and probably not any of the alternatives such as *video, Valium,* or *Venus!*

● **FIGURE 4.24** Two Perspectives on Britney Spears

Although one of these photos clearly has been altered, they look similar when viewed this way. However, turn the book upside down and look again.

Perceptual Set Another way learning serves as a platform from which context and expectation exert an influence on perception involves **perceptual set.** Under the influence of perceptual set we have a readiness to notice and respond to certain stimulus cues—like a sprinter anticipating the starter's pistol. In general, perceptual set involves a focused alertness for a particular stimulus in a given context. For example, a new mother is set to hear the cries of her child. Likewise, if you drive a sporty red car, you probably know how the highway patrol has a perceptual set to notice speeding sporty red cars.

Often, a perceptual set leads you to transform an ambiguous stimulus into the one you were expecting. To experience this yourself, read quickly through the series of words that follow in both rows:

FOX; OWL; SNAKE; TURKEY; SWAN; D?CK
BOB; RAY; DAVE; BILL; TOM; D?CK

Notice how the words in the two rows lead you to read D?CK differently in each row. The meanings of the words read prior to the ambiguous stimulus create a perceptual set. Words that refer to animals create a perceptual set that influences you to read D?CK as "DUCK." Names create a perceptual set leading you to see D?CK as DICK. Yet another illustration of perceptual set appears in the "Do It Yourself!" box "You See What You're Set to See."

Cultural Influences on Perception Cross-cultural psychologists have pointed to other ways that learning influences perception (Deregowski, 1980; Kitayama et al., 2003; Segall, 1994; Segall et al., 1966). Consider, for example, the famous Ponzo illusion, shown in Figure 4.25. In your opinion, which bar is longer: the one on top (marked A) or the one on the bottom (marked B)?

In actuality, both bars are the same length. (If you've developed a skeptical scientific attitude, you'll measure them!) Research shows, however, that responses to these figures depend strongly on culture-related experiences. Most readers of this book will report that the top bar is longer than the bottom bar, yet people from some cultural backgrounds are not so easily fooled. Why the difference?

The world you have grown up in probably included many structures featuring parallel lines that seemed to converge in the distance: long buildings, airport runways, and tunnels. You may even have stood on a straight railroad track and mused how the rails seem to meet at a faraway point. Psychologists call this *linear perspective* (which is yet another distance cue). Such experiences leave you vulnerable to images, such as the Ponzo illusion (see Figure 4.25), in which cues for size and distance are unreliable.

■ **Perceptual set** Readiness to detect a particular stimulus in a given context—as when a person who is afraid interprets an unfamiliar sound in the night as a threat.

DO IT YOURSELF! You See What You're Set to See

Labels create a context that can impose a perceptual set for an ambiguous figure. Have a friend look carefully at the picture of the "young woman" in part A of the accompanying figure, and have another friend examine the "old woman" in part B. (Cover the other pictures while they do this.) Then have them look together at part C. What do they see? Each will probably see something different, even though it's the same stimulus pattern. Prior exposure to the picture with a specific label will usually affect a person's perception of the ambiguous figure.

(A) Young woman

(B) Old woman

(C) Now what do you see?

But what about people from cultures where individuals have had far less experience with this cue for distance? Research on this issue has been carried out on the Pacific island of Guam, where there are no Ponzolike railroad tracks (Brislin, 1974, 1993). There, too, the roads are so winding that people have few opportunities to see roadsides "converge" in the distance. People who have spent their entire lives on Guam, then, presumably have fewer opportunities to learn the strong perceptual cue that converging lines indicate distance.

And, sure enough—just as researchers had predicted—people who had lived all their lives on the island of Guam were less influenced by the Ponzo illusion than were respondents from the mainland United States. That is, they were less likely to report that the top line in the figure was longer. These results strongly support the argument that people's experiences affect their perceptions—as Helmholz had theorized. Another example of how culture can affect perception comes from an experiment with Zulu tribes in Africa. In 1966, Segall, Campbell, and Herskovitz conducted an experiment in which they showed the Müller–Lyer illusion similar to that shown on page 141 (see Figure 4.19) to some Zulu tribes in Africa. At that time, the Zulu people they were testing lived in round huts with arched doorways. The people they tested were not as affected by the illusion as people living in Western cultures with lots of buildings and angles. Segall et al. argued that living in a "circular culture" affected perception.

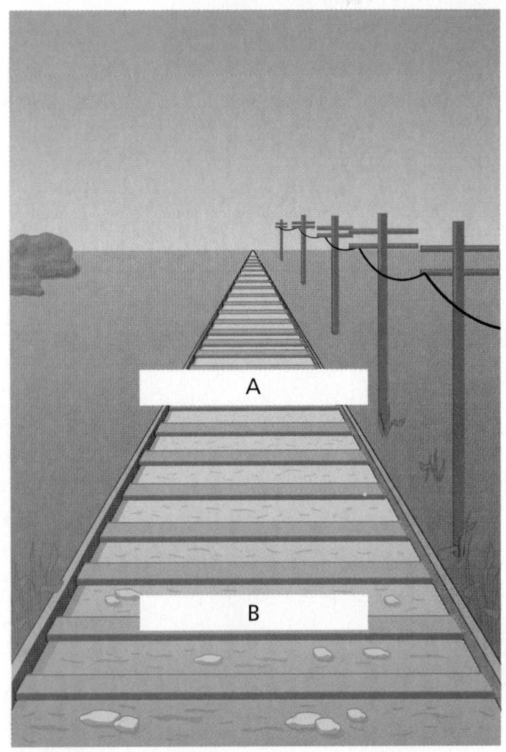
A
B

FIGURE 4.25 The Ponzo Illusion

The two white bars superimposed on the railroad track are actually identical in length. Because A appears farther away than B, we perceive it as longer.

Which of the two theories about perception that we have been discussing—Helmholtz's learning theory or the Gestaltists' innate theory—is correct? Both of them are. That is, our perceptual processes show the influence of both nature and nurture. Although both theories emphasize top-down processes, Gestalt theory proposes that the brain is innately disposed to influence perception in specific ways. But we can also say with confidence that perception is influenced by experience and learning, as Helmholtz concluded.

Attention is a key component of sensation and perception. Without attention and attentional processes, all the sensations in the world will not mean a thing. In fact, sensation and perception without attention are just light and noise. Think about being in a class and just drifting off. If the teacher is saying something important, and you are not paying attention, the information is gone. You sensed it, you even perceived that the teacher was talking, but because you were not paying attention, all of the body's automatic sensation and perception activities went for naught. In order for sensation and perception to have any value, there *must* be attention as well.

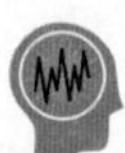

PSYCHOLOGY IN YOUR LIFE: SEEING AND BELIEVING

● Magicians count on the difference between appearance and reality.

If you assume, as most people do, that your senses give you an accurate and undistorted picture of the outside world, you are mistaken (Segall et al., 1990). Magicians, who base their careers on the difference between appearance and reality, count on fooling people for whom "seeing is believing." And you may have noticed that politicians and marketing experts rely on influencing people's interpretations of events, as well. So we hope that this chapter has shaken your faith in your senses and perceptions . . . just a bit.

Unlike magicians, politicians, and advertisers, perceptual psychologists are happy to reveal how sensation and perception play tricks on all of us (Hyman, 1989). They have developed a number of demonstrations that show how your vivid impressions of the world are really highly processed and interpreted images. We have already seen this in many visual illusions presented in the chapter. But, to drive the point home, consider this statement (which, unfortunately, was printed backwards):

.rat eht saw tac ehT

Please turn it around in your mind: What does it say? At first most people see a sensible sentence that says, "The cat saw the rat." But take another look. The difficulty lies in the power of expectations to shape your interpretation of stimulation.

This demonstration illustrates once again that we don't merely *sense* the world as it is, we *perceive* it. The goal of the process by which stimulation becomes sensation and, finally, perception is to find meaning in our experience. But it is well to remember that we impose our own meanings on sensory experience.

Differences in the ways we interpret our experiences explain why two people can look at the same sunset, the same presidential candidates, or the same religions and perceive them so differently. Perceptual differences make us unique individuals. An old Spanish proverb makes the point elegantly:

En este mundo traidor
No hay verdad ni mentira;
Todo es según el color
Del cristál con que se mira.

In this treacherous world
There is neither truth nor lie;
All is according to the color
Of the lens through which we spy.

● Did you see a woman committing suicide in the photo entitled "The Moment before Death" on page 147? Most people have difficulty identifying the falling woman in the center of the photo because of the confusing background and because they have no perceptual schema that makes them expect to see a person positioned horizontally in midair.

CHECK YOUR UNDERSTANDING

1. **RECALL:** Which of the following is an example of the kind of information that top-down processing contributes to perception?
   a. looking for a friend's face in a crowd
   b. constructing an object from memory
   c. hearing a painfully loud noise
   d. feeling a pinprick
   e. having to wait for your eyes to adjust to the dark in a theater

2. **RECALL:** The illusion in the Hermann grid (Figure 4.16) operates at the level of
   a. figure and ground.
   b. perception.
   c. sensation.
   d. stimulation.
   e. the subconscious.

3. **RECALL:** The Gestalt theory proposes that many of our perceptions are determined by
   a. ambiguity.
   b. bottom-up factors.
   c. top-down factors.
   d. illusions.
   e. innate factors.

4. **RECALL:** The faces/vase image (in Figure 4.17A) illustrates
   a. closure.
   b. attention as a gateway to consciousness.
   c. figure and ground.
   d. interposition
   e. similarity.

5. **APPLICATION:** When two close friends are talking, other people may not be able to follow their conversation because it has many gaps, which the friends can mentally fill in from their shared experience. Which Gestalt principle is illustrated by the friends' ability to fill in these conversational gaps?
   a. ambiguity
   b. similarity
   c. closure
   d. common fate
   e. proximity

6. **UNDERSTANDING THE CORE CONCEPT:** Which of the following best illustrates the idea that perception is not an exact internal copy of the world?
   a. the Ponzo illusion
   b. a bright light
   c. jumping in response to a pinprick
   d. bottom-up processing
   e. the sound of a familiar tune

ANSWERS: 1.a 2.c 3.e 4.c 5.c 6.a

SENSATION AND PERCEPTION: THE STATE OF THE ART

After more than a century of study, the details of sensation are pretty well known. Perception, on the other hand, has its murky spots. The one great, indisputable finding of perceptual psychology is this: Perception is not a duplicate of reality. And its corollary is the fact that most people still believe that their senses and perceptions don't deceive them. In addition, we know many specifics about the psychology of perception, as identified by Helmholtz, the Gestalt psychologist, and others following in their traditions. It's in the basic neuroscience of perception that the great gaps in our knowledge occur. In particular, the binding problem—the puzzle of how stimulus features, memories, and emotions are combined into a single percept—remains one of psychology's deepest mysteries.

USING PSYCHOLOGY TO LEARN PSYCHOLOGY

Studying for the Gestalt

One of the most mistaken notions about studying and learning is that students should set aside a certain amount of time for study every day. This is not to suggest that you shouldn't study regularly. Rather, it is to say that you shouldn't focus on just putting in your time. So where should you place your emphasis? (And what does this have to do with perceptual psychology?)

Recall the concept of *Gestalt*, the idea of the meaningful pattern, encountered in this chapter. The Gestalt psychologists taught that we have an innate tendency to understand our world in terms of meaningful patterns. Applied to your studying, this means that your emphasis should be on finding meaningful patterns—Gestalts—in your course work.

In this chapter, for example, you will find that your authors have helped you by dividing the material into three major sections. You can think of each section as a conceptual Gestalt, built around a Core Concept that ties it together and gives it meaning.

The psychological message is this: Organize your study around meaningful units of material. That is, identify a major concept or section of your book, and study that until it makes sense.

And forget about the clock.

CHAPTER SUMMARY

KEY QUESTION

CORE CONCEPT

• HOW DOES STIMULATION BECOME SENSATION?

The most fundamental step in sensation involves the transduction by the sense organs of physical stimuli into neural messages, which are sent onward in the sensory pathways to the appropriate part of the brain for further processing. Sensory adaptation occurs when the senses discontinue processing unchanging stimuli.

Not all stimuli become sensations, because some fall below the absolute threshold. Further, changes in stimulation are noticed only if they exceed the difference threshold, making a just-noticeable difference (JND). Classical psychophysics focused on identifying thresholds for sensations and for just-noticeable differences, but a newer approach, called signal detection theory, explains sensation as a process involving context, physical sensitivity, and judgment. And while subliminal perception of stimuli near the absolute threshold is possible under certain conditions, there is no evidence that it has been—or could be—used successfully in the mass media.

● **The brain senses the world indirectly because the sense organs convert stimulation into the language of the nervous system: neural messages.**

• HOW ARE THE SENSES ALIKE? AND HOW ARE THEY DIFFERENT?

All the senses involve transduction of physical stimuli into nerve impulses. In vision, photoreceptors in the retina transduce light waves into neural codes, which retain frequency and amplitude information. This visual information is then transmitted by the optic nerve to the brain's occipital lobes, which converts the neural signals into sensations of color and brightness. Both the trichromatic theory and the opponent process theory are required to explain how visual sensations are extracted. Vision makes use of only a tiny "window" in the electromagnetic spectrum.

In the ear, sound waves in the air are transduced into neural energy in the cochlea and then sent on to the brain's temporal lobes, where frequency and amplitude information are converted to sensations of pitch, loudness, and timbre. Neither our sensations of light or sound are properties of the original stimulus but are creations of the brain.

Other senses include position and movement (the vestibular and kinesthetic senses), smell, taste, the skin senses (touch, pressure, and temperature), and pain. Like vision and hearing, these other senses are especially attuned to detect changes in stimulation. Further, all sensation is carried to the brain by neural impulses, but we experience different sensations because the impulses are processed by different sensory regions of the brain.

The experience of pain can be the result of intense stimulation in any of several sensory pathways. While we don't completely understand pain, the gate-control theory explains how pain can be suppressed by competing sensations or other mental processes. Similarly, the ideal analgesic—one without unwanted side effects—has not been discovered, although placebos work exceptionally well for some people.

● **The senses all operate in much the same way, but each extracts different information and sends it to its own specialized sensory processing region in the brain.**

• WHAT IS THE RELATIONSHIP BETWEEN SENSATION AND PERCEPTION?

There is no exact dividing line between sensation and perception, but psychologists define perception as the stage at which meaning is attached to sensation. We derive meaning from "bottom-up" stimulus cues picked up by feature detectors and from "top-down" processes, especially those involving expectations. What remains unclear is how the brain manages to combine the output of many sensory circuits into a single percept: This is called the binding problem.

By studying illusions and constancies, researchers can learn about the factors that influence and distort the construction of perceptions. Illusions demonstrate that perception does not necessarily form an accurate representation of the outside world.

Perception has been explained by theories that differ in their emphasis on the role of innate brain processes versus learning—nature versus nurture. The Gestalt theory emphasizes innate factors that help us organize stimulation into sensation. In particular, the Gestaltists have described the processes that help us distinguish figure from ground, to identify contours and apply closure, and to group stimuli according to similarity, proximity, continuity, and common fate. Some aspects of depth perception, such as retinal disparity and convergence, may be innate as well. The theory of learning-based inference also correctly points out that perception is influenced by experience, such as context, perceptual set, and culture. Many aspects of depth perception, such as relative motion and atmospheric perspective, seem to be learned.

Despite all we know about sensation and perception, many people uncritically accept the evidence of their senses (and perceptions) at face value. This allows magicians, politicians, and marketers an opening through which they can manipulate our perceptions and, ultimately, our behavior.

- **Perception brings *meaning* to sensation, so perception produces an interpretation of the world, not a perfect representation of it.**

REVIEW TEST

For each of the following items, choose the single correct or best answer. The correct answers appear at the end.

1. What is the process that converts physical energy, such as sound waves, into neural signals?
   a. conduction
   b. kinesthesis
   c. sensory adaptation
   d. transduction
   e. psychophysics

2. Luisa agrees to look after her friends' new baby while they run an errand. Luisa tries to read with the stereo on but keeps listening for signs that the baby might be crying in the bedroom. Several times, Luisa thinks she can hear whimpering—but when she checks the baby, she usually finds her sound asleep. Which of the following best explains why Luisa's sensations are not always accurate?
   a. classical absolute threshold theory
   b. signal detection theory
   c. the law of Prägnanz
   d. Steven's power law
   e. Weber's law

3. Which of these sensory structures does not belong with the others?
   a. visual cortex
   b. rods
   c. retina
   d. ganglion cells
   e. basilar membrane

4. Place theory and frequency theory are explanations for processes involved in the sensation of
   a. different olfactory stimuli.
   b. the hue created by a light's wavelength.
   c. the pitch of sound.
   d. tactile stimuli.
   e. the timbre of sound.

5. Which one of the following is the only sense that does not relay information through the thalamus?
   a. the vestibular sense
   b. audition
   c. olfaction
   d. vision
   e. kinesthesis

6. At a crime scene, a detective finds a slip of paper with three symbols printed on it in ink. She cannot identify the source of the figures or which orientation is up. Thus she cannot determine whether the figures are the numbers 771 or the letters ILL. Because she has to guess at the meaning of the figures, her perception of them is
   a. bottom-up.
   b. data-driven.
   c. perception-driven.
   d. stimulus-driven.
   e. top-down.

7. Which one of the following is most commonly experienced when a stimulus is ambiguous, information is missing, elements are combined in unusual ways, or familiar patterns are not apparent?
   a. proximity
   b. a correct rejection
   c. a false alarm
   d. common fate
   e. an illusion

8. According to Gestalt explanations of how perceptual processes work, when a person encounters an unfamiliar collection of stimuli, he or she will try to
   a. analyze each stimulus component separately to ascertain its meaning.
   b. assemble the parts into a meaningful whole or pattern that makes sense.
   c. compartmentalize their findings.
   d. judge whether each stimulus matches a familiar signal.
   e. make guesses about its symbolism until finding a matching concept.

9. Research has shown that cultural factors can influence people's perception of
   a. distance.
   b. sensory adaptation.
   c. pitch.
   d. timbre.
   e. subliminal stimulation.

10. Although the markings in the ceiling tiles are of all different shapes and sizes, you notice that larger, darker spots seem to stand out against a background made up of smaller, lighter ones. Which principle of perceptual grouping explains this distinction?
    a. the principle of closure
    b. the law of common fate
    c. the law of Prägnanz
    d. the law of proximity
    e. the law of similarity

ANSWERS: 1. d 2. b 3. e 4. c 5. c 6. e 7. e 8. b 9. a 10. e

KEY TERMS

Sensation (p. 110)
Perception (p. 111)
Transduction (p. 112)
Sensory adaptation (p. 113)
Absolute threshold (p. 114)
Difference threshold (p. 114)
Just noticeable difference (JND) (p. 115)
Weber's law (p. 115)
Fechner's law (p. 115)
Steven's power law (p. 115)
Signal detection theory (p. 116)
Retina (p. 119)
Photoreceptors (p. 119)
Rods (p. 120)
Cones (p. 120)
Fovea (p. 120)
Optic nerve (p. 120)
Blind spot (p. 121)
Brightness (p. 121)
Color (p. 123)
Electromagnetic spectrum (p. 123)
Visible spectrum (p. 123)
Trichromatic theory (p. 124)
Opponent-process theory (p. 124)
Afterimages (p. 124)
Color blindness (p. 124)
Frequency (p. 126)
Amplitude (p. 126)
Tympanic membrane (p. 126)
Cochlea (p. 126)
Basilar membrane (p. 126)
Pitch (p. 127)
Loudness (p. 128)
Timbre (p. 128)
Conduction deafness (p. 128)
Nerve deafness (p. 128)
Vestibular sense (p. 130)
Kinesthetic sense (p. 130)
Olfaction (p. 130)
Pheromones (p. 130)
Gustation (p. 131)
Skin senses (p. 132)
Gate-control theory (p. 133)
Placebo effect (p. 134)
Percept (p. 135)
Feature detectors (p. 136)
Binding problem (p. 136)
Bottom-up processing (p. 136)
Top-down processing (p. 136)
Perceptual constancy (p. 137)
Illusion (p. 138)
Ambiguous figures (p. 139)
Gestalt psychology (p. 142)
Figure (p. 143)
Ground (p. 143)
Closure (p. 143)
Laws of perceptual grouping (p. 143)
Law of similarity (p. 144)
Law of proximity (p. 144)
Law of continuity (p. 144)
Law of common fate (p. 144)
Law of Prägnanz (p. 145)
Binocular cues (p. 145)
Monocular cues (p. 146)
Learning-based inference (p. 146)
Perceptual set (p. 148)

AP* REVIEW: VOCABULARY

Match each of the following vocabulary terms to its definition.

1. Sensation
2. Transduction
3. Sensory adaptation
4. Absolute threshold
5. Difference threshold
6. Trichromatic theory
7. Opponent-process theory
8. Feature detectors
9. Closure
10. Law of proximity

_____ **a.** Loss of responsiveness in receptor cells after stimulation has remained unchanged for a while.

_____ **b.** The smallest amount by which a stimulus can be changed and the difference be detected 50% of the time.

_____ **c.** The Gestalt principle that we tend to group objects together when they are near each other.

_____ **d.** The Gestalt principle that we tend to fill in gaps in figures and to see incomplete figures as complete.

_____ **e.** The idea that cells in the visual system process colors in complementary pairs, such as red or green or as yellow or blue.

_____ **f.** The process by which simulation of a sensory receptor produces neural impulses that the brain interprets as a sound, a visual image, an odor, a taste, a pain, or other sensory image.

_____ **g.** Cells in the cortex that specialize in extracting certain features of a stimulus.

_____ **h.** The amount of stimulation necessary for a stimulus to be detected 50% of the time.

_____ **i.** The idea that colors are sensed by three different types of cones sensitive to light in the red, blue, and green wavelengths.

_____ **j.** Transformation of one form of energy into another—especially, the transformation of stimulus information into nerve signals by the sense organs.

KEY 1.f 2.j 3.a 4.h 5.b 6.i 7.e 8.g 9.d 10.c

AP* REVIEW: ESSAY

Use your knowledge of the chapter concepts to answer the following essay question.

A common thread among all sensory modalities involves both sensation and perception. In a concise discussion, define and describe how each of the following applies to a sensory modality of your choice:

a. receptor

b. sensation

c. transduction

d. perception

e. resultant behavior

OUR RECOMMENDED BOOKS AND VIDEOS

BOOKS

Ackerman, D. (1990). *A natural history of the senses.* New York: Vintage. Poet Diane Ackerman's essays discuss smell, touch, taste, hearing, vision, and synesthesia (experiencing a sensation in the "wrong" sense, such as feeling a color or seeing a sound). The book is vivid and inspiring as well as informative.

Cytowic, R. L. (1998). *The man who tasted shapes.* Cambridge, MA: MIT Press. One in 100,000 people experience *synesthesia,* a condition of blended sensory perceptions: Different tastes have distinctive shapes, musical notes have color and form. Better understood than ever before, synesthesia demonstrates the active exploration of the brain and the literally memorable experiences of synesthetes themselves.

Sacks, O. (1998). *The island of the colorblind.* New York: Vintage Books. The latest by the author of *The Man Who Mistook His Wife for a Hat* and *An Anthropologist on Mars,* this fascinating, touching, and funny book describes Sacks's journey to a small island in Micronesia, where all the residents are colorblind yet experience and describe their world with richness, vividness, and acceptance.

Sheldrake, R. (2003). *The sense of being stared at: And other aspects of the extended mind.* New York: Crown Publishing. In a previous work, Rupert Sheldrake explored whether some dogs know when their owners are coming home. Here he extends his interest in supersensory awareness, examining people's claims of "knowing" when others are about to call them; parents' sensitivity to absent children's experiences; or, as the title suggests, our awareness of being watched and studied.

VIDEOS

Immortal Beloved. (1994, color, 125 min.). Directed by Bernard Rose; starring Gary Oldman, Jeroen Krabbe, Isabella Rossellini, Johanna Ter Steege. Ludwig van Beethoven's late-life deafness is explained in this musically rich biography, focusing on the question of the identity of the composer's great love. A few scenes are stunning to both watch and hear, a nice change from films with forgettable scores and soundtracks. (*Rating R*)

Rashomon. (1950, black-and-white, 88 min.; Japanese). Directed by Akira Kurosawa; starring Toshiro Mifune. A classic film by a master director, *Rashomon* tells the tale of a rape and murder from the perspectives of four very different witnesses, illustrating the intertwining of perception with motivation and emotion. What you see and remember is what you expect, based on your perception of the world—and of yourself. (*Rating PG-13*)

Key Question Chapter Outline

How Is Consciousness Related to Other Mental Processes?

Tools for Studying Consciousness

The Conscious and Nonconscious Minds

What Cycles Occur in Everyday Consciousness?

Daydreaming

Sleep: The Mysterious Third of Our Lives

Dreaming: The Pageants of the Night

What Other Forms Can Consciousness Take?

Hypnosis

Meditation

Psychoactive Drug States

Consciousness: The State of the Art

CORE CONCEPTS

Consciousness can take many forms, while other mental processes occur simultaneously outside our awareness.

Consciousness changes in cycles that correspond to our biological rhythms and to the patterns of stimulation in our environment.

An altered state of consciousness occurs when some aspect of normal consciousness is modified by mental, behavioral, or chemical means.

Psychology in Your Life

The Unconscious—Reconsidered

An empirical approach suggests a simpler unconscious than the one portrayed by Sigmund Freud.

Sleep Disorders

Insomnia, sleep apnea, narcolepsy, and daytime sleepiness can be hazardous to your health—and perhaps even to your life.

Dependence and Addiction

Psychoactive drugs alter brain chemistry, and they can produce physical or psychological addiction. But is addiction a disease or a character flaw?

USING PSYCHOLOGY TO LEARN PSYCHOLOGY:
Connecting Consciousness with Memory

Chapter

5

States of Consciousness

ONE RAINY SWISS SUMMER day in the early 19th century, a housebound trio of writers eagerly challenged each other to craft ghost stories. Yet, after several days of uninspired effort, Mary Wollstonecraft Shelley feared she would come up empty handed. Then one night, with the problem turning over in her mind, she went to bed and soon fell asleep, only to awaken some time later with horrific dream images in her head. She later recalled them clearly:

> My imagination, unbidden, possessed and guided me . . . I saw the pale student of unhallowed arts kneeling beside the thing he had put together. I saw the hideous phantasm of a man stretched out, and then . . . show signs of life, and stir with an uneasy, half vital motion . . . [The creator] would rush away from his odious handiwork, horror-stricken.

Early the next day she penned the words: "It was on a dreary night of November . . ." (Shelley, 1831, p. x). Thus began her "ghost story," *Frankenstein, or The Modern Prometheus.*

Mary Shelley was far from the first to have been inspired by a dream. From ancient times, dreams have been regarded as sources of insight, creativity, and prophecy. We can see this, for example, in the Old Testament story of the Israelite Joseph, who interpreted Pharaoh's dreams of fat and lean cattle as predicting first the years of plenty and then the years of famine that lay in store for the Egyptian kingdom (Genesis, 41:i–vii).

● Spanish painter Salvador Dali found inspiration for his work in his dreams. © 2004 Gala-Salvador Dali Foundation, Figueres, Spain, © Salvador Dali Museum, Inc. St. Petersburg, Florida, USA/Bridgeman Art Library

In more modern times, the English poet Samuel Taylor Coleridge attributed the imagery of his poem "Kubla Khan" to a dream (possibly drug-induced) that he experienced after reading a biography of the famed Mongol warrior. Likewise, painters such as surrealist Salvador Dali have found their dreams to be vivid sources of imagery. Composers as varied as Mozart, Beethoven, the Beatles, and Sting have all credited their dreams with inspiring certain works. And in the scientific world, chemist August Kekule's discovery of the structure of the benzene molecule was sparked by his dream of a snake rolled into a loop, grasping its own tail tucked in its mouth. Even the famous horror writer Stephen King claims to have harvested story ideas from his own childhood nightmares.

Dreaming represents just one of many states of consciousness that are possible for the human mind. Others include, of course, our familiar state of wakefulness and the less-familiar states of dreamless sleep, hypnosis, and meditation, as well as the chemically altered states produced by alcohol and other drugs. But that's not all. Behind these conscious states, the brain has other levels of processing that occur outside consciousness (Wallace & Fisher, 1999). These range from information readily available in memory (What is seven times nine?) to the operations occurring in the deep, primitive regions of the brain, which control basic biological functions, such as blood pressure and body temperature. Somewhere between these extremes are parts of the mind that somehow deal with our once-conscious memories and gut-level responses, as varied as this morning's breakfast and your most embarrassing moment. As we will see, this netherworld of nonconscious ideas, feelings, desires, and images has been a magnet for controversy ever since Freud suggested that dreams may reflect our unrecognized fears and desires. In this chapter we will evaluate this claim and others that have been made for consciousness and the "deeper" levels of processing in the mind.

KEY QUESTION

HOW IS CONSCIOUSNESS RELATED TO OTHER MENTAL PROCESSES?

In simplest terms, we can define **consciousness** as the process underlying the mental model we create of the world of which we are aware. It is also a part of the mind into which we can potentially retrieve a fact, an idea, an emotion, or a memory of an experience and recombine them in the processes we call "thinking." It's the part of the mind that helps us combine both reality and fantasy—the "movie" in your head. For example, if you see a doughnut when you are hungry, consciousness forms an image of the doughnut (based on external stimulation) and consults memory, which associates the image with food and also allows you to imagine eating the doughnut. Most likely, under these circumstances your consciousness will quickly fill with doughnutty imagery. But exactly *how* the brain does this is perhaps psychology's greatest mystery. How do the patterns in the firing of billions of neurons become the conscious image of a doughnut—or of the words and ideas on this page?

■ **Consciousness** The process by which the brain creates a model of internal and external experience.

Folk wisdom merely attributes consciousness to an *anima,* a spirit or inner life force, an explanation that takes us no closer to understanding how consciousness works. A Biblical variation on this theme connects consciousness to the soul—although the Bible also suggests that evil spirits or devils sometimes take over consciousness and cause bizarre behavior.

For psychologists, the big difficulty presented by consciousness is that it is so subjective and illusive—like searching for the end of the rainbow (Damasio, 1999, 2000). That lesson was driven home when the structuralists attempted to dissect conscious experience more than a century ago. As you will recall, the structuralists used a simple technique called introspection: People were asked to report on their own conscious experience. The slippery, subjective nature of consciousness quickly became obvious to nearly everyone, and psychologists began to despair that science would never find a way to study objectively something so private as conscious experience. (Think about it: How could you prove that you have consciousness?)

CONNECTION: CHAPTER 1
Wundt and the structuralists pioneered the use of introspection in their search for "the elements of conscious experience."

The problem seemed so intractable that, early in the 20th century, the notorious and influential behaviorist John Watson declared that the mind was out of bounds for the young science of psychology. Mental processes were little more than by-products of our actions, he said. (You don't cry because you are sad, you are sad because some event makes you cry.) Under Watson's direction, psychology became simply the science of behavior. And so, psychology not only lost its consciousness but also lost its mind!

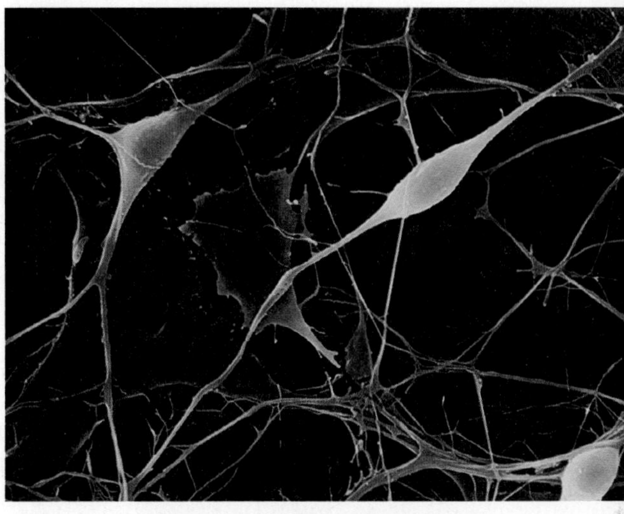

Francis Crick says that our consciousness is "no more than the behavior of a vast assembly of nerve cells and their associated molecules."

The psychology of consciousness remained in limbo until the 1960s, when a coalition of cognitive psychologists, neuroscientists, and computer scientists brought it back to life (Gardner, 1985). They did so for two reasons. First, many psychological issues had come to light that needed a better explanation than behaviorism could deliver: quirks of memory, perceptual illusions, drug-induced states (which were very popular in the 1960s). The second reason for the reemergence of consciousness came from technology. Scientists were acquiring new tools—especially computers, which allowed them to scan the brain and also gave them a model that could be used to explain how the brain processes information.

The combination of new tools and pressing problems, then, led to a multidisciplinary effort that became known as **cognitive neuroscience.** It includes scientists from a variety of fields, including cognitive psychology, neurology, biology, computer science, and linguistics—all interested in how the brain processes information and creates conscious experience. From the perspective of cognitive neuroscience, the brain acts like a biological computing device with vast resources—among them being 100 billion transistor-like neurons, each with thousands of interconnections—capable of creating the complex universe of imagination and experience we think of as consciousness (Chalmers, 1995; Churchland, 1995; Crick, 1994).

Cognitive neuroscience An interdisciplinary field involving cognitive psychology, neurology, biology, computer science, linguistics, and specialists from other fields who are interested in the connection between mental processes and the brain.

In this chapter we will see how neuroscientists have renewed the quest to understand the multiple conscious states of which we are capable, including sleep, dreaming, hypnosis, and drug-altered consciousness. We will also introduce you briefly to the mental processes that occur outside of consciousness, laying the groundwork for more in-depth exploration of that world in later chapters on emotion, motivation, perception, and memory. As we travel this path, please keep the following Core Concept readily available to your consciousness:

CORE CONCEPT

Consciousness can take many forms, while other mental processes occur simultaneously outside our awareness.

The big picture that emerges is one of a conscious mind that can take on a variety of roles, as we will see, but one that must focus sequentially, first on one thing and then on another, like a moving spotlight (see Tononi & Edelman,

1998). Consciousness is not good at multitasking: So, if you try to drive while talking on your cell phone, you must shift your attention back and forth between tasks (Rubenstein et al., 2001; Strayer et al., 2003). Meanwhile, **nonconscious processes** have no such restriction and can work on many jobs at once—which is why you can walk, chew gum, and breathe simultaneously. In more technical terms, consciousness must process information serially, while nonconscious brain circuits can processes many streams of information in parallel. We will begin our exploration of these multifarious mental states and levels with a look at some of the tools and techniques that have opened up this line of research.

Tools for Studying Consciousness

As you will recall from the previous chapter, high-tech tools, such as the MRI, PET, and EEG, have opened new windows through which researchers can look into the brain to see which regions are active during various mental tasks—showing us the "what" of consciousness. These imaging devices, of course, do not show the actual contents of conscious experience, but they quite clearly reveal distinct groups of brain structures that "light up" when we read or speak, for example. (See Figure 5.1.) The resulting images have left no doubt that conscious processing involves simultaneous activity in many brain circuits, especially in the cortex and in the pathways connecting the thalamus to the cortex. But, to glimpse the underlying mental processes—the "how" of consciousness—psychologists have devised other, even more ingenious, techniques. We will see many of these techniques throughout this chapter—in fact, throughout this book. For the moment, though, we will give you just two examples, as previews of coming attractions.

Mental Rotation A classic experiment by Roger Shepard and Jacqueline Metzler (1971) showed that it's not merely a metaphor when people speak of "turning things over" in their conscious minds. Using images like those in Figure 5.2, Shepard and Metzler asked volunteers to decide whether the two images in each pair show the same object in different positions. They reasoned that if the mind actually rotates these images when comparing them, people would take longer to respond when the difference between the angles of the images

■ **Nonconscious processes** Any brain process that does not involve conscious processing, including both preconscious memories and unconscious processes.

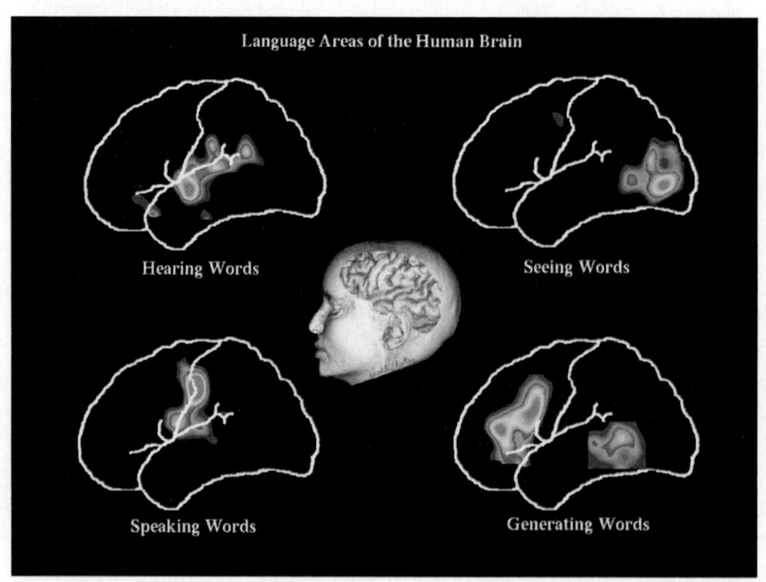
Language Areas of the Human Brain
Hearing Words
Seeing Words
Speaking Words
Generating Words

● **FIGURE 5.1** PET Scans of the Brain at Work

These PET scans show how different regions of the brain become active during different conscious tasks.

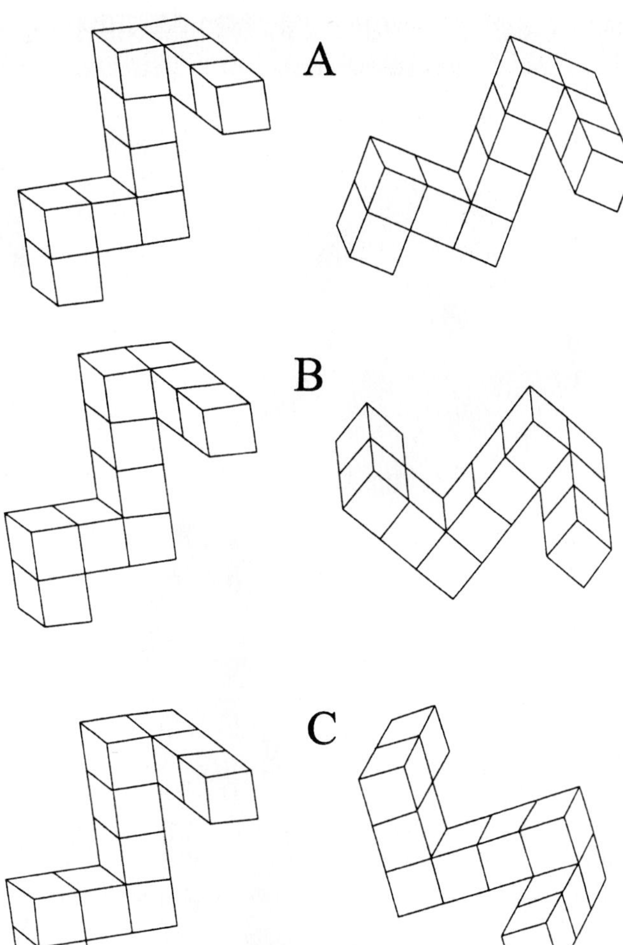
A
B
C

● **FIGURE 5.2** Figures for the Mental Rotation Experiment

These figures are similar to those used in Shepard and Metzler's mental rotation experiment. Results showed that people took longer to decide whether the images were the same or different, as the angles through which the images in each pair were rotated. You might try your own test to verify their findings.

in each pair is increased. And that is exactly what they found. If you try this experiment on your friends, it is likely that they, too, will respond more quickly to pair A—where the images have been rotated through a smaller angle—than to pairs B and C.

Zooming in with the Mind Another clever approach to the "how" of consciousness takes a different twist: Stephen Kosslyn found that we can use our conscious minds to "zoom in," camera-like, on the details of our mental images. To demonstrate this, Kosslyn (1976) first asked people to think of objects, such as an elephant or a cat or a chair. Then he asked questions about details of the imagined object (for example, "Is it a black cat?" or "Does it have a long tail?"), recording how long it took for his subjects to answer. He discovered that the smaller the detail he asked for, the longer subjects needed for a response. Subjects required extra time, Kosslyn proposed, to make a closer examination of their mental images. Both the Shepard and Metzler and the Kosslyn experiments suggest that we consciously manipulate our visual images in much the same way that we might manipulate physical objects in the outside world (Kosslyn, 1983). You can try this yourself with the demonstration in the accompanying box, "Do It Yourself! Zooming In on Mental Images."

DO IT YOURSELF! Zooming In on Mental Images

Ask a friend to close his or her eyes and imagine a house. Then, ask your friend to describe the color of the roof, the front door, and doorbell button. Using a watch or clock that displays seconds, record the amount of time it takes to get each answer. Based on Kosslyn's research, which item would you predict would require the longest response time? The shortest?

You will probably find that the smaller the detail you ask for, the longer it takes your friend to respond. Kosslyn interpreted this to mean that people need the extra time to "zoom in" on a mental image to resolve smaller features. In other words, we examine our mental images in the same way that we examine physical objects in the external world in order to perceive the "big picture" or the details.

● **FIGURE 5.3**

As we progress through the chapter, you will learn about other techniques used by neuroscientists to study consciousness and its allied mental processes. Now, let's see what picture has emerged from this work.

The Conscious and Nonconscious Minds

William James likened ordinary waking consciousness to a flowing stream that carries ever-changing sensations, perceptions, thoughts, memories, feelings, motives, and desires. This "stream of consciousness" can include awareness both of ourselves and of stimulation from our environment. And, as we have seen, it can also include physical sensations from within, such as hunger, thirst, pain, and pleasure.

Freud used another metaphor, comparing consciousness to the tip of an iceberg, which belies a much larger presence beneath the surface. A large body of evidence now confirms Freud's insight that much of the mind lurks and works out of sight, beneath the level of awareness—although probably not in exactly the way Freud believed, as we will see later. Most of the time our nonconscious machinery quietly operates in parallel with the conscious mind, but occasionally a nonconscious motive or emotion becomes so strong that it emerges into consciousness—as when a peculiar fragrance associated with an emotional memory suddenly brings that emotion to consciousness or when a growing hunger drive spills into awareness as a "Mac attack." To get a better perspective on these processes, we will first consider the major functions of consciousness. Then we will review what research and theory can tell us about the architecture that organizes the layers of mind below its surface.

What Consciousness Does for Us At this very moment, your consciousness is focused on these words, written in black letters on a white page. But the words don't stand alone. They have meaning, which also flows through consciousness as you read. You can, of course, shift the spotlight of your attention to something else—music in the background, perhaps—and as you do so, the words on the page slip into the fringes of awareness. You may be moving your eyes across the page, but the meaning does not really register. (Every student has had this experience.)

Now, if we can have your attention again, we'd like to remind you that consciousness has many functions. But three especially important ones were illustrated by the scenario in the previous paragraph (Solso, 2001; Tononi & Edelman, 1998):

- Consciousness restricts our attention. Because consciousness processes information serially, it limits what you notice and think about. In this way, consciousness keeps your brain from being overwhelmed by stimulation. It is also the property that will not let you concentrate on what you are reading when you shift your attention to music playing in the background.
- Consciousness provides a mental "meeting place," where sensation can combine with memory, emotions, motives, and a host of other psychological processes. Thus, consciousness is the canvas on which we create a meaningful picture from the stimulation offered by our internal and external worlds. This is the aspect of consciousness that links meaning to words on a page or connects the emotion of joy to the sight of an old friend's face.
- Consciousness allows us to create a mental model of the world that we can manipulate. Unlike simpler organisms, we are not prisoners of the moment: We don't just react reflexively to stimulation. Instead, we can use a conscious model of our world that draws on memory, bringing both the past and the future into awareness. With this model in mind, we can think and plan by manipulating our mental world to evaluate alternative responses and imagine how effective they will be. It is this feature of consciousness that helps you generate your own examples for concepts in this text—or keeps you from being too brutally honest with a friend wearing clothes you don't like.

These three features—restriction, combination, and manipulation—apply in varying degrees to all states of consciousness, whether dreaming, hypnosis, meditation, a drug state, or our "normal" waking state. On the other hand, nonconscious processes operate in a much different way, as we have said. To show you how this region of the mind works, let's begin by distinguishing two levels of nonconscious processing.

Levels of the Nonconscious Mind Sigmund Freud originally proposed that processing outside awareness could influence our conscious thoughts, feelings, dreams, fantasies, and actions. And, although many cognitive psychologists would reject most details of Freud's theory as little more than fantasies, they would retain the notion that the nonconscious mind has two main divisions, often called the *preconscious* and the *unconscious.*

The Preconscious Psychologists define memories of events (a date last weekend, for example) and facts (Salem is the capital of Oregon) that have once been the focus of attention as **preconscious memories.** They can return to consciousness with relative ease when something cues their recall. Otherwise, they lie in the background of the mind, just beyond the boundary of consciousness until needed. Preconsciousness doesn't operate under the serial, one-thing-at-a-time limitation of consciousness. On the other hand, it doesn't have the ability that consciousness has for actively manipulating information.

The Unconscious A dictionary might define the term *unconscious* as the absence of all consciousness, as in one who has fainted, has become comatose, or is under anesthesia. But there is another meaning for *unconscious:* cognition occurring without awareness. In this sense, the **unconscious** consists of many levels of processing that occur without awareness, ranging from brain systems that run on "automatic pilot" to those that can have subtle influences on consciousness and behavior (Kihlstrom, 1987). You can get some idea of how these unconscious processes affect us if you think about how you often follow a familiar route to work or school without apparent thought. Let us show you another way in which psychologists have demonstrated the existence of this sort of unconscious processing in the laboratory.

A Demonstration of Unconscious Processing Try filling in the blanks to make a word from the following stem:

D E F ___ ___ ___

Using a technique called priming, psychologists can have some influence on the answers people give to such problems without their being conscious that they were influenced. In the example just given, there are a number of possible ways to complete the word stem, including *defend, defeat, defect, defile, deform, defray, defuse,* and *define.* We don't know for sure what your answer was, but we have carefully set you up to increase the probability that you would pick the word *define.* To do so, we deliberately "primed" your response by twice using the word *define* in the two paragraphs preceding our test. With priming methods such as this, psychologists have a powerful tool for probing the interaction of conscious and unconscious processes.

■ **Preconscious memories** Information that is not currently in consciousness but can be recalled to consciousness voluntarily or after something calls attention to them.

■ **Unconscious** In classic Freudian theory, a part of the mind that houses memories, desires, and feelings that would be threatening if brought to consciousness. Many modern cognitive psychologists view the unconscious in less sinister terms, merely as a collection of mental processes that operate outside of awareness—but not typically suppressing information or working at odds with consciousness.

PSYCHOLOGY IN YOUR LIFE: THE UNCONSCIOUS—RECONSIDERED

As we have seen, the term *unconscious* can have many meanings. In Freud's psychoanalytic theory, for example, powerful unconscious forces actively work to block (or repress) sexual desires and traumatic memories (Freud, 1925). If allowed to break through into consciousness, these would cause extreme anxiety, Freud taught. In this view, the unconscious mind serves as a mental dungeon where terrible urges and threatening memories can be kept "locked up" outside of awareness.

Ever since Freud, the art and literature of the Western world have been captivated by the idea of an unconscious mind filled with dark and sinister motives and memories. For example, Joseph Conrad's novel *Heart of Darkness* tells the story of a person's internal and unconscious struggle with the most evil of desires for power, destruction, and death. Unconscious desires can be sexual, as well. What else could account for the dubious success of the titillating stories splashed so obviously across the pages of the tabloids and the screens of the "soaps"?

CONNECTION: CHAPTER 8

In Freud's *psychoanalytic theory,* the unconscious makes up the major part of the mind. In this view, it serves as the source of sexual and aggressive desires.

Freud also taught that we "forget" anniversaries because we have unconscious reservations about the relationship. He said that we choose mates who are, on an unconscious level, just substitutes for our fathers and mothers. And he gave us the concept of the "Freudian slip," which one wag defined as "saying one thing when you really mean your mother."

In essence, Freud's view is just a variation on the anima hypothesis mentioned earlier: He placed the ego—the rational decision-maker part of the mind—at the center of consciousness. There, said Freud, it assumes the responsibility of keeping the sexual and aggressive forces of the unconscious in check. But was he right? Although most psychologists today would say that Freud's views were better as metaphors than as objective science, his ideas are still widely accepted by the general public.

Advances in research methods (such as priming) have made it possible to analyze unconscious thought processes in ways never dreamed of by Freud (Kihlstrom, 1990; Kihlstrom et al., 1992; Rozin, 1976). As a result, the mind beneath consciousness does not appear to be so dramatic or sinister as Freud portrayed it. Rather, a cognitive view suggests a much simpler structure than the complicated censoring and repressing system that Freud proposed (Greenwald, 1992).

For the most part, the nonconscious mind seems to devote its resources to simple background tasks such as screening the incoming stream of sights, sounds, smells, and textures, rather than to repressing memories of traumatic experiences. This ability also provides a quick appraisal of events for their attractiveness or harmfulness (LeDoux, 1996). These unconscious pathways can even save your life, as when you react "without thinking" to a swerving car or a deadly snake on the path in front of you. In this fashion, the less-than-conscious mind works *with* consciousness, rather than against it. Ironically, the cognitive view of an unconscious that monitors, sorts, discards, and stores the flood of data we encounter may give the unconscious a larger role than Freud originally conceived.

CHECK YOUR UNDERSTANDING

1. **RECALL:** Who objected most strenuously to defining psychology as the science of consciousness?
   a. the behaviorists
   b. the cognitive psychologists
   c. the Freudians
   d. the humanists
   e. the neurologists

2. **RECALL:** According to cognitive neuroscience,
   a. consciousness has no relationship to the brain.
   b. consciousness is a product of the brain.
   c. creativity arises from altered states of consciousness.
   d. consciousness does not exist.
   e. the conscious mind has little access to the larger world of mental activity in the unconscious.

3. **APPLICATION:** Suppose you wanted to sample the contents of preconsciousness in a group of volunteers. Which technique would be most appropriate?
   a. Ask them to recall specific memories to consciousness.
   b. Ask them to recall a dream.
   c. Do a priming experiment.
   d. Have them undergo psychoanalysis.
   e. Give them MRI scans.

4. **UNDERSTANDING THE CORE CONCEPT:** Which of the following is a description of consciousness suggested by the Core Concept for this section?
   a. Consciousness processes information serially.
   b. Consciousness allows us to respond reflexively, without thinking.
   c. Consciousness controls the autonomic nervous system.
   d. Consciousness makes us more alert.
   e. Consciousness is just an abstract concept.

ANSWERS: 1. a 2. b 3. a 4. a

KEY QUESTION

WHAT CYCLES OCCUR IN EVERYDAY CONSCIOUSNESS?

If you are a "morning person," you are probably at your peak of alertness soon after you awaken. But this mental state doesn't last all day. Like most other people, you probably experience a period of mental lethargy in the afternoon. At this low point in the cycle of wakefulness, you may join much of the Latin world, which wisely takes a siesta. Later, your alertness increases for a time, only to fade again during the evening hours. Punctuating this cycle may be periods of heightened focus and attention (as when you are called on in class) and periods of reverie, known as daydreams. Finally, whether you are a "morning" or "night" person, you eventually drift into that third of your life spent asleep, where conscious contact with the outside world nearly ceases.

Psychologists have traced these cyclic changes in consciousness, looking for reliable patterns. Our Core Concept for this section of the chapter summarizes what they have found:

CORE CONCEPT

Consciousness changes in cycles that correspond to our biological rhythms and to the patterns of stimulation in our environment.

In this section we will devote most of our attention to the cyclic changes in consciousness involved in sleep and nocturnal dreaming. We begin, however, with another sort of "dreaming," that occurs while we are awake.

Daydreaming

In the mildly altered state of consciousness that we call **daydreaming,** attention turns inward to memories, expectations, and desires—often with vivid mental imagery (Roche & McConkey, 1990). Daydreaming occurs most often when people are alone, relaxed, engaged in a boring or routine task, or just about to fall asleep (Singer, 1966, 1975). But is daydreaming normal? You may be relieved to know that most people daydream every day. Research shows, however, that young adults report the most frequent daydreams, with the amount of daydreaming declining significantly with increasing age (Singer & McCraven, 1961).

● Daydreaming, common among people of all ages, may be a source of creativity.

Daydreams can serve valuable, healthy functions (Klinger, 1987). They often dwell on practical and current concerns in people's lives, such as classes, goals (trivial or significant), and interpersonal relationships. As we ruminate on these concerns, daydreaming can help us make plans and solve problems.

On the other hand, daydreams can feature persistent and unwelcome wishes, worries, or fantasies. What can you do if that happens? Suppose that you decide to stop entertaining a particular thought—fantasies of an old flame, a persistent tune running through your head, or worries about a grade. Studies suggest that deliberate efforts to suppress unwanted thoughts are likely to backfire. In the "white bear" experiment (Wegner et al., 1987), students were asked to speak into a tape recorder about anything that came to mind. They were instructed, however, not to think about "a white bear." The results: Despite the instructions, the students mentioned a white bear about once per minute! Obviously, trying to suppress a thought or put something out of your mind can result in an obsession with the very thought you seek to escape. Yet, when you don't try to censor your thoughts but, instead, allow your mind to roam freely, as daydreaming and fantasy naturally do, unwanted or upsetting thoughts usually become less intrusive and finally cease (Wegner, 1989).

■ **Daydreaming** A common (and quite normal) variation of consciousness in which attention shifts to memories, expectations, desires, or fantasies and away from the immediate situation.

And how do daydreams compare with dreams of the night? No matter how realistic our fantasies may be, daydreams are rarely as vivid as our most colorful night dreams. Neither are they as mysterious—because they are more under our control. Nor do they occur, like night dreams, under the influence of biological cycles and the strange world that we call sleep. It is to this world that we now turn our attention.

Sleep: The Mysterious Third of Our Lives

If you live to be 90, you will have slept for nearly 30 years. Even though this means we "lose" a third of our lives, most of us take this lengthy alteration of daily consciousness for granted. In fact, we often anticipate sleep with pleasure. But what is this mysterious mental state? Once the province of psychoanalysts, prophets, poets, painters, and psychics, the world of sleep has now become a vibrant field of study for scientific researchers, who have shown that sleep must be understood as one of our natural biological cycles (Beardsley, 1996). We begin our exploration of this realm of altered consciousness with an examination of these cycles.

Circadian Rhythms All creatures fall under the influence of nature's cyclic changes, especially the daily pattern of light and darkness. Among the most important for we humans are those known as **circadian rhythms,** bodily patterns that repeat approximately every 24 hours. (*Circadian* comes from the Latin *circa* for "about" + *dies* for "a day.") Internal control of these recurring rhythms resides in a "biological clock" that sets the cadence of such functions as metabolism, heart rate, body temperature, and hormonal activity. Although we don't know precisely how this clock works, we know its locus is the hypothalamus—the suprachiasmatic nucleus, to be exact (Pinel, 2003). This group of cells receives input from the eyes and so is especially sensitive to the light–dark cycles of day and night (Barinaga, 2002). From a biological perspective, then, the cycle of sleep and wakefulness is just another circadian rhythm.

For most individuals, the normal sleep–wakefulness pattern is naturally a bit longer than a day in length. When placed for long periods in an environment in which there are no time cues, most people settle into a circadian cycle of about 25 hours. But under more normal circumstances, the pattern undergoes daily readjustment by our exposure to light and by our habitual routines (Dement & Vaughan, 1999).

Anything that throws off your biological clock affects how you feel and behave. Work schedules that shift from day to night are notorious for such effects (Dement & Vaughan, 1999; Moore-Ede, 1993). Staying up all night studying for an exam will have similar consequences. Likewise, flying across several time zones results in jet lag because the internal circadian cycle is disrupted by your new temporal environment. If it is 1:00 A.M. to your body but only 10:00 P.M. to the people around you, you must use energy and resources to adapt to your surroundings. The resulting symptoms of jet lag include fatigue, irresistible sleepiness, and temporary cognitive deficits. Air travelers should note that our biological clocks can adjust more readily to longer days than to shorter ones. Therefore, traveling eastbound (losing hours in your day) creates greater jet lag than traveling westbound (gaining hours). Apparently, it is easier to stay awake a bit longer than it is to fall asleep sooner than usual.

The Main Events of Sleep Sleep has been a mystery for most of human history—until late one night in 1952. It was then that graduate student Eugene Aserinsky decided to make recordings of his sleeping son's brain waves and muscle movements of the eyes (Brown, 2003). The session proceeded uneventfully for about an hour and a half, with nothing but the slow rhythms of sleep

Circadian rhythms Physiological patterns that repeat approximately every 24 hours, such as the sleep–wakefulness cycle.

appearing as tracks on the EEG. Then suddenly, a flurry of eye movements appeared. The recording showed the boy's eyeballs darting back and forth, as though he were watching a fast-changing scene. At the same time, the brain wave patterns told Aserinsky that the boy was alert. Expecting to find that his son had awakened and was looking around, Aserinsky entered the bedroom and was surprised to see him lying quietly, with his eyes closed and fast asleep. What was going on? Wisely, the researcher ran more volunteers through the same procedure, and he found that essentially the same pattern occurred periodically throughout the night in all of them.

About every 90 minutes during sleep, we enter a stage called **REM sleep,** marked by rapid eye movements (REM) beneath closed eyelids. These take place for several minutes and then abruptly cease (Aserinsky & Kleitman, 1953). The interim periods, without rapid eye movements, are known as **non-REM (NREM) sleep.** And what happens in the mind and brain during these two different phases of sleep?

To find out, researchers awakened sleepers during either REM sleep or NREM sleep and asked them to describe their mental activity (Dement & Kleitman, 1957). The NREM reports typically contained either brief descriptions of ordinary daily events or no mental activity at all. By contrast, REM reports were usually filled with vivid cognitions, featuring fanciful, bizarre scenes. In other words, rapid eye movements were a sign of dreaming. Strangely, while the eyes dance during REM sleep, the voluntary muscles in the rest of the body are immobile—paralyzed—a condition now known as **sleep paralysis.** From an evolutionary perspective, we can see that this probably kept our ancestors from wandering out of their caves and into trouble while acting out their dreams. Sleepwalking and sleep talking don't occur during REM sleep but in the deepest stage of NREM sleep.) We'll have much more to say about dreaming in a moment. For now, let's see how REM sleep fits with the other phases of sleep.

The Sleep Cycle Imagine that you are a volunteer subject in a laboratory specializing in sleep research. Already connected to EEG recording equipment, you soon become comfortable with the wires linking your body to the machinery, and you are settling in for a night's sleep. While you are still awake and alert, the EEG shows your brain waves pulsing at a rate of about 14 cycles per second (cps). As you begin to relax and become drowsy, they slow to about 8 to 12 cps. When you fall asleep, the EEG shows further changes. Then, over the course of the night, your brain waves begin a cycle of activity much like the pattern you see in Figure 5.4—a cycle that repeats itself over and over through the night. A closer look at the recording of this cycle the next morning will show several distinct stages, each with a characteristic EEG signature (see Figure 5.5):

- In Stage 1 sleep, the EEG displays some slower (theta) activity, along with fast brain (beta) waves similar to those seen in the waking state.
- During the next phase, Stage 2, the generally slower EEG is punctuated by sleep spindles—short bursts of fast electrical activity that reliably signals the end of Stage 1.
- In the following two stages (3 and 4), the sleeper enters a progressively deeper state of relaxed sleep. The heart rate and breathing rate slow down. Brain waves also slow dramatically, with delta waves appearing for the first time. The deepest point in the sleep cycle occurs, in Stage 4, about a half hour after sleep onset.
- As Stage 4 ends, the electrical activity of the brain increases, and the sleeper climbs back up through the stages in reverse order.

REM sleep A stage of sleep that occurs approximately every 90 minutes, marked by bursts of rapid eye movements occurring under closed eyelids. REM sleep periods are associated with dreaming.

Non-REM (NREM) sleep The recurring periods, mainly associated with the deeper stages of sleep, when a sleeper is not showing rapid eye movements.

Sleep paralysis A condition in which a sleeper is unable to move any of the voluntary muscles, except those controlling the eyes. Sleep paralysis normally occurs during REM sleep.

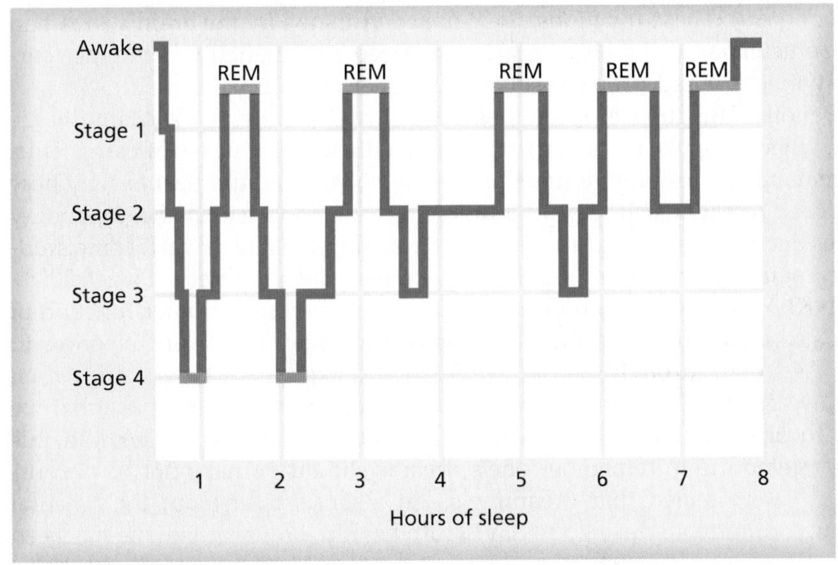
Awake
Stage 1
Stage 2
Stage 3
Stage 4
REM
REM
REM
REM
REM
1
2
3
4
5
6
7
8
Hours of sleep

● **FIGURE 5.4** Stages Of Sleep

In a typical night, the deepest sleep (Stages 3 and 4) occurs mainly in the first few hours. As the night progresses, the sleeper spends more and more time in the stages of light sleep and in REM sleep.

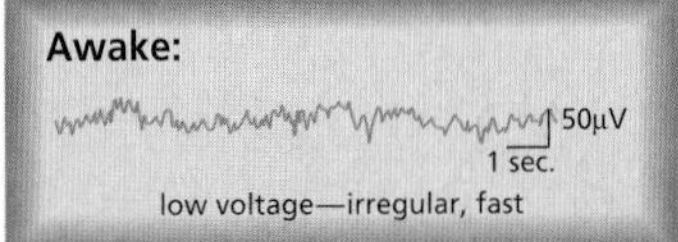
Awake:
50µV
1 sec.
low voltage—irregular, fast

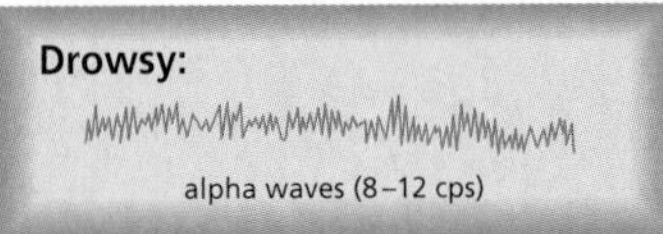
Drowsy:
alpha waves (8–12 cps)

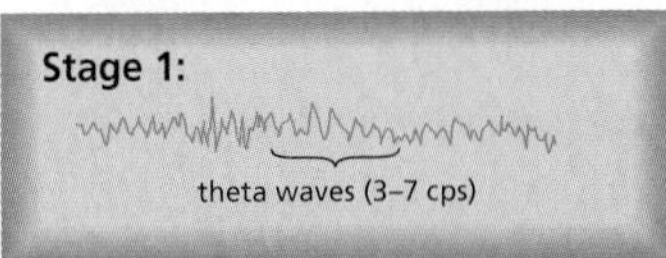
Stage 1:
theta waves (3–7 cps)

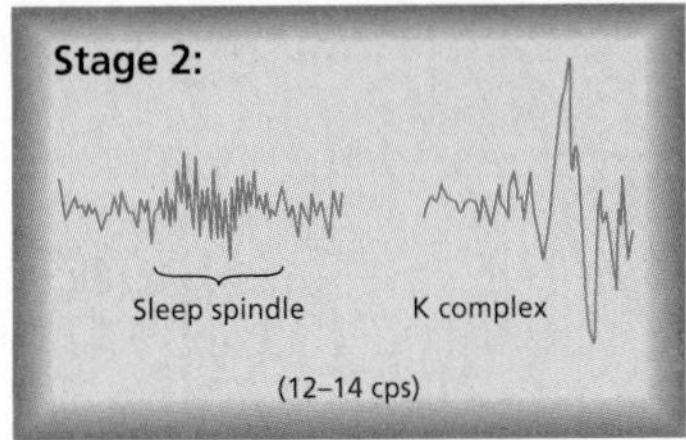
Stage 2:
Sleep spindle
K complex
(12–14 cps)

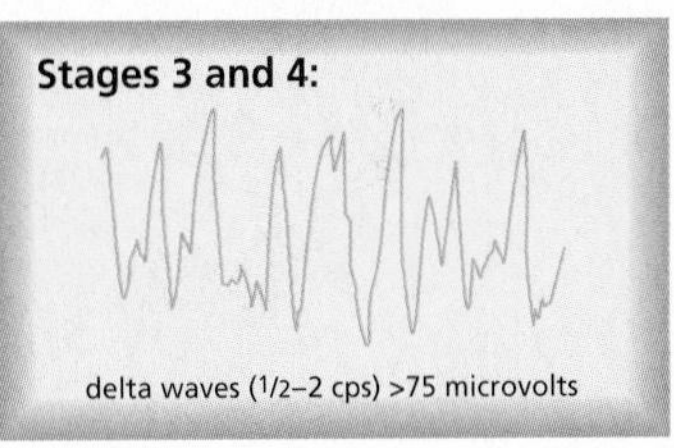
Stages 3 and 4:
delta waves (1/2–2 cps) >75 microvolts

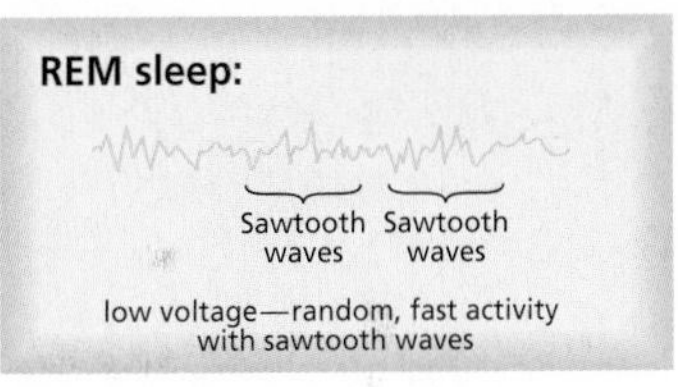
REM sleep:
Sawtooth waves
Sawtooth waves
low voltage—random, fast activity with sawtooth waves

● **FIGURE 5.5** EEG Patterns in Stages of Sleep

- As the sleeper reaches Stage 1 again, fast beta waves recorded by the EEG reappear. In addition, the sleeper now enters REM sleep for the first time. Then, after a few minutes of REMing, the entire cycle begins to repeat itself.

Over the course of an average night's sleep, most people make the circuit up and down through the stages of sleep four to six times. In each successive cycle, the amount of time spent in deep sleep (Stages 3 and 4) decreases, and the amount of time spent in REM sleep increases. During the first cycle, the REM period may last only 10 minutes, while in the last cycle, we may spend as much as an hour in REM sleep. A look at Figure 5.4 will show you how this pattern plays out through a typical night's sleep. Studying this pattern will not only help you understand your normal night's sleep but will also provide the framework for understanding the abnormal patterns found in most sleep disorders, which we will consider a little later. Again, please note the three most important features of normal sleep: (a) the 90-minute cycles, (b) the occurrence of deepest sleep near the beginning of the night, and (c) the increase in REM duration as sleep progresses.

What do you suppose would happen if a person were deprived of a substantial amount of REM sleep for a whole night? Laboratory studies show that REM-deprived subjects feel tired and irritable the next day. Then, during the following night, they spend much more time in REM sleep than usual, a condition known as **REM rebound.** This observation suggests that one of the functions of sleep is to satisfy a basic biological need for REM. Sleep-deprived college students take note: Because we get most of our REM sleep during the last few cycles of the night, we inevitably suffer some REM deprivation and REM rebound if we cut our night's sleep short.

The Function of Sleep Sleep is so common among animals that it surely must have some essential function, but sleep scientists disagree on what that function is (Maquet, 2001; Pinel, 2003; Rechtschaffen, 1998). There are several possibilities. Evolutionary psychology suggests that sleep may have evolved because it enabled animals to conserve energy and stay out of harm's way at times when there was no need to forage for food or search for mates (Dement &

■ **REM rebound** A condition of increased REM sleep caused by REM-sleep deprivation.

Vaughan, 1999). These functions, then, are coordinated by the brain's circadian clock. Some experiments also suggest that sleep aids mental functioning, particularly memory and problem solving (Wagner et al., 2004).

Yet another function of sleep was poetically described by William Shakespeare, when he spoke of "sleep that knits up the ravell'd sleave of care." Thus sleep may have a restorative function for the body and mind. But exactly how might sleep restore us? It may be a time when the body replenishes its energy supplies and purges itself of toxins built up during the day. In fact, some studies suggest that damaged brain cells do get repaired during sleep (Siegel, 2003).

In 1983, Francis Crick and Graeme Mitchison proposed another function of dream sleep. According to the Crick–Mitchison view, we dream in order to forget. As we go through the day we learn and experience things, and when we do, we create new neural networks. Crick and Mitchison propose that we dream to unravel those neural nets. In the words of Francis Crick, "In this model, attempting to remember one's dreams should perhaps not be encouraged. . . ." They stated that dreaming is, in a sense, taking out the "mental trash" we accumulate during the day. Truth be told, however, no one has been able to show how sleep actually restores us—although there's no doubt that it makes us feel restored (Dement & Vaughan, 1999).

The Need for Sleep How much sleep we need depends on several factors. For one thing, genetics sets broad sleep requirements that differ for each species. And although sleep duration is influenced by circadian rhythms, there is some individual variation (Barinaga, 1997b; Haimov & Lavie, 1996). Part of that variation is genetic, but the amount of sleep we require is linked to our personal characteristics and habits. For example, those who sleep longer than average tend to be more nervous, worrisome, artistic, creative, and nonconforming. Short sleepers tend to be more energetic and extroverted (Hartmann, 1973). And, it is no surprise that the amount of exercise a person gets influences the need for sleep. Oddly, however, strenuous physical activity during the day increases the amount of slow-wave sleep in Stage 4, but it has no effect on REM time (Horne, 1988).

From a developmental perspective, we see that sleep duration and the shape of the sleep cycle change over one's lifetime. As Figure 5.6 shows, newborns sleep about 16 hours per day, with half that time devoted to REM. Dur-

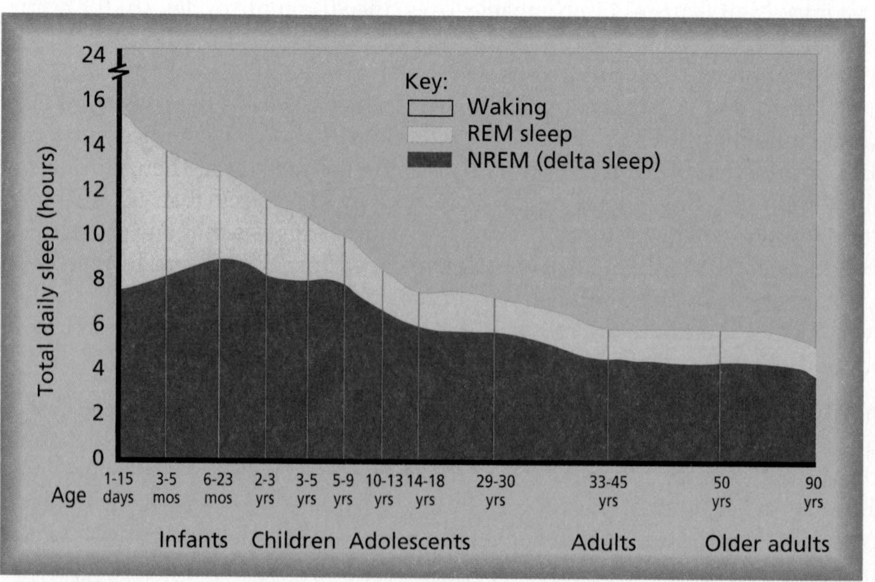

Total daily sleep (hours)
24
16
14
12
10
8
6
4
2
0
Key:
Waking
REM sleep
NREM (delta sleep)
Age
1-15 days
3-5 mos
6-23 mos
2-3 yrs
3-5 yrs
5-9 yrs
10-13 yrs
14-18 yrs
29-30 yrs
33-45 yrs
50 yrs
90 yrs
Infants
Children
Adolescents
Adults
Older adults

● **FIGURE 5.6** Patterns of Human Sleep Over a Lifetime

The graph shows changes with age in the total amounts of REM and NREM sleep and in the percentage of time spent in REM sleep. Note that, over the years, the amount of REM sleep decreases considerably, while NREM diminishes less sharply.

DO IT YOURSELF! How Much Sleep Do You Need?

Many college students operate in a chronic state of sleep deprivation. Because their schedules are crowded with study, work, and social events, students may convince themselves that they need only a few hours sleep each night. And, in fact, the average college student sleeps only about 6.8 hours a night (Hicks, 1990). Does too little sleep really make a difference in how well you perform in your classes? Psychologist Cheryl Spinweber (1990) has found that sleep-deprived undergraduates get lower grades than their counterparts who get enough sleep.

How can you tell if you need more sleep? Answer the following questions honestly:

1. Do you often get sleepy in your classes?
2. Do you sleep late on weekends?
3. Do you usually get sleepy when you get bored?
4. Do you often fall asleep while reading or watching TV?
5. Do you usually fall asleep within five minutes of going to bed?
6. Do you awake in the morning feeling that you are not rested?
7. Would you oversleep if you did not use an alarm clock to drive you out of bed?

If you answered "Yes" to any of these questions, chances are that you are shorting yourself on sleep. You may also be paying the price in the quality of your learning and in your grades.

ing childhood, those numbers gradually decline. Young adults typically sleep seven to eight hours (although they may need more), with about 20% REM. By old age, we sleep even less, with only 15% of sleep spent in REM. You can find out whether you are getting enough sleep by answering the questions in the above "Do It Yourself!" box.

Sleep Debt versus the Circadian Clock So, how much sleep do we humans need—and what happens if we don't get enough? Your mother was right: Most adults need to sleep about eight hours, or a bit more, to feel good and function efficiently. But that's only an average. For different individuals, the amount of sleep needed ranges from about six to nine hours (although most people need more sleep than they think they do). In the sleep laboratory, when volunteers are placed in a dark room and allowed to sleep without interruption and without reference to clocks, the average adult settles into a pattern that produces about eight and one-half hours of sleep each night. Yet, in their daily lives, most Americans get significantly less—night after night (Maas, 1999). This creates a sleep shortage that researcher William Dement calls a **sleep debt** (Dement & Vaughan, 1999).

People who pile up a chronic sleep debt usually don't realize it (Dement, 2000; Dement & Vaughan, 1999). They may be groggy and sleepy when the alarm clock rouses them in the morning. But they don't see this as a sign of a sleep debt because their circadian clocks make them "wake up" and begin to feel alert over the next few hours. Afternoon drowsiness may be attributed to a big lunch—which, in truth, does not cause sleepiness. (It's the clock, again.) They may also rationalize away their struggle to stay awake in a meeting or class by telling themselves that sleepiness is a normal response to boredom (Van Dongen et al., 2003). In fact, the normal response to boredom is restlessness—not sleepiness—unless one is sleep deprived.

What is actually happening is that the sleep-deprived individual gets caught in a daily tug-of-war between the pulls of a sleep debt and our relentless circadian rhythms. But our internal clocks can fool us, too. Even when we have not had enough sleep, the clock in the brain can make us feel relatively alert at certain times of the day—usually late morning and late afternoon. But this alertness can also be illusory. With a chronic sleep debt, you are never as alert and mentally efficient as you could be if the sleep debt were paid with a few good nights of sleep (Van Dongen et al., 2003). Unfortunately, the sleep debt is sometimes "paid" with a tragedy—as happened dramatically a few years ago, when *Exxon Valdez*, a giant tanker, ran aground, spilling oil across a pristine bay in the Alaskan wilderness. The ensuing investigation revealed

■ **Sleep debt** A sleep deficiency caused by not getting the amount of sleep that one requires for optimal functioning.

that a crew member who was steering the ship at the time had had only six hours of sleep in the previous two days.

Of special interest to students is this fact: Sleep deprivation can have a devastating effect on cognitive and motor functioning (Pilcher & Walters, 1997). In plainer language, William Dement says that a big sleep debt "makes you stupid" (Dement & Vaughan, 1999, p. 231). Evidence of this is found in a study that deprived one group of volunteers of sleep and gave another group enough alcohol to make them legally drunk (their blood alcohol content reached .1 percent). After 24 hours of sleep loss—like staying up all night studying for a test—the sleepy volunteers were performing just like the intoxicated group on tests of thinking and coordination (Fletcher et al., 2003).

Unfortunately, sleep-deprived people usually don't realize how impaired they actually are. Further, the pressures and opportunities of modern life commonly make us underestimate the amount of sleep we need. We may also believe that we can combat sleepiness and successfully reduce our need for sleep by dint of will power and caffeine. But such measures never give us the clarity of mind that a good night's sleep does. As a result, we may struggle much of our lives with a chronic sleep deficit, never realizing why we must wage a daily battle with drowsiness.

● Death-related images appear more often in dreams of Mexican American college students than in those of Anglo-American college students. This probably occurs because death is more prominently a part of Mexican culture, as can be seen in this figure, used in the Day of the Dead celebration.

Dreaming: The Pageants of the Night

Every night of your life, you experience a spectacular series of events staged only in your dreams. What produces these fantastic cognitive spectacles? And, what—if anything—do they mean? As we saw earlier, sleep scientists now know that dreams occur regularly throughout the night, most often in REM sleep. They have also identified the parts of the brain that control dreaming—including, especially, parts of the brain stem. What remains most mysterious about this stage of sleep is why we dream.

Sleep scientists have approached dreaming with this question: What function do dreams have? On a biological level, dreams may be necessary for healthy brain functioning, although the evidence for that is not certain (Siegel, 2003). From a cognitive perspective, some experts see dreams as meaningful mental events, serving pressing cognitive needs or reflecting important events or fantasies in the dreamer's mental world. Others argue that dreams are merely the brain's random activity during sleep—and, therefore, their content may have no special meaning. Let's look at both sides of this debate on the meaningfulness of dreams.

Dreams as Meaningful Events At the beginning of the 20th century, Sigmund Freud laid out the most complex and comprehensive theory of dreams and their meanings ever developed—a theory that has since enjoyed enormous influence, despite a lack of scientific evidence to support it (Squier & Domhoff, 1998). In this view, dreams represent "the royal road to the unconscious," lined with clues to an individual's hidden mental life. For this reason, Freud made the analysis of dreams the cornerstone of psychoanalysis, as set out in his classic book *The Interpretation of Dreams* (1900).

Freud's Theory of Dreams In psychoanalytic theory, dreams have two main functions: to *guard* sleep (by disguising disruptive thoughts with symbols) and to serve as sources of wish fulfillment. Freud believed that dreams play their guardian role by relieving psychic tensions created during the day. They serve their wish-fulfillment function by allowing the dreamer to work harmlessly through unconscious desires.

In his explanation of the meaning of dreams, Freud distinguished between the **manifest content**—the dream's story line—and the **latent content**—the (supposed) symbolic meaning of the dream. Psychoanalytic therapists, therefore, scrutinize the manifest content of their patients' dreams for clues that relate to latent motives and conflicts that may lurk in the unconscious. For example, clues relating to sexual conflicts might take the form of long rigid objects or containers, which, in Freudian theory, symbolize the male and female genitals.

Must you be a trained psychoanalyst to understand dreams? Not necessarily. The manifest content in many of our dreams has a fairly obvious connection to our waking lives. You have probably noticed that frightening dreams often relate to life stressors that have found their way into your sleeping thoughts. Research has lent support to such observations. For example, one study found that individuals depressed about divorce often had dreams that were fixed on past relationships (Cartwright, 1984). By analyzing the patterns and content of your own dreams, you may find it is not difficult to assign meaning to many of the images and actions you recall (Hall, 1953/1966; Van de Castle, 1994). We must emphasize, however, that there is no solid scientific support for Freudian interpretations of latent dream content.

Dreams Vary by Culture, Gender, and Age Freudian dream analysis has also been challenged on the grounds that Freud was not always scrupulous in his research. For example, he asserted that boys frequently dream of strife with their fathers—but he did no careful studies to verify his theoretical suspicions. Rather, on the basis of a few cases, he jumped to the conclusion that such dreams were signs of unconscious sexual jealousy. Many other explanations are possible, however, as anthropologists have shown by studying dreams of the Trobriand Islanders. Boys in that culture don't dream of their fathers so much as of their uncles, who act as the disciplinarians in that society (Malinowski, 1927; Segall et al., 1990). Freud's theory, then, may be an example of confirmation bias.

CONNECTION: CHAPTER 1
Confirmation bias leads us to notice evidence that agrees with our views and to ignore evidence that does not.

Modern sleep scientists have taken a more objective approach to dreams than Freud did (see Domhoff, 1996). They now know that the content of dreams varies by age, gender, and culture. Children are more likely to dream about animals than adults are, and the animals in their dreams are more likely to be large, threatening, and wild. In contrast, college students dream more usually of small animals, pets, and tame creatures. This may mean that children feel less in control of their world than adults do and so may find that world depicted in scarier imagery while they sleep (Van de Castle, 1983, 1994).

Women everywhere more commonly dream of children, while men more often dream of aggression, weapons, and tools (Murray, 1995). In a sample of over 1800 dreams collected by dream researcher Calvin Hall, American women dreamed about both men and women, while men dreamed about men twice as often as about women. In another sample of over 1300 dreams, Hall found that hostile interactions between characters outnumbered friendly exchanges and that 64% of dreamed emotions had a negative complexion, such as anger and sadness (Hall, 1951, 1984).

The highly specific effects of culture can be seen in reports from the West African nation of Ghana, where dreams often feature attacks by cows (Barnouw, 1963). Likewise, Americans frequently find themselves embarrassed by public nakedness in their dreams, although such reports rarely occur in cultures where people customarily wear few clothes. Images of death appear more often in the dreams of Mexican American college students than in the dreams of Anglo American students, probably because concerns about

■ **Manifest content** The story line of a dream, taken at face value without interpretation.

■ **Latent content** The symbolic meaning of objects and events in a dream. Latent content is usually an interpretation based on Freud's psychoanalytic theory or one of its variants. The latent content of a dream involving clocks might involve fear of the menstrual cycle and, hence, of one's sexuality.

death are more a part of life in Latin American cultures (Roll et al., 1974). In general, the cross-cultural research lends support to Rosalind Cartwright's hypothesis (1977) that dreams merely reflect life events that are important to the dreamer.

Dreams and Recent Experience Sleep research has also found—as we might expect—that dream content frequently connects with recent experience. If you're struggling with your taxes all day, you're likely to dream about your taxes at night, especially during your first REM period. Typically, the first dream of the night connects with events of the previous day. Then, dreaming in the second REM period (90 minutes later) may build on a theme that emerged during the first REM period. And so it goes through the night, like a rumor passed from one person to another: The final dream that emerges may have a connection—but only a remote one—to events of the previous day. But because the final dream of the night is the one most likely to be remembered, we may not recognize the link with the previous day's events (Cartwright, 1977; Kiester, 1980).

Dreams and Cognition The relationship between dreams and recent experience may belie yet another possible function of dreams. Comparisons of individuals who were selectively deprived of REM sleep with those deprived of NREM sleep suggest that REM sleep helps us remember—although we must add that this conclusion is still controversial (Kinoshita, 1992; Maquet, 2001; Siegel, 2001; Stickgold et al., 2001; Winson, 1990). It may be that REM sleep is a normal part of weaving new experiences into the fabric of old memories (Barinaga, 1994; Cartwright, 1978; Dement, 1980; Karni et al., 1994).

Dreams as Random Activity of the Brain Not everyone believes that dream content has any special meaning of consequence—certainly not any latent content that warrants psychoanalytic interpretation. In particular, the **activation-synthesis theory** says that dreams result when the sleeping brain tries to make sense of its own spontaneous bursts of activity (Leonard, 1998; Squier & Domhoff, 1998). In this view, dreams have their origin in periodic neural discharges emitted by the sleeping brain stem. As this energy sweeps over the cerebral cortex, the sleeper experiences impressions of sensation, memory, motivation, emotion, and movement. Although the cortical activation is random, and the images it generates may not be logically connected, the brain tries to make sense of the stimulation it receives. To do so, the brain synthesizes, or pulls together, the "messages" in these random electrical bursts by creating a coherent story. A dream, then, could merely be the brain's way of making sense out of nonsense.

The proponents of this theory, J. Allan Hobson and Robert McCarley (1977), argued that REM sleep furnishes the brain with an internal source of needed stimulation. This internal activation promotes the growth and development of the brain at the time when the sleeping brain has blocked out external stimulation. Dream content, therefore, results from brain activation, not unconscious wishes or other meaningful mental processes. Although Hobson (1988, 2002) claims that the story line in our dreams is added as a "brainstorm afterthought," he does acknowledge that dream content may nevertheless have some psychological meaning in that the dream story is influenced by culture, gender, personality factors, and recent events. Thus, when brain activations are synthesized, dreams seem familiar and meaningful.

Activation-synthesis theory The theory that dreams begin with random electrical *activation* coming from the brain stem. Dreams, then, are the brain's attempt to make sense of—to *synthesize*—this random activity.

Dreams as a Source of Creative Insights Even if Hobson and McCarley are right—that dreams have no special meaning other than an attempt by the brain to make sense out of nonsense—they could still be a source of creative ideas.

Sleep and dreaming have inspired much art, as we see here in Rousseau's *Sleeping Gypsy*.

In fact, it would be astonishing if we did not turn to such wild and sometimes wonderful scenes in the night for inspiration. As we have seen, writers, composers, and scientists have done just that.

PSYCHOLOGY IN YOUR LIFE: SLEEP DISORDERS

You may be among the more than 100 million Americans who get insufficient sleep or poor-quality sleep (Dement & Vaughan, 1999). Some of these sleep problems are job related. Among people who work night shifts, for example, more than half nod off at least once a week on the job. And it may be no coincidence that some of the world's most serious accidents—the disastrous radiation emissions at the Three Mile Island and Chernobyl nuclear plants and the massive toxic chemical discharge at Bhopal—have occurred during late evening hours when people are likely to be programmed for sleep. Sleep experts speculate that many accidents occur because key personnel fail to function optimally as a result of insufficient sleep—as we noted earlier in the case of the *Exxon Valdez* oil spill (Dement, 1980; Dement & Vaughan, 1999).

Along with these job-related sleep problems, there are several clinical sleep disorders that sleep researchers have studied in their laboratories. Some are common; others are both rare and bizarre. Some are relatively benign, and some are potentially life threatening. The single element that ties them together is a disruption in one or more parts of the normal sleep cycle.

Insomnia is usually the diagnosis when people feel dissatisfied with the amount of sleep they get. Its symptoms include chronic inability to fall asleep quickly, frequent arousals during sleep, or early-morning awakening. Insomnia sufferers number about one-third of all adults, making this the most common of sleep disorders (Dement & Vaughan, 1999).

Insomnia The most common of sleep disorders—involving insufficient sleep, the inability to fall asleep quickly, frequent arousals, or early awakenings.

An occasional bout of sleeplessness is normal, especially when you have exciting or worrisome events on your mind. These incidents pose no special danger in themselves, unless attempts are made to treat the problem with barbiturates or over-the-counter "sleeping pills." These drugs disrupt the normal sleep cycle by cutting short REM sleep periods (Dement, 1980). As a result, they can actually aggravate insomnia by making the user feel less rested and more sleepy. Much more effective is psychological treatment employing cognitive behavioral therapy, which has had remarkable success (Smith, 2001).

CONNECTION: CHAPTER 13

Cognitive behavioral therapy combines cognitive and behavioral techniques in treating psychological disorders.

Sleep apnea, another common disorder, may be apparent only in a person's complaints of daytime sleepiness and a sleep partner's complaints about snoring. Behind the curtain of the night, the cause can be found in an abnormal breathing pattern. The apnea sufferer actually stops breathing for up to a minute, as often as several hundred times each night! (In case you're concerned, the brief cessation of breathing a few times each hour during the night is normal.) Most commonly, this results from collapse of the airway when the sleeper's muscle tone relaxes. The result is another major symptom of sleep apnea: frequent loud snoring, occurring each time the patient runs short of oxygen and tries mightily to get air through the collapsed airway (Seligson, 1994). As breathing stops and the sleeper's blood oxygen level plummets, the body's emergency system kicks into gear, causing distress hormones to course through the body. In the process, the sleeper awakens briefly, begins breathing again, and then falls back to sleep. Because most of this happens in deep sleep, there is usually no memory of the episode.

● Insomnia is a complex disorder caused by a variety of psychological, environmental, and biological factors. This college student anxiously contemplates her inability to get enough rest for the next day's classes.

Failure to recognize the nature of the problem can cause sufferers—and their families and coworkers—to interpret unusual daytime behavior as laziness or neglect. Sleep apnea can also have harmful biological effects, including elevated blood pressure, and can put dangerous levels of stress on the blood vessels and heart (Anch et al., 1988; Stavish, 1994b).

Occasional episodes of sleep apnea are likely to occur in premature infants, who may need physical stimulation to start breathing again. Further, any tendency toward sleep apnea can be aggravated by putting a young child to bed on its stomach. (Sleep scientists strongly recommend "back to sleep.") Obviously, the problem can be lethal, and it is one possible cause of sudden infant death syndrome (SIDS). Until their underdeveloped respiratory systems mature, these infants must remain connected to breathing monitors. For adults with sleep apnea, permanent breathing failure is not a strong concern. In adults, treatment focuses on the hundreds of nightly apnea episodes, which can be alleviated by use of a device that pumps extra air into the lungs and keeps the airway open during sleep.

Night terrors, which occur primarily in children, pose no health threat. Typically, a night terror attack presents itself as the screaming of a terrified-looking child who is actually in Stage 4 sleep and very difficult to awaken. When finally alert, the child may still feel fearful but have no specific memory of what mental events might have caused the night terror. In fact, the whole experience is likely to be more memorable to the beleaguered family members than to the child.

Unlike garden-variety nightmares, sleep-terror episodes occur in deep sleep, rather than in REM sleep. In this respect they are like sleepwalking and sleep talking, which also occur in Stage 4. All three of these conditions seem to have a genetic component. In themselves, they are not dangerous, although sleepwalkers can inadvertently climb out of upper-story windows or walk into a busy street—so it pays to take some precautions. In most cases, sleepwalking and night terrors diminish or disappear in adulthood, but if they pose persistent and chronic problems, the individual should be evaluated by a sleep specialist.

■ **Sleep apnea** A respiratory disorder in which the person intermittently stops breathing many times while asleep.

■ **Night terrors** Deep sleep episodes that seem to produce terror, although any terrifying mental experience (such as a dream) is usually forgotten upon awakening. Night terrors occur mainly in children.

■ **Narcolepsy** A disorder of REM sleep, involving sleep-onset REM periods and sudden daytime REM-sleep attacks usually accompanied by cataplexy.

Narcolepsy, one of the most unusual of sleep disorders, produces sudden daytime sleep attacks, often without warning. But these are no ordinary waves of drowsiness. So suddenly do these sleep attacks develop that narcolepsy sufferers have reported falling asleep while driving a car, climbing a ladder, or scuba diving under 20 feet of water. Narcoleptic sleep attacks may also be preceded by a sudden loss of muscle control, a condition known as **cataplexy.**

Strangely, anything exciting can trigger a narcoleptic episode. For example, these patients commonly report that they fall asleep while laughing at a joke or even while having sex. Obviously, narcolepsy can be dangerous—and not so good for intimate relationships, either.

Assembling the pieces of this puzzle of symptoms, we find that narcolepsy is fundamentally a disorder of REM sleep. Specifically, a sleep recording will show that the narcolepsy victim has an abnormal sleep-onset REM period. That is, instead of waiting the usual 90 minutes to begin REMing, the narcoleptic person enters REM as sleep begins. You may have already guessed that the accompanying cataplexy is simply REM sleep paralysis.

Studies of narcoleptic animals show that the disorder is a genetic problem affecting the sleep-control circuitry in the brain stem (Harder, 2004). It has no known cure, but we have drugs that diminish the frequency of both the sleep attacks and the cataplexy. And now that we know that the cause is biological, narcoleptic patients are no longer sent to psychotherapy aimed at searching for the unconscious conflicts that were once assumed to underlie the disorder.

So, what should you do if you suspect that you have a serious sleep disorder, such as chronic insomnia, sleep apnea, or narcolepsy? An evaluation by a sleep expert is the place to start. Many hospitals have sleep disorder clinics to which your physician or clinical psychologist can refer you.

● The discovery of narcolepsy in dogs showed that the disorder has a biological basis.

■ **Cataplexy** Sudden loss of muscle control.

CHECK YOUR UNDERSTANDING

1. **RECALL:** Which statement is true about daydreaming?
   a. Daydreams help focus your attention.
   b. Most people daydream every day.
   c. Daydreams are usually more vivid than night dreams.
   d. Daydreams usually serve as an escape from the concerns of real life.
   e. Most people can easily suppress unwanted thoughts.

2. **RECALL:** All of the following are related to our circadian rhythms, except
   a. daydreaming.
   b. waking.
   c. dreaming.
   d. sleep.
   e. jet lag.

3. **RECALL:** Suppose that you are working in a sleep laboratory, where you are monitoring a subject's sleep recording during the night. As the night progresses, you would expect to see that
   a. dreaming becomes less frequent.
   b. the four-stage cycle gradually lengthens.
   c. Stage 3 and 4 sleep periods lengthen.
   d. REM periods become longer.
   e. Stage 1 keeps reappearing.

4. **RECALL:** According to the activation-synthesis theory, dreams are
   a. replays of events during the previous day.
   b. wish fulfillments.
   c. mental garbage.
   d. storylike episodes that provide clues about problems in the unconscious mind.
   e. an attempt by the brain to make sense of random activity in the brain stem.

5. **APPLICATION:** Which of the following symptoms suggests the presence of a sleep disorder?
   a. needing nine hours of sleep each night in order to feel rested
   b. napping during the day
   c. not remembering your dreams
   d. a REM period at the beginning of sleep
   e. a brief cessation of breathing once or twice a night

6. **UNDERSTANDING THE CORE CONCEPT:** Our Core Concept states that consciousness changes in cycles that normally correspond to our biological rhythms and to the patterns of our environment. Which of the following illustrates this concept?
   a. the Crick–Mitchison view
   b. priming
   c. consciousness, preconsciousness, and the unconscious
   d. sleep and dreaming
   e. REM rebound

ANSWERS: 1.b 2.a 3.d 4.e 5.d 6.d

WHAT OTHER FORMS CAN CONSCIOUSNESS TAKE?

A roller coaster ride is one way to alter your consciousness.

Children stand on their heads or spin around to make themselves dizzy. You may seek similar sensations on hair-raising theme-park rides or by sky diving. But why do people do these strange things to themselves? One view says that "human beings are born with a drive to experience modes of awareness other than the normal waking one; from very young ages, children experiment with techniques to change consciousness" (Weil, 1977, p. 37). So, sleep, dreams, fantasies, and thrilling experiences offer compelling alternatives to everyday conscious experience.

In this section of the chapter, we will see how certain psychological techniques, such as hypnosis and meditation, can alter consciousness, too. But, for some people, these conventional alternatives may not provide the states of consciousness they seek. Instead, they may turn to drugs that alter ordinary awareness. We will also examine this approach to changing consciousness. Our discussion of drugs will include both legal substances, such as alcohol, tobacco, and caffeine, and illegal drugs, such heroin, PCP, cannabis, and amphetamines. What is the theme that ties these altered states of consciousness together? The Core Concept of this section says:

An altered state of consciousness occurs when some aspect of normal consciousness is modified by mental, behavioral, or chemical means.

This may sound simplistic at first, but it carries the important implication that altered states do not involve any mysterious or paranormal phenomena that defy rational explanation. Rather, altered states are modifications of ordinary consciousness that we can study with the tools of science. Let's begin with what is known about hypnosis.

Hypnosis

The cartoon images have it wrong. Neither the hypnotist's eyes nor fingertips emit strange, mesmerizing rays that send subjects into a compliant stupor—nor does a dangling shiny bauble have the power to control people's minds.

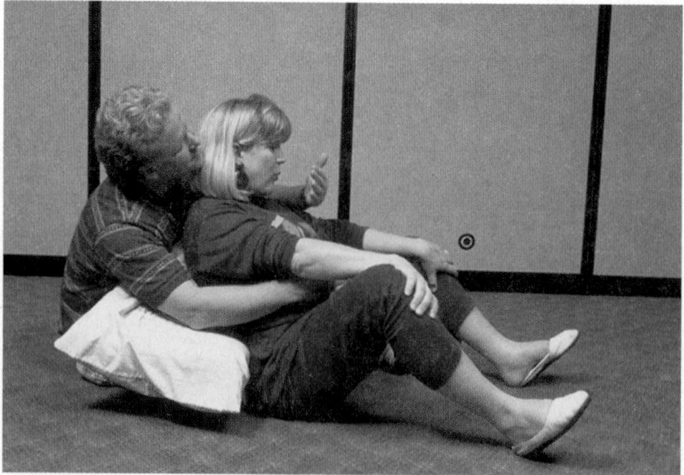

Hypnosis can help to control pain in many individuals. Here, a woman is learning hypnotic techniques that she will use in natural childbirth.

A more accurate (but much less dramatic) picture would show the hypnotist making suggestions to promote concentration and relaxation (Barber, 1976, 1986). Soon the subject appears to be asleep, although he or she can obviously hear suggestions and carry out requests. In some cases, the individual under hypnosis also seems to have amazing powers to ignore pain, remember long-forgotten details, and create hallucinations. But what mental processes make these things happen? To find out, we will explore several viewpoints on the nature of hypnosis. Then, we will consider some of its valid and practical uses by psychologists.

The term *hypnosis* derives from *Hypnos,* the name of the Greek god of sleep. Yet, the EEG record tells us that ordinary sleep plays no role in hypnosis, even though hypnotized individuals may appear to be in a relaxed, sleeplike state. (There is no unique EEG signature for hypnosis.) Most authorities would say **hypnosis** involves a state of awareness characterized by deep relaxation, heightened suggestibility, and focused attention.

When deeply hypnotized, some people have the special ability to respond to suggestion with dramatic changes in perception, memory, motivation, and sense of self-control (Orne, 1980). And, yes, stage hypnotists can make carefully selected volunteers quack like a duck or seem to like the taste of a bitter lemon. After the experience is over, people often report that they experienced heightened responsiveness to the hypnotist's suggestions and felt that their behavior was performed without intention or any conscious effort.

Hypnotizability Dramatic stage performances of hypnosis give the impression that hypnotic power lies with the hypnotist. However, the real star is the person who is hypnotized. The hypnotist is more like an experienced guide showing the way. Some individuals can even practice self-hypnosis, or autohypnosis, by inducing the hypnotic state through self-administered suggestions.

The single most important factor in achieving a hypnotic state is a participant's susceptibility. Experts call this hypnotizability, and they measure it by a person's responsiveness to standardized suggestions. Individuals differ in this susceptibility, varying from complete unresponsiveness to any suggestion, at one extreme, to total responsiveness to virtually every suggestion, at the other. A highly hypnotizable person may respond to suggestions to move their arms, walk about, experience hallucinations, have amnesia for important memories, and become insensitive to painful stimuli. And, we should add, because hypnosis involves heightened suggestibility, any "recovered memories" obtained by this means are highly suspect.

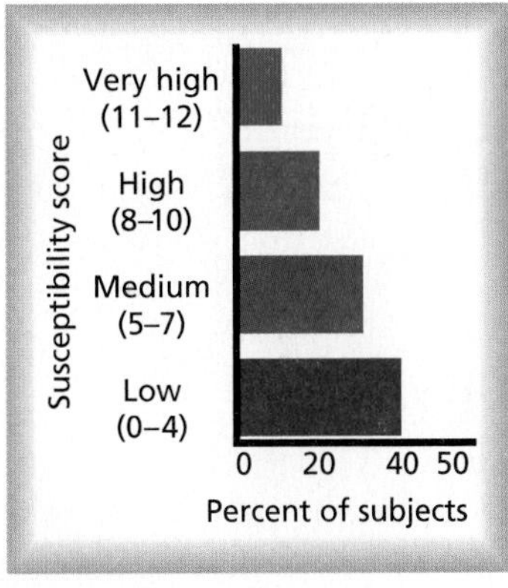
Very high
(11–12)
High
(8–10)
Medium
(5–7)
Low
(0–4)
Susceptibility score
0
20
40
50
Percent of subjects

● **FIGURE 5.7** Level of Hypnosis Reached at First Induction

This graph shows the results achieved by 533 subjects hypnotized for the first time. (Hypnotizability was measured by the 12-item Stanford Hypnotic Susceptibility Scale.)

Figure 5.7 shows the percentage of college-age people who achieved various levels of hypnotizability the first time they were given a hypnotic induction test. For example, a hypnotist may test a new subject's acceptance of suggestion by saying, "Your right hand is lighter than air," and observing whether the subject allows his or her arm to float upward. High scorers are more likely than low scorers to experience pain relief, or hypnotic analgesia, and to respond to hypnotic suggestions for experiencing perceptual distortions.

Hypnosis as an Altered State The experts disagree about the psychological mechanisms involved in hypnosis (Fromm & Shor, 1979; Kihlstrom, 1998; Kirsch & Lynn, 1995, 1998; Woody & Sadler, 1998). Some believe that hypnosis is a distinct state of consciousness, quite separate from sleep or our normal waking state (Fromm & Shor, 1979). Other experts propose that hypnosis is simply heightened motivation (Barber, 1979; Kirsch & Braffman, 2001). In this view, hypnotic subjects are not entranced but merely motivated to focus their attention and to channel more energy into suggested activities. They are hypnotized because they want or expect to be, so they focus on expressing and

■ **Hypnosis** An induced state of awareness, usually characterized by heightened suggestibility, deep relaxation, and highly focused attention.

achieving the responses the hypnotist tries to evoke. Still other experts think that hypnosis is usually a social process, involving role playing, often to please the hypnotist (Sarbin & Coe, 1972).

CONNECTION: CHAPTER 12

Extreme forms of dissociation are associated with clinical disorders, known as *dissociated states.* These include *dissociative identity disorder* (formerly called "multiple personality disorder").

A widely held view, originally proposed by researcher Ernest Hilgard (1992), portrays hypnosis as a dissociated state involving a "hidden observer" in the person's mind, operating in parallel with normal consciousness. Hilgard has shown that hypnotized individuals who say they feel no pain when their hand is placed in ice water will nevertheless respond affirmatively to the instruction, "If some part of you does feel pain, please raise your right index finger." Hilgard believed that attention to the painful sensation was shifted to the hidden observer, leaving normal consciousness blissfully unaware.

Recent theories have attempted to find common ground among these perspectives. And perhaps all have a bit of the truth. It may be that hypnosis, like the normal waking state, can cover a whole range of dissociated states, intensified motives, heightened expectations, and social interactions (Kirsch & Lynn, 1995; Woody & Sadler, 1998).

Practical Uses of Hypnosis Stage tricks aside, what is hypnosis good for? Because it can exert a powerful influence on psychological and body functions in some people, hypnosis can be a useful tool for researchers (Bowers, 1983; Hilgard, 1968, 1973; Miller & Bowers, 1993; Nash, 2001). By using normal volunteers under hypnosis, an experimenter can induce temporary mental conditions, such as anxiety, depression, or hallucinations, instead of having to find individuals who already have these problems. For example, in one study of the psychological issues associated with hearing loss, college students given the hypnotic suggestion to become deaf on cue reported feeling paranoid and excluded because they could not hear what other subjects were saying and assumed they were being deliberately whispered about and excluded (Zimbardo et al., 1981).

Hypnosis has uses in psychological treatment, too. For instance, it can be an effective tool in desensitizing phobic patients who are afraid of heights or spiders. It can also be a part of a relaxation training program designed to combat stress. In addition, therapists find it useful for eliminating unwanted behaviors, such as smoking. A frequently used technique calls for planting posthypnotic suggestions that can diminish a patient's cravings (Barnier & McConkey, 1998; Kihlstrom, 1985). By means of posthypnotic suggestion, a therapist can also induce the patient to forget events that occurred during or before the hypnotic session, an effect called *posthypnotic amnesia.*

Finally, hypnosis has a place in medical and dental treatment, especially for managing pain during procedures in which the patient wants to avoid the risks of anesthesia (Nash, 2001). For example, the Lamaze method of natural childbirth uses a hypnosis-like procedure as a primary means of pain control. However, it is important to note that not everyone can be hypnotized deeply enough for effective analgesia (Callahan, 1997; Miller & Bowers, 1993; Orne, 1980). Still, in some cases, hypnosis alone will allow patients to undergo treatments that would otherwise cause excruciating pain (Finer, 1980). And for some highly suggestible individuals, hypnosis may actually be superior to conventional anesthesia for controlling pain.

How does hypnosis produce pain relief? Hilgard's hidden-observer explanation is one possibility, although other scientists have taken a more biological approach to the problem. Currently there is no universally accepted explanation, although we can rule out one contender. Experiments have demonstrated that endorphins, which account for the pain-relieving property of placebos, are *not* responsible for hypnotic analgesia (Grevert & Goldstein, 1985; Mayer,

CONNECTION: CHAPTER 3

Endorphins are the body's own opiate-like substances.

1979; Watkins & Mayer, 1982). Another possibility, called the *gate-control theory,* was covered in the discussion of pain, in Chapter 4. For now, we will accept hypnosis as a valuable tool about which much remains to be learned concerning the ways in which it alters consciousness.

Meditation

Many religions and traditional psychologies of the Asian and Pacific cultures use forms of **meditation** to direct consciousness away from worldly concerns and temptations. Although the purpose of meditation varies among practitioners, many use it to seek some form of spiritual enlightenment and to increase self-knowledge and well-being. Although meditators may use a variety of techniques, they commonly begin by concentrating on a repetitive behavior (such as breathing), assuming certain body positions (yogic postures), and minimizing external stimulation. (You can see the similarities with hypnosis.)

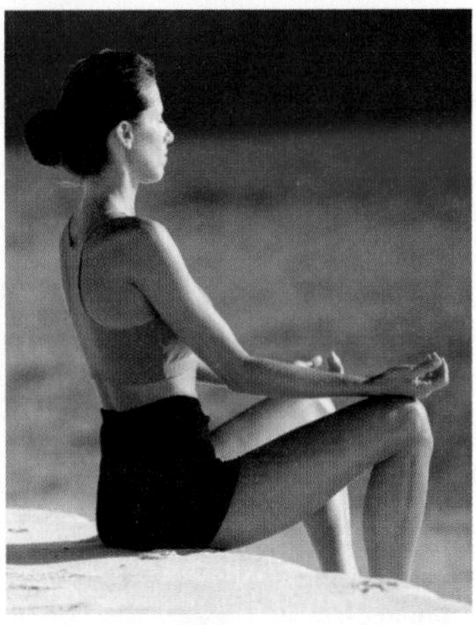

● Meditation produces relaxation and, perhaps, new insights.

To view meditation as an altered state of consciousness may reflect a particularly Western worldview, because Asian beliefs about the mind are typically different from those of Western cultures (Austin, 1998, Rosch, 1999). Buddhism, for example, teaches that the visible universe is an illusion of the senses. To become enlightened, a Buddhist tries to control bodily yearnings, to stop the ordinary experiences of the senses and mind, and to discover how to see things in their truest light. Thus, in the Buddhist view, meditation more accurately captures reality. In contrast, Western cognitive scientists often view meditation as an altered form of consciousness, and they aspire to understand it and to harness it for therapeutic purposes (Barinaga, 2003b).

What exactly are the mental and physical effects of meditation? Experienced meditators show changes in their brain-wave patterns (Kasamatsu & Hirai, 1966). Along the same lines, a recent study by Richard Davidson and his colleagues showed that meditation produces frontal lobe changes that are also associated with positive emotions (Davidson et al., 2003). Other studies have linked meditation with beneficial changes in blood pressure and stress hormones (Seeman et al., 2003). And, as still other studies have shown, meditation produces relaxation and reduces anxiety, especially in people who function in stress-filled environments (Benson, 1975; Bjork, 1991; Shapiro, 1985; van Dam, 1996). In many ways, then, meditating is like resting, because it has been found to reduce various signs of bodily arousal (Dillbeck & Orme-Johnson, 1987; Holmes, 1984; Morrell, 1986). As for some of the more subjective benefits attributed to meditation, such as its power to bring new understandings and meaning to one's life, such issues lie beyond the limits in which science can operate objectively.

Psychoactive Drug States

For millennia, humans have used alcohol, opium, cannabis, mescaline, coca, caffeine, and other drugs to alter their everyday perceptions of reality. Especially under stress, people throughout the world take drugs for pleasure, for relaxation, or just to avoid the unpleasantness of their lives. Some drugs, such as LSD, are taken by those seeking the hallucinations they produce. Other drugs (alcohol is an example) can act as "social lubricants" to help people feel comfortable with each other. Still other drugs are used by individuals seeking a euphoric "rush," a "buzz," a state of tranquility, or even stupor. What, if anything, do all these drugs have in common?

To some extent, all **psychoactive drugs** impair the brain mechanisms that usually help us make good decisions (Gazzaniga, 1998a). In addition, the most widely abused drugs—cocaine, heroin, and amphetamines—all stimulate the

■ **Meditation** A state of consciousness often induced by focusing on a repetitive behavior, assuming certain body positions, and minimizing external stimulation. Meditation may be intended to enhance self-knowledge, well-being, and spirituality.

■ **Psychoactive drugs** Chemicals that affect mental processes and behavior by their effects on the brain.

brain's "reward circuits." From an evolutionary perspective, we know that our brains are built to find pleasure in many substances (such as the taste of sweet or fatty foods) that helped our ancestors survive and reproduce. Cocaine, heroin, and amphetamines trick the brain by exploiting these same mechanisms with strong, direct, and pleasurable signals that make our bodies "think" that these substances are good for us (Nesse & Berridge, 1997).

Cultural trends influence drug-taking behavior, too. The United States saw this vividly during the 1960s and 1970s, when the country entered a period of casual experimentation with recreational drugs and other mind-altering techniques. By 1989, nearly 55% of American high school seniors had reported using one or more illegal drugs in their senior year (Johnston et al., 1989). Data from several sources, including emergency room visits, drug arrests, and surveys, indicate that overall illicit drug use has declined since the early 1990s. There has been, however, a rise in drug use among young teenagers (Martin, 1999). Credit for the overall decline in illicit drug use is often claimed by proponents of antidrug education programs, although the evidence does not show most of these programs to be especially effective (Murray, 1997).

Let us now have a closer look at the most commonly used and abused psychoactive drugs. We do so by grouping them in categories: *hallucinogens, opiates, depressants,* and *stimulants* (see Table 5.1). In general, we will find that all the drugs in each category have similar effects on the mind and brain.

Hallucinogens Drugs known as **hallucinogens** produce changes in consciousness by altering perceptions, creating hallucinations, and blurring the boundary between self and the external world. For example, an individual experiencing hallucinogenic effects might listen to music and suddenly feel that he or she is producing the music or that the music is coming from within. Most hallucinogenic drugs act in the brain at specific receptor sites for the neurotransmitter serotonin (Jacobs, 1987).

CONNECTION: CHAPTER 3

Serotonin is a neurotransmitter involved with reward, sleep, memory, and depression.

Commonly used hallucinogens include mescaline (made from a type of cactus), psilocybin (from a mushroom), LSD or "acid," and PCP (also called phencyclidine). Both LSD and PCP are synthetic drugs made in chemical laboratories. PCP, or "angel dust," was a favorite of young people who used hallucinogens until the word got around that the intensity and duration of its effects were quite unpredictable. The drug produces a strange dissociative reaction, in which the user feels disembodied or removed from parts of his or her personality. Users may become confused, grow insensitive to pain, and feel separated (dissociated) from their surroundings.

■ **Hallucinogens** Drugs that create hallucinations or alter perceptions of the external environment and inner awareness.

Cannabis, derived from the hemp plant (used, therefore, to make rope, as well as dope), also acts as a hallucinogen. Its active ingredient is THC (tetrahy-

● When psychologists talk about drugs, they include legal substances such as tobacco and caffeine, two extremely popular stimulants in most cultures.

TABLE 5.1	Psychoactive Drugs: Medical Uses, Effects, Likelihoods of Dependence		
		Dependence	
Category	Medical Uses	Psychological	Physical
Opiates			
Morphine	Painkiller, cough suppressant	High	High
Heroin	Under investigation	High	High
Codeine	Painkiller, cough suppressant	Moderate	Moderate
Methadone	Treatment of heroin addiction	Low	High
Hallucinogens			
Mescaline	None	None	Unknown
Psilocybin	None	Unknown	Unknown
LSD	None	None	None
PCP	Veterinary anesthetic	Unknown	High
Cannabis	Reduces nausea from chemotherapy	Low	Low
Depressants			
Barbiturates	Sedative, sleep, anticonvulsant, anesthetic	Moderate–high	Moderate–high
Benzodiazepines	Antianxiety, sleep, anticonvulsant, sedative	Low–moderate	Low–moderate
Alcohol	Antiseptic	Moderate	Moderate
Rohypnol	None in U.S. (elsewhere for sedation, anesthesia, and treatment of insomnia)	Low–moderate	Low–moderate
Stimulants			
Amphetamines	Weight control, counteract anesthesia	High	High
Methamphetamine	ADHD, weight control (rarely)	High	High
MDMA (ecstasy)	None (originally developed as an appetite suppressant)	Moderate	Moderate
Cocaine	Local anesthetic	High	High
Nicotine	Gum, patch for cessation of smoking	Low–high	Low–high
Caffeine	Weight control, stimulant in acute respiratory failure, analgesia	Low	Low

drocannabinol), found both in the plant's dried leaves and flowers (marijuana) and in its solidified resin (hashish). Most commonly it is smoked, although it can also be eaten.

The experience obtained from ingesting THC depends on its dose. Small doses may create mild, pleasurable highs, and larger doses can cause long hallucinogenic reactions. Unlike alcohol, its effects can last for many hours—and long after users feel themselves to be impaired (Julien, 2001). The pleasant effects include altered perception, sedation, pain relief, mild euphoria, and distortions of space and time—similar in some respects to the effects of heroin (Wickelgren, 1997). Alternatively, depending on the social context, and expectations, the effects can be an unpleasant mixture of fear, anxiety, and confusion. Cannabis also produces temporary failures in memory, as well as impairments in motor coordination (Julien, 2001). Those who work or drive under its influence suffer a higher risk of accidents (Moskowitz, 1985)—and those who study under its influence are likely to remember nothing.

Some habitual cannabis users become psychologically addicted to its pleasurable effects and may crave the drug so often that it interferes with other pursuits, including school or work. Nevertheless, the potential for physical dependence on this drug is lower than most other psychoactive substances (Grinspoon et al., 1997; Pinel, 2003).

What causes the mind-altering effects of this drug? In the brain, THC causes the release of dopamine, which suggests an effect on the brain's reward system (Carlson, 2004). Neuroscientists have also discovered cannabis receptors in the brain (Wilson & Nicoll, 2002). This suggests that the brain makes its own THC-like chemicals, which it uses to modulate information flow. So, marijuana and hashish produce their mind-altering effects by exploiting the natural chemistry of the brain. It is no wonder, then, that they can interfere with cognition, because these receptors are particularly abundant in pathways involving learning, thinking, and memory.

Opiates Another class of drugs, known as **opiates,** includes morphine, heroin, and codeine—all made from the opium poppy. These are highly addictive drugs that suppress physical sensation and response to stimulation, including painful stimulation. From a medical standpoint, morphine and codeine have particularly good analgesic (pain-relieving) properties that result from their similarity to the body's own pain-relieving chemicals, the endorphins.

Derived from morphine, heroin originally was developed in 19th-century Germany by the Bayer Company (of aspirin fame), but it was abandoned because it is even more highly addictive than morphine. For the intravenous heroin user, however, the drug is attractive because it gives a strong rush of pleasurable sensations. These feelings of euphoria supplant all worries and awareness of bodily needs, although—surprisingly—there are no major changes in cognitive abilities. Under the influence of these drugs, the user is usually able to converse normally and to think clearly. Unfortunately, serious addiction is likely once a person begins to inject heroin. To avoid heightened sensitivity to pain and the intense cravings of withdrawal, the addict must take the drug frequently—at least daily—making it a very expensive habit to maintain. Because addicts often steal to support their habit, the use of heroin underlies much of the property crime in cities around the world.

Methadone, a synthetic opiate, can be taken orally and therefore doesn't require injection. It has essentially the same euphoric, analgesic, and addictive effects as heroin, but when taken orally, methadone doesn't produce the same "rush" because the drug level in the brain increases slowly. This feature makes methadone useful as a substitute for heroin in drug treatment programs, in which the patient is switched to methadone and then gradually weaned from opiates altogether.

Paradoxically, patients who take opiates for pain control under medical supervision rarely become highly addicted. The reason for the difference in effects between the use of opiates for pleasure and for pain is unclear. It appears, however, that the presence of pain causes opiates to affect parts of the brain other than the "reward centers" involved in pleasure. The practical point is this: There is little to fear from the legitimate medical use of these drugs for controlling pain (Melzack, 1990).

Depressants Drugs that slow the mental and physical activity of the body by inhibiting activity in the central nervous system are collectively known as **depressants.** (Depressants don't necessarily make people feel clinically depressed, in the sense of "sad.") They include barbiturates (usually prescribed for sedation), benzodiazepines (antianxiety drugs), and alcohol (a social stimulant and nervous system depressant). By inhibiting the transmission of messages in the central nervous system, depressants tend to slow down the mental and physical activity of the body. In appropriate dosages, depressants can

■ **Opiates** Highly addictive drugs, derived from opium, that can produce a profound sense of well-being and have strong pain-relieving properties.

■ **Depressants** Drugs that slow down mental and physical activity by inhibiting transmission of nerve impulses in the central nervous system.

relieve symptoms of pain or anxiety, but overuse or abuse of depressants is dangerous because these drugs impair reflexes and judgment. They may also be addictive.

Barbiturates, commonly used in "sleeping pills," can induce sleep. Unfortunately, they have the side effect of reducing REM-sleep time. This leaves the user feeling unrested, despite a full night's sleep. In addition, withdrawal from barbiturates causes severe REM rebound, filling sleep with unpleasant dreams. Worse yet, overdoses of barbiturates may cause loss of consciousness, sometimes to the point of coma and even death. Fatal reactions to barbiturates are made all the more likely because the lethal dose is relatively close to the dose required for inducing sleep or other desired effects. The chance of accidental overdose can be compounded by alcohol or other depressant drugs, which magnify the depressant action of barbiturates (Maisto et al., 1995).

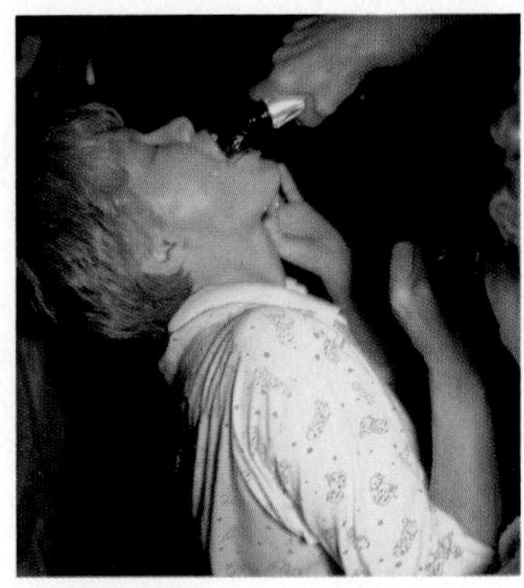

● Physical dependence, tolerance, and addiction to alcohol often begin with binge drinking, common on many college campuses.

The benzodiazepines (pronounced *BEN-zo-dye-AZ-a-peens*), commonly prescribed to treat anxiety, are safer than barbiturates. Physicians frequently prescribe them to calm patients without causing sleepiness or sedation. For this reason, they are often referred to as "minor tranquilizers"—the best known and most widely prescribed of which include Valium and Xanax. (The tranquilizing drugs used to treat psychotic disorders work differently and are not classified as depressants.)

CONNECTION: CHAPTER 13

Benzodiazepines are used to treat anxiety-related problems, such as panic disorder and obsessive–compulsive disorder.

While the benzodiazepines are relatively safe, compared to barbiturates, they can also be overused and abused. Addiction occurs and is of special concern because these drugs are so commonly prescribed. Overdoses produce poor muscle coordination, slurred speech, weakness, and irritability, while withdrawal symptoms include increased anxiety, muscle twitching, and sensitivity to sound and light. Significantly, the benzodiazepines are almost never taken by recreational drug users because people who are not suffering from anxiety usually do not like their effects (Wesson et al., 1992).

Alcohol, another drug that acts as a brain depressant, was one of the first psychoactive substances used by humankind. Under its influence, people have a variety of reactions that involve loosening of inhibitions. At first, this may seem like a contradiction: How can a depressant make people less inhibited? What actually happens is that the alcohol depresses activity in the brain circuits that normally control self-monitoring of our thoughts and behavior. The result depends on the context and the personality of the imbiber, who may become more talkative or quiet, friendly or abusive, ebullient—or, sometimes, psychologically depressed. Alcohol's effects also depend on whether other drugs, such as MDMA ("ecstasy") or rohypnol (the "date-rape drug"), are being used simultaneously. Such drugs are believed by users to enhance social interaction and empathy, although their effects can easily spin out of control, especially in combination with alcohol (Gahlinger, 2004).

Physically, alcohol in very small doses can induce relaxation and even slightly improve an adult's reaction time. In slightly larger amounts, it can impair coordination and mental processing—sometimes even when drinkers believe their performance has been improved. Moreover, it is quite easy for alcohol to accumulate in the system because the body may not metabolize it as fast as it is ingested. In general, the body breaks down alcohol at the rate of only one ounce per hour, and greater amounts consumed in short periods stay in the body and depress activity in the central nervous system. When the level of alcohol in the blood reaches a mere 0.1% (1/1000 of the blood), an individual experiences deficits in thinking, memory, and judgment, along with emotional instability and coordination problems. In most parts of the United States, this level of blood alcohol automatically qualifies a driver as being legally drunk.

Distillers, brewers, and wine makers spend millions of dollars annually depicting the social and personal benefits of alcoholic beverages. And, to be sure, many adults use alcohol prudently. Nevertheless, an estimated 5 to 10% of American adults who use alcohol drink to the extent that it harms their health, career, or family and social relationships (Julien, 2001). Physical dependence, tolerance, and addiction all develop with prolonged heavy drinking—of the sort that often begins with binge drinking, common on college campuses. When the amount and frequency of drinking alcohol interfere with job or school performance, impair social and family relationships, and create serious health problems, the diagnosis of alcoholism is appropriate (see Julien, 2001; Vallee, 1998).

Abuse of alcohol has become a significant problem for about 15 million Americans (Pinel, 2003). The effects of the problem are much more widespread, however. When ingested by pregnant women, alcohol can affect the fetus. In fact, alcohol use by expectant mothers is a leading cause of mental retardation (Committee on Substance Abuse, 2000). Estimates suggest that 40% of Americans see the effects of alcohol abuse in a family member (Vallee, 1998). For many Americans aged 15 to 25, the problem becomes a lethal one: Alcohol-related automobile accidents are the leading cause of death in this age group.

Stimulants In contrast with depressants, **stimulants** speed up central nervous system activity. The result is a boost in both mental and physical activity level. Surprisingly, stimulants can also increase concentration and reduce the hyperactive behavior seen in attention-deficit/hyperactivity disorder (ADHD). With narcoleptic patients, they also have a use in preventing sleep attacks.

CONNECTION: CHAPTER 13

ADHD is a relatively common disorder of attention span and behavior, usually diagnosed in children but sometimes found in adults.

Recreational users of certain stimulants seek still other effects: intense pleasurable sensations, increased self-confidence, greater energy and alertness, and euphoria. Cocaine, in particular, packs what may be the most powerfully rewarding punch of any illegal drug (Landry, 1997). Crack, an especially addictive form of cocaine, produces a swift, pleasurable high that wears off quickly. Amphetamine (often called "speed") and related drugs have effects comparable to cocaine. Among these, a particularly powerful variant known as methamphetamine came into widespread use during the 1990s. Still another stimulant known as MDMA (often called "ecstasy") has grown popular in the "rave" culture, where it has a reputation for creating a feeling of euphoria and for energizing young users to dance for hours, sometimes leading to dehydration, convulsions, and other unpleasant consequences (Gahlinger, 2004; Yacoubian et al., 2004). Ecstasy is also known to impair memory (Verbaten, 2003).

Stimulants Drugs that arouse the central nervous system, speeding up mental and physical responses.

Stimulant drugs hold other dangers, as well. Heavy amphetamine and cocaine users may experience frightening hallucinations and paranoid delu-

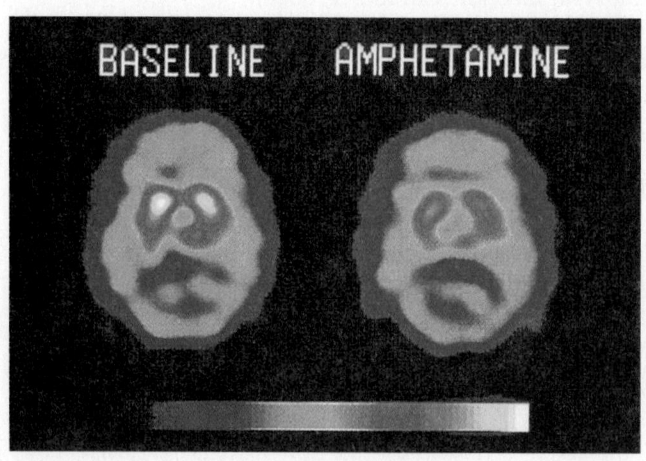
BASELINE
AMPHETAMINE

Brain changes during use of drugs can be seen on PET-scan images. Much less activity is seen in the limbic system of the brain under the influence of amphetamines.

sions—symptoms also associated with severe mental disorder. And these drugs can send users on an emotional roller coaster of euphoric highs and depressive lows. This leads users to increase the frequency and dosage, quickly making the abuse of these drugs spiral out of control. Yet another danger accrues to "secondhand" users: children who were exposed to cocaine in their mother's blood while in the womb. Studies show that such children are at increased risk for developing cognitive problems, emotional difficulties, and behavior-control disorders (Vogel, 1997b).

Two other stimulants that you may not even think of as psychoactive drugs are caffeine and nicotine—yet their effects on the brain are swift and powerful. Within 10 minutes, two cups of strong coffee or tea deliver enough caffeine to have a measurable effect on the heart, blood circulation, and signaling in the brain. Nicotine inhaled in tobacco smoke can have similar effects within just seconds. Both drugs are addictive, and both augment the effects of the natural rewarding chemicals released by the brain. In this way, nicotine and caffeine tease the brain's reward pathways into responding as if using these substances were associated with something beneficial for us. Fortunately, in the case of caffeine, the negative effects are minor for most people. Further, caffeine has a built-in "braking" action that limits its intake because high dosages also produce uncomfortable anxiety-like feelings.

In contrast to caffeine, nicotine is a much more dangerous drug for two reasons: Nicotine is highly addictive, and it has been associated with a variety of health problems, including cancer, emphysema, and heart disease. In fact, the negative impact of smoking on health is greater than that of all other psychoactive drugs combined—including heroin, cocaine, and alcohol. According to the U.S. Public Health Service, smoking is the leading cause of preventable disease, with a human cost of more than 350,000 deaths annually. As a result, the American Medical Association has formally recommended that the U.S. Food and Drug Administration regard nicotine as a drug to be regulated. Currently, however, nicotine is both legal and actively promoted—with a $2.7 billion budget from the tobacco industry. Although antismoking campaigns have been somewhat effective in reducing the overall level of smoking in the United States, some 47 million Americans still smoke. Most worrisome is the fact that more than 3 million teenagers smoke, and their numbers are increasing by about 3000 who start every day (Gardyn & Wellner, 2001; Julien, 2001).

PSYCHOLOGY IN YOUR LIFE: DEPENDENCE AND ADDICTION

We have seen that psychoactive drugs can alter the functioning of neurons in your brain and, as a consequence, temporarily change your consciousness. Once in your brain, they usually act on synapses to block or stimulate neural messages. In this way, drugs profoundly alter the brain's communication system, affecting perception, memory, mood, and behavior.

CONNECTION: CHAPTER 3

Most psychoactive drugs mimic neurotransmitters or enhance or dampen their effects at the synapses.

Significantly, a given dose of many psychoactive drugs comes to have a weaker consciousness-altering effect with continued use. As a result, the user needs larger and larger dosages to achieve the same effect. This reduced effectiveness with repeated use of a drug is called **tolerance.** Hand-in-hand with tolerance goes **physical dependence**—a process in which the body adjusts to and comes to need the substance, in part because the production of neurotransmitters in the brain is affected by the frequent presence of the drug (Wickelgren, 1998c). A person with a physical dependence requires the drug in his or her body and may suffer unpleasant withdrawal symptoms if the drug is not present. Further, a person who develops tolerance to a highly

■ **Tolerance** The reduced effectiveness a drug has after repeated use.

■ **Physical dependence** A process by which the body adjusts to, and comes to need, a drug for its everyday functioning.

● The line between substance use and abuse is easy to cross for those who become addicted.

addicting drug such as heroin becomes less sensitive to all sorts of natural reinforcers, including the pleasures of friendship, food, and everyday entertainment: The drug, in increasing dosages, becomes the only thing capable of providing pleasure (Helmuth, 2001a). **Addiction** is said to occur when the person continues to use a drug in the face of adverse effects on his or her health or life—often despite repeated attempts to stop.

Withdrawal involves uncomfortable physical and mental symptoms that occur when drug use is discontinued. It can include physical trembling, perspiring, nausea, increased sensitivity to pain, and, in the case of extreme alcohol withdrawal, even death. Although heroin and alcohol are the drugs that most commonly come to mind when we think of withdrawal symptoms, nicotine and caffeine, as well as certain sleeping pills and "tranquilizing" drugs, can also cause unpleasant withdrawal symptoms.

Individuals may find themselves craving or hungering for the drug and its effects, even though they are not physically dependent—a condition known as **psychological dependence** or psychological addiction. This usually results from the powerfully rewarding effects that many psychoactive drugs produce. Psychological dependence can occur with many drugs, including caffeine and nicotine, prescription medications, and over-the-counter drugs.

Addiction, whether biological or psychological, ultimately affects the brain (Gazzaniga, 1998a; Koob & Le Moal, 1997; Nestler, 2001). Consequently, in the view of many public health professionals, this makes both forms of addiction brain diseases (Leshner, 1997). On the other hand, the general public has been reluctant to view drug addicts as people who have an illness. Instead, the public often thinks of addicts as weak or bad individuals who should be punished (MacCoun, 1998).

What difference does our characterization of addiction make? When addicts are seen as persons suffering from a disease, they are most logically placed in treatment programs. By contrast, when they are seen as persons with character defects, addicts are sent to prison for punishment—which does little to break the cycle of drug use, crime, and addiction.

Strange as it may seem, some experts argue that viewing addiction as a disease may also interfere with the effective treatment of drug addicts. How could this be? The disease model of addiction, with its emphasis on biological causes and medical treatment, does little to deal with the social and economic context in which addictions develop. This may account for the fact that psychologically based treatment programs that treat alcohol abuse as a behavioral problem may work better than medically based programs (Miller & Brown, 1997).

We can also see the blind spots of the disease model in heroin addiction. Treatment programs have a notoriously poor record with heroin addicts who have picked up their habits on the streets of the United States. On the other hand, they had far greater success with the thousands of veterans who became addicted to the heroin that was readily available to troops in Vietnam. What made the difference? The addicted veterans did not remain in the environment where they had become addicted—which was the wartime culture of Vietnam. Instead, they returned home to an environment that was not usually so supportive of a heroin habit. In contrast, heroin users who become addicted in the United States tend to return, after treatment, to the same environment that originally led to their addiction.

Whether physical or psychological, disease or character flaw, drug addiction poses many personal and social problems. Clearly, this is a field that has much room for new ideas and new research.

■ **Addiction** A condition in which a person continues to use a drug despite its adverse effects–often despite repeated attempts to discontinue using the drug. Addiction may be based on physical or psychological dependence.

■ **Withdrawal** A pattern of uncomfortable or painful physical symptoms and cravings experienced by the user when the level of drug is decreased or the drug is eliminated.

■ **Psychological dependence** A desire to obtain or use a drug, even though there is no physical dependence.

CHECK YOUR UNDERSTANDING

1. **RECALL:** Hypnosis is sometimes used by psychological researchers to
   a. cure patients suffering from severe mental disorders.
   b. improve memory.
   c. create mental states, such as anxiety or euphoria.
   d. study the effects of psychoactive drugs.
   e. induce amnesia for traumatic experiences.

2. **RECALL:** Psychoactive drugs usually create their effects by ______ in the brain.
   a. causing delayed stress reactions
   b. stimulating reward circuits
   c. rewiring neural pathways
   d. disabling dendrites
   e. altering memories

3. **RECALL:** Which of the following statements is true?
   a. Research has proven conclusively that addiction is a brain disease.
   b. The reinforcing nature of drugs ensures low addiction rates.
   c. Some psychologists suggest that treating addiction as a disease ignores the social and economic factors that surround the problem.
   d. The cycle of addiction is most efficiently broken with a combination of punishment for relapses and drugs that counteract the effects of psychoactive drugs.
   e. Most public health professionals view addiction as a character weakness.

4. **APPLICATION:** Which of the following groups of drugs have the opposite effects on the brain?
   a. stimulants and depressants
   b. depressants and opiates
   c. hallucinogens and sedatives
   d. opiates and sedatives
   e. hallucinogens and stimulants

5. **UNDERSTANDING THE CORE CONCEPT:** An altered state of consciousness occurs when some aspect of normal consciousness is modified either by mental, behavioral, or chemical means. This suggests that
   a. some states of consciousness are mystical phenomena that cannot ever be explained.
   b. altered states of consciousness are the primary source of creativity in our minds.
   c. consciousness is immutable.
   d. all states of consciousness are controlled by unconscious needs, desires, and memories.
   e. psychologists can study altered states of consciousness with scientific methods.

ANSWERS: 1.c 2.b 3.c 4.a 5.e

CONSCIOUSNESS: THE STATE OF THE ART

We have seen that, aside from our familiar state of wakefulness, consciousness can occur in many forms. More surprising, perhaps, is the discovery that mental processing can also occur outside of consciousness. We have also seen that neuroscientists have developed techniques with which they can study these once private and subjective worlds that occur both in consciousness and in the preconscious and unconscious. Among their achievements with these techniques, scientists have flung open the gates of the sleeping and dreaming mind. They have also learned much about the workings of the mind under the influence of hypnosis, meditation, and drugs.

What remains to be learned? Still hotly debated and poorly understood is the function of dreams: Do they mean anything, or are they merely a by-product of an always-active brain cut off from the outside world? Also remaining to be discovered are better treatments for certain sleep disorders, such as narcolepsy and insomnia, as well as more effective treatments for addictions.

But the biggest and most elusive prize of all is a full understanding of consciousness itself. How can the activity of neurons "lighting up" in our brains produce the ongoing movie-of-the-mind that we call consciousness? At this point, no one really knows.

USING PSYCHOLOGY TO LEARN PSYCHOLOGY

Connecting Consciousness with Memory

Expand your consciousness? In the strictest sense, it is not really possible, because consciousness has a limited capacity. As we noted at the beginning of the chapter, consciousness can focus on only one thing at a time. What can be expanded, however, is the access your consciousness has to information you have stored in preconscious memory. Learning how to do this can be of tremendous help to students who need to absorb a large amount of information and to prove it on an exam.

You will, of course, have an advantage if you face an exam with your consciousness unimpaired by the massive sleep debt that students sometimes incur in an "all-nighter" study session. No amount of caffeine can bring your sleep-deprived consciousness back to optimum functioning. Just as your teachers have always preached, it is far better to spread your studying over several days or weeks, rather than trying to learn everything at once and losing sleep over it.

It can also help when we reach Chapter 7 to understand that consciousness is fundamentally the same as working memory, a mental "work space" that holds only a few items at once. Because of its severely limited capacity, you cannot possibly hold in consciousness all the information you need to remember for an exam. Most of the material must be stored outside of consciousness in preconscious long-term memory. The trick is to be able to bring it back into consciousness when needed. Here are some strategies that you may find helpful in doing this:

1. *Study for the gist.* Students sometimes think their professors ask "trick questions," although professors almost never do so intentionally. In reality, a good exam question will show whether students understand the meaning of a term—the gist—rather than having merely memorized a definition. A twofold study strategy can help you get the gist of a concept. First, paraphrase the definition given in the text or in class. Second, think of an example from your own experience that illustrates the concept.
2. *Look for connections among concepts.* Even if you have the gist of the concepts you have studied, you will probably need to know how those concepts are related to each other. The professor may ask you to explain, for example, what happens to the *sleep cycle* in people with *narcolepsy*. Therefore a good study strategy is to ask yourself, "How is this new concept related to what I learned previously?"
3. *Anticipate the most likely cues.* Just because you know the material doesn't mean that the exam questions will make the right answer spill from long-term memory back into consciousness. It pays, therefore, to spend some of your study time thinking about the kinds of questions your professor might ask. For example, you may have learned about the effects of various psychoactive drugs, but you could be stumped when the professor asks you to explain why alcohol is more like the barbiturates than the opiates. (Do you know?) You can often anticipate such questions by noting what the professor emphasizes in lecture. It also helps to think of the kinds of questions that your professor is known to favor. (A study partner helps a lot with this.) Some of the most frequently seen test questions begin with terms such as "Explain," "Evaluate," or "Compare and contrast."

In general, the relationship between consciousness and memory suggests that learning the kind of material required in your college classes requires that the material be actively processed while it is in consciousness. To do so effectively, it must be made meaningful. This requires making connections between new information and information that is already in your memory. It also requires organizing the information so that you see how it is interconnected. And, finally, it requires anticipating the cues that will be used to bring it back to consciousness.

CONNECTION: CHAPTER 7

Working memory (also called short-term memory) is a main component of consciousness, but it holds only a small number of items at any time.

CHAPTER SUMMARY

KEY QUESTION

CORE CONCEPT

• HOW IS CONSCIOUSNESS RELATED TO OTHER MENTAL PROCESSES?

Consciousness represents one of the major mysteries of psychology. Cognitive scientists agree that consciousness involves restricted attention. It also involves the mental model we create of our internal and external world. Consciousness employs mental processes that not only integrate all the mental activity in our awareness but also enable us to manipulate their contents. Moreover, consciousness exists in various states, including the normal waking state, states of sleep and dreaming, hypnosis, meditation, and drug states. Aspects of consciousness can be studied with the techniques of cognitive psychology.

In addition to consciousness, the mind has many nonconscious modes that can operate outside awareness. These include the preconscious and various levels of unconscious processing. Consciousness is limited to serial processing, but the mind can process information nonconsciously in parallel channels. New technologies and techniques have opened windows on conscious processes for researchers. Increasingly, cognitive scientists are disputing the Freudian concept of an unconscious that works in opposition to the conscious mind.

● **Consciousness can take many forms, while other mental processes occur simultaneously outside our awareness.**

• WHAT CYCLES OCCUR IN EVERYDAY CONSCIOUSNESS?

Consciousness shifts and changes in everyday life, commonly taking the form of daydreaming, sleep, and nocturnal dreams. Although the function of sleep is not altogether clear, everyone agrees that sleep and wakefulness are part of the circadian cycle. Sleep researchers have revealed the features of the normal sleep cycle, including the four stages of sleep, which undergo 90-minute cycles, including both REM and non-REM periods. Over the course of the night, each ensuing sleep cycle involves less deep sleep and more REM sleep. The sleep cycle also changes dramatically with age. Most adults need at least eight hours of sleep every night.

The function of dreams is also unclear, but they often occur in REM sleep. While Freud's dream theory has been influential, it has no empirical support. Dreams have, however, always been a source of inspiration and creativity for humankind.

Aberrations in the sleep cycle can produce various sleep disorders. Narcolepsy is a disorder of REM sleep, insomnia involves shortened sleep, and sleep apnea involves abnormalities in deep sleep. Other disorders of a less serious nature include night terrors, sleep talking, and sleepwalking.

● **Consciousness changes in cycles that correspond to our biological rhythms and to the patterns of stimulation in our environment.**

• WHAT OTHER FORMS CAN CONSCIOUSNESS TAKE?

Altered states of consciousness include hypnosis, meditation, and the effects of psychoactive drugs. From a cognitive-neuroscience perspective, these may involve changes in psychological processes rather than entirely new forms of awareness. Hypnosis remains a puzzle, although it is known to block pain and to have other uses in therapy and research. Likewise, experts dispute whether meditation is a distinct state of consciousness, even though it has measurable effects on arousal. To understand the effects of psychoactive drugs, it is helpful to group them as hallucinogens, opiates, depressants, and stimulants. Most psychoactive drugs that are abused produce sensations of pleasure and well-being that make the drugs especially attractive and potentially addictive.

● **An altered state of consciousness occurs when some aspect of normal consciousness is modified by mental, behavioral, or chemical means.**

REVIEW TEST

For each of the following items, choose the single correct or best answer. The correct answers appear at the end of the test.

1. What was the objection by Watson and other behaviorists to the study of consciousness?
   a. Consciousness is the result of an inner life force, which they did not have the tools to study.
   b. Consciousness is an essential component of learning.
   c. Consciousness could not be accessed by introspection.
   d. Consciousness is not affected by rewards and punishments.
   e. Conscious processes cannot be directly observed and measured.

2. Imaging techniques, such as MRI and PET scans, allow cognitive scientists to connect mental activity with
   a. cognition.
   b. behavior.
   c. learning.
   d. brain activity.
   e. priming.

3. Which of the following is *not* one of the functions of consciousness cited by your text?
   a. manipulating a mental image of the world
   b. relinquishing control to enhance self-awareness
   c. combining sensation with memory
   d. selecting pertinent information for further processing
   e. restricting attention to what is relevant

4. Which one of the following did Freud believe to be a function of the unconscious mind?
   a. regulation of sleep, wakefulness, blood pressure, heart rate, body temperature, and habit patterns
   b. the construction of grammatically correct sentences, without having to think consciously about the grammatical rules
   c. logical thinking
   d. the unconscious mind serves no purpose
   e. protecting consciousness from sexual desires and traumatic experiences
5. Rapid eye movements are reliable behavioral signs that
   a. a person is very low in hypnotizability.
   b. a sleeper is dreaming.
   c. one has achieved a genuine meditative state.
   d. an individual has reached the deepest level of sleep.
   e. an individual is under the influence of alcohol or other drugs.
6. Which one of the following is a sleep disorder characterized by brief interruptions when the sleeper stops breathing, wakens, resumes breathing, and falls back asleep?
   a. analgesia
   b. night terrors
   c. apnea
   d. daytime sleepiness
   e. insomnia
7. Which of the following statements about hypnosis is true?
   a. Anyone can be hypnotized if the hypnotist knows the most effective techniques to use.
   b. Hypnosis has no medical value.
   c. Hypnotizability relies on a person's ability to respond to suggestion.
   d. Hypnosis is actually a form of NREM sleep.
   e. The less intelligent or educated a person is, the more hypnotizable he or she will be.
8. Psychology has verified that meditation can be useful for producing
   a. heightened cognitive arousal.
   b. a deeper understanding of oneself.
   c. enlightenment.
   d. increased metabolic rates.
   e. a state of relaxation.
9. Which of the following drugs would be most likely to produce hallucinations (sensory experiences with no basis in reality)?
   a. benzodiazepines
   b. mescaline
   c. amphetamines
   d. alcohol
   e. nicotine
10. Three major effects sought by users of ______ are increased alertness, greater self-confidence, and euphoria.
   a. barbiturates
   b. stimulants
   c. depressants
   d. opiates
   e. hallucinogens

ANSWERS: 1. e 2. d 3. b 4. e 5. b 6. c 7. c 8. e 9. b 10. b

KEY TERMS

Consciousness (p. 158)
Cognitive neuroscience (p. 159)
Nonconscious processes (p. 160)
Preconscious memories (p. 164)
Unconscious (p. 164)
Daydreaming (p. 166)
Circadian rhythms (p. 167)
REM sleep (p. 168)
Non-REM (NREM) sleep (p. 168)
Sleep paralysis (p. 168)
REM rebound (p. 169)
Sleep debt (p. 171)
Manifest content (p. 173)
Latent content (p. 173)
Activation-synthesis theory (p. 174)
Insomnia (p. 175)
Sleep apnea (p. 176)
Night terrors (p. 176)
Narcolepsy (p. 176)
Cataplexy (p. 177)
Hypnosis (p. 179)
Meditation (p. 181)
Psychoactive drugs (p. 181)
Hallucinogens (p. 182)
Opiates (p. 184)
Depressants (p. 184)
Stimulants (p. 186)
Tolerance (p. 187)
Physical dependence (p. 187)
Addiction (p. 188)
Withdrawal (p. 188)
Psychological dependence (p. 188)

AP* REVIEW: VOCABULARY

Match each of the following vocabulary terms to its definition.

1. Consciousness
2. Nonconscious processes
3. Circadian rhythms
4. REM rebound
5. Manifest content
6. Latent content
7. Sleep apnea
8. Cataplexy
9. Tolerance
10. Withdrawal

_____ a. A condition of increased REM sleep caused by REM-sleep deprivation.

_____ b. The story line of a dream without interpretation.

_____ c. The process by which the brain creates a model of internal and external experience.

_____ d. The reduced effectiveness a drug has after repeated use.

_____ e. Sudden loss of muscle control.

_____ f. A respiratory disorder in which the person stops breathing many times while asleep.

_____ g. The symbolic meaning of objects and events in a dream.

_____ h. A physiological pattern that repeats approximately every 24 hours.

_____ i. A pattern of painful physical symptoms experienced by the user when the level of drug is decreased or eliminated.

_____ j. Any brain process that does not involve conscious processing.

KEY 1.c 2.j 3.h 4.a 5.b 6.g 7.f 8.e 9.d 10.i

AP* REVIEW: ESSAY

Use your knowledge of the chapter concepts to answer the following essay question.

Over time, contrasting theories of dreaming have evolved. Compare and contrast these theories, being sure that your response uses appropriate psychological terminology.

Identify the following theories: activation-synthesis hypothesis, Crick–Mitchison view, and memory consolidation. Compare and contrast them using the following:

1. Main concepts
2. Arguments for
3. Arguments against

OUR RECOMMENDED BOOKS AND VIDEOS

ARTICLE

Nash, M. R. (2001, July). The truth and hype of hypnosis. *Scientific American, 285,* 46–49, 52–55. Everyone has images of hypnosis: the shiny watch, the command to become "verrry sleepy . . ." Advances in cognitive science have left the fascination and much of the mystery intact, while answering questions about how hypnosis works in alleviating pain, retrieving memories, and other applications.

BOOKS

Coren, S. (1996). *Sleep thieves: An eye-opening exploration into the science and mysteries of sleep.* Free Press Paperbacks. Coren gives us the "A to ZZZZs of sleep," including whether dogs and cats dream, determining whether you are getting enough sleep, how to help children sleep better, and the dangers of Daylight Savings Time.

Hobson, A. (2002). *Dreaming: An introduction to the science of sleep.* New York: Oxford University Press. Have you wakened from realistic dreams, confused about what is real? Hobson identifies the qualities that distinguish one's dreaming from waking life and links these to specific brain processes.

Jaynes, J. (2001). *The origin of consciousness in the breakdown of the bicameral mind.* New York: Mariner Books/Houghton Mifflin. Reissued since its original publication in 1976, this continually popular and intriguing work examines how consciousness may have originally evolved when the brain's two hemispheres, connected but separate, "heard" each other—and were experienced by early humans as the voices of spirits, gods—and finally of the self. Don't be disheartened by the mega-title; it's highly readable and provocative.

Peacock, R., & Gorman, R. (Eds.). (1998). *Sleep: Bedtime reading.* Universe Publishing. Wide awake and trying not to worry about it? Try some bedtime reading by the best authors. Includes short works by authors ranging from Alice Walker to John Updike, along with poetry, pictures, and photographs—all designed to take your mind off what's keeping you awake so you can get some rest.

Samorini, M., Calliope, T., & Montgomery, R. (2002). *Animals and psychedelics: The natural world and the instinct to alter consciousness.* New York: Park Street Press. How natural is it for people to deliberately alter consciousness by ingesting psychoactive substances? From observations of our nonhuman relatives, pretty natural! Like humans, wild animals and insects seek out substances (e.g., caffeine, nectar) that alter perception, possibly expanding their behavioral responses—thus increasing adaptation and survival. How and why do substances stop expanding and begin impairing the mind?

VIDEOS

Mesmer. (1994, color, 107 min.). Directed by Roger Spottiswoode; starring Alan Rickman, Amanda Ooms. In 18th-century Vienna and Paris, Franz Anton Mesmer discovers the power of "animal magnetism" to heal the sick. Derided as a charlatan, his methods dubbed "mesmerism," Mesmer brings clinical hypnosis to Paris, where it becomes an entertainment for the bored aristocracy (in the doomed reign of Marie Antoinette). Mesmer's true story is interesting, here romanticized with subplots and piqued with terrific dialogue. (*Not rated*)

Key Question Chapter Outline

CORE CONCEPTS

Psychology in Your Life

What Sort of Learning Does Classical Conditioning Explain?

The Essentials of Classical Conditioning
Applications of Classical Conditioning

▼ Classical conditioning is a basic form of learning in which a stimulus that produces an innate reflex becomes associated with a previously neutral stimulus, which then acquires the power to elicit essentially the same response.

Taste Aversions and Chemotherapy

Your friend risks developing a food aversion when the medicine makes her feel sick.

How Do We Learn New Behaviors by Operant Conditioning?

Skinner's Radical Behaviorism
The Power of Reinforcement
The Problem of Punishment
Operant and Classical Conditioning Compared

▼ In operant conditioning, the consequences of behavior, such as rewards and punishments, influence the chance that the behavior will occur again.

A Checklist for Modifying Operant Behavior

For changing your own behavior or someone else's, a combination of reinforcement and extinction is usually the best bet.

How Does Cognitive Psychology Explain Learning?

Insight Learning: Köhler in the Canaries with the Chimps
Cognitive Maps: Tolman Finds Out What's on a Rat's Mind
Observational Learning: Bandura's Challenge to Behaviorism
Rethinking Behavioral Learning in Cognitive Terms
Brain Mechanisms and Learning
"Higher" Cognitive Learning

▼ According to cognitive psychology, some forms of learning must be explained as changes in mental processes, rather than as changes in behavior alone.

A Critical Look at "Learning Styles"

Many claims are made for different learning styles, but the evidence supporting them is weak.

Learning: The State of the Art

USING PSYCHOLOGY TO LEARN PSYCHOLOGY:
Operant Conditioning Can Help You Study More—and Enjoy It

Chapter

6

Learning

SABRA HAD JUST GRADUATED from college, with a degree in graphic arts, and landed a good job at an advertising firm in San Francisco. The work was interesting and challenging, and Sabra enjoyed her new colleagues. The only negative was that her supervisor had asked her to attend an upcoming conference in Hawaii—and take an extra few days of vacation there at the company's expense. The problem was Sabra's fear of flying.

She hadn't had to deal with her fear previously because there was always an alternative. All her life, Sabra had lived close enough to family members that she could easily drive to visit them. And when she went away to college, it was only a 300-mile journey, so she could drive or take the train. But there was no other way to get to Hawaii (except by boat—which would be much too slow for commuting to a business conference). What was she to do?

A friend mentioned having seen an article in the newspaper about a program initiated by one of the airlines to help people overcome their fear of flying. Fortunately, Sabra had a few weeks before the conference started, so she contacted the airline and signed up for three weekend treatment sessions to be held at a local airport.

Sabra arrived at the appointed time, full of expectations and apprehensions—most of which turned out to be wrong. Would she have to see a therapist who would probe her childhood experiences and fantasies? Would they prescribe tranquilizers? Or would they give her some sort of terror-inducing treatment, such as flying upside-down in a small airplane?

In fact, the sessions were organized by a behavioral psychologist who gathered the nine participants in a small conference room. The therapist began by saying that such fears are learned—much as you might learn to cringe when you hear a dentist's drill or the scraping of fingernails on a blackboard. She said that it was not important how such fears got started. This fear-of-flying program would focus on the present, not on the past. Sabra began to feel more relaxed.

After a brief description of the learning-based therapy to be used, the group took a tour of the airport, including the cabin of a passenger jet parked on the Tarmac. Then they went back to "class" to learn the basics of how airplanes work and the physical forces that keep them in the air. The group also watched some videos involving routine flights in a commercial airplane. All in all, this first session went smoothly, and everyone seemed much more at ease than when they started.

The second weekend began with more classroom discussion. Then, the class went back into the airliner, where they took seats and went through a series of relaxation exercises led by the therapist. This training included deep breathing and progressive relaxation of specific muscle groups all over the body. When everyone in the group reported feeling relaxed, they again watched videos of flight on the plane's TV monitors. This was followed by more relaxation exercises. The final activity for the second weekend involved starting the engines and going through the preflight routine—all the way up to takeoff . . . and more relaxation exercises.

The final weekend session was almost identical to the previous one. The only difference was that the "graduation" exercise was an actual flight—a 20-minute trip out over the local countryside and back to the airport. It was, of course, voluntary, but only one of the nine people in the class chose not to go. Sabra went, but not without some anxiety. The therapist, however, encouraged the group to focus on the relaxation exercises they had learned, rather than on their feelings of fear. To the amazement of all who participated, these learning-based techniques helped them through the flight exercise without losing control of their emotional responses. Although no one's fear had vanished completely, everyone was able to bring it under control.

The happiest result was that Sabra was able to go to her meeting in Hawaii—where, by the way, she had a productive conference and a wonderful time. For our purposes we should also note that Sabra has flown several times since then, and she reports that each trip gets just a little easier—just as the psychology of learning would predict.

A Definition of Learning The program that saved Sabra's job came out of research in *learning*—but not the sort of hit-the-books learning that usually comes to the minds of college students. Psychologists define **learning** broadly, as a process through which experience produces a lasting change in behavior or mental processes. According to this definition, then, Sabra's "flight training" was learning—just as much as taking golf lessons and reading this book are learning experiences.

To avoid confusion, two parts of our definition need some elaboration. First, we should underscore the idea that learning leads to a *lasting change* in behavior. Suppose that you go to your doctor's office and get a particularly unpleasant injection, during which the sight of the needle becomes associated with pain. As a result, the next time you need a shot, you wince when you first see the needle. This persistent change in responding involves learning. But, by the same standard, a simple, reflexive reaction, such as jumping when you hear an unexpected loud noise, does *not* qualify as learning because it produces no

■ **Learning** A lasting change in behavior or mental processes that results from experience.

lasting change—nothing more than a fleeting reaction, even though it does entail a change in behavior.

Second, we should elaborate on the part of the definition that says learning affects *behavior* or *mental processes*. In the doctor's office example above, it is easy to see how learning affects behavior. But mental processes are more difficult to observe. How could you tell, for example, whether a laboratory rat had simply learned the behaviors required to negotiate a maze (turn right, then left, then right . . .) or whether it was following some sort of mental image of the maze, much as you would follow a road map? (And why should we care what, if anything, was on a rat's mind?)

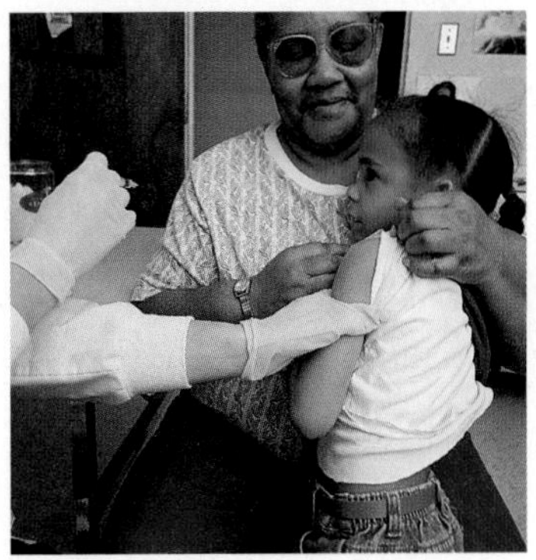

● Aversive conditioning has occurred when the mere sight of an object, such as a hypodermic needle, causes an avoidance reaction.

Behavioral Learning versus Cognitive Learning The problem of observing mental events, whether in rats or in people, underlies a long-running controversy between the behaviorists and the cognitive psychologists that threads through this chapter. For over 100 years, the behaviorists have maintained that psychology could be a true science only if it disregarded mental processes and focused exclusively on objective, observable stimuli and responses. On the other side of the issue, cognitive psychologists have contended that the behavioral view is far too limiting and that understanding learning requires that we make inferences about hidden mental processes. In the following pages, we will see that both sides in this dispute have made important contributions to our knowledge.

Learning versus Instincts So, what does learning—either behavioral or cognitive learning—do for us? Nearly every human activity, from working to playing to interacting with family and friends, involves some form of learning. Without learning, we would have no human language. We wouldn't know who our family or friends were. We would have no memory of our past or goals for our future. And without learning, we would be forced to rely on simple reflexes and a limited repertoire of innate behaviors, sometimes known as "instincts."

In contrast with learned responses, instinctive behavior (more properly known as *species-typical behavior*) is heavily influenced by genetic programming. It occurs in essentially the same way across different individuals in a species. We see instincts at work in bird migrations, animal courtship rituals, and a few human behavior patterns, such as nursing in newborns. All these examples involve responses that are influenced relatively little by experience, as compared to learned behaviors such as operating a computer, playing tennis, or wincing at the sight of a needle. In general, human behavior is much more influenced by learning and much less influenced by instincts than that of other animals. For us, learning confers the flexibility to adapt quickly to changing situations and new environments. In this sense, then, learning represents an evolutionary advance over instincts.

CONNECTION: CHAPTER 8

Instinct refers to motivated behaviors that have a strong innate basis.

Simple and Complex Forms of Learning Some forms of learning can be quite simple. For example, if you live near a busy street, you may learn to ignore the sound of the traffic. This sort of learning, known as **habituation,** involves learning *not to respond* to stimulation. It occurs in all animals that have nervous systems, including insects and worms. Another relatively simple form of learning is seen most obviously in humans: a preference for stimuli to which we have been previously exposed—whether or not the stimulus was associated with something pleasurable or even whether we were aware of the stimulus. This **mere exposure effect** probably accounts for the effectiveness of much advertising (Terry, 2000; Zajonc, 1968, 2001).

Other kinds of learning can be more complex. One involves learning a connection between two stimuli—as when a school child associates the 12 o'clock

■ **Habituation** Learning not to respond to the repeated presentation of a stimulus.

■ **Mere exposure effect** A learned preference for stimuli to which we have been previously exposed.

bell with lunch. And another occurs when we associate our actions with rewarding and punishing consequences, such as praise or a reprimand from the boss or an A or a D from a professor. The first two sections of the chapter will deal with these two types of **behavioral learning,** which we will call *classical conditioning* and *operant conditioning*.

In the third section of the chapter, the focus shifts from external behavior to internal mental processes. Our look at *cognitive learning* will consider how sudden "flashes" of insight and the imitative behavior require theories that go beyond behavioral learning—to explain how we solve puzzles or why children copy behavior they see on TV. We will also discuss the most complex type of learning, which involves the acquisition of concepts, the sort of learning you do in your college classes. Finally, the chapter will close on a practical note, by considering how to use the psychology of learning to help you study more effectively—and enjoy it. We begin, however, with a form of behavioral learning that accounts for many of your likes and dislikes—and, for one of your authors, an extreme dislike of olives.

KEY QUESTION

WHAT SORT OF LEARNING DOES CLASSICAL CONDITIONING EXPLAIN?

CONNECTION: CHAPTER 1
Structuralism and *functionalism* were two of the earliest schools of psychology.

Ivan Pavlov (1849–1936) would have been insulted if you had called him a psychologist. In fact, he had only contempt for the structuralist and functionalist psychology of his time, which he saw as being hopelessly mired in speculation about subjective mental life (Todes, 1997). Pavlov and the hundreds of student researchers who passed through Pavlov's Russian research "factory" were famous for their work on the digestive system, for which Pavlov eventually snared a Nobel prize (Fancher, 1979; Kimble, 1991).

Unexpectedly, however, the experiments on salivation (the first step in digestion) went awry, sending Pavlov and his crew on a detour into the psychology of learning—a detour that occupied Pavlov for the rest of his life. The problem was that the experimental animals began salivating even *before* food was put in their mouths (Dewsbury, 1997). In fact, saliva would start flowing when they saw the food or even when they heard the footsteps of the lab assistant bringing the food.

■ **Behavioral learning** Forms of learning, such as classical conditioning and operant conditioning, that can be described in terms of stimuli and responses.

This response was a puzzle. What, after all, was the biological function of salivating in anticipation of food? When Pavlov and his associates turned their attention to understanding these "psychic secretions," they made a series

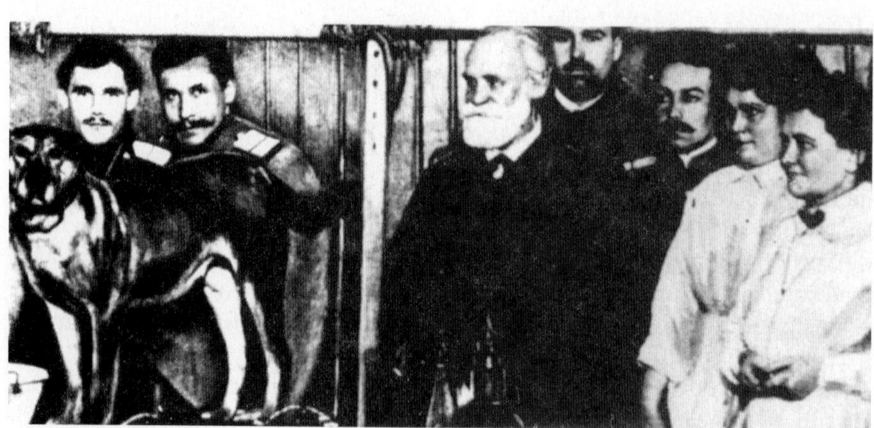

● **To study classical conditioning, Pavlov placed his dogs in a restraining apparatus. The dogs were then presented with a neutral stimulus, such as a tone. Through its association with food, the neutral stimulus became a conditioned stimulus eliciting salivation.**

of discoveries that would change the course of psychology (Pavlov, 1928; Todes, 1997). Quite by accident, they had stumbled upon an objective model of *learning*—one that could be manipulated in the laboratory to tease out the learned connections among stimuli and responses. This discovery, now known as **classical conditioning,** forms the Core Concept of this section:

CORE CONCEPT

Classical conditioning is a basic form of learning in which a stimulus that produces an innate reflex becomes associated with a previously neutral stimulus, which then acquires the power to elicit essentially the same response.

In the following pages we will see that classical conditioning accounts for some important behavior patterns found not only in animals but also in people. By means of classical conditioning, organisms learn about cues that help them avoid danger, as well as cues alerting them to food, sexual opportunity, and other conditions that promote survival. First, however, let's examine some of the fundamental features that Pavlov identified in classical conditioning.

The Essentials of Classical Conditioning

It is important to note that Pavlov's work on learning focused on simple, automatic responses known as *reflexes* (Windholz, 1997). Salivation and eye blinks are examples of such reflexes: They are normally triggered by stimuli that have biological significance. The blinking reflex, for example, protects the eyes; the salivation reflex aids digestion.

Pavlov's great discovery was that these reflexive responses could be associated with new stimuli—neutral stimuli that had previously produced no response. Thus, the connection between a reflex and a new stimulus could be *learned.* For example, Pavlov found he could teach his dogs to salivate upon hearing a certain sound, such as the tone produced by a tuning fork or a bell. You have experienced the same sort of learning if your mouth waters when you see a chocolate brownie.

To understand how these "conditioned reflexes" worked, Pavlov's team employed a simple experimental strategy. They first placed an untrained dog in a harness and set up a vial to capture the animal's saliva. Then, at intervals, a tone was sounded, after which the dog was given a bit of food. Gradually, over a number of trials, the dog began to salivate in response to the tone alone. In general, Pavlov and his students found that a **neutral stimulus** (one without any reflex-provoking power, such as a tone or a light), when paired with a natural reflex-producing stimulus (food), will by itself begin to elicit a learned response (salivation) that is similar to the original reflex. It's essentially the same conditioning process behind the association of romance with flowers or chocolate.

The main features of Pavlov's classical conditioning procedure are illustrated in Figure 6.1. At first glance, the terms may seem a bit overwhelming. Nevertheless, you will find it immensely helpful to study them carefully now so that they will come to mind easily later, when we analyze complicated, real-life learning situations, such as the acquisition and treatment of fears, phobias, and food aversions. Here we go . . .

Acquisition Classical conditioning always involves an **unconditioned stimulus (UCS),** a stimulus that automatically—that is, without conditioning—provokes a reflexive response. In Pavlov's experiments, food was used as the UCS because it produced a salivation reflex. In the language of classical conditioning, then, this response is called an *unconditioned reflex* or, more commonly, an **unconditioned response (UCR).** It is important to realize that the UCS–UCR connection involves no learning.

■ **Classical conditioning** A form of behavioral learning in which a previously neutral stimulus acquires the power to elicit the same innate reflex produced by another stimulus.

■ **Neutral stimulus** Any stimulus that produces no conditioned response prior to learning. When it is brought into a conditioning experiment, the researcher will call it a conditioned stimulus (CS). The assumption is that some conditioning occurs after even one pairing of the CS and UCS.

■ **Unconditioned stimulus (UCS)** In classical conditioning, the stimulus that elicits an unconditioned response.

■ **Unconditioned response (UCR)** In classical conditioning, the response elicited by an unconditioned stimulus without prior learning.

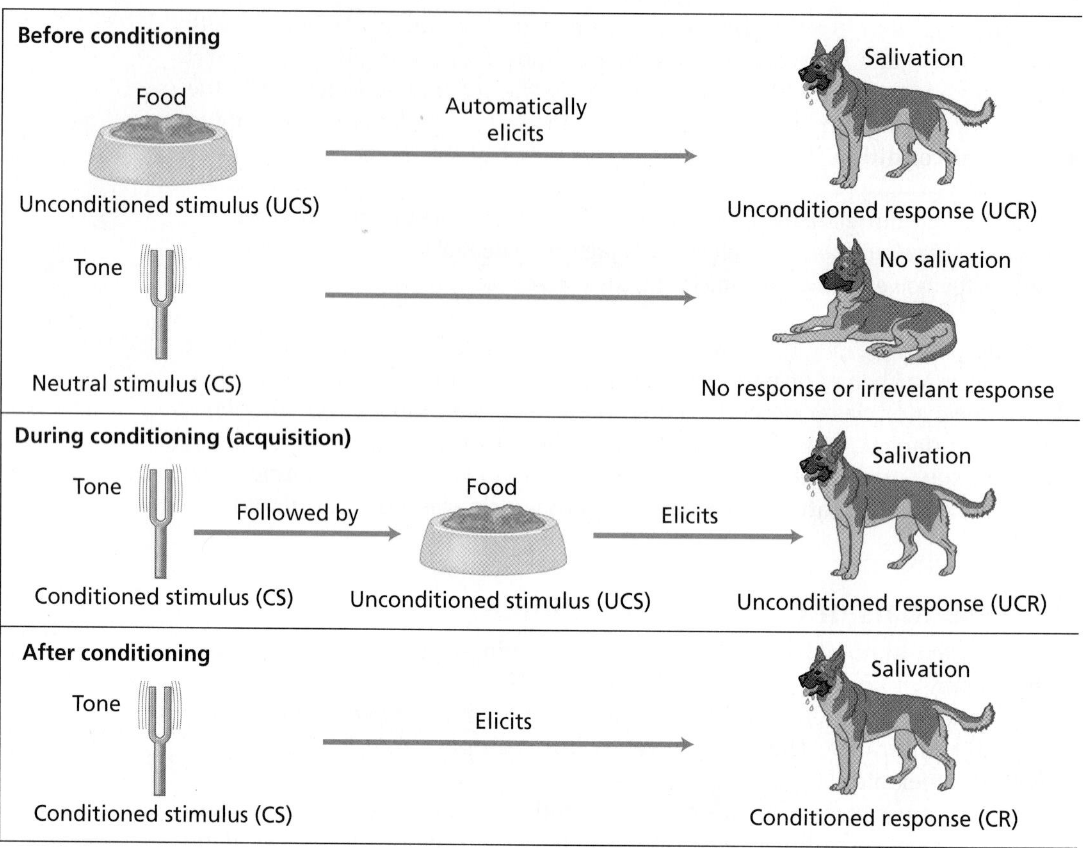
Before conditioning
Food
Automatically elicits
Salivation
Unconditioned stimulus (UCS)
Unconditioned response (UCR)
Tone
No salivation
Neutral stimulus (CS)
No response or irrevelant response
During conditioning (acquisition)
Tone
Followed by
Food
Elicits
Salivation
Conditioned stimulus (CS)
Unconditioned stimulus (UCS)
Unconditioned response (UCR)
After conditioning
Tone
Elicits
Salivation
Conditioned stimulus (CS)
Conditioned response (CR)

● **FIGURE 6.1** Basic Features of Classical Conditioning

Before conditioning, the food (UCS) naturally elicits salivation (UCR). A tone from a tuning fork is a neutral stimulus and has no effect. During conditioning (the acquisition phase), the tone is paired with the food, which continues to elicit the salivation response. Through its association with the food, the previously neutral tone becomes a conditioned stimulus (CS), gradually producing a stronger and stronger salivation response. (*Source:* From PSYCHOLOGY AND LIFE 15th ed. by P. G. Zimbardo and R. J. Gerrig. Copyright © 1999 by Pearson Education. Published and reprinted by permission of Allyn & Bacon, Boston, MA.)

During the **acquisition** or initial learning stage of classical conditioning, a neutral stimulus (a tone, for example) is paired with the unconditioned stimulus. Typically, after several trials the neutral stimulus will gradually come to elicit essentially the same response as does the UCS. So, in Pavlov's experiment in which the tone produced salivation, we say that this formerly neutral stimulus has become a **conditioned stimulus (CS).** Although the response to the conditioned stimulus is essentially the same as the response originally produced by the unconditioned stimulus, we now refer to it as the **conditioned response (CR).**

■ **Acquisition** The initial learning stage in classical conditioning, during which the conditioned response comes to be elicited by the conditioned stimulus.

■ **Conditioned stimulus (CS)** In classical conditioning, a previously neutral stimulus that comes to elicit the conditioned response. Customarily, in a conditioning experiment, the neutral stimulus is called a conditioned stimulus when it is first paired with an unconditioned stimulus (UCS).

■ **Conditioned response (CR)** In classical conditioning, a response elicited by a previously neutral stimulus that has become associated with the unconditioned stimulus.

With those terms firmly in mind, look at the graph of acquisition in a typical classical conditioning experiment, which appears in the first panel of Figure 6.2, where gradual acquisition of the conditioned response is reflected in the upward sweep of the line. Note that, at first, only weak responses are elicited by the conditioned stimulus. With continued CS–UCS pairings, however, the conditioned response increases in strength.

In conditioning, as in telling a joke, timing is critical. In most cases, the CS and UCS must be presented *contiguously* (close together in time) so that the organism can make the appropriate connection. The range of time intervals between the CS and UCS that will produce the best conditioning depends on the response being conditioned. For motor responses, such as eye blinks, a short interval of a second or less is best. For visceral responses, such as heart rate and salivation, longer intervals of 5 to 15 seconds work best. Conditioned

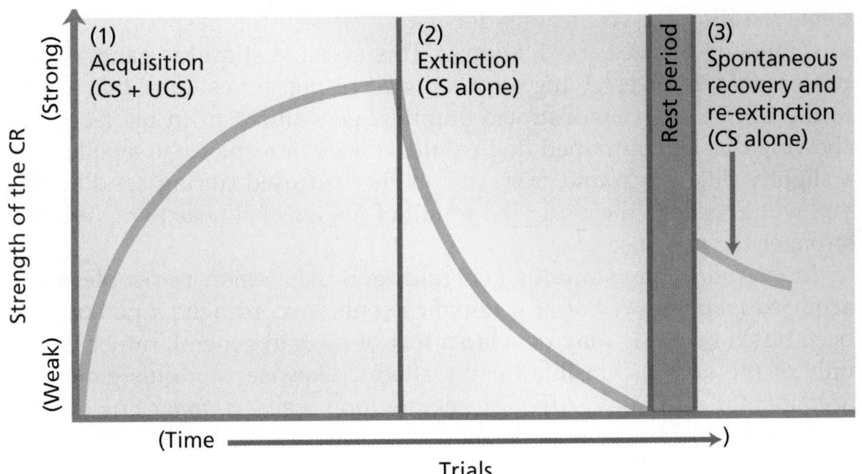

(1)
Acquisition
(CS + UCS)
(2)
Extinction
(CS alone)
Rest period
(3)
Spontaneous
recovery and
re-extinction
(CS alone)
Strength of the CR
(Strong)
(Weak)
(Time
)
Trials

● **FIGURE 6.2** Acquisition, Extinction, and Spontaneous Recovery

During acquisition (CS + UCS), the strength of the CR increases rapidly. During extinction, when the UCS no longer follows the CS, the strength of the CR drops to zero. The CR may reappear after a brief rest period, even when the UCS is still not presented; only the CS alone appears. The reappearance of the CR is called "spontaneous recovery." (*Source:* From PSYCHOLOGY AND LIFE 15th ed. by P. G. Zimbardo and R. J. Gerrig. Copyright © 1999 by Pearson Education. Published and reprinted by permission of Allyn & Bacon, Boston, MA.)

fear optimally requires longer intervals of many seconds or even minutes to develop. Taste aversions, we will see, can develop after even longer delays.

These, then, are the building blocks of classical conditioning: the CS, UCS, CR, UCR, and the timing that connects them. So, why did it take Pavlov three decades and 532 experiments to study such a simple phenomenon? There was more to classical conditioning than first met Pavlov's eyes. Along with acquisition, he also discovered the processes of *extinction, spontaneous recovery, generalization,* and *discrimination*—which we will now explore.

■ **Extinction (in classical conditioning)** The weakening of a conditioned response in the absence of an unconditioned stimulus.

■ **Spontaneous recovery** The reappearance of an extinguished conditioned response after a time delay.

Extinction and Spontaneous Recovery Suppose that, as a result of classical conditioning, your mouth waters at the sound of a bell on the ice cream wagon that cruises your neighborhood. Does such a conditioned response remain permanently in your behavioral repertoire? The good news, based on experiments by Pavlov's group, suggests that it does not. Conditioned salivation responses in Pavlov's dogs were easily eliminated by withholding the UCS (food) over several trials in which the CS (the tone) was presented alone. In the language of classical conditioning this is called **extinction.** It occurs when a conditioned response is eliminated by repeated presentations of the CS without the UCS. Figure 6.2 shows how the conditioned response (salivation) becomes weaker and weaker during extinction trials.

Now for the bad news: Let's imagine that your mouth-watering conditioned response has been extinguished. (The wagon repeatedly runs out of ice cream just before it gets to your house.) But after a time (the driver has been on a week's vacation), when you again hear the bell on the ice cream wagon, the conditioned response may reappear *spontaneously*. The same thing happened in Pavlov's dogs, which began salivating again when they again heard a bell, some time after undergoing extinction training. Pavlov termed this **spontaneous recovery.** Happily, when spontaneous recovery occurs, the conditioned response nearly always reappears at a lower intensity, as you can see in Figure 6.2. In practice, then, the CR can be brought under control, although sometimes this may require several extinction sessions.

The occurrence of spontaneous recovery is of considerable importance in behavior modification therapy for fears. But spontaneous recovery has theoretical importance, too. It tells us that extinction does not involve a complete elimination of the response from the organism's behavioral repertoire. Rather, extinction merely suppresses the conditioned response. What actually seems to be happening during extinction is the learning of a competing response *not to respond* to the conditioned stimulus.

CONNECTION: CHAPTER 13

Behavior modification therapies are based on classical conditioning and operant conditioning.

Generalization If you fear spiders, you will probably respond the same way to spiders of all sizes and markings. This is called **stimulus generalization,** a process that involves giving a conditioned response to stimuli that are similar to the CS. Pavlov demonstrated stimulus generalization in his laboratory by showing that a well-trained dog would salivate in response to a bell that made a slightly different sound from the one he had used during conditioning. As you would expect, the closer the sound of the new bell was to the original, the stronger the response.

In everyday life, stimulus generalization is common in people who have acquired fears as a result of traumatic events. Accordingly, a person who has been bitten by a dog may develop a fear of dogs in general, rather than a fear only of the dog responsible for the attack. Likewise, stimulus generalization accounts for an allergy sufferer's sneeze upon seeing a paper flower. In short, by means of stimulus generalization we learn to apply old reflexes in new situations.

Discrimination Learning Although you may have learned to salivate at the sound of the bell on the ice cream wagon, you probably don't drool when the doorbell rings—thanks to *stimulus discrimination.* Much the opposite of stimulus generalization, **stimulus discrimination** occurs when an organism learns to respond to one stimulus but not to stimuli that are similar. Pavlov and his students demonstrated this experimentally when they taught dogs to distinguish between two tones of different frequencies. Once again, their procedure was simple: One tone was followed by food, while another was not. Over a series of trials, the dogs gradually learned the discrimination, evidenced in salivation elicited by one tone and not by the other. Beyond the laboratory, discrimination learning can be found in our preferences for one commercial brand over another. Most obviously, perhaps, discrimination is involved in the continuing advertising battle between Pepsi and Coke.

Conditioning an Experimental Neurosis If you have ever had a class in which you couldn't guess what the teacher wanted, you have faced a vexing problem in discrimination learning. To study this problem in the laboratory, Pavlov confronted dogs with the seemingly simple task of distinguishing between a circle and an ellipse. One stimulus was always paired with food and the other was always paired with a painful electric shock. The task became more difficult, however, over a series of trials, when Pavlov gradually changed the ellipse to become more and more circular. And how did the dogs respond? As the discrimination became increasingly difficult, their responses grew more erratic. Finally, as the animals became more confused between the circle and the ellipse, they would snarl and snap at the handlers. Because such agitated responses resemble behavior of "neurotic" people who become irritable and defensive when they have difficult choices to make, this behavior pattern was dubbed **experimental neurosis.** Even today, this pattern stands as a model for the deterioration of behavior seen in both people and animals under stress.

Applications of Classical Conditioning

The beauty of classical conditioning is that it offers a simple explanation for many behaviors, from cravings to aversions. But it offers more than an explanation: It also gives us the tools for eliminating unwanted human behaviors—although Pavlov never attempted any therapeutic applications. It fell to the American behaviorist John Watson to first apply classical conditioning techniques to people.

The Notorious Case of Little Albert Conditioned fear in humans was first demonstrated experimentally by John Watson and Rosalie Rayner over 80

■ **Stimulus generalization** The extension of a learned response to stimuli that are similar to the conditioned stimulus.

■ **Stimulus discrimination** A change in responses to one stimulus but not to stimuli that are similar.

■ **Experimental neurosis** A pattern of erratic behavior resulting from a demanding discrimination learning task, typically one that involves aversive stimuli.

years ago (Brewer, 1991; Fancher, 1979). In an experiment that would be considered unethical today, Watson and Rayner (1920/2000) conditioned an infant named Albert to react fearfully to a white laboratory rat. They created the fear by repeatedly presenting the rat paired with an aversive UCS—the loud sound of a steel bar struck with a mallet. It took only seven trials for "Little Albert" to react with fear at the appearance of the rat (CS) alone. After Albert's response to the rat had become well established, Watson and Rayner showed that his fear readily generalized from the rat to other furry objects, such as a Santa Claus mask and a fur coat worn by Watson (Harris, 1979).

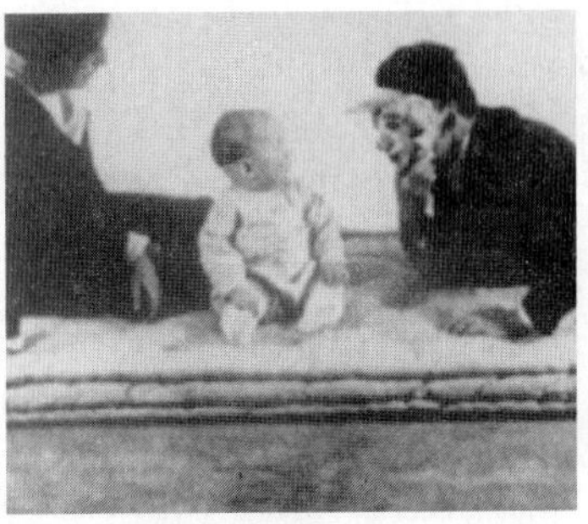

● John Watson and Rosalie Rayner conditioned Little Albert to fear furry objects like this Santa Claus mask (*Discovering Psychology*, 1990).

Most likely, the experiment caused Albert only temporary distress, because his fear extinguished rapidly. In fact, Watson and Rayner found it necessary to strengthen the child's response periodically. This need to recondition Albert threatened the whole experiment when, after five days, Watson and Rayner were attempting to show that the child's fear could be generalized to a dog, a rabbit, and a sealskin coat. Watson decided to "freshen the reaction to the rat" by again striking the steel bar. The noise startled the dog, which began to bark at Albert, frightening not only Little Albert but both experimenters (Harris, 1979).

Unlike Little Albert's short-lived aversion to furry objects, some fears learned under extreme conditions can persist for years (LeDoux, 1996). Many sailors were exposed to such conditions during World War II, when the signal used to call them to battle stations was a gong sounding at the rate of 100 rings a minute. For combat personnel aboard ship, this sound was strongly associated with danger—a CS for emotional arousal. The persistent effect of this learning was shown in a study conducted 15 years after the war, when Navy veterans who had experienced combat still gave a strong autonomic reaction to the old "call to battle stations" (Edwards & Acker, 1962).

CONNECTION: CHAPTER 3

The *autonomic nervous system* regulates the internal organs.

Like those veterans, any of us can retain a learned readiness to respond to old emotional cues. Fortunately, however, classical conditioning provides some tools for dealing with conditioned fears (Wolpe & Plaud, 1997). This process was first described by Mary Cover Jones in 1924, when she helped "uncondition" the fear that a 2-year old subject named Peter had toward a white rat and, by extension, a rabbit. Through a series of sessions in which she increased the "degrees of toleration," the fear began to decrease, until, at the end of the study, Peter stated that he liked the rabbit. A good therapeutic strategy combines extinction of the conditioned fear response with learning a relaxation response to the CS. This *counterconditioning* therapy, then, teaches patients to respond in a relaxed manner to the conditioned stimulus. The technique has been particularly effective in dealing with phobias. It was also part of the treatment used to help Sabra conquer her fear of flying.

Conditioned Food Aversions As young children, all four of your authors had bad experiences with specific foods. Phil got sick after eating pork and beans in the grade school lunchroom. Ann developed nausea after eating apple fritters. And it was Bob who became ill after overdosing on olives. In all three cases, we associated our distress with the distinctive sight, smell, and taste of the food—but not to anything else in our environment. Even today, the taste, smell, or appearance of the specific food is enough to cause a feeling of nausea.

Unpleasant as it can be, learning to avoid a food associated with illness has survival value. That's why humans and many other animals readily form an association between illness and food—much more readily than between illness and a nonfood stimulus, such as a light or a tone. And, although most forms of classical conditioning require only a short delay between the CS and the UCS, food aversions can develop when a distinctive taste has been separated by hours from the onset of illness. "Must have been something I ate!" we say.

John Garcia and Robert Koelling first recognized this selective CS–UCS connection when they noticed that rats avoided drinking from the water bottles

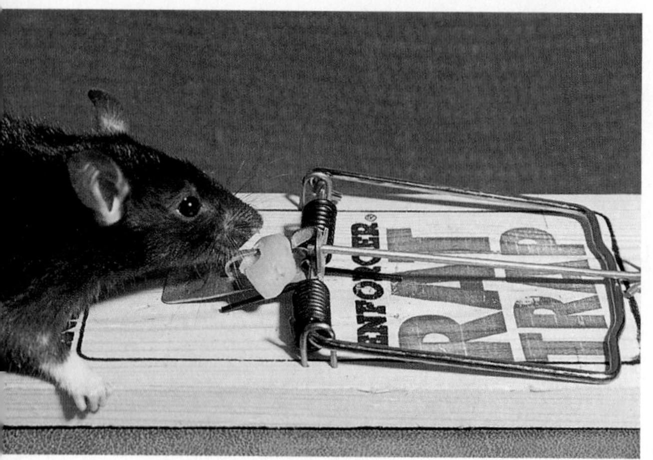
ENFORCER
RAT TRAP

● Bait shyness has survival value.

in the chambers where they had previously been made nauseated by radiation. Garcia and Koelling wondered: Could it be the taste of the water in those bottles that the rats were associating with being sick? Subsequent experiments confirmed their suspicions and led to yet another important discovery.

Garcia and Koelling (1966) found that rats readily learned an association between flavored water and illness, yet the rats could *not* be conditioned to associate flavored water with an electric shock delivered through a grid on the floor of the test chamber. This makes good "sense" from an evolutionary perspective, because illness can easily result from drinking (or eating) poisonous substances but rarely occurs following a sharp pain to the feet. On the other hand, the experiments found that rats easily learned to respond fearfully when bright lights and noise signaled an electric shock—but could *not* learn to connect those light/sound cues and subsequent illness.

■ **Taste-aversion learning** A biological tendency in which an organism learns, after a single experience, to avoid a food with a certain taste, if eating it is followed by illness.

A Challenge to Pavlov The problem that conditioned **taste-aversion learning** poses for classical conditioning is that it is not entirely learned. In fact, the tendency to develop taste aversions appears to be a part of our biological nature. And it is this biological basis for taste aversions that has caused psychologists to question some aspects of Pavlov's original theory of classical conditioning.

Unlike conditioning dogs to respond to a tone or a light, food aversions seem to require an innate (and therefore *unlearned*) disposition to associate sickness with food. We know this because people who develop food aversions don't normally make the same association to nonfood items that accompanied the food. For example, when Bob developed an aversion to olives, he did not also learn to avoid other objects in the room at the time, such as a light or a book on the table. It was solely the olives that became an effective conditioned stimulus. Taken together, such observations suggest that organisms have an inborn preparedness to associate certain stimuli with certain consequences, while other CS–UCS combinations are highly resistant to learning.

Moreover, food aversions can develop even when the time interval between eating and illness extends over several hours—as compared with just a few seconds in Pavlov's experiments. Again, this suggests that in food aversions we are not dealing with a simple classically conditioned response as Pavlov understood it but, instead, with a response that is based as much in nature (biology) as it is in nurture (learning).

● A conditioned taste aversion can make a coyote stop killing sheep.

Conditioning Coyotes: An Application The principles behind conditioned food aversion have been applied to practical problems in the world outside the laboratory. For example, John Garcia and his colleagues demonstrated how aversive conditioning can dissuade wild coyotes from attacking sheep. The researchers did so by wrapping toxic lamb burgers in sheepskins and stashing them on sheep ranches. When roaming coyotes found and ate these morsels, they became sick and—as predicted—developed a distaste for lamb meat. The result was a 30 to 50% reduction in sheep attacks. So powerful was this aversion for conditioned coyotes that, when captured and placed in a cage with a sheep, the coyotes would not get close to it. Some even vomited at the sight of a sheep (Garcia, 1990). Perhaps the most amazing result was this: Despite their success with coyotes, the scientists have been unable to modify the behavior of sheep ranchers to get them to apply the research. Apparently, sheep ranchers have a strong aversion to feeding lamb to coyotes!

So, what is the big lesson of taste aversions for our understanding of classical conditioning? Conditioning involves both nature and nurture. That is, conditioning depends not only on the learned relationship among stimuli and responses but also on the way an organism is genetically attuned to certain stimuli in its environment (Barker et al., 1978; Dickinson, 2001; Pinel, 2003). What any organism can—and cannot—learn in a given setting is to some extent a product of its evolutionary history (Garcia, 1993). This is a concept that Pavlov never understood.

If this child gets sick tonight, she may develop a taste aversion to this unusual flavor of ice cream.

PSYCHOLOGY IN YOUR LIFE: TASTE AVERSIONS AND CHEMOTHERAPY

Imagine that your friend Jena is about to undergo her first round of chemotherapy, just to make sure that any stray cells from the tumor found in her breast will be destroyed. To her surprise, the nurse enters the lab, not with the expected syringe, but with a dish of licorice-flavored ice cream. "Is this a new kind of therapy?" she asks. The nurse replies that it is, indeed. She explains that most patients who undergo chemotherapy experience nausea, which can make them "go off their feed" and quit eating, just when their body needs nourishment to fight the disease. "But," says the nurse, "We have found a way around the problem. If we give patients some unusual food before their chemotherapy, they will usually develop an aversion only to that food." She continued, "Did you ever hear of Pavlov's dogs?"

Cancer patients like Jena often develop aversions to normal foods in their diets to such an extent that they become anorectic and malnourished. The aversions are conditioned responses in which food (the CS) becomes associated with nausea. The problem is aggravated when chemotherapy treatments, which produce the nausea, are administered right after meals. Therapists trained to understand classical conditioning use their knowledge to prevent the development of aversions to nutritive foods by arranging for meals not to be given just before the chemotherapy. And, as in Jena's case, they also present a "scapegoat" stimulus. Thus, patients are given candies or ice cream with unusual flavors before the treatments so that the taste aversion becomes conditioned only to those special flavors. For some patients, this practical solution to problems with chemotherapy may make the difference between life and death (Bernstein, 1988, 1991).

CHECK YOUR UNDERSTANDING

1. **RECALL:** Classical conditioning is especially useful for understanding which one of the following examples of learning?
   a. a child who, after a painful dental visit, has learned to fear the dentist
   b. a dog that has learned to "sit up" for a food reward
   c. an executive who is afraid that she will lose her job
   d. a rat that has learned to run a maze
   e. a psychology student who is learning how memory works
2. **RECALL:** The responses in classical conditioning were originally
   a. new behaviors.
   b. premeditated behaviors.
   c. random acts.
   d. trained reflexes.
   e. innate reflexes.
3. **APPLICATION:** If you learned to fear electrical outlets after getting a painful shock, from plugging in a light, what would be the CS?
   a. the time period between seeing the outlet and getting the shock
   b. the prong on the light cord
   c. the electrical outlet
   d. the painful shock
   e. the fear
4. **UNDERSTANDING THE CORE CONCEPT:** Which of the following would be most likely to be an unconditioned stimulus (UCS) involved in classical conditioning?
   a. praise
   b. money
   c. music
   d. a flashing light
   e. food

ANSWERS: 1. a 2. e 3. c 4. e

HOW DO WE LEARN NEW BEHAVIORS BY OPERANT CONDITIONING?

With classical conditioning, you can teach a dog to salivate, but you can't teach it to sit up or roll over. Why? Salivation is a passive, involuntary reflex, while sitting up and rolling over are much more complex responses that we usually think of as voluntary. To a behavioral psychologist, however, such "voluntary" behaviors are really controlled by *rewards* and *punishments*—which have no role in classical conditioning. When rewards or punishments are involved, another important form of learning is at work. Psychologists call it *operant conditioning.* An **operant,** incidentally, is an observable behavior that an organism uses to "operate" in, or have an effect on, the environment. Thus, if you are reading this book to get a good grade on the next test, reading is an operant behavior.

You might also think of **operant conditioning** as a form of learning in which behavior change is brought about by the *consequences* of behavior. The Core Concept of this section puts the idea this way:

In operant conditioning, the consequences of behavior, such as rewards and punishments, influence the chance that the behavior will occur again.

Common rewarding consequences include money, praise, food, or high grades—all of which can encourage the behaviors they follow. By contrast, punishments such as pain, loss of privileges, or low grades can discourage the behaviors with which they are associated.

As you will see, the theory of operant conditioning is an important one for at least two reasons. First, operant conditioning accounts for a much wider spectrum of behavior than does classical conditioning. And second, it explains new behaviors—not just reflexive behaviors.

● Taking aspirin for pain usually results in negative reinforcement, because the pain diminishes.

Skinner's Radical Behaviorism

The founding father of operant conditioning, American psychologist B. F. Skinner (1904–1990), based his whole career on the idea that the most powerful influences on behavior are its *consequences.* Actually, it wasn't Skinner's idea, originally. He borrowed the concept of behavior being controlled by rewards and punishments from another American psychologist, Edward Thorndike, who had demonstrated how hungry animals would work diligently to solve a problem by trial and error to obtain a food reward. Gradually, on succeeding trials, erroneous responses were eliminated and effective responses were "stamped in." Thorndike called this the **law of effect.** (See Figure 6.3.)

The first thing Skinner did with Thorndike's psychology, however, was to rid it of subjective and unscientific speculation about the organism's feelings, intentions, or goals. What an animal "wanted" or the "pleasure" it felt was not important for an objective understanding of the animal's behavior. As a radical behaviorist, Skinner refused to consider what happens in an organism's mind, because such speculation cannot be verified by observation. For example, eating can be observed, but we can't observe the inner experiences of hunger, the desire for food, or pleasure at eating.

■ **Operant** An observable, voluntary behavior that an organism emits to "operate" on, or have an effect on, the environment.
■ **Operant conditioning** A form of behavioral learning in which the probability of a response is changed by its consequences–that is, by the stimuli that *follow* the response.
■ **Law of effect** The idea that responses that produced desirable results would be learned, or "stamped" into the organism.
■ **Reinforcer** A condition (involving either the presentation or removal of a stimulus) that occurs after a response and strengthens that response.

The Power of Reinforcement

While we often speak of "reward" in casual conversation, Skinner preferred the more objective term **reinforcer.** By this he meant any condition that follows and strengthens a response. Food, money, and sex serve this function for

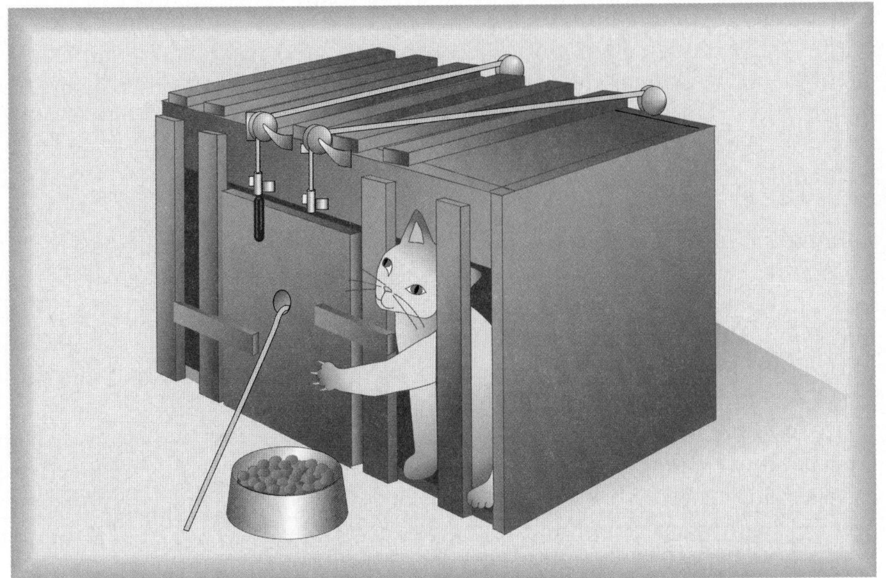

● **FIGURE 6.3** A Thorndike Puzzle Box
Unlike Pavlov's dogs, Thorndike's cats faced a problem: how to open the door in the puzzle box to get a food reward lying just outside. To solve this problem, the animals used *trial-and-error learning,* rather than simple reflexive responses. At first, their responses seemed random, but gradually they eliminated ineffective behaviors. And when the effects of their behavior were desirable (that is, when the door finally opened and the animals got the food), they used this strategy on subsequent trials. This change in behavior based on outcome of previous trials is called the *law of effect.* Much the same trial-and-error learning occurs when you learn a skill, such as shooting a basketball.

most people. So do attention, praise, or a smile. All are examples of **positive reinforcement,** which strengthens a response by occurring after the response and making the behavior more likely to occur again.

Most people know about positive reinforcement, of course, but few people understand the other main way to strengthen operant responses. It involves the reinforcement of behavior by the *removal* of an unpleasant or aversive stimulus. Psychologists call this **negative reinforcement.** (The word "negative" here is used in the mathematical sense of *subtract* or *remove,* while "positive" means *add* or *apply.*) Using an umbrella to avoid getting wet during a downpour is a behavior learned and maintained by negative reinforcement. That is, you use the umbrella to avoid or remove an unpleasant stimulus (getting wet). Likewise, when a driver buckles the seat belt, negative reinforcement occurs as the annoying sound of the seat-belt buzzer stops. Remember, it is the "subtraction" of the unpleasant stimulus that provides negative reinforcement.

● **B. F. Skinner is shown reinforcing the animal's behavior in an operant chamber, or "Skinner box." The apparatus allows the experimenter to control all the stimuli in the animal's environment.**

Reinforcing Technology: The "Skinner Box" One of B. F. Skinner's (1956) most important innovations was a simple device for studying the effects of reinforcers on laboratory animals: a box with a lever that an animal could press to obtain food, which he called an **operant chamber.** Nearly everyone else called it a "Skinner box," a term he detested. Over the intervening years, the apparatus has been used by thousands of psychologists to study operant conditioning.

The importance of the operant chamber was that it could be set to control the timing and the frequency of reinforcement. These factors, it turned out, are of huge importance in controlling behavior, as you will see in our discussion of *contingencies of reinforcement.* Moreover, the Skinner box could be programmed to conduct experiments at any time—even when the researcher was home in bed.

And speaking of beds, just to set the record straight, we'd like to mention a bit of trivia about the "baby tender" crib Skinner devised for his daughter, Deborah (Benjamin & Nielsen-Gammon, 1999). It consisted of an enclosed, temperature-controlled box—which unfortunately bore a superficial resemblance to the operant chambers used in his experiments. The public learned about the "baby tender" from an article by Skinner in the magazine *Ladies' Home Journal.* Many readers (and also those who did *not* read the article) jumped to wild

■ **Positive reinforcement** A stimulus presented after a response and increasing the probability of that response happening again.
■ **Negative reinforcement** The removal of an unpleasant or aversive stimulus, contingent on a particular behavior. Compare with *punishment.*
■ **Operant chamber** A boxlike apparatus that can be programmed to deliver reinforcers and punishers contingent on an animal's behavior. The operant chamber is often called a "Skinner box."

conclusions involving child neglect and heartless experimentation. The story of the "baby tender" took on a life of its own, and, years later, stories arose about Deborah Skinner's supposed psychotic breakdown, lawsuits against her father, and eventual suicide—none of which were true. In this case, the truth was not nearly as titillating as the fiction. In fact, Deborah grew up to be a well-adjusted individual who loved her parents.

● Chimpanzees will work for conditioned reinforcers. Here a chimp has earned plastic tokens, which it is depositing in a "chimp-o-mat" to obtain raisins, a primary reinforcer.

● Parents can use reinforcement contingencies to affect children's behavior.

■ **Reinforcement contingencies** Relationships between a response and the changes in stimulation that follow the response.

■ **Continuous reinforcement** A type of reinforcement schedule by which all correct responses are reinforced.

■ **Shaping** An operant learning technique in which a new behavior is produced by reinforcing responses that are similar to the desired response.

■ **Intermittent reinforcement** A type of reinforcement schedule by which some, but not all, correct responses are reinforced; also called *partial reinforcement.*

■ **Extinction (in operant conditioning)** A process by which a response that has been learned is weakened by the absence or removal of reinforcement. (Compare with *extinction in classical conditioning.*)

Contingencies of Reinforcement College and university students are reinforced for their studying with grade reports two or three times a year. Because that's too long between reinforcers for most students to maintain their academic behavior, professors schedule exams and award grades periodically throughout their courses. They want to encourage continual studying, rather than one big push at the end of the semester.

In any operant learning situation, the timing and frequency of rewards are crucial. How often will reinforcement be given? How much work is needed to earn a reinforcer? Will every response be reinforced—or will reinforcement occur only after a certain number of responses? These are the important questions we will pose in our discussion of **reinforcement contingencies,** which will deal with the many possible ways of associating responses and reinforcers. As you will see, the answers to these questions determine the behavior patterns of organisms, from laboratory rats to students (and their professors).

Continuous versus Intermittent Reinforcement Suppose you want to teach your dog a trick—say, sitting up on command. It would be a good idea to begin the training program with a reward for every correct response. Psychologists call this **continuous reinforcement.** It's a useful tactic early in the learning process, because rewarding every correct response gives feedback on how well each response was performed. In addition, continuous reinforcement is useful for **shaping** complex new behaviors, such as playing a musical instrument, because the teacher can continually "raise the bar," or increase the standard required for earning a reward, which tells the learner when performance has improved. In general, then, we can say that *continuous reinforcement is the best strategy for teaching and learning new behaviors.*

Continuous reinforcement does have some drawbacks, however. For one thing, an accidental failure to reward a correct response on one trial could easily be misinterpreted as a signal that the response was not correct. For another, continuous reinforcement typically loses its reinforcing quality as the organism becomes satiated, as you can imagine if someone were training you to shoot free throws by rewarding you with chocolate cake. Your first slice of chocolate cake may be highly rewarding, but by the time you have had 10 or 12 slices, the reward value is gone.

Happily, once the desired behavior is well established (for example, when your dog has learned to sit up), the demands of the situation change. The learner no longer needs rewards to discriminate a correct response from an incorrect one. Now is the time to shift to **intermittent reinforcement** (also called *partial reinforcement*), the rewarding of some, but not all, correct responses. A less frequent schedule of reward—perhaps, after every third correct response—can still serve as an incentive for your dog to sit up on command. In general, whether we're dealing with people or animals, *intermittent reinforcement is the most efficient way to maintain behaviors that have already been learned* (Robbins, 1971; Terry, 2000).

A big advantage of intermittent reinforcement comes from the resistance to *extinction* that it produces. Much like the extinction we saw in Pavlovian conditioning, **extinction** also occurs in operant conditioning. The operant version of extinction occurs when reinforcement is withheld, as when a gambler quits playing a slot machine that never pays off. Why do responses strengthened by partial reinforcement resist extinction much more strongly than responses that have been rewarded continuously? Imagine two gamblers and two slot machines. One machine inexplicably pays off on every trial, and another, a more typical machine, pays on an unpredictable, intermittent schedule. Now, suppose that both devices suddenly stop paying. Which gambler will catch on first? The one who has been rewarded for each pull of the lever (continuous reinforcement) will quickly notice the change, while the gambler who has won only occasionally (on partial reinforcement) may continue playing unrewarded for a long while.

● Continuous reinforcement is useful for *training* animals, but intermittent reinforcement is better for *maintaining* their learned behaviors.

Schedules of Reinforcement Now that you are convinced of the power of intermittent reinforcement, you should know that it occurs in two main forms or **schedules of reinforcement.** One, the **ratio schedule,** rewards a subject after a certain *number of responses.* The other, known as an **interval schedule,** provides a reward after a certain *time interval.* Let's look at the advantages and disadvantages of each.

■ **Schedules of reinforcement** Programs specifying the frequency and timing of reinforcements.

■ **Ratio schedule** A program by which reinforcement depends on the number of correct responses.

■ **Interval schedule** A program by which reinforcement depends on the time interval elapsed since the last reinforcement.

■ **Fixed ratio (FR) schedules** Programs by which reinforcement is contingent on a certain, unvarying number of responses.

■ **Variable ratio (VR) schedules** Reinforcement programs by which the number of responses required for a reinforcement varies from trial to trial.

■ **Fixed interval (FI) schedules** Programs by which reinforcement is contingent on a certain, fixed time period.

Ratio Schedules If you pay your employees based on the amount of work they perform, you are using a ratio schedule of reinforcement. Ratio schedules occur any time rewards are *based on the number of responses* (see Figure 6.4). Psychologists make a further distinction between two subtypes of ratio schedules: *fixed ratio* and *variable ratio* schedules.

Fixed ratio (FR) schedules are found in jobs where workers are paid on a piecework basis. Suppose that you own a tire factory, and you pay each worker a dollar for every 10 tires produced; you are using a fixed ratio schedule. Under this scheme, the amount of work (the number of responses) needed for a reward remains constant. Managers like FR schedules because the rate of responding is usually high (Terry, 2000; Whyte, 1972).

Variable ratio (VR) schedules are less predictable. Telemarketers—people who make sales pitches by telephone—work on a VR schedule: They never know how many phone calls they must make before they get the next sale. Slot machine players also respond on a variable ratio schedule. In both cases the variable ratio schedule keeps responses coming at a high rate—so high, in fact, that the VR schedule usually produces more responding than any other schedule of reinforcement. In the laboratory, Skinner demonstrated that a variable ratio schedule could entice a hungry pigeon to peck a disk 12,000 times an hour for rewards given, on the average, for every 110 pecks.

Interval Schedules Time is of the essence on an interval schedule. Accordingly, reinforcement is based on responses made within a certain *time period* (instead of on the number of responses given). (See Figure 6.4.) Psychologists distinguish two kinds of interval schedules: *fixed interval* and *variable interval* schedules.

Fixed interval (FI) schedules are common in the work world, where they may appear as a monthly paycheck. A student who studies for a weekly quiz is also on a fixed interval

● What schedule of reinforcement encourages this man to buy lottery tickets?

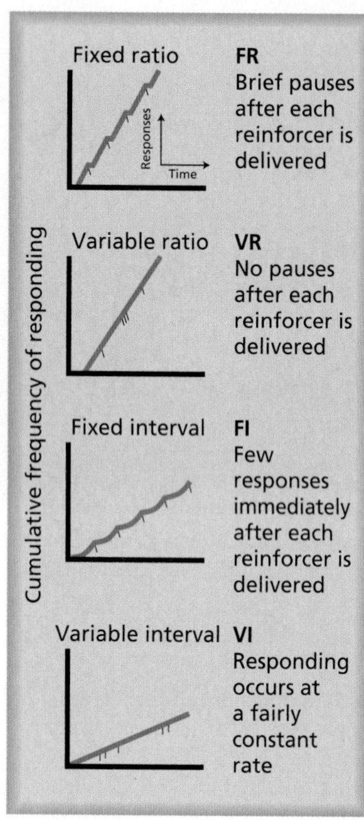
Fixed ratio
FR
Brief pauses after each reinforcer is delivered
Responses
Time
Variable ratio
VR
No pauses after each reinforcer is delivered
Fixed interval
FI
Few responses immediately after each reinforcer is delivered
Variable interval
VI
Responding occurs at a fairly constant rate
Cumulative frequency of responding

● **FIGURE 6.4** Reinforcement Schedules

These graphs show typical patterns of responding produced by four different schedules of reinforcement. (The hatch marks indicate when reinforcement is delivered.) Notice that the steeper angle of the top two graphs shows how the ratio schedules usually produce more responses over a given period of time than do the interval schedules.

schedule. Because the interval is invariant, the time period between rewards remains constant. You may have already guessed that fixed interval reinforcement usually results in a low response rate. Ironically, this is the schedule most widely adopted by business. Even a rat in a Skinner box programmed for a fixed interval schedule soon learns that it must produce only a limited amount of work during the interval in order to get its reward. Lever presses beyond the required minimum are just wasted energy. Thus, both rats and humans on fixed interval schedules may display only modest productivity until near the end of the interval, when the response rate increases rapidly. (Think of college students facing a term paper deadline.) Graphically, in Figure 6.4 you can see the "scalloped" pattern of behavior that results from this flurry of activity near the end of each interval.

Variable interval (VI) schedules are, perhaps, the most unpredictable of all. On a VI schedule, the time interval between rewards varies. The resulting rate of responding can be low or high, although not usually as high as for the VR schedule. For a pigeon or a rat in a Skinner box, the variable interval schedule may be a 30-second interval now, 3 minutes next, and a 1-minute wait later. On the job, random visits by the boss occur on a variable interval schedule. Fishing represents still another example: You never know how long it will be before the fish start biting again, but the occasional, unpredictable fish delivers reward enough to encourage fishing behavior over long intervals. And, while waiting for an elevator, it is fun to note which of your companions presses the button as if it controlled the arrival of the elevator on a VI schedule.

Primary and Secondary Reinforcers It is easy to see why stimuli that fulfill basic biological needs or desires will provide reinforcement: Food reinforces a hungry animal, and water reinforces a thirsty one. Similarly, the opportunity for sex becomes a reinforcer for a sexually aroused organism. Psychologists call such stimuli **primary reinforcers.**

But you can't eat money or drink it. So why does money act as a powerful reinforcer for most people? Neutral stimuli that are associated with primary reinforcers may also acquire a reinforcing effect and become **conditioned reinforcers** or **secondary reinforcers** for operant responses. And that's where money enters the picture; the system works similarly with grades, praise, smiles of approval, gold stars, and various kinds of status symbols. In fact, virtually any stimulus can become a secondary or conditioned reinforcer by being associated with a primary reinforcer. With strong conditioning, secondary reinforcers such as money, status, or awards can even come to be ends in themselves.

The power of conditioned reinforcers has been tapped by mental institutions that have set up so-called *token economies* to encourage desirable and healthy patient behaviors. Under a **token economy,** grooming or taking medication, for example, may be reinforced by plastic tokens awarded by the staff when patients perform these desired behaviors. The tokens can later be exchanged by patients for a wide array of rewards and privileges (Ayllon & Azrin, 1965; Holden, 1978). As an adjunct to other forms of therapy, token economies can help mental patients learn useful strategies for acting effectively in the world (Kazdin, 1994).

■ **Variable interval (VI) schedules** Programs by which the time period between reinforcements varies from trial to trial.

■ **Primary reinforcers** Reinforcers, such as food and sex, that have an innate basis because of their biological value to an organism.

■ **Conditioned reinforcers** or **secondary reinforcers** Stimuli, such as money or tokens, that acquire their reinforcing power by a learned association with primary reinforcers.

■ **Token economy** A therapeutic method, based on operant conditioning, by which individuals are rewarded with tokens, which act as secondary reinforcers. The tokens can be redeemed for a variety of rewards and privileges.

Preferred Activities as Reinforcers: The Premack Principle The opportunity to perform desirable activities can reinforce behavior just as effectively as food or drink or other primary reinforcers. For example, people who work out regularly might use a daily run or fitness class as a reward for getting other tasks done. Likewise, teachers have found that young children will learn to sit still if that behavior is reinforced with the opportunity to run around and make noise (Homme et al., 1963).

The principle at work here says that a preferred activity (running around and making noise) can be used to reinforce a less preferred one (sitting still and listing to the teacher). Psychologists call this the **Premack principle,** after its discoverer, David Premack (1965). He first demonstrated this in thirsty rats, which increased their running in an exercise wheel when they learned that the running would be followed by an opportunity to drink. And, just as Premack had anticipated, another group of rats that were exercise deprived, but not thirsty, increased the amount they drank when drinking was followed by a chance to run in the wheel. In exactly the same way, then, parents can use the Premack principle to get children to engage in otherwise unlikely behavior. For example, the opportunity to play with friends (a preferred activity) could be used to reinforce the less-preferred activity of making the bed or doing the dishes.

● Foods that many people around the world enjoy may not be a source of reinforcement for the typical North American.

Reinforcement across Cultures The laws of operant learning apply to all animals with a brain. The biological mechanism underlying reinforcement is, apparently, much the same across species. On the other hand, exactly what serves as a reinforcer varies wildly. Experience suggests that food for a hungry organism and water for a thirsty one will act as reinforcers because they satisfy basic needs related to survival. But what any particular individual will choose to satisfy those needs may depend as much on learning as on survival instincts—especially in humans, where secondary reinforcement is so important. For us, culture plays an especially powerful role in determining what will act as reinforcers. So, while some people would find eating a cricket reinforcing, most people of Euro-American ancestry would not. Similarly, disposing of a noisy cricket might seem both sensible and rewarding to a Baptist and aversive to a Buddhist. And, just to prove our point, we note that watching a game of cricket would most likely be rewarding to a British cricket fan—although punishingly dull to most Americans.

So, culture shapes preferences in reinforcement, but reinforcement also shapes culture. When you first walk down a street in a foreign city, all the differences that catch your eye are merely different ways that people have found to seek reinforcement or avoid punishment. A temple houses cultural attempts to seek rewards from the deity. Clothing may reflect attempts to seek a reinforcing mate or to feel comfortable in the climate. And a culture's cuisine evolves from learning to survive on the native plants and animals. It is in this sense, then, that we can see culture broadly as a set of behaviors originally *learned* by operant conditioning and shared by a group of people.

The Problem of Punishment

Punishment as a means of influencing behavior poses several difficulties, as schoolteachers and prison wardens will attest. In some respects, punishment acts as the opposite of reinforcement. Thus, punishment is an *aversive* consequence used to *weaken* the behavior it follows. But, like reinforcement, punishment comes in two main forms. One, called **positive punishment,** requires the *application of an aversive stimulus*—as, when you touch a hot plate, the painful consequence reduces the likelihood of your repeating that behavior. The other main form of punishment, known as **omission training** or **negative punishment,** results from the *removal of a reinforcer*—as when parents take away a misbehaving teen's car keys.

■ **Premack principle** The concept, developed by David Premack, that a more-preferred activity can be used to reinforce a less-preferred activity.

■ **Punishment** An aversive stimulus which, occurring after a response, diminishes the strength of that response. (Compare with *negative reinforcement.*)

■ **Positive punishment** The application of an aversive stimulus after a response.

■ **Omission training (negative punishment)** The removal of an appetitive stimulus after a response, leading to a decrease in behavior.

● As Calvin realizes, the probability of someone repeating a response can be decreased if the first response is followed by an aversive consequence, such as a loud noise or angry complaint.

Calvin and Hobbes
by Bill Watterson
HELLO, IS YOUR DAD THERE?
NO, HE ISN'T.
OK. WILL YOU WRITE DOWN MY NUMBER AND HAVE HIM CALL ME?
HOLD ON. I NEED A PEN.
POW!
AGHH! I'VE BEEN SHOT!
I HATE TAKING MESSAGES.

Calvin & Hobbes by Bill Watterson/Universal Press Syndicate.

Unlike reinforcement, however, punishment must be administered consistently. Intermittent punishment is far less effective than punishment delivered after every undesired response. In fact, *not punishing* an occurrence of unwanted behavior can have the effect of rewarding it—as when a supervisor overlooks the late arrival of an employee.

Punishment versus Negative Reinforcement You have probably noted that punishment and negative reinforcement both involve unpleasant stimuli. So, to avoid confusion, let's see how punishment and negative reinforcement differ, using the following examples (Figure 6.5). Suppose that an animal in a Skinner box can turn off a loud noise by pressing a lever: This action provides negative reinforcement. Now compare that with the other animal in Figure 6.5 for which the loud noise serves as a punishment for pressing the lever.

Please note that punishment and negative reinforcement are used to produce opposite effects on behavior (Baum, 1994). Punishment is used to *decrease* a behavior or reduces its probability of recurring. In contrast, negative reinforcement—like positive reinforcement—always *increases* a response's probability of occurring again.

And remember that the descriptors "positive" and "negative" mean "add" and "remove." Thus, both positive reinforcement and positive punishment involve administering or "adding" a stimulus. On the other hand, negative reinforcement and negative punishment always involve withholding or removing a stimulus. For a concise summary of the distinctions between positive and negative reinforcement and punishment, please see Table 6.1.

● **FIGURE 6.5** Negative Reinforcement and Punishment Compared

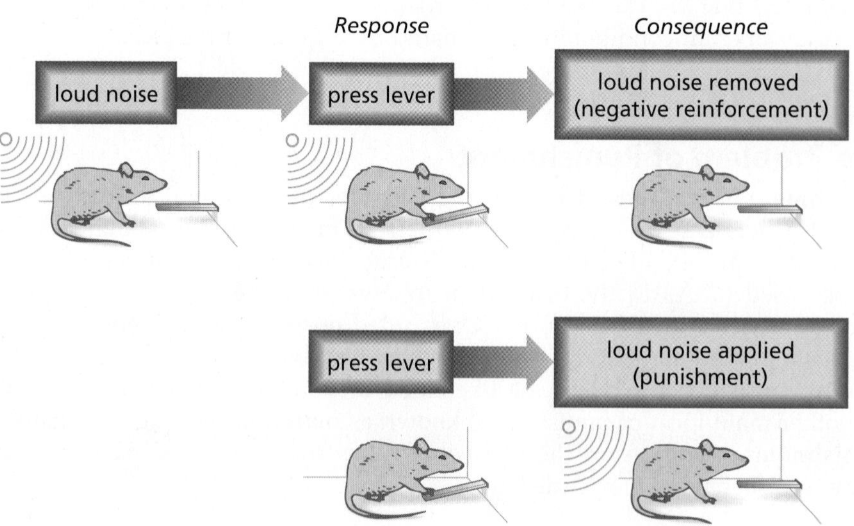

Response
Consequence
loud noise
press lever
loud noise removed (negative reinforcement)
press lever
loud noise applied (punishment)

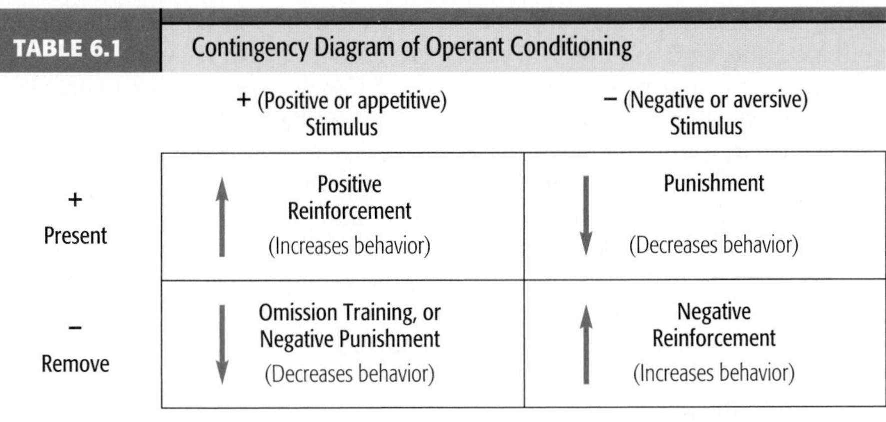

TABLE 6.1 Contingency Diagram of Operant Conditioning

	+ (Positive or appetitive) Stimulus	– (Negative or aversive) Stimulus
+ Present	↑ Positive Reinforcement (Increases behavior)	↓ Punishment (Decreases behavior)
– Remove	↓ Omission Training, or Negative Punishment (Decreases behavior)	↑ Negative Reinforcement (Increases behavior)

Three important points to keep in mind as you study this table:

1. The terms "positive" and "negative" mean that a stimulus (consequence) has been added (presented) or subtracted (removed). They have nothing to do with "good" or "bad."
2. We can often predict what effect a particular consequence will have, but the only way to know for sure whether it will be a reinforcer or a punisher is to observe its effect on behavior. For example, although we might guess that a spanking would punish a child, it might actually serve as a reinforcer to strengthen the unwanted behavior.
3. From a cognitive viewpoint, we can see that reinforcement consists of the presentation of a pleasant stimulus or the removal of an unpleasant one. Similarly, punishment entails the presentation of an unpleasant stimulus or the removal of a pleasant one, as in the case of omission training.

The Uses and Abuses of Punishment Our society relies heavily on punishment and the threat of punishment to keep people "in line." We put people in jail, fine them, spank them, and give them bad grades, parking tickets, and disapproving looks. And what is the result? Punishment often produces an immediate change in behavior—which, ironically, is reinforcing to the punisher and a major reason why the use of punishment is so widespread. Several other factors also encourage a punishment habit. For one, punishers may feel good while delivering the punishment, sensing that they are "settling a score" or "getting even" or making the other person "pay." This is why we speak of revenge as being "sweet."

● Prison riots and other aggressive behavior may result from highly punitive conditions.

But, punishment usually doesn't work as well in the long run as punishers would like (Terry, 2000). Punished children may continue to misbehave, reprimanded employees may still arrive late for work, and, in the United States, many people still commit crimes, despite the fact that we imprison criminals in numbers that far exceed those of any other Western society. Why is punishment so difficult to use effectively? There are several reasons.

First, *the power of punishment to suppress behavior usually disappears when the threat of punishment is removed* (Skinner, 1953). Drivers will observe the speed limit when they know the highway patrol is watching. Johnny will refrain from hitting his little brother when his parents are within earshot. And you will probably give up your wallet to a mugger who points a gun at you. That is, most people will comply with a demand accompanied by the threat of strong and certain punishment. But they may act quite differently when they know punishment is unlikely. This explains why motorists rarely slow down for "construction speed" signs on the highways: They know that the police rarely enforce these zones. In general, you can be certain of controlling someone's behavior through punishment or threat of punishment only if you can control the environment all of the time. Such total control is usually not possible, even in a prison.

Second, *punishment triggers escape or aggression.* When punished, organisms usually try to flee from or otherwise avoid further punishment. But if escape is blocked, they are likely to become aggressive. Corner a wounded animal, and it may savagely attack you. Put two rats in a Skinner box with an electrified floor grid, and the rats will attack each other (Ulrich & Azrin, 1962). Put humans in a harsh prison environment, and they may riot—or, if they are prison guards, they may abuse the prisoners (Zimbardo, 2004c).

Further, in a punitive environment, whether it be a prison, a school, or a home, people learn that punishment and aggression are legitimate means of influencing others, which may explain the smiling faces of the guards seen in the prisoner-abuse photos from Iraq. The punishment–aggression link also explains why abusing parents so often come from abusive families and why aggressive delinquents so often come from homes where aggressive behavior toward the children is commonplace (Golden, 2000). Unfortunately, the well-documented fact that punishment so often leads to aggression remains widely unknown to the general public.

Here's the third reason why punishment is so often ineffective: *Punishment makes the learner apprehensive, which inhibits learning new and better responses.* Unable to escape punishment, an organism may give up its attempts at flight or fight and surrender to an overwhelming feeling of hopelessness. This passive acceptance of a punitive fate produces a behavior pattern called *learned helplessness* (Overmier & Seligman, 1967). In people, this reaction can produce the mental disorder known as depression (Terry, 2000).

CONNECTION: CHAPTER 12

Depression is one of the most common mental disorders.

From the standpoint of a punisher seeking to produce a constructive change in attitudes and behavior, learned helplessness and depression are undesirable outcomes. Whether it produces escape, aggression, or learned helplessness, punishment focuses learners' attention on their own misery—which interferes with new learning. It also fails to help learners see what to do because it focuses attention on what not to do. By contrast, individuals who have not been punished feel much freer to experiment with new behaviors.

And the fourth reason why punitive measures may fail: *Punishment is often applied unequally,* even though that violates our standards of fair and equal treatment. For example, boys are punished more often than girls. Then, too, children (especially grade school children) receive more physical punishment than do adults. And, to give one more example, our schools—and probably our society at large—more often use punishment to control members of racial minority groups than they do to control members of the Caucasian majority (Hyman, 1996; Hyman et al., 1977).

Does Punishment Ever Work? In limited circumstances, punishment can work remarkably well (Terry, 2000). For example, punishment can halt the self-destructive behavior of autistic children who may injure themselves severely by banging their heads or chewing the flesh off their fingers. In these cases, a mild electric shock or a splash of cold water in the face can quickly put a stop to the unwanted behavior, although the effects may be temporary (Holmes, 2001; Linsheid et al., 1990; Lovaas, 1977; Lovaas et al., 1974).

Before you decide on punishment, we suggest you consider extinction and the rewarding of desirable alternative responses. But, if punishment seems to be the only option, it should at least meet the following conditions (Walters & Grusec, 1977):

- *Punishment should be swift*—that is, immediate. Any delay will decrease its effectiveness, so "You'll get spanked when your father gets home" is a poor punishment strategy.
- *Punishment should be certain*—that is, consistently administered every time the unwanted response occurs. When "bad" behavior goes unpunished, the unintended effect can actually be rewarding.
- *Punishment should be limited in duration and intensity*—just enough to stop the behavior but appropriate enough to "make the punishment fit the crime."

- *Punishment should clearly target the behavior,* not the character of the person.
- *Punishment should be limited to the situation in which the response occurred.*
- *Punishment should not give mixed messages* to the punished person (such as, "You are not permitted to hit others, but I am allowed to hit you").
- *The most effective punishment is usually omission training* (*negative punishment*), such as loss of privileges, rather than the application of unpleasant stimuli, such as pain.

Operant and Classical Conditioning Compared

Now that we have looked at the main features of operant and classical conditioning, let's compare them side by side. As you can see in Table 6.2 and the diagrams in Figure 6.6 it is, most obviously, the *consequences* of behavior—especially, rewards and punishments—that make operant conditioning different from classical conditioning. One note of caution: You can see in the diagram of operant learning that food rewards the dog for sitting up. But you will also see food being presented to the dog as an unconditioned stimulus, in the classical conditioning portion of Figure 6.6. The important thing to observe, however, is that in classical conditioning the food comes *before* the response—and therefore it cannot serve as a reward.

Classical conditioning and operant conditioning also differ in the sequence of stimulus and response. Classically conditioned behavior is largely a response to *past stimulation,* while operant behavior is directed at attaining some *future* reinforcement or avoiding a punishment. To say it another way, operant conditioning requires a stimulus that follows the response, whereas classical conditioning ends with the response. (See Figure 6.7.)

The rewards given in operant conditioning can be especially effective in encouraging *new behaviors*—whether they be pulling slot machine levers, making beds, brushing teeth, going to work, or studying for an exam. Classical conditioning, on the other hand, emphasizes eliciting the *same responses to new stimuli*—such as salivating at the sound of a bell or flinching at the sound of a dentist's drill.

You will also note that extinction works in slightly different ways in the two forms of learning. In classical conditioning, it requires withholding the unconditioned stimulus, while in operant

Animals can learn to do surprising things with a little help from operant conditioning techniques, such as shaping.

TABLE 6.2 Classical and Operant Conditioning Compared

Classical conditioning	Operant conditioning
Behavior is controlled by stimuli that *precede* the response (by the CS and UCS).	Behavior is controlled by consequences (rewards, punishments, etc.) that *follow* the response.
No reward or punishment is involved (although pleasant and aversive stimuli may be used).	Often involves reward (reinforcement) or punishment.
Through conditioning, a new stimulus (the CS) comes to produce "old" (reflexive) behavior.	Through conditioning, a new stimulus (a reinforcer) produces new behavior.
Extinction is produced by withholding the UCS.	Extinction is produced by withholding reinforcement.
Learner is passive (responds reflexively): Responses are involuntary. That is, behavior is *elicited* by stimulation.	Learner is active (operant behavior): Responses are voluntary. That is, behavior is *emitted* by the organism.

● **FIGURE 6.6** The Same Stimulus Plays Different Roles in Classical Conditioning and Operant Conditioning

The same stimulus (food) can play vastly different roles, depending on which type of conditioning is involved. In classical conditioning, it can be the UCS, while in operant conditioning it can serve as a reinforcer for operant behavior. Note also that classical conditioning involves the association of two stimuli that occur *before* the response. Operant conditioning involves a reinforcing (rewarding) or punishing stimulus that occurs *after* the response.

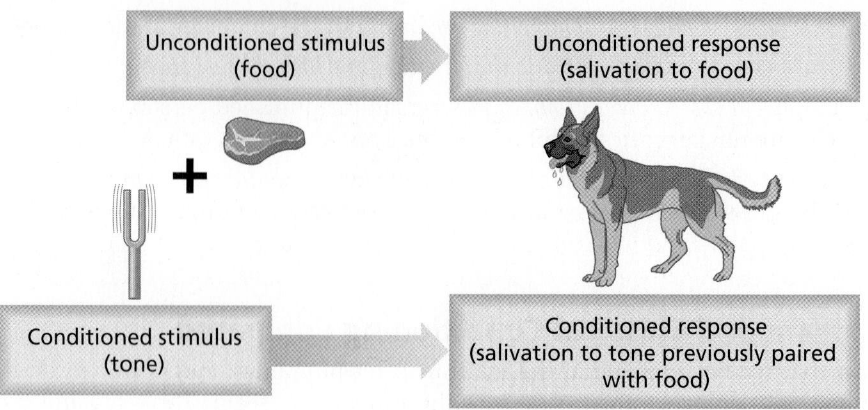

Unconditioned stimulus (food)
Unconditioned response (salivation to food)
+
Conditioned stimulus (tone)
Conditioned response (salivation to tone previously paired with food)

Classical Conditioning

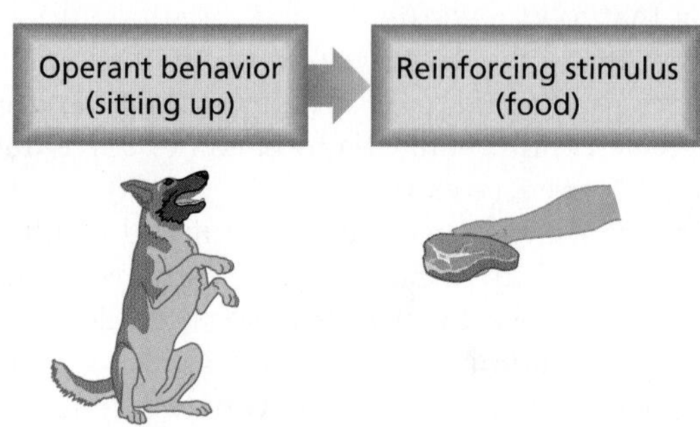

Operant behavior (sitting up)
Reinforcing stimulus (food)

Operant Conditioning

conditioning the reinforcer must be withheld. In both cases, however, the result is a gradual fading of the response.

Operant conditioning and classical conditioning differ in several other important ways that you see in Table 6.2. For one, operant behavior is not based on an automatic reflex action, as was the dog's salivation or Little Albert's crying. Accordingly, operant behavior seems more "voluntary"—more under the

● **FIGURE 6.7** Classical and Operant Conditioning Can Work Together

A response originally learned through classical conditioning can be maintained and strengthened by operant reinforcement.

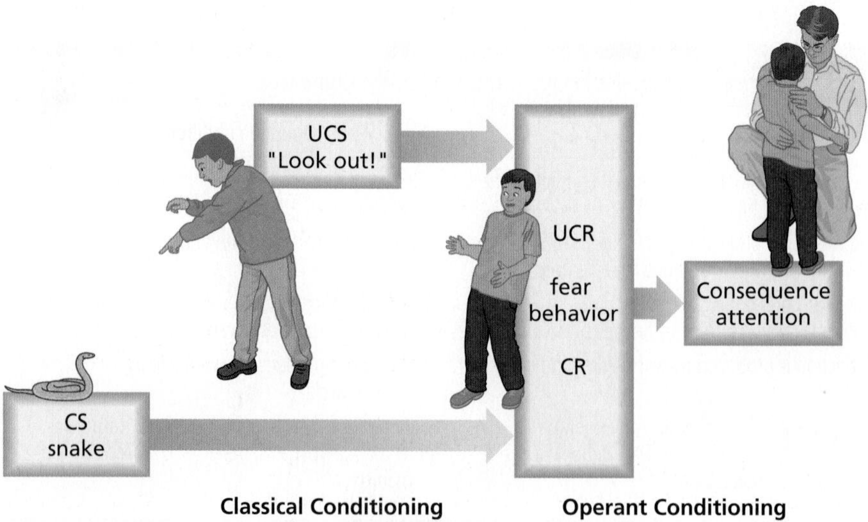

UCS
"Look out!"
UCR
fear
behavior
CR
Consequence
attention
CS
snake
Classical Conditioning
Operant Conditioning

control of the responder. To paraphrase a proverb: You can stimulate a dog to salivation (a reflex), but you can't make it eat (an operant behavior).

But don't make the mistake of thinking that classical and operant conditioning are competing explanations for learning. They can be complementary. In fact, responses that were originally learned by classical conditioning will often be maintained later by operant conditioning. How might this happen? Consider a snake phobia. Suppose that the fear of snakes was originally learned by classical conditioning when a snake (CS) was paired with a frightening UCS (someone yelling, "Look out!"). Once the phobic response is established, it could be maintained and strengthened by operant conditioning, as when bystanders give attention to the fearful person (see Figure 6.7). Similarly, the attention Bob, one of your authors, gets from refusing to eat olives encourages the aversion that he originally learned by classical conditioning.

PSYCHOLOGY IN YOUR LIFE: A CHECKLIST FOR MODIFYING OPERANT BEHAVIOR

Think of someone whose behavior you would like to change. For the sake of illustration, let's focus on your nephew Johnny's temper tantrums, which always seem to occur when you take him out in public. Operant conditioning offers a variety of tools that can help, provided you have some control over stimuli that are important to Johnny. Let's consider a checklist of these operant tools: positive reinforcement, punishment, negative reinforcement, and extinction.

- *Positive reinforcement* is a good bet, especially if you can find some desirable behavior to reinforce before the unwanted behavior occurs. And don't overlook the Premack principle, by which Johnny gets to do something he likes if he refrains from temper outbursts. Remember, too, that attention can be a powerful reinforcer for unwanted behavior.
- *Punishment* may be tempting, but it is always chancy. In addition, it usually has a bad effect on the relationship between punisher and the person being punished. It is also difficult to employ because, unlike positive reinforcement, punishment must be done with unfailing consistency. If you do decide to punish Johnny for his tantrums, make sure you do so swiftly, certainly, and without undue harshness. As we said earlier, restriction or loss of privileges (negative punishment) is usually more effective than the application of some aversive consequence (positive punishment).
- *Negative reinforcement* has many of the same drawbacks as punishment because it involves unpleasant stimulation. Parents may try—most often unsuccessfully—to use negative reinforcement as a means of encouraging unlikely behavior, such as doing homework, taking out the garbage, or feeding the dog. In its most common form, the parents attempt to use nagging (an aversive stimulus) until the desired behavior occurs, whereupon the nagging presumably stops (negative reinforcement). This tactic rarely works to anyone's satisfaction. (Ironically, Johnny's screaming fit is his own intuitive attempt to manipulate people with negative reinforcement.) The only time negative reinforcement predictably works well is when the aversive conditions were imposed naturally and impersonally—as when you have headache and take aspirin, which produces negative reinforcement when your headache goes away.
- *Extinction* is a guaranteed solution, but only if you control all the reinforcers. In Johnny's case, extinction simply means not giving in to the temper tantrum and not letting him have what he wants (attention or candy, for

example). Instead, you simply allow the tantrum to burn itself out. This may be embarrassing because children often pick the most public places for such displays—a good sign that they are doing so for attention. One big problem with extinction, however, is that it may take a while, so extinction is not a good option if the subject is engaging in dangerous behavior, such as playing in a busy street. Another problem, only recently recognized, is that extinction can unleash a flurry of new trial-and-error behaviors aimed at getting the expected reinforcement (Carpenter, 2001b).

The best approach—often recommended by child psychologists—is to use a combination of tactics. In Johnny's case, they would probably recommend both reinforcing his desirable behaviors and extinguishing his undesirable ones.

We recommend memorizing the four items on this checklist: positive reinforcement, punishment, negative reinforcement, and extinction. Then, whenever you are dealing with someone whose behavior is undesirable, go through the list and see whether one or more of these operant tactics might do the trick. And remember: The behavior you may want to change could be your own!

CHECK YOUR UNDERSTANDING

1. **RECALL:** Thorndike's *law of effect* said that an organism will learn to perform responses that are
   a. preceded by a conditioned stimulus.
   b. reflexive.
   c. prompted.
   d. preceded by a neutral stimulus.
   e. rewarded.

2. **APPLICATION:** Which one of the following is an example of negative reinforcement?
   a. taking away a child's favorite toy when the child misbehaves
   b. making a child watch while another child is punished
   c. giving a child a toy for misbehaving.
   d. going to the dentist and having a toothache relieved
   e. spanking a child for swearing

3. **APPLICATION:** Suppose that you have taught your dog to roll over for the reward of a dog biscuit. Then one day you run out of dog biscuits. Which schedule of reinforcement would keep your dog responding longer without a biscuit?
   a. noncontingent reinforcement
   b. positive reinforcement.
   c. negative reinforcement
   d. intermittent reinforcement
   e. continuous reinforcement

4. **RECALL:** Which one of the following is a conditioned reinforcer for most people?
   a. a sharp pain in the back
   b. water
   c. money
   d. sex
   e. food

5. **UNDERSTANDING THE CORE CONCEPT:** Operant conditioning, in contrast with classical conditioning, emphasizes events (such as rewards and punishments) that occur
   a. after the behavior.
   b. concurrently with another response.
   c. at the same time as another stimulus.
   d. during the behavior.
   e. before the behavior.

ANSWERS: 1. e 2. d 3. d 4. c 5. a

KEY QUESTION
?

HOW DOES COGNITIVE PSYCHOLOGY EXPLAIN LEARNING?

According to J. D. Watson's (1968) account in *The Double Helix,* the genetic code was cracked one day in a flash of insight following months of trial and error. You may have had a similar, if less famous, experience when solving a problem of your own. Such insightful events present difficulties for behavioral learning because they are hard to explain in terms of Pavlovian reflexes or Skinnerian shaping.

Many psychologists believe that an entirely different process, called *cognitive* learning, is responsible for such "flashes of insight." From this perspective, learning does not always show itself immediately in behavior. Instead, learning may be reflected in mental activity alone. And, to the chagrin of behaviorists, the cognitive view maintains that such mental processes can be examined objectively—as the Core Concept for this section says:

CORE CONCEPT

According to cognitive psychology, some forms of learning must be explained as changes in mental processes, rather than as changes in behavior alone.

Let's see how psychologists have approached this task of examining the covert mental processes behind learning. To do so, we first take you on a trip to the Canary Islands, off the coast of northern Africa.

Insight Learning: Köhler in the Canaries with the Chimps

CONNECTION: CHAPTER 4
Gestalt psychology is best known for its work on perception.

Isolated on Tenerife in the Canary Islands during World War I, Gestalt psychologist Wolfgang Köhler (*KER-ler*) had time to think long and hard about learning. He was disenchanted with the behaviorists' explanation for learning, which he found too limiting, and so he sought to develop his own theories. To Köhler's way of thinking, mental processes had to be an essential component of learning, even though they had been spurned as unscientific speculation by the behaviorists. To press his point, Köhler took advantage of a primate research facility on Tenerife to study chimpanzee behavior in situations that he contrived to make cognitive learning reveal itself (Sharps & Wertheimer, 2000; Sherrill, 1991).

In one famous study, Köhler showed that his chimps could solve complex problems by combining simpler behaviors they had previously learned separately. This was illustrated by Sultan, the brightest chimp, who had learned to pile up boxes and scramble on top of them to reach fruit suspended high in his cage and to use sticks to obtain fruit that was just out of reach. So, when Köhler presented Sultan with a novel situation, fruit suspended even higher in the air, the chimp first attacked it unsuccessfully with sticks, in trial-and-error fashion. In apparent frustration, Sultan eventually threw the sticks away, kicked the wall, and sat down. According to Köhler's report, the animal then scratched his head and began to stare at some boxes nearby. Suddenly, he jumped up and

● The sort of learning displayed by Köhler's chimps defied explanation by the behaviorists—in terms of classical conditioning and operant conditioning. Here you see Sultan, Köhler's smartest animal, solving the problem of getting the bananas suspended out of the reach by stacking the boxes and climbing on top of them. Köhler claimed that Sultan's behavior demonstrated *insight learning*.

dragged a box and a stick underneath the fruit, climbed on the box, and knocked down his prize with the stick. Remarkably, Sultan had never before seen or used this combination of responses. This suggested to Köhler that the animals were not mindlessly using conditioned behaviors but were learning by reorganizing their *perceptions* of problems. He ventured that such behavior shows how apes, like humans, learn to solve problems by suddenly perceiving familiar objects in new forms or relationships—a decidedly mental process, rather than a behavioral one. He called this **insight learning** (Köhler, 1925).

Remarkably, behaviorism had no convincing stimulus–response explanation for Köhler's demonstration, except to criticize it as poorly controlled. No stretch of the imagination could plausibly explain Sultan's behavior in stimulus–response terms, as a product merely of classical or operant conditioning. The feats of Köhler's chimps demanded the cognitive explanation of perceptual reorganization. In a similar fashion, rats in Edward Tolman's lab began behaving in ways that also flew in the face of accepted behavioral doctrine. Let's see what they were up to—next.

Cognitive Maps: Tolman Finds Out What's on a Rat's Mind

If you have ever given directions to someone or walked through your house in the dark, you have some idea of the *cognitive map* that Edward Tolman (1886–1959) proposed. Technically, a **cognitive map** is a mental image that an organism uses to navigate through a familiar environment. But could such a simple-minded creature as a rat have such complex mental imagery? And, if so, how could the existence of these cognitive maps be demonstrated?

Mental Images–Not Behaviors A cognitive map, Tolman argued, was the only way to account for a rat quickly selecting an alternative route in a maze when the preferred path to the goal is blocked. In fact, rats will often select the shortest detour around a barrier, even though taking that particular route was never previously reinforced. Rather than blindly exploring different parts of the maze through trial and error (as would be predicted by behavioral theory), Tolman's rats behaved as though they had a mental representation of the maze. (Figure 6.8 shows the arrangement of a maze such as Tolman used.)

■ **Insight learning** A form of cognitive learning, originally described by the Gestalt psychologists, in which problem solving occurs by means of a sudden reorganization of perceptions.

■ **Cognitive map** A mental representation of physical space.

S. GROSS

"Well, you don't look like an experimental psychologist to me."

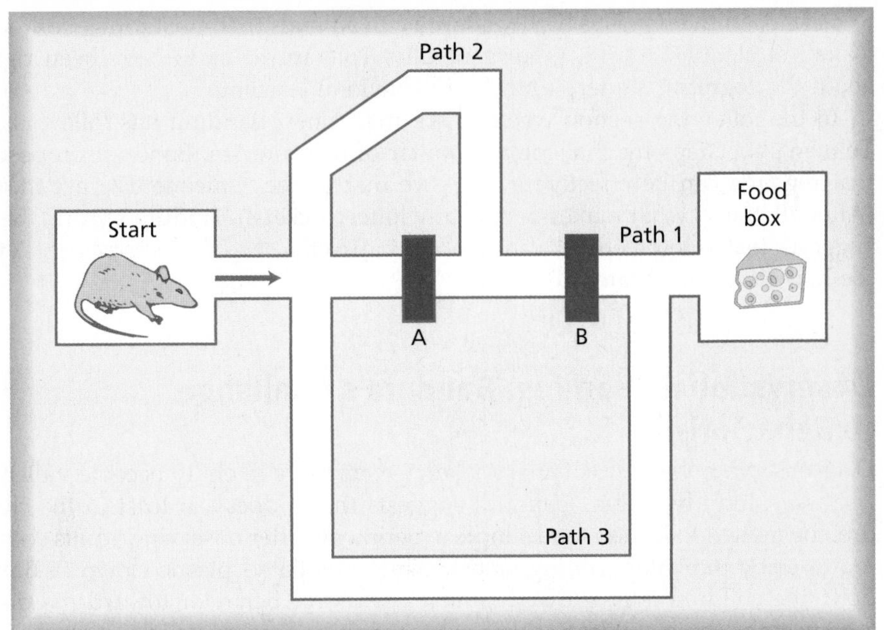
Path 2
Start
Food
box
Path 1
A
B
Path 3

● **FIGURE 6.8** Using Cognitive Maps in Maze Learning

Subjects preferred the direct path (Path 1) when it was open. When it was blocked at A, they preferred Path 2. When Path 2 was blocked at B, rats usually chose Path 3. Their behavior indicated that they had a cognitive map of the best route to the food box. (*Source:* From "Degrees of Hunger, Reward and Nonreward, and Maze Learning in Rats" by E. C. Tolman and C. H. Honzik, *University of California Publication of Psychology,* Vol. 4, No. 16, December 1930.)

In further support of his claim that learning was mental, not behavioral, Tolman offered another experiment. After rats had learned to run a maze, he flooded it with water and showed that the rats were quite capable of swimming though the maze. Again, this demonstrated that what the animals had learned were not behaviors. Instead of learning merely a sequence of right and left turns, Tolman argued, they had acquired a more abstract mental representation of the maze's spatial layout (Tolman & Honzik, 1930; Tolman et al., 1946).

Learning Without Reinforcement In yet another simple study that attacked the very foundations of behaviorism, Tolman (1948) allowed his rats to wander freely about a maze for several hours, during which they received no reinforcement at all. Yet, despite the lack of reinforcement (which behaviorists supposed to be essential for maze learning), the rats later were able to negotiate the maze for a food reward more quickly than rats that had never seen the maze before. Tolman called this *latent learning*.

The Significance of Tolman's Work What made Tolman's work both significant and provocative was its challenge to the prevailing behavioral views of Pavlov, Watson, and (later) Skinner. While Tolman accepted the idea that psychologists must study observable behavior, he showed that simple associations between stimuli and responses could not explain the behavior observed in his experiments. Tolman's cognitive explanations, therefore, presented a daring challenge to behaviorism (Gleitman, 1991; Kesner & Olton, 1990; Olton, 1992; Tolman, 1932). We should note, in passing, that Jean Piaget's work in developmental psychology (which we describe in Chapter 9) was simultaneously challenging behaviorism on another cognitive front.

Subsequent experiments on cognitive maps in rats, chimpanzees, and humans have broadly supported Tolman's work (Menzel, 1978; Moar, 1980; Olton, 1979). More recently, brain imaging has pointed to the hippocampus as a structure involved in "drawing" the cognitive map in the brain (Jacobs & Schenk, 2003). So, it seems clear that Tolman was right: Organisms learn the spatial layout of their environments by exploration, and they do so even if they are not reinforced for exploring. From an evolutionary perspective, this ability to make cognitive maps is highly adaptive in animals that must forage for food (Kamil et al., 1987). And, more generally, Tolman seems to have been right about the cognitive underpinnings of behavioral learning.

In the following section we shall see that Albert Bandura has followed in Tolman's footsteps by challenging a pillar of behaviorism. Bandura proposed that rewards can be effective even if we merely see someone else get them. (After all, this is what makes people buy lottery tickets!) Bandura's work, then, suggests that reinforcement can operate indirectly, through *observation.* Let's see how he demonstrated this idea.

● In the BoBo doll experiment, a boy and girl imitate the aggressive behavior that they have seen an adult exhibit.

Observational Learning: Bandura's Challenge to Behaviorism

Does observing violent behavior make viewers more likely to become violent? A classic study by Albert Bandura suggests that it does—at least in the children he invited to his lab for a simple experiment. After observing adults seeming to enjoy punching, hitting, and kicking an inflated plastic clown (a BoBo doll), the children later showed similar aggressive behavior toward the doll. Significantly, these children were more aggressive than those in a control condition who had not observed the aggressive models (Bandura et al., 1963). Subsequent studies showed that children will also imitate aggressive behaviors they have seen on film, even when the models were merely cartoon characters.

Learning by Observation and Imitation An important implication of Bandura's BoBo doll study is that imitation can serve us in situations where we have not had a chance to gather personal experience. Thus, we learn by imitation or observation, by watching the behavior of another person, or model. If the model's actions appear successful—that is, if the model seems to find it reinforcing—we may seek to behave in the same way. You can think of learning by observation and imitation as an extension of operant conditioning, in which we observe someone else getting rewarded but act as though we had also received a reward.

Psychologists simply call this **observational learning** or *social learning*. It accounts for children learning aggressive behavior by imitating aggressive role models who are perceived as successful or admirable or who seem to be enjoying themselves. And it accounts for changes in clothing fashions and the rapid spread of slang expressions, as well as many other learned behaviors. Observational learning is also seen in nonhuman species, as when a mother cat teaches her kittens how to hunt. One study demonstrated that even a creature as simple-brained as the octopus can learn by example from watching the behavior of other octopi (Fiorito & Scotto, 1992). And, not to be outdone, a clever bowerbird in an Australian national park has achieved some notoriety through observational learning by fooling tourists with its imitation of a cell phone ringing (Winters, 2002).

■ **Observational learning** A form of cognitive learning in which new responses are acquired after watching others' behavior and the consequences of their behavior.

Effects of Media Violence As you might have guessed, much of the research on observational learning has focused on the impact of violence in film and video (Bushman & Anderson, 2001; Huesmann et al., 2003; Johnson et al., 2001). Predictably, the issue is a controversial one (Anderson & Bushman, 2002; Bloom, 2002; Ferguson, 2002; Freedman, 1984, 1996). What we have is *correlational* evidence from more than 50 studies shows that observing violence is associated with violent behavior and more than 100 *experimental* studies pointing to a causal relationship (Huesmann & Moise, 1996; Primavera & Heron, 1996). In addition, we have experimental evidence that viewers of media violence show a reduction in emotional arousal and distress, when they subsequently observe violent acts—a condition known as *psychic numbing* (Murray & Kippax, 1979). Finally, notes social psychologist Elliot Aronson, extensive media violence is undoubtedly one factor contributing to violent tragedies, such as the Columbine High School shootings (Aronson, 2000).

Not all imitation is harmful, of course. By imitation we also learn about charitable behavior, comforting others in distress, and driving on the correct side of the road. In general, we can say that people learn much—both prosocial (helping) and antisocial (hurting) behaviors—through observation of others. This capacity to learn from watching enables us to acquire behaviors efficiently, without going through tedious trial and error. So, while observational learning seems to be a factor in violent behavior, it also enables us to learn socially useful behaviors by profiting from the mistakes and successes of others.

Rethinking Behavioral Learning in Cognitive Terms

In the last few decades of the 20th century, cognitive psychologists ventured deep into the territory of classical and operant conditioning, giving those theories a cognitive tweak (Leslie, 2001). One of the big issues they raised concerns the adaptive value of classical conditioning for an animal (Hollis, 1997). Specifically, Robert Rescorla has shown that the crucial feature of the conditioned stimulus is its *informativeness*—its value in predicting the onset of the unconditioned stimulus (Rescorla, 1972, 1988; Rescorla & Wagner, 1972). We saw this, for example, in food aversions, where a certain taste can serve as a warning of illness.

Research by Leon Kamin extends Rescorla's idea. Kamin (1969) has shown that a learner will form a CS–CR connection only if the CS seems to provide unique information about the UCS. In his laboratory, an aversive unconditioned stimulus, such as a shock, was preceded by multiple warning cues, such as lights, tones, and tastes. Yet, his animal subjects paid attention only to the stimuli that provided the best information about the UCS.

In the wild, the unique wing markings of monarch butterflies serve as conditioned stimuli for butterfly-eating birds that have a learned aversion for monarch butterflies. (They taste awful.) To give a more personal example, you may see smoke as well as smell the acrid odor of something burning before you actually see the flames of a fire. But you may have learned from experience that smoke is not always visible during a fire, whereas the smell of something burning is a telltale sign of fire. The smell then provides better information about whether there is a fire, so you learned to pay closer attention to the smell than to the sight of smoke.

Following the lead of Bandura, Kamin, and Rescorla, attempts are also being made by cognitive psychologists to broaden the scope of operant conditioning to include mental processes (Church, 2001; DeGrandpre, 2000; Ohlsson, 1996). From this perspective, reinforcement changes not only behavior but also the individual's *expectations* for future rewards or punishments in similar situations. An example will probably help: If you are rewarded with a better grade for attending your psychology class, this reward changes your future behavior by changing your expectation that attending future classes will also be rewarding. We will see more of this work in Chapter 14, where we will look at *social cognition.* (See Table 6.3.)

Brain Mechanisms and Learning

On a neural level, learning apparently involves physical changes that strengthen the synapses in groups of nerve cells—a process called **long-term potentiation** (Antonova et al., 2001; Carlson, 2004; Kandel, 2000). In operant conditioning, the

Long-term potentiation
A biological process, involving physical changes that strengthen the synapses in groups of nerve cells, which is believed to be the neural basis of learning.

TABLE 6.3	Behavioral Learning and Cognitive Learning Compared
Behavioral Learning	**Cognitive Learning**
Focuses on observable events (stimuli and responses) only	Makes inferences about mental processes that are not directly observable
Learning as associations among stimuli and responses	Learning as information processing: The learner seeks useful information from stimuli
Main forms of learning are habituation, classical conditioning, and operant (instrumental) conditioning	Learning also involves insight, observational learning, cognitive maps, and other more complex forms of learning
Developed as a rebellion against the subjective methods of structuralism and functionalism: Behaviorism became the dominant perspective for much of the 20th century.	Developed as a rebellion against the narrow perspective of behaviorism: Cognitive psychology became the dominant perspective at the end of the 20th century.
Big names: Pavlov, Thorndike, Watson, Skinner	Big names: Köhler, Tolman, Bandura, Rescorla

brain's reward circuitry also comes into play, especially parts of the limbic system and associated brain structures. These circuits are rich in dopamine receptors, leading many experts to believe that this transmitter is crucial to the brain's sensing of reward (Fiorillo et al., 2003; Shizgal & Avanitogiannis, 2003). In support of this view, we remind you that the highly reinforcing sensations produced by cocaine and amphetamines are due to their action as dopamine agonists.

CONNECTION: CHAPTER 3

An *agonist* is a chemical that mimics or enhances the effects of a neurotransmitter.

Neuroscientists Eric Kandel and Robert Hawkins (1992) have made a proposal that may connect behavioral learning and cognitive learning at the level of brain pathways. Their theory rests on the discovery that animals with relatively simple nervous systems have a single type of nerve circuit that enables them to learn simple behavioral responses. In the more complex brains of mammals, however, neuroscientists have found a second type of learning circuitry that apparently facilitates higher forms of learning, such as memory for events.

What is the significance of these findings? Kandel and Hawkins speculated that the two types of learning circuits may divide the task of learning along the same line that has long separated behavioral psychologists and cognitive psychologists. Some other psychologists now tentatively agree (Clark & Squire, 1998; Jog et al., 1999). The simpler circuit seems to be responsible for the sort of "mindless" learning that occurs when a dog drools at the sound of a bell or when a person acquires a motor skill, such as riding a bike or swinging a golf club. This kind of learning occurs slowly and improves with repetition over many trials. Significantly, classical conditioning and much of operant learning fit this description. By contrast, the second type of learning circuit seems to be responsible for more complex forms of learning that require conscious processing—the sort of learning that interests cognitive psychologists: concept formation, insight learning, observational learning, and memory for specific events. If further research verifies that this division reflects a fundamental distinction in the nervous system, we will be able to say that those on the behavioral and cognitive extremes were both (partly) right. They were talking about fundamentally different forms of learning.

"Higher" Cognitive Learning

Whatever the neuroscientists finally decide, it seems clear that the learning required in college classes, where you must learn abstract ideas, is different from the stimulus–response learning that Pavlov, Watson, and Skinner studied. Acquiring knowledge about the field of psychology, for example, involves building mental images, assimilating concepts, and pondering ways they can be related, compared, and contrasted. By the same token, Sabra's classes taught her *concepts* about flight and about emotional responses. It's not that behavioral conditioning isn't involved in human learning—after all, students *do* work for grades and salivate when they see a pizza—but the principles of behavioral learning don't tell the whole story of "higher" cognitive learning.

● Learning is not efficient when the learner is "multitasking"–trying to perform several tasks that demand attention at the same time.

The next two chapters will take us deeper into this realm of cognition, where we will discuss memory, thinking, concept formation, problem solving, and intelligence. There you will find out more about the mental structures that underlie cognitive learning. The problem we will face there is exactly the one that the behaviorists were hoping to avoid: In studying cognition, we must make inferences about processes that we cannot measure directly. Cognitive learning is always about processes that are one step removed from observable behavior. We will find, however, that cognitive psychologists have developed some very clever methods for obtaining objective data on which to base their inferences. The newest of these—coming fully on line in the last decade or so—is brain imaging, which, as we will see, has brought psychologists very close to an objective glimpse at private mental processes.

But, before we move on to these topics in the next chapter, let's pause for a critical look at a learning fad that has swept through college classrooms in recent years.

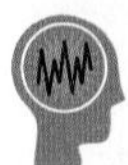

PSYCHOLOGY IN YOUR LIFE: A CRITICAL LOOK AT "LEARNING STYLES"

There is no doubt that people differ in the ways in which they approach learning. You can see by looking at your classmates that everyone brings a different set of interests, abilities, temperamental factors, developmental levels, social and cultural experiences, and emotions to bear on learning tasks. But, can we say that these constitute distinct "learning styles"?

Some educators have made claims about learning styles that go far beyond any supporting evidence (Terry, 2000). For example, much has been made of a supposed difference between "left-brained" and "right-brained" learners. But, as we saw in Chapter 3, this dichotomy is based on a fundamental misinterpretation of split-brain research. (In a person with an intact corpus callosum, both hemispheres work cooperatively.) What the proponents of left-brain/right-brain learning styles usually mean is that some people *prefer* learning verbally, whereas others *prefer* materials that are more visual–spatial. And, like all typologies, this one assumes that people fall neatly into distinct groups, even though it would be more accurate to see people as gradually shading from one end of the spectrum to the other. This questionable assumption may be one reason why little solid evidence exists to show that people who are described as having different learning styles actually do learn differently.

Many other learning-style schemes have been proposed, and with them paper-and-pencil tests have appeared on the market for assessing students' learning styles. Unfortunately, most of these schemes have little supporting data to show that people with different scores learn in different ways. An exception may be an ambitious program developed by Sternberg and Grigorenko to assess students on their abilities for logical, creative, and practical thinking—arguably, three distinct forms of "intelligence" (Sternberg, 1994;

Sternberg & Grigorenko, 1997). Students in an introductory psychology course were divided into groups that received instruction emphasizing the form of intelligence on which they had scored highest. (A control group of students was deliberately mismatched.) Tests at the end of the course indicated that students did best when the teaching emphasis matched their intellectual style. As a practical matter, however, such a fine-tuned approach is probably not feasible for implementation on a large scale.

On a more positive note, interest in learning styles has alerted teachers and professors to the fact that their material can usually be taught in a variety of ways. Further, the available research suggests that everyone learns better when the material can be approached in more than one way—both visual and verbal, as well as through hands-on active learning (see, for example, McKeachie, 1990, 1997, 1999). In recent years, this has led to the development of a variety of teaching methods to augment the lecture-only method that had previously been used extensively in classes.

The practical lesson here is to be skeptical of tests that purport to identify your learning style. Beware also of people who might tell you that you are a visual learner, a reflective learner, or some other such type. This sort of thinking erroneously suggests that each person learns in only one way. It also erroneously suggests that the way we learn is fixed and unchanging. In fact, your college experience presents a wonderful opportunity to learn to think and learn in new and unaccustomed ways.

CHECK YOUR UNDERSTANDING

1. **RECALL:** When their goal path was blocked, Tolman's rats would take the shortest detour around the barrier. This, said Tolman, showed that they had developed
   a. observational learning.
   b. operant behavior.
   c. trial-and-error learning.
   d. classical responses.
   e. cognitive maps.
2. **RECALL:** Cognitive psychologist Robert Rescorla has reinterpreted the process of classical conditioning. In his view, the conditioned stimulus (CS) serves as a
   a. stimulus that follows the UCS.
   b. punisher.
   c. cue that signals the onset of the UCS.
   d. negative reinforcement.
   e. cognitive map.
3. **APPLICATION:** If you were going to use Bandura's findings in developing a program to prevent violence among middle school children, you might
   a. have children role-play nonaggressive solutions to interpersonal problems.
   b. have children watch videos of aggressive children who are not being reinforced for their aggressive behavior.
   c. reward children for nonviolent acts.
   d. punish children for aggressive acts performed at school.
   e. have children punch a BoBo doll to "get the aggression out of their system."
4. **UNDERSTANDING THE CORE CONCEPT:** Which of the following proved to be difficult to explain in purely behavioral terms?
   a. a child learning to read
   b. a pigeon learning to press a lever in a Skinner box for a food reward
   c. a chimpanzee using a pile of boxes and a stick to obtain food hung high in its cage
   d. a dog salivating at the sound of a bell
   e. a trained seal doing a trick for a fish

ANSWERS: 1. e 2. c 3. b 4. c

LEARNING: THE STATE OF THE ART

Psychologists now understand the essential features of behavioral learning: habituation, classical conditioning, and operant conditioning. Arguably, they know more about such learning than about any other facet of psychology. Is there anything left to learn about learning? Here are three important frontiers that need much more exploration:

- We know only a little about the neuroscience behind learning: the nerve circuits, the neurotransmitters, and how they represent our experience (Kandel, 2000). At the most basic level, what *is* learning?
- We need more work that bridges the gap between behavioral and cognitive learning. The tools of neuroscience have removed many of the old (and, at the time, valid) objections the behaviorists voiced about the objective study of mental processes. But is cognitive learning just an elaboration of classical conditioning, operant conditioning, and habituation—or is it something fundamentally different?
- Third, we have just scratched the surface in our understanding of how we learn about concepts, ideas, and images. This is not only a theoretical issue but also a question of urgent practical importance: How can we facilitate such learning in our schools and colleges?

Plenty of work on learning remains to be done by a new generation of researchers who can ask the right questions and look beyond the old controversies.

USING PSYCHOLOGY TO LEARN PSYCHOLOGY

Operant Conditioning Can Help You Study More—and Enjoy It

You may have tried the Premack principle to trick yourself into studying more, perhaps by denying yourself TV time or a trip to the refrigerator until your homework was done. It works for some people, but if it doesn't work for you, try making the studying itself more enjoyable and more reinforcing.

For most of us, being with people we like is reinforcing, regardless of the activity. So, make some (not all) of your studying a social activity. That is, schedule a time when you and another classmate or two can get together to identify and clarify important concepts and to try to predict what will be on the next test.

Don't focus just on vocabulary. Rather, try to discover the big picture—the overall meaning of each section of the chapter. The Core Concepts are a good place to start. Then you can discuss with your friends how the details fit in with the Core Concepts. You will most likely find that the social pressure of an upcoming study group will help motivate you to get your reading done and identify murky points. When you get together for your group study session, you will find that explaining what you have learned reinforces your own learning. The real reinforcement comes, however, from spending some time—studying—with your friends!

CHAPTER SUMMARY

KEY QUESTION

CORE CONCEPT

Learning produces lasting changes in behavior or mental processes, giving us an advantage over organisms that rely more heavily on reflexes and instincts. Some forms of learning, such as habituation, are quite simple, while others, such as classical conditioning, operant conditioning, and cognitive learning, are more complex.

● WHAT SORT OF LEARNING DOES CLASSICAL CONDITIONING EXPLAIN?

The earliest learning research focused on classical conditioning, beginning with Ivan Pavlov's discovery that conditioned stimuli (after being paired with unconditioned stimuli) could elicit reflexive responses. His experiments on dogs showed how conditioned responses could be acquired, extinguished, and undergo spontaneous recovery in laboratory animals. He also demonstrated stimulus generalization and discrimination learning. John Watson extended Pavlov's work to people, notably in his famous experiment on the conditioning of fear in Little Albert. More recent work, particularly studies of taste aversions, suggests, however, that classical conditioning is not a simple stimulus–response learning process but also has a biological component. In general, classical conditioning affects basic, survival-oriented responses. Therapeutic applications of Pavlovian learning include the prevention of harmful food aversions in chemotherapy patients.

● **Classical conditioning is a basic form of learning in which a stimulus that produces an innate reflex becomes associated with a previously neutral stimulus, which then acquires the power to elicit essentially the same response.**

● HOW DO WE LEARN NEW BEHAVIORS BY OPERANT CONDITIONING?

A more active form of learning, called instrumental conditioning, was first explored by Edward Thorndike, who established the law of effect, based on his study of trial-and-error learning. B. F. Skinner expanded Thorndike's work, now called operant conditioning, to explain how responses are influenced by their environmental consequences. His work identified and assessed various consequences, including positive and negative reinforcement, punishment, and an operant form of extinction. The power of operant conditioning involves producing new responses. To do so, Skinner and others examined continuous reinforcement, as well as several kinds of intermittent reinforcement contingencies, including FR, VR, FI, and VI schedules.

As for punishment, research has shown that it is more difficult to use than reward because it has several undesirable side effects. There are, however, alternatives, including operant extinction and rewarding of alternative responses, application of the Premack principle, and prompting and shaping new behaviors.

● **In operant conditioning, the consequences of behavior, such as rewards and punishments, influence the chance that the behavior will occur again.**

● HOW DOES COGNITIVE PSYCHOLOGY EXPLAIN LEARNING?

Much research now suggests that learning is not just a process that links stimuli and responses: Learning is also cognitive. This was shown in Köhler's work on insight learning in chimpanzees, in Tolman's studies of cognitive maps in rats, and in Bandura's research on observational learning and imitation in humans—particularly the effect of observing aggressive models, which spawned many studies on media violence. All of this cognitive research demonstrated that learning did not necessarily involve changes in behavior nor did it require reinforcement. In the past three decades, cognitive scientists have worked on reinterpreting behavioral learning, especially operant and classical conditioning, in cognitive terms, as well as searching for the neural basis of learning. Some educators have, however, taken new developments in learning far beyond the evidence: Specifically, there is little empirical support for most of the claims in the "learning style" literature.

● **According to cognitive psychology, some forms of learning must be explained as changes in mental processes, rather than as changes in behavior alone.**

REVIEW TEST

For each of the following items, choose the single correct or best answer. The correct answers appear at the end.

1. Which one of the following taught that psychology should involve only the analysis of observable stimuli and responses?
   a. Albert Bandura
   b. B. F. Skinner
   c. Sigmund Freud
   d. John Garcia
   e. Wolfgang Köhler

2. According to Thorndike, rewarded responses are gradually "stamped in," while unrewarded or punished responses are eliminated. He called this
   a. classical conditioning.
   b. the law of effect.
   c. negative punishment.
   d. observational learning.
   e. extinction.

3. Which one of the following illustrates a reinforcement contingency?
   a. When I get home late, dinner is cold.
   b. Money is reinforcing because it buys me things I need and want, such as food, clothes, and entertainment.
   c. I get $500 for a week's work.
   d. If I don't show up for work, I will be fired.
   e. I always work harder in the morning than I do in the afternoon.

4. "The best part of going to the beach," your friend exclaims as you start your vacation, "is getting away from all the stress of work and school." If this is true, then your friend's vacation-taking behavior has been influenced by
   a. extinction.
   b. omission training.
   c. punishment.
   d. positive reinforcement.
   e. negative reinforcement.

5. Which of the following is *not* a good way to make punishment effective?
   a. Make it swift and brief.
   b. Focus it on the undesirable behavior.
   c. Make it intense.
   d. Deliver it immediately.
   e. Limit it to the situation in which the response occurred.
6. According to the Premack principle, a reinforcer can be
   a. the opportunity to engage in any behavior frequently performed by the organism.
   b. an automatic response to a stimulus.
   c. anything that rewards rather than penalizes behavior.
   d. changes in behavior from its past norms.
   e. a stimulus that becomes associated with an unconditioned stimulus.
7. In his research with rats running mazes, Edward C. Tolman concluded that his animals had
   a. made a CS–UCS connection.
   b. utilized positive reinforcement.
   c. displayed spontaneous recovery.
   d. adapted to positive and negative reinforcement.
   e. developed a cognitive map.
8. In Bandura's experiment with the BoBo doll, aggressive behavior resulted from
   a. observational learning.
   b. painful stimulation.
   c. punishment.
   d. negative reinforcement.
   e. insults.
9. During classical conditioning, for an organism to learn a conditioned association between two stimuli, the UCS must seem to
   a. predict the CS.
   b. mimic the NS.
   c. be predicted by the CS.
   d. be independent of the CS.
   e. follow the UCR.
10. The biggest problem with the concept of "learning styles" is that
    a. most people are visual learners—hardly anyone is an auditory learner.
    b. most educators don't believe in learning styles.
    c. auditory learning styles are underutilized.
    d. the ways people learn don't fall neatly into distinct learning-style categories.
    e. people who think with the right brain don't fit into any known learning style.

ANSWERS: 1.b 2.b 3.c 4.e 5.c 6.a 7.e 8.a 9.c 10.d

KEY TERMS

Learning (p. 196)
Habituation (p. 197)
Mere exposure effect (p. 197)
Behavioral learning (p. 198)
Classical conditioning (p. 199)
Neutral stimulus (p. 199)
Unconditioned stimulus (UCS) (p. 199)
Unconditioned response (UCR) (p. 199)
Acquisition (p. 200)
Conditioned stimulus (CS) (p. 200)
Conditioned response (CR) (p. 200)
Extinction (in classical conditioning) (p. 201)
Spontaneous recovery (p. 201)
Stimulus generalization (p. 202)
Stimulus discrimination (p. 202)
Experimental neurosis (p. 202)
Taste-aversion learning (p. 204)
Operant (p. 206)
Operant conditioning (p. 206)
Law of effect (p. 206)
Reinforcer (p. 206)
Positive reinforcement (p. 207)
Negative reinforcement (p. 207)
Operant chamber (p. 207)
Reinforcement contingencies (p. 208)
Continuous reinforcement (p. 208)
Shaping (p. 208)
Intermittent reinforcement (p. 208)
Extinction (in operant conditioning) (p. 208)
Schedules of reinforcement (p. 209)
Ratio schedule (p. 209)
Interval schedule (p. 209)
Fixed ratio (FR) schedules (p. 209)
Variable ratio (VR) schedules (p. 209)
Fixed interval (FI) schedules (p. 209)
Variable interval (VI) schedules (p. 210)
Primary reinforcers (p. 210)
Conditioned reinforcers or **secondary reinforcers** (p. 210)
Token economy (p. 210)
Premack principle (p. 211)
Punishment (p. 211)
Positive punishment (p. 211)
Omission training (negative punishment) (p. 211)
Insight learning (p. 220)
Cognitive map (p. 220)
Observational learning (p. 222)
Long-term potentiation (p. 223)

AP* REVIEW: VOCABULARY

Match each of the following vocabulary terms to its definition.

1. Classical conditioning
2. Conditioned stimulus (CS)
3. Spontaneous recovery
4. Law of effect
5. Ratio schedule
6. Interval schedule
7. Token economy
8. Premack principle
9. Omission training
10. Observational learning

_____ **a.** The reappearance of an extinguished conditioned response after a time delay.

_____ **b.** The concept that a more-preferred activity can be used to reinforce a less-preferred activity.

_____ **c.** A program by which reinforcement depends on the time elapsed since the last reinforcement.

_____ **d.** A previously neutral stimulus that comes to elicit the conditioned response.

_____ **e.** A therapeutic method by which individuals are rewarded with items that serve as secondary reinforcers.

_____ **f.** A form of cognitive learning in which new responses are acquired after watching others' behavior and the resulting consequences.

_____ **g.** The idea that responses that produced desirable results would be learned, or "stamped" into the organism.

_____ **h.** The removal of an appetitive stimulus following a response, which leads to a decrease in behavior.

_____ **i.** A program by which reinforcement depends on the number of correct responses.

_____ **j.** A form of behavior learning in which a previously neutral stimulus acquires the power to elicit the same innate reflex produced by another stimulus.

AP* REVIEW: ESSAY

Use your knowledge of the chapter concepts to answer the following essay question.

Albert Bandura designed one of the seminal experiments regarding Observational Learning. Support or refute his conclusions regarding children and violence being sure that your argument addresses each of the following:

a. positive reinforcement

b. negative reinforcement

c. punishment

d. omission training

OUR RECOMMENDED BOOKS AND VIDEOS

BOOKS

Artiss, K. L. (1996). *Mistake making.* Lanham, MD: University Press of America. Why doesn't everyone learn from experience? Some experiences may not be memorable—but certain types of people may also have difficulty making the adjustments necessary for each lesson; and, failing to learn, they end up suffering relentless punishment by repeating their errors and failures. Here's why it may happen—and what to do about it.

Greven, P. (1992). *Spare the child: The religious roots of punishment and the psychological impact of child abuse.* New York: Vintage Books. Imagine a world in which hitting a child is not only politically incorrect, it is also against the law of both man and God. Greven documents the great weight of evidence against any rationale for corporal punishment of children and asserts that we have a moral obligation to develop humane alternatives to beating our kids.

Martel, Yann. (2003). *Life of Pi.* Orlando, FL: Harcourt. No, this is not a math book. It's a fantastic (in both senses) novel about religion . . . and animal learning and behavior. Pi is a young boy from India, where his parents own a zoo and where he becomes a Hindu, a Christian, and a Moslem. When the zoo is sold, the family heads to Canada on a steamer, along with many of their animals. A storm sends the ship to the bottom, and the only survivors are Pi, a wounded zebra, a seasick orangutan, a hyena, and Richard Parker, a Bengal tiger—all in the same lifeboat. That's where Pi's deep understanding of animals comes in handy.

Nierenberg, G. I. (1996). *Doing it right the first time: A short guide to learning from your most memorable errors, mistakes, and blunders.* New York: Wiley. Mainly aimed at managers, this book also offers valuable advice to students (and professors) about how to first become aware of and then detect patterns in our own repeated errors. Some strategies involve focusing attention, learning from others' mistakes, and building accuracy.

Wright, J. (2003). *There must be more than this: Finding more life, love, and meaning by overcoming your soft addictions.* New York: Broadway Books. Educator Judith Wright finds that most people indulge—too much—in "soft addictions" such as watching TV, surfing the Net, gossiping, or shopping. Time spent in these tempting but ultimately unfulfulling activities leaves us needier than before. The key to change is in understanding why these time-wasters feel rewarding and how to find positive reinforcement instead in truly meaningful activity such as interacting with friends or completing valued work.

VIDEOS

A Clockwork Orange. (1971, color, 137 min.). Directed by Stanley Kubrick; starring Malcolm McDowell, Patrick Magee, Adrienne Corri. A classic and still powerful rendition of Anthony Burgess's novel about a futuristic society's efforts to reform a psychopathic criminal by applying aversive conditioning—with unexpected results. (*Rating R*)

Key Question Chapter Outline

What Is Memory?

Memory's Three Basic Tasks

How Do We Form Memories?

The First Stage: Sensory Memory
The Second Stage: Working Memory
The Third Stage: Long-Term Memory
The Biological Basis of Memory

How Do We Retrieve Memories?

Implicit and Explicit Memory
Retrieval Cues
Other Factors Affecting Retrieval

Why Does Memory Sometimes Fail Us?

Transience: Fading Memories Cause Forgetting
Absent-Mindedness: Lapses of Attention Cause Forgetting
Blocking: Interference Causes Forgetting
Misattribution: Memories in the Wrong Context
Suggestibility: External Cues Distort or Create Memories
Bias: Beliefs, Attitudes, and Opinions Distort Memories
Persistence: When We Can't Forget
The Advantages of the "Seven Sins" of Memory

How Do Children Acquire Language?

What are the Components of Thought?

Concepts
Imagery and Cognitive Maps
Thought and the Brain

What Abilities Do Good Thinkers Possess?

Problem Solving
Judging and Making Decisions

Memory: The State of the Art

CORE CONCEPTS

Human memory is an information-processing system that works constructively to encode, store, and retrieve information.

Each of the three memory stages encodes and stores memories in a different way, but they work together to transform sensory experience into a lasting record that has a pattern or meaning.

Whether memories are implicit or explicit, successful retrieval depends on how they were encoded and how they are cued.

Most of our memory problems arise from memory's "seven sins"—which are really by-products of otherwise adaptive features of human memory.

Infants and children face an especially important developmental task with the acquisition of language.

Thinking is a cognitive process in which the brain uses information from the senses, emotions, and memory to create and manipulate mental representations, such as concepts, images, schemas, and scripts.

Good thinkers not only have a repertoire of effective strategies, called algorithms and heuristics, they also know how to avoid common impediments to problem solving and decision making.

Psychology in Your Life

Would You Want a "Photographic" Memory?

This ability is rare, and those who have it say that the images can sometimes interfere with their thinking.

"Flashbulb" Memories: Where Were You When . . . ?

These especially vivid memories usually involve emotionally charged events. Surprisingly, they aren't always accurate.

On the Tip of Your Tongue

It is maddening when you know the word, but you just can't quite say it. But you're not alone. Most people experience this about once a week.

Improving Your Memory with Mnemonics

There are lots of tricks for learning lists, but another technique works better for mastering the concepts you'll meet in college.

Learning a New Language

Whether acquiring a new language occurs early in your academic or personal life, the knowledge is invaluable.

Schemas and Scripts Help You Know What to Expect . . .

But sometimes they fill in the blanks—without your knowing it.

On Becoming a Creative Genius

Such individuals have expertise, certain personality traits, and lots of motivation, but their thought processes are essentially the same as everyone else's.

USING PSYCHOLOGY TO LEARN PSYCHOLOGY:
How to Avoid Memory Failure on Exams

Chapter

7

Cognition

SOME 20 YEARS AGO, 12-year-old Donna Smith began to suffer from severe migraine headaches, which left her sleepless and depressed. Her parents, Judee and Dan, agreed to get her psychiatric help. During an evaluation recommended by her therapist, Donna disclosed—for the first time—that she had been sexually molested at the age of 3 by a neighbor. It was concluded that memories of the assault, buried in her mind for so long, were probably responsible for some of Donna's current problems, so she continued with therapy.

As a teenager, Donna began work with a new therapist, a private social worker specializing in child abuse. In their first session, the therapist asked Donna if she had been sexually abused by her father. Donna denied this but did mention the neighbor's assault. The therapist, however, believed there might be more behind Donna's problems. For many months, she repeatedly asked Donna whether her father had abused her. Finally, Donna told her a lie, claiming her father had once "touched" her, hoping this false claim would enable her therapy to move on. The therapist immediately reported Donna's father to the local sheriff and to the Maryland Department of Social Services (ABC News, 1995).

When Donna realized the drastic consequences of her false claim, she tried to set the record straight, but the therapist dismissed the confession, saying that all abuse victims recant their accusations once they learn their therapists are required to report such claims. The therapist was persuasive, and eventually Donna began to entertain the idea that her conscious memory was a self-delusion—a trick of her mind trying to protect itself from the "real" truth. Reluctantly, she concluded that it must have been her father, not the neighbor, who had assaulted her as a toddler. When the therapist convinced her to tell the story to county authorities, Donna was removed from her home and placed in foster care.

To her parents, these sudden accusations were "like a bomb"—and it got worse. Still in therapy, Donna became convinced her father had been a chronic abuser, and she began to hate him "wholeheartedly." Committed to a psychiatric hospital, she was diagnosed as having several different personalities, one of which claimed that her parents practiced ritual satanic abuse of Donna's younger brothers. The courts forbade Donna's parents to have contact with her. Judee Smith lost her license to run a day care center. Dan Smith, a retired naval officer, was arrested at his home and handcuffed in front of their two young sons. Financially ruined, he was tried on charges of abuse, based solely on his daughter's testimony. His two-week trial ended in a hung jury, and Dan Smith went free.

Shortly after the trial, Donna moved to Michigan with her foster family. In these new surroundings, far away from the system that had supported her fabricated story, she gradually regained perspective and found the courage to tell the truth. She admitted the charges had all been fabrications, and her doctor recommended that she be sent back to her family. The Smiths had a tearful reunion and began the slow process of rebuilding lost relationships and trust. "She's been a victim of this system, as much as we've been a victim," says Dan Smith. "You know, there's a lot of healing to be done."

According to Johns Hopkins psychiatrist Paul McHugh, erroneous recovered memories are fabricated from suggestions therapists offer in order to blame psychological problems on long-hidden trauma (ABC News, 1995). Memory expert Elizabeth Loftus agrees, noting that some clinicians are all too ready to accept their clients' memories, even fantastic tales of ritualistic abuse (Loftus, 2003a, b). In the book *Making Monsters,* social psychologist Richard Ofshe argues that clients can unknowingly tailor their recollections to fit their therapists' expectations. He adds that "therapists often encourage patients to redefine their life histories based on the new pseudomemories and, by doing so, redefine their most basic understanding of their families and themselves" (Ofshe & Watters, 1994, p. 6).

Today Donna and her family are "in wonderful shape, back together." Still, the memories of the Smith family's ordeal will remain painful shadows in the background of their lives forever. Fortunately, the same flexibility in human learning and remembering that created these problems can also provide the key to forgiving and healing.

We should emphasize that sexual abuse of children does occur, and it is a serious problem. While estimates vary considerably, it appears that from 4% to 20% of children in the United States experience at least one incident of sexual abuse (McAnulty & Burnette, 2004; Rathus et al., 2000). The issue raised by Donna's case, however, involves false claims of sexual abuse based on faulty "recovered memories." And, while such problems are relatively rare, they have surfaced often enough to alarm psychologists about the widespread misunderstanding people have about memory. Psychologists know that memory does not always make an accurate record of events—even when people are very confident about their recollections.

WHAT IS MEMORY?

In fact, Donna's memory works very much like your own. Memory is but one of the topics you will learn about in this chapter. As you will discover in this section, everyone has a memory capable of distortion. You will also learn about memory's inner workings and some extraordinary memory abilities. Finally, we will end this discussion on a practical note by considering some steps you can take to improve your memory.

As we have seen in the previous chapters, the operation of the brain and the components of learning are very complex. This chapter will show you how the functions of memory, language, and thought interact to enable people to recall information and to express and develop their individuality. Although this complexity may seem overwhelming to you now, in the remaining chapters you will be applying all of the concepts you have learned thus far about sensation and perception, the biological basis of behavior, consciousness, and motivation.

This chapter includes memory, language, and thought, and although each is presented separately, all work together as an integrated process that we call cognition.

The best defense against the tricks that memory can play comes from an understanding of how memory works. So let's begin building that defense with a definition: Cognitive psychologists view **memory** as a system that encodes, stores, and retrieves information—a definition, by the way, that applies equally to an organism or a computer. Unlike a computer's memory, however, human memory is a *cognitive* system, in the sense of the term's Latin root, *cognoscere,* which means "to know" or "to understand." That is, human memory works closely with the perceptual system, which takes information from the senses and selectively converts it into meaningful patterns that can be stored and accessed later when needed. These memory patterns, then, form the raw material for thought and behavior—allowing you to recognize a friend's face, ride a bicycle, recollect a trip to Disneyland, and (if all goes well) recall the concepts you need during a test. More generally, our Core Concept characterizes the memory system this way:

CORE CONCEPT

Human memory is an information-processing system that works constructively to encode, store, and retrieve information.

And how is memory related to *learning*? You might think of human memory as the cognitive system that processes, encodes, and stores information as we learn and then allows us to retrieve that learned information later. Accordingly, this chapter is an extension of our discussion of cognitive learning in Chapter 6. The focus here, however, will be on more complex *human* learning and memory, as contrasted with the simpler forms of animal learning and conditioning that we studied earlier.

A look at Figure 7.1 will make you aware of the reconstructive process of memory. Which image in the figure is the most accurate portrayal of a penny? Although pennies are common in our everyday experience, you will probably find that identifying the real penny image is not easy. Unless we are coin collectors, most of us pay little attention to the details of these familiar objects.

Memory Any system–human, animal, or machine–that encodes, stores, and retrieves information.

● FIGURE 7.1 The Penny Test

(*Source:* From "Long-Term Memory for a Common Object," by Nickerson and Adams in *Cognitive Psychology,* Vol. 11, Issue #1, 1979, pp. 287–307. Copyright © 1979. Reprinted by permission of Elsevier.)

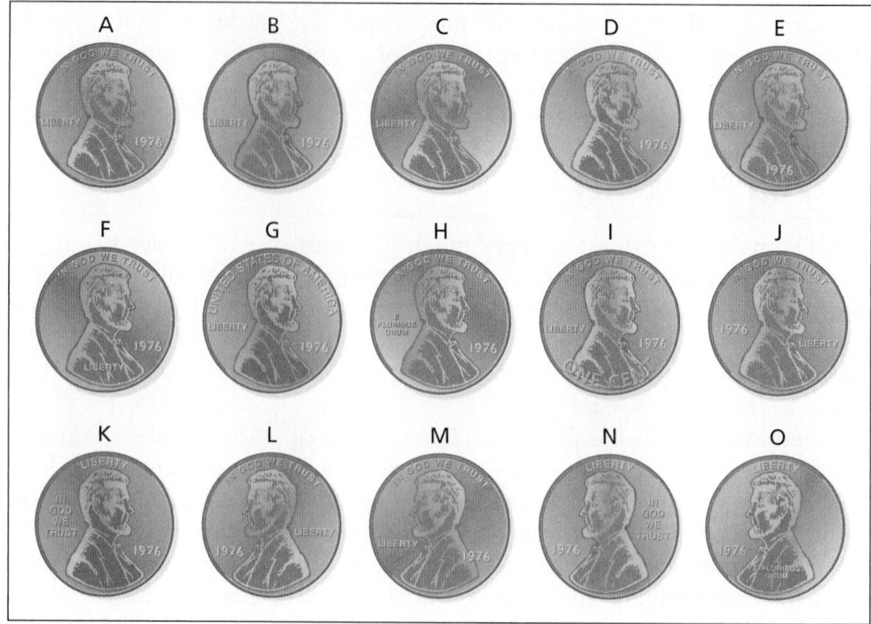
A
B
C
D
E
F
G
H
I
J
K
L
M
N
O

The result is a vague memory image that serves well enough in everyday life but is sparse on details. So, when retrieving the image of a penny, we automatically fill in the gaps and missing details—without realizing how much of the memory we are actually creating. (The right answer, by the way, is A.)

Memory's Three Basic Tasks

In simplest terms, human memory takes essentially meaningless sensory information (such as the sound of your professor's voice) and changes it into meaningful patterns (words, sentences, and concepts) that you can store and use later. This process is referred to by cognitive psychologists as the **information-processing model** of memory. To do so, memory must first *encode* the incoming sensory information in a useful format. **Encoding** requires that you *select* some stimulus event from among the vast array of inputs assaulting your senses. Is it a sound, a visual image, or an odor? Then you *identify* the distinctive features of that input. If it's a sound, is it loud, soft, or harsh? Does it fit some pattern, such as a car horn, a melody, a voice? Is it a sound you have heard before? Finally, you mentally tag, or *label,* an experience to make it meaningful. ("It's Dr. Weber. She's my psychology professor!")

For most of our everyday experiences, encoding can be so automatic and rapid that we have no awareness of the process. For example, you can probably recall what you had for breakfast this morning, even though you didn't deliberately try to make the experience "stick" in your mind. Emotionally charged experiences, such as an angry exchange with a colleague, are even more likely to lodge in memory without any effort on our part (Dolan, 2002).

On the other hand, memories for concepts, such the basic principles of psychology that you are learning about in this book, usually require a deliberate encoding effort, called *elaboration,* in order to establish a usable memory. During this elaboration, you connect a new concept with existing information in memory. One way to do this is to link it with concrete examples, such as when you associate the term *negative reinforcement* with the removal of pain when you take an aspirin. (As an aid to elaboration, this book provides many such examples that we hope will connect with your experience.) In another form of

■ **Information-processing model** A cognitive understanding of memory, emphasizing how information is changed when it is encoded, stored, and retrieved.

■ **Encoding** One of the three basic tasks of memory, involving the modification of information to fit the preferred format for the memory system.

elaboration, you connect the new idea to old concepts already in memory. This happens, for example, when you realize that "elaboration" is essentially the same process that Piaget called *assimilation.*

CONNECTION: CHAPTER 9

In Piaget's theory, *assimilation* involves absorbing new information into existing schemes.

Storage, the second essential memory task, involves the retention of encoded material over time. But as we get deeper into the workings of memory, you will learn that memory consists of three *stages,* each of which stores memories for different lengths of time and in different forms. The "trick" of getting difficult-to-remember material into long-term storage, then, is to recode the information before the time clock runs out. For example, while listening to a lecture, you have just a few seconds to find some pattern or meaning in the sound of your professor's voice before the information is lost.

Retrieval, the third basic memory task, is the payoff for your earlier efforts in encoding and storage. When you have a properly encoded memory, it takes only a split second for a good cue to access the information, bring it to consciousness, or, in some cases, to influence your behavior at an unconscious level. (Let's test the ability of your conscious retrieval machinery to recover the material we just covered: Can you remember which of the three memory tasks comes before *storage*?)

Alas, retrieval doesn't always go well, because the human memory system—marvelous as it is—sometimes makes errors, distorts information, or even fails us completely. In the last section of the chapter, we will take a close look at these problems, which memory expert Daniel Schacter (1996) calls the seven sins of memory. The good news is that there are effective techniques that you can use to combat memory's "sins."

■ **Storage** One of the three basic tasks of memory, involving the retention of encoded material over time.

■ **Retrieval** The third basic task of memory, involving the location and recovery of information from memory.

PSYCHOLOGY IN YOUR LIFE: WOULD YOU WANT A "PHOTOGRAPHIC" MEMORY?

Suppose that your memory were so vivid and accurate that you could use it to "read" paragraphs of this book out of memory during the next psychology exam. Such was the power of a 23-year-old woman tested by Charles Stromeyer and Joseph Psotka (1970). For example, she could look at the meaningless configuration of dots in the left-hand pattern in the accompanying "Do It Yourself!" box and combine it mentally with the right-hand image.

DO IT YOURSELF! A Test of Eidetic Imagery

Look at the dot pattern on the left in the figure for a few moments and try to fix it in your memory. With that image in mind, look at the dot pattern on the right. Try to put the two sets of dots together by recalling the first pattern while looking at the second one. If you are the rare individual who can mentally combine the two patterns, you will see something not apparent in either image alone. Difficult? No problem if you have eidetic imagery–but impossible for the rest of us. If you want to see the combined images, but can't combine them in your memory, look at Figure 7.2.

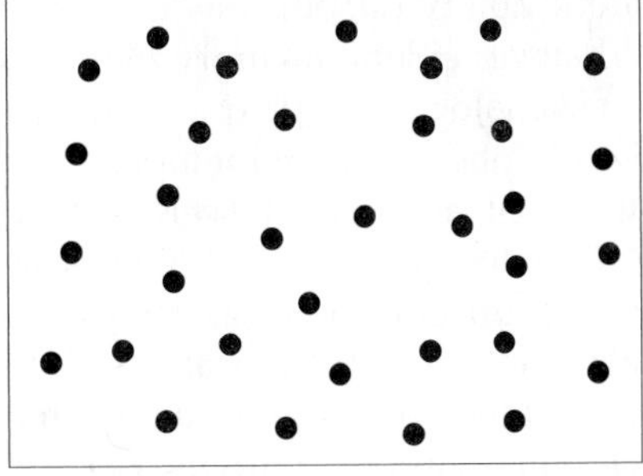

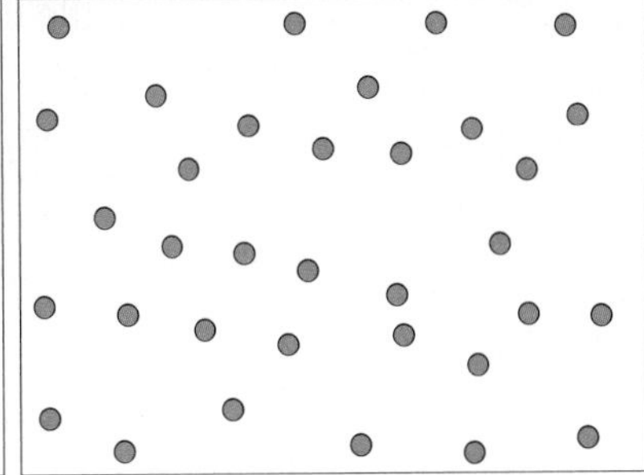

● **A Test of Eidetic Imagery** People with good eidetic imagery can mentally combine these two images to see something that appears in neither one alone.

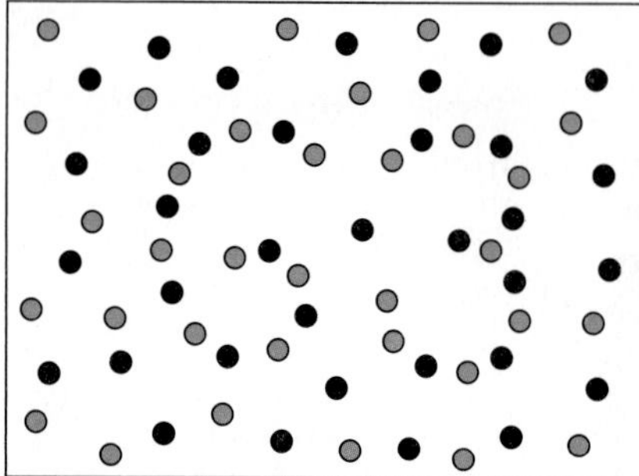

● **FIGURE 7.2** What an Eidetiker Sees
The combined images from the "Do It Yourself" box form a number pattern. (*Source:* From HUMAN MEMORY: Structures and Processes 2nd ed., by Roberta Klatzky. Copyright © 1980. Reprinted by permission of W. H. Freeman and Company/Worth Publishers.)

The combined pattern was the image shown in Figure 7.2. (Did you see the number "63"?) Wouldn't it be great to have such a "photographic" memory? Not entirely, it turns out.

The technical term for "photographic memory" is **eidetic imagery.** Psychologists prefer this term because eidetic images are, in many important respects, different from images made by a camera (Haber, 1969, 1980). For example, a photographic image renders everything in minute detail, while an eidetic image portrays the most interesting and meaningful parts of the scene most accurately.

Eidetic memories also differ in several respects from the normal memory images that most of us experience. For one thing, *eidetikers* describe their memory images as having the vividness of the original experience (Neisser, 1967). For another, eidetic images are visualized as being "outside the head," rather than inside in the "mind's eye." (Even though they see the image "outside," eidetikers realize that it is a mental image.) Further, an eidetic image can last for several minutes—even for days, in some cases. For example, the woman tested by Stromeyer and Psotka could pass the dot-combining test even when the two patterns were shown to her 24 hours apart. Remarkable as this is, however, the persistence of eidetic images can be a curse. Eidetikers report that their vivid imagery can clutter their minds and interfere with other things they want to think about (Hunter, 1964).

Eidetic imagery appears most commonly in children but only rarely in adults. One estimate says that up to 5% of children show some eidetic ability—although in most it's not good enough to pass the dot-combining test (Gray & Gummerman, 1975). While no one knows why eidetic imagery tends to disappear in adults, it may follow some sort of developmental sequence—like losing one's baby teeth. Possibly its disappearance is related to the child's development of formal operational thinking, which often begins at about age 11 or 12.

CONNECTION: CHAPTER 9
In Piaget's theory, the *formal operational stage* marks the appearance of abstract thought.

Alternatively, case studies suggest a connection between the decline of eidetic imagery and the development of language skills: Eidetikers report that describing an eidetic image in words makes the image fade from memory, and they learn to exploit this fact to control their intrusive imagery (Haber, 1969, 1970). A cross-cultural study from Nigeria further supports the idea that the loss of eidetic ability may result from a conflict between language skills and visual imagery. In this research, eidetic imagery was found to be common, not only among children, but also among adults of the Ibo tribe who were living in rural villages. Although the villagers could correctly draw details of images seen sometime earlier, tests showed that members of the same tribe who had moved to the city and had learned to read evidenced little eidetic ability (Doob, 1964).

Whatever eidetic memory may be, it is clearly rare—so rare, in fact, that some psychologists have questioned its existence (Crowder, 1992). The few studies of "photographic memory" have portrayed it as different from everyday memory, as we have seen. But the fact is that we know relatively little about the phenomenon, and few psychologists are currently studying it.

Eidetic imagery presents not only a practical problem for those rare individuals who possess it but also a theoretical problem for cognitive psychologists. If eidetic imagery exists, what component of memory is responsible? On the other hand, if it proves to be a unique form of memory, it doesn't fit well with the widely accepted three-stage model of memory—which we will discuss next.

■ **Eidetic imagery** An especially clear and persistent form of memory that is quite rare; sometimes known as "photographic memory."

CHECK YOUR UNDERSTANDING

1. **ANALYSIS:** Which of the following is a major objection to the "video recorder" theory of memory?
   a. Like perception, memory is an interpretation of experience.
   b. Memories are never accurate.
   c. Unlike a video recorder, memory takes in and stores an enormous quantity of information from all the senses, not just vision.
   d. Unlike a tape-recorded video memory, human memory cannot be edited and changed at a later time.
   e. Memories do not degrade.

2. **RECALL:** Which of the following are the three essential tasks of memory?
   a. eidetic imagery, short-term memory, and recall.
   b. sensory, working, and long-term memory
   c. remembering, forgetting, and repressing
   d. recall, recognition, and relearning
   e. encoding, storage, and retrieval

3. **ANALYSIS:** When you get a new cat, you will note her unique markings, so that you can remember what she looks like in comparison with other cats in the neighborhood. What would a cognitive psychologist call this process of identifying the distinctive features of your cat?
   a. eidetic imagery
   b. encoding
   c. recollection
   d. retrieval
   e. storage

4. **UNDERSTANDING THE CORE CONCEPT:** Which one of the following memory systems reconstructs material during retrieval?
   a. computer memory
   b. human memory
   c. video recorder memory
   d. information recorded in a book
   e. eidetic memory.

ANSWERS: 1. a 2. e 3. b 4. b

HOW DO WE FORM MEMORIES?

KEY QUESTION
?

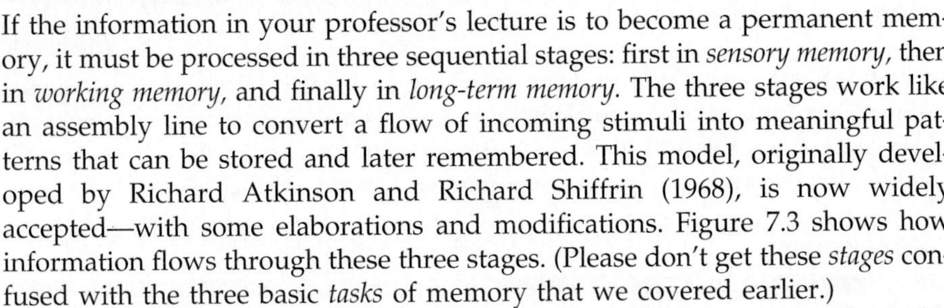

If the information in your professor's lecture is to become a permanent memory, it must be processed in three sequential stages: first in *sensory memory,* then in *working memory,* and finally in *long-term memory.* The three stages work like an assembly line to convert a flow of incoming stimuli into meaningful patterns that can be stored and later remembered. This model, originally developed by Richard Atkinson and Richard Shiffrin (1968), is now widely accepted—with some elaborations and modifications. Figure 7.3 shows how information flows through these three stages. (Please don't get these *stages* confused with the three basic *tasks* of memory that we covered earlier.)

Sensory memory, the most fleeting of the three stages, typically holds sights, sounds, smells, textures, and other sensory impressions for only a fraction of a second. You have experienced a sensory memory as you watched a moving Fourth of July sparkler leave a fading trail of light or heard the flow of one note into another as you listen to music. One function of these short-lived images is to maintain incoming sensory information long enough to be screened for possible entry into working memory.

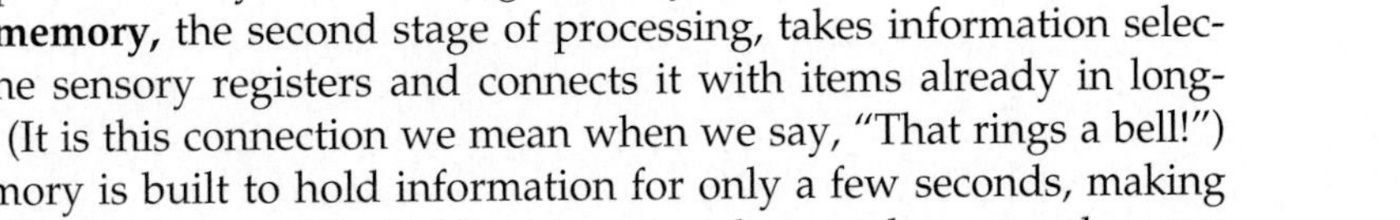

Working memory, the second stage of processing, takes information selectively from the sensory registers and connects it with items already in long-term storage. (It is this connection we mean when we say, "That rings a bell!") Working memory is built to hold information for only a few seconds, making it a useful buffer for temporarily holding items, such as a phone number you

■ **Sensory memory** The first of three memory stages, preserving brief sensory impressions of stimuli.

■ **Working memory** The second of three memory stages, and the most limited in capacity. It preserves recently perceived events or experiences for less than a minute without rehearsal.

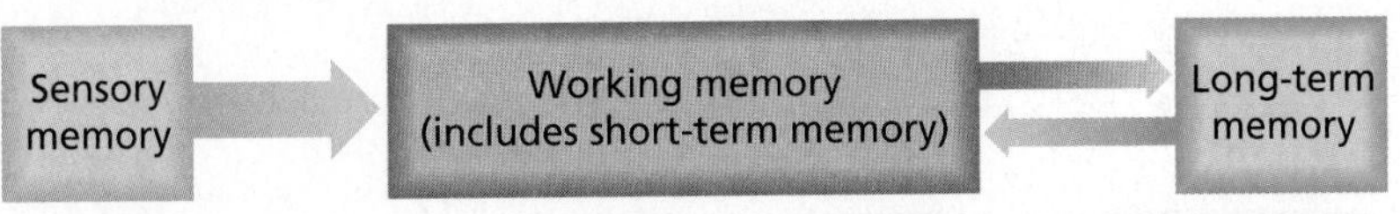
Sensory memory
Working memory (includes short-term memory)
Long-term memory

● **FIGURE 7.3** The Three Stages of Memory (Simplified)

The "standard model," developed by Atkinson and Shiffrin, says that memory is divided into three stages. Everything that goes into long-term storage must first be processed by sensory memory and working memory.

have just looked up. Originally, psychologists called this stage short-term memory (STM), a term still in use (Beardsley, 1997b; Goldman-Rakic, 1992). The newer term *working memory* emphasizes some elaborations on the short-term stage originally proposed in Atkinson and Shiffrin's model (Baddeley, 2001; Engle, 2002), as we will discuss below.

It is noteworthy that everything entering consciousness passes into working memory. The opposite is also true: We are conscious of everything that enters working memory. Because of this intimate relationship, some psychologists have suggested that working memory is actually the long-sought seat of consciousness that we discussed in Chapter 5 (LeDoux, 1996).

Long-term memory (LTM), the final stage of processing, receives information from working memory and can store it for much longer periods—sometimes for the rest of a person's life. Information in long-term memory constitutes our knowledge about the world and holds material as varied as an image of your mother's face, the lyrics to your favorite song, and the year that Wilhelm Wundt established the first psychology laboratory. (You remember: That was in 18??) Long-term memory holds each person's total knowledge of the world and of the self.

These, then, are the three stages of memory—which this section of the chapter will explore in detail. As you read, you should attend to the differences in the ways each stage processes and stores information. With these differences in mind you will begin to discover ways of exploiting the quirks of each stage to enhance your own memory abilities. In briefer terms, our Core Concept says:

CORE CONCEPT

Each of the three memory stages encodes and stores memories in a different way, but they work together to transform sensory experience into a lasting record that has a pattern or meaning.

■ **Long-term memory (LTM)** The third of three memory stages, with the largest capacity and longest duration; LTM stores material organized according to meaning.

In this section you will find out just how each of the three stages makes a unique contribution to the final memory product. (See Table 7.1.) As we consider each stage, we will look at its storage *capacity,* its *duration* (how long it retains information), its *structure and function,* and its *biological basis.*

TABLE 7.1 The Three Stages of Memory Compared

	Sensory memory	Working memory (STM)	Long-term memory (LTM)
Function	Briefly holds information awaiting entry into working memory	Involved in control of attention Attaches meaning to stimulation Makes associations among ideas and events	Storage of information
Encoding	Sensory images: no meaningful encoding	Encodes information (especially by meaning) to make it acceptable for long-term storage	Stores information in meaningful mental categories
Storage capacity	12–16 items	"Magic number 7" ± 2 chunks	Unlimited
Duration	About ¼ second	About 20–30 seconds	Unlimited
Structure	A separate sensory register for each sense	Central executive Phonological loop Sketchpad	Procedural memory and declarative memory (further subdivided into semantic and episodic memory)
Biological Basis	Sensory pathways	Involves the hippocampus and frontal lobes	Cerebral cortex

The First Stage: Sensory Memory

One of the big problems memory must confront is this: Your senses take in far more information than you can possibly use. While reading this book, your senses serve up the words on the page, sounds in the room, the feel of your clothes on your skin, the temperature of the air, the slightly hungry feeling in your stomach . . . And how do you deal with all of this? It's the job of sensory memory to hold the barrage of incoming sensation just long enough (about ¼ second) for your brain to scan it and decide which stream of information needs attention. But just how much information can sensory memory hold? Cognitive psychologist George Sperling answered this question by devising one of psychology's simplest and most clever experiments.

The Capacity and Duration of Sensory Memory In brief, Sperling found that this first stage of memory holds far more information than ever reaches consciousness. His method involved an array of letters, like the one below, flashed on a screen for a fraction of a second. (You might try glancing at the array briefly and then seeing how many you can recall.)

D J B W
X H G N
C L Y K

The sensory image of a friend's face is quickly taken into working memory. There it is elaborated with associations drawn from long-term storage.

In the experiment, Sperling first asked volunteers to report as many of the letters as they could remember from the array (as you just did). As expected, most people could remember only three or four items from such a brief exposure.

But, Sperling conjectured, it might be possible that far more information than these three or four items enters a temporary memory buffer and then vanishes before it can be reported. To test this possibility, he modified the task in the following way. Immediately after the array of letters appeared, an auditory cue signaled which row of letters the subject was to report: A high-pitched tone indicated the top row, a medium tone the middle row, and a low tone meant the bottom row. Thus, immediately after seeing a flash of letters and hearing a beep, respondents were to report items *from only one row,* rather than items from the whole array.

Under this *partial report* condition, most people achieved almost perfect accuracy—no matter which row was signaled. That is, Sperling's subjects could accurately report *any* single row, but not *all* rows. This result suggested that the actual storage capacity of sensory memory can be 12 or more items—even though all but three or four items usually disappear from sensory memory before they can enter consciousness (Sperling, 1960, 1963).

Would it be better if our sensory memories lasted longer, so we would have more time to scan them? Probably not. New information is constantly coming in, and it must also be monitored. Sensory memories last just long enough to dissolve into one another and give us a sense of flow and continuity in our experience. But they usually do not last long enough to interfere with new incoming sensory impressions (Loftus et al., 1992).

The Structure and Function of Sensory Memory You might think of sensory memory as having something like a movie screen, where images are "projected" fleetingly and then disappear. In fact, it is this blending of images in

FIGURE 7.4 Multiple Sensory Stores
We have a separate sensory memory for each of our sensory pathways. All feed into working (short-term) memory.

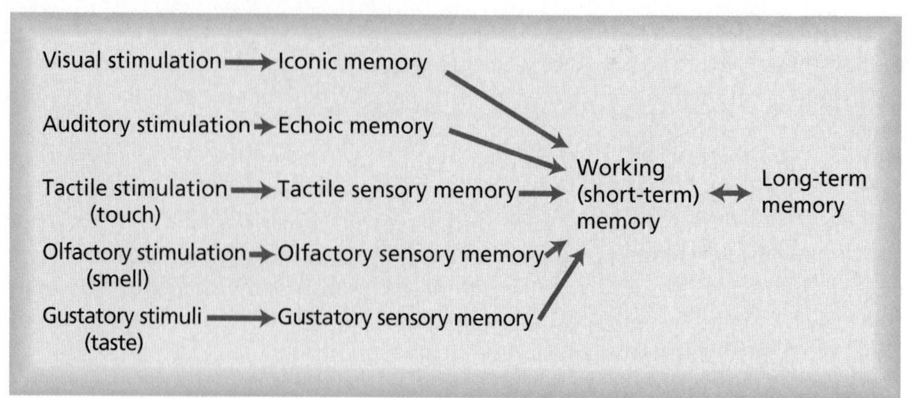
Visual stimulation → Iconic memory
Auditory stimulation → Echoic memory
Tactile stimulation (touch) → Tactile sensory memory
Olfactory stimulation (smell) → Olfactory sensory memory
Gustatory stimuli (taste) → Gustatory sensory memory
Working (short-term) memory
Long-term memory

sensory memory that allows us to have the impression of motion in a "motion picture"—which is really just a rapid series of still images.

But, not all sensory memory consists of visual images. There is a separate *sensory register* for each sense, with each register holding a different kind of sensory information, as you can see in Figure 7.4. The register for vision, called *iconic memory,* stores the encoded light patterns that we see as visual images. Similarly, the sensory memory for hearing, known as *echoic memory,* holds encoded auditory stimuli. Experiments have shown that echoic memory, like iconic memory, holds more information than can pass on into working memory (Darwin et al., 1972).

We should also emphasize that the sensory images have no meaning attached to them, just as an image on photographic film has no meaning to a camera. The job of sensory memory is simply to store the images briefly. As we will see, it's the job of the next stage, working memory, to add meaning to sensation.

The Biological Basis of Sensory Memory The biology of sensory memory appears to be relatively simple. Psychologists now believe that in this initial stage, memory images take the form of nerve impulses in the sense organs and their pathways to the brain. In this view, sensory memory consists merely of the rapidly fading trace of stimulation in our sensory systems (Bower, 2000b; Glanz, 1998). Working memory, then somehow "reads" these fading traces, as it decides which information to admit into the spotlight of attention and which to ignore and allow to disappear. It is this transition step—the handoff between sensory and working memory—that we only vaguely understand.

The Second Stage: Working Memory

The second stage, working memory, is where you process conscious experience (LeDoux, 1996). It is the buffer in which you put the new name you have just heard. It is the temporary storage site for the words at the first part of this sentence as you read toward the end. Thus, working memory is the mechanism that selects information from sensory memory.

Working memory also provides a mental "work space" where we sort and encode information before adding it to long-term memory (Shiffrin, 1993). In doing so, it accesses and retrieves information from long-term storage. So, it is also the register into which a long-term memory of yesterday's psychology class can be retrieved as you review for tomorrow's test.

You might think of working memory, then, as the "central processing chip" for the entire memory system. In this role, it typically holds information for about 20 seconds—far longer than does sensory memory. If you make a spe-

DO IT YOURSELF! Finding Your STM Capacity

Look at the following list of numbers and scan the four-digit number, the first number on the list. Don't try to memorize it. Just read it quickly; then look away from the page and try to recall the number. If you remember it correctly, go on to the next longer number, continuing down the list until you begin to make mistakes. How many digits are in the longest number that you can squeeze into your STM?

7 4 8 5
3 6 2 1 8
4 7 9 1 0 3
2 3 8 4 9 7 1
3 6 8 9 1 7 5 6
7 4 7 2 1 0 3 2 4
8 2 3 0 1 3 8 4 7 6

The result is your digit span, or your working (short-term) memory capacity for digits. Studies show that, under ideal testing conditions, most people can remember five to seven digits. If you remembered more, you may have been using special "chunking" techniques.

cial effort to rehearse the material, it can keep information active even longer, as when you repeat a phone number to yourself before dialing. It is also the mental work space in which we consciously mull over ideas and images pulled from long-term storage, in the process that we call "thinking." In all of these roles, then, working memory acts much like the central processing chip in a computer—not only as the center of mental action but also as a go-between for the other components of memory.

The Capacity and Duration of Working Memory This stage of memory is associated with the "magic number" seven (Miller, 1956). That is, working memory holds about seven items (give or take two)—a fact that caused lots of complaints when phone companies began requiring callers to add an area code to the old 7-digit phone number. Working memory's storage capacity does vary slightly from person to person, so you may want to assess how much yours can hold by trying the test in the "Do It Yourself!" box. Although there is some variation in STM capacity for different kinds of material, that variation is not large. Whatever your capacity is, it will be roughly the same whether you are dealing with letters, numbers, words, shapes, or sounds. Seven items of nearly any sort will fill up short-term memory for most people.

When we try to overload working memory, earlier items are usually lost to accommodate more recent ones. On the other hand, when working memory is filled with information that demands attention, we may not notice new information that we might otherwise think was important. This limited capacity of working memory, in the opinion of some experts, makes it unsafe to talk on your cell phone while driving (Wickelgren, 2001).

It's important to note that working memory's meager storage capacity is significantly smaller than that of sensory memory. In fact, working memory has the smallest capacity of the three memory stages. This limitation, combined with a tendency to discard information after about 20 seconds, makes this part of memory the information "bottleneck" of the memory system. (See Figure 7.5.) As you might have suspected, the twin problems of limited capacity and short duration are obstacles for students, who must process and remember large amounts of information when they hear a lecture or read a book. Fortunately, there are ways to work around these difficulties, as we will see below.

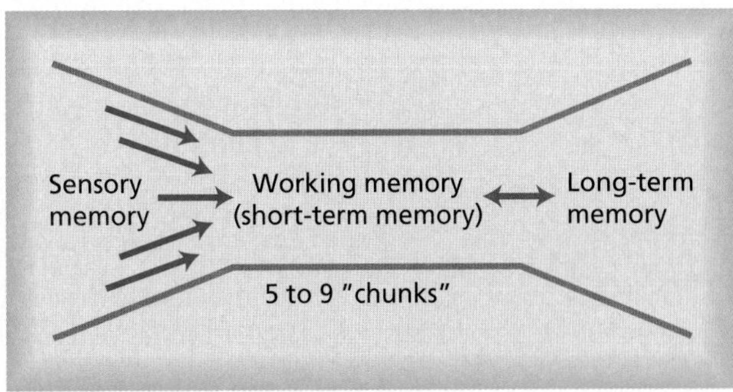
Sensory memory
Working memory (short-term memory)
Long-term memory
5 to 9 "chunks"

● **FIGURE 7.5** The STM Bottleneck
Caught in the middle, with a much smaller capacity than sensory and long-term memories, working memory (short-term memory) becomes an information bottleneck in the memory system. As a result, much incoming information from sensory memory is lost.

The Structure and Function of Working Memory Three important parts of working memory are shown

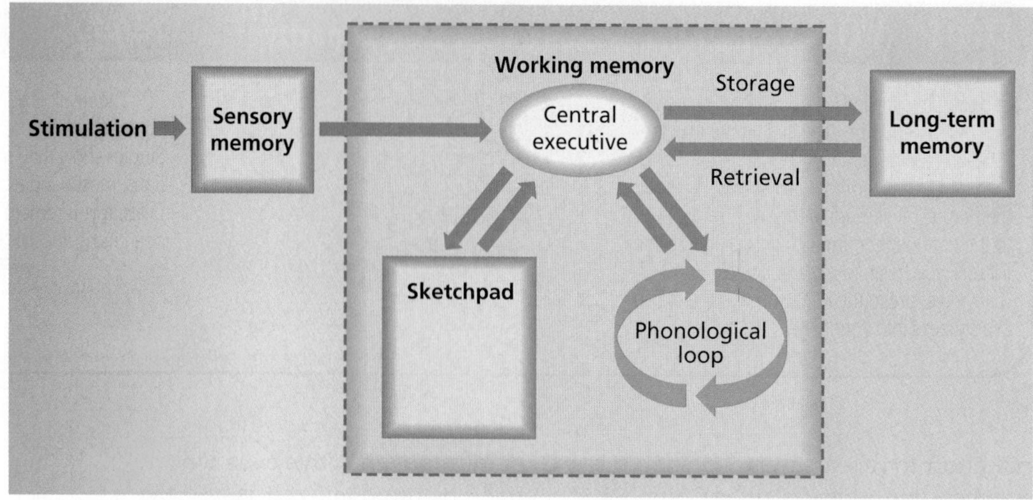
Working memory
Stimulation
Sensory memory
Central executive
Storage
Retrieval
Long-term memory
Sketchpad
Phonological loop

● **FIGURE 7.6** A Model of Working Memory

Atkinson and Shiffrin's original model divided memory into three stages. Events must first be processed by *sensory memory* and *short-term memory* (now called working memory) before they finally go into *long-term memory* storage—from which they can later be retrieved back into working memory. Baddeley's (2001) updated version of working memory, shown here, includes a *central executive* that directs attention, a *sketchpad* for visual and spatial information, and a *phonological loop* for sounds. (*Source:* Adapted from "Episodic Buffer: A New Component of Working Memory?" by A. Baddeley, *Trends in Cognitive Sciences* (2002), 4, pp. 417–423, American Psychological Association.)

in Figure 7.6. A *central executive* directs attention to material retrieved from long-term memory or to important input from sensory memory, such as someone calling a name. A second component consists of a *phonological loop,* which temporarily stores sounds—helping you to remember the mental "echo" of a name or to follow a melody. The third part of working memory is known as the *sketchpad,* used to store and manipulate visual images, as when you are imagining the route between your home and class.

Even with these tools, however, working memory still must face the twin limitations of limited capacity and short duration. For this purpose, it has two options, known as *chunking* and *rehearsal.* Successful students know how to use both strategies.

Chunks and Chunking In memory, a *chunk* is any pattern or meaningful unit of information. A chunk can be a single letter or number, a name, or even a concept. For example, the sequence 1–4–5–9 consists of four digits that could constitute four chunks. However, if you recognize this sequence as the last four digits of your social security number—which is already available in your long-term memory—the four numbers need occupy only one chunk in STM. By **chunking** you can get more material into the seven slots of working memory.

The phone company figured this out years ago—which is why they put hyphens in phone numbers. So, when they group the seven digits of a phone number (e.g., 6735201) into two shorter strings of numbers (673-5201), they have helped us arrange seven separate items into two chunks—which leaves room for the area code.

■ **Chunking** Organizing pieces of information into a smaller number of meaningful units (or chunks)—a process that frees up space in working memory.

■ **Maintenance rehearsal** A working-memory process in which information is merely repeated or reviewed to keep it from fading while in working memory. Maintenance rehearsal involves no active elaboration.

The Role of Rehearsal Speaking of phone numbers, suppose that you have just looked up the number mentioned in the preceding paragraph. To keep it alive in working memory, you probably repeat the digits to yourself over and over. This technique is called **maintenance rehearsal,** and it serves well for maintaining information temporarily in working memory. Maintenance rehearsal not only keeps information fresh in working memory but also prevents competing inputs from crowding it out. However, it is not an efficient way to transfer information to long-term memory—although it is a strategy commonly used for this purpose by people who don't know how memory operates. So, the student who "crams" for a test using simple repetition (maintenance rehearsal) probably won't remember much of the material.

A better strategy for getting information into long-term memory involves **elaborative rehearsal.** With this method, information is not merely repeated but is actively connected to knowledge already stored. Suppose that you are an ophthalmologist, and you want your patients to remember your phone number. Because numbers are notoriously difficult to remember, you can help your customers with their elaborative rehearsal by using a "number" that makes use of the letters on the phone buttons, such as 1-800-EYE-EXAM. The same principle can be used with more complex material, such as you are learning in psychology. For example, when you read about *echoic* memory, you may have elaborated it with a connection to "echo," also an auditory sensation.

Acoustic Encoding: The Phonological Loop While reading words like "whirr," "pop," "cuckoo," and "splash," you can hear in your mind the sounds they describe. Much the same thing happens, less obviously, even with words that don't have imitative sounds because working memory converts them into the sounds of spoken language in its phonological loop. There, verbal patterns in working memory acquire an acoustic (sound) form, whether they come through our eyes or our ears (Baddeley, 2001). And this can cause some interesting memory errors. When people are asked to recall lists of letters they have just seen, the mistakes they make tend to involve confusions of letters that have a similar sound—such as D and T—rather than letters that have a similar look—such as E and F (Conrad, 1964). Mistakes aside, however, this **acoustic encoding** has its advantages. Specifically, it seems to have a role in learning and using language (Baddeley et al., 1998; Schacter, 1999).

Visual and Spatial Encoding: The Sketchpad Serving much the same role for visual and spatial information, the sketchpad in working memory encodes visual images and mental representations of objects in space (Baddeley, 2001). For example, it holds the visual images you mentally rummage through when you're trying to imagine where you left your car keys. Neurological evidence suggests that the sketchpad involves the coordination of several brain systems, including the frontal and occipital lobes, while the phonological loop uses the temporal lobes.

Levels of Processing in Working Memory The more connections you can make with new information while it is in working memory, the more likely you are to remember it later (Craik, 1979). Obviously this requires an interaction between working memory and long-term memory. According to the **levels-of-processing theory** proposed by Fergus Craik and Robert Lockhart (1972), "deeper" processing—establishing more connections with long-term memories—makes new information more meaningful and more memorable. An experiment will illustrate this point.

Craik and his colleague Endel Tulving (1975) had volunteer subjects examine a list of 60 common words presented on a screen one at a time. As each word appeared, the experimenters asked questions designed to control how deeply subjects processed each word. For example, when BEAR appeared on the screen, the experimenters would ask one of three questions: "Is it in capital letters?" "Does it rhyme with 'chair'?" "Is it an animal?" Craik and Tulving theorized that merely scanning the word for capital letters would not require processing the word as deeply as would comparing its sound with that of another word. But the deepest level of processing, they believed, would

■ **Elaborative rehearsal** A working-memory process in which information is actively reviewed and related to information already in LTM.

■ **Acoustic encoding** The conversion of information, especially semantic information, to sound patterns in working memory.

■ **Levels-of-processing theory** The explanation for the fact that information that is more thoroughly connected to meaningful items in long-term memory (more "deeply" processed) will be remembered better.

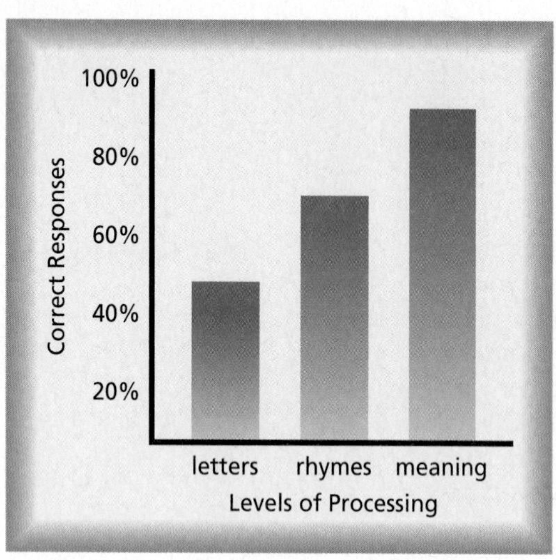
100%
80%
60%
40%
20%
Correct Responses
letters
rhymes
meaning
Levels of Processing

■ **FIGURE 7.7** Results of Levels-of-Processing Experiment
Words that were processed more deeply (for meaning) were remembered better than words examined for rhymes or for target letters.

occur when some aspect of the word's *meaning* was analyzed, as when they asked whether BEAR was an animal. Thus, Craik and Tulving predicted that items processed more deeply would leave more robust traces in memory. And their prediction was correct. When the subjects were later asked to pick the original 60 words out of a larger list of 180, they remembered the deeply processed words much better than words processed more superficially, as the graph in Figure 7.7 shows.

The Biological Basis of Working Memory Although the exact biological mechanism is not clear, working memory probably holds information in actively firing nerve circuits. Brain-imaging studies suggest a likely location for these short-term circuits is in the frontal cortex, regions that are active across a variety of working-memory tasks (Beardsley, 1997b; Smith, 2000). And, as we might expect, the working-memory circuits have connections with all the sensory parts of the brain and to areas known to be involved in long-term storage.

The research also suggests that the frontal regions house some "executive processes" that are involved in focusing attention and thinking about the information in short-term storage. These mental processes involve attention, priorities, planning, updating the contents of working memory, and monitoring the time sequence of events. Brain imaging studies indicate that the executive processes of working memory are anatomically distinct from the sites of short-term storage (Smith & Jonides, 1999).

The Third Stage: Long-Term Memory

Can you remember who discovered classical conditioning? What is the name of a play by Shakespeare? How many birthdays have you had? Such information, along with everything else you know, is stored in your long-term memory (LTM), the last of the three memory stages.

Given the vast amount of data stored in LTM, it is a marvel that so much of it is so easily accessible. The method behind the marvel involves a special feature of long-term memory: Words and concepts are encoded by their meanings, which interconnects them with other items that have similar meanings. Accordingly, you might picture LTM as a huge web of interconnected associations. The result is that good retrieval cues (stimuli that prompt the activation of a long- term memory) can help you quickly locate the item you want amid all the data stored there. Computer scientists would very much like to understand this feature of LTM and use it to increase the search and retrieval speed of their machines.

The Capacity and Duration of Long-Term Memory How much information can long-term memory hold? As far as we know, it has unlimited storage capacity. (No one has yet maxed it out, so you don't have to conserve memory by cutting back on your studying.) LTM uses its capacity to store all the experiences, events, information, emotions, skills, words, categories, rules, and judgments that have been transferred to it from working memory. Thus your LTM contains your total knowledge of the world and of yourself. And, unless it falls victim to injury or dementia, long-term memory is potentially capable of storing information for a lifetime—which makes long-term memory clearly the champion in both duration and storage capacity among the three stages of memory. How does LTM manage to have unlimited capacity? That's still an unsolved mystery of memory, but we do know that the metaphor of LTM being like a computer's hard drive is somewhat misleading. Instead, we suggest that you conceive of LTM as a sort of mental scaffold, so the more associations you make, the more information it can hold.

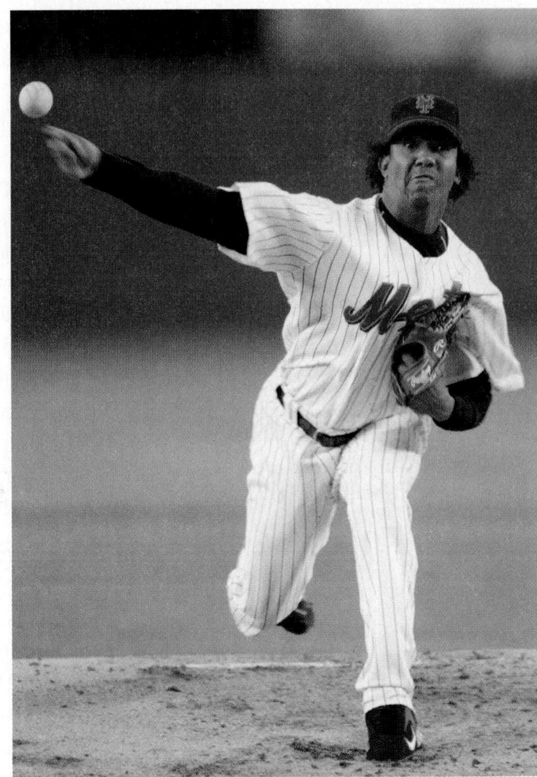

● Procedural memory allows experts like pitcher Pedro Martinez to perform complex tasks automatically, without conscious recall of the details.

The Structure and Function of Long-Term Memory With a broad overview of LTM in mind, let's look at some of the details. First, let's examine the two main parts of LTM, each distinguished by the sort of information it holds. One, a register for the things we know how to *do,* is called *procedural memory.* The other, which acts as storage for the information that we can *describe*—the facts we know and the experiences we remember—is called *declarative memory.*

Procedural Memory Mental directions, or "procedures," for how things are done are stored in **procedural memory.** (See Figure 7.8.) We use it to remember the "how to" skills we have learned, such as riding a bicycle, tying shoelaces, or playing a musical instrument (Anderson, 1982; Tulving, 1983). Most often, we are conscious of the details of our performance only during the early phases of acquisition, when we must think about every move we make. Later, after the skill is thoroughly learned, it occurs mainly at or beyond the fringes of awareness, as when a concert pianist performs a piece without consciously recalling the details.

Declarative Memory The other major division of LTM, **declarative memory,** stores specific information, such as facts and events. Recalling the directions for driving to a specific location requires declarative memory (although knowing how to drive a car depends on procedural memory). In contrast with procedural memory, declarative memory more often requires some conscious mental effort. You may be able to see evidence of this when people roll their eyes or make facial gestures while searching their memories. As they do so, they are looking in one of declarative memory's two subdivisions: *episodic memory* and *semantic memory.*

Episodic memory is the portion of declarative memory that stores personal experiences: your memory for events, or "episodes" in your life. It also stores *temporal coding* (or time tags) to identify *when* the event occurred and *context coding* that indicates *where* it took place. For example, memories of your recent vacation or of an unhappy love affair are stored in episodic memory, along with codes for where and when these episodes occurred. Thus, episodic memory acts as your internal diary or *autobiographical memory.* You consult it when

■ **Procedural memory** A division of LTM that stores memories for how things are done.

■ **Declarative memory** A division of LTM that stores explicit information; also known as fact memory. Declarative memory has two subdivisions: episodic memory and semantic memory.

■ **Episodic memory** A subdivision of declarative memory that stores memory for personal events, or "episodes."

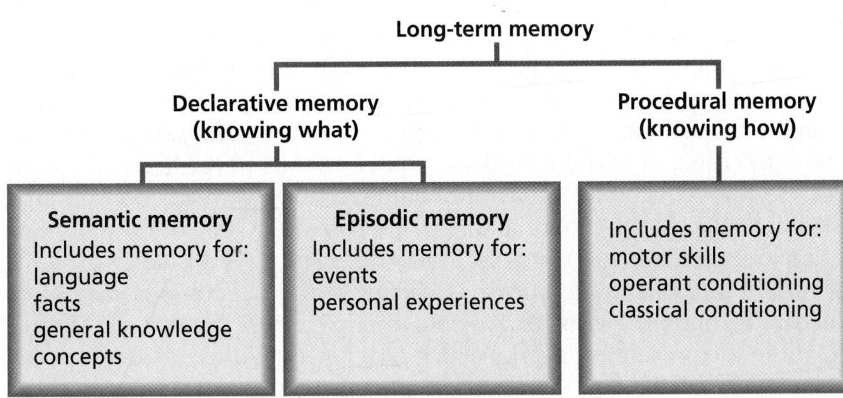
Long-term memory
Declarative memory (knowing what)
Procedural memory (knowing how)
Semantic memory
Includes memory for:
language
facts
general knowledge
concepts
Episodic memory
Includes memory for:
events
personal experiences
Includes memory for:
motor skills
operant conditioning
classical conditioning

● **FIGURE 7.8** Components of Long-Term Memory

Declarative memory involves knowing specific information—knowing "what." It stores facts, personal experiences, language, concepts—things about which we might say, "I remember!" *Procedural memory* involve knowing "how"—particularly motor skills and behavioral learning.

JEOPARDY!
LANE
JULIE
ROBERT

● From which division of declarative memory are facts retrieved by *Jeopardy* contestants?

someone says, "Where were you on New Year's Eve?" or "What did you do in class last Tuesday?"

Semantic memory is the other division of declarative memory. (Refer again to Figure 7.8 if this is becoming confusing.) It stores the basic meanings of words and concepts. Usually, semantic memory retains no information about the time and place in which its contents were acquired. Thus you keep the meaning of "cat" in semantic memory—but probably not a recollection of the occasion on which you first learned the meaning of "cat." In this respect, semantic memory more closely resembles an encyclopedia or a database than an autobiography. It stores a vast quantity of facts about names, faces, grammar, history, music, manners, scientific principles, and religious beliefs. All the facts and concepts you know are stored there, and you consult its registry when someone asks you, "Who was the third president?" or "What are the two divisions of declarative memory?"

The Biological Basis of Long-Term Memory The search for the **engram,** the biological basis of long-term memory has taken two approaches. One has involved looking for the neural circuitry used by memory in the brain. The other looks on the level of synapses and biochemical changes that are believed to represent the physical *memory trace* in nerve cells.

Using the first tactic, pioneering brain researcher Karl Lashley searched surgically for the engram by removing portions of rats' brains and later testing the animals to see if they had lost memory for a task learned prior to the operation. After years of such work, a frustrated Lashley finally gave up his quest for a special locus in the brain for the engram, in the belief that any part of the brain could store memories (Bruce, 1991; Lashley, 1950).

Clues from the Tragic Case of H. M. A breakthrough came in the form of a tragic figure, known only by his initials. H. M. lost most of his ability to form new declarative memories as a result of a botched brain operation (Hilts, 1995). Since 1953, he has been unable to create new memories of the events in his life. New experiences slip away before he can store them in long-term memory—although his memory for events prior to the operation remains normal. Ironically, one of the few things he has been able to learn is that he has a memory problem. At this writing, H. M. still lives in a nursing home near Boston, where he has resided for decades. Throughout his post-operative life, he has maintained generally good spirits and worked extensively with psychologist Brenda Milner (whom he still cannot recognize). We owe much of our understanding of memory to their relationship.

On H. M.'s medical record, the condition is called **anterograde amnesia,** but to put the problem in cognitive terms, H. M.'s ability to transfer new concepts and experiences from short-term storage to long-term memory is severely impaired. From a biological perspective, the cause was removal of the hippocampus and amygdala on both sides of the brain. This was done during surgery for the severe epileptic seizures from which he suffered as a young man (see Figure 7.9). Although his seizures diminished, he was left with a terrible and permanent disability. H. M. has never been able to recognize the people who have taken care of him in the 50+ years after his surgery. The 9/11 attacks, the moon landings, the computer revolution—all have left no apparent trace in his mind. Likewise, he is always shocked to see an aging face when he looks in the mirror, expecting to see the younger man he was a half century ago (Milner et al., 1968; Rosenzweig, 1992). In brief, H. M. is a man caught in the present moment—which fades away without being captured by memory.

CONNECTION: CHAPTER 12

Retrograde amnesia involves loss of memory for information acquired in the past.

■ **Semantic memory** A subdivision of declarative memory that stores general knowledge, including the meanings of words and concepts.

■ **Engram** The physical changes in the brain associated with a memory. It is also known as the *memory trace.*

■ **Anterograde amnesia** The inability to form memories for new information (as opposed to retrograde amnesia, which involves the inability to remember information previously stored in memory).

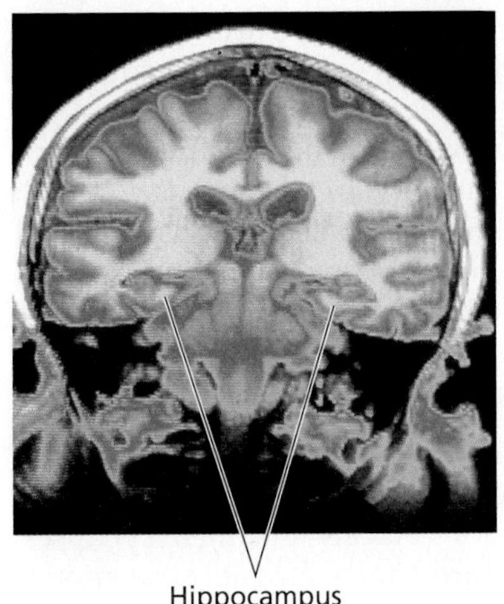
Hippocampus

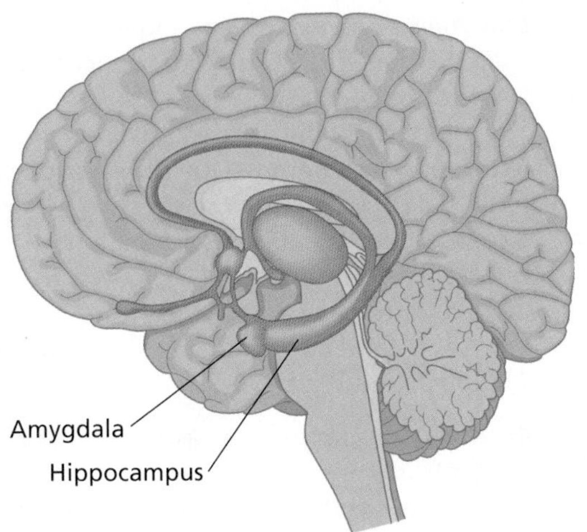
Amygdala
Hippocampus

● **FIGURE 7.9** The Hippocampus and Amygdala

The hippocampus and amygdala were surgically removed from both sides of H. M.'s brain. To help yourself visualize where these structures lie, compare the drawing with the MRI image. The MRI shows the brain in cross section, with a slice through the hippocampus visible on each side.

What have we learned from H. M.? Again speaking biologically, H. M. has taught us that the hippocampus and amygdala that were removed from H. M.'s brain are crucial to laying down new episodic memories, although they seem to have no role in retrieving old memories (Bechara et al., 1995; Wirth et al., 2003). Further, as we will see in a moment, Milner has been able to show that H. M. retains the ability to form some *procedural* memories, even though he cannot lay down new *episodic* traces. Just as important, H. M.'s case also brought renewed interest in finding the biological underpinnings of memory.

Parts of the Brain Associated with Long-Term Memory In the last two decades, neuroscientists have added much detail to the picture that H. M. has given us of human memory (Eichenbaum, 1997; Schacter, 1996). We now know that deterioration of the hippocampus accounts for many symptoms of Alzheimer's disease—which, as we saw in Chapter 3, involves loss of ability to make new memories. We have also learned that most long-term memories make an intermediate stop in the hippocampus on their way to their final destination in long-term storage (McClelland et al., 1995). In a process called **consolidation,** the intermediate hippocampal memories are gradually changed into relatively permanent memories stored in the cortex.

Neuroscientists have also discovered that the hippocampus's neural neighbor, the amygdala, has the job of strengthening memories that have strong emotional associations (Bechara et al., 1995). These emotional associations, it seems, act as an aid for access and retrieval (Dolan, 2002). The amygdala, then, is probably the mechanism responsible for the persistent and troubling memories reported by soldiers and other who have experienced violent assaults. In some cases, these memories can be so vivid that they constitute a condition known as *posttraumatic stress disorder.*

CONNECTION: CHAPTER 12

Lasting biological changes may occur in the brains of individuals having *posttraumatic stress disorder.*

As we have seen, the brain uses some of the same circuits for memory that it uses for sensation, perception, and motor responses (Kandel & Squire, 2000). For example, studies show that the brain's visual cortex is involved in generating visual memory images (Barinaga, 1995; Ishai & Sagi, 1995, 1997; Kosslyn et al., 1995). Further, neuroscientists have found that a person who sustains damage to a part of the brain involving sensations may lose memories for those sensations. For example, as we saw in artist Jonathan I.'s case (Chapter 4), damage to the regions that process color vision may cause memory loss for colors—even to the point of being incapable of imagining what colors might look like (Sacks, 1995; Zeki, 1992). The general principle seems to be

■ **Consolidation** The process by which short-term memories are changed to long-term memories over a period of time.

that memories of sensory experiences involve the same parts of the brain used to perceive those experiences in the first place (Martin et al., 1995; Wheeler et al., 2000).

In the preceding paragraphs, then, we have explored one fruitful approach to locating the engram—the physical trace of memory. In that approach, which has focused on brain structures, H. M. and a few others like him have played a central role. The discoveries made by studying H. M., plus all the subsequent research on the brain, have shown that different aspects of memory clearly involve different parts of the brain. Now, let's turn to another approach—one requiring that we zoom in closer to see memory at the level of neurons, synapses, and chemicals.

Memories, Neurons, and Synapses The second approach to the engram has concentrated on the biology and chemistry of neurons and their synapses. We'll spare you the details, but the big picture shows long-term memories forming at the synapse as fragile chemical traces that gradually consolidate into more permanent synaptic changes over time (Balter, 2000; Beardsley, 1997b; Haberlandt, 1999; Kandel, 2001; McGaugh, 2000; Travis, 2000a). This explains why a blow to the head or an electric shock to the brain can cause loss of recent memories that have not yet consolidated. (The diagnosis in this case would be **retrograde amnesia,** or loss of prior memory traces.) Certain drugs. too, can interfere with the formation of long-term memories (Lynch & Staubli, 1991). The picture that emerges from such observations shows that memories form when activity in nerve circuits causes biochemical changes that make those circuits in the brain more likely to respond again in the future. We called this *long-term potentiation* in the previous chapter. Many thousands, if not millions, of neurons are probably involved in encoding and storing a single memory.

● Memories can be enhanced by emotional arousal: It is unlikely that Halle Berry will forget this moment.

While memories are consolidating, they can also be strengthened by the person's emotional state—which accounts for our especially vivid memories of emotionally arousing experiences. From an evolutionary perspective, this is highly adaptive. If you survive a frightening encounter with a bear, for example, you are quite likely to remember to avoid bears in the future. The underlying biology involves emotion-related chemicals, such as epinephrine (adrenalin) and certain stress hormones, which act to enhance memory for emotion-laden experiences (Cahill et al., 1994; LeDoux, 1996; McGaugh, 2000).

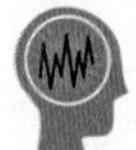

PSYCHOLOGY IN YOUR LIFE: "FLASHBULB" MEMORIES: WHERE WERE YOU WHEN . . . ?

The closest most people will come to having a "photographic memory" is a **flashbulb memory,** an exceptionally clear recollection of an important emotion-packed event—a very vivid episodic memory (Brown & Kulik, 1977). You probably have a few such memories: a tragic accident, a death, a graduation, a victory. It's as though you had made a flash picture in your mind of the striking scene. (The term was coined in the days when flash photography required a new "flashbulb" for each picture.)

■ **Retrograde amnesia** The inability to remember information previously stored in memory. (Compare with anterograde amnesia.)

■ **Flashbulb memory** A clear and vivid long-term memory of an especially meaningful and emotional event.

Many people have formed essentially the same flashbulb memories of certain events in the news, such as the December 2004 tsunami, the September 11 attacks, Princess Diana's death, or the shootings at Columbine high school. Researchers have also found that the attempted assassination of President Reagan (Pillemer, 1984) and the O. J. Simpson trial verdict (Schmolck et al., 2000) caused large numbers of people to develop flashbulb memories. Typically, these memories record precisely where the individuals were at the time they received the news, what they were doing, and the emotions they felt.

Despite their strong emotional involvement, flashbulb memories can be remarkably accurate (Schmolck et al., 2000). Yet studies have shown that flashbulb memories can become distorted over time (Neisser, 1991). For example, on the morning after the Challenger space shuttle explosion, psychology professors asked their students to describe the circumstances under which they had heard the news. Three years later the same students were again asked to recall the event. Of the latter accounts, about one-third gave substantially different stories, mostly about details on which they had previously not focused their attention at the time. It is also noteworthy that even those whose recollections were erroneous reported a high level of confidence in their memories (Winograd & Neisser, 1992). The general pattern appears to be this: Up to a year later, most flashbulb memories are nearly identical to reports given immediately after the event, while recollections gathered after two or three years show substantial distortions (Schmolck et al., 2000). What doesn't change, oddly enough, is people's confidence in their recollections.

● The attacks on the World Trade Center and the Pentagon were shocking events, and many Americans have "flashbulb" memories that include where they were and what they were doing when they learned of the attacks.

CHECK YOUR UNDERSTANDING

1. **RECALL:** Which part of memory has the smallest capacity? (That is, which part of memory is considered the "bottleneck" in the memory system?)
   a. sensory memory
   b. working memory
   c. long-term memory
   d. implicit memory
   e. explicit memory

2. **RECALL:** Which part of long-term memory stores autobiographical information?
   a. semantic memory
   b. procedural memory
   c. recognition memory
   d. episodic memory
   e. eidetic memory

3. **RECALL:** In order to get material into permanent storage, it must be made meaningful while it is in
   a. sensory memory.
   b. working memory.
   c. long-term memory.
   d. recall memory.
   e. immediate memory.

4. **APPLICATION:** As you study the vocabulary in this book, which method would result in the deepest level of processing?
   a. learning the definition given in the marginal glossary
   b. marking each term with a highlighter each time it occurs in a sentence in the text
   c. thinking of an example of each term
   d. having a friend read a definition, with you having to identify the term in question form, as on the TV show *Jeopardy*
   e. glossing over it , knowing you will see it later

5. **UNDERSTANDING THE CORE CONCEPT:** As the information in this book passes from one stage of your memory to the next, the information becomes more
   a. important.
   b. meaningful.
   c. interesting.
   d. accurate.
   e. astute.

ANSWERS: 1. b 2. d 3. b 4. c 5. b

KEY QUESTION

HOW DO WE RETRIEVE MEMORIES?

The whole point of encoding and storing memories in meaningful categories is to facilitate their speedy and accurate retrieval. But, as we will see, memory has several surprising tricks it can play during retrieval. One involves the possibility of retrieving a memory that you didn't know you had—which tells us that some memories can be successfully encoded and stored without our awareness. Another quirk involves our being both quite confident of a memory and quite wrong—as we saw in flashbulb memories. Our Core Concept summarizes the retrieval process this way:

CORE CONCEPT

Whether memories are implicit or explicit, successful retrieval depends on how they were encoded and how they are cued.

Implicit and Explicit Memory

We will begin our exploration of retrieval with another lesson from H. M. Surprisingly, H. M. has retained the ability to learn new motor skills, according to Brenda Milner, the psychologist who has become his guardian and protector (Milner et al., 1968; Raymond, 1989). For example, Milner has taught H. M. the difficult skill of mirror writing—writing while looking at his hands in a mirror. In general, his *procedural* memory for such motor tasks is quite normal, even though he cannot remember learning these skills and doesn't know that he knows how to perform them.

But you don't have to have brain damage like H. M. to have memories of which you are unaware. A normal memory has disconnected islands of information, too. For over a hundred years, psychologists have realized that people with no memory defects can know something without knowing that they know it (Roediger, 1990). Psychologist Daniel Schacter (1992, 1996) calls this **implicit memory:** memory that can affect your behavior but which you did not deliberately learn or of which you currently have no awareness. By contrast, **explicit memory** involves awareness.

Procedural memories are often implicit, as when golfers remember how to swing a club without thinking about how to move their bodies. Likewise, H. M.'s mirror writing was a procedural memory. But implicit memories are not limited to procedural memory—nor is explicit memory synonymous with declarative memory. Information in your semantic store can be either *explicit* (such as in remembering the material you have studied for a test) or *implicit* (such as knowing the color of the building in which your psychology class is held). The general rule is this: A memory is implicit if it can affect behavior or mental processes without becoming fully conscious. Explicit memories, on the other hand, always involve consciousness during retrieval.

Retrieval Cues

For accurate retrieval, both implicit and explicit memories require good *cues.* You have some feeling for these if you've used search terms in Google or another Internet search engine: Make a poor choice of terms, and you can come up either with nothing or with Internet garbage. Things work in much the same way in long-term memory, where a successful search requires good mental **retrieval cues,** which are the "search terms" used to activate a memory. Sometimes the only retrieval cue required to bring back a long-dormant experience is a certain odor, such as the smell of fresh-baked cookies that you asso-

■ **Implicit memory** A memory that was not deliberately learned or of which you have no conscious awareness.

■ **Explicit memory** Memory that has been processed with attention and can be consciously recalled.

■ **Retrieval cues** Stimuli that are used to bring a memory to consciousness or into behavior.

ciated with visiting Grandma's house. At other times the retrieval cue might be an emotion, as when a person struggling with depression gets caught in a maelstrom of depressing memories. On the other hand, some memories are not so easily cued. During a test, for example, you can draw a blank if the wording of a question doesn't jibe with the way you thought about the material as you were studying—that is if the question isn't a good retrieval cue for the associations you made in memory. As you can see, then, whether a retrieval cue is a good one depends on the type of memory being sought and the web of associations in which the memory is embedded.

In the following paragraphs, we will illustrate how retrieval cues can activate or *prime* implicit memories. Then we will return to the more familiar territory of explicit memory to show how recognition and recall are cued. Later in the chapter, we will discuss the failure of retrieval cues in the context of forgetting.

Retrieving Implicit Memories by Priming A quirk of implicit memory landed former Beatle George Harrison in court (Schacter, 1996). Lawyers for a singing group known as the Chiffons claimed that the melody in Harrison's song "My Sweet Lord" was nearly identical to that of the Chiffon classic, "He's So Fine." Harrison denied that he deliberately borrowed the melody but conceded that he had heard the Chiffons's tune prior to writing his own. The court agreed, stating that Harrison's borrowing was a product of "subconscious memory." Everyday life abounds with similar experiences, says Daniel Schacter (1996). You may have proposed an idea to a friend and had it rejected, but weeks later your friend excitedly proposed the same idea to you, as if it were entirely new.

In such real-life situations it is often hard to say what cues an implicit memory to surface. Psychologists have, however, developed ways to "prime" implicit memories in the laboratory (Schacter, 1996). To illustrate, imagine that you have volunteered for a memory experiment. First, you are shown a list of words for several seconds:

assassin, octopus, avocado, mystery, sheriff, climate

Then, an hour later, the experimenter asks you to examine another list and indicate which items you recognize from the earlier list: *twilight, assassin, dinosaur,* and *mystery.* That task is easy for you. But then the experimenter shows you some words with missing letters and asks you to fill in the blanks:

ch _ _ _ _ nk, o _ t _ _ _ us, _ og _ y _ _ _, _ l _ m _ te

It is likely that answers for two of these pop readily into mind, *octopus* and *climate.* But chances are that you will be less successful with the other two words, *chipmunk* and *bogeyman.* The reason for this difference has to do with **priming,** the procedure of providing cues that stimulate memories without awareness of the connection between the cue and the retrieved memory. Because you had been primed with the words *octopus* and *climate,* they more easily "popped out" in your consciousness than did the words that had not been primed.

CONNECTION: CHAPTER 4

Priming is also a technique for studying nonconscious processes.

Retrieving Explicit Memories Anything stored in LTM must be "filed" according to its pattern or meaning. Consequently, the best way to add material to long-term memory is to associate it, while in working memory, with material already stored in LTM. We have called that process *elaborative rehearsal.* Encoding many such connections by elaborative rehearsal gives you more ways of accessing the information, much as a town with many access roads can be approached from many directions.

Priming A technique for cuing implicit memories by providing cues that stimulate a memory without awareness of the connection between the cue and the retrieved memory.

Meaningful Organization Remembering the *gist* of an idea rather than the actual words you heard demonstrates the role that *meaning* has in long-term memory. For example, you may hear the sentence "The book was returned to the library by Mary." Later, you are asked if you heard the sentence "Mary returned the book to the library." You may indeed mistakenly remember having "heard" the second sentence, because even though the two sentences are different utterances, they mean the same thing. This again shows that human LTM stores meaning, rather than an exact replica of the original event (Bransford & Franks, 1971). This is exactly what you would expect from a memory system that relies on the same cognitive processes and brain pathways as our perceptual system.

If you'll forgive us for repeating ourselves, your authors want to underscore the practical application of LTM being organized according to meaning: *If you want to store new information in your LTM, you must make it meaningful while it is in working memory.* This requires you to associate new information with things you already know. That's why it is important in your classes (such as your psychology class) to think of personal examples of the concepts you want to remember.

Recall and Recognition Retrieval of explicit memories can be cued in two main ways. One involves the retrieval method required on essay tests, the other involves the method needed on multiple choice tests. **Recall** (on an essay test) is a retrieval task in which you must create an answer almost entirely from memory, with the help of only minimal cues from the question. This is a recall question: "What are the three memory stages?" **Recognition,** on another hand, is the method required by multiple-choice tests. It is a retrieval task in which you merely identify whether a stimulus has been previously experienced. Normally, recognition is less demanding than recall because the cues available for a recognition task are much more complete. Incidentally, the reason why people say, "I'm terrible with names, but I never forget a face" is that recall (names) is much tougher than recognition (faces).

Recognition is also the method used by police when they ask an eyewitness to identify a suspected robber in a lineup. The witness is required only to match an image from memory (the robber) against a present stimulus (a suspect in the lineup). And what would be a comparable recall task? A witness working with a police artist to make a drawing of a suspect must recall, entirely from memory, the suspect's facial characteristics.

Other Factors Affecting Retrieval

We have seen that the ability to retrieve information from explicit declarative memory depends on whether information was encoded and elaborated to make it meaningful. You won't be surprised to learn that alertness, stress level, drugs, and general knowledge also affect retrieval. Less well known, however, are influences related to the context in which you encoded a memory and also the context in which you are remembering.

Encoding Specificity Perhaps you have encountered your psychology professor at the grocery store, and you needed a moment to recognize who it was. On the other hand, you may have been talking to a childhood friend, and something she said cued a flood of memories that you hadn't thought about for years. These experiences are contrasting examples of the **encoding specificity principle.** That is, they involve situations in which the context affected the way a memory was encoded and stored—influencing its retrieval at a later time. In general, researchers have found that *the more closely the retrieval cues*

■ **Recall** A retrieval method in which one must reproduce previously presented information.

■ **Recognition** A retrieval method in which one must identify present stimuli as having been previously presented.

■ **Encoding specificity principle** The doctrine that memory is encoded and stored with specific cues related to the context in which it was formed. The more closely the retrieval cues match the form in which the information was encoded, the better it will be remembered.

match the form in which the information was encoded, the better the information will be remembered.

It seems that context has a bigger effect under some circumstances than others (Bjork & Richardson-Klavehn, 1989). Happily, you don't have to worry about context effects when you study in one setting and take a test in another (Fernandez & Glenberg, 1985; Saufley et al., 1985). Of far more importance are the kinds of test questions you face and the approach to learning you have used. If the exam questions are quite different from anything you have thought about, then you may find the exam difficult. For this reason, psychologist Robert Bjork (2000) suggests that teachers introduce "desirable difficulties" into their courses. By this he means that students should be given assignments that make them come to grips with the material in many different ways—project, papers, problems, and presentations—rather than just memorizing the material and parroting it back. By doing so, the professor is helping students build more connections into the web of associations into which a memory is embedded—and the more connections there are, the easier it becomes to cue a memory.

Mood and Memory Information processing isn't just about facts and events, it's also about emotions and moods. We use the expressions "feeling blue" and "looking at the world through rose-colored glasses" to suggest that moods can bias our perceptions. Our moods can also affect what we pull out of memory. If you have ever had an episode of uncontrollable giggling (usually in a totally inappropriate situation), you know how a euphoric mood can trigger one silly thought after another. And at the other end of the mood spectrum, people who are depressed often report that *all* their thoughts have a melancholy aspect. Thus depression perpetuates itself through biased retrieval of depressing memories. In general, the kind of information we retrieve from memory heavily depends on our moods (Bower, 1981; Gilligan & Bower, 1984; Lewinsohn & Rosenbaum, 1987; MacLeod & Campbell, 1992). This phenomenon is known as **mood-congruent memory** (Terry, 2000).

Mood-congruent memory A memory process that selectively retrieves memories that match (are congruent with) one's mood.

Not just a laboratory curiosity, mood-congruent memory can also have important health implications. Says memory researcher Gordon Bower, "Doctors assess what to do with you based on your complaints and how much you complain" (McCarthy, 1991). Because depressed people are likely to emphasize their medical symptoms, they may receive treatment that is much different from that dispensed to more upbeat individuals with the same disease. This, says Bower, means that physicians must learn to take a person's psychological state into consideration when deciding on a diagnosis and a course of therapy.

PSYCHOLOGY IN YOUR LIFE: ON THE TIP OF YOUR TONGUE

Try to answer as many of the following questions as you can:

- What is the North American equivalent of the reindeer?
- What do artists call the board on which they mix paints?
- What is the name for a tall, four-sided stone monument with a point at the top of its shaft?
- What instrument do navigators use to determine latitude by sighting on the stars?
- What is the name of the large metal urns used in Russia to dispense tea?
- What is the name of a small Chinese boat usually propelled with a single oar or pole?

The Washington Monument is an example of a tapered stone object that is topped by a pyramid-shaped point. Can you recall the name for such objects? Or, is it "on the tip of your tongue"?

Our guess is that your responses to these questions were of three kinds: (a) you recalled the correct word, (b) you didn't have a clue, or—most interesting for our purposes—(c) you couldn't retrieve the word, but you had a strong sense that you have it somewhere in memory. In the last case, the answer was "on the tip of your tongue," an experience that psychologists call the **TOT phenomenon** (Brown, 1991). Surveys show that most people have this experience about once a week.

The most common TOT experiences center on names of personal acquaintances, names of famous persons, and familiar objects (Brown, 1991). About half the time, the target words finally do pop into mind, usually within about one agonizing minute. Most subjects report that the experience is uncomfortable (Brown & McNeill, 1966).

What accounts for the TOT phenomenon? A likely explanation involves *interference:* when another memory blocks access or retrieval, as when you were thinking of Jan when you unexpectedly meet Jill (Schacter, 1999). (You will read more about interference and other causes of forgetting in the next section of the chapter.) And, even though you were unable to *recall* some of the correct words (caribou, palette, obelisk, sextant, samovar, sampan), you could probably *recognize* most of them. It's also likely that some features of the sought-for words abruptly popped to mind ("I know it begins with an *s!*"), even though the words themselves eluded you. So, the TOT phenomenon occurs during a recall attempt, when there is a poor match between retrieval cues and the encoding of the word in long-term memory.

And, we'll bet you can't name all Seven Dwarfs.

■ **TOT phenomenon** The inability to recall a word, while knowing that it is in memory. People often describe this frustrating experience as having the word "on the tip of their tongue."

CHECK YOUR UNDERSTANDING

1. **APPLICATION:** Remembering names is usually harder than remembering faces because names require ______, while faces require ______.
   a. short-term memory/long-term memory
   b. declarative memory/procedural memory
   c. encoding/retrieval
   d. recall/recognition
   e. storage/recall

2. **APPLICATION:** At a high school class reunion you are likely to experience a flood of memories that would be unlikely to come to mind under other circumstances. What memory process explains this?
   a. implicit memory
   b. anterograde amnesia
   c. encoding specificity
   d. the TOT phenomenon
   e. retrograde amnesia

3. **RECALL:** A person experiencing the TOT phenomenon is unable to ______ a specific word.
   a. recognize
   b. recall
   c. encode
   d. learn
   e. store

4. **UNDERSTANDING THE CORE CONCEPT:** An implicit memory may be activated by priming, and an explicit memory may be activated by a recognizable stimulus. In either case, a psychologist would say that these memories are being
   a. cued.
   b. recalled.
   c. stored.
   d. chunked.
   e. learned.

ANSWERS: 1. d 2. c 3. b 4. a

KEY QUESTION

WHY DOES MEMORY SOMETIMES FAIL US?

We forget appointments and anniversaries. During today's test we can't remember the terms we studied the night before. Or a familiar name seems just out of our mental reach. Yet, ironically, we sometimes cannot rid memory of an unhappy event. Why does memory play these tricks on us—making us remember what we would rather forget and forget what we want to remember?

According to memory expert Daniel Schacter, the blame falls on what he terms the "seven sins" of memory: *transience, absent-mindedness, blocking, misattribution, suggestibility, bias,* and unwanted *persistence* (Schacter, 1999, 2001). Further, he claims that these seven problems are really the consequences of some very useful features of human memory. They are features that stood our ancestors in good stead and so are passed down and preserved in our own memory system. Our Core Concept puts this notion more succinctly:

CORE CONCEPT

Most of our memory problems arise from memory's "seven sins"—which are really by-products of otherwise adaptive features of human memory.

As we look into the "seven sins," we will also have the opportunity to consider such practical problems as the reliability of eyewitness testimony and ways in which memory contributes to certain mental disorders, such as depression. In this section we will also revisit the "memory wars," involving disputes about recovered memories of trauma and sexual abuse—the problem that we encountered in Donna Smith's case at the beginning of the chapter. Finally, we will look at some strategies for improving our memories by overcoming some of Schacter's "seven sins." We begin, however, with the frustration of fading memories.

Transience: Fading Memories Cause Forgetting

Memories seem to weaken with time. (How would you do on a rigorous test of the course work you took a year ago?) Although no one has directly observed a human memory trace fade and disappear, much circumstantial evidence points to the **transience,** or impermanence, of long-term memory—the first of Schacter's "sins."

■ **Transience** The impermanence of a long-term memory. Transience is based on the idea that long-term memories gradually fade in strength over time.

In a classic study of transience, pioneering psychologist Hermann Ebbinghaus (1908/1973) learned lists of *nonsense syllables* (such as POV, KEB, and RUZ) and tried to recall them over varying time intervals. This worked well to assess his retention over short periods up to a few days. But to measure memory after long delays of weeks or months, when recall had failed completely, Ebbinghaus had to invent another method that measured the number of trials required to *relearn* the original list. If it took fewer trials to relearn the list than were required to learn it originally, the difference indicated a "savings" that could serve as a measure of memory. (If the original learning required 10 trials and relearning required 7 trials, the savings was 30%.) By using the *savings method,* Ebbinghaus could trace what happened to memory over long periods of time. The curve obtained from his data is shown in Figure 7.10. There you can see how the graph initially plunges steeply and then flattens out over longer intervals. This represents one of Ebbinghaus's most important discoveries: *For relatively meaningless material, there is a rapid initial loss of memory, followed by a declining rate of loss.* Subsequent

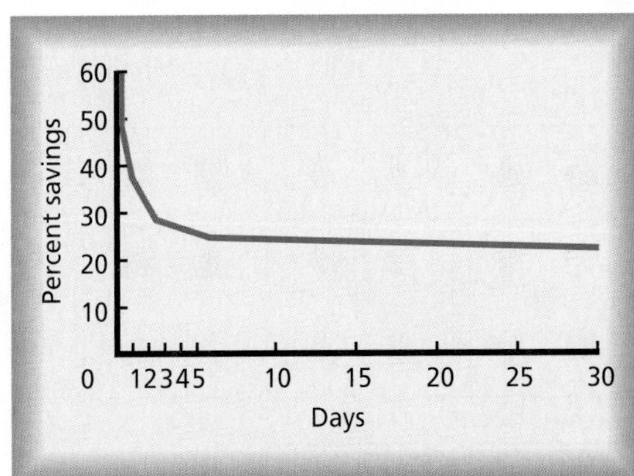
Percent savings
60
50
40
30
20
10
0
1 2 3 4 5
10
15
20
25
30
Days

● **FIGURE 7.10** Ebbinghaus's Forgetting Curve

Ebbinghaus's forgetting curve shows that the savings demonstrated by relearning drops rapidly and reaches a plateau, below which little more is forgotten. The greatest amount of forgetting occurs during the first day after learning. (*Source:* From PSYCHOLOGY AND LIFE 15th ed. by P. G. Zimbardo and R. J. Gerrig. Copyright © 1999 by Pearson Education. Reprinted by permission of Allyn & Bacon, Boston, MA.)

research shows that this **forgetting curve** captures the pattern of transience by which we forget much of the verbal material we learn.

Modern psychologists have built on Ebbinghaus's work, but they are now more interested in how we remember *meaningful* material, such as information you read in this book. Meaningful memories seem to fade, too—just not as rapidly as did Ebbinghaus's nonsense syllables. Much of this modern work uses brain scanning techniques, such as fMRI and PET, to visualize diminishing brain activity during forgetting (Schacter, 1996, 1999).

CONNECTION: CHAPTER 3

PET and *fMRI* are brain scanning techniques that form images of especially active regions in the brain.

Some memories, however, do not follow the classic forgetting curve as closely. Motor skills, for example, are often retained substantially intact in procedural memory for many years, even without practice—"just like riding a bicycle." The same goes for certain especially memorable emotional experiences, such as "flashbulb" incidents or certain childhood events (although they may become distorted, as we have seen). Obviously, the transience hypothesis—that memories fade over time—doesn't describe the fate of all our memories. As we will see next, even some memories that seem to be forgotten haven't faded away completely. Instead, they may only be temporarily lost.

● Misplacing your car keys results from a shift in attention. Which of the seven "sins" does this represent?

Absent-Mindedness: Lapses of Attention Cause Forgetting

When you misplace your car keys or forget an anniversary, you have had an episode of **absent-mindedness.** It's not that the memory has disappeared from your brain circuits. Rather, you have suffered a retrieval failure caused by shifting your attention elsewhere. In the case of a forgotten anniversary, the attention problem occurred on the retrieval end—when you were concentrating on something that took your attention away from the upcoming anniversary. And as for the car keys, your attentive shift probably occurred during the original encoding—when you should have been paying attention to where you laid the keys. In college students, this form of absent-mindedness commonly comes from listening to music or watching TV while studying.

For a demonstration of this sort of encoding error, please see our magic trick in Figure 7.11. The same process was at work in the "depth of processing" experiments, in which people who encoded information shallowly (retrieval cue: Does the word contain an *e*?) were less able to recall the target word (Craik & Lockhart, 1972). Another example can be found in demonstrations of *change blindness:* In one study, participants viewed a movie clip in which one actor who was asking directions was replaced by another actor while they were briefly hidden by two men carrying a door in front of them. Amazingly, fewer than half of the viewers noticed the change (Simons & Levin, 1998).

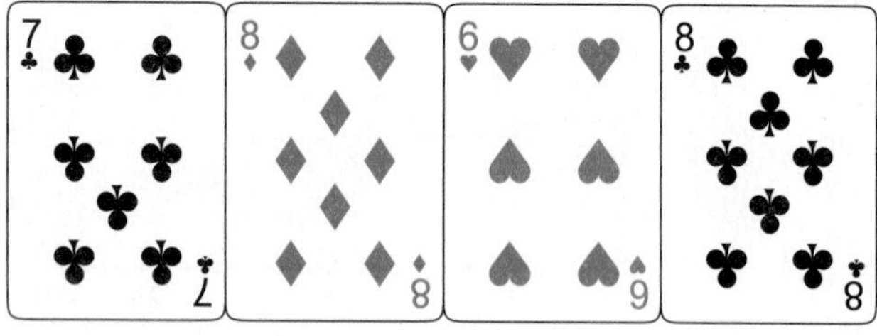

● **FIGURE 7.11** The "Magic" of Memory

Pick one of the cards. Stare at it intently for at least 15 seconds, being careful not to shift your gaze to the other cards. Then turn the page.

Blocking: Interference Causes Forgetting

You are most likely to notice this next memory "sin" when you have a "tip-of-the-tongue" experience. It also occurs when you attempt to learn two conflicting things in succession, such as would happen if you had a French class followed by a Spanish class. In general, **blocking** occurs when information has encountered *interference*—that is, when one item acts as an obstacle to accessing and retrieving another memory. And what is likely to cause interference? Three main factors top the list:

1. The greater the similarity between two sets of material to be learned, the greater the interference between them is likely to be. French and Spanish classes are more likely to interfere with each other than are psychology and accounting.
2. Meaningless material is more vulnerable to interference than meaningful material. Because LTM is organized by meaning, you will have more trouble remembering your locker combination than you will a news bulletin.
3. Emotional material is a powerful cause of interference. So, if you broke up with your true love last night, you will probably forget what your literature professor says in class today.

A common source of interference comes from an old habit getting in the way of a new one. This can happen, for example, when people switch from one word-processing program to another. Interference also accounts for the legendary problem old dogs have in learning new tricks. Everyday life offers many more examples, but interference theory groups them in two main categories: *proactive interference* and *retroactive interference.*

Proactive Interference When an old memory disrupts the learning and remembering of new information, **proactive interference** is the culprit. An example of proactive interference occurs when, after moving to a new home, you still look for items in the old places where you used to store them, although no such locations exist in your new environment. *Pro-* means "forward," so in *pro*active interference, old memories act forward in time to block your attempts at new learning.

Retroactive Interference When the opposite happens—when newly learned information prevents the retrieval of previously learned material—we can blame forgetting on **retroactive interference.** *Retro-* means "backward"; the newer material reaches back into your memory to block access to old material. Retroactive interference explains what happens when you drive a car with an automatic transmission and then forget to use the clutch when you return to one with a "stick shift." That is, recent experience retroactively interferes with your ability to retrieve an older memory. (See Figure 7.12.)

The Serial Position Effect In yet another example of blocking, you may have noticed that the first and last parts of a poem or a vocabulary list are easier to learn and remember than the middle portion—which receives interference from both ends. In general, the *primacy effect* refers to the relative ease of remembering the first items in a series, while the *recency effect* refers to the robustness of memory for the most recent items. Together, with diminished memory for the middle portion, we term this the **serial position effect.** You can see it at work when you meet a series of people: You are more likely to remember the names of those you met first and last than you are those you met in between (other factors being equal, such as the commonness of their names, the distinctiveness of their appearance, and their personalities).

Forgetting curve A graph plotting the amount of retention and forgetting over time for a certain batch of material, such as a list of nonsense syllables. The typical forgetting curve is steep at first, becoming flatter as time goes on.

Absent-mindedness Forgetting caused by lapses in attention.

Blocking Forgetting that occurs when an item in memory cannot be accessed or retrieved. Blocking is caused by *interference.*

Proactive interference A cause of forgetting by which previously stored information prevents learning and remembering new information.

Retroactive interference A cause of forgetting by which newly learned information prevents retrieval of previously stored material.

Serial position effect A form of interference related to the sequence in which information is presented. Generally, items in the middle of the sequence are less well remembered than items presented first or last.

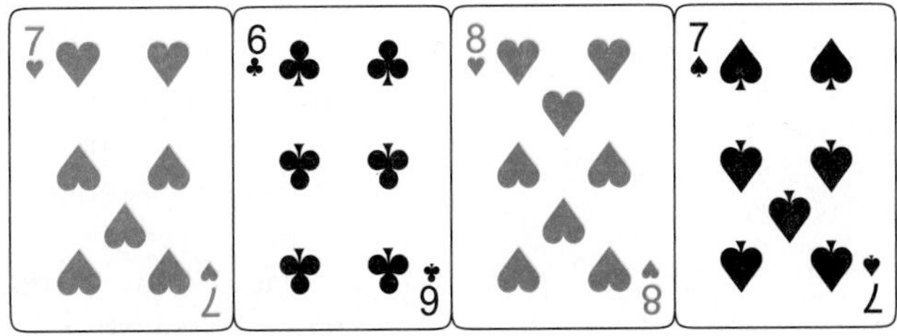

FIGURE 7.11 The "Magic" of Memory (*continued*)

Your card is gone! How did we do it? We didn't read your mind; it was your own *reconstructive memory* and the "sin" of *absent-mindedness* playing card tricks on you. If you don't immediately see how the trick works, try it again with a different card.

● **FIGURE 7.12** Two Types of Interference

In proactive interference, earlier learning (Spanish) interferes with memory for later information (French). In retroactive interference, new information (French) interferes with memory for information learned earlier (Spanish).

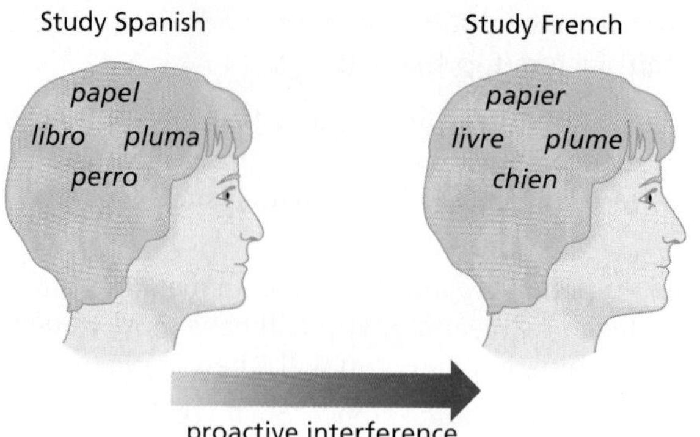
Study Spanish
papel
libro pluma
perro
Study French
papier
livre plume
chien
proactive interference

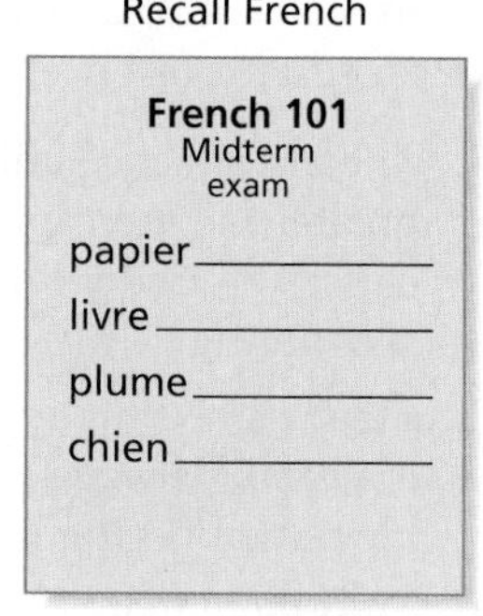
Recall French
French 101
Midterm
exam
papier
livre
plume
chien

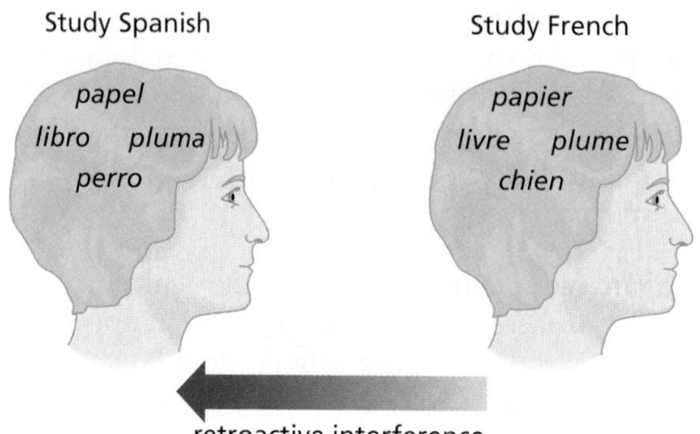
Study Spanish
papel
libro pluma
perro
Study French
papier
livre plume
chien
retroactive interference

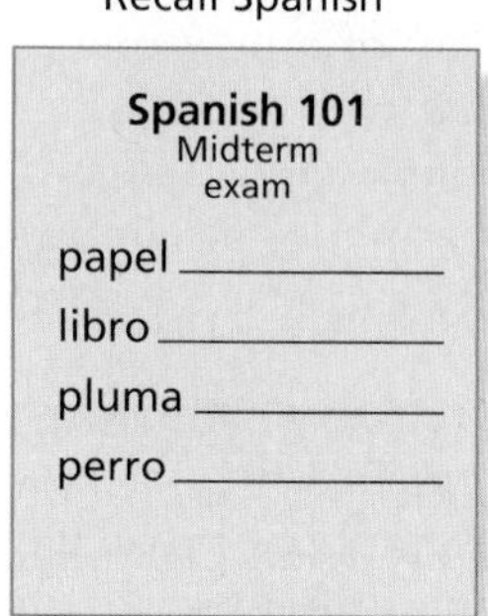
Recall Spanish
Spanish 101
Midterm
exam
papel
libro
pluma
perro

How does interference theory explain the serial position effect? Unlike the material at the ends of the poem or list, the part in the middle is exposed to a double dose of interference—both retroactively and proactively. That is, the middle part receives interference from both directions, while material at either end gets interference from only one side. (This suggests that you might find it helpful to pay special attention to the material in the middle of this chapter.)

Misattribution: Memories in the Wrong Context

All three "sins" discussed so far make memories inaccessible. Sometimes, however, memories are retrievable, but they are associated with the wrong time, place, or person. Schacter (1999) calls this **misattribution.** This is caused by the reconstructive nature of long-term memory. In the penny demonstration at the beginning of the chapter, you learned that memories are typically retrieved as fragments that we reassemble in such a way as to make them meaningful to us. This opens the way to connecting information with the wrong, but oh-so-sensible, context.

Here's an example: Psychologist Donald Thompson was accused of rape, based on a victim's detailed, but mistaken, description of her assailant (Thompson, 1988). Fortunately for Thompson, his alibi was indisputable. At the time of the crime he was being interviewed live on television—about memory distortions. The victim, it turned out, had been watching the interview just before she was raped and had misattributed the assault to Thompson.

Misattribution also can cause people to believe mistakenly that other people's ideas are their own. This sort of misattribution occurs when a person hears an idea and keeps it in memory, while forgetting its source. Unintentional plagiarism comes from this form of misattribution, as we saw earlier in the case of Beatle George Harrison.

■ **Misattribution** A memory fault that occurs when memories are retrieved but are associated with the wrong time, place, or person.

Yet another type of misattribution can cause people to remember something they did not experience at all. Such was the case with volunteers who were asked to remember a set of words associated with a particular theme: *door, glass, pane, shade, ledge, sill, house, open, curtain, frame, view, breeze, sash, screen,* and *shutter*. Under these conditions, many participants later remembered *window,* even though that word was not on the list (Roediger & McDermott, 1995, 2000). This result again shows the power of context cues in determining the content of memory. It also demonstrates how people tend to create and retrieve memories based on meaning.

Suggestibility: External Cues Distort or Create Memories

Memories can also be distorted or created by suggestion, a possibility of particular importance to the law. Witnesses may be interviewed by attorneys or by the police, who may make suggestions about the facts of a case—either deliberately or unintentionally—which might alter a witness's testimony. Such concerns about **suggestibility** prompted Elizabeth Loftus and John Palmer to investigate the circumstances under which eyewitness memories can be distorted.

Memory Distortion Participants in the classic Loftus and Palmer study first watched a film of two cars colliding. Then, the experimenters asked them to estimate how fast the cars had been moving. The witnesses' responses depended heavily on how the questions were worded (Loftus, 1979, 1984; Loftus & Palmer, 1973). Half were asked, "How fast were the cars going when they *smashed* into each other?" Their estimates, it turned out, were about 25% higher than those given by respondents who were asked, "How fast were the cars going when they *hit* each other?" This distortion of memory caused by misinformation is known, appropriately enough, as the **misinformation effect.**

Clearly, the Loftus and Palmer study shows that memories can be distorted and embellished by cues and suggestions given at the time of recall. Memories can even be created by similar methods—all without the individual's awareness that memory has been altered. We'll show you how.

■ **Suggestibility** The process of memory distortion as the result of deliberate or inadvertent suggestion.

■ **Misinformation effect** The distortion of memory by suggestion or misinformation.

● Our criminal justice system relies heavily on eyewitness identifications and descriptions. How well does this system work? You can judge for yourself in the case of a Catholic priest, Father Pagano (right), who was arrested and accused of a series of robberies. The police and the prosecutor were certain that they had the right man, because seven witnesses had identified him as the culprit. Father Pagano was finally exonerated during his trial, when the real robber (left)—hardly a look-alike—confessed.

Fabricated Memories To create entirely false memories, Elizabeth Loftus and her colleagues contacted the parents of college students and obtained lists of childhood events, which the students were asked to recall. Added to those lists were plausible events that never happened, such as being lost in a shopping mall, spilling the punch bowl at a wedding, meeting Bugs Bunny at Disneyland (impossible because Bugs is not a Disney character), or experiencing a visit by a clown at a birthday party (Braun et al., 2002; Hyman et al., 1995; Loftus, 1997a, 1997b; Loftus & Ketcham, 1994). After repeated recall attempts over a period of several days, many of the students claimed to remember the bogus events. All that was required were some credible suggestions.

Factors Affecting the Accuracy of Eyewitnesses In the wake of studies such as these, much attention has focused on the accuracy of eyewitness recall. You can verify this by typing "eyewitness" into the PsychInfo database or looking up the following sources: Bruck and Ceci, 1997; Lindsay, 1990, 1993; Loftus, 1992, 1993, 2003b; Loftus and Ketcham, 1991, 1994; and Weingardt and colleagues, 1995. Here are the most important factors this research has identified:

- People's recollections are less influenced by leading questions if they are forewarned that interrogations can create memory bias.
- When the passage of time allows the original memory to fade, people are more likely to misremember information.
- Each time a memory is retrieved, it is reconstructed and then restored (much like a word-processing document that is retrieved, modified, and saved), increasing the chances of error.
- The age of the witness matters: Younger children and adults over 65 may be especially susceptible to influence by misinformation in their efforts to recall.
- Confidence in a memory is not a sign of an accurate memory. In fact, misinformed individuals can actually come to believe the misinformation in which they feel confidence.

The Recovered Memory Controversy At the beginning of the chapter, the Smith family's ordeal began with Donna Smith's claim that she had been sexually abused by her father. Subsequently, Donna came to believe her own claims, although she later stated that they were all fabrications. And now we see that research on eyewitness memory confirms the notion that suggestion can lead people not only to report false memories but to believe them (Hyman et al., 1995; Loftus, 1997a, 1997b).

Are all recovered memories suspect? The truth is that we frequently recover memories—accurate memories—of long-forgotten events. A chance remark, a peculiar odor, or an old tune can cue vivid recollections that haven't surfaced in years. The ones to be especially suspicious of, however, are memories cued by suggestion or leading questions—as were Donna Smith's recollections.

One notorious source of suggestion that pops up in many recovered memory cases is a book: *The Courage to Heal.* This book suggests repeatedly that forgotten memories of incest and abuse may lie behind people's feelings of powerlessness, inadequacy, vulnerability, and a long list of other unpleasant thoughts and emotions (Bass & Davis, 1988). The authors state, "If you . . . have a feeling that something abusive happened to you, it probably did" (pp. 21–22).

The belief that buried memories of traumatic experiences can cause mental and physical symptoms was originally proposed by Sigmund Freud. In his theory of *repression,* Freud taught that threatening or traumatic memories can be stored in the unconscious mind, where they indirectly influence our thoughts and behavior. He also taught that the only way to be free of these repressed memories is to root them out during therapy—bringing them into

CONNECTION: CHAPTER 10

Psychoanalyst *Sigmund Freud* taught that most of the mind is not accessible to consciousness.

the daylight of consciousness, where they could be dealt with rationally. Freud, however, never offered more than anecdotes and testimonials to support his repression theory.

In fact, modern cognitive research suggests just the opposite. Emotionally arousing events, including threatening ones, are usually remembered vividly (McNally et al., 2003; Shobe & Kihlstrom, 1997). Most people, however, are unaware of this fact, retaining a strong but unfounded belief in repression and in the Freudian unconscious. Likewise, many people also hold a strong belief that memory makes an accurate record of events, even though psychological science has abundant evidence showing that memory is prone to error (Neimark, 2004).

We are not suggesting that all therapists use suggestive techniques to recover repressed memories, although some still do (Poole et al., 1995). Patients should be especially wary of therapists who go "fishing" for unconscious causes of mental problem, using such techniques as hypnosis, dream analysis, and repeated leading questions about early sexual experiences. There is no evidence to support the validity of these methods for the recovery of accurate memories.

We should also note that the issue of recovered memories is both complex and charged with emotion. It is also one that strikes many people close to home. Thus, it remains controversial, even among psychologists, where it has caused bitter dispute between therapists and experimental psychologists. Yet, despite the controversy, most experts agree on the following points.

- Sexual abuse of children *does* occur, and it is more prevalent than most professionals had suspected just a generation ago (McAnulty & Burnette, 2004).
- Memories cued by suggestion are particularly vulnerable to distortion and fabrication (Loftus, 2003a).
- Early memories, especially those of incidents that may have happened in infancy, are likely to be fantasies or misattributions. Episodic memories of events before age 3 are extremely rare (Schacter, 1996).
- There is no infallible way to be sure about memories of sexual abuse (or any other memories) without independent supporting evidence (Ceci & Bruck, 1993).
- Although traumatic events can be forgotten, they are much more likely to form persistent and intrusive memories that people would rather forget. Moreover, such events can permanently alter the structure of the hippocampus (Teicher, 2002).
- There is no solid evidence for repression, in the Freudian sense of an unconscious memory that can cause physical and mental symptoms (Schacter, 1996).

Bias: Beliefs, Attitudes, and Opinions Distort Memories

The sixth memory "sin," which Schacter calls bias, refers to the influence of personal beliefs, attitudes, and experiences on memory. Lots of domestic arguments of the "Did not! Did, too!" variety owe their spirited exchanges to bias. Naturally, it's easier to see in another person than in ourselves. Here are two other, more subtle forms that memory bias can take.

Expectancy Bias Suppose that you are among a group of volunteers for an experiment in which you read a story about Bob and Margie, a couple who plan to get married. Part of the story reveals that Bob doesn't want to have children, and he is worried how Margie is going to take this disclosure. When he does tell her, Margie is shocked, because she desperately wants children. Then, after reading the story, you are informed that Bob and Margie did get married. Another group of volunteers is told that the couple ended their relationship. Will those in the two groups remember the Bob and Margie story differently?

Those who heard the unexpected ending (the condition in which Bob and Margie decided to get married) gave the most erroneous reports. Their errors made sense, however because what they recalled made the outcome fit their expectations (Schacter, 1999; Spiro, 1980). One person, for example, "remembered" that Bob and Margie had separated but decided their love could overcome their differences. Another related that the couple had decided on adoption, as a compromise. This **expectancy bias** stems from an unconscious tendency to remember events as being congruent with our expectations.

Self-Consistency Bias People abhor the thought of being inconsistent, even though research suggests that they are kidding themselves. This Schacter calls the **self-consistency bias.** It showed itself, for example, in one study that found people are less consistent than they remembered themselves being in their support for political candidates (Levine, 1997). Another study showed that people believe themselves to be more consistent than they actually are on their stands concerning equality of women, aid to minority groups, and the legalization of marijuana (Marcus, 1986).

The self-consistency bias appears in emotional memories, as well as in memories for attitudes and beliefs (Levine & Safer, 2002). Earlier in the chapter we saw that our moods could affect which memories we retrieve. Here, however, we are more interested in how our emotions can distort our memories. For example, a study of dating couples who were interviewed twice, two months apart, found that memories could be biased by how well the relationship had progressed over the interval. Those who had grown to like each other more remembered their initial evaluations of their partners as more positive than they actually were, while those whose relationships had become more negative had the opposite response (Scharfe & Bartholomew, 1998). In each of these studies, whether they involve attitudes, beliefs, opinions, or emotions, we see that our biases act as a sort of distorted mirror in which our memories are reflected.

Persistence: When We Can't Forget

The seventh "sin" of memory, **persistence,** reminds us that memory sometimes works all too well, especially when intense negative emotions are involved. In fact, intrusive recollections of unpleasant events lie at the heart of certain psychological disorders. Depressed people can't stop ruminating about unhappy events in their lives. Similarly, patients with *phobias* may become obsessed by fearful memories about snakes, dogs, crowds, spiders, or lightning. All of this again points to the powerful role that emotion plays in memory. Neuroscientists believe that it does so by strengthening the physical changes in the synapses that hold our memories (LeDoux, 1996).

CONNECTION: CHAPTER 12

People with *phobias* have extreme and unreasonable fears of specific objects or situations.

The Advantages of the "Seven Sins" of Memory

Despite the grief they cause us, the "seven sins" are actually by-products of adaptive features of memory, argues Daniel Schacter (1999). Thus, transience—maddening as it is to the student taking a test—is actually a way the memory system prevents itself from being overwhelmed by information that is no

■ **Expectancy bias** In memory, a tendency to distort recalled events to make them fit one's expectations.

■ **Self-consistency bias** The commonly held idea that we are more consistent in our attitudes, opinions, and beliefs than we actually are.

■ **Persistence** A memory problem in which unwanted memories cannot be put out of mind.

longer needed. Similarly, blocking may be viewed as a process that usually allows only the most relevant information (the information most strongly associated with the present cues) to come to mind. Again, this is a process that prevents us from a flood of unwanted and distracting memories.

In contrast, absent-mindedness is the by-product of the useful ability to shift our attention. Similarly, misattributions, biases, and suggestibility result from a memory system built to deal with *meaning* and discard details. (The alternative would be a computer-like memory filled with information at the expense of understanding.) And, finally, we can see that the "sin" of persistence is really a feature of a memory system that is especially responsive to emotional experiences, particularly those involving fear. In general, then, the picture that emerges of memory's "failures" is also one of a system that is well adapted to the conditions people have faced for thousands of years.

PSYCHOLOGY IN YOUR LIFE: IMPROVING YOUR MEMORY WITH MNEMONICS

To improve your memory, try using some mental strategies called *mnemonics* (pronounced *ni-MON-ix,* from the Greek word meaning "remember"). **Mnemonics** are methods memory experts use for encoding information to be remembered by associating it with information already in long-term memory. To illustrate, we will take a detailed look at two mnemonic strategies: the *method of loci* and *natural language mediators.*

● Mnemonic strategies help us remember things by making them meaningful. Here an elementary school teacher helps students remember the letter *K* by showing that "*K* does karate."

The Method of Loci Dating back to the ancient Greeks, the **method of loci** (pronounced *LOW-sye,* from the Latin *locus,* "place"), is literally one of the oldest tricks in this book. It was originally devised to help orators remember the major points of their speeches. You will also find it a practical means of learning and remembering lists.

To illustrate, imagine a familiar sequence of places, such as the bed, desk, and chairs in your room. Then, using the method of loci, mentally move from place to place in your room, and as you go, imagine putting one item from your list in each place. To retrieve the series, you merely take another mental tour, examining the places you used earlier. There you will "see" the item you have put in each locus. To remember a grocery list, for example, you might mentally picture a can of *tuna* on your bed, *shampoo* spilled on your desktop, and a box of *eggs* open on a chair. Bizarre or unconventional image combinations are usually easier to remember; a can of tuna in your bedroom will make a more memorable image than tuna in your kitchen (Bower, 1972).

The mental images used in this technique work especially well because they employ both verbal and visual memories (Paivio, 1986). It's worth noting, by the way, that visual imagery is one of the most effective forms of encoding: You can easily remember things by associating them with vivid, distinctive mental pictures. In fact, you could remember your grocery list by using visual imagery alone. Simply combine the mental images of tuna, shampoo, and eggs in a bizarre but memorable way. So, you might picture a tuna floating on an enormous fried egg in a sea of foamy shampoo. Or you might imagine a politician you dislike eating tuna from the can, her hair covered with shampoo suds, while you throw eggs at her.

Natural Language Mediators Memory aids called **natural language mediators** associate meaningful word patterns with new information to be remembered. For instance, you can make up a story to help you remember a grocery list (the same one, consisting of tuna, shampoo, and eggs). The story might link the items this way: "The cat discovers I'm out of *tuna* so she interrupts

■ **Mnemonics** Techniques for improving memory, especially by making connections between new material and information already in long-term memory.

■ **Method of loci** A mnemonic technique that involves associating items on a list with a sequence of familiar physical locations.

■ **Natural language mediators** Words associated with new information to be remembered.

me while I'm using the *shampoo* and meows to *egg* me on." Similarly, advertisers know that rhyming slogans and rhythmic musical jingles can make it easier for customers to remember their products and brand names ("Oscar Mayer has a way with . . ."). The chances are that a teacher in your past used a simple rhyme to help you remember a spelling rule ("*I* before *E* except after *C*") or the number of days in each month ("Thirty days has September . . ."). In a physics class you may have used a natural language mediator in the form of an *acronym*—a word made up of initials—to learn the colors of the visible spectrum in their correct order: "Roy G. Biv" stands for red, orange, yellow, green, blue, indigo, violet.

Remembering Names The inability to remember people's names is one of the most common complaints about memory. So, how could you use the power of association to remember names? In the first place, you must realize that remembering names doesn't happen automatically. People who do this well must work at it by making associations between a name and some characteristic of the person—the more unusual the association, the better.

Suppose, for example, you have just met a man whose name is Bob. You might visualize his face framed in a big "O," taken from the middle of his name. To remember his friend Ann, think of her as "Queen Ann," sitting on a throne. And, as for their companion Phil, you might visualize putting a hose in Phil's mouth and "fill"-ing him with water. (It is usually best not to tell people about the mnemonic strategy you are using to remember their names.)

In general, the use of mnemonics teaches us that memory is flexible, personal, and creative. It also teaches us that *memory ultimately works by meaningful associations.* With this knowledge and a little experimentation, you can devise techniques for encoding and retrieval that work well for you based on your own personal associations and, perhaps, on your own sense of humor.

CHECK YOUR UNDERSTANDING

1. **RECALL:** Which one of the following statements best describes forgetting, as characterized by Ebbinghaus's forgetting curve?
   a. We forget at a constant rate.
   b. We forget slowly at first and then more rapidly as time goes on.
   c. We forget rapidly at first and then more slowly as time goes on.
   d. Ebbinghaus's method of relearning showed that we never really forget.
   e. We never forget.

2. **APPLICATION:** Which kind of forgetting is involved when the sociology I studied yesterday makes it more difficult to learn and remember the psychology I am studying today?
   a. proactive interference
   b. retroactive interference
   c. decay
   d. retrieval failure
   e. heuristics

3. **RECALL:** What is the term for the controversial notion that memories can be blocked off in the unconscious, where they may cause physical and mental problems?
   a. interference
   b. repression
   c. persistence
   d. absent-mindedness
   e. transience

4. **RECALL:** Which one of the seven "sins" of memory is disputed by those who believe that memories of childhood abuse can, in many cases, be recovered during adulthood?
   a. transience
   b. persistence
   c. absent-mindedness
   d. suggestibility
   e. decay

5. **UNDERSTANDING THE CORE CONCEPT:** Which one of the "sins" of memory probably helps us avoid dangerous situations we have encountered before?
   a. suggestibility
   b. bias
   c. persistence
   d. misattribution
   e. absent-mindedness

ANSWERS: 1. c 2. a 3. b 4. d 5. c

HOW DO CHILDREN ACQUIRE LANGUAGE?

KEY QUESTION
?

One of the defining characteristics of humans is the use of complex *language*—our ability to communicate through spoken and written words and gestures. From a developmental perspective, human language acquisition is awe-inspiring: Newborn children know no words at all, yet in only a few years virtually all of them become fluent speakers of any language they hear spoken regularly—or *see*, in the case of gestural languages such as American Sign Language. What makes them such adept language learners? Developmental specialists believe that human infants possess innate (inborn) abilities that help them with this task (Pinker, 1994). Here's how our Core Concept states the main idea of this section:

CORE CONCEPT

Infants and children face an especially important developmental task with the acquisition of language.

Language Structures in the Brain According to the *innateness theory of language,* children acquire language not merely by imitating but also by following an inborn program of steps to acquire the vocabulary and grammar of the language in their environment. Psycholinguist Noam Chomsky (1965, 1975) has proposed that children are born with mental structures—built into the brain—that make it possible to comprehend and produce speech. Many experts agree with Chomsky that innate mental machinery orchestrates children's language learning (Hauser, Chomsky, & Fitch, 2002). Indeed, research based on the Human Genome Project has provided evidence that the foundations of language are, in part, genetic (Liegeois et al., 2001). One such mechanism, we have seen, lies in Broca's area, the motor speech "controller" in the cerebral cortex. Chomsky refers to these speech-enabling structures collectively as a **language acquisition device** or **LAD.**

In Chomsky's theory, the LAD—like a computer chip—contains some very basic rules, common to all human languages. One such rule might be the distinction between nouns (for names of things) and verbs (for actions). These innate rules, Chomsky argues, make it easier for children to discover patterns in languages to which they are exposed.

What other evidence does Chomsky have to suggest that the foundations of language are innate? Children worldwide proceed through very similar stages of learning their native languages. A logical hypothesis for explaining this pattern would be that children possess inborn "programs" for language development that automatically run at certain times in the child's life. Despite the cross-cultural similarities in the sequence, however, language learning is not precisely the same across cultures. Such variations suggest that children's built-in capacity for language is not a rigid device but a set of "listening rules" or guidelines for perceiving language (Bee, 1994; Slobin, 1985a, b). For example, babies pay attention to the sounds and rhythms of the sound strings they hear others speak (or, in sign language, see), especially the beginnings, endings, and stressed syllables. Relying on their built-in "listening guides," young children deduce the patterns and rules for producing their own speech.

In general, language researchers have been impressed with the fact that most young children are both ready to acquire language and flexible about its final form and context. This is equally true for children exposed to any of the world's 4000 spoken languages, as well as to gestural communication systems, such as American Sign Language. Such adaptability suggests that the LAD in children is flexible, not rigidly programmed (Goldin-Meadow & Mylander, 1990; Meier, 1991). Recent research also suggests that the effect can go the other

■ **Language acquisition device or LAD** A biologically organized mental structure in the brain that facilitates the learning of language because (according to Chomsky) it is innately programmed with some of the fundamental rules of grammar.

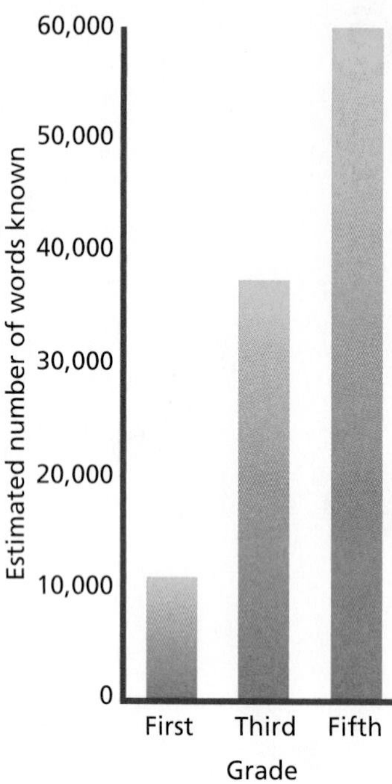
60,000
50,000
40,000
30,000
20,000
10,000
0
Estimated number of words known
First
Third
Fifth
Grade

FIGURE 7.13 Growth in Grade-School Children's Vocabulary

The number of words in a child's vocabulary increases rapidly during the grade school years—an even faster rate of increase than during the preschool years. The chart shows total vocabulary, including words that a child can use (production vocabulary) and words that a child can understand (comprehension vocabulary). These data were reported in 1995 by J. M. Anglin of the University of Waterloo, Ontario, Canada.

way as well: The language we learn as children also fine-tunes the structure of the brain, as when English speakers "wire" their brains to distinguish the sounds /r/ and /l/, sounds that cannot be distinguished by many Japanese speakers (Iverson et al., 2003).

Babbling: A Foundation for Language Besides their ability to perceive speech sounds, infants have a natural ability to produce language sounds. Part of this tendency arises from a vocal apparatus that is biologically adapted for speech. As a result, infants babble, producing speechlike sounds and syllables such as "mamama" or "beebee" well before they begin to use true words. Infants at this stage may also follow conversational "rules," such as taking turns with vocalizations (Jaffe et al., 2001). Amazingly, during this *babbling stage,* babies make nearly all sounds heard in all languages. Eventually, however, learning narrows the repertoire down to the sounds of the language that the baby hears (Clark & Clark, 1977; Mowrer, 1960).

Acquiring Vocabulary and Grammar Inborn language abilities don't tell the whole story, for children must *learn* the words and the structure of a particular language. Accordingly, learning the basic grammar and vocabulary in the native language represents an important project for children in their first few years of life—and they are excellent language learners. At age 2, the average child has a vocabulary of nearly a thousand different words (Huttenlocher et al., 1991). By the age of 6, that number has burgeoned to an astounding 10,000 words (Anglin, 1993, 1995). Assuming that most of these words are learned after the age of 18 months, this works out to about nine new words a day, or almost one word per waking hour (Bower, 1998c; Carey, 1978). Even more surprising, the pace of vocabulary acquisition picks up between about ages 6 and 10, as you can see in Figure 7.13.

What is the pattern by which children develop vocabulary and grammar? Developmental psychologists recognize three initial stages: the *one-word stage,* the *two-word stage,* and *telegraphic speech.* During the *one-word stage,* which begins at about 1 year of age, children utter single concrete nouns or verbs, such as *Mama* or *drink.* Later, they learn to put words together to express more complex ideas.

The Naming Explosion At around 18 months of age, children's word learning accelerates rapidly. At this age, children may delight in pointing to objects and naming them. Researchers have called this phase the "naming explosion" because children begin to acquire new words, especially names for objects, at a rapidly increasing rate. Soon they also discern that some words are not names but actions (verbs) that describe how named objects and persons affect each other.

After about six months, the naming explosion subsides and children begin to use one-word utterances in different sequences to convey more complex meanings. When these words come in pairs, they are said to enter the *two-word stage,* and the range of meanings children can convey increases tremendously. Studies of different languages show that, around the world, children's two-word utterances begin to divide their experience into certain categories. For example, children speaking languages as diverse as English, Samoan, Finnish, Hebrew, and Swedish were found to talk mostly about three categories of ideas: movers, movable objects, and locations (Braine, 1976). When young Alexis kicks a ball, for example, the mover is Alexis and the movable object is the ball. Alexis can express this relationship in the two-word sequence, "Alexis ball." It is in the two-word stage, at about 2 years, that children first develop the language rules called *grammar.* This allows them to move past simple naming and combine words into sentences.

The Rules of Grammar: Putting Words Together Even if you have a limited vocabulary, you can combine the same words in different sequences to convey a rich variety of meanings. For example, "I saw him chasing a dog" and "I saw a dog chasing him" both use exactly the same words, but switching the order of the words *him* and *dog* yields completely different meanings. **Grammar** makes this possible: It is a language's set of rules about combining and ordering words to make understandable sentences (Naigles, 1990; Naigles & Kako, 1993). Different languages may use considerably different rules about grammatical combinations. In Japanese, for example, the verb always comes last, while English is much more lax about verb position.

In their early two- and three-word sentences, children's speech is *telegraphic:* short, simple sequences of nouns and verbs without plurals, tenses, or function words like *the* and *of*. For example, "Ball hit Evie cry" is *telegraphic speech.* To develop the ability to make full sentences, children must learn to use other forms of speech, such as modifiers (adjectives and adverbs) and articles (the, those), and they must learn how to put words together—grammatically. In English, this means recognizing and producing the familiar subject-verb-object order, as in "The lamb followed Mary."

Finally, children need to acquire grammatical skill in using **morphemes,** the meaningful units that make up words. Morphemes mark verbs to show tense (walk*ed,* walk*ing*) and mark nouns to show possession (Maria*'s,* the people*'s*) and plurality (fox*es,* child*ren*). Often, however, children make mistakes because they do not know the rule or apply an inappropriate one (Marcus, 1996). One common error, known as **overregularization,** applies a rule too widely and creates incorrect forms. For example, after learning to make past tense verb forms by adding *-d* or *-ed,* children may apply this "rule" even to its exceptions, the irregular verbs, creating such nonwords as *hitted* and *breaked.* Learning to add *-s* or *-es* to make plurals, children may apply the rule to irregular nouns, as in *foots* or *mouses.*

Other Language Skills Words and the grammatical rules for combining them are only some of the ingredients of communication. To communicate well, children also need to learn the social rules of conversation. They must learn how to join a discussion, how to take turns talking and listening, and how to make contributions that are relevant. Adult speakers use body language, intonation, and facial expressions to enhance their communication. They also use feedback they get from listeners and are able to take the perspective of the listener. Children must master these skills in order to become successful communicators—to become part of a human language community.

As they grow older, children also begin to express abstract meanings, especially as their thoughts extend beyond the physical world and into their psychological world. For example, after the age of 2, children begin to use words such as *dream, forget, pretend, believe, guess,* and *hope,* as they talk about internal states (Shatz et al., 1983). They also use words such as *happy, sad,* and *angry* to refer to emotional states. Finally, after cognitive advances that occur later in childhood, they understand and use highly abstract words such as *truth, justice,* and *idea.*

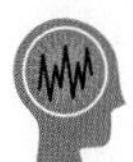

PSYCHOLOGY IN YOUR LIFE: LEARNING A NEW LANGUAGE

Learning a new language is something that (almost) every high school student has to do. Some schools require two years of a language, some three, while some may even require four. The developmental perspective suggests that children learn languages best early in life, long before they reach high

■ **Grammar** The rules of a language, specifying how to use words, morphemes, and syntax to produce understandable sentences.

■ **Morphemes** The meaningful units of language that make up words. Some whole words are morphemes (example: *word*); other morphemes include grammatical components that alter a word's meaning (examples: *-ed, -ing,* and *un-*).

■ **Overregularization** Applying a grammatical rule too widely and thereby creating incorrect forms.

school. Lennenberg (1967) argued that languages should be learned early in life when people are most receptive to acquiring languages. This explains why adolescents and adults who learn languages speak it with an accent, whereas those who learn non-native languages before puberty have no accent!

Given the research and findings on learning languages, the question becomes, "Why do we teach languages so late (comparatively) in the educational program?" Although second languages have been taught beginning in 7th or 8th grade for years, the recent focus on testing competes with time in the day spent teaching languages at the elementary and middle school levels. There are some schools and school systems, such as Fairfax County, Virginia, that have immersion programs beginning in kindergarten which extend through middle school. These schools and systems have committed to bilingual education to the extent that at least half of the instructional day is taught in a second language (usually a school focuses on one particular language). Whether you learned a second language earlier or later in your academic career, the knowledge remains a valuable asset to your future endeavors.

CHECK YOUR UNDERSTANDING

1. **RECALL:** Noam Chomsky has presented evidence supporting his theory that
   a. children learn language by imitating their parents.
   b. children are born with some rules of grammar programmed into their brains.
   c. vocabulary is innate, but grammar is learned.
   d. different languages may have entirely different rules of grammar.
   e. grammar interferes with a child's ability to learn languages.
2. **RECALL:** A child's acquisition of grammar first becomes apparent at
   a. the babbling stage.
   b. the one-word stage.
   c. the two-word stage.
   d. the concrete operational stage.
   e. adolescence.
3. **UNDERSTANDING THE CORE CONCEPT:** There are many developmental tasks that children must face in the area of language. Can you name two?

ANSWERS: 1. b 2. c 3. Vocabulary and grammar.

A Look Ahead

In the next section of the chapter, we will focus on the processes underlying thought, especially in decision making and problem solving. One of the most common methods used to describe how thinking and problem solving work is called the **computer metaphor.** This metaphor likens the brain to an information processor such as those found in a computer hard drive. While this may seem simple and logical to some, as we progress through this section, you will see that the brain and its capabilities go far beyond the "plugging and chugging" of information that computers provide. Our brains can create *concepts* and new thoughts and ideas that are more than simply a regurgitation of information from our long-term memory. We will examine the building blocks of cognition, called *concepts, images, schemas,* and *scripts.* You will also find that the tools psychologists use to study cognition include both time-honored psychological methods and the rapidly developing techniques of brain imaging. This excursion into thinking will also give us the opportunity to look at the related topic of creativity and that mysterious quality known as "genius."

■ **Computer metaphor** The idea that the brain is an information-processing organ that operates, in some ways, like a computer.

WHAT ARE THE COMPONENTS OF THOUGHT?

KEY QUESTION

Solving a math problem, deciding what to do Friday night, and indulging a private fantasy all involve *thinking.* More generally, we can conceive of thinking as a complex act of information processing in the brain, by which we deal with our world of ideas, feelings, desires, and experience. Our Core Concept notes that this information can come from within and from without, but it always involves some form of mental representation:

CORE CONCEPT

Thinking is a cognitive process in which the brain uses information from the senses, emotions, and memory to create and manipulate mental representations, such as concepts, images, schemas, and scripts.

These mental representations, then, are the building blocks of cognition, which thinking organizes in meaningful ways. The ultimate results can be the higher thought processes that we call reasoning, imagining, judging, deciding, problem solving, expertise, creativity, and—sometimes—genius.

Concepts

You may have had an experience known as *déjà vu* (from the French for "seen before"). The term refers to the strange feeling that your present experience jibes with a previous experience, even though you cannot retrieve the explicit memory. Perhaps you have visited a new place that seems oddly familiar or had a social conversation that seemed repetitive. While this *déjà vu* feeling can be an illusion, it also reflects the brain's ability to treat new stimuli as instances of familiar categories, even if the stimuli are slightly different from anything it has encountered before. Here's the point: The ability to assimilate experiences into familiar mental categories—and to take the same action toward them or give them the same label—is regarded as one of the most basic attributes of thinking organisms (Mervis & Rosch, 1981).

● Only humans—because of their ability for thinking about what might be—can indulge in flights of fancy.

The mental categories that we form in this way are called **concepts.** Concepts are among the building blocks of thinking, because they enable us to organize knowledge in systematic ways (Goldman-Rakic, 1992). Concepts may be mental representations for classes of objects, activities, or living organisms, such as "chairs," "birthday parties," or "birds." They may also represent properties (such as "red" or "large"), abstractions (such as "truth" or "love"), relations (such as "smarter than"), procedures (such as how to tie your shoes), or intentions (such as the intention to break into a conversation) (Smith & Medin, 1981). Because concepts are mental structures, researchers cannot observe them directly but have had to infer their influence in people's thinking indirectly by studying their observable effects on behavior or on brain activity. For example, you cannot be sure that another person shares your concept of "red," but you can observe whether he or she responds in the same way you do to stimuli that you both call "red." Likewise, in Google, an index consisting of a huge set of search terms represents the concepts on which a user can run a search.

Two Kinds of Concepts Everyone conceptualizes the world in a unique way, so our concepts define who we are. Yet behind this individual uniqueness lie similarities in the ways that people form concepts. Many cognitive psychologists believe that we all distinguish between two different types of concepts: *natural concepts* and *artificial concepts* (Medin et al., 2000).

■ **Concepts** Mental representations of categories of items or ideas, based on experience.

Natural concepts are rather imprecise mental classifications that develop out of our everyday experiences in the world. You may possess a natural concept of "bird" based on your experiences with birds. You probably also have natural concepts associated with Chevrolets, your mother's face, artichokes, and the Statue of Liberty. While each of these examples may involve words, natural concepts also can involve visual images, emotions, and other nonverbal memories.

Your own natural concept of "bird" invokes a mental **prototype,** a generic image that represents a typical bird from your experience (Hunt, 1989; Medin, 1989; Mervis & Rosch, 1981; Rosch & Mervis, 1975). To determine whether some object is a bird or not, you mentally compare the object to your bird prototype. The more sophisticated your prototype, the less trouble you will have with flightless birds, such as ostriches and penguins, or with birdlike flying creatures, such as bats, or with turtles and platypuses, which lay eggs, as do birds. Natural concepts are sometimes called "fuzzy concepts" because of their imprecision (Kosko & Isaka, 1993).

Research support for the idea of a prototype comes from studies showing that people respond more quickly to typical members of a category than to more unusual ones—that is, their reaction times are faster. For example, it takes less time to say whether a robin is a bird than to say whether an ostrich is a bird, because robins resemble most people's prototype of a bird more closely than ostriches do (Kintsch, 1981; Rosch et al., 1976). The prototype is formed on the basis of frequently experienced features. These features are stored in memory, and the more often they are perceived, the stronger their overall memory strength is. Thus, the prototype can be rapidly accessed and recalled.

By comparison, **artificial concepts** are those defined by a set of rules or characteristics, such as dictionary definitions or mathematical formulas. The definition of "rectangle" that you learned in math class is an example. Artificial concepts represent precisely defined ideas or abstractions, rather than actual objects in the world. So, if you are a zoology major, you may also have an artificial concept of "bird," which defines it as a "feathered biped." Like these textbook definitions of birds and rectangles, most of the concepts you learn in school are artificial concepts. "Cognitive psychology" is also an artificial concept; so is the concept of "concept"!

Most of the concepts in our everyday lives, however, are natural concepts. We can identify clusters of properties that are shared by different instances of a concept (for example, robins, penguins, and ostriches all are birds and all have feathers), but there may be no one property that is present in all instances. Still, we consider some instances as more representative of a concept—more typical of our mental prototype (more "birdlike")—than others.

Concept Hierarchies We organize much of our declarative memories into **concept hierarchies,** from general to specific, as seen in Figure 7.14. For most people, the broad category of "animal" has several subcategories, such as "bird" and "fish," which are subdivided, in turn, into their specific forms, such as "canary," "ostrich," "shark," and "salmon." The "animal" category may itself be a subcategory of the still larger category of "living beings." We can think of these concepts and categories as arranged in a hierarchy of levels, with the most general and abstract at the top and the most specific and concrete at the bottom, as shown in Figure 7.14. They are also linked to many other concepts: Some birds are edible, some are endangered, some are national symbols. It may help you to understand this if you use the following conceptual model: The connections among concepts seem to work much like the links you see on web pages.

Culture, Concepts, and Thought Most of the research on concept formation has been done by Euro-American psychologists, who have studied how con-

■ **Natural concepts** Mental representations of objects and events drawn from our direct experience.

■ **Prototype** An ideal or most representative example of a conceptual category.

■ **Artificial concepts** Concepts defined by rules, such as word definitions and mathematical formulas.

■ **Concept hierarchies** Levels of concepts, from most general to most specific, in which a more general level includes more specific concepts—as the concept of "animal" includes "dog," "giraffe," and "butterfly."

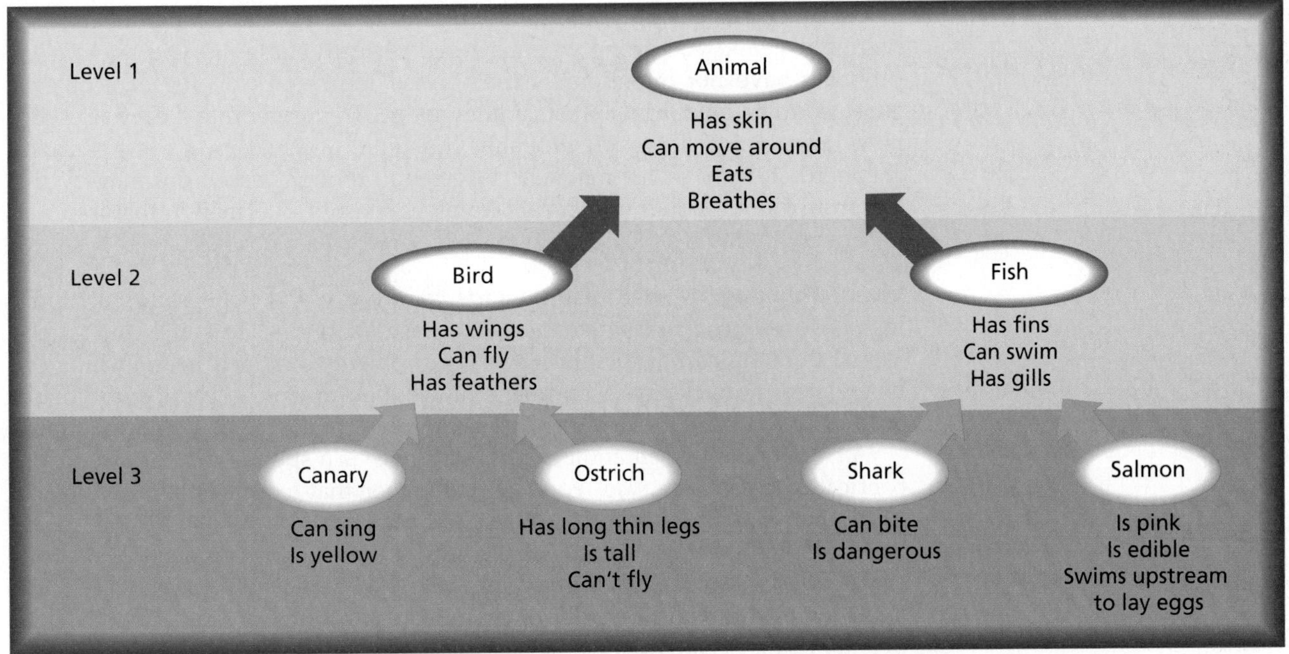
Level 1
Animal
Has skin
Can move around
Eats
Breathes
Level 2
Bird
Has wings
Can fly
Has feathers
Fish
Has fins
Can swim
Has gills
Level 3
Canary
Can sing
Is yellow
Ostrich
Has long thin legs
Is tall
Can't fly
Shark
Can bite
Is dangerous
Salmon
Is pink
Is edible
Swims upstream
to lay eggs

● **FIGURE 7.14** Hierarchically Organized Structure of Concepts

cepts are used in their own culture. But recent work by cross-cultural psychologists cautions us not to assume that thinking works exactly the same way in all parts of the globe. For example, Americans have learned from recent conflicts with cultures in the Middle East that the concepts of "democracy" and "freedom" may carry vastly different connotations in different parts of the world.

One big cultural difference involves the use of logic: Many groups do not value the use of logical reasoning as much as do Europeans and North Americans (Bower, 2000a; Nisbett et al., 2001). Even in the United States, many people place higher value on qualities variously known as "common sense" or "intuition"—which refer to thinking based on experience, rather than on logic.

Another cultural difference involves concept formation. Although people everywhere do form concepts, most Asian cultures tend to place less importance on precise definitions and clear-cut conceptual categories than do the dominant cultures of Europe and North America (Nisbett, 2000; Peng & Nisbett, 1999). From an Asian perspective, conceptual boundaries tend to be more fluid, and the focus is more on the relationships among concepts, rather than on their definitions. Thus, a person who grew up in Bankok might be more interested than would a native of Boston in the ways in which the terms "masculine" and "feminine" are contrasting ideas, rather than defining the exact meaning of each term.

Imagery and Cognitive Maps

Do you think only in words, or do you sometimes think in pictures and spatial relationships or other sensory images? If you take a moment to think of a face, a tune, or the smell of fresh bread, the answer is obvious. Sensory mental imagery revives information you have previously perceived and stored in memory. This revival may take place without immediate sensory input, yet it produces internal representations of events and concepts in sensory forms, such as visual images.

Consider, for example, the following question: What shape are a German shepherd's ears? Assuming you answered correctly, how did you know? You probably have not intentionally memorized the shapes of dog ears or ever expected to be quizzed about such knowledge. To answer that a German shepherd has pointed ears, you probably consulted a visual image of a German shepherd stored in your memory. In general, thought based on imagery differs from verbal thought because it involves sensory information that is stored in sensory pathways of the brain (Kosslyn, 1983; Paivio, 1983).

Visual Thinking Visual imagery adds complexity and richness to our thinking, as do images that involve the other senses (sound, taste, smell, and touch). Visual thinking can be useful in solving problems in which relationships can be grasped more clearly in an image rather than in words. That is why books such as this one often encourage visual thinking with pictures and diagrams.

A cognitive representation of physical space is a special form of visual concept called a *cognitive map*. You will remember that learning theorist Edward C. Tolman was the first to hypothesize that people (and other animals) form mental maps of their environment, which they use to guide their actions toward desired goals. Cognitive maps help you get to your psychology class, and they enable you to give another person directions to a nearby theater or deli. By using cognitive maps, people can move through their homes with their eyes closed or go to familiar destinations even when their usual routes are blocked (Hart & Moore, 1973; Thorndyke & Hayes-Roth, 1979).

Cultural Influences on Cognitive Maps Mental maps also seem to reflect our subjective impressions of physical reality. And thus the maps we have in our minds mirror the view of the world that we have developed from the perspective of our own culture. For example, if you were asked to draw a world map, where would you begin and how would you represent the size, shape, and relations between various countries? This task was given to nearly 4000 students from 71 cities in 49 countries as part of an international study of the way people of different nationalities visualize the world. The study found that the majority of maps had a Eurocentric world view: Europe was placed in the center of the map, and the other countries were arranged around it (probably due to the dominance for many centuries of Eurocentric maps in geography books). But the study also yielded many interesting culture-biased maps, such as the ones by a Chicago student (Figure 7.15) and an Australian student (Figure 7.16). American students, incidentally, did poorly on this task, often misplacing countries. Students from the former Soviet Union and Hungary made the most accurately detailed maps (Saarinen, 1987).

Thought and the Brain

As they have studied the inner world of thought, cognitive researchers have been forced to invent ways of mapping the mind itself. We will see that these methods can now bring us close to the long-standing goal of connecting mental activity to brain activity (Ashby & Waldron, 2000; Beardsley, 1997a; Behrmann, 2000; Freedman et al., 2001; Thorpe & Fabre-Thorpe, 2001). For example, with the help of the computer, biological scientists have demonstrated that certain thoughts, such as "dog" or "pencil," can be associated with specific electrical wave patterns in the brain (Garnsey, 1993; Osterhout & Holcomb, 1992). They have demonstrated this by presenting a repeated stimulus (such as the word *dog* flashed on a screen) to a volunteer "wired" to record the brain's electrical responses. While the brain waves on just one trial may show no clear pattern, a computer can average many brain wave responses to

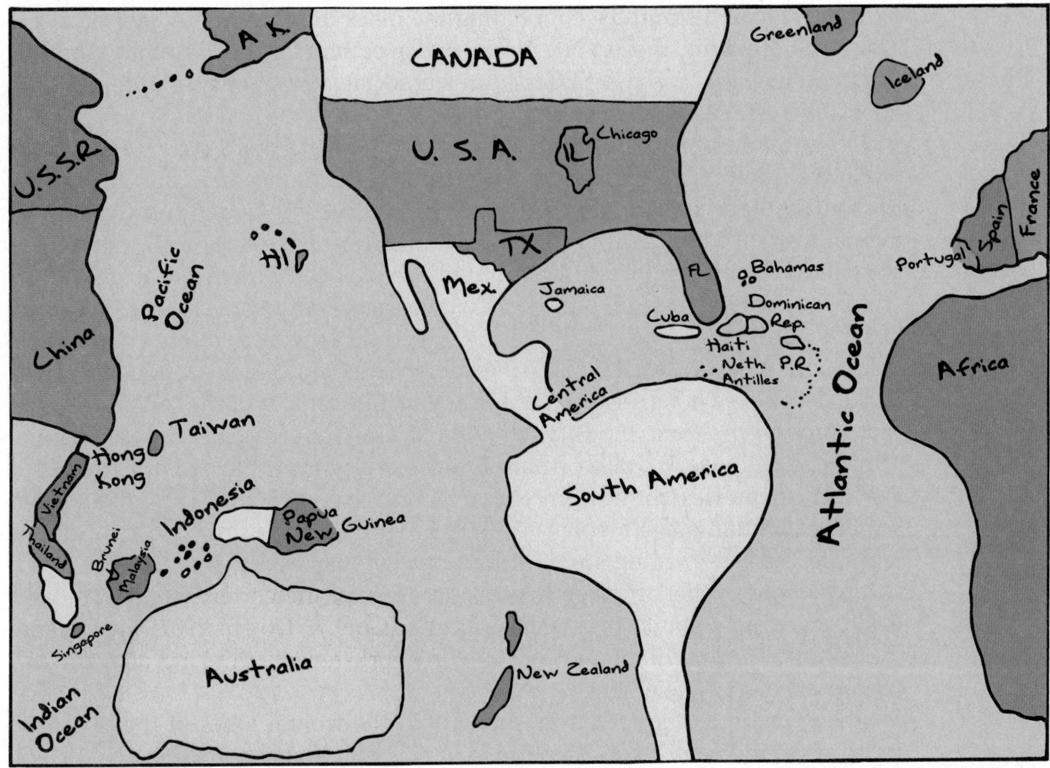

A.K.
CANADA
Greenland
Iceland
U.S.S.R
U. S. A.
IL
Chicago
TX
Mex
FL
Bahamas
Jamaica
Cuba
Dominican Rep.
Haiti
P.R.
Neth. Antilles
Portugal
Spain
France
Africa
Pacific Ocean
HI
China
Central America
Atlantic Ocean
Taiwan
Hong Kong
Vietnam
Indonesia
Papua New Guinea
Thailand
Brunei
Malaysia
South America
Singapore
Australia
New Zealand
Indian Ocean

● **FIGURE 7.15** Chicagocentric View of the World

How does this sketch compare with your view of the world? (*Source:* From COGNITIVE PSYCHOLOGY 5th ed. by Robert L. Solso. Copyright © 1998 by Allyn & Bacon. Reprinted by permission of Allyn and Bacon, Boston, MA.)

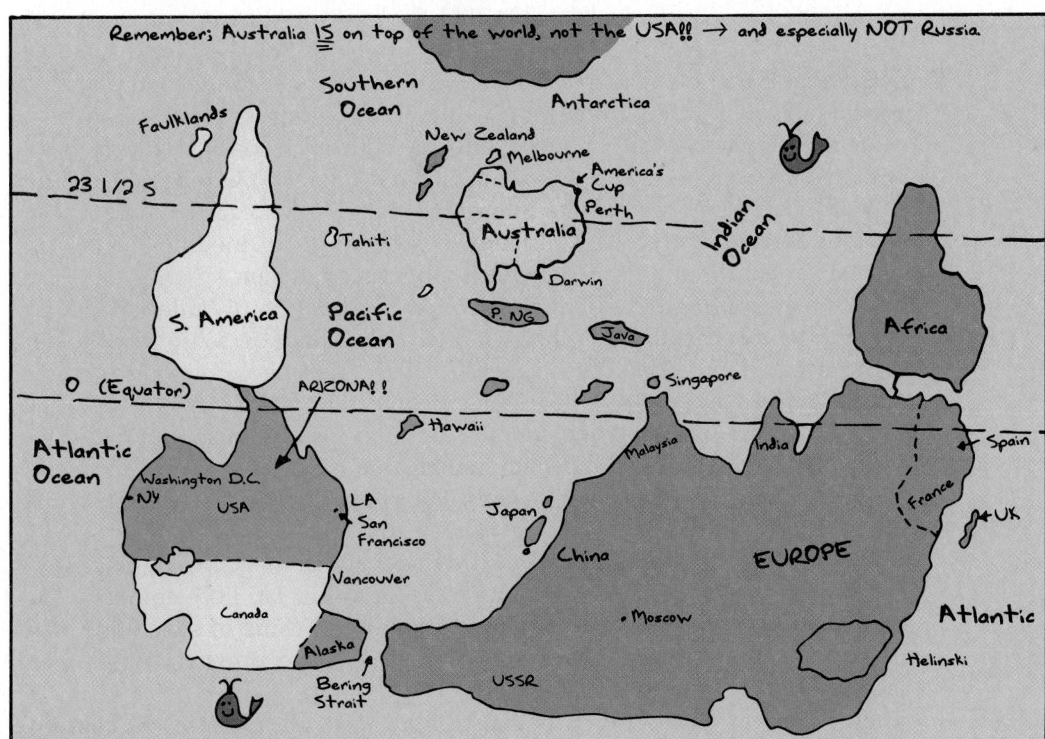

Remember; Australia IS on top of the world, not the USA!! → and especially NOT Russia.
Southern Ocean
Antarctica
Faulklands
New Zealand
Melbourne
America's Cup
Perth
23 1/2 S
Tahiti
Australia
Indian Ocean
Darwin
S. America
Pacific Ocean
P. NG
Java
Africa
0 (Equator)
ARIZONA!!
Singapore
Hawaii
Atlantic Ocean
Malaysia
India
Spain
Washington D.C.
NY
USA
LA
San Francisco
Japan
France
UK
China
EUROPE
Vancouver
Canada
Moscow
Atlantic
Alaska
Helinski
Bering Strait
USSR

● **FIGURE 7.16** Australiocentric View of the World

Now who's "down under"? It probably would not occur to most Americans to draw a map "upside down" like this one, with Australia near the center of the world. (*Source:* From COGNITIVE PSYCHOLOGY 5th ed. by Robert L. Solso. Copyright © 1998 by Allyn & Bacon. Reprinted by permission of Allyn and Bacon, Boston, MA.)

a single, repeated stimulus, eliminating the random background "noise" of the brain and isolating the unique brain wave pattern evoked by that stimulus (Kotchoubey, 2002). These EEG patterns associated with particular stimuli are called **event-related potentials.**

Other methods can also tell us which parts of the brain switch on and off while we think. With PET scans and magnetic resonance imaging (MRI) neuroscientists have identified brain regions that become active during various mental tasks. Two broad findings have come from this work. First, thinking is an activity involving widely distributed areas of the brain—not just a single "thinking center." Second, brain scans have revealed the brain as a community of highly specialized modules, each of which deals with different components of thought (Cree & McRae, 2003; Posner & McCandliss, 1993; Raichle, 1994; Solso, 2001). As we have seen, the brain generates many of the images used in thought with the same modular circuitry it uses for sensation and perception. Thus, visual imagery drawn from memory arises from the visual cortex, and auditory memories come from the auditory cortex (Behrmann, 2000). Even thinking with language involves different regions, depending on the topic. For example, a brain-imaging study of humor demonstrated that most jokes crack us up mainly in the language processing areas of the cortex, while puns also tickle the brain's sound-processing circuits (Goel & Dolan, 2001). In general, the picture of thought coming out of this work reveals thinking as a process composed of many elements.

Recent neuroscience research shows that the frontal lobes of the brain are especially important in coordinating mental activity when we think, make decisions, and solve problems (Helmuth, 2003a; Koechlin et al., 2003). To do so, the prefrontal cortex takes on three different tasks: keeping track of the *episode* (the situation in which we find ourselves), understanding the *context* (the meaning of the situation), and responding to a specific *stimulus* in the situation. Here's how it works: Suppose that the phone rings (the stimulus). Normally—at your own house—you would answer it. But suppose further that you are at a friend's house (a different context). Under those conditions, you would probably let the phone ring without answering it. Now suppose that your friend, who has just hopped into the shower, has asked you to take a message if the phone happens to ring (the episode); you will answer it. From a neuroscience perspective, the interesting thing is that each of these tasks is performed cooperatively by different combinations of modules in the prefrontal cortex. It's an impressive and sophisticated system.

Another exciting development involves the location of brain circuits that seem to be associated with what we often call "common sense," or the ability to act on "intuition" (Bechara et al., 1997; Gehring & Willoughby, 2002; Vogel, 1997). Psychologists have long known that when people make decisions—whether about buying a house or choosing a spouse—they draw on feelings as well as reason. This emotional component of thinking apparently involves regions of the frontal lobes just above the eyes. These structures allow us unconsciously to add emotional "hunches" to our decisions in the form of information about past rewards and punishments. Individuals with severe damage to this area of the brain seem to display little emotion. They may also lack "intuition"—the ability to know the value of something without conscious reasoning—and they frequently make unwise choices when faced with decisions (Damasio, 1994).

In brief, various forms of brain scanning provide glimpses of cognitive processes through new windows. The task ahead is to figure out what this new information is telling us about cognition. The "big picture" of human cognitive processes is thus still emerging, piece by piece, just as one might assemble a jigsaw puzzle.

■ **Event-related potentials**
Brain waves shown on the EEG in response to stimulation.

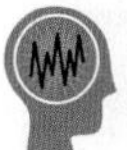

PSYCHOLOGY IN YOUR LIFE: SCHEMAS AND SCRIPTS HELP YOU KNOW WHAT TO EXPECT

Much of your knowledge is stored in your brain as schemas (Oden, 1987). A **schema** is a cluster of related concepts that provides a general conceptual framework for thinking about a topic, an event, an object, people, or a situation in one's life. You probably have schemas that represent "college" and "music," for example. Some of these schemas could contain an entire hierarchy of concepts. Let's look at some important ways in which schemas are used.

CONNECTION: CHAPTER 9
Piaget said that cognitive development involves changes in *schemas.*

Expectations Schemas are one of the attributes that Google and other search engines lack, so they have no real understanding of "birthday" or "psychology" or "nonfat mocha." But for us, schemas provide contexts and expectations about the features likely to be found when you encounter familiar people, situations, images, and ideas (Baldwin, 1992). For example, to an airline passenger the word *terminal* probably conjures up a schema that includes scenes of crowds, long corridors, and airplanes. For a heart attack victim, however, the schema for *terminal* might include feelings of anxiety and thoughts of death. And for an auto mechanic, *terminal* might mean a connection for a battery cable.

Making Inferences New information, which is often incomplete or ambiguous, makes more sense when you can relate it to existing knowledge in your stored schemas. So schemas enable you to make inferences about missing information, as the following example will demonstrate. Consider this statement:

> Tanya was upset to discover, upon opening the basket, that she'd forgotten the salt.

With no further information, what can you infer about this event? *Salt* implies that the basket is a picnic basket containing food. The fact that Tanya is upset that the salt is missing suggests that the food in the basket is food that is usually salted, such as hard-boiled eggs or vegetables. You automatically know what other foods might be included and, equally important, what definitely is not: Everything in the world that is larger than a picnic basket and anything that would be inappropriate to take on a picnic—from a boa constrictor to bronze-plated baby shoes. The body of information you now have has been organized around a "picnic-basket" schema. Relating the statement about Tanya to your preestablished schema gives the statement meaning.

How important are schemas to you? According to researchers Donald Norman and David Rumelhart, schemas are the primary units of meaning in the human information-processing system (1975). You comprehend new information by integrating new input with what you already know, as when your favorite pizza parlor advertises a new spicy Thai chicken curry pizza. (Piaget called this *assimilation.*) If you find a discrepancy between new input and existing schemas, you overcome it by changing what you know (*accommodation*) or ignoring the new input, as when the concept of "telephone" was revolutionized by the introduction of cell phones.

Scripts as Event Schemas We have schemas not only about objects and events but also about persons, roles, and ourselves. These schemas help us to decide what to expect or how people should behave under specific circumstances. An *event schema* or **script** consists of knowledge about sequences of interrelated, specific events and actions expected to occur in a certain way in particular settings (Baldwin, 1992). We have scripts for going to a restaurant, using the library, listening to a lecture, going on a first date, and even making love.

■ **Schema** A knowledge cluster or general conceptual framework that provides expectations about topics, events, objects, people, and situations in one's life.

■ **Script** A cluster of knowledge about sequences of events and actions expected to occur in particular settings.

DO IT YOURSELF! Your Memory for Concepts

Read the following passage carefully:

> Chief Resident Jones adjusted his face mask while anxiously surveying a pale figure secured to the long gleaming table before him. One swift stroke of his small, sharp instrument and a thin red line appeared. Then the eager young assistant carefully extended the opening as another aide pushed aside glistening surface fat so that the vital parts were laid bare. Everyone stared in horror at the ugly growth too large for removal. He now knew it was pointless to continue.

Now, without looking back, please complete the following exercise: Circle below the words that appeared in the passage:

patient	scalpel	blood	tumor
cancer	nurse	disease	surgery

In the original study, most of the subjects who read this passage circled the words *patient, scalpel,* and *tumor.* Did you? However, none of the words were there! Interpreting the story as a medical story made it more understandable, but also resulted in inaccurate recall (Lachman et al., 1979). Once the subjects had related the story to their schema for hospital surgery, they "remembered" labels from their schema that were not present in what they had read. Drawing on a schema not only gave the subjects an existing mental structure to tie the new material to but also led them to change the information to make it more consistent with their schema-based expectations.

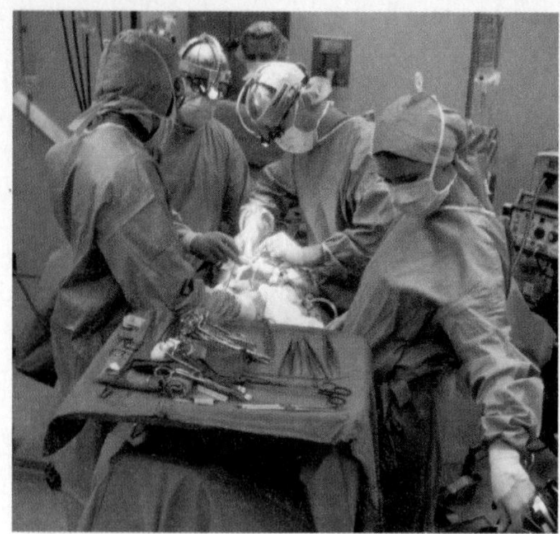

Even though they may not be prejudiced, people may avoid interactions with those of other ethnic groups because they don't understand each other's scripts.

Cultural Influences on Scripts Scripts used in other cultures may differ substantially from ours. For example, during the Persian Gulf War, American women stationed in Arab locales discovered that many behaviors they might take for granted at home—such as walking unescorted in public, wearing clothing that showed their faces and legs, or driving a car—were considered scandalously inappropriate by citizens of their host country. To maintain good relations, these servicewomen had to change their habits and plans to accommodate local customs. We can see from such examples that the scripts found in diverse cultures have developed from distinct schemas for viewing the world.

Conflicting Scripts When people who follow similar scripts get together, they feel comfortable because they have comprehended the "meaning" of the situation in the same way and have the same expectations of each other (Abelson, 1981; Schank & Abelson, 1977). When people do not all follow similar scripts, however, they may be made uncomfortable by the script "violation" and may have difficulty understanding why the scene was "misplayed." Unfortunately, when scripts clash, people may say, "I tried to interact, but it was so awkward that I don't want to try again" (Brislin, 1993).

CHECK YOUR UNDERSTANDING

1. **APPLICATION:** A dictionary definition would be an example of
   a. an artificial concept.
   b. a natural concept.
   c. a core concept.
   d. an abstract concept.
   e. a concrete concept.

2. **APPLICATION:** Which one of the following lists represents a concept hierarchy?
   a. cat, dog, giraffe, elephant
   b. animal, mammal, dog, cocker spaniel
   c. woman, girl, man, boy
   d. lemur, monkey, chimpanzee, human
   e. beaver, fox, cat, cougar

3. **APPLICATION:** Knowing how to check out a book at the library is an example of
   a. a natural concept.
   b. an event-related potential.
   c. a cognitive map.
   d. a script.
   e. a core concept.

4. **UNDERSTANDING THE CORE CONCEPT:** All of the following are components of thought, *except*
   a. concepts.
   b. images.
   c. schemas.
   d. stimuli.
   e. scripts.

ANSWERS: 1. a 2. b 3. d 4. d

KEY QUESTION

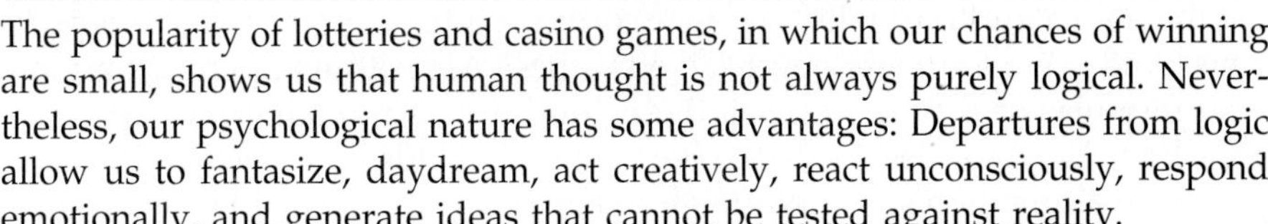

WHAT ABILITIES DO GOOD THINKERS POSSESS?

The popularity of lotteries and casino games, in which our chances of winning are small, shows us that human thought is not always purely logical. Nevertheless, our psychological nature has some advantages: Departures from logic allow us to fantasize, daydream, act creatively, react unconsciously, respond emotionally, and generate ideas that cannot be tested against reality.

We are, of course, capable of careful reasoning. After all, our species did invent that most logical of devices, the computer. Still, the psychology of thinking teaches us that we should not expect people always to behave in a strictly logical manner or that good judgment will be based on reason alone. This ability to think *psycho*logically enhances our ability to solve problems and make effective decisions. And, as we will see, good thinkers also know how to use effective thinking strategies and the avoidance of ineffective or misleading strategies. Our Core Concept puts this in more technical language:

CORE CONCEPT

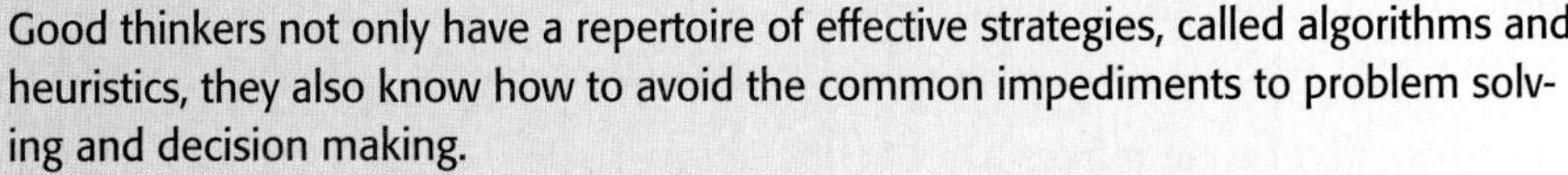

Good thinkers not only have a repertoire of effective strategies, called algorithms and heuristics, they also know how to avoid the common impediments to problem solving and decision making.

We will see that thinking is more useful than mere logic, because it helps us make decisions rapidly in a changing world that usually furnishes us incomplete information.

Problem Solving

Artists, inventors, Nobel Prize winners, great presidents, successful business executives, world-class athletes, and successful college students—all must be effective problem solvers. And what strategies do these effective problem solvers use? No matter what their field, those who are most successful share certain characteristics. They, of course, possess the requisite knowledge for solving the problems they face. In addition, they are skilled at (a) *identifying the problem* and (b) *selecting a strategy* to attack the problem. In the next few pages we will examine these two skills, with the aid of some examples.

Identifying the Problem A good problem solver learns to consider all the relevant possibilities, without leaping to conclusions. Suppose that you are driving along the freeway, and your car suddenly begins sputtering and then quits. As you coast over to the shoulder, you notice that the gas gauge says "empty." What do you do? Your action in this predicament depends on the problem you think you are solving. If you assume that you are out of fuel, you may hike to the nearest service station for a gallon of gas. But you may be disappointed. By representing the problem as "out of gas," you may fail to notice a loose battery cable that interrupts the supply of electricity both to the spark plugs and to the gas gauge. The good problem solver considers all the possibilities before committing to one solution.

Selecting a Strategy The second ingredient of successful problem solving requires selecting a strategy that fits the problem at hand (Wickelgren, 1974). For simple problems, a trial-and-error approach will do—as when you search in the dark for the key to open your front door. More difficult problems require better methods. Problems in specialized fields, such as engineering or medicine, may require not only specialized knowledge but special procedures or formulas. Such step-by-step procedures and formulas are called *algorithms.* In addition, expert problem-solvers have a repertoire of more intuitive, but less precise, strategies called *heuristics.* Let's look more closely at both of these methods.

Algorithms Whether you are a psychology student or a rocket scientist, selecting the right algorithms will guarantee correct solutions for many of your problems. And what are these never-fail strategies? **Algorithms** are nothing more than formulas or procedures, like those you learned in math classes or in science labs. They are designed to solve particular kinds of problems for which you have all the necessary information. For example, you can use algorithms to balance your checkbook, figure your gas mileage, and calculate your grade-point average. If applied correctly, an algorithm *always* works because you merely follow a step-by-step procedure that leads directly from the problem to the solution.

Despite their usefulness, however, algorithms cannot solve every problem you face. Problems that involve subjective values or have too many unknowns (Will you be happier with a red car or a white car? Or which is the best airline to take to Denver?) and problems that are just too complex for a formula (How can you get a promotion? What will the fish bite on today?) do not lend themselves to the use of algorithms. And that is why we also need the more intuitive and flexible strategies called heuristics.

■ **Algorithms** Problem-solving procedures or formulas that guarantee a correct outcome, if correctly applied.

■ **Heuristics** Cognitive strategies or "rules of thumb" used as shortcuts to solve complex mental tasks. Unlike algorithms, heuristics do not guarantee a correct solution.

Heuristics Everyone makes a collection of heuristics while going through life. Examples: "Don't keep bananas in the refrigerator." "If it doesn't work, see if it's plugged in." "Feed a cold and starve a fever" (or is it the other way around?). **Heuristics** are simple, basic rules—so-called "rules of thumb" that help us cut through the confusion of complicated situations. Unlike algorithms, heuristics do not guarantee a correct solution, but they often give us a good start in the right direction. Some heuristics require special knowledge, such as training in medicine or physics or psychology. Other heuristics, such as those you will learn in the following paragraphs, are more widely applicable—and well worth remembering.

● **FIGURE 7.17** Working Backward

Mazes and math problems often lend themselves to the heuristic of working backward. Try solving this maze, as the mouse must do, by starting at what would normally be the finish (in the center) and working backward to the start.

Some Useful Heuristic Strategies Here are three essential heuristics that should be in every problem solver's tool kit. They require no specialized knowledge, yet they can help you in a wide variety of puzzling situations. The common element shared by all three of these heuristics involves getting the problem solver to approach a problem from a different perspective.

Working Backward Some problems, such as the maze seen in Figure 7.17, may baffle us because they present so many possibilities we don't know where to start. A good way to attack this sort of

● Watson and Crick used the analogy of a spiral staircase to help them understand the structure of the DNA molecule and crack the genetic code.

puzzle is by beginning at the end and *working backward.* (Who says that we must always begin at the beginning?) This strategy can eliminate many of the false starts and dead ends that we would otherwise stumble into by trial and error.

In general, working backward is an excellent strategy for problems in which the end-state or goal is clearly specified, such as mazes or certain math problems. This approach can be especially valuable when the initial conditions are vague.

Searching for Analogies If a new problem is similar to another you have faced before, you may be able to employ a strategy that you learned previously. For example, if you are an experienced cold-weather driver, you use this strategy to decide whether to install tire chains on a snowy day: "Is the snow as deep as it was the last time I needed chains?" The trick is to recognize the similarity, or *analogy,* between the new problem and the old one—a skill that takes practice (Medin & Ross, 1992).

Breaking a Big Problem into Smaller Problems Are you facing a huge problem, such as an extensive term paper? The best strategy may be to break the big problem down into smaller, more manageable steps, often called *subgoals.* In writing a paper, for example, you might break the problem into the steps of selecting a topic, doing your library research, outlining the paper, writing the first draft, and revising the paper. In this way, you will begin to organize the work and develop a plan for attacking each part of the problem. And tackling a problem in a step-by-step fashion makes big problems seem more manageable. Any large, complex problem—from writing a paper to designing an airplane—may benefit from this approach. In fact, the Wright Brothers deliberately used this heuristic to break down their problem of powered human flight into its components. By using a series of kites, gliders, and models, they studied the component problems of lift, stability, power, and directional control. Later they put their discoveries together to solve the larger problem of powered human flight (Bradshaw, 1992).

Obstacles to Problem Solving Having a good repertoire of strategies is essential to successful problem solving, but people may also get stuck because they latch onto an ineffective strategy. For this reason, problem solvers must learn to recognize when they have encountered an obstacle that demands a new approach. In fact, becoming a successful problem solver has as much to do with recognizing such obstacles as it does with selecting the right algorithm or heuristic. Here are some of the most troublesome of the obstacles problem solvers face.

Mental Set Sometimes you may persist with a less-than-ideal strategy simply because it has worked on other problems in the past. In psychological terms, you have an inappropriate **mental set**—the tendency to respond to a new problem in the same way you approached a similar problem previously. You have "set" your mind on a single strategy, but this time you've chosen the wrong analogy or algorithm. Let's illustrate this with the following puzzle.

Each of the groups of letters in the columns below is a common, but scrambled, word. See if you can unscramble them:

nelin	frsca	raspe	tnsai
ensce	peshe	klsta	epslo
sdlen	nitra	nolem	naoce
lecam	macre	dlsco	tesle
slfal	elwha	hsfle	maste
dlchi	ytpar	naorg	egran
neque	htmou	egsta	eltab

(adapted from Leeper & Madison, 1959)

Check your answers against the key in Figure 7.18.

Most people, whether they realize it or not, eventually solve the scrambled word problem with an algorithm by rearranging the order of the letters in all the words in the same way, using the formula 3-4-5-2-1. Thus,

nelin	becomes	linen
12345		34521

■ **Mental set** The tendency to respond to a new problem in the manner used for a previous problem.

■ **Functional fixedness** The inability to perceive a new use for an object associated with a different purpose; a form of mental set.

Notice, however, that when you use that algorithm, your answers for the last two columns won't agree with the "correct" ones given in Figure 7.18. The mental set that you developed while working on the first two columns prevented you from seeing that there is more than one answer for the last 14 items. The lesson of this demonstration is that a mental set can make you approach new problems in old but restricted ways. While a mental set often does produce results, you should occasionally stop to ask yourself whether you have slipped into a rut that prevents your seeing another answer. (Now can you find some other possible answers to the scrambled words in the last two columns?)

linen	scarf	pears	stain
scene	sheep	talks	poles
lends	train	melon	canoe
camel	cream	colds	steel
falls	whale	shelf	meats
child	party	groan	anger
queen	mouth	gates	bleat

● **FIGURE 7.18** Unscrambled Words

The words you found to solve the scrambled word problem may not jibe with the ones listed here—especially in the third and fourth columns. Most people, whether they are aware of it or not, develop an algorithm as they work on the first two columns. While the formula will work on all the words, it interferes with the problem solver's ability to see alternative solutions for the words in the last two columns.

Functional Fixedness A special sort of mental set occurs when you think you need a screwdriver, but you don't realize that you could tighten the bolt with a dime. Psychologists call this **functional fixedness.** Under this condition, the function of a familiar object becomes so set, or fixed, in your mind that you cannot see a new function for it. To illustrate, consider this classic problem:

Your psychology professor has offered you $5 if you can tie together two strings dangling from the ceiling (see Figure 7.19) without pulling them down. But when you grab the end of one string and pull it toward the other one, you find that you cannot quite reach the other string. The only objects available to you in the room are on the floor in the corner: a Ping-Pong ball, five screws, a screwdriver, a glass of water, and a paper bag. How can you reach both strings at once and tie them together?

Read the following if you want a hint: In this problem you may have had functional fixedness with regard to the screwdriver. Did you realize that you could use the screwdriver as a pendulum weight to swing one of the strings toward you?

Self-Imposed Limitations We can be our own worst enemies when we impose unnecessary limitations on ourselves. The classic nine-dot problem in Figure 7.20 illustrates this neatly. To solve this one, you must connect all nine dots with no more than four connecting straight lines—that is, drawn without lifting your pencil from the paper. The instructions allow you to cross a line, but you may not retrace a line.

Most people who confront this problem impose an unnecessary restriction on themselves by assuming that they cannot draw lines beyond the square made by the dots. Literally, they don't "think outside the box." Figure 7.21 gives two possible correct answers. Translating this into personal terms, we can find many instances in which people impose unnecessary restrictions on themselves. Students may assume that they have no talent for math or science—thereby eliminating the possibility of a technical career. Or, because of gender stereotypes, a man may never consider that he could be a nurse or a grade school teacher, and a woman may assume that she must be a secretary, rather than an administrator. What real-life problems are you working on in which you have imposed unnecessary limitations on yourself?

Other Obstacles There are many other obstacles to problem solving that we will simply mention, rather than discuss in detail. These include lack of specific knowledge required by the problem, lack of interest, low self-esteem,

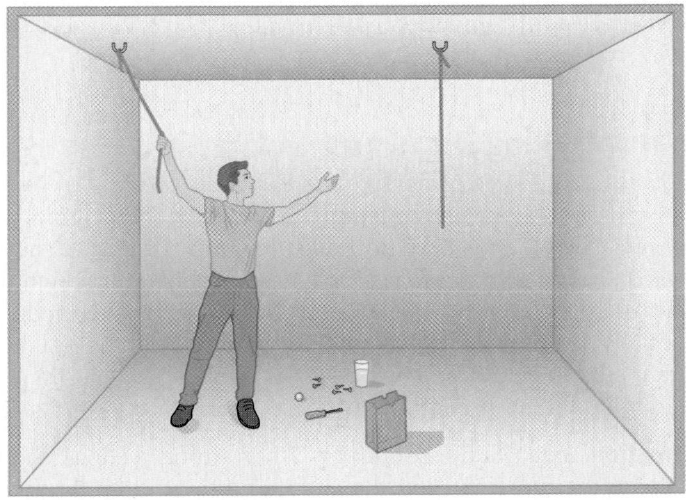

● **FIGURE 7.19** The Two-String Problem

How could you tie the two strings together, using only the objects found in the room?

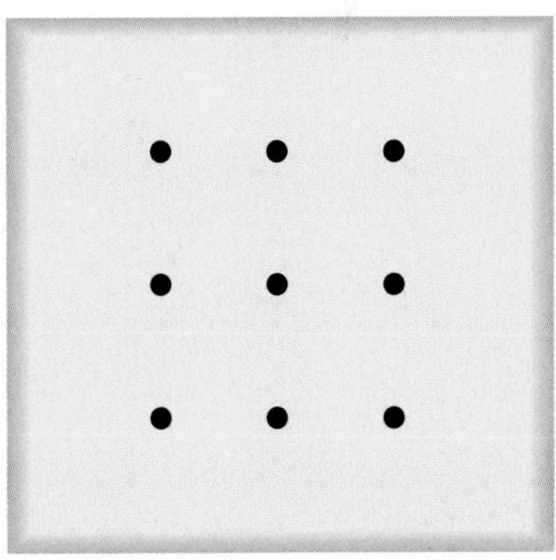

● **FIGURE 7.20** The Nine-Dot Problem

Can you connect all nine dots with four connecting straight lines without lifting your pencil from the paper? (*Source:* Adapted from "Can You Solve It?" in HOW TO SOLVE MATHEMATICAL PROBLEMS: Elements of a Theory of Problems and Problem Solving by Wayne A. Wickelgren. Copyright © 1974 by W. H. Freeman and Company. Reprinted by permission of Dover Publications and the author.)

FIGURE 7.21 Two Solutions to the Nine-Dot Problem

(*Source:* From HOW TO SOLVE MATHEMATICAL PROBLEMS: Elements of a Theory of Problems and Problem Solving by Wayne A. Wickelgren. Copyright © 1974 by W. H. Freeman and Company. Reprinted by permission of Dover Publications and the author.)

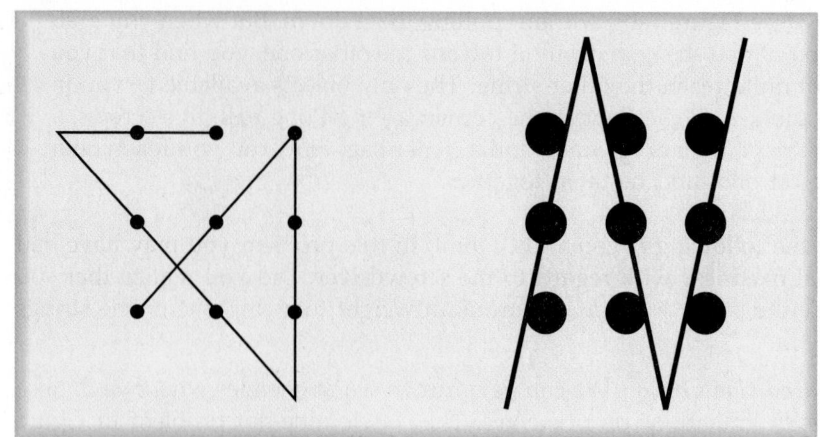

fatigue, and drugs (even legal drugs, such as cold medicines or sleeping pills). Arousal and the accompanying stress represent another important stumbling block for would-be problem solvers. When you study emotion and motivation in the next chapter, you will see that there is an optimum arousal level for any task, be it basketball, brain surgery, or making a presentation in class. Beyond that critical point, further arousal causes performance to deteriorate. Thus, moderate levels of arousal actually facilitate problem solving, but high stress levels can make problem solving impossible.

In general, our discussion of problem solving shows that we humans are thinkers who readily jump to conclusions, based on our knowledge and biased by our motives, emotions, and perceptions. In view of this, it is surprising that our thinking so often serves us well in day-to-day life. Yet, from another perspective, it makes perfect sense: Most of our problem-solving efforts involve drawing on past experience to make predictions about future rewards and punishments. If you think about this for a moment, you will realize that this is exactly what operant conditioning is all about—which suggests that this mode of thinking is a fundamental part of our nature. Many of the "flaws" in our reasoning abilities, such as functional fixedness, are actually part of an adaptive (but necessarily imperfect) strategy that helps us use our previous experience to solve new problems.

CONNECTION: CHAPTER 6

Operant conditioning involves the control of behavior by rewards and punishments.

Judging and Making Decisions

Whether you are a student, a professor, or a corporate president, you will make decisions every day. "How much should I invest?" "What grade does this paper deserve?" "How much time do I need to study tonight?" You can think of each decision as the solution to a problem—a problem for which there may not be a clearly right answer, but a problem requiring judgment. Unfortunately, especially for those who have not studied the psychology of decision making, judgment can be clouded by biases—which are really just faulty heuristics. Let's examine the most common of these causes of poor judgment.

The Confirmation Bias Suppose that Fred has strong feelings about raising children: "Spare the rod and spoil the child," he says. How do you suppose Fred will deal with the news that punishment can actually encourage aggressive behavior? Chances are that he will be swayed by the *confirmation bias* to ignore or find fault with information that doesn't fit with his opinions and to seek information with which he agrees. He will probably give you examples of spoiled children who didn't get much punishment for their transgressions or

CONNECTION: CHAPTER 1

The *confirmation bias* makes us pay attention to events that confirm our beliefs and ignore evidence that contradicts them.

upstanding adults, like himself, who owe their fine character to harsh discipline. A great deal of evidence shows that the confirmation bias is a powerful and all-too-human tendency (Aronson, 2004; Nickerson, 1998). In fact, we all act like Fred sometimes, especially on issues on which we hold strong opinions.

The Hindsight Bias A friend tells you that she lost money investing in "dot-com" stocks. "I thought the Internet was the wave of the future," she says. "I knew the boom in Internet stocks would turn into a bust," you reply. You are guilty of the **hindsight bias,** sometimes called the "I-knew-it-all-along effect" (Fischhoff, 1975; Hawkins & Hastie, 1990). Just as guilty of hindsight bias are the Monday morning quarterbacks who know what play should have been called at the crucial point in yesterday's big game. This form of distorted thinking appears after an event has occurred and people overestimate their ability to have predicted it. Hindsight bias can flaw the judgment of jurors, historians, newscasters, and anyone else who second-guesses other people's judgments after all the facts are in.

The Anchoring Bias Ask a few of your friends, one at a time, to give a quick, off-the-top-of-the-head guess at the answer to the following simple math problem:

$$1 \times 2 \times 3 \times 4 \times 5 \times 6 \times 7 \times 8 = ?$$

Make them give you an estimate without actually doing the calculation; give them only about five seconds to think about it. Then pose the problem in reverse to some other friends:

$$8 \times 7 \times 6 \times 5 \times 4 \times 3 \times 2 \times 1 = ?$$

Are the results different for the two groups?

Nobody will give precisely the right answer, of course, but it's likely that your friends will respond as volunteers did in Amos Tversky and Daniel Kahneman's experiment (Kahneman & Tversky, 2000; Tversky & Kahneman, 1973, 1974). (See also Jacowitz & Kahneman, 1995.) It turns out that the answers to such questions, where people usually don't have a good "ballpark" answer, depend on whether the problem begins with larger or smaller numbers. Those who saw the first problem gave a lower estimate than did those who were given the second problem. In Tversky and Kahneman's study, the average answer for the first group was 512, while the average for the second group was 2250. Apparently, their "first impression"—larger or smaller numbers at the beginning of the problem—biased their responses.

Tversky and Kahneman have explained the difference between the two groups on the basis of an **anchoring bias.** That is, people apparently use this flawed heuristic to "anchor" their thinking to the higher or lower numbers that appear at the beginning of the problem. The anchoring bias can also influence what we decide to pay for a car or a house, depending on the price of the first one we are shown.

The Representativeness Bias If you assume that blondes are mentally challenged or ministers are prudish or math professors are nerdish, you not only have some prejudices but your judgment has been clouded by **representativeness bias.** One reason why people succumb to such prejudices is that the representativeness bias simplifies the task of social judgment. Once something is "categorized," it shares all the features of other members in that category. The fallacy in this heuristic, of course, is that people, events, and objects do not "belong" to categories simply because we find it mentally convenient to

■ **Hindsight bias** The tendency, after learning about an event, to "second guess" or believe that one could have predicted the event in advance.

■ **Anchoring bias** A faulty heuristic caused by basing (anchoring) an estimate on a completely unrelated quantity.

■ **Representativeness bias** A faulty heuristic strategy based on the presumption that once people or events are categorized, they share all the features of other members in that category.

give them labels. By relying on category memberships to organize our experiences, we risk ignoring or underestimating the tremendous diversity of individual cases and complexity of people.

When estimating the likelihood that a specific individual belongs to a certain category—"vegetarian," for example—we look to see whether the person possesses the features found in a typical category member. For example, is your new acquaintance, Holly, a vegetarian? Does she resemble your prototype of a "typical" vegetarian? Perhaps you believe that most vegetarians wear sandals, ride bicycles, and support liberal social causes. If so, you might judge that Holly represents enough of the characteristics of your concept of "vegetarians" to belong to the same group.

But such an analysis is not entirely reasonable. Although some—perhaps many—vegetarians wear sandals, ride bicycles, and hold liberal views, the opposite may not be true: Because vegetarians are a minority group in the general population, it is unlikely that any particular individual who supports liberal social causes, wears sandals, and rides a bicycle is also vegetarian. That is, by ignoring the base rate information—the probability of a characteristic occurring in the general population—you have drawn an erroneous conclusion. Holly may in fact be an omnivore like most of your acquaintances, although if you invite her to dinner she will probably accept the cheese pizza and salad you offer her without complaint. While your representativeness bias—judging Holly by what seems to be her "type"—may not be especially important in this case, the same error underlies the more serious prejudices that result when people classify others solely on the basis of group membership.

The Availability Bias Yet another faulty heuristic comes from our tendency to judge probabilities of events by how readily examples come to mind. Psychologists call this the **availability bias.** We can illustrate this by asking you: Do more English words begin with *r* than have *r* in the third position? Most people think so because it is easier to think of words that begin with *r*. That is, words beginning with *r* are more available to us from long-term memory. Similarly, through observational learning, people who watch a lot of violent crime on television have violent images readily *available* in their memories. As a result, such people usually judge their chances of being murdered or mugged as being much higher than do people who watch little television (Singer et al., 1984).

PSYCHOLOGY IN YOUR LIFE: ON BECOMING A CREATIVE GENIUS

Everyone would agree that Einstein was a creative genius. So were Aristotle and Bach. And we can make a case that Brin and Page, the Google guys, are geniuses, too. But what about your Aunt Mabel who does watercolors? Such questions illustrate the big problem in creativity research: The experts cannot agree on an exact definition of creativity. Most, however, would go along with the slightly fuzzy notion that **creativity** is a process that produces novel responses that contribute to the solutions of problems. Most would also agree that a "genius" is someone whose insight and creativity are so great that they set that individual apart from ordinary folk. As with the idea of creativity, the boundary for genius is not well defined.

Let's follow the lead of psychologist Robert Weisberg, who offers a view of "genius" that goes against the commonly held assumption that geniuses are completely different from the rest of us. In brief, he argues that geniuses are merely good problem solvers who also possess certain helpful—but entirely human—characteristics.

■ **Availability bias** A faulty heuristic strategy that estimates probabilities based on information that can be recalled (made available) from personal experience.
■ **Creativity** A mental process that produces novel responses that contribute to the solutions of problems.

Creative Genius as Not So Superhuman Here's how Weisberg (1986) characterizes most people's assumptions about the quality we call "genius":

> Our society holds a very romantic view about the origins of creative achievements. . . . This is the genius view, and at its core is the belief that creative achievements come about through great leaps of imagination which occur because creative individuals are capable of extraordinary thought processes. In addition to their intellectual capacities, creative individuals are assumed to possess extraordinary personality characteristics which also play a role in bringing about creative leaps. These intellectual and personality characteristics are what is called "genius," and they are brought forth as the explanation for great creative achievements. (p. 1)

But, according to Weisberg and some other scholars in this area (Bink & Marsh, 2000), there is surprisingly little evidence supporting this view. In fact, the notion that creative geniuses are a breed apart may actually discourage creativity by making people feel that it is out of their reach. A more productive portrait, suggests Weisberg, views the thinking of people we call geniuses to be "ordinary thought processes in ordinary individuals" (p. 11). What produces extraordinary creativity, he says, is extensive knowledge, high motivation, and certain personality characteristics—not superhuman talents.

● There was no question but that Albert Einstein was bright. He also had an independent streak, a sense of humor, an intense interest in the complex problem of gravity, and a willingness to restructure the problem. He also sought the stimulation of other physicists. But he probably did not use thought processes that were altogether different from those used by other thinkers.

Everyone agrees with Weisberg on one point: The most highly creative individuals have a highly developed understanding of the basic knowledge in their fields (Gardner, 1993; Klahr & Simon; Who Wants to Be a Genius?, 2001). In fact, you cannot become highly creative without first becoming an *expert:* having extensive and organized knowledge of the field in which you will make your creative contribution. But such mastery is not easily achieved, because it requires a high level of motivation that can sustain the individual through years of intense training and practice. Studies indicate that about 10 years of work are required to master the knowledge and skills required for full competence in virtually any field, be it skiing, sculpture, singing, or psychology (Ericsson et al., 1993; Sternberg & Lubart, 1991, 1992). Further, such factors as time pressures and a hypercritical supervisor, teacher, or parent can suppress the creative flow (Amabile et al., 2002).

Aptitudes, Personality Characteristics, and Creativity In opposition to Weisberg, psychologist Howard Gardner (1993) argues that the extraordinary creativity that we see in the work of Freud, Einstein, Picasso, and others is a combination of several factors that include not only expertise and motivation but certain patterns of abilities and personality characteristics. Highly creative individuals, he says, have **aptitudes**—largely innate potentialities—specific to certain domains. (These potentialities, of course, must be developed by intensive study and practice.) Freud, for example, had a special facility for creating with words and understanding people; Einstein was remarkably good at logic and spatial relationships; and Picasso's creativity arose from a combination of aptitudes comprising spatial relationships and interpersonal perceptiveness.

But at the same time, creative people usually possess a certain cluster of personality traits. The literature emphasizes the following ones (Barron & Harrington, 1981; Csikszentmihalyi, 1996):

- *Independence:* Highly creative people have the ability to resist social pressures to conform to conventional ways of thinking, at least in their area of creative interest (Amabile, 1983, 1987). That is, they have the confidence to

■ **Aptitudes** Innate potentialities (as contrasted with abilities acquired by learning).

strike out on their own. Because of this, perhaps, many creative people describe themselves as loners.

- *Intense interest in a problem:* Highly creative individuals also must have an all-consuming interest in the subject matter with which they will be creative (Amabile, 2001). They are always tinkering, in their minds, with problems that fascinate them (Weisberg, 1986). External motivators, such as money or a Nobel Prize, may add to their motivation, but the main motivators are internal, otherwise they could not sustain the long-term interest in a problem necessary for an original contribution.
- *Willingness to restructure the problem:* Highly creative people not only grapple with problems, but they often question the way a problem is presented. (Recall our earlier discussion about identifying the problem.) For example, students from the School of the Art Institute of Chicago who later became the most successful creative artists among their class members had one striking characteristic in common: They were always changing and redefining the assignments given by their instructors (Getzels and Csikszentmihalyi, 1976).
- *Preference for complexity:* Creative people seem drawn to complexity—to what may appear messy or chaotic to others. Moreover, they revel in the challenge of looking for simplicity in complexity. Thus highly creative people may be attracted to the largest, most difficult, and most complex problems in their fields (Sternberg & Lubart, 1992).
- *A need for stimulating interaction:* Creativity of the highest order almost always grows out of an interaction of highly creative individuals. Early in their careers, creative people usually find a mentor—a teacher who brings them up to speed in their chosen field. Highly creative individuals then go on to surpass their mentors and then find additional stimulation from the ideas of others like themselves. Often, this means leaving behind family and former friends (Gardner, 1993).

What, then, is the take-home message for our understanding of creativity? Those who have looked closely at this domain agree on two main points. First, creativity requires well-developed knowledge of the field in which the creative contribution will be made. Second, high-level creativity requires certain personal characteristics, such as independence and the motivation required to sustain an interest in an unsolved problem over a very long period of time. That is your formula for becoming a creative genius.

Oh . . . and what about intelligence: Is a high IQ necessary for creativity or genius? The answer to that question is a bit complicated. Low intelligence inhibits creativity—although we will see that there are some special cases, known as *savants,* who may have a highly developed skill despite their mental handicaps. On the other end of the IQ spectrum, we find that having high intelligence does not necessarily mean that the individual will be creative: There are lots of very bright people who never produce anything that could be called groundbreaking or highly original and insightful. In general, we can say that intelligence and creativity are distinct abilities (Barron & Harrington, 1981; Kershner & Ledger, 1985). We can find plodding, unimaginative persons at all IQ levels, and we can find highly creative persons with only average IQ scores. To understand the reasons why creativity and intelligence are different, it will be helpful to know what intelligence is and how it is measured.

CHECK YOUR UNDERSTANDING

1. **RECALL:** What is the first step in problem solving?
   a. selecting a strategy
   b. avoiding pitfalls
   c. searching for analogies
   d. identifying the problem
   e. developing algorithms

2. **APPLICATION:** A math problem calls for finding the area of a triangle. You know the formula, so you multiply $\frac{1}{2}$ the base times the height. You have used
   a. an algorithm.
   b. a heuristic.
   c. functional fixedness.
   d. intuition.
   e. an analogy.

3. **RECALL:** Good problem solvers often use "tricks of the trade" or "rules of thumb" known as
   a. algorithms.
   b. heuristics.
   c. trial and error.
   d. deductive reasoning.
   e. scripts.

4. **APPLICATION:** Which one of the following would be an example of confirmation bias at work?
   a. Mary ignores negative information about her favorite political candidate.
   b. Aaron agrees with Joel's taste in music.
   c. Natasha refuses to eat a food she dislikes.
   d. Bill buys a new RV, even though his wife was opposed to the purchase.
   e. Frank buys a lottery ticket because he read about a lotto winner.

5. **RECALL:** Which of the following is *not* a characteristic that is consistently found among highly creative people?
   a. independence
   b. a high level of motivation
   c. willingness to restructure the problem
   d. extremely high intelligence
   e. open-mindedness

6. **UNDERSTANDING THE CORE CONCEPT:** Heuristic strategies show that our thinking is often based on
   a. logic rather than emotion.
   b. experience rather than logic.
   c. trial and error rather than algorithms.
   d. common sense rather than learning.
   e. logic rather than creativity.

ANSWERS: 1.d 2.a 3.b 4.a 5.d 6.b

MEMORY: THE STATE OF THE ART

The three-stage model, with the modifications we have discussed, gives a good snapshot of memory taken from the information-processing perspective. It is widely accepted by cognitive psychologists but relatively unknown by the general public. What surprises and frightens the public most, however, are the distortions and errors that our memories are heir to. In fact, these "sins" of memory are among the hottest topics for research at the moment.

Two other topics can also be found at the cutting edge of current memory research. One involves the apparently vast and poorly explored domain of implicit memory. What, cognitive psychologists wonder, does memory do while it is "off line"? The other hot topic centers on the biological basis of memory, especially the changes that take place as our synapses lay down long-term memories. And, once the biology of memory becomes clearer, the ultimate goal of memory researchers will come into view: making a connection between the biology and all the quirks of memory we have studied in this chapter.

USING PSYCHOLOGY TO LEARN PSYCHOLOGY

How to Avoid Memory Failure on Exams

Mnemonic strategies designed for memorizing lists of unrelated items won't help much with the material you need to learn in your psychology class. There the important material consists of concepts—often abstract concepts, such as "operant conditioning" or "retroactive interference." Such material calls for different mnemonic strategies geared both to concept learning and to avoiding the two memory "sins" feared most by college students: *transience* and *blocking*. So, let's see what advice cognitive psychologists would give to students for avoiding these two quirks of memory.

Studying to Avoid Transience

- *Make the material meaningful to you.* Many studies have shown that memories will remain stronger if the information is approached in a way that makes it meaningful, rather than as just a collection of facts and definitions (Baddeley, 1998; Haberlandt, 1999; Terry, 2000). One strategy for doing this involves using the **whole method,** a technique often used by actors who must learn a whole script in a short time. With this approach, the learner begins by getting an overview of all the material to be learned—the "big picture" into which the details can be assimilated. Suppose, for example, that you have a test on this chapter coming up next week. Using the whole method, you would look over the chapter outline and summary, along with all the Key Questions and Core Concepts on the chapter-opening page, before beginning to read the details of the chapter. This approach erects a mental framework on which you can hang the details of encoding, interference, retrieval, and other memory topics.
- *Spread your learning out over time.* A second way to build strong memories that are resistant to transience involves **distributed learning** (Baddeley, 1998; Terry, 2000). In less technical terms, the research suggests that you should study your psychology frequently (distributed, or spaced, learning), rather than trying to learn it all at once in a single "cram" session ("massed" learning). This approach avoids the lowered efficiency of learning brought about by fatigue and seems to strengthen memories that are in the process of consolidation. One study found that students could double the amount of information they learned in a given amount of time and also increase their understanding of the material by studying in two separate sessions, rather than in one session (Bahrick et al., 1993). Studies have also shown that distributed learning results in the material being retained longer (Schmidt & Bjork, 1992).

Studying to Avoid Blocking on the Test

The strategies mentioned above will help you get to the test with a strong memory for the material you need to know. But you also will want to avoid blocking, the inability to find and retrieve what you have in memory. To help you achieve this, we suggest some techniques that apply four ideas you have learned in this chapter: *interference theory, repetition, elaborative rehearsal,* and *encoding specificity:*

- *Take active steps to minimize interference.* You can't avoid interference altogether, but you can avoid studying for another class after your review session for tomorrow's psychology test. And you can make sure that you understand all the material and that you have cleared up any potentially conflicting points well before you go to the test. If, for example, you are not sure of the difference between *declarative memory* and *semantic memory,* you should discuss this with your instructor.
- *Rehearse and relearn what you have already learned.* Students often think that, just because they have read and understood the material, they will remember it. With complex concepts and ideas, you will probably need to use *repetition* in a form called **overlearning.** With this method, you continue to review the material, even after you think you understand it. Overlearning not only boosts the strength of a memory but also gives you repeated opportunities to link it with other ideas in LTM (which is our next point).
- *Elaborate on the material by thinking of examples and other associations.* One of the best ways of doing *elaborative rehearsal* when studying for a test is to

■ **Whole method** The mnemonic strategy of first approaching the material to be learned "as a whole," forming an impression of the overall meaning of the material. The details are later associated with this overall impression.

■ **Distributed learning** A technique whereby the learner spaces learning sessions over time, rather than trying to learn the material all in one study period.

■ **Overlearning** A strategy whereby the learner continues to study and rehearse the material after it has been initially brought to mastery.

create your own examples of the concepts. So, as you study about proactive interference, think of an example from your own experience. And don't forget to think of examples involving the Core Concepts, too. This approach will help to prevent blocking because adding associations to the material you are learning adds more ways in which the material can be accessed when you need it.

- *Test yourself with retrieval cues you expect to see on the examination.* Finally, by using the principle of *encoding specificity*, you can learn the material in a form that is most likely to be cued by the questions your psychology professor puts on the test. To do this, it is helpful to work with a friend who is also studying for the same test. We also recommend that you get together for this purpose a day or two before the test, after both of you have studied the material thoroughly enough to feel you understand it. Your purpose, at this point, will not be to learn new material but to anticipate the most likely test items. Does your professor prefer essay questions? Short-answer questions? Multiple-choice? Try to think up and answer as many questions as you can of the type most likely to appear on the test. Don't overlook the Key Questions throughout the chapter.

And please don't overlook the other mnemonic features we have included throughout this book to guide you in your study. These include the "Check Your Understanding" quizzes and "Chapter Review" tests, as well as the "Do It Yourself!" demonstrations. All these mnemonic devices are based on well-established principles of learning and memory. Studying this way may sound like a lot of work—and it is. But the results will be worth the mental effort.

CHAPTER SUMMARY

KEY QUESTION
?

CORE CONCEPT

• WHAT IS MEMORY?

Any memory system involves three important processes: encoding, storage, and retrieval. Eidetic imagery is a rare and poorly understood form of memory that produces especially vivid and persistent memories that may interfere with thought.

• Human memory is an information-processing system that works constructively to encode, store, and retrieve information.

• HOW DO WE FORM MEMORIES?

The memory system is composed of three distinct stages: sensory memory, working memory, and long-term memory. The three stages work together sequentially to convert incoming sensory information into useful patterns or concepts that can be retrieved for later use.

Sensory memory holds 12 to 16 visual items for about 1/4 second. A separate sensory register for each sense holds material just long enough for important information to be selected for further processing.

Working memory draws information from sensory memory and long-term memory and processes it consciously. It has at least three components: a central executive, a phonological loop, and a sketch pad. We can cope with its limited duration and capacity by chunking, rehearsal, and acoustic encoding.

Long-term memory has apparently unlimited storage capacity and duration. It has two main partitions: declarative memory (for facts and events) and procedural memory (for perceptual and motor skills). Declarative memory can be further divided into episodic memory and semantic memory. Semantic information is encoded, stored, and retrieved according to the meaning and context of the material.

Flashbulb memories are common for highly emotional experiences. Although most people have a great deal of confidence in such vivid memories, studies have shown that these memories can be distorted over time, especially memories of material that was not the focus of attention.

• Each of the three memory stages encodes and stores memories in a different way, but they work together to transform sensory experience into a lasting record that has a pattern or meaning.

• HOW DO WE RETRIEVE MEMORIES?

H.M.'s case demonstrates that information can be stored as explicit or implicit memories. Implicit memories can be cued by priming. Explicit memories can be cued by recall or recognition tasks. The accuracy of memory retrieval depends on several factors, including specificity and mood.

• Whether memories are implicit or explicit, successful retrieval depends on how they were encoded and how they are cued.

• WHY DOES MEMORY SOMETIMES FAIL US?

Memory failures involve the "seven sins" of memory. These include forgetting, resulting from weakening memory traces (transience), lapses of attention (absent-mindedness), and inability to retrieve a memory (blocking). Much forgetting can also be attributed to a form of blocking called interference. The final "sin" occurs when unwanted memories persist in memory, even though we would like to forget them.

Some causes of forgetting can be overcome by mnemonic strategies such as the method of loci, natural language mediators, and other associative methods.

● **Most of our memory problems arise from memory's "seven sins"—which are really by-products of otherwise adaptive features of human memory.**

● HOW DO CHILDREN ACQUIRE LANGUAGE?

Young children are biologically equipped to learn language and motivated to communicate. Many experts believe that children have "language acquisition devices" hard-wired into their brains. Psychologists find that language development proceeds in a predictable sequence, involving the babbling stage, the one- and two-word stages, and telegraphic speech, as children acquire vocabulary at an almost unbelievable rate. Grammar appears when the child begins to put words together.

● **Infants and children face an especially important task in the area of language acquisition.**

● WHAT ARE THE COMPONENTS OF THOUGHT?

Cognitive scientists often use the computer metaphor to conceive of the brain as an information-processing organ. Natural concepts and artificial concepts are building blocks of thinking; they are formed by identifying properties that are common to a class of objects or ideas. Concepts are often arranged in hierarchies ranging from general to specific. Other mental structures that guide thinking include schemas, scripts, and visual imagery such as mental maps.

● **Thinking is a cognitive process in which the brain uses information from the senses, emotions, and memory to create and manipulate mental representations, such as concepts, images, schemas, and scripts.**

● WHAT ABILITIES DO GOOD THINKERS POSSESS?

Two of the most crucial thinking skills involve identifying the problem and selecting a problem-solving strategy. Useful strategies include algorithms, which produce a single correct answer, and heuristics, or "rules of thumb." Among the most useful heuristics are working backward, searching for analogies, and breaking a bigger problem into smaller ones. Common obstacles to problem solving include mental set, functional fixedness, and self-imposed limitations. Moreover, judging and decision making can be flawed by biases and faulty heuristics. These include confirmation bias, hindsight bias, anchoring bias, representativeness bias, and availability bias (heuristic). Those who are often called creative geniuses are highly motivated experts who often have a certain cluster of traits, such as independence and a need for stimulating interaction. They appear, however, to use ordinary thinking processes, although the role of natural talent is the subject of dispute.

● **Good thinkers not only have a repertoire of effective strategies, called algorithms and heuristics, but also know how to avoid the common impediments to problem solving and decision making.**

REVIEW TEST

For each of the following items, choose the single correct or best answer. The correct answers appear at the end.

1. Unlike a video recorder, human memory is
   a. accurate.
   b. digital.
   c. fast.
   d. reconstructive.
   e. temporary.
2. Which of the following is one of the three essential tasks of memory?
   a. accuracy
   b. consistency
   c. elaboration
   d. encoding
   e. misattribution
3. H. M.'s ________ memory was more profoundly affected by the surgery than his ________ memory.
   a. eidetic/sensory
   b. episodic/procedural
   c. implicit/explicit
   d. recognition/recall
   e. short-term/long-term
4. Elise used to live in a house with a large kitchen, where all the silverware was stored in a drawer to the right of the sink. Since she moved to her new apartment, she finds that she habitually looks for the silverware in a drawer to the right of the sink, although no such drawer exists. Her behavior reflects forgetting due to
   a. absence of retrieval cues.
   b. availability heuristic.
   c. proactive interference.
   d. repression.
   e. retroactive interference.
5. Studies of eyewitness testimony and recovery of "repressed" memories show that
   a. distorted memories are a sign of mental disorder.
   b. memories can be severely distorted, even when we have confidence in them.

c. memory is infallible.
d. our unconscious minds remember events as they actually happened.
e. the more confident we are of a memory, the more likely it is to be true.

6. Which of the following utterances illustrates overregularization in language development?
   a. "babababa."
   b. "Drink milk, all gone."
   c. "House."
   d. "Me gots two foots and two handses."
   e. "Want cookie."

7. Which of the following statements about thinking is true?
   a. It cannot be observed from observable behavior.
   b. It stores, but does not manipulate, knowledge.
   c. It transforms available information into new mental representations.
   d. All of the above.
   e. None of the above.

8. An alien being from another galaxy has landed on Earth and is overwhelmed by the sensory input it must process. Eventually the alien simplifies its thinking by categorizing sets of experiences and objects according to common features. In other words, the alien learns to form
   a. algorithms.
   b. concepts.
   c. heuristics.
   d. hypotheses.
   e. scripts.

9. A mental _________ outlines the proper sequence in which actions and reactions might be expected to happen in a given setting, such as when you visit a new grocery store.
   a. algorithm
   b. heuristic
   c. map
   d. prototype
   e. script

10. Because you watch a lot of violent videos, you think your chances of being mugged are quite high. Your judgment is flawed by
   a. anchoring bias.
   b. functional fixedness.
   c. hindsight bias.
   d. availability bias.
   e. stereotyping.

ANSWERS: 1.d 2.e 3.b 4.c 5.a 6.d 7.c 8.b 9.e 10.d

KEY TERMS

Memory (p. 235)
Information-processing model (p. 236)
Encoding (p. 236)
Storage (p. 237)
Retrieval (p. 237)
Eidetic imagery (p. 238)
Sensory memory (p. 239)
Working memory (p. 239)
Long-term memory (LTM) (p. 240)
Chunking (p. 244)
Maintenance rehearsal (p. 244)
Elaborative rehearsal (p. 245)
Acoustic encoding (p. 245)
Levels-of-processing theory (p. 245)
Procedural memory (p. 247)
Declarative memory (p. 247)
Episodic memory (p. 247)
Semantic memory (p. 248)
Engram (p. 248)
Anterograde amnesia (p. 248)
Consolidation (p. 249)
Retrograde amnesia (p. 250)
Flashbulb memory (p. 250)
Implicit memory (p. 252)
Explicit memory (p. 252)
Retrieval cues (p. 252)
Priming (p. 253)
Recall (p. 254)
Recognition (p. 254)
Encoding specificity principle (p. 254)
Mood-congruent memory (p. 255)
TOT phenomenon (p. 256)
Transcience (p. 257)
Forgetting curve (p. 259)
Absent-mindedness (p. 259)
Blocking (p. 259)
Proactive interference (p. 259)
Retroactive interference (p. 259)
Serial position effect (p. 259)
Misattribution (p. 260)
Suggestibility (p. 261)
Misinformation effect (p. 261)
Expectancy bias (p. 264)
Self-consistency bias (p. 264)
Persistence (p. 264)
Mnemonics (p. 265)
Method of loci (p. 265)
Natural language mediators (p. 265)
Language acquisition device (LAD) (p. 267)
Grammar (p. 269)
Morphemes (p. 269)
Overregularization (p. 269)
Computer metaphor (p. 270)
Concepts (p. 271)
Natural concepts (p. 272)
Prototype (p. 272)
Artificial concepts (p. 272)
Concept hierarchies (p. 272)
Event-related potentials (p. 276)
Schemas (p. 277)
Script (p. 277)
Algorithms (p. 280)
Heuristics (p. 280)
Mental set (p. 282)
Functional fixedness (p. 282)
Hindsight bias (p. 285)
Anchoring bias (p. 285)
Representativeness bias (p. 285)
Availability bias (p. 286)
Creativity (p. 286)
Aptitudes (p. 287)
Whole method (p. 290)
Distributed learning (p. 290)
Overlearning (p. 290)

AP* REVIEW: VOCABULARY

Match each of the following vocabulary terms to its definition.

1. Maintenance rehearsal
2. Elaborative rehearsal
3. Procedural memory
4. Episodic memory
5. Morpheme
6. Overregularization
7. Concepts
8. Prototype
9. Schema
10. Functional fixedness

_____ **a.** Meaningful units of language that make up words.

_____ **b.** A most representative example of a conceptual category.

_____ **c.** A working-memory process in which information is merely repeated to keep it from fading.

_____ **d.** Mental representations of categories of items or ideas.

_____ **e.** The inability to perceive a new use for an object.

_____ **f.** A knowledge cluster that provides expectations about topics, objects, people, and the like in one's life.

_____ **g.** A working-memory process in which information is actively related to information already in LTM.

_____ **h.** A subdivision of declarative memory that stores memory for personal events.

_____ **i.** A division of LTM that stores memories for how things are done.

_____ **j.** Applying a grammatical rule too widely.

AP* REVIEW: ESSAY

Use your knowledge of the chapter concepts to answer the following essay question.

Describe the information-processing model of memory, and provide a specific example of each of the following: sensory storage, short-term memory, and long-term memory.

OUR RECOMMENDED BOOKS AND VIDEOS

BOOKS

Gardner, H. (1999). *Intelligence reframed: Multiple intelligences for the 21st century.* New York: Basic Books. Psychologist Howard Gardner elaborates and suggests how to apply his theory that each of us possesses seven or more basic types of intelligence to varying degrees: the familiar linguistic and logical-mathematical types that are the focus of traditional education and testing, but also intelligences of music, movement, spatial awareness, and other abilities—including new discoveries such as naturalistic intelligence (awareness of the living environment).

Gould, S. J. (1981). *The mismeasure of man.* New York: Norton. Stephen Jay Gould's book is a classic indictment of flawed assessment and testing, especially when used to discriminate against or oppress social groups.

Kerr, P. (1992). *A philosophical investigation.* New York: Penguin. In the future world of this mystery novel, governments test all men for a sex-linked gene predicting whether one might become a serial killer—until one unidentified suspect uses his expertise in computers and philosophy to kill those who test positive.

Keyes, D. (1995). *Flowers for Algernon.* New York: Harcourt Brace. The reissued novelization of the classic 1960 science fiction story that inspired the 1968 Oscar-winning movie *Charly* and the 2000 TV movie *Flowers for Algernon.* A young retarded man undergoes experimental surgery to increase his intelligence—with astonishing and tragic results.

Perkins, D. (2000). *Archimedes' bathtub: The art and logic of breakthrough thinking.* New York: W. W. Norton. Ancient Greek philosopher Archimedes shouted "Eureka!" ("I have found it") when, lowering himself into a bath, he recognized the process of water displacement. This author explains practical and entertaining strategies for producing creative inspiration in our own lives.

Plous, S. (1993). *The psychology of judgment and decision making.* Philadelphia: Temple University Press. Psychologist Scott Plous argues that common sense is an unreliable guide in modern living, showing the silly choices we make and recommending how judgments can be more logical and successful.

VIDEOS

i am sam. (2001, color, 132 min.). Directed by Jessie Nelson; starring Sean Penn, Michelle Pfeiffer. A gentle retarded man, threatened by a social services agency with losing custody of his young daughter, is helped in his battle by a high-powered attorney whose own life is also troubled. (*Rating PG-13*)

Little Man Tate. (1991, color, 99 min.). Directed by Jodie Foster; starring Jodie Foster, Dianne Wiest, Adam Hann-Byrd, David Hyde Pierce, Harry Connick, Jr. A single, working-class mother must decide how best to bring up her young son, a child genius whose abilities challenge the good intentions and abilities of the adults who care about him. (*Rating PG*)

The Luzhin Defense. (2000, color, 112 min.). Directed by Marleen Gorris; starring John Turturro, Emily Watson. In the 1920s, a socially naive but intellectually brilliant Grand Master of chess, protected all his life by his manager, attends a world tournament where he meets the love of his life but finds he is emotionally unprepared to face the real world. (*Rating PG-13*)

Searching for Bobby Fischer. (1993, color, 110 min.). Directed by Steve Zaillian; starring Joe Mantegna, Max Pomeranc, Joan Allen, Ben Kingsley. In this absorbing drama based on true story, a father encourages his talented son to compete for a championship title, revealing the rewards and risks of child genius. (*Rating PG*)

Key Question Chapter Outline

CORE CONCEPTS

Psychology in Your Life

What Do Our Emotions Do For Us?

- The Evolution of Emotions
- Cultural Universals in Emotional Expression
- Counting the Emotions

Core Concept: Emotions have evolved to help us respond to important situations and to convey our intentions to others.

Emotional Differences Between Men and Women Depend on Culture

Men and women differ in their emotional experiences, both within and across cultures.

Where Do Our Emotions Come From?

- The Neuroscience of Emotion
- Psychological Theories of Emotion: Resolving Some Persistent Issues

Core Concept: The discovery of two distinct brain pathways for emotional arousal has clarified the connections among the many biological structures involved in emotion and has offered solutions to many long-standing issues in the psychology of emotion.

Arousal, Performance, and the Inverted U

Up to a point, arousal can increase performance, but either too little or too much arousal will prevent one from achieving peak performance.

How Much Control Do We Have Over Our Emotions?

- Developing Emotional Intelligence
- Detecting Deception

Core Concept: Although emotional responses are not always consciously regulated, we can learn to control them.

Controlling Anger

Instead of "venting" anger, which may only intensify those feelings, keep your feelings to yourself until you can be more rational about the nature of your complaint and how to resolve it.

Motivation: What Makes Us Act As We Do?

- How Psychologists Use the Concept of Motivation
- Types of Motivation
- Theories of Motivation

Core Concept: Motivation takes many forms, but all involve inferred mental processes that select and direct our behavior.

Rewards Can (Sometimes) Squelch Motivation

Extrinsic rewards can sometimes remove the intrinsic motivation.

How Are Achievement, Hunger, and Sex Alike? Different?

- Achievement Motivation
- Hunger Motivation
- Sexual Motivation
- Motives in Conflict

Core Concept: Achievement, hunger, and sex exemplify other human motives because they differ not only in the behavior they produce but also in the mix of biological, mental, behavioral, and social/cultural influences on them.

The Origins of Sexual Orientation

Research in this area remains controversial because, among other things, the data collected thus far are correlational, rather than experimental, so cause and effect cannot be established.

How and Why Do We Experience Stress?

- Stressors, Ancient and Modern
- Traumatic Stressors
- The Physical Stress Response
- The General Adaptation Syndrome
- Stress and the Immune System

Core Concept: The human stress response to perceived threat activates thoughts, feelings, behaviors, and physiological arousal that normally promote adaptation and survival.

Developing Resilience

Six specific processes have been developed to identify characteristics of resiliency.

USING PSYCHOLOGY TO LEARN PSYCHOLOGY:
Motivating Yourself

Chapter

8

Emotion and Motivation

ELLIOT PRESENTED A PUZZLE. His life was unraveling, yet he maintained an attitude of composure. Once a model employee, he had let the quality of his work slip to the point that he finally lost his job. If anything, said his supervisors, Elliot had developed a habit of working almost too well. He often latched onto a small task, such as sorting a client's paperwork, and spent the whole afternoon on various classification schemes—never quite getting to the real job he had been assigned (Damasio, 1994).

His personal life also fell apart. A divorce was followed by a short marriage and another divorce. Several attempts at starting his own business involved glaringly flawed decisions that finally ate up all his savings.

Yet, surprisingly, in most respects Elliot seemed normal. He had a pleasant personality and an engaging sense of humor. He was obviously smart—well aware of important events, names, and dates. He understood the political and economic affairs of the day. In fact, examinations revealed nothing wrong with his movements, memory, perceptual abilities, language skills, intellect, or ability to learn.

Complaints of headaches led the family doctor to suspect that the changes in Elliot might be the result of a brain lesion. Tests proved the suspicion correct. Brain scans showed a mass the size of a small orange that was pressing on the frontal lobes just above Elliot's eyes.

The tumor was removed, but not before it had done extensive damage. The impact was limited to the frontal lobes—in a pattern that was remarkably similar to that seen in the famous case of Phineas Gage nearly 150 years earlier (see Chapter 3). Like Gage, Elliot had undergone a profound change as the result of frontal lobe damage. But the effects in Elliot were more subtle than in Gage. As a psychologist who examined him said, "We might summarize Elliot's predicament as *to know but not to feel*" (Damasio, 1994, p. 45). His reasoning abilities were intact, but damage to the circuitry of his frontal lobes disrupted his ability to attach values to the objects, events, and people in his life. In short, Elliot had been emotionally crippled.

One of the most pernicious misunderstandings about the human mind is the idea that emotion is the opposite of reason. But the case of Elliot, taken from Antonio Damasio's 1994 book *Descartes' Error,* makes it clear that emotion is a vital ingredient in making effective personal decisions. With a disruption in his ability to connect concepts and emotions, Elliot could not value one course of action over another.

Emotions can, of course, spin out of control, producing the extreme and unwise behavior we see in jealous lovers, severely depressed individuals, and drivers crazed by "road rage." Yet, as Elliot's case shows, pure reason unmodulated by emotion can also have devastating effects.

So, what is this thing called *emotion*? In brief, **emotion** is a four-part process consisting of *physiological arousal, cognitive interpretation, subjective feelings,* and *behavioral expression.* We will illustrate with that most thoroughly studied of all emotions: fear.

Suppose you are frightened by an aggressive, snarling dog. The physiological component of the fear response sets off an alarm that is broadcast simultaneously through the autonomic nervous system and the endocrine system. The result is a visceral fear response, that includes draining of the blood from the stomach (which we describe as a "knot" in the belly) and constriction of the blood vessels in the face (which makes a fearful person pale).

The second component of emotion, a cognitive interpretation of events and feelings, involves both a conscious and an unconscious recognition of the dangerous situation and the consequent feelings of fear. In fact, the more you think about it, the more fearful you may become. Such thoughts, then, can drive both your subjective feelings and physical arousal to new heights.

The "feeling" component of emotions comes from two sources. One involves the brain sensing the body's state of arousal (Damasio, 1994, 2003). The other comes from memories of the body's state in similar situations in the past. So, when you encounter the snarling dog, your brain may retrieve a memory of how you felt during previous encounters with hostile dogs.

Finally, emotions can also produce behavior. In response to the aggressive dog, this could manifest itself in the so-called "fight-or-flight" response, as well as in emotion-laden facial expressions and vocalizations, such as crying, grimacing, or shouting. Angry responses might also be accompanied by voluntary gestures, such as waving a fist or pointing out one's state of mind with the middle finger. In such ways, emotions can act as motives, in the sense that they organize and direct our behavior.

How, then is motivation linked to emotion? Note that both words share a common root, "*mot-*," from the Latin *motus,* meaning "move." The psychology of motivation and emotion has retained this meaning by viewing emotion and motivation as complementary processes. The concept of *emotion* emphasizes arousal, both physical and mental, while *motivation* emphasizes how this arousal becomes action.

■ **Emotion** A four-part process that involves physiological arousal, subjective feelings, cognitive interpretation, and behavioral expression—all of which *interact,* rather than occurring in a linear sequence. Emotions help organisms deal with important events.

WHAT DO OUR EMOTIONS DO FOR US?

The death of a parent, an insult, winning an award, losing a lover to a rival: All induce strong feelings—sorrow, anger, joy, jealousy. But what do these states have in common? That is, why do we put them all in the same category called "emotion"? The common thread is this: All emotions involve a state of mental and physical arousal focused on some event of importance to the individual.

And what functions do these emotional responses serve? Surely emotions must do more than just adding variety or "color" to our mental lives. The brief answer to the question is given by our Core Concept:

CORE CONCEPT

Emotions have evolved to help us respond to important situations and to convey our intentions to others.

In this section, we will first consider the adaptive functions of emotions from an evolutionary perspective. Next, we will add a social/cultural perspective to see how the language of emotional expression tells others of our emotional state. Finally, at the end of this section, we will consider the issue of gender differences in emotion and how they are shaped by culture.

The Evolution of Emotions

Whether they occur in humans, hyenas, cats, or kangaroos, emotions serve as arousal states that help organisms cope with important recurring situations (Dolan, 2002; LeDoux, 1996). Accordingly, emotions have survival value and so have been shaped by natural selection (Gross, 1998). Fear, for example, undoubtedly helped individuals in your family tree react to situations that could have made them a meal instead of an ancestor. Similarly, the emotion we call "love" may commit us to a family, which helps to continue our genetic line. Likewise, sexual jealousy can be seen as an emotion that evolved to deal with the biologically important problem of mate infidelity, which threatens the individual's chances of producing offspring (Buss & Schmitt, 1993). Humor, too, seems to have evolved to serve, in part, a social purpose, as we can surmise from the "in-jokes" and rampant laughter among people in tightly knit social groups (Panksepp, 2000).

It is an important biological fact that individuals vary tremendously in emotional responsiveness (Davidson, 2000b). Some of these individual differences arise from random genetic variations that inevitably occur as organisms reproduce (Gabbay, 1992). We see this, for example, in the differing tendencies people have for depression. Evolution, then, takes advantage of these random genetic variations.

We should emphasize, however, that emotions are not entirely programmed by genetics. They also involve learning. Particularly important in setting our emotional temperament are experiences that occur early in life, as well as experiences that have evoked particularly strong emotional responses (Barlow, 2000; LeDoux, 1996). Thus, learned emotional responses, along with a biological disposition for emotionality, can be important components of many psychological disorders, including depression, panic attacks, and phobic reactions—to name just a few.

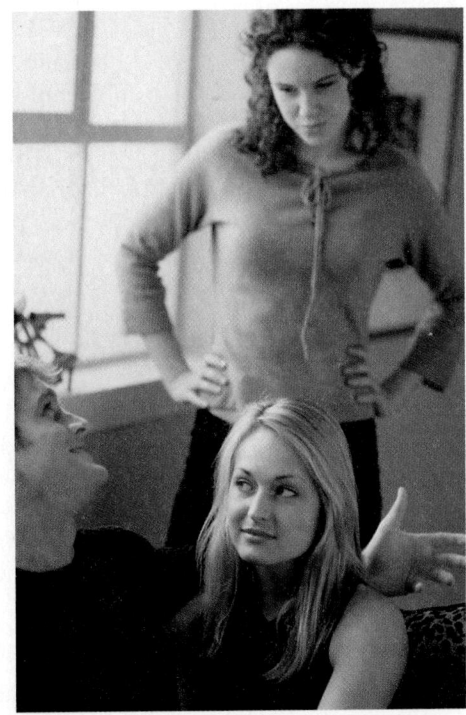

● Sexual jealousy probably has an evolutionary basis because mate infidelity threatens the individual's chances of producing offspring.

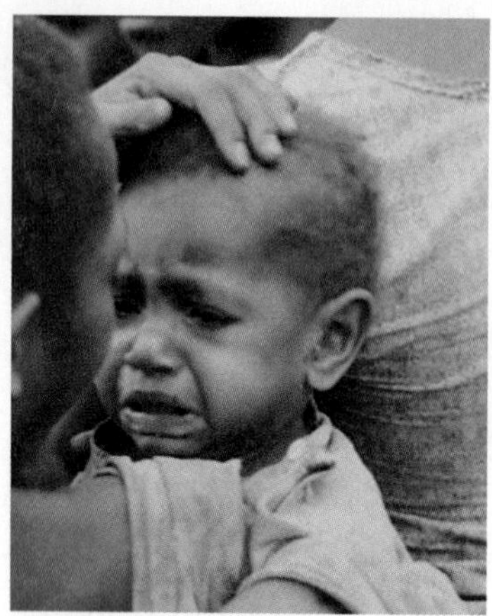

Facial expressions convey universal messages. Although their culture is very different, it is probably not hard for you to tell how this child from New Guinea is feeling.

Cultural Universals in Emotional Expression

You can usually tell when your friends are happy or angry by the looks on their faces or by their actions. This is useful because reading their emotional expressions helps you to know how to respond to them: As our Core Concept suggests, emotional expressions aid social interaction. But does raising the eyebrows and rounding the mouth say the same thing in Minneapolis as it does in Madagascar? Much research on emotional expression has centered on such questions.

According to Paul Ekman, the leading researcher in this area, people speak and understand substantially the same "facial language" the world around (Ekman, 1984, 1992, 2003; Ekman & Rosenberg, 1997). Studies by Ekman's group have demonstrated that humans share a set of universal emotional expressions that testify to the common biological heritage of the human species. Smiles, for example, signal happiness and frowns indicate sadness on the faces of people in such far-flung places as Argentina, Japan, Spain, Hungary, Poland, Sumatra, the United States, Vietnam, the jungles of New Guinea, and the Eskimo villages north of the Arctic Circle (Biehl et al., 1997; Ekman et al., 1987; Izard, 1994).

Ekman and his colleagues claim that people everywhere can recognize at least seven basic emotions: sadness, fear, anger, disgust, contempt, happiness, and surprise (Ekman, 1993; Ekman & Friesen, 1971, 1986; Ekman et al., 1969, 1987; Keating, 1994). There are, however, huge differences across cultures in both the context and the intensity of emotional displays—the so-called **display rules.** In many Asian cultures, for example, children are taught to control emotional responses—especially negative ones—while many American children are encouraged to express their feelings more openly (Matsumoto, 1994, 1996).

Regardless of culture, however, emotions usually show themselves, to some degree, in people's behavior. From their first days of life, babies produce facial expressions that communicate their feelings (Ganchrow et al., 1983). And the ability to read facial expressions develops early, too. Very young children pay close attention to facial expressions, and by age 5 they nearly equal adults in their skill at reading emotions in people's faces (Nelson, 1987). You can check your own skill at interpreting facial expressions by taking the quiz in the "Do It Yourself!" box.

This evidence all points to a biological underpinning for our abilities to express and interpret a basic set of human emotions. Moreover, as Charles Darwin pointed out over a century ago, some emotional expressions seem to appear across species boundaries. Darwin especially noted the similarity of our own facial expressions of fear and rage to those of chimpanzees and wolves (Darwin, 1998/1862; Ekman, 1984).

But are *all* emotional expressions universal? No. Cross-cultural psychologists tell us that certain emotional responses carry different meanings in different cultures (Ekman, 1992, 1994; Ellsworth, 1994). These, therefore, must be learned rather than innate. For example, what emotion do you suppose might be conveyed by sticking out the tongue? For Americans this might indicate disgust, while in China it can signify surprise. Likewise, a grin on an American face may indicate joy, while on a Japanese face it may just as easily mean embarrassment. Clearly, culture influences emotional expression.

Counting the Emotions

How many emotions are there? A long look in the dictionary turns up more than 500 emotional terms (Averill, 1980). Most experts, however, see a more limited number of basic emotions. Often mentioned is Ekman's list of seven—anger, disgust, fear, happiness, sadness, contempt, and surprise—based on the

Display rules The permissible ways of displaying emotions in a particular society.

DO IT YOURSELF! Identifying Facial Expressions of Emotion

Take the facial emotion identification test to see how well you can identify each of the seven emotions that Ekman claims are culturally universal. Do not read the answers until you have matched each of the following pictures with one of these emotions: disgust, happiness, anger, sadness, surprise, fear, and contempt. Apparently, people everywhere in the world interpret these expressions in the same way. This tells us that certain facial expressions of emotion are probably rooted in our human genetic heritage.

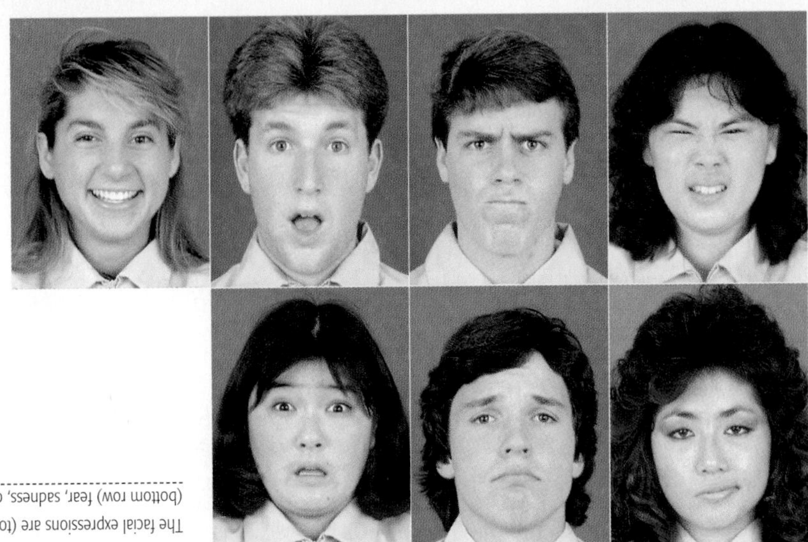

- What emotion is being expressed in each face?

ANSWERS:
The facial expressions are (top row from left) happiness, surprise, anger, disgust; (bottom row) fear, sadness, contempt.

universally recognized facial expressions. Robert Plutchik (1980, 1984) has argued for eight basic emotions that emerged from a mathematical analysis of people's ratings of a large number of emotional terms. You will see in Figure 8.1 that, even though Plutchik and Ekman approached the problem in very different ways, Plutchik's list is remarkably similar to Ekman's.

But what about emotions that appear on none of these basic lists? What of envy, regret, pride, or mirth? From the perspectives of Ekman, Plutchik, and others who argue for a simplified list of basic emotions, a larger palette of human emotions involves complex blends of the more basic emotions.

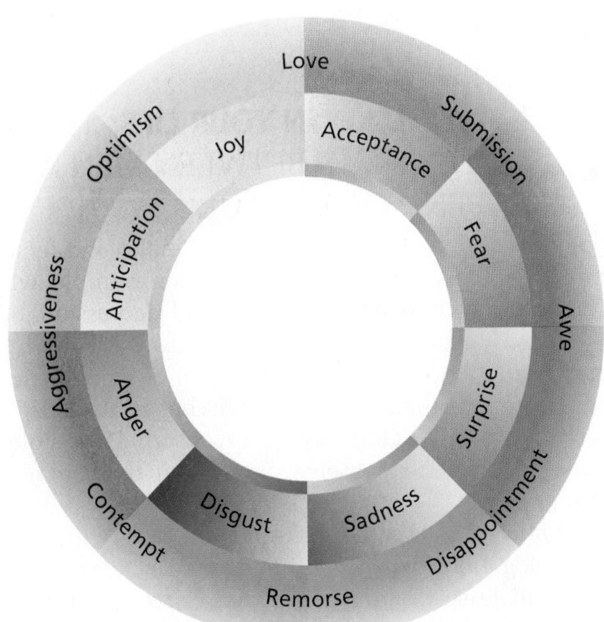

Love
Submission
Awe
Disappointment
Remorse
Contempt
Aggressiveness
Optimism
Joy
Acceptance
Fear
Surprise
Sadness
Disgust
Anger
Anticipation

FIGURE 8.1 The Emotion Wheel

Robert Plutchik's emotion wheel arranges eight primary emotions on the inner ring of a circle of opposite emotions. Pairs of adjacent emotions can combine to form more complex emotions noted on the outer ring of the figure. For example, love is portrayed as a combination of joy and acceptance. Still other emotions, such as envy or regret (not shown) emerge from still other combinations of more basic emotions portrayed on the wheel. (*Source:* Figure, "The Emotion Wheel," from "A Language for the Emotions," by R. Plutchik, *Psychology Today,* February 1980. Copyright © 1980 by Sussex Publishers, Inc. Reprinted by permission of Sussex Publishers, Inc.)

DO IT YOURSELF! Are You a Sensation Seeker?

Different people seem to need different levels of emotional arousal. Marvin Zuckerman argues that "sensation seekers" have an unusually high need for stimulation that produces arousal. In addition to the need for thrills, sensation seekers may be impulsive, prefer new experiences, and be easily bored (Kohn et al., 1979; Malatesta et al., 1981; Zuckerman, 1974).

From your score on the Sensation Seeking Scale below you can get a rough idea of your own level of sensation seeking. You may also want to give this scale to some of your friends. Do you suppose that most people choose friends who have sensation-seeking tendencies similar to their own? Wide differences in sensation-seeking tendencies may account for strain on close relationships, when one person is reluctant to take the risks that the other actively seeks.

THE SENSATION-SEEKING SCALE

Choose A or B for each item, depending on which response better describes your preferences. The scoring key appears at the end.

1. A I would like a job that requires a lot of traveling.
   B I would prefer a job in one location.
2. A I am invigorated by a brisk, cold day.
   B I can't wait to get indoors on a cold day.
3. A I get bored seeing the same old faces.
   B I like the comfortable familiarity of everyday friends.
4. A I would prefer living in an ideal society in which everyone is safe, secure, and happy.
   B I would have preferred living in the unsettled days of our history.
5. A I sometimes like to do things that are a little frightening.
   B A sensible person avoids activities that are dangerous.
6. A I would not like to be hypnotized.
   B I would like to have the experience of being hypnotized.
7. A The most important goal of life is to live it to the fullest and experience as much as possible.
   B The most important goal of life is to find peace and happiness.
8. A I would like to try parachute jumping.
   B I would never want to try jumping out of a plane, with or without a parachute.
9. A I enter cold water gradually, giving myself time to get used to it.
   B I like to dive or jump right into the ocean or a cold pool.
10. A When I go on a vacation, I prefer the comfort of a good room and bed.
    B When I go on a vacation, I prefer the change of camping out.
11. A I prefer people who are emotionally expressive even if they are a bit unstable.
    B I prefer people who are calm and even-tempered.
12. A A good painting should shock or jolt the senses.
    B A good painting should give one a feeling of peace and security.
13. A People who ride motorcycles must have some kind of unconscious need to hurt themselves.
    B I would like to drive or ride a motorcycle.

KEY

Each of the following answers earns one point: 1A, 2A, 3A, 4B, 5A, 6B, 7A, 8A, 9B, 10B, 11A, 12A, 13B. Compare your point total with the following norms for sensation-seeking:

0–3	Very low
4–5	Low
6–9	Average
10–11	High
12–13	Very high

Source: From "The Search for High Sensation" by M. Zuckerman, *Psychology Today,* February 1978.

PSYCHOLOGY IN YOUR LIFE: EMOTIONAL DIFFERENCES BETWEEN MEN AND WOMEN DEPEND ON CULTURE

Some emotional differences between males and females undoubtedly have a biological basis. This would explain, for example, why certain emotional disturbances, such as panic disorder and depression, occur more commonly in women. Biological differences may also explain why men show more anger and display more physiological signs of emotional arousal during interpersonal conflicts than do women (Fischer et al., 2004; Gottman, 1994; Gottman & Krokoff, 1989; Gottman & Levenson, 1986; Polefrone & Manuck, 1987; Rusting & Nolen-Hoeksema, 1998). Men also commit most of the world's violent acts.

Other gender differences, however, may depend as much on culture as on biology. For instance, in the United States, males and females often learn different lessons about emotional control. Gender stereotypes dictate that men and boys receive reinforcement for emotional displays of dominance, anger, and aggressive behavior (Fischer, 1993). On the other hand, they may be punished for emotional displays that show weakness: crying, depression, and sadness (Gottman, 1994). Meanwhile, the pattern of reinforcement and punishment may be reversed for females. Women and girls receive encouragement for emotions that show vulnerability. But they may be punished for displaying emotions that suggest dominance.

Not only does culture affect the emotional displays of men and women differently, but different cultures teach the sexes different *display rules*—the permissible ways of showing emotions (Ekman, 1984). In actuality, researchers have found neither sex to be more emotionally expressive overall. Instead, they have discovered that cultures differ in emotional expression much more than do the sexes.

In Israel and Italy, for example, men more often than women hide their feelings of sadness. The opposite holds true in Britain, Spain, Switzerland, and Germany, where women are more likely than men to hide their emotions. In many Asian cultures both sexes learn to restrain all their emotional expressions (Wallbott et al., 1986).

A note of caution: It is always tricky to distinguish biological from cultural influences. We know that men and women often give different emotional interpretations to the same situation—a crying child, for example—but only when the situation involves both a man and a woman (Lakoff, 1990; Stapley & Haviland, 1989).

Overall, we can say that the sexes often differ in their emotional experiences, both within and across cultures. We cannot conclude, however, that one sex has more emotional intensity than the other (Baumeister et al., 1990; Fischer et al., 1993; Oatley & Duncan, 1994; Shaver & Hazan, 1987; Shields, 1991).

CHECK YOUR UNDERSTANDING

1. **RECALL:** From the evolutionary perspective, we can understand emotions as helping organisms identify
   a. others of their own gender.
   b. sources of danger.
   c. beauty and wonder in the world around them.
   d. locations in which to find food and mates.
   e. important and recurring situations.

2. **RECALL:** Which one of the following is *not* one of the culturally universal emotions identified by Ekman's research?
   a. anger
   b. surprise
   c. contempt
   d. regret
   e. fear

3. **ANALYSIS:** Plutchik would say that *regret* is
   a. one of a thousand distinct emotions of which people are capable.
   b. one of the most basic human emotions.
   c. a combination of more basic emotions.
   d. not really an emotion, because it does not appear on the emotion wheel.
   e. the basis for other emotions.

4. **RECALL:** In which respect do men and women differ in their emotional expressions?
   a. Women are, overall, more emotionally expressive than men.
   b. Certain emotional disorders, such as depression, occur more often in women.
   c. In Asian countries, men are more open about their feelings than are women.
   d. Men are more rational than women.
   e. Women are more rational than men.

5. **UNDERSTANDING THE CORE CONCEPT:** According to this section of the chapter, what is the adaptive value of communicating our emotional states?
   a. It helps us to understand our own needs better.
   b. It allows us to deceive others about our emotional states and get what we want.
   c. It allows us to anticipate each other's responses and so to live more easily in groups.
   d. Communicating our emotional state helps us get rid of strong negative emotions, such as fear and anger.
   e. It helps us achieve self-awareness.

ANSWERS: 1. e 2. d 3. c 4. b 5. c

WHERE DO OUR EMOTIONS COME FROM?

Suppose that you are touring a "haunted house" at Halloween, when a filmy figure startles you with ghostly "Boo!" Your emotional response is immediate. It may involve an outward reaction, such as jumping, gasping, or screaming. At the same time, you respond internally, with changes in body chemistry, the function of internal organs, along with arousal in certain parts of the brain and autonomic nervous system. Moreover, these gut-level responses, such as an accelerated heart beat, can persist long after the you realize that you were really in no danger—after you realize that you were fooled by someone dressed in a sheet.

This suggests that emotion operates both on a visceral level and on a conscious level. And, in fact, that idea connects to one of the great recent discoveries in psychology: the existence of two pathways in the brain that process emotion-provoking information. This, then, is the focus of our Core Concept for this section:

The discovery of two distinct brain pathways for emotional arousal has clarified the connections among the many biological structures involved in emotion and has offered solutions to many of the long-standing issues in the psychology of emotion.

In the following pages we will see how the young neuroscience of emotion has begun to identify the machinery that produces our emotions. The details are not yet entirely clear, but we do have a broad-brush picture of the emotion pathways in the brain and their connections throughout the body. In this section we will look first at the basic neuroscience of emotion. Then we will see how the discoveries in this area have resolved some long-standing disputes in the field. At the end of this section, we will turn to a practical application, to see how emotional arousal can affect our performance—say, on a final examination or in an important athletic contest.

The Neuroscience of Emotion

People who suffer from phobias, such as a fear of snakes, usually know that their responses are irrational. What causes a person to hold two such conflicting mind sets? The answer lies in two distinct emotion processing systems in the brain (LeDoux, 1996, 2000). One—a fast response system—operates mainly at an unconscious level, where it quickly screens incoming stimuli and helps us respond quickly to cues of potentially important events, even before they reach consciousness. This system, linked to the implicit memory system, acts as an early-warning defense that produces, for example, a near-instantaneous fright response to a loud noise in the middle of the night (Bechara et al., 1995; Helmuth, 2003b; Johnson, 2003). It relies primarily on deep-brain circuitry that operates automatically, without requiring deliberate conscious control. (See Figure 8.2.)

CONNECTION: CHAPTER 7

Implicit memories involve material of which we are unaware—but that can affect behavior.

Remarkably, these unconscious emotion circuits seem to have a built-in, innate sensitivity to certain cues—which explains why fears of spiders and snakes are more common than fears of, say, electricity (which actually causes more deaths than spiders and snakes). In addition, this quick-response system can easily learn emotional responses through classical conditioning. But it can also be slow to forget. Thus, a person may quickly learn to fear dogs after being bitten, yet the emotional memory of the incident may be quite difficult to extinguish.

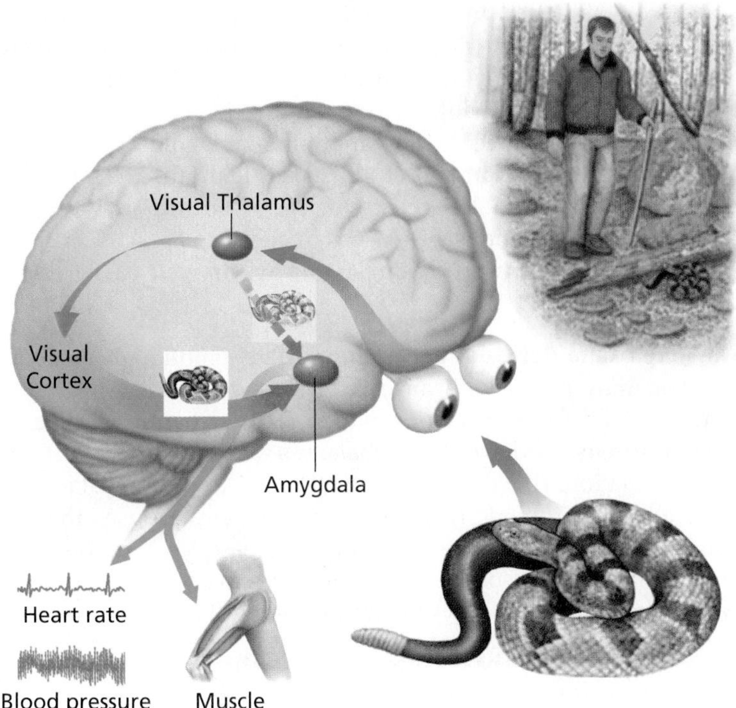
Visual Thalamus
Visual
Cortex
Amygdala
Heart rate
Blood pressure
Muscle

● **FIGURE 8.2** Two Emotion-Processing Pathways

Two emotion systems are at work when the hiker sees a snake. One is fast and unconscious; the other operates more slowly and consciously. The fast system routes incoming visual information through the visual thalamus to the amygdala (dashed pathway), which quickly initiates fear and avoidance responses–all occurring unconsciously. The slower pathway involves the visual cortex, which makes a more complete appraisal of the stimulus and also sends an emotional message to the amygdala and other lower brain structures. The result of this is a conscious perception of the situation and a conscious feeling of fear.

The other emotional system—the one that involves conscious processing—is linked to explicit memory (LeDoux, 1996). Its circuitry can create, for example, the fear that grows in your mind when you anticipate giving a speech or the excitement you experience as you consciously process the thrilling sensations of your first whitewater rafting trip. This system generates emotions more slowly than the unconscious pathways, but it delivers more complete information to consciousness. It attaches emotional reactions to concepts and experiences that you find especially interesting, attractive, or repulsive. Relying heavily on the cerebral cortex, its view of events can differ significantly from that of the unconscious processing system. Thus, the phobic person can feel fear, despite "knowing" that there is no sensible basis for the feeling.

As you can see, then, the brain has no "emotion center" (Davidson, 2000a). Rather, it has many emotion-related circuits that serve the two distinct emotion systems. And, to complicate matters, these two systems also interact. So, the feelings that we associate with an emotion such as fear, for example, can well up into consciousness from the unconscious system (LeDoux, 1996). Alternatively, the conscious emotional system can signal the unconscious circuits, which might produce, for example, the knot you feel in your stomach just before giving a speech. The interplay of these two systems apparently gives rise to the feelings that we call "intuition" (Myers, 2002).

Let us take a more detailed look at these biological mechanisms at work behind our emotions.

The Role of the Limbic System Both emotion pathways rely on circuits in the brain's limbic system. Situated in the layer above the brain stem, the limbic structures undoubtedly evolved as control systems for behaviors used in attack, defense, and retreat: the "fight-or-flight" response (Caldwell, 1995; LeDoux, 1994, 1996). Evidence for this comes from lesioning (cutting) or electrically stimulating parts of the limbic system, which can produce dramatic changes in emotional responding. Tame animals with altered limbic systems may become killers, while prey and predators with limbic lesions may become peaceful companions (Delgado, 1969). Particularly well documented is the importance of the amygdala in the emotion of fear (LeDoux, 1996; Whalen, 1998). (See Figure 8.2.) Like a guard dog, the amygdala is continuously alert for threats, although recent research hints at a role for the amygdala in positive emotions, too (Hamann et al., 2002; Helmuth, 2003a). As you can see in the figure, the amygdala appears to occupy an important position in the processing of our emotions because it receives messages from the quick-and-unconscious emotion-processing pathway, as well as the longer-and-slower conscious pathway.

The Role of the Reticular Formation Many emotional reactions such as anger and fear may begin with an early warning sounded by the brain's built-in alarm system: the reticular formation. This structure, strategically located in the brain stem, works with the thalamus and the amygdala to monitor incoming information. If it detects a potential threat, the reticular formation sets off a cascade of automatic responses that not only arouses the brain but makes your heart accelerate, your respiration increase, your mouth get dry, and your muscles become tense. All these responses evolved long ago in our ancestral past to mobilize the body quickly for the fight-or-flight emergency reaction.

The Role of the Cerebral Cortex The cerebral cortex—the outermost layer of brain tissue and our "thinking cap"—plays the starring role in the conscious emotion pathway, where it interprets events and associates them with memories and feelings. Just as distinct patches of cortex produce different sensations, positive and negative emotions are associated with different cortical regions. In general, the right hemisphere specializes in negative emotions, such as anger and depression, while the left processes more positive, joyful emotions (Davidson, 1992a, b; 2000a, b; Heller et al., 1998; Kosslyn et al., 2002).

The notion that the two cerebral hemispheres specialize in different classes of emotion has been dubbed **lateralization of emotion.** The evidence is found in EEG recordings of normal people's emotional reactions, as well as in studies relating brain damage in the right or left hemisphere to specific disturbances in emotional expression (Adolphs et al., 2001; Ahern & Schwartz, 1985; Borod et al., 1988).

The Role of the Autonomic Nervous System What makes your heart race when you are startled? The messages that you "take to heart" (and to your other internal organs) when you become emotionally aroused are routed through the autonomic nervous system (Levenson, 1992). The parasympathetic division usually dominates in pleasant emotions. But when you are startled or when you experience some unpleasant emotion, the sympathetic division becomes more active (see Table 8.1).

Suppose an emergency—or merely the memory of an emergency—occurs (a speeding car is coming directly at you!). As you will recall from Chapter 3, the brain alerts the body by means of messages carried along pathways of the sympathetic system. Some messages direct the adrenal glands to release stress hormones. Others make the heart race and blood pressure rise. At the same time, the sympathetic system directs certain blood vessels to constrict, diverting energy to the voluntary muscles and away from the stomach and intestines. (This causes the feeling of a "knot" in your stomach.) Then, when the emergency has passed, the parasympathetic division takes over, carrying instructions that counteract the emergency orders of a few moments earlier. You may, however, remain aroused for some time after experiencing a strong emotional activation because hormones continue to circulate in the bloodstream. If the emotion-provoking situation is prolonged (as when you work every day for a

■ **Lateralization of emotion**
Different influences of the two brain hemispheres on various emotions. The left hemisphere apparently influences positive emotions (for example, happiness), and the right hemisphere influences negative emotions (anger, for example).

TABLE 8.1 Responses Associated with Emotion

Component of emotion	Type of response	Example
Physiological arousal	Neural, hormonal, visceral, and muscular changes	Increased heart rate, blushing, becoming pale, sweating, rapid breathing
Subjective feelings	The private experience of one's internal affective state	Feelings of rage, sadness, happiness
Cognitive interpretation	Attaching meaning to the emotional experience by drawing on memory and perceptual processes	Blaming someone, perceiving a threat
Social/behavioral reactions	Expressing emotion through gestures, facial expressions, or other actions	Smiling, crying, screaming for help

boss whom you detest), the emergency response can sap your energy and cause both physical and mental deterioration.

The Role of Hormones Your body produces dozens of hormones, but among the most important for your emotions are serotonin, epinephrine (adrenalin), and norepinephrine. Serotonin is associated with feelings of depression. Epinephrine is the hormone produced in fear. Norepinephrine is more abundant in anger. Steroid hormones (sometimes abused by bodybuilders and other athletes) can also exert a powerful influence on emotions. In addition to their effects on muscles, steroids act on nerve cells, causing them to change their excitability. This is a normal part of the body's response to emergency situations. But when additional doses of steroid drugs are ingested over extended periods, these potent chemicals can produce dangerous side effects, including tendencies to rage or depression (Daly et al., 2003; Majewska et al., 1986; Miller et al., 2002). The mood changes associated with stress, pregnancy, and the menstrual cycle may also be related to the effects that steroid hormones have on brain cells.

CONNECTION: CHAPTER 13

Drugs that inhibit the reuptake of *serotonin* are often used to treat depression.

Psychological Theories of Emotion: Resolving Some Persistent Issues

The tools of neuroscience have provided evidence that has helped psychologists resolve some long-disputed issues in the field of emotion. How do biology, cognition, and behavior interact to produce an emotion? Is one the cause of the others? Are emotion and cognition separate? Let's look briefly at these controversies and at how insights drawn from neuroscience have begun to resolve them.

Do Our Physical Responses Cause Our Emotions? In the early days of psychology, just over a century ago, William James taught that our physical responses underlie our emotions. "We feel sorry *because* we cry, angry *because* we strike, afraid *because* we tremble," James said (1890/1950, p. 1006). This view, simultaneously proposed by the Danish psychologist Carl Lange, became known as the **James–Lange theory.**

Other scientists, notably Walter Cannon and Philip Bard, objected that physical changes in our behavior or our internal organs occur too slowly to account for split-second emotional reactions, such as those we feel in the face of danger. They also objected that our physical responses are not varied enough to account for the whole palate of human emotion. In their view,

■ **James–Lange theory** The proposal that an emotion-provoking stimulus produces a physical response that, in turn, produces an emotion.

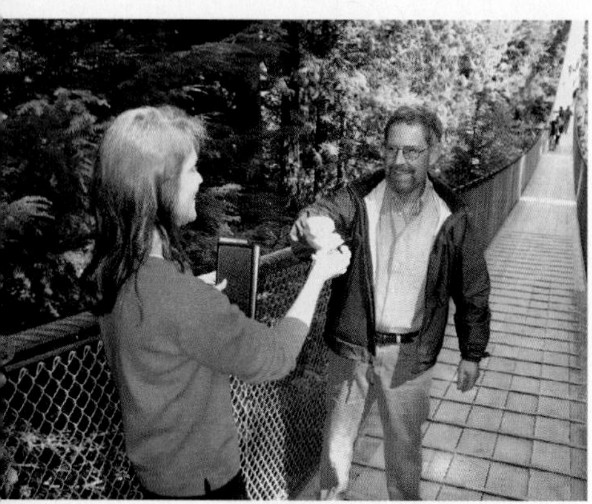

● Here on the Capilano Bridge, psychologists Bob Johnson (one of your authors) and Dr. Susan Horton of Mesa Community College reenact the Dutton study described in the text.

referred to as the **Cannon–Bard theory,** the emotional feeling and the internal physical response occurred simultaneously.

Which side was right? Both had part of the truth. On the one hand, modern neuroscience has confirmed that our physical state can influence our emotions—much as the James–Lange theory argued (LeDoux, 1996). You may have noted edgy feelings after drinking too much coffee or grumpiness when hungry. Similarly, psychoactive drugs, such as alcohol or nicotine, can influence the physical condition of our brains and, hence, alter our moods. These emotional responses arise from circuits deep in the brain responding unconsciously to our physical condition.

An important new twist on the James–Lange theory comes from the idea that the brain maintains memories of physical states that are associated with events. So, when you see a snake on the path in front of you, your brain can quickly conjure up a body-memory of the physical response it had previously in a similar situation (Damasio, 1994). This idea, then, effectively counters Walter Cannon's objection that physical changes in the body occur too slowly to cause our feelings.

On the other hand, our physical responses are not the sole cause of our emotions. Emotions can also be aroused by external cues detected by our unconscious emotional system, as we have seen. Thus, an unexpected loud noise or the sight of blood can trigger a reflexive emotional response that simultaneously makes you jump and produces a visceral response. Many psychologists now believe that depression and phobic reactions can result from conditioned responses of this unconscious emotional system.

What's the Role of Cognition in Emotion? You can make yourself emotional just by thinking, as any student with "test anxiety" will testify. The more you think about the dire consequences of failing a test, the more the anxiety builds. "Method" actors, like the late Marlon Brando, have long exploited this fact to make themselves feel real emotions on stage. They do so by recalling an incident from their own experience that produced the emotion they want to portray, such as grief, joy, or anger.

Stanley Schachter's (1971) **two-factor theory,** also known as Schachter–Singer theory, adds an interesting complication to the role of cognition in emotion. This theory suggests that the emotions we feel depend on our appraisal of both (a) our internal *physical state* and (b) the external *situation* in which we find ourselves. Strange effects occur when these two factors conflict—as they did in the following classic study of emotion, which enterprising students may want to adapt in order to spice up their romantic lives.

An attractive female researcher interviewed male subjects who had just crossed one of two footbridges. One was a safe, sturdy structure; the other a wobbly suspension bridge across a deep canyon—the latter selected to elicit physical arousal. The researcher, pretending to be interested in the effects of scenery on creativity, asked the men to write brief stories about a picture of a woman. She also invited them to call her if they wanted more information about the research. As predicted, those men who had just crossed the wobbly bridge (and were, presumably, more physically aroused by the experience) wrote stories containing more sexual imagery than those who used the safer structure. And four times as many of them called the female researcher "to get more information"! Apparently, the men who had crossed the shaky bridge misinterpreted their increased arousal as emotional attraction to the female researcher (Dutton & Aron, 1974).

Before you rush out to find the love of your life on a wobbly bridge, we must caution you, numerous attempts to test the two-factor theory have produced conflicting results (Leventhal & Tomarken, 1986; Sinclair et al., 1994). So,

■ **Cannon–Bard theory** The counterproposal that an emotional feeling and an internal physiological response occur at the same time: One is not the cause of the other. Both were believed to be the result of cognitive appraisal of the situation.

■ **Two-factor theory** The proposal claiming that emotion results from the cognitive appraisal of both physical arousal (Factor 1) and an emotion-provoking stimulus (Factor 2).

under what conditions are we most likely to misinterpret our emotions? Normally, external events confirm what our biology tells us, without much need for elaborate interpretation—as when you feel disgust at an unpleasant odor or joy when seeing an old friend. But what happens when we experience physical arousal from not-so-obvious sources, such as exercise, heat, or drugs? When we know (or think we know) that one of these is the source of our feelings, we will most likely make no emotional interpretation. Misattribution is not inevitable, but it is much more likely in a complex environment where many stimuli are competing for our attention, as in the bridge study, above. It is also likely in an environment where we have faulty information about our physical arousal, as when the unsuspected caffeine in a soft drink makes us edgy. Obviously, however, we need more research on the misattribution of emotions. (See Figure 8.3.)

STARBUCKS COFFEE

● The two-factor theory would predict that a decaffeinated-coffee drinker who accidentally drank coffee with caffeine could mistake the resulting physical arousal for emotion.

Another approach to emotion is called the **cognitive appraisal theory** of emotion. According to this theory, advocated by both Frijda (1986) and Lazarus (1991c), after the event has occurred we make a conscious decision about how we should feel. The "appraisal" aspect of this comes into play when we decide whether the event was in our favor and what we believe the cause to be. An example of this is reading the narrative comments your teacher made on an essay you wrote. Your assessment of those comments tells you whether they are positive. In *primary* appraisal we look at how the event affects us, and in *secondary* appraisal we look at how we deal with the event.

Next we will examine the **opponent-process theory** of emotion. In this theory, emotions work in pairs. When we trigger one emotion, its opposite is suppressed. This theory has been expanded to describe drug use, in that the high associated with the use of a drug is later replaced by a low, or withdrawal symptom. In later stages of drug use, following habituation, individuals take a drug not for the high associated with it when they started using drugs, but rather to avoid the lows.

■ **Cognitive appraisal theory** Theory of emotion which theorizes that individuals decide on an appropriate emotion following the event.

■ **Opponent-process theory** Theory of emotion which theorizes that emotions have pairs. When one is triggered, the other is suppressed (for example, when we feel happy, sad is the suppressed emotion).

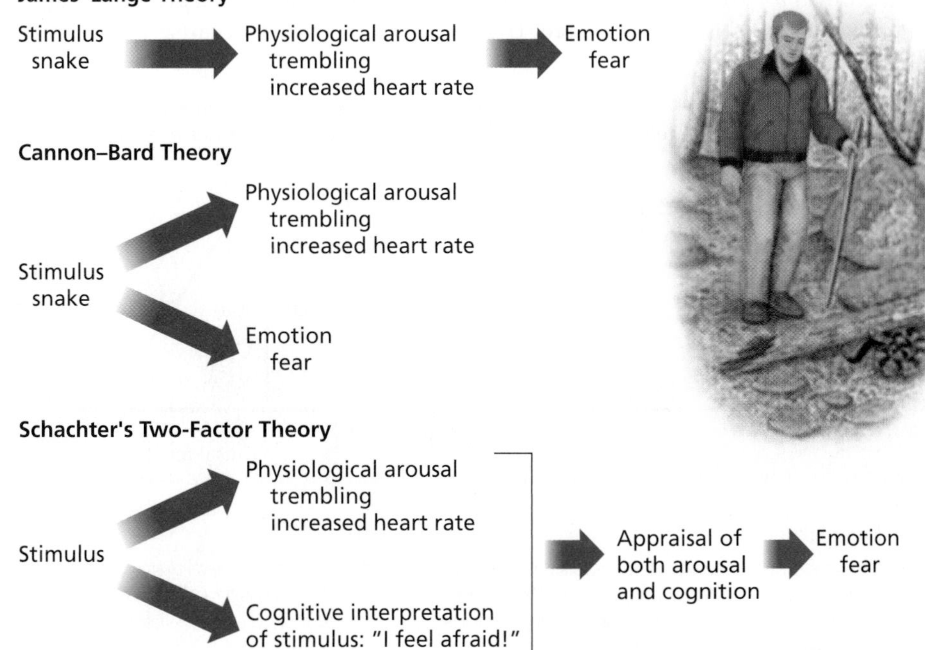
James–Lange Theory
Stimulus snake
Physiological arousal trembling increased heart rate
Emotion fear
Cannon–Bard Theory
Physiological arousal trembling increased heart rate
Stimulus snake
Emotion fear
Schachter's Two-Factor Theory
Physiological arousal trembling increased heart rate
Stimulus
Appraisal of both arousal and cognition
Emotion fear
Cognitive interpretation of stimulus: "I feel afraid!"

● **FIGURE 8.3** Theories of Emotion Compared

Sorrow

● Depression is more common in women, but men are more prone to violence. This sketch is by Vincent Van Gogh, no stranger to depression himself.

Can We Separate Cognition and Emotion? Some theorists have argued that emotion and cognition are separate, independent brain processes (Izard, 1989, 1993; Zajonc, 1980, 1984). In panic disorder, for example, panic attacks can occur suddenly and without warning—in the absence of a threatening situation and without emotion-provoking thoughts.

An opposing view has been set forth by those who specialize in cognitive psychotherapy. This perspective asserts that cognition and emotion have an intimate connection. Richard Lazarus (1984, 1991a), for example, argues that we can conquer negative emotional responses by changing the way we think about events. In this view, cognition and emotion are components of a single mental system.

Again, insights from neuroscience can again help us resolve this conflict. And again, both sides have part of the truth (LeDoux, 1996). Whether emotion and cognition are separate or intertwined depends on which of the two main emotion circuits in the brain is involved. The emotion-and-cognition-are-separate view has recognized the distinction between the conscious and the unconscious emotion systems. In contrast, the emotion-and-cognition-are-connected view has focused on the conscious emotion pathways.

PSYCHOLOGY IN YOUR LIFE: AROUSAL, PERFORMANCE, AND THE INVERTED U

Athletes always want to be "up" for a game—but how far up should they be? Cheering sports fans might think that increased arousal will always improve performance—but that is not necessarily true. Too much arousal can make an athlete "choke" and her or his performance falter. The same is true for you when you face an examination. Up to a point, increasing levels of arousal can motivate you to study and facilitate your recall during the test, but higher levels can produce test anxiety and a drop in your grade.

This complex relationship between arousal and behavior has been studied both in laboratory animals and in humans. For hungry and thirsty rats used in experiments on learning, the curve of performance first rises and then later declines with the intensity of arousal. The same pattern holds for humans in a variety of circumstances, including athletes under pressure. Psychologists call this the **inverted U function** (so named because the graph

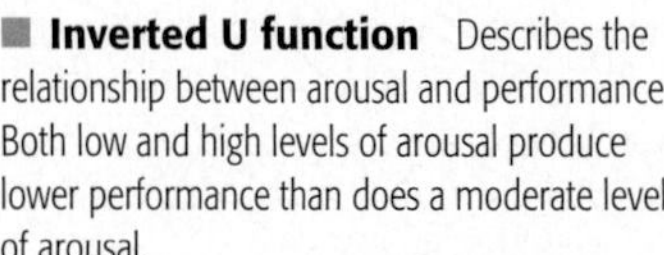

■ **Inverted U function** Describes the relationship between arousal and performance. Both low and high levels of arousal produce lower performance than does a moderate level of arousal.

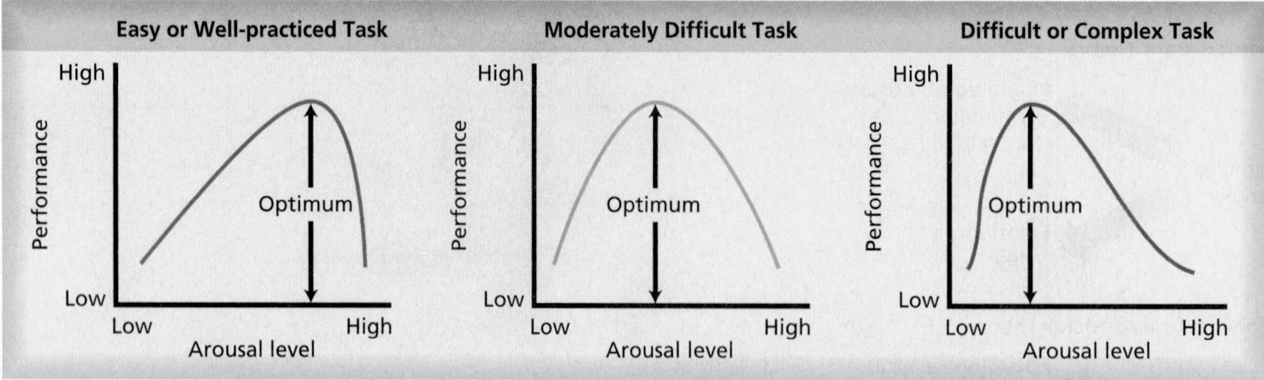
Easy or Well-practiced Task
Moderately Difficult Task
Difficult or Complex Task
High
Low
Performance
Optimum
Low
High
Arousal level

The Inverted U

Performance varies with arousal level and task difficulty. For easy or well-practiced tasks, a higher level of arousal increases performance effectiveness. However, for difficult or complex tasks, a lower level of arousal is optimal. A moderate level of arousal is generally best for tasks of moderate difficulty. These inverted U-shaped functions show that performance is worst at both low and high extremes.

resembles an upside-down letter U, as you can see in the figure). It suggests that either too little or too much arousal can impair performance. Think about it: How much pressure would you want your brain surgeon to feel? Which brings us to a second important point.

The optimum amount of arousal varies with the task. As you can see in the figure, it takes more arousal to achieve peak performance on simple or well-practiced tasks than it does on complex tasks that require much thinking and planning. Thus, cheers may boost performance at basketball games but not in brain surgery.

The amount of stimulation needed to produce optimal arousal also varies with the individual. In fact, some people seem to thrive on the thrill of dangerous sports, such as rock climbing and skydiving—activities that would produce immobilizing levels of arousal in most of us (Zuckerman et al., 1978, 1980, 1993). Marvin Zuckerman (1995, 2004), who has studied people he calls **sensation seekers,** believes that such individuals have a biological need for high levels of stimulation. Research suggests that the underlying biology involves the brain's dopamine pathways (Bevins, 2001). You can test your own sensation-seeking tendencies with Zuckerman's scale, found in the "Do It Yourself!" box on page 302.

■ **Sensation seekers** In Zuckerman's theory, individuals who have a biological need for higher levels of stimulation than do other people.

CHECK YOUR UNDERSTANDING

1. **RECALL:** During emotional arousal, the ______ nervous system sends messages to the internal organs.
   a. somatic
   b. sensory
   c. autonomic
   d. cerebellar
   e. afferent
2. **APPLICATION:** We would be most likely to misattribute the source of our arousal when
   a. taking a drug, such as a diet pill, that has the unexpected side effect of physical arousal.
   b. taking a drug, such as caffeine, that we know produces arousal.
   c. winning a race.
   d. feeling depressed after the death of a loved one.
   e. losing a race.
3. **RECALL:** In the field of emotion, theorists have long debated whether
   a. feelings are associated with emotional responses.
   b. we are aware of our emotions.
   c. cognition and emotion are independent of each other.
   d. men are sensitive to women's emotions.
   e. emotions are valid.
4. **UNDERSTANDING THE CORE CONCEPT:** Emotions result from an interaction of biological arousal, subjective feelings, cognitive interpretation, and behavioral expression. Which two of these are emphasized in the two-factor theory of emotion?
   a. subjective feelings and behavioral expression
   b. cognitive interpretation and behavioral expression
   c. biological arousal and cognitive interpretation
   d. biological arousal and subjective feelings
   e. subjective feelings and cognitive interpretation

ANSWERS: 1. c 2. a 3. c 4. c

KEY QUESTION
?

HOW MUCH CONTROL DO WE HAVE OVER OUR EMOTIONS?

Your supervisor says something critical of your work—unfairly, you think. Suddenly anger and defensiveness well up inside you. You can't express these emotions to the boss, but your face betrays your feelings. Is such a response as automatic and uncontrollable as the knee-jerk reflex? Richard Lazarus (1991a, b) has shown that training can help people not only to modify and control their private feelings but also to control the expression of them.

In many situations, aside from work, it can be desirable to mask or modify what you are feeling. If you dislike a professor, you might be wise not to show your true emotions. And, if you have strong romantic feelings toward someone—more than he or she realizes—it might be safest to reveal the depth of your feelings gradually, lest you frighten the person away with too much too soon. Similarly, in business negotiations, you will do better if you can prevent yourself from signaling too much emotional arousal. Even in leisure activities like playing poker or planning your next move in chess, you will be most successful if you keep your real feelings, beliefs, and intentions a secret. All of these examples testify that emotional control has an important role in our ability to interact with other people.

In this section, then, we look at the issues involved in emotional control. We begin with the concept of "emotional intelligence," the ability to modulate your own emotions and to understand and react appropriately to those of others. Then we will look at the other side of emotional control: the detection of deception—which is really a problem in detecting emotional responses that someone is trying to hide. Then, in the final part of this section, we will examine the control of anger. Here is the Core Concept that ties these topics together:

CORE CONCEPT

Although emotional responses are not always consciously regulated, we can learn to control them.

The practical, takeaway message from this section is that, while emotions do sometimes slip out of control, we are not simply at their mercy. Emotional understanding and control are skills that can be learned.

Developing Emotional Intelligence

It takes a certain sort of "smarts" to understand and control one's emotions. Psychologists Peter Salovey and John Mayer have called this **emotional intelligence** (Mayer & Salovey, 1997; Salovey & Mayer, 1990). Their goal is to raise emotional intelligence to the same level in our awareness as the much-better-known academic forms of intelligence assessed by traditional IQ tests—which you will recall from the previous chapter.

The Predictive Power of Emotional Intelligence Those with high emotional intelligence are not only tuned in to their own emotions and those of others but they can also manage their negative feelings and curtail inappropriate expression of their impulses. The power of this ability can be seen in the results of the "marshmallow test," says Daniel Goleman (1995):

> Just imagine you're four years old, and someone makes the following proposal: If you'll wait until after he runs an errand, you can have two marshmallows for a treat. If you can't wait until then, you can have only one—but you can have it right now.

How did the children in this experiment respond to the temptation of the marshmallow that sat before them, within reach, while the researcher was away? Goleman continues:

> Some four-year-olds were able to wait what must surely have seemed an endless fifteen to twenty minutes for the experimenter to return. To sustain themselves in their struggle they covered their eyes so they wouldn't have to stare at temptation, or rested their heads in their arms, talked to themselves, sang, played games with their hands and feet, even tried to go to sleep. These plucky preschoolers got the two-marshmallow

■ **Emotional intelligence** The ability to understand and control emotional responses.

> reward. But others, more impulsive, grabbed the one marshmallow, almost always within seconds of the experimenter's leaving the room on his "errand." (pp. 80–81)

But the amazing predictive power of the marshmallow test was revealed when these same children were tracked down in adolescence. As a group, those who had curbed their impulse to grab the single marshmallow were better off on all counts. They were more self-reliant, more effective in interpersonal relationships, better students, better able to handle frustration and stress. By contrast, the children who had given in to temptation had lives marked by troubled relationships, shyness, stubbornness, and indecisiveness. They also were much more likely to hold low opinions of themselves, to mistrust others, and to be easily provoked by frustrations. In the academic sphere, they were more likely to be uninterested in school. Goleman notes that the marshmallow test also correlated clearly with SAT scores: Those who, as 4-year-olds, were able to delay gratification scored, on the average, 210 points higher than did their counterparts who had grabbed the single marshmallow years earlier.

Emotional intelligence, however, is not a perfect predictor of success, cautions John Mayer (1999). Nor should we think of it as a replacement for traditional IQ scores. Rather, says Mayer, emotional intelligence is merely another variable that can help us refine our understanding and our predictions of behavior.

Detecting Deception

You might think you can spot deception when someone fails to "look you in the eye" or fidgets nervously. If so, you could be setting yourself up to be duped. Most of us are poor lie detectors—or truth detectors, for that matter. One reason is that social interactions often occur in familiar situations, where we pay little attention to nonverbal cues. Nevertheless, experts who study deception find that a person who deliberately tries to hoodwink us may "leak" uncontrolled nonverbal signals of deception. Knowing how to read these cues could help you decide whether a salesperson or politician is lying to you or whether a physician might be concealing something about your medical condition.

Deception Cues The real key to effective deception detection lies in perceiving patterns of a person's behavior over time. Without the chance for repeated observations, you are much less able to judge a person's honesty (Marsh, 1988). Still, you may find yourself in a situation where even a little help in deception detection might be better than none at all—such as when buying a used car or listening to a political speech. Here are some helpful guidelines that psychology can offer (from DePaulo et al., 2003; Kleinke, 1975; Marsh, 1988; Zuckerman et al., 1981):

- Some lies involve false information, as when a used-car salesperson tells you that a junker is in good working order. In such cases, the effort to hide the truth costs the liar some cognitive effort. This results in heightened attention (evident in dilation of the pupils), longer pauses in speech (to choose words carefully), and more constrained movement and gesturing (in an attempt to avoid "giving away" the truth).
- On the other hand, when a lie involves hiding one's true feelings—as a good poker player does when holding a straight flush—the liar may become physically and behaviorally more aroused. This becomes evident in postural shifts, speech errors, nervous gestures (such as preening by touching or stroking the hair or face), and shrugging (as if to dismiss the lie).

- The face is easier to control than the body, so a deceiver may work on keeping a "poker face" but forget to restrain bodily clues. A smart deception detective might therefore concentrate on a speaker's body movements: Are they rhythmic? Are they calculated? Do the hands move freely or nervously? (Gamblers and those who study gambling may refer to such an unconscious habit as a "tell.") The eyes, also, can sometimes give deceivers away—especially when they're using the common social deception of trying to look happy or amused, when they are not. While our attention may more naturally focus on a smile as an indicator of happiness or amusement, that can be manipulated much more easily than the muscles around the eyes. Only in genuine grins do the eye muscles crinkle up the skin around the eyes. You can test your ability to tell a real from a fake smile in the "Do It Yourself!" box on the facing page.
- The ability to "look you straight in the eye" is, in fact, a reasonably good indicator of truth-telling—but only when dealing with people who usually tell the truth. When they do lie, their amateurish efforts to deceive often show up in averted gaze, reduced blinking (indicating concentration of attention elsewhere), and less smiling. A practiced liar, however, can look straight at you while telling complete fiction.

Do "Lie Detectors" Really Work? The **polygraph,** often called a "lie detector," relies on the assumption that people will exhibit physical signs of arousal when lying. The device really acts as an emotional arousal detector, rather than a direct indicator of truth or lies. Most polygraph machines make a record of the suspect's heart rate, breathing rate, perspiration, and blood pressure. Occasionally, voice-print analysis is also employed.

Critics have pointed out several problems with the polygraphic procedure (Aftergood, 2000; Holden, 2001b; Saxe, 1991, 1994). For example, subjects know when they are suspects, so some will give heightened responses to the critical questions, whether they are guilty or innocent. Some people, however, can give deceptive responses because they have learned to control or distort their emotional responses. To do so they may employ simple physical movements, drugs, or biofeedback training—a procedure in which people are given moment-to-moment information on certain biological responses, such as perspiration or heart rate (Saxe et al., 1985). Either way, a polygraph examiner risks incorrectly identifying innocent people as guilty and failing to spot the liars.

A Few Fibs from the Polygrapher To minimize these problems, polygraphers typically employ several tricks of their trade. They may start the interview by persuading the subject that the machine is highly accurate. A common ploy is to ask a series of loaded questions designed to provoke obvious emotional reactions. For example, "Did you ever, in your life, take anything that did not belong to you?" In another favorite technique, the examiner uses a deceptive stimulation procedure, or "stim test," in which the subject draws a card from a "stacked" deck. Then the examiner pretends to identify the card from the subject's polygraph responses (Kleinmuntz & Szucko, 1984).

When the actual interrogation begins, it will consist of an artistic mix of *critical questions, irrelevant questions,* and *control questions.* The irrelevant questions ("Are you sitting down right now?") are designed to elicit truthful answers accompanied by a physical response consistent with truth-telling. The control questions ("Did you ever lie to your parents?") are designed to elicit an anxious, emotionally aroused response pattern. Then the examiner can compare the subject's responses to these two types of questions with responses to the critical questions ("Did you steal the jewels?"). It is assumed that a guilty sub-

Polygraph A device that records or graphs many ("poly") measures of physical arousal, such as heart rate, breathing, perspiration, and blood pressure. A polygraph is often called a "lie detector," even though it is really an arousal detector.

DO IT YOURSELF! The Eyes Have It

Can you tell if people are sincere when they smile at you? Smiles aren't made just with the mouth, but with the whole face, especially the eyes. A real smile is different from a fake one, primarily around the eyes. Specifically, when we feel genuine joy or mirth, the *orbicularis occuli* muscles wrinkle up the skin around the eyes.

With this in mind, take a look at these two pictures of smiling faces and see if you can tell which ones is the real smile and which one is forced. See the text for the tell-tale signs of a faked smile.

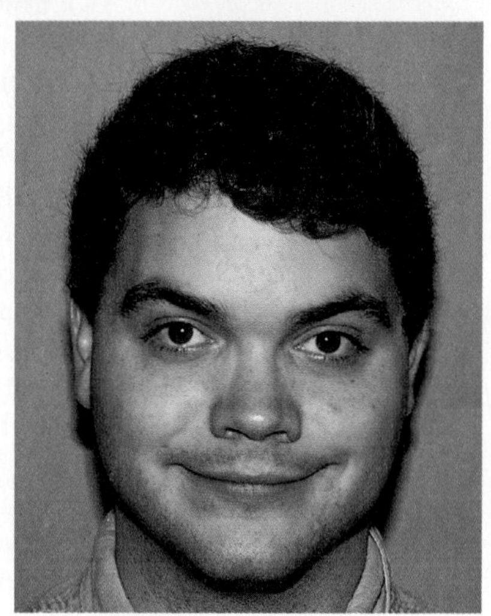

ject will give a stronger response to the critical questions than to the irrelevant and control questions.

Serious Concerns About Accuracy Sensible as this seems, several issues call the polygraph procedure into question. Consider, for example, the problem of accuracy. Even if the examination were 95% accurate, the 5% error rate could lead to the misidentification of many innocent people as being guilty. Imagine that your company arranges for all 500 of your employees to take a "lie detector" test to find out who has been stealing office supplies. Imagine also that only about 4% (20 out of 500 people) are really stealing, which is not an unreasonable estimate. If the lie detector test is 95% accurate, it will correctly spot 19 of these 20 thieves. But the company will still have a big problem. The test will also give 5% *false positives,* falsely fingering 5% of the innocent people. Of the 480 innocent employees, the polygraph will inaccurately implicate 24 as liars. That is, *you could end up with more people falsely accused of lying than people correctly accused of lying.* This was borne out in field study of suspected criminals, who were later either convicted or declared innocent. The polygraph results were no better than a random coin flip (Brett et al., 1986).

● The polygraph, often called a "lie detector," relies on the assumption that people display physical signs of arousal when lying.

An equally serious concern with polygraphy is that there are no generally accepted standards either for administering a polygraph examination or for interpreting its results. Different examiners could conceivably come to different conclusions in the same case.

For these reasons, the U.S. Congress has outlawed most uses of polygraph tests in industry and in the government. About half of the states do not admit lie detector evidence in court (Patrick & Iacono, 1991). And the National Academies of Science (2003) has recently released a report saying that the polygraph is too crude to be useful for screening people to identify possible terrorists or other national security risks.

Alternative Approaches to Deception Detection The reining in of polygraph testing has spurred the development of alternative means of detecting dishonesty (Sackett, 1994). Much of this work has been devoted to paper-and-pencil instruments that are often called "integrity tests." How well do these instruments work? Not very well, according to reports by the American Psychological Association and by the U.S. government's Office of Technology Assessment. In general, like the polygraph, these instruments seem to be more accurate than mere interviews, but they also suffer from a high false-positive rate (Camara & Schneider, 1994).

More recently, researchers have turned to brain-scanning techniques to see if they can catch liars (Ross, 2003). A certain brain wave pattern known as P300 has been linked with a variety of attention-getting cues, such as hearing one's name, but studies show it can also be evoked by fibbing. In addition, fMRI images show that lying activates all the brain areas involved in telling the truth, plus several more (Langleben et al., 2002). This suggests that lying is not something completely separate from the truth but an operation the liar must perform on the truth, says psychiatrist Daniel Langleben.

The potential advantage of such techniques is that they bypass the anxiety-response pathway used by polygraphy. By registering neural activity, they get much closer to the person's actual thoughts. But how well do these new techniques work? Not well enough for the police and the courts—yet.

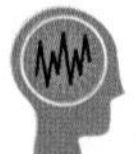

PSYCHOLOGY IN YOUR LIFE: CONTROLLING ANGER

Anger has a bad reputation because of its association with aggression and violence. But, says anger expert Howard Kassinove, aggression accompanies anger only about 10% of the time (DeAngelis, 2003). And, say psychologists, anger can—if properly controlled—have a positive effect by communicating feelings, helping people stand up for their rights, and clarifying problems in a relationship. Says Carol Tavris (1989), "Imagine what the women's suffrage movement would have been like if women had said, 'Guys, it's really so unfair, we're nice people and we're human beings too. Won't you listen to us and give us the vote?' "

Most people feel angry a few times a week and manage to keep their anger in bounds, so the results are usually positive (Kassinove et al., 1997). On the other hand, a few people go much too far, say anger researcher Raymond Tafrate and his colleagues (2002). Anger episodes that occur frequently—to the point of being a personality trait—are pathological and need treatment. Likewise, violence that causes harm to someone is never normal or acceptable. That said, however, there is no clinically recognized category for abnormal levels of anger, which can be a problem for clinicians who are trying to bill insurance companies for anger management therapy.

So, what happens in therapy for anger? According to Colorado State University's Jerry Deffenbacher, the best treatment strategies involve some combination of relaxation training, cognitive therapy, and skill development (J. D. Holloway, 2003a). During therapy, patients practice relaxation techniques until they can quickly put themselves in a relaxed mood during an anger-producing situation (a common one involves being cut off by another car on the road).

The cognitive therapy component involves learning alternative ways of interpreting situations that would otherwise cause anger. The motorist who is cut off by another driver might learn to think, "There's an accident waiting to happen, and I don't want to be part of it."

The third part of the therapy—skill development—involves practical applications. For the angry driver, this might mean practicing safe driving techniques, as an alternative to aggressive driving. In this phase, the therapist might shift the treatment setting out of the office and onto the road.

"Anger has long been a problem for me," writes anger management trainer Melvyn Fein. "Over the years it has cost me a great deal of pain and denied me much happiness" (1993, p. ix). Failing at various efforts to control and constructively express his anger, Fein himself became a clinician and developed an approach to anger disorders. Fein's program, Integrated Anger Management (I.A.M.), adds three more components to Deffenbacher's list:

1. Learning to express anger safely, so that it will not spin out of control
2. Identifying the underlying source of one's anger, such as frustration with injustice or the inability to achieve a valued goal
3. Letting go of unrealistic goals that feed the anger, such as the naive belief that expressing anger will motivate others to "do the right thing"

All the experts agree that the public subscribes to some dangerous myths about anger. On television shows, for example, you can see people attacking and humiliating others, as if the public venting of feelings and the act of revenge will eliminate their anger. In fact, retaliation for a real or imagined wrong is likely to bring only the most fleeting feeling of satisfaction.

It's far more likely that venting one's anger will increase the tendency to become enraged at ever smaller provocations. Solid psychological research indicates that when you are angry with someone, "getting it off your chest" by aggressively confronting or hurting that individual will not neutralize your bad feelings. Instead it will almost certainly intensify them. Thus, retaliation is likely not to end a feud but rather to feul it—a reality obvious throughout human history, filled with wars about pride, power, status, and honor. A saner and safer strategy is to keep your feelings to yourself, at least until the passion of your anger has subsided and you can be more rational about the nature of your real complaint and what might be done to solve the problem (Tavris, 1989, 1995). Often, all it takes to defuse a tense and angry situation is to communicate the facts and your feelings to the person toward whom you feel anger.

CHECK YOUR UNDERSTANDING

1. **RECALL:** People with emotional intelligence
   a. feel no emotions.
   b. are extremely emotionally responsive.
   c. know how to control their emotional responses.
   d. can always deceive a polygrapher.
   e. sense others' feelings.
2. **RECALL:** When lying by giving false information, you are likely to
   a. become more animated in your gesturing.
   b. become more constrained in your gesturing.
   c. control your body more easily than you control your face.
   d. look someone "straight in the eye."
   e. shift your eyes to the left.
3. **RECALL:** "Lie detectors" detect
   a. feelings.
   b. emotion.
   c. motivation.
   d. untruthfulness.
   e. physical arousal.
4. **APPLICATION:** Psychological research suggests that it might be best to handle your feelings of anger toward a friend by
   a. hitting a punching bag.
   b. venting your anger by yelling at your friend.
   c. calmly telling your friend that you feel angry.
   d. doing nothing except "stewing" in your angry feelings.
   e. engaging in other, unrelated activities.
5. **UNDERSTANDING THE CORE CONCEPT:** Research suggests that the ability to control one's emotional responses is
   a. a personality trait that cannot be changed.
   b. largely a matter of hormones.
   c. closely connected to IQ.
   d. a skill that can be learned.
   e. a genetic predisposition.

ANSWERS: 1. c 2. b 3. e 4. c 5. d

MOTIVATION: WHAT MAKES US ACT AS WE DO?

Why do some people climb mountains, while others rob banks or join the Peace Corps? What drives anorectic individuals to starve themselves—sometimes to their deaths? Why do some of us feel a need to achieve, while others seek security? Such questions lie in the domain of the psychology of motivation, which deals with the internal processes that cause us to move toward a goal or away from a situation we judge to be unpleasant. As you will remember, motivation is the complement of emotion. While emotion arouses us physically and mentally, motivation channels that arousal into goal-directed action.

Motivation is the general term for all the processes involved in starting, directing, and maintaining physical and psychological activities. Motivational processes determine which of many possible responses you will select at any moment—although the selection is not always a deliberate, conscious one. Will it be laughing or crying? Fight or flight? Studying or playing? The motivational menu always offers multiple choices. The Core Concept for this section puts it this way:

Motivation takes many forms, but all involve inferred mental processes that select and direct our behavior.

We begin our study of motivation with a look at the ways in which we use the concept of motivation.

How Psychologists Use the Concept of Motivation

Professors may think that students who do poorly on exams are "not well motivated." Sports commentators speculate that winning teams were "hungrier" or "more motivated" than their opponents. Detectives seek to establish a motive in building a case against a criminal suspect. In everyday language, we use the term *motivation* to refer to a variety of responses that seem to arise from a person's internal mental state rather than from the external situation.

Psychologists, too, often need to make inferences about internal processes that select and direct behavior. Such inferences are formalized in the concept of motivation, which psychologists find especially useful in the following circumstances:

CONNECTION: CHAPTER 14

On the other hand, the common mistake of attributing behavior to internal characteristics, rather than the situation, is known as the *fundamental attribution error.*

- *Motivation connects observable behavior to internal states:* When we see someone eating, we may infer that a hunger drive is at work. We must be careful about drawing such inferences too quickly, though, because eating might be caused by something else (e.g., social pressure, the availability of a favorite food, or a desire to gain weight). So a motive, such as hunger, can be identified with confidence only when other influences have been ruled out.
- *Motivation accounts for variability in behavior:* Psychologists use motivational explanations when the variations in people's performances are not obviously due to differences in physical or mental abilities or to differing environmental demands. For example, the intensity of your motivation may explain why you play tennis well one day but poorly another. It also may explain why some people do better than others of comparable skill in competitive situations, such as in a basketball game. Thus, differences in motivation explain differences in the same individual or between individuals.
- *Motivation explains perseverance despite adversity:* Motivation helps us understand why organisms continue to perform reliably even under difficult or variable conditions. Motivation gets you to work on time, even when

Motivation All the processes involved in starting, directing, and maintaining physical and psychological activities.

you had a sleepless night or had to drive through a blizzard. When highly motivated, you persist, even if you realize the chances of success are slim—as does a determined quarterback whose team is down by 20 points in the final quarter.

- *Motives relate biology to behavior:* We are biological organisms with complex internal mechanisms that automatically regulate bodily functions to promote survival. States of deprivation (such as needing fluids) automatically trigger these mechanisms, which then influence bodily functioning (such as feeling thirsty), creating motivational states.

In each of these cases, an internal motivational process channels the organism's energies into a particular pattern of behavior.

The fact that some people do better in competition than others can be explained in part by different degrees of motivation. These men are participating in the international Games for the Disabled.

Types of Motivation

Psychologists often distinguish between motives and drives. They prefer the term **drive** for motivation that is assumed to have a strong biological component and, therefore, plays an important role in survival or reproduction. Hunger and thirst are examples of biological drives. In contrast, many psychologists reserve the term **motive** for urges that are mainly learned, such as the need for achievement or the desire to play video games. Obviously, however, many motivated behaviors—such as eating, drinking, and sexual behavior—can have roots in both biology and learning.

Psychologists also distinguish between *intrinsic* and *extrinsic* motivation. **Intrinsic motivation** comes from within the individual who engages in an activity for its own sake, in the absence of external reward. Leisure activities, such as cycling, kayaking, or playing the guitar, are usually intrinsically motivated. Intrinsic motivation arises from inner qualities, such as personality traits or special interests. On the other hand, **extrinsic motivation** comes from outside the person. It involves behavior aimed at some external consequence, such as money, grades, or praise, rather than at satisfying an internal need.

In addition, motives and drives can arise from either **conscious motivation** or **unconscious motivation.** That is, motivated individuals may or may not be aware of the drives or motives underlying their behavior—much as emotional arousal can occur on a conscious or unconscious level. Freud took this idea a step further, suggesting that the unconscious mind harbors complex motives arising from traumatic experiences and sexual conflicts. Modern-day psychologists, however, stand divided on Freud's teachings (see, for example, Bruner, 1992; Erdelyi, 1992; Greenwald, 1992; Jacoby et al., 1992; Kihlstrom et al., 1992; Loftus & Klinger, 1992).

Theories of Motivation

We have no comprehensive theory that accounts for the whole gamut of human motives and drives. Sex, for example, seems to obey very different motivational rules from those regulating hunger or thirst or regulation of body temperature, even though all are rooted in biology: You can die from lack of food or warmth, but not from lack of sex. Much of the difficulty in explaining diverse types of motivation arises because of our dual nature: We are simultaneously creatures driven by our biology (as when you are ravenous because you haven't eaten all day) and by learning (as when you associate the lunch bell with food). In the following pages, we will look at several theories of motivation, beginning with *instinct theory,* the grandparent of all modern motivational theories.

- **Drive** Biologically instigated motivation.
- **Motive** An internal mechanism that selects and directs behavior. The term *motive* is often used in the narrower sense of a motivational process that is learned, rather than biologically based (as are drives).
- **Intrinsic motivation** The desire to engage in an activity for its own sake, rather than for some external consequence, such as a reward.
- **Extrinsic motivation** The desire to engage in an activity to achieve an external consequence, such as a reward.
- **Conscious motivation** Having the desire to engage in an activity and being aware of the desire.
- **Unconscious motivation** Having a desire to engage in an activity but being consciously unaware of the desire. Freud's psychoanalytic theory emphasized unconscious motivation.

Instinct Theory According to **instinct theory,** organisms are born with a set of biologically based behaviors, called instincts, that generally promote their survival. Instinct accounts reasonably well for regular cycles of animal activity, as seen in salmon that travel thousands of miles back to the stream where they were spawned. Although such instinctive behavior does not depend heavily on learning, experience can often modify the behavior. We see this when bees communicate the location of food to each other, when army ants embark on synchronized hunting expeditions, and when birds use landmarks in their annual migrations.

In recent years, the term *instinct* has migrated from the scientific vocabulary to the speech of everyday life. So we speak casually of "maternal instincts," of an athlete who "instinctively catches the ball," and of a "killer instinct" in a competitive entrepreneur. In fact, we use the term in so many ways that its meaning has become vague and imprecise—a mere label, rather than an explanation for behavior. As a result, the term *instinct* has dropped out of favor among psychologists (Deckers, 2001). Ethologists, who study animal behavior in natural habitats, now prefer the term **fixed-action patterns,** more narrowly defined as unlearned behavior patterns that occur throughout a species and are triggered by identifiable stimuli. Examples of fixed-action patterns include such diverse behaviors as bird migration and dominance displays in baboons.

Do instincts—perhaps in their new guise as fixed-action patterns—explain any part of human behavior? They do seem to account for some responses, such as nursing, that we see in newborns. But we stand on shakier ground when using the term to explain more complex human behaviors. So, while we might speculate that the motivation of a hard-driving executive could involve some basic biological instinct, this explanation is weak, at best. Similarly, it is simplistic to think about sex as an unlearned instinct—as we shall see in a few pages.

Drive Theory The concept of *drive* originated as an alternative to instinct. It was defined as the hypothetical state of energy or tension that moves an organism to meet a biological need (Woodworth, 1918). Thus, an animal that needs water is driven to drink. Likewise, a need for food drives organisms to eat. Thus, in *drive theory,* it's a biological **need** that produces a drive—which, in turn, is seen as an urge or motivated state of tension directed at meeting that need. The drive, then, motivates the animal to act to reduce the drive level, a process called *drive reduction.* You have felt this buildup and release of tension if you have been extremely cold and then felt driven to find shelter.

According to drive theory, the desirable state that organisms seek is a balanced condition called **homeostasis** (Hull, 1943, 1952). Organisms that have a biological imbalance (caused, say, by lack of fluids) are driven to seek a homeostatic balance (by drinking). Similarly, we can understand hunger as an imbalance in the body's energy supply. This imbalance drives an animal that has been deprived of food to eat in order to restore a condition of equilibrium.

Unfortunately for drive theory, the story of motivation has proved not to be that simple. For instance, drive theory cannot explain why, in the absence of any apparent deprivation or drives, organisms act merely to increase stimulation. Thus both humans and animals engage in play—behavior that is satisfying in itself, rather than a means of reducing a drive. And in the laboratory, rats will cross an electrified grid to reach nothing on the other side except a novel environment. Even animals deprived of food and water, when placed in unfamiliar surroundings with plenty of opportunities to eat or drink, may choose to explore instead. Only after they have satisfied their curiosity do they begin to satisfy their hunger and thirst (Berlyne, 1960; Fowler, 1965; Zimbardo & Montgomery, 1957). And, as for human motivation, it is hard to imagine a basic need or a biological drive that could propel people out of airplanes or force them to climb the face of Yosemite's El Capitán. Apparently, for both

■ **Instinct theory** The now-outmoded view that certain behaviors are completely determined by innate factors. The instinct theory was flawed because it overlooked the effects of learning and because it employed instincts merely as labels, rather than as explanations for behavior.

■ **Fixed-action patterns** Genetically based behaviors, seen across a species, that can be set off by a specific stimulus. The concept of fixed-action patterns has replaced the older notion of instinct.

■ **Need** In drive theory, a need is a biological imbalance (such as dehydration) that threatens survival if the need is left unmet. Biological needs are believed to produce drives.

■ **Homeostasis** The body's tendency to maintain a biologically balanced condition, especially with regard to nutrients, water, and temperature.

people and animals, exploring and taking an interest in the world are rewarding experiences in themselves. For these reasons, psychologists have concluded that drive theory does not hold all the answers to motivation. Still, they have been reluctant to abandon the concept of drive, which, as we noted earlier, has come to mean a biologically based motive that plays an important role in survival or reproduction.

Cognitive Theory and Locus of Control We have seen that many of our motives depend more on learning and thinking than on biological drives or instincts. Watching TV, reading a book, listening to music, climbing a mountain—all owe their motivational push to cognitive processes that we have studied earlier in this book. One of the most influential cognitive theories emphasizes the importance of expectations in motivating behavior.

In his cognitive *social-learning theory* (1954), Julian Rotter (pronounced *ROH-ter*) asserted that the likelihood of our selecting a certain behavior (such as studying instead of partying) is determined by two factors: (1) the expectation of attaining a goal (getting a good grade) and (2) the personal value of the goal. But what determines these expectations? Rotter says that they depend largely on our **locus of control,** our belief about our ability to control the events in our lives. If, for example, you believe that studying hard will lead to good grades, you have an *internal locus of control,* and you will behave differently from those who have an *external locus of control* and believe that grades depend on luck or on the teacher's biases. Rotter's theory would also predict that people who exercise, save money, or use seat belts have an internal locus of control. On the other hand, the theory also predicts that those who buy lottery tickets or smoke cigarettes have an external locus of control. Such predictions have been supported by thousands of studies that you can find simply by typing "locus of control" into the PsychInfo database.

Freud's Psychodynamic Theory By contrast with all the other views we have considered, Sigmund Freud taught that motivation comes mainly from the murky depths of the unconscious mind, which he called the *id.* There, he said, lurked two basic desires: *eros,* the desire for sex, and *thanatos,* the aggressive, destructive impulse. Virtually everything we do is based on one or the other of these urges—or the maneuvers that the other parts of the mind use to keep these desires in check. Because these urges are always building, we continually need to find acceptable outlets for our sexual and aggressive needs. Thus, a creative artist is merely finding an acceptable output for the sex drive, while prizefighters and soldiers use their professions as a psychologically safe outlet for their destructive tendencies.

Eros and thanatos are often portrayed as instincts. But it would oversimplify Freud's theory to think of it as just another instinct theory. He wasn't trying to explain the everyday, biologically based behaviors that we find in eating, drinking, mating, nursing, and sleeping. Rather, he was trying to explain the symptoms we find in mental disorders such as phobias or depression.

We will discuss Freud's theory in much more detail when we get to the chapter on personality. Aside from introducing you here to Freud's views on motivation and noting that there is not a great deal of evidence supporting his views, we would like to make one other point. Among the principal theories of motivation discussed in this chapter, Freud's is the only one that takes a developmental approach to motivation. That is, Freud theorized about the ways our motives change from childhood to adulthood. As we mature, our sexual and aggressive desires become less conscious. Meanwhile we develop more and more subtle and sophisticated ways of letting off these two kinds of motivational "steam"—ways that are usually both socially acceptable and acceptable to our conscious minds. For example, according to the Freudian

■ **Locus of control** An individual's sense of where his or her life influences originate–internally or externally.

TABLE 8.2	Theories of Motivation Compared					
Theories	Biological needs	Cognitive needs	Unconscious desires	Developmental changes	Social needs	Self-actualization
Instinct theory *Main idea:* Specific biological mechanisms govern our behaviors.	X					
Drive theory *Main idea:* Needs produce specific drives that motivate behavior until the drive is reduced.	X					
Cognitive theories *Main idea:* Many of our motives are the result of perception and learning, rather than biological processes.		X				
Maslow's theory *Main idea:* Motivation is based on needs, which occur in a priority (hierarchical) order, so more basic needs are met first.	X				X	X
Freud's theory *Main idea:* Motivation stems from *eros* and *thanatos,* but as we mature we gain more control over these urges.			X	X		

perspective, a person with a weight problem may be overeating to satisfy an unconscious self-destructive urge. (See Table 8.2.)

Maslow's Humanistic Theory What happens when you must choose between meeting a biological need and fulfilling a desire based on learning? How do you choose whether to eat, sleep, visit friends, or study? Abraham Maslow (1970) said that you act on your most pressing needs, which occur in a natural *hierarchy,* or order of importance. Unlike the other theories of motivation we have considered, Maslow's humanistic theory attempts to span a wide range of human motivation from biological drives to social motives to creativity. Specifically, Maslow's theory proposes a **hierarchy of needs:** a listing of needs arranged in order of priority (Figure 8.4). The "higher" needs have little influence on our behavior, said Maslow, until the more basic need are fulfilled.

■ **Hierarchy of needs** In Maslow's theory, the notion that needs occur in priority order, with the biological needs as the most basic.

- *Biological needs,* such as hunger and thirst, fall at the base of the hierarchy and must be satisfied before higher needs make themselves felt. When biological needs are pressing, other concerns are put on hold.
- *Safety needs* motivate us to avoid danger, when biological needs are reasonably well satisfied. Note that a hungry animal (with unmet biological needs) may risk its physical safety for food,
until it gets its belly full; then the safety needs take over.
- *Attachment and affiliation needs* energize us when we are no longer concerned about danger. These needs make us want to belong, to affiliate with others, to love, and to be loved.

- *Esteem needs* follow next in the hierarchy. These include the needs to like oneself, to see oneself as competent and effective, and to do what is necessary to earn the respect of oneself and others.
- *Self-actualization* lies at the top of the needs hierarchy, motivating us to seek the fullest development of our creative human potential. Self-actualizing persons are self-aware, self-accepting, socially responsive, spontaneous, and open to novelty and challenge.

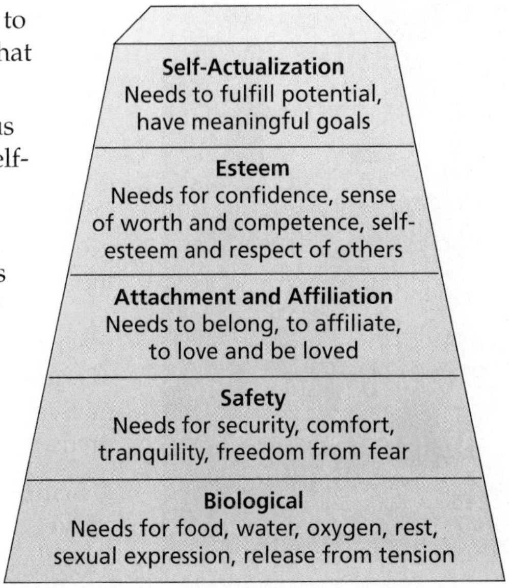

How does Maslow's theory square with observation? It does explain why we may neglect our friends or our career goals in favor of meeting pressing biological needs signaled by pain, thirst, sleepiness, or sexual desire. Yet—in contradiction to Maslow's theory—people frequently neglect their basic biological needs in favor of social ones, as we saw in rescue workers during the terrorist attack on New York. To Maslow's credit, however, he called our attention to the important role of social motivation in our lives. A great body of work now demonstrates this need we have for relationships with others (Baumeister & Leary, 1995; Brehm, 1992; Hatfield & Rapson, 1993; Kelley et al., 1983; Weber & Harvey, 1994a, b).

Self-Actualization
Needs to fulfill potential, have meaningful goals

Esteem
Needs for confidence, sense of worth and competence, self-esteem and respect of others

Attachment and Affiliation
Needs to belong, to affiliate, to love and be loved

Safety
Needs for security, comfort, tranquility, freedom from fear

Biological
Needs for food, water, oxygen, rest, sexual expression, release from tension

● **FIGURE 8.4** Maslow's Hierarchy of Needs

According to Maslow, needs at the lower level of the hierarchy dominate an individual's motivation as long as they are unsatisfied. Once these are adequately satisfied, the higher needs occupy an individual's attention.

Exceptions to Maslow's theory have also been pointed out by cross-cultural psychologists, who see his ideas as applicable only to self-oriented (individualistic) cultures, rather than to group-oriented (collectivistic) cultures. Other critics point out that some important human behaviors do not fit Maslow's hierarchy. It fails to explain, for example, why you might miss a meal when you are absorbed in an interesting book. It fails to explain why sensation seekers, as we saw earlier, would pursue risky interests (such as whitewater kayaking) that override their safety needs. And it fails to explain the behavior of people who deliberately take their own lives. The critics will admit, however, that Maslow's theory was, at least, a step toward a comprehensive theory of motivation.

Overall, Maslow's influence has been greater in the spheres of psychotherapy and education than in motivational research. Business, too, has been especially receptive to Maslow's ideas. Many dollars have been made by consultants using this theory as the basis for seminars on motivating employees. The main idea they have promoted is that humans have an innate need to grow and actualize their highest potentials. Such an upbeat approach was also welcomed by psychologists who had wearied of the negative motivational emphasis on hunger, thirst, anxiety, and fear.

PSYCHOLOGY IN YOUR LIFE: REWARDS CAN (SOMETIMES) SQUELCH MOTIVATION

It's likely that, at some time or another, you have had to take a test in a subject that didn't interest you. If you were a conscientious student, you learned the material anyway in order to get a good grade or, perhaps, to avoid disappointing your parents. Psychologists say that such behavior is extrinsically motivated because it aims at getting an external reward (or avoiding aversive consequences). Teachers often use grades as extrinsic motivators, hoping to get students more involved in their studies. Extrinsic motivation also explains why people take vitamins, marry for money, pay their taxes, and use deodorant.

But what do you suppose would happen if people were given extrinsic rewards (praise, money, or other incentives) for intrinsically motivated behavior—doing things that they already find enjoyable? Would the reward make the activity even more—or less—enjoyable?

● Overjustification occurs when extrinsic rewards for doing something enjoyable take the intrinsic fun out of the activity. It is likely that this person would not enjoy video games as much if he were paid for playing.

Overjustification To find out, psychologists studied two groups of school children who enjoyed drawing pictures (Lepper et al., 1973). One group agreed to draw pictures for a reward certificate, while a control group made drawings without the expectation of reward. Both groups made drawings enthusiastically. Some days later, however, when given the opportunity to draw pictures again, the rewarded children were significantly less enthusiastic about drawing than those who had not been rewarded. In contrast, the group who had received no rewards were actually more interested in drawing than they had been before!

The experimenters concluded that external reinforcement had squelched the internal motivation in the group that had been rewarded. They called this **overjustification.** As a result of overjustification, they reasoned, the children's motivation had changed from intrinsic to extrinsic. Consequently, the children were less interested in making pictures in the absence of reward.

A Justification for Rewards But do rewards always have this effect? Many studies of this issue have been done since the drawing study, and it is now clear that rewards do not always interfere with intrinsic motivation (Covington, 2000; Eisenberger & Cameron, 1996). This is consistent with the fact that many professionals both love their work and get paid for it.

Specifically, the newer research shows that overjustification occurs only when the reward is given without regard for quality of performance. In fact, this is just what happened to the children who were all given certificates for their drawings. The same effect can occur in a business when employees are given year-end bonuses regardless of their work. Happily, we now have proof that rewards can be used effectively to motivate people—if the rewards are given not as a bribe but for a job well done.

What's the practical application of these discoveries? If your child doesn't like to practice the piano, wash the dishes, or do homework, no amount of reward is going to change his or her attitude. On the other hand, if the child enjoys piano practice, feel free to give praise, or a special treat, when the job is well done. Such rewards can make a motivated person even more motivated. Likewise, if you have disinterested employees, don't bother trying to motivate them with pay raises (unless, of course, the reason they're unmotivated is that you are paying them poorly). But impromptu praise, an unexpected certificate, or some other small reward when it is deserved may make good employees even better. The danger of rewards seems to occur when the rewards are extrinsic and they are given without regard to the level of performance.

So, how do you think professors should reward their students?

■ **Overjustification** The process by which extrinsic (external) rewards can sometimes displace internal motivation, as when a child receives money for playing video games.

CHECK YOUR UNDERSTANDING

1. **RECALL:** Psychologists use the concept of motivation in several important ways. Which of the following is *not* among them?
   a. to connect observable behavior to internal states
   b. to account for variability in behavior
   c. to explain perseverance despite adversity
   d. to explain reflexive responses
   e. to relate behavior and internal feelings

2. **RECALL:** One reason the term instinct has dropped out of favor with psychologists is that
   a. human behavior has no genetic basis.
   b. all behavior is learned.
   c. the term became a label for behavior, rather than an explanation for behavior.
   d. instinct applies to animal behavior, but not to human behavior.
   e. instincts are the root of all behavior.

3. **ANALYSIS:** What makes Maslow's theory of motivation different from most other theories?
   a. It deals with biological motives.
   b. It deals with a wide range of motives.
   c. It helps us understand both animal behavior and human behavior.
   d. It deals with both emotion and motivation.
   e. It preceded all other theories.

4. **UNDERSTANDING THE CORE CONCEPT:** Motivation takes many forms, but all involve inferred mental processes that select and direct our behavior. Thus, the psychology of motivation attempts to explain why a certain _______ is selected.
   a. emotion
   b. action
   c. sensation
   d. reward
   e. perception

ANSWERS: 1. d 2. c 3. b 4. b

HOW ARE ACHIEVEMENT, HUNGER, AND SEX ALIKE? DIFFERENT?

Now that we have reviewed some essential motivational concepts and theories, we will shift our focus to three diverse and important motives: achievement, hunger, and sex. We will see how each of these motives differs from the others, not just in the behavior it produces, but in deeper ways as well. The Core Concept expresses the point:

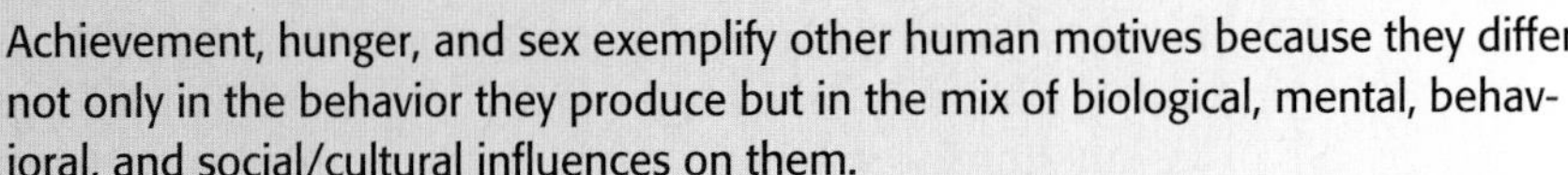

Achievement, hunger, and sex exemplify other human motives because they differ not only in the behavior they produce but in the mix of biological, mental, behavioral, and social/cultural influences on them.

Each of the motives to be discussed in this section differs in its blend of nature and nurture. They also differ in their sensitivity to internal and environmental cues, in the reinforcers that satisfy them, and in the social/cultural influences to which they respond. So far, no one—not even Maslow—has been clever enough to devise a theory that encompasses the whole range of motivations, takes all these factors into account, and still fits the facts.

Recent developments in evolutionary psychology, however, show promise in explaining diverse drives heavily rooted in biology, such as hunger and the sex drive (Buss, 1999, 2001). Evolutionary theory suggests that each motivational mechanism evolved in response to different environmental pressures. And as we will see, the evolutionary perspective has offered some particularly strong and controversial proposals to explain gender differences.

But even with these tools, we still have no complete and comprehensive theory of motivation. For the moment, then, psychologists must be content with an array of specific theories, each of which explains a different motive. The contrasts between hunger, sex, and achievement will make this point clear.

Achievement Motivation

Before you read the caption for Figure 8.5, imagine what might be happening in the picture. The story you tell yourself about the boy and his violin may reveal some of your dominant motives, especially your *need for achievement.* It's a psychological motive that accounts for a wide range of behaviors in our culture. Achievement, of course, can be motivated by a desire for recognition, fame, praise, money, or other extrinsic incentives. But, for most of us, there is an intrinsic satisfaction that comes with meeting a challenge and attaining a goal of personal significance. Whatever its source, the need for achievement is an important source of human motivation.

● **FIGURE 8.5** Alternative Interpretations of a TAT Picture

Story Showing High *n Ach:* The boy has just finished his violin lesson. He's happy at his progress and is beginning to believe that all his sacrifices have been worthwhile. To become a concert violinist, he will have to give up much of his social life and practice for many hours each day. Although he knows he could make more money by going into his father's business, he is more interested in being a great violinist and giving people joy with his music. He renews his personal commitment to do all it takes to make it.

Story Showing Low *n Ach:* The boy is holding his brother's violin and wishes he could play it. But he knows it isn't worth the time, energy, and money for lessons. He feels sorry for his brother, who has given up all the fun things in life to practice, practice, practice. It would be great to wake up one day and be a top-notch musician, but it doesn't happen that way. The reality is boring practice, no fun, and the likelihood that he'll become just another guy playing a musical instrument in a small-town band.

Measuring the Need for Achievement Psychologists Henry Murray and David McClelland pioneered the measurement of achievement motivation with an instrument called the *Thematic Apperception Test (TAT)*. On this test, people are asked to tell stories in response to a series of ambiguous pictures, like the one of the boy with the violin. Each story, Murray and McClelland theorized, represents a *projection* of the respondent's psychological needs. That is, they assumed that the stories would reflect the themes that were psychologically important for the storyteller. From responses to several of these TAT pictures, Murray and McClelland worked out measures of the **need for achievement (*n Ach*),** which they saw as the desire to attain a difficult, but desired, goal.

Now read the caption for Figure 8.5, which shows an example of how a high *n Ach* individual and a low *n Ach* individual might interpret a TAT picture. We these examples in mind, you can judge where your own story fits on a scale from low to high *n Ach*.

What characteristics distinguish people with a high need for achievement? People high in *n Ach* show more persistence on difficult tasks than do people with low achievement needs (Cooper, 1983; French & Thomas, 1958; McClelland, 1987b). In school, those with high *n Ach* tend to get better grades (Raynor, 1970); they also tend to have higher IQ scores (Harris, 2004). In their career paths, they take more competitive jobs (McClelland, 1965), assume more leadership roles, and earn more rapid promotions (Andrews, 1967). As entrepreneurs, those with high *n Ach* become more successful (McClelland, 1987a, 1993).

A Cross-Cultural Perspective on Achievement From a global viewpoint, American psychology's emphasis on achievement motivation may reflect a Western bias. Cross-cultural psychologist Harry Triandis points out that cultures differ in the value they place on achievement motivation. This difference, in turn, involves a fundamental psychological distinction among cultures: their emphasis on *individualism* or *collectivism* (1990). Western cultures, including the United States, Canada, Britain, and Western Europe, emphasize **individualism.** People growing up in these cultures learn to place a high premium on individual achievement (along with the companion concepts of freedom and equality). By contrast, says Triandis, the cultures of Latin America, Asia, Africa, and the Middle East often emphasize **collectivism,** the values of group loyalty and subordination of self to the group. This means that the collectivistic cultures often discourage individual achievement. Even in the collectivist cultures of Japan, Hong Kong, and South Korea, where very high values are placed on doing well in school and business, the expectation is not of achieving individual honors but of bringing honor to the family.

Without a cross-cultural perspective, it would be easy for Americans to jump to the erroneous conclusion that motivation for individual achievement is a "natural" part of the human makeup. But Triandis's insight suggests that this is not true. Rather, collectivist cultures seem to value group achievement over individual achievement. More generally, cross-cultural research tells us that a complete understanding of motives—particularly those that involve learning—must always take cultural influences into account. (See Table 8.3.)

■ **Need for achievement (*n Ach*)** In Murray and McClelland's theory, a mental state that produces a psychological motive to excel or to reach some goal.

■ **Individualism** The view, common in the Euro-American world, that places a high value on individual achievement and distinction.

■ **Collectivism** The view, common in Asia, Africa, Latin America, and the Middle East, that values group loyalty and pride over individual distinction.

TABLE 8.3 A Comparison of Three Motives

Motive	Distinguishing features
Achievement	Primarily a psychological motive; no major biological influences known Operates primarily at a conscious level Affected by the culture's emphasis on individualism or collectivism
Hunger	A biological drive, but also influenced by learning A deficiency motive; aroused by deprivation May involve unconscious processes
Sex	A biological drive, but also influenced by learning Not primarily a deficiency motive May involve unconscious processes

Hunger Motivation

You will survive if you don't achieve, but you will die if you don't eat. Unlike achievement motivation, hunger serves as part of our biological maintenance and survival mechanisms (Rozin, 1996). And if eating were a behavior that had to be entirely learned, many people might starve to death before they mastered its complexities. Instead, when food is available and we are hungry, eating seems to come naturally. But biology isn't the whole story: Hunger motivation and eating behavior have turned out to be far more complex than had originally been thought. So psychologists now incorporate the complexities of hunger and eating into a view we will call the *multiple-systems approach.*

The Multiple-Systems Approach to Hunger Your brain combines hunger-related information of many kinds: your body's energy requirements and nutritional state, your food preferences, food cues in your environment, and cultural demands. For example, your readiness to eat a slice of pizza depends on factors such as how long it has been since you last ate, whether you like pizza, what time of day it is (breakfast?), whether your friends are encouraging you to have a slice, and whether pizza is an acceptable food in your culture. Assembling all these data, the brain sends signals to neural, hormonal, organ, and muscle systems to start or stop food-seeking and eating. Here are the main biological factors involved (see also Figure 8.6):

- Receptors in the brain monitor sugar and fat levels in the blood, sending signals to the *lateral hypothalamus.* If the sugar level in your blood is low, for example, this brain structure sends out signals that produce the feeling of hunger (Nisbett, 1972).
- An internal biological "scale" continually weighs the body's fat stores and informs the central nervous system of the result. Whenever deposits stored in specialized fat cells fall below a certain level, or **set point,** signals trigger eating behavior—a homeostatic process (Keesey & Powley, 1975). Research suggests that one cause of obesity may involve certain chemicals (e.g., the hormone *ghrelin*) that signal hunger and others (e.g., *leptin* and *peptide YY3-36*) that signal when the set point has been reached. Animals lacking leptin, for example, continue to eat even when not hungry (Gura, 2000; Woods et al., 1998).
- Pressure detectors in the stomach signal fullness or a feeling of emptiness. These messages are sent to the brain, where they combine with information about blood nutrients and the status of the body's fat cells.

■ **Set point** Refers to the tendency of the body to maintain a certain level of body fat and body weight.

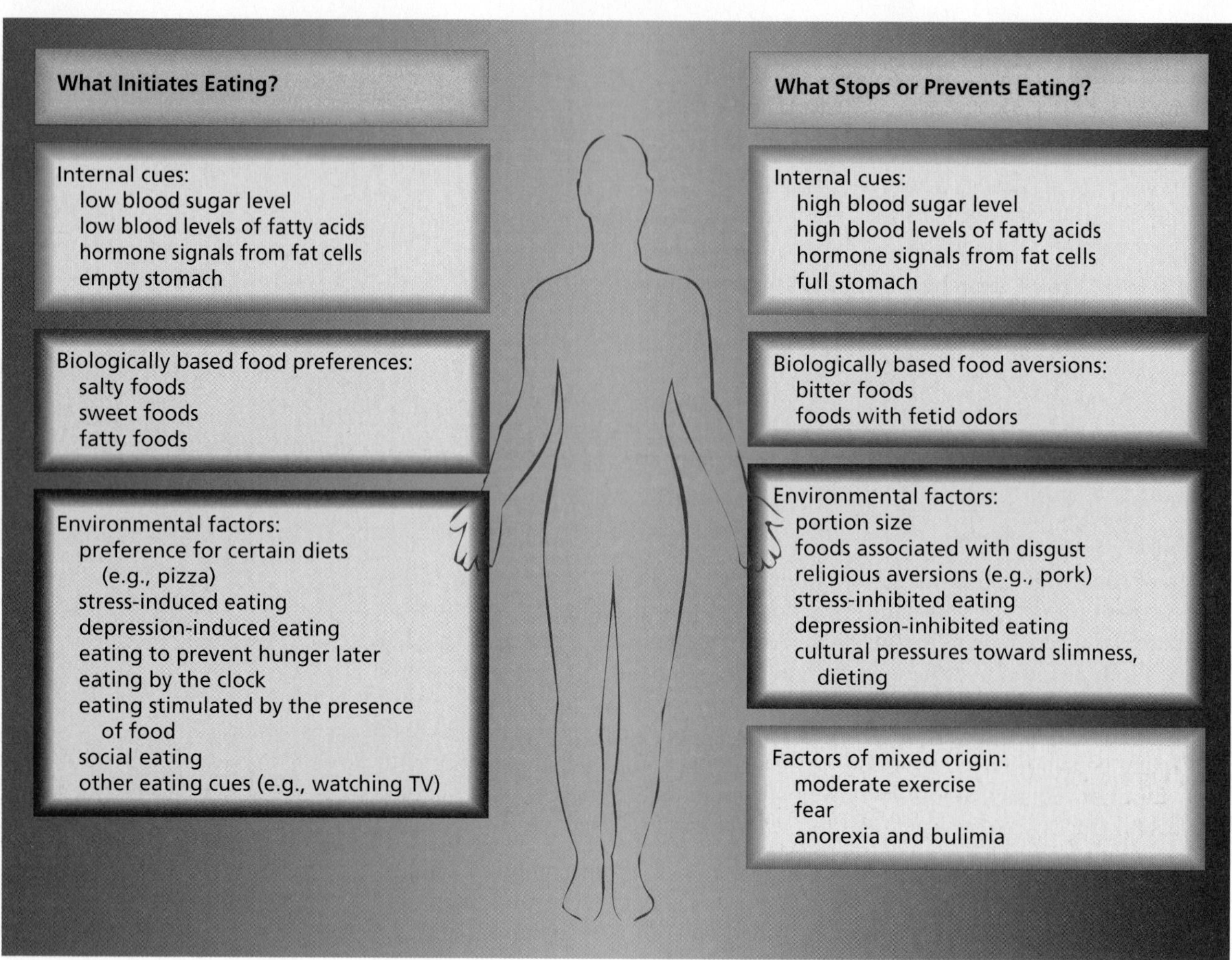
What Initiates Eating?
Internal cues:
low blood sugar level
low blood levels of fatty acids
hormone signals from fat cells
empty stomach
Biologically based food preferences:
salty foods
sweet foods
fatty foods
Environmental factors:
preference for certain diets (e.g., pizza)
stress-induced eating
depression-induced eating
eating to prevent hunger later
eating by the clock
eating stimulated by the presence of food
social eating
other eating cues (e.g., watching TV)
What Stops or Prevents Eating?
Internal cues:
high blood sugar level
high blood levels of fatty acids
hormone signals from fat cells
full stomach
Biologically based food aversions:
bitter foods
foods with fetid odors
Environmental factors:
portion size
foods associated with disgust
religious aversions (e.g., pork)
stress-inhibited eating
depression-inhibited eating
cultural pressures toward slimness, dieting
Factors of mixed origin:
moderate exercise
fear
anorexia and bulimia

● **FIGURE 8.6** Multiple-Systems Model of Hunger and Eating

- Other mechanisms give us preferences for sweet and high-fat foods. These preferences have a biological basis that evolved to steer our ancestors toward the calorie-dense foods that enabled them to survive when food supplies were unpredictable. This tendency has been exploited in modern times by the manufacturers of sweet and fatty snack foods.
- Physical activity also contributes to hunger and satiation. Extreme exercise provokes hunger, but studies show that moderate exercise actually suppresses appetite (Hill & Peters, 1998).

These hunger mechanisms usually work together to keep fat stores and body weight within a narrow range specified by the biological set point. The set point doesn't always keep weight in a desirable range, however. According to the Centers for Disease Control, half of the U.S. population is overweight, and nearly a quarter is clinically obese (Taubes, 1998; Wickelgren, 1998c).

In addition to the biological mechanisms we have been discussing, our emotional state can encourage or discourage eating. For example, both humans and animals refrain from eating when they are fearful. Stress and depression can affect appetite, too, although the effects are variable: Some people respond by eating more, some by eating less.

We also associate certain situations with eating, so we feel hungry regardless of our biological needs. This explains why you may feel hungry when you notice that the clock says it is lunch time. It also explains why you may feel a desire to snack when you watch TV or want a third helping at Thanksgiving dinner.

Likewise, culture can influence hunger and eating. This can be seen in societies, such as the United States, where social norms promote thinness or in Oceania, where larger bodies are often considered more attractive (Newman, 2004). Images of ultrathin fashion models can especially influence women and girls to believe they are "supposed" to look as if they do not eat much—a distorted ideal that has been linked to self-destructive eating disorders (Haller, 1992).

Eating Disorders When a person weighs less than 85% of the desirable weight and still worries about being fat, the likely diagnosis is *anorexia nervosa.* This condition may also be accompanied by *bulimia nervosa,* characterized by periods of binge eating followed by purging measures, which may include vomiting, fasting, or using laxatives. In the United States, these disorders are estimated to occur about 10 times as often in females as in males, with the greatest risk being in adolescent girls and young women.

Much attention has focused on the social pressures on girls and women to look thin. Recent work on anorexia and bulimia, however, has questioned the assumption that social pressures play the dominant role—focusing instead on possible genetic factors (Grice et al., 2002; Kaye et al., 2004; Keel & Klump, 2003). This makes sense from an evolutionary standpoint, says clinical psychologist Shan Guisinger (2003). She points out the hyperactivity often seen in anorexic individuals—as opposed to the lethargy common in most starving persons—suggesting that hyperactivity under conditions of starvation may have been an advantage that motivated the ancestors of modern-day anorectic individuals to leave famine-impoverished environments.

Other scientists, too, have questioned the assumption that anorexia is a "culture-bound" syndrome occurring primarily in the United States and other Western nations—where obesity seems to be a result of overeating. A careful examination of the available data suggests, however, that the disorder is not limited to Western countries. Rather, it occurs in cultures around the world, where the disorder has previously gone unrecognized. Moreover, it is now seen as an extremely serious disorder, posting the highest mortality rate of any recognized mental disorder (Agras et al., 2004).

Weight Control Among Americans, the problem of obesity has grown at an alarming rate since the early 1980s, with the result that 30% of American adults are now classified as obese (Abelson & Kennedy, 2004; Marx, 2003; Newman, 2004; Taubes, 1998; Wickelgren, 1998c). The real problem, of course, is not obesity but the associated health risks for such problems as heart disease, stroke, and diabetes. Worse yet, people in most industrialized nations are following the American lead. Unfortunately, the fundamental causes of this obesity epidemic are not altogether clear. No one in the field of obesity research believes that the condition results from the lack of "will power" (Friedman, 2003). Most experts believe, however, that the causes include lack of exercise, poor diet (including an increasing amount of "junk food"), and genetic factors (Comuzzie & Allison, 1998; Gura, 1998; Hill & Peters, 1998; Levine et al., 1999; Ravussin & Danforth, 1999).

From an evolutionary standpoint, humans are Stone Age creatures adapted to deal with periods of feast and famine. So, we tend to eat more than we need when food is abundant, as a hedge against future periods of starvation. Unfortunately, this Stone Age strategy is not well suited to life in a modern world—where most people in developed countries have no need to expend energy running down game or digging roots. Nor are we well suited to a world of french fries, milkshakes, candy bars, and nachos, which appeal to our

Volumetric thirst A drop in extracellular fluid levels.

Osmotic thirst A drop in intracellular fluid levels.

deeply ingrained tastes for salty, fatty, and sweet foods—which just happen to be calorie-rich (Pinel et al., 2000). In many respects, the typical school or office bears far less resemblance to the environment in which humans evolved than to afeedlot, where animals are fattened with abundant food and little opportunity for exercise.

The problem is not lack of concern. Americans, especially, seem obsessed by weight and weight loss, as a glance at the magazine headlines on the newsstand will show. At any given time, one-third of adult Americans say that they are on some sort of weight-control diet (Callaway, 1987; Gibbs, 1996; Jeffery, 1987).

In spite of all we know about hunger and weight control, no one has yet discovered a weight-loss scheme that really works. Notwithstanding nationally advertised claims, no diet, surgical procedure, drug, or other weight-loss gimmick has ever produced long-term weight loss for a majority of the people who have tried it. It is encouraging to know, however, that some potentially effective weight-control chemicals are being tested as you read this, although it may be several years before any come to market (Campfield et al., 1998; Gura, 2003). In the meantime, the experts suggest that the best pathway to long-term weight control involves maintaining a well-balanced diet and a program of moderate exercise (Institute of Medicine, 2002).

Thirst and Pain Much as hunger can direct behavior that moves us *toward* certain stimuli that will satisfy that hunger, thirst directs activity that moves us *toward* substances that will satisfy that thirst. On a biological level, the thirst drive takes two forms: *volumetric thirst* and *osmotic thirst*. **Volumetric thirst** is caused by a drop in blood plasma levels, as a result of decreased extracellular fluid (fluid outside the cells in your body, as in the blood). **Osmotic thirst** results from water moving through the cell walls of your body and escaping in the form of sweat, urine, feces, mucus, or the moisture in your breath. Your body detects a drop in intracellular fluid and extracellular fluid as the sensation of thirst—a highly motivating condition increases. When we *rehydrate* by drinking water, a sports drink, or some other thirst-quenching fluid, we are replenishing both intracellular and extracellular fluids.

Pain, by contrast with thirst and hunger, usually produces a drive to *avoid* or *remove,* rather than seek, a stimulus. Consider a pin prick, for example. (Pain is like thirst, however, in that the drive produced by pain has survival value.) Although we avoid most painful stimulation when we can, there are some people who actively seek painful stimuli such as those who consume hot peppers or salsa.

Sexual Motivation

You may have noticed that sex is a most unusual drive. Unlike hunger or thirst, arousal of the sex drive is usually pleasurable. Even so, sexually aroused individuals typically seek to reduce the tension by sexual activity. And again unlike hunger and thirst, sex is not a homeostatic drive because it does not return the body to an equilibrium condition. Sexual motivation, however, can serve many other goals, including pleasure, reproduction, and social bonding.

Our cultural lessons and life experiences influence the meaning of sex in our lives.

In one respect, sexual motivation does have a kinship with hunger and thirst: It has its roots in survival. But even in this respect, sex is unique among biological drives because lack of sex poses no threat to the individual's survival. We can't live for long without food or water, but some people live their lives without sexual activity (although others would say that that's not really living!). Sexual motivation involves the survival of the species, not the individual.

All the biological drives—sex included—exert such powerful influences on behavior that they have led to numerous social constraints and taboos, such as prohibitions on eating certain meats or drinking alcohol. In the realm of sexuality, we find extensive culture-specific rules and sanctions involving a wide variety of sexual practices. In fact, all societies regulate sexual activity, but the restrictions vary widely. For example, homosexuality has been historically suppressed in American culture, but it is widely accepted in Polynesian cultures. Even the discussion of sex can become mired in taboo, misinformation, and embarrassment. Scientists who study human sexuality have felt intense social and political pressures, which show no signs of abating in the present. The result is that the scientific understanding of sexuality, which we examine below, has been hard won.

The Scientific Study of Sexuality The first major scientific study of human sexuality was initiated by Alfred Kinsey and his colleagues (1948, 1953) in the mid-20th century, with interviews of some 17,000 Americans concerning their sexual behavior. To a generally shocked public, these researchers revealed that certain behaviors (oral sex, for example) previously considered rare, and even abnormal, were actually quite widespread—or at least reported to be. While Kinsey's data are now over 50 years old, his interviews continue to be considered an important source of information about human sexual behavior, especially since no one else has interviewed such a large and varied sample.

In the 1990s, another large survey of American sexuality was described in *The Social Organization of Sexuality: Sexual Practices in the United States* (Laumann et al., 1994) and in a smaller, more readable companion volume called *Sex in America* (Michael et al., 1994). (See Table 8.4.) This project, known as the National Health and Social Life Survey (NHSLS), involved interviews of 3432 adults, ages 18 to 59. While there were some built-in sources of bias (for example, only English-speaking persons were interviewed), the NHSLS managed to get a remarkable response rate: 79% of those recruited for the survey agreed to participate.

But it was sex researchers William Masters and Virginia Johnson (1966, 1970, 1979) who really broke with tradition and taboo by bringing sex into their laboratory. There they studied sex by directly observing and recording the

TABLE 8.4 Sexual Preferences and Behaviors of Adult Americans

Frequency of intercourse	Not at all	A few times per year	A few times per month	Two or more times per week
Percentage of men	14	16	37	34
Percentage of women	10	18	36	37

Number of sexual partners since age 18	0	1	2–4	5–10	10–20	21+
Percentage of men	3	20	21	23	16	17
Percentage of women	3	31	31	20	6	3

Infidelity while married	
Men	15.1%
Women	2.7%

Sexual orientation	Males	Females
Heterosexual	96.9	98.6
Homosexual	2.0	0.9
Bisexual	0.8	0.5

Source: Adapted from Michael et al., 1994. Table based on survey of 3432 scientifically selected adult respondents.

Sexual response cycle The four-stage sequence of arousal, plateau, orgasm, and resolution occurring in both men and women.

physiological patterns of people engaging in sexual activity of various types, including masturbation and intercourse. By doing so, they discovered not what people *said* about sex (which carries obvious problems of response bias) but how people actually *reacted physically* during sex. In the wake of Masters and Johnson's daring departure from tradition, the study of human sexual behavior has become much more accepted as a legitimate field of scientific inquiry.

Based on their observations, Masters and Johnson described four phases of human sexual responding, which they collectively called the **sexual response cycle** (see Figure 8.7). These are the distinguishing events of each phase:

- In the *excitement phase,* blood vessel changes in the pelvic region cause the clitoris to swell and the penis to become erect. Blood and other fluids also become congested in the testicles and vagina.
- During the *plateau phase,* a maximal level of arousal is reached. Rapid increases occur in heartbeat, respiration, blood pressure, glandular secretions, and muscle tension.
- When they reach the *orgasm phase,* males and females experience a very intense and pleasurable sense of release from the cumulative sexual tension. Orgasm, characterized by rhythmic genital contractions, culminates in ejaculation of semen in men and can involve clitoral and vaginal sensations in women.
- During the *resolution phase,* the body gradually returns to its preexcitement state, as fluids dissipate from the sex organs. At the same time, blood pressure and heart rate, which had increased dramatically, drop to their customary levels. Note how similar men's and women's physical responses are at each phase of the cycle.

Note also that Masters and Johnson focused on physiological arousal and responses. They did not emphasize the psychological aspects of sexuality—for example, emotional responses, sexual desire, or the motivation to seek out a partner or make oneself available for sexual experience. Still, from their biological observations of subjects' sexual behavior, Masters and Johnson drew several significant conclusions:

- Men and women have remarkably similar patterns of biological response, regardless of the source of sexual arousal—whether it be intercourse or masturbation. This is clearly seen in the four phases of the sexual response cycle.
- Although the phases of the sexual response cycle are similar in the two sexes, women tend to respond more slowly but often remain aroused longer.

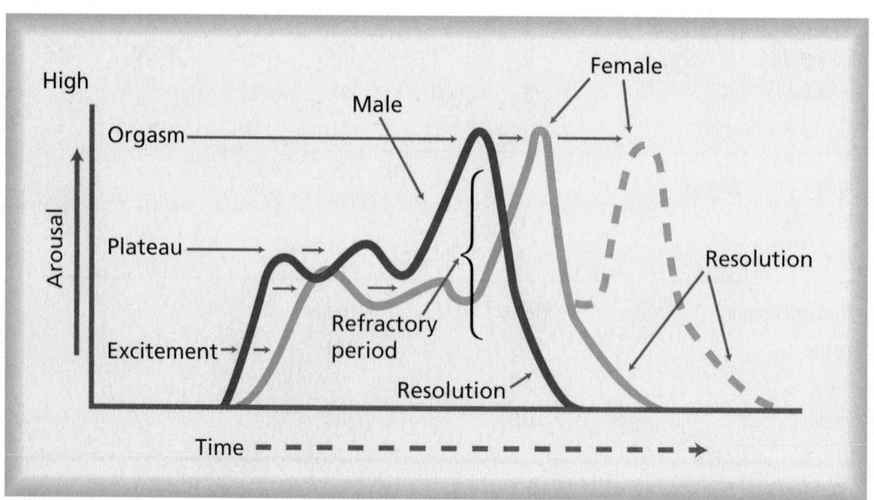
High
Arousal
Orgasm
Plateau
Excitement
Male
Female
Refractory period
Resolution
Resolution
Time

● **FIGURE 8.7** Phases of Human Sexual Response

The phases of sexual response in males and females have similar patterns. The primary differences are in the time it takes for males and females to reach each phase and in the greater likelihood that females will achieve multiple orgasms. (*Source:* From HUMAN SEXUALITIES by S. H. Gagnon. Copyright © 1977 by HarperCollins Publishers, Inc. Reprinted by permission of the publisher.)

- Many women can have multiple orgasms in a short time period; men rarely do.
- Size of the genitals or other physical sex characteristics (such as vagina, breasts, penis) is generally unrelated to any aspect of sexual performance (except, perhaps, attitude about one's sexual capability).

In addition, Masters and Johnson used their discoveries about sexual behavior to develop effective behavioral therapies for a variety of sexual disorders, including male erectile disorder (inability to achieve or maintain an erection), premature ejaculation, and female orgasmic disorder.

CONNECTION: CHAPTER 13

The behavior therapies focus on what people *do,* rather than on what they think or feel. Such treatments are effective for a variety of problems, including phobias and other anxiety disorders.

While Masters and Johnson focused on the physiological side of sex, other researchers have studied the cognitive and social components. Much of this work has emphasized how our sexual lives are influenced by learning. We see this, for example, in responses to cues that provoke sexual arousal.

Sexual Cues Human sexual motivation does not come primarily from the genitals. In fact, the brain is the major human sex organ. What turns you on is what your brain finds sexually arousing, and how you respond is determined both by your inherited sexual tendencies and by what your brain has learned. The sequence of sexual activities that may lead to orgasm can begin with a single unconditioned stimulus—usually touch—but may also include a variety of conditioned stimuli, such as sights, sounds, and smells. In the form of genital caresses, touch is a universal component of sexual foreplay (Ford & Beach, 1951). Virtually any stimulus that becomes associated with genital touch and orgasm can become a conditioned stimulus that motivates sexual activity—whether the stimulus is present physically or only in memory or fantasy.

Visual stimuli can be arousing to both men and women (Murnen & Stockton, 1997). Exactly what a person finds sexually stimulating, however, is often determined by stimuli (such as erotic pictures) and sexual fantasies experienced during masturbation (Storms, 1980, 1981). Inanimate objects, textures, sounds, visual images, odors—any tangible or imagined stimulus—can become the focus of arousal through this conditioned association. For reasons that are poorly understood, some people learn to become aroused only by specific stimuli, such as pain or the sight of undergarments (Rachman, 1966).

Sexual Scripts Generalized sexual arousal can be channeled into specific behaviors (such as kissing or masturbation) that depend on how the individual has learned to think about sexual matters. **Sexual scripts** are socially learned programs of sexual interpretation and responsiveness. How do you know how you are "supposed" to feel when aroused? What do you do when you feel that way? Your culture provides you with many clues from which you develop the sexual scripts for your own behavior. Images from movies and television suggest the importance of kissing and touching, and how to engage in these activities—or at least how beautiful actors and actresses (with many hours of "method" rehearsal) manage to engage in these displays. Advertisements, music videos, and conversations with friends also contribute to many young people's sexual scripts. Unfortunately, while these scripts suggest images and goals, they can provide unreliable and unrealistic information. We assemble aspects of these scripts through social interaction over a lifetime. The attitudes and values embodied in one's sexual scripts define one's general approach to sexuality.

CONNECTION: CHAPTER 7

In general, *scripts* are the expectations we have for events in various situations, such as classrooms, restaurants, traffic jams, and picnics. Scripts often involve social situations–including sexual relationships.

When people have different scripts for an interaction, problems can develop. For example, touch can differ in meaning for men and women. Whether they are mates or coworkers, one person's comment or "friendly touch" may be perceived by the other as a "sexual advance." In fact, research supports the idea that men and women frequently perceive sexually related behaviors differently (U.S. Merit Systems Protection Board, 1995).

- **Sexual scripts** Socially learned ways of responding in sexual situations.

An Evolutionary Perspective on Sexuality While the theory of sexual scripts says that sexual behavior patterns can be learned, the evolutionary perspective looks for the origins of sexual motivation in our genes. Some observers (Archer, 1996; Buss, 1999, 2001; Buss & Schmitt, 1993) argue that genetic pressures have resulted in different mating strategies, and therefore different gender roles, for males and females. (These views are a matter of emphasis: All theorists recognize that both learning and genetics affect our sexual behaviors.)

Biologically speaking, the goal of both sexes is to leave as many offspring as possible. Yet, the potential physical costs of mating differ for males and females (Bjorklund & Shackelford, 1999). As a result, the sexes have evolved different—and sometimes conflicting—mating strategies, say the evolutionary psychologists. Because females can produce only a few children over a lifetime and because they make a huge biological investment in pregnancy and a substantial commitment of time and energy in child rearing, the best sexual strategy for females involves caution in mate selection. For males, however, the costs and benefits are much different because they cannot become pregnant. For males, the theory says, the biggest payoff results from copulating as often as possible with mates who are in prime breeding condition. As a result, men tend to seek young and physically well-developed partners, while females may seek somewhat older mates who can offer resources, status, and protection for offspring. Not incidentally, these agendas often produce conflict, promiscuity, and sexual jealousy.

Although the evolutionary perspective may seem cold and harsh in its view of sexual motivation, it does account for many gender differences in mating behaviors, such as the larger number of sexual partners typically reported by men than women. (See Table 8.4.) Even so, biology does not prohibit the learning of alternative sex roles and scripts, nor does it explain the social and cultural pressures that cast men and women in different roles (Eagly & Wood, 1999). Moreover, it does not explain why most people remain with their mates over extended periods of time (Hazan & Diamond, 2000). A complete understanding of sexual motivation must include both its evolutionary roots and, especially in humans, the many variations that occur through learning.

Motives in Conflict

As we have seen, there are many different motives and many ways in which people's behavior can be influenced. Most of the motives we have covered in this chapter have involved biological processes, however, there are cognitive factors that influence behavior as well. A good way to look at the role of cognition with respect to motives is to look at how we resolve conflicts. There are four primary ways to look at conflict (Miller, 1959): approach–approach conflict, approach–avoidance conflict, avoidance–avoidance conflict, and multiple approach–avoidance conflict.

In **approach–approach conflict,** one must choose between two equally attractive options, such as going to the movies with friends or attending another friend's party. This differs from **approach–avoidance conflict,** in which there are both appealing and negative aspects to the decision you have to make, for example, telling the truth about a friend cheating on a test. (The positive is that in doing so, you would ensure that everyone was graded on their merits; the negative is that you might be afraid that you would lose a friend.) In **avoidance–avoidance conflict,** one has to choose between two equally unattractive options. For example, do you take out the trash or clean up the kitchen? Neither is something you want to do, but you have to do one of them. The last type of conflict is **multiple approach–avoidance conflict.** Here, one has

Approach–approach conflict A conflict in which one must choose between two equally attractive options.

Approach–avoidance conflict A conflict in which there are both appealing and negative aspects to the decision to be made.

Avoidance–avoidance conflict A conflict in which one has to choose between two equally unattractive options.

Multiple approach–avoidance conflict A conflict in which one must choose between options that have both many attractive and many negative aspects.

TABLE 8.5 Motives in Conflict

Motive	Choice
Approach–approach	Two equally attractive options
Approach–avoidance	Equally attracted to and repelled by the same option
Avoidance–avoidance	Two equally unattractive options
Multiple approach–avoidance	Many positive and negative aspects affecting choice among options

to choose between both attractive and negative aspects of the available alternatives. A good example of this is choosing a college. Each one has plusses and minuses, so deciding which one to attend can be very difficult.

PSYCHOLOGY IN YOUR LIFE: THE ORIGINS OF SEXUAL ORIENTATION

Heterosexuality and homosexuality represent two forms of **sexual orientation,** which refers to the direction or object of one's sexual interests. Ever since Alfred Kinsey's first reports, we have known that human sexual orientation is a complex issue. To complicate matters, cross-cultural studies reveal considerable variability in the ways that sexual orientation occurs. In parts of New Guinea, for example, the culture dictates that homosexual behavior is universal among young males, who then switch to a heterosexual orientation when they marry (Money, 1987). Among Americans, estimates put the figure between about 1 and 10%—depending on whether homosexuality is defined as one's primary orientation (see Table 8.4 on p. 331) or, more broadly, as any same-sex erotic behavior during one's lifetime.

What does the available evidence tell us about the origins of sexual orientation? We know several factors that are *not* involved. Speaking biologically, we know that sexual orientation is *not* caused by variations in levels of testosterone in adults, although the issue of testosterone or estrogen influences in the fetus is still an open question (McAnulty & Burnette, 2004). From a social perspective, we also know that certain parenting styles or family configurations do *not* cause children to turn toward heterosexuality or homosexuality (see Bailey et al., 1995; Bell et al., 1981, Golombok & Tasker, 1996; Isay, 1990). Similarly, researchers have come up empty-handed in their attempts to link human sexual orientation to early sexual experiences.

● The origins of sexual orientation are unclear, although some evidence points to biological factors. What is clear is that research on sexual orientation often generates controversy.

A controversial theory proposed by Daryl Bem, however, asserts that we become attracted to the sex that we, as young children, consider most unlike us. Bem has amassed considerable evidence in support of this "exotic becomes erotic" theory (Bem, 1996, 2001). (For an opposing viewpoint, however, see Peplau et al., 1998, who dispute Bem's interpretation of the evidence and argue that his theory does not take women's experiences into account.)

On a more positive note, attempts to identify biological origins of sexual feelings in the genes and the brain have shown some promise. For example, Richard Pillard and Michael Bailey (1991) studied sexual orientation of male identical twins. They discovered that when one twin is homosexual, the chances of the other being homosexual is about 50%—as compared with an incidence of roughly 5 or 6% in the general population. This study also found that the rate drops to 22% for fraternal twins and 11% for adoptive brothers

■ **Sexual orientation** One's erotic attraction toward members of the same sex (a homosexual orientation), the opposite sex (a heterosexual orientation), or both sexes (a bisexual orientation).

of homosexuals. Encouraged by these results, the researchers later studied female twin pairs—with essentially the same results (Bower, 1992).

Looking through a different biological window on sexual orientation, neurobiologist Simon LeVay (1991; LeVay & Hamer, 1995) found that a part of the hypothalamus in the brains of homosexual men was smaller than the same structure in heterosexual men. Critics of LeVay's research warn of confounding factors, arising from the fact that most of his homosexual subjects were AIDS victims and that the disease may have affected the structure under study.

Research in this area remains controversial because of the strong feelings, political issues, and prejudices involved (Herek, 2000). Further, it has attracted scientific criticism because it is correlational—rather than experimental—so the data cannot establish cause and effect with certainty. Moreover, some observers object that gay men and lesbians should not feel pressured to justify their behavior by seeking a biological basis for it (Byne, 1995).

Where does this leave us in our understanding of sexual orientation? Attitudes toward minority forms of sexual orientation, such as homosexuality, differ sharply among cultures around the world, with Americans among the most divided on issues such as gay marriage. Most experts—but not all—would say that the research strongly supports some biological influence on sexual orientation. Just how biology might influence our behavior in the bedroom, however, remains a mystery.

CHECK YOUR UNDERSTANDING

1. **RECALL:** Which of the following is often considered a biological drive?
   a. hunger
   b. safety
   c. *n Ach*
   d. fear
   e. all of the above

2. **RECALL:** How did Murray and McClelland measure *n Ach*?
   a. with a polygraph
   b. with the Thematic Apperception Test
   c. by measuring achievement-related hormones in the blood
   d. by using grade-point averages (GPAs)
   e. by using AP tests

3. **RECALL:** Which motive seems to regulate behavior in order to maintain a certain physical condition in the body, known as a *set point*?
   a. achievement
   b. hunger
   c. sex
   d. homeostasis
   e. all of the above

4. **ANALYSIS:** Which of the following motives would most likely be influenced by living in an individualistic culture versus a collectivist culture?
   a. hunger
   b. thirst
   c. sex
   d. homeostasis
   e. *n Ach*

5. **UNDERSTANDING THE CORE CONCEPT:** In which of the following would biological factors be *least* important in accounting for the motivational differences between individuals?
   a. hunger
   b. thirst
   c. *n Ach*
   d. sex
   e. homeostasis

ANSWERS: 1. a 2. b 3. b 4. e 5. c

KEY QUESTION
?

HOW AND WHY DO WE EXPERIENCE STRESS?

What images come to mind when you hear the word *stress*? Most people think of the pressures in their lives: difficult jobs, unhappy relationships, financial woes, health problems, and final exams. You may have some visceral associations with stress, too: a churning stomach, perspiration, headache, or high blood pressure. And, as we have noted, stress is also linked with physical illness. In fact, stress is associated with many aspects of modern society, and it is also associated with our internal reactions. This is what makes stress a slippery concept.

We use the word *stress* loosely in everyday conversation, referring to a *situation* that confronts us (Lazarus et al., 1985). For example, if your employer or professor has been giving you a difficult time, you may say that you are "under stress," as though you were being squashed by a heavy object. In this conversational sense, stress means an external threat or pressure, an unpleasant event.

However, psychologists use the term in a more specific way: For them, stress is not a situation but a *response.* They see **stress** as referring to the physical and mental changes that occur in response to a challenging or threatening situation (Krantz et al., 1985). It is useful to make a distinction between, on the one hand, stressful stimuli or situations, which we call **stressors,** and, on the other hand, the arousal we call stress or the *stress response.* Thus a stressor is the large, angry man climbing out of the car you just bashed into; stress is your response to that large, angry man: your racing heart, shaky hands, and sudden perspiration. Your demanding boss is the stressor; your upset stomach is part of your stress response.

This section of the chapter begins with a review of the stressors that have drawn the most attention from psychologists. These include everything from petty hassles to relationship problems to terrorist attacks. The Core Concept for this section emphasizes the essentially adaptive nature of the stress response to stressors that vary dramatically in nature and intensity:

CORE CONCEPT

The human stress response to perceived threat activates thoughts, feelings, behaviors, and physiological arousal that normally promote adaptation and survival.

Whether stress comes from the 9/11 disaster, a long illness, or a traffic jam, how we respond depends on an interaction of the same basic elements that you see in Figure 8.8: the stressor, our personal characteristics, the resources we have available. Many of the individual differences seen in responses stem from how we consciously and unconsciously evaluate the stressor and assess our resources for coping with it. Together these two sets of perceptions—identifying the threat and determining how one will cope—make up the process of *cognitive appraisal.*

The stress response has the same components as the emotional response. This means that it has four major components, shown in Figure 8.8. In addition to cognitive appraisal, the stress response includes a physiological response (such as a "knot" in the stomach), subjective feelings (such as fear), and behavior (such as aggression). But stress is not just another emotion. In its most worrisome form, it is an emotional response that people can experience for long periods—which makes the physiological arousal potentially so dangerous. You cannot remain in a state of arousal for months or years without some dire consequences. As we will see, however, cognitive appraisal can be turned to our advantage, as one of the most effective tools for coping with stress.

Stressors, Ancient and Modern

Early humans survived mortal dangers by responding quickly and decisively to potentially lethal attacks by predators or hostile tribes, and some of the ways we respond to stressors in modern times are the result of our ancestors' evolutionary legacy. Modern life, of course, adds some new dangers: demanding jobs, financial worries, and computer crashes. Most recently we have faced the

■ **Stress** A physical and mental response to a challenging or threatening situation.
■ **Stressor** A stressful stimulus, a condition demanding adaptation.

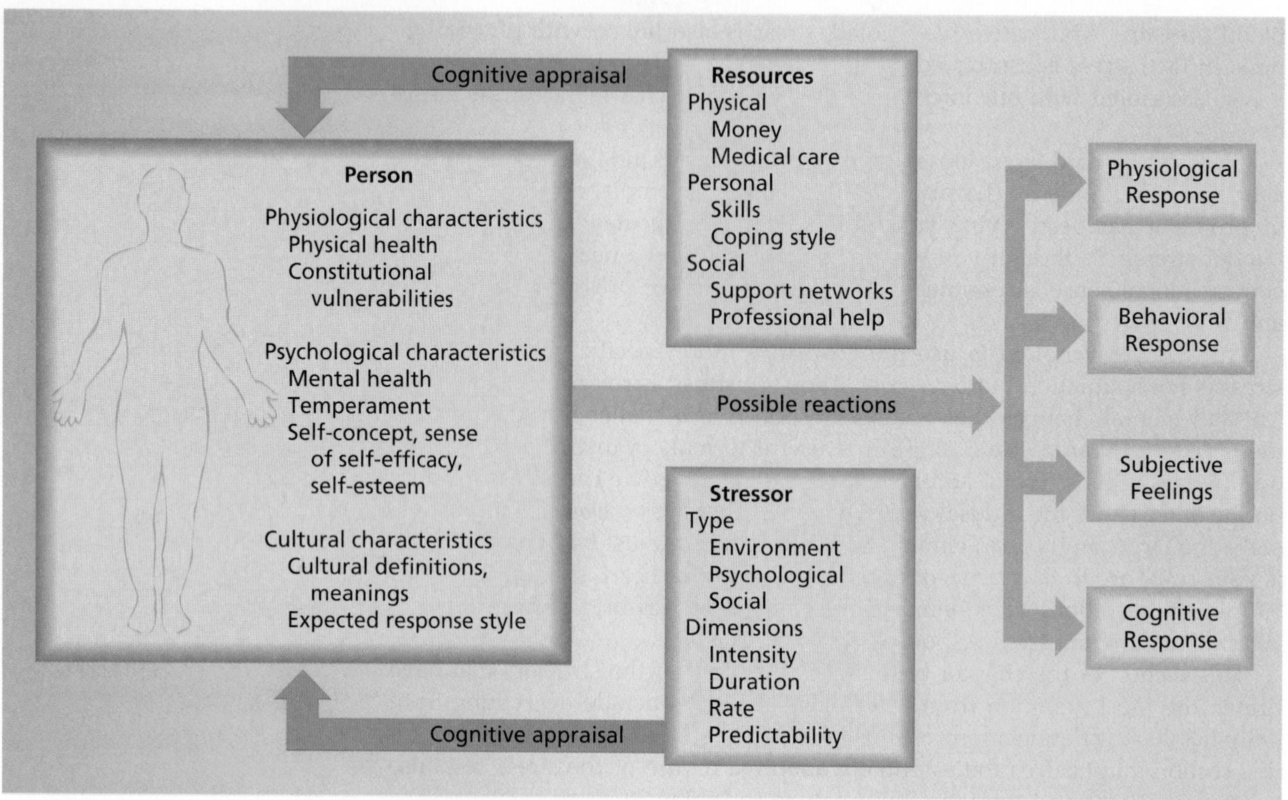
Cognitive appraisal
Resources
Physical
Money
Medical care
Personal
Skills
Coping style
Social
Support networks
Professional help
Person
Physiological characteristics
Physical health
Constitutional vulnerabilities
Psychological characteristics
Mental health
Temperament
Self-concept, sense of self-efficacy, self-esteem
Cultural characteristics
Cultural definitions, meanings
Expected response style
Possible reactions
Stressor
Type
Environment
Psychological
Social
Dimensions
Intensity
Duration
Rate
Predictability
Cognitive appraisal
Physiological Response
Behavioral Response
Subjective Feelings
Cognitive Response

● **FIGURE 8.8** A Model of Stress

Cognitive appraisal of the stress situation interacts with the stressor and the physical, social, and personal resources available for dealing with the stressor. Individuals respond to threats on various levels–physical, behavioral, emotional, and cognitive. Some responses are adaptive, and others are maladaptive or even lethal.

stressors of international terrorism. Yet while we are exposed to new stressors, our stress response reflects the body's millennia-old ability to become quickly aroused to meet emergencies. So, when the power company threatens to cut off your power or your boss criticizes your work, an ancient response pattern occurs, as your muscles tighten, your hormones surge, and you feel an urge to flee or fight. Unfortunately, these old remedies don't always work as well with the new problems.

Some of the serious stressors confronting our ancestors, such as catastrophe or combat, do continue to face us today. Thus we begin our review with a look at primitive threats to survival and the responses that evolved to meet them. Next we contrast sudden, traumatic stressors with more gradual chronic stressors. Finally, we consider stress of adapting to normal life-changing events.

Primitive Stressors Human beings have adapted to an enormous variety of living environments and environmental conditions worldwide, confronting climate extremes, scarce reources, and hostile neighbors. Those who responded most quickly and effectively to danger survived and passed those responsive genes to their offspring; slower or less clever individuals were less likely to survive in the course of human evolution. In all the variety of challenges humans faced, three mortal threats continually demanded quick action: the danger of *starvation, exposure* to the elements, and mortal *attack.* Wherever we have lived, whatever we have done, we always must find a way to feed ourselves, to obtain shelter and protection, and to defend ourselves. While these goals are unmet, there is no time to waste; we must be quick to appraise the problem and solve it. The quicker we are to feel fear or anger and take appropriate action, the better our chances of success and survival.

Responding to Threat Thus we are the descendants of ancestors who were best suited to *fight or flee* when faced with threats to survival. This evolutionary script is retained in our body's automatic responses to frightening or enraging conditions. If someone insults you, your face feels hot and your fists seem to clench by themselves, readying you for a physical contest. Facing a very different sort of "threat": Suppose you are unprepared for class discussion, but the instructor calls on *you*. Your heart races, your knees get wobbly, and you feel the urge to run away. These examples illustrate the two poles of the fight-or-flight response, a sequence of internal processes triggered when a threat is perceived, preparing the organism for either struggle or escape.

An individual's fight-or-flight pattern depends on an innate "program" built into the brain. However, responses to different stressors are also affected by how an individual has *learned* to deal with threat. The built-in impulse to either fight or flee from a stressor can cause you to overreact to a mild problem, one that cannot be solved with either action. You may feel intimidated by an unwanted phone call, but running away won't make the caller stop pursuing you. Or an obnoxious television talk show might upset you, but yelling or throwing the remote control at the set won't change the host's politics. Thus you find what works and what doesn't work and refine your responses to various stressors accordingly.

Since prehistoric times, humans have been individually challenged by loss and catastrophe. As people collected into communities, societal issues and group conflict has also led us to "worry ourselves sick" by anticipating what might go wrong, from minor irritants to major traumas (Sapolsky, 1994). Both traumatic events and chronic stressors continue to challenge us today.

Traumatic Stressors

Catastrophic events such as natural disaster and major terrorist attacks both qualify as types of **traumatic stressors,** situations that threaten your own or others' physical safety, arousing feelings of fear, horror, or helplessness. On a more personal level, the loss of a loved one constitutes a trauma, despite the fact that death and separation are likely to affect everyone at some time. We examine traumatic stress by considering first natural and human-made catastrophes, then the power of personal loss, and finally the complexity of post-traumatic stress.

Catastrophe Stress and loss in the extreme accompany *catastrophic events*—sudden, violent calamities, including both natural disasters, such as the 2004 tsunami in Southeast Asia, and human-made tragedies such as terrorist attacks and warfare. Anyone caught up in such a catastrophic event can lose loved ones or possessions; less obvious is the fact that one's *response* to a catastrophe can have devastating effects on physical and mental health. For example, firefighters and emergency workers find themselves reliving the events in nightmares and in daytime flashbacks.

Studies of catastrophe survivors have taught psychologists how individuals who have undergone such traumas and losses respond to these ordeals (Asarnow et al., 1999; Baum, 1990; Sprang, 1999). Such research is difficult: Ethics prevent psychologists from creating disastrous events in order to study their effects on volunteer subjects. The only way to study these events is to be on the scene after the catastrophe, getting the story from the survivors while it is fresh in their minds.

■ **Traumatic stressor** A situation that threatens one's physical safety, arousing feelings of fear, horror, or helplessness.

● Catastrophic events, like the September 11, 2001, terrorist attack on the World Trade Center, are particularly stressful because they are life threatening, out of our control, and difficult to explain.

Natural disasters are violent, destroying life and property in the affected area. But human-made catastrophes such as massive crime and terrorism have an added dimension of threat, because they are produced intentionally by other people. *Terrorism* has been defined as a type of disaster caused by "human malevolence" with a goal of disrupting society by creating fear and danger (Hall et al., 2002).

Psychological responses to extreme natural and human-caused disasters have been theorized to occur in stages, as victims experience shock, feel intense emotion, and struggle to reorganize their lives (Beigel & Berren, 1985; Horowitz, 1997). Cohen and Ahearn (1980) identified five stages that we pass through:

1. Immediately after the event, victims experience *psychic numbness,* including shock and confusion, and for moments to days cannot comprehend what has happened.
2. During a phase of *automatic action,* victims have little awareness of their own experiences and later show poor recall for what occurred. This phase is worsened by a lack of preparedness, delaying rescue and costing lives.
3. In a third stage of *communal effort,* people pool resources and collaborate, proud of their accomplishments but also weary and aware that they are using up precious energy reserves. Without better planning, many survivors lose hope and initiative for rebuilding their lives.
4. In the fourth phase, survivors may experience a *letdown* as, depleted of energy, they comprehend and feel the tragedy's impact. Public interest and media attention fade, and survivors feel abandoned although the state of emergency continues.
5. An extended final period of *recovery* follows as survivors adapt to the changes created by the disaster. The fabric of the community will change as the natural and business environments are altered. On the national scale after 9/11, survivors demanded to know how the attacks could have happened in the first place—reflecting a basic need to know "why?" and to find meaning in loss.

Stage theories of stress response are useful because they help us to anticipate what survivors will go through and what kinds of assistance they need. To learn from and make sense of catastrophic loss, we formulate *accounts,* narratives that explain what happened and why. These stories help us to explain ourselves to each other; sharing them may even reflect a more general human need to tell our stories and be understood by those close to us (Harvey, 1996; Harvey et al., 1990). When an event is surprising or unpleasant, we are especially likely to formulate explanations (Holtzworth-Munroe & Jacobson, 1985). By confiding our stories to others, we begin to work through the pain of loss (Harvey, 2000; Weber & Harvey, 1994b).

People who undergo any sort of trauma generally become more susceptible to physical illness. The power of stories holds even here, however: Survivors who discuss their experiences in detail with others suffer fewer health problems (Niederhoffer & Pennebaker, 2002; Pennebaker, 1990; Pennebaker & Harber, 1991; Pennebaker et al., 1988, 1989).

Newsworthy events such as natural disasters merit news coverage, broadcasting the sounds and images of others' pain. Viewers are not immune to such programs, however, and may experience a sort of "second-hand" traumatization.

Posttraumatic Stress Individuals who have undergone severe ordeals—rape, combat, beatings, torture—may experience a belated pattern of stress symptoms that can appear months, or even years, after their trauma. In **posttraumatic stress disorder (PTSD),** the individual reexperiences mental and physical responses that accompanied the trauma. Nearly one adult in 12 in the United States has suffered from PTSD at some time in his or her life—a higher rate than many experts had assumed, with symptoms lasting more than 10 years for over one-third of cases. Traumas described by PTSD victims most frequently include having witnessed another person's being killed or badly injured, having lived through a natural disaster, and having survived a life-threatening accident. Men cite more experiences of physical attack, military combat, threat with a weapon, or being held captive or hostage; women cite more experiences of rape, sexual molestation, physical abuse, and neglect during childhood (Bower, 1995a).

CONNECTION: CHAPTER 12

Posttraumatic stress disorder is categorized as an *anxiety disorder,* along with panic, phobic, and obsessive–compulsive disorders.

A little-acknowledged threat to combat soldiers is killing the enemy. Soldiers who had killed in combat were found to suffer higher rates of PTSD than other troops, a special syndrome dubbed *perpetration-induced traumatic stress* (PITS) (MacNair, 1999, 2002). Training and commanding troops to kill, argues one scholar, is a major factor in eventual breakdown. Such trauma can be reduced if individual soldiers are taught mentally to confront the act of killing—an unlikely policy as long as the military itself cannot confront it (Grossman, 1996). Although military authorities "have produced reams of studies on every other aspect of combat trauma—grief, survivor's guilt, fear, and so on—the aftereffects of taking an enemy's life are almost never studied" (Baum, 2004, p. 46).

Victims of posttraumatic stress disorder typically become distracted, disorganized, and experience memory difficulties (Arnsten, 1998). They suffer a psychic numbing to everyday events (a reaction also called *diminished hedonic capacity*). They may also feel alienated from other people. The emotional pain of this reaction can result in various symptoms, such as problems with sleeping, guilt about surviving, difficulty concentrating, and an exaggerated "startle response" (wide-eyed, gasping, surprised behavior displayed when one perceives a sudden threat). Rape survivors, for example, may experience a barrage of psychological aftereffects, including feelings of betrayal by people close to them, anger about having been victimized, and fear of being alone (Baron & Straus, 1985; Cann et al., 1981).

■ **Posttraumatic stress disorder (PTSD)** Delayed stress reaction in which an individual involuntarily reexperiences emotional, cognitive, and behavioral aspects of past trauma.

Posttraumatic stress disorder can also have lasting biological consequences (Arnsten, 1998; Caldwell, 1995; Crowell, 2002; Mukerjee, 1995; Sapolsky, 1998). The brain may undergo physical changes when the stress is extreme in intensity or duration. Stress can cause the brain's hormone-regulating system to develop hair-trigger responsiveness, making the victim of posttraumatic stress overreact to mild stressors or even harmless but surprising stimulation. Based on these clues, researchers are searching for a treatment that might counteract these malfunctioning brain pathways.

● Confiding in others is helpful in working through feelings generated by trauma and loss.

A recent study of the mental health of troops returning from the Middle East showed the overall rate of mental health concerns, including PTSD as well as depression and anxiety, was close to 15%, whereas about twice as many veterans of Vietnam reported nightmares and other PTSD symptoms. Authors of the study found a significant risk of mental health problems, exacerbated because various barriers prevent troops from obtaining care and treatment, "particularly the perception of stigma among those most in need of such care" (Hoge et al., 2004, p. 13). The soldiers with the worst symptoms resist seeking treatment *even after returning home,* for fear it will cause them embarrassment or harassment. Such harsh judgment constitutes a "worst-care scenario" that demands immediate attention (Friedman, 2004, p. 76).

We have seen that stress has many sources, and it can have serious health consequences. Now we will learn how it works on us both biologically and psychologically.

The Physical Stress Response

There is no scientific evidence that mental power alone can alter external physical events, such as the roll of the dice or dealing of cards. The mind can control matter outside our bodies only by controlling our behavior. Mental influence on internal events, however, is another story: Evidence for this internal mind-over-matter effect abounds in psychology and medicine. How this works during stress—to our advantage and disadvantage—is the subject of this section of the chapter, where we look at the physical components of stress.

Firefighters usually report that they love their work, and for some the job is a family tradition. But these individuals' camaraderie and commitment cannot lessen the threat, the risk of injury and death—the stress they experience—when they must answer the alarm, race into harm's way, grieve, and adapt. Even for an experienced firefighter, how does the body respond to the perception of that stressor?

The physical response to nearly any stressor follows the same sequence:

1. An initial arousal
2. A protective behavioral reaction, often taking the form of the fight-or-flight response
3. Internal responses of the autonomic nervous system (ANS) and endocrine system
4. A decrease in the effectiveness of the immune system

As we examine each physical response, note that these are the same processes we reviewed in the experience of emotion in the last chapter. As we have stated, the stress response is a form of emotional response.

Arousal When a stressful situation begins suddenly—as when a professional firefighter first hears the alarm—the stress response is likely to begin with abrupt and intense physiological arousal, including accelerated heart rate, quickened breathing, increased blood pressure, and profuse perspiration. This response involves the same unconscious brain circuits involved in emotional arousal (recall Figure 8.2). This scenario illustrates a case of **acute stress,** a temporary pattern of stressor-activated arousal with a distinct onset and limited duration.

Sometimes, however, arousal may merely fester, or it may grow slowly, as when jealousy first tugs at you, then distracts you, and finally disrupts your life with fear or outrage. This sort of long-term arousal is an example of **chronic stress.** It involves a continuous state of stressful arousal persisting over time, a state in which the demands may be greater than one's resources for dealing with them.

Arousal does us no good if it creates panic and confusion that keep us from responding to a threat. Fortunately, the human brain evolved to coordinate several simultaneous reactions involving the nervous system, the endocrine system, and the muscles. As a result, we are biologically equipped to make efficient and effective responses to changing environmental demands. So, when one perceives an external threat, these bodily mechanisms are set in motion. Many are automatic or reflexive because instant action and extra strength may be required if the organism is to survive. As introduced earlier, this basic pattern of internal activity constitutes the *fight-or-flight response.*

Fight or Flight Imagine you are attending a meeting with your coworkers. Suddenly the department head criticizes you and claims that you have failed to attend to tasks that were really someone else's responsibility. As everyone's eyes quickly turn your way, you feel your face getting hot, your jaw tightening, and your fists clenching. You would not dream of shouting or hitting anyone—but you feel like it.

Now imagine another stressful scenario: You walk into class a few moments late, only to find everyone putting their books and notes away, apparently clearing their desks for a test you did not realize was scheduled for today. Your heart seems to stop, your mouth is dry, and your knees feel weak. Momentarily you consider hurrying back out the door. Why does this feel like a threat? Your life is not really in danger, and running away won't solve your problem. So why do you feel a physical urge to escape?

These two scenarios illustrate the two poles of the **fight-or-flight response,** a sequence of internal processes that prepares the aroused organism for struggle or escape. It occurs when a situation is *interpreted* as threatening. When a fight-or-flight reaction does occur, its pattern depends on how the organism has learned to deal with threat, as well as on an innate fight-or-flight "program" built into the brain. Thus you have an *internal* urge to flee from an unexpected test, but you have *learned* from experience that, sooner or later, you'll have to face the music and make up the missed work—so fleeing does no good and could even worsen your problem.

While the fight-or-flight response can be acquired or influenced by learning, it is essentially an innate reaction operating largely outside consciousness. This autonomic response was first recognized early in the 20th century by physiologist Walter Cannon, whose research revealed that a threat stimulates a sequence of activities in the organism's nerves and glands (Cannon, 1914; 1936). We now know that the amygdala and the hypothalamus control this response by initiating a cascade of events in the autonomic nervous system (ANS), endocrine system, and immune system (Jansen et al., 1995; LeDoux, 1996).

As you recall, the autonomic nervous system (ANS) regulates the activities of our internal organs. When an individual perceives a situation as threatening, the hypothalamus sends an emergency message to the ANS, which sets in motion several bodily reactions to stress. See Figure 8.9 for an account of how

● In cases of acute stress, such as this woman faces as a fire races through her house, the stressful situation arises suddenly, and the stress response begins with abrupt and intense physiological arousal.

CONNECTION: CHAPTER 3

The *autonomic nervous system* operates outside of consciousness and sends messages to the internal organs.

■ **Acute stress** A temporary pattern of stressor-activated arousal with a distinct onset and limited duration.

■ **Chronic stress** Continuous stressful arousal persisting over time.

■ **Fight-or-flight response** Sequence of internal processes preparing an organism for struggle or escape.

● **FIGURE 8.9** Bodily Reactions to Stress

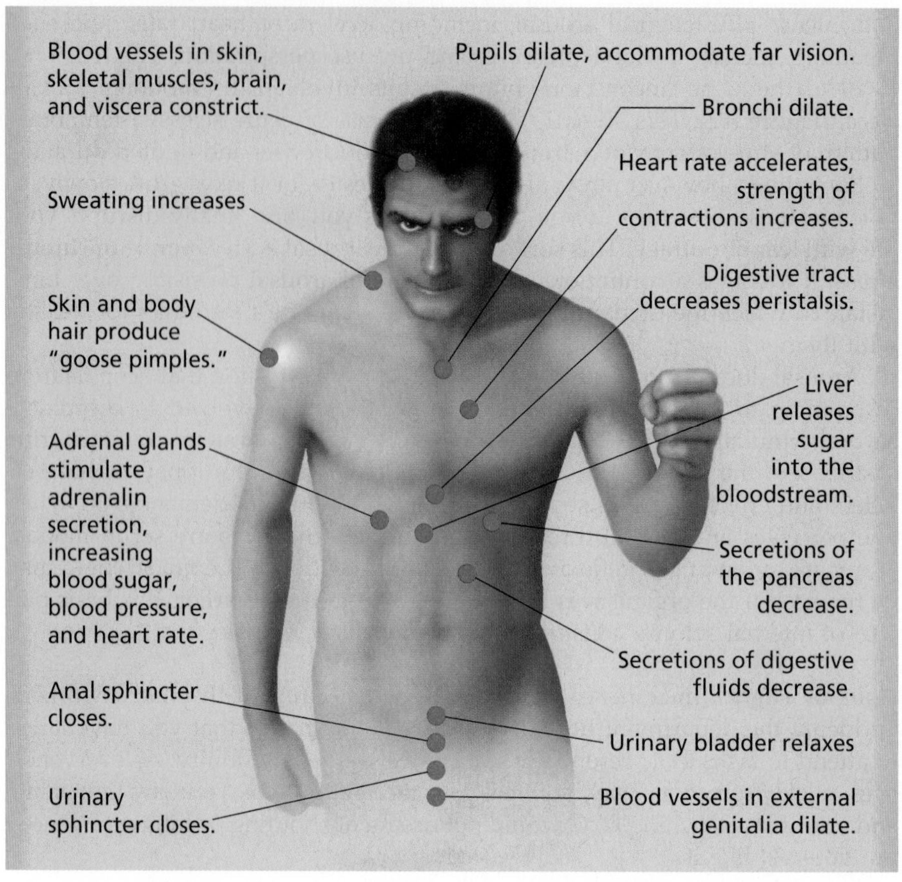
Blood vessels in skin, skeletal muscles, brain, and viscera constrict.
Pupils dilate, accommodate far vision.
Bronchi dilate.
Heart rate accelerates, strength of contractions increases.
Sweating increases
Digestive tract decreases peristalsis.
Skin and body hair produce "goose pimples."
Liver releases sugar into the bloodstream.
Adrenal glands stimulate adrenalin secretion, increasing blood sugar, blood pressure, and heart rate.
Secretions of the pancreas decrease.
Secretions of digestive fluids decrease.
Anal sphincter closes.
Urinary bladder relaxes
Urinary sphincter closes.
Blood vessels in external genitalia dilate.

the body is prepared for an emergency response by the ANS and endocrine system (system of internal glands). The response can be helpful when you need to escape a mudslide, confront a hostile rival, or protect your children from a tsunami, and it served our ancestors well. But it has a cost. Staying physiologically "on guard" against a threat eventually wears down the body's natural defenses. In this way, suffering from frequent stress—or frequently interpreting experiences as stressful—can create a serious health risk: An essentially healthy stress response can become distress.

In sudden emergencies, these automatic responses can be helpful, producing effective action without requiring the time and effort of complex thinking and planning. But, as we have seen, modern living has produced a different class of stressors—*psychosocial stressors*—that act over far longer periods and threaten not our immediate survival but our status, lifestyle, health, or self-respect. In the face of chronic psychological stressors, our emergency response may offer little help—or may even backfire. The automatic response that evolved for quick action and to ensure survival can, when prolonged, exhaust bodily resources and actually *impede* survival. Stress researcher Robert Sapolsky notes that our powerful stress-response system works effectively for short-term emergencies, "but we turn it on for months on end, worrying about mortgages, relationships, and promotions" (1998, p. 7).

While fight-or-flight behaviors—efforts to counterattack or flee—are visible in our behavior, the accompanying autonomic and endocrine responses occur invisibly inside us. Like the fight-or-flight response, these internal responses are adaptive for dealing with acute, life-threatening stressors. But if a stressor is chronic and long-term, or is not a definable external threat, then our internal stress response can become prolonged, producing physical weakness and illness—even death.

The General Adaptation Syndrome

How do victims of stress and persistent negative emotions become candidates for disease? Our understanding of how stress causes illness began in the early 20th century with the work of Canadian endocrinologist Hans Selye (pronounced *SELL-yeh*). In brief, he discovered that different stressors trigger essentially the same systemic reaction, or general physical response, which mobilizes the body's resources to deal with the threat. Moreover, he found, all stressors provoke some attempt at adaptation, or adjustment of the body to the stressor. Because the bodily response was a general rather than a specific adaptation effort, Selye dubbed it the **general adaptation syndrome (GAS).** (See Figure 8.10.) Normally, these responses are helpful, but under chronically stressful conditions, they can lead to heart disease, asthma, headache, gastric ulcers, arthritis, and a variety of other disorders (Carlson, 2004; Friedman & Booth-Kewley, 1988; Salovey et al., 2000).

Selye's model of the GAS describes a three-stage response to any threat, consisting of an *alarm reaction,* a *stage of resistance,* and a *stage of exhaustion* (Hughes et al., 1984; Johnson, 1991; Selye, 1956, 1991).

The Alarm Reaction. In the first stage of stress, the body's warning system activates and begins to mobilize its resources against the stressor. In this **alarm reaction,** the hypothalamus sets off an emergency response in the hormone system, especially in the adrenal glands, through the pathway shown in Figure 8.11. The result is a flood of steroid hormones into the bloodstream—chemicals that support strength and endurance (the reason why some athletes risk dangerous side effects by abusing steroids).

At the same time, the hypothalamus sends emergency messages through the sympathetic division of the autonomic nervous system to internal organs and glands, arousing the body for action. This mechanism probably underlies

■ **General adaptation syndrome (GAS)** Pattern of general physical responses that take essentially the same form in responding to any serious chronic stressor.

■ **Alarm reaction** First stage of the GAS, during which the body mobilizes its resources to cope with a stressor.

Stage 1: Alarm reaction	*Stage 2: Resistance*	*Stage 3: Exhaustion*
General arousal caused by: • increase of adrenal hormones. • reaction of sympathetic nervous system. If stressor is not removed, organism moves to Stage 2.	Arousal subsides because of: • decrease in adrenal output. • counter reaction of parasympathetic nervous system. If stressor is not removed, the organism moves to Stage 3.	General arousal of Stage 1 reappears. Powerful parasympathetic response opposes arousal. If stressor is not removed in time, death occurs.

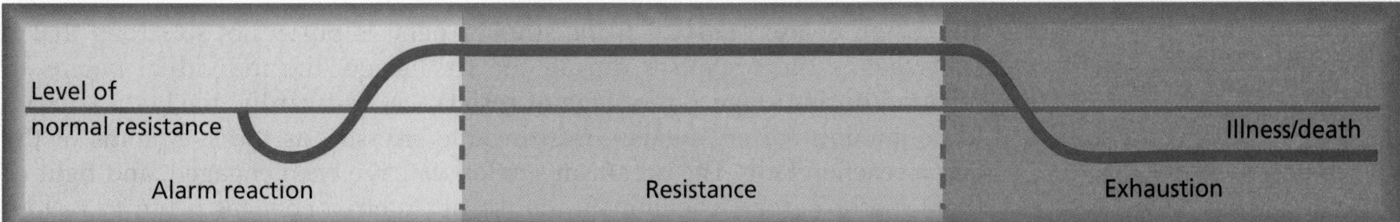
Level of
normal resistance
Illness/death
Alarm reaction
Resistance
Exhaustion

● **FIGURE 8.10** The General Adaptation Syndrome

In Stage 1, the body produces an emergency arousal response to a stressor. Then, in Stage 2, the body adapts to the continuing presence of the stressor. In Stage 3, if the stressor is not reduced, an arousal response begins again even though the body's defenses are depleted–with dangerous results.

● **FIGURE 8.11** The Alarm Reaction Pathway

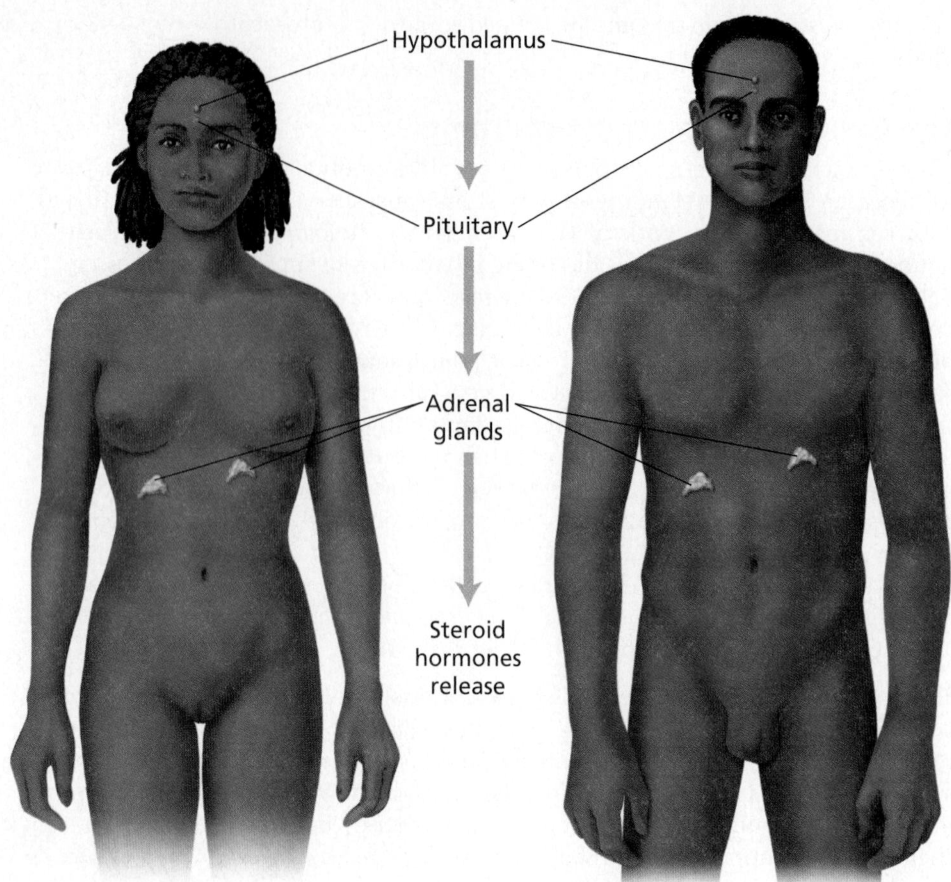
Hypothalamus
Pituitary
Adrenal glands
Steroid hormones release

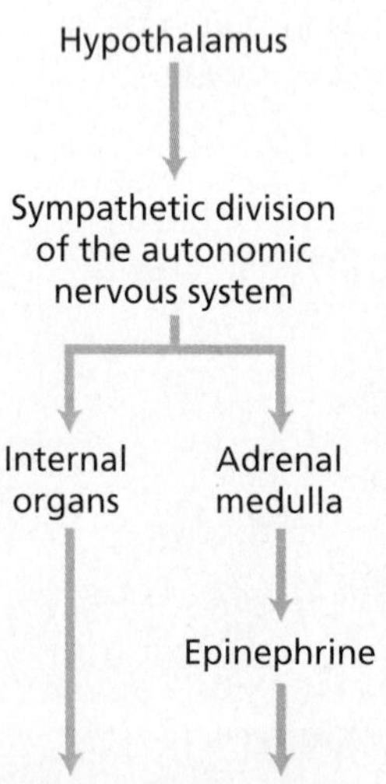
Hypothalamus
Sympathetic division of the autonomic nervous system
Internal organs
Adrenal medulla
Epinephrine
• Heart rate increases.
• Blood pressure increases.
• Blood sugar rises.
• Blood flow to gut decreases.
• Blood flow to heart, brain, and muscles increases.
• Perspiration increases.
• Pupils dilate.

● **FIGURE 8.12** Diagram of Sympathetic Pathways for Responses to Stress

stories of people in emergencies exhibiting amazing strength, speed, or prowess in feats they could not duplicate later. This autonomic response follows the pathways listed in Figure 8.12.

As our Core Concept notes, if the stressor persists over a long period, this initially adaptive alarm reaction can become distress, as it depletes much of the body's energy and defensive resources. It can also cause high blood pressure, deterioration of the immune system, fatty deposits in the blood vessels, bleeding ulcers, and a variety of other symptoms. These reactions also make the stressed person a prime candidate for infections or other diseases. In addition, studies suggest that prolonged or repeated stress may produce long-term changes in the brain that provoke depression (Sapolsky, 1998; Schulkin, 1994). Stress hormones can also damage the brain and interfere with its ability to regenerate neurons, especially in the hippocampus (Gould et al., 1998; Sapolsky, 1998).

The Stage of Resistance. If the stressor persists but is not so strong that it overwhelms the organism during the first stage, the individual begins to rebound during stage 2, the **stage of resistance.** Outwardly, the body appears to be gaining the advantage—resisting the stressor, as the symptoms of the alarm reaction fade. The organism's defenses have been engaged, and fight or flight might reduce or eliminate the threat. Internal changes begin to restore homeostasis. Previously swollen, the adrenal glands now return to normal size and diminish steroid output, although hormone response continues at a lower level, as an internal struggle against the stressor continues.

Surprisingly, the resistance that the body displays in this stage applies only to the *original* stressor, the challenge that first raised the alarm. In his research,

Selye found that if an experimental animal had adapted to one stressor (e.g., electric shock), but a second stressor was introduced (e.g., extreme cold), the animal soon died. The animal's resources were apparently so depleted that it could not mobilize a defense against the new stressor. In general, if a second stressor is introduced in the second stage of the GAS, the organism may not be able to adapt. A tragic human example is found in a soldier who collapses and dies in response to the new stress of a prison camp after surviving months of stressful combat.

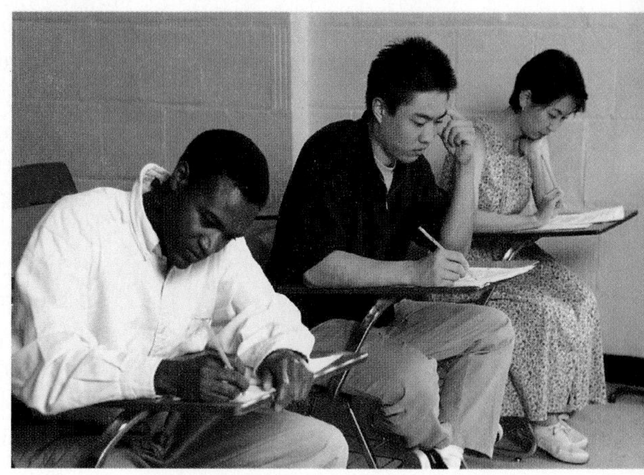

● After responding to one stressor, such as finishing a difficult test, you may find your bodily resources somewhat depleted, leaving you less able to deal with another, unexpected stressor.

Alarm and resistance activities use bodily energy. They reduce the levels of resources available for dealing with additional stressors. The body now requires time and rest to build up its energy reserves again. Imagine yourself as the star of an action movie, pursued by an evil archenemy. You race your old car a long distance to escape your pursuer. But the engine oil was low to begin with, and now it's worse. Just when it seems you have a good lead and can safely pull over to add some oil, another evildoer's vehicle appears in your rear view mirror! You must go on—but how long can you run like this before you burn out your engine?

Now imagine your body responding to a stressful scenario: You've just completed a grueling test; you went without sleep, studying day and night, surviving on junk food and caffeine. Now it's over. You can relax and rest at last. But the phone rings: It's the welcome voice of the love of your life, with an unwelcome note of some negative emotion. Before you can announce the good news that you survived the test, the voice says, "I don't know how to say this, but—look, we have to talk . . ." This is probably not *good* news but may signal serious trouble, even a breakup—definitely a stressor. Already exhausted by your test-taking experience, how will you handle this important conversation? You feel stricken, frightened, and even angry: Why this threat? Why now?

The Stage of Exhaustion. Running on empty, overreacting to a stressor that is "too much," these examples illustrate the experience of physiological *exhaustion.* In Selye's GAS model, if the stage of resistance fails to relieve stress, then the symptoms of the alarm reaction inevitably reappear. This time, however, a powerful autonomic response accompanies them. In this third stage, the **stage of exhaustion,** the autonomic nervous system overcompensates in its attempt to moderate resurging hormone activity. Soon the organism may approach the point of no return: Exhaustion and eventual death overtake it if the stressor is not removed quickly. You can also see why prolonged use of steroids—which are really stress hormones—is dangerous (except under certain medical conditions): They effectively put the body into a state of exhaustion, producing perilous deterioration.

Can you die from the stress of a broken heart? Well, you can certainly get *sick* from a broken heart! And, should it occur in the final stage of the GAS, a broken heart might indeed be fatal.

So we see that Selye's GAS model offers a useful explanation of how stress can lead not only to the initial fight-or-flight reaction but also to chronic and debilitating conditions. In particular, it has enlightened medical and psychological researchers about the connections between stressful experiences and physical ailments. Before we look more closely at the details of the chronic stress response, let's first consider two intriguing alternatives to fight-or-flight: withdrawal and nurturance.

Withdrawal Fight-or-flight is not always possible: An individual can become *entrapped* when efforts to fight or run away are blocked at every turn (Gilbert

■ **Stage of resistance** Second stage of the GAS, during which the body adapts to and uses resources to cope with a stressor.

■ **Stage of exhaustion** Third stage of the GAS, during which the body depletes its resources in responding to an ongoing stressor.

& Gilbert, 2003). Or a stressor maybe just too much for an individual to cope with, and no action is taken at all: The individual might "freeze like a deer in the headlights." Of course, nonhuman animals have not yet evolved to cope with human inventions like automobiles speeding through the countryside. But human beings may also "freeze" in the face of threat. This pattern of adaptation is the *passive fear response,* in which the individual responds to threat by becoming emotionally withdrawn and disengaged (Eisler & Levine, 2002).

For prey species such as rabbits and deer, it makes good biological sense to freeze momentarily, so no sound or movement betrays its location to a predator. For humans, however, withdrawing from others cannot hide us from emotional stressors, yet it can be protective by discouraging unwanted contact. This response can be learned, but biology may also predispose some individuals to passivity—including reduced activity and movement, a lower rate of metabolism, and slowing of the heart rate. Either way, regular reliance on passivity produces a *general inhibition syndrome (GIS)* of withdrawal rather than active response to stress. The GIS is more likely when an organism perceives itself to be helpless and defenseless in the presence of danger (Hamilton, 1989). The "freeze" pattern may also be a symptom of anxiety, major depression, and other mental disorders.

Tend and Befriend We have seen that fight and flight are alternative reactions to stress and that passivity or withdrawal represents another possibility. But there is yet another—which has only recently been recognized.

Psychologist Shelley Taylor noticed that the fight-or-flight model was developed by male theorists doing research with male subjects—male rats, mice, and humans. But, she suggests, fear and aggression may characterize the responses of males more than those of females (Taylor, 2003; Taylor et al., 2000). Taylor has proposed an alternative **tend-and-befriend** model of stress response that may better explain the behavior of females in response to threats to themselves and their offspring. This theory argues that because females are the primary caretakers of offspring, priority must be given to protecting the survival of the young. Aggression ("fight") can cause injury to oneself or one's children; escape ("flight") leaves children defenseless. Neither response promotes adaptation and survival from the female caretaker's point of view (Volpe, 2004).

The tend-and-befriend model proposes that females are biologically predisposed—through brain and hormonal activity—to respond to threat by nurturing and protecting their offspring and seeking social support (Eisler & Levine, 2002; Ennis et al., 2001; Taylor et al., 2000). This pattern, also called the *bonding response,* is common to all female mammals—part of the caregiving pattern that is necessary for infant attachment to develop.

CONNECTION: CHAPTER 9

Infants apparently have an inborn need for *attachment*.

One study in support of the tend-and-befriend model examined men's and women's hormonal changes and self-reports prior to an important examination. While reported anxiety levels did not differ, men had significantly higher levels of cortisol excretion than women—an important steroid in the fight-or-flight response (Ennis et al., 2001). In times of crisis, a more adaptive response for a woman may be to tend the children and befriend others who can provide strength in numbers to insure adaptation and survival of her offspring. There is also evidence that support providers benefit, too, as seen in a lower mortality rate for older adults who give help and emotional support to friends, relatives, and neighbors (Brown et al., 2003).

■ **Tend-and-befriend model** Stress response model proposing that females are biologically predisposed to respond to threat by nurturing and protecting offspring and seeking social support.

The picture emerging from these complementary responses to stressful situations—fight-or-flight, passivity, and tend-and-befriend—is of a more complex stress response that works both to defend and to nurture, promoting the survival not only of the individual but also of offspring, family, and community. Thus, we can see that the hormonal systems and brain processes have evolved to enable both self-protection and reaching out to others in times of danger (Pitman, 2003). Tending-and-befriending powerfully complements the fight-or-flight pattern, together accounting for the survival of not only individuals but relationships and communities.

Stress and the Immune System

Originally, Selye's research examined only the effects of various *physical* stressors on animals' bodily responses. Since that time, further research has revealed how *mental* processes, such as perception and worry, also affect one's health and resources. We now know that any threat or stressor has similar effects—and one of the most interesting is the effect of stress on the **immune system,** the body's elaborate set of physical defenses against disease. Research has shown, for example, that the stress of loss that occurs when relationships end in death or divorce can produce both depression and *immunosuppression* (impairment in the function of the immune system), leaving people more vulnerable to disease (Cohen & Syme, 1985; Kiecolt-Glaser & Glaser, 1987, 2001).

Obviously, the immune system can be important to both our physical and our mental health, so the connection between stress and the immune system deserves a closer look. This connection involves the discovery of links between thought processes and brain function. Together these connections define a field known as **psychoneuroimmunology** (Ader & Cohen, 1993; Maier et al., 1994; Solvason et al., 1988).

The human immune response, which evolved to respond to short-term stressors, may react to chronic stressors by breaking down and turning on itself (Segerstrom & Miller, 2004). Thus, a person who faces, for example, the long-term stress of caring for a parent with Alzheimer's disease runs the risk of dangerous immunosuppression—which increases vulnerability to physical disease. Ironically, immune function can also be accompanied by less serious problems that we *interpret* as stressors. When next you feel upset over seemingly uncontrollable events or possible future problems, such as grades, career choices, or relationships, consider the signals you are sending to your brain and immune system. You may literally be worrying yourself sick. (Which, of course, can be just one more thing to worry about, if you are a chronic worrier!)

How do mental processes affect the immune system? The central nervous system and immune systems maintain a communication "loop" in response to stress, injury, or infection—a cold virus, for example (Maier & Watkins, 1999). In response to a stressor, the brain sends messages to the autonomic nervous system and endocrine system, which have links to organs that produce the immune response. (Components of the immune system include the blood, bone marrow, the liver, and the thymus gland.) The brain then receives feedback from the immune system via neural and endocrine pathways (Maier & Watkins, 2000). Among the chemical messengers shuttling between the brain and the immune system are proteins known as **cytokines.** After these hormonelike chemicals alert the brain to distress in the body, the brain releases its own cytokines to reduce energy output, causing symptoms like fever and listlessness—responses that usually help fight disease but can sometimes get out of control (DeAngelis, 2002a). In addition to tiredness, cytokines may produce feelings of depression, involving a spiral of negative emotion and thought. Such a response can prolong stress and illness (National Public Radio, 2004a).

One of the main factors that determine whether an immune reaction will harm rather than support health is the nature of the stressor (Pert, 1997). Many physical stressors, such as strenuous exercise or an attack by an aggressive animal, begin and end abruptly. These *acute* stressors trigger *natural immunity*

■ **Immune system** Bodily organs and responses that protect the body from foreign substances and threats.

■ **Psychoneuroimmunology** Multidisciplinary field that studies the influence of mental states on the immune system.

■ **Cytokines** Hormonelike chemicals facilitating communication between brain and immune system.

● A basketball coach displays some Type A behaviors.

responses, which help reduce the risk of injury. In contrast, *chronic* psychological stressors—a difficult marriage, a bad supervisor, an unfair professor—emerge gradually, last a long time, and are not readily solved with fight or flight or with an immune response. There is no physical enemy to battle, no safe haven to seek—no quick fix. Bodily responses become maladaptive, the body becomes more vulnerable to infection and injury, and eventually immune disorders can develop. This immunosuppression, a diminished effectiveness of the immune response, entails serious health risks.

In fact, many chronic stressors are conditions that challenge our emotional well-being or social status. We have seen that such conditions can cause physical disease just as surely as can viruses, bacteria, and physical trauma. Not surprisingly, then, it has been psychology rather than medicine that has had the most to say about the ways people cope with stress, both successfully and unsuccessfully.

Type A and Type B Patterns Cardiologists Meyer Friedman and Ray Rosenman (1974) hired an upholsterer to repair the furnishings in their waiting room. When the upholsterer pointed out that for most of the chairs, it was the front edges of the seats that showed unusually high wear, the two doctors realized that their patients' heart problems might be related to a certain style of coping with stress. It was as if these heart patients were always "on the edge of their seats." When the patients were interviewed about their habits, their behaviors revealed a striking pattern of impatience, competitiveness, aggressiveness, and hostility—all stress-related responses. Many also admitted they were notorious workaholics. Friedman and Rosenman later found this collection of attitudes and behaviors predictive of heart disease, dubbing it the **Type A** pattern. In fact, the Type A individual had twice as much risk of heart disease as the **Type B,** an individual who takes a relaxed approach to life (Matthews, 1982).

While the speed, perfectionism, and time-urgency of Type A's are valued in our competitive society and may promote success in professional and social life, there is a price to pay. Type A businessmen are stricken with coronary heart disease more than twice as often as men in the general population (Friedman & Rosenman, 1974; Jenkins, 1976); Type A's are at greater risk for all forms of cardiovascular disease, including heart attack and stroke (Dembroski et al., 1978; Dembroski & Costa, 1987; Haynes & Feinleib, 1980). Besides cardiovascular risks, other illnesses have been linked with Type A habits: allergies, head colds, headaches, stomach disorders, and mononucleosis (Suls & Marco, 1990; Suls & Sanders, 1988). In the long run, the "successful" Type A style can actually be dysfunctional, unhealthy, and self-defeating.

A tendency toward anger and hostility is suspected to be the riskiest component of the Type A pattern (Clay, 2001; Whiteman & Fowkes, 1997). It is reasonable to feel irritated when a slow-moving vehicle blocks you in traffic, but feeling enraged is irrational and dangerous. Likewise, the Type A's perfectionism has been linked to anxiety (about reaching impossible goals) and depression (from failing to reach them) (Joiner & Schmidt, 1995). How does the Type A behavior pattern get translated into a heart attack or other physical disease? The details are not yet clear, but Friedman and Ulmer (1984) found that as deadlines approached for one group of working subjects, blood tests showed increased cholesterol and clotting factors—similar to the alarm reaction of Selye's general adaptation syndrome.

The majority of us have personality patterns that do not fit either of these extremes. However, understanding the link between Type A behavior and heart disease can help in developing more effective disease prevention. One study showed heart attack survivors given stress-management training had

■ **Type A** Behavior pattern characterized intense, angry, competitive, or perfectionistic responses to challenging situations.

■ **Type B** Behavior pattern characterized by relaxed, unstressed approach to life.

half as many heart attacks in the next three years as a control group who had received no such training (Friedman & Ulmer, 1984). The researchers concluded, "No drug, food, or exercise program ever devised, not even a coronary bypass surgical program, could match the protection against recurrent heart attacks" afforded by learning to manage stress (p. 141).

While such reports have caused a stir among health professions and the press, the last line has not yet been written about the link between personality and disease (Lesperance & Frasure-Smith, 1996). At this moment, it appears that those who are most at risk may be the ones who are depressed, those who display lots of anger, and (paradoxically) those who *suppress* their negative emotions (Clay, 2001; Friedman et al., 1994; Whiteman & Fowkes, 1997; Wright, 1988).

Learned Helplessness Earlier we examined an alternative to the fight-or-flight response to stress, which often produces a retreat to passivity or fear. Anyone might freeze at some point in life, but what if such inhibition became a chronic pattern? To illustrate, imagine a child who has grown up in a dysfunctional or abusive family—a child who received no emotional or intellectual support. All his life he has been told how "dumb" he is, and when he gets to school, he stumbles on his initial attempts with words and numbers. The teacher gives him poor grades; the other kids make fun of him. After only a few more such attempts he gives up permanently. This passive resignation following recurring failure or punishment is termed **learned helplessness.**

● In hospitals and nursing homes, patients may learn to feel helpless, because they cannot make decisions or exert control over their own lives.

Evidence of learned helplessness originally came from animal studies performed by Martin Seligman and his colleagues. This work showed that dogs receiving inescapable electric shocks soon gave up their attempts to avoid the punishment and passively resigned themselves to their fate (Seligman, 1975, 1991; Seligman & Maier, 1967). Later, when given the opportunity to escape, the dogs typically did nothing but whimper and take the shock. In contrast, a control group of dogs that had not been subjected to previous punishment were quick to escape. Seligman concluded that the experimental group of animals had already learned that nothing they did mattered or altered the consequences, so they "gave up and lay down" (Seligman, 1991, p. 23) and passively accepted their fate (Seligman & Maier, 1967).

An experiment by Donald Hiroto (1974) employed human subjects in a variation of Seligman's dog research. Students were placed in a very noisy room, but some quickly found a way to turn off the noise; for others the noise controls did not work. When the subjects were placed in a new room and afflicted with a different irritating noise, those who had successfully turned off the noise in the previous room quickly found the simple solution in the second room. In contrast, those who had failed to shut off the noise earlier just sat in the new room, making no effort to stop the latest stressor. They had already learned to be helpless. Seligman and other scholars see symptoms of the same learned helplessness syndrome in human populations, such as abused and discouraged children, battered wives, prisoners of war, depressed patients—and some college students in introductory psychology (Finamore, 2000; Overmier, 2002; Seligman, 1975, 1998; Yee et al., 2003).

In nursing homes and hospitals, too, patients may learn to feel and act helpless (Baltes, 1995; Buie, 1988). Some nursing homes caring for large numbers of residents may not encourage patients to make decisions or take control of their lives. Such independence takes too much staff time—and time is seen as money. So residents are awakened, fed, bathed, toileted, cached in front of television sets, and cycled back to bed, on a routine that offers little variety or choice. But such treatment robs patients of individual responsibility and makes them seem incapable of even the simplest tasks.

■ **Learned helplessness** Pattern of failure to respond to noxious stimuli after an organism learns its responses are ineffective.

But what do you suppose would happen if nursing-home patients were given more control over their lives? Researchers Judith Rodin and Ellen Langer arranged for one group of elderly patients to make more choices about day-to-day events, such as meals and activities. For a control group the staff took full charge of their care, as usual. After 18 months, the "more responsible" residents were more active and alert and reported a more positive outlook than the controls. That outcome was predicted—but there was an even more intriguing result. During the follow-up period, 25% of the control group died, while death claimed only 15% of the group given increased responsibility (Rodin, 1986). Other research has extended the conclusion that a sense of personal control and mastery can alleviate learned helplessness and improve the quality of life in a broad range of institutional settings, including hospitals, prisons, and schools (Faulkner, 2001; Schill & Marcus, 1998; Sommer, 2000; Zarit & Pearlin, 2003).

PSYCHOLOGY IN YOUR LIFE: DEVELOPING RESILIENCE

Perhaps you have already survived adversity in your life and recognize in yourself some of the qualities that enabled you to bounce back from adversity. If not, you probably feel grateful not to have faced such pain or difficulty. But if you were to face major obstacles in life, how could you begin now to develop greater resilience?

Robert Brooks and Sam Goldstein (2004) list number of processes as part of experiencing the *resilient mindset,* including:

- Feeling in control of your life
- Communicating and interacting effectively with others
- Establishing realistic goals and expectations
- Learning from both successes and failures
- Feeling empathy and compassion for others
- Feeling special (but not self-centered)

While a mindset sounds "set" or inflexible, Brooks and Goldstein note that *"mindsets can be changed"* (2003, p. 3). To that end, they offer a workbook to help you review the specific attitudes, habits, and experiences that contribute to your present level of resilience, with suggestions for making the changes you need to make. Here are several questions to ask yourself (adapted from Brooks & Goldstein, 2004). Review your answers and identify one or two changes you might begin to undertake right away. Make achieving greater resilience one of those goals about which to be realistic right from the start!

1. Identify a self-defeating behavior you would like to change. What can you change about the way you think that will help you make this change?
2. List several sources of meaning and energy in your life. How do these help you to overcome setbacks?
3. What are some differences between how you would like others to see you, and how you see yourself? How can you close the gap in order to be as you would like others to see you?
4. Do you make mistakes that prevent you from communicating well with others? What could you do to make these mistakes less frequently?
5. Describe your ideal self. Which ideal traits are least like your present self? In what ways are you already closest to your ideal self?

Remember that the goal of this and other self-review exercises is to change behavior in order to become healthier and more resilient—not to change things about yourself that you believe in and value. By learning about other resilient people—reading about them or listening to people you probably already know—you will identify the most realistic goals for this effort and the best ways to meet those goals.

EMOTION AND MOTIVATION: THE STATE OF THE ART

Recent advances in neuroscience have produced deep insights into our emotions. Long neglected by behaviorists and purely cognitive psychologists, emotions can now be seen as vital components of our thought processes—even those we once thought of as purely rational. Yet, many details of emotion remain unclear, particularly the details of the brain's emotional circuitry. Another major area that cries out for new research involves ways of treating emotional disorders, such as depression and various anxiety-related disorders, which represent major health problems all over the world. And, while we're at it, we also need effective ways of helping people develop the "emotional intelligence" needed to control anger and other impulsive behavior.

As for motivation, the basic neural processes have received relatively little attention—compared to the explosion in research in emotion in the past decade. The state of the art is a somewhat detailed understanding of individual motives, but only a fragmentary "big picture" of how diverse motives, such as hunger, sexuality, and achievement, go together. Thus, motivation is a field of psychology that is ripe for a revolution.

USING PSYCHOLOGY TO LEARN PSYCHOLOGY

Motivating Yourself

The world's greatest achievements in music, art, science, business, and countless other pursuits often stem from the intrinsic motivation of people pursuing ideas in which they are deeply interested. You achieve this state of mind when focusing intently on some problem or activity that makes you lose track of time and become oblivious to events around you. Psychologist Mihaly Csikszentmihalyi calls this **flow** (1990, 1998).

Although some people turn to drugs or alcohol to experience an artificial feeling of flow, meaningful work produces more satisfying and more sustained flow experiences. In fact, one type of flow experience identified by Csikszentmihalyi (1990) is very similar to the goal of *n Ach* as identified by McClelland (1987b), namely the pleasure of mastering a challenging task.

■ **Flow** In Csikszentmihalyi's theory, an intense focus on an activity, accompanied by increased creativity and near-ecstatic feelings. Flow involves intrinsic motivation.

What is the link with studying and learning? If you find yourself lacking in motivation to learn the material for some class, the extrinsic promise of grades may not be enough to prod you to study. You may, however, be able to trick yourself into developing intrinsic motivation and flow by posing this question: What do people who are specialists in this field find interesting? Among other things, the experts are fascinated by an unsolved mystery, a theoretical dispute, or the possibility of an exciting practical application. A psychologist, for example, might wonder: "What motivates violent behavior?" Or, "How can we increase people's motivation to achieve?" Once you find such an issue, try to find out what solutions have been proposed. In this way, you will share the mind set of those who are leaders in the field. And—who knows?—perhaps you will become fascinated with the field, too.

CHAPTER SUMMARY

KEY QUESTION

CORE CONCEPT

WHAT DO OUR EMOTIONS DO FOR US?

Emotion and motivation are complementary processes that arouse the organism and direct its behavior. Emotions are normally adaptive, but if too intense or prolonged, they may be destructive. From an evolutionary standpoint, the function of motives and emotions is to help organisms make responses that promote their survival and reproduction. Socially, emotional expressions serve to communicate feelings and intentions.

At least seven basic facial expressions of emotion are universally understood across cultures. There is no consensus on the number of emotions humans can experience; most experts believe that there are a small number of basic emotions, which can mix to produce more complex emotions.

Some emotional differences between males and females probably have a biological basis. This is seen in differential rates of certain emotional disorders. On the other hand, cultural differences demonstrate that some gender differences in emotion are learned. Specifically, different cultures teach men and women different display rules about controlling emotional expression. In general, neither sex can be said to be more emotional than the other.

Emotions have evolved to help us respond to important situations and to convey our intentions to others.

WHERE DO OUR EMOTIONS COME FROM?

Neuroscience has revealed two distinct emotion systems in the brain. One operates mainly at an unconscious level and relies on deep limbic structures, especially the amygdala; the other involves conscious processing in the cortex. Emotions also involve visceral changes in response to messages transmitted by the autonomic nervous system and the hormone system. Understanding how the two emotion systems work has begun to resolve some controversies involving the roles of physical responses and cognition in emotion—particularly the interplay among physical responses, cognitions, and feelings of emotion.

The inverted U theory describes the complex relationship between arousal and performance: Increasing arousal produces improved performance, but only up to a certain level of optimum arousal, which depends on the complexity of the task. Sensation seekers seem to have an especially high need for arousal.

The discovery of two distinct brain pathways for emotional arousal has clarified the connections among the many biological structures involved in emotion and has offered solutions to many long-standing issues in the psychology of emotion.

HOW MUCH CONTROL DO WE HAVE OVER OUR EMOTIONS?

Emotional intelligence, the ability to keep one's emotions from getting out of control, is vital for maintaining good social relationships. It is distinct from the characteristics measured by traditional IQ tests. Emotional control can be achieved by learning, which has been demonstrated in anger management programs.

People can also control their emotions to deceive, and no sure method of detecting such deception exists, even though the use of "lie detectors" is widespread. The polygraph industry is built on the dubious premise that people who are lying will show certain signs of emotional arousal, although no verified and accepted standards exist for such examinations.

While aggression can be the result of anger, people usually hold aggression in check. In fact, the expression of anger without aggression often has positive results, as in the women's suffrage movement. Some people, however, have trouble managing anger and aggression and can benefit from cognitive therapy. The commonsense view that it is always good to vent anger and aggression is a dangerous myth.

Although emotional responses are not always consciously regulated, we can learn to control them.

MOTIVATION: WHAT MAKES US ACT AS WE DO?

The concept of motivation refers to inferred internal processes that guide behavior. The concept of motivation helps explain behavior that cannot be explained by the circumstances alone. Psychologists often distinguish psychological motives from biological drives, intrinsic motivation from extrinsic motivation, and conscious motivation from unconscious motivation.

Theorists have explained motivation in terms of instincts, drives, and cognitive states, such as perceived locus of control. Freud taught that our primary motives are unconscious and based on sexual and aggressive instincts. Maslow attempted to tie together a wide range of human motivation—from biological drives to psychological motives—into a hierarchy of needs. Many exceptions to his theory have been pointed out, however.

Extrinsic rewards are widely used as motivators. Research has shown, however, that extrinsic rewards can dampen intrinsic motivation, especially when rewards are given without regard for the quality of performance.

Motivation takes many forms, but all involve inferred mental processes that select and direct our behavior.

HOW ARE ACHIEVEMENT, HUNGER, AND SEX ALIKE? DIFFERENT?

Some motives rely heavily on learning, while others depend more heavily on biological factors. Moreover, motives differ in their sensitivity to environmental cues, reinforcers, and social/cultural influences. No comprehensive theory of motivation takes all these factors into account, although an evolutionary perspective suggests that each distinct motive evolved independently, in response to environmental pressures.

Achievement is a psychological motive that accounts for an important segment of human behavior, both in school and on the job. Societies vary in the intensity of their need for achievement, depending on their tendencies toward individualism or collectivism. In contrast, hunger and eating are motivated at many levels—by biological processes, external cues, social influences, and learning. Many Americans seek to control their appetite and body weight, although no weight-loss scheme is effective for most people over the long run. Unlike hunger and weight control, the sex drive is not homeostatic, even though sexual motivation is heavily influenced by biology. Sexual behavior in humans also depends on learning—of various sexual scripts. Most evidence suggests, however, that sexual orientation also has its origins in biology.

● **Achievement, hunger, and sex exemplify other human motives because they differ not only in the behavior they produce but also in the mix of biological, mental, behavioral, and social/cultural influences on them.**

● HOW AND WHY DO WE EXPERIENCE STRESS?

At the root of most stress is change and the need to adapt to environmental, physical, psychological, and social demands. Primitive stressors included mortal threats such as the struggle to survive, catastrophe, and loss. Modern stressors include posttraumatic stress and daily hassles.

Stress begins with arousal triggered by interpreting an event or condition as a stressor. The autonomic nervous system produces bodily responses to adapt to such experiences. Both acute threats and chronic conditions can trigger a fight-or-flight response, expressing aggression or fear. Hans Selye identified three stages in the general adaptation syndrome: alarm, resistance, and exhaustion. Other theories propose a passive withdrawal or entrapment response, and a tend-and-befriend pattern more characteristic of women. Stress can either excite or suppress the body's immune response.

Individuals' psychological reactions to stress vary according to what those stressors mean. Those with Type A personality traits risk adverse stress reactions, while Type B's are more relaxed. As a result of experiencing failure, learned helplessness produces passive resignation in the face of threat. Personal qualities can also reduce stress. People who have learned a pattern of cognitive hardiness are more resistant to stress. From an early age, some individuals demonstrate resilience, a capacity to "bounce back" from and overcome adversity. A more resilient mindset can be developed by increasing your sense of control, effectiveness, confidence, and realism.

● **The human stress response to perceived threat activates thoughts, feelings, behaviors, and physiological arousal that normally promote adaptation and survival.**

REVIEW TEST

For each of the following items, choose the single best answer. The answer key appears at the end.

1. While emotion emphasizes ______, motivation emphasizes ______.
   a. behavior/cognition
   b. arousal/action
   c. neural activity/hormones
   d. needs/drives
   e. drives/needs

2. Which of the following is the region of the brain most involved in emotions, attack, self-defense, and flight?
   a. the occipital cortex
   b. the limbic system
   c. the endocrine system
   d. the cerebellum
   e. the parietal lobe

3. Which theory of emotion first called attention to the idea that our physical responses can influence our emotions?
   a. the instinct theory
   b. Maslow's theory
   c. Ekman's theory
   d. the Schachter–Singer theory
   e. the James–Lange theory

4. Unlike achievement motivation, hunger and sex have a strong ______ basis.
   a. cognitive
   b. environmental
   c. biological
   d. perceptual
   e. genetic

5. People who are high in the need for achievement have been found to be more likely to
   a. demand immediate gratification for their desires.
   b. persist in monotonous tasks.
   c. have excellent interpersonal skills.
   d. get better grades in school.
   e. have a high IQ.

6. According to psychologists, which of the following experiences would be considered an example of *stress?*
   a. an earthquake that destroys your home and possessions
   b. an angry neighbor who demands that you turn down your stereo
   c. a pop quiz your instructor announces just as you take your seat
   d. the death of a beloved grandparent
   e. your arousal and behaviors when you are threatened by a stranger

7. Like the experience of emotion, the physical response to stress almost always begins with
   a. a protective behavior.
   b. a state of arousal.
   c. a reduction in immune effectiveness.
   d. fear.
   e. humor.

8. In the ___ stage of Selye's GAS, the organism's defenses are fully engaged and the organism shows signs of recovery from the initial stress.
   a. alarm
   b. withdrawal
   c. resistance
   d. exhaustion
   e. recovery

9. Which of the following stressors is the type that would most likely cause the immune system to malfunction and even cause harm?
   a. accidentally slipping and falling on an icy surface
   b. caring for a dying family member for a prolonged period
   c. being rejected by someone you are romantically interested in
   d. receiving a bad grade on a test in an important college course
   e. waking up in a bad mood

10. Amanda possesses many Type A personality traits; this means Amanda has a higher probability of suffering from ___ than non–Type A individuals.
   a. heart disease
   b. colds and flu
   c. accidents
   d. cancer
   e. schizophrenia

ANSWERS: 1. b 2. b 3. e 4. c 5. d 6. e 7. b 8. c 9. b 10. a

KEY TERMS

Emotion (p. 298)
Display rules (p. 300)
Lateralization of emotion (p. 306)
James–Lange theory (p. 307)
Cannon–Bard theory (p. 308)
Two-factor theory (p. 308)
Cognitive appraisal theory (p. 309)
Opponent-process theory (p. 309)
Inverted U function (p. 310)
Sensation seekers (p. 311)
Emotional intelligence (p. 312)
Polygraph (p. 314)
Motivation (p. 318)
Drive (p. 319)
Motive (p. 319)
Intrinsic motivation (p. 319)
Extrinsic motivation (p. 319)
Conscious motivation (p. 319)
Unconscious motivation (p. 319)
Instinct theory (p. 320)
Fixed-action patterns (p. 320)
Need (p. 320)
Homeostasis (p. 320)
Locus of control (p. 321)
Hierarchy of needs (p. 322)
Overjustification (p. 324)
Need for achievement (*n Ach*) (p. 326)
Individualism (p. 326)
Collectivism (p. 326)
Set point (p. 327)
Volumetric thirst (p. 330)
Osmotic thirst (p. 330)
Sexual response cycle (p. 332)
Sexual scripts (p. 333)
Approach–approach conflict (p. 334)
Approach–avoidance conflict (p. 334)
Avoidance–avoidance conflict (p. 334)
Multiple approach–avoidance conflict (p. 334)
Sexual orientation (p. 335)
Stress (p. 337)
Stressor (p. 337)
Traumatic stressor (p. 339)
Posttraumatic stress disorder (PTSD) (p. 341)
Acute stress (p. 343)
Chronic stress (p. 343)
Fight-or-flight response (p. 343)
General adaptation syndrome (GAS) (p. 345)
Alarm reaction (p. 345)
Stage of resistance (p. 347)
Stage of exhaustion (p. 347)
Tend-and-befriend model (p. 348)
Immune system (p. 349)
Psychoneuroimmunology (p. 349)
Cytokines (p. 349)
Type A (p. 350)
Type B (p. 350)
Learned helplessness (p. 351)
Flow (p. 353)

AP* REVIEW: VOCABULARY

Match each of the following vocabulary terms to its definition.

1. James–Lange theory
2. Cannon–Bard theory
3. Schachter–Singer theory
4. Emotional intelligence
5. Drive
6. Motive
7. Osmotic thirst
8. Volumetric thirst
9. Stress
10. Stressor

_____ a. Emotion-producing stimulus produces a physical response which produces an emotion.

_____ b. An internal mechanism that selects and directs behavior.

_____ c. Emotional feeling and internal responses take place at the same time.

_____ d. A drop in intracellular fluid levels.

_____ e. A condition demanding adaptation.

_____ f. A drop in extracellular fluid levels.

_____ g. The ability to understand and control emotional responses.

_____ h. Emotion results from the cognitive appraisal of both physical arousal and an emotion-provoking stimulus.

_____ i. Biologically instigated motivation.

_____ j. A physical and mental response to a challenging or threatening situation.

AP* REVIEW: ESSAY

Use your knowledge of the chapter concepts to answer the following essay question.

Compare and contrast the following theories of motivation. Be sure that your analysis includes the definition of each theory and a valid, theoretically based criticism. Be specific.

a. James–Lange theory

b. Drive reduction

c. Cognitive appraisal

OUR RECOMMENDED BOOKS AND VIDEOS

BOOKS

Barer-Stein, T. (1999). *You eat what you are: People, culture, and food traditions.* Toronto: Culture Concepts. Barer-Stein explores how our culture determines not only what we eat but what we want to eat, how we hunger, and the role of food in our individual lives.

Evans, D. (2001). *Emotion: The science of sentiment.* Oxford, UK: Oxford University Press. A philosopher explores the role of feelings in life and in our lives, including discussions of complex states such as love and happiness and whether nonemotional intellect is superior—or disabled.

Groopman, J. (2003). *The anatomy of hope: How people prevail in the face of illness.* New York: Random House. Surveying cancer patients and lab researchers, the author, a medical doctor, uses stories and personalities to explore the origins of hope and its impact on healing, doctors' impact on their patients' optimism, and why some severely or terminally ill persons are able to hang on to hope—while others let go and give up.

Jamison, K. R. (1999). *On moods.* New York: Random House. The doctor-author who revolutionized writing about manic–depressive illness (bipolar disorder) in her book *An Unquiet Mind* now explores the range and power of lasting emotions and moods in general.

McEwen, B. S., & Lasley, E. N. (2004). *The end of stress as we know it.* Washington, DC: The Dana Press. Not another pop-psych book for consumers of quick techniques, this book offers updated research and applied neuroscience for understanding how the brain and immune system interact, with the ironic result that stress *protects* you from temporary stressors but can *harm* you in responding to chronic stressors.

Pyszczynsky, T., Solomon, S., & Greenberg, J. (2003). *In the wake of 9/11: The psychology of terror.* Washington, DC: American Psychological Association. Relying on terror management theory, the authors show how the threat of death triggers the thoughts and emotions produced by terrorist attack.

Ridley, M. (1995). *The Red Queen: Sex and the evolution of human nature.* New York: Penguin. In Lewis Carroll's *Through the Looking Glass,* the Red Queen had to keep running just to stay in place. Likewise, author Matt Ridley argues, with wit and insight, sex is the human species's best strategy for changing and adapting to ever-changing world conditions.

Taylor, S. E. (2003). *The tending instinct: Women, men, and the biology of relationships.* New York: Owl Books. Psychologist Shelley Taylor, disagreeing with theories that all survival depends on a self-preservation instinct, argues that human survival thrives on social motivations, including cooperation, caregiving, and altruism—especially for women.

Videos

The Fight Club. (1999, color, 139 min.) Directed by David Fincher; starring Edward Norton, Brad Pitt, Meat Loaf. An unusual new acquaintance introduces a disillusioned young man to a new way of life—through fighting. Does manhood (or personhood) depend on a willingness to harm and be harmed? The unusual story, with a surprising psychological twist, made for a surprisingly popular film. (*Rating R*)

The Fisher King. (1991, color, 137 min.). Directed by Terry Gilliam; starring Robin Williams, Jeff Bridges, Amanda Plummer, Mercedes Ruehl, Michael Jeter. When a talk-radio announcer's flip remark to an unstable caller has tragic consequences, he seeks to make amends by helping one of the victims. The film includes powerful imagery of fantastic visions, paranoid delusions, and posttraumatic stress—with poignant and comic moments, too. (*Rating R*)

Patch Adams. (1998, color, 103 min.). Directed by Tom Shadyac; starring Robin Williams, Monica Potter, Daniel London, Bob Gunton, Peter Coyote. The film is based on the true story of Hunter "Patch" Adams, M.D., who became a physician despite his irreverence regarding the power and money of modern medicine and his desire to make medical care reassuring and even fun for patients. (*Rating PG-13*)

Shine. (1999, color, 105 min.). Directed by Scott Hicks; starring Geoffrey Rush, Sonia Todd, Armin Mueller-Stahl. Based on the true story of concert pianist David Helfgott, this film shows his recuperation from a crushing breakdown by reviewing the stress and abuse of his early life and choosing to prevail and work toward an acclaimed comeback. (*Rating PG-13*)

Key Question Chapter Outline

CORE CONCEPTS

Psychology in Your Life

How Do Psychologists Explain Development?

The Nature–Nurture Interaction
Gradual versus Abrupt Change

Development is a process of growth, change, and consistency brought about by an interaction of heredity and environment.

Psychological Traits in Your Genes

While genes contribute to your thoughts and behaviors, you shouldn't assume that biology is everything.

What Capabilities Does the Child Possess?

Prenatal Development
The Neonatal Period: Abilities of the Newborn Child
Infancy and Childhood: Building on the Neonatal Blueprint

Newborns have innate abilities for finding nourishment, interacting with others, and avoiding harmful situations, while the developing abilities of infants and children rely more on learning.

Does Your Child Measure Up?

The developmental milestones are averages, but children show great variation in their development.

What Are the Developmental Tasks of Infancy and Childhood?

Cognitive Development: Piaget's Theory
Social and Emotional Development

Infants and children face especially important developmental tasks in the areas of cognition and social relationships—tasks that lay a foundation for further growth in adolescence and adulthood.

Childhood Influences on Your Personality

Erikson's theory says that your personality is shaped by a series of developmental crises.

What Changes Mark the Transition of Adolescence?

Adolescence and Culture
Physical Maturation in Adolescence
Cognitive Development in Adolescence
Social and Emotional Issues in Adolescence
Sexual Issues in Adolescence

Adolescence offers new developmental challenges growing out of physical changes, cognitive changes, and socioemotional pressures.

The Development of Moral Thinking

Moral dilemmas reveal stages of moral reasoning—but not necessarily moral behavior.

What Developmental Challenges Do Adults Face?

Erikson's Theory of Young Adulthood: Intimacy versus Isolation
The Challenge of Midlife: Generativity versus Stagnation
New Perspectives on Women, Men, Work, and Family

Nature and nurture continue to produce changes throughout life, but in adulthood these changes include both growth and decline.

The Last Developmental Challenges You Will Face

The final years of life present a challenge, but a new picture of aging is emerging.

Developmental Psychology: The State of the Art

USING PSYCHOLOGY TO LEARN PSYCHOLOGY:
Cognitive Development in College

Chapter

9

Psychological Development

WHAT COULD GRAB PUBLIC interest more effectively than a story of twins separated at birth and reunited as adults? Many such tales have come out of the twin-study project at the University of Minnesota. But what really attracts journalists are the reports of uncanny similarities between identical twins who were raised by different parents, taught by different teachers, influenced by different peers and siblings, and sometimes even raised in different cultures.

Take, for example, the "Jim Twins." Separated just a few weeks after they were born, identical twins Jim Springer and Jim Lewis were adopted separately and raised apart. Yet something drove them on parallel paths, even though those paths didn't cross again for 39 years. At their reunion, the "Jim twins" discovered some remarkable correspondences in their habits, preferences, and experiences. Some examples:

- They achieved nearly identical scores on tests of personality, intelligence, attitudes, and interests.
- Medically, both have mildly high blood pressure and have had spells that they mistakenly thought were heart attacks; both have had vasectomies; both suffer from migraine headaches.
- Both chain-smoke Salem cigarettes and drink Miller Lite beer.

- Both had been indifferent students: Jim Lewis had dropped out in the 10th grade, while Jim Springer had managed to graduate from high school.
- Both had been married twice, and both of their first wives were named Linda. Both of their second wives were named Betty. Both men like to leave love notes around the house.
- Lewis had three sons, including one named James Alan. Springer had three daughters, plus a son named James Allan.
- Both had owned dogs named Toy.
- Both drive Chevrolets, chew their fingernails, like stock-car racing, and dislike baseball.
- Both had been sheriff's deputies.
- Both do woodworking as a hobby. Lewis likes to make miniature picnic tables, and Springer makes miniature rocking chairs. Both had built white benches around trees in their yards.

When he first read about the two Jims in a newspaper, psychologist Thomas Bouchard knew their case presented a rare opportunity to study the relative effects of heredity and environment and how they unfold over time in the process we call *development* (Holden, 1980a, b; Jackson, 1980; Lykken et al., 1992). The Jims agreed to participate and so became the first of some 115 pairs of reunited twins (plus four sets of reared-apart triplets) to be studied over the next 20 years at the University of Minnesota.

Another remarkable pair, Oskar Stör and Jack Yufe, were also separated at birth, and from that point on their lives went in almost unbelievably different directions. Stör was raised by his grandmother in Czechoslovakia and attended a Nazi-run school during World War II, while Yufe was taken to Trinidad, where he was raised as a Jew by his biological father. Oskar is now married, a strong union man, and a devoted skier, while Jack is separated, a businessman, and a self-styled workaholic. Still, alongside these huge differences, the researchers again found some striking similarities in seemingly trivial behavior patterns. Both twins wear neatly clipped moustaches; both read magazines from back to front; both have a habit of storing rubber bands on their wrists; both flush the toilet before using it; both like to dunk buttered toast in coffee; and both think it is funny to sneeze loudly in public.

A Critical Look at the Twin Studies As compelling as these correspondences are, we must interpret them with care (Phelps et al., 1997). Let's begin that interpretation by putting on our critical thinking caps and confronting the same questions that puzzled Bouchard and his colleagues: What might account for the remarkable similarities they were uncovering in the lives of reunited identical twins? How much was genetics? How much was coincidence? Were there any other explanations that could account for their results? As so often happens in psychology, the answers are complex.

To see these two twin pairs in a broader perspective, you need to know that they are "outliers"—extreme among the twins studied at Minnesota, even though they have received the lion's share of media coverage. Although Bouchard and his colleagues found many unexpected developmental similarities between individuals in all the twin pairs they studied, most were not nearly so much alike as Oskar and Jack or the Jims. Bouchard acknowledges that many of the similarities are just coincidences (The Mysteries, 1998). Yet it is precisely such coincidences that make the news and catch our eye. Even so, cautions twin researcher Richard Rose, "If you bring together strangers who were born on the same day in the same country and ask them to find similarities between them, you may find a lot of seemingly astounding coincidences" (Horgan, 1993). While mere coincidence does not offer a very dazzling explanation, the alternatives seem absurd. No one seriously suggests, for example, that the names of Betty and Linda could have been written into the genes of the two Jims or that heredity really specifies storing rubber bands on one's wrists.

The real story, then, is both less dramatic and more important: Identical twins do show remarkable similarities, but mainly in the characteristics you might expect: intelligence, temperament, gestures, posture, and pace of speech—all of which do make sense as traits that could be genetically influenced. And the fact that fraternal twins and other siblings show fewer similarities also suggests that hereditary forces are at work—in all of us, whether we are twins or not. Bouchard (1994) himself takes a rather extreme position, suggesting that heredity accounts for up to 80% of the similarities observed among identical twins (What We Learn, 1998). Critics aren't so sure.

3
F D

● Twin studies are one way to study the relative importance of nature and nurture, but they must be interpreted with caution. This photo shows the identical "Bob Twins," who, like the "Jim Twins," grew up not knowing of each other's existence. Both sport mustaches and smoke a pipe; both have engineering degrees; and both married teachers named Brenda. It is unlikely that all the similarities—striking as they may be—are caused by genetics.

Identical Twins Are Not Identical What objections do the critics raise concerning the twin studies Bouchard and his colleagues have been conducting? First, they note that, stunning as the similarities between identical twins may seem, the effect of the environment also shows up in each pair of twins. None of the twin pairs displays behavior that is identical across the board. And the fact that twins reared together typically are more alike than those reared apart provides further testimony to the effect of environment. The additional fact that the personalities of most twin pairs become less alike as they age provides still further evidence that the environment, as well as heredity, is at work (McCartney et al., 1990). We should note, too, that many of the twin pairs studied by Bouchard had been reunited for some time before he found them—an environmental condition that could easily accentuate, or even *create,* similarities. This was true, for example, of Oskar Stör and Jack Yufe, the Nazi and Jew twins, who met five months before Bouchard got to them. In fact, says psychologist Leon Kamin, Bouchard's twins face strong incentives to exaggerate their similarities and minimize their differences in order to please the research team and to attract media attention (Horgan, 1993). (Since their story broke in the press, Stör and Yufe have hired agents, made paid appearances on TV, and sold their story to a Hollywood film producer.)

A second sort of criticism points out that because identical twins look alike, people often treat them alike. This is an environmental factor that can easily account for many similarities in behavior. For example, some people's faces look good with moustaches, and if a pair of twins have such faces, people may encourage them to grow moustaches—whether or not they have been raised together. The resulting similarity, then, can be due as much to environment as to heredity.

Finally, the critics also remind us that scientists' hopes and expectations can influence their conclusions in this sort of research. Because Bouchard and other investigators of identical twins expect to find some hereditary influences, their attention will be drawn more to similarities than to differences. In fact, this is what people often do when they meet: Their conversation jumps from topic to topic until they discover common interests, attitudes, experiences, or activities.

CONNECTION: CHAPTER 1

The *expectancy bias* can distort perceptions and research findings.

Is there any point of consensus about the twin studies and about the effects of heredity and environment? Bouchard and his critics all would say that neither heredity nor environment ever acts alone to produce behavior or mental processes. They always *interact.* That is, from a developmental perspective, heredity and environment work together throughout a person's life. In addition, most would agree that the important findings coming out of the Minnesota twin research have nothing to do with unique and amazing similarities between particular twins. Rather, they have to do with the similarities found across all the identical twin pairs they studied: Twins show extraordinary similarities with each other in personality, attitudes, facial expressions, and temperament—almost everything, oddly enough, except their choice of mates: The spouses of identical twins were no more similar to each other than were people who would have been chosen at random (El-Hai, 1999). What the twin studies really did was to remind us that we are products of *both* heredity and environment—nature *and* nurture.

KEY QUESTION

HOW DO PSYCHOLOGISTS EXPLAIN DEVELOPMENT?

Broadly speaking, **developmental psychology** is the psychology of growth, change, and consistency through the lifespan. It asks how thinking, feeling, and behavior change through infancy, childhood, adolescence, and adulthood. It also seeks to understand how the brain changes, how our bodies change, and what effects these changes have on sensation, perception, cognition, motivation, emotion, and personality. And developmental psychology seeks to discover the threads of consistency—the "who we are"—that provide continuity throughout our lives. Beyond describing change and consistency, developmental psychologists also want to understand the fundamental forces that *cause* development. And that, of course, is where the two broad influences of heredity and environment come in. For developmental psychology, the big questions about heredity and environment are (a) How much weight does each wield? and (b) How do they interact?

Psychologists often refer to this as the **nature–nurture issue:** *Nature* refers to the effects of heredity and *nurture* to the influence of environment. Because this issue is so central to developmental psychology, we have highlighted it in the first Core Concept of this chapter:

CORE CONCEPT

Development is a process of growth, change, and consistency brought about by an interaction of heredity and environment.

The most important word here is **interaction:** Heredity and environment are always entwined in an inseparable relationship. The story of development, then, is the story of the *nature–nurture interaction* over the lifespan.

■ **Developmental psychology** The psychological specialty that studies how organisms change over time as the result of biological and environmental influences.

■ **Nature–nurture issue** The long-standing discussion over the relative importance of nature (heredity) and nurture (environment) in their influence on behavior and mental processes.

■ **Interaction** A process by which forces work together or influence each other–as in the interaction between the forces of heredity and environment.

The Nature–Nurture Interaction

It was probably Shakespeare who first brought the terms *nature* and *nurture* together (Gottesman, 1997), when Prospero describes the futility of his efforts to civilize his beastlike servant Caliban:

> A devil, a born devil, on whose nature
> Nurture can never stick; on whom my pains,
> Humanely taken, all, all lost, quite lost . . .
>
> —*The Tempest,* Act 4, Scene 1

More important, Shakespeare seems to have grasped the idea that nature and nurture can work in partnership—the idea of *interaction* that has not always been obvious to others. Those who had missed this important point have long argued over which of these forces—nature *or* nurture—is the more important influence on our thoughts and behaviors. It also reappears in the debate over racial differences and gender differences, as we will see a few chapters hence.

Although people continue to ask, "Is it nature *or* nurture?" psychologists today are more interested in understanding how heredity and environment *work together* to produce our personalities and our mental abilities (Bronfenbrenner & Ceci, 1994; Dannefer & Perlmutter, 1990). We know that virtually every human characteristic (with the trivial exceptions of certain physical traits, such as eye color) is shaped by both an individual's biological inheritance and experience (de Waal, 1999). That is, *nature and nurture interact.* If you are good at, say, math or music, your ability is really the result of a combination of genetic potential and experience. Heredity establishes your potential, but experience determines how your potential will be realized. To put it yet another way: Nature *pro*poses, and nurture *dis*poses.

Still, we may ask: Which of our traits does heredity affect most? And which are most heavily influenced by learning or other environmental factors (such as disease or nutrition)? And it's worth noting that answering such questions can pose some hazards. For example, we know that in the genetic disorder known as Down syndrome, biology has a strong influence. In this condition, the output of abnormal chromosomes leads to mental retardation—and there is no cure. The hazard of knowing about the genetic basis for Down syndrome is that the parents or teachers of children with such disorders may simply conclude that biology determines the child's destiny and give up hope. By focusing on the genetic side of the disorder, they may overlook effective learning-based treatments that can measurably improve the living skills of these individuals.

Mindful of such dangers, psychologists have nevertheless forged ahead in the study of hereditary and environmental contributions to thought and behavior. To do so, they have invented several clever methods for weighing the effects of nature and nurture. These include studies of twins and studies of adopted children. Briefly, we will examine how these two methods work, as well as their strengths and weaknesses.

Twin Studies Twins, as we have seen in Bouchard's studies, can give us some tantalizing clues about the relative contribution of nature and nurture, especially when the twins have been separated since birth. But identical twins separated at birth and later reunited are a scarce resource. For that reason, psychologists have also devised ways to tease out the effects of nature and nurture from studies comparing identical and fraternal twins who were reared together. Because **identical twins** have precisely the same genotype and **fraternal twins** have (on the average) 50% of their genes in common, hereditary effects should show up more strongly in identical twins. (In studies comparing these two twin types, the fraternal twins serve as a sort of *control group*). Such studies have given us valuable information on the genetics of mental and behavioral disorders, including alcoholism, Alzheimer's disease, schizophrenia, depression, and panic disorder (Eley, 1997; Plomin et al., 1994; Pool, 1997).

■ **Identical twins** A pair who started life as a single fertilized egg, which later split into two distinct individuals. Identical twins have exactly the same genes.

■ **Fraternal twins** A pair who started life as two separate fertilized eggs that happened to share the same womb. Fraternal twins, on the average, have about 50% of their genetic material in common.

CONNECTION: CHAPTER 2

The *control group* in a study serves as a standard against which other groups can be compared.

Adoption Studies If you adopted a baby, would he or she grow up to resemble you more than the biological parents? This is the sort of question asked by psychologists who do adoption studies. By comparing the characteristics of adopted children with those of their biological and adoptive family members, developmental psychologists have yet another method for separating the effects of heredity and environment. Similarities with the biological family point to the effects of nature, while similarities with the adoptive family suggest the influence of nurture. This work, in concert with twin studies, has revealed genetic contributions to a variety of psychological characteristics, such as intelligence, sexual orientation, temperament, and impulsive behavior (Bouchard, 1994; Dabbs, 2000; Hamer, 1997; Saudino, 1997; Wright & Mahurin, 1997).

Gradual versus Abrupt Change

Most of us cringe with embarrassment when our parents tell stories on us, especially about the "cute" things we said or did as children. What makes children's antics so cute, of course, is that they don't think like adults. But how do children *become* adults? Is there a predictable *pattern* they follow as their thought and language and social relationships become more and more adult-like? Such questions raise a second issue related to our Core Concept: whether the developmental changes produced by nature and nurture happen abruptly or gradually—whether we go through clearly defined "stages" or change more gradually and continually throughout our lives.

According to the **continuity view,** change is gradual. Children become more skillful in thinking, talking, or acting in much the same way that they become taller: through a gradual developmental process. We know that skilled behaviors often develop in this fashion, as you can see in the trial-and-error process of a child learning to walk or eat with a spoon. The more interesting question, of course, is whether complex mental processes, such as development of thought and language, follow the same pattern.

■ **Continuity view** The perspective that development is gradual and continuous—as opposed to the discontinuity (stage) view.

■ **Discontinuity view** The perspective that development proceeds in an uneven (discontinuous) fashion—as opposed to the continuity view.

Psychologists who take the opposing **discontinuity view** see development as more abrupt—as a succession of changes that produce different behaviors in different age-specific life periods, or *stages,* such as infancy, childhood, and adolescence. In this view, development can occur in bursts. That is, development can be *discontinuous.* You can observe this discontinuous process at work in beginning readers who suddenly discover the connection between letters and sounds. (For a graphical comparison of the continuity and discontinuity views, see Figure 9.1.)

You may have heard parents dismissing a child's misbehavior or moodiness as "just going through a

● In a remarkable series of self-portraits, we see developmental changes in the face of the painter Rembrandt.

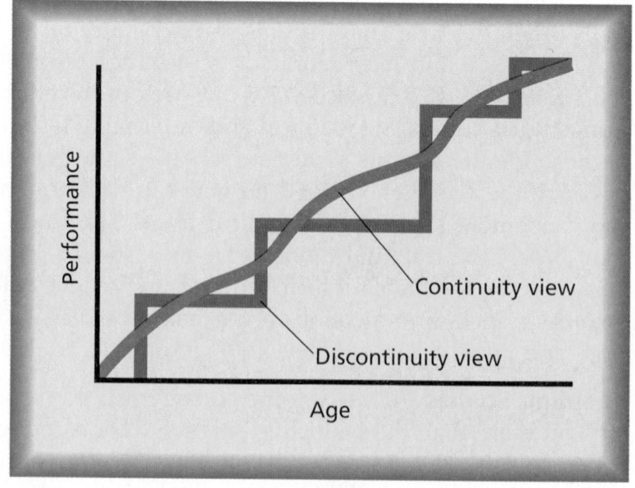
Performance
Continuity view
Discontinuity view
Age

● **FIGURE 9.1** Continuity versus Discontinuity

The continuity view sees development as a process of continual change, while the discontinuity view sees development as a series of steps, or stages.

stage," such as the "terrible twos," when children are becoming more mobile and independent. But for psychologists who subscribe to the discontinuity view, stages are not simply difficult times. These psychologists define **developmental stages** as periods of life initiated by distinct transitions (changes) in physical or psychological functioning. From a stage perspective, specific abilities, such as walking, talking, or abstract reasoning, appear at specific ages or life periods because different developmental processes come into play. In general, developmental psychologists who take the discontinuity view find that people go through the same stages in the same order—but not necessarily at the same rate.

■ **Developmental stages** Periods of life initiated by significant transitions or changes in physical or psychological functioning.

PSYCHOLOGY IN YOUR LIFE: PSYCHOLOGICAL TRAITS IN YOUR GENES

Eye color and the shape of your earlobes are purely genetic traits. Even some food aversions, such as a distaste for broccoli, can be anchored in the genes. But as far as we know, heredity by itself determines none of our more complex psychological characteristics (Horgan, 1993). Where personality traits, temperament, interests, and abilities are concerned, heredity always acts in combination with environment. Outgoing people, for example, aren't just born that way; they have also been encouraged to let their tendencies to extraversion show. Still, it's fair for developmental psychologists and biopsychologists to ask which psychological characteristics have strong genetic links.

A genetic contribution to general intelligence, for example, is well established—although psychologists disagree over the magnitude of heredity's role (Plomin et al., 1994). There is also a good possibility that genes contribute to your sexual orientation (Hamer et al., 1993). And it just may be that an interest in skydiving, rock climbing, or other risky behavior has a substantial genetic component (Hamer, 1997). The evidence suggests that genes also contribute to your basic temperament and personality, including all of the "Big Five" personality factors (Bouchard, 1994; Plomin, 1997).

CONNECTION: CHAPTER 10

The *Big Five* are fundamental traits that reliably distinguish different personality patterns among people in all cultures.

Likewise, some clinical disorders are associated with genetic abnormalities (Eley, 1997; Gibbs, 1995; Mann, 1994; Plomin et al., 1994). One of the first to be discovered was Huntington's disease, a rare problem that causes aggressive behavior and mental deterioration beginning in midlife (Cattaneo et al., 2002). Depression, a far more common problem, can also have genetic roots (although this doesn't mean that everyone who gets depressed has a genetic problem). Similarly, twin studies have revealed a strong genetic contribution to schizophrenia, a major mental disorder. Fear, too, can have a hereditary basis, especially in those who suffer from a condition known as panic disorder. So can anxiety, the basis for repetitive "neurotic" rituals, such as compulsively checking and rechecking the alarm clock setting, seen in obsessive–compulsive disorder. There's also evidence that the violence that may occur in an antisocial personality and the uncontrollable outbursts of Tourette's syndrome stem ultimately from the genes. And, if you are older, you may worry that every instance of forgetting is a sign of Alzheimer's disease, which (in some forms) arises from a genetic flaw that takes first the memory and then the rest of the mind.

Thus we see that many psychological traits, both desirable and undesirable, have a connection to our genes, as well as in our experience. But, at the risk of playing the same tune too often, we must emphasize: Genetics is not everything. While heredity is involved in nearly all we do, human behaviors also are shaped by environment. And by "environment" we mean not only the influence of learning (including the impact of all our experiences) but also physical factors such as nutrition and physical stress (Brown, 1999).

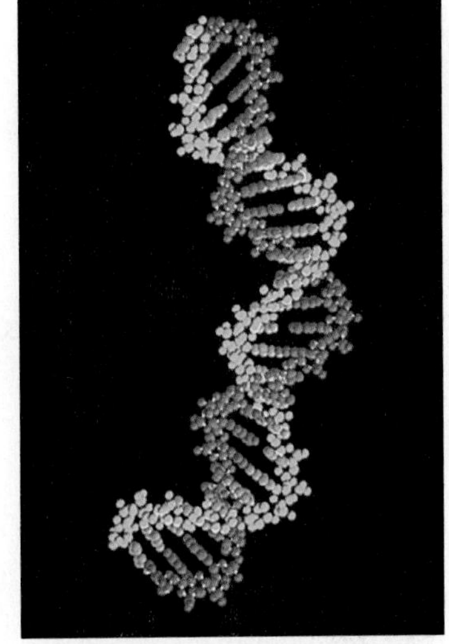

● The genetic code, written in DNA, contains our complete hereditary blueprint, grouped into genes and chromosomes.

Unfortunately, people sometimes go to extremes by seeing hereditary effects everywhere. A strong hereditarian stance can, for example, lead to unfair labeling of people as having "bad blood" if they come from troubled or abusive families. Just as disturbing, hereditarian expectations can create complacency and self-centeredness in those whose parents have desirable characteristics, such as high intelligence or good looks. Either way, expectations about genetic influences can create a self-fulfilling prophecy, which leads people to live up (or down) to their expectations. If you expect to be smart and successful (or stupid and a failure), chances are you won't be disappointed.

CHECK YOUR UNDERSTANDING

1. **RECALL:** Psychologists have resolved the nature–nurture controversy by saying that we are the products of
   a. heredity.
   b. environment.
   c. both heredity and environment.
   d. neither heredity nor environment.
   e. all our experiences.

2. **APPLICATION:** Which of the following statements is most accurate with regard to the "Jim twins"?
   a. They are no more similar than other siblings.
   b. It is reasonably certain that their similarities come from shared early experiences.
   c. It has been proved that their similarities are just chance.
   d. They are similar because they were raised in the same family environment.
   e. We cannot say for certain that their similarities are mainly genetic.

3. **RECALL:** Which perspective says that developmental change is a gradual process?
   a. the continuity view
   b. the discontinuity view
   c. the hereditarian view
   d. the environmental view
   e. the longitudinal view

4. **UNDERSTANDING THE CORE CONCEPT:** Which one of the following best exemplifies a developmental change that results from an interaction of heredity and environment?
   a. the appearance of facial hair in a teenage boy
   b. eye color
   c. a child learning to talk
   d. winning the lottery
   e. hair color

ANSWERS: 1. c 2. e 3. a 4. c

KEY QUESTION

WHAT CAPABILITIES DOES THE CHILD POSSESS?

People used to think that babies began life as a "blank slate"—with an empty brain and no abilities. In modern times, however, that picture has changed. We now see newborns as possessing a remarkable set of abilities that they acquired through their genes. They are social creatures, also adept at locating food and avoiding potential harm. These *innate* (inborn) abilities are the focus of the Core Concept for this section:

CORE CONCEPT

Newborns have innate abilities for finding nourishment, interacting with others, and avoiding harmful situations, while the developing abilities of infants and children rely more on learning.

To be sure, the newborn's capabilities are limited—but they are effective enough to promote survival. The newborn arrives in the world already "knowing," for example, how to get nourishment by suckling and how to get attention by cooing and crying. Still, it is helpful to think of the newborn's basic abilities as a sort of scaffold to which new and more complex abilities are added as the child grows and develops.

To explain where these abilities come from and how they develop, we will organize our discussion around three important developmental periods: the *prenatal* period, the *neonatal* (newborn) period, and *infancy.* You will notice that, in each phase, development builds on the abilities and structures laid down earlier.

Prenatal Development

The **prenatal period** spans the nine months between conception and birth. As every mother has sensed, it is a time of furious developmental activity that readies the organism for life on its own outside the womb. In this prenatal period, it passes successively through three stages, which we will describe in a bit more detail.

Shortly after conception, the fertilized egg, also known as a **zygote,** begins to grow through cell division. First one cell becomes two; then two become four; and when the number reaches about 150, the zygote implants itself in the lining of the uterus—a process that is completed about 10 days after conception. At this point it becomes an **embryo** (along with those cells that will form into the placenta and other supportive structures).

During the embryonic phase, the genetic plan determines how all the organs that will later be found in the newborn infant begin to form. In this stage, the embryo's cells begin to specialize as components of particular organ systems, a process known as *differentiation.* (Before differentiation, certain cells in the embryo, known as *embryonic stem cells,* are capable of forming into any organ of the body.)

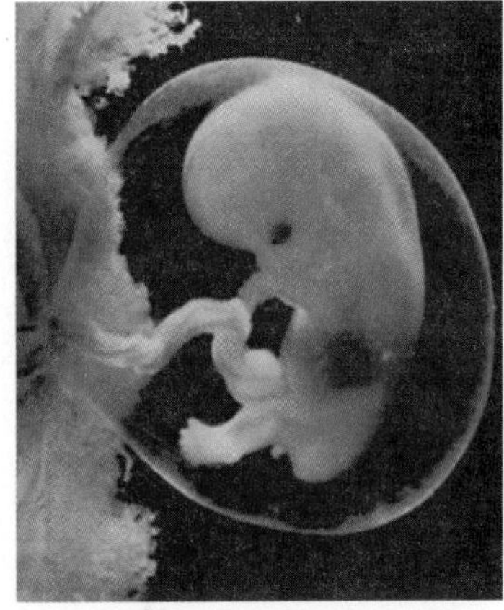

● As the brain grows in the developing embryo, it forms as many as 250,000 new neurons per minute.

At first, the embryo's cells form distinct layers. Those in the outer layer become the nervous system and the skin. Cells in the middle layer become muscles, bones, blood vessels, and certain internal organs. Those in the inner layer differentiate on a path that will eventually make them into the digestive system, lungs, and glands. By the end of the first month the initial single cell of the zygote has developed into an embryo with millions of specialized cells. Eventually this process of cell division and differentiation, which continues throughout the prenatal period, produces all the tissues and organs of the body.

The first rudimentary "behavior"—a heartbeat—appears when the embryo is about three weeks old and one-sixth of an inch long. A few weeks later, when it is not yet an inch in length, the embryo makes reflexive responses to stimulation. These behaviors occur long before the brain has developed to the point where it can think or direct behaviors.

After the eighth week, the developing embryo is called a **fetus.** Spontaneous movements commanded by the somatic nervous system begin at about this time, although the mother doesn't usually feel these movements until the 16th week after conception (Carmichael, 1970; Humphrey, 1970). By this point, the fetus has grown to about 7 inches long (the average length at birth is 20 inches).

Teratogens: Prenatal Toxins Specialists used to think that the womb shielded the developing organism from nearly all environmental assaults, but we now know better. Although the **placenta** (an organ that develops between the embryo/fetus and the mother) screens out some potentially dangerous substances, many can pass through this interface. These toxic substances, called **teratogens,** include viruses (including HIV, the AIDS virus), certain drugs, and other chemicals. Among the most common teratogens are nicotine and alcohol.

The effects of these teratogens vary from slight to devastating, depending on the type, amount of exposure, and stage of prenatal development in which exposure occurs. Fetal alcohol syndrome is one of the more worrisome disorders that can occur in children of mothers who drink heavily during pregnancy. The symptoms can include mental retardation, poor motor coordination, impaired attention, and hyperactivity.

■ **Prenatal period** The developmental period before birth.
■ **Zygote** A fertilized egg.
■ **Embryo** In humans, the name for the developing organism during the first eight weeks after conception.
■ **Fetus** In humans, the term for the developing organism between the embryonic stage and birth.
■ **Placenta** The organ interface between the embryo or fetus and the mother. The placenta separates the bloodstreams, but it allows the exchange of nutrients and waste products.
■ **Teratogens** Substances from the environment, including viruses, drugs, and other chemicals, that can damage the developing organism during the prenatal period.

Prenatal Development of the Brain Prenatally, the brain grows new neurons at the amazing rate of up to 250,000 per minute. By birth it has produced some 100 billion (Dowling, 1992). All originate from a proliferation of cells at the top of the embryo's hollow *neural tube.* (Your own brain and spinal cord have a hollow core that harks back to your embryonic days.) These furiously multiplying cells eventually become the brain; but to do so, they must embark on a once-in-a-lifetime journey. As new brain cells are produced, they actually migrate out of the neural tube and then extend their axons and dendrites to make connections with other newly formed neurons. Exactly how they manage to make the proper connections to form a functioning brain is still the subject of much research. The basic plan for "wiring" the brain, however, must be contained in the genetic code.

The Neonatal Period: Abilities of the Newborn Child

What is the sensory world like for the newborn? The father of American psychology, William James, guessed that everything must be an overwhelming jumble of stimuli—"One great blooming, buzzing confusion" (James, 1890). We now know that his views grossly underestimated infants' capabilities. Long before babies achieve motor coordination and locomotion, they take in vast amounts of information about their surroundings, filtering and processing stimulation that attracts, interests, or upsets them. They also have an amazing behavioral repertoire that they use to respond to and manipulate their environment.

During the **neonatal period** (newborn period), which covers the time from birth to one month of age, neonates are capable of responding to stimulation from all of their senses. For example, newborn babies will turn their heads toward anything that strokes their cheeks—a nipple or a finger—and begin to suck it. They can also respond to taste: the sweeter the fluid, the more continuously and forcefully an infant will suck (Lipsitt et al., 1976). They smile when they smell banana essence, and they prefer salted to unsalted cereal (Bernstein, 1990; Harris et al., 1990). However, they recoil from the taste of lemon or shrimp or the smell of rotten eggs. And, as early as 12 hours after birth, they show distinct signs of pleasure at the taste of sugar water or vanilla. All these responses are part of the ability the newborn has to seek nourishment—as the Core Concept for this section suggested.

What else can newborns do with their senses? Minutes after birth, their eyes scan their surroundings, although their vision is not, at first, especially sharp. In fact, babies are born rather nearsighted, with an optimal focus of about 12 inches—ideal for looking at faces. Their distance vision, however, is poor, with a visual acuity of about 20/500 (which means that they can discriminate at 20 feet stimuli that most older children can see clearly at 500 feet). Moreover, good vision requires the operation and coordination of a great many receptor cells in the eye's retina, in the visual pathways, and in the occipital cortex of the brain. At birth, relatively few of these connections are laid down. But these immature systems develop very rapidly, and the baby's visual abilities soon become quite effective (Banks & Bennett, 1988).

Early on, infants can perceive large objects that display a great deal of contrast. By the age of one month, a child can detect contours of a head at close distances. At seven weeks, the baby can scan the features of the caregiver's face, and, as the caregiver talks, the baby can contact his or her eyes. Just as heredity biases infants to prefer human voices over other sounds, it programs them to prefer human faces to most other visual patterns (Fantz, 1963). Although newborns can see colors, their ability to differentiate colors, such as red from orange from blue, becomes dramatically better a month or two after

■ **Neonatal period** In humans, the neonatal (newborn) period extends through the first month after birth.

birth (Teller, 1998). At three months, the baby can perceive depth and is well on the way to enjoying the visual abilities of adults. And it may surprise you to know that infants seem to possess a rudimentary ability to "count" objects they see: They know, for example, the difference between two dolls and three (Wynn, 1992, 1995). Such *core knowledge* serves as the foundation for the later development of more complex skills, such as are required for arithmetic (Spelke, 2000). They also have strong auditory preferences, one being a greater attraction to female voices than to those of men. Neonates also shift their attention to sound patterns they have heard before, and within a few weeks of birth they begin to recognize their mothers' voice (Carpenter, 1973; DeCasper & Fifer, 1980; DeCasper & Spence, 1986; Spelke & Owsley, 1979).

Aside from their sensory abilities, babies are born with a remarkable set of behavioral reflexes that provide a biological platform for later development. Among these reflexes, the *postural reflex* allows babies to sit with support, and the *grasping reflex* enables them to cling to a caregiver. And, in their cooing and crying, babies also have some rudimentary tools for social interaction. These and other innate responses equip newborns with the essential tools for survival and "instinctive" know-how. In addition, babies have built-in safety features that help them avoid or escape from unpleasant stimulation, such as loud noises, bright lights, strong odors, and painful stimuli. All of this, of course, makes much evolutionary sense because these abilities are highly adaptive and promote survival.

Infancy and Childhood: Building on the Neonatal Blueprint

Following the neonatal period, the child enters **infancy,** a period that lasts until approximately 18 months of age—the time when speech has become well developed. (The Latin root *infans* means "incapable of speech.") It is a time of rapid, genetically programmed growth and still-heavy reliance on the repertoire of reflexes and "instinctive" behaviors that we discussed above. All of these abilities arise from a nervous system that continues to develop at a furious pace. At birth and for the first few years of life, many potential brain circuits are not fully connected, a fact that helps to explain why most people have a poor memory for events that occurred before they were about 3½ years of age (Bauer, 2002; Howe & Courage, 1993). In order to complete the process of forming the brain's circuitry, the neonatal brain shifts its emphasis from producing new cells to a different mode of growth. The genetic program now emphasizes the branching of axons and dendrites (Kolb, 1989). As the dendrites and axons grow and connect, the total mass of neural tissue in the brain continues to increase rapidly—by 50% in the first two years. By 4 years of age it has nearly doubled its birth size.

As nerve fibers grow and connections form in the young brain, stimulation is necessary to make them permanent and functional. Those connections that are not used are lost through a process called *synaptic pruning.* This destruction of unused connections does not destroy the neurons themselves. Rather it returns them to an uncommitted state, awaiting a role in future development (Johnson, 1998). In some cases, however, vital neural connections may be broken, as can happen in children born with congenital cataracts of the eyes. If the cataracts are not treated early, neural connections in the visual system are irretrievably lost.

The genetic program (along with the physical limitations imposed by the size of the skull) does not allow the tremendous growth of brain circuitry to continue indefinitely. So, the neural growth rate gradually diminishes. Finally, by about 11 years of age, the brain attains its ultimate mass.

■ **Infancy** In humans, infancy spans the time between the end of the neonatal period and the establishment of language–usually at about 18 months to 2 years.

Learning Assumes a Role in Development Infancy is also a period during which youngsters begin to exploit their abilities for *learning*. Babies start to build up their knowledge of the world by observing relations between important sensory events, as when a certain tone of the mother's voice signals it is time to eat. This involves a fundamental form of learning that psychologists call *classical conditioning* (it's the same sort of learning that makes your mouth water at the sight of a pizza or makes some people faint at the sight of blood). This form of learning in babies was demonstrated by an experiment in which newborns were taught to anticipate pleasurably sweet sensations by first stroking the babies' foreheads and then giving them sugar water. After several trials, the stroking alone would cause the babies to turn their heads in the direction from which the sweet fluid had been delivered—a learned anticipation of more of the same (Blass, 1990).

CONNECTION: CHAPTER 6

Classical conditioning is a form of learning, originally studied by Pavlov, in which one event signals the occurrence of another.

Infants also use their learning ability to expand their social interaction skills. We have seen, for example, that young babies can learn to distinguish their mother's voice. Likewise, they learn to associate their caregiver with certain odors. And, as any parent will tell you, babies quickly learn how to manipulate their parents by cooing, smiling, and crying. Learning and memory also underlie the surprising ability of newborns to imitate simple facial expressions, such as sticking out the tongue or rounding the mouth (Meltzoff, 1998; Meltzoff & Prinz, 2002). In general, as development proceeds through infancy, learning assumes an ever-larger role in producing even more complex behaviors.

Social Abilities As the foregoing discussion suggests, infants are built for social interaction, and they not only respond to, but also interact with, their caregivers from the moment of birth. Film studies of this interaction reveal a remarkable degree of *synchronicity:* close coordination between the gazing, vocalizing, touching, and smiling of mothers and infants (Martin, 1981). And while babies respond and learn, they also send out messages to those willing to listen to and love them. The result of this interaction can be seen in studies showing how the feelings of mothers and infants are coordinated (Fogel, 1991). So, a 3-month-old infant may laugh when his or her mother laughs and frown or cry in response to her display of negative emotion (Tronick et al., 1980).

Attachment Ideally, social development begins with the establishment of a close emotional relationship between a child and a parent figure. Psychologists call this **attachment,** although the popular media often refer to it as "bonding." By either name, this relationship is especially important because it lays the foundation for all other relationships that follow.

CONNECTION: CHAPTER 8

Instinct is a common but imprecise term that refers to behaviors that have a strong genetic basis.

Attachment behaviors appear to occur "instinctively" in many species, although they are not necessarily limited to the infant's interactions with the biological parents. One striking example occurs in **imprinting,** the powerful attraction of infants of some species (notably in birds) to the first moving object or individual they see. A baby chick hatched by a mother duck will form an attachment to its surrogate mother—even though it is a chicken, not a duck. The imprinted chick will even follow its duck-mother right up to the water's edge when she and her ducklings go for a swim. (You may also recall *The Ugly Duckling,* the children's tale about imprinting.) Thus, the imprinting tendency is an innate predisposition, although the organism's environment and experience determine what form it will take. While imprinting occurs most clearly in birds, a similar, but more complex, process may account for the attachment between human infants and their caregivers.

■ **Attachment** The enduring social-emotional relationship between a child and a parent or other regular caregiver.

■ **Imprinting** A primitive form of learning in which some young animals follow and form an attachment to the first moving object they see and hear.

Although humans apparently have an inborn need for attachment, there is no guarantee that parents will always respond to this need. What, then, can babies do to increase the chances of getting the contact they want? Unlike a baby chick, human babies are not mobile enough at birth to use their own locomotion to get closeness or attention from a caregiver. When they want to get close to the attachment figure (e.g., their mother), they cannot simply crawl or move toward her. But they can emit signals—such as smiling, crying, and vocalizing—to promote responsive behavior (Campos et al., 1983). And few can resist a baby's smile! According to John Bowlby (1973), infants will form attachments to any individual who consistently and appropriately responds to their signals.

● Konrad Lorenz (1903–1989), a researcher who pioneered the study of imprinting, dramatically demonstrated what can happen when young birds become imprinted on an object other than their mother.

Some observers have suggested that attachment begins as early as the first few weeks (Ainsworth, 1973; Ainsworth et al., 1978; Bowlby, 1969, 1973). One study found, for example, that when mothers left the room, their 2- to 4-month-old babies' skin temperature dropped, a sign of emotional distress (Mizukami et al., 1990). In these youngsters, skin temperature dropped even more when a stranger replaced the mother. In contrast, skin temperature remained steady if the mother stayed in the room—even if the stranger was present. Apparently, children only a few months old rely on their caretakers as a "safe base," even before they can indicate attachment with crying or locomotion (Bee, 1994).

The Strange Situation Developmental psychologist Mary Ainsworth spent a career studying the various forms attachment takes. She did this by observing young children in a variety of carefully contrived "strange situations." For example, she separated children from their mothers by a barrier or placed them alone in an unfamiliar room (Ainsworth, 1989; Ainsworth et al., 1978; Ainsworth & Wittig, 1969; Lamb, 1999). Using such methods in a variety of cultures, Ainsworth found that the children's responses fell into two main categories, reflecting either secure attachment or insecure attachment. Securely attached children felt close to their mothers, safe, and more willing to explore or tolerate a novel experience—confident that they could cry out for help or be reunited with the missing parent. Insecurely attached children were more likely to react to the "strange situation" in one of two ways: with anxiety and ambivalence or with avoidance. The anxious-ambivalent children wanted contact but cried with fear and anger when separated and proved difficult to console even when reunited with their mothers. The avoidant children acted as though they were unconcerned about being separated from their mothers, not crying when they left and not seeking contact when they returned. Avoidant children may be showing the effects of repeated rejection, no longer seeking attachment because their efforts have failed in the past (Shaver & Hazan, 1994).

Attachment fascinates researchers because patterns established in infancy may persist in a variety of childhood and even adult behaviors, influencing later-life job satisfaction, relationship choices, and intimacy experiences—although the current research carries mixed messages on this issue. (See Berk, 2004, for a more detailed review.) As children grow up and become adults, they no longer restrict their attachment to their primary caregiver. While they may retain their childhood attachment style, they gradually widen their attachments to include peers, friends, teachers, coworkers, and others in their community. We should emphasize, however, that—powerful as attachment is—individuals who lack healthy attachments in infancy and childhood are not necessarily doomed to failure in life. Attachment problems are good predictors of later problems with social relationships, but many people do succeed in overcoming attachment difficulties (Kagan, 1996, 1998). Further, cross-cultural psychologists have cautioned us that attachment patterns may differ somewhat from culture to culture. For example, Japanese mothers make more physical

● Children become attached to their caregivers, and parents likewise become attached to their children. Love and responsibility help offset the daily struggles for survival faced by poor families the world over.

DO IT YOURSELF! What's Your Attachment Style?

Indicate which one of the following three self-descriptions you most agree with (adapted from Shaver & Hazan, 1994):

1. I am somewhat uncomfortable being close to others; I find it difficult to trust them completely, difficult to allow myself to depend on them. I am nervous when anyone gets too close, and love partners often want me to be more intimate than I feel comfortable being.
2. I find that others are reluctant to get as close as I would like. I often worry that my partner doesn't really love me or won't want to stay with me. I want to get very close to my partner, and this sometimes scares people away.
3. I find it relatively easy to get close to others and am comfortable depending on them. I don't often worry about being abandoned or about someone getting too close to me.

WHAT YOUR CHOICE MEANS

We realize that it is probably obvious to you which of the statements above is "best." Nevertheless, just considering the alternatives should help you understand attachment styles–and, perhaps, yourself–a little better. Here's our interpretation: If you selected the first statement, you agreed with the attitude that reflects an avoidant, insecure attachment. This style was chosen by 25% of Shaver and Hazan's respondent sample. The second statement reflects an anxious-ambivalent, insecure attachment style, selected by 20% of the sample. The third statement reflects a secure attachment style, the most common pattern identified, accounting for 55% of respondents (Shaver & Hazan, 1994).

What do these styles signify for later life? Through interviews, observations, and questionnaires, researchers have identified several consequences of attachment style, secure or insecure, in adulthood (see Ainsworth, 1989; Collins & Read, 1990; Hazan & Shaver, 1990; Kirkpatrick & Shaver, 1992; Shaver & Hazan, 1993, 1994; Simpson, 1990):

- Secure individuals have more positive self-concepts and believe that most other people are good-natured and well-intentioned. They see their personal relationships as trustworthy and satisfying.
- Secure respondents are satisfied with their job security, coworkers, income, and work activity. They put a higher value on relationships than on work and derive their greatest pleasure from connections to others.
- Insecure, anxious-ambivalent persons report emotional extremes and jealousy. They feel unappreciated, insecure, and unlikely to win professional advancement. They make less money than those with other attachment styles, working more for approval and recognition than for financial gain. They fantasize about succeeding but often slack off after receiving praise.
- Avoidant people fear intimacy and expect their relationships to fail. They place a higher value on work than on relationships and generally like their work and job security. They follow a workaholic pattern, but (not surprisingly) they are dissatisfied with their coworkers.
- Secure individuals tend to choose as partners others who are secure. After breakups, avoidant individuals claim to be less bothered by the loss of the relationship, although this may be a defensive claim, with distress showing up in other ways (e.g., physical symptoms).

contact with infants, while American mothers make more eye contact (Rothbaum et al., 2000b). With such caveats in mind, we now invite you to take the quiz in the "Do It Yourself!" box "What's Your Attachment Style?"

Contact Comfort Why do infants become attached to caregivers in the first place? An evolutionary explanation says that attachment safeguards an infant's survival by assuring the support and protection it requires. Through natural selection, individuals with genetic tendencies to "attach" will survive, thrive, and pass those tendencies along to their own offspring.

In addition to affording protection, could attachment also be the child's way of encouraging the parents to provide food—its most basic physical need? This idea has been dubbed the "cupboard theory": Infants become attached to those who provide the "cupboard" containing the food supply. This theory has been a favorite of those who believe that nursing is the basis for healthy relationships. But does the cupboard theory really explain the parent–child bond?

To understand how psychologists have dealt with this issue, we have to imagine the way many people looked at child rearing in the 1940s and 50s, when the cupboard theory prevailed. Freud had convinced most physicians that young infants and children were so mentally undeveloped that the only thing of real importance in their lives was the breast or the bottle. Nothing like adult social relationships entered their little minds—which explains why no one worried about the lack of touching or other displays of affection given premature infants in incubators or older children in orphanages (Blum, 2002; Sapolsky, 2002).

Psychologists Harry and Margaret Harlow guessed that a more fundamental cause of attachment involves physical contact (Harlow, 1965; Harlow &

Harlow, 1966). To see if they were right, they decided to test this idea against the cupboard theory in an animal model, using infant monkeys who had been separated from their mothers at birth. The Harlows placed orphaned baby monkeys in cages where they had access to two artificial *surrogate mothers.* One was a simple wire figure that provided milk through a nipple—a "cupboard," but little else. The other was a cloth-covered figure providing no milk but offering abundant stimulation from its soft terry-cloth cover. Confirming their expectations, the Harlows observed that their baby monkeys spent many hours nestled close to the cloth mother but little time with the wire model, despite the nourishment the latter provided. Moreover, when the baby monkeys were frightened, they sought comfort by clinging to the cloth figure. They also used it as a base of operations when exploring new situations. With these observations, then, the Harlows were able to show that the infant monkeys become attached to and prefer a "mother" figure that provides **contact comfort,** the stimulation and reassurance derived from physical touch.

● One of Harlow's monkeys and its artificial terry-cloth mother. Harlow found that the contact comfort mothers provide is essential for normal social development.

Human infants need contact comfort, too. The lack of a close, loving relationship in infancy even affects physical growth. We know this from observations of children in emotionally detached or hostile family environments: Such children have slower growth and bone development. They may grow again if removed from the poor environment, but their growth is stunted again if they are returned to it, a phenomenon known as *psychosocial dwarfism.* A related condition, which has no organic basis but results from lack of parental love and nurturing, is known as *failure to thrive,* seen in wasted-looking, withdrawn, and apathetic infants. Accordingly, in some hospitals that recognize the power of contact comfort, premature infants and others born at risk are scheduled to receive regular holding and cuddling by staff members and volunteers. Clearly, a close, interactive relationship with loving adults is a child's first step toward healthy physical growth and normal socialization.

Maturation and Physical Abilities Sitting, crawling, and walking—like the growth of the brain, the growth spurt of puberty, and the onset of menopause—all occur on their own biological time schedules. Psychologists use the term **maturation** for the unfolding of these genetically programmed processes of growth and development over time. When organisms are raised under adequate environmental conditions, their maturation follows a predictable pattern. In humans, maturation generates all of the sequences and patterns of behavior seen in Figure 9.2.

Even when maturation takes the leading role, we must keep in mind the *interaction* of biology and environment. Thus, in the sequence for motor control shown in Figure 9.2, a child learns to walk without special training, following a time-ordered pattern that is typical of all physically capable members of our species. Indeed, in cultures where children are carried in cradle boards, walking occurs on a similar schedule (Dennis & Dennis, 1940). Despite this hereditary pattern, however, we find that environmental influences can sometimes play a part. In the West Indies, where infants receive vigorous massage after the daily bath and frequent practice in moving their legs while being held, children sit and walk a little earlier, on the average, than do children in the United States (Hopkins & Westra, 1988). On the other hand, lack of human contact can have the opposite effect, as in children who had spent their lives lying in cribs in Iranian orphanages were observed to be very slow in learning to sit and walk (Dennis, 1960).

Harking back to our discussion of continuity and discontinuity, physical growth in humans has always been viewed as a *continuous* process whose rate changes with age, slowing over time after a rapid start in the early years. This picture of continuous physical growth has been qualified, however, as the

■ **Contact comfort** Stimulation and reassurance derived from the physical touch of a caregiver.

■ **Maturation** The process by which the genetic program manifests itself over time.

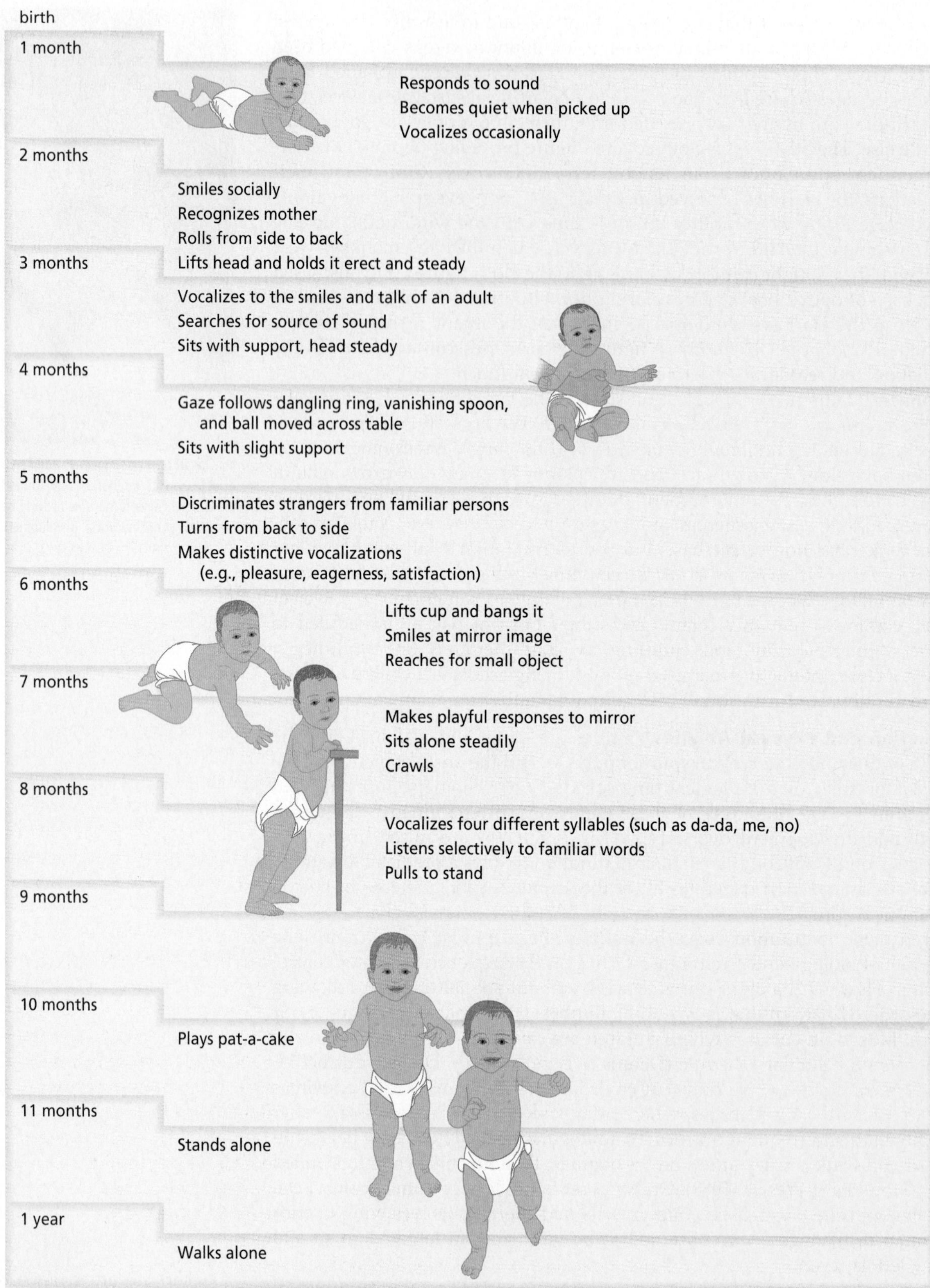

birth
1 month
Responds to sound
Becomes quiet when picked up
Vocalizes occasionally
2 months
Smiles socially
Recognizes mother
Rolls from side to back
3 months
Lifts head and holds it erect and steady
Vocalizes to the smiles and talk of an adult
Searches for source of sound
Sits with support, head steady
4 months
Gaze follows dangling ring, vanishing spoon, and ball moved across table
Sits with slight support
5 months
Discriminates strangers from familiar persons
Turns from back to side
Makes distinctive vocalizations (e.g., pleasure, eagerness, satisfaction)
6 months
Lifts cup and bangs it
Smiles at mirror image
Reaches for small object
7 months
Makes playful responses to mirror
Sits alone steadily
Crawls
8 months
Vocalizes four different syllables (such as da-da, me, no)
Listens selectively to familiar words
Pulls to stand
9 months
10 months
Plays pat-a-cake
11 months
Stands alone
1 year
Walks alone

● **FIGURE 9.2** Maturational Timetable for Motor Control

This figure shows average ages at which each behavior is performed. There are considerable individual differences in the *rate* of development, so the time at which each response occurs is variable. Most infants, however, follow the *sequence* of development outlined here.

result of reports showing that growth in the length of infants' bodies occurs in discontinuous "bursts." Developmentalists call this *saltation* (from the Latin *saltare*, "to leap"). In fact, all through infancy and childhood, physical growth involves an alternation between active and inactive growth phases (Lampl et al., 1992). Typically, infants go for several days showing no growth at all, and then suddenly they enter a growth spurt, in which they can add as much as one-half inch in length in 24 hours!

To summarize, we have seen that neonates come equipped to accomplish three basic tasks of survival: finding sustenance (feeding), maintaining contact with people (for protection and care), and defense against harmful stimuli (withdrawing from pain or threat). Such tasks require a set of innate abilities, and these abilities, in turn, form a foundation on which learning and physical maturation build the perceptual skills, the ability to understand experiences, and basic thinking skills that continue to develop during infancy, childhood, and throughout life (von Hofsten & Lindhagen, 1979).

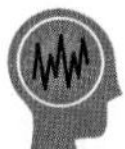

PSYCHOLOGY IN YOUR LIFE: DOES YOUR CHILD MEASURE UP?

It is risky to discuss the ages by which a child "should" achieve certain physical and mental skills. Children show great variation in their development. Some children walk by 11 months, about half do so by their first birthdays, and nearly all achieve this milestone by 15 months of age. So if your child, or a child you know, hasn't started walking and talking by age 1, you shouldn't panic. Likewise, you shouldn't be worried if your child isn't talking by the average time suggested in the baby books. Einstein was slow to talk, too.

On the other hand, large differences from the averages should not be ignored. If a child still isn't beginning to walk and talk by age 2, the caregiver should consult a specialist, such as a pediatrician or developmental psychologist, to see whether something is wrong. It is well to remember, also, that a delay in one area, such as the onset of speech, does not mean that the child is "retarded" or will be generally slow in other areas. Not only are there great variations among children, but variations occur normally within an individual child.

What developmental standards would a specialist use? Certainly, a child should be responsive to people almost from the moment of birth. All the major reflexes discussed in the previous section should be present. (These should be checked by the pediatrician.) Then, as the child develops, you will want to watch at the appropriate times for the abilities listed in Figure 9.2. Doing so will not only help you follow the child's progress but also make you more knowledgeable about the process of psychological development.

CHECK YOUR UNDERSTANDING

1. **RECALL:** Which of the following does not appear before birth?
   a. the heartbeat
   b. movement of limbs
   c. growth and migration of neurons
   d. vocalizations
   e. all appear before birth

2. **RECALL:** After birth, brain development emphasizes the
   a. migration of neurons.
   b. development of connections among neurons.
   c. development of the brain stem.
   d. multiplication of neurons.
   e. function of individual neurons

3. **APPLICATION:** You are a psychologist working in a pediatric hospital. What would you recommend as one of the most important things that the staff could do for newborn babies to promote their healthy development?
   a. Talk to them.
   b. Begin toilet training them.
   c. Make eye contact with them.
   d. Feed them on a fixed schedule.
   e. Touch them.

4. **APPLICATION:** You would expect your newborn baby to
   a. quickly learn to recognize the sound of his or her name.
   b. react negatively to a taste of lemon.
   c. prefer the father's deeper voice to the mother's higher voice.
   d. smile when eating.
   e. mimic facial expressions.

5. **RECALL:** Mary Ainsworth found two main types of attachment,
   a. shy and bold.
   b. introverted and extraverted.
   c. secure and insecure.
   d. strong and weak.
   e. nature and nurture.

6. **UNDERSTANDING THE CORE CONCEPT:** Which one of the following is an innate ability that promotes survival?
   a. the grasping reflex
   b. recognition of the mother's face
   c. toilet training
   d. sharp vision
   e. smell

ANSWERS: 1. d 2. b 3. e 4. b 5. c 6. a

KEY QUESTION

WHAT ARE THE DEVELOPMENTAL TASKS OF INFANCY AND CHILDHOOD?

Two of the greatest accomplishments of your life are developing your ability to think and reason, and forming relationships with the important people in your life. (Another is acquiring your native language, which we discuss in Chapter 7.) Each of these serve as the basis for further development later in life. And we will see that as children work through these tasks, they undergo profound psychological changes. Here's how our Core Concept states the main idea of this section:

CORE CONCEPT

Infants and children face especially important developmental tasks in the areas of cognition and social relationships—tasks that lay a foundation for further growth in adolescence and adulthood.

As we will see below, the developmental differences between children and adults are huge, but the differences in thought and socialization are not simply the result of adults' greater experience or store of information. The differences between children and adults also involve the unfolding of crucial maturational processes. Let us first consider cognitive development.

Cognitive Development: Piaget's Theory

If you have ever known a toddler going through the naming explosion, you have seen that children have an insatiable appetite for labeling things they know. Behind this labeling is their emerging ability for thinking, perceiving, and remembering. The next few pages will focus on the ways in which these mental abilities emerge, a process called *cognitive development.*

Psychologists interested in cognitive development ask such questions as: When do children realize that objects still exist even when they can't see them? Do they know that it is possible to hold ideas that aren't true? Can they understand that people have desires and dreams, but objects do not? Developmental psychologists investigate not only *what* children think but *how* they think.

In this section we will emphasize the pioneering work on cognitive development by the late Swiss psychologist Jean Piaget (although there are other points of view). For nearly 50 years, Piaget observed children's intellectual development and formulated his observations into a comprehensive theory.

Piaget began this quest to understand the child's mind by carefully observing the behavior of his own three children. His methods were simple: He would pose problems to them, observe their responses, slightly alter the situations, and once again observe their responses. Piaget attended especially to the developmental transitions and changes in his children's thinking, reasoning, and problem solving. This focus led to a *discontinuous stage model* of development, which emphasized Piaget's view that children undergo a revolution in thought at each stage. We will see below that three key ideas distinguish Piaget's approach: (1) *schemas,* (2) the interaction of *assimilation* and *accommodation,* and (3) the *stages of cognitive development.*

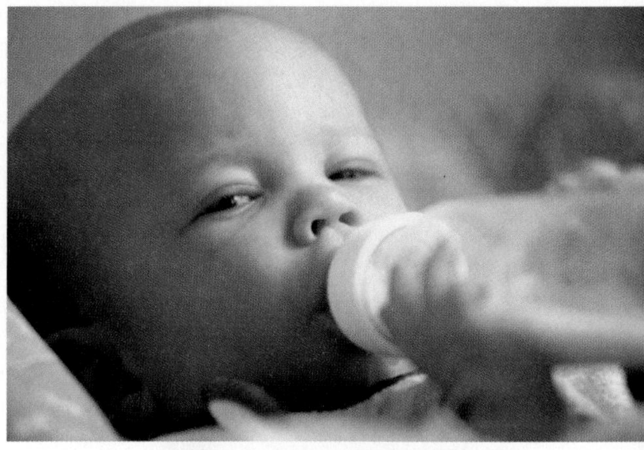

● Although an infant will begin to suck a bottle just the way he or she sucked a breast (assimilation), the infant will soon discover that some changes are necessary (accommodation). The child will make an even greater accommodation in the transitions from bottle to cup.

Schemas To illustrate the concept of schemas, think of some four-legged animals. Now think of some that are friendly. Then think of one that barks. You might have started by imagining elephants, tigers, cats, and dogs (all four-legged), then narrowed your choices down to cats and dogs (four-legged and friendly), and finally to just dogs (which bark). You could do this easily only because you have developed mental structures (mental programs) that enable you to interpret concepts and events. Piaget termed such mental structures **schemas.** We have schemas for concepts, such as "dog" and "development." We have schemas for actions, such as eating with chopsticks. We also have schemas for solving problems, such as finding the area of a circle or dealing with a crying baby. In general, schemas are mental structures that guide thinking. According to Piaget, they are also the building blocks of development. Schemas form and change as we develop and organize our knowledge to deal with new experiences and predict future events. As you read this, you are building a schema about schemas!

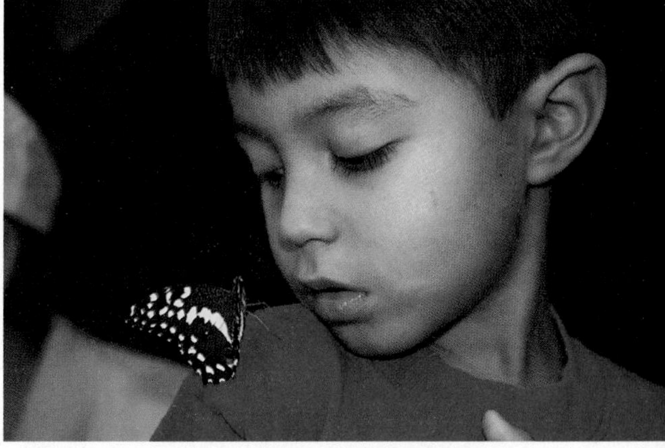

● Accommodation occurs when this child learns that a butterfly does not fit his schema for "bird."

Assimilation and Accommodation In Piaget's system, two dynamic processes underlie all cognitive growth: *assimilation* and *accommodation.* **Assimilation** is a mental process that modifies new information to fit with existing schemas—with what is already known. A baby who knows how to suck from a nipple will use assimilation to deal with new objects such as a finger or a new toy. Likewise, an older child might assimilate a new word such as "pepperoni" to describe a favorite kind of pizza. You, too, experience assimilation when you read about a favorite actor's new film or gain skill in using a new program on your computer.

By contrast, **accommodation** is a process of *restructuring or modifying schemas* to incorporate new information. For example, a child's simplistic "bird" schema, which includes any flying object, undergoes accommodation when the child learns that a butterfly is not a bird. Adults experience accommodation of their mental schemas, too. For example, the Internet has caused widespread accommodation in the schemas people use to conceptualize shopping and communicating. You, too, may need to modify a schema when the professor in your psychology course says something that surprises you—such as, "Children have innate language abilities," when you had always assumed that language was acquired entirely by learning. As a result, your schema about newborn children may change to accommodate your new knowledge.

■ **Schemas** In Piaget's theory, mental structures or programs that guide a developing child's thought.

■ **Assimilation** A mental process that modifies new information to fit it into existing schemas.

■ **Accommodation** A mental process that restructures existing schemas so that new information is better understood.

Object permanence, the perception that objects exist independently of one's own actions or awareness, develops gradually during the first stage of cognitive development and is solidly formed before age one. The baby in these pictures clearly believes that the toy no longer exists once it is obscured by the screen.

For Piaget, cognitive development results from the continual interweaving of assimilation and accommodation. Through these two processes, the individual's behavior and knowledge become less dependent on concrete external reality and more reliant on internal thought. In general, *assimilation* makes new information fit our existing views of the world, and *accommodation* changes our views to fit new information.

Piaget's Stages of Cognitive Development The way a child thinks about the world progresses through four revolutionary changes. Piaget described these changes in terms of four stages of cognitive growth: the *sensorimotor stage* (infancy), the *preoperational stage* (early childhood), the *concrete operational stage* (middle childhood), and the *formal operational stage* (adolescence). At each stage, distinct styles of thinking emerge as the child progresses from sensory reaction to logical thought. It is important to note that all children progress through these stages in the same sequence, although one child may take longer to pass through a given stage than does another child.

The Sensorimotor Stage (Birth to about age 2) We have seen that children enter the world equipped with many innate and reflexive behaviors, such as those for clinging, sucking, and crying. None of these require thought—in the sense of the complex mental activity seen in problem solving later in childhood. Instead, children in the **sensorimotor stage** give mainly reflexive or "instinctive" motor responses to stimulation, with very little "thinking" involved. Piaget called this *sensorimotor intelligence.* Not everything is automatic, however. As we have seen, children at this stage are also capable of simple learning, even though the circuitry in the cortex is not yet well connected. They learn to recognize people they see frequently. And they learn to coordinate their body parts to grasp and explore attractive objects (a rattle, perhaps) or to avoid things that they dislike (such as the taste of a lemon wedge).

A major development of significance for later thinking and learning appears in the second year: the ability to make mental images, or internal mental representations, of objects. With the power of **mental representation,** children can now form mental images of objects and events and begin to use them in thinking and problem solving.

Gradually, the child takes mental representation one step farther by realizing that objects continue to exist even when they are out of sight. This ability, called **object permanence,** liberates the child from the present and from his or her immediate surroundings. (This makes the game of peekaboo interesting to a young child.) The basics are in place by one year of age, but the ability for object permanence continues to develop through the second year (Flavell, 1985). At the same time, language begins to appear, and so words become another way to make mental representations. Together these forms of representational thought become the major accomplishment of the sensorimotor stage.

The Preoperational Stage (from about 2 to 6 or 7 Years of Age) The cognitive advances in the next developmental stage, the **preoperational stage,** grow out of the ability to represent objects mentally. One of these advances involves the emerging sense of self as distinctive from other people and objects in the environment. Another advance involves the ability to solve simple problems using mental representation (such as searching different places for a lost toy). Yet despite these abilities, the child cannot solve problems requiring logical thought. Other important limiting features of the child's mind in this period are *egocentrism, animistic thinking, centration,* and *irreversibility.*

- **Egocentrism,** a self-centered focus, causes children to see the world only in terms of themselves and their own position. Further, they assume that others see the world in the same way they do. So, when you are talking to a

- **Sensorimotor stage** The first stage in Piaget's theory, during which the child relies heavily on innate motor responses to stimuli.
- **Mental representation** The ability to form internal images of objects and events.
- **Object permanence** The knowledge that objects exist independently of one's own actions or awareness.
- **Preoperational stage** The second stage in Piaget's theory, marked by well-developed mental representation and the use of language.
- **Egocentrism** In Piaget's theory, the self-centered inability to realize that there are other viewpoints beside one's own.

preoperational child on the phone, she may say, "Look at my new dollie!" assuming you can see things on her end of the line. As a result of this egocentrism, preoperational children are not yet able to fully empathize with others or take others' points of view. For this reason, children may act in ways that have destructive or hurtful consequences, even though they don't intend to upset or harm others. Egocentrism also makes it difficult for a child at this stage to share toys or food.

- **Animistic thinking** involves the belief that inanimate objects have life and mental processes, just as people do. For example, if a child slips and bangs her head on the table, she might complain about the "bad table," blaming it for hurting her.
- **Centration** involves the inability to understand an event because the child focuses attention too narrowly, while ignoring other important information. That is, the child can "center" on only one bit of information at a time. So, for example, a thirsty child may insist on drinking a "big glass" of juice, preferring a tall narrow container to a short wide one, mistakenly assuming that the height of the glass ensures that it will hold more juice, while ignoring the other relevant dimension of width. (See the "Do It Yourself!" box "Playing with Children—Piagetian Style.")
- **Irreversibility** is the inability to think through a series of events or the steps involved in solving a problem and then to reverse course, returning to the mental starting point. In short, preoperational children lack the ability to do and then undo an act in their minds. To give a concrete example, Sam might see Mary spill a box of raisins on the table and think, "Wow! Mary has lots more raisins than I have in my little box." But preoperational Sam cannot mentally reverse the process and think, "If she put them all back in the box, it would look like the same amount I have in mine." This inability—to do a mental "experiment," then undo it and mentally try another approach—represents the biggest obstacle to logical thinking in the preoperational child.

● This 5-year-old girl is aware that the two containers have the same amount of colored liquid. However, when the liquid from one is poured into a taller narrow container, she indicates that there is more liquid in the taller one. She has not yet grasped the concept of conservation, which she will understand by age 6 or 7.

While we might see these as limitations, keep in mind that they are also the characteristics that make children at this stage most charming and interesting—and different from older children and adults.

The Concrete Operational Stage (from about 7 to about 11 Years of Age) At the next stage, children break through the barrier of *irreversibility* to understand, for the first time, that many things may stay essentially the same, even when their superficial appearance changes. In this **concrete operational stage,** they can understand that a short, wide glass can hold as much juice as a tall, narrow one or that the spilled raisins must fit back in the box. So the problems that defeated the preoperational child now yield to a new understanding of the way that volume is *conserved.* Similarly, they now understand that a string of red beads is not longer than an identical string of blue beads, even though the red beads are stretched out in a line while the blue beads lie in a small pile. They realize that the beads *look* different in their grouping, but this does not mean that they *are* different in number. This new ability, called **conservation,** represents one of the most important cognitive breakthroughs that most 7-year-olds have made.

Along with the new ability to understand conservation, children at this stage acquire the capability for performing **mental operations.** They have overcome the problem of irreversibility, so they now can solve problems by manipulating concepts entirely in their minds. This allows the concrete operational child to think things through before taking action. As a result, they may be less impulsive. They are also less gullible, giving up many "magical" notions, such as the belief in Santa Claus, that they now know to be impossible.

■ **Animistic thinking** A preoperational mode of thought in which inanimate objects are imagined to have life and mental processes.

■ **Centration** A preoperational thought pattern involving the inability to take into account more than one factor at a time.

■ **Irreversibility** The inability, in the preoperational child, to think through a series of events or mental operations and then mentally reverse the steps.

■ **Concrete operational stage** The third of Piaget's stages, when a child understands conservation but still is incapable of abstract thought.

■ **Conservation** The understanding that the physical properties of an object or substance do not change when appearances change but nothing is added or taken away.

■ **Mental operations** Solving problems by manipulating images in one's mind.

DO IT YOURSELF! Playing with Children–Piagetian Style

If you have access to a child, you can try out some of the problems Piaget posed for his children in order to study their thinking. For example, with a preoperational or concrete operational child, it's always fun to give a conservation problem that involves pouring liquid from a tall, narrow container into a short, wide one. Begin by pouring the same amounts into two identical vessels, such as glass measuring cups. Get the child to agree that you are starting with the same amount in each. Then pour the liquid from one vessel into a shallow pan. Ask the child, "Does one of these have more than the other, or are they both the same?" Then see if your child's responses fit with Piaget's observations.

Piaget found that the concrete operational child–who understands conservation–will know that the volume of liquid remains the same, regardless of the shape of the container. The preoperational child will think that the shallow pan has less because the liquid does not come up as far on the container. This shows that the younger child does not know that volume is conserved, regardless of the shape of the container. Piaget claimed that it also showed that the younger child cannot reason about both height and width simultaneously.

Using their ability for performing mental operations, concrete operational children begin to use simple reasoning to solve problems. The symbols they use in reasoning are, however, still mainly symbols for concrete objects and events, not abstractions. The limitations of their concrete thinking are shown in the familiar game of "20 questions," the goal of which is to determine the identity of an object by asking the fewest possible yes/no questions of the person who thinks up the object. A child of 7 or 8 usually sticks to very specific questions ("Is it a bird?" "Is it a cat?"), but does not ask the higher-level questions that more efficiently narrow down the possibilities for the correct answer ("Does it fly?" "Does it have fur?").

The *formal operational stage,* Piaget's final stage of cognitive development, we will save for our discussion of adolescence, when the individual overcomes the limitations of the previous stages, undergoing yet another cognitive revolution. Suffice it to say for now that this final stage involves the development of abstract thought.

Beyond Piaget: Other Perspectives on Cognitive Development Most psychologists accept the broad picture that Piaget painted of development (Beilin, 1992; Flavell, 1996; Lourenço & Machado, 1996). However, newer research suggests that the transition between one stage and another is less abrupt—more continuous—than Piaget's theory implies. Also, researchers have shown that children are, in some ways, more intellectually sophisticated at each stage than Piaget had found (Munakata et al., 1997). Studies show, for example, that some mental representation occurs as early as three months of age, rather than in the second year, as Piaget had thought (Gulya et al., 1998). Recent research also shows that by one year of age, infants develop the complex idea that people have intentions that may differ from their own (Baldwin, 2000; Tomasello, 2000).

Some psychologists believe that what Piaget saw as limitations on preoperational thought may actually be the inability to *express* thoughts (Bauer, 2002). Thus preoperational children may actually *understand* some of the same concepts that older children do, but they may still lack the skills to perform accordingly. For example, a 5-year-old child who has watched her father prepare breakfast in the past can watch him and understand what he is cooking but may not be able to describe it to her visiting grandmother or express why she likes her pancakes "the way Daddy fixes them." Researchers have found, in contrast with Piaget's notion of centration, that young children (ages 3 and 4) understand that the "insides" of objects, although they are invisible, are not necessarily identical to their external appearances (Gelman & Wellman, 1991). And, in contrast with Piaget's claims about animistic thinking, 3- to 5-year-old children, when pressed to do so, are consistently able to distinguish between real and purely mental (imaginary) entities (Wellman & Estes, 1986). Finally, studies of emotional development have shown that preoperational children can understand that other people have internal emotional responses that do not always jibe with their outward expressions (Bower, 1997b).

Other developmental psychologists counter that Piaget's theory is not as rigid as its critics claim. Rather, it is flexible enough to accommodate new findings. And, say Piaget's supporters, it underwent continual change throughout his long career (Lourenço & Machado, 1996).

What is really needed, says Robert Siegler, is a new metaphor for development (Siegler, 1994). Instead of the abrupt changes implied by stage theories, he proposes that we think of "waves." The wave metaphor, he says, better fits both the scientific data and our everyday experience, which shows the variability of children's behavior. For example, a child may, during a single day, use several different strategies to solve the same linguistic problem: "I ate," "I eated," and "I ated." This is not the pattern we would find if a child were making a sudden leap from one stage to another. Instead, says Siegler, this is a pattern of overlapping developmental waves, where each wave can be thought of as the ebb and flow in the strength of a cognitive strategy (Azar, 1995).

Social and Emotional Development

Our health, happiness, and even our survival depend on forming meaningful, effective relationships, in the family, with peers—and, later in life, on the job. This means that children need to begin the long process of learning the rules their society uses for governing its members' social and political interactions. They must also learn to monitor their own feelings and behavior and understand those of others.

As we have seen, Piaget taught that the preoperational child assumes other people share his or her view of the world. To grow beyond this egocentric perspective, the child must develop a **theory of mind.** This consists of an awareness that others may have beliefs, desires, and emotions different from one's own and that these mental states underlie their behavior (Frith & Frith, 1999). The theory of mind is also a set of expectations about how people will act in certain situations—such as when given a present or when spoken to angrily. This accomplishment is fundamental to successful social interaction, whether it be play, work, or establishing friendships and partnerships.

Smiling is one simple but important way people begin social and emotional interactions. So essential is a smile to human communication that a baby's first smile is probably generated automatically by genetically controlled processes. In fact, smiles occur in babies throughout the world (Gazzaniga, 1998a). The delight parents take in a baby's first smile represents the beginning of lifelong lessons in social behavior. People smile not only as a sign of positive feelings but also because their audience expects such a facial expression (Fridlund, 1990). However, social and emotional development involves much more than a winning smile. On the "nature" side, psychologists have found that an innate disposition or *temperament* influences our responsiveness to others. And on the "nurture" side, psychologists have found many environmental factors that influence socialization. We will analyze these two important concepts more deeply.

Temperament Psychologists use the term **temperament** for an individual's inherited, "wired-in" pattern of personality and behavior. Harvard researcher Jerome Kagan, who has studied temperament in thousands of children, observed that about 10 to 15% of infants are "born shy" or "born bold" (Kagan,

■ **Theory of mind** An awareness that other people's behavior may be influenced by beliefs, desires, and emotions that differ from one's own.

■ **Temperament** An individual's characteristic manner of behavior or reaction—assumed to have a strong genetic basis.

1994a, b; Kagan et al., 1986; Kagan & Snidman, 1991). In response to physical and social stimulation, shy babies are more easily frightened and less socially responsive than bold babies. Because of a baby's temperament, people are less likely to interact and be playful with the shy baby, accentuating the child's initial disposition.

Although basic temperaments can be recognized almost at birth, they are not written in stone (Kagan, 1996). (Remember: Nature always interacts with nurture.) Experience and parenting styles can modify the way temperament expresses itself. For example, a bold child reared by bold parents will certainly experience and respond to the world differently from a bold child reared by timid or fearful parents. Likewise, if a shy baby's parents recognize the child's withdrawal and gently play with her and encourage her to interact, the child may become more outgoing than her temperament would otherwise have predicted. Thus family members and friends can teach every individual a variety of responses to the world, all within his or her temperamental range. Nor is one temperament ideal for all situations. We should "remember that in a complex society like ours, each temperamental type can find its adaptive niche" (Kagan, quoted in Gallagher, 1994, p. 47).

Related to this are the ideas of Lev Vygotsky, who described a theory of social-cognitive development. Vygotsky maintained that social interaction plays a basic and key role in the development of cognition. In addition to the role of a supportive environment, he said, children have a **zone of proximal development** (Vygotsky, 1978) in which they may develop at either end of the zone (quickly or slowly), depending on the support and guidance available.

Socialization To help children find the most adaptive niches for their abilities and temperaments, parents socialize their offspring. *Socialization,* however, doesn't just happen it childhood. It is the lifelong process of shaping an individual's behavior patterns, values, standards, skills, attitudes, and motives to conform to those regarded as desirable in a particular society (Hetherington & Parke, 1975). We first learn about these things, of course, from our parents, so developmental psychologists have looked at the effects of various *parenting styles* on children's personalities and social behaviors. Aside from parents, many individuals and institutions exert pressure on the child to adopt socially approved values. Among these, the school and leisure-time influences, such as television and peers, have tremendous impact. And increasingly, many preschool children are shaped by their experiences in day care. Let's first take a look at parenting styles.

Four Parenting Styles and Their Effects Most approaches to child rearing fall into one of four distinct parenting styles that developmental psychologists have found in families all over the world (Baumrind, 1967, 1971; Darling & Steinberg, 1993; Russell et al., 2002). (As you read about these, you might try to imagine how you would have turned out differently if your parents had used one of the other approaches.) *Authoritarian parents* often live by the slogan "Spare the rod and spoil the child." They demand conformity and obedience, and they tolerate little discussion of rules, which they enforce with punishment or threats of punishment. In an alternative approach, *authoritative parents* can be demanding, too. They have high expectations of their children, which they enforce with consequences. But unlike authoritarian parents, they combine high standards with warmth and respect for the child's views: They are quite willing to listen to a child's ideas and feelings, and they often encourage a democratic family atmosphere. Authoritative parents usually place a heavy emphasis on reasoning and explaining in order to help their children learn to anticipate the consequences of their behavior. Taking a third approach, *permissive parents* set few rules and allow the children to make their own deci-

■ **Zone of proximal development** The difference between what a child can do with help and what the child can do without any help or guidance.

TABLE 9.1 Features of the Four Parenting Styles

Style	Emotional involvement	Authority	Autonomy
Authoritative	Parent is warm, attentive, and sensitive to child's needs and interests.	Parent makes reasonable demands for the child's maturity level; explains and enforces rules.	Parent permits child to make decisions in accord with developmental readiness; listens to child's viewpoint.
Authoritarian	Parent is cold and rejecting; frequently degrades the child.	Parent is highly demanding; may use coercion by yelling, commanding, criticizing, and reliance on punishment.	Parent makes most decisions for the child; rarely listens to child's viewpoint.
Permissive	Parent is warm but may spoil the child.	Parent makes few or no demands–often out of misplaced concern for child's self-esteem.	Parent permits child to make decisions before the child is ready.
Uninvolved	Parent is emotionally detached, withdrawn, and inattentive.	Parent makes few or no demands–often lacking in interest or expectations for the child.	Parent is indifferent to child's decisions and point of view.

Source: From DEVELOPMENT THROUGH THE LIFESPAN 3rd ed. by L. E. Berk. Copyright © 2004 by Pearson Education. Published and reprinted by permission of Allyn & Bacon, Boston, MA.

sions. Like authoritative parents, they are caring and communicative, but permissive parents give most decision-making responsibility to their children. Permissive parents believe that children can learn better from the consequences of their own actions than they can from following rules set by their parents. *Uninvolved parents* tend to be either indifferent or rejecting, sometimes to the point of neglect or abuse (Maccoby & Martin, 1983). Typically parents in this group lead such stress-filled lives that they have little time or energy for their children. (See Table 9.1.)

You can probably guess the usual outcomes of these different parenting styles. Research shows that children with authoritative parents tend to be confident, self-reliant, and enthusiastic—overall, happier, less troublesome, and more successful. Those with authoritarian parents tended to be anxious and insecure. Those with permissive or uninvolved parents are typically less mature, more impulsive, more dependent, and more demanding. Thinking back to our earlier discussion of attachment, these findings shouldn't be surprising. Generally speaking, authoritative parents take a more involved, interactive role in their children's lives—forming a stronger social-emotional attachment—than do the other three types of parents. This lays a strong foundation for prosocial behavior in the developing child.

Effects of Day Care As working parents make increasing use of day care for their children, we should ask the following question: How necessary is it to have a full-time caregiver? The question is an urgent one in the United States and Canada, where over half of all mothers with children under age 3 are employed, and more children are cared for by paid providers than by relatives (Scarr, 1997, 1998; Statistics Canada, 2002; U.S. Bureau of the Census, 2002).

The research on this issue sends mixed messages. First the good news: Most children thrive in day care. They do as well—sometimes better—both intellectually and socially as children raised at home by a full-time parent. Now the bad news: Some poor-quality day care experiences influence children to be aggressive, depressed, or otherwise maladjusted. Fortunately, the overwhelming majority of day care centers do a fine job (Bower, 1996; Clarke-Stewart, 1989; NICHD Early Child Care Research Network, 2003).

Given how important day care is in our society, it is comforting to note that having alternative caregivers does not in itself cause psychological problems. Rather, difficulties appear most often in poorly staffed centers where large numbers of children get little attention from only a few adults (Howes et al., 1988; NICHD Early Child Care Research Network, 2000). Another source of difficulty results from the unfortunate fact that children who are placed in the poorest-quality day care programs are most often from the poorest, most disorganized, and most highly stressed families. Developmental psychologist Laura Berk (2004) concludes that this volatile combination of inadequate day care and family pressure places some children at high risk for emotional and behavioral problems. Yet, she says, using this evidence to curtail day care services would be a mistake, because forcing a parent on a marginal income to stay home may expose children to an even greater level of risk.

All this means that day care is, in itself, neither good nor bad. It is the quality of care, whether given by a parent or a paid provider, that makes all the difference. Development expert Sandra Scarr (1998) says,

> There is an extraordinary international consensus among child-care researchers and practitioners about what quality child care is: It is warm, supportive interactions with adults in a safe, healthy, and stimulating environment, where early education and trusting relationships combine to support individual children's physical, emotional, social, and intellectual development. . . . (p. 102)

School and Leisure Influences Children and adolescents in the United States and other industrialized countries have much more free time than children elsewhere in the world. In nonindustrialized societies, children average some six hours a day working at some sort of chores or labor. By comparison, the typical American child spends less than one-half hour at such tasks. Moreover, the amount of free time available to U.S. children has increased dramatically over the last several generations (Larson, 2001). While long, hard work may teach discipline and responsibility, there is little evidence that it produces positive changes in cognitive development.

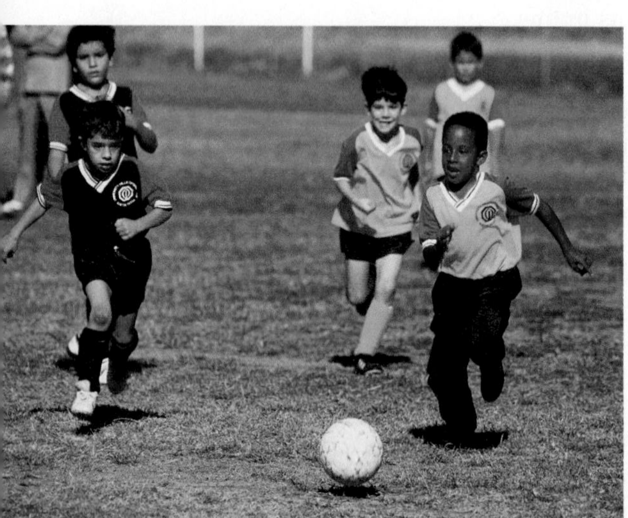

● Children and adolescents in industrialized societies average about six hours a day of discretionary time. Many choose to spend this time in organized activities, such as sports, although the most popular pursuit is "hanging out" with friends.

On the other hand, American children also spend more time (on the average) doing schoolwork than did children in years past—although not as much as their foreign counterparts in other industrialized countries. Still, there is time left over: How is it spent? Much is taken up watching television, talking on the telephone, or surfing the Internet (the consequences of which are largely unknown at present). The largest amount of discretionary time, however, is spent "hanging out" with friends. Surprisingly, however, many children spend the majority of their "free" time in structured activities, such as clubs and other organizations, art and music lessons, and sports—although this varies greatly from child to child (Larson, 2000).

Is the time of our nation's children well spent? Certainly some of it is unproductive or even counterproductive. For example, spending a great deal of time watching violent TV is predictive of aggressive behavior (Strasburger, 1995). Still, only the most unfeeling person would argue that all a child's time should be accounted for in developmentally productive activities. Clearly, the increase in leisure time, as well as increased access to information and the media, is a trend that is sweeping over industrialized nations. Where it may lead will be a subject for future research.

Gender Differences in Socialization Anyone who has watched young boys and girls playing has noticed gender differences in their social interaction. The sexes usually prefer to segregate themselves—a pattern that holds across cultures (Maccoby, 1998, 2000). In their play, boys are typically more aggressive than girls, although there are certainly exceptions. Girls tend to organize themselves into small, cooperative groups. By contrast, boys often form larger groups that have a hierarchical structure, or "pecking order." In these groups, individual boys continually compete for higher-ranking positions. They frequently resort to aggressive tactics, such as hitting, shoving, and verbal threats. Evolutionary psychologists believe that these gender differences have an innate basis (Buss, 1999), which may be related, in part, to gender differences in testosterone levels (Dabbs, 2000). This does not mean, of course, that environmental factors, such as parenting styles and peer influences, make no difference. Social-cognitive theorists like Kay Bussey and Albert Bandura (1999) attempt to counter this view by reminding us that children also *learn* gender roles and gender-related behaviors, such as aggressiveness, competitiveness, or cooperation.

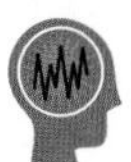

PSYCHOLOGY IN YOUR LIFE: CHILDHOOD INFLUENCES ON YOUR PERSONALITY

Your personality and your social relationships are a unique blend of your temperament, your attachment style, and many other forces that have acted on you through life. But are there common problems that everyone faces at certain points in life—problems that generate predictable personality changes across the lifespan? A theory of personality proposed by psychoanalyst Erik Erikson says yes.

As a middle-aged immigrant to America, Erik Erikson (1963) became aware of conflicts and choices he faced because of his new status. This caused him to reflect on the many such conflicts every individual must face in the continuing process of development. Before reading further, please take a moment to do as Erikson did: Recall some of the conflicts or challenges you have experienced in childhood. These will give you a vantage point from which to understand Erikson's theory—and your own personality.

Erikson's Theory of Psychosocial Development Erikson saw human development as a sequence of **psychosocial stages,** defined by common problems that emerge throughout life, from infancy to old age. As the term implies, all involve our social relationships. When people face these challenges, he said, they make choices that influence the growth of their personalities. Good choices lay the foundation for healthy growth during later stages.

Erikson identified eight such stages. With each succeeding stage, a new challenge comes into focus, as shown in Table 9.2. The problem must be satisfactorily resolved at a given stage if an individual is to cope successfully with the new problems that present themselves in later stages. Here we will review the psychosocial stages of childhood; later in the chapter we will review the issues experienced in adolescence and adulthood.

Trust versus Mistrust In the first stage of psychosocial development, you needed to develop a basic sense of trust in your environment and in those who cared for you. This trust is a natural accompaniment to a strong attachment relationship with a caregiver who provides food, warmth, and the comfort of physical closeness. But if these basic needs were not met, Erikson suggested, you experienced a developmental crisis that he called *trust versus mistrust*. At this stage, inconsistent parenting, lack of physical closeness and warmth, or the frequent absence of a caring adult may produce a lasting sense

■ **Psychosocial stages** In Erikson's theory, the developmental stages refer to eight major challenges that appear successively across the lifespan, which require an individual to rethink his or her goals and relationships with others.

TABLE 9.2 Erikson's Psychosocial Stages

Age/Period (approximate)	Principal Challenge	Adequate Resolution	Inadequate Resolution
0 to 1½ years	Trust vs. mistrust	Basic sense of safety, security; ability to rely on forces outside oneself	Insecurity, anxiety
1½ to 3 years	Autonomy vs. self-doubt	Perception of self as agent; capable of controlling one's own body and making things happen	Feelings of inadequacy about self-control, control of events
3 to 6 years	Initiative vs. guilt	Confidence in oneself as being able to initiate, create	Feeling of lack of self-worth
6 years to puberty	Competence vs. inferiority	Adequacy in basic social and intellectual skills; acceptance by peers	Lack of self-confidence; feelings of failure
Adolescence	Identity vs. role confusion	Comfortable sense of self as a person, both unique and socially accepted	Sense of self as fragmented, shifting, unclear sense of self
Early adulthood	Intimacy vs. isolation	Capacity for closeness and commitment to another	Feeling of aloneness, loneliness, separation; denial of intimacy needs
Middle adulthood	Generativity vs. stagnation	Focus of concern beyond oneself, to family, society, future generations	Self-indulgent concerns; lack of future orientation
Late adulthood	Ego-integrity vs. despair	Sense of wholeness; basic satisfaction with life	Feelings of futility, disappointment

of mistrust, insecurity, and anxiety. Children facing such conditions will not be prepared for the second stage in their psychological development. The healthy personality requires a foundation of trust from which the individual can become more adventurous.

Autonomy versus Self-Doubt In the second stage, as you acquired skills in walking and talking, you also expanded your ability to interact with objects and people. If you entered this stage with a sense of trust in others, these new abilities should have brought you a comfortable sense of autonomy (independence) and of being a capable and worthy person. Too much restriction or criticism at this stage may have led to self-doubts—hence the term for this stage: *autonomy versus self-doubt*. Harsh demands made on you beyond your ability—such as attempting toilet training too early—could have discouraged your efforts to persevere in mastering new tasks. Such demands also can lead to stormy scenes of confrontation, disrupting the supportive parent–child relationship. In contrast, the 2-year-old who insists on the right to do something without help, in response to appropriate demands, acts out of a need to affirm his or her autonomy and adequacy.

Initiative versus Guilt If you developed a basic sense of trust and autonomy during your preschool days, you probably entered the grade school years as a child who could comfortably initiate intellectual and motor tasks. For example, children in this stage want to do things for themselves, such as choose what to wear or what to eat. The danger at this stage comes from overcontrolling adults, who demand an impossible degree of self-control ("Why can't you sit still?"), with the result that the child is overcome by feelings of inadequacy and guilt. The term for this stage reflects these two alternatives:

initiative versus guilt. Caregivers' responses to self-initiated activities either encourage or discourage the freedom and self-confidence needed for the next stage.

Competence versus Inferiority If you successfully resolved the crises of the three earlier stages, you were ready to develop your skills and competencies in a more systematic way. During the elementary school years, school activities and sports offer arenas for learning more complex intellectual and motor skills, while peer interaction offers the chance to develop social skills. Successful efforts in these pursuits lead to feelings of competence. Some youngsters, however, become discouraged spectators rather than performers, or they experience failure that leaves them with a sense of inferiority. The term for this stage, therefore, is *competence versus inferiority.*

A Critical Reflection on Erikson's Theory How much confidence should we place in Erikson? Although widely respected, his developmental theory does have some shortcomings. Based mainly on clinical observation, it lacks a rigorous scientific basis. Moreover, as some critics point out, Erikson's list of developmental issues does not adequately capture the problems faced by girls and women. Nonetheless, your authors suggest that Erikson's work should be seen as a comprehensive pioneering effort that has encouraged us to look at the life cycle as a whole, putting into perspective both the unfolding changes and the continuity of life experience.

CONNECTION: CHAPTER 2

Clinical observation is a form of the *case study* method.

CHECK YOUR UNDERSTANDING

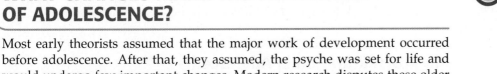

1. **RECALL:** Match the ability/limitation with the Piagetian stage at which it becomes an important characteristic of thinking.
   a. centration — i. sensorimotor stage
   b. abstract thought — ii. preoperational stage
   c. innate schemas — iii. concrete operational stage
   d. conservation — iv. formal operational stage
2. **APPLICATION:** Imagine that you are a family counselor. Which parenting style would you encourage parents to adopt in order to encourage their children to become confident and self-reliant?
   a. authoritative
   b. authoritarian
   c. permissive
   d. uninvolved
   e. both a and b
3. **UNDERSTANDING THE CORE CONCEPT:** There are many developmental tasks that children must face in the areas of thought and social interaction. Can you name one in each of these areas?

ANSWERS: 1. a. ii, b. iv, c. i, d. iii 2. a 3. Thought processes: for example, young children are not capable of abstract reasoning. (Piaget's theory suggests other differences at each stage.) Social relationships: attachment, development of a theory of mind.

WHAT CHANGES MARK THE TRANSITION OF ADOLESCENCE?

KEY QUESTION

Most early theorists assumed that the major work of development occurred before adolescence. After that, they assumed, the psyche was set for life and would undergo few important changes. Modern research disputes these older views. Modern psychologists agree that we have a remarkable capacity for developmental change throughout our lifespan (Kagan, 1996, 1998). Again in adolescence the big changes lie in three important areas—as our Core Concept says:

CORE CONCEPT

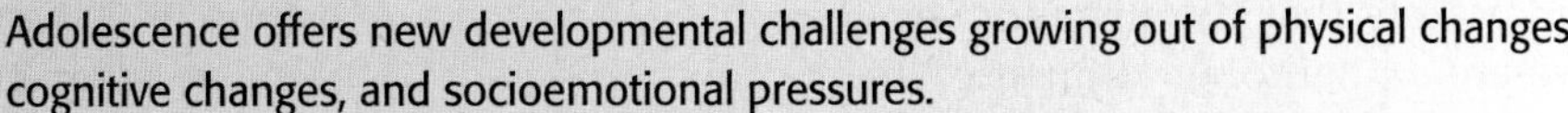

Adolescence offers new developmental challenges growing out of physical changes, cognitive changes, and socioemotional pressures.

Just when does *adolescence* begin? Or, to put the question more personally, what event first made you think of yourself as an adolescent? Chances are that it had something to do with your sexual maturation, such as a first menstrual period or a nocturnal ejaculation. Psychologists mark the beginning of **adolescence** as the onset of *puberty,* when sexual maturity, or the ability to reproduce, is attained. However, they cannot so precisely identify the point at which adolescence ends and adulthood begins.

Adolescence and Culture

Variations among cultures compound the difficulty of specifying the span of adolescence. Although the physical changes that take place at this stage are universal, the social and psychological dimensions of adolescence depend on the cultural context. For example, if you enter your teen years in a society that celebrates puberty as the entry to adulthood and rewards you with the power to make responsible choices, you will have a very different experience from someone whose culture condemns teenagers as confused and potentially dangerous troublemakers.

In fact, most nonindustrial societies do not identify an adolescent stage as we know it. Instead, children in these societies move directly into adulthood with **rites of passage.** These rituals usually take place at about the time of puberty and serve as a public acknowledgment of the transition from childhood to adulthood. Rites of passage vary widely among cultures, from extremely painful rituals to periods of instruction in sexual and cultural practices or periods of seclusion involving survival ordeals. For example, in some tribal groups, the young person may be asked to take a meditative journey alone or to submit to symbolic scarring or circumcision surrounded by friends and family. Once individuals have completed the passage, there is no ambiguity about their status: They are adults, and the ties to their childhood have been severed.

Our own society has few transition rituals to help children clearly mark their new adolescent status or for adolescents to know when they have become young adults. One such rite of passage for many middle-class teenagers in America is qualifying for a driver's license. Another is high school graduation. Both provide a young person with an added measure of freedom and independence that is not available to children.

Although many issues are important in adolescence, we will focus on a few of the most important developmental tasks that confront adolescents in the United States and the industrialized Western world: coming to terms with physical maturity, a new level of cognitive development, redefining social roles and emotional issues, dealing with sexual opportunities and pressures, and the development of moral standards. Each of these issues is just one component of the central task of establishing one's identity. We begin with the physical changes that mark the end of childhood and the onset of adolescence.

■ **Adolescence** In industrial societies, a developmental period beginning at puberty and ending (less clearly) at adulthood.

■ **Rites of passage** Social rituals that mark the transition between developmental stages, especially between childhood and adulthood.

■ **Puberty** The onset of sexual maturity.

■ **Primary sex characteristics** The sex organs and genitals.

■ **Secondary sex characteristics** Gender-related physical features that develop during puberty, including facial hair and deepening voice in males, widened hips and enlarged breasts in females, and the development of pubic hair in both sexes.

Physical Maturation in Adolescence

One of the first signs of approaching adolescence is the *pubescent growth spurt.* Two to three years after the onset of the growth spurt, **puberty,** or sexual maturity, is reached. Puberty for males begins with the production of live sperm (usually at about age 14 in the United States), while for girls it begins at *menarche,* the onset of menstruation (usually between ages 11 and 15). These serve as indicators that the **primary sex characteristics**—the sex organs and genitals—are undergoing dramatic change, accompanied by equally dramatic changes in the **secondary sex characteristics,** the enlargement of breasts and the widening of hips in girls, the deepening of the voice and appearance of facial hair in boys, and the sprouting of pubic hair in both sexes.

Simultaneously, boys and girl generally become more aware of their own appearance, often judging themselves harshly by the standards they think other people may be applying to them. And, unfair as it may be, physical attractiveness does influence the way people think about each other (Hatfield & Rapson, 1993). Thus, one of the most formidable tasks of adolescence involves coming to terms with one's physical self by developing a realistic yet accepting *body image* (one's personal and subjective view of one's own appearance). This image is dependent not only on measurable features, such as height and weight, but also on perceptions of other people's assessments and on cultural standards of physical beauty. During adolescence, dramatic physical changes and heightened emphasis on peer acceptance (especially acceptance by sexually attractive peers) intensifies concern with one's body image.

● Body image becomes especially important in the teenage years.

Approximately 44% of American adolescent girls and 23% of boys claimed that they have "frequently felt ugly and unattractive"; similar data have been found across many cultures (Offer et al., 1981, 1988). Physical appearance is clearly one of the biggest concerns among adolescents (Perkins & Lerner, 1995). Girls' self-concepts are particularly tied to perceptions of their physical attractiveness, while boys seem more concerned with their physical prowess, athletic ability, and effectiveness in achieving goals (Lerner et al., 1976; Wade, 1991). In general, girls and women are more dissatisfied with their weight and shape than are males, and they experience more conflict about food and eating (Rolls et al., 1991). These differences probably mirror a cultural preoccupation with female beauty and male strength—an inevitable source of concern because not all adolescents can embody the cultural ideals of attractiveness. There are also cultural influences on self-concept; some research indicates that the self-esteem of white adolescents of both sexes is more tied to physical attractiveness than is that of black adolescents (Wade, 1991). Over time, adolescents seem to become more accepting of their appearances. Nonetheless, the attainment of acceptable body images can be a difficult task.

Cognitive Development in Adolescence

Adolescence brings with it Piaget's final stage of cognitive growth, involving the capacity for abstract and complex thought. In this **formal operational stage,** the individual begins to ponder introspective problems involving ways of becoming better accepted by peers, along with abstract and intangible issues, such as fairness, love, and reasons for existence. With these formal operational reasoning powers, adolescents and adults now approach life's problems in a way that demonstrates their ability to use abstractions and to adopt thinking strategies that are not merely random guesswork. In the "20 questions" game we mentioned earlier, they impose their own structures on the task, starting with broad categories and then formulating and testing hypotheses in light of their knowledge of categories and relationships. Their questioning moves from general categories ("Is it an animal?") to subcategories ("Does it fly?") and then to specific guesses ("Is it a bird?") (Bruner et al., 1966).

Behind these changes in thinking are some profound changes occurring inside the body. Concentrations of the hormones estrogen and testosterone rise to high levels. At the same time, the frontal lobes of the brain, a region involved in social and emotional behaviors, is undergoing a "remodel," involving growth of new circuits, loss of some old ones, and changes in the balance of neurotransmitters (Spear, 2000). All of this probably contributes to increases among adolescents in sensation-seeking and risk-taking behaviors, as well as to increasing preoccupation with body image, sex, and social-emotional issues.

■ **Formal operational stage** The last of Piaget's stages, during which abstract thought appears.

● According to Erikson, during the "identity crisis" adolescents must define their identities as individuals even as they seek the comfort and feeling of belonging that comes from being with friends and family. One compromise might be to experiment with different norms–such as clothing or hairstyles–within the security of supportive relationships with companions, cliques, or romantic partners.

Social and Emotional Issues in Adolescence

Erik Erikson asserted that the essential problem of adolescence is discovering one's true identity amid the confusion of playing many different roles for different audiences in an expanding social world. Resolving this problem of identity helps the individual develop a sense of a coherent self. While it is normal and healthy for one's identity to change throughout life, failure of the adolescent to find a satisfactory resolution for his or her identity issues may result in a self-concept that lacks a stable core. Resolution of this issue is both a personal process and a social experience (Erikson, 1963).

The Increasing Influence of Peers Several factors influence the move toward an emerging self-identity. Family ties become stretched as the adolescent spends more time outside the home (Paikoff & Brooks-Gunn, 1991). In industrialized countries such as the United States, much of that time is spent in school. What adolescents do with that time, however, depends on gender (Buhrmester, 1996). Friendships among girls are built on emotional closeness, with girls often getting together "just to talk." By contrast, friendships among boys emphasize activities, with talk centering on personal achievements or those of others.

Some developmental experts argue that the effects of parents, family, and childhood become nearly lost as the adolescent peer group gains influence (Harris, 1995). In American society, the adolescent encounters new values, receives less structure and adult guidance, and feels a strong need for peer acceptance. As a result, adolescents report spending more than four times as much time talking to peers as to adults (Csikszentmihalyi et al., 1977; Larson, 2001). With their peers, adolescents refine their social skills and try out different social behaviors. Gradually, they define their social identities, the kind of people they choose to be, and the sorts of relationships they will pursue.

Is Adolescence a Period of Turmoil? Problems with loneliness, depression, and shyness can also become significant during adolescence, which is one reason for the sharp increase in suicide among teenagers (Berk, 2004; U.S. Bureau of the Census, 2002; Zimbardo, 1990). Studies of adolescent suicide show that the triggering experience for such a tragedy is often a shaming or humiliating event, such as failure in some achievement or a romantic rejection (Garland & Zigler, 1993). The intensity of a young person's social and personal motives can make it hard to keep perspective and recognize that even difficult times will pass and that everyone makes mistakes.

Many parents worry that their teenagers will endanger themselves in proving their loyalty to unreasonable friends or norms. Fortunately, research suggests that most adolescents are able to "look before they leap" by considering the wisdom of committing risky acts (Berndt, 1992). Adolescents who have poor relationships with their parents are at greater risk for trouble.

Another factor also has a huge influence on adjustment: the biological changes associated with puberty—for which many teenagers are unprepared. Awakening interest in sexuality is amplified by the hormonal surges of adolescence. High levels of testosterone, particularly in boys, have been associated with risky and antisocial behavior. Again, however, relationships with parents are crucial: Testosterone-related problems are much more likely in teens who lack the stabilizing force of a solid relationship with their parents (Booth et al., 2003).

But is adolescence inevitably a period of turmoil? It is a period in which individuals are likely to have conflicts with their parents, experience extremes of mood, and engage in risky behaviors (Arnett, 1999). For some, adolescence certainly presents overwhelming problems in relationships and in self-esteem. As a survey of the research has concluded, "The adolescent years mark the beginning of a downward spiral for some individuals" (Eccles et al., 1993, p. 90). Yet for most teens, these years are *not* a time of anxiety and despair (Myers & Diener, 1995). While many parents anticipate that the relationship with their children will encounter a rocky road when the children enter adolescence, the more typical experience is relatively tranquil. In fact, the majority of adolescent youth say that they feel close to their parents (Galambos, 1992). In general, those who have the least trouble are adolescents with authoritative parents—who are responsive and, at the same time, hold their children to high standards. Those adolescents who have the most difficulty are most likely to come from homes where parenting is either permissive or authoritarian (Collins et al., 2000).

Delinquency Only a small proportion of teens and young adults (about 6%) are at high risk for crime, and most of them are males in the 15- to 25-year age range (Lykken, 2001). Nevertheless, this small group accounts for about half of all crimes committed. What causes these individuals to turn to criminal behavior? There is no single, simple answer, but one of the important correlates has to do with family structure. Please realize that many other factors are undoubtedly also at work, including poverty, abuse, media influences, lack of job opportunities, and lack of education.

We focus here on family structure because it is the single strongest correlate of delinquency. Several studies have found that more than two-thirds of all delinquent males come from single-parent families—almost always involving a mother but no father (Beck et al., 1988; Forgatch et al., 1994; Snyder & Sickmund, 1995). A similar percentage of teenage girls who have babies out of wedlock also come from single-mother families (Kristol, 1994). The common thread seems to be fatherless, single-parent families.

We hasten to remind you that these data were not obtained by experiments. They are correlations. Obviously, then, they do not prove that fatherlessness *causes* delinquency. Yet, because we have no other obvious alternatives that connect so strongly with delinquency, fatherlessness remains a chief suspect. Further, the rise in delinquency over the last several decades parallels the increase in divorce and out-of-wedlock births during the same period (Lykken, 2001).

What can be done about delinquency? Few would go as far as psychologist David Lykken (2001), who has suggested—perhaps with tongue in cheek—licensing people to become parents. But when we think about the social forces that work against the family structure, many possibilities suggest themselves, including a welfare system and a tax system that have built-in disincentives for families, along with an educational system that too often does little to prepare students for dealing with the problems of family relationships. As you can see, this is an area ripe for both research and action.

Sexual Issues in Adolescence

A new awareness of sexual feelings and impulses accompanies physical maturity. In one large study, the majority of American adolescent males and females said that they often think about sex (Offer et al., 1981). Yet many still lack adequate knowledge or have misconceptions about sex and sexuality—even if they are sexually active. Sex is a topic parents find difficult to discuss with children, so adolescents tend to be secretive about sexual concerns, making exchange of information and communication even more difficult. The development of a sexual identity that defines sexual orientation and guides sexual behavior thus becomes an important task of adolescence.

Masturbation is the most common orgasmic expression of sexual impulses in adolescence (Wilson & Medora, 1990). By age 16, almost 90% of boys and 60% of girls in the United States report that they have masturbated (Janus &

Janus, 1993). But the figures we have could well be low. You can imagine the problems scientists face in trying to get good data on such private sexual practices. Sex research typically involves anonymous surveys, which may not give a complete picture of behaviors that are often associated with shame and guilt. Thus, one should realize that the statistics reported are estimates—often likely to be underestimates.

Same-Sex Orientation in Adolescence The same cautions that apply to the data on masturbation also apply to the research on adolescents who report they are gay, lesbian, or bisexual. Moreover, the data we have are somewhat sparse because funds for research on sexual behavior have been cut drastically in recent years. One study, however, involved data on some 83,000 youth in grades 7 through 12, obtained by combining information from several smaller surveys (Reis & Saewyc, 1999). Overall, the study found that same-sex sexual activity was reported by between 1% and 5.3% of the respondents.

Same-sex sexual behavior does not necessarily mean that the individual considers him- or herself to be homosexual or bisexual. Some experiment with same-sex activity yet think of themselves as heterosexual. For others, however, such experiences do fit with a gay, lesbian, or bisexual orientation—or with indecision about their orientation. Indeed, one sample from the study cited above found that 8.5% of the respondents identified themselves as gay, lesbian, bisexual, or undecided.

Exclusively homosexual feelings are difficult to resolve during adolescence, when individuals are intensely concerned with the conventions and norms of their society. While most gay and lesbian individuals first become aware of their sexual orientation in early adolescence, many may not attain self-acceptance of their sexual identities until their middle or late 20s (Newman & Muzzonigro, 1993). The time lag undoubtedly reflects the relative lack of social support for a homosexual orientation and exemplifies the importance of society's role in all aspects of identity development.

Heterosexual Behavior in Adolescence The overwhelming majority of adolescents have a predominantly heterosexual orientation. And do they practice their preferences? The proportion of American adolescents engaging in sexual intercourse rose substantially during the 1970s and 1980s but then leveled off (Chilman, 1983; London et al., 1989; Reinisch, 1990; Zeman, 1990). The 1990s, however, saw a drop in adolescent intercourse of about 10% (Centers for Disease Control, 2000). In a 1995 study, about half of all young Americans had engaged in intercourse by age 17, and about 75% had done so by the age of 20 (Harvey & Spigner, 1995).

There is evidence that the initial sexual experiences of males and females differ substantially. For the vast majority of females, emotional involvement is an important ingredient of sexual attraction. In contrast, for most males, personal relationships appear to be less important than the sex act itself. In fact, the average male reports little emotional involvement with his first sexual partner (Miller & Simon, 1980; Sprecher et al., 1995).

PSYCHOLOGY IN YOUR LIFE: THE DEVELOPMENT OF MORAL THINKING

Is there a pattern in the development of our sense of right and wrong? The best-known psychological approach to moral development comes from the late Lawrence Kohlberg (1964, 1981), who based his theory on Piaget's view

TABLE 9.3	Kohlberg's Stages of Moral Reasoning
Levels and Stages	**Reasons for Moral Behavior**
I. Preconventional morality	
Stage 1: Egocentric pleasure/pain/profit orientation	Avoid pain or avoid getting caught
Stage 2: Cost/benefit orientation; reciprocity ("I'll scratch your back if you'll scratch mine")	Achieve/receive rewards or mutual benefits
II. Conventional morality	
Stage 3: "Good child" orientation	Gain acceptance, avoid disapproval
Stage 4: Law-and-order orientation	Follow rules, avoid penalties
III. Postconventional (principled) morality	
Stage 5: Social contract orientation	Promote the welfare of one's society
Stage 6: Ethical principle orientation (e.g., Gandhi, Jesus, Mohammed)	Achieve justice, be consistent with one's principles, avoid self-condemnation

of cognitive development. After all, reasoned Kohlberg, moral thinking is just a special form of cognition. Mirroring Piaget's stages, each stage in Kohlberg's theory of moral reasoning is based on a different moral standard. Table 9.3 summarizes these stages.

It is important to understand that Kohlberg was more interested in the ways that people *think* about moral problems than in what they will *do* when led into temptation (Alper, 1985; Kohlberg, 1968). Accordingly, Kohlberg probed people's moral thinking by presenting people with a series of *moral dilemmas,* such as the following:

> In Europe a woman was near death from a very special kind of cancer. There was one drug that the doctors thought might save her. It was a form of radium that a druggist in the same town had recently discovered. The drug was expensive to make, but the druggist was charging ten times what the drug cost him to make. He paid $200 for the radium and charged $2000 for a small dose of the drug. The sick woman's husband, Heinz, went to everyone he knew to borrow the money, but he could only get together about $1000, which is half of what it cost. He told the druggist that his wife was dying, and asked him to sell it cheaper or let him pay later. But the druggist said, "No, I discovered the drug and I'm going to make money from it." So Heinz got desperate and broke into the man's store to steal the drug for his wife. Should Heinz have done that? Why? (Colby et al., 1983, p. 77)

Think about your own response to this situation before you read further.

It is important to understand that it made no difference to Kohlberg whether a person said that Heinz should or should not have stolen the drug. The problem is a genuine dilemma, so a well-reasoned case can be made on either side. For Kohlberg and his colleagues, the interesting part of an individual's answer was the moral thinking behind it. They found that the reasons given fell into six categories, corresponding to the following stages. See if you can tell where your own response to the Heinz problem fits.

- *Stage 1:* People reasoning at this stage think only of reward and punishment. They show no concern for others. In response to the Heinz dilemma they might say, "He should take the drug because he might get in trouble if he let his wife die." Or, on the other hand, "He shouldn't steal the drug because he might get caught and go to jail."
- *Stage 2:* The first sign of awareness of other perspectives shows itself at the second stage of moral reasoning. Still concerned about reward and punishment, the stage 2 person may seek personal gain by appealing to another person's self-interest, saying, in effect: "You scratch my back, and I'll scratch yours." Here is a sample stage 2 response to the Heinz case: "He should steal the drug because he is poor and needs his wife to help him make a living."
- *Stage 3:* The main concerns at this stage are seeking social approval and keeping everyone happy. Decisions are based on personal relationships rather than on principle. A typical stage 3 response: "They won't blame him for stealing the drug, but everyone would think he is bad if he let his wife die."
- *Stage 4:* Maintaining social order is paramount at stage 4. In this stage people often emphasize laws, rules, policies, promises, duty, or respect for authority in their responses. Someone at stage 4 might say, "He shouldn't steal the drug because it would violate the Ten Commandments," or "He should steal the drug because his first obligation is to his wife."
- *Stage 5:* Kohlberg called this the "social contract" stage because it emphasized the idea that rules and laws are flexible and can be changed by social consensus and by legislation. Emphasis at this stage is on fairness, rather than on the blind obedience of the previous stage. A possible stage 5 response to the Heinz dilemma: "He should take the drug, and the law should be interpreted to allow an exception under such desperate circumstances."
- *Stage 6:* At this stage the individual bases a decision on universal principles of conscience that he or she would apply to all people in all situations. These are abstract and general principles, which often refer to the dignity and worth of each person, rather than concrete rules such as the Ten Commandments. A possible stage 6 response: "He should take the drug because if he doesn't, he is putting a greater value on property than on human life."

You can see how Kohlberg's stages of moral reasoning parallel the stages of Piaget's theory, as the individual moves from concrete, egocentric reasons to more other-oriented, abstract ideas of right and wrong. Accordingly, at the first stages, a child may not steal a cookie for fear of punishment, while at a more advanced level, the child may resist stealing for fear of not living up to the parents' expectations. In general, the earliest stages of moral reasoning are based on self-interest, while later, more advanced stages center on others' expectations or on broader standards of social good. Unfortunately, not all people attain the later, least egocentric stages. In fact, Kohlberg found that many adults never even reach stage 4.

Culture and Morality Does moral development follow the same developmental sequence everywhere? Yes, said Kohlberg. Cross-cultural work shows that individuals attain the same stages in the same order in all cultures studied, including Turkey, Taiwan, Guatemala, Japan, and the United States (Eckensberger, 1994). However, this research also hints at some limitations of the theory in explaining moral development in other cultural contexts: The higher stages, as defined by Kohlberg, have not been found in all cultures. Even in his native United States, Kohlberg found that stages 5 and 6 do not always emerge. Their emergence appears to be associated with high levels of verbal ability and formal education (Rest & Thoma, 1976).

Gender and Morality One of the most stinging criticisms of Kohlberg's theory has come from Carol Gilligan (1982), a colleague at Kohlberg's own campus. Gilligan argued that the theory has a male bias and ignores uniquely feminine conceptions of morality. For women, says Gilligan, morality is embedded in social relationships and personal caring, which makes them appear to reach a plateau at stage 3. To his credit, Kohlberg responded by taking a fresh look at his data for stage 3 and stage 4. As a result, he redefined stage 4 by moving militant law-and-order responses (most often given by males) to stage 3. Most subsequent studies have found no significant sex differences in moral reasoning (Walker, 1989, 1991; Walker & de Vries, 1985; Walker et al., 1987).

A more telling critique suggests that research on moral reasoning may have limited practical value. Studies have found no close connection between people's moral reasoning and their behavior. Moreover, most moral reasoning comes after people have intuitively decided how to act. Moral reasoning, then, may be little more than rational justification for an emotional decision, claims psychologist Jonathan Haidt (2001). In the arena of morality, says Haidt, it's the "emotional dog" that wags its "rational tail," not the other way around.

CHECK YOUR UNDERSTANDING

1. **RECALL:** Which one of the following would be considered a secondary sex characteristic?
   a. deepening of the voice in males
   b. production of semen
   c. menarche
   d. maturation of the genitals
   e. ovulation
2. **RECALL:** Which one is a stage of life that is not recognized by some cultures?
   a. childhood
   b. adolescence
   c. adulthood
   d. old age
   e. infancy
3. **RECALL:** Which one is associated with a major challenge of adolescence, according to Erikson?
   a. ego-integrity
   b. intimacy
   c. generativity
   d. stagnation
   e. identity
4. **RECALL:** Which one of the following groups becomes most influential in the lives of adolescents?
   a. parents
   b. teachers
   c. peers
   d. celebrities
   e. children
5. **RECALL:** According to Kohlberg, as moral reasoning advances, individuals become less
   a. emotional.
   b. self-centered.
   c. ruled by instinct.
   d. attached to their parents.
   e. questioning
6. **UNDERSTANDING THE CORE CONCEPT:** Which of the following is a cognitive change appearing in adolescence that affects one's ability to think more deeply and abstractly about the social pressures of adolescence?
   a. depression
   b. formal operational thought
   c. conservation
   d. assimilation and accommodation
   e. nature and nurture

ANSWERS: 1. a 2. b 3. e 4. c 5. b 6. b

WHAT DEVELOPMENTAL CHALLENGES DO ADULTS FACE?

The transition from adolescence to young adulthood is marked by decisions about advanced education, career, and intimate relationships. Making such decisions and adjusting to the consequences are major tasks of adulthood because they shape the course of adult psychological development. But development doesn't stop there. Continuing pressures of careers, families, and friends, along with the relentless physical maturation (and eventual decline) of the body continually throw up new developmental challenges, as noted in the Core Concept for our discussion of adulthood:

Nature and nurture continue to produce changes throughout life, but in adulthood these changes include both growth and decline.

To see how developmental changes unfold in adulthood, let's begin with personality—where, for once, we find an area of agreement between Freud and psychologists who came after him.

Freud taught that adult development is driven by two basic needs: *love* and *work.* Abraham Maslow (1970) described these needs as love and belonging, which, when satisfied, allow the emergence of the needs for esteem and fulfillment. Other theorists divide the basic needs of adulthood into affiliation or social acceptance needs, achievement or competence needs, and power needs (McClelland, 1975, 1985; McClelland & Boyatzis, 1982). And in Erikson's theory, the early and middle adult years focus on needs for intimacy and "generativity." It is noteworthy that nearly every theorist has proposed some sort of social or affiliative need as a fundamental theme running through adulthood. But, because Erikson gave the most comprehensive account of adult personality, we will again concentrate on his theory.

Erikson's Theory of Young Adulthood: Intimacy versus Isolation

Young adulthood, said Erikson, poses the challenge of establishing close relationships with other adults (see Table 9.2 on p. 386). He described *intimacy* as the capacity to make a full commitment—sexual, emotional, and moral—to another person. The individual must resolve the conflict between wanting to establish closeness to another and fearing the vulnerability and risks such closeness can bring. Making intimate commitments requires compromising personal preferences, accepting responsibilities, and yielding some privacy and independence—but it can also bring great rewards. Failure to resolve this crisis leads to isolation and the inability to connect to others in meaningful ways.

Much research supports this notion of the need for close relationships with others. And it is the basis for one of the most practical applications that you can take with you from this text: *Anything that isolates us from sources of social support—from a reliable network of friends and family—puts us at risk for a host of physical ills, mental problems, and even social pathologies.* We are social creatures, and we need each other's help and support to be effective and healthy (Basic Behavioral Science Task Force, 1996).

For Erikson, a young adult must consolidate a clear and comfortable sense of identity (by resolving the crisis of adolescence) before being able to cope successfully with the risks and benefits of adult intimacy. In essence, you must know who and what you are before you can begin to love someone else and share your life with that person. However, the sequence from identity to intimacy that Erikson described may not accurately reflect present-day realities. The trend in recent years has been for young adults to live together before marrying, to delay making contractual commitments to lifelong intimacy with one person. In addition, many individuals today must struggle with identity issues (for example, career choices) at the same time they are trying to deal with intimacy issues. We don't yet know how these changes will affect people or society in the long run. In general, however, we can say that life for young adults today offers more choices and more complications than did the same period of life for the generation described by Erikson.

To complicate matters, marriage (one common route to the successful resolution of the search for intimacy) often occurs more than once in an individual's life. In fact, married adults in the United States are now divorcing at a rate four times greater than adults did 50 years ago. Half of all U.S. marriages end in divorce (U.S. Bureau of the Census, 2002). Moreover, an increasing number of couples are cohabitating rather than getting married (Doyle, 2002b). This rise in divorce may result from individuals seeking intimacy before they resolve their own identities. It may also result from unrealistic expectations that members of a couple have of each other and of what constitutes an ideal marriage and family structure (Cleek & Pearson, 1985). On the other hand, there is evidence that communication and affection between spouses is now better than it was in earlier times and that those who have learned good communications skills have substantially improved their chances of avoiding divorce (Caplow, 1982; Markman & Notarius, 1993).

Married people are now more likely to see each other as partners and friends and less likely to feel constrained by the stereotype of what society expects of a "husband" or "wife." Partners in "peer marriages" talk with and help each other in ways that work best for their relationship, irrespective of traditional ideas about the man being "boss" or the wife being responsible for "women's work" (Schwartz, 1994). The key to such a fair and satisfying relationship is communication in which both partners feel able to openly express their hopes and fears (Klagsbrun, 1985). A mushrooming of knowledge on how good communication can maintain relationships has helped our culture to view marriage as a worthwhile investment and therapy as a valuable option for supporting such efforts (Gottman, 1994; Notarius, 1996). In brief, relating is no longer viewed as a set of skills that "comes naturally" with the establishment of intimacy. Instead, close relationships are seen as lifelong works in progress, worthwhile investments of time and energy whose quality can be improved with clearer self-understanding, effective conflict resolution, and good communication.

The Challenge of Midlife: Generativity versus Stagnation

According to Erikson, the next major opportunity for growth lies in the path to **generativity** during adult midlife. For those who have successfully met the earlier challenges of identity and intimacy, generativity involves a commitment to make a contribution to family, work, society, or future generations—a crucial challenge of one's 30s, 40s, and 50s. Thus, people in this phase of life broaden their focus beyond self and partner, often as volunteers in community service groups. Research confirms that adults who express a strong sense of being generative and productive also report high life satisfaction (McAdams et al., 1993). In contrast, those who have not resolved earlier crises of identity and intimacy may experience a "midlife crisis." Such people question past choices, becoming cynical and stagnant or, at the other extreme, self-indulgent

■ **Generativity** In Erikson's theory, a process of making a commitment beyond oneself to family, work, society, or future generations.

and reckless. The good news is that most people do not undergo a midlife emotional upheaval or suffer the "empty nest syndrome" (Clay, 2003a, b).

A brief summary of all of the theories we have discussed is shown in Table 9.4 on page 399.

New Perspectives on Women, Men, Work, and Family

Life in many 21st century households would astonish Freud and other theorists of yesteryear, say psychologists Rosalind Barnett and Janet Hyde (2001). For one thing, dual-career families are now the norm. For another, women are receiving professional training at an unprecedented level. A third change involves the increasing fluidity among roles as worker and family member: Men no longer (at least, not as often) define themselves only as workers and family providers, and women are less likely to define themselves solely as wives and mothers. For most people this provides an expanded source of social support and an increased sense of well-being.

At this writing, same-gender couples are visibly forming family units, getting married, and raising children. And, as every reader of this book will be aware, this has become highly politicized. You can be sure that research on gay and lesbian families is forthcoming from psychologists, but at present we have only a few dozen studies. They almost uniformly suggest that same-sex couples can have healthy, nurturing relationships, and that their children are as well-adjusted as children from heterosexual couples (APA Online, 2004; see also Redding, 2001, 2002; Rooney, 2002).

Finally, we should note that the population is becoming older, as increasing numbers of people live long enough to become elderly. Moreover, *baby boomers* (those born in the "baby boom" right after World War II) are retiring, and retirement is becoming both an issue and an opportunity for more people. The research says that women (as a group) are less prepared for retirement than are men, although among retirees the majority report being happier than they were during their working years (Kim & Moen, 2001). If our society is to face the problems of an older population, with even more time on their hands than teenagers have, we will need far more extensive research dealing with this group.

PSYCHOLOGY IN YOUR LIFE: THE LAST DEVELOPMENTAL CHALLENGES YOU WILL FACE

At the beginning of the 20th century, only 3% of the U.S. population was over 65. One hundred years later that figure is about 13%. When the baby boom generation reaches this age over the next few years, nearly one-fourth of our population will be in this oldest group.

If you are now a 17-year-old high school student, you will be in your early 40s by the year 2030, and you will have witnessed a profound demographic shift (change in population characteristics). By that time, more than 80 million Americans will be over 60 years of age. For the first time in history, the number of people in the 60-plus age group will outnumber those under 20 years of age. This will represent a dramatic reversal of all previous demographics and a potentially significant shift away from today's youth-oriented culture (Pifer & Bronte, 1986). Among the effects: Tattoos and body piercings will become common in nursing homes, and there will also be far fewer people to pay the Social Security and Medicare bills.

With drastic changes in our society's age distribution looming, it is more crucial than ever to understand the nature of aging as well as the abilities

TABLE 9.4 Overview of Developmental Theories

Theorist	Continuity/ Discontinuity	Topic/Area of Coverage	Key Concept
Piaget	Discontinuity	Cognitive development	Formal operations
Kagan	N/A	Social development	Temperament
Vygotsky	Discontinuity	Social/cognitive development	Zone of proximal development
Erikson	Discontinuity	Psychosocial development	Conflicts
Kohlberg	Discontinuity	Moral development	Reasoning
Kübler-Ross	Discontinuity	Social development	Thanatology

and needs of the elderly (Roush, 1996). The problem of dealing with an aging population is even more pressing in Third World countries, where incomes and standards of living are low and where health care resources are minimal (Holden, 1996a). And, on a personal level, it may be helpful to anticipate some of the developmental challenges you will face in the last phase of your life.

Ego-Integrity versus Despair According to Erikson, an increasing awareness of your own mortality and of the changes in your body, behavior, and social roles will set the stage for late adulthood. Erikson called the crisis he identified at this stage *ego-integrity versus despair.* Ego-integrity, the healthy end of this dimension, involves the ability to look back on life without regrets and to enjoy a sense of wholeness. For those whose previous crises had unhealthy solutions, however, aspirations may remain unfulfilled, and these individuals may experience futility, despair, and self-deprecation. Sadly, they often then fail to resolve the crisis successfully at this final developmental stage.

In general, Erikson characterizes old age as a time of new challenges. What are the tasks of old age, and what resources and limitations must we confront as we look ahead to the autumn of our lives? In a series of interviews with middle-aged and older men and women, Ryff (1989) found that nearly everyone of both sexes defined "well-being" in terms of relationships with others: being a caring, compassionate person and having a good social support network. Respondents also emphasized the value of accepting change, enjoying life, and cultivating a sense of humor.

New Perspectives on Aging From a biological perspective, aging typically means decline: Energy reserves are reduced, cell machinery functions less efficiently, and muscle tone diminishes. From a cognitive perspective, however, we will see that aging is no longer synonymous with decline (Qualls & Abeles, 2000). In fact, many abilities, including expert skills and some aspects of memory, may improve with age (Azar, 1996; Krampe & Ericsson, 1996). A lifetime's accumulation of experience may finally culminate in wisdom—if the mind remains open and active. Thus, we see that theories of aging are models of balance or trade-offs: In old age, a person may lose energy reserves but gain an ability to control emotional experiences and thereby conserve energy. In other words, we can expect two kinds of changes—gains and losses—as we grow older (Baltes, 1987).

Some of the most obvious changes that occur with age affect people's physical appearances and abilities. As we age, we can expect our skin to wrinkle, our hair to thin and gray, and our height to decrease an inch or two. Our hearts and lungs operate less efficiently, so we can expect decreased physical stamina. We can also expect some of our senses to dull. These changes occur and develop gradually, so we have ample opportunity to gauge them

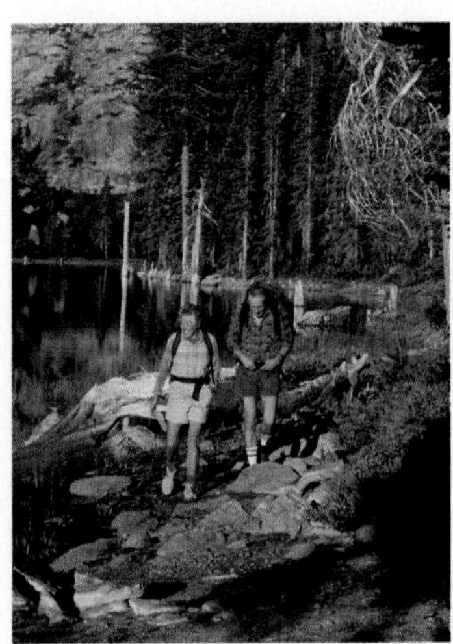

● Older people who pursue high levels of environmental stimulation tend to maintain higher levels of cognitive abilities.

and try to adjust. Successful aging takes into consideration both individual potential and realistic limits (Baltes, 1993). Consider how an individual might make the most of the following resources he or she has, given each of the changes accompanying aging:

- *Vision:* As we age, the lenses in our eyes become discolored and less flexible, affecting both color vision and distance vision. Most people over 65 experience some loss of visual acuity, and without corrective lenses half of the elderly would be considered legally blind. Glasses do aid in adjusting to these changes in vision, however, especially for night driving or close work such as reading.
- *Hearing:* Diminished hearing is common among those 60 and older, especially the ability to hear high-frequency sounds. Problems can ensue if the loss is undetected or denied (Maher & Ross, 1984; Manschreck, 1989). A person may come to believe that others are deliberately whispering to avoid being heard, leading to a mild form of paranoia (belief that one is being victimized). Those with a hearing loss might explain others' actions inaccurately because they lack information and blame their misinterpretations on evil intentions instead of simple bad hearing (Zimbardo et al., 1981). Fortunately, early hearing-aid therapy can be more effective than later psychotherapy. Hearing aids can compensate for much of one's hearing loss. In addition, those close to someone with a probable hearing loss can help them by speaking in lower-pitched tones, enunciating clearly, and reducing background noise.
- *Thinking, learning, and problem-solving:* A great fear about aging is that it is accompanied by the loss of mental abilities. But is this fear justified? Certain parts of the brain, particularly the frontal lobes, do lose mass as we age, but there is little evidence that this causes a general mental decline in healthy adults. Performance on tasks requiring imagination, such as vivid imagery strategies for memorizing, does seem to decline with age (Baltes & Kliegl, 1992). And people do acquire information more slowly by the time they are in their 70s and 80s. By that age, many older people—but not all—begin to show some decline in cognitive abilities. The older the group, the more variation we find (Kramer & Willis, 2002). On the other hand, the decline for the average person may not be as severe as folk wisdom had assumed (Helmuth, 2003c). Brain-imaging studies suggest that older people's brains compensate by processing information differently, bringing more regions into play (Cabeza, 2002; Helmuth, 2002). In fact, there is new research showing that moderate physical fitness training improves cognitive abilities in older adults and may forestall or even prevent age-related mental decline (Colcombe et al., 2004). Moreover, the evidence suggests that some abilities actually improve with age. Vocabulary, for example, is consistently better in older adults, as are social skills. And, accomplished with regard to skilled performance, musicians have been shown to improve well into their 90s (Krampe & Ericsson, 1996). Psychologists are now exploring age-related gains in wisdom, such as expertise in practical knowledge and life experience (Baltes, 1990).
- *Memory:* A common complaint among older adults is that their ability to remember things is not as good as it used to be. Most of these age-related memory difficulties appear in a part of the memory system that processes and stores new information (Poon, 1985). Aging does *not* seem to diminish access to knowledge or events that occurred long ago, so an elderly person may have to ask the name of a new acquaintance once or twice before finally remembering it but may have no trouble recalling the names of old friends or celebrities. A more important concern might be that people

explain memory loss differently depending on the age of the forgetful person. Using a double standard, younger adults attribute other young adults' memory failures to lack of effort but those of older adults to loss of ability (Parr & Siegert, 1993).

Particularly worrisome to older people is **Alzheimer's disease,** a degenerative disorder of the brain that produces both diminished thinking abilities and memory problems. Ultimately, it can cause death. Alzheimer's disease is estimated to occur in about 4% of the population over the age of 65, with the incidence increasing with age, to over 50% in people beyond age 85 (National Institute on Aging, 2004). One of the early signs involves memory problems, causing many older persons to become anxious when they are unable to remember a name or an event—a difficulty to which they would have given little thought when younger. It is an especially frightening disorder because it can render people helpless, rob them of their ability to make new memories, and make them forget loved ones.

- *Sexual functioning:* One myth about aging is that elderly people cannot or should not be sexually active. Belief in such a myth can be a greater obstacle than any physical limitations to experiencing satisfying sex in late adulthood. There is no age, for either men or women, at which the capability for arousal or orgasm ceases. (This is particularly true now that drugs, such as the well-advertised Viagra, have enhanced erectile ability for millions of older men.) And while sex loses its reproductive functions in late adulthood, it doesn't lose its capacity for providing pleasure. Regular sexual practice also enhances healthy aging because it provides arousal, aerobic exercise, fantasy, and social interaction (Ornstein & Sobel, 1989). Experience and creativity clearly compensate for minor physical changes or losses of physical stamina.
- *Social interaction:* An unfortunate consequence of living a long life is outliving some friends and family members. In addition, the reduced mobility associated with aging can make people become somewhat less active socially in later adulthood. While older adults reduce the extent of their social contacts, they remain more invested in those ties they choose to keep. Maintaining even a single intimate relationship can markedly improve personal health, as can living with a beloved pet (Siegel, 1990). Research shows that as people age, they tend to engage in **selective social interaction,** maintaining only the most rewarding contacts for the investment of precious physical and emotional energy (Carstensen, 1987, 1991; Lang & Carstensen, 1994).
- *Emotions:* While old age is often seen as a time of depression and restriction of emotions, the evidence doesn't support this view in healthy older adults, although age often improves people's ability to *control* their emotions—when they want to (Lawton, 2001). Moreover, older individuals report experiencing more positive emotions and fewer negative emotions than do younger adults (Mroczek, 2001).

What can be done for those who experience trouble or personal difficulty in aging? Many elderly people have discovered particular strategies that help them age successfully. For example, older adults can remain both active and close to people by doing volunteer work in the community, joining clubs and classes, or spending time with grandchildren. In addition, we might learn lessons from other cultures where older citizens are well respected and venerated for their wisdom. Before this happens, however, people must overcome stultifying stereotypes of the elderly as incapable and incompetent (Brewer et al., 1981).

Alzheimer's disease
A degenerative brain disease usually noticed first by its debilitating effects on memory.

Selective social interaction
Choosing to restrict the number of one's social contacts to those who are the most gratifying.

One other important development theory to consider as we look toward later adulthood was proposed by Elisabeth Kübler-Ross. In her 1969 book *On Death and Dying,* she described the developmental changes that terminally ill and/or dying individuals experience. Kübler-Ross identified five stages of death and dying: **denial, anger, bargaining, depression,** and **acceptance.** Although in her early writings she stated that each patient goes through them in order, as time went on she was shocked to learn that some health care providers were actually trying to force patients through the stage at set points in time. She later came to assert that each individual experiences the stages differently according to his or her own experience. As we have seen throughout development, not everyone develops in the same way or in the same timeframe, and Kübler-Ross argued that this is true for death and dying as well.

What, then, would be a good strategy for dealing with the challenges of aging? Perhaps successful aging consists of making the most of gains while minimizing the impact of losses (Schulz & Heckhausen, 1996). Additionally, it is helpful to realize that losses of specific abilities need not represent threats to one's sense of self. As one's physical and psychological resources change, so do one's goals (Carstensen & Freund, 1994). In this fashion, late adulthood may be a time not of increasing frustration, but of increasing fulfillment.

DEVELOPMENTAL PSYCHOLOGY: THE STATE OF THE ART

Developmental psychology has shown beyond doubt that development—physical, cognitive, social, and emotional—continues throughout the lifespan. And the older we get, the more diversity we find among our age mates, even though we are facing many of the same issues or "life crises."

The most recent research has shown us that people at all ages have more abilities than previous generations of developmental psychologists believed. We now know, for example, that newborns can imitate facial expressions, that infants can count, and that thinking can be sharp in the elderly.

Much remains to be discovered, however. Highly effective treatments for many disorders connected to development, such as autism and Alzheimer's disease, remain just out of reach. The decoding of the human genome also promises insights into developmental problems—but those problems, too, remain unsolved. And finally (although this developmental "to-do" list is incomplete), the major social changes occurring in our society—including the redefinition of work and family, retirement, increased leisure time, instant access to information, and gender equality—all are having their effects on development in ways that we don't yet fully understand.

■ **Denial** Refusing to believe the individual is sick.

■ **Anger** Patient displays anger that they are sick, "why me!"

■ **Bargaining** Making a deal, in return for a cure, they will fulfill promises.

■ **Depression** Generally depressed affect includes sleep, loss of appetite, etc.

■ **Acceptance** Patient realizes death is inevitable and accepts fate.

CHECK YOUR UNDERSTANDING

1. **RECALL:** According to Erikson, a person who successfully faces the issue of intimacy versus isolation will have
   a. a meaningful career.
   b. children.
   c. a thirst for knowledge.
   d. social support.
   e. a robust sense of self.

2. **RECALL:** According to Erikson, people at midlife most want to
   a. have the freedom and independence to pursue their leisure interests.
   b. hang out with their friends.
   c. develop independence.
   d. maintain or improve their physical appearance.
   e. make a contribution to their career, society, or future generations.

3. **APPLICATION:** A major demographic shift is now in progress. This change involves
   a. a culture that is increasingly focusing on youth.
   b. an increase in the average age of the population.
   c. the roles of worker and parent becoming more rigidly defined.
   d. fewer women assuming professional roles.
   e. fewer men becoming primary caregivers.

4. **UNDERSTANDING THE CORE CONCEPT:** Old age eventually means that the person will experience decline in
   a. thinking and problem-solving abilities.
   b. social support from family.
   c. vision and hearing.
   d. emotional well-being.
   e. ego-integrity.

ANSWERS: 1. d 2. e 3. b 4. c

USING PSYCHOLOGY TO LEARN PSYCHOLOGY

Cognitive Development in College

Does your arrival at the formal operational stage, in the middle or high school years, signal the end of the cognitive line? Or will your thinking abilities continue to develop as you go on to college? A study by developmental psychologist William Perry suggests that your perspective on learning will change and mature as your college experience unfolds. This prediction is based on a sample of students that Perry followed through their undergraduate years at Harvard and Radcliffe. Specifically, he found that students' views of psychology and their other social science courses changed radically, as did their view of what they were there to learn (Perry, 1970, 1994).

At first, students in Perry's study had the most difficulty coming to grips with the diverse and conflicting viewpoints they encountered in their courses. For example, many confronted, for the first time, the idea that reasonable people can disagree—even about their most cherished "truths" concerning good and evil, God, nature, and human nature:

> A few seemed to find the notion of multiple frames of reference wholly unintelligible. Others responded with violent shock to their confrontation in dormitory bull sessions, or in their academic work, or both. Others experienced a joyful sense of liberation. (Perry, 1970, p. 4)

In dealing with this academic culture shock, Perry's students passed through a series of distinct intellectual stages that were reminiscent of Piaget's stages. And, although they arrived at college at different levels of cognitive maturity and continued to develop at different rates, all progressed through the same intellectual stages in the same sequence. Here are some of the highlights of this intellectual journey:

- Students at first typically see a college or university as a storehouse of information—a place to learn the Right Answers. Thus, they believe it is the professor's job to help students find these answers.
- Sooner or later, students discover an unexpected—perhaps shocking—diversity of opinion, even among the experts. At this stage, college students are likely to attribute conflicting opinions to confusion among poorly qualified experts.
- Eventually, students begin to accept diverse views as legitimate—but only in the fuzzy areas (such as psychology, other social sciences, and humanities) where experts haven't yet found the Right Answers. They decide that in subjects where the Right Answers haven't been nailed down, professors grade them on "good expression" of their ideas.
- Next, some students (not all) discover that uncertainty and diversity of opinion are everywhere—not just in the social sciences and humanities. They typically solve this problem in their minds by dividing the academic world into two realms: (a) one in which Right Answers exist (even though they haven't all been discovered) and (b) another in which anyone's opinion is as good as anyone else's. Often, at this stage, they perceive math and the "hard" sciences as the realm of Right Answers, leaving the social sciences and humanities in the realm of opinion.
- Finally, the most mature students come to see that multiple perspectives exist in all fields of study.

The students who achieve the final stage begin to see "truth" as tentative. They now realize that knowledge is always building and changing—even in the "hard" sciences. And they realize that a college education is not just learning an endless series of facts. Rather, it is learning about the important *questions* and major *concepts* of a field. In this book we have called them "Key Questions" and "Core Concepts."

At what stage will you find yourself?

CHAPTER SUMMARY

KEY QUESTION

CORE CONCEPT

● HOW DO PSYCHOLOGISTS EXPLAIN DEVELOPMENT?

Developmental psychologists study change and growth in physical and mental functioning throughout the lifespan. They have resolved the old nature–nurture issue by pointing out that nature and nurture always interact. Nevertheless, the issue continues to be debated. To weigh the relative contributions of heredity and environment, psychologists employ a variety of methods, including observations of identical twins, fraternal twins, and adopted children. The resulting studies show that many complex behaviors have a genetic component. Another controversy in developmental psychology involves continuity versus discontinuity. Psychologists who speak of developmental stages are taking the discontinuity view.

● **Development is a process of growth, change, and consistency brought about by an interaction of heredity and environment.**

● WHAT CAPABILITIES DOES THE CHILD POSSESS?

While the newborn mind was once considered a "blank slate," we now know that newborns possess certain innate abilities that help them survive. During the prenatal period, the organism progressively becomes a zygote, an embryo, and a fetus. Teratogens can damage the organism at any of these stages. Development of the brain proceeds at a rapid pace during the prenatal period, laying the foundation for the neonate's abilities to find food, interact with others, and avoid harm. Developmental research shows that infants are born with many sensory capabilities, preferences, and motor reflexes, plus the abilities to learn new responses that develop throughout childhood.

Developmental psychologists have been especially interested in the relationship between child and mother (or other caregiver). Ainsworth found that children may become either securely or insecurely attached. Attachment patterns established in infancy often persist into adulthood. Harlow's research suggests that infants seek contact comfort in the relationship with the mother.

Developmental psychologists have also looked carefully at the sequence of physical maturation and the influence of experience—particularly social interaction and physical contact—on the times at which various physical abilities, such as sitting and walking, develop.

● **Newborns have innate abilities for finding nourishment, interacting with others, and avoiding harmful situations, while the developing abilities of infants and children rely more on learning.**

● WHAT ARE THE DEVELOPMENTAL TASKS OF INFANCY AND CHILDHOOD?

Piaget's theory says that assimilation and accommodation are the two basic processes affecting our mental schemes and so underlie cognitive development. Piaget also proposed that children's cognitive development goes through four stages: the sensorimotor, the preoperational, the concrete operational, and the formal operational stages. New abilities, such as mental representation, object permanence, conservation, and mental operations, mark the emergence of successive stages. Newer theory and research have, however, modified many of Piaget's ideas.

Social and emotional development require that the child learn the rules of society and also develop a theory of mind. The basis for socialization is an innate temperament, which can be modified by experience, particularly by the four parenting styles: authoritative, authoritarian, permissive, and uninvolved. Day care is ever more frequently used in the United States, and research shows it can have positive effects on children. Children are also influenced by peers, school, and the media. Gender differences in socialization appear in the types of friendships formed by boys and girls.

Certain developmental disorders, including mental retardation, autism, dyslexia, and ADHD, are most frequently seen in childhood. In most cases, existing treatments can help, but they are far from cures for these disorders.

Erikson's theory proposes that personality develops through a series of crises, each focused on resolving an issue about oneself and others. These issues define four stages of psychosocial development in childhood, characterized by these issues: trust versus mistrust, autonomy versus self-doubt, initiative versus guilt, and competence versus inferiority.

● **Infants and children face especially important developmental tasks in the areas of cognition and social relationships—tasks that lay a foundation for further growth in adolescence and adulthood.**

● WHAT CHANGES MARK THE TRANSITION OF ADOLESCENCE?

The meaning of adolescence varies from culture to culture, although developmental psychologists define adolescence as a stage that starts at puberty. For Americans, the transitions of adolescence typically focus on rapid physical maturation and the development of a sexual, social, and gender identity, although there are few distinct rites of passage. Cognitive development in adolescence involves emerging abstract thought, which accompanies the formal operational stage. Peers become increasingly influential, and, for most, the family diminishes in influence. Some become delinquent. For the majority, the journey through adolescence is not unduly traumatic, but for some it is marked by loneliness or even suicide.

Sexual issues are especially important in adolescence, whether the individuals are homosexual or heterosexual. For the latter group, the past decade has witnessed a decline in sexual intercourse among adolescents.

Kohlberg's theory of moral reasoning, built on Piaget's foundation, is also a stage theory. In Kohlberg's view, lower stages involve concerns with personal consequences, and higher stages have a broader focus on principles of ethical living. It seems to be applicable across a variety of cultures, although some critics have raised issues of gender bias in the theory.

● Adolescence offers new developmental challenges growing out of physical changes, cognitive changes, and socioemotional pressures.

● WHAT DEVELOPMENTAL CHALLENGES DO ADULTS FACE?

The challenges of adulthood focus on social needs, particularly achieving intimacy and a sense of generativity. In recent years, major social changes in sex roles and the configuration of the family, career paths, and retirement have occurred, all of which affect the course of psychological development. In later adulthood, individuals must maintain a sense of integrity despite some physical changes and losses.

Erikson believed that successful resolution of earlier life crises can enable one to face the end of life with acceptance and even a sense of satisfaction. New perspectives on aging, however, show that this period of life is marked by both gains and losses, notably in vision, hearing, intelligence, memory, sexual functioning, and social interaction. For some aging is very difficult, but for others it is a time of increasing fulfillment.

● Nature and nurture continue to produce changes throughout life, but in adulthood these changes include both growth and decline.

REVIEW TEST

For each of the following items, choose the single correct or best answer. The correct answers appear at the end.

1. The term *nature* refers to the effects of ______, and *nurture* refers to the effects of ______.
   - **a.** continuity; discontinuity
   - **b.** parents; peers
   - **c.** assimilation; accommodation
   - **d.** heredity; environment
   - **e.** acceptance; bargaining
2. A psychologist taking the discontinuity view might see development as
   - **a.** a gradual process.
   - **b.** a matter of learning.
   - **c.** entirely genetic.
   - **d.** a series of stages.
   - **e.** strictly the result of parenting style.
3. About eight weeks after conception, the developing human organism is known as
   - **a.** a zygote.
   - **b.** an embryo.
   - **c.** an infant.
   - **d.** a neonate.
   - **e.** a fetus.
4. Which of the following is(are) true of the physical abilities of the newborn infant?
   - **a.** At birth, babies already have preferences for particular tastes and smells and dislikes for others.
   - **b.** Just moments after birth, a neonate may turn in the direction of a voice or reach out an exploring hand.
   - **c.** While babies are born with poor eyesight, they soon learn to detect large objects and high-contrast patterns.
   - **d.** All of the above are true.
   - **e.** None of the above is true.
5. Which of the following utterances illustrate(s) overregularization in language development?
   - **a.** "Babababa."
   - **b.** "Me gots two foots and two handses."
   - **c.** "Drink milk, all gone."
   - **d.** "Want cookie."
   - **e.** All of the above illustrate overregularization.
6. "Hey! That's not fair," complains Judi. "Tonio has more ice cream than me." Actually, both Judi and Tonio received a single scoop, but Tonio has stirred his around so it seems to fill the dish, while Judi's scoop is more compact. Judi's complaint indicates that she has not yet acquired the concept of ______ that affects how children think about the physical properties of things.
   - **a.** centration
   - **b.** egocentrism
   - **c.** conservation
   - **d.** object permanence
   - **e.** ego-integrity
7. Harry and Margaret Harlow conducted landmark studies of the behaviors of baby monkeys who were separated from their mothers and had access only to mother "dummies" in their cages. This work confirmed that
   - **a.** genuine attachment is possible only with the infant's biological mother.
   - **b.** contact comfort and physical touch are important for healthy early development.
   - **c.** the "cupboard theory of attachment" is true for both humans and nonhumans.
   - **d.** nonhuman infants will imprint on and restrict social behavior to the first visually prominent thing they see after birth.
   - **e.** all animal research is generalizable to humans.
8. For Erikson, the psychosocial crisis of ______ is addressed by skill development and social interaction during the elementary school years, when children must explore their abilities, talents, and peer relationships.
   - **a.** trust versus mistrust
   - **b.** autonomy versus doubt
   - **c.** competence versus inferiority
   - **d.** identity versus role confusion
   - **e.** ego-integrity versus despair

9. The briefest summary of the concerns and issues of adult development might simply be
   a. success and security.
   b. power and conquest.
   c. youth and beauty.
   d. death and dying.
   e. love and work.

10. In late adulthood, loss of ______ has often been associated with feelings of paranoia and social isolation.
    a. intellectual abilities
    b. sexual functioning
    c. one's spouse
    d. hearing
    e. sensory modalities

ANSWERS: 1. d 2. d 3. e 4. d 5. b 6. c 7. b 8. c 9. e 10. d

KEY TERMS

Developmental psychology (p. 362)
Nature–nurture issue (p. 362)
Interaction (p. 362)
Identical twins (p. 363)
Fraternal twins (p. 363)
Continuity view (p. 364)
Discontinuity view (p. 364)
Developmental stages (p. 365)
Prenatal period (p. 367)
Zygote (p. 367)
Embryo (p. 367)
Fetus (p. 367)
Placenta (p. 367)
Teratogens (p. 367)
Neonatal period (p. 368)
Infancy (p. 369)
Attachment (p. 370)
Imprinting (p. 370)
Contact comfort (p. 373)
Maturation (p. 373)
Schemas (p. 377)
Assimilation (p. 377)
Accommodation (p. 377)
Sensorimotor stage (p. 378)
Mental representation (p. 378)
Object permanence (p. 378)
Preoperational stage (p. 378)
Egocentrism (p. 378)
Animistic thinking (p. 379)
Centration (p. 379)
Irreversibility (p. 379)
Concrete operational stage (p. 379)
Conservation (p. 379)
Mental operations (p. 379)
Theory of mind (p. 381)
Temperament (p. 381)
Zone of proximal development (p. 382)
Psychosocial stages (p. 385)
Adolescence (p. 388)
Rites of passage (p. 388)
Puberty (p. 388)
Primary sex characteristics (p. 388)
Secondary sex characteristics (p. 388)
Formal operational stage (p. 389)
Generativity (p. 397)
Alzheimer's disease (p. 401)
Selective social interaction (p. 401)
Denial (p. 402)
Anger (p. 402)
Bargaining (p. 402)
Depression (p. 402)
Acceptance (p. 402)

AP* REVIEW: VOCABULARY

Match each of the following vocabulary terms to its definition.

1. Nature–nurture
2. Continuity view
3. Discontinuity view
4. Attachment
5. Assimilation
6. Accommodation
7. Temperament
8. Generativity
9. Selective social interaction
10. Neonatal period

_____ a. Mental process that modifies new information into existing schemas.

_____ b. In humans, this period extends though the first month after birth.

_____ c. An individual's characteristic manner of behavior or reaction.

_____ d. The view that development is gradual.

_____ e. A process of making a commitment beyond oneself to family, work, etc.

_____ f. Mental process that restructures existing schemas so that new information is better understood.

_____ g. Choosing to restrict the number of one's social contacts to those who are the most gratifying.

_____ h. The enduring social-emotional relationship between a child and parent/caregiver.

_____ i. Discussion about the relative importance of heredity and environment in development.

_____ j. The view that development proceeds in irregular "fits and starts."

AP* REVIEW: ESSAY

Use your knowledge of the chapter concepts to answer the following essay question.

Development involves the processes of growth and change from conception across the lifespan, including changes in physical, cognitive, and social behaviors. Focusing on the period of adolescence, give examples of the physical, cognitive, and social changes that occur. State how each of these three examples would be interpreted by the two sides of *either* the nature–nurture debate *or* the continuity–discontinuity controversy.

OUR RECOMMENDED BOOKS AND VIDEOS

ARTICLE

Sapolsky, R. (2001, November). The loveless man . . . who invented the science of love. *Scientific American,* 95–96. This is a review of Blum's *Love at Goon Park,* a study of attachment theorist Harry Harlow, the depressed yet disciplined scientist who isolated and studied miserable, lonely monkeys and discovered the importance to them (and to us) of touch, connection, and mother love.

BOOKS

Blum, D. (2002). *Love at Goon Park: Harry Harlow and the science of affection.* Boulder, CO: Perseus Books. Today we take for granted the importance of touch in expressing consolation, closeness, and sexual attraction, but the concept became commonplace only in the 1950s, with psychologist Harry Harlow's work on "contact comfort" among infant monkeys. From Harlow's controversial research and poignant photographs of frightened baby monkeys came research on human attachment as well as applications to romantic love. ("Goon Park" was the nickname for the often misread address of Harlow's University of Wisconsin laboratory at "600 N. Park").

Colapinto, J. (2001). *As nature made him: The boy who was raised as a girl.* New York: HarperPerennial. When a newborn boy lost his penis in a botched circumcision, his parents were advised by an "expert" to raise him as a girl, with a girl's name, clothing, and new gender instruction. Originally presented as a successful effort in identity shaping, the treatment became a developmental nightmare for the growing child, who at 14 decided to live life as a male instead. Presenting family with sympathy and doctors with disdain, the narrative becomes a gripping story of an individual in the crossfire of nature and nurture.

Kilbourne, J. (2000). *Can't buy my love: How advertising changes the way we think and feel.* New York: Free Press. The average American is exposed to over 3000 advertisements a day, all promising that love, sex, power, or self-esteem can be acquired simply by purchasing clothing, cosmetics, shoes, or cars. Educational psychologist and media expert Jean Kilbourne explores these manipulative messages and the damage they do—especially to young women and girls.

Snowdon, D. (2001). *Aging with grace: What the nun study teaches us about leading longer, healthier, and more meaningful lives.* New York: Bantam Doubleday Dell. In the late 1980s, the author undertook a study of aging and disability in a community of elderly Catholic nuns; but he eventually found he could not maintain a scholarly distance from them and began to care and learn about them individually. Here he presents the lessons he learned from them about the blend of community, commitment, activity, and health.

VIDEOS

Marvin's Room. (1996, color, 98 min.). Directed by Jerry Zaks; starring Meryl Streep, Diane Keaton, Leonardo DiCaprio. Estranged sisters face family crises as one, who is sick, calls on help from the other, who is losing a battle with her teenaged son. This cinematic tangle of family tensions, insights, and oversights captures the "messiness" of real-life family relationships. (*Rating PG-13*)

Welcome to the Dollhouse. (1996, color, 87 min.). Directed by Todd Solondz; starring Heather Matarazzo, Brandon Sexton, Jr., Daria Kalinina, Matthew Faber. The pain of puberty is depicted through the eyes of a young woman whose suburban parents are amazingly unsympathetic and favor her baby sister and whose school experience seems to be the Seventh Grade from Hell. The film has good performances and a lot of humor. (*Rating R*)

Key Question Chapter Outline

CORE CONCEPTS

Psychology in Your Life

What Forces Shape Our Personalities?

Psychodynamic Theories
Humanistic Theories
Social-Cognitive Theories
Current Trends

According to the psychodynamic, humanistic, and cognitive theories, personality is a continuously changing process, shaped by our internal needs and cognitions and by external pressures from the social environment.

Explaining Unusual People and Unusual Behavior

You don't need a theory of personality to explain why people do the expected.

What Persistent Patterns Are Found in Personality?

Personality and Temperament
Personality as a Composite of Traits

Another approach describes personality in terms of stable patterns known as temperaments, traits, and types.

Finding Your Type

When it comes to classifying personality according to types, a little caution may be in order.

What "Theories" Do People Use to Understand Each Other?

Implicit Personality Theories
Personality across Cultures

People everywhere develop implicit assumptions ("folk theories") about personality, but these assumptions vary in important ways across cultures.

Developing Your Own Theory of Personality

You'll probably want to be eclectic.

Personality: The State of the Art

USING PSYCHOLOGY TO LEARN PSYCHOLOGY:
Your Academic Locus of Control

Chapter 10

Personality

WHAT DROVE MARGARET SANGER? A psychologist trying to understand this powerful and charismatic figure might conclude that the balance in her life shifted on a sweltering day in July of 1912. She had responded to a call from the slums in New York City's Lower East Side, where Jake Sachs had found his wife, Sadie, unconscious and bleeding on the kitchen floor. The cause: Sadie had attempted to give herself an abortion. It was Sanger's job as an emergency-response nurse to save Sadie's life.

In those days, unwanted pregnancy—and botched abortions—were often the result of ignorance. Giving medical advice on sex was illegal, and birth control devices, such as condoms and diaphragms, were nearly impossible to obtain. As a result, some 100,000 illegal abortions were performed in the state every year—many of them by dangerous quack practitioners. People like Sadie, the poor and uneducated—those least able to bear the costliness of many children—had nowhere to turn for competent help with reproduction and family planning (Asbell, 1995).

Thanks to swift action by Margaret Sanger, Sadie Sachs survived. Nevertheless, Sanger was angry that she could do nothing to help prevent unwanted pregnancies. She was limited by the law to providing after-the-fact treatment for the victims of incompetent abortionists. It only added fuel to her inner fire when she later heard Sachs ask the doctor, "What can I do to stop having babies?" and heard his sarcastic reply, "Better tell Jake to sleep on the roof" (Sanger, 1971).

Sanger saw Sadie Sachs only one more time: Three months later, pregnant once again, Sadie died of another abortion attempt. This needless death spurred Sanger to seek an answer to her patients' pleas for safe contraception, "no matter what it might cost" (Sanger, 1938, in Conway, 1992, p. 567).

The cost was high. Sanger left the nursing profession and put her own family in the background as she began to research and promote contraception full time. In 1914 the threat of a prison term for "indecency" forced her to flee for England, where she spent a year waiting for the charges to be dropped. But she couldn't avoid jail altogether: In 1916, when she opened a public birth-control clinic, Sanger had to serve several jail sentences for illegally distributing information about contraception.

For 40 years, Sanger persistently challenged laws making contraception a criminal act and insisted that women take control of—and responsibility for—their bodies, sexuality, and childbearing (Kennedy, 1970; Sanger, 1971). But her single-minded focus on the birth-control cause eventually cost her a marriage to a man who had adored her and supported her work. Finally, in 1952, Sanger, then in her 70s, joined forces with philanthropist Katharine McCormick to commission the development of an oral contraceptive. The result: The first birth-control pills for women were approved for prescription eight years later.

Personality The psychological qualities that bring continuity to an individual's behavior in different situations and at different times.

The pattern of dogged determination seen in Sanger across these 40 years of struggle illustrates the central idea of this chapter: **Personality** consists of the psychological qualities that bring continuity to an individual in different situations and at different times. So, the *theories* of personality we will discuss in this chapter are "big picture" explanations that attempt to tie together all the important influences on an individual's thoughts and behavior. Thus, we might think of personality as the thread of consistency that runs through our lives (Cervone & Shoda, 1999). And when the "thread" of personality breaks, we see certain mental disorders involving extreme inconsistencies in personality: bipolar disorder, schizophrenia, and so-called "multiple personality" disorder.

CONNECTION: CHAPTER 12

Multiple personality and *split personality* are older terms for *dissociative identity disorder.*

What processes were at work to produce the pattern and consistency that we see in the life of Margaret Sanger? Was her personality shaped primarily by the people and events in her life? Those events were often so chaotic that we are forced to consider another possibility—that her strength and determi-

Personality is the thread of continuity in an individual in different situations.

nation arose from internal traits—from her basic makeup. You may recognize these alternatives as another instance of the nature–nurture question. The answer, of course, lies with *both:* Experience *and* innate factors shaped Margaret Sanger's personality, just as they shape our own.

In this chapter we will examine a number of theoretical explanations for personality. As we do so, you will find that some place more emphasis on nature and others on nurture. You will also find that particular theories are suited to dealing with particular kinds of issues:

- If your goal is to understand a depressed friend, a troublesome child—any individual—as a developing, changing being, you will probably find one of the *psychodynamic, humanistic,* or *cognitive theories* of personality most helpful. These theories are described in the first part of the chapter.
- If what you need is a snapshot of a person's current personality characteristics—as you might want if you were screening job applicants for your company—a theory of *temperaments, traits,* or *types* may be your best bet. You will find these in the second section of the chapter.
- If you are most interested in how people understand each other—as you might be if you were doing marriage counseling or conflict management—you will want to know the assumptions people make about each other. That is, you will want to know their *implicit theories of personality.* These will be discussed in the final section of the chapter.
- And, if you are wondering whether people understand each other in the same ways the world around, you will want to know about the *cross-cultural* work in personality. Such issues are also discussed in the final section of the chapter.

WHAT FORCES SHAPE OUR PERSONALITIES?

KEY QUESTION
?

If you have ever attended a family or high school reunion, you know that people change and grow relentlessly. They develop new interests and new friends, they move to new places, and they have new experiences. In this section we will consider three ways of accounting for the paths their personalities take: the *psychodynamic,* the *humanistic,* and the *cognitive theories.* Each describes personality from a different perspective, but all portray it as a dynamic, developing process. And all emphasize the interplay of internal mental processes and external social interactions—as our Core Concept says:

CORE CONCEPT

According to the psychodynamic, humanistic, and cognitive theories, personality is a continuously changing process, shaped by our internal needs and cognitions and by external pressures from the social environment.

Although the three viewpoints we will consider in this section of the chapter—the psychodynamic, humanistic, and cognitive theories—share some common ground, each emphasizes a different combination of factors. Most *psychodynamic theories* of personality call attention to motivation, especially unconscious motives, and the influence of past experiences on our mental health. *Humanistic theories* emphasize our present, subjective reality: What we believe is important now and how we think of ourselves in relation to others. Because the humanistic and psychodynamic theories were influenced so much by clinical practice—psychologists working with people who seek counseling and therapy—we grouped them together as the *clinical perspective* in Chapter 1.

The *social-cognitive theories* come out of the research experiments in psychology, rather than clinical practice. They are based on the idea that personality is influenced by learning, perception, and social interaction. In some respects, however, the social-cognitive theories complement rather than contradict the clinical perspective: All agree that our lives include past, present, and future; that our minds have both conscious and unconscious levels; and that our behaviors are sometimes emotional and impulsive and at other times cooler and more calculated. (As you are coming to see, it is impossible to place these theories in neat and tidy categories.) Which theory you choose will depend, to some extent, on what aspect of personality and behavior you want to explain. So, let us look more closely at each perspective.

Psychodynamic Theories

● Sigmund Freud was the founder of psychoanalysis and the psychodynamic perspective. He is seen here walking with his daughter Anna Freud, who later became a psychoanalyst in her own right.

The psychodynamic approach originated in the late 1800s with a medical puzzle called *hysteria,* now known as *conversion disorder.* In this condition, the physician finds physical symptoms, such as a muscle weakness, loss of sensation in a part of the body, or even paralysis—but no apparent physical cause, such as nerve damage. The psychological nature of hysteria finally became apparent when the French physician Jean Charcot demonstrated that he could make hysterical symptoms disappear by suggestion. He did this while his patients were in a hypnotic trance.

Sigmund Freud (1856–1939), a young and curious doctor, heard of Charcot's work and traveled to Paris to watch his renowned hypnotic demonstrations. Inspired, Freud returned to Vienna, resolving to try the hypnotic cure on his own patients. But to his dismay, Dr. Freud found that many could not be hypnotized deeply enough to affect their symptoms. Moreover, even the ones who lost their symptoms under hypnosis regained them after the trance was lifted. Finally, a frustrated Freud resolved to find another way to understand and treat the mysterious illness. The new approach he created became known as **psychoanalysis** or **psychoanalytic theory.** Technically, *psychoanalytic theory* is the term for Freud's explanation of personality and mental disorder, while *psychoanalysis* refers to his system of treatment for mental disorder. In practice, however, it has always been difficult to separate Freud's theory from his therapeutic procedures. Thus the term *psychoanalysis* is often used to refer to both (Carver & Scheier, 2000).

Freud's Psychoanalytic Theory At center stage in the personality, Freud placed the concept of the **unconscious.** He saw this hidden part of the mind as the source of powerful impulses, instincts, motives, and conflicts that energize the personality. We are normally unaware of this psychic domain, said Freud, because its contents are too threatening and anxiety-provoking. Only by using the special techniques of psychoanalysis would we find that a person who had, for example, been sexually molested in childhood still holds these memories in the unconscious. But these memories attempt to escape from the unconscious and reemerge in disguised form—perhaps as a dream or a symptom of a mental disorder, such as depression or a phobia. Even in the healthiest of us, said Freud, behavior originates in unconscious drives that we don't want to acknowledge. Consequently, we go about our daily business without knowing the real motives behind our behavior. Today, many psychologists consider this concept of the unconscious to be Freud's most important contribution to psychology. (See Figure 10.1.)

■ **Psychoanalysis** Freud's system of treatment for mental disorders. The term is often used to refer to psychoanalytic theory, as well.

■ **Psychoanalytic theory** Freud's theory of personality.

■ **Unconscious** In Freudian theory, this is the psychic domain of which the individual is not aware but that is the storehouse of repressed impulses, drives, and conflicts unavailable to consciousness.

Drives and Instincts The actions of the unconscious mind are powered by psychological energy—that is, by motives, drives, and desires. In one of his graphic analogies, Freud described the personality as the mental equivalent of steam in a boiler. Psychoanalysis focuses on how the mind's energy is exchanged, transformed, and expressed. For example, the "mental steam" of the sex drive could be expressed directly through sexual activity or indirectly through joking or creative pursuits. Freud named this drive *Eros,* for the Greek god of passionate love. And the energy behind this drive he called **libido,** from the Latin word for "lust." It is libidinal energy that fuels not only our sexual behavior but also our work and our leisure activities: drawing, dancing, reading, body building—nearly everything we do.

But Eros did not explain everything that fascinated Freud. Specifically, it did not explain acts of human aggression and destruction. It also did not explain the symptoms of the war veterans he saw who continued to relive their wartime traumas in nightmares and hallucinations. Such misery could only be explained with another drive, which he called *Thanatos* (from the Greek word for "death"). Freud conceived of Thanatos as the "death instinct" that drives the aggressive and destructive acts that humans commit against each other and themselves.

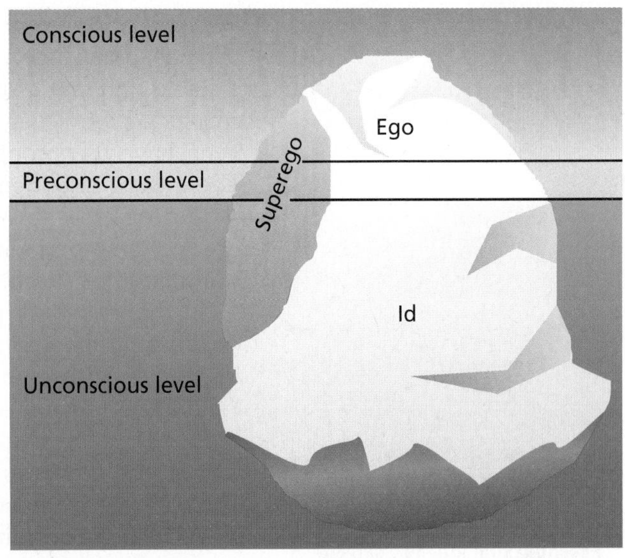

Conscious level
Ego
Preconscious level
Superego
Id
Unconscious level

● **FIGURE 10.1** Freud's Model of the Mind

In another famous metaphor, Freud likened the mind to an iceberg, because only a small portion appears "above the surface"–in consciousness. Meanwhile, the vast unconscious mind lurks "beneath the surface" of our awareness.

Was Freud right about Eros and Thanatos? You might gauge his theory against your own experience. Have you observed any human behavior that could not, broadly speaking, be assigned to one of these two categories: life and death—or, if you prefer, creation and destruction?

Personality Structure Freud pictured a continuing battle between two antagonistic parts of the personality, the *id* and the *superego.* This conflict is moderated by yet another part of the mind, the *ego.* (See Figure 10.1.)

He conceived of the **id** as the primitive, unconscious reservoir that houses the basic motives, drives, and instinctive desires that determine our personalities. Like a child, the id always acts on impulse and pushes for immediate gratification—especially sexual, physical, and emotional pleasures—to be experienced here and now without concern for consequences. It is the *only* part of the personality present at birth.

By contrast, the superego serves as the mind's "police force" in charge of values and morals learned from parents and from society. The **superego** corresponds roughly to our common notion of conscience. It develops as the child forms an internal set of rules based on the external rules imposed by parents and other adults. It is the inner voice of "shoulds" and "should nots." The superego also includes the *ego ideal,* an individual's view of the kind of person he or she should strive to become. Understandably, the superego frequently conflicts with the id's desires because the id wants to do what feels good, while the superego insists on doing what is right and moral.

Resolving the conflicts between id and superego is the job of the third major part of the personality's trinity, the **ego**—the conscious, rational portion of the mind. The ego must choose actions that will gratify the id's impulses but without violating one's moral principles or incurring undesirable consequences. For example, if you found that you had been given too much change at the grocery store, the superego would insist that you give it back, while the id might urge you to spend it on ice cream. The ego, then, would try to find a compromise, which might include returning the money and buying ice cream with your own money. That is, when the id and superego conflict, the ego tries to satisfy both. However, as pressures from the id, superego, and environment intensify, it becomes more difficult for the ego to find workable compromises. The result may be the conflicted or disturbed thoughts and behaviors that signify mental disorder.

■ **Libido** The Freudian concept of psychic energy that drives individuals to experience sensual pleasure.

■ **Id** The primitive, unconscious portion of the personality that houses the most basic drives and stores repressed memories.

■ **Superego** The mind's storehouse of values, including moral attitudes learned from parents and from society; roughly the same as the common notion of the conscience.

■ **Ego** The conscious, rational part of the personality, charged with keeping peace between the superego and the id.

Personality Development and Early Experiences As Freud talked with his patients about their past, he began to understand that personality follows predictable patterns of development throughout childhood and adolescence. He concluded, however, that "forgotten" experiences in infancy and early childhood have the strongest impact on personality formation and later behavior. These early experiences continue to influence the unconscious mind as the child progresses through a series of **psychosexual stages.** These stages consist of successive periods in which the developing child associates pleasure with stimulation of specific bodily areas.

In the *oral stage,* pleasure is associated with the mouth: suckling, crying, spewing. In the *anal stage,* pleasure comes from stimulating parts of the body associated with elimination. Next, in the *phallic stage,* pleasure comes from "immature" sexual expression, such as masturbation. (This also explains the humor popular with the prepubescent set.) Finally, after a quiet period of *latency,* the adult *genital stage* brings (to some) mature sexual relationships. These stages are detailed in Table 10.1.

■ **Psychosexual stages** Successive, instinctive patterns of associating pleasure with stimulation of specific bodily areas at different times of life.

Why such a seemingly bizarre theory of psychosexual development? Among the issues that Freud was trying to understand with his theory of psychosexual development were those of gender identity and gender roles. Why is it that boys usually develop a masculine identity, even though most boys are raised

TABLE 10.1 Freud's Stages of Psychosexual Development

Psychosexual Stage		Later Signs of Problems Beginning at This Stage	
Oral Stage (1st year)		Smoking	Obesity
Desires:	Oral stimulation by sucking, eating, crying, babbling	Nail-biting	Talkativeness
Challenge:	Overcoming dependency	Chewing	Dependency
		Gluttony	Gullibility
Anal Stage (approximately 1–3 years)		Messiness	Excessive cleanliness
Desires:	Anal stimulation by bladder and bowel function	Temper tantrums	Stinginess
Challenge:	Toilet training	Destructiveness	Coldness, distance, aloofness
	Self-control	Cruelty	
Phallic Stage (approximately 3–6 years)		Masturbation (not considered abnormal by modern psychology and psychiatry; see Chapter 9)	
Desires:	Stimulation of genitals	Jealousy	
Challenge:	Resolving Oedipus complex, involving erotic attraction to parent of opposite sex and hostility to parent of same sex	Egocentric sex	
		Sexual conquests	
		Problems with parents	
Latency (approximately 6 years to puberty)		Excessive modesty	
Desires:	Repression of sexual and aggressive desires, including those involved in the Oedipus complex	Preference for company of same sex	
Challenge:	Consciously: learning modesty and shame	Homosexuality (considered by Freud to be a disorder, but not by modern psychology and psychiatry; see Chapter 9)	
	Unconsciously: dealing with repressed Oedipal conflict		
Genital Stage (puberty and adulthood)		(none)	
Desires:	Mature sexual relationships		
Challenge:	Displacing energy into healthy activities		
	Establishing new relationship with parents		

primarily by their mothers? Why do girls, as they become adults, most often develop a sexual attraction to males—and boys to females? And why do some not follow this pattern?

Freud's answers to these questions were convoluted and, many psychologists would say, contrived. His inside-the-mind perspective ignored the influence of vastly different forms of socialization for boys and girls. It also ignored the possibility of differences in genetic programming, about which little was known in Freud's day. Instead, he invoked the notion of the **Oedipus complex,** whereby boys feel an erotic attraction toward their mothers. Successful resolution of the Oedipal conflict requires boys to *displace* (shift) their attraction to females of their own age and, at the same time, develop an **identification** with their fathers. Girls, he proposed, develop **penis envy** (because they don't have one!) and are usually attracted to males (who do). Most psychologists today reject these Freudian notions of psychosexual development because they lack scientific support. It is important, however, to remember two things: First, these Freudian concepts—strange as they may seem—continue to have a wide impact outside psychology, particularly in the humanities. Second, while Freud may have been wrong about the details of psychosexual development, he may have been right about other aspects of human personality (Bower, 1998b).

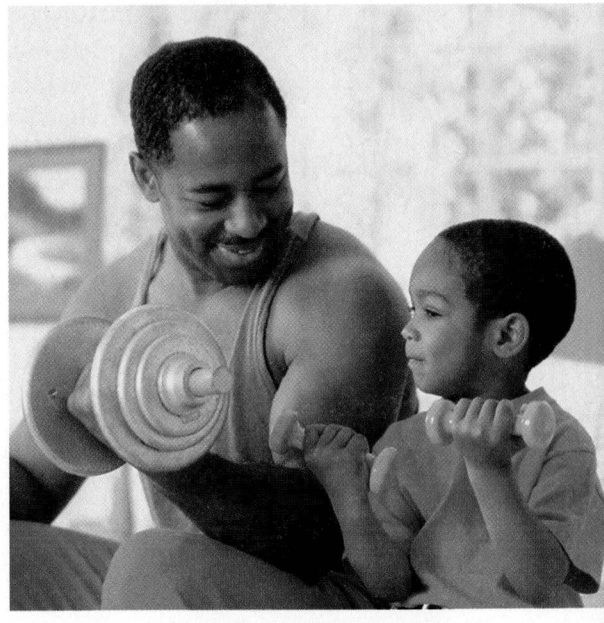

● During the phallic stage, a child must resolve feelings of conflict and anxiety by identifying more closely with the same-sex parent–said Freud.

Freud might have been right, for example, in his assertion that certain difficulties early in life lead to **fixation:** arrested psychological development. An *oral stage* fixation, caused by a failure to throw off the dependency of the first year of life, may lead to dependency on others in later childhood and adulthood. We also see an oral fixation in certain behaviors involving the mouth, such as overeating, alcoholism, and tendencies toward sarcasm. Among these diverse problems we find a common theme: using the mouth as the way to connect with what one needs. Fixation in the *anal* stage is presumed to come from problems associated with the second year of life when toilet training is a big issue. Anal fixations can result in a stubborn, compulsive, stingy, or excessively neat pattern of behavior—all related to common themes of "holding on" and not losing control of one's body or life. In Table 10.1 you will find examples of fixation at other developmental stages.

Ego Defenses The ego has an arsenal of **ego defense mechanisms** for dealing with conflict between the id's impulses and the superego's demand to deny them. All operate, said Freud, at the *preconscious level*—just beneath the surface of consciousness. Under mild pressure from the id we may, for example, rely on simple ego defenses, such as *fantasy* or *rationalization.* But if unconscious desires become too insistent, the ego may solve the problem by "putting a lid on the id." To do so, the ego must push extreme desires and threatening memories out of conscious awareness and into the recesses of the unconscious mind.

Repression is the name for the ego defense mechanism that excludes unacceptable thoughts and feelings from awareness. For example, repression may explain the behavior of a student who suspects she failed an important test and "forgets" to attend class the day the graded tests are returned. This memory lapse protects her from feeling upset or anxious—at least temporarily. In fact, that is the problem with repression and most of the other ego defense mechanisms, said Freud: They solve the problem only for the moment, leaving the underlying conflict unresolved.

Freud also taught that repression can block access to feelings, as well as memories. For example, if a child has strong feelings of anger toward her

■ **Oedipus complex** According to Freud, a largely unconscious process whereby boys displace an erotic attraction toward their mother to females of their own age and, at the same time, identify with their fathers.
■ **Identification** The mental process by which an individual tries to become like another person, especially the same-sex parent.
■ **Penis envy** According to Freud, the female desire to have a penis–a condition that usually results in their attraction to males.
■ **Fixation** Occurs when psychosexual development is arrested at an immature stage.
■ **Ego defense mechanisms** Largely unconscious mental strategies employed to reduce the experience of conflict or anxiety.
■ **Repression** An unconscious process that excludes unacceptable thoughts and feelings from awareness and memory.

"All right, deep down it's a cry for psychiatric help—but at one level it's a stick-up."

father—which, if acted out, would risk severe punishment—repression may take over. The repressed hostile impulse can no longer operate consciously. But although the impulse is not consciously felt, it is not gone, said Freud. At an unconscious level it continues to influence behavior, but in less direct ways, perhaps disguised as dreams, fantasies, or symptoms of mental disorder.

Freud—always the keen observer of human behavior—proposed many other ego defense mechanisms in addition to fantasy, rationalization, and repression. Here are some of the most important:

- *Denial:* "I don't have a problem." This defense avoids a difficult situation by simply denying that it exists. Denial is a defense frequently seen, for example, in alcoholics, child abusers, people who have problems managing anger, and people who engage in risky behavior, such as casual, unprotected sex.
- *Rationalization:* People using this defense mechanism give socially acceptable reasons for actions that are really based on motives that they believe to be unacceptable. A student who feels stressed by academic pressures may decide to cheat on a test, rationalizing it by saying that "everyone does it."
- *Reaction formation:* This ego defense mechanism occurs when people act in exact opposition to their true feelings. Accordingly, those troubled by their own sexual desires may initiate a crusade against "dirty books" in the city library. Or a child with low self-esteem may become a bully.
- *Displacement:* When your boss makes you angry, you may later displace your anger by yelling at your mate or kicking the dog. This ego defense mechanism involves shifting your reaction from the real source of your distress to a safer individual or object.
- *Regression:* Under stress, some people hide; others cry, throw things, or even wet their pants. That is, they adopt immature, juvenile behaviors that were effective ways of dealing with stress when they were younger.
- *Sublimation:* Gratifying sexual or aggressive desires in ways that are acceptable in one's culture, as in acting or sports.
- *Projection:* When we are upset or aroused, we may use the defense of projection to attribute our own unconscious desires to other people or objects. An example frequently seen in small children involves each accusing the other of starting a conflict.

This latter concept—projection—led to the development of *projective tests,* which have been used extensively in clinical psychology for evaluating personality and mental disorders. We take a brief detour at this point to introduce you to these projective techniques.

Projective Tests What do you see in Figure 10.2? Ambiguous images such as these are the basis for **projective tests.** Freudian clinicians often employ such instruments to probe their patients' innermost feelings, motives, conflicts and desires. The assumption is that people will *project* their hidden motives and conflicts onto the images. In fact, you may have noticed that, when gazing at the clouds, different people see different images, and the images people report seem to reflect their own personalities.

In the most famous of projective techniques, the **Rorschach inkblot technique** (pronounced *ROAR-shock*), the ambiguous stimuli are symmetrical inkblots (Rorschach, 1942). The technique calls for showing the blots one at a time and asking the respondent, "What do you see? What does this seem to be?" The examiner usually interprets responses in light of psychoanalytic theory by noting how they might reflect unconscious sexual and aggressive impulses (Erdberg, 1990).

■ **Projective tests** Personality assessment instruments, such as the Rorschach and TAT, which are based on Freud's ego defense mechanism of projection.

■ **Rorschach inkblot technique** A projective test requiring subjects to describe what they see in a series of ten inkblots.

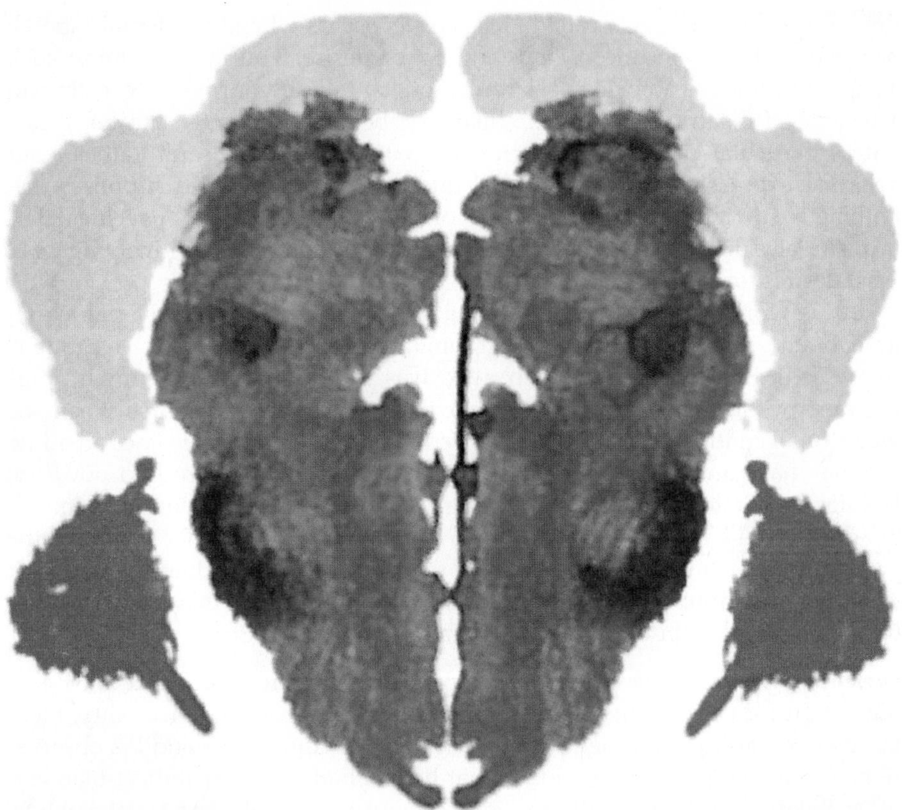

● **FIGURE 10.2** An Inkblot Similar to Those Used in the Rorschach Test

The Rorschach's value as a testing instrument has been questioned because objective studies of its accuracy have been disappointing (Anastasi, 1988; Lilienfeld et al., 2000a, b; Wood et al., 1996). Moreover, critics claim that the test is based on theoretical concepts (such as unconscious motives) that are impossible to demonstrate objectively. Despite these criticisms, many clinicians have continued to champion the Rorschach, arguing that it can provide unique insights as part of a broader personality assessment (Exner, 1974, 1978; Exner & Weiner, 1982; Hibbard, 2003).

■ **Thematic Apperception Test (TAT)** A projective test requiring subjects to make up stories that explain ambiguous pictures.

By comparison, the **Thematic Apperception Test (TAT),** developed by Henry Murray, is a projective test that stands on somewhat firmer scientific ground. This test consists of ambiguous pictures, for which respondents are instructed to generate a story (see Figure 10.3). The story should describe what the characters in the scenes are doing and thinking, what led up to each event, and how each situation will end. According to the theory behind the TAT, the respondent perceives the elements in the actual picture and further *apperceives* (fills in) personal interpretations and explanations, based on his or her own thoughts, feelings, and needs. The examiner then interprets the responses by looking for psychological themes, such as aggression, sexual needs, and relationships among people mentioned in the stories. Unlike the Rorschach, the TAT has proved its mettle, especially for assessing achievement motivation, as we saw in Chapter 8 (McClelland, 1987b).

● **FIGURE 10.3** Sample Card from the TAT

Psychic Determinism To the Freudian analyst, everything a person does has meaning. In particular, mental symptoms such as fears and phobias are interpreted as signs of unconscious difficulties. Similarly, a so-called *Freudian slip* occurs when "accidental" speech or behavior belies an unconscious conflict or desire. You might commit such a slip, as you leave a boring social function, by telling your host, "I really had a terrible—I mean *terrific*—time." Likewise, being consistently late for a date with a particular person is no accident, Freud would have said. Rather, your behavior expresses the way you feel unconsciously. This idea supposes that nothing we do is accidental. Rather, according to his principle of **psychic determinism,** all our acts are determined by unconscious processes involving traumas, desires, or conflicts.

In his work with hysterical patients, Freud observed that physical symptoms often seemed connected to a traumatic event that had been "forgotten" (repressed). For instance, a patient who was hysterically "blind" might, during therapy, suddenly recall seeing her parents having intercourse when she was a small child. How had this produced blindness? As she becomes an adult, she may have anticipated her first sexual encounter, which aroused powerful feelings associated with that upsetting memory. Thus, the young woman's blindness could represent an unconscious attempt to undo her vision of the original event—and to deny her own sexual feelings. Blindness would also bring her attention, comfort, and sympathy from others. In this way, her inner psychic motives both determine and maintain her condition.

Evaluating Freud's Work Whatever your feelings about Freud, you must give him credit for developing the first comprehensive theory of personality, mental disorder, and psychotherapy. His writing was compelling and his observations astute—so perceptive, in fact, that he has had a greater impact than any other theorist on the way all of us think about personality and mental abnormality (Fisher & Greenberg, 1985).

Nevertheless, psychologists today give Freud mixed reviews (Azar, 1997; McCullough, 2001). One problem is that many Freudian concepts, such as "libido," "anal stage," or "repression," are vague. Because they lack clear operational definitions, much of the theory is impossible to evaluate scientifically.[1] In an earlier chapter we saw the results of this lack of objectivity in the controversy over recovery of repressed memories—a notion that arises directly from Freud's ideas but that has no solid empirical support. Elizabeth Loftus warns that, by blithely accepting vague Freudian notions of repression and "recovery" of memories, society risks dangerous levels of paranoia, persecution of the innocent, and self-inflicted misery (Loftus & Ketcham, 1991, 1994). It should be noted, however, that valiant efforts are being made to put Freud's concepts on a scientific footing (Cramer, 2000).

CONNECTION: CHAPTER 1

Operational definitions are stated in objective, observable, and measurable terms.

A second criticism says that Freudian "theory" is a seductive explanation for the past but a poor predictor of future responses. That is, its focus is on retrospective explanation. By overemphasizing historical origins of behavior, psychoanalysis directs attention away from current events that may be responsible for maintaining the behavior.

A third criticism says that Freud gave short shrift to women. For example, we have seen that he portrayed women as suffering from "penis envy." In fact, Freud's theory may simply describe the attitudes that permeated the male-dominated world of his time.

■ Psychic determinism Freud's assumption that all our mental and behavioral responses are caused by unconscious traumas, desires, or conflicts.

A final criticism claims that the unconscious mind is not as smart or purposeful as Freud believed (Loftus & Klinger, 1992). In this newer view, the unconscious acts reflexively, sometimes based on innate response patterns and

[1]Because many of Freud's ideas are not testable, his psychoanalytic theory is not a *scientific* theory, as we defined the term in Chaper 1. Here we follow common usage, which calls it a theory.

sometimes based on conditioned responses. Research in the neuroscience of emotion has, as we saw in Chapter 3, supported this new view of an unconscious emotional processing system in the brain—much less malign and deliberate than anything that Freud imagined (LeDoux, 1996).

Despite these shortcomings, Freud's ideas have found a receptive audience with the public at large (Gray, 1993, p. 47). Much of his appeal may be explained by his accessibility to nonpsychologists and by his emphasis on sexuality, a topic that grabs everyone's interest. As a result, Freudian images and symbols abound in the art and literature of the 20th century. His ideas have had an enormous influence on marketing as well. For example, advertisers often promote new products by associating them with a sexy model and hinting that the product will bring sexual satisfaction to its owner. Alternatively, some advertisers capitalize on Freud's destructive instinct. In this vein, television commercials for everything from antibacterial soap and other "personal products" to life insurance remind us of threats to our happiness (social rejection, irregularity, untimely death) and then offer products and services to reduce our anxiety and restore hope.

Let us end our discussion of Freud by seeing whether his explanation of personality can give us a useful perspective on Margaret Sanger. A psychoanalyst interpreting her drive and sense of mission would scrutinize her childhood, looking for conflicts with parents and anxiety about sexual feelings. The analyst might also focus on her mother's death, which occurred when Sanger was 19, and on her later claim that she blamed her father for exhausting her mother with so many births. Unresolved anger toward her mother (a vestige of the phallic stage of psychosexual development) would be transformed into guilt over her mother's death. By projecting blame onto her father, she removed her conscious sense of guilt. Perhaps Sanger took up the banner of birth control in order to deal with the presence of her now-unconscious guilt and anxiety about unhappy family experiences. Or perhaps she identified with her mother's sacrifice and sought to punish her father and other would-be fathers by depriving them of their control over women's reproductive fate. As is usual with psychoanalysis, these guesses are guided by hindsight—and cannot be either proved or disproved.

The Neo-Freudians Freud was always a controversial figure—an image he liked to promote (Sulloway, 1992). As such, he attracted many followers. But he brooked no criticism of the basic principles in his theories. As a result, several of Freud's equally strong-willed disciples broke away from the psychoanalytic fold to establish their own systems of personality, mental disorder, and treatment. Whatever these **neo-Freudians** (literally, "new Freudians") changed in Freud's theory, they always retained a *psychodynamic* emphasis. That is, they kept Freud's idea of personality as a process driven by motivational energy—although they often disagreed about the specific motives that energize personality: Are our motives primarily sexual or social? Conscious or unconscious? The next few pages will give you a sense for the divergent paths followed by these neo-Freudians.

Carl Jung: Extending the Unconscious Freud attracted many disciples, but none more famous than Carl Jung (pronounced *YOONG*), a member of the inner circle of colleagues who helped Freud develop and refine psychoanalytic theory during the first decade of the 1900s. For a time, Freud viewed the somewhat younger Jung as his "crown prince" and probable successor. But Freud's paternal attitude increasingly vexed Jung, who was developing theoretical ideas of his own (Carver & Scheier, 1992). Eventually this personality conflict—which Freud interpreted as Jung's unconscious wish to usurp his fatherly authority—caused a split in their relationship.

■ **Neo-Freudians** Literally "new Freudians"; refers to theorists who broke with Freud but whose theories retain a psychodynamic aspect, especially a focus on motivation as the source of energy for the personality.

● Jungian archetypes abound in art, literature, and film. This photo, from *The Lord of the Rings,* shows Gandalf, who embodies the archetype of magician or trickster. The same archetype is evoked by the coyote in Native American legends and by Merlin in the King Arthur legends.

For Jung, the break with Freud centered on two issues. First, Jung thought that his mentor had overemphasized sexuality at the expense of other unconscious needs and desires that Jung saw at the heart of personality. He believed spirituality, for example, to be a fundamental human motive, coequal with sexuality. Moreover, he disputed the very structure of the unconscious. This new vision of the unconscious, Jung's most famous invention, warrants closer examination.

The Collective Unconscious In place of the Freudian id, Jung installed a two-part unconscious, consisting of both a *personal unconscious* and a *collective unconscious.* While the Jungian **personal unconscious** spanned essentially the same territory as the Freudian id, its collective twin was another matter—and wholly a Jungian creation. He saw in the **collective unconscious** a reservoir for instinctive "memories" held by people everywhere—in much the same way that humans all share a common genetic code. These collective memories tie together countless generations of human history and give us the ancient images, called **archetypes,** that appear and reappear in art, literature, and folktales around the world (Jung, 1959).

■ **Personal unconscious** Jung's term for that portion of the unconscious corresponding roughly to the Freudian id.

■ **Collective unconscious** Jung's addition to the unconscious, involving a reservoir for instinctive "memories," including the archetypes, which exist in all people.

■ **Archetypes** The ancient memory images in the collective unconscious. Archetypes appear and reappear in art, literature, and folktales around the world.

■ **Introversion** The Jungian dimension that focuses on inner experience–one's own thoughts and feelings–making the introvert less outgoing and sociable than the extravert.

■ **Extraversion** The Jungian personality dimension involving turning one's attention outward, toward others.

Among these archetypal memories, Jung identified the *animus* and the *anima,* which represent the masculine and feminine sides of our personality. Other archetypes give us the universal concepts of mother, father, birth, death, the hero, the trickster, God, and the self. On the darker side of the self lurks the *shadow* archetype, representing the destructive and aggressive tendencies that we don't want to acknowledge in our personalities. You can recognize your shadow at work the next time you take an instantaneous dislike to someone: This occurs when the other person reminds you of your shadow characteristics.

For Jung, the causes of mental disorder include not only repressed traumas and conflicts in the personal unconscious but also failure to acknowledge the archetypes we find unacceptable in our collective unconscious. Applying Jungian theory to the case of Margaret Sanger, a therapist might suspect that Sanger's determination originated in conflicts between the masculine and feminine sides of her nature: the animus and anima. Another Jungian possibility would be that her mother's early death made her deny her own maternal archetype, resulting in her obsession with birth control.

Personality Types Jung's *principle of opposites* portrays each personality as a balance between opposing pairs of tendencies or dispositions, which you see in Table 10.2. Jung taught that most people tend to favor one or the other in each pair. The overall pattern of such tendencies, then, was termed a *personality type,* which Jung believed to be a stable and enduring aspect of the individual's personality.

TABLE 10.2 Jung's Opposing Tendencies in Personality
conscious–unconscious
extravert–introvert
rational–irrational
thinking–feeling
intuition–sensation
good–bad
masculine–feminine

The most famous of these pairs is **introversion** and **extraversion.** Extraverts turn attention outward, on external experience. As a result, extraverts are more in tune with people and things in the world around them than they are with their inner needs. They tend to be outgoing and unaffected by self-consciousness. Introverts, by contrast, focus on inner experience—their own thoughts and feelings—which makes them seem more shy and less sociable. Few people have all pairs of forces in perfect balance. Instead, one or another dominates, giving rise to personality types (Fadiman & Frager, 2001).

Evaluating Jung's Work Like Freud, Jung's influence is strongest outside of psychology, especially in literature and the popular press. Psychology has not found Jung so attractive, mainly because his ideas, like Freud's, do not lend themselves to objective observation and testing. In two respects, however, Jung has had a big impact on psychological thinking. First, he challenged Freud and thereby opened the door to a spate of alternative personality theories. Second, his notion of *personality types* makes Jung not only a psychodynamic theorist but also a pillar of the temperament/trait/type approach that we will review in the middle segment of this chapter. There you will see that Jung's type theory is the basis for the most widely used psychological test in the world, the *Myers–Briggs Type Indicator.*

Karen Horney: A Feminist Voice in Psychodynamic Psychology Karen Horney (*HORN-eye*) and Anna Freud, Sigmund Freud's daughter, represent virtually the only feminine voices within the early psychoanalytic movement. In this role Horney disputed the elder Freud's notion of the Oedipus complex and his assertion that women must suffer from penis envy (Horney, 1939). Instead, Horney maintained that women want the same opportunities and rights that men enjoy and that many personality differences between males and females result from social roles, not from unconscious urges. She also disputed Freud's contention that personality is determined mainly by early childhood experiences. For Horney, normal growth involves the full development of social relationships and of one's potential. This development, however, may be blocked by a sense of uncertainty and isolation that she called **basic anxiety.** It is this basic anxiety that leads to adjustment problems and mental disorder. In Horney's view, the neurotic person—the individual who is unhappy and anxious—suffers from "unconscious strivings developed in order to cope with life despite fears, helplessness, and isolation" (1942, p. 40).

Neurotic Needs When people feel anxious and unsafe, healthy psychological development is thwarted, and they become *neurotic.* In Horney's theory, the signs of unhealthy development and neurosis involve ten **neurotic needs,** which are normal desires taken to extremes. You can see these neurotic needs listed in Table 10.3.

Horney also identified three patterns of attitudes and behavior that people use to deal with basic anxiety, either in a healthy or neurotic way: moving *toward others, against others,* or *away from others.* Those who move toward others in a neurotic fashion have a pathological need for constant reminders of love and approval. Such persons may need someone to help, to take care of, or for whom to "sacrifice" themselves. Alternatively, they may seek someone on whom they can become dependent. They may end up behaving passively and feeling victimized. In contrast, those who move against others earn power and respect by competing or attacking successfully, but they risk being feared and ending up "lonely at the top." Those who take the third route, moving away from others to protect themselves from imagined hurt and rejection, are likely to close themselves off from intimacy and support.

What analysis would Horney have made of Margaret Sanger? We suspect that she would have focused on Sanger's achievements, attempting to determine whether they were the result of a healthy drive to fulfill her potential or a neurotic need for power, status, self-respect, achievement, and independence. Undoubtedly, Horney would have reminded us that society often praises these needs in men and punishes them in women. So, from this

■ **Basic anxiety** An emotion, proposed by Karen Horney, that gives a sense of uncertainty and loneliness in a hostile world and can lead to maladjustment.
■ **Neurotic needs** Signs of neurosis in Horney's theory, these 10 needs are normal desires carried to a neurotic extreme.

TABLE 10.3 Horney's Ten Neurotic Needs

1. Need for affection and approval
2. Need for a partner and dread of being left alone
3. Need to restrict one's life and remain inconspicuous
4. Need for power and control over others
5. Need to exploit others
6. Need for recognition or prestige
7. Need for personal admiration
8. Need for personal achievement
9. Need for self-sufficiency and independence
10. Need for perfection and unassailability

● How would Karen Horney have interpreted Margaret Sanger's personality? Margaret Sanger had a flair for publicity. Here she has her lips sealed with tape so that she cannot be accused of illegally preaching birth control in Boston. Instead, she will write her message on a blackboard.

point of view, it is likely that Horney may have seen in Sanger a robust and healthy personality.

Evaluating Horney's Work Neglect engulfed Karen Horney's ideas during midcentury (Monte, 1980). Then her 1967 book *Feminine Psychology* appeared at just the right time to elevate her among those seeking a feminist perspective within psychology and psychiatry. But, having attracted renewed interest, will Horney eventually slip again into oblivion? Her theory suffers from the same flaw that plagues the other psychodynamic theories: a weak scientific foundation. It awaits someone to translate her concepts into verifiable form so that they can be put to a scientific test.

Alfred Adler: An early split from Psychoanalysis Another Neo-Freudian, Alfred Adler proposed theories encompassing birth order, theories about lifestyle, and his most famous theoretical construct, the **inferiority complex.** Developing in childhood, the inferiority complex is a feeling of inferiority that is largely unconscious. According to Adler, the causes of this complex can be as simple as being told you are dumb or not good at something to the extent that you believe it, regardless of your level of skill or talent. Out of this complex comes **compensation,** where one attempts to make up for these deficiencies (real or imagined) in some way (Ansbacher & Ansbacher, 1964). The strengths of this theory are that it is remarkably complete and describes a vast array of behaviors.

■ **Inferiority complex** A feeling of inferiority that is largely unconscious, with its roots in childhood

■ **Compensation** Making up for one's real or imagined deficiencies

Other Neo-Freudian Theorists Sigmund Freud's revolutionary ideas attracted many others to the psychoanalytic movement—some of whom, like Erik Erikson and Alfred Adler, also broke with Freud to develop their own ideas. For the most part, the post-Freudian theorists accepted the notions of psychic determinism and unconscious motivation. But they did not always agree with Freud on the details, especially about the sex and death instincts or the indelible nature of early life experiences. In general, the post-Freudians made several significant changes in the course of psychoanalysis:

- They put greater emphasis on ego functions, including ego defenses, development of the self, and conscious thought as the major components of the personality—whereas Freud focused primarily on the unconscious.
- They viewed social variables (culture, family, and peers) as having an important role in shaping personality—whereas Freud focused mainly on instinctive urges and conflicts.
- They extended personality development beyond childhood to include the entire lifespan—whereas Freud focused mainly on early childhood experiences.

In doing so, the post-Freudians broke Freud's monopoly on personality theory and paved the way for new ideas from the humanistic and cognitive theorists.

Humanistic Theories

With their emphasis on internal conflict and mental disorder, the Freudians and neo-Freudians had compelling explanations for mental disorders, but they largely failed to provide a usable theory of the healthy, "normal" personality. And so the humanistic approach grew to fill that need.

The humanistic theories are optimistic about the core of human nature. For humanists, personality is not driven by unconscious conflicts and defenses against anxiety but rather by needs to adapt, learn, grow, and excel. They retained the idea of motivation as one of the central components of personality, but they accentuated the positive rather than negative motives. Mental disorders, when they do occur, are seen as stemming from unhealthy *situations* that cause low self-esteem and unmet needs, rather than from unhealthy *individuals.*

Thus, the humanists emphasized the positive in human nature. Once people are freed from negative situations, such as a abusive relationships, and negative self-evaluations, such as "I'm not smart," the tendency to be healthy should actively guide them to life-enhancing choices. These ideas brought a new focus on the individual's self-concept and subjective interpretation of reality, rather than the external perspective of an observer or therapist.

Traits Stable personality characteristics that are presumed to exist within the individual and guide his or her thoughts and actions under various conditions.

Central traits According to trait theory, traits that form the basis of personality.

Secondary traits In trait theory, preferences and attitudes.

Cardinal traits Personality components that define people's lives; Very few individuals have cardinal traits.

Self-actualizing personalities Healthy individuals who have met their basic needs and are free to be creative and fulfill their potentialities.

Gordon Allport and the Beginnings of Humanistic Psychology Gordon Allport developed one of the first complete theories in humanistic psychology, with his trait/dispositional theory. Trait theory assumes individuals possess three types of **traits**: central traits, secondary traits, and cardinal traits. Traits are stable personality characteristics that are presumed to exist within the individual and guide his or her thoughts and actions under various conditions. **Central traits** are characteristics that form the core of one's personality. Examples include the descriptors such as happy, sad, and moody. The next component of Allport's theory is what he called **secondary traits.** These are components such as preferences and attitudes. The final component of trait theory is known as cardinal traits. The **cardinal traits** are the ones that define people's lives (examples of this include things like greed, avarice, and sadism). Allport postulated that very few individuals actually possess cardinal traits—and that those who do, develop them relatively later in life. It is not clear why this is so.

Abraham Maslow and the Healthy Personality Abraham Maslow referred to the humanistic view as psychology's "third force," to contrast his ideas with the psychoanalytic and behavioristic movements that had dominated psychology during most of his lifetime. He was especially concerned by the Freudian fixation on mental disturbance and maladjustment. Instead, Maslow argued, we need a theory that describes mental health as something more than just the absence of illness. That theoretical need became his life's quest. He sought the ingredients of the healthy personality where no one had ever looked for them before: in people who had lived especially full and productive lives (Maslow, 1968, 1970, 1971).

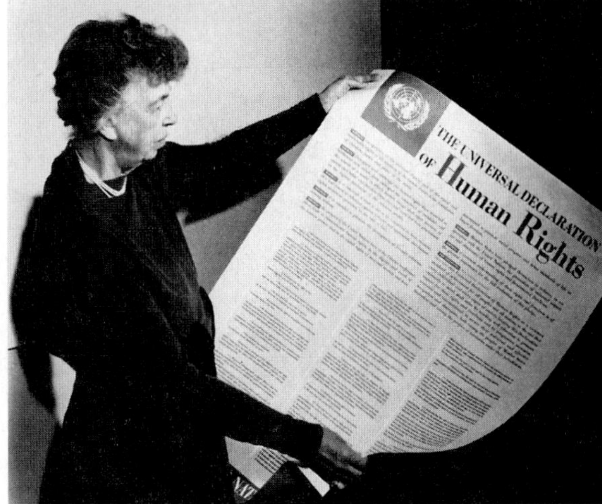
The Universal Declaration of Human Rights
Maslow considered Eleanor Roosevelt to be a self-actualizing person.

Maslow's subjects included the historical figures Abraham Lincoln and Thomas Jefferson, plus several persons of stature during his own lifetime: Albert Einstein, Albert Schweitzer, and Eleanor Roosevelt. In these individuals Maslow found personalities whose basic needs had been met (e.g., needs for food, shelter, love, and respect) and who had become free to pursue an interest in "higher" ideals, such as truth, justice, and beauty—a penchant that sometimes engaged them in causes about which they felt deeply. (We hope you're thinking about Margaret Sanger at this point.) They could act independently because they had no neurotic need for the approval of others. Maslow called these people **self-actualizing personalities.** He found his self-actualizers to be creative, full of good humor, and given to spontaneity—but, at the same time, accepting of their own limitations and those of others. In brief, self-actualizers are those who feel free to fulfill their potentialities.

Although Maslow was most interested in the healthy, self-actualizing personality, his theory of a *hierarchy of needs* also offers an explanation of maladjustment. A long-unfulfilled "deficiency" need, such as a need for love or esteem, can produce maladjustment, while freedom from such needs allows the person to pursue interests that promote growth and fulfillment. Indeed, the research shows that people who are self-accepting lead happier lives, while

CONNECTION: CHAPTER 8
Maslow's *hierarchy of needs* claims that motives occur in a priority order.

people who have low self-esteem may go through life feeling fearful, angry, or depressed (Baumeister, 1993; Brown, 1991).

Carl Rogers's Fully Functioning Person In contrast with Maslow, Carl Rogers was a therapist who often worked with dysfunctional people rather than self-actualizers (1951, 1961, 1980). Yet he did not overlook the healthy personality, which he called the **fully functioning person.** Such an individual has a self-concept that is *positive* and *congruent* with reality. That is, the fully functioning person has high self-esteem, which is consistent (congruent) with the messages he or she receives from others, who express their approval, friendship, and love. Negative experiences, however, can produce *incongruence,* a threat to one's self-esteem. For example, a boy who thinks of himself as "smart" has a positive self-concept, but he experiences incongruence when the teacher returns his paper with a C on it.

Rogers insisted that psychology recognize the reality of perceptions and feelings, which he called the **phenomenal field.** We respond, he said, to this subjective experience, not to an objective reality. That is why a student's reaction to a grade depends entirely on the student's perception. Receiving a C may shock a student who is used to receiving As but thrill one who has been failing: Both are reacting to their subjective phenomenal fields. In Rogers's system, then, the phenomenal field becomes a part of the personality, as a sort of filter for our experience. It contains our interpretations of both the external and internal worlds. It also contains the *self,* the humanists' version of the Freudian ego, which is the part of the phenomenal field that defines who we are.

Rogers also believed that everyone has the capacity for growth in a supportive and nurturing environment. This assumption probably grew (if you'll allow us a neo-Freudian interpretation) from his reaction to an isolated and unhappy childhood dominated by the rigid rules of his parents' strict religious beliefs. So restrictive was this environment that he even felt "wicked" when he first tasted a bottle of pop without his parents' knowledge (Rogers, 1961). Later, from an adult perspective, Rogers concluded that children from homes where parental love is *conditional* (dependent) on good behavior may grow up with anxiety and a strong sense of guilt that leads to low self-esteem and mental disorder. Instead of guilt-mongers, he believed, we need people who can give us *unconditional positive regard*—love without conditions attached.

Unlike the psychodynamic theorists who focused on unhealthy, self-destructive motives, Rogers, Maslow, and other humanistic personality theorists believe that our deepest motives are for positive growth. In its healthiest form, self-actualization is a striving to realize one's potential—to develop fully one's capacities and talents. (Examples might include Picasso, Einstein, or your favorite musician.) According to the humanistic theorists, this innate quest is a constructive, guiding force that moves each person toward positive behaviors and the enhancement of the self.

How would humanistic theorists characterize Margaret Sanger? They would probably begin by asking, "How does Margaret Sanger see her world? What matters to her? Where is she, where does she want to be, and how does she believe she can get there?" The answers to these questions would identify her motives. Perhaps Sanger saw her life as an opportunity to change the miserable and often deadly consequences of unwanted pregnancy. But why, then, did she claim credit for the success of the birth-control movement, despite the fact that it was a team effort? A humanistic perspective would not assume that her motives were necessarily self-centered. If she believed the cause needed a figurehead, she may have felt that too many personalities associated with the movement would diffuse the effort. Ultimately, they would judge her healthy if her motives were healthy, that is, if she were self-actualizing. In everyday language this means moving toward fulfilling her potential.

■ **Fully functioning person** Carl Rogers's term for a healthy, self-actualizing individual, who has a self-concept that is both positive and congruent with reality.

■ **Phenomenal field** Our psychological reality, composed of one's perceptions and feelings.

Evaluating the Humanistic Theories The upbeat humanistic view of personality brought a welcome change for many therapists who had become weary of the pessimistic Freudian perspective, with its emphasis on unspeakable desires and repressed traumas. They liked its focus on making one's present and future life more palatable, rather than dredging up painful memories of an unalterable past. They also liked its attention to mental health rather than mental disorder.

But not everyone jumped on the humanists' bandwagon. Many criticized humanistic concepts for being fuzzy: What exactly is "self-actualization," they asked? Is it an inborn tendency or is it created by one's culture? Experimental psychologists contended that too many concepts in humanistic psychology are so unclear that they defy objective testing. And the psychoanalytic theorists criticized the humanistic emphasis on present conscious experience, arguing that the humanistic approach does not recognize the power of the unconscious. Cross-cultural psychologists, too, have criticized the humanists' emphasis on the self—as in *self*-concept, *self*-esteem, and *self*-actualization. This "self-centered" picture of personality may simply be the viewpoint of observers looking through the lens of an individualistic Western culture (Heine et al., 1999).

Recently, the whole notion of self-esteem as the basic ingredient for mental health has been brought under the lens of research . . . and found wanting. The finding is important because many programs designed to improve school performance, combat drug abuse, and discourage teen sex and violence are based on boosting self-esteem. After a review of the research, psychologist Roy Baumeister and his colleagues (2003) report that low self-esteem causes none of these problems—as shown by the fact that bullies and drug users often have high self-esteem. This, rather than seeing high self-esteem as an end in itself, Baumeister and his colleagues urge us to see it as a by-product of achievement.

Recently, a movement known as **positive psychology** has formed to pursue essentially the same goals established by the humanists. The difference is that those allied with positive psychology are more concerned than were the humanists about laying a scientific foundation for their theories. This effort has produced the solid work we have seen on optimism, happiness, social support, and health (Buss, 2000; Diener, 2000; Myers, 2000; Peterson, 2000; Seligman & Csikszentmihalyi, 2000; Volz, 2000). But, despite these successes, the positive psychology movement is limited as an explanation of personality by its restricted focus on desirable aspects of human functioning.

So, is there an alternative view that overcomes the problems we have seen in the psychodynamic, humanistic, and the new positive psychology theories? Let's consider the cognitive approach.

Social-Cognitive Theories

Neither the humanists nor psychoanalysts showed much interest in putting their ideas on a firm experimental foundation. Their work came largely out of a clinical tradition of working with individuals who sought their help. Cognitive psychology, however, arose from a different source—a solidly scientific tradition with an emphasis on research (Cervone, 2004). The trade-off is that the cognitive theories are not as comprehensive as those of the humanists or psychodynamic theorists. The cognitive approach zeroes in on specific influences on personality and behavior, without assuming to explain everything, as we shall see in our sampling of cognitive ideas below.

Observational Learning and Personality: Bandura's Theory In Albert Bandura's view, we are driven not by inner forces or environmental influences alone but also by our *expectations* of how our actions might affect other people, the environment, and ourselves (Bandura, 1986). A distinctive feature of

■ **Positive psychology** A recent movement within psychology, focusing on desirable aspects of human functioning, as opposed to an emphasis on psychopathology.

Children develop a clearer sense of identity by observing how men and women behave in their culture.

the human personality is the ability to foresee the consequences of actions. We don't have to yell "Fire!" in a crowded theatre to know what would happen if we did. In addition, we can learn *vicariously* (by observing other people) to see what rewards and punishments their behaviors bring. Thus, our personalities are shaped by our interactions with others.

Perhaps the most important contribution of Bandura's theory is this focus on social learning, or **observational learning,** the process by which people learn new responses by watching each others' behavior. When we see Billy hit his brother, we also learn whether the result is rewarding or punishing for Billy. Thus, through observational learning we can see what works and what does not work, without having to go through trial-and-error for ourselves. In Bandura's view, then, personality is a collection of *learned* behavior patterns, many of which we have borrowed from others.

Through observational learning, children and adults acquire an enormous range of information about their social environment—what gets rewarded and what gets punished or ignored. Skills, attitudes, and beliefs may be acquired simply by noting what others do and the consequences that follow. In this way, children may learn to say "Please" and "Thank you," to be quiet in libraries, and to refrain from public nose picking. Alternatively, psychological problems can be acquired by observing poor role models, such as a relative with a fear of spiders, or by exposure to environments that reward unhealthy attitudes and behaviors, like prejudice and drug abuse.

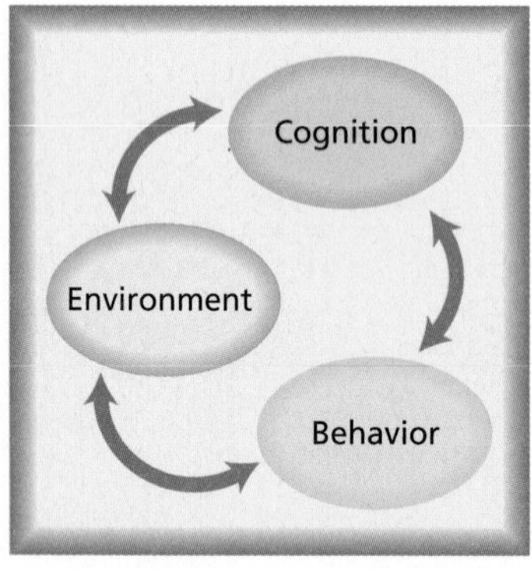

Cognition
Environment
Behavior

FIGURE 10.4 Reciprocal Determinism
In reciprocal determinism, the individual's cognitions, behavior, and the environment all interact.

In Bandura's theory, cognitions are another a major component of our personalities. But cognition doesn't occur in a vacuum: Cognitive processes involve an ongoing relationship between the individual and the environment—an interaction of our behavior, our environment, and our cognitions. Bandura calls this **reciprocal determinism** (Bandura, 1981, 1999). The simple but powerful relationship of these variables is summarized in Figure 10.4.

How does reciprocal determinism work in real life? If, for example, you like psychology, your interest (a cognition) will probably lead you to spend time in the psychology department on campus (an environment) interacting with students and faculty (social behavior) who share your interest. To the extent that you find this stimulating and rewarding, this activity will reciprocally strengthen your interest in psychology and encourage you to spend more time with your friends in the psychology department. This, then, is one instance of the reciprocal determinism among cognition (interest in psychology), environment (the psychology department) and behavior (interacting with others who like psychology).

Locus of Control: Rotter's Theory Another cognitive psychologist, Julian Rotter (rhymes with *voter*) tells us that the way we act depends on our sense of personal power or **locus of control.** To illustrate, we ask you this question: Do you feel you can control the grade you achieve in your psychology class? If you do, you have an *internal* locus of control, and you probably work hard to get good grades. On the other hand, if you have the feeling that the professor will arbitrarily give you whatever she or he wants you to have—regardless of how much studying you do or the quality of your work—you have an *external* locus of control, and you probably study relatively little.

Scores on Rotter's *Internal–External Locus of Control Scale* correlate with people's emotions and behavior in many situations (Rotter, 1990). For example,

Observational learning The process of learning new responses by watching others' behavior.

Reciprocal determinism The process in which cognitions, behavior, and the environment mutually influence each other.

Locus of control An individual's sense of where his or her life influences originate.

DO IT YOURSELF! Finding Your Locus of Control

Julian Rotter (1966) has developed a test that assesses a person's sense of internal or external control over events. The test items consist of pairs of contrasting statements, and subjects must choose one statement with which they most agree from each pair. This format is called a forced-choice test. Unlike many other personality tests, the scoring for each item on Rotter's Internal–External Scale is transparent: The test-taker can easily tell in which direction most items are scored. Here are some items from a preliminary version of the test (Rotter, 1971).

You can see which direction you lean by counting the number of statements with which you agreed in each column. Agreement with those in the left column suggests an internal locus of control.

1a. Promotions are earned through hard work and persistence.	1b. Making a lot of money is largely a matter of getting the right breaks.
2a. In my experience I have noticed that there is usually a direct connection between how hard I study and the grades I get.	2b. Many times the reactions of teachers seem haphazard to me.
3a. If one knows how to deal with people they are really quite easily led.	3b. I have little influence over the way other people behave.
4a. People like me can change the course of world affairs if we make ourselves heard.	4b. It is only wishful thinking to believe that one can really influence what happens in society at large.
5a. I am the master of my fate.	5b. A great deal that happens to me is probably a matter of chance.

those with an internal locus of control are not only more likely to get good grades, but they also are more likely to exercise and watch their diets than are externals (Balch & Ross, 1975; Findley & Cooper, 1983). As you might expect, externals are more likely to be depressed (Benassi et al., 1988).

While we may feel more in control of certain situations than others, many studies suggest that locus of control is an important characteristic of our personalities. That is, people tend to approach different situations with assumptions about their ability to control their fate. Therefore, an internal or external disposition seems to be a reliable personality characteristic—although Rotter resists calling this a *trait* because he believes the term conveys the erroneous idea that internality–externality is fixed and unchangeable. You can evaluate your own locus of control by following the instructions in the "Do It Yourself!" box above.

Evaluating the Social-Cognitive Approach to Personality Critics argue that the cognitive theories generally overemphasize rational information processing and overlook both emotion and unconscious processes as important components of personality. So, for those who feel that emotions and motives are central to the functioning of human personality, the cognitive approaches to personality have a blind spot. However, because emotion and associated unconscious processes have assumed a greater role in cognitive psychology recently, we can anticipate a new generation of cognitive theories of personality that do take these aspects of personality into account (Mischel & Shoda, 1995).

A real strength of the social-cognitive theories is their foundation of solid psychological research—unlike most of the ideas proposed by the Freudians, neo-Freudians, and humanists. You will recall, for example, Bandura's famous Bobo doll experiment, which we discussed in Chapter 6. The price paid for the social-cognitive theories, however, is that they are much less comprehensive than the old and grand theories of personality proposed by Freud and his followers. The payoff, however, has come in the form of both explanations and treatments for a number of mental disorders that often seem to involve observational learning, particularly anxiety-based disorders, such as phobias, and behavior disorders in children.

CONNECTION: CHAPTER 12

Other anxiety disorders include *panic disorder* and *obsessive–compulsive disorder.*

How, then, would a cognitive psychologist explain Margaret Sanger? A cognitive interpretation of Sanger's work and personality would focus on how she interpreted the rewards and punishments she experienced and how these interpretations shaped her behavior. Each time she gave a public lecture about birth-control methods or printed and distributed an illegal pamphlet, Sanger's actions brought punitive consequences—but she was also rewarded with public attention and admiration, press coverage, and ultimately the revocation of unjust laws. Margaret Sanger learned that by enduring hardships, she raised public awareness and changed the social climate. In turn, these successes shaped her, making her less a private citizen and more a public figure.

A cognitive personality theorist would also call attention to the lessons Sanger learned in her social relationships. As she became a celebrity—someone whom others saw as a symbol of a movement rather than a mere individual—she acquired a sense of personal power and an internal locus of control that had eluded her in her early efforts to speak about health education. In her 1938 autobiography, she styled herself as a heroine and martyr, interweaving fanciful stories with accurate information about her life. A cognitive theorist would wonder whether she had come to believe the legendary side of the personality that she had strived to create.

Current Trends

Gone are the days when Freud, Jung, Horney, and others were building the grand, sweeping theories of personality that attempted to explain everything we humans do. The humanistic and cognitive theorists arose and pointed out blind spots in the older psychodynamic theories. Now the emphasis has shifted again, as psychologists have brought elements of the psychodynamic, humanistic, and cognitive perspectives together with new knowledge about the impact of culture, gender, and family dynamics. You should be especially aware of three important trends in our thinking about personality.

In *family systems theory,* for example, the basic unit of analysis is not the individual but the family (Gilbert, 1992). This perspective says that personality is shaped by the ways people interacted first in the family and, later, in the peer group. While Freud and others did recognize that parents influence children, the new emphasis is on *interaction*—on the ways that members of the family or the peer group influence each other. This has led to viewing people with psychological problems as individuals embedded in dysfunctional groups, rather than as "sick" persons. This emphasis has also given us a new interpersonal language for personality. We often speak now of *codependence* (instead of *dependent* personalities) and *communication* (instead of mere *talk*). We also have a heightened awareness of relationships and process (the changes that occur as relationships develop).

A second trend comes from psychology's increasing awareness of cultural differences. An increasing number of publications on personality come from psychologists around the world—not just from Europe and America (Quiñones-Vidal et al., 2004). As Stanley Sue (1991) reminds us, our society is becoming ethnically more diverse. No longer can we assume that everyone shares the same cultural experience or the same values. And Harry Triandis (1995) has warned us, for example, that people who grow up in *collectivistic* societies may not have the need for individual achievement learned by those who grow up in *individualistic* societies. Triandis also tells us that no culture's approach is superior to the others: They are merely different. We will consider the question of personality differences across cultures in more detail near the end of this chapter.

A third trend comes from an increasing appreciation of gender influences. While we do not know the weights to assign nature and nurture in our attempts to understand gender differences, we do know that males and females often perceive situations differently (Tavris, 1991). For example, males tend to be more physically aggressive than females. Females tend to form close relationships in small, equal-status groups, while males tend to connect in larger groups (teams) organized hierarchically with leaders and followers.

Together these three trends have enlarged our understanding of the forces that shape personality. The new emphasis is on diversity and group processes, rather than on commonalities and individuals. As a result, the picture of personality has become much more complex—but it has undoubtedly become far more accurate.

PSYCHOLOGY IN YOUR LIFE: EXPLAINING UNUSUAL PEOPLE AND UNUSUAL BEHAVIOR

A theory of personality is helpful in understanding unusual personalities.

You don't need a theory of personality to explain why people usually get to work on time, sing along at concerts, or spend weekends with their family and friends. That is, you don't need a theory of personality to explain why people do what you would expect them to do. But when they behave in odd and unexpected ways, a personality theory becomes handy. A good theory can help you understand interesting and unusual people whom you read about in the newspaper—those who risk their lives to save another, politicians embroiled in scandal, a serial killer, the charismatic leader of a religious cult, and the controversial CEO of a Fortune 500 company.

Which approach to personality offers the best explanations? Unfortunately, none has the whole truth. But each perspective we have covered so far—the psychodynamic, the humanistic, and the cognitive—can help you see personality from a different angle, so you will need to use them all to get the whole picture. To illustrate, let's suppose that you are a counseling psychologist, working at a college counseling center, and a client, a young woman, tells you that she is contemplating suicide. How can your knowledge of personality help you understand her?

The cognitive perspective, with its emphasis on perception and social learning, suggests that her difficulty may lie in her interpretation of some depressing or threatening event. It also alerts you to the possibility that her suicidal thoughts reflect a suicidal role model—perhaps a friend or a family member.

The humanistic view suggests that you explore her unmet needs, such as feeling alone, unloved, or not respected. This view also calls your attention to the possibility of suicidal thoughts arising from low self-esteem.

The psychodynamic perspective suggests that you consider your client's internal motivation. Is she a hostile person who has turned her hostility on herself? Does she have some unfinished emotional business from an earlier developmental stage, such as guilt for angry feelings toward her parents? Does she have an unresolved identity crisis?

No one has a simple answer to the problem of understanding why people do what they do. That is for the counselor and client to work out together. What these theories of personality *can* do, however, is call your attention to factors you might otherwise overlook.

CHECK YOUR UNDERSTANDING

1. **RECALL:** The psychodynamic theories emphasize
   a. behavior.
   b. consciousness.
   c. learning.
   d. motivation.
   e. the logical basis of behavior.

2. **RECALL:** Freud believed that mental disorders stem from conflicts and drives that are repressed in the
   a. ego.
   b. superego.
   c. id.
   d. Eros.
   e. Thanatos.

3. **APPLICATION:** Which of the following behaviors would a Freudian say is driven by Thanatos?
   a. a violent assault
   b. dreaming
   c. eating
   d. flying an airplane
   e. sexual intercourse

4. **RECALL:** What is the ego defense mechanism on which the Rorschach and TAT are based?
   a. displacement
   b. fantasy
   c. projection
   d. reaction formation
   e. regression

5. **APPLICATION:** If you react strongly to angry outbursts in others, you may be struggling with which Jungian archetype?
   a. the anima
   b. the animus
   c. the hero
   d. introversion
   e. the shadow

6. **RECALL:** Karen Horney believed that the main forces behind our behaviors are
   a. aggressive and destructive.
   b. the result of the Oedipus complex.
   c. sexual.
   d. social.
   e. unconscious.

7. **RECALL:** The humanistic theorists were very different from the psychodynamic theorists because of their emphasis on
   a. the cognitive forces behind behavior.
   b. emotional intelligence.
   c. the healthy personality.
   d. mental disorder.
   e. the role of the unconscious.

8. **RECALL:** Our expectations of reward and punishment play a major role in
   a. the cognitive theories.
   b. the humanistic theories.
   c. the psychodynamic theories.
   d. none of the above theories of personality.
   e. all of the above.

9. **UNDERSTANDING THE CORE CONCEPT:** What do the psychodynamic, humanistic, and cognitive theories of personality have in common?
   a. They all view personality as largely unconscious.
   b. They all acknowledge the internal mental processes underlying our personality characteristics.
   c. They all say that men and women have entirely different motives underlying their behaviors.
   d. They all have a strong basis in psychological research.
   e. They have nothing in common.

ANSWERS: 1.d 2.c 3.a 4.c 5.e 6.d 7.c 8.a 9.b

KEY QUESTION

WHAT PERSISTENT PATTERNS ARE FOUND IN PERSONALITY?

Two thousand years before academic psychology appeared, people were classifying each other according to four *temperaments,* based on a theory proposed by the Greek physician Hippocrates (*Hip-POCK-rah-tees*). A person's temperament, he suggested, resulted from the balance of the four **humors,** or fluids, secreted by the body. A *sanguine,* or cheerful, person was characterized by strong, warm blood. A *choleric* temperament, marked by anger, came from yellow bile (called *choler*), believed to flow from the liver. Hippocrates thought that the liver also produced black bile, from which arose a *melancholic,* or depressed, temperament. Finally, if the body's dominant fluid is phlegm, or mucus, the person will have a *phlegmatic* temperament: cool, aloof, slow, and unemotional. Hippocrates' biology may have been a little off the mark, but his notion of tem-

■ **Humors** Four body fluids—blood, phlegm, black bile, and yellow bile—that, according to an ancient theory, control personality by their relative abundance.

peraments established themselves as "common sense." Even today you will occasionally encounter his terms used to describe people's personalities.

Since the days of Hippocrates, many other personality classification systems have been developed. The most simplistic ones are just streeotypes: If fat, then jolly; if an engineer, then conservative; if female, then sympathetic. Unfortunately, they oversimplify the very complicated problem of understanding the patterns found in personality. In fact, even you may be guilty of such oversimplifications, if you group people strictly according to college class, major, sex, ethnicity, and qualities such as honesty, shyness, or sense of humor.

Still, something in human nature seems to encourage us to group people by categories, according to certain distinguishing features. In modern psychology, some personality theorists describe people in terms of *temperaments:* global dispositions of personality, such as "outgoing" or "shy." Others prefer to look for *traits,* which are more specific characteristics in the personality, such as "cautious." Still others group people according to their personality *types,* which are clusters of traits. As you will see, however, most agree on certain fundamental dimensions of personality. Our Core Concept says:

CORE CONCEPT

Another approach describes personality in terms of stable patterns known as temperaments, traits, and types.

As you can see, the terms *temperament, trait,* and *type* overlap—which allows us to use the generic term *trait perspective* for this general approach to understanding human personality.

CONNECTION: CHAPTER 1
The *trait perspective* is one of the seven major viewpoints in modern psychology.

What makes these theories different from mere stereotypes—the conservative engineer, the macho male, or the dismal economics professor? It's all in the science. A good temperament, trait, or type theory has a solid research base. Let's look a few prominent examples.

Personality and Temperament

Psychologists define **temperament** as the inherited personality dispositions that are apparent in early childhood and that establish the tempo and mood of the individual's behaviors (Hogan et al., 1996; Mischel, 1993). When they speak of temperaments, psychologists are usually referring to a single, dominant "theme," such as shyness or moodiness, that characterizes a person's personality. Modern psychology has, of course, abandoned the four-humors theory of temperament, but it has retained its most basic concept: *Biological dispositions do affect our basic personalities.* In support of this view, psychologists can point to structures in the brain that are known to regulate fundamental aspects of personality (Canli et al., 2002; Carpenter, 2001a; Craik et al., 1999; Davidson, 2002; LeDoux, 2002; Zuckerman, 1995). You will recall, for example, the case of Phineas Gage, who received an accidental lobotomy and thereby demonstrated the role of the frontal lobes in social interaction and the suppression of impulsive behavior.

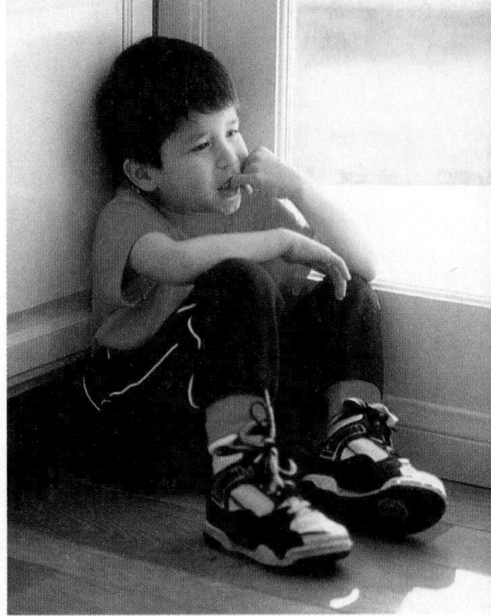

Some shyness is inherited, and some is learned through experience.

Temperament The basic and pervasive personality dispositions that are apparent in early childhood and that establish the tempo and mood of the individual's behaviors.

Biological psychologists now suspect that some individual differences in disposition also arise from the balance of chemicals in the brain, which may have a genetic basis (Azar, 2002; Sapolsky, 1992). In this sense, the theory of humors still lives, but in a different guise: Modern biological psychology has replaced the humors with neurotransmitters. So depression—which characterizes most suicidal people—may result from an imbalance of certain transmitters. Likewise, anxiety, anger, and euphoria may each arise from other neurochemical patterns. As developmental psychologist Jerome Kagan says (in Stavish, 1994a), "We all have the same neurotransmitters, but each of us has a slightly different mix" (p. 7). That, says Kagan, is what accounts for many of the temperamental differences among people, especially with regard to negative traits, such as fearfulness, sadness, and shyness.

In fact, Kagan runs a fascinating research program focusing on the inherited basis of shyness (Kagan et al., 1994). This program has clearly demonstrated that on the very first day of life, newborns already differ in the degree to which they are "inhibited" or "uninhibited"—that is, shy versus bold. About 10 to 15% of all children appear to be born shy or introverted, while a similar percentage appear to be born bold or extraverted, as assessed by a variety of measures. These initial differences in temperament persist over time, with the majority of children being classified with the same temperament in measurements taken over an 11-year interval. On the other hand, we know that the percentage of shy college-age students—40% or more—is much higher than the percentage of shy children (Zimbardo, 1990). It is thus reasonable to assume that some shyness is inherited, while even more is learned through negative experiences in one's social life. It is also the case that if a child is withdrawn, startles easily, is unlikely to smile, and is fearful of both strangers and novelty, then that child will create an environment that is not friendly, playful, or supportive. In this way, heredity and environment interact, with initially inherited characteristics becoming amplified—or perhaps muted—over time, because they produce social signals telling others to either approach or stay away.

So does biology determine your destiny? An inherited temperament may set the *range* of your responses to some life situations. However, temperament by itself does not fully determine your life experiences (Kagan & Snidman, 1998). Even among your biological relatives, your unique family position, experiences, and sense of self guarantee that your personality pattern is unlike that of anyone else (Bouchard et al., 1990).

Personality as a Composite of Traits

If you were to describe a friend, you might speak of temperament—a single dominant theme in his or her personality. But you might also describe your friend on several dimensions, using the language of *traits:* moody, cheerful, melancholy, enthusiastic, volatile, friendly, or smart. Traits are stable personality characteristics that are presumed to exist within the individual and to guide his or her thoughts and actions under various conditions. In this sense, then, traits work to channel the way our motives are expressed in behavior (Winter et al., 1998).

The "Big Five" Traits: The Five-Factor Theory By restricting the definition of personality to motivational and emotional characteristics (excluding such attributes as IQ, skills, and creativity), trait theorists are building a consensus on the major components of personality. Using the mathematical tool of *factor analysis* (which helps an investigator look for relationships, or clusters, among personality test items), many researchers have found five dominant personality factors, sometimes called the *Big Five* (Carver & Scheier, 2000; Digman, 1990; Goldberg, 1981, 1993). As yet, we have no universally accepted names for these factors, although the first term in the list below may be the most widely used. (You will note that each dimension is *bipolar,* describing a range from high to low on that trait. The first term we have listed is a label referring to the "high" pole for each trait.)

- *Openness to experience* (also called inquiring intellect, curiosity, independence, or, at the opposite pole, closed-mindedness)
- *Conscientiousness* (also called dependability, cautiousness, perseverance, superego strength, prudence, or constraint, and, at the opposite pole, impulsiveness, carelessness, or irresponsibility)

- *Extraversion* (also called social adaptability, assertiveness, sociability, boldness, or self-confidence, and, at the opposite pole, introversion)
- *Agreeableness* (also called conformity, likeability, friendly compliance, warmth, or, at the opposite pole, coldness or negativity)
- *Neuroticism* (also called anxiety or emotionality and, at the opposite pole, emotional stability or emotional control)

As an aid to remembering these dimensions, think of the acronym *OCEAN,* standing for *O*penness, *C*onscientiousness, *E*xtraversion, *A*greeableness, and *N*euroticism.

This **five-factor theory** is important because it greatly simplifies a formerly confusing picture. Various theorists, such as Freud, Jung, Adler, Horney, Erikson, and Maslow, had suggested a wide array of "fundamental" personality dimensions. In addition, the dictionary gives us several hundred terms commonly used to describe personality (Allport & Odbert, 1936). While psychologists had attempted to simplify this daunting list of personality characteristics, it wasn't until the last decade or so that agreement has emerged on which traits were fundamental. Although debate still continues about the details, a broad coalition of theorists has now concluded that we can describe people with reasonable accuracy by specifying their position on each of these five dimensions. The five-factor theory also offers the advantage of describing personality in the familiar terms of everyday language.

Significantly, the five-factor model also seems to have validity across cultures. An Israeli sample produced the same five factors as those found in Americans (Birenbaum & Montag, 1986). A study drawing on people from Canada, Germany, Finland, and Poland also supported the five-factor theory (Paunonen et al., 1992), as did still other studies of individuals from Germany, Portugal, Israel, China, Korea, and Japan (McCrae & Costa, 1997), as well as Japanese university students (Bond et al., 1975) and Filipino students (Guthrie & Bennet, 1970). Note that the same five factors stood out in each of these cultures as the basic framework of personality. Digman (1990) notes that these strikingly consistent results, coming in from such diverse cultures, lead to the suspicion "that something quite fundamental is involved here" (p. 433).

Raymond Cattell and the 16PF (Personality Factor) Trait theory was further advanced by the work of Raymond Cattell. Utilizing statistics, Cattell identified sixteen personality factors that he believed constituted the building blocks of each individual's personality. It was the degree to which each person possessed these factors that formed their complete personality. Cattell proposed that we all have the same basic personality traits, such as vigilance and sensitivity, but each of us has unique degrees of those traits.

Assessing Traits If you were a clinical or counseling psychologist, you would have your choice of dozens of instruments for measuring personality. We have already met some of these in our discussion of the Rorschach inkblot technique, along with its projective cousin, the TAT, which came to us from the psychodynamic perspective. Now let us examine some of the personality tests spawned in part by the theories of traits, types, and temperaments.

One of the newer trait-based instruments comes from the five-factor theory: the NEO-PI or "Big Five Inventory" (Caprara et al., 1993; Costa & McCrae, 1992a, b). This personality assessment device has been used to study personality stability across the lifespan and the relationship of personality characteristics to physical health and various life events.

One of the most widely used of the personality inventories is the *Minnesota Multiphasic Personality Inventory,* usually called the **MMPI-2.** (The "2" means it is a revised form of the original *MMPI.*) Strictly speaking, it doesn't measure

■ **Five-factor theory** A trait perspective suggesting that personality is composed of five fundamental personality dimensions: openness to experience, conscientiousness, extraversion, agreeableness, and neuroticism.

■ ***MMPI-2*** A widely used personality assessment instrument that gives scores on ten important clinical traits. Also called the *Minnesota Multiphasic Personality Inventory.*

enduring personality traits. Rather, its ten clinical scales were developed to measure serious mental problems, such as depression and schizophrenia (Butcher et al., 1989; Butcher & Williams, 1992; Greene, 1991; Helmes & Reddon, 1993). It consists of 567 statements dealing with attitudes, habits, fears, preferences, physical health, beliefs, and general outlook, such as:

- I am often bothered by thoughts about sex.
- Sometimes I like to stir up some excitement.
- If people had not judged me unfairly, I would have been far more successful.

Respondents are asked to indicate whether each statement describes them, and their answers are scored on the ten clinical dimensions listed in Table 10.4.

Attempting to fake a good or bad score on the *MMPI-2* is not a smart idea. The test has four "lie" scales that will most likely signal that something is amiss. All are sensitive to unusual responses. Here are some items similar to those on the lie scales:

- Sometimes I put off doing things I know I ought to do.
- On occasion I have passed on some gossip.
- Once in a while, I find a dirty joke amusing.

Too many attempts to make yourself look good or bad will boost your lie scale scores into the questionable range.

From a scientific standpoint, the *MMPI-2* is an exemplary instrument for two reasons. First, it has **reliability.** This means that it provides consistent and stable scores. So, for example, when a person takes the test on two different occasions, the scores are likely to be much the same. Any good test must have reliability; otherwise, the scores would be erratic and undependable.

Second, the *MMPI-2* has **validity**—which means that it actually measures what it was designed to measure: indicators of mental disturbance. The instrument does a credible job, for example, of identifying depressed or psychotic persons (Greene, 1991). So, as a diagnostic instrument, the *MMPI-2* has a good record—although it must be used with care in non-Western cultures because some of its items have culture-specific content (Lonner, 1990). Clinicians should also be cautious when giving the *MMPI-2* to members of ethnic minorities in the United States, because minority groups were not well represented in the original sample used in developing the test (Butcher & Williams, 1992; Graham, 1990).

■ **Reliability** An attribute of a psychological test that gives consistent results.
■ **Validity** An attribute of a psychological test that actually measures what it is being used to measure.

Evaluating Temperament and Trait Theories Several criticisms have been leveled at the temperament and trait theories and the tests they have spawned.

TABLE 10.4 MMPI-2 Clinical Scales

Hypochondriasis (Hs): Abnormal concern with bodily functions
Depression (D): Pessimism; hopelessness; slowing of action and thought
Conversion hysteria (Hy): Unconscious use of mental problems to avoid conflicts or responsibility
Psychopathic deviate (Pd): Disregard for social custom; shallow emotions; inability to profit from experience
Masculinity–femininity (Mf): Differences between men and women
Paranoia (Pa): Suspiciousness; delusions of grandeur or persecution
Psychasthenia (Pt): Obsessions; compulsions; fears; low self-esteem; guilt; indecisiveness
Schizophrenia (Sc): Bizarre, unusual thoughts or behavior; withdrawal; hallucinations; delusions
Hypomania (Ma): Emotional excitement; flight of ideas; overactivity
Social introversion (Si): Shyness; disinterest in others; insecurity

For one, these theories give us a "snapshot" of personality—a picture that portrays personality as fixed and static, rather than as a dynamic and changing process. Another criticism is that they oversimplify our complex natures by describing personality on just a few dimensions. As evolution scholar Stephen Jay Gould remarked, "The world does not come to us in neat little packages" (1996, p. 188). And what would we gain, for example, by judging Margaret Sanger as "passionate" or by finding that she scored high on traits such as outgoingness and dominance but low on agreeableness or conventional thinking? Such judgments would validate others' observations of her and even her own self-descriptions. But brief labels and concise categories also leave out important detail. Although many women may have possessed similar traits, no one else did what Margaret Sanger did. A simple sketch of personality cannot provide the insight of a more complex portrait.

On the positive side, trait theories give us some ability to *predict* behavior in common situations, such as work settings—to select employees who are well trained and to screen out those who might cause problems. But trait theories suffer from the same difficulty as the instinct theories. Both *describe* behavior with a label but do not *explain* it. For example, we can attribute depression to a depressive trait or an outgoing personality to extraversion without really understanding the behavior. In short, trait theories identify common traits, but they do not tell us much about their source or how traits interact (McAdams, 1992; Pervin, 1985). Moreover, because most people display a trait only to a moderate degree, we must ask how useful traits are for understanding all but the extreme cases. In contrast, dynamic theories of personality (which we examined in the first part of this chapter) emphasize changing, developing forces within the individual and the environment.

THE FAR SIDE® By GARY LARSON
© 1990 FarWorks, Inc. All Rights Reserved/Dist. by Creators Syndicate
The glass is half full!
The glass is half empty.
Half full... No! Wait! Half empty!.. No, half... What was the question?
Hey! I ordered a cheeseburger!
Larson

The four basic personality types

Finally, with trait theory we again encounter the problem of the *self-fulfilling prophecy*. When given trait labels, people may begin to act as those labels suggest, making it more difficult for them to change. A child labeled "shy," for example, may have to struggle against both the label and the trait.

CONNECTION: CHAPTER 7
The original *self-fulfilling prophecy* involved students whose academic performance was altered by teachers' expectations.

Traits and the Person–Situation Debate Cognitive theorist Walter Mischel dropped a scientific bombshell on the trait theorists with evidence suggesting that we behave far less consistently from one situation to another than most had assumed (1968, 1973). A person who is extraverted in one situation can become shy and retiring in another; an emotionally stable person may fall apart when the situation changes radically. Therefore, Mischel argued, knowledge of the *situation* is more important in predicting behavior than knowing a person's traits. The ensuing tumult within the field has become known as the **person–situation controversy** (Pervin, 1985).

In fact, Mischel's position challenged the very foundations of most personality theories. After all, if people do act inconsistently in different situations, then what good is a theory of personality? Critics mounted withering attacks on Mischel's thesis, pointing out that his methods underestimated a thread of consistency across situations (Epstein, 1980). Bem and Allen (1974) have also pointed out that some people behave more consistently than others. Moreover, people are most consistent when others are watching (Kenrick

Person–situation controversy A theoretical dispute concerning the relative contribution of personality factors and situational factors in controlling behavior.

● Often the situation is a more powerful predictor of behavior than are personality traits.

& Stringfield, 1980) and when in familiar situations (Funder, 1983a, b; Funder & Ozer, 1983).

Nevertheless, it is true that personality traits as measured by personality tests typically account for less than 10% of all the factors that affect behavior (Digman, 1990)—a small number, indeed! But don't make the mistake of assuming that the situation accounts for the remaining 90%. Correlations between situations and behaviors are relatively weak, too. The lesson to be learned here is that the majority of factors affecting behavior simply cannot be assigned to one category or the other. Behavior seems to result from an *interaction* of trait and situational variables (Kenrick & Funder, 1988). In fact, Mischel has never suggested that we abandon theories of personality. Rather, he sees behavior as a function of the situation, the individual's *interpretation* of the situation, and personality (1990; Mischel & Shoda, 1995).

Mischel has argued that personality variables have their greatest impact on behavior when cues in the situation are *weak* or *ambiguous.* When situations are strong and clear, there will be less individual variation in response. For example, suppose that one day when you are in class, a student collapses, apparently unconscious, onto the floor. After a stunned silence, the instructor asks the class to keep their seats and then points *at you,* demanding loudly, "Use your cell phone to call 911, and get an ambulance here!" What do you do? This is a "strong" situation: Someone is in control, an instructor you already see as an authority figure; that person has told you unambiguously what to do. You are likely to comply—as would most people in that situation. In Mischel's characterization of person–situation interactions, there would be very little variation in how individuals respond to these circumstances.

But now suppose that you are walking leisurely through campus and you see a crowd gathered around a student who has collapsed on the sidewalk. Will you go for help? This is a "weak" situation, and your actions are likely to depend more strongly on your past experience and on such personality variables as independence and extraversion.

PSYCHOLOGY IN YOUR LIFE: FINDING YOUR TYPE

The notion of **type** refers to especially important dimensions or clusters of traits that are found in essentially the same pattern in many people. As we saw earlier, Carl Jung made the concept of type a feature of his theory of personality. (Thus, we could classify Jung as both a psychodynamic theorist and a trait/type theorist.) Jung's typology scheme, especially his notions of introversion and extraversion, have enjoyed wide influence and, as we have seen, is now recognized as one of the Big Five trait dimensions. Of particular importance is the use of Jung's typology as the foundation for the world's most widely used test of personality: the *Myers–Briggs Type Indicator.*

■ **Type** Refers to especially important dimensions or clusters of traits that are not only central to a person's personality but are found with essentially the same pattern in many people.

■ ***Myers–Briggs Type Indicator (MBTI)*** A widely used personality test based on Jungian types.

You are likely to have taken the ***Myers–Briggs Type Indicator (MBTI)*** because it is given to nearly two million people each year (Druckman & Bjork, 1991). It is used in many college counseling centers, where students may be advised to select a career that fits with their personality type. It is also used in relationship counseling, where couples are taught to accommodate to each other's personality styles. And the *MBTI* is commonly used by consultants in management training sessions to convey the message that people have distinct personality patterns that suit them for different kinds of jobs.

We pause to give the *MBTI* a close look for two reasons. First, as the only objective measure of personality based on Jung's type theory, it presents an opportunity to examine some of his ideas critically. Second, as one of the most widely used of psychological instruments, the *MBTI* deserves critical scrutiny. We suggest that there are some good reasons to be cautious when interpreting the results on an *MBTI* profile.

● Extraversion is thought by some to represent a major personality type.

On the Myers–Briggs test, examinees answer a series of questions about how they make judgments, perceive the world, and relate to others (Myers, 1962, 1976, 1987; Myers & Myers, 1995). Based on these responses, a scoring system assigns an individual to a four-dimensional personality type, derived from the Jungian dimensions of Introversion–Extraversion, Thinking–Feeling, Sensation–Intuition, and Judgment–Perception. You will recall that according to Jung, personality types are stable patterns over time.

What does the *Myers–Briggs Type Indicator* tell us about the stability or *reliability* of types? Remember that reliable test gives consistent results. But the research suggests that the reliability of the *MBTI* is questionable. One study found that fewer than half of those tested on the *MBTI* had exactly the same type when retested five weeks later (McCarley & Carskadon, 1983). Another study found a change in at least one of the four type categories in about 75% of respondents (see Druckman & Bjork, 1991). Such results certainly raise questions about the fundamental concept of "type."

A second issue concerns the *validity* of the Myers–Briggs test (Pittenger, 1993). We have said that a valid test actually measures what it is being used to measure. And again the research on the *MBTI* gives a mixed picture (Druckman & Bjork, 1991). As you might expect, people who work with people—entertainers, counselors, managers, and sellers—tend to score higher on extraversion. By comparison, librarians, computer specialists, and physicians number many introverts in their ranks. The danger lies, however, in turning averages into stereotypes. In fact, the data show a diversity of types within occupations. Further, we find a conspicuous lack of evidence documenting a relationship between personality type and occupational success. Although proponents of the *MBTI* claim it to be useful in vocational counseling, a review of the literature by a team from the National Academy of Sciences found no relationship between personality type, as revealed by the *MBTI,* and performance on a particular job (Druckman & Bjork, 1991). This report has, however, been vigorously disputed by users of the instrument (Pearman, 1991). Clearly, the *Myers–Briggs Type Indicator* needs more validity work before we can confidently encourage people to make life choices on the basis of its results.

Counselors using the *Myers–Briggs* to assess Jungian personality types often argue that its value lies not in its accuracy but in its ability to suggest new avenues for exploration—previously unknown personality patterns that might suggest career possibilities that might never have come to the individual's attention. Moreover, those who take the test often report that they have gained insight into themselves from the experience. Thus the instrument may have some value in counseling, especially when counselors resist the temptation to interpret the results rigidly. Unfortunately, no research has been done that documents these benefits over the long term. Says the National Academy of Sciences Report (Druckman & Bjork, 1991), "Lacking such evidence, it is a curiosity why the instrument is used so widely" (p. 99).

CHECK YOUR UNDERSTANDING

1. **RECALL:** *Temperament* refers to personality characteristics that
   a. have their roots in the unconscious.
   b. are learned, especially from one's parents and peers.
   c. cause mental disorders.
   d. cause people to be "nervous" or unpredictable.
   e. have a substantial biological basis.

2. **APPLICATION:** A friend of yours always seems agitated and anxious, even when nothing in the circumstances would provoke such a response. Which one of the Big Five traits applies to this characteristic of your friend?
   a. agreeableness
   b. conscientiousness
   c. extraversion
   d. introversion
   e. neuroticism

3. **RECALL:** Walter Mischel argues that ______ is (are) less important than ______.
   a. the conscious mind/the unconscious
   b. emotions/reason
   c. the situation/emotions
   d. traits/the situation
   e. traits/temperament

4. **UNDERSTANDING THE CORE CONCEPT:** What is found in most psychodynamic, humanistic, and cognitive theories but is not found in most temperament, trait, and type theories?
   a. a description of the components of the personality
   b. labels for common mental disorders
   c. concepts that are useful for individuals involved in personnel selection decisions
   d. a description of the processes of development and change underlying personality
   e. nothing, because these theories all share the same components

ANSWERS: 1. e 2. e 3. d 4. d

KEY QUESTION

WHAT "THEORIES" DO PEOPLE USE TO UNDERSTAND EACH OTHER?

We have seen how psychologists view personality. But how do people who are *not* psychologists think about people? This is an important matter because we all regularly make assumptions—right or wrong—about other people's personalities. You do so when you meet someone new at a party, when you apply for a job, and when you form your first impression of a professor or classmate. Do people make similar assumptions about each other in other cultures? These questions are significant because the "folk theories," or *implicit personality theories,* that people use to understand each other can support or undermine relationships among individuals—or even among nations. Our Core Concept says:

CORE CONCEPT

People everywhere develop implicit assumptions ("folk theories") about personality, but these assumptions vary in important ways across cultures.

In this section we will examine the assumptions commonly found in implicit theories of personality. Then, at the end, we will help you discover what implicit assumptions you make about others.

Implicit Personality Theories

Think of someone who has been a role model for you. Now think of someone you can't stand to be around. In both cases, what immediately springs to mind are personal attributes—traits—that you have learned to use to describe people: honesty, reliability, sense of humor, generosity, outgoing attitude, aggressiveness, moodiness, or pessimism, for example. Even as a child, you had a rudimentary system for appraising personality. You tried to determine which new acquaintances would be friend or foe; you worked out ways of dealing with your parents or teachers based on how you read their personalities. You have probably also spent a great deal of time trying to get a handle on who you are—on what qualities distinguish you from others, which ones to develop, and which to discard.

In each case, your judgments were personality assessments reflecting your **implicit personality theory,** your personal explanation of how people's qualities and experiences influence their response patterns. Like the implicit memories we studied in Chapter 7, implicit theories of personality operate in the background, largely outside of our awareness. There they simplify the task of understanding other people (Fiske & Neuberg, 1990; Macrae et al., 1994).

Implicit theories often rely on naive assumptions about traits. For example, people tend to assume that certain clusters of traits go together—creativity and emotional sensitivity, for example. Consequently, when they observe one of these traits, they may assume that the person possesses the other (Hochwalder, 1995). People's personal experiences and motives can also influence their judgment of others. So, if you have had your heart broken by someone who was attractive but unwilling to make a commitment, you may quickly judge other attractive persons to be "insincere" or "untrustworthy."

In judging people, Americans and Europeans also tend to make the **fundamental attribution error.** This error in judgment relies on the assumption that another person's behavior, especially clumsy, inappropriate, or otherwise undesirable behavior, is the result of a flaw in the personality rather than in the situation. For example, if you trip and fall as you enter a psychology class at an American college or university, other students are likely to assume that you are a clumsy person. But if you were stumbling into a psychology class in China or Japan, the students would be more likely to assume that your bizarre behavior had some external cause, such as someone bumping you or an irregularity in the floor tiles. Cross-cultural research shows that the fundamental attribution error is less common in group-oriented, *collectivistic* cultures, such as are found in China and India (Lillard, 1997; Miller, 1984; Morris & Peng, 1994).

Personality across Cultures

The very concept of personality theory is a Western (Euro-American) invention, said cross-cultural psychologist Juris Draguns (1979). Therefore, it is not surprising that all formal theories of personality have been created by people trained in the framework of the Western social sciences, with a built-in bias toward individualism (Guisinger & Blatt, 1994; Segall et al., 1999). Other cultures, however, address many of the same issues in their own ways. Most of these non-Western perspectives have originated in religion (Walsh, 1984). Hindus, for example, see personality as a union of opposing characteristics (Murphy & Murphy, 1968). The Chinese concept of complementary opposite forces, yin and yang, provides a similar perspective (which influenced Carl Jung's *principle of opposites*).

Individualism, Collectivism, and Personality According to Harry Triandis (1989, 1990, 1994; Triandis & Gelfand, 1998), cultures differ most fundamentally on the dimension of *individualism* versus *collectivism,* which we alluded to above. For those raised in the Euro-American tradition, the individual is the basic unit of society, while those raised in many Asian and African cultures emphasize the family or other social groups. In collectivistic cultures people tend to form identities that blend harmoniously with the group, and they expect that others are motivated to do the same. In individualistic cultures, a person tends to form a unique identity and assume that others are similarly motivated to stand out from the crowd (Pedersen, 1979). Thus, for Euro-Americans

■ **Implicit personality theory** Assumptions about personality that are held by people (especially nonpsychologists) to simplify the task of understanding others.

■ **Fundamental attribution error** The assumption that another person's behavior, especially clumsy, inappropriate, or otherwise undesirable behavior, is the result of a flaw in the personality, rather than in the situation.

● Most Asian cultures have a collectivist tradition that affirms the group, rather than the individual, as the fundamental social unit.

the self is a whole, while for many Asians and Africans the self is only a part (Cohen & Gunz, 2002; Gardiner et al., 1998; Markus & Kitayama, 1994). For Euro-Americans, a group is composed of separate individuals; when they work together they become a "team." By contrast, for Asians and Africans the group is the natural unit; the individual is incomplete without the group. Much of the conflict and misunderstanding arising from business dealings and political negotiations across cultures stems from different expectations about personality and the individual's relationship to the group.

Many aspects of peoples' personalities and behavior are related to their culture's position on the individualism-versus-collectivism dimension. We have already seen how the fundamental attribution error is more common in individualistic cultures. Two other topics related to individualism versus collectivism and to personality have received special emphasis by cross-cultural psychologists: (1) competition versus cooperation and (2) the need for achievement. In brief, when given the choice of competition or cooperation, individualistic Americans characteristically choose to compete (Aronson, 2004; Gallo & McClintock, 1965). Americans, on the average, also score higher on measures of need for achievement than do people in collectivist cultures.

Other Cultural Differences Cultures differ on other personality-related dimensions that are not so obviously related to individualism–collectivism. These include:

- *Status of different age groups and sexes:* The status of the elderly is higher in many Asian cultures than in the United States; women have second-class status in many traditional societies (Segall et al., 1999).
- *Romantic love:* The assumption that romantic love should be the basis for marriage is a historically recent European invention and is most often found in individualistic cultures (Rosenblatt, 1966).
- *Stoicism:* Asian cultures teach people to suppress the expression of intense feelings (Tsai & Uemura, 1988), while Euro-Americans are much more likely to express strong emotions (although there are pronounced gender differences).
- *Locus of control:* Persons in industrialized nations, such as the United States and Canada, more often have an internal locus of control than do those in developing countries, such as Mexico or China (Berry et al., 1992; Draguns, 1979; Shiraev & Levy, 2004).
- *Thinking versus feeling:* Many cultures (e.g., in Latin America) do not make the strong distinction between thoughts and emotions that Americans do (Fajans, 1985; Lutz, 1988).

Cultures even differ in their views of the ideal personality (Matsumoto, 1996). In the Western psychological tradition, mental health consists of integrating opposite and conflicting parts of the personality. This can be seen especially clearly in Freudian and Jungian theory. By contrast, some Asian psychologies, particularly those associated with Buddhism, seek the opposite: to dissociate consciousness from sensation and from memories of worldly experience (Gardiner et al., 1998; Pedersen, 1979).

Despite these differences, can we say that people are fundamentally the same the world over? On the level of neurons and brain circuits, the answer is certainly "Yes." But personality is also locked in the embrace of culture, so a more comprehensive answer would be "No—but perhaps they can be described on the same Big Five dimensions." In the words of Erika Bourguignon (1979), "It is one of the major intellectual developments of the twentieth century to call into question the concept of a universal human nature."

Even though personality and culture are partners in a perpetual dance, we can make this distinction between them:

> "Culture" refers to those aspects of a society that all its members share, are familiar with, and pass on to the next generation. "Personality" refers to unique combinations of traits (which all people in a culture know about, even though a given trait does not describe a given person) which differentiate individuals within a culture. (Brislin, 1981, pp. 51–52)

But don't forget that culture and personality interact. A culture shapes the personalities of the individuals within it, just as individuals can influence a culture. Your personality is, to a certain extent, a product of your society's values, attitudes, beliefs, and customs about morality, work, child rearing, aggression, achievement, competition, death, and dozens of other matters important to humans everywhere. And in a larger sense, a culture is the "personality" of a society (Benedict, 1934).

In addition to the theories of personality described earlier in this chapter, one more researcher is worth noting. Hans Eysenck's theory examined two dimensions of temperament, **neuroticism** and **extraversion–introversion.** Note that for Eysenck, neuroticism was a scale on which people could be rated for their *susceptibility* to neurotic problems such as panic attacks or other nervous disorders, not the disorders themselves. But when he refers to extraversion and introversion, Eysenck is using these terms the way people with no background in psychology think of them. These are pervasive ways in which a person interacts with the environment (extraverts are gregarious and outgoing, introverts quiet and reserved).

PSYCHOLOGY IN YOUR LIFE: DEVELOPING YOUR OWN THEORY OF PERSONALITY

Each of the theories we have examined has its limitations and strengths. Consequently, most psychologists become **eclectic.** That is, they either switch theories as the situation requires or construct a theory of personality by borrowing ideas from many perspectives. While an eclectic approach may appear to offer the easiest route, it presents difficulties that arise from certain fundamental conflicts among theories. To give one example: How could we reconcile Freud's concept of our behavior being driven by primitive instincts with humanism's assumption of the innate goodness of our nature?

It may help to think of a personality theory as a map showing the major pathways through a person's psychological landscape. As you formulate your own theory, you must decide how to weight the forces that determine which paths we select—the forces of conditioning, motivation and emotion, heredity and environment, individualism and collectivism, cognition, traits, culture, self-concept, and potential. We propose the following questions, which will help you sort out the assumptions in your implicit theory of personality.

- In your opinion, are people more rational and logical (as the cognitive theories contend), or do they more often act on the basis of feelings and emotions (as the psychodynamic theories argue)?
- Are people usually conscious of the reasons for their behavior, as many of the post-Freudians claimed? Or are their actions mainly caused by unconscious needs, desires, and urges (as Freud suggested)?

Neuroticism Susceptibility to neurotic problems.

Extraversion A personality descriptor indicating the "outgoing" nature of some individuals.

Introversion A personality descriptor indicating the quiet and reserved nature of some individuals.

Eclectic Either switching theories to explain different situations or building one's own theory of personality from pieces borrowed from many perspectives.

● Do you think these people are conscious of the reasons for their behavior? Some views of personality assert that anger comes from an inner drive that arises in the unconscious mind. Other views emphasize conscious cognitions of environmental stimuli.

- What do you see as the basic motives behind human behavior: sex, aggression, power, love, spirituality . . . ?
- Are human motives essentially egocentric and self-serving? Or are they altruistic, unmotivated by the desire for personal gain (as the humanists suggest)?
- When you try to understand another person's actions, which of the following do you consider to be most important: the situation (as Mischel says); the person's inner needs, drives, motives, and emotions (as the psychodynamic theories say); or the person's basic personality characteristics (as the trait and type theories say)?
- Is our basic, inner nature essentially healthy and good (as the humanists see it) or composed of primitive and self-serving desires (as Freud saw it)?

No one has yet found the "right" answers, but the answers you give say a great deal about your own personality.

CHECK YOUR UNDERSTANDING

1. **APPLICATION:** You would expect to find the concept of self emphasized in
   a. a collectivistic culture.
   b. the culture of an industrialized society.
   c. an individualistic culture.
   d. a poor culture.
   e. a wealthy culture.

2. **RECALL:** Cross-cultural psychologists say that a basic distinction among cultures is their emphasis on
   a. capitalism or socialism.
   b. external or internal locus of control.
   c. individualism or collectivism.
   d. nature or nurture.
   e. thoughts or feelings.

3. **APPLICATION:** You are making the *fundamental attribution error* when
   a. you decide to dislike someone who speaks angrily to you.
   b. you see someone who is nice-looking and assume that she is self-centered and arrogant.
   c. you go to a foreign country and assume that everyone thinks the same way you do.
   d. you think someone is clumsy when he trips and drops his books.
   e. you swap one emotion for one that is less threatening.

4. **UNDERSTANDING THE CORE CONCEPT:** Implicit personality theories involve
   a. assumptions about themselves that people want to hide from others.
   b. the assumptions that people make about each other's motives, intentions, and behaviors.
   c. conclusions that are obvious.
   d. opinions that people privately hold about others but will not express openly.
   e. unconscious instincts, memories, and conflicts.

ANSWERS: 1. c 2. c 3. d 4. b

PERSONALITY: THE STATE OF THE ART

Everyone acknowledges that no single theory explains everything we lump under "personality" as the enduring psychological characteristics that provide continuity to our behavior and distinguish one person from another. Modern theories have a more scientific base than did those of Freud, Jung, Horney, and their contemporaries. Moreover, as Mischel tells us, the situation may be even more influential than the personality in determining what we do.

So where does that leave the cutting edges in the science of personality? Some researchers are looking for genetic connections to temperament and the major personality traits. There have been no "breakthroughs" yet—but stay tuned. Others, as we have noted, are exploring how families, cultures, and gender influence personality. Our guess is that one of the most volatile areas for personality research in the coming decade is going to involve neuroscience. We will gain a deeper understanding of how personality is manifested in the brain, especially in brain chemistry. We hope, however, that an emphasis on the *nature* of personality doesn't make researchers loose sight of its *nurture*—of how experience can alter the very circuits and chemicals that the brain uses to create personality.

USING PSYCHOLOGY TO LEARN PSYCHOLOGY

Your Academic Locus of Control

Although an internal or external locus of control can be a central feature of your personality, your perceived locus of control can also change from situation to situation. When you are speaking in front of a group, for example, you may feel that the situation is beyond your control, but when you are on skis you may feel that your are fully the master of your fate. And what about your education? Do you have a sense of internal or external control with regard to—say—your grade in psychology?

An external locus of control concerning grades poses a danger for the high school student because high school life is so full of distractions and temptations. If you believe that your grades are largely beyond your control, you can easily be driven by the enticements of the moment and let your studies slide. This attitude can, of course, become a self-fulfilling prophecy that ruins your grades not only in psychology but across the board.

The following questions will help you discover your academic locus of control:

- On a test do you often find that, even if you know the material, anxiety wipes the information from your memory?
- On a test do you often know the material well but find that the test is unfair or covers material that the teacher did not indicate would be on the test?
- Do you feel poorly motivated to cope with college-level work?
- Are you so easily distracted that you can never quite get around to studying?
- Do you believe that some people are born to be good students and some are not?
- Do you feel that you have no control over the grades you receive?
- Do you feel that you are not smart enough to cope with college-level work?
- Do you feel that success in college will be largely a matter of luck?

If you answered "yes" to several of these questions, then you probably have an *external* locus of control with respect to your college work—an attitude that can hamper your chances of success. What can be done? Nothing, if you are completely convinced that your success is beyond your control. If, however, you are open to the idea of establishing more control over your educational experience, here are several suggestions:

- Get help with test anxiety from your counseling center or learning resources center.
- Find a tutor either among friends or at your learning resources center.
- Talk to your teachers individually: Ask them to give you some pointers on what they consider to be especially important (and testable) in their classes.
- Go to your high school's learning resources center and get an assessment of your strengths and weaknesses and of your interest patterns. Then make a plan to correct your weaknesses (e.g., with remedial classes in your weak areas) and build on your strengths. Select a major that capitalizes on your strengths and interests.

We would wish you good luck—but of course that's only of concern to externalizers!

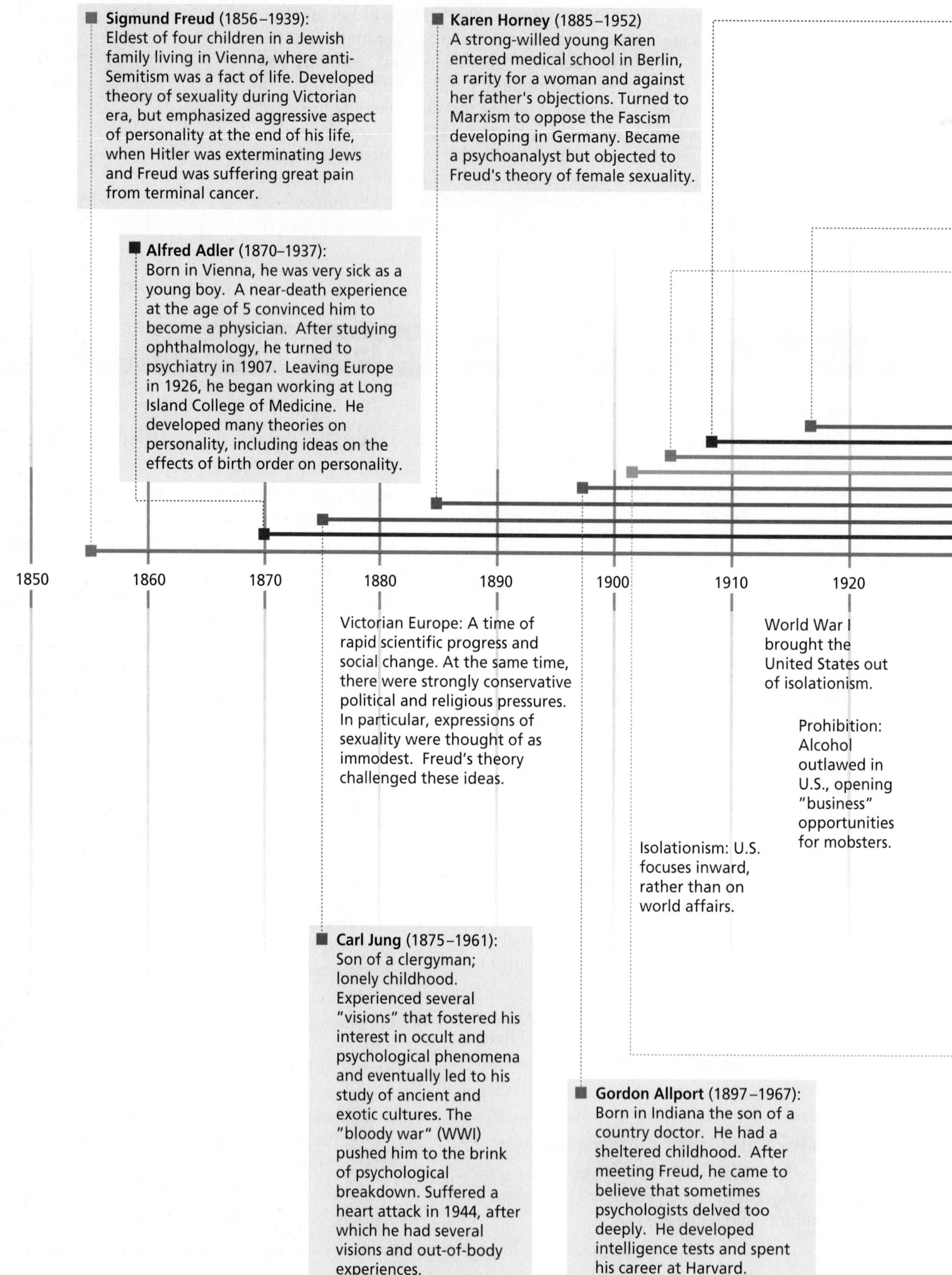

Sigmund Freud (1856–1939):
Eldest of four children in a Jewish family living in Vienna, where anti-Semitism was a fact of life. Developed theory of sexuality during Victorian era, but emphasized aggressive aspect of personality at the end of his life, when Hitler was exterminating Jews and Freud was suffering great pain from terminal cancer.
Karen Horney (1885–1952)
A strong-willed young Karen entered medical school in Berlin, a rarity for a woman and against her father's objections. Turned to Marxism to oppose the Fascism developing in Germany. Became a psychoanalyst but objected to Freud's theory of female sexuality.
Alfred Adler (1870–1937):
Born in Vienna, he was very sick as a young boy. A near-death experience at the age of 5 convinced him to become a physician. After studying ophthalmology, he turned to psychiatry in 1907. Leaving Europe in 1926, he began working at Long Island College of Medicine. He developed many theories on personality, including ideas on the effects of birth order on personality.
1850
1860
1870
1880
1890
1900
1910
1920
Victorian Europe: A time of rapid scientific progress and social change. At the same time, there were strongly conservative political and religious pressures. In particular, expressions of sexuality were thought of as immodest. Freud's theory challenged these ideas.
World War I brought the United States out of isolationism.
Prohibition: Alcohol outlawed in U.S., opening "business" opportunities for mobsters.
Isolationism: U.S. focuses inward, rather than on world affairs.
Carl Jung (1875–1961):
Son of a clergyman; lonely childhood. Experienced several "visions" that fostered his interest in occult and psychological phenomena and eventually led to his study of ancient and exotic cultures. The "bloody war" (WWI) pushed him to the brink of psychological breakdown. Suffered a heart attack in 1944, after which he had several visions and out-of-body experiences.
Gordon Allport (1897–1967):
Born in Indiana the son of a country doctor. He had a sheltered childhood. After meeting Freud, he came to believe that sometimes psychologists delved too deeply. He developed intelligence tests and spent his career at Harvard.

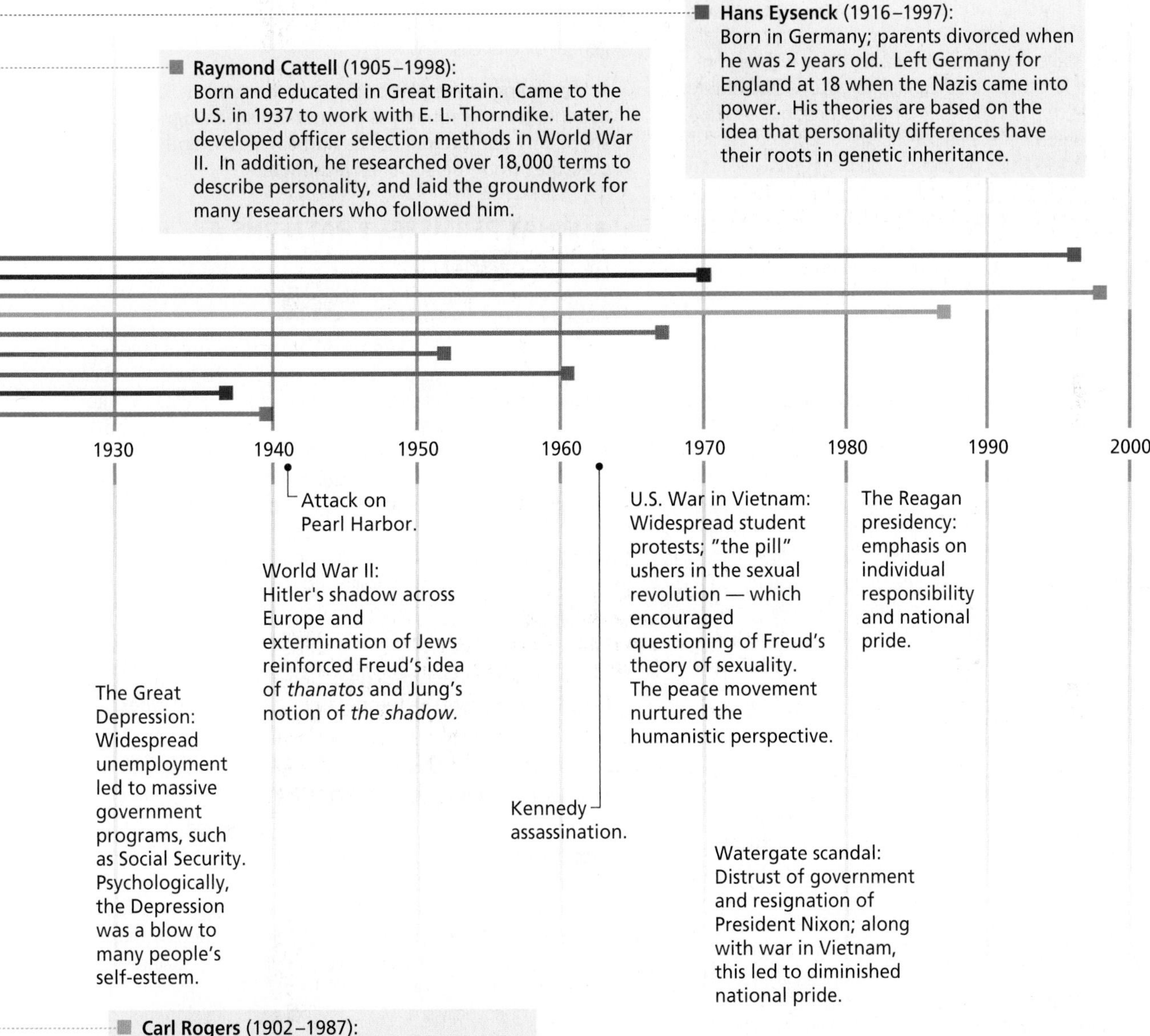

Abraham Maslow (1908–1970):
The son of Russian-Jewish immigrants to New York; remembered his childhood as unhappy, lonely, isolated, depressing. A good student, his focus moved from music and drama to psychology, in which he became fascinated with behaviorism — which he later rejected. Early in his career as a psychology professor in New York, he came in contact with many of the finest Jewish scholars who had fled Nazi persecution in Europe during World War II. He became interested in ways that psychology could be used to promote world peace.
Hans Eysenck (1916–1997):
Born in Germany; parents divorced when he was 2 years old. Left Germany for England at 18 when the Nazis came into power. His theories are based on the idea that personality differences have their roots in genetic inheritance.
Raymond Cattell (1905–1998):
Born and educated in Great Britain. Came to the U.S. in 1937 to work with E. L. Thorndike. Later, he developed officer selection methods in World War II. In addition, he researched over 18,000 terms to describe personality, and laid the groundwork for many researchers who followed him.
1930
1940
1950
1960
1970
1980
1990
2000
Attack on Pearl Harbor.
World War II: Hitler's shadow across Europe and extermination of Jews reinforced Freud's idea of *thanatos* and Jung's notion of *the shadow.*
The Great Depression: Widespread unemployment led to massive government programs, such as Social Security. Psychologically, the Depression was a blow to many people's self-esteem.
Kennedy assassination.
U.S. War in Vietnam: Widespread student protests; "the pill" ushers in the sexual revolution — which encouraged questioning of Freud's theory of sexuality. The peace movement nurtured the humanistic perspective.
The Reagan presidency: emphasis on individual responsibility and national pride.
Watergate scandal: Distrust of government and resignation of President Nixon; along with war in Vietnam, this led to diminished national pride.

Carl Rogers (1902–1987):
The fourth of six children in a very strict Protestant family from rural Illinois. A good student, but unhappy and lonely during childhood — worried that he had mental problems. Studied for the ministry for a time but instead became a counselor and therapist. His person-centered ideas struck a responsive chord with students in the 1960s, who were rebelling against paternalistic attitudes of colleges and universities, as well as against the war in Vietnam.

● **FIGURE 10.5** The Historical Context of Personality Theories

Theories of personality have often been influenced by the historical context in which they were developed.

CHAPTER SUMMARY

KEY QUESTION

CORE CONCEPT

• WHAT FORCES SHAPE OUR PERSONALITIES?

The psychodynamic, humanistic, and cognitive theories all seek to explain the influences that mold our personalities. Freud's psychoanalytic theory states that the personality is shaped by unconscious desires and conflicts. None of our thoughts or behaviors happen by accident, according to the principle of psychic determinism. Early childhood experiences also have a strong influence on personality, as the child goes through predictable psychosexual stages in which conflicts are dealt with unconsciously. Freud believed that the personality consisted of three main structures, the id (the reservoir of unconscious desires), the ego (the largely conscious part of the mind), and the superego (which contains the conscience and the ego ideal). Part of the ego, involving the ego defense mechanisms, operates outside of consciousness. One of these defense mechanisms, projection, is the basis for widely used projective tests.

Freud's theory has been extremely influential. Still, critics fault Freud's work for being scientifically unsound, a poor basis for prediction, and unfair to women. Modern psychology also suggests that the unconscious mind is less clever and purposeful than Freud believed.

Other psychodynamic theories, such as those proposed by Jung and Horney, also assume that personality is a dynamic process that involves strong and often-conflicting motives and emotions. Each of these neo-Freudians, however, emphasizes different aspects of personality. Jung proposed a collective unconscious, populated by archetypes. He also proposed that people fall into certain personality types, characterized especially by tendencies to introversion and extraversion. Horney, on the other hand, emphasized conscious processes, basic anxiety, and feminist issues in personality theory. Healthy people, she said, move toward others, while neurotic people move against others.

The humanistic theories, such as those of Maslow and Rogers, argue that people are naturally driven toward self-actualization, but this tendency can be suppressed by unhealthy conditions and perceptions. Maslow emphasized a hierarchy of needs, suggesting that when the deficiency needs are met, a person is more likely to pursue self-actualization. Rogers taught that the fully functioning person has a positive self-concept that is congruent with reality, while mental disorder arises from incongruence. High self-esteem is more likely when a child comes from a family that provides unconditional positive regard. The humanistic theories have had considerable impact on psychotherapy, but they have been criticized for lacking a strong scientific base.

The social-cognitive theories, by contrast, do have a scientific basis. Bandura's theory suggests that personality is shaped by observational learning. This occurs in an interaction of cognition, behavior, and the environment known as reciprocal determinism. According to Rotter's locus-of-control theory, those with an internal locus are more likely to feel they can control events in their lives than those who have an external locus of control. The social-cognitive theories are much more limited in scope than the psychodynamic or humanistic theories.

Modern theories of personality, unlike those of Freud, Jung, Horney, and the other psychodynamic theorists, have not attempted to provide comprehensive explanations for all aspects of personality. Emphasis has turned to the individual acting in a social environment, such as the family. Other emphases include cultural influences on personality, as well as an awareness of gender differences.

• According to the psychodynamic, humanistic, and cognitive theories, personality is a continuously changing process, shaped by our internal needs and cognitions and by external pressures from the social environment.

• WHAT PERSISTENT PATTERNS ARE FOUND IN PERSONALITY?

Temperament, trait, and type theories are descriptive approaches to personality with a long history stretching back to the ancient Greeks. Modern trait/type/temperament theories are frequently used as the basis for diagnosis, personnel selection, and psychological testing. *Temperament* refers to innate personality dispositions, which may be tied to factors in the brain. Traits give personality consistency across situations and may be influenced by both heredity and learning. Many psychologists now agree on the Big Five traits. Trait assessment is the basis for many psychological tests. The person–situation controversy, however, has raised questions about the relative contribution of personality traits and situations to behavior. Type theory is seen especially in the contro-versial and widely used MBTI, based on Jung's personality typology.

• Another approach describes personality in terms of stable patterns known as temperaments, traits, and types.

• WHAT "THEORIES" DO PEOPLE USE TO UNDERSTAND EACH OTHER?

People everywhere deal with each other on the basis of their implicit personality theories, which simplify the task of understanding others. Implicit theories may rely on naive assumptions, such as the fundamental attribution error. Moreover, cross-cultural psychologists have found that the assumptions people make about personality and behavior vary widely across cultures—depending especially on whether the culture emphasizes individualism or collectivism. Most psychologists develop their own eclectic theories of personality by combining ideas from various perspectives.

• People everywhere develop implicit assumptions ("folk theories") about personality, but these assumptions vary in important ways across cultures.

REVIEW TEST

For each of the following items, choose the single best answer. The correct answers appear at the end.

1. Which sort of personality theory would most likely emphasize unconscious motivation?
   a. psychodynamic theory
   b. trait theory
   c. humanistic theory
   d. cognitive theory
   e. cognitive-behavioral theory

2. Which one of the following is an ego defense mechanism that may cause us to forget unpleasant or threatening experiences?
   a. displacement
   b. projection
   c. regression
   d. repression
   e. reaction formation

3. Critics fault Freud's psychoanalytic theory because it
   a. does not explain the source of mental disorders.
   b. has no theory of psychological development.
   c. has little basis in scientific research.
   d. has had little impact on popular culture.
   e. does not account for the role of the unconscious.

4. One of the biggest differences between Freud and Jung can be seen in Jung's idea of
   a. the collective unconscious.
   b. locus of control.
   c. implicit personality theories.
   d. shyness.
   e. dispositions.

5. The humanistic theorists were the first to emphasize
   a. unconscious motives.
   b. mental disorder.
   c. the healthy personality.
   d. how people are similar to other animals.
   e. repressed sexual desires.

6. According to Rogers, children may grow up with feelings of guilt and anxiety in homes where
   a. parents are not good role models.
   b. one of the parents is absent most of the time.
   c. parental love is conditional on good behavior.
   d. the parents are in conflict with each other.
   e. genetic inheritance from parents predisposes them to guilt.

7. Reciprocal determinism involves the interaction of
   a. the id, ego, and superego.
   b. self-actualization, unconditional positive regard, and the phenomenal field.
   c. the conscious mind, the conscience, and the collective unconscious.
   d. cognitions, behavior, and the environment.
   e. genetics, the environment, and dispositions.

8. Explaining why a new classmate does not seem attractive, your friend remarks, "I don't much like thin people, because they're too nervous!" This assumption reveals that your friend favors a ______ theory of personality.
   a. humanistic
   b. psychodynamic
   c. cognitive
   d. collectivistic
   e. type

9. Which of the following is *not* one of the Big Five personality factors?
   a. neuroticism
   b. intelligence
   c. conscientiousness
   d. openness to experience
   e. extraversion

10. Your implicit theory of personality would help you
    a. know that a friend needs comforting when she loses her job.
    b. laugh at a joke.
    c. shout at a friend when you are angry at your employer.
    d. feel rewarded when you receive your paycheck.
    e. gain a sense of accomplishment for a good grade.

ANSWERS: 1.a 2.d 3.c 4.a 5.c 6.c 7.d 8.e 9.b 10.a

KEY TERMS

Personality (p. 410)
Psychoanalysis (p. 412)
Psychoanalytic theory (p. 412)
Unconscious (p. 412)
Libido (p. 413)
Id (p. 413)
Superego (p. 413)
Ego (p. 413)
Psychosexual stages (p. 414)
Oedipus complex (p. 415)
Identification (p. 415)
Penis envy (p. 415)
Fixation (p. 415)
Ego defense mechanism (p. 415)
Repression (p. 415)
Projective tests (p. 416)
Rorschach inkblot technique (p. 416)
Thematic Apperception Test (TAT) (p. 417)
Psychic determinism (p. 418)
Neo-Freudians (p. 419)
Personal unconscious (p. 420)
Collective unconscious (p. 420)
Archetypes (p. 420)
Introversion (p. 420)
Extraversion (p. 420)
Basic anxiety (p. 421)
Neurotic needs (p. 421)
Inferiority complex (p. 422)

Compensation (p. 422)
Traits (p. 423)
Central traits (p. 423)
Secondary traits (p. 423)
Cardinal traits (p. 423)
Self-actualizing personalities (p. 423)
Fully functioning person (p. 424)
Phenomenal field (p. 424)
Positive psychology (p. 425)
Observational learning (p. 426)
Reciprocal determinism (p. 426)
Locus of control (p. 426)
Humors (p. 430)
Temperament (p. 431)
Five-factor theory (p. 433)
MMPI-2 (p. 433)
Reliability (p. 434)
Validity (p. 434)
Person–situation controversy (p. 435)
Type (p. 436)
Myers–Briggs Type Indicator (MBTI) (p. 436)
Implicit personality theory (p. 439)
Fundamental attribution error (p. 439)
Neuroticism (p. 441)
Extraversion (p. 441)
Introversion (p. 441)
Eclectic (p. 441)

AP* REVIEW: VOCABULARY

Match each of the following vocabulary terms to its definition.

1. Personality
2. Ego
3. Superego
4. Projection
5. Personal unconscious
6. Locus of control
7. Temperament
8. Traits
9. Five-factor theory
10. Type

_____ **a.** When we are upset or aroused, we may use this defense mechanism to attribute our own unconscious desire to other people or objects.

_____ **b.** The psychological qualities that bring continuity to an individual's behavior in different situations and at different times.

_____ **c.** An individual's sense of where his or her life influences originate.

_____ **d.** A trait perspective suggesting that personality is composed of five fundamental personality dimensions: openness to experience, conscientiousness, extraversion, agreeableness, and neuroticism.

_____ **e.** Refers to especially important dimensions or clusters of traits that are central to a person's personality and are found with essentially the same pattern in many people.

_____ **f.** The basic and pervasive personality dispositions that are apparent in early childhood and that establish the tempo and mood of the individual's behaviors.

_____ **g.** The conscious, rational part of the personality, charged with keeping peace between the superego and the id.

_____ **h.** The mind's storehouse of values, including moral attitudes learned from parents and from society; roughly the same as the common notion of the conscience.

_____ **i.** Stable personality characteristics that are presumed to exist within the individual and to guide his or her thoughts and actions under various conditions.

_____ **j.** Jung's term for that portion of the unconscious that corresponds roughly to the Freudian id.

AP* REVIEW: ESSAY

Use your knowledge of the chapter concepts to answer the following essay question.

In personality theory, there are a number of differing approaches. One of the most unique is the cognitive-behavioral approach. In a well-thought-out and concise essay, describe the research of Rotter and Bandura. Be sure that your essay includes the following:

a. locus of control

b. reciprocal determinism

c. observational learning

d. trait

OUR RECOMMENDED BOOKS AND VIDEOS

BOOKS

Carducci, B. J., with Golant, S. (1999). *Shyness: A bold new approach.* New York: HarperCollins. Not a workbook for "changing" shy people into extroverts, this book is rather a set of strategies for living a "successfully shy life," including managing shyness when meeting others, working, falling in love, making small talk, and caring for shy children.

Janda, L. H. (1996). *The psychologist's book of self-tests: 25 love, sex, intelligence, career, and personality tests developed by professionals to reveal the real you.* New York: Perigee/Berkley. Just remember that any self-report technique depends on *your* responses—meaning that, to a large extent, you already know or can somewhat control the "outcome." Nonetheless, well constructed, valid, and reliable psychological assessments can cast individual data in a new light according to various theories of development, individual difference, and aptitude.

Kagan, J. (1995). *Galen's prophecy: Temperament in human nature.* Boulder, CO: Westview Press. Since ancient times, healers have believed each human being is born one of a few types: introvert or extrovert; sanguine, choleric, melancholy, or phlegmatic—and dozens of other typologies based on bodily shape or humors. The author, a renowned child psychologist, examines the scientific evidence for two basic types—shy (introverted) and bold—and how these inborn patterns determine one's life experiences in adjustment, work, and love.

VIDEOS

Catch Me If You Can. (2002, color, 141 min.). Directed by Steven Spielberg; starring Leonardo DiCaprio, Tom Hanks, Christopher Walken. Based on the best-selling memoir of con artist Frank Abagnale, Jr. (subtitled *The True Story of a Real Fake*), this is the story of a young man who succeeded in impersonating an airline pilot, pediatrician, hospital supervisor, assistant attorney general, and college professor—but was he motivated by greed or by love for his failed father? (*Rating PG-13*)

Identity. (2003, color, 90 min.). Directed by James Mangold; starring John Cusack, Ray Liotta, Amanda Peet, Alfred Molina. Ten strangers, trapped together in a storm-bound motel, deal in dramatically different ways with the threat of a killer among them—and all seem to have some mysterious connection with a legal proceeding taking place in a distant location. (*Rating R*)

The Talented Mr. Ripley. (1999, color, 139 min.). Directed by Anthony Minghella; starring Matt Damon, Gwyneth Paltrow, Jude Law. A poor, amoral young man, sent to retrieve a wayward heir from his European adventures, soon befriends the heir and tragically envies his target's beautiful life. Based on the late Patricia Highsmith's novel, the original U.S. film title listed Ripley's many personality traits and states: "The Mysterious, Yearning, Secretive, Sad, Lonely, Troubled, Confused, Loving, Musical, Gifted, Intelligent, Beautiful, Tender, Sensitive, Haunted, Passionate, Talented Mr. Ripley." (*Rating R*)

Key Question Chapter Outline

CORE CONCEPTS

Psychology in Your Life

How Do We Measure Individual Differences?

Validity and Reliability
Standardization and Norms
Types of Tests
Ethics and Standards in Testing

Measuring individual differences is an essential component of psychology, but strict guidelines and ethical standards must be followed to ensure that results and conclusions are valid and appropriate.

Testing in Education

"Tracking" and "mainstreaming" are two very different approaches to high school education.

How Is Intelligence Measured?

Binet and Simon Invent a School Abilities Test
American Psychologists Borrow Binet and Simon's Idea
IQ Testing Today
Problems with the IQ Formula

Intelligence testing has a history of controversy, but most psychologists now view intelligence as a normally distributed trait that can be measured by performance on a variety of tasks—both verbal and nonverbal.

What Can You Do for an Exceptional Child?

In both mental retardation and giftedness, children should be encouraged to capitalize on their abilities.

What Are the Components of Intelligence?

Psychometric Theories of Intelligence
Cognitive Theories of Intelligence
Cultural Definitions of Intelligence

Some psychologists believe that the essence of intelligence is a single, general factor, while others believe that intelligence is best described as a collection of distinct abilities.

Test Scorers and the Self-Fulfilling Prophecy

An IQ score can create expectations that have a life of their own.

How Do Psychologists Explain IQ Differences Among Groups?

Intelligence and the Politics of Immigration
What Evidence Shows That Intelligence Is Influenced by Heredity?
What Evidence Shows That Intelligence Is Influenced by Environment?
Heritability and Group Differences

▼

While most psychologists agree that both heredity and environment affect intelligence, they disagree on the source of IQ differences among racial and social groups.

Helping Others Think Critically about Group Differences

There are many reasons why the heritability of intelligence doesn't mean that group differences are genetic.

USING PSYCHOLOGY TO LEARN PSYCHOLOGY:
Developing Expertise in Psychology—or Any Other Subject

Chapter

11

Testing and Individual Differences

R = 0 2

AL WAS A STUDENT who enjoyed mathematics and the violin. At the age of 16 he took and failed an entrance exam for a prestigious university, which prevented him from studying to become an electrical engineer, his lifelong goal. Following this setback, he enrolled at a less renowned college and, at the age of 21, graduated as a teacher of math and physics.

Al applied for a teaching job at a college but was rejected. He even asked some well-connected friends to try and help him secure a position, all to no avail. For over a year he wrote to different colleges seeking a teaching job, but he eventually gave up his ambition to teach college math. Taking a low-level government job while working on furthering his education part-time, he eventually earned a doctoral degree. While in his government post, he continued to write and study and began publishing a number of papers in scientific journals.

A few years later he earned a position at a university, and he excelled there. From Al's early history, it would be impossible to tell that the little boy who failed his first college entrance exam would persevere and go on to become one of the most influential thinkers of the 20th century, and arguably one of the most well known—Albert Einstein.

What does this story tell us about testing and individual differences? Clearly, one thing it tells us is that testing can be flawed. There are some psychologists, known as psychometricians, who study testing and measurement to help improve these systems of assessment. What happened to Einstein was most likely an error in determining and measuring individual differences. The entrance exam that Albert took was designed to measure a student's ability to succeed in an academic setting and to determine the differences among students. This leads to the first key question of the present chapter.

KEY QUESTION

HOW DO WE MEASURE INDIVIDUAL DIFFERENCES?

As you can see from what happened to Einstein, testing can be used ineffectively and inappropriately. Testing can also serve useful and valuable purposes. The essential aspect of testing in psychology is best evaluated by looking at our core concept for this section:

CORE CONCEPT

Measuring individual differences is an essential component of psychology, but strict guidelines and ethical standards must be followed to ensure results and conclusions are valid and appropriate.

Validity and Reliability

When psychologists measure or test individual differences or aptitudes, psychologists use two methods to determine whether the results have significance. They assess the validity and reliability of the tests used to make these measurements. **Validity** is the term we use when asking whether the test actually measures what it purports to measure. For example, if you were to take a psychology test on which all the questions were related to chemistry, it would have a very low validity score. Psychologists also look at **reliability,** which reflects whether a test yields the same results over time. If you were to take a test twice and get 70% right the first time and 30% right the second time, that test would be revealed to have very low reliability.

Psychologists have developed a number of ways to test for both validity and for reliability. When we look at validity, we first examine what is called **face validity.** That is, does it appear, "on the face of it," that the test tests what it is supposed to test? If your test were written in a language you did not understand, it would have no face validity. The second type of validity we look at is called **content validity.** In this type of validity, each item is representative of the larger body of knowledge about a subject. Consider, for example, the AP Psychology Exam. It does not test everything in psychology but, rather, has questions that are representative of the knowledge that constitutes mastery of the subject. This type of validity is measured by a methodology called **item analysis.** In item analysis, each question is specifically examined to see how it is related back to the learning objectives being tested. Another form of validity is **criterion validity.** In tests with this form of validity, performance on the test is measured against a performance goal. In other words, in order to get a particular score, you have to meet a certain criterion, or level of proficiency. A simple way to think about criterion validity is to associate it with an achievement test (which measures knowledge) rather than an aptitude test (which ostensibly measures native abilities).

Next we look at reliability, the second measure of a good test. In essence, reliability means consistency. The important thing here is to ensure that on a particular test, a test taker would get about the same score each time he or she takes it. There are a number of ways to determine whether a test is reliable. Perhaps the most basic type of reliability is **test–retest reliability.** In this

- **Validity** A property exhibited by a test that measures what it purports to measure.
- **Reliability** A property exhibited by a test that yields the same results over time.
- **Face validity** Measures whether a test looks like it tests what it is supposed to test.
- **Content validity** A property exhibited by a test in which each item is representative of the larger body of knowledge about the subject that the test covers.
- **Item analysis** The process of examining each question on a test to see how it is related to the objectives being tested.
- **Criterion validity** A property exhibited by a test that accurately measures performance of the test taker against a specific learning goal.
- **Test–retest reliability** A property exhibited by a test on which people get about the same scores when they take the test more than once.

method, we simply give the test again to check and see whether people get the same score when they retake the test. Of course, you can only take your AP exam once, so we need alternative methods to test for reliability. The methodology used most in this situation is called **split-half reliability.** To apply the split-half method, you would take a test, split it into two parts, and compare the scores that an individual got on the two halves. For example, the AP Psychology Exam has 100 questions. To measure reliability, you would take the score someone had on the odd-numbered questions and compare it to the score the same person earned on the even-numbered questions. If the scores were the same (or very similar), the test would have a high degree of reliability.

Standardization and Norms

Now that we have established both validity and reliability, we need to see how a test can be used to compare individuals. The way we do that is to look at standardization and norms. You have heard the term *standardized test.* What does that mean? In the most basic sense, it means (1) that the administration and scoring guidelines are the same for each student and (2) that the results of the test can be used to draw conclusions about the test takers in regard to the objectives of the test.

One of the main questions that arises here is "How can results between test takers be compared?" Well, to answer that, we need to discuss norms and norm setting. The method used most frequently to establish norms relies on the statistics we discussed in Chapter 2. We use statistics to establish what is called a normal curve, or bell curve. This standard curve can be used to describe most phenomena. In our examples we will use women's height and, later in the chapter, intelligence quotient (IQ). If you sample enough women, you will find that the majority of women (roughly 67%) fall within a range of 5 feet 1 inch to 5 feet 9 inches tall, with an average height of 5 feet 5 inches. As you move further away from the average, there are fewer and fewer people. For example there are many women who are 5 feet 5 inches, but very few who are 6 feet 4 inches. (See Figure 11.1.)

When the normal curve is applied to testing, in order to establish norms (and the curve) a test must be pretested and then the scores plotted. When a statistically significant sample of the population has been tested, you can feel confident in drawing conclusions. The most readily available example of this is in IQ scores.

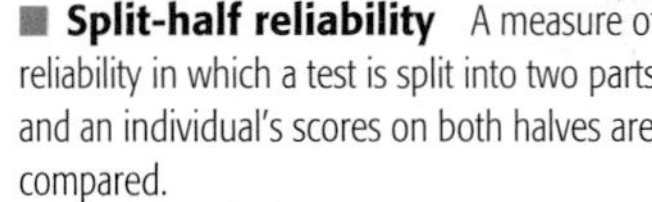

■ **Split-half reliability** A measure of reliability in which a test is split into two parts and an individual's scores on both halves are compared.

■ **Normal range** Scores falling near the middle of a normal distribution.

Applying this same concept to intelligence, psychologists find that people's IQ test scores (like the women's heights we considered above) fit a normal distribution. (See Figure 11.2.) More precisely, when IQ tests are given to large numbers of individuals, the scores of those at each age level are normally distributed. (Adults are placed in their own group, regardless of age, and the distribution of their scores also fits the bell-shaped curve.) Instead of using the old IQ formula, IQs are now determined from tables that indicate where test scores fall on the normal curve. The scores are statistically adjusted so that the average for each age group is set at 100. Scores near the middle of the distribution (usually between 90 and 110) are considered to be in the **normal range** (see Figure 11.2). At the extreme ends of the distribution, scores below 70 are often said to be in the *mentally retarded range,* and those above 130 are sometimes said to indicate *giftedness.*

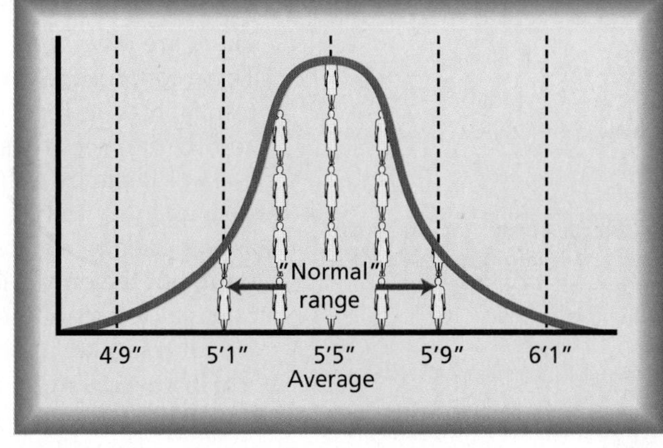
"Normal"
range
4′9″
5′1″
5′5″
Average
5′9″
6′1″

● **FIGURE 11.1** An (Imaginary) Normal Distribution of Women's Heights

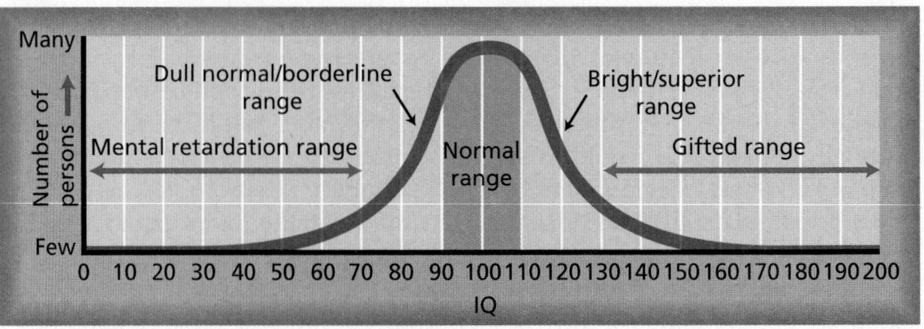
Many
Few
Number of persons
Dull normal/borderline range
Bright/superior range
Mental retardation range
Normal range
Gifted range
0 10 20 30 40 50 60 70 80 90 100 110 120 130 140 150 160 170 180 190 200
IQ

● **FIGURE 11.2** The Normal Distribution of IQ Scores Among a Large Sample (*Source:* from WESCHLER'S MEASUREMENT AND APPRAISAL OF ADULT INTELLIGENCE, 5th ed., by Joseph D. Matarazzo. Copyright © 1972 by Oxford University Press. Reprinted by permission of Oxford University Press, Inc.)

Thus IQ scores are no longer calculated by dividing mental age by chronological age. The concept of a "ratio" expressed as a multiple of 100 (a percentage-like number that is easy to understand) is retained, however. This solves the problem of calculating adult IQs by comparing adults with adults.

Types of Tests

When we look at assessment in general, aside from intelligence testing, we find two general types of tests: objective tests and subjective tests. **Objective tests** are generally multiple-choice/selected-response tests that can be scored easily by machine. The Minnesota Multiphasic Personality Inventory (MMPI) and the Myers Briggs Type Indicator (MBTI) are good examples of objective tests. These tests can be easily scored and the results presented and interpreted quite quickly. The second type of test is called a **subjective test,** in which individuals are given an ambiguous figure and asked to describe what they see, or are given an open-ended situation and asked to finish a story about it. Examples of subjective tests include the Thematic Apperception Test (TAT) developed by David McClelland and the Rorschach Inkblot test. In these tests individuals are either shown a picture and asked to describe/write down what is taking place (TAT), or shown an inkblot and asked to tell the examiner what they see. In the case of the Rorschach, how the subjects pick up, hold, and look at the card, and how long it takes them to make a response, are also considered.

One of the issues that arises with subjective tests is **inter-rater reliability,** a measure of how similarly two different test scorers would score the test. Some studies of the Rorschach suggest that its inter-rater reliability is very low, while others dispute this claim.

Ethics and Standards in Testing

There are other very important and fundamental questions related to testing. These concern the confidentiality of the information elicited on tests and of test results, how to report the results, how to use the tests to compare individuals, and the impact of tests on society as a whole.

Let's begin by examining what to do with the results of a test. In most cases, such as in IQ testing, individual results are never released. Individual results are reported to test developers and scorers to ensure that IQ scales remain constant, but the only data that are released are group data, and, except for a confidential report of his or her own scores supplied to each test taker, the individual test taker's scores cannot be identified.

However, simply sending results back to the test taker without describing or explaining their significance or relevance should be avoided. For example, if you were told that you earned a 48 on your latest psychology test, what would that mean to you? Is that a raw score of 48? What was the mean? Was

■ **Objective tests** Tests that can be scored easily by machine, such as multiple-choice tests and selected-response tests.

■ **Subjective tests** Tests in which individuals are given an ambiguous figure or an open-ended situation and asked to describe what they see or finish a story.

■ **Inter-rater reliability** A measure of how similarly two different test scorers would score a test.

it the high score? Was it the low one? All of those questions are very important when trying to measure your actual performance.

In addition, for a test to be useful, it needs to be interpreted properly. As you will see when we discuss *The Bell Curve* later in this chapter, sometimes tests and their results can be interpreted improperly and/or inaccurately. Aside from the negative impact on the individual test takers, tests used improperly can affect how people look at, value, and relate to others in a larger context. This social impact has to be considered very carefully. In fact, a great deal of IQ testing, as well as the SAT II and AP exams have been scrutinized to control for culture bias or anything else that may skew the results of a test.

What does this have to do with ethics and standards in testing? In all testing, results need to be properly and appropriately reported and interpreted to test takers and also to other interested parties (such as colleges, as in the case of the AP Psychology Exam). Ethics in a testing situation refers not only to how tests are administered (the standards component) but also to how they are used and by whom. And abuses *have* occurred. In the early 20th century, for example, the eugenics movement misused and misinterpreted test results.

PSYCHOLOGY IN YOUR LIFE: TESTING IN EDUCATION

Years ago, testing used to be used in order to not only assess students, but to track them into educational programs which were designed to fit their educational needs and potential. Over time, it has been argued that "tracking" or placing students in classes based on their assessed ability is not necessarily the best way to approach education. Over the last few years, a movement toward inclusion has taken hold. While inclusion has been used mostly in the special education community to ensure that students with special needs can spend as much time in "mainstreamed" classes as possible, the idea of an inclusive classroom has been expanded to, in some cases, do away with honors-level classes. The logic behind this effort is as follows: If all classes incorporate all students, those at the top of the performance curve will be able to assist and help students at the lower ends.

Think about how this would (or does) affect your education? Would you be better off in a class having all levels of students or one which is solely geared for AP/College-Bound, high-achieving students? What role does or should testing play in this debate?

CHECK YOUR UNDERSTANDING

1. **APPLICATION:** When we check to see whether a test will yield the same results over time, we are assessing its
   - **a.** reliability.
   - **b.** validity.
   - **c.** normality.
   - **d.** objectivity.
   - **e.** subjectivity.

2. **APPLICATION:** The Thematic Apperception Test is a(n) _____ test?
   - **a.** short-answer
   - **b.** essay
   - **c.** multiple-choice
   - **d.** objective
   - **e.** subjective

3. **UNDERSTANDING THE CORE CONCEPT:** All of the following are components of ethical testing *except*
   - **a.** item analysis.
   - **b.** validity.
   - **c.** reliability.
   - **d.** objectivity.
   - **e.** instinct.

ANSWERS: 1. a 2. e 3. e

KEY QUESTION

HOW IS INTELLIGENCE MEASURED?

Psychologists have long been fascinated by the ways people differ in their abilities to reason, solve problems, and think creatively. The assessment of individual differences, however, did not begin with modern psychology. Historical records show that sophisticated mental testing methods were used in ancient China. Over 4000 years ago, the Chinese employed a program of civil service testing that required government officials to demonstrate their competence every third year at an oral examination. Later, applicants were required to pass written civil service tests to assess their knowledge of law, the military, agriculture, and geography. British diplomats and missionaries assigned to China in the early 1800s described the selection procedures so admiringly that the British, and later the Americans, adopted modified versions of China's system for the selection of civil service personnel (Wiggins, 1973).

Unlike the historical Chinese, however, modern Americans seem to be more interested in how "smart" people are, than in how much they have learned. It is the interest in this sort of "native intelligence" that spurred the development of intelligence testing as we know it today. But despite the long history of mental testing and the widespread use of intelligence tests in our society, the exact meaning of the term *intelligence* is still disputed (Neisser et al., 1996). Most psychologists would probably agree with the general definition that we gave earlier—that intelligence involves abilities to acquire knowledge, reason, and solve problems. They would also agree that a complete picture of an individual's intelligence must be obtained from measurements across a variety of tasks. However, they disagree on exactly what these abilities are or whether they are many or few in number.

● Even though the SAT tests are far from perfect predictors of college success, they are widely used. Many items on the SAT are similar to those found on intelligence tests.

Everyone does agree that intelligence is relative. That is, an individual's level of intelligence is defined in relation to the same abilities in a comparison group, usually of the same age range. Everyone also agrees that intelligence is a *hypothetical construct:* a characteristic that is not directly observable, but is, instead, inferred from behavior. In practice, this means that intelligence is measured from an individual's responses on an intelligence test. The individual's scores are then compared to those of a reference group. Exactly what these tests should assess is the source of much controversy—and the focus of this section of this chapter. Our Core Concept says:

CORE CONCEPT

Intelligence testing has a history of controversy, but most psychologists now view intelligence as a normally distributed trait that can be measured by performance on a variety of tasks—both verbal and nonverbal.

We begin our survey of intelligence and intelligence testing by introducing you to the people who founded the field of intelligence testing.

Binet and Simon Invent a School Abilities Test

Alfred Binet (*Bi-NAY*) and his colleague Théodore Simon stepped into history in 1904. At that time, a new law required all French children to attend school, and the government needed a means of identifying those who needed remedial help. Binet and Simon were asked to design a test for this purpose. They responded with 30 problems sampling a variety of abilities that seemed necessary for school (Figure 11.3). The new approach was a success. It did, indeed, predict which children could, or could not, handle normal schoolwork.

Four important features distinguish the Binet-Simon approach (Binet, 1911):

1. Binet and Simon interpreted scores on their test as an estimate of *current performance,* not as a measure of innate intelligence.
2. They wanted the test scores to be used to identify children who needed special help, not merely to categorize or label them as bright or dull.
3. They emphasized that training and opportunity could affect intelligence, and they wanted to identify areas of performance in which special education could help the children identified by their test.
4. They constructed the test *empirically*—based on how children were observed to perform—rather than tying the test to a particular theory of intelligence.

On the original Binet-Simon test, a child was asked to perform tasks such as the following:

- Name various common objects (such as a clock or a cat) shown in pictures.
- Repeat a 15-word sentence given by the examiner.
- Give a word that rhymes with one given by the examiner.
- Imitate gestures (such as pointing to an object).
- Comply with simple commands (such as moving a block from one location to another).
- Explain the differences between two common objects.
- Use three words (given by the examiner) in a sentence.
- Define abstract terms (such as *friendship*).

● **FIGURE 11.3** Sample Items from the First Binet-Simon Test

French children of various ages were assessed with this test, and the average for children at each age was computed. Then each child's performance was compared to the averages for children of various ages. Scores were expressed in terms of **mental age (MA):** the average age at which individuals achieve a particular score. So, for example, when a child's score was the same as the average score for a group of 5-year-olds, the child was said to have a mental age of 5, regardless of his or her actual **chronological age (CA),** the number of years since the individual's birth. Binet and Simon decided that those most needing remedial help were students whose MA was two years behind CA.

American Psychologists Borrow Binet and Simon's Idea

Less than a decade after the French began testing their school children, American psychologists imported the Binet-Simon test of school abilities and changed it into the form we now call the *IQ test.* They did this by first modifying the scoring procedure, expanding the test's content, and obtaining scores from a large normative group of people, including adults. Soon "intelligence testing" was widely accepted as a technique by which Americans were defining themselves—and each other.

The Appeal of Intelligence Testing in America Why did tests of intelligence become so popular in the United States? Three forces that were changing the face of the country early in the 20th century conspired to make intelligence testing seem like an orderly way out of growing turmoil and uncertainty. First, the United States was experiencing an unprecedented wave of immigration, resulting from global economic, social, and political crises. Second, new laws requiring universal education—schooling for all children—were flooding schools with students. And third, when World War I began, the military needed a way of assessing and classifying the new recruits. Together, these events resulted in a need for large numbers of people to be identified, documented, and classified (Chapman, 1988). Assessment of intelligence was seen not only as a way to bring some order to the tumult of rapid social change, but also as an inexpensive and democratic way to separate those who could benefit from education or military leadership training from those who could not.

One consequence of the large-scale group-testing program in America was that the public came to accept the idea that intelligence tests could accurately differentiate people in terms of their mental abilities. This acceptance soon led

■ **Mental age (MA)** The average age at which normal (average) individuals achieve a particular score.

■ **Chronological age (CA)** The number of years since the individual's birth.

to the widespread use of tests in schools and industry. Another, more unfortunate consequence was that the tests were used to reinforce prevailing prejudices. Specifically, Army reports suggested that differences in test scores were linked to race and country of origin (Yerkes, 1921). Of course, the same statistics could have been used to demonstrate that environmental disadvantages limit the full development of people's intellectual abilities. Instead, immigrants with limited facility in English or even little understanding of how to take such tests were labeled "morons," "idiots," and "imbeciles" (terms used at the time to specify different degrees of mental retardation).

While these problems are more obvious to us now (with the help of hindsight), at the time they were obscured by the fact that the tests did what most people wanted: They were simple to administer, and they provided a means of assessing and classifying people according to their scores. Never mind that there were some built-in biases and that some people were treated unfairly. In general, the public perceived the tests as objective and democratic.

The Stanford-Binet Intelligence Scale The most respected of the new American tests of intelligence was developed by Stanford University professor Lewis Terman. His approach was to adapt the Binet and Simon test for U.S. schoolchildren by standardizing its administration and its age-level norms. The result was the Stanford-Binet Intelligence Scale (Terman, 1916), which soon became the standard by which other measures of intelligence were judged. Because it had to be administered individually, Terman's test was less economical than the group tests. Nevertheless, it was better suited for spotting learning problems. Even more important, the Stanford-Binet test was designed both for children and adults.

With his new test Terman introduced the concept of the **intelligence quotient (IQ),** a term coined originally by German psychologist William Stern in 1914. The IQ was the ratio of mental age (MA) to chronological age (CA), multiplied by 100 (to eliminate decimals):

$$\text{IQ} = \frac{\text{Mental Age}}{\text{Chronological Age}} \times 100$$

Please follow us through the IQ equation with these examples: Consider a child with a chronological age of 8 years whose test scores reveal a mental age of 10. Dividing the child's mental age by chronological age (MA/CA = 10/8) gives 1.25. Multiplying that result by 100, we obtain an IQ of 125. In contrast, another 8-year-old child who performs at the level of an average 6-year-old (MA = 6) has an IQ of 6/8 × 100 = 75, according to Terman's formula. Those whose mental age is the same as their chronological age have IQs of 100, which is considered to be the average or "normal" IQ.

Within a short time, the new Stanford-Binet test became a popular instrument in clinical psychology, psychiatry, and educational counseling. With the publication of this test, Terman also promoted his belief that intelligence is largely innate and that his IQ test could measure it precisely. The implicit message was that an IQ score reflected something fundamental and unchanging about people.

Although the Stanford-Binet became the "gold standard" of intelligence testing, it had its critics. The loudest objection was that it employed an inconsistent concept of intelligence because it measured different mental abilities at different ages. For example, 2- to 4-year-olds were tested on their ability to manipulate objects, whereas adults were tested almost exclusively on verbal items. Test makers heeded these criticisms, and as the scientific understanding of intelligence increased, psychologists found it increasingly important to measure multiple intellectual abilities at all age levels. A modern revision of

Intelligence quotient (IQ)
A numerical score on an intelligence test, originally computed by dividing the person's mental age by chronological age and multiplying by 100.

the Stanford-Binet now provides separate scores for several mental skills (Vernon, 1987).

IQ Testing Today

The success of the Stanford-Binet test encouraged the development of other IQ tests. As a result, psychologists now have a wide choice of instruments for measuring intelligence. The most prominent of these alternatives are the Wechsler Adult Intelligence Scale (WAIS), the Wechsler Intelligence Scale for Children (WISC), and the Wechsler Preschool and Primary Scale of Intelligence (WPPSI). With these instruments, psychologist David Wechsler offers a family of tests that measure many skills that are presumed to be components of intelligence, including vocabulary, verbal comprehension, arithmetic ability, similarities (the ability to state how two things are alike), digit span (repeating a series of digits after the examiner), and block design (the ability to reproduce designs by fitting together blocks with colored sides). As our Core Concept noted, these tests measure intelligence by assessing performance on a variety of tasks.

● A psychologist administers an intelligence test to a 4-year-old child. The performance part of this test includes a block design task, an object completion task, and a shape identification task.

Like the Stanford-Binet, the Wechsler tests are *individual* tests. That is, they are given to one person at a time. Also available are *group* tests of intelligence that can be administered to large numbers of students simultaneously. Unlike the Stanford-Binet and the Wechsler tests, these group tests are primarily paper-and-pencil measures, involving booklets of questions and computer-scorable answer sheets. The convenience of group tests—even though they are not as precise as individual tests—has made IQ testing, along with other forms of academic assessment, widespread. It is quite likely that you took such tests several times as you went through grades 1 through 8, perhaps without realizing what they were. The items in the "Do It Yourself!" box are similar to items in many commonly used group tests of mental abilities.

DO IT YOURSELF! Sample IQ Test Items

Try your hand at the following items adapted from group tests of intelligence. Some of the items are more challenging than others. You will find the correct answers at the end.

VOCABULARY: Select the best definition for each word:

1. **viable**
   a. traveled b. capable of living
   c. V-shaped d. can be bent
2. **imminent**
   a. defenseless b. expensive
   c. impending d. notorious

ANALOGIES: Examine the relationship between the first two words. Then, find an answer that has the same relationship with the word in **bold letters:**

3. Washington: Lincoln
   July: a. January b. April
   c. May d. October
4. ocean: canoe
   verse: a. poem b. pen
   c. water d. serve

SIMILARITIES: Which letter on the right belongs to the same category as the one on the left?

5. **J** A M S Z T
6. **A** S D U V X

SEQUENCES: Choose the answer that best completes the sequence:

7. a z b y c x d? e s u w f
8. 1 3 6 10 15? 16 18 21 27 128

MATHEMATICAL REASONING

9. Portland and Seattle are actually 150 miles apart, but on a map they are two inches apart. If Chicago and Norfolk are five inches apart on the same map, what is the actual distance between those two cities?
   a. 125 miles b. 250 miles
   c. 375 miles d. 525 miles

ANSWERS: 1. b 2. c 3. d (October comes after July) 4. d (*verse* and *serve* have the same letters) 5. S (the only one with a curve in it) 6. U (the only vowel) 7. W 8. 21 9. c

Problems with the IQ Formula

A problem in calculating IQ scores became apparent as soon as psychologists began to use their formula with adults. Here's what happens: By the mid- to late teenage years, gains in mental age scores usually level off, as people develop mentally in many different directions. Consequently, mental growth, as measured by a test, appears to slow down. So Terman's formula for computing IQs makes normal children appear to become mentally retarded adults—at least as far as their test scores are concerned! Note what happens to the average 30-year-old's score if mental age, as measured by a test, stays at the same level as it was at age 15:

$$\text{IQ} = \frac{\text{Mental Age}}{\text{Chronological Age}} = \frac{15}{30} \times 100 = 50$$

Psychologists quickly realized that this paints an erroneous picture of adult mental abilities. People do not grow less intelligent as they become adults (even though their children sometimes think so). Rather, adults develop in different directions, which their IQ scores do not necessarily reflect. Prudently, psychologists decided to abandon the original IQ formula and to find another means of calculating IQs. Their solution was similar to the familiar practice of "grading on the curve."

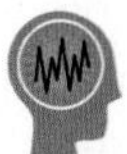

PSYCHOLOGY IN YOUR LIFE: WHAT CAN YOU DO FOR AN EXCEPTIONAL CHILD?

■ **Mental retardation** Often conceived as representing the lower 2% of the IQ range, commencing about 30 points below average (below about 70 points). More sophisticated definitions also take into account an individual's level of social functioning and other abilities.

■ **Giftedness** Often conceived as representing the upper 2% of the IQ range, commencing about 30 points above average (at about 130 IQ points).

As we have noted, mental retardation and giftedness lie at the opposite ends of the intelligence spectrum. As traditionally conceived, **mental retardation** occupies the IQ range below IQ 70—taking in the scores achieved by approximately 2% of the population (see Figure 11.2). Arbitrarily, **giftedness** begins 30 points above average, at 130 IQ points, comprising another 2% of the population. Now, bearing in mind all we have learned about the limitations of IQ tests, let's take a brief look at these two categories.

Mental Retardation The current view of mental retardation deemphasizes IQ scores by focusing on practical abilities to get along in the world (Baumeister, 1987; Detterman, 1999; Greenspan, 1999; Robinson et al., 2000). In fact, the American Association of Mental Retardation now offers a definition of mental retardation that does not even mention an IQ cutoff score. According to this new perspective, mental retardation involves "significantly subaverage intellectual functioning" that becomes apparent before age 18. It also involves limitations in at least two of the following areas: "communication, self-care, home living, social skills, community use, self-direction, health and safety, functional academics, leisure and work" (Turkington, 1993, p. 26).

CONNECTION: CHAPTER 1

Down syndrome produces both physical symptoms and mental retardation; it arises from a chromosomal defect.

Causes of Mental Retardation Mental retardation has many causes (Daily et al., 2000; Scott & Carran, 1987). Some are known to be genetic because we can point to a specific genetically controlled defect. This is the case, as we have noted, in people who have Down syndrome. Some causes are environmental, as in fetal alcohol syndrome, which involves brain damage incurred before birth, resulting from the mother's abuse of alcohol during pregnancy. Other environmental causes include postnatal accidents that damage the cognitive regions of the brain. Still other causes involve conditions of deprivation or neglect, which fail to give the developing child the experiences needed for advancement up the intellectual ladder. Some cases have no known cause.

Dealing with Mental Retardation We have no cures, although research has found some preventive measures for certain types of mental retardation. For example, a simple test performed routinely on newborn babies can identify a hidden genetic disorder known as PKU. If detected early, the mental retardation usually associated with PKU can be prevented by a special diet. More generally, genetic counseling, pregnancy care services, and education of new parents are other preventive strategies (Scott & Carran, 1987).

Aside from prevention, special education programs can help those who develop mental retardation to learn vocational and independent living skills. Meanwhile, biological scientists hope that one day they will be able to treat genetically based forms of mental retardation with therapies that are just now being conceived. Genetic treatment may involve splicing a healthy gene into a benign virus that would "infect" all of a retarded person's cells and replace the defective gene. At present, genetic therapy is being tried experimentally for the treatment of certain physical diseases, but it is at least a few years away in the treatment of mental retardation.

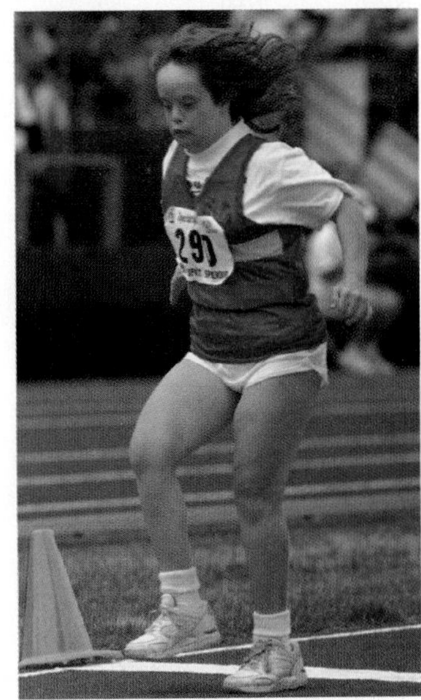

● The Special Olympics offers mentally retarded children (and others with disabilities) an opportunity to capitalize on their abilities and to build self-esteem.

For now, what can you do if you have a mentally retarded child? Dealing with mental retardation usually means making the best of a difficult situation. Parents of a retarded child should realize that, because the nervous system is so immature at birth and because so much physical and mental development occurs during the first years of life, interventions that begin early will have the greatest payoffs. Realistically, however, the most intellectual improvement one can expect from an optimal educational program is an IQ gain of about 15 points (Robinson et al., 2000).

Psychological approaches that involve sensory stimulation and social interaction can be enormously important. In fact, an enriched environment may be just as helpful to a mentally retarded child as it is to a gifted child. Teams of special education teachers, speech therapists, educational psychologists, physicians, and other specialists can devise programs that enable mentally retarded persons to capitalize on the abilities they have, rather than being held prisoner of their disabilities (see Schroeder et al., 1987). Behavior modification programs have been especially successful. As a result, many retarded citizens have learned to care for themselves and have learned vocational skills that enable them to live independently (Landesman & Butterfield, 1987).

CONNECTION: CHAPTER 13

Behavior modification therapies are based on behavioral learning principles derived from operant and classical conditioning.

Giftedness At the other end of the intelligence spectrum we find the "gifted," with their especially high IQs, typically defined as being in the top 1 or 2% (Robinson et al., 2000). But, you might wonder, what do such people eventually do with their superior intellectual abilities? Does a high IQ give its owner an advantage in life? A long look at gifted individuals suggests that it does.

Terman's Studies of Giftedness The most extensive project ever undertaken to study gifted individuals began in 1921 under the direction of Lewis Terman, the same person who brought Binet and Simon's IQ test to the United States (Leslie, 2000). From a large pool of children tested in the California schools, Terman selected 1528 children who scored near the top of the IQ range. His longitudinal research program followed these children as they went through school and on into adulthood. Periodically through their lives, Terman retested them and gathered other information on their achievements and adjustment patterns. The resulting decades of data have taught us much about the nature of giftedness. Almost uniformly, Terman's gifted children excelled in school—as one might expect from the strong correlation between IQ and academic achievement. Terman also remarked on the good health and happiness of the children in his sample, although newer evidence suggests that highly gifted children are susceptible to certain physical and psychological disorders (Winner, 2000).

As they moved into adulthood, the gifted group continued on the path of success. An unusually high number of scientists, writers, and professionals emerged from its ranks. Together they published more than 2000 scientific articles, patented 235 inventions, and wrote 92 books. By middle age, more than 86% of the men in Terman's sample had entered high-status professions (Terman & Oden, 1959).

Yet, for all their achievements, no one in this high-IQ sample achieved the level of an Einstein, a Picasso, or a Martha Graham. Nor did a high IQ turn out to be a guarantee of wealth or stature. In fact, many from Terman's sample led ordinary, undistinguished lives. The ones who were most visibly successful seemed to have, in addition to their high IQs, extraordinary motivation and someone at home or at school who was especially encouraging to them (Goleman, 1980; Oden, 1968). You will remember that we previously found these same characteristics to be markers of "genius."

Dealing with Giftedness Imagine that you are the parent of a child with a very high IQ score, say 145. Which one of the following would be the best course of action?

- Enroll your child in special after-school classes.
- Hire a tutor to help the child with his or her homework.
- Send the child to a private school.
- Do nothing special.

What do the experts say?

Don't rush out to enroll your child in special classes or provide other "help" because of his or her IQ score (Csikszentmihalyi et al., 1993; Wong & Csikszentmihalyi, 1991). Parents can destroy the spark of curiosity by pushing a child toward goals that do not hold the child's interest. Chances are you have already provided an environment in which your child's native ability could thrive. So do not make any rash and radical changes.

Above all, avoid making the child feel like a freak because of his or her unusual abilities and high IQ score. In part because of the personality traits common in gifted children—especially a tendency to spend time alone, working on their interests—they are more likely than other children to suffer social and emotional disorders (Winner, 2000). Nor should you feel smug about your genetic contribution to your child's intellect. Remember that IQ tests sample only a small fraction of human abilities. Other people's kids may have equally amazing abilities in untested regions of their intellects. In fact, many gifted individuals may go unrecognized by the schools because they have an outstanding talent that shows up primarily in art or music—domains in which formal abilities testing is rarely done.

Remember, also, that a high IQ is no guarantee of high motivation, high creativity, or success in life. All it guarantees is an intellectual opportunity. So, what should you do with a bright child? Nothing special that you would not have done before you knew the IQ score.

CHECK YOUR UNDERSTANDING

1. **RECALL:** One of Binet's great ideas was that of mental age, which was defined as
   a. the average age at which people achieve a particular score on an intelligence test.
   b. an individual's biological age plus the score he or she achieves on a mental test.
   c. an individual's level of emotional maturity, as judged by the examiner.
   d. the variability in scores seen when an individual is tested repeatedly.
   e. a means of measuring performance on a test against a specific learning goal.

2. **APPLICATION:** You have tested a 12-year-old child and found that she has a mental age of 15. Using the original IQ formula, what is her IQ?
   a. 50
   b. 75
   c. 100
   d. 115
   e. 125

3. **RECALL:** A problem with the original IQ formula is that it gave a distorted picture of the intellectual abilities of
   a. adults.
   b. children.
   c. retarded persons.
   d. gifted students.
   e. the elderly.

4. **UNDERSTANDING THE CORE CONCEPT:** If intelligence is a normally distributed characteristic, then you would expect to find it
   a. to be different abilities in different people.
   b. to be spread throughout the population, but with most people clustered near the middle of the range.
   c. to a significant degree only in people whose IQ scores are above 100.
   d. to be determined entirely by hereditary factors.
   e. to be determined entirely by environmental factors.

ANSWERS: 1. a 2. e 3. a 4. b

WHAT ARE THE COMPONENTS OF INTELLIGENCE?

KEY QUESTION

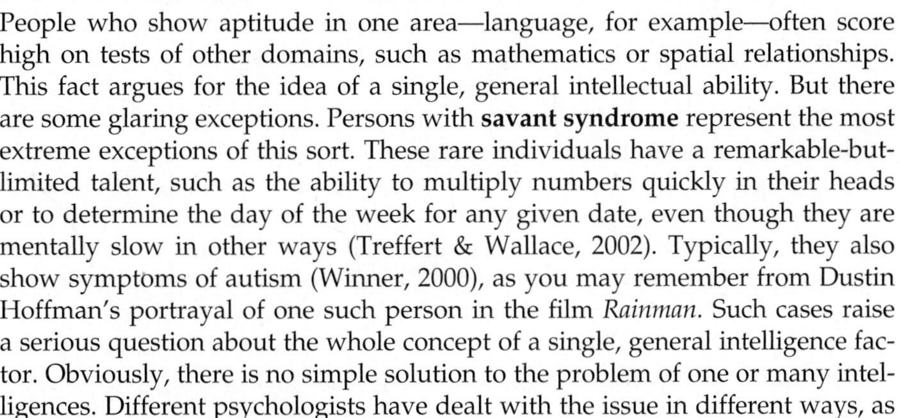

People who show aptitude in one area—language, for example—often score high on tests of other domains, such as mathematics or spatial relationships. This fact argues for the idea of a single, general intellectual ability. But there are some glaring exceptions. Persons with **savant syndrome** represent the most extreme exceptions of this sort. These rare individuals have a remarkable-but-limited talent, such as the ability to multiply numbers quickly in their heads or to determine the day of the week for any given date, even though they are mentally slow in other ways (Treffert & Wallace, 2002). Typically, they also show symptoms of autism (Winner, 2000), as you may remember from Dustin Hoffman's portrayal of one such person in the film *Rainman.* Such cases raise a serious question about the whole concept of a single, general intelligence factor. Obviously, there is no simple solution to the problem of one or many intelligences. Different psychologists have dealt with the issue in different ways, as our Core Concept suggests:

CORE CONCEPT

Some psychologists believe that the essence of intelligence is a single, general factor, while others believe that intelligence is best described as a collection of distinct abilities.

We will first examine this issue from the viewpoint of psychologists in the *psychometric tradition:* those who have been interested in developing tests to measure mental abilities. Following that excursion, we will look at intelligence from the standpoint of cognitive psychologists who have recently brought a fresh perspective to the problem.

Psychometric Theories of Intelligence

Psychometrics is the field of "mental measurements." It is the psychological specialty that has given us most of our IQ tests, along with achievement tests,

■ **Savant syndrome** Found in individuals who have a remarkable talent (such as the ability to determine the day of the week for any given date) even though they are mentally slow in other domains.

CONNECTION: CHAPTER 1

Psychologists in the specialty of psychometrics often subscribe to the *trait perspective*.

personality tests, the SAT, and a variety of other assessment instruments. Many pioneers in psychology carved their professional niches with contributions to psychometrics, including Alfred Binet and Lewis Terman. Yet another famous figure in this field was Charles Spearman, a psychologist who is best known for his work suggesting that intelligence is a single factor.

Spearman's *g* Factor By the 1920s, there were many tests of intelligence available, and British psychologist Charles Spearman was able to show that individuals' scores on different tests, involving problems of many kinds, are often highly correlated (1927). This, he said, points to a single, common factor of *general intelligence* underlying performance across all intellectual domains. Spearman did not deny that some people have outstanding talents or deficits in certain areas. But, he said, these individual differences should not blind us to a single general intelligence factor at work behind all our mental activity. Spearman called this general intellectual ability the ***g* factor.** He assumed that this general factor is innate, and most psychologists at the time agreed with him (Tyler, 1988, p. 128).

Recently, neuroscientists have found some support for Spearman's theory. John Duncan and his colleagues (2000) have shown that various tests of *g* all involve a portion of the brain's frontal lobes. This suggests, they say, a single brain mechanism that controls various forms of intelligent behavior. Could this site be the locus of *g*? Although Duncan and his group think so, others believe this explanation oversimplifies both the nature of intelligence and that of the brain (McArdle et al., 2002; Sternberg, 1999, 2000b).

Cattell's Fluid and Crystallized Intelligence Using sophisticated mathematical techniques, Raymond Cattell (1963) determined that general intelligence can be broken down into two relatively independent components that he called *crystallized* and *fluid intelligence.* **Crystallized intelligence** consists of the knowledge a person has acquired, plus the ability to access that knowledge. Thus, crystallized intelligence reflects the person's ability to store and retrieve information from semantic memory. It is measured by tests of vocabulary, arithmetic, and general information. In contrast, **fluid intelligence** is the ability to see complex relationships and solve problems—abilities that involve using algorithms and heuristics, which we discussed earlier in this chapter. Fluid intelligence is often measured by tests of block design and spatial visualization, tests that do not rely on the individual possessing certain "crystallized" background information in order to solve a problem. For Cattell, both types of intelligence were essential to adaptive living.

CONNECTION: CHAPTER 7

Much of our general knowledge is stored in *semantic memory,* a partition of long-term memory.

Cognitive Theories of Intelligence

Late in the 20th century, when the cognitive view emerged as a major force in psychology, it produced some radical new ideas about intelligence. In brief, the cognitive view of intelligence went well beyond the emphasis on vocabulary, logic, problem solving, and other skills that had been measured to predict school success (see Table 11.1). *Intelligence,* said cognitive psychologists, involves cognitive processes that contribute to success in many areas of life—not just school (Sternberg, 2000b). We will focus on two of these cognitive theories.

Sternberg's Triarchic Theory You may know someone who seems to have plenty of "book smarts" but who has never been very successful in life. Such people often don't know how to "read" others or to deal with unexpected events. Psychologist Robert Sternberg says that they lack **practical intelligence:** the ability to cope with the people and events in their environment. Practical intelligence is sometimes called "street smarts," although it applies just as well

■ ***g* factor** A general ability, proposed by Spearman as the main factor underlying all intelligent mental activity.
■ **Crystallized intelligence** The knowledge a person has acquired, plus the ability to access that knowledge.
■ **Fluid intelligence** The ability to see complex relationships and solve problems.
■ **Practical intelligence** According to Sternberg, the ability to cope with the environment; sometimes called "street smarts."

TABLE 11.1 Theories of Intelligence Compared

Spearman	Cattell	Sternberg	Gardner
"*g*" factor	Crystallized intelligence		
	Fluid intelligence	Analytical intelligence	Naturalistic intelligence Logical-mathematical intelligence Linguistic intelligence
		Creative intelligence	Spatial intelligence Musical intelligence Bodily-kinesthetic intelligence
		Practical intelligence	Interpersonal intelligence Intrapersonal intelligence
			Spiritual intelligence Existential intelligence

Note: Different theorists see intelligence as having different components, as shown in the columns of this table. The rows show roughly comparable components of intelligence described by various theories (although the reader should be aware that the correspondences are not exact). For example, Sternberg's *practical intelligence* is similar to Gardner's two components called *interpersonal intelligence* and *intrapersonal intelligence,* while Spearman's *g* ignores these abilities.

at home, on the job, or at school as it does on the street. One study suggests that it can also be thought of as "horse sense": Researchers found that, among regular visitors to racetracks, those who were most successful at picking winning horses had IQs no higher than those who were less successful. This suggests that this very practical ability to pick winners is something different from the form of intelligence measured on standard IQ tests (Ceci & Liker, 1986).

In contrast with practical intelligence, Sternberg refers to the ability measured by most IQ tests as **analytical intelligence** (also called *logical reasoning*). It includes the ability to analyze problems and find correct answers. Your grades in college are likely to be closely related to your logical reasoning abilities.

Creative intelligence, a third form of intelligence described by Sternberg's theory, helps people develop new ideas and see new relationships among concepts. Creative intelligence is what Picasso used to develop the new form of painting called *cubism.* It is also the form of intelligence that Sternberg used to develop his new theory of intelligence.

This formulation is often called the **triarchic theory** because it combines three (*tri* = three) intelligences. For Sternberg each one in this trio of abilities—practical intelligence, analytical intelligence, and creative intelligence—is relatively independent of the others. That is, a person's ability in one of the three areas doesn't necessarily predict his or her intelligence in the other two. Each represents a different dimension for describing and evaluating human performance. This theory reminds us that it is inaccurate to think of a single IQ score as summarizing all that is important or valuable about people's mental abilities (Sternberg, 1999; Sternberg et al., 1995).

Gardner's Multiple Intelligences Like Sternberg, Harvard psychologist Howard Gardner believes that traditional IQ tests measure only a limited range of human mental abilities. But he argues that we have at least seven separate

■ **Analytical intelligence** According to Sternberg, the ability measured by most IQ tests; includes the ability to analyze problems and find correct answers.

■ **Creative intelligence** According to Sternberg, the form of intelligence that helps people see new relationships among concepts; involves insight and creativity.

■ **Triarchic theory** The term for Sternberg's theory of intelligence; so called because it combines three ("tri-") main forms of intelligence.

One of Gardner's seven intelligences is bodily-kinesthetic intelligence, the ability to coordinate one's body movements with grace and control, as demonstrated by dancers, athletes, and surgeons.

CONNECTION: CHAPTER 8

Emotional intelligence involves the ability to understand and use emotions effectively.

mental abilities, which he calls **multiple intelligences** (Ellison, 1984; Gardner, 1983, 1999b):

1. *Linguistic intelligence:* Often measured on traditional IQ tests by vocabulary tests and tests of reading comprehension
2. *Logical-mathematical intelligence:* Also measured on most IQ tests with analogies, math problems, and logic problems
3. *Spatial intelligence:* The ability to form mental images of objects and to think about their relationships in space
4. *Musical intelligence:* The ability to perform, compose, and appreciate musical patterns, including patterns of rhythms and pitches
5. *Bodily-kinesthetic intelligence:* The ability for controlled movement and coordination, such as that needed by a dancer or a surgeon
6. *Interpersonal intelligence:* The ability to understand other people's intentions, emotions, motives, and actions, as well as to work effectively with others
7. *Intrapersonal intelligence:* The ability to know oneself, to develop a satisfactory sense of identity, and to regulate one's life

Each of these intelligences arises from a separate module in the brain, Gardner claims. The latter two, interpersonal and intrapersonal intelligence, are similar to a capacity that some psychologists call *emotional intelligence.* People who are high in emotional intelligence are good at "reading" other people's emotional states, as well as being especially aware of their own emotional responses.

In addition to these, Gardner's book *Intelligence Reframed* (1999a) proposes three more intelligences. *Naturalistic intelligence* allows people to classify living things as members of diverse groups (e.g., dogs, petunias, bacteria). *Spiritual intelligence* involves the ability to think in abstract spiritual terms and to put oneself in a spiritual frame of mind. And, finally, *existential intelligence* permits individuals to think about the largest and smallest components of the universe, the purpose of existence, and the meaning of death and to deal with profound emotional experiences such as love. The evidence that these latter three involve independent abilities based in specific brain modules, however, is not as strong as for the previous seven intelligences.

Like Sternberg, Gardner sees all the components of intelligence as equally important. Yet the value of each is also culturally determined, according to what is needed by, useful to, and prized by a given society. Gardner notes that Western society promotes the first two intelligences, while other societies value one or more of the other kinds of intelligence. For example, in small, isolated communities, people often place a high value on getting along with others (Gardner's *interpersonal ability*). In these restricted social settings, people have no place to go if they get into a quarrel and want to escape or part ways. In such societies, people generally avoid quarrels by recognizing potential problems at an early stage and modifying behaviors to solve problems quickly.

Assessing these newly recognized kinds of intelligence demands more than the usual paper-and-pencil tests. Gardner's approach requires that examinees be observed and assessed in a variety of life situations. On its face, the notion of multiple intelligences appears to be sound, but it awaits verification through tests that are still in the process of development.

Cultural Definitions of Intelligence

Multiple intelligences A term used to refer to Gardner's theory, which proposes that there are seven (or more) forms of intelligence.

If you had been socialized in a Pacific island culture, which would matter more: your SAT scores or your ability to navigate a boat on the open ocean? With such examples, cross-cultural psychologists have called our attention to the notion that "intelligence" can have different meanings in different cultures (Kleinfeld, 1994; Neisser et al., 1996; Rogoff, 1990; Segall et al., 1999; Serpell, 1994; Vernon, 1969). In fact, many languages have no word at all for intelligence as we conceive of it: the mental processes associated with logic, vocabulary, mathematical ability, abstract thought, and academic success (Matsumoto, 1996).

On the other hand, people in all cultures prize certain mental abilities—although those abilities are not the same in different cultures. Western cultures often associate intelligence specifically with *quick* solutions to problems. This contrasts with the Buganda people in Uganda, who associate intelligence with slow and thoughtful responses. Yet another view is found among the Djerma-Sonhai in Niger (West Africa), who think of intelligence as a combination of social skills and good memory. And for the Chinese, intelligence involves, among other things, extensive knowledge, determination, social responsibility, and ability for imitation.

A Native American Concept of Intelligence John Berry (1992) has extensively studied the kinds of mental abilities considered valuable among Native Americans. He began by asking adult volunteers among the Cree in northern Ontario to provide him with Cree words that describe aspects of thinking, starting with examples like "smart" or "intelligent." The most frequent responses translate roughly to "wise, thinks hard, and thinks carefully."

Although Cree children attend schools introduced by the dominant Anglo (English-European) culture, the Cree themselves make a distinction between "school" intelligence and the kind of "good thinking" valued in the Cree culture. Such thinking seems to center on being "respectful." As one respondent explained, intelligence "is being respectful in the Indian sense. You need to really know the other person and respect them for what they are" (Berry, 1992, p. 79). This attitude of "respect for others" is widespread in Native American cultures, Berry found.

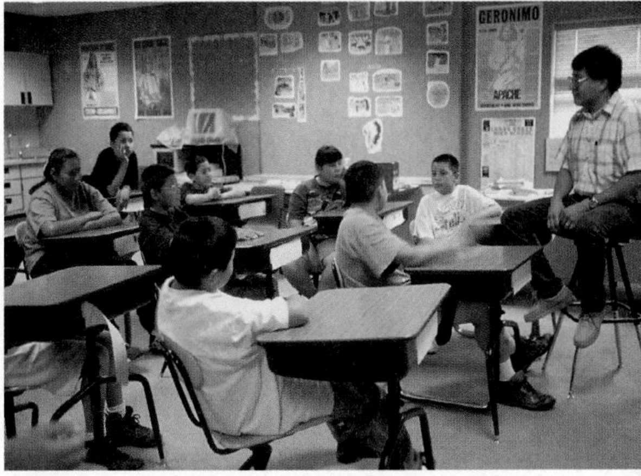
GERONIMO

● For this Native American teacher and his students, "intelligence" may have a different meaning from that used by Anglo Americans. In the Cree culture, intelligence involves wisdom and respect for others.

"Backwards Knowledge" One term Berry's respondents offered as an example of the opposite of intelligence translates as "lives like a white." This refers disparagingly to behaviors the Cree have observed among some Anglo people. The Cree define "lives like a white" as a combination of being "stupid" and having "backwards knowledge." A "stupid" person does not know the necessary skills for survival and does not learn by respecting and listening to elders. One has "backwards knowledge" if he or she disrupts relationships, creating disharmony instead of encouraging smooth interactions with others. Such disruption is not necessarily intentional or malicious. For example, an English teacher may ask Cree students to write an essay that would persuade others to change certain behaviors. However, in the Cree culture the concept of "persuading" can interfere with the traditional Cree value of "accepting others as they are." By encouraging such questioning of elders and traditions—a common practice in Anglo education—the teacher promotes disruption, which may be a path to "wisdom" in Anglo culture but is "backwards" in Cree views of intelligence.

As you can see from these examples, different cultures may define intelligence quite differently (Sternberg, 2000b). In order to understand and cooperate with people of diverse heritages, we would be most "intelligent" if we resisted the impulse to impose our own definition of "intelligence" on others. Within psychology, cross-cultural psychologists have led the way in urging us to see what is valued—and what devalued—in other people's experience.

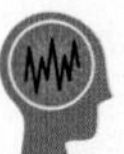

PSYCHOLOGY IN YOUR LIFE: TEST SCORES AND THE SELF-FULFILLING PROPHECY

If you have ever been called "dumb" or "slow," "shy," "plain," "bossy," or "uncoordinated," you know, first hand, the powerful effect that labels and expectations can have. An IQ score is a label too, and in our test-conscious society, an IQ score can alter the course of a life. As a nation of test takers, we sometimes forget that test scores are, at best, statistical measures of current functioning. People too often think of themselves as being "an IQ of 110" or "a B student," as if scores or grades were labels stamped permanently on their brains. Such labels may become barriers to advancement, as people come to believe that their mental and personal qualities are unchangeable—that they dictate their lot in life. Two classic studies will bring this fact into stark relief.

Expectations Influence Rat Performance Robert Rosenthal and Lenore Jacobson (1968a, b) asked psychology students to run rats through a maze and record their times. The experimenters told some students that their rats were especially bright; other students heard that their rats were slow learners. (In fact, Rosenthal and Jacobson had randomly assigned rats to the "bright" and "dull" groups.) Amazingly, the students' data showed that rats that were *believed* to be bright outperformed their supposedly duller littermates. Obviously, expectations had influenced the students' observations.

Expectations Also Influence Student Performance So, Rosenthal and Jacobson wondered, could a teacher's expectations similarly affect evaluations of a student's performance in school? To find out, they arranged to give grade school teachers erroneous information about the academic potential of about 20% of their students (approximately five in each classroom). Specifically, the teachers heard that some students had been identified by a standardized test as "spurters," who would blossom academically during the coming year. In fact, testing had revealed no such thing; the "spurters" had been randomly selected by the experimenters.

Knowing what happened to the rats, you can guess what happened to these children. Those whom the teachers expected to blossom did so. The teachers rated the "spurters" as being more curious and having more potential for success in life than the other children. Socially, the teachers saw these children as happier, more interesting, better adjusted, more affectionate, and needing less social approval. Significantly, when the children again took the original test (actually an IQ test) a year later, the children in the experimental group (who had been arbitrarily assigned a high expectation of mental growth) made substantial gains in IQ points. The gains were especially pronounced among first and second graders. Rosenthal and Jacobson call this effect a **self-fulfilling prophecy.** You can see it operating anywhere that people live up to the expectations of others—or of themselves.

The Effects of Negative Expectations Did the self-fulfilling prophecy apply to the students not labeled as possible academic "spurters"? Many of these children also gained IQ points during the year of the experiment, but they gained fewer points, and they were rated less favorably by their teachers. Apparently, not receiving a promising prophecy can create negative expectations, just as a positive label can create positive expectations.

Please remember the self-fulfilling prophecy the next time you are tempted to place a label on someone.

■ **Self-fulfilling prophecy** Observations or behaviors that result primarily from expectations.

CHECK YOUR UNDERSTANDING

1. **APPLICATION:** From the perspective of Cattell's theory, the ability to use algorithms and heuristics would be an aspect of
   a. convergent thinking.
   b. crystallized intelligence.
   c. logical thinking.
   d. divergent thinking.
   e. fluid intelligence.

2. **APPLICATION:** A friend tells you that he has found a way to improve his grades by stopping by his psychology teacher's room once a week to ask questions about the reading. If this is successful, you could say that your friend has shown
   a. practical intelligence.
   b. logical reasoning.
   c. experiential intelligence.
   d. convergent thinking.
   e. divergent thinking.

3. **RECALL:** Which of Gardner's seven intelligences is most like that measured on standard IQ tests?
   a. linguistic ability
   b. bodily-kinesthetic ability
   c. interpersonal ability
   d. intrapersonal ability
   e. spatial ability

4. **RECALL:** A self-fulfilling prophecy comes true because of
   a. innate factors.
   b. most people's lack of substantial logical-mathematical ability.
   c. the lack of precision of IQ tests.
   d. people's expectations.
   e. cultural norms.

5. **UNDERSTANDING THE CORE CONCEPT:** Which of the following most aptly characterizes the current debate about intelligence?
   a. mental age versus chronological age
   b. single versus multiple
   c. practical versus logical
   d. cognitive versus behavioral
   e. fluid versus crystalized

ANSWERS: 1. e 2. a 3. a 4. d 5. b

KEY QUESTION

HOW DO PSYCHOLOGISTS EXPLAIN IQ DIFFERENCES AMONG GROUPS?

It is a fact that a gap of approximately 15 points exists between the average IQ scores of African Americans and Caucasian Americans (Neisser et al., 1996; Vincent, 1991). A similar IQ gap separates children from middle-income homes and low-income homes (Jensen & Figueroa, 1975; Oakland & Glutting, 1990). Nobody disputes that these gaps exist. What the experts disagree about are the *causes* of these IQ discrepancies. As we will see, the disagreement is another example of the nature–nurture controversy. Our Core Concept describes the issue this way:

CORE CONCEPT

While most psychologists agree that both heredity and environment affect intelligence, they disagree on the source of IQ differences among racial and social groups.

The controversy over the source of intelligence is potentially of great importance for people's lives—and a politically hot issue. If we assume that intelligence is primarily the result of innate (hereditary) factors, we will most likely conclude that it is fixed and unchangeable. This leads some to the mistaken conclusion that a group having low IQ scores must be innately inferior and should be treated as second-class citizens. On the other hand, if we conclude that intelligence is shaped largely by experience (environment), we are more likely to make a range of educational opportunities available for everyone and to view people of all ethnic, cultural, and economic groups as equals. Either way, our conclusion may become a self-fulfilling prophecy.

In fact, neither the hereditarian nor the environmentalist view is completely right. Repeatedly in this book we have seen that psychologists now recognize that both heredity and environment play a role in all our behavior and mental processes. But there is more to the issue of group differences than this. In

● The IQ scores of identical twins show a strong influence of genetics. The identical twins in this photo have gathered for the Twins Days Festival in Twinsburg, Ohio.

this chapter we add another important dimension to the heredity–environment interaction: While every individual's intelligence is determined, in part, by heredity, this fact does not mean that the IQ differences among groups have some biological basis. On the contrary, many psychologists have argued that group differences are totally environmental—although this, too, is disputed, as our Core Concept suggests. You will find out why this is so in the following pages.

Intelligence and the Politics of Immigration

In the early 1900s, Henry Goddard, an influential psychologist who believed that intelligence is a hereditary trait, proposed mental testing for all applicants for immigration and the exclusion of those who were found to be "mentally defective" (Strickland, 2000). With encouragement from Goddard and some other assessment-minded psychologists, Congress passed the 1924 Immigration Restriction Act, designed to restrict immigration of groups and nationalities in which people had been "proved" to be of inferior intellect—based largely on Goddard's data. Among the groups restricted were Jews, Italians, and Russians. What Goddard and the U.S. Congress ignored was the fact that the tests were given in English—often to people with little familiarity with the English language and the culture in which the tests were conceived. Of course many of these immigrants received low scores!

Today we are more aware of the shortcomings of intelligence tests. We also know that, while heredity has an effect on an individual's intelligence, experience does, too. And we know that Goddard used faulty reasoning when he concluded that heredity accounts for group differences in intelligence. To understand how heredity could affect individual differences but not group differences, we need to look first at the evidence supporting the hereditarian and environmentalist arguments.

What Evidence Shows That Intelligence Is Influenced by Heredity?

Many lines of research point to a hereditary influence on intelligence. For example, studies comparing the IQ scores of identical twins with fraternal twins and other siblings show a strong genetic correlation. Another common approach compares adopted children with their biological and adoptive families. These studies find that the correlation between the IQs of children and their biological parents is greater than that with their adoptive parents (Plomin & DeFries, 1998). As Table 11.2 shows, the closer the genetic relationship—from cousins to siblings to twins—the closer the relationship of IQ scores. In general, work on twins and adopted children shows genetic influences on a wide range of attributes as diverse as heart functioning (Brown, 1990), personality traits (Tellegen et al., 1988), hypnotizability (Morgan et al., 1970), and intelligence (Chorney et al., 1998; McClearn et al., 1997; Neisser et al., 1996; Petrill et al., 1998). Work coming out of the Human Genome Project has also lent support to the notion that intelligence has a genetic component. Scientists are careful to point out, however, that the genetic basis of intelligence is complex because it involves the interaction of many genes (Chorney et al., 1998).

While psychologists agree that heredity plays an important part in determining an individual's IQ scores, they also agree that it remains difficult to estimate the relative weights of heredity and environment (Plomin, 1989; Scarr, 1998; Stevenson et al., 1987). One reason for this is that children who live in

TABLE 11.2 Correlation of IQ Scores with Genetic Relationship

Genetic relationship	Correlation Between IQ scores
Identical twins	
Reared together	0.86
Reared apart	0.86
Fraternal twins	
Reared together	0.60
Siblings	
Reared together	0.47
Reared apart	0.24
Parent/child	0.40
Foster parent/child	0.31
Cousins	0.15

Note: A correlation shows the degree of association between variables–in this case, between the IQs of pairs of individuals. The closer to 1.0, the closer the connection. For example, we can see that the IQ scores of identical twins reared together are more closely correlated (.86) than the IQs of mere siblings reared together (.47). The data strongly suggest a genetic component that contributes to intelligence. (*Source:* From "Familial Studies of Intelligence: A Review," by Bouchard and McGue in *Science,* 1981, Vol. 212, pp. 1055–1059. Copyright © 1981 by the American Association for the Advancement of Science. Reprinted by permission of AAAS.)

the same family setting do not necessarily share precisely the same psychological environment. First-born children, for example, are treated differently from the youngest. You probably are aware of this fact if you have siblings.

What Evidence Shows That Intelligence Is Influenced by Environment?

The evidence that the environment influences intellectual development is persuasive, too. Even when we look for genetic effects, we find greater similarities of IQ among people who have been reared together than those reared apart. And in laboratory animals, a stimulus-enriched habitat early in life has been shown to result in a more complex, complete development of brain cells and cortical regions. The superior performance of these animals on a range of tasks persists through life. In other experiments, we find that young monkeys that are trained to solve problems and are also offered the companionship of other monkeys display more active curiosity and higher intelligence than those reared without this environmental stimulation.

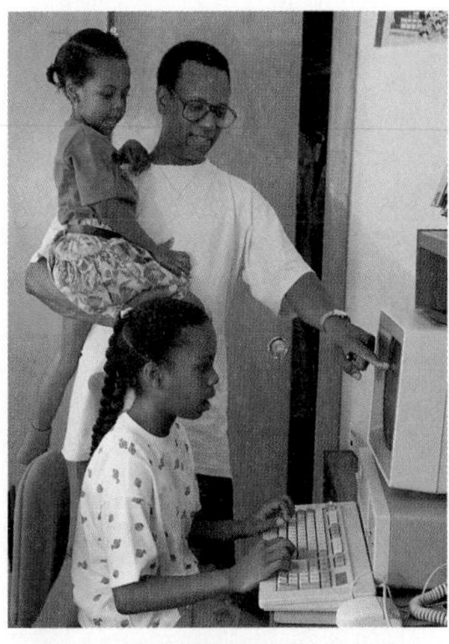

● The personal attention children receive can affect their intelligence. This contemporary parent is deeply involved in his children's education.

Such findings hint that we might boost the intellectual functioning of human infants by enriching their environments. Indeed, we will see that early enrichment programs can raise children's IQ scores. Regular schooling also may boost IQ scores. In fact, the total amount of schooling children get is directly correlated with their IQ scores (Ceci & Williams, 1997). Even in adulthood, environmental factors, such as the cognitive complexity and intellectual demands of one's job, can influence mental abilities throughout life (Dixon et al., 1985).

Heritability and Group Differences

Let us acknowledge, then, that heredity has an influence—perhaps a substantial influence—on intelligence. But we should also be clear about another term: *heritability*. This concept is crucial for understanding the idea that hereditary differences among *individuals* do not imply that heredity accounts for the differences we observe among *groups.* In other words, heritability is not the same thing as heredity. Specifically, **heritability** refers to the amount of trait variation within a group that can be attributed to genetic differences. Thus, it is important to realize that *we can speak of heritable differences only within a group of individuals who have shared the same environment.*

To illustrate, suppose that we examined a group of children who were all raised in an intellectually stimulating environment, with devoted parents who spent lots of time interacting with them and reading to them—things we know improve intellectual abilities. Among these children, we would find variation in intellectual abilities. Because they were all treated in essentially the same fashion, however, we could attribute much of the differences in their IQ scores to the effects of heredity. In this group, IQ would have a high heritability.

In contrast, suppose that we examined a group of children who had been raised under conditions of neglect (given mere custodial care in an orphanage, with no intellectual stimulation from their caregivers). We would most likely find that these children have relatively little variability among their IQ scores because they are all intellectually stunted. For this group, intelligence would have low heritability—because the poor environment did not offer an opportunity for these children's genetic potential to be realized.

Now, what about the differences *between* the two groups? The IQ differences would be real. But—this is the important part—our observations could tell us nothing about the genetic differences (if any) between the groups. For all we know they might have the same genetic potential. But because the environments were so different, we cannot tell what role genetics played in determining their IQ scores. By applying this notion to groups of people who are exposed to different cultural traditions or experience different levels of wealth or discrimination, you can see that we have no way to evaluate what proportion of the differences between the groups should be attributed to heredity or to environment. To reiterate: *Heritability is a concept that refers to within-group differences, not between-group differences.* Just because intelligence may be highly heritable does not mean that the environment has no impact (Dickens & Flynn, 2001; Neisser et al., 1996).

The Jensen Controversy Despite the concerns we have just cited, a few psychologists remain unconvinced that group differences in IQ can be accounted for by environmental factors. In particular, Harvard psychologist Arthur Jensen (1969) stirred up a hornets' nest of controversy with his contention that racial differences in IQ have a genetic basis. We can boost IQ scores to some extent, said Jensen, by helping the poor and disadvantaged, but there are limits imposed by heredity.

In support of his thesis, Jensen cited several studies showing a strong influence of heredity on IQ. He also presented a complex statistical argument that showed only a weak environmental effect on IQ and achievement. Then, turning his attention to government programs that had attempted to give extra help to disadvantaged black children, Jensen claimed that, although most had shown some positive effects, none had erased racial differences in performance. What remained must be a genetic difference in abilities, he maintained.

Over the next five years, more than 100 published articles responded to Jensen's challenge. Sometimes it seemed that the Jensen controversy had generated far more heat than light. The protest occasionally became ugly, with charges of bigotry and racism nearly drowning the scientific debate. Nevertheless, it did have the positive effect of stimulating a new wave of research and theory aimed at gaining greater understanding of black–white IQ differences.

■ **Heritability** The amount of trait variation within a group, raised under the same conditions, that can be attributed to genetic differences. Heritability tells us nothing about between-group differences.

Critics pointed out several factors that Jensen had minimized or ignored, including the effects of racism, lower teacher expectations for black children, lack of opportunity, low self-esteem, and a white, middle-class bias built into IQ and achievement tests (Neisser, 1997; Neisser et al., 1996). While Jensen holds to his original position (Jensen, 1980, 1985, 1998, 2000), many (but not all) psychologists now agree that a combination of environmental factors can explain the differences on which Jensen built his case. Let us now look at some of the post-Jensen discoveries, beginning with a study of children whose environment had been altered by adoption.

The Scarr and Weinberg Adoption Study A monumental study by Sandra Scarr and Richard Weinberg confronted the issue head-on by comparing black and white children who had been adopted into similar home environments (1976, 1978). Their research focused on educational records and IQ test scores from both the biological families and the adoptive families of 115 white children and 176 black children who had been adopted in Minnesota during the 1950s. All the children had been adopted into white families. For both groups of children, the biological parents had average IQ scores (near 100), while the adoptive parents' IQs were somewhat higher, averaging above 115.

What did Scarr and Weinberg find when they reexamined the IQ scores of these two groups of adoptees in late adolescence? There were no differences! Both the black group and the white group of adoptees had scores that averaged about 110, significantly higher than their biological parents, although not quite as high as their adoptive parents. Such results testify to a powerful effect of the environment on IQ. The results also contradict Jensen's claim that group differences are genetic.

Social Class and IQ Research on the relationship between social class and IQ shows similar environmental effects. Socioeconomic class (as reflected in an individual's financial status and lifestyle) is clearly correlated with IQ. While affluence is associated with higher IQ scores, groups with the lowest average IQ scores are those for whom poverty, illiteracy, and hopelessness are most widespread. Supporters of the environmental position claim that racism and discrimination initially landed many minorities in the impoverished inner cities, and these same factors continue to keep them there today.

How does social class affect IQ? Poverty creates circumstances that limit individual potential in many ways, particularly in terms of nutrition, health care, and education (Brown & Pollitt, 1996; Neisser et al., 1996). Poverty means less-adequate health care, so it should not surprise you that researchers have traced poor health during pregnancy and low birth weight to low mental ability in children. Poverty also means less of other factors known to promote intellectual development. Poor nutrition, lack of access to books and computers, and job schedules that leave parents little time to stimulate a child's intellect all correlate with poverty and can be detrimental to performance on tasks such as those demanded by IQ tests (for example, vocabulary or sentence comprehension). Research also shows that a significant proportion of children with low IQs have been adversely affected by "environmental insults," such as living in homes with lead-based paint chips peeling from walls, causing toxic lead levels in children who ingest this material (Needleman et al., 1990).

Poverty has other crippling effects, too. In most parts of the United States, public schools are funded by revenue from local property taxes. Thus, wealthy neighborhoods can provide bigger and better school facilities and amenities, while poorer districts may suffer from crowding, physically deteriorating structures, threats to personal safety, and few "extras" such as media centers or computers. In such environments, even children with the aptitude to learn may find it difficult to rise above their circumstances. Proponents of the view that environment has a strong influence on intelligence usually support equal-opportunity legislation, better schools, and intervention programs that help disadvantaged children build self-confidence and learn the skills necessary to succeed in school (Tirozzi & Uro, 1997; Zigler & Muenchow, 1992; Zigler & Styfco, 1994).

Head Start: A Successful Intervention Program One such intervention program is *Head Start,* originally implemented over 40 years ago to provide educational enrichment for disadvantaged children. It grew from the assumption that many children from deprived families need an intellectual boost to prepare them for school. The program is intended to head off problems on several fronts by serving children's physical as well as mental needs with nutritional and medical support, plus a year or two of preschool education. Wisely, Head Start also involves parents in making policy, planning programs, working in classrooms, and learning about parenting and child development. Head Start centers around the country currently serve about 800,000 children yearly—estimated to be 40% of the number who need it (Ripple et al., 1999).

Does it work? Again, there is some controversy (Jensen, 1969; Kantrowitz, 1992), although a great deal of research suggests that Head Start does, indeed, help disadvantaged children get ready for school (Lazar & Darlington, 1982; Lee et al., 1988; Ripple et al., 1999; Ripple & Zigler 2003; Schweinhart & Weikart, 1986; Smith, 1991). Children who were enrolled in the program score higher on IQ tests and have higher school achievement during the early grades than a matched control group who received no such intervention (Zigler & Styfco, 1994). More important, their head start lasts. Although the differences between the Head Start children and the control group diminish over time, the effects are still detectable in adolescence. Compared to the control group, Head Start children are less likely to be placed in special education classes, less likely to fail a grade, and more likely to graduate from high school.

It now appears, however, that such attempts to raise IQ by special environmental interventions may not start early enough. Studies indicate that early educational intervention, starting in the first months of life, can raise infants' scores on intelligence tests by as much as 30% compared to control groups (Ramey & Ramey, 1998a, b; Wickelgren, 1999). Although the gains may diminish with time, especially if supportive programs are withdrawn, significant differences remain when intervention starts in infancy. The best way to summarize these and other relevant findings is to say that the earlier the individual is immersed in an enriched environment, the better.

Test Biases Still other forces influence IQ scores and contribute to differences among groups. A portion of the difference between the average IQ scores of black and white children may be attributable to problems with the IQ tests themselves. Many psychologists argue that IQ test questions have built-in biases toward a middle- or upper-class background—biases that favor the white child (Garcia, 1981; Helms, 1992; Miller-Jones, 1989). For an opposing view, however, that holds that test bias does *not* contribute to group differences in IQ scores, see Jensen (2000) and Reynolds (2000).

One source of possible bias stems from the fact that most IQ tests rely heavily on vocabulary level. This gives a big advantage to children who have been read to and who are encouraged to read. We can see a related bias in a well-known IQ test that asks for a definition of "opulent" (rich), a term one is far less likely to hear in a poor household.

Because expectations can also affect IQ scores, psychologists have argued that lowered expectations among some minority groups about their own potential can contribute to racial differences in IQ scores (Schwartz, 1997). One study found that merely being asked to identify their race produced lower scores for minority students on a test of academic abilities (Steele, 1997). In another study, a group of black women faltered on an IQ test when they were told that white women usually do better on the test. These women, who expected to do poorly, received IQ scores that averaged a full 10 points lower than another group who were told that black women usually receive high scores (Thomas, 1991).

Yet another source of bias has to do with the examiner. Not only does the examiner's attitude influence IQ scores, but so do his or her gender and race. Studies have found that black children receive higher scores when tested by a black examiner (Bodmer & Cavalli-Sforza, 1970; Sattler, 1970). In brief, test takers do best when they perceive the examiner to be similar to themselves.

Finally, Janet Helms (1992) has pointed out that the attempt to explain why African American children deviate from the Caucasian norm may, itself, rest on the biased assumption that one culture is superior to another. Specifically, she says, it "assumes that white-American culture defines the most intellectually rich environment" (p. 1086). Seldom do we ask how well white children learn the norms of other cultures. Helms asks: Why should the Caucasian American norm be the standard by which everyone else is judged?

The Bell Curve: Another Hereditarian Offensive The dispute over causes of racial differences in IQ flared again in 1994. At issue was a book, *The Bell Curve: Intelligence and Class Structure in American Life,* by Richard Herrnstein and Charles Murray. The name echoes the bell-shaped "normal distribution" of IQ scores (see shape of the graph in Figure 11.2). In this volume, Herrnstein and Murray argued that racial differences in IQ have a strong genetic basis. If these innate differences were accepted, the nation could move on to more enlightened and humane social policies, they said. Critics immediately identified not only a racist bias but pointed to unsound "science" at the core of *The Bell Curve.*

How is *The Bell Curve*'s argument flawed? The answer will be familiar to you by now: While there is no doubt that heredity influences individual intelligence, Herrnstein and Murray, like hereditarians before them, have offered no proof that differences *between groups* exposed to different environments have a hereditary basis (see Coughlin, 1994; Fraser, 1995). Further, much of the "evidence" they offer is suspect (Kamin, 1994). One study cited by Herrnstein and Murray claimed to document the low IQs of black Africans, but it employed tests given in English—a language in which the Zulu subjects of the study were not fluent (Kamin, 1995). The test used in that study also assumed that subjects were familiar with electrical appliances found in urban middle-class homes (rather than Zulu villages) and equipment, such as microscopes, not typically found in Zulu schools.

Compounding the problems in their analysis of the evidence, Herrnstein and Murray commit another scientific error about which you learned early in this book: They confuse correlation with causation. In fact, the Herrnstein and Murray argument is just as plausible when turned around: Poverty and all of the social and economic disadvantages that go with it could just as well be important causes of low IQ scores.

Despite its flaws, *The Bell Curve* has struck a chord with many Americans. It resonates with the preference for simple genetic "causes" for behavior, rather than more complex explanations. It also fits with our cultural biases about educational achievement. This is seen in a study that asked Americans and Asians to account for a child's academic success. Predictably, American respondents emphasized "innate ability," whereas Asian respondents emphasized the importance of "studying hard" (Stevenson et al., 1993).

PSYCHOLOGY IN YOUR LIFE: HELPING OTHERS THINK CRITICALLY ABOUT GROUP DIFFERENCES

If someone you know were to claim that the discrepancy between IQ scores of whites and blacks is proof of the genetic intellectual superiority of whites, how would you respond? You might begin with the argument that the influence of genetics on individual intelligence tells us nothing about the influence of genetics on group differences. You could also point to the evidence showing that, while the group average IQ for African Americans is as much as 10 to 15 IQ points below the group average for U.S. whites, there is much overlapping of scores. That is, the difference *between* groups is small compared to the spread of scores of individuals *within* each group (Neisser et al., 1996). And you could say that biologists have taught us that "race" is not a valid biological concept (Beutler et al., 1996; Cohen, 1998; Yee et al., 1993). Even if we use a social definition, where people define their own racial group, the differences between the gene pools of people who claim to be of different racial groups are very small compared to the genetic differences among individual members of the same group (Bamshad & Olson, 2003; Gould, 1996; Zuckerman, 1990).

In the "separate but equal" schoolroom of 1940s Tennessee, African American children received little attention and a poor education.

Perhaps the most persuasive argument against the genetic interpretation of group differences is that many other variables are confounded with race, including racism, poverty, self-fulfilling prophecies, and differential opportunities for education—each of which can influence IQ scores. For example, in a large-scale, longitudinal study of more than 26,000 children, the best predictors of a child's IQ at age 4, for both black and white children, were the family's socioeconomic status and the level of the mother's education (Broman et al., 1975). When opportunities are made more equal, as we saw in the Scarr-Weinberg study, the differences disappear.

Unfortunately, the fact of group differences in IQ scores has been interpreted as a genetic difference and used to justify racist views. Even today, such data are used to justify discrimination against the disadvantaged poor, women, minorities, and immigrants in providing educational and career opportunities and in formulating public policy (Gould, 1996; Hirsch et al., 1990; Kamin, 1974). In the extreme, racist interpreters of the genetic argument support **eugenics** programs that would limit "breeding" by "undesirable" groups, laws restricting the immigration of certain groups, and legal inequality that favors the group in power. But the science just doesn't support such actions or the beliefs behind them.

Eugenics A philosophy and a political movement that encouraged biologically superior people to interbreed and sought to discourage biologically inferior people from having offspring.

CHECK YOUR UNDERSTANDING

1. **RECALL:** Most early American psychologists working on intelligence believed that the dominant influence on intelligence was
   a. heredity.
   b. experience.
   c. gender.
   d. the size of one's brain.
   e. environment.

2. **ANALYSIS:** It is most accurate to say that
   a. intelligence is influenced more by heredity than by environment.
   b. intelligence is influenced more by environment than by heredity.
   c. intelligence is the result of an interaction of heredity and environment.
   d. the influence of environment on intelligence is most powerful in the children of minority groups.
   e. intelligence is influenced more by family makeup than by any interactions of heredity and environment.

3. **RECALL:** The concept of heritability refers to genetic variation
   a. within an individual's sperm cells or ova.
   b. between one group and another.
   c. within an individual's immediate family.
   d. within a group of individuals who have had the same environment.
   e. between family members.

4. **UNDERSTANDING THE CORE CONCEPT:** Although everyone agrees that heredity affects ______ intelligence, there is no evidence that it accounts for differences among ______.
   a. individual /groups
   b. group/individuals
   c. high/the mentally retarded
   d. academic/practical intelligence
   e. fluid/individuals

ANSWERS: 1.a 2.c 3.d 4.a

TESTING AND INDIVIDUAL DIFFERENCES: THE STATE OF THE ART

Recent years have brought advances in our understanding of concept formation, particularly from brain imaging studies. But we still know very little about the biological basis for "higher" thinking processes, such as creativity, expertise, and intelligence—the qualities that Brin and Page used to create Google. Nor do we have precise knowledge about what environment most effectively nurture these characteristics.

Psychology in the 21st century has also seen the field of intelligence testing—once considered one of psychology's unqualified great achievements—shrouded in controversy over the extent to which it is influenced by our hereditary nature and to what degree is it is nurtured by our environment. On the brighter side, psychologists have broadened our understanding of intelligence with the concept of multiple intelligences and with the notion that intelligence has different meanings in different cultural groups.

So, where is psychology headed in the field that encompasses thinking, intelligence, creativity, expertise, and problem solving? The hottest areas of research lie in neuroscience—finding the links between thinking and brain function. The most-needed areas of research, however, may lie in finding practical applications for the home and classroom.

USING PSYCHOLOGY TO LEARN PSYCHOLOGY

Developing Expertise in Psychology—or Any Other Subject

Obviously, **experts** are people who know a lot about a particular subject. Unlike a novice, an expert confronting a problem does not have to start from scratch. Experts can often see a solution quickly because they have seen many similar problems before. That is, they are especially good at using the heuristic of finding analogies.

Another quality distinguishing expert thinkers from beginners lies in the way their knowledge is organized. While the novice possesses only a collection of disjointed facts and observations, experts have organized their knowledge into elaborate schemas (Bédard & Chi, 1992; Bransford et al., 1986; Chi et al., 1982; Glaser, 1990; Greeno, 1989; Klahr & Simon, 2001). We can see this quite clearly in a famous study of world-class chess players.

■ **Experts** Individuals who possess well-organized funds of knowledge, including the effective problem-solving strategies, in a field.

A Study of Chess Experts

Dutch psychologist Adriaan de Groot found some striking differences when he compared the ways a group of grand master chess players and another group of merely good players responded to a chess problem. Allowed five seconds to view a configuration of pieces as they might appear on a chess board during a match, the grand masters were able to reproduce the pattern far more accurately than the less-expert subjects (de Groot, 1965). Does that mean that the grand masters had better visual memories? No. When confronted with a random pattern of pieces on the chess board—a pattern that would never happen in a match—the grand masters did no better than the other subjects. This suggests that the experts were able to draw on familiar patterns in memory, rather than trying to recall individual pieces and positions.

How to Become an Expert

Are experts born, or is expertise learned? As we saw with creativity, there is little evidence that inborn talent plays a substantial role in expert performance (Ericsson & Charness, 1994). To be objective, however, we should say that there is an opposing view that recognizes innate talent (Simonton, 2001): It is likely, from this view, that people don't usually make the huge commitment of time and energy to become an expert in a field for which they do not have some initial aptitude.

So, could you, for example, become an expert—in psychology, perhaps? The research shows that, no matter what the field, experts learn their expertise (Bédard & Chi, 1992). Aside from facts and specific skills, they also acquire a repertoire of multipurpose heuristics, such as those we discussed earlier. And they know the special problem-solving techniques, or "tricks of the trade," that are unique to their field of expertise. These heuristics help them find solutions more quickly, without having to follow so many blind alleys (Gentner & Stevens, 1983; Simon, 1992).

Expertise as Organized Knowledge

Research on experts also shows that learning facts and skills is not enough to produce real expertise (Bransford et al., 1986; Glaser, 1984; Greeno, 1989; Mayer, 1983). In addition, experts also possess a great deal of well-organized information about a field and its important concepts, which gives the expert both a fund of knowledge to apply to a problem and a familiarity with the field's common problems and solutions. That is, they know not only the facts but also how the facts are interrelated and used.

How, then, do you become an expert? A supportive environment, with good teachers and mentors, helps (Barab & Plucker, 2002). Beyond that, it's study and practice! But don't just focus on the details. Learn the important schemas and problem-solving strategies in your chosen field, too. How long will it take? Research shows that achieving world-class status in any of a wide gamut of fields—from athletics to academics to chess to music—requires about 10 years of intensive study and practice (Ericsson et al., 1993; Gardner, 1993).

What does this suggest for your learning of psychology and other disciplines? You can take the first steps in developing your expertise by attending to the way your professors and your texts organize the information they present (Gonzalvo et al., 1994). Consider such questions as the following:

- What are the terms that your psychology professor keeps mentioning over and over? These might be such concepts as "cognitive science," "behaviorism," "developmental," or "theoretical perspectives." For you they may be, at first, unfamiliar and abstract, but for the professor they may represent the core of the course. Make sure you know what the terms mean and why they are important.
- Around what concepts is the course syllabus organized? What are the new terms that are associated with the main topics?
- Around what concepts is the textbook organized? You may be able to tell this quickly by looking at the table of contents. Alternatively, the authors may lay out the organizing points in the preface at the beginning of the book. (In this book, we have attempted to help you identify the organizing principles of each chapter in the form of Core Concepts.)

If you can identify the organizing principles for the course, they will simplify your studying. This makes sense, of course, in terms of our earlier study of memory. Long-term memory (as you will remember!) is organized by meaningful associations. Accordingly, when you have a simple and effective way of organizing the material, you will have a framework that will help you store and retain it in long-term memory.

CHAPTER SUMMARY

KEY QUESTION

CORE CONCEPT

● HOW DO WE MEASURE INDIVIDUAL DIFFERENCES?

Utilizing validity and reliability, we can develop and use tests which accurately assess the information we need, and do it consistently and accurately over time. There are several types of validity, content and criterion as well as reliability, test–retest and split-half. Standardization and norms are also an essential aspect of assessment, as they allow us to clearly establish how a score compares with others in a population. Ethics not only refer to what tests test, but how the scores can be, and should be used. The ethical considerations in testing cannot be understated.

● **Measuring individual differences is an essential component of psychology, but strict guidelines and ethical standards must be followed to ensure that results and conclusions are valid and appropriate.**

● HOW IS INTELLIGENCE MEASURED?

The measurement of intelligence is both common and controversial. Assessment of mental ability has an ancient human history but was not based on scientific practice until the 20th century. In 1904, Binet and Simon developed the first workable test of intelligence, based on the assumption that education can modify intellectual performance. In America, IQ testing became widespread for the assessment of Army recruits, immigrants, and schoolchildren. The original IQ calculation was abandoned in favor of standard scores based on the normal distribution. IQ scores are a key ingredient in identifying mental retardation and giftedness, which are often seen as occupying the extremes of the IQ distribution.

● **Intelligence testing has a history of controversy, but most psychologists now view intelligence as a normally distributed trait that can be measured by performance on a variety of tasks—both verbal and nonverbal.**

● WHAT ARE THE COMPONENTS OF INTELLIGENCE?

Among the first psychometric theories of intelligence, Spearman's analysis emphasized a single, common factor known as *g*. Later, Cattell separated *g* into two components: fluid and crystallized intelligence. Modern cognitive psychologists have conceived of intelligence as a combination of several abilities. In particular, Gardner and Sternberg have taken the lead in extending the definition of intelligence beyond school-related tasks. Sternberg's triarchic theory proposes analytic, creative, and practical intelligences, while Gardner's theory of multiple intelligences has claimed at least seven components of intelligence—and possibly three more. Meanwhile, cross-cultural psychologists have shown that "intelligence" has different meanings in different cultures. In the United States much emphasis is placed on mental tests. In such a climate, however, a big danger lies in test scores becoming mere labels that influence people's behavior through the self-fulfilling prophecy.

● **Some psychologists believe that intelligence comprises one general factor, *g*, while others believe that intelligence is a collection of distinct abilities.**

● HOW DO PSYCHOLOGISTS EXPLAIN IQ DIFFERENCES AMONG GROUPS?

Hereditarian arguments maintain that intelligence is substantially influenced by genetics, a belief endorsed by the U.S. government, which at one time used IQ tests to restrict immigration. Environmental approaches argue that intelligence can be dramatically shaped by influences such as health, economics, and education. While most psychologists now agree that intelligence is heritable, they also know that heritability refers to variation within a group and does not imply that between-group differences are the result of hereditary factors. Nevertheless, the dispute over the nature and nurture of group differences in intelligence flared up again in 1969, when Jensen argued that the evidence favored a strong genetic influence. This argument was echoed in the 1994 book *The Bell Curve.* Critics have pointed out that much of the research cited by those taking the extreme hereditarian position is flawed. In addition, intelligence testing itself may be biased in favor of those with particular language and cultural experiences. Hereditarian claims, however, have stimulated much research, such as Scarr and Weinberg's research on adopted children and follow-up studies of the Head Start program. This research has shown that the racial and class differences in IQ scores can be eliminated by environmental changes.

● **While most psychologists agree that both heredity and environment affect intelligence, they disagree on the source of IQ differences among racial and social groups.**

REVIEW TEST

For each of the following items, choose the single correct or best answer. The correct answers appear at the end.

1. Tests that yield relatively consistent results are said to be
   a. valid.
   b. reliable.
   c. normed.
   d. standardized.
   e. consistent.

2. Howard Gardner's approach to intelligence could be best represented by which of the following:
   a. multiple intelligences
   b. mental retardation is a purely genetic component
   c. general intelligence (g)
   d. IQ has no application to our daily lives
   e. IQ varies over time

3. The AP Exam relies on which test of reliability?
   a. split-half
   b. test–retest
   c. content
   d. face
   e. criterion
4. Objective tests use _____, while subjective tests use _____.
   a. ambiguous figures/selected responses
   b. images/objects
   c. hand scoring techniques/machine scoring techniques
   d. objects/images
   e. selected responses/ambiguous figures
5. Binet and Simon assumed that
   a. intelligence is inherited.
   b. mental age does not increase as fast as chronological age.
   c. social class differences in intelligence should be remedied by governmental programs.
   d. education could affect intelligence.
   e. age and intelligence are not related.
6. According to Lewis Terman's formula, a 9-year-old child with an IQ of 100 would have a mental age of
   a. 9.
   b. 10.
   c. 18.
   d. 90.
   e. 100.
7. According to Howard Gardner, there are at least seven "intelligences." Which one of these is most like an ability assessed by traditional IQ tests?
   a. musical
   b. kinesthetic
   c. linguistic
   d. intrapersonal
   e. instinctual
8. The fact that intelligence is heritable has sometimes been misunderstood by those taking an extreme hereditarian view as meaning that ______ explains ______ differences in IQ scores.
   a. environment/individual
   b. heredity/group
   c. environment/group
   d. heredity/individual
   e. nature/natural
9. The Scarr and Weinberg study supports the idea that racial differences in IQ scores are the result of
   a. genetic differences.
   b. environmental differences.
   c. test biases.
   d. unknown factors.
   e. brain mass.
10. The characteristic that most distinguishes the expert from the novice is
   a. intelligence.
   b. talent.
   c. organized knowledge.
   d. speed of problem solving.
   e. education.

ANSWERS: 1. b 2. a 3. a 4. e 5. d 6. a 7. c 8. b 9. b 10. c

KEY TERMS

Validity (p. 452)
Reliability (p. 452)
Face validity (p. 452)
Content validity (p. 452)
Item analysis (p. 452)
Criterion validity (p. 452)
Test–retest reliability (p. 452)
Split-half reliability (p. 453)
Normal range (p. 453)
Objective test (p. 454)
Subjective test (p. 454)
Inter-rater reliability (p. 454)
Mental age (MA) (p. 457)
Chronological age (CA) (p. 457)
Intelligence quotient (IQ) (p. 458)
Mental retardation (p. 460)
Giftedness (p. 460)
Savant syndrome (p. 463)
***g* factor** (p. 464)
Crystallized intelligence (p. 464)
Fluid intelligence (p. 464)
Practical intelligence (p. 464)
Analytical intelligence (p. 465)
Creative intelligence (p. 465)
Triarchic theory (p. 465)
Multiple intelligences (p. 466)
Self-fulfilling prophecy (p. 468)
Heritability (p. 472)
Eugenics (p. 476)
Experts (p. 477)

AP* REVIEW: VOCABULARY

Match each of the following vocabulary terms to its definition.

1. Validity
2. Reliability
3. Test–retest
4. Split-half
5. Inter-rater reliability
6. Mental age
7. Chronological age
8. Normal range
9. Crystallized intelligence
10. Fluid intelligence

_____ a. A measure of reliability in which a test is split into two parts and the scores on the halves of the test are compared.

_____ b. A property of a test that actually measures what it purports to measure.

_____ c. The average age at which normal (average) individuals achieve a particular score.

_____ **d.** A property of a test will yield consistent results over time.

_____ **e.** The ability to see complex relationships and solve problems.

_____ **f.** Scores falling near the middle of a distribution.

_____ **g.** The number of years since an individual's birth.

_____ **h.** A measure of how two different test scorers would score a test.

_____ **i.** The knowledge a person has acquired, plus the ability to access that knowledge.

_____ **j.** A measure of reliability in which a test is given again to check and see if people get the same scores when they take the test again.

AP* REVIEW: ESSAY

Use your knowledge of the chapter concepts to answer the following essay question.

If you were developing an AP test, how would the following factor into your design?

a. Face validity

b. Item analysis

c. Split-half reliability

OUR RECOMMENDED BOOKS AND VIDEOS

BOOKS

Gardner, H. (1999). *Intelligence reframed: Multiple intelligences for the 21st century.* New York: Basic Books. Psychologist Howard Gardner elaborates and suggests how to apply his theory that each of us possesses seven or more basic types of intelligence to varying degrees: the familiar linguistic and logical-mathematical types that are the focus of traditional education and testing, but also intelligences of music, movement, spatial awareness, and other abilities—including new discoveries such as naturalistic intelligence (awareness of the living environment).

Gould, S. J. (1981). *The mismeasure of man.* New York: Norton. Stephen Jay Gould's book is a classic indictment of flawed assessment and testing, especially when used to discriminate against or oppress social groups.

Perkins, D. (2000). *Archimedes' bathtub: The art and logic of breakthrough thinking.* New York: W. W. Norton. Ancient Greek philosopher Archimedes shouted "Eureka!" ("I have found it") when, lowering himself into a bath, he recognized the process of water displacement. This author explains practical and entertaining strategies for producing creative inspiration in our own lives.

Plous, S. (1993). *The psychology of judgment and decision making.* Philadelphia: Temple University Press. Psychologist Scott Plous argues that common sense is an unreliable guide in modern living, showing the silly choices we make and recommending how judgments can be more logical and successful.

VIDEOS

i am sam. (2001, color, 132 min.). Directed by Jessie Nelson; starring Sean Penn, Michelle Pfeiffer. A gentle retarded man, threatened by a social services agency with losing custody of his young daughter, is helped in his battle by a high-powered attorney whose own life is also troubled. (*Rating PG-13*)

The Luzhin Defense. (2000, color, 112 min.). Directed by Marleen Gorris; starring John Turturro, Emily Watson. In the 1920s, a socially naive but intellectually brilliant Grand Master of chess, protected all his life by his manager, attends a world tournament where he meets the love of his life but finds he is emotionally unprepared to face the real world. (*Rating PG-13*)

Searching for Bobby Fischer. (1993, color, 110 min.). Directed by Steve Zaillian; starring Joe Mantegna, Max Pomeranc, Joan Allen, Ben Kingsley. In this absorbing drama based on true story, a father encourages his talented son to compete for a championship title, revealing the rewards and risks of child genius. (*Rating PG*)

Key Question Chapter Outline

CORE CONCEPTS

Psychology in Your Life

What Is Psychological Disorder?

Changing Concepts of Psychological Disorder

Indicators of Abnormality

The medical model takes a "disease" view, while psychology sees psychological disorder as an interaction of biological, mental, social, and behavioral factors.

A Caution to Readers

If you find that you have some signs of psychological disorder, don't jump to conclusions.

How Are Psychological Disorders Classified?

Overview of the *DSM-IV* Classification System

Mood Disorders

Anxiety Disorders

Somatoform Disorders

Dissociative Disorders

Eating Disorders

Schizophrenia

Personality Disorders

Developmental Disorders

Adjustment Disorders and Other Conditions

The *DSM-IV,* the most widely used system, classifies disorders by their mental and behavioral symptoms.

Shyness

If you have it, it doesn't have to be permanent. (And, by the way, it's not a mental disorder.)

What Are the Consequences of Labeling People?

Diagnostic Labels Can Compound the Problem

The Cultural Context of Psychological Disorder

Ideally, accurate diagnoses lead to proper treatments, but diagnoses may also become labels that depersonalize individuals and ignore the social and cultural contexts in which their problems arise.

The Plea of Insanity

It's not a psychological or psychiatric term, and, contrary to popular opinion, it is a defense that is seldom used.

Psychological Disorders: The State of the Art

USING PSYCHOLOGY TO LEARN PSYCHOLOGY:
Diagnosing Your Friends and Family

Chapter 12

Psychological Disorders

THE VOLUNTEERS KNEW they were on their own. If they managed to get into the hospital, the five men and three women could get out only by convincing the staff that they were sane. None had ever been diagnosed with a mental illness, but perhaps they were not so "normal" after all: Would a normal person lie to get into such a place? In fact, all were collaborators in an experiment designed to find out whether normality would be recognized in a mental hospital.

The experimenter, David Rosenhan—himself one of the pseudopatients—suspected that terms such as *sanity, insanity, schizophrenia, mental illness,* and *abnormal* might have fuzzier boundaries than the psychiatric community thought. He also suspected that some strange behaviors seen in mental patients might originate in the abnormal atmosphere of the mental hospital, rather than in the patients themselves. To test these ideas, Rosenhan and his collaborators decided to see how mental hospital personnel would deal with patients who were not mentally ill.

Individually, they applied for admission at different hospitals, complaining that they had recently heard voices that seemed to say "empty," "hollow," and "thud." Aside from this, they claimed no other symptoms of disorder. All used false names, and the four who were mental health professionals gave false occupations—but apart from these fibs, the subjects answered all questions truthfully. They tried to act normally, although the prospect of entering the alien hospital environment made them feel anxious; they also worried about not being admitted and—worse yet—being exposed as frauds.

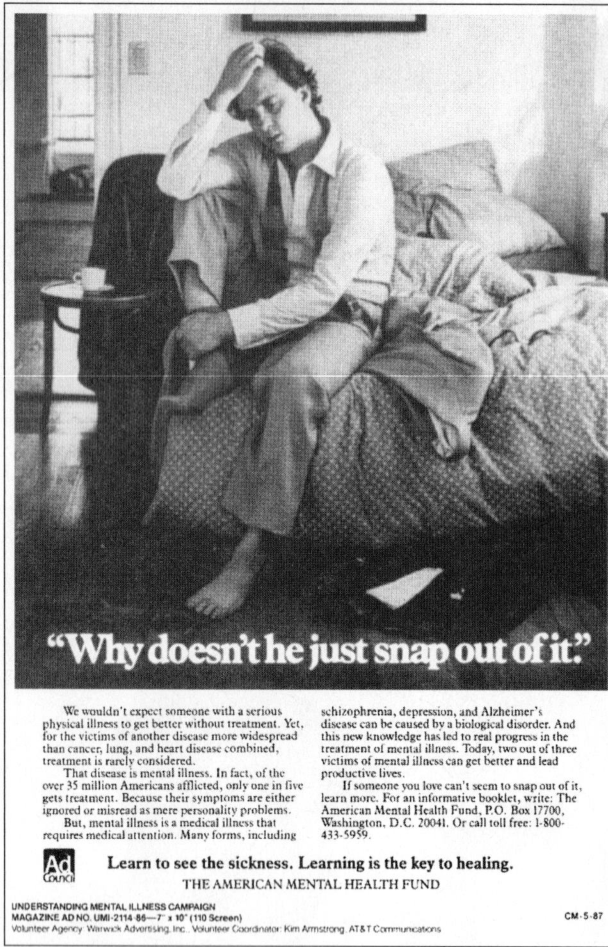
"Why doesn't he just snap out of it."
We wouldn't expect someone with a serious physical illness to get better without treatment. Yet, for the victims of another disease more widespread than cancer, lung, and heart disease combined, treatment is rarely considered.
That disease is mental illness. In fact, of the over 35 million Americans afflicted, only one in five gets treatment. Because their symptoms are either ignored or misread as mere personality problems.
But, mental illness is a medical illness that requires medical attention. Many forms, including schizophrenia, depression, and Alzheimer's disease can be caused by a biological disorder. And this new knowledge has led to real progress in the treatment of mental illness. Today, two out of three victims of mental illness can get better and lead productive lives.
If someone you love can't seem to snap out of it, learn more. For an informative booklet, write: The American Mental Health Fund, P.O. Box 17700, Washington, D.C. 20041. Or call toll free: 1-800-433-5959.
Ad Council
Learn to see the sickness. Learning is the key to healing.
THE AMERICAN MENTAL HEALTH FUND
UNDERSTANDING MENTAL ILLNESS CAMPAIGN
MAGAZINE AD NO. UMI-2114-86—7" x 10" (110 Screen)
CM-5-87
Volunteer Agency: Warwick Advertising, Inc., Volunteer Coordinator: Kim Armstrong, AT&T Communications

Advertisements like the one shown here have gone a long way toward correcting our views of mental illness and creating sympathy for its sufferers.

Their concerns about fraud vanished quickly, for all readily gained admittance at 12 different hospitals (some did it twice). All but one were diagnosed with "schizophrenia," a major psychological disorder often accompanied by hearing imaginary voices.

After admission, the pseudopatients made no further claims of hearing voices or any other abnormal symptoms. Indeed, all wanted to be on their best behavior to gain release. Their only apparent "deviance" involved taking notes on the experience—at first privately and later publicly, when they found that the staff paid little attention. The nursing records indicated that when the staff did notice, they interpreted the note-taking as part of the patient's illness. (One comment: "Patient engages in writing behavior.") But in spite of the absence of abnormal symptoms, it took an average of 19 days for the pseudopatients to convince the hospital staff that they were ready for discharge. One unfortunate individual wasn't released for almost two months.

Two main findings from this classic study jarred the psychiatric community to its core. First, *no professional staff member at any of the hospitals ever realized that any of Rosenhan's pseudopatients was a fraud.* Of course, the staff may have assumed that the patients had been ill at the time of admission and had improved during their hospitalization. But that possibility did not let the professionals off Rosenhan's hook: Despite apparently normal behavior, not one pseudopatient was ever labeled as "normal" or "well" while in the hospital. And upon discharge, they were still seen as having schizophrenia—but "in remission."

The mistaken diagnosis does not suggest that the hospital staff members were unskilled or unfeeling. The fact that they did not detect the pseudopatients' normal behavior is probably because they spent little time observing and interacting with the patients. Most of the time they kept to themselves in a glassed-in central office that patients called "the cage." As Rosenhan (1973) said,

> It could be a mistake, and a very unfortunate one, to consider that what happened to us derived from malice or stupidity on the part of the staff. Quite the contrary, our overwhelming impression of them was of people who really cared, who were committed and who were uncommonly intelligent. Where they failed, as they sometimes did painfully, it would be more accurate to attribute those failures to the environment in which they, too, found themselves than to personal callousness. Their perceptions and behavior were controlled by the situation . . . (p. 257)

CONNECTION CHAPTER 14

Social psychology has taught us about the *power of the situation*—that is, the powerful and often unrecognized influence that the social context has on our behavior.

A second finding tells us volumes about the patients and the nature of psychological disorder itself: *To everyone's surprise, the hospital patients readily detected the ruse, even though the professional staff did not.* The pseudopatients reported that the other patients regularly voiced their suspicions: "You're not crazy. You're a journalist or a professor. . . . You're checking up on the hospital." In his report of this experience, entitled

"On Being Sane in Insane Places," Rosenhan (1973) noted dryly, "The fact that the patients often recognized normality when staff did not raises important questions" (p. 252). You will hear the echo of these "important questions" as we critically examine the medical view of mental disorder in this chapter.

Please note that Rosenhan did not deny the existence of psychological disorders. People do suffer the anguish of **psychopathology** (also called *mental disorder* or *mental illness*). According to a study conducted by the National Institutes of Mental Health, about 15.4% of the population suffers from diagnosable mental health problems. Another study found that during any given year, the behaviors of over 56 million Americans meet the criteria for a diagnosable psychological disorder (Carson et al., 1996; Regier et al., 1993). Over the lifespan, as many as 32% of Americans will suffer from some psychological disorder (Regier et al., 1988).

Neither did Rosenhan deny that the initial diagnoses given his pseudopatients were justified. After all, they claimed to be hearing voices—a strong indicator of abnormality. Rosenhan's interest in mental hospitals centered on the assumptions made there about people who have been diagnosed with a "mental illness." These conditions, he argued, blinded caregivers to the needs of their patients. As we look at the problem of diagnosing and describing psychological disorder in this chapter, it will be helpful to keep Rosenhan's study in mind. Even though this research was done some 30 years ago, the terms *abnormal, disorder,* and *mental illness* still carry meanings that can prevent us from seeing people with psychological problems as individuals.

KEY QUESTION

WHAT IS PSYCHOLOGICAL DISORDER?

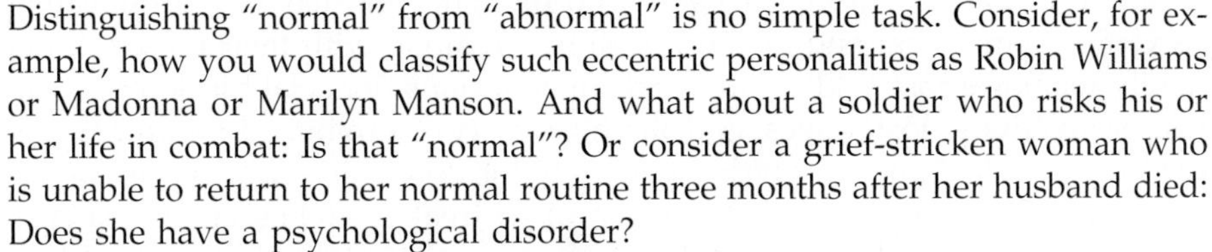

Distinguishing "normal" from "abnormal" is no simple task. Consider, for example, how you would classify such eccentric personalities as Robin Williams or Madonna or Marilyn Manson. And what about a soldier who risks his or her life in combat: Is that "normal"? Or consider a grief-stricken woman who is unable to return to her normal routine three months after her husband died: Does she have a psychological disorder?

More extreme disorders are more easily detected. Clinicians (specialists in the treatment of psychological problems) look for three classic symptoms of severe psychopathology: *hallucinations, delusions,* and extreme *affective disturbances.* **Hallucinations** are false sensory experiences, such as hearing nonexistent voices (as Rosenhan's pseudopatients said they did). **Delusions** are extreme disorders of thinking that involve persistent false beliefs. If you think you are the president of the United States (and you are not), you have a symptom of psychopathology. Or if you think people are out to "get" you, you may also have a delusional disorder. Similarly, those whose **affect** (emotion) is characteristically depressed, anxious, or manic—or those who seem to have no emotional response at all—have other possible signs of severe psychological disorder.

Beyond such extreme signs of distress, the experts do not always agree, however. What is abnormal and what is not become a judgment call, a judgment made more difficult because no sharp boundary separates normal from abnormal thought and behavior. It may be helpful to think of psychological disorder as part of a continuum ranging from the absence of disorder to severe disorder, as shown in Table 12.1. The big idea here is that people with

■ **Psychopathology** Any pattern of emotions, behaviors, or thoughts inappropriate to the situation and leading to personal distress or the inability to achieve important goals. Other terms having essentially the same meaning include *mental illness, mental disorder,* and *psychological disorder.*

■ **Hallucinations** False sensory experiences that may suggest mental disorder. Hallucinations can have other causes, such as drugs or sensory isolation.

■ **Delusions** Extreme disorders of thinking, involving persistent false beliefs. Delusions are the hallmark of paranoid disorders.

■ **Affect** A term referring to emotion or mood.

TABLE 12.1 The Spectrum of Mental Disorder

Mental disorder occurs on a spectrum that ranges from the absence of signs of pathology to severe disturbances, such as are found in major depression or schizophrenia. The important point is that there is no sharp distinction that divides those with mental disorders from those who are "normal."

No Disorder	Mild Disorder	Moderate Disorder	Severe Disorder
Absence of signs of psychological disorder	Few signs of distress or other indicators of psychological disorder	Indicators of disorder are more pronounced and occur more frequently	Clear signs of psychological disorder, which dominate the person's life
Absence of behavior problems	Few behavior problems; responses usually appropriate to the situation	More distinct behavior problems; behavior is often inappropriate to the situation	Severe and frequent behavior problems; behavior is usually inappropriate to the situation
No problems with interpersonal relationships	Few difficulties with relationships	More frequent difficulties with relationships	Many poor relationships or lack of relationships with others

psychological disorders are not in a class by themselves. Rather, their disorders are an exaggeration of normal responses.

In this section of the chapter, we will focus on two contrasting views of psychological disorder. One, coming to us from medicine, is sometimes called the medical model. It portrays mental problems much as it does physical disorders: as sickness or disease. The other view, a psychological view, sees psychological disorders as the result of multiple factors that can involve both nature and nurture. As our Core Concept puts it:

CORE CONCEPT

The medical model takes a "disease" view, while psychology sees psychological disorder as an interaction of biological, mental, social, and behavioral factors.

No matter how we conceptualize psychopathology, nearly everyone agrees that psychological disorder is common. It touches the daily lives of millions. It can be insidious, working its way into thoughts and feelings, diminishing its victims' emotional and physical well-being, along with their personal and family relationships. And it can create an enormous financial burden through lost productivity, lost wages, and the high costs of prolonged treatment. Yet the way people think of psychopathology does have a consequence: As we will see, it determines how they attempt to treat it—whether with drugs, charms, rituals, talk, torture, brain surgery, hospitalization, or commitment to an "insane asylum."

In this section of the chapter, we will find that the two main ways of looking at psychopathology, the medical model and the psychological view, are often at odds. Some of this conflict is territorial, resulting from professional infighting. But some of the conflict has historical roots, as we shall see next.

Changing Concepts of Psychological Disorder

Before December 10, 1973, homosexuality was considered an illness. But on that day the American Psychiatric Association voted to drop homosexuality from its list of officially recognized disorders. The membership had decided that this sexual orientation was not associated with mental problems, a decision that has since been shown repeatedly to be accurate—with the understandable exception of problems related to the stress of discrimination (Cochran et al., 2003; Meyer, 2003). This change, however, was only one of the most recent in a continuously evolving concept of mental disorder that stretches back thousands of years.

Historical Roots In the ancient world, people assumed that supernatural powers were everywhere, accounting for good fortune, disease, and disaster. In this context, psychopathology was believed to be caused by demons and spirits that had taken possession of the person's mind and body (Sprock & Blashfield, 1991). If you had been living in the ancient world, your daily routine would have included rituals aimed at outwitting or placating these supernatural beings.

In about 400 B.C., the Greek physician Hippocrates took humanity's first step toward a scientific view of mental disturbance when he declared that abnormal behavior has physical causes. He taught his disciples to interpret the symptoms of psychopathology as an imbalance among four body fluids called "humors": blood, phlegm (mucus), black bile, and yellow bile (see Figure 12.1). Those with an excess of black bile, for example, were inclined to melancholy or depression, while those who had an abundance of blood were sanguine, or warmhearted. With this revolutionary idea, Hippocrates incorporated mental disorder into medicine, and his view influenced educated people in the Western world until the end of the Roman Empire.

CONNECTION CHAPTER 10

Hippocrates' humor theory was a theory of *temperaments*.

Then, in the Middle Ages, superstition eclipsed the Hippocratic model of mental disorder. Under the influence of the medieval Church, physicians and clergy reverted to the old ways of explaining abnormality in terms of demons and witchcraft. In these harsh times, the Inquisition was driven by the belief that unusual behavior was the work of the Devil. The "cure" involved attempts to drive out the demons who possessed the unfortunate victim's soul. As a

Humors	Origin	Temperament
blood	heart	sanguine (cheerful)
choler (yellow bile)	liver	choleric (angry)
melancholer (black bile)	spleen	melancholy (depressed)
phlegm	brain	phlegmatic (sluggish)

● **FIGURE 12.1** Hippocrates' Humor Theory

In Hippocrates' view, mental disorder was caused by an excess of the body fluids, or "humors."

● A painting of the witchcraft trials held in Salem, Massachusetts, in 1692. Twenty people were executed before the hysteria subsided.

result, thousands of mentally disturbed people were tortured and executed all across the European continent. And in 1692, the same view of mental disorder led the young colony in Salem, Massachusetts, to convict and execute several of its residents for witchcraft (Karlsen, 1998). A group of young girls had frightened the community with a rash of convulsions and reports of sensory disturbances that were interpreted as signs of demonic possession. A modern analysis of the Salem witch trials has concluded that the girls were probably suffering from poisoning by a fungus growing on rye grain—the same fungus that produces the hallucinogenic drug LSD (Caporeal, 1976; Matossian, 1982, 1989).

The Medical Model In the latter part of the 18th century, the "disease" view that originated with Hippocrates reemerged with the rise of science. The resulting **medical model** held that mental disorders are *diseases* of the mind that, like ordinary physical diseases, have objective causes and require specific treatments. People began to perceive individuals with psychological problems as sick (suffering from illness), rather than as demon-possessed or immoral. And what a difference a new theory made! Treating mental disorders by torture and abuse no longer made sense. The new view of mental illness brought sweeping reforms that were implemented in "asylums" for the "insane." In this supportive atmosphere, many patients actually improved—even thrived—on rest, contemplation, and simple but useful work (Maher & Maher, 1985). Unfortunately, political pressures eventually turned the initially therapeutic asylums into overcrowded warehouses of neglect.

Despite such problems, however, the medical model was unquestionably an improvement over the demon model. Yet modern psychologists think that the medical model has its own weaknesses. They point out that the assumption of "disease" leads to a doctor-knows-best approach in which the therapist takes all the responsibility for diagnosing the illness and prescribing treatment. Under this assumption, the patient may become a passive recipient of medication and advice, rather than an active participant in treatment. Psychologists believe that this attitude wrongly encourages dependency on the doctor, encourages unnecessary drug therapy, and does little to help the patient develop good coping skills.

Not incidentally, a doctor-knows-best approach also takes responsibility away from psychologists and gives it to psychiatrists. Psychologists bristle at the medical model's implication that their treatment of mental "diseases" should be done under the supervision of a physician. In effect, the medical model assigns psychologists to second-class professional status. As you can see, ownership of the whole territory of psychological disorder is hotly contested.

CONNECTION: CHAPTER 1

Psychiatrists, but not psychologists, are trained in medicine.

Psychological Models What does psychology have to offer in place of the medical model? Most clinical psychologists have now turned to a combination of psychological perspectives that derive from *behaviorism, cognitive psychology, social learning,* and *biological psychology.* We will look at these more closely.

The Social–Cognitive–Behavioral Approach Modern psychologists often combine ideas from perspectives that were once considered incompatible: cognitive psychology and behaviorism. In brief, cognitive psychology looks inward, emphasizing mental processes, while behaviorism looks outward, emphasizing the influence of the environment. As we saw in the chapter on learning,

■ **Medical model** The view that mental disorders are diseases that, like ordinary physical diseases, have objective physical causes and require specific treatments.

bridges between these perspectives were built by social-learning theorists and others. As a result, a major shift in psychological thinking in recent years now views these traditions as complementary, rather than competitive. Moreover, both sides now acknowledge that cognition and behavior usually occur in a social context, requiring a *social perspective*.

The *behavioral perspective* tells us that abnormal behaviors can be acquired in the same fashion as healthy behaviors—through behavioral learning. This view focuses on our behavior and the environmental conditions, such as rewards, punishments, and social pressures, that maintain it. For example, the behavioral perspective would suggest that a fear of public speaking could result from a humiliating public speaking experience and a subsequent avoidance of any opportunity to develop public speaking skills.

The *cognitive perspective*, by contrast, suggests that we must also consider how people *perceive* or *think about* themselves and their relations with other people. Among the important cognitive variables are these: whether people believe they have control over events in their lives (an internal or external locus of control), how they cope with threat and stress, and whether they attribute behavior to situational or personal factors (Bandura, 1986).

The **social–cognitive–behavioral approach,** then, is a psychological alternative to the medical model, combining three of psychology's major perspectives. Typical of this approach is Albert Bandura's theory of *reciprocal determinism*, which proposes that behavior, cognition, and social/environmental factors all influence each other. From this viewpoint, a fear of public speaking can be understood as a product of behavioral learning, cognitive learning, and social learning.

● Phillippe Pinel was one of the first to humanely treat inmates with mental disorders. He is best known for removing the shackles from from mental patients at La Bicêtre hospital in Paris in 1792. To almost everyone's amazement, the patients responded favorably.

The Biopsychology of Mental Disorder Although most psychologists have reservations about the medical model, they do not deny the influence of biology on thought and behavior. Modern biopsychology assumes that some mental disturbances involve the brain or nervous system in some way, and this view is taking an increasingly prominent position. An explosion of research in neuroscience during the past decade confirms the role of the brain as a complex organ whose mental functions depend on a delicate balance of chemicals and ever-changing circuits. Subtle alterations in the brain's tissue or in its chemical messengers—the neurotransmitters—can profoundly alter thoughts and behaviors. Genetic factors, brain injury, infection, and learning are a few factors that can tip the balance toward psychopathology.

On the heredity front, the Human Genome Project has specified the complete human genetic package. Many psychologists see this accomplishment as a ripe opportunity for specialists in behavioral genetics who are searching for genes associated with specific psychological disorders (Plomin, 2003). It won't be easy, however. So far, only a few genetic abnormalities have been linked with specific mental problems, despite the fact that some of the most severe pathologies, such as schizophrenia and bipolar disorder, do run in families. Most such disorders are likely to result from multiple genes interacting with forces in the environment (Boomsma et al., 1997). Watch the news for further developments.

Indicators of Abnormality

While clinicians sometimes disagree about the *etiology* (causes) of psychological disorders, they usually agree broadly on the indicators of abnormality (Rosenhan & Seligman, 1995). What are these indicators? Earlier we noted that hallucinations, delusions, and extreme affective changes are signs of severe mental disorder. But many psychological problems don't reveal themselves in

■ **Social–cognitive–behavioral approach** A psychological alternative to the medical model that views psychological disorder through a combination of the social, cognitive, and behavioral perspectives.

such stark ways. Accordingly, clinicians also look for the following more subtle signs that may also indicate psychological disturbances, ranging from mild to severe (see Table 12.1):

- *Distress:* Does the individual show unusual or prolonged levels of unease or anxiety? For example, almost anyone will get nervous before an important test, but feeling so overwhelmed with unpleasant emotions that concentration becomes impossible for long periods is a sign of abnormality.
- *Maladaptiveness:* Does the person act in ways that make others fearful or interfere with his or her well-being? We can see this, for example, in someone who drinks so heavily that she or he cannot hold down a job or drive a car without endangering others.
- *Irrationality:* Does the person act or talk in ways that are irrational or incomprehensible to others? A woman who converses with her long-dead sister, whose voice she hears in her head, is behaving irrationally. Likewise, behavior or emotional responses that are inappropriate to the situation, such as laughing at the scene of a tragedy, show irrational loss of contact with one's social environment.
- *Unpredictability:* Does the individual behave erratically and inconsistently at different times or from one situation to another, as if experiencing a loss of control? For example, a child who suddenly smashes a fragile toy with his fist for no apparent reason is behaving unpredictably. Similarly, a manager who treats employees compassionately one day and abusively the next is acting unpredictably.
- *Unconventionality and undesirable behavior:* Does the person behave in ways that are statistically rare and violate social norms of what is legally or morally acceptable or desirable? Being merely "unusual" is not a sign of abnormality—so feel free to dye your hair red and green at Christmastime. But if you decide to act beyond the bounds of social acceptability by strolling naked in the mall, that would be considered abnormal.

Is the presence of just one indicator enough to demonstrate abnormality? It's a judgment call. Clinicians are more confident in labeling behavior as "abnormal" when two or more of the indicators are present. And the more extreme and prevalent the indicators are, the more confident psychologists can be about identifying an abnormal condition. Moreover, none of these criteria is a condition shared by all forms of disorder that we will describe later in this chapter. Different diagnoses, we shall see, include different combinations from the above list.

While these indicators may suggest a disorder, the clinician still must decide which disorder it is. This can be difficult, because psychopathology takes many forms. Some diagnoses may have a familiar ring: *depression, phobias,* and *panic disorder.* You may be less well acquainted with others, such as *conversion disorder* or *catatonic schizophrenia.* In all, a bewildering 300-plus specific varieties of psychopathology are described in the *Diagnostic and Statistical Manual of Mental Disorders* (4th edition), known by clinicians and researchers as the *DSM-IV* ("DSM-four") and used by mental health professionals of all backgrounds to describe and diagnose psychopathology. So influential is this system that we will devote the entire middle section of this chapter to an explanation of it.

● Behaviors that make other people feel uncomfortable or threatened may be a sign of abnormality.

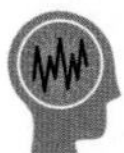

PSYCHOLOGY IN YOUR LIFE: A CAUTION TO READERS

As you read about the symptoms of psychological disorder, you are likely to wonder about your own mental health. All students studying abnormal psychology face this hazard. To see what we mean, you might answer the following questions, which are based on the indicators of abnormality discussed earlier.

1. Have you had periods of time when you felt "blue" for no apparent reason? (distress)
2. Have you ever gone to a party on a night when you knew you should be studying? (maladaptiveness)
3. Have you had an experience in which you thought you heard or saw something that wasn't really there? (irrationality)
4. Have you had a flash of temper in which you said something that you later regretted? (unpredictability)
5. Have you had unusual thoughts that you told no one about? (unconventionality)
6. Have you made someone fearful or distressed because of something you said or did? (maladaptiveness)

The fact is that almost everyone will answer "yes" to at least one—and perhaps all—of these questions. This does not necessarily mean abnormality. Whether you, or anyone else, is normal or abnormal is a matter of degree and frequency—and clinical judgment.

So, as we take a close look at specific psychological disorders in the next section of the chapter, you will most likely find some symptoms that you have experienced. So will your classmates. Even though they may not say so, most other students will find themselves in one or more of the disorders that we will be studying. (A similar problem is common among medical students, who begin to notice that they, too, have symptoms of the physical diseases they learn about.) You should realize that *this is normal.* One reason, of course, why you may see yourself in this chapter arises from the fact that no sharp line separates psychopathology from normalcy. All psychological disorders involve exaggerations of normal tendencies. Moreover, people who are basically healthy may occasionally become depressed, for example—although they do not *stay* depressed or develop the depths of despair that clinically depressed people do. We are not suggesting that concerns about psychological disorder should be taken lightly, however. If, after reading this chapter, you suspect that you may have a problem, you should discuss it with a professional.

● Sadness or crying is not necessarily a sign of abnormality. Some occasions call for sadness and tears.

CHECK YOUR UNDERSTANDING

1. **RECALL:** In Rosenhan's study, who discovered that the "pseudopatients" were feigning mental illness?
   a. psychiatrists
   b. psychologists
   c. nurses and aides working on the ward
   d. other patients
   e. other physicians

2. **APPLICATION:** Which of the following symptoms most clearly suggests the presence of abnormality?
   a. hallucinations
   b. worries
   c. unusual behavior
   d. creativity
   e. distraction

(*continues*)

3. **RECALL:** Hippocrates proposed that mental disorder was caused by
   a. possession by demons.
   b. an imbalance in four body fluids.
   c. a fungus growing on rye grain.
   d. traumatic memories in the unconscious.
   e. the taking of potions.

4. **RECALL:** The behavioral perspective emphasizes the influence of ______, while the cognitive perspective emphasizes ______.
   a. genetics/conscious processes
   b. conscious processes/unconscious processes
   c. heredity/environment
   d. medical factors/psychological factors
   e. the environment/mental processes

5. **UNDERSTANDING THE CORE CONCEPT:** Which of the following would be least likely to be noticed by a clinician using strictly the medical model of mental disorder?
   a. delusions
   b. severe disturbances in affect
   c. an unhealthy family environment
   d. a degenerative brain disease
   e. hallucinations.

ANSWERS: 1.d 2.a 3.b 4.e 5.c

HOW ARE PSYCHOLOGICAL DISORDERS CLASSIFIED?

Imagine that you have entered a music store looking for a particular CD. Anything you could possibly want is there, but the employees do not bother grouping albums by musical category: They just dump everything randomly into the bins. With so many selections, but no organization, shopping there would be impossible—which is why music stores never operate this way. Instead, they organize selections into categories, such as rock, blues, classical, rap, country, and jazz. In much the same way, the *Diagnostic and Statistical Manual of Mental Disorders* (4th ed.) brings order to the more than 300 recognized mental disorders. Usually called simply the ***DSM-IV,*** this manual represents the most widely used system for classifying such disorders. We will use it as the scheme for organizing the disorders we have selected for discussion in this chapter.

What is the organizing pattern employed by the *DSM-IV?* It groups nearly all recognized forms of psychopathology into categories, according to mental and behavioral symptoms, such as anxiety, depression, sexual problems, and substance abuse. Our Core Concept states:

The DSM-IV, the most widely used system, classifies disorders by their mental and behavioral symptoms.

It would be impossible to cover all the recognized psychological disorders in this chapter. Therefore, we must focus on those that you are most likely to encounter in daily life and in the study of psychopathology in more advanced courses.

Overview of the *DSM-IV* Classification System

The fourth edition of the *Diagnostic and Statistical Manual of Mental Disorders,* the *DSM-IV,* was published in 1994 by the American Psychiatric Association. Then, in 2000, that volume was given a midedition update, the *DSM-IV-TR* (TR means *Text Revision*). It offers practitioners a common and concise language for the description of psychopathology. It also contains criteria for diagnosing each of the disorders it covers. Even though the manual was developed primarily by psychiatrists, its terminology has been adopted by clinicians of all stripes, including psychiatrists, psychologists, and social workers. In addi-

■ ***DSM-IV*** The fourth edition of the *Diagnostic and Statistical Manual of Mental Disorders,* published by the American Psychiatric Association; the classification system most widely accepted psychiatric in the United States.

tion, most health insurance companies use *DSM-IV* standards in determining what treatments they will pay for—a fact that gives this manual enormous economic clout.

The *DSM-IV* also helps psychologists and psychiatrists look at the entire person as they make their evaluation. This process is known as *multiaxial diagnosis.* In multilaxial diagnosis, professionals consider not only the "abnormal" behavior but also general medical conditions (Axis 3, see Table 12.2), psychosocial and environmental problems (Axis 4), and global assessment of functioning (Axis 5). By looking beyond just the disorder, psychologists and psychiatrists can treat the whole person, and not just the individual's symptoms.

The fourth edition of the *DSM* has brought with it some big changes. For example, it has banished the term *neurosis* from the official language of psychiatry (although you will frequently hear the term used in more casual conversation). Originally, a **neurosis** or *neurotic disorder* was conceived of as a relatively common pattern of subjective distress or self-defeating behavior that did not show signs of brain abnormalities or grossly irrational thinking. In short, a "neurotic" was someone who might be unhappy or dissatisfied but was not considered dangerously ill or out of touch with reality. In the *DSM-IV,* the term *neurosis* has been dropped or replaced by the term *disorder* (Carson et al., 1996; Holmes, 2001). So, for example, "obsessive–compulsive neurosis" is now simply *obsessive–compulsive disorder.*

Dutch artist Vincent Van Gogh showed signs of bipolar disorder. This problem seems to have a high incidence among very creative people.

In contrast, a **psychosis** was previously thought to differ from neurosis in both the quality and the severity of symptoms. A condition was frequently designated as *psychotic* if it involved profound disturbances in perception, rational thinking, or affect (emotion)—the three classic signs we discussed earlier. As a result, a clinician using previous editions of the *DSM* would have been more likely to diagnose severe depression, for example, as "psychotic." In the *DSM-IV*, the term *psychotic* is restricted mainly to a loss of contact with reality, as is found in the *schizophrenic disorders,* which we shall discuss below (Carson et al., 1996; Holmes, 2001).

TABLE 12.2 Multiaxial Diagnosis

Axis 1	Clinical disorders
Axis 2	Personality disorders Mental retardation
Axis 3	General medical conditions
Axis 4	Psychosocial and environmental problems
Axis 5	Global assessment of functioning

As you may have surmised from its origins in psychiatry, the *DSM-IV* has close ties to the medical model of mental illness. Its language is the language of medicine—symptoms, syndromes, diagnoses, and diseases—and its final form is a curious mixture of science and tradition. (Note: It contains no diagnosis of "normal.") Yet, in contrast with early versions of the manual, which had a distinctly Freudian flavor, the *DSM-IV* manages, for the most part, to avoid endorsing theories of cause or treatment. It also differs from early versions of the *DSM* in giving extensive and specific descriptions of the symptoms of each disorder. So, while the *DSM-IV* has its critics, the need for a common language of psychological disorder has brought it wide acceptance.

Mood Disorders: Extremes of Mood, from Mania to Depression

- Major depression
- Bipolar disorder

Let us turn now to a sampling of disorders described in the *DSM-IV.* A look at the chart in the margin will give you an overview of the scheme the manual uses to classify these disorders. We begin with those that involve sustained extremes of emotion: the *mood disorders.*

Mood Disorders

Everyone, of course, experiences occasional strong or unpleasant emotional reactions. Emotionality is a normal part of our ability to interpret and adapt to our world. However, when moods careen out of control, soaring to extreme elation or plunging to deep depression, the diagnosis will probably be one of the **mood disorders.** The clinician will also suspect an affective disorder when

Neurosis Before the *DSM-IV,* this term was used as a label for subjective distress or self-defeating behavior that did not show signs of brain abnormalities or grossly irrational thinking.

Psychosis A disorder involving profound disturbances in perception, rational thinking, or affect.

Mood disorders Abnormal disturbances in emotion or mood, including bipolar disorder and unipolar disorder. Mood disorders are also called affective disorders.

■ **Major depression** A form of depression that does not alternate with mania.

an individual's moods are consistently inappropriate to the situation. Here we will discuss the two best-known of these affective disturbances: *major depression* and *bipolar disorder.*

Major Depression If you fail an important examination, lose a job, or lose a love, it is normal to feel depressed for a while. If a close friend dies, it is also normal to feel depressed. But if you remain depressed for weeks or months, long after the depressing event has passed, then you may have the clinically significant condition called **major depression** or *major depressive disorder,* which is among the commonest of all major mental disturbances.

Novelist William Styron (1990) writes movingly about his own experience with severe depression. The pain he endured convinced him that clinical depression is much more than a bad mood: He characterized it as "a daily presence, blowing over me in cold gusts" and "a veritable howling tempest in the brain" that can begin with a "gray drizzle of horror." Major depression does not give way to manic periods.

Incidence Psychologist Martin Seligman (1973, 1975) has called depression the "common cold" of psychological problems. Nearly everyone has, at some time, suffered either major depression or a milder form that clinicians call *dysthymia.* In the United States, depression accounts for the majority of all mental hospital admissions, but it is still believed to be underdiagnosed and undertreated (Kessler et al, 2003; Robins et al., 1991). The *Wall Street Journal* estimates that depression costs Americans about $43 billion each year, including the costs of hospitalization, therapy, and lost productivity (Miller, 1993). But the human cost cannot be measured in dollars. Countless people in the throes of depression may feel worthless, lack appetite, withdraw from friends and family, have difficulty sleeping, lose their jobs, and become agitated or lethargic. In severe cases, they may also experience psychotic distortions of reality. You can give yourself a quick evaluation for signs of depression in the box "Do It Yourself! A Depression Check," on the facing page.

Most worrisome of all, suicide claims one in 50 depression sufferers (Bostwick & Pankratz, 2000). Significantly, suicide is a greater risk when a depressed person is on the way down in a depressive episode—or is on the mend. That is, in the depths of depressive despair, there is usually no energy or will to do *anything,* much less carry out a plan for suicide.

Incidentally, we advise that a suicide threat always be taken seriously, even though you may think it is just a bid for attention—and even if you see no further signs of depression. Other factors may be at work. Abuse of alcohol or other drugs, for example, multiplies the likelihood of suicide, as do chronic physical diseases or brain abnormalities (Ezzell, 2003; Shneidman, 1987). You should direct any person who suggests he or she is thinking about suicide to a competent professional for help.

Cross-cultural studies indicate that depression is the single most prevalent form of disability around the globe (Holden, 2000a), although the incidence of major depression varies widely throughout the world, as Table 12.3 shows. While some of the variation may be the result of differences in reporting and in readiness or reluctance to seek help for depression, other factors seem to be at work, too. In Taiwan and Korea, for example, these factors include low rates of marital separation and divorce—factors known to be associated with high risk of depression in virtually all cultures. On the other hand, the stresses of war have undoubtedly inflated the rate of depression in the Middle East (Horgan, 1996; Weissman et al., 1996).

TABLE 12.3 Lifetime Risk of a Depressive Episode Lasting a Year or More

Taiwan	1.5%
Korea	2.9%
Puerto Rico	4.3%
United States	5.2%
Germany	9.2%
Canada	9.6%
New Zealand	11.6%
France	16.4%
Lebanon	19%

DO IT YOURSELF! | A Depression Check

Most people think that depression is marked by outward signs of sadness, such as weeping. But depression affects other aspects of thought and behavior as well. For a quick check on your own tendencies to depression, please answer "yes" or "no" to each of the following questions, all adapted from the signs of depression listed in the *DSM-IV:*

1. Do you feel deeply depressed, sad, or hopeless most of the day?
2. Do you feel you have lost interest in most or all activities?
3. Have you experienced any major change in appetite or body weight, though not from dieting?
4. Have you experienced a significant change in your sleeping patterns?
5. Do you feel more restless than usual—or more sluggish than usual?
6. Do you feel more fatigued than you ought to?
7. Do you feel persistently hopeless or inappropriately guilty?
8. Have you been finding it increasingly difficult to think or concentrate?
9. Do you have recurrent thoughts of death or suicide?

Your answers to these items do not constitute any proof that you are, or are not, depressed. While there is no "magic number" of items you must answer "yes" in order to qualify as depressed, if you answered "yes" to some of them and if you are concerned, you might want to seek a professional opinion. Remember that a diagnosis of depression is a clinical judgment call, based on the signs listed in the *DSM-IV:* Essentially, it is the pattern and the quality of your life, your feelings, and your behavior that determine whether or not you are depressed. Remember also that self-report is always subject to some bias. If you are concerned after considering the signs of depression in your life, we recommend an examination by a competent mental health professional, who will take into account not only your self-descriptions but also your behavior, your social context, and the rewards and aversive circumstances in your life.

Causes of Depression Some cases of major depression almost certainly involve a genetic predisposition. Severe bouts with depression often run in families (Andreasen et al., 1987; Plomin et al., 1994; Weissman et al., 1986). Further indication of a biological basis for depression comes from the favorable response that many depressed patients have to drugs that affect the brain's neurotransmitters norepinephrine, serotonin, and dopamine (Ezzell, 2004; Hirschfeld & Goodwin, 1988; Nemeroff, 1998). Evidence also indicates that depression is related to lower brain wave activity in the left frontal lobe (Davidson, 1992a, b, 2000; Robbins, 2000). In a few cases, depression may be caused by viral infection (Bower, 1995b). Such evidence leads some observers to believe that depression is really a collection of disorders having a variety of causes (Kendler & Gardner, 1998).

A special form of depression seems to be related to sunlight deprivation. It appears most frequently during the long, dark winter months among people who live in high latitudes (Wehr & Rosenthal, 1989). (See Figure 12.2.) This aptly named **seasonal affective disorder** (technically defined as seasonal pattern specifier), or **SAD,** is related to levels of the light-sensitive hormone melatonin, which regulates our internal biological clocks (Campbell & Murphy, 1998; Oren & Terman, 1998). Based on this knowledge, researchers have

■ **Seasonal affective disorder (SAD)** Technically *Seasonal pattern specifier,* this *DSM-IV* course specifier for mood disorders is believed to be a form of depression caused by deprivation of sunlight. The term "Course Specifier" is used to describe how a disorder progresses.

CONNECTION CHAPTER 5

The "biological clock," located in the hypothalamus, regulates our *circadian rhythms.*

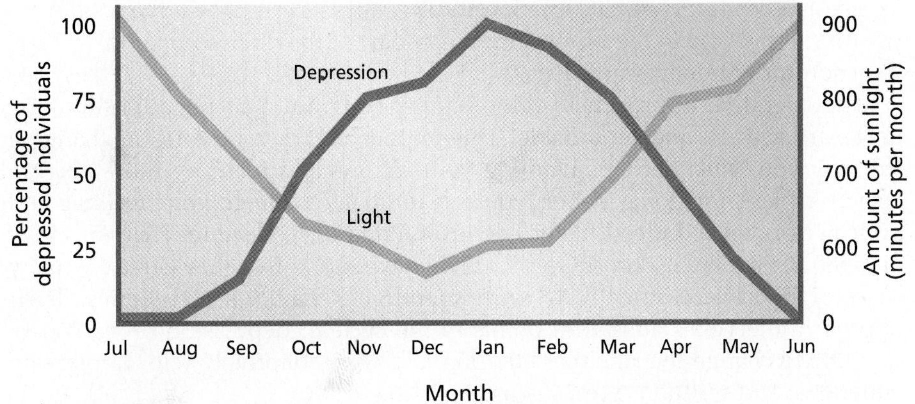
Percentage of depressed individuals
100
75
50
25
0
Depression
Light
900
800
700
600
0
Amount of sunlight (minutes per month)
Jul
Aug
Sep
Oct
Nov
Dec
Jan
Feb
Mar
Apr
May
Jun
Month

● **FIGURE 12.2** Seasonal Affective Disorder

People who suffer from seasonal affective disorder are most likely to experience symptoms of depression during months with shortened periods of sunlight. (*Source:* Adaptation of Fig. 1, p. 74 from "Seasonal Affective Disorder: A Description of the Syndrome and Preliminary Findings with Light Therapy" by N. E. Rosenthal et al., *Archives of General Psychiatry, 41* (1984), pp. 72–80. American Medical Association.

● **FIGURE 12.3** The Cognitive–Behavioral Cycle of Depression

As you follow Fred around the cycle, note how his depression feeds on itself.

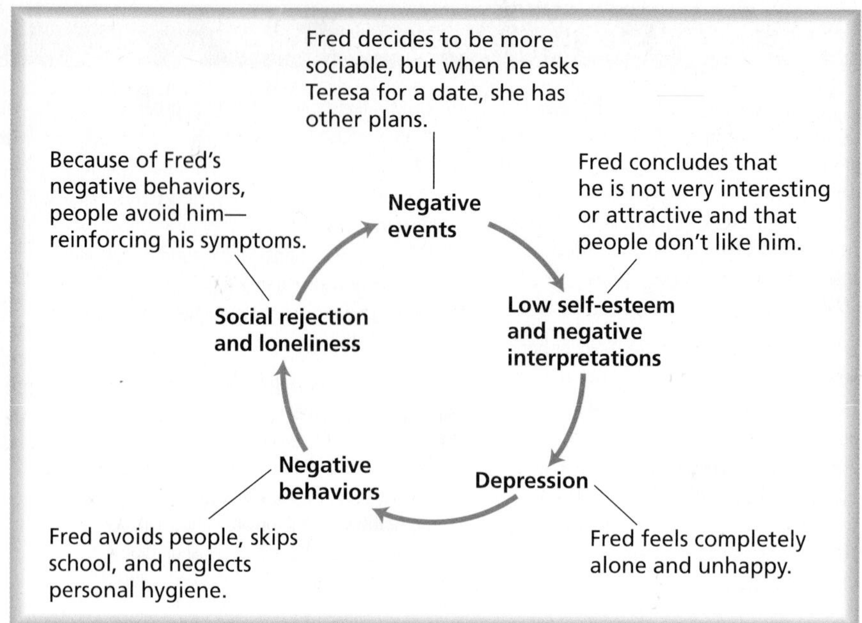
Fred decides to be more sociable, but when he asks Teresa for a date, she has other plans.
Negative events
Fred concludes that he is not very interesting or attractive and that people don't like him.
Low self-esteem and negative interpretations
Depression
Fred feels completely alone and unhappy.
Negative behaviors
Fred avoids people, skips school, and neglects personal hygiene.
Social rejection and loneliness
Because of Fred's negative behaviors, people avoid him—reinforcing his symptoms.

developed an effective therapy that regulates melatonin by exposing SAD sufferers daily to bright artificial light (Lewy et al., 1987).

Biology alone cannot entirely explain depression, however. We must also understand it as a mental, social, and behavioral condition. Initially, a negative event, such as losing a job, can make anyone feel depressed, but low self-esteem and a pessimistic attitude can fuel a cycle of depressive thought patterns (Abramson et al., 1989; Sweeney et al., 1986; Wood et al., 1990a, b). (See Figure 12.3.) Probably because of low self-esteem, depression-prone people are more likely to perpetuate the depression cycle by attributing negative events to their own personal flaws or external conditions that they feel helpless to change (Azar, 1994; Robins, 1988; Seligman, 1991; Seligman et al., 1979). Martin Seligman calls this *learned helplessness.* The resulting negative self-evaluation generates a depressed mode, which leads in turn to negative behaviors such as crying. These behaviors encourage others to avoid the depressed individual. Consequently, depressed people feel rejected and lonely, which also feeds the cycle of their despair (Coyne et al., 1991).

If you think this description of depression sounds a lot like the definition of stress that we gave in Chapter 8—you're right! One of the most promising approaches to research on this disorder sees depression as fundamentally a stress disorder (Holden, 2003b). Specifically, stress hormones adversely affect neurons, especially in the hippocampus—a part of the brain known to be a site of action for antidepressant drugs.

The cognitive approach to depression points out that negative thinking styles are learned and modifiable. This implies that if you work on changing the way you *think,* perhaps blaming yourself less and focusing more on constructive plans for doing better, you can ultimately change your feelings and your performance. Indeed, Peter Lewinsohn and his colleagues (Lewinsohn et al., 1980, 1990; Lewinsohn & Gottlib, 1995) have found that they can treat many cases of depression effectively with cognitive–behavioral techniques. Their approach intervenes at several points in the cycle of depression to teach people how to change their helpless thinking, to cope adaptively with unpleasant situations, and to build more rewards into their lives.

Who Becomes Depressed? Clinicians have noted that depression rates are higher for women than for men (Leutwyler, 1995; Strickland, 1992; Weissman et al., 1996). According to Susan Nolen-Hoeksema (1987, 1990, 2001), the difference may lie in the differing response styles of men and women who are experiencing negative moods. When women experience sadness, she says, they tend to think about the possible causes and implications of their feelings. In contrast, men attempt to distract themselves from depressed feelings, either by shifting their attention to something else or by engaging in a physical activity that will take their minds off their mood. This model suggests that the more *ruminative* response of women—characterized by a tendency to concentrate on problems—increases women's vulnerability to depression (Shea, 1998).

The incidence of depression and the age at which it strikes are changing—at least in the United States. According to Martin Seligman, depression is between 10 and 20 times as common as it was 50 years ago (National Press Club, 1999). In the mid-1900s, most casualties of depression were middle-aged women, but now depression is more often a teenage problem—still more prevalent in females than in males (NIMH, 2000). Seligman, who has studied depression extensively, blames this increase in occurrence and decrease in age to three factors: (1) an out-of-control individualism and self-centeredness that focuses on individual success and failure, rather than group accomplishments; (2) the self-esteem movement, which has taught a generation of schoolchildren that they should feel good about themselves, irrespective of their efforts and achievements; and (3) a culture of *victimology,* which reflexively points the finger of blame at someone or something else.

Bipolar Disorder Another mood disorder also involves periods of depression—but, in addition, alternating periods of extreme elation. Formerly known as *manic–depressive disorder,* the condition is now listed in the *DSM-IV* as **bipolar disorder.** The alternating periods of *mania* (excessive elation or manic excitement) and the profound sadness of depression represent the two "poles."

During the manic phase, the individual becomes euphoric, energetic, hyperactive, talkative, and emotionally wound tight like a spring. It is not unusual for people, swept up in mania, to spend their life savings on extravagant purchases or to engage promiscuously in a number of sexual liaisons or other potentially high-risk actions. When the mania diminishes, they are left to deal with the damage they have created during their frenetic period. Soon, in the depressive phase, a dark wave of melancholy sweeps over the mind, producing symptoms indistinguishable from the "unipolar" form of depression we discussed earlier. Biologically speaking, however, these two forms of depression differ: We know this because the antidepressant drugs that work well on major depression are not usually effective for bipolar disorder.

A genetic component in bipolar disorder is well established, although the exact genes involved have not been pinpointed (Bradbury, 2001; Plomin et al., 1994). While only 1% of the general population has bipolar attacks, having an identical twin afflicted with the problem inflates one's chances to about 70% (Allen, 1976; Tsuang & Faraone, 1990). The fact that bipolar disorder usually responds well to medication also suggests biological factors at work.

Anxiety Disorders

Would you pick up a snake or let a tarantula rest on your shoulder? For some people the mere thought of snakes or spiders is enough to send chills of fear down their spines. Everyone, of course, has experienced anxiety or fear in threatening or dangerous situations. But pathological anxiety is far more severe than the normal anxiety associated with life's challenges. It is also relatively

■ **Bipolar disorder** A mental abnormality involving swings of mood from mania to depression.

Anxiety Disorders: Fear, Anxiety, Panic Attacks

- Generalized anxiety disorder
- Panic disorder
- Agoraphobia
- Specific phobias
- Obsessive–compulsive disorder

common—even more common than major depression (Barlow, 2000). One estimate says that 15% of the general population has, at some time, experienced symptoms that are serious enough to qualify as one of the **anxiety disorders** recognized in the *DSM* (Regier et al., 1988).

Here we will review four major disorders that have anxiety as their main feature: (1) generalized anxiety disorder, (2) panic disorder, (3) phobic disorder, and (4) obsessive–compulsive disorder. You will note that the major differences among them have to do with the focus and duration of anxiety: Is anxiety present only occasionally or most of the time? Does the anxiety seem to come from nowhere—unrelated to the individual's environment or behavior? Does it come from an external object or situation, such as the sight of blood or a snake? Does it involve the victim's own ritualistic behavior, as in a person who compulsively avoids stepping on cracks in the sidewalk? (See the chart in the margin.)

Generalized Anxiety Disorder Some people spend months or years of their lives coping with anxiety. Charles, a heavy-equipment operator, says he has dizzy spells, headaches, cold sweats, and frequent feelings of anxiety. But he has no clue why he feels anxious. It's free-floating anxiety, as clinicians sometimes call it, and they would diagnose his condition as **generalized anxiety disorder.** People with this disorder have a pervasive and persistent sense of anxiety. They are not just worried or fearful about specific situations or objects, such as heights or spiders. Nor does the anxiety come in waves, punctuated by periods of relative calm. Such patterns of anxiety signify different anxiety disorders, to which we turn next.

Panic Disorder While you are calmly eating lunch, an unexpected wave of panic sweeps over you, seemingly from nowhere. Your heart races, your body shakes, you feel dizzy, your hands become clammy and sweaty, you are afraid that you might be dying. You are having a *panic attack.*

The distinguishing feature of **panic disorder** is a strong feeling of anxiety that has no connection with present events (Barlow, 2001). As in generalized anxiety disorder, the feeling is one of "free-floating anxiety." Attacks usually last for only a few minutes and then subside (McNally, 1994). Because of the unexpected nature of these "hit-and-run" attacks, *anticipatory anxiety* often develops as an added complication. The dread of the next attack and of being helpless and suddenly out of control can lead a person to avoid public places, and yet fear being left alone. Cognitive–behavioral theorists view panic attacks as conditioned responses to physical sensations that may have initially been learned during a period of stress (Antony et al., 1992).

CONNECTION CHAPTER 8

The brain has two main *emotional pathways;* one operates mainly at an unconscious level.

Biologically, we have evidence of a genetic influence in panic disorder (Plomin et al., 1994). However, the brain mechanism responsible for this condition probably lies in the limbic system—especially in the amygdala, which appears abnormal on PET scans of many patients (Barlow, 2000, 2001; Resnick, 1992). Significantly, it is this part of the brain that houses the unconscious emotional-arousal pathway described by Joseph LeDoux (1996). Overstimulation of these circuits can produce lasting physical changes that make the individual more susceptible to anxiety attacks in the future (Rosen & Schulkin, 1998).

To complicate matters, many victims of panic disorder have additional symptoms of **agoraphobia.** This condition involves panic that develops when they find themselves in situations from which they cannot easily escape, such as crowded public places or open spaces (Antony et al., 1992; Magee et al., 1996). The term *agoraphobia* is a literal translation from the ancient Greek for "fear of the marketplace." Victims of agoraphobia often fear that if they experience an attack in one of these locations, help might not be available or the

■ **Anxiety disorders** Mental problems characterized mainly by anxiety. Anxiety disorders include panic disorder, specific phobias, and obsessive–compulsive disorder.

■ **Generalized anxiety disorder** A psychological problem characterized by persistent and pervasive feelings of anxiety, without any external cause.

■ **Panic disorder** A disturbance marked by panic attacks that have no obvious connection with events in the person's present experience. Unlike generalized anxiety disorder, the victim is usually free of anxiety between panic attacks.

■ **Agoraphobia** A fear of public places and open spaces, commonly accompanying panic disorder.

situation will be embarrassing to them. These fears deprive afflicted persons of their freedom, and some become prisoners in their own homes. If the disorder becomes this extreme, they cannot hold a job or carry on normal daily activities.

You may know someone who has panic disorder or agoraphobia. These problems occur in about 2% of the population (McNally, 1994), and they are much more common in women than in men. Fortunately, the treatment outlook is good. Medical therapy involves antianxiety drugs to relieve the panic attacks. Purely psychological treatment is also effective: Studies have shown that cognitive–behavioral therapy may equal or outperform drug therapy in combating panic attacks ("Cognitive–Behavior Therapy," 1991; Craske et al., 1991).

METRO
NETWORKS

A common form of social phobia involves an extreme fear of public speaking.

Phobic Disorders In contrast with panic disorder, **phobias** involve a persistent and irrational fear of a specific object, activity, or situation—a response all out of proportion to the circumstances. (These are sometimes called *specific phobias,* as contrasted with the broader fears found in agoraphobia.) Many of us respond fearfully to certain stimuli, such as spiders or snakes—or perhaps to multiple-choice tests! But these emotional responses become full-fledged phobic disorders only when they cause substantial disruption to our lives.

Phobias are relatively common. Studies suggest that 12.5% of Americans suffer from a phobic disorder at some point in their lives (Regier et al., 1988). Some specific phobias are quite rare, as in a fear of a certain type of insect. Others, such as fear of public speaking, are quite common—so common that they seem almost normal (Stein et al., 1996). (See Table 12.4.) Among the most common phobic disorders are *social phobias,* irrational fears of normal social situations (Magee et al., 1996). Phobic responses to heights (acrophobia), snakes (ophidiophobia), and closed-in spaces (claustrophobia) are also common.

What causes phobias? Long ago, John Watson and Rosalie Rayner demonstrated that fears can be learned. We also have abundant evidence that fears and phobias can be unlearned through cognitive–behavioral therapy based on conditioning. But learning may not tell the whole story. Martin Seligman (1971) has argued that humans are biologically predisposed to learn some kinds of fears more easily than others. This **preparedness hypothesis** suggests that we carry an innate biological tendency, acquired through natural selection, to respond quickly and automatically to stimuli that posed a survival threat to our ancestors (Öhman & Mineka, 2001). This explains why we develop phobias for snakes and lightning much more easily than we develop fears for automobiles and electrical outlets—objects that have posed a danger only in recent times.

CONNECTION CHAPTER 6

Watson and Rayner's infamous experiment with Little Albert showed that fears could be learned by *classical conditioning.*

Obsessive–Compulsive Disorder Seventeen-year-old Jim seemed to be a normal adolescent with many talents and interests. Then, almost overnight, he was transformed into a lonely outsider, excluded from social life by his psychological disabilities. Specifically, he developed an obsession with washing. Haunted by the notion that he was dirty—in spite of what his senses told him—Jim began to spend more and more time cleansing himself. At first his ritual ablutions were confined to weekends and evenings, but soon they consumed all his time, forcing him to drop out of school (Rapoport, 1989).

Jim had developed **obsessive–compulsive disorder,** or *OCD,* a condition characterized by patterns of persistent, unwanted thoughts and behaviors. Obsessive–compulsive disorder affects about 2.5% of Americans at some point during their lives (Regier et al., 1988). Nearly everyone has had some of its symptoms in a mild form.

The *obsession* component of OCD consists of thoughts, images, or impulses that recur or persist despite a person's efforts to suppress them. For example, a person with an obsessive fear of germs may avoid using bathrooms outside

Phobias A group of anxiety disorders involving a pathological fear of a specific object or situation.

Preparedness hypothesis The notion that we have an innate tendency, acquired through natural selection, to respond quickly and automatically to stimuli that posed a survival threat to our ancestors.

Obsessive–compulsive disorder A condition characterized by patterns of persistent, unwanted thoughts and behaviors.

TABLE 12.4	Phobias	
DSM-IV Category	Object/Situation	Incidence
Agoraphobia	Crowds, open spaces	Common (3.5–7% of adults)
Social phobias	Fear of being observed or doing something humiliating	common (11–15%)
Specific phobias	Varies by category	(up to 16% of adults)
Animals	Cats (ailurophobia)	
	Dogs (cynophobia)	
	Insects (insectophobia)	
	Spiders (arachnophobia)	
	Birds (avisophobia)	
	Horses (equinophobia)	
	Snakes (ophidiophobia)	
	Rodents (rodentophobia)	
Inanimate objects or situations	Closed spaces (claustrophobia)	
	Dirt (mysophobia)	
	Thunder (brontophobia)	
	Lightning (astraphobia)	
	Heights (acrophobia)	
	Darkness (nyctophobia)	
	Fire (pyrophobia)	
Bodily conditions	Illness or injury (nosophobia)	
	Sight of blood (hematophobia)	
	Cancer (cancerophobia)	
	Venereal disease (venerophobia)	
	Death (thanatophobia)	
Other specific phobias	Numbers (numerophobia)	
	The number 13 (triskaidekaphobia)	
	Strangers, foreigners (xenophobia)	
	String (linonophobia)	rare
	Books (bibliophobia)	rare
	Work (ergophobia)	rare

Note: Hundreds of phobias have been described and given scientific names; this table provides only a sample. Some of the rare and strange-sounding phobias may have been observed only in a single patient.

his or her home or refuse to shake hands with strangers. And, because sufferers realize that their obsessive thoughts and compulsive rituals are senseless, they often go to great lengths to hide their compulsive behavior from other people. This, of course, places restrictions on their domestic, social, and work lives. Not surprisingly, OCD patients have extremely high divorce rates.

You probably have had some sort of mild obsessional experience, such as petty worries ("Did I remember to lock the door?") or a haunting phrase or melody that kept running through your mind. Such thoughts are normal if they occur only occasionally and have not caused significant disruptions of your life. As we have noted in other disorders, it is a matter of degree.

Compulsions, the other half of obsessive–compulsive disorder, are repetitive, purposeful acts performed according to certain private "rules," in response to an obsession. Victims feel that their compulsive behavior will reduce the tension associated with their obsessions. Typical compulsions include irresistible urges to clean, to check that lights or appliances have been turned off, and to count objects or possessions. When they are calm, people with obsessive–compulsive disorder view the compulsion as senseless, but when their anxiety rises, they can't resist performing the compulsive behavior ritual to relieve tension. Part of the pain experienced by people with this problem is that they are frustrated by the irrationality of their obsessions and their powerlessness to eliminate them.

The tendency for OCD to run in families suggests a genetic link. Another hint comes from the finding that many people with OCD also display *tics,* unwanted involuntary movements, such as exaggerated eye blinks. In these patients, brain imaging often shows oddities in the deep motor control areas, suggesting something amiss in the brain (Resnick, 1992). OCD expert Judith Rapoport tells us to think of compulsions as "fixed software packages" programmed in the brain. Once activated, she theorizes, the patient gets caught in a behavioral "loop" that cannot be switched off (Rapoport, 1989).

● Obsessive–compulsive disorder makes people engage in senseless, ritualistic behaviors, such as repetitive hand washing.

Curiously, certain drugs that are commonly prescribed for depression can alleviate both the obsessions and the compulsive rituals (Poling et al., 1991). In further support of a biological basis for OCD, investigators have found that these drugs can reverse compulsive behavior in dogs that display a preoccupation with grooming themselves (Ross, 1992).

Again, however, we must note that biology cannot explain everything. Some victims of OCD have clearly *learned* that their anxiety-provoking thoughts are connected to harmful consequences (Barlow, 2000). Further evidence that learning plays a role can be seen in the results of behavioral therapy, which is effective in reducing compulsive actions. The behavioral strategy for treating compulsive hand-washing, for example, calls for a form of extinction, in which the therapist soils the patient's hands and prevents him or her from washing for progressively longer periods. Indeed, behavioral therapy can produce changes that show up in PET scans of OCD sufferers' brains (Schwartz et al., 1996). Thus, when we change behavior, we inevitably change the wiring of the obsessive–compulsive brain. This disorder shows us, once again, that biology and behavior are inseparable.

Somatoform Disorders

"Soma" means *body.* Thus, we use the term **somatoform disorders** for psychological problems appearing in the form of bodily symptoms or physical complaints, such as weakness or excessive worry about disease. The somatoform disorders are not especially common, occurring in about 2% of the population (Holmes, 2001). Yet despite their rarity, they have captured the popular imagination under their more common names: "hysteria" and "hypochondria." (See the chart in the margin.)

Somatoform Disorders: Physical Symptoms or Overconcern with One's Health

- Conversion disorder
- Hypochondriasis

The *DSM-IV* recognizes several types of somatoform disorders, but we will cover only two: *conversion disorder* and *hypochondriasis.* And, while we're talking about somatoform disorders, please note their potential for confusion with *psychosomatic disorders,* in which mental conditions—especially stress—lead to actual physical disease. The *DSM-IV* places psychosomatic disorders under a separate heading, "Psychological Factors Affecting Medical Condition."

■ **Somatoform disorders** Psychological problems appearing in the form of bodily symptoms or physical complaints, such as weakness or excessive worry about disease. The somatoform disorders include conversion disorder and hypochondriasis.

■ **Conversion disorder** A type of somatoform disorder, marked by paralysis, weakness, or loss of sensation but with no discernible physical cause.

Conversion Disorder Paralysis, weakness, or loss of sensation—with no discernible physical cause—distinguishes **conversion disorder** (formerly called "hysteria"). Patients with this diagnosis may, for example, be blind, deaf,

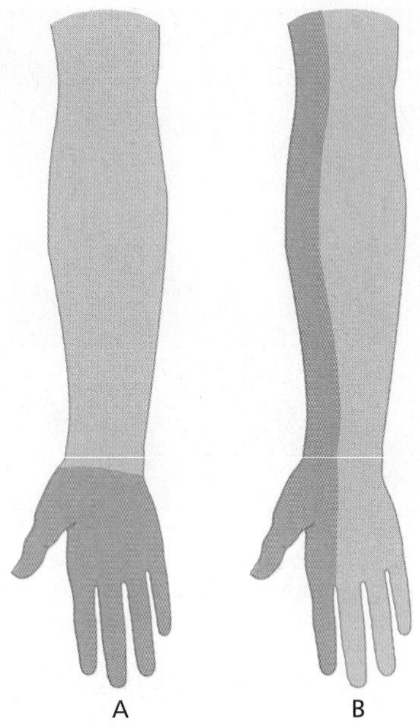
A
B

● **FIGURE 12.4** Glove Anesthesia
The form of conversion disorder known as "glove anesthesia" (A) involves a loss of sensation in the hand, as though the patient were wearing a thick glove. This cannot be a neurological disorder because the pattern of "anesthesia" does not correspond to the actual pattern of nerves in the hand, shown in (B).

unable to walk, or insensitive to touch in part of their bodies. Yet they have no organic disease that shows up on neurological examinations, laboratory tests, or X rays. In conversion disorder, the problem really is "all in the mind."

"Glove anesthesia" represents a classic form of conversion disorder. As you can see in Figure 12.4, the pattern of insensitivity to touch or pain fits the patient "like a glove." The tip-off that the problem is *psychogenic,* not physical, comes from the pattern of the patient's symptoms: They do not match any possible pattern of nerve impairment. Other cases, however, are not always so clear-cut. Some physicians may rush too quickly to diagnose conversion disorder when they are confronted with baffling symptoms or especially difficult patients. Concluding that the problem is "all in their heads" conveniently tosses it into somebody else's lap. Women, particularly, have charged that physicians dismiss their physical complaints as "just a hysterical reaction" and refer the patient to a psychiatrist.

We should point out that the term *conversion disorder* carries with it some baggage from our Freudian past. Originally, the term implied an unconscious displacement (or *conversion*) of anxiety into physical symptoms—although many clinicians no longer subscribe to that explanation. Some cases of conversion disorder are now thought to be physical stress responses.

Mysteriously, conversion disorder was much commoner a century ago in Europe and the United States. The problem has declined in industrialized countries, probably due to increased public understanding of physical and mental disorders (American Psychiatric Association, 1994; Nietzel et al., 1998). It is still relatively common in economically undeveloped regions, such as China (Spitzer et al., 1989) and Africa (Binitie, 1975) and among poorly educated persons in the United States (Barlow & Durand, 2005).

Hypochondriasis "Hypochondriacs" worry about getting sick. Every ache and pain signals a disease. Because of their exaggerated concern about illness, patients with **hypochondriasis** often bounce from physician to physician until they find one who will listen to their complaints and prescribe some sort of treatment—often minor tranquilizers or placebos. Naturally, these individuals represent easy marks for health fads and scams. They also find their way to the fringes of the medical community, where they may buy extensive treatment packages from disreputable practitioners.

The other side of the problem is a mistaken diagnosis of hypochondriasis (similar to the problem we found with conversion disorder). Clinicians may sometimes be too ready to conclude that the patient's concerns are imaginary. This can have disastrous consequences, such as overlooking the symptoms of very real and very serious physical diseases, such as cancer or a chronic infection.

■ **Hypochondriasis** A somatoform disorder involving excessive concern about health and disease; also called *hypochondria.*

■ **Dissociative disorders** A group of pathologies involving "fragmentation" of the personality, in which some parts of the personality have become detached, or dissociated, from other parts.

Dissociative Disorders: Nonpsychotic Fragmentation of the Personality

- Dissociative amnesia
- Dissociative fugue
- Depersonalization disorder
- Dissociative identity disorder

Dissociative Disorders

The common denominator for all the **dissociative disorders** is "fragmentation" of the personality—a sense that parts of the personality have detached (dissociated) from others. Among the dissociative disorders we find some of the most fascinating forms of mental pathology, including dissociative fugue, depersonalization disorder, and the controversial dissociative identity disorder (formerly called "multiple personality"), made famous by the fictional Dr. Jekyll and Mr. Hyde. Unfortunately, the underlying causes of dissociative disorders remain unclear. (See the chart in the margin.)

Dissociative Amnesia Sometimes memory loss is too extensive or too specific to be explained by normal forgetting. In some such cases we call it *amnesia.* You may know an amnesia victim who has suffered a memory loss as the result of a severe blow to the head, perhaps in an auto accident. Sometimes, however, people may sustain a purely psychological form of amnesia, known as **dissociative amnesia,** as the result of a traumatic or highly stressful experience. In this disorder, the memory loss involves a specific event or series of events—usually a threatening experience in childhood.

CONNECTION CHAPTER 7

Compare with *anterograde amnesia* in the case of H. M.

You can see that dissociative amnesia is closely related to *posttraumatic stress disorder,* which we discussed in Chapter 8. In both cases, memory loss is related to a stressful incident or period in the person's life. We should also note, however, that dissociative amnesia can be a controversial diagnosis when it is associated with recovered memories of childhood abuse. As we discussed in Chapter 7, some psychologists have raised important questions about the accuracy of such recovered memories. And, as the *DSM-IV* states, dissociative amnesia may have "been overdiagnosed in individuals who are highly suggestible" (p. 479).

Dissociative Fugue Now consider the case of "Jane Doe," a woman with *dissociative fugue.* She was found near death in a Florida park, where she was incoherent and suffering the effects of exposure. In contrast with victims of dissociative amnesia, discussed above, Jane Doe had a pervasive memory loss: no memory of her identity and no ability to read or write. Therapy revealed general information about the kind of past she must have had, but no good clues to her origins. After a nationwide television appeal, Jane Doe and her doctors were flooded with calls from possible relatives, the most promising of which was an Illinois couple, certain she was their daughter. They had not heard from her for over four years, since she had moved from Illinois to Florida. Despite their confidence that they had found her, she was never able to remember her past or what had happened to her (Carson et al., 1996).

Jane Doe had **dissociative fugue,** which is a combination of fugue, or "flight," and *amnesia.* In such persons amnesia takes the form of a lost sense of identity. They also flee their homes, families, and jobs—which is why the disorder is termed *fugue.* Some victims appear disoriented and perplexed. Others may travel to distant locations and take up new lives, appearing unconcerned about the unremembered past. Usually the fugue state lasts only hours or days, followed by complete and rapid recovery. A few cases may continue for months—or, as with Jane Doe, for years.

Heavy alcohol use may predispose a person to dissociative fugue. This suggests that it may involve some brain impairment—although no certain cause has been established. Like dissociative amnesia, fugue occurs more often in those under prolonged high stress, especially in times of war and other calamities. Some psychologists also suspect that memory dissociation and repression accompany instances of sexual and physical childhood abuse (Spiegel & Cardeña, 1991). As with dissociative amnesia, however, this conjecture is disputed.

Depersonalization Disorder Yet another form of dissociation involves a sensation that mind and body have separated. Patients with **depersonalization disorder** commonly report "out-of-body experiences" or feelings of being external observers of their own bodies. Some patients feel as if they are in a dream. (Fleeting, mild forms of this are common, so there is no cause for alarm!) A study of 30 such cases found that obsessive–compulsive disorder and certain personality disorders often accompany this condition (Simeon et al., 1997). The causes are unknown.

People undergoing severe physical trauma, such as a life-threatening injury in an auto accident, may also report symptoms of depersonalization. So do some patients who have had near-death experiences. Usually the sensation

■ **Dissociative amnesia** A psychologically induced loss of memory for personal information, such as one's identity or residence.

■ **Dissociative fugue** Essentially the same as dissociative amnesia, but with the addition of "flight" from one's home, family, and job. *Fugue* (pronounced *FEWG*) means "flight."

■ **Depersonalization disorder** An abnormality involving the sensation that mind and body have separated, as in an "out-of-body" experience.

● These two paintings by Sybil, a dissociative identity disorder (DID) victim, illustrate the differences among the personalities. The painting on the left was done by Peggy, Sybil's angry, fearful personality. The painting above was done by Mary, a home-loving personality.

passes quickly, although it can recur. In such individuals, investigators have attributed the disorder to hallucinations and to natural changes in the brain that occur during shock (Siegel, 1980).

Dissociative Identity Disorder Robert Louis Stevenson's famous story of Dr. Jekyll and Mr. Hyde has become a misleading stereotype of **dissociative identity disorder.** In reality, most such cases occur in women, and most display more than two identities (Ross et al., 1989). Unlike the homicidal Mr. Hyde, rarely do they pose a danger to others.

Although it was once thought to be rare, some specialists now believe that dissociative identity disorder has always been common but hidden or misdiagnosed. It usually first appears in childhood (Vincent & Pickering, 1988), and its victims frequently report having been sexually abused (Putnam et al., 1986; Ross et al., 1990). The formation of multiple identities or selves may be a form of defense by the dominant self to protect itself from terrifying events.

Dissociative identity disorder (DID) has now become a familiar diagnosis because of its portrayal in books such as *Sybil* (Schreiber, 1973) and *The Flock* (Casey & Wilson, 1991) and in films such as the 1996 production *Primal Fear.* Each emerging personality contrasts in some significant way with the original self. For example, the new personality might be outgoing if the original personality is shy, tough if the original is weak, and sexually assertive if the other is fearful and sexually naive. These alternate personalities, each with its own consciousness, emerge suddenly—usually under stress.

What lies behind this mysterious disturbance? Psychodynamic theories explain it as a fracturing of the ego, as a result of ego defense mechanisms that do not allow energy from conflicts and traumas to escape from the unconscious mind. Cognitive theories see it as a form of role-playing or mood-state dependency, a form of memory bias in which events experienced in a given mood are more easily recalled when the individual is again in that mood state (Eich et al., 1997). Others suggest that at least some cases are frauds (as in the case of a student, charged with plagiarizing a term paper, who claimed that he had multiple personalities and that one of them copied the paper without the knowledge of his dominant personality). Some observers have even sug-

■ **Dissociative identity disorder** A condition in which an individual displays multiple identities, or personalities; formerly called "multiple personality disorder."

gested that the disorder exists only in the minds of a few therapists (Piper, 1998). In this view, patients may initially be led by the suggestive questioning of their therapists, who seek to uncover what they suspect are repressed memories of trauma and molestation (Loftus, 1993; Loftus & Ketcham, 1994; Ofshe & Watters, 1994).

In an unfortunate choice of terms, dissociative identity disorder is sometimes called "split personality." This causes confusion because schizophrenia (which literally means "split mind") has no relationship to dissociative identity disorder. In schizophrenia, the "split" refers to a psychotic split from reality, not to a fracturing of one personality into many personalities. Dissociative identity disorder, on the other hand, is *not* a psychotic disorder. We suggest that the reader avoid confusion by entirely avoiding the term "split personality."

● Billboards, magazines, TV, the fashion world, and the movies promote images of body shapes that are unrealistic for most people—yet people often judge themselves against these standards.

Eating Disorders

Like a drug addiction, Carla's eating disorder is so powerful that she cannot resume healthy eating patterns without great difficulty. She (it is usually a she) has always felt overweight, and recently she has put herself on a severe diet—a starvation diet. Little does Carla realize that she has become the victim of an eating disorder that will ultimately alter her body in undesirable, and even lethal, ways. After some months, she may become dangerously underweight. Food has become repugnant. She feels "full" after eating only a bite or two. The original motivation may have been the same with Carla's friend Jennifer, but Jennifer has resorted to another extreme method of weight control: She often overeats, but she makes herself vomit after a meal. Eventually, her teeth and the tissues in her mouth and esophagus come under attack by the action of refluxed stomach acid. And she, like Carla, may become dangerously malnourished.

Significantly, such eating disorders are most prevalent in Western cultures in which hunger is not widespread. They are especially likely to develop among middle- and upper-middle-class young women. Here we examine the two best-known eating disorders, exemplified above: *anorexia nervosa* and *bulimia nervosa.* (See the chart in the margin at the bottom of the page.)

Anorexia Nervosa The condition called *anorexia* (persistent lack of appetite) may develop as a consequence of certain physical diseases or conditions, such as shock, nausea, or allergic reactions. However, when loss of appetite that endangers an individual's health stems from emotional or psychological causes, the syndrome is called **anorexia nervosa** ("nervous anorexia"). A person suffering from anorexia nervosa may act as though she is unconcerned with her condition, although she is emaciated. Commonly, anorexia nervosa is associated with extreme dieting, as in Carla's case. (Most dieters, by contrast, have an increased desire for food.)

■ **Anorexia nervosa** An eating disorder that involves persistent loss of appetite that endangers an individual's health and stems from emotional or psychological reasons rather than from organic causes.

What causes anorexia nervosa? A strong hint comes from the finding that most anorectic persons are young white females from middle-class American homes. They typically have backgrounds of good behavior and academic success, but they starve themselves, hoping to become acceptably thin and attractive (Grice et al., 2002; Kaye et al, 2004; Keel & Klump, 2003). While cultural ideals of feminine beauty change over time, in recent decades the mass media—including fashion magazines and MTV—have promoted extremely slim models and celebrities (Andersen & DiDomenico, 1992; Rolls et al., 1991). Especially during adolescence, when people tend to evaluate themselves in terms of physical attractiveness, they judge themselves harshly for failing to live up to cultural ideals (Conger & Petersen, 1984). A victim of anorexia typically

Eating Disorders
- Anorexia nervosa
- Bulimia nervosa

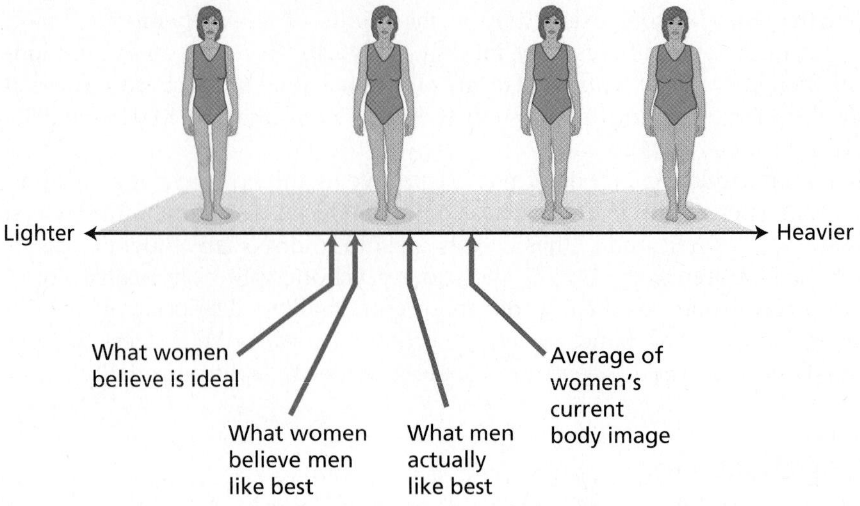

● **FIGURE 12.5** Women's Body Images
April Fallon and Paul Rozin (1985) asked female college students to give their current weight, their ideal weight, and the weight they believed men would consider ideal. The results showed that the average woman felt that her current weight was significantly higher than her ideal weight–and higher than the weight she thought men would like. To make matters worse, women also see their bodies as looking larger than they actually are (Thompson, 1986). When men were asked to rate themselves on a similar questionnaire, Fallon and Rozin found no such discrepancies between ideal and actual weights. But when asked what they saw as the ideal weight for women, they chose a higher weight than women did. No wonder women go on diets more often than men and are more likely to have a major eating disorder (Mintz & Betz, 1986; Striegel-Moore et al., 1993).

Lighter
Heavier
What women believe is ideal
What women believe men like best
What men actually like best
Average of women's current body image

◀ **CONNECTION** CHAPTER 8
Genetic factors may also be at work in anorexia nervosa and bulimia nervosa.

embraces a distorted body image, believing herself to be unattractively fat, and rejects others' reassurances that she is not overweight (Bruch, 1978; Fallon & Rozin, 1985). In an effort to lose imagined "excess" weight, the anorectic victim rigidly suppresses her appetite, feeling rewarded for such self-control when she does lose pounds and inches—but never feeling quite thin enough. (See Figure 12.5.)

Bulimia In the "binge-and-purge" syndrome known as **bulimia nervosa,** the sufferer overeats (binges) and then attempts to lose weight (purges) by means of self-induced vomiting, laxative use, or fasting (Rand & Kuldau, 1992). Those who suffer from bulimia usually keep their disorder inconspicuous and may even be supported in their behavior patterns by peers and by competitive norms in their academic, social, and athletic lives (Polivy & Herman, 1993; Rodin et al., 1985; Squire, 1983; Striegel-Moore et al., 1993).

Eating disorders are commonly associated with other forms of psychopathology. For example, bulimia nervosa is a predictor of depression (Walters et al., 1992). It has been observed that anorectic and bulimic individuals apparently take little joy in their thinner profiles, even though their original rationale might have been to lose weight. Further, while hungry normal people look forward to eating and enjoying a good meal, eating-disordered individuals do not associate pleasure with food and may even dread having to eat. Corroborating this observation, bulimic patients in one study took longer to begin eating a scheduled meal, ate more slowly, and reported significantly more negative moods during eating than did control subjects (Hetherington et al., 1993).

Cognitive explanations for eating disorders analyze how the individual sees herself and thinks about food, eating, and weight. Accordingly, many successful treatments of eating disorders employ strategies that alter self-perception and boost feelings of self-efficacy (Baell & Wertheim, 1992).

Schizophrenia

■ **Bulimia nervosa** An eating disorder characterized by eating binges followed by "purges" induced by vomiting or laxatives; typically initiated as a weight-control measure.
■ **Schizophrenia** (pronounced *skits-o-FRENNY-a*) A psychotic disorder involving distortions in thoughts, perceptions, and/or emotions.

Literally, the word *schizophrenia* means "split or broken mind"—and the "split" is from reality. In psychological terms, **schizophrenia** is a severe form of psychopathology in which personality seems to disintegrate and perception is distorted. Schizophrenia is the disorder that people have in mind when they use the terms "madness," "psychosis," or "insanity."

For the victim of schizophrenia, the mind can be twisted in terrible ways. The world may become bleak and devoid of meaning, or it may become so filled with sensation that everything appears in a confusion of multiple realities layered with hallucinations and delusions. In schizophrenia, emotions often become blunted, thoughts turn bizarre, and language takes strange twists. Memory may also become fragmented (Danion et al., 1999). The disorder breaks the unity of the mind, sending its victims on meaningless mental detours, sometimes riding trains of "clang" associations (associations involving similar-sounding words), and producing confused verbalizations that clinicians call "word salads." (See the chart in the margin.) Here is an example of schizophrenic speech:

> The lion will have to change from dogs into cats until I can meet my father and mother and we dispart some rats. I live on the front of Whitton's head. You have to work hard if you don't get into bed . . . It's all over for a squab true tray and there ain't no squabs, there ain't no men, there ain't no music, there ain't no nothing besides my mother and my father who stand alone upon the Island of Capri where is no ice. Well it's my suitcase sir. (Rogers, 1982)

Schizophrenia: **Psychotic Deterioration of the Personality, Including Disturbances in Affect, Thinking, and Socialization**

- Disorganized type
- Catatonic type
- Paranoid type
- Undifferentiated type
- Residual type

In a lifetime, more than one of every 100 Americans—more than 2 million over the age of 18—will become afflicted (Holmes, 2001; McGuire, 2000; NIMH, 2003; Regier et al., 1993). For as yet unknown reasons, the first appearance of schizophrenia typically occurs for men before they are 25 and for women between 25 and 45 years of age.

For years, schizophrenia has consistently been the primary diagnosis for about 40% of all patient admissions to public mental hospitals—far out of proportion to all other categories of mental illness (Manderscheid et al., 1985). Because schizophrenic patients require prolonged or recurrent treatment, they can be expected to occupy about half of all mental hospital beds in the nation (American Psychiatric Association, 2000; Carson et al., 2000). Most sobering, about one-third of all schizophrenic patients will never fully recover, even with the best therapy available.

Major Types of Schizophrenia Many investigators consider schizophrenia a constellation of separate disorders. Here are the five most common:

- *Disorganized type* represents everyone's image of mental illness, featuring incoherent speech, hallucinations, delusions, and bizarre behavior. A patient who talks to imaginary people most likely has this diagnosis.
- *Catatonic type,* involving a spectrum of motor dysfunctions, appears in two forms. Persons with the more common *catatonic stupor* may remain motionless for hours—even days—sometimes holding rigid, statuelike postures. In the other form, called *catatonic excitement,* patients become agitated and hyperactive.
- *Paranoid type* features delusions and hallucinations but no catatonic symptoms and none of the incoherence of disorganized schizophrenia. The paranoid delusions of persecution or of grandiosity (highly exaggerated self-importance) found in this type of schizophrenia are less well organized—more illogical—than those of the patient with a purely delusional disorder.
- *Undifferentiated type* serves as a catchall category for schizophrenic symptoms that do not clearly meet the requirements for any of the other categories above.
- *Residual type* is the diagnosis for individuals who have suffered from a schizophrenic episode in the past but currently have no major symptoms such as

hallucinations or delusional thinking. Instead, their thinking is mildly disturbed, or their emotional lives are impoverished. The diagnosis of residual type may indicate that the disease is entering remission, or becoming dormant. (This diagnosis was assumed in most of Rosenhan's pseudopatients, whom we met at the beginning of the chapter.)

Our understanding of schizophrenia suffers from the fact that most schizophrenic patients display such a hodgepodge of symptoms that they drop into the "undifferentiated" category. Trying to make more sense of the problem, many investigators now merely divide the symptoms of schizophrenia into *positive* and *negative* categories (Javitt & Coyle, 2004; Sawa & Snyder, 2002). Positive symptoms refer to active processes, such as delusions and hallucinations, while negative symptoms refer to passive processes and deficiencies, such as social withdrawal and poverty of thinking. Patient responses to drug therapy support this division: Those with positive schizophrenia usually respond to antipsychotic drugs, while those with negative schizophrenia do not (Andreasen et al., 1995; Heinrichs, 1993). But even this distinction has its problems. Negative schizophrenia often looks like major depression. In addition, both positive and negative symptoms may occur in a single patient. All these difficulties have led some researchers to conclude that schizophrenia is a name for many separate disturbances.

CONNECTION CHAPTER 13

Antipsychotic drugs work by reducing the activity of the neurotransmitter dopamine in the brain.

Possible Causes of Schizophrenia No longer do most theorists look through the Freudian lens to see schizophrenia as the result of defective parenting or repressed childhood trauma (Johnson, 1989). Studies show that adopted children with *no* family history of the disorder run no increased risk of developing schizophrenia when placed in a home with a schizophrenic parent (Gottesman, 1991). Thus, an emerging consensus among psychiatrists and psychologists views schizophrenia as fundamentally a brain disorder—or a group of disorders (Sawa & Snyder, 2002).

Support for this brain disorder view comes from many quarters. As we have noted, the antipsychotic drugs (sometimes called *major tranquilizers*)—which interfere with the brain's dopamine receptors—can suppress the symptoms of positive schizophrenia (Carlsson, 1978; Snyder, 1986). On the other hand, drugs that stimulate dopamine production (e.g., the amphetamines) can actually produce schizophrenic symptoms (Dracheva et al., 2001; Lewis et al., 2001; Smith et al., 2001). Recently, attention has turned to deficiencies in the neurotransmitter glutamate (Javitt & Coyle, 2004). Other evidence of a biological basis for schizophrenia comes in the form of brain abnormalities shown by computerized imaging techniques (Mesulam, 1990; Raz & Raz, 1990; Resnick, 1992; Suddath et al., 1990). (See Figure 12.6.)

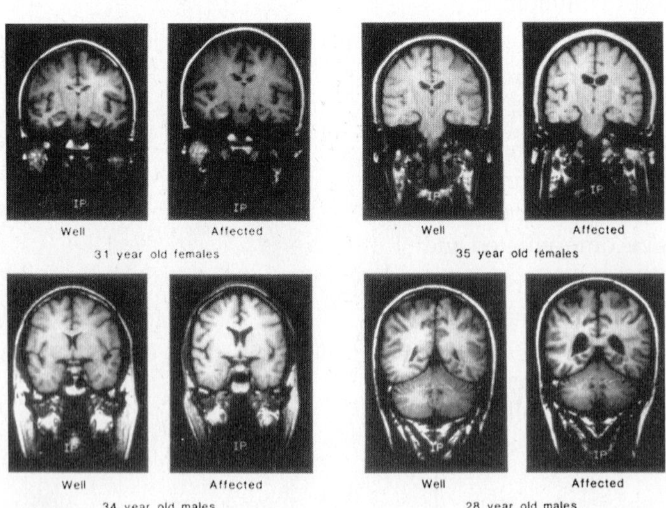
Well
Affected
31 year old females
Well
Affected
35 year old females
Well
Affected
34 year old males
Well
Affected
28 year old males

● **FIGURE 12.6** MRI Scans of a Twin with Schizophrenia and a Twin without Schizophrenia

The normal twin is on the left. Note the enlarged ventricles (fluid-filled spaces) in the brain of the schizophrenic twin on the right.

Yet another line of evidence for the biological basis of schizophrenia comes from family studies (Holden, 2003a; Lencer et al., 2000; Plomin et al., 1994). As we found with the mood disorders, the closer one's relationship to a person with schizophrenia, the greater one's chances of developing it (Gottesman, 1991, 2001; Heston, 1970; Nicol & Gottesman, 1983). This conclusion comes from impressive studies of identical twins reared apart and from adoption studies of children having schizophrenic blood relatives. While only about

1% of us in the general population become schizophrenic, the child of a schizophrenic parent incurs a risk about 14 times higher. The worst case would be to have an identical twin who has developed the condition. In that event, the other twin's chances of becoming schizophrenic jump to nearly 50%.

As with the mood disorders, biology does not tell the whole story of schizophrenia. We can see the effect of the environment, for example, in the fact that 90% of the relatives of schizophrenic patients do not have schizophrenia (Barnes, 1987). Even in identical twins who share *exactly* the same genes, the *concordance rate* (the rate at which the disorder is shared by both) for schizophrenia is only about 50%. That is, in half the cases in which schizophrenia strikes identical twins, it leaves one twin untouched. A hopeful Finnish study found that being raised in a healthy family environment can actually lower the risk of schizophrenia in adopted children who have a genetic predisposition to the disease (Tienari et al., 1987). Apparently, schizophrenia requires a biological predisposition plus some unknown environmental agent to "turn on" the hereditary tendency (Cromwell, 1993; Iacono & Grove, 1993). This agent could be a chemical toxin, stress, or some factor we have not yet dreamed of. Taken as a whole, this research suggests that genetic factors may not themselves be sufficient for the disorder to develop (Nicol & Gottesman, 1983). (See Figure 12.7.) Despite all the biological evidence, we must remember that psychological disorder is always an interaction of biological, cognitive, and environmental factors, as our first Core Concept of the chapter suggested.

This broader perspective is often called the **diathesis–stress hypothesis.** It says that biological factors may place the individual at risk for schizophrenia (as well as many other disorders), but environmental stressors transform this potential into an actual disorder (Walker & Diforio, 1997). (The word *diathesis* refers to a predisposition or physical condition that makes one susceptible to

■ **Diathesis–stress hypothesis** In reference to schizophrenia, the proposal that says that genetic factors place the individual at risk while environmental stress factors transform this potential into an actual schizophrenic disorder.

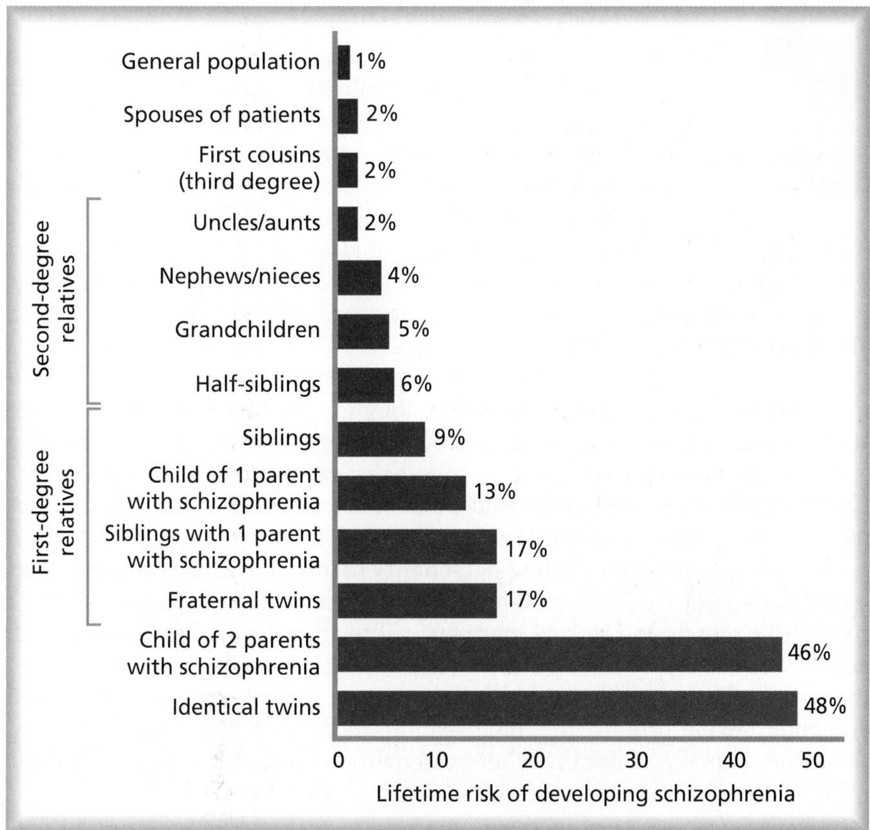
General population
1%
Spouses of patients
2%
First cousins (third degree)
2%
Uncles/aunts
2%
Nephews/nieces
4%
Grandchildren
5%
Half-siblings
6%
Siblings
9%
Child of 1 parent with schizophrenia
13%
Siblings with 1 parent with schizophrenia
17%
Fraternal twins
17%
Child of 2 parents with schizophrenia
46%
Identical twins
48%
Second-degree relatives
First-degree relatives
0
10
20
30
40
50
Lifetime risk of developing schizophrenia

● **FIGURE 12.7** Genetic Risk of Developing Schizophrenia

The graph shows average risks for developing schizophrenia in persons with a schizophrenic relative. Data were compiled from family and twin studies conducted in European populations between 1920 and 1987; the degree of risk correlates highly with the degree of genetic relatedness. (*Source:* Fig. 10, p. 96, "Genetic Risk of Developing Schizophrenia," from SCHIZOPHRENIA GENESIS: The Origins of Madness by Irving Gottesman. Copyright © 1991. Reprinted by permission of W. H. Freeman and Company/Worth Publishers.)

disease.) Thus schizophrenia can be seen as a stress response by one who is predisposed to the disorder. In this view, then, susceptible individuals may never develop schizophrenia if they are spared certain damaging conditions or stressors that might push them "over the edge."

Personality Disorders: Chronic Patterns of Maladjustment That May Extend through the Whole Personality

- Narcissistic personality disorder
- Antisocial personality disorder
- Borderline personality disorder

Personality Disorders

The **personality disorders** show themselves in a chronic history of poor judgment, disordered thinking, emotional disturbances, disrupted social relationships, or lack of impulse control. The key is that the condition derives from a personality pattern of long standing. These patterns can seriously impair an individual's ability to function in social or work settings.

Ten types of personality disorder are recognized in the *DSM-IV* (see the chart in the margin). Here we will consider three of the better known: *narcissistic personality disorder, antisocial personality disorder,* and *borderline personality disorder.*

People with a **narcissistic personality disorder** have an exaggerated sense of self-importance, a need for constant attention or admiration, and often a preoccupation with fantasies of success or power. These people often respond inappropriately to criticism or minor defeat, either by acting indifferent or by overreacting. They have problems in interpersonal relationships, feel entitled to favors without obligations, exploit others selfishly, and have difficulty understanding how others feel. For example, an individual with narcissistic personality disorder might express annoyance—but not empathy—when a friend has to cancel a date because of a death in the family.

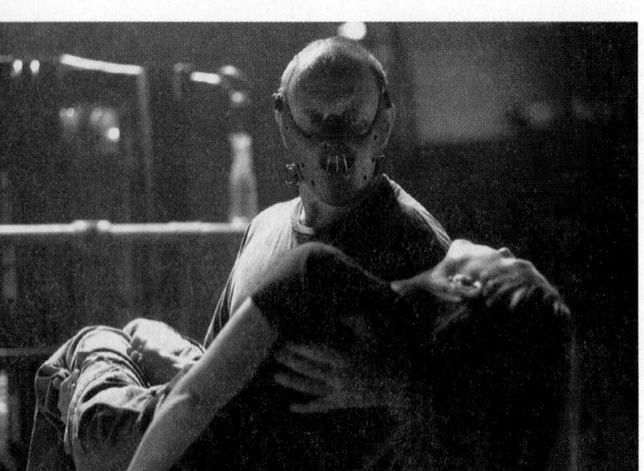

● The films *Silence of the Lambs* and *Hannibal* portray an extreme antisocial personality in the character of Hannibal Lecter.

Another personality disorder, **antisocial personality disorder,** is marked by a long-standing pattern of irresponsible or harmful behavior that indicates a lack of conscience and a diminished sense of responsibility to others. Chronic lying, stealing, and fighting are common signs. People with antisocial personality disorder may not experience anxiety, shame, or any other sort of intense emotion. They can "keep cool" in situations that would arouse and upset normal people. Violations of social norms begin early in their lives—disrupting class, getting into fights, and running away from home. Individuals who show a criminal pattern of antisocial personality disorder, such as committing murders and other serious crimes, are popularly referred to as "psychopaths" or "sociopaths."

Although carriers of the antisocial type of personality disorder can be found among street criminals and con artists, they are also well represented among successful politicians and businesspeople who put career, money, and power above everything and everyone. Two to three percent of the population in the United States may have antisocial personality disorder. Men are four times more likely to be so diagnosed than women (Regier et al., 1988, 1993).

The main signs of **borderline personality disorder** are instability and impulsivity (Carson et al., 2000; Holmes, 2001). People with this diagnosis have unpredictable moods and stormy interpersonal relationships, often becoming upset and abusive in response to perceived slights. They also have little tolerance for frustration. Their impulsivity may be seen in a tendency for substance abuse, gambling, sexual promiscuity, binge eating, reckless driving, self-mutilation, or suicide attempts. As with the other personality disorders, the treatment outlook for borderline personality disorder is guarded. (See Table 12.5.)

■ **Personality disorders** Conditions involving a chronic, pervasive, inflexible, and maladaptive pattern of thinking, emotion, social relationships, or impulse control.

■ **Narcissistic personality disorder** Characterized by a grandiose sense of self-importance, a preoccupation with fantasies of success or power, and a need for constant attention or admiration.

■ **Antisocial personality disorder** Characterized by a long-standing pattern of irresponsible behavior indicating a lack of conscience and a diminished sense of responsibility to others.

■ **Borderline personality disorder** An unstable personality given to impulsive behavior.

TABLE 12.5	Types of Personality Disorders
Type clusters*	**Dominant feature**
Odd or eccentric	
Paranoid personality disorder	Unwarranted suspicion and mistrust of people
Schizoid personality disorder	Lack of interest in people or social relationships
Schizotypal personality disorder	Symptoms of schizophrenia, but not severe enough to be considered psychotic
Erratic or Emotional	
Borderline personality disorder	Instability and impulsivity
Histrionic personality disorder	Need for attention; shallow social relationships
Narcissistic personality disorder	Preoccupation with self; exaggerated sense of self-importance
Antisocial personality disorder	Antisocial behavior, without anxiety or guilt
Anxious or Fearful	
Avoidant personality disorder	Hypersensitivity to social rejection
Dependent personality disorder	Excessive reliance on others; reluctance to make independent decisions
Obsessive–compulsive personality disorder	Rigid need for perfection, order, and control; preoccupation with details

*Based on categories in the *DSM-IV*, with cluster names suggested by Holmes (2001).

Developmental Disorders

Developmental problems can appear at any age, but several common ones are first seen in childhood, including *autism, attention-deficit hyperactivity disorder (ADHD),* and *dyslexia.* Here we will give you a brief description of these disorders, because you have already encountered them in earlier chapters. (See the chart in the margin.)

Autism A complex and poorly understood disorder, **autism** involves an impoverished ability to "read" other people, use language, and interact socially. To illustrate, imagine the following situation: Sally and Anne are playing together, when Sally puts a piece of candy in a box and then leaves the room. While Sally is gone, Anne opens the box, removes the candy, and stashes it in her purse. When Sally comes back, where will she look for the candy? Normal children will say that Sally will look in the box. Autistic children are most likely to say (if they communicate at all) that Sally will look in the purse. Thus, the autistic child lacks a *theory of mind* (Frith, 1993). Severely autistic children cannot imagine themselves in Sally's place, believing something they know is not the case. As a result of this deficit, the autistic child has difficulty in social relationships, usually existing in a world of extreme social isolation.

Besides the theory-of-mind deficiencies and social isolation, most autistic persons also have language difficulties. In fact, many never achieve functional language at all. Perhaps because of all these difficulties, many are classified as mentally retarded (although most mentally retarded persons are *not* autistic). In severe cases, such children may engage in destructive self-stimulation, such as head-banging. Often they will also display repetitive behavior, such as rocking, for extended periods.

Developmental Disorders: **Disorders Usually First Diagnosed in Infancy, Childhood, or Adolescence**

- Autism
- Dyslexia
- Attention-Deficit Hyperactivity Disorder (ADHD)

CONNECTION CHAPTER 1

Facilitated communication was a discredited attempt to communicate with autistic individuals.

■ **Autism** A developmental disorder marked by disabilities in language, social interaction, and the ability to understand another person's state of mind.

Autism occurs in about 1 in 500 children and often is first suspected at about 1½ to 2 years of age, when the child fails to develop language (Kabot, Masi, & Segal, 2003). Most experts believe that autism is fundamentally a brain disorder, with a genetic basis. At present there is no cure, although there are treatment programs that can improve socialization and speech—but they are intensive and relatively expensive.

Dyslexia Reading is a key that opens many doors in a modern, information-driven society. But those doors can remain closed for people who have difficulty in reading—people with **dyslexia.** The disorder affects about 1 of 5 children to some degree, often leading to poor school performance. And, because school is so important in our society, it often leads to diminished self-esteem and eventually to lost career opportunities (Shaywitz, 1996).

Contrary to popular presumption, dyslexia is not a visual disorder. It doesn't cause letters and words to "jump around" or reverse themselves. Research over the last 15 years suggests, instead, that the disorder involves the abnormalities in the brain's language-processing circuits (Breier et al., 2003). Ironically, another "cause" may be language itself: Speakers of English—with its bizarre spelling menagerie, containing some 1120 ways to spell only 40 different sounds—are much more likely to be dyslexic than are Italian speakers, who must contend with only 33 combinations of letters for 25 sounds (Helmuth, 2001c; Paulesu et al., 2001).

In a sense, dyslexia may not even be a distinct disorder. Researcher Sally Shaywitz and her colleagues have made a case that there is no marker that sets dyslexic individuals entirely apart from others who are merely average readers. She argues that dyslexia is simply the diagnosis we give to an arbitrarily defined group of people occupying the lower end of the reading-abilities spectrum (Shaywitz et al., 1990).

Everyone does agree that dyslexia involves reading difficulties. Everyone also agrees that recent years have seen great strides made in understanding the neurological basis of the disorder, debunking some of the myths surrounding dyslexia (smart people, like Einstein, *can* have dyslexia), and developing treatments. Currently, the most effective treatments are special reading programs that emphasize the matching of sounds to letter combinations.

Attention-Deficit Hyperactivity Disorder (ADHD) Some children have more trouble than others sitting still and focusing attention on a task, such as solving a math problem or listening to directions from the teacher. Many things can cause these symptoms, including distracting problems at home, abuse from peers, or merely a cultural tradition that places low value on the tasks that demand quiet attention. Besides those, there seems to be a brain-based condition, known as **attention-deficit hyperactivity disorder (ADHD),** that can interfere with even the best of intentions to focus attention and sit quietly (Barkley, 1998). The disorder is estimated to affect some 3 to 5% of school-age children (Brown, 2003b). (Contrary to a belief widely held among the general public, hyperactivity is *not* caused by eating sugar [Wolraich et al., 1995].)

ADHD is a controversial diagnosis, and its treatment is even more controversial (Sax & Kautz, 2003). Critics have claimed that ADHD is overdiagnosed, often being used to describe normal rambunctiousness or to blame children for the mistakes made by unskilled parents and teachers. In addition, drug treatment consisting of stimulant drugs strikes many people as being wrongheaded. On the other hand, many careful studies have demonstrated that properly administered drug therapy, along with behavioral therapy, can improve attention and diminish hyperactivity in a majority (about 70%) of

■ **Dyslexia** A reading disability, thought by some experts to involve a brain disorder.
■ **Attention-deficit hyperactivity disorder (ADHD)** A developmental disability involving short attention span, distractibility, and extreme difficulty in remaining inactive for any period.

individuals diagnosed with ADHD (Daley, 2004; MTA Cooperative Treatment Group, 2004).

Adjustment Disorders and Other Conditions

Although the large majority of everyday psychological problems involve making choices and dealing with confusion, frustration, and loss, the *DSM-IV* gives these problems short shrift under *adjustment disorders* and under the awkwardly named category *other conditions that may be a focus of clinical attention.* Together, these categories represent a catch basin for relatively mild problems that do not fit well under other headings. They span a diverse range of conditions that include mild depression, physical complaints, marital problems, academic problems, job problems, parent–child problems, bereavement, and even *malingering* (faking an illness). Consequently, the largest group of people suffering from mental problems may fit these headings—even though the *DSM-IV* devotes disproportionately little space to them. Ironically, because these adjustment difficulties are so prevalent, sufferers who turn to psychologists and psychiatrists account for a large proportion of the patient load seen by professionals in private practice.

BEK

"Wait! Come back! I was just kidding about wanting to be happy."

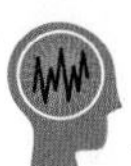

PSYCHOLOGY IN YOUR LIFE: SHYNESS

Being shy is a common problem, but it is not a *DSM-IV* disorder. Rather, *shyness* is a distressing pattern of avoiding or withdrawing from social contact. At the extreme, shy behavior may resemble a social phobia or avoidant personality disorder, as afflicted individuals seek to limit or escape from social interactions. As we have seen many times before, it is a matter of degree. Shy people are not utterly incapacitated by fear, yet they may suffer from loneliness and from lost opportunities to pursue interests and relationships.

What are the origins of this painful problem? For some people it may begin at birth: Shyness is one of three basic temperaments that have been observed among infants and traced through adult life (Kagan et al., 1988, 1994a). Jerome Kagan has also recently proposed that shyness may have its origin in an overly excitable amygdala (Kagan, 2001). But shyness and other forms of social anxiety are also *learned* responses, so that even those who are not "born shy" can acquire shy behavior patterns.

On a hopeful note, shyness does not have to be a permanent condition. Many people overcome it on their own. Organizations such as Toastmasters help people build verbal skills and confidence in social situations. And many others have found the help they need in cognitive–behavioral therapy groups. If you suffer from shyness, we recommend Phil Zimbardo's (1990) book *Shyness* as a good place to look for help.

● Shyness may be painful, but it is not a *DSM-IV* disorder.

CHECK YOUR UNDERSTANDING

1. **RECALL:** The *DSM-IV* is based on the
   a. cognitive perspective.
   b. behavioral perspective.
   c. eclectic view.
   d. psychoanalytic view.
   e. medical model.

2. **RECALL:** Which disorder involves extreme swings of mood from elation to depression?
   a. panic disorder
   b. bipolar disorder
   c. schizophrenia
   d. unipolar depression
   e. PTSD

3. **APPLICATION:** According to the preparedness hypothesis, which one of the following phobias would you expect to be most common?
   a. fear of snakes (ophidiophobia)
   b. fear of books (bibliophobia)
   c. fear of horses (equinophobia)
   d. fear of the number 13 (triskaidekaphobia)
   e. fear of water (aquaphobia)

4. **RECALL:** Which of the following disorders involves a deficiency in memory?
   a. phobia
   b. antisocial personality
   c. dissociative fugue
   d. obsessive–compulsive disorder
   e. schizophrenia

5. **RECALL:** Which of the following is a disorder in which the individual displays more than one distinct personality?
   a. schizophrenia
   b. depersonalization disorder
   c. bipolar disorder
   d. phobia
   e. dissociative identity disorder

6. **RECALL:** Which of the following is primarily a disorder of young American women?
   a. bipolar disorder
   b. schizophrenia
   c. anorexia nervosa
   d. antisocial personality disorder
   e. phobia

7. **RECALL:** Hallucinations and delusions are symptoms of
   a. schizophrenia.
   b. somatoform disorders.
   c. anxiety disorders.
   d. depersonalization disorder.
   e. panic disorders.

8. **RECALL:** Which category of disorder is most common?
   a. schizophrenia
   b. dissociative disorders
   c. eating disorders
   d. the adjustment disorders and "other conditions that may be a focus of clinical attention"
   e. mood disorders

9. **UNDERSTANDING THE CORE CONCEPT:** The *DSM-IV* groups most mental disorders by their
   a. treatments.
   b. causes.
   c. symptoms.
   d. theoretical basis.
   e. cures.

ANSWERS: 1. e 2. b 3. a 4. c 5. e 6. c 7. a 8. d 9. c

DO IT YOURSELF! The Insanity Plea: How Big Is the Problem?

How often is the plea of insanity used? Before you read about the insanity defense in the next part of the chapter, try to guess the approximate percentage of accused criminals in the United States who use a plea of insanity in court: _______%. You will find the correct answer in the "Psychology in Your Life" section on p. 516. (An answer within 10% indicates that you have an exceptionally clear grasp of reality!)

Hint: Research shows that the public has an exaggerated impression of the problem.

KEY QUESTION
?

WHAT ARE THE CONSEQUENCES OF LABELING PEOPLE?

"Mad." "Maniac." "Mentally ill." "Crazy." "Insane." "Disturbed." "Neurotic." These, along with all the official diagnostic terms that appear in the *DSM-IV*, are labels used by the public, the courts, and mental health professionals to describe people who display mental disturbances. Ideally, an accurate diagnosis leads to an effective treatment program for the afflicted individual. Sometimes, however, labels create confusion and hurt. They can turn people into stereotypes, masking their personal characteristics and the unique circumstances that contribute to their disorders. And, if that is not enough, labels can provoke prejudices and social rejection.

In this section we will begin with the problem of labeling as it affects the individual. Then we will pursue the issue of labeling in a larger context: Does psychological disorder mean the same thing in all cultures? Finally, we will look critically at the label "insanity" as used by the courts. The Core Concept, around which all of this is organized, says:

CORE CONCEPT

Ideally, accurate diagnoses lead to proper treatments, but diagnoses may also become labels that depersonalize individuals and ignore the social and cultural contexts in which their problems arise.

Diagnostic Labels Can Compound the Problem

Labeling a person as mentally disturbed can have both serious and long-lasting consequences, aside from the mental disturbance itself. A person may suffer a broken leg or an attack of appendicitis, but when one recovers, the diagnosis moves into the past. Not so with mental disorders. A label of "depression" or "mania" or "schizophrenia" can be a stigma that follows a person forever (Farina et al., 1996; Wright et al., 2000). But what about a mistaken diagnosis? As Rosenhan pointed out, a mistaken diagnosis of cancer is cause for celebration, but almost never is a diagnosis of mental disorder found to be wrong. As you will recall in the "pseudopatient" study, discussed at the beginning of the chapter, the glaring fact of normalcy never emerged, in part, because of the label *schizophrenia.*

The diagnostic label may also become part of a cycle of neglect resulting from the inferior status accorded people with mental disorders. Sadly, in our society, to be mentally disordered is to be devalued. This, of course, lowers self-esteem and reinforces disordered behavior. Thus, society extracts costly penalties from those who deviate from its norms—and in the process it perpetuates the problem of mental disorder.

Perhaps the most extreme reaction against labeling has come from radical psychiatrist Thomas Szasz, who claimed that mental illness is a "myth" (1961, 1977). Szasz argued that the symptoms used as evidence of mental illness are merely medical labels that give professionals an excuse to intervene in what are really social problems: deviant people violating social norms. Once labeled, these people can be treated for their "problem of being different," with no threat of disturbing the existing order.

We must keep in mind, therefore, that the goal of diagnosis is not simply to fit a person into a diagnostic box. Instead, a diagnosis should initiate a process that leads to a greater understanding of a person and to the development of a plan to help. A diagnosis should be a beginning, not an end.

The Cultural Context of Psychological Disorder

Few other clinicians would go as far as Thomas Szasz, but many advocate an *ecological model* that takes the individual's external world into account (Levine & Perkins, 1987). In this model, abnormality is viewed as an interaction between individuals and the social and cultural context. Disorder results from a mismatch between a person's behavior and the needs of the situation. If you are a private investigator, for example, it might pay to have a slightly suspicious, or "paranoid," complexion to your personality, but if you are a nurse, this same characteristic might be called "deviant."

In support of an ecological model, studies show that culture influences both the prevalence of psychological disorders and the symptoms that disturbed people display (Jenkins, 1994; Manson, 1994; Matsumoto, 1996). For example, work done by the World Health Organization (1973, 1979) in Colombia, Czechoslovakia, Denmark, India, Nigeria, Taiwan, Britain, the United States, and the then-USSR established that the incidence of schizophrenia varies substantially from culture to culture. It also showed that schizophrenic symptoms, such as auditory hallucinations, show cultural variability.

Psychiatry, too, is beginning to note the effects of culture on psychopathology. The *DSM-IV,* in fact, has a section devoted to culture-specific disorders (although this section recognizes no disorders that are found specifically in the United States). According to psychiatrists Arthur Kleinman and Alex Cohen (1997), psychiatry has clung too long to three persistent myths:

1. The myth that psychological disorders have a similar prevalence in all cultures
2. The myth that biology creates psychological disorder, while culture merely shapes the way a person experiences it
3. The myth that culture-specific disorders occur only in exotic places, rather than here at home

But are cultural differences so great that a person who hallucinates might be labeled schizophrenic in our culture but visionary or shaman (a healer or seer) in another? Jane Murphy (1976) set out to answer this question in a study of two non-Western groups, the Eskimos of northwest Alaska and the Yorubas of rural tropical Nigeria, societies selected because of their wide geographic separation and cultural dissimilarity. In both groups she found separate terms and distinct social roles for the shaman and for the psychotic individual. Similar findings have since come from studies of cultures all over the world (Draguns, 1980). If mental illness is a socially defined myth, as psychiatrist Thomas Szasz asserts, it is a myth nurtured by cultures everywhere.

Still, the incidence of specific psychological disorders varies among cultures. Abundant evidence shows that, even though schizophrenia, for example, can be found everywhere, American clinicians use the diagnosis far more frequently than their counterparts in other countries. In the United States we apply the schizophrenic label to nearly all patients with psychotic symptoms (Sprock & Blashfield, 1991).

PSYCHOLOGY IN YOUR LIFE: THE PLEA OF INSANITY

Now let's look at a closely related issue: the plea of insanity. What is your opinion: Does the insanity plea really excuse criminal behavior and put thousands of dangerous people back on the streets? Let's look at the facts.

In 1843, Daniel M'Naughten, a deranged woodcutter from Glasgow, thought he had received "instructions from God" to kill the British Prime Minister, Robert Peel. Fortunately for Peel, this would-be assassin struck down his secretary by mistake. Apprehended and tried, M'Naughten was found "not guilty by reason of insanity." The court reasoned that M'Naughten's mental condition prevented him from knowing right from wrong. The public responded with outrage. Neither did the public like the modern-day insanity ruling involving John Hinckley, the young man who shot and wounded then-President Ronald Reagan.

Such infamous cases have molded a low public opinion of the insanity defense. The citizenry blames psychologists and psychiatrists for clogging the courts with insanity pleas, allowing homicidal maniacs back on the streets, and letting criminals go to hospitals for "treatment" instead of prisons for punishment. But this public image of insanity has several problems.

For one thing, "insanity" appears nowhere among the *DSM-IV* listing of disorders recognized by psychologists and psychiatrists. Technically, **insanity** is neither a psychological nor a psychiatric term. It is a *legal* term, which only a court—not psychologists or psychiatrists—can officially apply. By law, insanity can include not only psychosis, but jealous rage, mental retardation, and a wide variety of other conditions in which a person might not be able to control his or her behavior or distinguish right from wrong (Thio, 1995).

Why, then, can we not simply abolish the laws that allow this technicality? The answer to that question turns on the definition of a crime. Legally, a crime requires two elements: (a) an illegal act (just wanting to commit a crime is not enough) and (b) the *intent* to commit the act. Merely wishing your boss dead is no crime (because you committed no illegal act). Neither is flattening the boss who accidentally steps in front of your moving car in the parking lot (assuming you had not planned the deed). But if you plot and plan and then lie in wait to willfully run over the boss, you have committed an intentional and illegal act—and the courts can convict you of murder. From this example, you can see why no one wants to give up the legal requirement of intent. But you can also see why this safeguard leaves the door open for the controversial plea of insanity.

With these things in mind, take a moment to recall your estimate of the percentage of accused criminals who use the insanity plea. (See the earlier "Do It Yourself!" box.) In reality, accused criminals use the insanity defense far less often than the public realizes. According to David Rosenhan (1983), it occurs in only about two of 1000 criminal cases, and of this tiny number, only a fraction are successful. Also contrary to popular belief, most successful insanity pleas do not occur in murder cases. Still, public concern about abuses of the insanity plea have led several states to experiment with alternatives. Some now require separate verdicts on the act and the intent, allowing a jury to reach a verdict of "guilty but mentally ill" (Savitsky & Lindblom, 1986).

● The plea of insanity is rare–and it is usually unsuccessful.

■ **Insanity** A legal term, not a psychological or psychiatric one, referring to a person who is unable, because of a mental disorder or defect, to conform his or her behavior to the law.

CHECK YOUR UNDERSTANDING

1. **RECALL:** Which one of the following statements is true?
   a. Mental disorders have a similar prevalence in all cultures.
   b. In general, biology creates mental disorder, while culture merely shapes the way a person experiences it.
   c. Culture-specific stressors occur primarily in developing countries.
   d. Cultures around the world seem to distinguish between people with mental disorders and people who are visionaries or prophets.
   e. Mental disorders are more prevalent in Eastern cultures.

2. **RECALL:** *Insanity* is a
   a. psychological term.
   b. psychiatric term, found in the *DSM-IV* under "psychotic disorders."
   c. legal term.
   d. term that refers either to "neurotic" or "psychotic" symptoms.
   e. a classification for those seeking treatment.

3. **UNDERSTANDING THE CORE CONCEPT:** Which unfortunate consequence of diagnosing mental disorders is emphasized in this section of the chapter?
   a. the inaccuracy of diagnosis
   b. stigmatizing those with mental disorders
   c. adding to the already overcrowded conditions in mental hospitals
   d. that some cultures do not recognize mental disorders
   e. the importance of the insanity defense

ANSWERS: 1. d 2. c 3. b

PSYCHOLOGICAL DISORDERS: THE STATE OF THE ART

We have seen that our understanding of psychological disorders has some huge gaps. In particular, there are fundamental pieces missing from the puzzles of depression and schizophrenia. Certain other disorders, such as phobias, are reasonably well understood.

Much of the confusion centers on the *DSM-IV,* which classifies some disorders by symptom and some by presumed cause. This is not to fault the developers of this highly influential manual. Rather, we are, in the beginning of the 21st century, just starting to develop a scientific understanding around which the next editions of the *DSM* can be organized.

By the way, don't rush out to buy a copy of the *DSM-IV.* The next edition, the *DSM-V,* is due off the presses in 2011.

USING PSYCHOLOGY TO LEARN PSYCHOLOGY

Diagnosing Your Friends and Family

Don't do it! Don't use your new knowledge of psychological disorders to diagnose your family and friends. This is a common source of grief among psychology students.

We realize how tempting it is to apply what you are learning to the people in your life. Some of the disorders that we have considered here are common, so it would be surprising if they sounded completely alien. As you go through this chapter, you will almost certainly notice signs of anxiety, paranoia, depression, mania, and various other impairments of perception, memory, or emotion in your friends and relatives. It is a variation on the tendency, discussed earlier, to see signs of psychological disorder in oneself. You should recognize this as a sign that you are acquiring some new knowledge about psychological disorder. But we suggest that you keep these thoughts to yourself.

You must remember that reading one chapter does not make you an expert on psychopathology, so you should be cautious about making amateur diagnoses. What you especially should *not* do is to tell someone that you think he or she is schizophrenic, bipolar, obsessive–compulsive—or any other diagnostic label.

Having said that, we should also note that erring too far in the opposite direction by ignoring signs of pathology could also be hazardous. If someone you know is struggling with significant mental problems—and if he or she asks for your opinion—you should refrain from putting a label on the problem, but you can encourage that person to see a competent professional for diagnosis and possible treatment. We will discuss more about how that is done—in the next chapter.

CHAPTER SUMMARY

KEY QUESTION
?

CORE CONCEPT

• WHAT IS PSYCHOLOGICAL DISORDER?

Three classic signs suggest severe psychological disorder: hallucinations, delusions, and severe affective disturbances. But beyond these, the signs of disorder are more subtle, and a diagnosis depends heavily on clinical judgment.

Our modern conception of abnormality has evolved from attributing disorders to demon possession or imbalances of humors to the current medical model, which sees psychopathology as "illness" and with which many psychologists disagree. The broader psychological model includes mental, behavioral, and social factors as well as biological ones. Aside from the three classic signs of disorder, psychopathology is usually judged by the degree to which a person exhibits distress, maladaptiveness, irrationality, unpredictability, and unconventionality.

It is normal to experience symptoms of psychological disorders on occasion, so psychology students are often unjustifiably concerned that they have a mental disorder. Frequent signs of abnormality, however, should prompt a consult with a mental health professional.

● **The medical model takes a "disease" view, while psychology sees psychological disorder as an interaction of biological, mental, social, and behavioral factors.**

● HOW ARE PSYCHOLOGICAL DISORDERS CLASSIFIED?

The most widely used system for classifying mental disorders is the *DSM-IV,* which derives from psychiatry and has a bias toward the medical model. The *DSM-IV* recognizes more than 300 specific disorders, categorized by symptom patterns, but it has no category for "normal" functioning.

Among the *DSM-IV* categories are the *mood disorders,* which involve emotional disturbances. *Major depression* is the most common affective disorder, while *bipolar disorder* occurs less commonly. The *anxiety disorders* include *generalized anxiety disorder, panic disorder, phobic disorders,* and *obsessive–compulsive disorder.* The *somatoform disorders* involve the mind–body relationship in various ways. Those with *conversion disorder* have physical symptoms but no organic disease, while those with *hypochondriasis* suffer from exaggerated concern about illness. The *dissociative disorders* include *dissociative amnesia, dissociative fugue, depersonalization disorder,* and *dissociative identity disorder.* All disrupt the integrated functioning of memory, consciousness, or personal identity. Two patterns of *eating disorder* are common: *anorexia nervosa* (self-starvation) and *bulimia nervosa* (binging and purging). Both are related to unrealistic, negative body images and are difficult to treat. *Schizophrenia* is a psychotic disorder characterized by extreme distortions in perception, thinking, emotion, behavior, and language. Schizophrenia takes five forms: *disorganized, catatonic, paranoid, undifferentiated,* and *residual* types. Evidence for the causes of schizophrenia has been found in a variety of factors, including genetics, abnormal brain structure, and biochemistry. *Personality disorders* are patterns of perception, thinking, or behavior that are long-standing and inflexible and that impair an individual's functioning. They include the *narcissistic, antisocial,* and *borderline personality disorders.* The *DSM-IV* also lists a variety of *developmental disorders,* including *autism, dyslexia,* and *attention-deficit hyperactivity disorder.*

The most common forms of disorder are classified in the *DSM-IV* as the *adjustment disorders* and *"other conditions that may be a focus of clinical attention."* These include a wide range of problems in living. *Shyness* is a widespread problem—and a treatable one—but it is not officially a disorder, unless it goes to the extreme of a social phobia or avoidant personality disorder.

● **The *DSM-IV,* the most widely used system, classifies disorders by their mental and behavioral symptoms.**

● WHAT ARE THE CONSEQUENCES OF LABELING PEOPLE?

Labeling someone as psychologically or mentally disordered is ultimately a matter of human judgment. Yet even professional judgments can be biased by prejudices. Those labeled with psychological disorders may be depersonalized in ways that most physically ill people are not. Culture has an effect on whether a behavior is called normal, abnormal, or merely unusual. Cross-cultural research suggests that people everywhere distinguish between psychotic individuals and those whom they label shamans, prophets, or visionaries.

"Insanity" is a special sort of label that is awarded by the courts. Insanity, however, is not a psychological or psychiatric term. In fact, the insanity defense is not often used, much less used successfully—although a few high-profile cases have captured public attention.

● **Ideally, accurate diagnoses lead to proper treatments, but diagnoses may also become labels that depersonalize individuals and ignore the social and cultural contexts in which their problems arise.**

REVIEW TEST

For each of the following items, choose the single correct or best answer. The answer key appears at the end.

1. The medical model views mental disorder as
   - **a.** a character defect.
   - **b.** a disease or illness.
   - **c.** an interaction of biological, cognitive, behavioral, social, and cultural factors.
   - **d.** normal behavior in an abnormal context.
   - **e.** maladaptive contingencies of reinforcement.
2. Which of the following is *not* one of the six indicators of possible abnormality agreed upon by psychologists?
   - **a.** distress
   - **b.** observer discomfort
   - **c.** unconventionality
   - **d.** irrationality
   - **e.** chronic physical illness
3. The *DSM-IV* is
   - **a.** a personality inventory.
   - **b.** the most widely used classification system for mental disorders.
   - **c.** the neurochemical implicated in anxiety disorders.
   - **d.** a class of psychoactive drugs effective in the treatment of schizophrenia.
   - **e.** a pattern specifier for depression.
4. A long-standing pattern of irresponsible behavior that hurts others without causing feelings of guilt or remorse is typical of
   - **a.** an obsessive–compulsive disorder.
   - **b.** an antisocial personality disorder.
   - **c.** a narcissistic personality disorder.
   - **d.** paranoid schizophrenia.
   - **e.** dissociative fugue.

5. A young woman wanders into a hospital, claiming not to know who she is, where she came from, or how she got there. Her symptoms indicate that she might be suffering from a(n) ______ disorder.
   a. anxiety
   b. affective
   c. personality
   d. dissociative
   e. mood

6. Which of the following statements about phobic disorders is true?
   a. Any extreme and irrational fear of a situation or thing, such as of spiders, is considered a phobia.
   b. The preparedness hypothesis suggests that some people learn their fears from their parents at an early age.
   c. Phobias represent one form of affective disorders.
   d. They are rarely diagnosed outside the United States.
   e. All of the above are true.

7. ______ has been called the "common cold of psychopathology," because it occurs so frequently and because almost everyone has experienced it, at least briefly, at some time.
   a. Obsessive–compulsive disorder
   b. Bipolar disorder
   c. Depression
   d. Paranoid schizophrenia
   e. Autism

8. A person who suffers from ______ cannot eat normally but engages in a ritual of "binging"—periodic binges of overeating—followed by "purging" with induced vomiting or use of laxatives.
   a. anorexia nervosa
   b. bulimia nervosa
   c. inhibition
   d. mania
   e. depression

9. The ______ type of schizophrenia is characterized by delusions.
   a. residual
   b. catatonic
   c. paranoid
   d. undifferentiated
   e. disorganized

10. Rosenhan believes that his "pseudopatients" were not recognized as normal because
   a. the staff members in the mental hospitals were incompetent.
   b. the staff members in the mental hospitals were just as disturbed as the patients.
   c. mental illness is a myth.
   d. staff members did not expect patients to be normal.
   e. he denied the existence of psychological disorders.

ANSWERS: 1. b 2. e 3. b 4. b 5. d 6. a 7. c 8. b 9. c 10. d

KEY TERMS

Psychopathology (p. 485)
Hallucinations (p. 485)
Delusions (p. 485)
Affect (p. 485)
Medical model (p. 488)
Social–cognitive–behavioral approach (p. 489)
DSM-IV (p. 492)
Neurosis (p. 493)
Psychosis (p. 493)
Mood disorders (p. 493)
Major depression (p. 494)
Seasonal pattern specifier or (**SAD**) (p. 495)
Bipolar disorder (p. 497)
Anxiety disorders (p. 498)
Generalized anxiety disorder (p. 498)
Panic disorder (p. 498)
Agoraphobia (p. 498)
Phobias (p. 499)
Preparedness hypothesis (p. 499)
Obsessive–compulsive disorder (p. 499)
Somatoform disorders (p. 501)
Conversion disorder (p. 501)
Hypochondriasis (p. 502)
Dissociative disorders (p. 502)
Dissociative amnesia (p. 503)
Dissociative fugue (p. 503)
Depersonalization disorder (p. 503)
Dissociative identity disorder (p. 504)
Anorexia nervosa (p. 505)
Bulimia nervosa (p. 506)
Schizophrenia (p. 506)
Diathesis–stress hypothesis (p. 509)
Personality disorders (p. 510)
Narcissistic personality disorder (p. 510)
Antisocial personality disorder (p. 510)
Borderline personality disorder (p. 510)
Autism (p. 511)
Dyslexia (p. 512)
Attention-deficit hyperactivity disorder (ADHD) (p. 512)
Insanity (p. 517)

AP* REVIEW: VOCABULARY

Match each of the following vocabulary terms to its definition.

1. Hallucinations
2. Delusions
3. Medical model
4. Mood disorders
5. Anxiety disorders
6. Somatoform disorders
7. Dissociative disorders
8. Diathesis–stress hypothesis
9. Borderline personality disorder
10. Autism

______ a. Extreme disorders of thinking, involving persistent false beliefs.

______ b. A developmental disorder marked by disabilities in language and in social interaction.

______ c. A class of disorders including bipolar disorder.

_____ d. A class of disorders including panic disorder.

_____ e. A disorder characterized by an unstable personality given to impulsive behavior.

_____ f. A class of disorders including depersonalization disorder.

_____ g. A class of disorders including conversion disorder.

_____ h. False sensory experiences that may suggest a mental disorder.

_____ i. The view that mental disorders are diseases that have objective physical causes and require specific treatments.

_____ j. The proposal that genetic factors place the individual at risk while environmental stress factors transform this potential into schizophrenic disorder.

AP* REVIEW: ESSAY

Use your knowledge of the chapter concepts to answer the following essay question.

Dissociative disorders and personality disorders are two relatively common forms of abnormality. Compare and contrast them, being sure to include the following for each abnormality:

a. characterization of the abnormalities involved

b. diagnostic criteria

c. axis of diagnosis

OUR RECOMMENDED BOOKS AND VIDEOS

BOOKS

Casey, N. (Ed.). (2002). *Unholy ghost: Writers on depression.* New York: Perennial. In this "reader on depression"—including observations and stories by writers including Russell Banks, Susanna Kaysen, William Styron, and Anne Beattie—the selections offer vivid descriptions of how depression feels, the behaviors it causes, its effects on others, and the wide-ranging treatments of depression.

Gregory, J. (2003). *Sickened: A memoir of a Munchausen by proxy childhood.* New York: Bantam. In search of attention, excitement, or purpose, Julie Gregory's disordered mother made and kept her sick, then dragged her to doctors and hospitals in search of drugs and surgery for nonexistent ailments. Even as an adult, Gregory never recognized she had been abused until she heard a lecture on MBP.

Porter, R. (2003). *Madness: A brief history.* Oxford, U.K.: Oxford University Press. Today the attitude is widespread that most people struggle with some degree of mental illness at some point in life. But for most of history, the mentally ill have been ostracized as unacceptably different, persecuted, imprisoned, "treated" with torture, or at best dismissed as "sick." This engaging account traces how attitudes shifted over centuries of recognizing and responding to mental illness in human societies.

Torrey, E. F., & Miller, J. (2002). *The invisible plague: The rise and fall of mental illness from 1750 to the present.* Rutgers, NJ: Rutgers University Press. Here is a comprehensive and well-presented history of mental illness in the Western world, with no pat answers about causes or treatment, with a lighter and more literary tone than you'd expect in a sad history.

VIDEOS

A Beautiful Mind. (2001, color, 135 min.). Directed by Ron Howard; starring Russell Crowe, Jennifer Connelly, Ed Harris. This absorbing, Oscar-winning film is based on the true story of the early career of Nobel Prize–winning mathematician John Forbes Nash, who suffered life-long from paranoid schizophrenia. (*Rating PG-13*)

As Good as It Gets. (1997, color, 138 min.). Directed by James Brooks; starring Jack Nicholson, Helen Hunt, Greg Kinnear, Cuba Gooding, Jr., Shirley Knight. An obsessive–compulsive writer becomes entangled, much against his will and inclinations, in the lives of a neighbor, a waitress, and their families, in his efforts to keep his world predictable and protected. For all its funny as well as tragic moments, the film makes clear the struggle of those who suffer from anxiety disorders. (*Rating PG-13*)

K-Pax. (2001, color, 120 min.). Directed by Iain Softley; starring Kevin Spacey, Jeff Bridges. A mental hospital patient, claiming actually to be visitor from another planet, baffles his psychiatrist, whose own life is touched by the "alien's" abilities as he searches for clues to the patient's true past. (*Rating PG-13*)

The Three Faces of Eve. (1957, black-and-white, 91 min.). Directed by Nunnally Johnson; starring Joanne Woodward, Lee J. Cobb, David Wayne. This classic film is based on the true story of a woman found to have at least three distinct personalities and the efforts she and her therapists made to find the source—and the resolution—of her dissociative disorder. Woodward won an Oscar for her astonishing performance. (*Not rated*)

Vertigo. (1958, color, 128 min.). Directed by Alfred Hitchcock; starring James Stewart, Kim Novak, Barbara Bel Geddes. A police detective with a fear of heights (acrophobia) is lured first into a mysterious romance and then into a crime in this dramatic cinematic portrayal of anxiety and terror. (*Rating PG*)

Key Question Chapter Outline

What Is Therapy?

- Entering Therapy
- The Therapeutic Relationship and the Goals of Therapy
- Therapy in Historical and Cultural Context

How Do Psychologists Treat Psychological Disorders?

- Insight Therapies
- Behavior Therapies
- Cognitive–Behavioral Therapy: A Synthesis
- Evaluating the Psychological Therapies

How Is the Biomedical Approach Used to Treat Psychological Disorders?

- Drug Therapy/Psychopharmacology
- Other Medical Therapies for Mental Disorder
- Hospitalization and the Alternatives

Therapies: The State of the Art

CORE CONCEPTS

Therapy for psychological disorders takes a variety of forms, but all involve some relationship focused on improving a person's mental, behavioral, or social functioning.

Psychologists employ two main forms of treatment: the insight therapies (focused on developing understanding of the problem) and the behavior therapies (focused on changing behavior through conditioning).

Biomedical therapies seek to treat psychological disorders by changing the brain's chemistry with drugs, its circuitry with surgery, or its patterns of activity with pulses of electricity or powerful magnetic fields.

Psychology in Your Life

Paraprofessionals Do Therapy, Too.

Some studies show that the therapist's level of training is not the main factor in therapeutic effectiveness.

Where Do Most People Get Help?

A lot of therapy is done by friends, hairdressers, and bartenders.

What Sort of Therapy Would You Recommend?

There is a wide range of therapeutic possibilities to discuss with a friend who asks for your recommendation.

USING PSYCHOLOGY TO LEARN PSYCHOLOGY:
How Is Education Like Therapy?

Chapter

13

Therapies for Psychological Disorders

"You are a very sick rabbit."

LAURA, A PETITE WOMAN in her 40s with a contagious smile, speaks intently about her profession as a psychotherapist. "Yes," she says, "Once your therapeutic practice is established, you might enjoy greater flexibility, autonomy, and meaningfulness than in many other careers. But no, it's not easy work, and it demands both an intellectual and an emotional investment. Moreover," Laura protests, dispelling a common myth about therapy, "A therapist is not a 'paid friend'! A therapist is a trained professional who knows the art of establishing a helping relationship and knows how to apply the knowledge of psychology to an individual struggling with problems and choices."

Laura's orientation is in humanistic therapy, an approach aimed at helping clients see themselves clearly. Humanistic therapies are designed for individuals who seek to be more adaptive, healthy, and productive in their lives. "Early in the therapeutic relationship, my role might be somewhat parental," Laura explains. "Perhaps my client never had the opportunity to grow up with real support. As a child, this client may have created a way to function that worked for her. But now, she needs to be an adult—not a child—and she gets pushed back into those old ways of reacting. It becomes self-sabotaging. The client feels stuck." Laura sits quietly for a few moments, then goes on. "Since I've been there myself, I recognize it. When the client finally trusts me enough, I point these issues out to her, and she can begin to take charge of her life in a healthier way."

Today, practicing psychotherapists may hold any of dozens of degrees and certifications, choosing from scores of therapeutic techniques. For all that training, however, Laura insists that working as a therapist is not purely a science. "Therapy is also an art," asserts Laura, "It's experiential. We may know the skills required to be an effective therapist, like listening well. And we know the central issues, like trust between therapist and client. But these aren't enough to make someone a good therapist. You also need personal experience and insight. You need to be able to sense what your client cannot communicate. And there's no science for that—it's intuitive."

But there's still more to having a psychotherapy practice, Laura points out: "It's not only challenging cases that are difficult! Sometimes it's the hassles of dealing with health insurance that get to you." Laura grins. "But when the therapeutic relationship is real, and our work together progresses, it's very satisfying—even, sometimes, fun! Once we finally 'get it,' my client and I can laugh together.

"I do love it. I love the intensity of it," Laura concludes. "As a therapist, I am there for my clients—*with* my clients. I see them clearly. They come to me with the gift of their trust. It's awe-inspiring. And they wouldn't come if they didn't have the strength and the love to keep going and keep growing."

■ **Therapy** A general term for any treatment process; in psychology and psychiatry, *therapy* refers to a variety of psychological and biomedical techniques aimed at dealing with mental disorders or coping with problems of living.

As Laura makes clear, therapists work at the interface between the science and art of helping. Her approach to therapy, as you will see in this chapter, is just one of many ways to be a therapist. Yet, despite the diversity of approaches that Laura and her colleagues bring to their work, the overwhelming majority of people who enter **therapy** receive significant help. Not everyone becomes a success case, of course. Some people wait too long, until their problems become intractable. Some do not end up with the right sort of therapy for their problems. And, unfortunately, many people who could benefit from therapy do not have access to it because of financial constraints. Still, the development of a wide range of effective therapies is one of the success stories in modern psychology.

In this next-to-last chapter of our journey together through psychology, we begin an overview of therapy by considering what therapy is, who seeks it, what sorts of problems they bring to it, and who administers it. Here we will also see how therapeutic practices have been influenced by history and culture. In the second section of the chapter, we will consider the major types of psychological treatments currently used and how well they work. Then, in the final section, we will look at medical treatments for mental disorders, including drug therapy, psychosurgery, and "shock treatment." There we will also compare hospital treatment for mental disorder with community-based treatment.

As you read through this chapter, we hope you will weigh the advantages and disadvantages of each therapy. Keep in mind, too, that you may sometime be asked by a friend or relative to use what you have learned here to recommend an appropriate therapy. It's even possible that you may sometime need to select a therapist for yourself.

● Many people could benefit from some form of therapy. Most people who enter therapy receive significant help.

WHAT IS THERAPY?

KEY QUESTION

When you think of "therapy," chances are that a stereotype pops into mind, absorbed from countless cartoons and movies: a "neurotic" patient lying on the analyst's couch, with a bearded therapist sitting at the patient's head, scribbling notes and making interpretations. In fact, this is a scene from classic Freudian psychoanalysis, which is a rarity today, although it dominated the first half of the 20th century.

The reality of modern therapy differs from the old stereotype on several counts. First, most therapists don't have their patients (or *clients*) lie on a couch. Second, people now seek therapeutic help for a wide range of problems besides the serious *DSM-IV* disorders: People also go to counselors or therapists for help in making difficult choices, dealing with academic problems, and coping with losses or unhappy relationships. And here's a third way in which the stereotype of therapy is false: Some forms of therapy now involve as much action as they do talk and interpretation—as you will see shortly.

"You are a very sick rabbit."

At first, the therapeutic menu may appear to offer a bewildering list of choices, involving talk and interpretation, behavior modification, drugs, and, in some cases, even "shock treatment" or brain surgery. No matter what form therapy takes, however, there is one constant, as our Core Concept suggests:

CORE CONCEPT

Therapy for psychological disorders takes a variety of forms, but all involve some relationship focused on improving a person's mental, behavioral, or social functioning.

In this chapter, as we examine a sample from the therapeutic universe, we will see that each form of therapy is based on different assumptions about mental disorder. Yet all involve relationships designed to change a person's functioning in some way. Let's begin our exploration of therapy by looking at the variety of people who enter treatment and the problems they bring with them to the therapeutic relationship.

Entering Therapy

Why would you go into therapy? Why would anyone? Most often, people enter therapy when they have a problem that they are unable to resolve by themselves. They may seek therapy on their own initiative, or they may be advised to do so by family, friends, a physician, or a coworker.

Cathy □ Cathy Guisewite

MY DOG IS SEEING A THERAPIST, MOM !!
OH, CATHY, THAT'S NOTHING TO BE ASHAMED OF.
REALLY ?
THERAPISTS HELP MILLIONS OF PEOPLE. THERE'S NO REASON THEY CAN'T HELP ANIMALS.
EVERYONE CAN BENEFIT FROM A LITTLE OBJECTIVE ADVICE NOW AND THEN !
THANKS, MOM. THAT'S JUST WHAT MY THERAPIST SAID.
AACK ! MY DAUGHTER IS SEEING A THERAPIST !!!

Cathy by Cathy Guisewite/Universal Press Syndicate

CONNECTION CHAPTER 12

The *medical model* assumes that mental disorders are similar to physical diseases.

Obviously, you don't have to be "crazy" to seek therapy. If you do enter therapy, however, you may be called either a patient or a client. Practitioners who take a biological or medical approach to treatment commonly use the term *patient.* On the other hand, *client* is often used by professionals who think of psychological disorders not as mental *illnesses* but as *problems in living* (Rogers, 1951; Szasz, 1961).

Access to therapy can be affected by a variety of factors. As we have noted, therapy is far easier to obtain if you have money or adequate health insurance. For the poor, especially poor ethnic minorities, economic obstacles block access to professional mental health care (Bower, 1998d; Nemecek, 1999). Another problem can be lack of qualified therapists. In many communities, it is still much easier to get help for physical health problems than for psychological problems. Even the nature of a person's psychological problems can interfere with getting help. An individual with agoraphobia, for example, finds it hard, even impossible, to leave home to seek therapy. Similarly, paranoid persons may not seek help because they don't trust mental health professionals. Obviously, many problems remain to be solved before all those who need therapy can get it.

The Therapeutic Relationship and the Goals of Therapy

Sometimes you only need to talk out a problem with a sympathetic friend or family member, perhaps to "hear yourself think" or to receive reassurance that you are still worthwhile or likeable. But friends and family have needs and agendas of their own that may interfere with helping you. In fact, they may sometimes be part of the problem. For whatever reason, when the people you are close to cannot offer the help and support you need, it may be appropriate to seek the help of a professionally trained therapist. You might also want professional help if you wish to keep your problems and concerns confidential. Moreover, professional therapists have expertise in identifying mental disorders and in using therapeutic techniques that a friend would probably not know about and certainly would not have the skills to employ. In all these ways, a professional relationship with a therapist differs from friendship or kinship.

What Are the Components of Therapy? In nearly all forms of therapy there is some sort of *relationship* between the therapist and the patient/client seeking assistance—as our Core Concept indicates. (There are computer-therapy programs, where the idea of a "relationship" is stretching the point.) Trust is one of the essential ingredients of a good therapeutic relationship. You and your therapist must be able to work together as allies, on the same side and toward the same goals, joining forces to cope with and solve the problems that have brought you to therapy (Horvath & Luborsky, 1993). It also helps if you *believe* that therapy will be effective for your problem.

In addition to the relationship between therapist and client, depending on the specific approach used, the therapeutic process typically involves some or all of the following processes:

1. *Identifying the problem:* This may mean merely agreeing on a simple description of circumstances or feelings to be changed, or, in the case of a *DSM-IV* disorder, this step may call for a formal diagnosis about what is wrong.
2. *Identifying the cause of the problem or the conditions that maintain the problem:* In some forms of therapy, this involves searching for the source of the patient's or client's discomfort. Alternatively, other forms of therapy emphasize the present causes—that is, the conditions that are keeping the problem alive.
3. *Deciding on and carrying out some form of treatment:* This involves selecting a specific type of therapy designed to minimize or eliminate the troublesome symptoms.

Who Does Therapy? Although more people seek out therapy now than in the past, people usually turn to trained mental health professionals only when their psychological problems become severe or persist for extended periods. When they do, those seeking therapy usually choose one of seven main types of professional helpers: counseling psychologists, clinical psychologists, psychiatrists, psychoanalysts, psychiatric nurse practitioners, clinical (psychiatric) social workers, or pastoral counselors. The differences among these specialties are detailed in Table 13.1. As you examine that table, note that each specialty has its area of expertise. For example, the only therapists who are widely licensed to prescribe drugs are psychiatrists, psychoanalysts (with medical degrees), and psychiatric nurse practitioners.

Currently, through their professional organizations, clinical psychologists are seeking to obtain prescription privileges (Sternberg, 2003). Already, a few military psychologists have been trained, in a highly acclaimed program, to prescribe drugs (Dittmann, 2004; Newman et al., 2000; Rabasca, 1999). And in 2002, New Mexico became the first state to grant prescription privileges to psychologists who have completed a rigorous training program, including 850 hours of course work and supervised internship (Dittmann, 2003). Similar legislation has been introduced in a dozen other states. Nevertheless, prescription privileges for psychologists remains a highly political issue, hotly contested by the medical profession (Clay, 1998; Hayes & Heiby, 1996; Sleek, 1996).

Therapy in Historical and Cultural Context

How you deal with mental disorder depends on how you think about mental disorder. If you believe, for example, that mental problems are diseases, you will treat them differently than another person who believes they indicate a flaw in one's character or a sign of influence by evil spirits. Likewise, the way society treats people with mental disorders has always depended on its prevailing beliefs.

History of Therapy As we saw in the previous chapter, people in medieval Europe often interpreted mental disorder as the work of devils and demons.

TABLE 13.1	Types of Mental Health Care Professionals	
Professional title	**Specialty and common work settings**	**Credentials and qualifications**
Counseling psychologist	Provides help in dealing with the common problems of normal living, such as relationship problems, child rearing, occupational choice, and school problems. Typically counselors work in schools, clinics, or other institutions.	Depends on the state: typically at least a master's in counseling, but more commonly a PhD (Doctor of Philosophy), EdD (Doctor of Education), or PsyD (Doctor of Psychology)
Clinical psychologist	Trained primarily to work with those who have more severe disorders, but may also work with clients having less severe problems. Usually in private practice or employed by mental health agencies or by hospitals. Not typically licensed to prescribe drugs.	Usually required to hold PhD or PsyD; often an internship and state certification required.
Psychiatrist	A specialty of medicine; deals with severe mental problems–most often by prescribing drugs. May be in private practice or employed by clinics or mental hospitals.	MD (Doctor of Medicine); may be required to be certified by medical specialty board.
Psychoanalyst	Practitioners of Freudian therapy. Usually in private practice.	MD (some practitioners have doctorates in psychology, but most are psychiatrists who have taken additional training in psychoanalysis).
Psychiatric nurse practitioner	A nursing specialty; licensed to prescribe drugs for mental disorders. May work in private practice or in clinics and hospitals.	Requires RN (Registered Nurse) credential, plus special training in treating mental disorders and prescribing drugs.
Clinical or psychiatric social worker	Social workers with a specialty in dealing with mental disorders, especially from the viewpoint of the social and environmental context of the problem.	MSW (Master of Social Work)
Pastoral counselor	A member of a religious order or ministry who specializes in treatment of psychological disorders. Combines spiritual guidance with practical counseling.	Varies

In that context, then, the job of the "therapist" was to perform an exorcism or to "beat the devil" out of the disordered person—to make the body an inhospitable place for a spirit or demon. In more recent times, however, reformers have urged that the mentally ill be placed in institutions called *asylums,* where they could be shielded from the stresses of the world—and from the brutal "therapies" that had been all too customary. Unfortunately, the ideal of the insane asylums was not often realized.

One of the most infamous of the asylums was also one of the first: Bethlehem Hospital in London, where for a few pence on the weekend sightseers could go to observe the inmates, who often put on a wild and noisy "show" for the curious audience. As a result, "Bedlam," the shortened term Londoners used for "Bethlehem," became a word used to describe any noisy, chaotic place.

In most asylums, inmates received, at best, only custodial care; at worst they were neglected or put in cruel restraints, such as cages and straightjackets. Some even continued to receive beatings, cold showers, and other forms of abuse. It's not hard to guess that such treatment rarely produced improvement in people suffering from psychological disorders.

Modern Approaches to Therapy Modern mental health professionals have abandoned the old demon model and frankly abusive treatments in favor of therapies based on psychological and biological theories of mind and behavior. Yet, as we will see, even modern professionals disagree on the exact causes and the most appropriate treatments—a state of the art that gives us a wide variety of therapies from which to choose. To help you get an overview of this cluttered therapeutic landscape, here is a preview of things to come.

The **psychological therapies** are often collectively called simply *psychotherapy.*[1] They focus on changing disordered thoughts, feelings, and behavior using psychological techniques (rather than biomedical interventions). And they come in two main forms. *Insight therapy* focuses on helping people understand their problems and change their thoughts, motives, or feelings. *Behavior therapy* focuses primarily on behavior change.

■ **Psychological therapies** Therapies based on psychological principles (rather than on the biomedical approach); often called "psychotherapy."

■ **Biomedical therapies** Treatments that focus on altering the brain, especially with drugs, psychosurgery, or electroconvulsive therapy.

In contrast with psychotherapy, the **biomedical therapies** focus on treating mental problems by changing the underlying biology of the brain. To do so, a physician or nurse practitioner can employ a variety of drugs, including antidepressants, tranquilizers, and stimulants. Occasionally the brain may be treated directly with electromagnetic stimulation or even surgery.

Disorder and Therapy in a Cultural Context Ways of thinking about and treating mental disorder vary widely across cultures (Matsumoto, 1996). Individualistic Western (European and North American) views and practices generally regard psychological disorders to be the result of disease processes, abnormal genetics, distorted thinking, unhealthy environments, or stressors. But collectivist cultures often have quite different perspectives (Triandis, 1990; Zaman, 1992). Asian societies may think of mental disorder as a disconnect between the person and the group. Likewise, many Africans believe that mental disorder results when an individual becomes estranged from nature and from the community, including the community of ancestral spirits (Nobles, 1976; Sow, 1977). In such cultures, treating mentally disturbed individuals by removing them from society is unthinkable. Instead, healing takes place in a social context, emphasizing a distressed person's beliefs, family, work, and life environment. An African use of group support in therapy has

● In this painting from the 1730s, we see the chaos of a cell in the London hospital St. Mary of Bethlehem. Here the upper classes have paid to see the horrors, the fiddler who entertains, and the mental patients chained, tortured, and dehumanized. The chaos of Bethlehem eventually became synonymous with the corruption of its name—Bedlam.

[1]No sharp distinction exists between *counseling* and *psychotherapy.* In general, however, counseling is a shorter process, more likely to be focused on a specific problem, while psychotherapy characteristically involves a longer-term and wider-ranging exploration of issues.

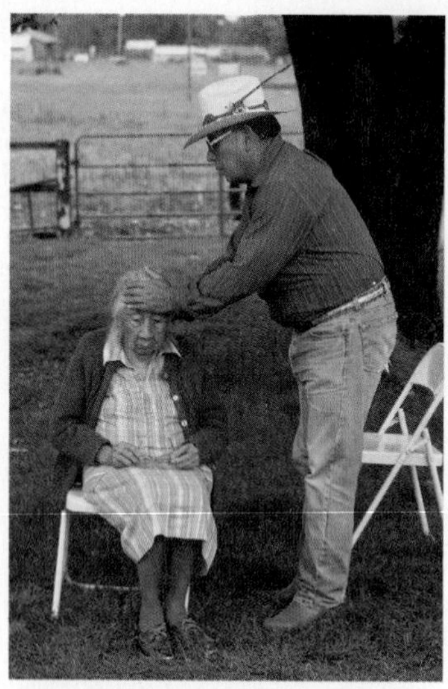

In many cultures, treatments for mental and physical disorders are closely allied with religious beliefs. Here, a Native American healer concentrates on spiritual forces that are presumed to have a role in the woman's discomfort.

developed into a procedure called "network therapy," where a patient's entire network of relatives, coworkers, and friends becomes involved in the treatment (Lambo, 1978).

In many places around the world, the treatments of both mental and physical problems is also bound up with religion and the supernatural—much as in medieval Europe, although their treatments are not usually so harsh. Certain persons—priests, ministers, shamans, sorcerers, and witches—are assumed to have special mystical powers to help distressed fellow beings. Their methods involve ceremonies and rituals that bring emotional intensity and meaning into the healing process. Combined with the use of symbols, they connect the individual sufferer, the shaman, and the society to supernatural forces to be won over in the battle against madness (Devereux, 1981; Wallace, 1959).

PSYCHOLOGY IN YOUR LIFE: PARAPROFESSIONALS DO THERAPY, TOO

Does the best therapy always require a highly trained (and expensive) professional? Or can *paraprofessionals*—who may have received on-the-job training in place of graduate training and certification—be effective therapists? If you are seeking treatment, these questions are important because hospitals, clinics, and agencies are increasingly turning to paraprofessionals as a cost-cutting measure: Those who lack full professional credentials can be hired at a fraction of the cost of those with professional degrees. They are often called "aides" or "counselors" (although many counselors do have professional credentials).

Surprisingly, a review of the literature has found no substantial differences in the effectiveness of the two groups across a wide spectrum of psychological problems (Christensen & Jacobson, 1994). This is good news in the sense that the need for mental health services is far greater than the number of professional therapists can possibly fill. And, because paraprofessional therapists can be effective, highly trained professionals may be freed for other roles, including prevention and community education programs, assessment of patients, training and supervision of paraprofessionals, and research. The reader should be cautioned about overinterpreting this finding, however. Professionals and paraprofessionals have been found to be equivalent only in the realm of the insight therapies, which we will discuss in a moment (Zilbergeld, 1986). Such differences have not yet been demonstrated in the areas of behavior therapies, which require extensive knowledge of operant and classical conditioning and of social-learning theory.

More and more therapy is being done by paraprofessionals.

CHECK YOUR UNDERSTANDING

1. **RECALL:** People in collectivist cultures are likely to view mental disorder as a symptom of something wrong in
   a. the unconscious mind.
   b. a person's behavior, rather than in the mind.
   c. a person's relationship with family or community.
   d. a person's character.
   e. a person's attitude.

2. **RECALL:** A therapist, but not necessarily a friend, can be relied on to
   a. maintain confidentiality.
   b. give you good advice.
   c. offer sympathy when you are feeling depressed.
   d. be available when needed.
   e. all of the above.

3. **APPLICATION:** Which of the following therapists would be most likely to treat an unwanted response, such as nail biting, as merely a bad habit, rather than as a symptom of an underlying disorder?
   a. a psychoanalyst
   b. a psychiatrist
   c. an insight therapist
   d. a group therapist.
   e. a behavioral therapist

4. **UNDERSTANDING THE CORE CONCEPT:** In what respect are all therapies alike?
   a. All may be legally administered only by licensed, trained professionals.
   b. All make use of insight into a patient's problems.
   c. All involve the aim of altering the mind, behavior, or social relationships.
   d. All focus on discovering the underlying cause of the patient's problem, which is often hidden in the unconscious mind.
   e. All involve a change in an individual's behavior.

ANSWERS: 1. c 2. a 3. e 4. c

KEY QUESTION

HOW DO PSYCHOLOGISTS TREAT PSYCHOLOGICAL DISORDERS?

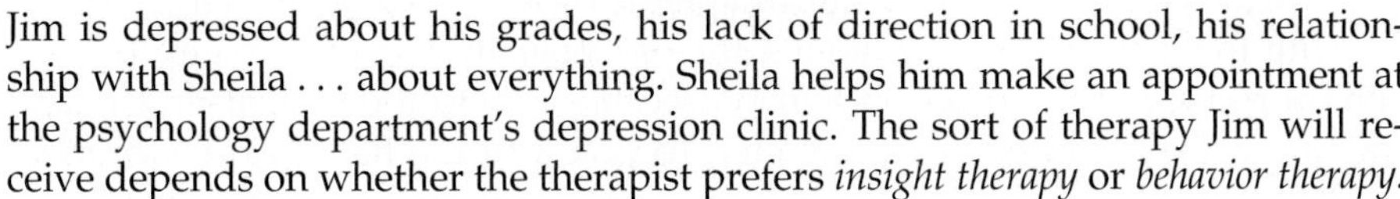

Jim is depressed about his grades, his lack of direction in school, his relationship with Sheila . . . about everything. Sheila helps him make an appointment at the psychology department's depression clinic. The sort of therapy Jim will receive depends on whether the therapist prefers *insight therapy* or *behavior therapy.*

Insight therapy, as you will see, helps the individual gain an understanding of the problem. Various forms of insight therapy are based on the theories of personality we discussed in Chapter 10 and on the cognitive theories of perception, learning, and memory we discussed in Chapters 4, 6, and 7. The behavior therapies, on the other hand, put less emphasis on understanding and insight, while focusing more directly on changing behavior. They draw mainly on the work of Pavlov (classical conditioning) and Skinner (operant conditioning). Our Core Concept puts these ideas together in fewer words:

CORE CONCEPT

Psychologists employ two main forms of treatment: the insight therapies (focused on developing understanding of the problem) and the behavior therapies (focused on changing behavior through conditioning).

The insight therapies, we shall see, were the first truly psychological treatments developed, and for a long time they were the only psychological therapies available. In recent years they have been joined by the behavior therapies, which are now among the most effective tools we have. But it is with the insight therapies that we begin.

Insight Therapies

The **insight therapies** attempt to change people on the *inside*—changing the way they think and feel. Sometimes called **talk therapies,** these methods share the assumption that distressed persons need to develop an understanding of the disordered thoughts, emotions, and motives that underlie their mental difficulties.

The insight therapies come in dozens of different "brands," but all take a *clinical perspective,* using various techniques for revealing and changing a patient's disturbed mental processes through discussion and interpretation. Some, such as Freudian psychoanalysis, assume that problems lie hidden deep in the unconscious, so they employ elaborate and time-consuming techniques to draw them out. Others, such as Carl Rogers's nondirective therapy, minimize the importance of the unconscious and look for problems in the ways people think and interact with each other. Most modern insight therapies require much less time—usually weeks or months—than the years demanded by traditional

■ **Insight therapies** Psychotherapies in which the therapist helps patients/clients understand (gain insight into) their problems.
■ **Talk therapies** Psychotherapies that focus on communicating and verbalizing emotions and motives to understand their problems.

Insight Therapies

- Freudian psychoanalysis
- Neo-Freudian therapies
- Humanistic therapies
- Cognitive therapies
- Group therapies

Freudian psychoanalysis. We have space here to examine only a sampling of the most influential ones, beginning with the legendary methods developed by Sigmund Freud. (See the chart in the margin.)

Freudian Psychoanalysis In the classic Freudian view, psychological problems arise from tension created in the unconscious mind by forbidden impulses and threatening memories. Therefore, Freudian therapy, known as **psychoanalysis,** probes the unconscious in an attempt to bring these issues into the "light of day"—that is, into consciousness, where they can be rendered harmless. The major goal of psychoanalysis, then, is to reveal and interpret the contents of the unconscious mind.

To get at unconscious material, Freud needed ways to get around the defenses the ego has erected to protect itself. One ingenious method called for free association, by which the patient would relax and talk about whatever came to mind, while the therapist would listen, ever alert for veiled references to unconscious needs and conflicts. Another method involved *dream interpretation,* which you will recall from Chapter 3.

CONNECTION CHAPTER 12

The ego defense mechanisms include *repression, regression, projection, denial, rationalization, reaction formation, displacement,* and *sublimation.*

With these and other techniques, the psychoanalyst gradually developed a clinical picture of the problem and proceeded to help the patient understand the unconscious causes for symptoms. To give you the flavor of this process, we offer Freud's interpretation of a fascinating case involving a 19-year-old girl diagnosed with "obsessional neurosis" (now listed in the *DSM-IV* as *obsessive–compulsive disorder*). Please bear in mind that Freud's ideas no longer represent the mainstream of either psychology or psychiatry. But they remain important because many of Freud's techniques have carried over into newer forms of therapy. They are also important because many of Freud's concepts, such as *ego, repression, the unconscious, identification,* and *Oedipus complex,* have become part of our everyday vocabulary. The following case, then—in which you may find Freud's interpretations shocking—will give you a sense of the way psychotherapy began about a century ago.

With these cautions in mind, then, let's meet Freud's patient. When the girl entered treatment, she was causing her parents distress with a strange bedtime ritual that she performed each night. As part of this ritual, she first stopped the large clock in her room and removed other smaller clocks, including her wrist watch. Then she placed all vases and flower pots together on her writing table, so—in her "neurotic" way of thinking—they could not fall and break during the night. Next, she ensured that the door of her room would remain half open by placing various objects in the doorway. After these precautions, she turned her attention to the bed, where she made certain that the bolster did not touch the headboard and that a pillow lay diagonally in the center of the bolster. Then she shook the eiderdown in the quilt until all the feathers sank to the foot-end, after which she meticulously redistributed them evenly again. And finally, she would crawl in bed and attempt to sleep with her head precisely in the center of the diagonal pillow.

The ritual did not proceed smoothly, however. She would do and then redo first one and then another aspect of the ritual, anxious that she had not performed everything properly—although she acknowledged to Freud that all aspects of her nightly precautions were irrational. The result was that it took the girl about two hours to get everything ready for bed each night.

As we mentioned above, establishing a relationship with the patient is essential to psychoanalysis, and through this, Freud made some dramatic claims about her behavior. Not the least of which centered around unfulfilled sexual desires. These revelations came about through free-association, having the patient say the first that comes to mind, and by looking at resistances, which are topics and ideas that the patient avoids talking about in therapeutic sessions.

■ **Psychoanalysis** The form of psychodynamic therapy developed by Sigmund Freud. The goal of psychoanalysis is to release conflicts and memories from the unconscious.

● Sigmund Freud's study, including the famous couch (right), is housed in London's Freud Museum. The 82-year-old Freud fled to London in 1938 upon the Nazi occupation of Austria and died there the following year.

In the final stage of psychoanalysis, patients learn how the relationship they have established with the therapist reflects the unresolved problems they had with their parents. This projection of parental attributes onto the therapist is called transference, and the final phase of therapy is known as the **analysis of transference.** According to psychoanalytic theory, patients will recover when they are finally released from the repressive mental restraints established in the relationship with their parents during early childhood (Munroe, 1955).

Neo-Freudian Psychodynamic Therapies Please pardon us for doing a bit of analysis on Freud: He had a flair for the dramatic, and he also possessed a powerful, charismatic personality—or, as he himself might have said, a strong ego. Accordingly, Freud encouraged his disciples to debate the principles of psychoanalysis, but he would tolerate no fundamental changes in his doctrines. This inevitably led to conflicts with some of his equally strong-willed followers, such as Alfred Adler, Carl Jung, and Karen Horney, who eventually broke with Freud to establish their own schools of therapy.

In general the neo-Freudian renegades retained many of Freud's basic ideas and techniques, while adding some and modifying others. In the true psychodynamic tradition, the **neo-Freudian psychodynamic therapies** have retained Freud's emphasis on motivation. Most now have abandoned the psychoanalyst's couch and treat patients face-to-face. Most also see patients once a week for a few months, rather than several times a week for several years, as in classical psychoanalysis.

So how do the neo-Freudian therapists get the job done in a shorter time? Most have shifted the emphasis from the unconscious to conscious motivation—so they don't spend so much time probing for hidden conflicts and repressed memories. Most have also made a break with Freud on one or more of the following points:

- The significance of the self or ego (rather than the id)
- The influence of life experiences occurring after childhood (as opposed to Freud's emphasis on early-childhood experience)
- The role of social needs and interpersonal relationships (rather than sexual and aggressive desires)

■ **Analysis of transference** The Freudian technique of analyzing and interpreting the patient's relationship with the therapist, based on the assumption that this relationship mirrors unresolved conflicts in the patient's past.

■ **Neo-Freudian psychodynamic therapies** Therapies for mental disorder that were developed by psychodynamic theorists who embraced some of Freud's ideas but disagreed with others.

And, as we saw in Chapter 11, each constructed a theory of disorder and therapy that had different emphases. We do not have space here to go into these approaches in greater detail, but let's briefly consider how a neo-Freudian therapist might have approached the case of the obsessive girl that Freud described. Most likely a modern psychodynamic therapist would focus on the current relationship between the girl and her parents, perhaps on whether she has feelings of inadequacy for which she is compensating by becoming the center of her parents' attention for two hours each night. And, instead of working so intensively with the girl, the therapist might well work with the parents on changing the way they deal with the problem.

Humanistic Therapies The primary symptoms for which college students seek therapy include low self-esteem, feelings of alienation, failure to achieve all they feel they should, difficult relationships, and general dissatisfaction with their lives. These problems in everyday existence are commonly called *existential crises.* This term underscores the idea that many problems deal with questions about the meaning and purpose of one's existence. The humanistic psychologists have developed therapies aimed specifically at these problems—and this is the approach preferred by Laura, the therapist we met at the beginning of the chapter.

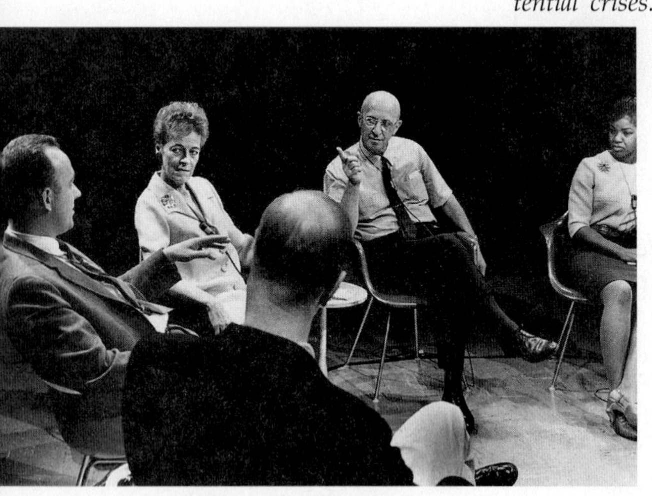

● Humanistic therapist Carl Rogers (right center) facilitates a therapy group.

Humanistic therapists believe that people are generally motivated by healthy needs for growth and psychological well-being. Thus, they dispute Freud's assumption of a personality divided into conflicting parts, dominated by a selfish id, and driven by hedonistic instincts and repressed conflicts. Rather, the humanists emphasize the concept of a *whole* person engaged in a continual process of change. Humanistic therapists also assume that mental disorder occurs only when conditions interfere with normal development and produce low self-esteem. **Humanistic therapies,** therefore, attempt to help clients confront their problems by recognizing their own freedom, enhancing their self-esteem, and realizing their fullest potential (see Schneider & May, 1995). A humanistic therapist (if there had been one around a century ago) would probably have worked with Freud's patient to explore her self-concept and her feelings about her parents. There would have been no attempt at interpreting the girl's symptoms.

Among the most influential of the humanistic therapists, Carl Rogers (1951, 1977) developed a method called **client-centered therapy,** which assumes that all people have the need to self-actualize—that is, to realize their potential. But healthy development can be hindered by a conflict between one's desire for a positive self-image and criticism by self and others. This conflict creates anxiety and unhappiness. The task of Rogerian therapy, then, is to create a nurturing environment in which clients can work through their conflicts to achieve self-enhancement and self-actualization.

■ **Humanistic therapies** Treatment techniques based on the assumption that people have a tendency for positive growth and self-actualization, which may be blocked by an unhealthy environment that can include negative self-evaluation and criticism from others.

■ **Client-centered therapy** A humanistic approach to treatment developed by Carl Rogers, emphasizing an individual's tendency for healthy psychological growth through self-actualization.

■ **Reflection of feeling** Carl Rogers's technique of paraphrasing the clients' words, attempting to capture the emotional tone expressed.

One of the main techniques used by Rogerian therapists involves **reflection of feeling** (also called *reflective listening*) to help clients understand their emotions. With this technique therapists paraphrase their clients' words, attempting to capture the emotional tone expressed and acting as a sort of psychological "mirror" in which clients can see themselves. Notice how the Rogerian therapist uses reflection of feeling in the following excerpt from a therapy session with a young woman (Rogers, 1951, p. 152):

CLIENT: It probably goes all the way back into my childhood. . . . My mother told me that I was the pet of my father. Although I never realized it—I mean, they never treated me as a pet at all.

And other people always seemed to think I was sort of a privileged one in the family. . . . And as far as I can see looking back on it now, it's just that the family let the other kids get away with more than they usually did me. And it seems for some reason to have held me to a more rigid standard than they did the other children.

THERAPIST: You're not so sure you were a pet in any sense, but more that the family situation seemed to hold you to pretty high standards.

CLIENT: M-hm. That's just what has occurred to me; and that the other people could sorta make mistakes, or do things as children that were naughty . . . but Alice wasn't supposed to do those things.

THERAPIST: M-hm. With somebody else it would be just—oh, be a little naughtiness; but as far as you were concerned, it shouldn't be done.

CLIENT: That's really the idea I've had. I think the whole business of my standards . . . is one that I need to think about rather carefully, since I've been doubting for a long time whether I even have any sincere ones.

THERAPIST: M-hm. Not sure whether you really have any deep values which you are sure of.

CLIENT: M-hm. M-hm.

In stark contrast with psychoanalysis, the Rogerian therapist assumes that people have basically healthy motives. These motives, however, can be stifled or distorted by social pressures and low self-esteem. The therapist's task is mainly to remove barriers that limit the expression of this natural positive tendency and help the client clarify and accept his or her own feelings. This is accomplished within an atmosphere of *genuineness, empathy,* and *unconditional positive regard*—nonjudgmental acceptance and respect for the client. And although such concepts may seem to some as mere "feel-good" theorizing, they have solid scientific support. A recent American Psychological Association task force, charged with finding research-based practices that contribute to the effectiveness of therapy, combed the research literature and found evidence that therapy is most likely to be successful when the therapist provides the Rogerian qualities of empathy, positive regard, genuineness, and feedback (Ackerman et al., 2001). (See Figure 13.1.)

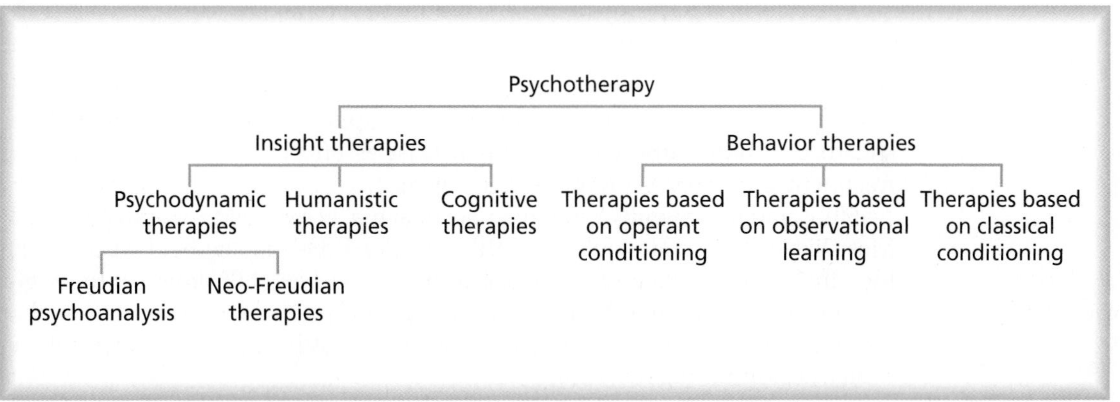
Psychotherapy
Insight therapies
Behavior therapies
Psychodynamic therapies
Humanistic therapies
Cognitive therapies
Therapies based on operant conditioning
Therapies based on observational learning
Therapies based on classical conditioning
Freudian psychoanalysis
Neo-Freudian therapies

● **FIGURE 13.1** Types of Psychotherapy

Each of the two major branches of psychotherapy has many variations.

● A cognitive therapist would say that this student, depressed about a poor grade, may well stay depressed if he berates his own intelligence rather than reattributing the blame to the situation—a tough test.

Cognitive Therapies The insight therapies we have discussed so far focus primarily on people's emotions or motives. **Cognitive therapy,** on the other hand, sees rational *thinking* as the key to therapeutic change. The assumption is that psychological problems arise from erroneous thinking. Cognitive therapy takes several forms, but we will give you some of its flavor with one example: Aaron Beck's cognitive therapy for depression.

Beck, who was originally trained in classical psychoanalysis, broke with the Freudian tradition when he began noticing that the dreams and free associations of his depressed patients were filled with negative thoughts. Commonly they would make such self-deprecating statements as "Nobody would like me if they really knew me" and "I'm not smart enough to make it in this competitive school." Gradually Beck came to believe that depression occurs because of this negative self-talk. So, says Beck, "The therapist helps the patient to identify his warped thinking and to learn more realistic ways to formulate his experiences" (Beck, 1976, p. 20).

Here's a sample of Beck's approach, taken from a therapy session with a college student (Beck et al., 1979, pp. 145–146):

CLIENT: I get depressed when things go wrong. Like when I fail a test.

THERAPIST: How can failing a test make you depressed?

CLIENT: Well, if I fail, I'll never get into law school.

THERAPIST: Do you agree that the way you interpret the results of the test will affect you? You might feel depressed, you might have trouble sleeping, not feel like eating, and you might even wonder if you should drop out of the course.

CLIENT: I have been thinking that I wasn't going to make it. Yes, I agree.

THERAPIST: Now what did failing mean?

CLIENT: (tearful) That I couldn't get into law school.

THERAPIST: And what does that mean to you?

CLIENT: That I'm just not smart enough.

THERAPIST: Anything else?

CLIENT: That I can never be happy.

THERAPIST: And how do these thoughts make you feel?

CLIENT: Very unhappy.

THERAPIST: So it is the meaning of failing a test that makes you very unhappy. In fact, believing that you can never be happy is a powerful factor in producing unhappiness. So, you get yourself into a trap—by definition, failure to get into law school equals "I can never be happy."

As you can see from this exchange, the cognitive therapist helps the individual confront the destructive thoughts that support depression. Studies have shown that Beck's approach can be at least as effective as medication in the treatment of depression (Antonuccio, 1995).

How might a cognitive therapist approach a 19-year-old obsessive patient? Most likely the focus would be on the irrational beliefs she held, such as the idea that flower pots and vases could, by themselves, fall down in the night and break. A cognitive therapist would also challenge the assumption that something catastrophic might happen (such as not being able to sleep!) if she didn't perform a nightly ritual.

■ **Cognitive therapy** Emphasizes rational thinking (as opposed to subjective emotion, motivation, or repressed conflicts) as the key to treating mental disorder.

■ **Group therapy** Any form of psychotherapy done with more than one client/patient at a time. Group therapy is often done from a humanistic perspective.

Group Therapies All the treatments we have discussed to this point involve one-to-one relationships between a patient or client and therapist. However, **group therapy** can have value in treating a variety of concerns, particularly problems with social behavior and relationships. This can be done in many ways—with couples, families, or groups of people who have similar problems, such as drug addictions. Usually they meet together once a week, but some innovative therapy groups are even available on the Internet (Davison et al., 2000). Most commonly, group approaches employ a humanistic perspective, although psychodynamic groups are common, too. Among the benefits of group therapy, clients have opportunities to observe and imitate new social behaviors in a forgiving, supportive atmosphere. We will touch on only a small sample of group therapies below: *self-help groups* and *marital and family therapy.*

Self-Help Support Groups Perhaps the most noteworthy development in group therapy has been the surge of interest in **self-help support groups.** It is estimated that there are more than 500,000 such groups, which are attended by some 15 million Americans every week (Leerhsen, 1990). Many are free, especially those that are not directed by a health care professional. Such groups give people a chance to meet under nonthreatening conditions to exchange ideas with others who are having similar problems and are surviving and sometimes even thriving (Christensen & Jacobson, 1994; Jacobs & Goodman, 1989; Schiff & Bargal, 2000).

One of the oldest, Alcoholics Anonymous (AA), pioneered the self-help concept, beginning in the mid-1930s. Central to the original AA process is the concept of "12 steps" to recovery from alcohol addiction, based not on psychological theory but on the trial-and-error experience of early AA members. The first step begins with recognizing that one has become powerless over alcohol; the second affirms that faith in a "greater power" is necessary for recovery. In the remaining steps the individual seeks help from God and sets goals for making amends to those who have been hurt by his or her actions. Members are urged and helped by the group to accept as many of the steps as possible in order to maintain recovery.

The feminist consciousness-raising movement of the 1960s brought the self-help concept to a wider audience. As a result, self-help support groups now exist for an enormous range of problems, including

- Managing life transition or other crises, such as divorce or death of a child
- Coping with physical and mental disorders, such as depression or heart attack
- Dealing with addictions and other uncontrolled behaviors, such as alcoholism, gambling, overeating, sexual excess, and drug dependency
- Handling the stress felt by relatives or friends of those who are dealing with addictions

Group therapy also makes valuable contributions to the treatment of terminally ill patients. The goals of such therapy are to help patients and their families live their lives as fully as possible, to cope realistically with impending death, and to adjust to the terminal illness (Adams, 1979; Yalom & Greaves, 1977). One general focus of such support groups for the terminally ill is to help them learn "how to live fully until you say goodbye" (Nungesser, 1990).

Couples and Family Therapy Sometimes the best setting in which to learn about relationships is in a group of people struggling with relationships. *Couples counseling* (or therapy), for example, may involve one or more couples who are learning to clarify their communication patterns and improve the quality of their interaction (Napier, 2000). By seeing couples together, a therapist can help the partners identify the verbal and nonverbal styles they use to dominate, control, or confuse each other. Each party is taught how to reinforce desired responses in the other and withdraw reinforcement for undesirable reactions. Couples are also taught nondirective listening skills to help

Self-help support groups Groups, such as Alcoholics Anonymous, that provide social support and an opportunity for sharing ideas about dealing with common problems. Such groups are typically organized and run by laypersons, rather than professional therapists.

the other person clarify and express feelings and ideas (Dattilio & Padesky, 1990; O'Leary, 1987).

Couples therapy typically focuses not on the personalities involved but on the *processes* of their relationship, particularly their patterns of conflict and communication (Gottman, 1994; Greenberg & Johnson, 1988; Notarius & Markman, 1993). Difficult as this may be, changing a couple's interaction patterns can be more effective than individual therapy with one person at a time (Gottman, 1994).

In *family therapy,* the "client" is an entire nuclear family, and each family member is treated as a member of a system of relationships (Fishman, 1993). A family therapist helps troubled family members perceive the issues or patterns that are creating problems for them. The focus is on altering the psychological "spaces" between people and the interpersonal dynamics among people (Foley, 1979; Schwebel & Fine, 1994).

Family therapy can not only reduce tensions within a family, but it can also improve the functioning of individual members by helping them recognize their roles in the group. Virginia Satir, a pioneer of family therapy, noted that the therapist, too, has roles to play during therapy. Among them, the therapist acts as an interpreter and clarifier of the interactions that take place in the therapy session, as well as an advisor, mediator, and referee (Satir, 1983; Satir et al., 1991). As in couples therapy, family therapy focuses on the *situational* rather than the *dispositional* aspects of a problem. That is, the therapist helps family members look at how they interact, rather than at individual's motives and intentions. For example, the therapist might point out how one family member's unemployment affects everyone's feelings and relationships—rather than seeking to assign blame or label anyone as lazy or selfish. The goal of a family therapy meeting, then, is not to have a "gripe session," but to develop the family's ability to come together for constructive problem solving.

Behavior Therapies

Behavior Therapies

- Systematic desensitization
- Aversion therapy
- Contingency management
- Token economies
- Participant modeling

If the problem is overeating, bed-wetting, shyness, antisocial behavior, or anything else that can be described in purely behavioral terms, the chances are good that it can be modified by one of the behavior therapies (also known as **behavior modification**). Based on the assumption that these undesirable behaviors have been *learned* and therefore can be *un*learned, **behavior therapy** relies on the principles of operant and classical conditioning. In addition to those difficulties listed above, behavior therapists report success in dealing with fears, compulsions, depression, addictions, aggression, and delinquent behaviors.

Behavior therapists focus on problem behaviors (rather than inner thoughts, motives, or emotions). They determine how these behaviors might have been learned and, more important, how they can be eliminated and replaced by more effective patterns. To see how this is done, we will look first at the therapy techniques borrowed from classical conditioning. (See the chart in the margin.)

Classical Conditioning Therapies The first example of behavior therapy came from psychologist Mary Cover Jones (1924). Working with a fearful small boy named Peter, she was able to desensitize the boy's intense fear of a rabbit, over a period of weeks, by gradually bringing the rabbit closer and closer while the boy was eating. Eventually, Peter was able to allow the rabbit to sit on his lap while he petted it. (You may notice the similarity to John Watson's experiments on Little Albert. Indeed, Jones was an associate of Watson and knew of the Little Albert study. Unlike Albert, however, Peter came to treatment already possessing an intense fear of rabbits and other furry objects.)

■ **Behavior modification** Another term for behavior therapy.
■ **Behavior therapy** Any form of psychotherapy based on the principles of behavioral learning, especially operant conditioning and classical conditioning.

Surprisingly, it was another 14 years before behavior therapy reappeared, this time as a treatment for bed-wetting (Mowrer & Mowrer, 1938). The method involved a fluid-sensitive pad placed under the patient. When moisture set off an alarm, the patient would awaken. The treatment was effective in 75% of cases—an amazing success rate, in view of the dismal failure of psychodynamic therapy to prevent bed-wetting by talking about the meaning of the symptom. Yet it took another 20 years before behavior therapy entered the mainstream of psychological treatment. Why the delay? The old Freudian idea—that every symptom has an underlying, unconscious cause that must be discovered and eradicated—was extremely well rooted in clinical lore. Therapists dared not attack symptoms (behaviors) directly for fear of *symptom substitution:* the idea that when one symptom was eliminated, another, which might be much worse, could take its place. It took the psychiatrist Joseph Wolpe to challenge that entrenched notion.

THE FAR SIDE® By GARY LARSON
© 1986 FarWorks, Inc. All Rights Reserved/Dist. by Creators Syndicate
The Far Side® by Gary Larson © 1986 FarWorks, Inc. All Rights Reserved. Used with permission.
Professor Gallagher and his controversial technique of simultaneously confronting the fear of heights, snakes, and the dark.

Systematic Desensitization Wolpe reasoned that the development of irrational fear responses and other undesirable emotionally based behaviors seems to follow the classical conditioning model. As you will recall, classical conditioning involves the association of a new stimulus with an unconditioned stimulus, so that the person responds the same way to both. Wolpe also realized another simple truth: The nervous system cannot be relaxed and agitated at the same time, because these two incompatible processes cannot be activated simultaneously. These two ideas, then, became the basis for **systematic desensitization** (Wolpe, 1958, 1973).

CONNECTION CHAPTER 6

In *classical conditioning,* a CS comes to produce essentially the same response as the UCS.

His method begins with a training program that teaches his patients to relax their muscles and their minds (Rachman, 2000). While patients are in this deeply relaxed state, he helps them extinguish their fears by having them imagine fearful situations. They do so in gradual steps that move from remote associations of the feared situation to direct images of it.

In the process of systematic desensitization, the therapist and client first identify the stimuli that provoke anxiety and arrange them in a *hierarchy* ranked from weakest to strongest (Shapiro, 1995). For example, a patient suffering from severe fear of public speaking constructed the hierarchy of unconditioned stimuli shown in Table 13.2. During desensitization, the relaxed client vividly imagines the *weakest* anxiety stimulus on the list. If the stimulus can be

■ **Systematic desensitization** A behavioral therapy technique in which anxiety is extinguished by exposing the patient to an anxiety-provoking stimulus.

TABLE 13.2 A Sample Anxiety Hierarchy

The following is typical of anxiety hierarchies that a therapist and a patient might develop to desensitize a fear of public speaking. The therapist guides the deeply relaxed patient in imagining the following situations:

1. Seeing a picture of another person giving a speech
2. Watching another person give a speech
3. Preparing a speech that I will give
4. Having to introduce myself to a large group
5. Waiting to be called upon to speak in a meeting
6. Being introduced as a speaker to a group
7. Walking to the podium to make a speech
8. Making a speech to a large group

● In "virtual reality," phobic patients can confront their fears safely and conveniently in the behavior therapist's office. On a screen inside the headset, the patient sees computer-generated images of feared situations, such as seeing a snake, flying in an airplane, or looking down from the top of a tall building.

visualized without discomfort, the client goes on to the next stronger one. After a number of sessions, the client can imagine the most distressing situations on the list without anxiety (Lang & Lazovik, 1963)—hence the term *systematic* desensitization. In some forms of systematic desensitization, called **exposure therapy,** the therapist may actually have the patient confront the feared object or situation, such as a spider or a snake, rather than just imagining it. You will recall that Sabra, whom you met in the story opening Chapter 6, went through a form of desensitization to deal with her fear of flying.

A number of studies have shown that desensitization works remarkably well with phobic patients (Smith & Glass, 1977). Desensitization has also been successfully applied to a variety of fears, including stage fright and anxiety about sexual performance (Kazdin, 1994; Kazdin & Wilcoxin, 1976). Recently, psychologists have added a high-tech twist by using computer-generated images that expose phobic patients to fearful situations in a safe virtual-reality environment (Hoffman, 2004; Rothbaum & Hodges, 1999; Rothbaum et al., 2000a).

Aversion Therapy Clearly, desensitization therapy helps clients deal with stimuli that they want to *avoid.* But what about the reverse? What can be done to help those who are attracted to stimuli that are harmful or illegal? Examples include drug addiction, certain sexual attractions, and tendencies to violence—all problems in which deviant behavior is elicited by some specific stimulus. **Aversion therapy** tackles these problems with a conditioning procedure designed to make tempting stimuli less provocative by pairing them with unpleasant (aversive) stimuli. For example, the aversive stimuli could be electric shocks or nausea-producing drugs, whose effects are highly unpleasant but not in themselves dangerous to the client. In time, the negative reactions (unconditioned responses) associated with the aversive stimuli come to be associated with the conditioned stimuli (such as an addictive drug), and the person develops an aversion that replaces the desire.

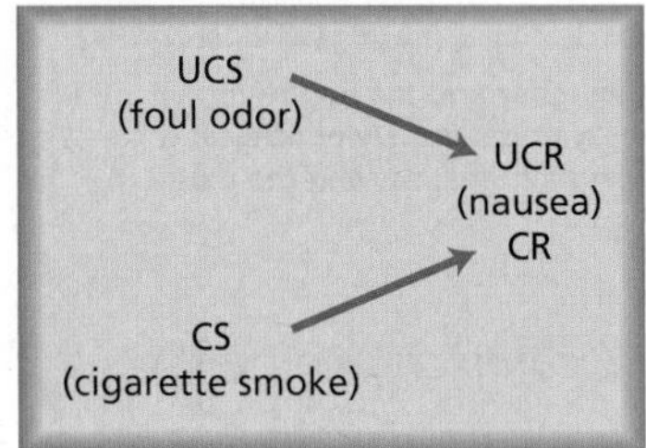
UCS
(foul odor)
UCR
(nausea)
CR
CS
(cigarette smoke)

● **FIGURE 13.2** Conditioning an Aversion for Cigarette Smoke

Aversion therapy for smoking might simultaneously pair a foul odor with cigarette smoke blown in the smoker's face. The foul odor (such as rotten eggs) produces nausea. This response then becomes the conditioned response associated with cigarette smoke. (*Source:* From THE PRACTICE OF BEHAVIOR THERAPY 4th ed. by Joseph Wolpe. Copyright © 1990 by Allyn & Bacon. Reprinted by Allyn & Bacon, Boston, MA)

To give another example, if you were to elect aversion therapy to help you quit smoking, you might be required to chain-smoke cigarettes while having a foul odor blown in your face—until you develop a strong association between smoking and nausea. (see Figure 13.2). A similar conditioning effect occurs in alcoholics who drink while taking Antabuse, a drug often prescribed to encourage sobriety.

In some ways, aversion therapy resembles nothing so much as torture. So why would anyone submit voluntarily to it? Usually people do so only because they have unsuccessfully tried other treatments. In some cases, people may be required to enter aversion therapy by the courts or as part of a treatment program while in prison.

CONNECTION CHAPTER 6

In *operant conditioning,* behavior changes because of consequences, such as rewards and punishments.

Operant Conditioning Therapies Johnny has a screaming fit when he goes to the grocery store with his parents and they refuse to buy him candy. His behavior is an example of a problem that has been acquired by operant conditioning—he has been rewarded when his parents have given in to his demands. In fact, many behavior problems found in both children and adults have been shaped by rewards and punishments. Consider, for example, the similarities between Johnny's case and the employee who chronically arrives late for work or the student who waits until the last minute to study for a test. Behavior therapists argue that changing such behaviors requires operant conditioning techniques. Let's look at two variations on this theme.

■ **Exposure therapy** A form of desensitization therapy in which the patient directly confronts the anxiety-provoking stimulus (as opposed to imagining the stimulus).

■ **Aversion therapy** As a classical conditioning procedure, aversive counterconditioning involves presenting individuals with an attractive stimulus paired with unpleasant (aversive) stimulation in order to condition revulsion.

Contingency Management Johnny's parents may learn to extinguish his fits at the grocery store by simply withdrawing their attention—no easy task, by the way. In addition, the therapist may coach them to "catch Johnny being good"

DO IT YOURSELF! Behavior Self-Modification

Is there a behavior you would like to engage in more often than you do–studying, initiating conversations with others, exercising to keep fit? Write this in behavioral terms on the line below. (No fair using mentalistic words, such as "feeling" or "wanting." Behaviorists require that you keep things objective by specifying only an observable behavior.)

The desired new behavior: ___________

____

When or under what conditions would you like to engage in this new behavior? On the line below, write in the time or stimulus conditions when you want to initiate the behavior (for example: in class, when relaxing with friends, or at a certain time every morning).

The time or conditions for the new behavior: ___________________

____

To increase your likelihood of producing the desired response, apply some positive reinforcement therapy to yourself. Choose an appropriate reward that you will give yourself when you have produced the desired behavior at the appropriate time. Write the reward that you will give yourself on the line below.

Your reward: ___________________

____

Give yourself feedback on your progress by keeping a daily record of the occurrence of your new behavior. This could be done, for example, on a calendar or a graph. In time, you will discover that the desired behavior has increased in frequency. You will also find that your new habit carries its own rewards, such as better grades or more satisfying social interactions (Kazdin, 1994).

and give him the attention he needs then. Over time, the changing contingencies will work to extinguish the old, undesirable behaviors and help to keep the new ones in place. This approach is an example of **contingency management:** changing behavior by modifying its consequences. It has proved effective in managing behavior problems found in many settings, including families, schools, prisons, the military, and mental hospitals. To give another example, the careful application of reward and punishment can dramatically reduce the self-destructive behaviors in autistic children (Frith, 1997). You can also apply contingency management techniques to yourself, if you would like to change some undesirable habit: See the accompanying box, "Do It Yourself! Behavior Self-Modification."

Winston
America's Best.
Pleasure is where you find it.
More
HABIT HELPER

● A patient undergoes a simplified form of aversion therapy in which overexposure to smoke makes her nauseous. The smell of smoke and smoking behavior then take on unpleasant associations.

One caution is in order: Although some people misbehave merely because they want attention, simply giving more attention can be counterproductive. For example, overzealous parents and teachers may be tempted to praise children lavishly, even when their performance has been mediocre—under the mistaken impression that the extra praise will increase low self-esteem and boost performance. In such cases, parents and teachers can aggravate behavior problems by increasing rewards (Viken & McFall, 1994). How could this be? What the child actually learns is that more rewards can be "earned" by producing fewer and fewer desirable behaviors. One must, therefore, take care in simply piling on more rewards. The key to success lies in tying rewards more closely to (making them *contingent on*) desirable behaviors.

Token Economies The special form of therapy called a **token economy** is the behavioral version of group therapy. It commonly finds application in classrooms and institutions (Ayllon & Azrin, 1968; Martin & Pear, 1999). The method takes its name from the plastic tokens sometimes awarded by therapists or teachers as immediate reinforcers for desirable behaviors. In a classroom, earning a token might mean sitting quietly for several minutes, participating in a class discussion, or turning in an assignment. Later, recipients may redeem the tokens for food, merchandise, or privileges. Often, "points" or play money are used in place of tokens. The important thing is that the individual receive something as a reinforcer immediately after giving desired responses.

■ **Contingency management** An operant conditioning approach to changing behavior by altering the consequences, especially rewards and punishments, of behavior.

■ **Token economy** An operant technique applied to groups, such as classrooms or mental hospital wards, involving the distribution of "tokens" or other indicators of reinforcement contingent on desired behaviors. The tokens can later be exchanged for privileges, food, or other reinforcers.

■ **Participant modeling** A social-learning technique in which a therapist demonstrates and encourages a client to imitate a desired behavior.

■ **Cognitive–behavioral therapy** A newer form of psychotherapy that combines the techniques of cognitive therapy with those of behavior therapy.

The token economy approach has also been found to work well in encouraging prosocial behaviors among mental patients and prisoners (Schaefer & Martin, 1966). In these settings, the token reinforcers might be exchanged for cigarettes, reading material, or better living conditions. A PsychInfo search reveals that in the last 10 years alone, over 100 published studies attest to the effectiveness of the token economy in shaping desirable behavior.

Participant Modeling: An Observational-Learning Therapy "Monkey see—monkey do," we say. And sure enough, monkeys learn fears by observation and imitation. One study showed that laboratory monkeys with no previous aversion to snakes could acquire a simian version of *ophidiophobia* by observing their parents reacting fearfully to real snakes and toy snakes. (You don't remember that one? Look back at Table 12.3 on page 494.) The more disturbed the parents were at the sight of the snakes, the greater the resulting fear in their offspring (Mineka et al., 1984). A follow-up study showed that such fears were not just a family matter. When other monkeys that had previously shown no fear of snakes were given the opportunity to observe unrelated adults responding to snakes fearfully, they quickly acquired the same response, as you can see in Figure 13.3 (Cook et al., 1985).

CONNECTION CHAPTER 6

Participant modeling is based on Bandura's theory of *observational learning.*

Like monkeys, people also learn fears by observing the behavior of others. **Participant modeling** takes advantage of this propensity for observational learning by having the client, or *participant,* observe and imitate another person who is *modeling* desirable behaviors. Coaches, of course, often use participant modeling to teach their athletes new skills. Likewise, participant modeling has proved of value in therapy, where the therapist may model the behavior and encourage the client to imitate it. For example, in treating a phobia for snakes, a therapist might first approach a caged snake, then touch the snake, and so on. (Because snake phobias are so common, they are often the subject of behavior therapy demonstrations.) The client then imitates the modeled behavior but at no time is forced to perform. If the therapist senses resistance, the client may return to a previously successful, less-threatening behavior. As you can see, the procedure is similar to systematic desensitization, with the important addition of observational learning. In fact, participant modeling draws on concepts from both operant and classical conditioning.

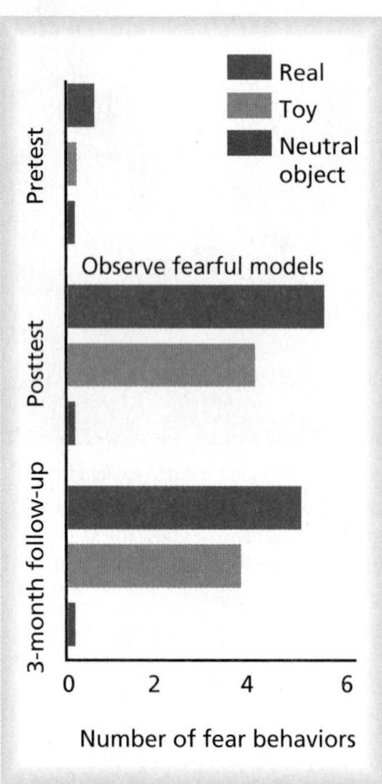

Real
Toy
Neutral object
Pretest
Observe fearful models
Posttest
3-month follow-up
0
2
4
6
Number of fear behaviors

● **FIGURE 13.3** Fear Reactions in Monkeys

After young monkeys raised in laboratories observe unrelated adult monkeys showing a strong fear of snakes, they are vicariously conditioned to fear real snakes and toy snakes with an intensity that persists over time. (*Source:* From "Observational Conditioning of Snake Fear in Unrelated Rhesus Monkeys" by M. Cook, S. Mineka, B. Wokenstein, and K. Laitsch, *Journal of Abnormal Psychology, 94,* pp. 591–610. Copyright © 1985 by American Psychological Association. Reprinted by permission of American Psychological Association.)

The power of participant modeling in eliminating snake phobias can be seen in a study that compared the participant modeling technique with several other approaches: (1) *symbolic modeling,* a technique in which subjects receive indirect exposure by watching a film or video in which models deal with a feared situation; (2) desensitization therapy, which, as you will remember, involves exposure to an imagined fearful stimulus; and (3) no therapeutic intervention (the control condition). As you can see in Figure 13.4, participant modeling was the most successful. The snake phobia was eliminated in 11 of the 12 subjects in the participant modeling group (Bandura, 1970).

Cognitive–Behavioral Therapy: A Synthesis

Suppose you are having difficulty controlling feelings of jealousy every time your mate is friendly with someone else. Chances are that the problem originates in your cognitions about yourself and the others involved ("Marty is stealing Terry away from me!") These thoughts may also affect your behavior, making you act in ways that could drive Terry away from you. A dose of therapy aimed at *both* your cognitions and your behaviors may be a better bet than either one alone.

In brief, **cognitive–behavioral therapy** combines a cognitive emphasis on thoughts and attitudes with the behavioral strategies that we discussed earlier. This dual approach assumes that an irrational self-statement often underlies

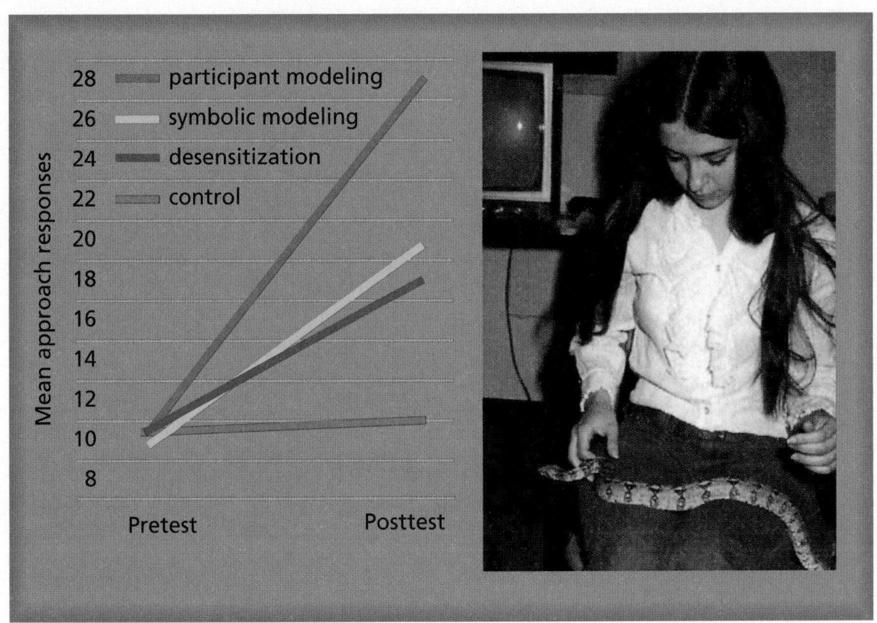
28
26
24
22
20
18
16
14
12
10
8
participant modeling
symbolic modeling
desensitization
control
Mean approach responses
Pretest
Posttest

● **FIGURE 13.4** Participant Modeling Therapy

The subject shown in the photo first watches a model make a graduated series of snake-approach responses and then repeats them herself. Eventually, she can pick up the snake and let it move about on her. The graph compares the number of approach responses subjects made before and after receiving participant modeling therapy (most effective) with the behavior of those exposed to two other therapeutic techniques and a control group. (*Source:* From "Modeling Therapy" by D. Albert Bandura. Reprinted by permission of the author.)

maladaptive behavior. For example, an addicted smoker might automatically tell himself, "One more cigarette won't hurt me" or "I'll go crazy if I don't have a smoke now." These irrational self-statements must be changed or replaced with rational, constructive coping statements before the unacceptable behavior pattern can be modified. Here is an example of healthier thinking: "I can get through this craving if I distract myself with something else I like to do, like going to a movie."

In cognitive–behavioral treatment, the therapist and client work together to modify irrational self-talk, set attainable behavioral goals, develop realistic strategies for attaining them, and evaluate the results. In this way, people change the way they approach problems and gradually develop new skills and a sense of self-efficacy (Bandura, 1986, 1992; Schwarzer, 1992).

Rational–Emotive Behavior Therapy: Challenging the "Shoulds" and "Oughts" One of the most famous (some would say "notorious") forms of cognitive–behavioral therapy was developed by the colorful Albert Ellis (1987, 1990, 1996) to help people eliminate self-defeating thought patterns. Ellis has dubbed his treatment **rational–emotive behavior therapy (REBT),** a name derived from its method of challenging certain "irrational" beliefs and behaviors.

What are the irrational beliefs challenged in REBT, and how do they lead to maladaptive feelings and actions? According to Ellis, maladjusted individuals base their lives on a set of unrealistic values and unachievable goals. These "neurotic" goals and values lead people to hold unrealistic expectations that they should *always* succeed, that they should *always* receive approval, that they should *always* be treated fairly, and that their experiences should *always* be pleasant. (You can see the most common irrational beliefs in the accompanying box, "Do It Yourself! Examining Your Own Beliefs.") For example, in your own daily life, you may frequently tell yourself that you "should" get an A in math or that you "ought to" spend an hour exercising every day. Further, he says, if you are unable to meet your goals and seldom question this neurotic self-talk, it may come to control your actions or even prevent you from choosing the life you want. If you were to enter REBT, your therapist would teach you to recognize such assumptions, question how rational they are, and replace faulty ideas with more valid ones. Don't "should" on yourself, warns Ellis.

CONNECTION: CHAPTER 10

Compare with Karen Horney's *neurotic trends*.

■ **Rational–emotive behavior therapy (REBT)** Albert Ellis's brand of cognitive therapy, based on the idea that irrational thoughts and behaviors are the cause of mental disorders.

DO IT YOURSELF! Examining Your Own Beliefs

It may be obvious that the following are not healthy beliefs, but Albert Ellis finds that many people hold them. Do you? Be honest: Put a check mark beside each of the following statements that accurately describes how you feel about yourself.

_______ 1. I must be loved and approved by everyone.

_______ 2. I must be thoroughly competent, adequate, and achieving.

_______ 3. It is catastrophic when things do not go the way I want them to go.

_______ 4. Unhappiness results from forces over which I have no control.

_______ 5. People must always treat each other fairly and justly; those who don't are nasty and terrible people.

_______ 6. I must constantly be on my guard against dangers and things that could go wrong.

_______ 7. Life is full of problems, and I must always find quick solutions to them.

_______ 8. It is easier to evade my problems and responsibilities than to face them.

_______ 9. Unpleasant experiences in my past have had a profound influence on me. Therefore, they must continue to influence my current feelings and actions.

_______ 10. I can achieve happiness by just enjoying myself each day. The future will take care of itself.

In Ellis's view, all these statements are irrational beliefs that can cause mental problems. The more items you have checked, the more "irrational" your beliefs. His cognitive approach to therapy, known as rational–emotive behavior therapy, concentrates on helping people see that they can "drive themselves crazy" with such irrational beliefs. For example, a student who parties rather than studying for a test holds irrational belief #8. A person who is depressed about not landing a certain job holds irrational belief #3. You can obtain more information on Ellis's system from his books.

How might a cognitive–behavioral therapist have dealt with Freud's obsessive patient? First, donning a cognitive "thinking cap," the therapist would challenge the girl's irrational beliefs, as we suggested earlier. Then, switching to a behaviorist's hat, the therapist might teach the girl relaxation techniques to use when she began to get ready for bed each evening. These techniques then would substitute for the obsessive ritual. It is also likely that the therapist would work with the parents (as might the psychodynamic therapist), focusing on helping them learn not to reward the girl with attention for her ritual behavior.

Changing the Brain by Changing the Mind Research now shows that cognitive–behavioral therapy may not only help people change their minds but also change the brain itself. In one study, patients who suffered from obsessions about whether they had turned off their stoves or locked their doors, for example, were given cognitive behavior modification (Schwartz et al., 1996). When they felt an urge to run home and check on themselves, they were trained to relabel their experience as an obsession or compulsion—not a rational concern. They then focused on waiting out this "urge" rather than giving in to it, by distracting themselves with other activities for about 15 minutes. Positron emission tomography (PET) scans of the brains of subjects who were trained in this technique indicated that, over time, the part of the brain responsible for that nagging fear or urge gradually became less active. As this study shows, the mind can fix the brain!

Evaluating the Psychological Therapies

Now that we have looked at a variety of psychological therapies (see Figure 13.5), let us step back and ask how well therapy works. Does it really make a difference? The answer to this question hasn't always been clear (Kopta et al., 1999; Shadish et al., 2000).

Think about it: How could you tell whether therapy works? Lots of evidence says that people who have undergone therapy *like* it. This was shown in a survey involving thousands of subscribers to *Consumer Reports* (1995). Respondents indicated how much their treatment helped, how satisfied they

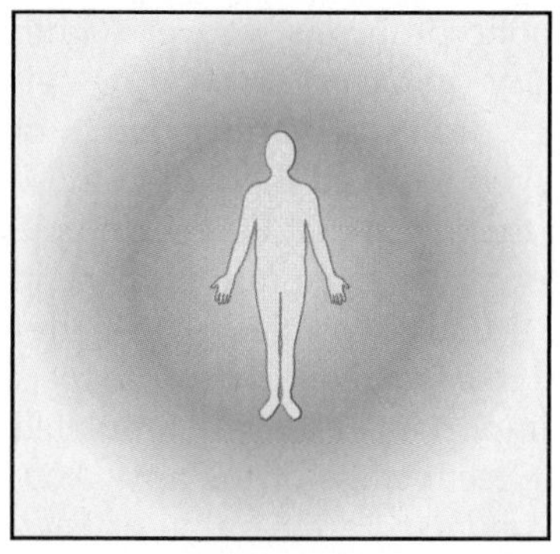

Behavior therapies
aim to change things *outside the individual*—rewards, punishments, and cues in the environment—in order to change the person's external behaviors

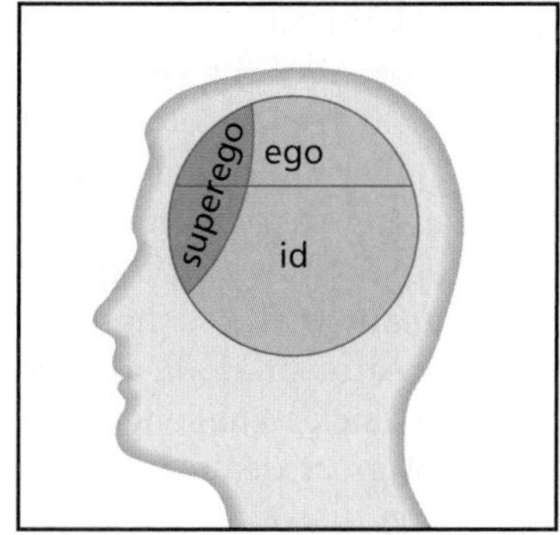
superego
ego
id

Psychodynamic therapies
aim to make changes *inside the person's mind*, especially the unconscious.

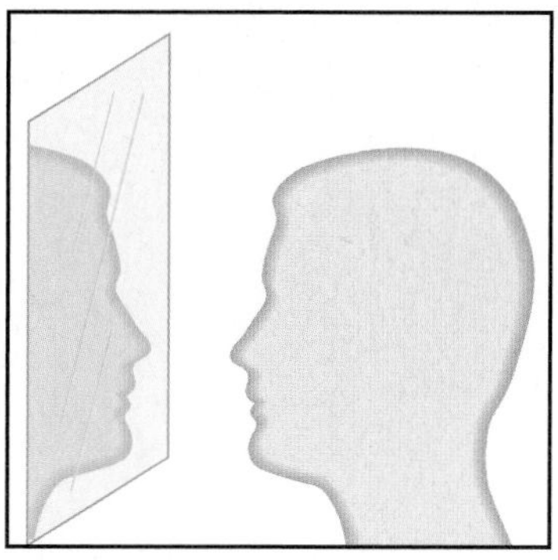

Humanistic therapies
aim to change the way people *see themselves*.

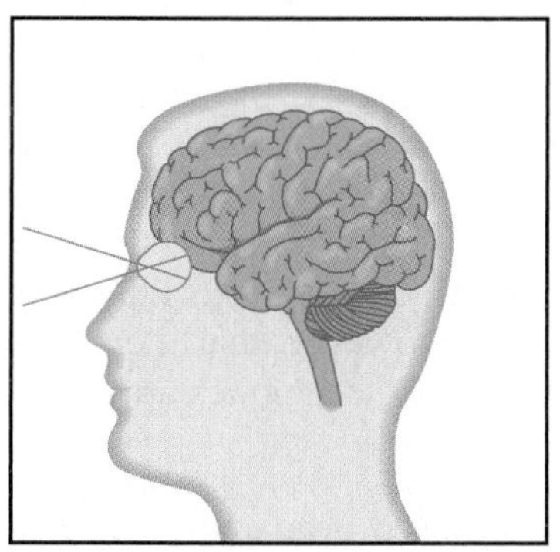

Cognitive therapies
aim to change the way people *think and perceive*.

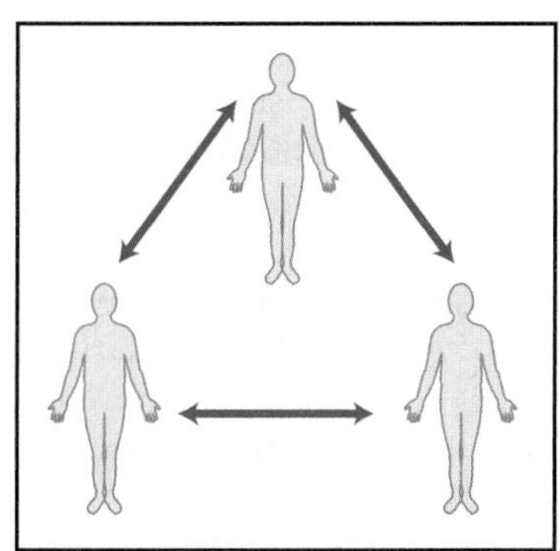

Group therapies
aim to change the way people *interact*.

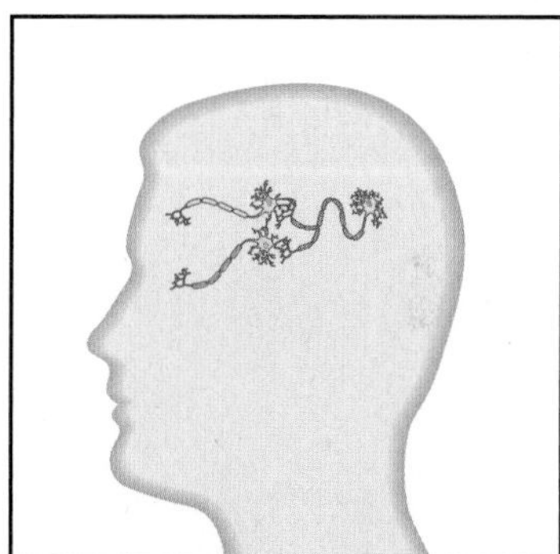

Biomedical therapies
aim to change the structure or function of the brain.

● **FIGURE 13.5** A Comparison of Different Types of Therapy

were with the therapist's treatment of their problems, how much their "overall emotional state" changed following therapy, as well as what kind of therapy they had undergone. For about 3000 of the 7000 respondents, therapy consisted of talking to friends, to relatives, or to clergy (as might be expected from our discussion earlier in this chapter). Another 2900 saw a mental health professional; the rest saw family doctors or support groups. Among the results: (a) Therapy works—that is, it was perceived to have helped clients diminish or eliminate their psychological problems; (b) long-term therapy is better than short-term therapy; and (c) all forms of therapy are about equally effective for improving clients' problems (see Jacobson & Christensen, 1996; Kazdin, 1986; Seligman, 1995).

We can't give a thumbs-up to therapy, however, merely because people say they like it or that it helped them (Hollon, 1996). Testimonials don't make for good science—which is why psychologists now demand that therapy be judged by studies having a *comparison group* or *control group*. Let's turn, therefore, to the controlled studies of therapy's effectiveness.

CONNECTION CHAPTER 2
A *control group* is treated exactly as the *experimental group*, except for the crucial *independent variable*.

Eysenck's Controversial Proclamation The issue of therapy's effectiveness came to a head in 1952. After reviewing the existing evidence, British psychologist Hans Eysenck shook the therapeutic world with the claim that roughly two-thirds of all people with nonpsychotic problems recover within two years of the onset of the problem, *whether they get therapy or not*. The evidence came from a review of several outcome studies of various kinds of insight therapy, all of which compared patients who received therapy to those who were on waiting lists, awaiting their turn in therapy. What Eysenck noted, then, is that people on the waiting lists got better at the same rate as those in therapy. This meant that psychotherapy is essentially worthless—no better than having no treatment at all. To say the least, this wasn't a happy prospect for therapists. Eysenck's challenge had a most important result: It stimulated therapists to do a great deal of research on the effectiveness of therapy. And, as we will see, the discoveries that were made underscore the value of *replication* of research as a crucial part of the scientific method.

In Response to Eysenck Major reviews of the accumulating evidence on therapy began to be reported in 1970 (by Meltzoff & Kornreich), in 1975 (by Luborsky et al.), and in 1977 (by Smith and Glass). Overall, this literature—numbering some 375 studies—supported two major conclusions. First, therapy is, after all, more effective than no therapy. And second, Eysenck had overestimated the improvement rate in no-therapy control groups.

Gradually, then, a consensus supporting the value of psychotherapy emerged (Meredith, 1986; VandenBos, 1986). Moreover, the newest research began to show that therapy was effective not only in Western industrialized countries (in the United States, Canada, and Europe) but also in a variety of cultural settings throughout the world (Beutler & Machado, 1992; Lipsey & Wilson, 1993). A number of writers have cautioned, however, that therapists must be sensitive to cultural differences and adapt their techniques appropriately (Matsumoto, 1996; Shiraev & Levy, 2001).

New Questions The new studies have, however, raised new questions. Are some therapies better than others? Can we identify therapies that are best suited for treating specific disorders? The Smith and Glass survey (1977) hinted that the answers to those questions were "Yes" and "Yes." Smith and Glass found that the behavior therapies seemed to have an advantage over insight therapies for the treatment of many anxiety disorders. More recent evaluations have found that insight therapies can also be used effectively to treat certain problems, such as marital discord and depression. Indeed, there is a clear trend toward matching specific therapies to specific conditions. It is important to realize, however, that these therapeutic techniques do not necessarily "cure" psychological disorders. In the treatment of schizophrenia, mental retardation, or autism, for example, psychological therapies may be deemed effective when people suffering from these afflictions learn more adaptive behaviors (Hogarty et al., 1997; Lovaas, 1993; Wolpe, 1985).

Consensus and Controversy on Effective Therapies The American Psychological Association has sponsored a special task force charged with evaluating psychological therapies (Chambless et al., 1996; Nathan, 1998; "Task Force," 1993). The thrust of their findings is that more and more specific disorders—literally dozens of them—can be treated successfully by specific therapies that have been validated in well-designed experiments (Barlow, 1996). Here are some examples of therapies pronounced effective by this group:

- Behavior therapy for specific phobias, enuresis (bedwetting), autism, and alcoholism
- Cognitive–behavioral therapy for chronic pain, anorexia, bulimia, agoraphobia, and depression
- Insight therapy for couples' relationship problems

More recently, a report by the American Psychological Association focused specifically on evidence-based treatments for depression (Hollon et al., 2003). That document asserts that several varieties of psychotherapy can be effective. These include cognitive, behavior, and family therapy. The APA report also acknowledged that there is a legitimate role for both drug and electroconvulsive therapies in the treatment of depression. In fact, some studies suggest that for depression, a combination of cognitive–behavioral therapy and drug therapy can have a greater effect than either treatment alone (Keller et al., 2000).

Surprisingly, perhaps, the movement to identify therapies that work has generated spirited discussion among therapists (Glenn, 2003). Researchers find that a common element in successful therapy is a caring, hopeful relationship and a new way of looking at oneself and the world (Barker et al., 1988; Jones et al., 1988). This conclusion has been supported by a more recent study that found the effectiveness of therapy to depend less on the *type* of therapy used and more on the *quality of the relationship* between therapist and client (Blatt, Sanislow, & Pilkonis, 1996). Some practitioners fear that they will become locked into a therapeutic straitjacket by insurance companies, which will be unwilling to pay for any treatments not on the official list or for any deviations from "approved" treatments, no matter what the needs of the individual patient. On the other side of the issue are those who fear that nonmedical therapists will be squeezed out of the picture by drug-prescribing physicians.

To end this discussion on a more encouraging note: A recent study of 200 practitioners found that psychologists tend to modify their approach to treatment to fit the needs of their clients, as the situation unfolds during counseling or psychotherapy (Holloway, 2003b). That is, despite our emphasis in this chapter on conflicting opinions about treatment of psychological disorders, most practitioners are quite willing to adapt their methods to the individual client, rather than holding rigidly to a particular theoretical orientation. And that is good news, indeed, coming from a field that has traditionally had strongly divided allegiances. It appears that the emphasis on science-based practice is finally breaking down the old therapeutic boundaries.

PSYCHOLOGY IN YOUR LIFE: WHERE DO MOST PEOPLE GET HELP?

The effectiveness of psychotherapy for a variety of problems seems to be established beyond doubt. Having said that, we should again acknowledge that *most people experiencing mental distress do not turn to professional therapists for help.* Rather they turn to "just people" in the community (Wills & DePaulo, 1991). Those suffering from mental problems often look to friends, clergy, hairdressers, bartenders, and others with whom they have a trusting relationship. In fact, for some types of problems—perhaps the commonest problems of everyday living—a sympathetic friend may be just as effective as a trained professional therapist (Berman & Norton, 1985; Christensen & Jacobson, 1994).

To put the matter in a different way: Most mental problems are not the crippling disorders described in the previous chapter. Rather, the psychological difficulties most of us face result from lost jobs, difficult marriages, misbehaving children, friendships gone sour, loved ones dying . . . In brief, the most familiar problems involve chaos, confusion, choice, frustration, stress, and loss. People who find themselves in the throes of these adjustment difficulties may not need extensive psychotherapy, medication, or some other special treatment. They need someone to help them sort through the pieces of their problems. Usually this means that they turn to someone like you.

What can you do when someone asks you for help? First, you should realize that some problems do indeed require immediate professional treatment. These include a suicide threat or an indication of intent to harm others. You should not delay finding competent help for someone with such tendencies. Second, you should remember that most therapy methods require special training, especially those calling for cognitive–behavioral therapy techniques or psychodynamic interpretations. We urge you to learn as much as you can about these methods—but we strongly recommend that you leave them to the professionals. Some other techniques, however, are simply extensions of good human relationships, and they fall well within the layperson's ability to administer mental "first aid." Briefly, we will consider three of these:

- *Listening:* You will rarely go wrong if you just listen. Sometimes listening is all the therapy a person in distress needs. It works by encouraging the speaker to organize a problem well enough to communicate it. As a result, those who talk out their problems frequently arrive at their own solutions. As an **active listener,** you take the role a step further by giving the speaker feedback: nodding, maintaining an expression that shows interest, paraphrasing, and asking for clarification when you don't understand. As we saw in the client-centered therapy excerpt on pages 534–535, active listening lets the speaker know that the listener is interested and *empathetic* (in tune with the other person's feelings). At the same time, you will do well to avoid the temptation to give advice. Advice robs the recipient of the opportunity to work out his or her own solutions.
- *Acceptance:* Nondirective therapists call this a *nonjudgmental attitude.* It means accepting the person and the problem as they are. It also means suppressing shock, disgust, or condemnation that would create a hostile climate for problem solving.
- *Exploration of alternatives:* People under stress may see only one course of action, so you can help by identifying other potential choices and exploring the consequences of each. (You can point out that *doing nothing* is also a choice.) Remember that, in the end, the choice of action is not up to you but to the individual who owns the problem.

Beyond these basic helping techniques lies the territory of the trained therapist. Again, we strongly advise you against trying out the therapy techniques discussed in this chapter for any of the serious psychological disorders discussed in the previous chapter or listed in the *DSM-IV.*

■ **Active listener** A person who gives the speaker feedback in such forms as nodding, paraphrasing, maintaining an expression that shows interest, and asking questions for clarification.

CHECK YOUR UNDERSTANDING

1. **RECALL:** Counterconditioning is based on the principles of
   a. operant conditioning.
   b. classical conditioning.
   c. social learning.
   d. cognitive learning.
   e. observational learning.
2. **APPLICATION:** You could use contingency management to change the behavior of a child who comes home late for dinner by
   a. pairing food with punishment.
   b. having the child observe someone else coming home on time and being rewarded.
   c. pairing food with rewards.
   d. having the child relax and imagine being home on time for dinner.
   e. refusing to let the child have dinner.

3. **RECALL:** A primary goal of psychoanalysis is to
   a. change behavior.
   b. reveal problems in the unconscious.
   c. overcome low self-esteem.
   d. help the client learn how to get along with others.
   e. alter interior thought processes.

4. **RECALL:** Carl Rogers invented a technique to help people see their own thinking more clearly. Using this technique, the therapist paraphrases the client's statements. Rogers called this
   a. client-centered therapy.
   b. reflection of feeling.
   c. unconditional positive regard.
   d. self-actualization.
   e. analysis.

5. **RECALL:** Which form of therapy directly confronts a client's self-defeating thought patterns?
   a. humanistic therapy
   b. behavioral therapy
   c. participant modeling
   d. psychoanalytic therapy
   e. rational–emotive behavior therapy

6. **RECALL:** Eysenck caused a furor with his claim that people who receive psychotherapy
   a. are just looking for a paid friend.
   b. really should seek medical treatment for their disorders.
   c. are usually just pampered rich people who have nothing better to do with their lives.
   d. get better no more often than people who receive no therapy at all.
   e. respond only to psychoanalysis.

7. **UNDERSTANDING THE CORE CONCEPT:** A phobia would be best treated by ______, whereas a problem of choosing a major would be better suited for ______.
   a. behavioral therapy/insight therapy
   b. cognitive therapy/psychoanalysis
   c. insight therapy/behavioral therapy
   d. humanistic therapy/behavioral therapy
   e. psychoanalysis/humanistic therapy

ANSWERS: 1.b 2.e 3.b 4.b 5.e 6.d 7.a

HOW IS THE BIOMEDICAL APPROACH USED TO TREAT PSYCHOLOGICAL DISORDERS?

KEY QUESTION
?

The mind exists in a delicate biological balance. It can be upset by irregularities in our genes, hormones, enzymes, and metabolism, as well as by damage from accidents and disease. When something goes wrong with the brain, we can see the consequences in abnormal patterns of behavior or peculiar cognitive and emotional reactions. The biomedical therapies, therefore, attempt to treat these mental disorders by intervening directly in the brain. Our Core Concept specifies the targets of these therapies:

CORE CONCEPT

Biomedical therapies seek to treat psychological disorders by changing the brain's chemistry with drugs, its circuitry with surgery, or its patterns of activity with pulses of electricity or powerful magnetic fields.

Each of the biomedical therapies emerges from the *medical model* of abnormal mental functioning, which assumes an organic basis for mental illnesses and treats them as diseases—as we saw in Chapter 12. We begin our examination of these biomedical therapies with the powerful arsenal of prescription psychoactive drugs.

Drug Therapy/Psychopharmacology

In the history of the treatment of mental disorder, nothing has ever rivaled the revolution created by the discovery of drugs that could calm anxious patients, restore contact with reality in withdrawn patients, and suppress hallucinations in psychotic patients. This brave new therapeutic era began in 1953 with the introduction of the first antipsychotic drugs (often called tranquilizers). As

■ **Psychopharmacology** The prescribed use of drugs to help treat symptoms of mental illness ostensibly to ensure that individuals are more receptive to talk therapies.

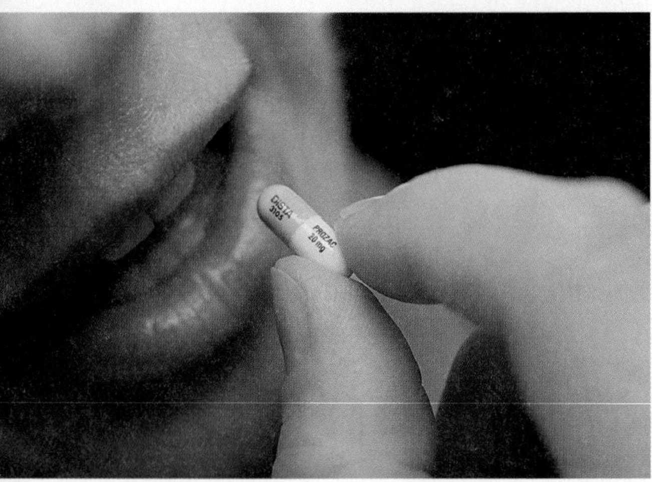
PROZAC
20 mg

● What will be the effect of prescribing mood-altering drugs such as Prozac to millions of people?

these drugs found wide application, many unruly, assaultive patients almost miraculously became cooperative, calm, and sociable. In addition, many thought-disordered patients, who had previously been absorbed in their delusions and hallucinations, began to respond to the physical and social environment around them.

The effectiveness of drug therapy had a pronounced effect on the census of the nation's mental hospitals. In 1955, over half a million Americans were living in mental institutions, each staying an average of several years. Then, with the introduction of tranquilizers, the numbers began a steady decline. In just over 10 years, fewer than half the number of the country's formerly hospitalized mental patients actually resided in mental hospitals, and those who did were usually kept for only a few months.

Drug therapy has long since steamrolled out of the mental hospital and into our everyday lives. Currently, millions of people take drugs for anxiety, stress, depression, hyperactivity, insomnia, fears and phobias, obsessions and compulsions, addictions, and numerous other problems. Clearly, a drug-induced revolution has occurred. But what are these miraculous drugs?

Drug Therapies

- Antipsychotic drugs
- Antidepressants and mood stabilizers
- Antianxiety drugs
- Stimulants

You have probably heard of Prozac and Valium, but those are just two of scores of psychoactive drugs that can alter your mood, your perceptions, your desires, and perhaps your basic personality. Here we will consider four major categories of drugs used today: *antipsychotics, antidepressants and mood stabilizers, antianxiety drugs,* and *stimulants.* (See the chart in the margin.)

Antipsychotic Drugs The purpose of the **antipsychotic drugs** is to treat the symptoms of psychosis: delusions, hallucinations, social withdrawal, and agitation (Dawkins et al., 1999; Gitlin, 1990; Holmes, 2001; Kane & Marder, 1993). Most work by reducing the activity of the neurotransmitter dopamine in the brain—although the precise reason why this has an antipsychotic effect is not known. For example, *chlorpromazine* (sold under the brand name Thorazine) and *haloperidol* (brand name: Haldol), for example, are known to block dopamine receptors in the synapse between nerve cells. A newer antipsychotic drug, *clozapine* (Clozaril), both decreases dopamine activity and increases the activity of another neurotransmitter, serotonin, which inhibits the dopamine system (Javitt & Coyle, 2004; Sawa & Snyder, 2002). These drugs reduce overall brain activity, but they do not merely "tranquilize" the patient. Rather, they reduce the positive symptoms of psychosis, although they do little for the social distance, jumbled thoughts, and poor attention spans seen in patients with negative symptoms of schizophrenia (Wickelgren, 1998b).

CONNECTION CHAPTER 12

Positive symptoms of *schizophrenia* include active hallucinations, delusions, and extreme emotions; negative symptoms include withdrawal and "flat" emotions.

Unfortunately, long-term administration of antipsychotic drugs can have several negative side effects. Physical changes in the brain have been noted (Gur & Maany, 1998). Most worrisome is **tardive dyskinesia,** which produces an incurable disturbance of motor control, especially of the facial muscles. Although the newer drug, clozapine, has reduced motor side effects because of its more selective dopamine blocking, its use involves a small risk of *agranulocytosis,* a blood disease caused by bone marrow dysfunction. With the possibility of such side effects, are antipsychotic drugs worth the risk? There is no easy answer. The risks must be weighed against the severity of the patient's current suffering.

■ **Antipsychotic drugs** Medicines that diminish psychotic symptoms, usually by their effect on the dopamine pathways in the brain.

■ **Tardive dyskinesia** An incurable disorder of motor control, especially involving muscles of the face and head, resulting from long-term use of antipsychotic drugs.

Antidepressants and Mood Stabilizers The drug therapy arsenal also includes several compounds that have revolutionized the treatment of depression and bipolar disorder. As with other psychoactive drugs, neither the antidepressants nor the mood stabilizers can provide a "cure." Their use, however, has made a big difference in the lives of many people suffering from mood disorders.

Antidepressant Drugs All three major classes of **antidepressant drugs** work by "turning up the volume" on messages transmitted over certain brain pathways, especially those using norepinephrine and serotonin (Holmes, 2001). *Tricyclic* compounds such as Tofranil and Elavil reduce the neuron's reabsorption of neurotransmitters after they have been released in the synapse between brain cells—a process called *reuptake*. A second group includes the famous antidepressant Prozac (fluoxetine). These drugs are known as *SSRIs* (selective serotonin reuptake inhibitors) because they selectively focus on preventing the reuptake of serotonin. As a result, SSRIs keep serotonin available in the synapse longer by preventing its inactivation and removal. For many people, this prolonged serotonin effect dramatically lifts depressed moods (Hirschfeld, 1999; Kramer, 1993). The third group of antidepressant drugs are *monoamine oxidase (MAO) inhibitors,* which limit the activity of the enzyme MAO, a chemical that breaks down norepinephrine in the synapse. When MAO is inhibited, more norepinephrine is available to carry neural messages across the synapse.

CONNECTION CHAPTER 3

Reuptake is a process by which neurotransmitters are taken intact from the synapse and cycled back into the terminal buttons of the axon. Reuptake, therefore, "tones down" the message being sent from one neuron to another.

The possibility of suicide is a special concern when considering antidepressant therapy. It usually takes a few weeks for antidepressants to have an effect—a long time to wait if the patient has suicidal tendencies, which are common in depressed patients. This delayed effect may account for the findings of a new study that shows an alarming increase in suicides in the month after patients begin taking antidepressants (Jick et al., 2004). Even more worrisome, according to some critics, is the possibility that the drugs themselves may sometimes contribute to suicidal thoughts by making depression worse before it gets better (Bower, 2004). While we wait for more research on this important issue, the U.S. Food and Drug Administration currently requires makers of antidepressant medications to warn physicians that patients taking these medications need close monitoring for suicidal tendencies.

Controversy over SSRIs In his book *Listening to Prozac,* psychiatrist and Prozac advocate Peter Kramer (1993) encourages the use of the drug to deal not only with depression but also with general feelings of social unease and fear of rejection. Such claims have brought heated replies from therapists who fear that drugs may merely mask the psychological problems that people need to face and resolve. Some worry that the wide use of antidepressants may produce changes in the personality structure of a huge segment of our population—changes that could bring unanticipated social consequences (Breggin & Breggin, 1994; Sleek, 1994). In fact, more prescriptions are being written for antidepressants than there are people who are clinically depressed (Coyne, 2001). The problem seems to be especially acute on college and university campuses, where increasing numbers of students are taking antidepressants (Young, 2003). At present, no one knows what the potential dangers might be of altering the brain chemistry of large numbers of people over long periods.

Mood Stabilizers A simple chemical, *lithium* (in the form of **lithium carbonate**) has proved highly effective as a mood stabilizer in the treatment of bipolar disorder (Schou, 1997). Lithium is not just an antidepressant, however. It affects both ends of the emotional spectrum, dampening swings of mood that would otherwise range from uncontrollable periods of hyperexcitement to the lethargy and despair of depression. But lithium, unfortunately, has a serious drawback: In high concentrations, it is toxic. Physicians have learned that safe therapy requires that small doses be given to build up therapeutic concentrations in the blood over a period of a week or two. Then, as a precaution, patients must have periodic blood analyses to ensure that lithium concentrations have not risen to dangerous levels. In a welcome development, researchers have

■ **Antidepressant drugs** Medicines that affect depression, usually by their effect on the serotonin and/or norepinephrine pathways in the brain.

■ **Lithium carbonate** A simple chemical compound that is highly effective in dampening the extreme mood swings of bipolar disorder.

found a promising alternative to lithium for the treatment of bipolar disorder (Azar, 1994; Walden et al., 1998). Divalproex sodium (brand name: Depakote), originally developed to treat epilepsy, seems to be more effective than lithium for most patients, and with fewer dangerous side effects (Bowden et al., 2000).

Antianxiety Drugs To reduce stress and suppress anxiety associated with everyday hassles, untold millions of Americans take **antianxiety drugs.** Many psychologists believe, however, that these drugs—like the antidepressants—are too often prescribed for problems that people should face, rather than mask with chemicals. Nevertheless, antianxiety compounds can be useful in helping people deal with specific situations, such as anxiety prior to surgery or an airplane flight.

The most commonly prescribed classes of antianxiety compounds are *barbiturates* and *benzodiazepines.* Barbiturates act as central nervous system depressants, so they have a relaxing effect. But barbiturates can be dangerous if taken in excess or in combination with alcohol. By contrast, the benzodiazepines, such as Valium and Xanax, work by increasing the activity of the neurotransmitter GABA, thereby decreasing activity in brain regions more specifically involved in feelings of anxiety. The benzodiazepines are sometimes called "minor tranquilizers."

CONNECTION CHAPTER 3
GABA is the major *inhibitory* neurotransmitter in the brain.

Here are some cautions to bear in mind about the antianxiety drugs (Hecht, 1986):

- In general, the antianxiety drugs work by sedating the user; if used over long periods, these drugs can be physically and psychologically addicting (Holmes, 2001; Schatzberg, 1991).
- These medicines should not be taken to relieve anxieties that are part of the ordinary stresses of everyday life.
- When used for extreme anxiety, these drugs should not normally be taken for more than a few days at a time. If used longer than this, their dosage should be gradually reduced by a physician. Abrupt cessation after prolonged use can lead to withdrawal symptoms, such as convulsions, tremors, and abdominal and muscle cramps.
- Because the antianxiety drugs depress the central nervous system, they can impair one's ability to drive, operate machinery, or perform other tasks that require alertness (such as studying or taking exams).
- In combination with alcohol (also a central nervous system depressant) or with sleeping pills, antianxiety drugs can lead to unconsciousness and even death.

Finally, we should mention that some antidepressant drugs have also been found useful for reducing the symptoms of certain anxiety disorders, such as panic disorders, agoraphobia, and obsessive–compulsive disorder. (A modern psychiatrist might well have prescribed antidepressants for Freud's obsessive patient.) Because these problems may arise from low levels of serotonin, they may also respond well to drugs like Prozac that specifically affect serotonin function.

Stimulants Ranging from caffeine to nicotine to amphetamines to cocaine—any drug that produces excitement or hyperactivity falls into the category of **stimulants.** We have noted that stimulants find some use in the treatment of narcolepsy. They also have an accepted niche in treating **attention-deficit/hyperactivity disorder (ADHD)**. While it may seem strange to prescribe stimulants (a common one is Ritalin) for hyperactive children, studies comparing stimulant therapy with behavior therapy and with placebos have shown a clear role for stimulants (American Academy of Pediatrics, 2001; Henker & Whalen, 1989; Poling et al., 1991; Welsh et al., 1993). Although the exact mechanism is

- **Antianxiety drugs** A category of drugs that includes the barbiturates and benzodiazepines, drugs that diminish feelings of anxiety.
- **Stimulants** Drugs that normally increase activity level by encouraging communication among neurons in the brain. Stimulants, however, have been found to suppress activity level in persons with attention-deficit/hyperactivity disorder.
- **Attention-deficit/hyperactivity disorder (ADHD)** A common problem in children who have difficulty controlling their behavior and focusing their attention.

unknown, stimulants may work in hyperactive children by increasing the availability of dopamine, glutamate, and/or serotonin in their brains (Barkley, 1998; Gainetdinov et al., 1999; Wu, 1998).

As you can imagine, the use of stimulants to treat ADHD has generated controversy (O'Connor, 2001). Some objections, of course, stem from ignorance of the well-established calming effect these drugs have in children with this condition. Other worries have more substance. For some, the drug will interfere with normal sleep patterns. Additionally, there is evidence that stimulant therapy can slow the growth of children (NIMH, 2004). There are also legitimate concerns that a potential for abuse exists in the temptation to see every child's behavior problem as a symptom of ADHD (Angold et al., 2000; Marshall, 2000; Smith, 2002). Critics also suggest that the prescription of stimulants to children might encourage later drug abuse (Daw, 2001).

Evaluating the Drug Therapies The drug therapies have caused a revolution in the treatment of severe mental disorders, starting in the 1950s, when virtually the only treatments available were talk therapies, hospitalization, restraints, "shock treatment," and lobotomies. Of course, none of the drugs discovered so far can "cure" any mental disorder. Yet in many cases they can alter the brain's chemistry to suppress symptoms.

But is all the enthusiasm warranted? According to neuroscientist Elliot Valenstein, a close look behind the scenes of drug therapy raises important questions (Rolnick, 1998; Valenstein, 1998). Valenstein believes that much of the faith in drug therapy for mental disorders rests on hype. He credits the wide acceptance of drug therapy to the huge investment drug companies have made in marketing their products. Particularly distressing are concerns raised recently about the willingness of physicians to prescribe drugs for children—even though the safety and effectiveness of many drugs have not been established in young people (K. Brown, 2003a).

Few question that drugs are the proper first line of treatment for certain conditions, such as bipolar disorder and schizophrenia. In other cases, however, the apparent advantages of drug therapy are quick results and low cost. Yet some research raises doubts about simplistic time-and-money assumptions. Studies show, for example, that treating depression, anxiety disorders, and eating disorders with cognitive–behavioral therapy—alone or in combination with drugs—may be both more effective and economical in the long run than relying on drugs alone (Barlow, 1996; Clay, 2000; Hollon, 1996).

Other Medical Therapies for Psychological Disorder

Describing a modern-day counterpart to Phineas Gage, the headline in the *Los Angeles Times* read, "Bullet in the Brain Cures Man's Mental Problem" (February 23, 1988). The article revealed that a 19-year-old man suffering from severe obsessive–compulsive disorder had shot a .22 caliber bullet through the front of his brain in a suicide attempt. Remarkably, he survived, his pathological symptoms were gone, and his intellectual capacity was not affected.

CONNECTION CHAPTER 3
Phineas Gage survived–with a changed personality–after a steel rod was blasted through his frontal lobe.

We don't recommend this form of therapy, but the case illustrates the potential effects of physical intervention in the brain. Accordingly, we will look briefly at two medical alternatives to drug therapy that were conceived to alter the brain's structure and function: psychosurgery and direct stimulation of the brain.

Psychosurgery With scalpels in place of bullets, surgeons have long aspired to treat mental disorders by severing connections between parts of the brain or by removing small sections of brain. In modern times, **psychosurgery,** the general term for such procedures, is usually considered a method of last resort.

■ **Psychosurgery** The general term for surgical intervention in the brain to treat psychological disorders.

Nevertheless, psychosurgery has a long history, dating back at least to medieval times, when surgeons might open the skull to remove "the stone of folly" from an unfortunate madman. (There is, of course, no such "stone"—and there was no anesthetic except alcohol for these procedures.)

In modern times, the best-known form of psychosurgery involved the now-abandoned *prefrontal lobotomy.* This operation, developed by Portuguese psychiatrist Egas Moñiz,[2] severed certain nerve fibers connecting the frontal lobes with deep brain structures, especially those of the thalamus and hypothalamus—much as happened by accident to Phineas Gage, whom we discussed in Chapter 3. The original candidates for Moñiz's scalpel were agitated schizophrenic patients and patients who were compulsive and anxiety-ridden. The effects of this rather crude operation were often a dramatic reduction in agitation and anxiety. On the other hand, the operation permanently destroyed basic aspects of the patients' personalities. Frequently, they emerged from the procedure with loss of interest in their personal well-being and their surroundings. Further, a lobotomy usually produced an inability to plan ahead, an indifference to the opinions of others, childlike actions, and the intellectual and emotional flatness of a person without a coherent sense of self. Not surprisingly, when the new drug therapies promised to control psychotic symptoms with less risk of permanent loss, the era of lobotomy came to a close in the 1950s (Valenstein, 1980).

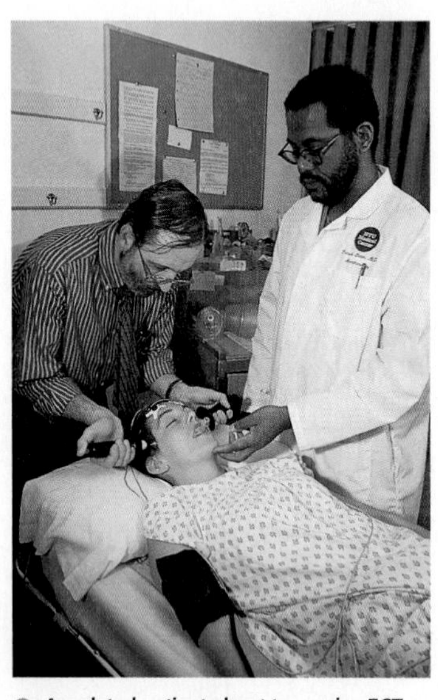

● A sedated patient about to receive ECT. Electroconvulsive therapy involves a weak electrical current to a patient's temples, causing a convulsion. Some psychiatrists have found ECT successful in alleviating symptoms of severe depression, but most therapists regard it as a treatment of last resort.

Psychosurgery is still occasionally done, but it is now much more limited to precise and proven procedures for very specific brain disorders. In the "split-brain" operation, for example, severing the fibers of the corpus callosum can reduce life-threatening seizures in certain cases of epilepsy, with relatively few side effects. Psychosurgery is also done on portions of the brain involved in pain perception in cases of otherwise intractable pain. Today, however, no *DSM-IV* diagnoses are routinely treated with psychosurgery.

Brain-Stimulation Therapies Electrical stimulation of the brain in the form known as **electroconvulsive therapy (ECT)** is still widely used, especially in patients who have not responded to drug treatment for depression. ECT induces a convulsion by applying an electric current (75 to 100 volts) to a patient's temples briefly—from one-tenth to a full second. The convulsion usually runs its course in less than a minute. Patients are prepared for this traumatic intervention by sedating them with a short-acting barbiturate and a muscle relaxant. This renders them unconscious and minimizes violent, uncontrolled physical spasms during the seizure (Abrams, 1992; Malitz & Sackheim, 1984). Within half an hour the patient awakens but has no memory of the seizure or of the events preparatory to treatment.

Does it work? Crude as this treatment may seem—sending an electric current through the skull and brain—studies have shown ECT to be a useful tool in treating depression, especially in patients with suicidal tendencies that demand an intervention that works more rapidly than medication or psychotherapy (Glass, 2001; Holden, 2003; Hollon et al., 2002; Sackheim et al., 2000). Typically, the symptoms of depression are reduced in a three- or four-day course of treatment, in contrast with the one- to two-week period required for drug therapy to be effective. Speed can be a major concern in depression, where suicide is always a possibility.

■ **Electroconvulsive therapy (ECT)** A treatment used primarily for depression and involving the application of an electric current to the head, producing a generalized seizure. Sometimes called "shock treatment."

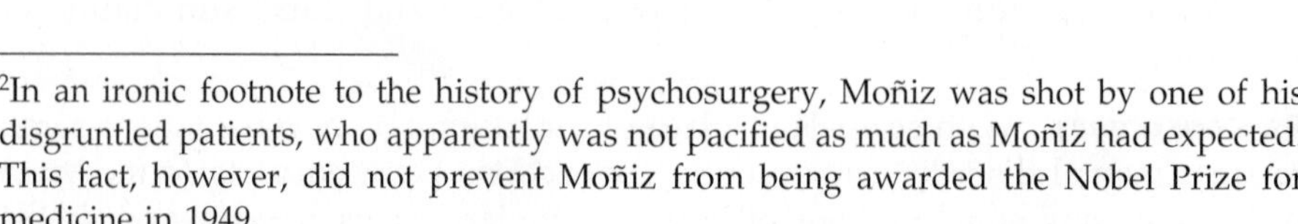

[2]In an ironic footnote to the history of psychosurgery, Moñiz was shot by one of his disgruntled patients, who apparently was not pacified as much as Moñiz had expected. This fact, however, did not prevent Moñiz from being awarded the Nobel Prize for medicine in 1949.

Some critics fear that ECT might be abused to silence dissent or punish patients who are uncooperative (Holmes, 2001). Other worries about ECT stem from the fact that its effects are not well understood. To date no definitive theory explains why inducing a mild convulsion should alleviate disordered symptoms.

Most worrisome, perhaps, are the memory deficits sometimes caused by electroconvulsive therapy (Breggin, 1979, 1991). Proponents claim, on the other hand, that patients generally recover full memory functions within months of the treatment (Calev et al., 1991). In the face of such concerns, the National Institute of Mental Health (1985) investigated the use of ECT and gave it a cautious endorsement for treating a narrow range of disorders, especially severe depression. Then, in 1990, the American Psychiatric Association also proclaimed ECT to be a valid treatment option. To minimize even short-term side effects, however, ECT is usually administered "unilaterally"—and only to the right temple, in order to reduce the possibility of speech impairment (Scovern & Kilmann, 1980).

CONNECTION CHAPTER 3

Speech is controlled by the left hemisphere in most people.

A promising new therapeutic tool for stimulating the brain with magnetic fields may offer all the benefits of ECT without the unwanted side effects of memory loss. Still in the experimental stages, **transcranial magnetic stimulation (TMS)** involves directing high-powered magnetic stimulation to specific parts of the brain. Studies indicate that TMS may be useful for treating not only depression but also schizophrenia and bipolar disorder (George, 2003; George et al., 1999; Helmuth, 2001b; Travis, 2000b; Wassermann & Lisanby, 2001). Because most applications of TMS therapy do not require the induction of a seizure, researchers hope also that it offers a safer alternative to ECT.

Hospitalization and the Alternatives

We have seen that mental hospitals were originally conceived as places of refuge—"asylums"—where disturbed people could escape the pressures of normal living. In fact, they often worked very well (Maher & Maher, 1985). But by the 20th century these hospitals had become overcrowded and, at best, little more than warehouses for the disturbed with nowhere else to go. Rarely were people of means committed to mental hospitals; instead, they were given private care, including individual psychotherapy (Doyle, 2002a). By contrast, in the large public mental hospitals, a feeble form of "group therapy" was often done with a whole ward—perhaps 50 patients—at a time. But too many patients and too few therapists meant that little, if any, real therapy occurred. The drugs that so profoundly altered treatment in mental hospitals did not appear until the 1950s, so prior to that time institutionalized patients were often controlled by straitjackets, locked rooms, and, sometimes, lobotomies. It's too bad that Maxwell Jones didn't come to the rescue a half-century earlier, with his frontal attack on the mental hospital system.

The Therapeutic Community In 1953—at about the time antipsychotic drugs were introduced—psychiatrist Maxwell Jones proposed replacing traditional hospital "treatment" for mental disorders with a **therapeutic community** designed to bring meaning to patients lives. He envisioned the daily hospital routine itself structured as a therapy that would help patients learn to cope with the world outside. With these goals in mind, he abolished the dormitory accommodations that had been typical of mental hospitals and gave patients more private living quarters. He required that they make decisions about meals and daily activities. Then, as they were able to take more responsibilities, patients assumed the tasks of everyday living, including laundry, housekeeping,

■ **Transcranial magnetic stimulation (TMS)** A treatment that involves magnetic stimulation of specific regions of the brain. Unlike ECT, TMS does not produce a seizure.

■ **Therapeutic community** Jones's term for a program of treating mental disorder by making the institutional environment supportive and humane for patients.

and maintenance. Further, Jones involved them in helping to plan their own treatment, which included not only group psychotherapy but occupational therapy and recreational therapy as well (Jones, 1953).

Eventually, variations on the therapeutic community concept were adopted across the United States, Canada, Britain, and Europe—sometimes more on paper than in reality, as we saw in Rosenhan's "pseudopatient" study. But the changes did not come cheaply. The newer approach obviously required more staff and more costly facilities. The high costs led to a search for still another alternative, which came in the form of community-based treatment—which began to look more and more attractive with the increasing availability of drug therapies.

Deinstitutionalization and Community Mental Health For mental health professionals of all stripes, the goal of **deinstitutionalization** was to remove patients from mental hospitals and return them to their communities for treatment in a more familiar and supportive environment. The concept of deinstitutionalization also gained popularity with politicians, who saw large sums of money being poured into mental hospitals (filled, incidentally, with nonvoting patients). Thus, by the 1970s, a consensus formed among politicians and the mental health community that the major locus of treatment should shift from mental hospitals back to the community. There both psychological and drug therapies would be dispensed from outpatient clinics, and recovering patients could live with their families, in foster homes, or in group homes. This vision became known as the **community mental health movement.**

Self Realization

● Deinstitutionalization put mental patients back in the community—but often without adequate resources for continued treatment.

Unfortunately, the reality did not match the vision (Doyle, 2002a; Torrey, 1996, 1997). Community mental health clinics—the centerpieces of the community mental health movement—rarely received the full funding they needed. Chronic patients were released from mental hospitals, but they often returned to communities that could offer them few therapeutic resources and to families ill-equipped to cope with them (Arnhoff, 1975; Smith et al., 1993). Then, as patients returned to the community and needed care, they entered psychiatric wards at local general hospitals—rather than mental hospitals. As a result, hospital care has continued to consume most funding for mental health in the United States. Currently, mental patients account for about 25% of all hospital days (Kiesler, 1993).

Some disturbed individuals, who would have been hospitalized in an earlier time, have now all but disappeared from view within their communities. An estimated 150,000 persons, especially those with chronic schizophrenia, have ended up homeless, with no network of support (Torrey, 1997). Although estimates vary widely, up to 52% of homeless men and 71% of homeless women in the United States probably suffer from psychological disorders, and many of them are former mental hospital patients (Fischer & Breakey, 1991; Lamb, 1998). Many also have problems with alcohol or other drugs (Drake et al., 1991). Under these conditions, they survive by shuttling from agency to agency. With no one to monitor their behavior, they usually stop taking their medication, and so their condition deteriorates until they require a period of rehospitalization.

■ **Deinstitutionalization** The policy of removing patients, whenever possible, from mental hospitals.

■ **Community mental health movement** An effort to deinstitutionalize mental patients and to provide therapy from outpatient clinics. Proponents of community mental health envisioned that recovering patients could live with their families, in foster homes, or in group homes.

Despite the dismal picture we have painted, community treatment has not proved altogether unsuccessful. After a review of ten studies in which mental patients were randomly assigned to hospital treatment or to various community-based programs, Kiesler (1982a) reported that patients more often improved in the community treatment programs. Further, those given community-based treatment were less likely to be hospitalized at a later date. When community health programs have adequate resources, they can be highly effective (McGuire, 2000).

PSYCHOLOGY IN YOUR LIFE: WHAT SORT OF THERAPY WOULD YOU RECOMMEND?

Now that we have looked at both the psychological and biomedical therapies, consider the following situation. A friend tells you about some personal problems he or she is having and requests your help in finding a therapist. Because you are studying psychology, your friend reasons, you might know what kind of treatment would be best. How do you respond?

First, you can lend a friendly ear, using the techniques of active listening, acceptance, and exploration of alternatives, which we discussed earlier in the chapter. In fact, this may be all that your troubled friend needs. But if your friend wants to see a therapist or if the situation looks in any way like one that requires professional assistance, you can use your knowledge of mental disorders and therapies to help your friend decide what sort of therapist might be most appropriate. To take some of the burden off your shoulders, both of you should understand that any competent therapist will always refer the client elsewhere if the required therapy lies outside the therapist's specialty.

A Therapy Checklist Here, then, are some questions you will want to consider before you recommend a particular type of therapist:

- *Is medical treatment needed?* While you should not try to make a diagnosis, you should encourage your friend to see a psychiatrist for medical treatment if you suspect that the problem involves psychosis, mania, or bipolar disorder. Medical evaluation is also indicated if you suspect narcolepsy, sleep apnea, epilepsy, Alzheimer's disease, or other problems recognized to have a biological basis. If your suspicion is confirmed, the psychiatrist may employ a combination of drug therapy and psychotherapy.
- *Is there a specific behavior problem?* For example, does your friend want to eliminate a fear of spiders or a fear of flying? Is the problem a rebellious child? A sexual problem? Is she or he depressed—but not psychotic? If so, behavior therapy or cognitive–behavioral therapy with a counseling or clinical psychologist is probably the best bet. (Most psychiatrists and other medical practitioners are not trained in these procedures.) You can call the prospective therapist's office and ask for information on specific areas of training and specialization.
- *Would group therapy be helpful?* Many people find valuable help and support in a group setting, where they can learn not only from the therapist but also from other group members. Groups can be especially effective in dealing with shyness, lack of assertiveness, and addictions, and with complex problems of interpersonal relationships. (As a bonus, group therapy is often less expensive than individual therapy.) Professionals with training in several disciplines, including psychology, psychiatry, and social work, run therapy groups. Again, your best bet is a therapist who has had special training in this method and about whom you have heard good things from former clients.
- *Is the problem one of stress, confusion, or choice?* Most troubled people don't fall neatly into one of the categories that we have discussed in the previous

paragraphs. More typically, they need help sorting through the chaos of their lives, finding a pattern, and developing a plan to cope. This is the territory of the insight therapies.

Some Cautions We now know enough about human biology, behavior, and mental processes to know some treatments to avoid. Here are some particularly important examples:

- *Drug therapies to avoid:* The minor tranquilizers are too frequently prescribed for patients leading chronically stressful lives (Alford & Bishop, 1991). As we have said, because of their addicting and sedating effects, these drugs should only be taken for short periods—if at all. Similarly, some physicians ignore the dangers of sleep-inducing medications for their patients who suffer from insomnia. Although these drugs have legitimate uses, many such prescriptions carry the possibility of drug dependence and of interfering with the person's ability to alter the conditions that may have caused the original problem.
- *Advice and interpretations to avoid:* Although psychodynamic therapy can be helpful, patients should also be cautioned that some such therapists may give ill-advised counsel in problems of anger management. Traditionally, Freudians have believed that individuals who are prone to angry or violent outbursts harbor deep-seated aggression that needs to be vented. But, as we have seen, research shows that trying to empty one's aggressions through aggressive behavior, such as shouting or punching a pillow, may actually increase the likelihood of later aggressive behavior.

With these cautions in mind, then, your friend can contact several therapists to see which has the skills and the manner that offer the best fit for her or his problem and personality.

CHECK YOUR UNDERSTANDING

1. **RECALL:** Which class of drugs blocks dopamine receptors in the brain?
   a. antipsychotics
   b. antidepressants
   c. antianxiety drugs
   d. stimulants
   e. depressants
2. **RECALL:** A controversial treatment for attention-deficit/hyperactivity disorder involves
   a. antipsychotics.
   b. antidepressants.
   c. antianxiety drugs.
   d. stimulants.
   e. depressants.
3. **RECALL:** Which of the following medical treatments for mental disorder has now been largely abandoned as ineffective and dangerous?
   a. electroconvulsive therapy
   b. lithium
   c. prefrontal lobotomy
   d. the "split-brain" operation
   e. antipsychotics
4. **RECALL:** The community mental health movement followed a deliberate plan of ______ mental patients.
   a. hospitalizing
   b. deinstitutionalizing
   c. administering insight therapy to
   d. removing stressful events in the lives of
   e. lobotomizing
5. **UNDERSTANDING THE CORE CONCEPT:** Drug therapies, psychosurgery, and ECT all are methods of treating mental disorder
   a. by changing the chemistry of the body.
   b. by removing stress in the patient's life.
   c. that always succeed.
   d. that have no scientific basis.
   e. by directly altering the function of the brain.

ANSWERS: 1. a 2. d 3. c 4. b 5. e

THERAPIES: THE STATE OF THE ART

Prompted initially by questions about the effectiveness of therapy and later by a shift to managed health care, the mental health professions have begun to identify specific psychological and biomedical treatments that are effective for specific disorders. The disorders for which real help now exists include depression, phobias and other anxiety disorders, certain schizophrenias, ADHD, and autism. We can expect to see more and more such treatments identified, especially in the realm of drug therapies.

On the negative side, some drug therapies are overprescribed, as physicians and patients seek quick fixes for mental problems. The reality is that most *DSM-IV* disorders have no easy cures. For these, time is required for counseling or psychotherapy that may be necessary to sort through problems and examine alternative solutions.

USING PSYCHOLOGY TO LEARN PSYCHOLOGY

How Is Education Like Therapy?

Consider the ways in which psychotherapy is like your classroom experiences:

- Most therapists, like most teachers, are professionals with special training in what they do.
- Most patients/clients are like students in that they are seeking professional help to change their lives in some way.
- Much of what happens in therapy and in the classroom involves learning: new ideas, new behaviors, new insights, new connections.

It may help you learn psychology (and other subjects, as well) to think of teaching and learning in therapeutic terms. As we have seen, therapy seems to work best when therapist and client have a good working relationship and when the client believes in the value of the experience—and the same is almost certainly true for the student–teacher relationship. You can take the initiative in establishing a personal-but-professional relationship with your psychology teacher by doing the following two things: (1) asking questions or otherwise participating in class (at appropriate times and without dominating, of course) and (2) seeking your instructor's help on points you don't understand or on course-related topics you would like to pursue in more detail (doing so during regular office hours). The result will be learning more about psychology, because you will be taking a more active part in the learning process. Incidentally, an active approach to the course will also help you stand out from the crowd in the teacher's mind, which could be helpful if you later need a teacher recommendation for college.

Now consider a parallel between education and group therapy. In group therapy, patients learn from each other, as well as from the therapist. Much the same can occur in your psychology course, if you consider other students as learning resources. As we noted earlier in this book, the most successful students often spend part of their study time sharing information in groups.

One other tip for learning psychology we can borrow from the success of behavior therapies: the importance of changing behavior, not just thinking. It is easy to "intellectualize" a fact or an idea passively when you read about it or hear about it in class. But you are likely to find that the idea has little impact on you ("I know I *read* about it, but I can't *remember* it!") if you don't use it. The remedy is to do something with your new knowledge: Tell someone about it, come up with illustrations from your own experience, or try acting in a different way. For example, after reading about active listening in this chapter, try it the next time you talk to a friend. Educators sometimes speak of this as "active learning." And it works!

CHAPTER SUMMARY

KEY QUESTION

CORE CONCEPT

• WHAT IS THERAPY?

People seek therapy for a variety of problems, including *DSM-IV* disorders and problems of everyday living. Treatment comes in many forms, both psychological and biomedical, but most involve diagnosing the problem, finding the source of the problem, making a prognosis, and carrying out treatment. A variety of professionals work under this model. In earlier times, treatments for those with mental problems were usually harsh and dehumanizing, often based on the assumption of demon possession. Only recently have people with emotional problems been treated as individuals with "illnesses," which has led to more humane treatment.

Currently in the United States, there are two main approaches to therapy: the psychological and the biomedical therapies. Psychological therapies include insight therapy and behavior therapy—each of which, in turn, come in several forms. Other cultures often have different ways of understanding and treating mental disorders, often making use of the family and community. In the United States there is a trend toward increasing use of paraprofessionals as mental health care providers, and the literature generally supports their effectiveness.

● **Therapy for psychological disorders takes a variety of forms, but all involve some relationship focused on improving a person's mental, behavioral, or social functioning.**

• HOW DO PSYCHOLOGISTS TREAT PSYCHOLOGICAL DISORDERS?

The first of the insight therapies, psychoanalysis grew out of Sigmund Freud's theory of personality. Using such techniques as free association and dream interpretation, its goal is to bring repressed material out of the unconscious, where it can be interpreted and neutralized, particularly in the analysis of transference. Neo-Freudians typically emphasize the patient's current social situation, interpersonal relationships, and self-concept.

Among other insight therapies, humanistic therapy focuses on individuals becoming more fully self-actualized. In one form, client-centered therapists strive to be nondirective in helping their clients establish a positive self-image.

Another form of insight therapy, cognitive therapy concentrates on changing negative or irrational thought patterns about oneself and one's social relationships. The client must learn more constructive thought patterns in reference to a problem and apply the new technique to other situations. This has been particularly effective for depression.

Group therapy can take many approaches. Self-help support groups, such as AA, serve millions, even though they are not usually run by professional therapists. Family therapy and couples therapy usually concentrate on situational difficulties and interpersonal dynamics as a total system in need of improvement, rather than on internal motives.

The behavior therapies apply the principles of learning—especially operant and classical conditioning—to problem behaviors. Among the classical conditioning techniques, systematic desensitization is commonly employed to treat fears. Aversion therapy may also be used for eliminating unwanted responses. Operant techniques include contingency management, which especially involves positive reinforcement and extinction strategies. And, on a larger scale, behavior therapy may be used to treat or manage groups in the form of a token economy. Participant modeling, based on observational learning therapy, may make use of both classical and operant principles, involving the use of models and social-skills training to help individuals practice and gain confidence about their abilities.

In recent years a synthesis of cognitive and behavior therapies has emerged, combining the techniques of insight therapy with methods based on observational learning theory. Rational–emotive behavior therapy helps clients recognize that their irrational beliefs about themselves interfere with life and helps them learn how to change those thought patterns.

The effectiveness of therapy was challenged in the 1950s by Eysenck. Since that time, however, research has shown that psychotherapy can be effective for a variety of psychological problems. Often it is more effective than drug therapy. As the research on mental disorders becomes more refined, we are learning to match specific psychotherapies to specific disorders.

Most people do not get psychological help from professionals. Rather, they get help from teachers, friends, clergy, and others in their community who seem sympathetic. Friends can often help through active listening, acceptance, and exploration of alternatives, but serious problems require professional assistance.

● **Psychologists employ two main forms of treatment: the insight therapies (focused on developing understanding of the problem) and the behavior therapies (focused on changing behavior through conditioning).**

• HOW IS THE BIOMEDICAL APPROACH USED TO TREAT PSYCHOLOGICAL DISORDERS?

Biomedical therapies concentrate on changing the physiological aspects of mental illness. Drug therapy includes antipsychotic, antidepressant, mood stabilizing, antianxiety, and stimulant medicines. Most affect the function of neurotransmitters, but the precise mode of action is not known for any of them. Nevertheless, such drugs have caused a revolution in the medical treatment of mental disorder, such as schizophrenia, depression, bipolar disorder, anxiety disorders, and ADHD. Critics, however, warn of their abuse, particularly in treating the ordinary stress of daily living.

Psychosurgery has lost much of its popularity in recent years because of its radical, irreversible side effects. Electroconvulsive therapy, however, is still widely used—primarily with depressed patients—although it remains controversial. A new and promising alternative involves transcranial magnetic stimulation of specific brain areas. Meanwhile, hospitalization has been a mainstay of medical treatment, although the trend is away from mental hospitals to community-based treatment. The policy of deinstitutionalization was based on the best intentions, but many mental patients have been turned back into their communities with few resources and little treatment. When the resources are available, however, community treatment is often successful.

If someone asks your advice on finding a therapist, you can refer him or her to any competent mental health professional. You should avoid trying to make a diagnosis or attempting therapy for mental disorders, but you may use your knowledge of psychology to steer the person toward a medical specialist, a behavior therapist, group therapy, or some other psychological treatment that you believe might be appropriate. There are, however, some specific therapies and therapeutic techniques to avoid.

● **Biomedical therapies seek to treat psychological disorders by changing the brain's chemistry with drugs, its circuitry with surgery, or its patterns of activity with pulses of electricity or powerful magnetic fields.**

REVIEW TEST

For each of the following items, choose the single correct or best answer. The answer key appears at the end of the test.

1. Despite the differences between various types of therapy, all therapeutic strategies are designed to
   a. make the client feel better about him- or herself.
   b. help the individual fit better into his or her society.
   c. change the individual's functioning in some way.
   d. educate the person without interfering with his or her usual patterns of behavior.
   e. utilize medication in arriving at a final therapy.

2. While professionals with somewhat different training and orientations can provide similar forms of therapy in which all of the following groups are trained practitioners, only ______ on the list below are qualified to prescribe medications for the treatment of mental or behavioral disorders.
   a. neuropharmacologists
   b. psychiatric social workers
   c. psychologists
   d. psychotherapists
   e. psychiatrists

3. Because a central goal of the therapist is to guide a patient toward understanding the connections between past origins and present symptoms, psychodynamic therapy is a form of ______ therapy.
   a. insight
   b. cognitive
   c. behavior
   d. rational–emotive behavior
   e. group

4. Lola has an irrational fear of speaking in front of others. With the support of her instructor and her entire psychology class, Lola confronts her fear by standing alone in front of her classmates and talking about her phobia. This strategy of placing the individual in the dreaded situation is called
   a. exposure therapy.
   b. catharsis.
   c. insight therapy.
   d. social-learning therapy.
   e. group.

5. To teach his young daughter not to be afraid to swim, a father tells her to "Watch me!" as he wades into the surf, then rolls with the waves, and finally invites her to join him if she wants to try. In behavioral therapy, this technique is known as
   a. clinical ecology.
   b. counterconditioning.
   c. behavioral rehearsal.
   d. participant modeling.
   e. systematic desensitization.

6. A patient finds herself feeling personally fond of her therapist, who reminds her of her father. This is an example of the psychoanalytic process known as
   a. resistance.
   b. reaction formation.
   c. regression.
   d. negative transference.
   e. transference.

7. Which of the following problems might best be corrected through rational–emotive behavior therapy (REBT)?
   a. An addicted smoker wants to quit.
   b. A young man has an extreme fear of heights.
   c. An average-weight woman diets constantly, believing that she must be thin in order to have anyone love her.
   d. A patient complains of continual "voices" in his head telling him that people are trying to harm him.
   e. An elderly male has memory problems.

8. In recent years, psychotherapy research has found
   a. drugs to be more effective than cognitive–behavioral therapy.
   b. insight therapy to be more effective than behavioral therapy for most disorders.
   c. most mental problems to have their roots in unconscious motives or emotions.
   d. specific therapies that are highly effective for specific disorders.
   e. that nearly all individuals eventually "get better" with or without therapy.

9. Valium, a drug with a high "abuse potential," is classified as an ______ medication.
   a. antianxiety
   b. antidepressant
   c. antipsychotic
   d. antihistamine
   e. stimulant

10. Which of the following statements about electroconvulsive therapy (ECT) is true?
    a. Proper ECT applies a very strong electric current directly to a patient's brain without the need for sedatives or anesthetic medication.
    b. Some studies have found ECT to be effective in the treatment of severe depression.
    c. ECT is known to work by increasing the stimulation of a particular neurotransmitter in the brain.
    d. ECT works best with manic patients.
    e. ECT is a sure way to "cure" resistant depression.

ANSWERS: 1. c 2. e 3. a 4. a 5. d 6. b 7. c 8. d 9. a 10. b

KEY TERMS

Therapy (p. 524)
Psychological therapies (p. 529)
Biomedical therapies (p. 529)
Insight therapies (p. 531)
Talk therapies (p. 531)
Psychoanalysis (p. 532)
Analysis of transference (p. 533)
Neo-Freudian psychodynamic therapies (p. 533)
Humanistic therapies (p. 534)
Client-centered therapy (p. 534)
Reflection of feeling (p. 534)
Cognitive therapy (p. 536)
Group therapy (p. 536)
Self-help support groups (p. 537)
Behavior modification (p. 538)
Behavior therapy (p. 538)
Systematic desensitization (p. 539)
Exposure therapy (p. 540)
Aversion therapy (p. 540)
Contingency management (p. 541)
Token economy (p. 541)
Participant modeling (p. 542)
Cognitive–behavioral therapy (p. 542)
Rational–emotive behavior therapy (REBT) (p. 543)
Active listener (p. 548)
Psychopharmacology (p. 549)
Antipsychotic drugs (p. 550)
Tardive dyskinesia (p. 550)
Antidepressant drugs (p. 551)
Lithium carbonate (p. 551)
Antianxiety drugs (p. 552)
Stimulants (p. 552)
Attention-deficit/hyperactivity disorder (ADHD) (p. 552)
Psychosurgery (p. 553)
Electroconvulsive therapy (ECT) (p. 554)
Transcranial magnetic stimulation (TMS) (p. 555)
Therapeutic community (p. 555)
Deinstitutionalization (p. 556)
Community mental health movement (p. 556)

AP* REVIEW: VOCABULARY

Match each of the following vocabulary terms to its definition.

1. Psychoanalysis
2. Client-centered therapy
3. Cognitive therapy
4. Behavior therapy
5. Aversion therapy
6. Psychopharmacology
7. REBT
8. Antianxiety drugs
9. Stimulant

_____ a. This therapy is essentially based on operant and classical conditioning.

_____ b. This therapy involves the prescribed use of drugs to help treat symptoms of mental illness so that individuals are more receptive to talk therapies.

_____ c. This therapy emphasizes an individual's tendency for healthy psychological growth.

_____ d. This is the category of drugs that includes benzodiazepines and barbiturates.

_____ e. This type of therapy is based on Albert Ellis's form of cognitive therapy.

_____ f. The goal of this therapy is to release conflicts and memories from the unconscious.

_____ g. This therapy pairs an attractive stimulus with an aversive one in order to condition revulsion.

_____ h. Chemical compounds that increase activity level by encouraging communication among neurons in the brain.

_____ i. This therapy focuses on rational thinking as the key to treating mental disorders.

AP* REVIEW: ESSAY

Use your knowledge of the chapter concepts to answer the following essay question.

Compare and contrast the ways in which a psychopharmacologist and a rational–emotive behavior therapy (REBT) therapist would treat a patient with bipolar disorder. Be sure that your response addresses diagnosis, methodology, and differences between the two therapies.

OUR RECOMMENDED BOOKS AND VIDEOS

BOOKS

Beam, A. (2001). *Gracefully insane: The rise and fall of America's premier mental hospital.* New York: PublicAffairs. This is a history of McLean Hospital outside Boston, Massachusetts, the mental hospital equivalent of a luxury hotel, which over the years offered "spa" treatments and retreat for wealthier patients and celebrities, including author Sylvia Plath, poet Anne Sexton, musicians Ray Charles and James Taylor, and Susanna Kaysen of the memoir and movie *Girl, Interrupted,* about her two-year stay in McLean.

Berger, L., & Vuckovic, A. (1995). *Under observation: Life inside the McLean Psychiatric Hospital.* New York: Penguin Books. This vivid portrayal of life in psychiatric institutions is illustrated with case histories and the personal stories of patients who emerge not as characters but as real people, disturbingly familiar and similar to ourselves.

Davidson, J., & Dreher, H. (2003). *The anxiety book: Developing strength in the face of fear.* New York: Riverhead Books/Penguin. This guide to identifying the level and sources of your own anxiety assesses its impact on your life and discusses using cognitive techniques, physical exercise, and professional resources for treatment.

Hesley, J. W., & Hesley, J. G. (2001). *Rent two films and let's talk in the morning: Using popular movies in psychotherapy,* 2nd edition. New York: John Wiley & Sons. The authors offer a wonderful guide to using therapeutic "videowork" to get more out of feature films whose plots and messages provide information and imagery of psychological disorders and treatment.

VIDEOS

Analyze This. (1999, color, 103 min.). Directed by Harold Ramis; starring Robert DeNiro, Billy Crystal, Lisa Kudrow. This is a comedy about an arrogant mob boss, overwhelmed by emotional reactions to his "work," who insists on the help of a psychotherapist reluctant to hear his tale of criminal woe. A funny satire, with insights into the ethical challenges of therapy, this film is better than its lame 2002 sequel, *Analyze That.* *(Rating R)*

Good Will Hunting. (1997, color, 126 min.). Directed by Gus Van Sant; starring Matt Damon, Robin Williams, Ben Affleck. A troubled working-class youth—and mathematical genius—is helped by a renowned MIT professor and an offbeat psychologist (Williams in his Oscar-winning role) to confront his painful past and discipline his talents. *(Rating R)*

Spellbound. (1945, black-and-white, 111 min.). Directed by Alfred Hitchcock; starring Gregory Peck, Ingrid Bergman, Leo G. Carroll. The classic mystery concerns an amnesic who may or may not be a murderer, helped by the psychoanalyst with whom he has fallen in love. The surreal dream sequences were designed by artist Salvador Dali. *(No Rating)*

What About Bob? (1991, color, 99 min.). Directed by Frank Oz; starring Bill Murray, Richard Dreyfuss, Julie Hagerty. A professional psychiatric patient proves the undoing of a pompous psychiatrist, pursued by the needy, neurotic man to his family summer vacation—where the patient proceeds to charm everyone, clarifying the psychiatrist's own inabilities as a father and husband. The film is a sometimes disturbing comedy about the artificial barriers blocking the unique therapist–client relationship. *(Rating PG)*

Key Question Chapter Outline

CORE CONCEPTS

Psychology in Your Life

How Does the Social Situation Affect Our Behavior?

- Social Standards of Behavior
- Conformity
- Obedience to Authority
- The Bystander Problem: The Evil of Inaction

We usually adapt our behavior to the demands of the social situation, and in ambiguous situations we take our cues from the behavior of others in that setting.

On Being "Shoe" at Yale

How college students dress may be a matter of their "taste," but it may also be a matter of unconscious social influence to dress like the "in crowd" dresses.

Constructing Social Reality: What Influences Our Judgments of Others?

- Interpersonal Attraction
- Making Cognitive Attributions
- Prejudice and Discrimination
- Other Topics in Social Psychology

The judgments we make about others depend not only on their behavior but also on our interpretation of their actions within a social context.

Loving Relationships

The end of a relationship can be difficult for everyone. Social psychologists have begun to study what it takes to keep people caring about each other.

What Are the Roots of Violence and Terrorism?

- The Social Psychology of Aggression and Violence
- The Robbers Cave: An Experiment in Conflict
- Fuel for Terrorism

The power of the situation can help us understand violence and terrorism, but a broader understanding requires multiple perspectives that go beyond the boundaries of traditional psychology.

Multiple Perspectives on Terrorism

A field experiment on groups of Boy Scouts holds lessons for dealing with conflict in the Middle East.

Social Psychology: The State of the Art

A Personal Endnote

USING PSYCHOLOGY TO LEARN PSYCHOLOGY:
Psychology: Persuasion in the Classroom

Chapter

14

Social Psychology

ON A SUMMER SUNDAY in California, a siren shattered the serenity of college student Tommy Whitlow's morning. A police car screeched to a halt in front of his home. Within minutes, Tommy was charged with a felony, informed of his constitutional rights, frisked, and handcuffed. After he was booked and fingerprinted at the city jail, Tommy was blindfolded and transported to the Stanford County Prison, where he was stripped and issued a smock-type uniform with an I.D. number on the front and back. Tommy became "Prisoner 647." Eight other college students were also arrested and assigned numbers during that mass arrest by the local police.

The prison guards were anonymous in their khaki military uniforms, reflector sunglasses, and nameless identity as "Mr. Correctional Officer," but with symbols of power shown off in their big night sticks, whistles, and handcuffs. To them, the powerless prisoners were nothing more than their worthless numbers.

The guards insisted that prisoners obey all of their many arbitrary rules without question or hesitation. Failure to do so led to losses of privileges. At first, privileges included opportunities to read, write, or talk to other inmates. Later, the slightest protest resulted in the loss of "privileges" of eating, sleeping, washing, or having visitors during visiting nights. Failure to obey rules also resulted in a variety of unpleasant tasks

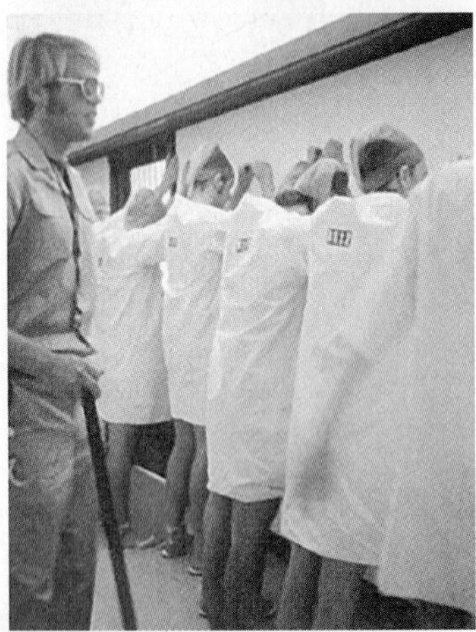

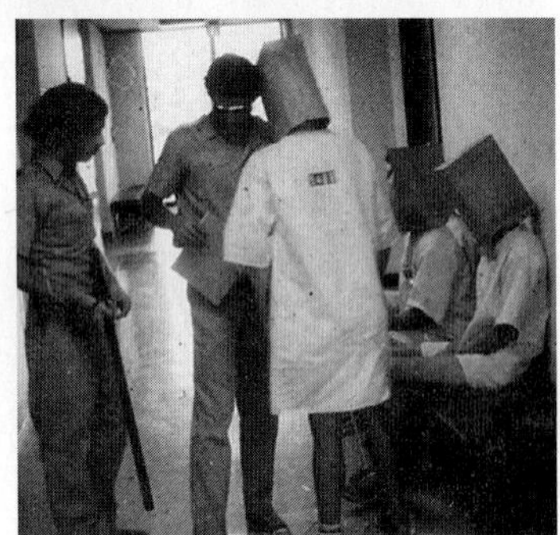

● Scenes from the Stanford prison experiment.

such as endless push-ups, jumping jacks, and number count-offs that lasted for hours on end. Each day saw an escalation of the level of hostile abuse by the guards against their prisoners: making them clean toilets with bare hands, do push-ups while a guard stepped on the prisoner's back, spend long hours naked in solitary confinement, and finally engage in degrading forms of sexual humiliation. "Prisoner 647" encountered some guards whose behavior toward him and the other prisoners was sadistic, taking apparent pleasure in cruelty; others were just tough and abusive, but none of the few "good" guards ever challenged the extremely demeaning actions of the "perpetrators of evil."

Less than 36 hours after the mass arrest, "Prisoner 8412," the ringleader of an aborted prisoner rebellion that morning, had to be released because of an extreme stress reaction of screaming, crying, rage, and depression. On successive days, three more prisoners developed similar stress-related symptoms. A fifth prisoner developed a psychosomatic rash all over his body when the parole board rejected his appeal, and he too was released from the Stanford County Jail.

At night, "Prisoner 647" tried to remember what Tommy Whitlow had been like before he became a prisoner. He also tried to imagine his tormentors before they became guards. He reminded himself that he was a college student who had answered a newspaper ad and agreed to be a subject in a two-week psychological experiment on prison life. He had thought it would be fun to do something unusual, and he could always use some extra money.

Everyone in the prison, guard and prisoner alike, had been selected from a large pool of student volunteers. On the basis of extensive psychological tests and interviews, the volunteers had been judged as law-abiding, emotionally stable, physically healthy, and "normal-average" on all psychological measures. In this mock prison experiment, assignment of participants to the independent variable treatment of "guard" or "prisoner" roles had been determined by random assignment. Thus, in the beginning there were no systematic differences between the "ordinary" college males who were in the two different conditions. By the end of the study, there were no similarities between these two alien groups. The prisoners lived in the jail around the clock, and the guards worked standard eight-hour shifts.

As guards, students who had been pacifists and "nice guys" in their usual life settings behaved aggressively—sometimes even sadistically. As prisoners, psychologically stable students soon behaved pathologically, passively resigning themselves to their unexpected fate of learned helplessness. The power of the simulated prison situation had created a new social reality—a functionally real prison—in the minds of both the jailers and their captives. The situation became so powerfully disturbing that the researchers were forced to terminate the two-week study after only six days.

Although Tommy Whitlow said he wouldn't want to go through it again, he valued the personal experience because he learned so much about himself and about human nature. Fortunately, he and the other students were basically healthy, and extensive debriefing showed that they readily bounced back from the prison experience. Follow-ups over many years revealed no lasting negative effects on these students. The participants had all learned an important lesson: Never underestimate the power of a bad situation to overwhelm the personalities and good upbringing of even the best and brightest among us (Haney et al., 1973; Haney & Zimbardo, 1998; Zimbardo, 1973,

1975; Zimbardo et al., 1999; replicated in Australia by Lovibond et al., 1979). For detailed information about this study and its relationship to recent abuses of Iraqi prisoners by American military police guards, see *www.prisonexperiment.org.*

Suppose *you* had been a subject in the Stanford prison experiment. Would you have been a good guard—or a sadist? A model compliant prisoner—or a rebel? Could you have resisted the pressures and stresses of these circumstances? We'd all like to believe we would be good guards and heroic prisoners; we would never step across that line between good and evil. And, of course, we all believe that we would be able to keep things in perspective, knowing that it was "just an experiment," only role-playing and not real. But the best bet is that most of us would react the same way as these participants did. This disturbing study raises many questions about how well we really know ourselves, our inner dispositional qualities, and how much we appreciate the subtle powers of external forces on us, the situational qualities.

● **Scene at the Abu Ghraib prison.**

Welcome to social psychology, the field that investigates how individuals affect each other. It may be a relief to hear that not all of social psychology brings such bad news about ourselves as does the Stanford prison experiment. This exciting field of psychology also explores the forces that bring people together for friendships and loving relationships. As you study **social psychology** in this chapter, you will learn how people's thoughts, feelings, perceptions, motives, and behavior are influenced by interactions with others. Social psychologists try to understand behavior within its *social context.* Defined broadly, the **social context** includes the real, imagined, or symbolic *presence of other people;* the *activities and interactions* that take place among people; the *settings* in which behavior occurs; and the *expectations* and social *norms* governing behavior in a given setting (Sherif, 1981).

Most of all, the Stanford prison experiment conducted by Philip Zimbardo (one of your authors) underscores the *power of social situations* to control human behavior. This is a major theme to emerge from social psychological research of the past 50 years. In the first part of this chapter, you will see how seemingly minor features of social settings can have a huge impact on what we think and how we feel and act. In these studies you will see how the situation can produce conformity to group standards—even when the group is clearly "wrong." Other studies will demonstrate how situational forces can lead many average people to blindly follow orders—even orders to harm others.

Yet, as powerful as the situation can be, psychologists know that it is not *objective reality* to which we respond. Rather, we respond to our *subjective interpretation* of the situation—to our perception—which can differ significantly from person to person. This, then, is the second great theme in social psychology: the construction of a *subjective social reality.* We must grasp this world of expectations and perceptions in order to understand the attractive forces at work in building friendships and romantic relationships, as well as the repulsive forces underlying prejudice and violence.

Our examination of prejudice will set the stage for a third theme that will combine the first two. We will see how social psychologists have experimented with altering the situation to change subjective social reality that, in turn, helps *to promote the human condition.* This, we will discover, has important implications for understanding violence and terrorism and for resolving conflicts among individuals, groups, and even nations. We begin now with the first of these three themes, the power of the situation.

■ **Social psychology** The branch of psychology that studies the effects of social variables and cognitions on individual behavior and social interactions.

■ **Social context** The combination of (a) people, (b) the activities and interactions among people, (c) the setting in which behavior occurs, and (d) the expectations and social norms governing behavior in that setting.

KEY QUESTION

HOW DOES THE SOCIAL SITUATION AFFECT OUR BEHAVIOR?

Suppose that you find yourself in an interview, with the possibility of being hired for the job of your dreams. Afterward, the interview suggests that you go to lunch together in the company cafeteria. Will you order a sandwich, a salad, or a full-course meal? Will you leave the plastic tray under your plate as you eat? Will you put the tiny paper napkin in your lap? Will you shift your fork from your left hand to your right hand as you put the food you cut into your mouth? Even in this simple social situation, there are many social and cultural rules governing what is appropriate and acceptable behavior. If you are like most people in an unfamiliar situation such as this, you will take your cues from those around you.

Social psychologists believe that, even when the situation is a familiar one, such as a college classroom, the primary determinant of individual behavior is the social situation in which that behavior occurs. So powerful is the situation that it can sometimes dominate our personalities and override our past history of learning, values, and beliefs. We will see that the pressures of the situation can create powerful psychological effects, such as prejudice, blind obedience, and violence. Social roles, rules, how we are dressed, competition, or the mere presence of others can profoundly influence how we behave. Often, these subtle situational variables affect us in many ways even without our awareness. Our Core Concept emphasizes this point:

CORE CONCEPT

We usually adapt our behavior to the demands of the social situation, and in ambiguous situations we take our cues from the behavior of others in that setting.

In this section, we will review some research that explores this concept, called **situationism.** Situationism assumes that the environment, or the behavioral context, can have both subtle and forceful effects on people's thoughts, feelings, and behaviors. Situationism is contrasted with *dispositionism,* the tendency to attribute behavior to internal factors, such as genes, traits, and character qualities. Here we will look particularly at the power of the situation to create conformity, obedience, and sometimes even the willingness to inflict harm on others.

Social Standards of Behavior

A job interview, such as the one described above, provides an example of a situational influence on your behavior as you try to do "what is right" in front of your prospective employer. You will also notice the power of the situation when you compare the way students talk to their friends versus their professors. Most people learn to size up their social circumstances and make their behavior conform to situational demands. The responses most people make depend heavily on two factors: the social roles they play and the social norms of the group. Let us look at both of these closely.

Social Roles Whether you are at a concert, in a department meeting, at a pizza parlor, or in a rock concert mosh pit, you will see that people operate by rules that depend on their *social roles.* You can see this more clearly by responding to the question: Who are you? Almost certainly you and other readers of this book are students or teachers of psychology—social roles that imply different sets of behaviors. (One, for example, takes exams; the other grades them.) It is

■ **Situationism** The view that environmental conditions influence people's behavior as much as or more than their personal dispositions do.

likely that you take on many other social roles in different parts of your life. Are you a part-time employee? Someone's child? A cyclist? A musician? A friend? A lover? A spammer? A **social role** is one of several socially defined patterns of behavior that are expected of persons in a given setting or group. The roles you assume may result from your interests, abilities, and goals—or they may be imposed on you by the group or by cultural, economic, or biological conditions beyond your control. In any case, social roles prescribe your behavior by making obvious what you should do, how you should do it, and when.

■ **Social role** One of several socially defined patterns of behavior that are expected of persons in a given setting or group.

■ **Script** A cluster of knowledge about the sequences of events and actions expected to occur in a particular setting.

■ **Social norms** A group's expectations regarding what is appropriate and acceptable for its members' attitudes and behaviors.

The situations in which you live and function also determine the roles that are available to you and the behaviors others expect of you. Being a college student, for example, is a social role that carries certain implicit assumptions about attending classes, studying, and handing in papers before deadline. In addition, the adoption of this role makes other roles less likely. Thus, your role as college student diminishes the chances that you will assume the role of homeless person, drug pusher, or witch doctor, for example. By the same token, because you have college experience, numerous other roles (such as manager, teacher, attorney, doctor, and politician) are available to you.

GOFF

"GOSH, ACKERMAN, DIDN'T ANYONE IN PERSONNEL TELL YOU ABOUT OUR CORPORATE CULTURE?"

The Stanford prison experiment cast guards and prisoners in different social roles. Yet, just a week before, their roles (college students) were very similar. Chance, in the form of random assignment, had decided their new roles as guards or prisoners, and these roles created status and power differences that influenced everyone's behavior in that prison situation.

Remember that no one taught the participants to play their roles. Each student called upon *scripts* about those roles. A **script** involves a person's knowledge about the sequence of events and actions that are expected of a particular social role. So, if an individual understands the role of "guard" as someone who uses coercive rules to limit the freedom of "prisoners," then that person is likely to use a script derived from that schema to become an authoritarian guard under conditions such as the Stanford prison experiment. In fact, many students in the guard role were surprised at how easy it was for them to enjoy controlling and dominating other people, just as did guards whom they read about or saw in films.

CONNECTION: CHAPTER 7

Schemas are cognitive structures that integrate knowledge and expectations about a topic or concept.

In trying to understand what happened in the Stanford prison experiment, we should note that all the prisoners and guards were male. Would it have made any difference if women had been in the roles of prisoner and guard? We will never know because the unanticipated negative impact of the experiment on both the guards and prisoners would make it unethical to do the experiment again. The possibility of gender differences, however, is raised by this fact: The experiment was called off after a graduate student, Christina Maslach, visited the "prison" and was shocked by what she saw. Immediately she conferred with Dr. Zimbardo, whom she implored to end the study. After some intense discussion, he agreed to do so. (Drs. Maslach and Zimbardo were later married and have lived happily ever after.)

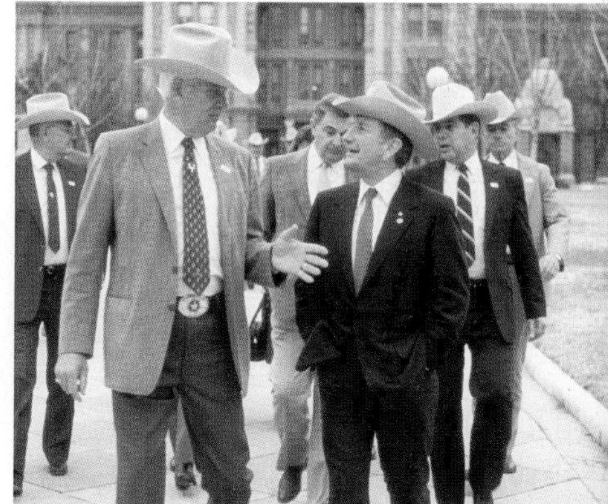

● Social norms can define rigid dress codes for group members.

Social Norms In addition to specific social roles, groups develop many "unwritten rules" for the ways that members should act. These expectations, called **social norms,** dictate socially appropriate attitudes and behaviors. Social norms can be broad guidelines, such as ideas about which political or religious attitudes are considered acceptable. Social norms can also be quite specific, embodying standards of conduct such as being quiet in the library or shining your shoes for a job interview. Norms can guide conversation, as when they restrict discussion of sensitive or taboo subjects in the presence of certain company. And norms can define dress codes, whether requiring uniforms or business suits or prohibiting shorts and tank tops. In the Stanford prison experiment, the guards quickly developed norms for abusive behavior. That norm was not already present in the situation, it was an *emergent norm,* one that emerged out of the transactions between guards and prisoners in that situation. Some norms exist in unwritten rules that are built into various situations, such as when teachers are lecturing, students are expected to listen and not talk simultaneously. However, what about the norms governing your behavior in elevators? We bet you always face the front of the elevator and either stop talking to a friend or talk lower when others are there as well. Why? Where are those rules written? How did you learn them? What will happen the next time when you enter an elevator filled with other people and *you face the rear?* Try that little experiment and see how others react.

CONNECTION: CHAPTER 6

Bandura demonstrated that we acquire many social behaviors through *observational learning.*

When a person joins a new group, such as a work group or a group of friends, there is always an adjustment period during which the individual tries to discover how best to fit in. Adjustment to a group typically involves discovering its social norms. Individuals experience this adjustment in two ways: by first noticing the *uniformities and regularities* in certain behaviors, and then by observing the *negative consequences* when someone violates a social norm. For example, a new student in your school who carries books and notes in an attaché case will be seen as "out of it" if backpacks are in, and vice versa in other schools.

Social Norms Influence Students' Political Views Social scientist Theodore Newcomb wanted to know if the political views of faculty can influence those of their students. The college: Vermont's Bennington College. The time: the 1930s. The students: from wealthy, conservative homes with decidedly conservative values. The faculty: young, dynamic, and liberal. Bennington's campus culture had a prevailing norm of political and economic liberalism. Social psychologist Theodore Newcomb wondered: Which forces most shape the attitudes of these students, their family's or their faculty's? His data showed that the norms of the campus won the war of influence against the norms of the family. In most women, their initial conservative attitude was transformed as they progressed through their college years, so that by their senior year they had clearly converted to liberal thinking and causes (Newcomb, 1943). But was that shift in attitudes enduring?

Twenty years later, the social influence of the Bennington experience was still evident. Women who had graduated as liberals were still liberals; the minority who had resisted the prevailing liberal norm had remained conservative. This was accomplished in part by marrying their "own kind" politically. Most of the women had married husbands with values similar to their own—either liberal or conservative—and created supportive new home environments that sustained those different ideologies. The liberal Bennington allegiance was evident in the 1960 presidential election when 60% of the class Newcomb had investigated voted for liberal John Kennedy, rather than conservative Richard Nixon—in contrast to less than 30% support for Kennedy among graduates of comparable colleges at that time (Newcomb et al., 1967).

Campus culture is not the only source of norms and group pressure, of course. One's workplace, neighborhood, religious group, and family all communicate standards for behavior—and threaten sanctions (such as firing, social rejection, or excommunication) for violating those norms. But a college or university environment can have a powerful impact on young people. This is especially true if they have had narrow life experiences and have not previously encountered attitudes radically different from their own. For example, new college students commonly adopt classmates' political opinions, as in the Bennington study, and also frequently take on religious beliefs of classmates, as well as attitudes about sex and alcohol (see Prentice & Miller, 1993; Schroeder & Prentice, 1995).

Conformity

How powerful are these social pressures? We can see the effects of social pressure in people's moods, clothing styles, and leisure activities (Totterdell, 2000; Totterdell et al., 1998). This tendency to mimic other people is called the *chameleon effect* (Chartrand & Bargh, 1999). A personal example of the effects of pervasive social pressures in a college environment on the way students dress can be seen in the study outlined in the "Psychology in Your Life" feature at the end of this section.

We have seen how social pressure in political attitudes influenced Bennington College students. But can social influence be strong enough to make people follow a group norm that is clearly and objectively wrong? Could the power of that situation prove stronger than the evidence of your own eyes?

The Asch Effect Solomon Asch (1940, 1956) set out to answer just such questions by having a group of his confederates challenge the perception of individual students by making them think that their eyes were deceiving them. In Asch's study, male college students were told they would be participating in a study of visual perception. They were shown cards with three lines of differing lengths and asked to indicate which of the three lines was the same length as a separate, standard line (see Figure 14.1). The problem was simple: The lines were different enough so that mistakes were rare when volunteers responded alone. But when those same individuals were put in a group of other students who had been coached to give wrong answers, well, everything changed.

CONNECTION: CHAPTER 4

Asch made us realize that *perceptual interpretation* involves the social situation.

Here's how the experiment worked. On the first three trials, everyone agreed on the correct answer. But the first person to respond on the fourth trial reported an obviously incorrect judgment, reporting as equal two lines that were clearly different. So did the next person, and so on, until all members of the group but the remaining one (the only real subject in the experiment) had unanimously agreed on an erroneous judgment. That person then had to decide whether to go along with everyone else's view of the situation and conform or remain independent, standing by the objective evidence of his own eyes. This group pressure was imposed on 12 of the 18 trials.

What did he and other participants in his position finally do? As you might expect, nearly everyone showed signs of disbelief and discomfort when faced with a majority who saw the world so differently from the way they did. But despite their distress, the group pressure usually prevailed. Three-quarters of those subjected to group pressure conformed to the false judgment of the group one or more times, while only one-fourth remained completely independent on all trials. In various related studies, between 50 and 80% conformed with the majority's false estimate at least once; a third yielded to the majority's wrong judgments on half or more of the critical trials.

Social psychologists call this the **Asch effect:** the influence of a group majority on the judgments of an individual. The Asch effect has become the classic illustration of **conformity**—the tendency for people to adopt the behavior and opinions presented by other group members. Even though individuals were judging matters of fact, not merely personal opinions, most caved in to conformity pressures.

At the same time, we should recognize that the Asch effect, powerful as it is, still does not make everyone conform. Conformity researchers do regularly find "independents," individuals who are bothered and even dismayed to find themselves in disagreement with the majority, but who nonetheless stand their ground and "call 'em as they see 'em"—even to the point of deliberately giving a wrong answer when the group gives a correct one (Friend et al., 1990). As we will see in a host of other studies in this chapter, more often than not

■ **Asch effect** A form of conformity in which a group majority influences individual judgments.

■ **Conformity** The tendency for people to adopt the behaviors, attitudes, and opinions of other members of a group.

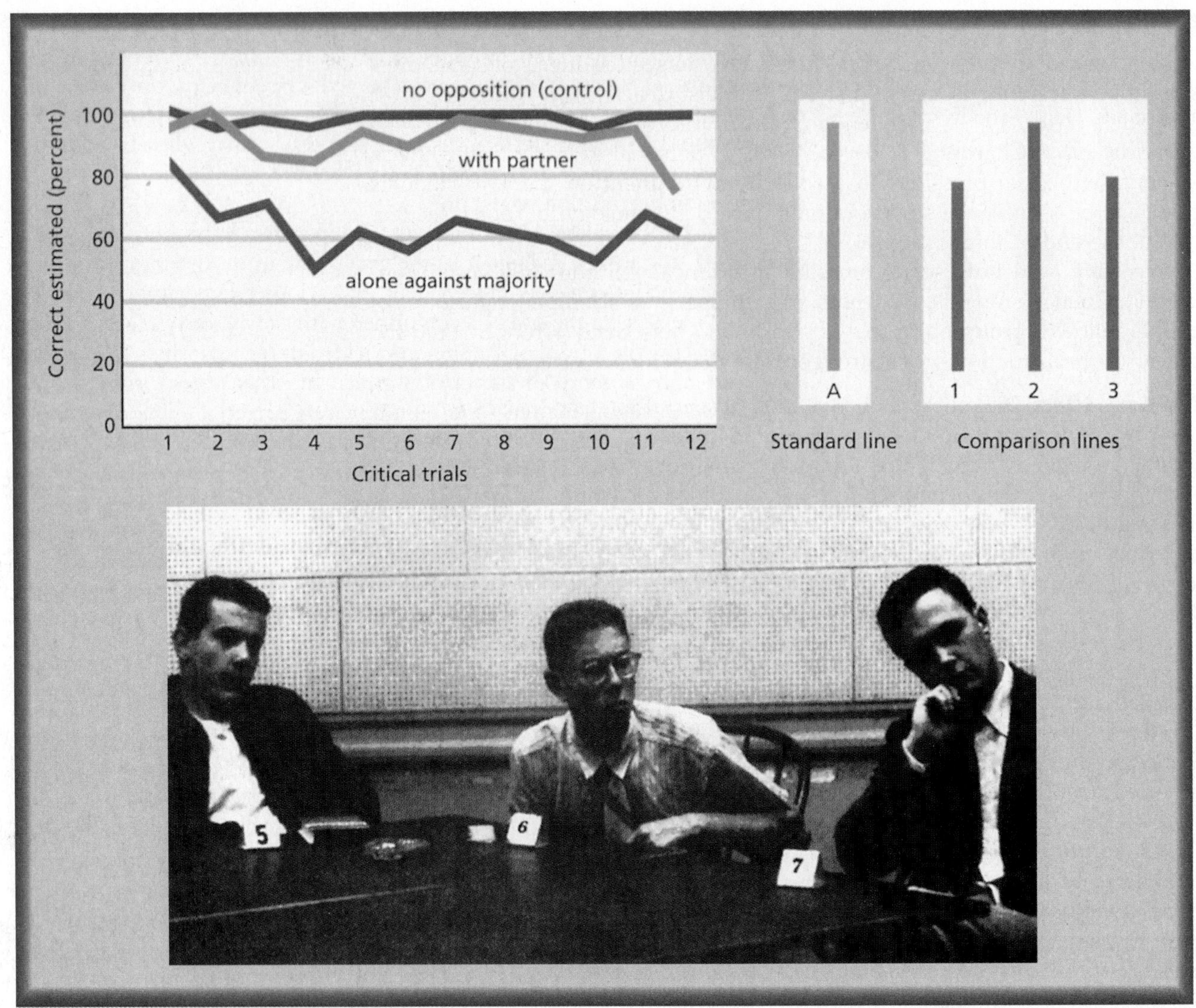
no opposition (control)
with partner
alone against majority
Correct estimated (percent)
100
80
60
40
20
0
1 2 3 4 5 6 7 8 9 10 11 12
Critical trials
A
1 2 3
Standard line
Comparison lines
5
6
7

● **FIGURE 14.1** Conformity in the Asch Experiments

In this photo from Asch's study, the naive individual, number 6, displays obvious concern about the majority's erroneous judgment. At top right, you see a typical stimulus array. At top left, the graph illustrates conformity across 12 critical trials, when individuals were grouped with a unanimous majority or had the support of a single dissenting partner. (A lower percentage of correct estimates indicates a greater degree of conformity with the group's false judgment.)

the majority conforms, complies, and gives up personal standards for group standards. However, this situational power faces one challenge, that of *individual heroic defiance. Heroes* are people who are able to resist situational forces that overwhelm their peers and remain true to their personal values. They are the "whistle blowers" who challenge corrupt or immoral systems by not going along with the company norm. Sherron Watkins (Schwartz & Watkins, 2003), a vice president at Enron Corporation, did that when she exposed the illegal transactions of Enron, and Army Reservist Joe Darby exposed the horrendous abuses of prisoners by his buddies at Iraq's Abu Ghraib Prison. But these "heroes" are often despised by their former colleagues and made to pay a high price for not being a silent "team player." Darby, for example, had to go into hiding under protective custody for many months because of death threats against him by soldiers in his battalion for humiliating them by exposing the photos of sadistic abuse of prisoners.

Group Characteristics That Produce Conformity In further experiments, Asch identified three factors that influence whether a person will yield to group pressure: (1) *the size of the majority,* (2) *the presence of a partner who dis-*

sented from the majority, and (3) *the size of the discrepancy* between the correct answer and the majority's position. He found that individuals tended to conform with a unanimous majority of as few as three people, but not if they faced only one or two. However, even in a large group, giving the person one ally who dissented from the majority opinion sharply reduced conformity (as shown in Figure 14.1). With such a "partner," nearly all subjects resisted the pressures to conform. Remarkably, however, some individuals continued to yield to the group even with a partner present. All who yielded underestimated the influence of the social pressure and the frequency of their conformity; a few even claimed that they really had seen the lines as the majority had claimed and so were not conforming, only reporting accurately what they were seeing (Asch, 1955, 1956).

● Sharron Watkins, an executive at Enron, realized that illegal activities were taking place and exposed the mess publicly; she is a heroic whistle blower.

Numerous studies have revealed additional factors that influence conformity. (These experiments have included both females and males.) Specifically, a person is more likely to conform under the following circumstances:

- When a judgment task is difficult or ambiguous (Deutsch & Gerard, 1955; Lott & Lott, 1961; Saltzstein & Sandberg, 1979).
- When the group members are perceived as especially competent.
- When responses are given publicly rather than privately.
- When the group majority is unanimous—but once that unanimity is broken, the rate of conformity drops dramatically (Allen & Levine, 1969; Morris & Miller, 1975).

So now imagine you are about to vote openly in a group, as is common in clubs or on boards of directors. You will probably conform to the group majority if (a) the issue being decided is complex or confusing, (b) others in the group seem to know what they are talking about, (c) you must vote by raising your hand instead of casting an anonymous ballot, (d) the entire group casting their votes before you all vote in a certain way, and especially if (e) the leader votes first.

Groupthink Groups can also be pressured to conform. This important social psychological process that encourages conformity in the thinking and decision making of individuals when they are in groups, such as committees, has been termed "groupthink" by psychologist Irving Janis (1972; Janis & Mann, 1977). In *groupthink,* members of the group attempt to conform their opinions to what each believes to be the consensus of the group. This conformity bias leads the group to take actions that each member might normally consider unwise. Seven conditions likely to promote groupthink are

CONNECTION: CHAPTER 7

Our judgments are often affected by personal *biases*.

- Isolation of the group
- High group cohesiveness
- Directive leadership
- Lack of norms requiring methodical procedures
- Homogeneity of members' social background and ideology
- High stress from external threats with low hope of a better solution than that of the group leader

This concept was first developed to help understand bad decisions made by the U.S. government regarding the bombing of Pearl Harbor, the Vietnam War, and the invasion of Cuba's Bay of Pigs. Later, others have cited groupthink as a factor that contributed to the faulty decisions in the space shuttle disasters, the bankruptcy of Enron Corporation, and, more recently, the 2003 decision to wage war against Iraq (see Schwartz & Wald, 2003). The U.S.

CONNECTION: CHAPTER 10

Most personality theories focus on internal processes, while social psychology now emphasizes the external situation.

Senate Intelligence Committee investigating the justifications for the Iraq War cited groupthink as one of the processes involved in that decision. It is interesting to note the use of this social psychological concept in an official report of that government committee:

> The Intelligence Community (IC) has long struggled with the need for analysts to overcome analytic biases . . . . This bias that pervaded both the IC's analytic and collection communities represents 'group think,' a term coined by psychologist Irving Janis in the 1970's to describe a process in which a group can make bad or irrational decisions as each member of the group attempts to conform their opinions to what they believe to be the consensus of the group. IC personnel involved in the Iraq WMD issue demonstrated several aspects of groupthink: examining few alternatives, selective gathering of information, pressure to conform within the group or withhold criticism, and collective rationalization. (U.S. Senate, 2004, p. 4)

Obedience to Authority

So far, we have seen how groups influence individuals. But the arrow of influence also points the other way: Certain individuals, such as leaders and authorities, can command the obedience of groups—or even large masses of people. The ultimate demonstration of this effect was seen in the World War II era, with the emergence of Adolf Hitler in Germany and Benito Mussolini in Italy. These dictators transformed the rational citizens of whole nations into mindlessly loyal followers of a fascist ideology bent on world conquest.

Modern social psychology had its origins in this wartime crucible of fear and prejudice. It was natural, then, that many of the early social psychologists focused on the personalities of people drawn into fascist groups. Specifically, they looked for an *authoritarian personality* behind the fascist group mentality (Adorno et al., 1950). But that dispositional analysis failed to recognize the social, economic, historical, and political realities operating on those populations at that time. To clarify this point, let us reflect for a moment on some more recent examples of unquestioning obedience to authority.

In 1978, a group of American citizens left California to relocate their Protestant religious order, called "Peoples Temple," in the South American jungle of Guyana. There, following the orders of their charismatic leader, the Reverend Jim Jones, over 900 members of the Peoples Temple willingly administered lethal doses of cyanide to hundreds of their children, then to their parents, and then to themselves. Then, in 1993, 100 members of a religious sect in Waco, Texas, joined their leader, David Koresh, in defying federal agents who had surrounded their compound. After a standoff of several weeks, the Branch Davidians set fire to their quarters rather than surrender. In the resulting conflagration, scores of men, women, and children perished. Four years later, the college-bred members of another group calling itself "Heaven's Gate" followed their leader's command to commit mass suicide in order to achieve a "higher plane" of being. And on September 11, 2001, followers of Osama bin Laden commandeered commercial airliners and piloted them into the Pentagon and the World Trade Center. In addition to murdering thousands of people on those planes and working at those sites, they knowingly committed suicide. And even more recently, scores of suicide bombers, both men and women, have blown themselves apart as "revolutionary martyrs" in the Palestinian campaign against Israel. Were these people mentally deranged, stupid, and totally strange creatures—unlike us? Are there any conditions under which *you* would blindly obey an order from a person you love and respect (or fear) to do such extreme deeds? Would you, for example, obey an authority figure who told you to electrocute a stranger? Of course, you are saying to yourself, "No way," "Not me," "I am not that kind of person." But think about what each of the people we have described above must have been thinking *before* they were caught up in their obedience trap—the same thing as you, probably.

After reading this chapter, you may be more likely to answer, "I hope not—but I have a better understanding of the social forces that can pressure ordinary people like me to commit horrible acts." And, your authors hope, your study of social psychology will make you more resistant to the forces that produce unquestioning obedience and conformity. We want you to be one of the thoughtful heroes and not one of the mindless majority.

On that note, let us now turn to the most convincing demonstration of situational power ever created in the laboratory. In a dramatic experiment, social psychologist Stanley Milgram (1965, 1974) showed that a willingness of people to follow the orders of an authority, even potentially lethal ones, is not confined to a few extreme personalities or deranged individuals. This finding, along with certain ethical issues that the experiment raises, places Milgram's work at the center of one of the biggest controversies in psychology (Blass, 1996; Miller, 1986; Ross & Nisbett, 1991). Let us begin with a look at the controversial methods Milgram used.

Milgram's Obedience Experiment The experiment was first conducted on Yale College students where Milgram was teaching at the time. After his initial surprising results, he advertised for more paid volunteers among ordinary citizens in several towns in Connecticut and conducted variations of his original paradigm on more than 1000 participants from a variety of backgrounds. The volunteers thought that they were participating in a scientific study of memory and learning. Specifically, they were led to believe that the research aimed to help improve learning and memory by punishing errors as soon as they were made, as well as rewarding correct responding. Cast in the role of "teacher," a volunteer subject was instructed to punish memory errors made by another person (actually a confederate of the experimenter) playing the role of "learner." To administer punishment, the teacher was told to throw a switch that would deliver an electric shock to the learner each time the learner made an error. Moreover, the teacher was told to increase the level of shock by a fixed amount for every new error. Overseeing the whole procedure was a white-coated experimenter. This authority figure presented the rules, arranged for the assignment of roles (by a rigged drawing of lots), and ordered the teachers to do their job whenever they hesitated or dissented.

The real question driving the experiment was this: How far would people go before they defied the authority figure by refusing to obey? The dependent variable was the teacher's response, measured by the highest shock level he was willing to deliver. The level of shock could be clearly seen on a "shock generator" that featured a row of 30 switches that apparently could deliver shocks in 30-volt steps from a weak start of 15 volts all the way up to 450 volts, marked on the generator as "XXX."

To make the situation realistic, Milgram gave each "teacher" a mild sample shock. This convinced them that the apparatus was actually delivering shocks and that they would be causing the "learner" increasing pain and suffering each time they flipped a switch. Except for this demonstration shock, however, no shocks were actually administered: You will remember that the learner was actually a part of the experimental team.

The part of the learner was played by a pleasant, mild-mannered man about 50 years old. He mentioned having a "heart condition" but said he was willing to go along with the procedure. The experimenter obliged by strapping

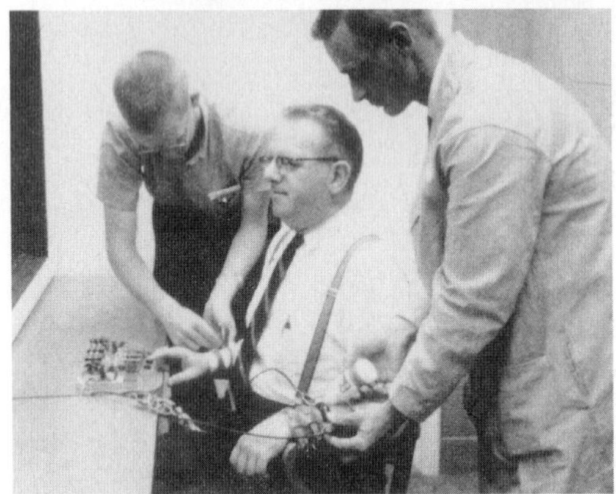

● Milgram's obedience experiment. Top, generator; bottom, the "learner" being strapped into his electrified chair. Experts incorrectly predicted the behavior of the "teachers" because they failed to consider the influence of the special situation created in the experiment. Although many of the participants in Milgram's study dissented verbally, the majority obeyed.

him into an "electric chair" in an adjacent room. As the learner, his task was to memorize pairs of words and then choose the correct response for each stimulus word from a multiple-choice listing. Following the experimental script, the learner soon began making mistakes.

At 75 volts, the script called for the learner to moan and grunt; at 150 volts he would demand to be released from the experiment. At 180 volts he would cry out that he could not stand the pain any longer. The plan then called for the learner's protests to increase with increasing shock levels. For any teachers still delivering punishment at the 300-volt level, the learner would shout that he would no longer take part in the experiment and must be freed. As you might imagine, this situation was stressful. If the teacher hesitated or protested about delivering the required shock at any level, the experimenter interrupted, stating that the experiment "must continue," demanding that the teacher "please continue." Most volunteers dissented often; when they asked who would be responsible for the consequences, the authority figure said he would assume full responsibility. But when the shock level rose to 375 volts, the "learner" screamed out, and there was a thud and then silence. Virtually all of the participants stopped shocking but then continued when the authority reminded them that failure to respond was an error that also had to be punished. The experiment ended only when the shock level reached the 450-volt maximum—or when the "teacher" refused to obey.

The Shocking Results Suppose for a moment that you were the "teacher." Ask yourself the following questions:

- How far up the shock scale would you go?
- At which level would you refuse to continue?

In Milgram's experiment, nearly two-thirds delivered the maximum 450 volts to the learner. Most of those who refused to give the maximum shock obeyed until reaching about 300 volts. And no one who got within five switches of the end refused to go all the way. By then their resistance was broken; they had resolved their own conflicts and just tried to get it over with as quickly as possible. Most verbally dissented but behaviorally obeyed the white-coated authority. These same results were found with the Yale College students as with the many ordinary citizens from all walks of life.

These were not sadistic people who obeyed happily. They dissented verbally, even though they continued to deliver shocks. One person complained to the unwavering experimenter, "He can't stand it! I'm not going to kill that man in there! You hear him hollering? He's hollering . . . Who is going to take the responsibility if anything happens to that gentleman?" Clearly upset, this individual added, "You mean I've got to keep going up with that scale? No sir, I'm not going to kill that man!" (Milgram, 1965, p. 67). But the shocks continued. When the learner simply stopped responding to the questions, some teachers called out to him, urging him to get the answer right so they would not have to continue shocking him. All the while they protested loudly to the experimenter, but the experimenter responded with stern commands: "You have no other choice, you *must* go on." Even when there was only silence from the learner's room, the teacher was ordered to keep shocking him more and more strongly, all the way up to the button that was marked "Danger: Severe Shock XXX (450 volts)." Most people obeyed.

Of course, no shocks were ever delivered to the learner. The "victim" of the "shocks" was an accomplished actor who congenially chatted with his "teacher" after the experiment and assured him he was fine and had never felt any shocks. All of his comments during the study had been tape recorded to standardize the procedure across the many trials and variations of the study. Moreover, the powerful authority figure in the white lab coat was not a "real" authority—not Milgram himself, but a hired actor. And for all the "teachers" knew, once the learner fell silent he might have been unconscious or dead—but in any case his memory could not be improved by further shocks. Nevertheless, hundreds of people, young and old, educated or not, mindlessly obeyed and continued doing as ordered even though it would have made no sense had they thought rationally about what they were doing.

The controversy about Milgram's research concerns the ethics of deception and the potentially disturbing effects on those in the role of teacher.

This Chinese man risked his life by defying authority. Would you have done the same?

Why Do We Obey Authority? From the many variations Milgram conducted on his original study, we can conclude that people tended to be obedient under the following conditions (Milgram, 1965, 1974; Rosenhan, 1969):

- *When a peer modeled obedience* by complying with the authority figure's commands
- *When the victim was remote from the "teacher"* and could not be seen or heard
- *When the "teacher" was under direct surveillance of the authority figure* so that he was aware of the authority figure's presence
- *When a participant acted as an intermediary bystander,* merely "assisting" the one who was delivering the shock, rather than actually throwing the switches
- *When the authority figure had higher relative status,* as when the participant was a student and the experimenter was billed as "professor" or "doctor"

What are the lessons to be learned? If you carefully review these conditions (Figure 14.2), you can see that the obedience effect results from *situational* variables and not *personality* variables. In fact, personality tests administered to the subjects did *not* reveal any traits that differentiated those who obeyed from those who refused, nor did they identify any psychological disturbance or abnormality in the obedient punishers. These findings enable us to rule out personality as a variable in obedient behavior. And what about gender? Milgram later found that women were just as obedient as men (Milgram, 1974).

Like the Stanford prison study, obedience research challenges the myth that evil lurks in the minds of evil people—that the bad "they" differ from the good "us" who would never do such things. The purpose in recounting these findings is not to debase human nature or to excuse evil deeds but to make it clear that even normal, well-meaning individuals can give in to strong situational and social influences to behave wrongly when they know very well how they should behave. In a sense, this reflects one view of "evil" as knowing better but doing worse.

Before moving on to our next major issue, there is an important matter for us to add. Although you should remember the Milgram effect as "two-thirds

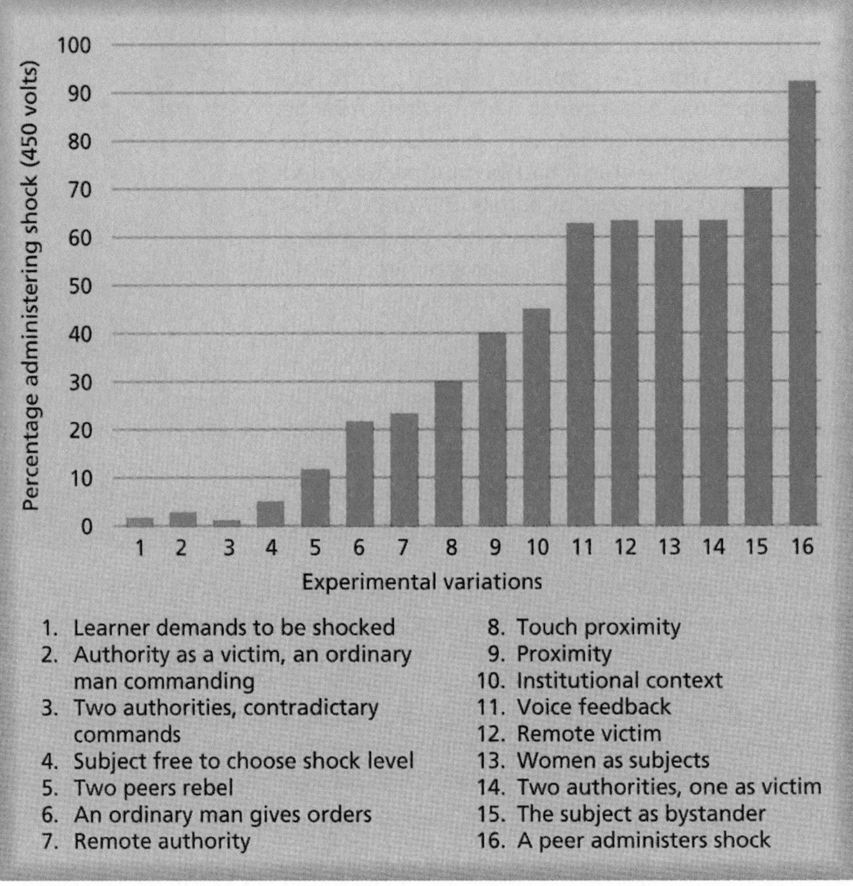
Percentage administering shock (450 volts)
100
90
80
70
60
50
40
30
20
10
0
1 2 3 4 5 6 7 8 9 10 11 12 13 14 15 16
Experimental variations
1. Learner demands to be shocked
2. Authority as a victim, an ordinary man commanding
3. Two authorities, contradictary commands
4. Subject free to choose shock level
5. Two peers rebel
6. An ordinary man gives orders
7. Remote authority
8. Touch proximity
9. Proximity
10. Institutional context
11. Voice feedback
12. Remote victim
13. Women as subjects
14. Two authorities, one as victim
15. The subject as bystander
16. A peer administers shock

● **FIGURE 14.2** Obedience in Milgram's Experiments

The graph shows a profile of weak or strong obedience effects across situational variations of Milgram's study of obedience to authority. (*Source:* From THE OBEDIENCE EXPERIMENTS: A Case Study of Controversy in the Social Sciences by A. G. Miller. Copyright © 1986 by Praeger Publishers, Inc. Reprinted by permission of Greenwood Publishing Group, Inc., Westport, CT.)

CONNECTION: CHAPTER 9

Moral judgments depend not only on the situation but also on one's stage of *moral development.*

went all the way," in the many variations he conducted obedience went all the way up to 90% if the teacher first observed others going all the way, although it dropped to only 10% when the teacher saw peers refusing to go all the way. The other take-home message from these experiments is that social models can have an enormous impact on how you behave and that you should be aware that you are a social model for others. And just to make you more aware when such influence may be at work, in Table 14.1 we have listed some general tactics of influence that can get good people to do harmful deeds (Zimbardo, 2004b).

TABLE 14.1 Getting Good People to Do Bad Things

- Provide people with an ideology to justify beliefs for actions.
- Make people take a small first step toward a harmful act with a minor, trivial action, and then gradually increase those small actions.
- Make those in charge seem like a "just authority."
- Slowly transform a once compassionate leader into a dictatorial figure.
- Provide people with vague and ever-changing rules.
- Relabel the situation's actors and their actions to legitimize the ideology.
- Provide people with social models of compliance.
- Allow verbal dissent but only if people continue to comply behaviorally with orders.
- Encourage dehumanizing the victim.
- Make exiting the situation difficult.

The Bystander Problem: The Evil of Inaction

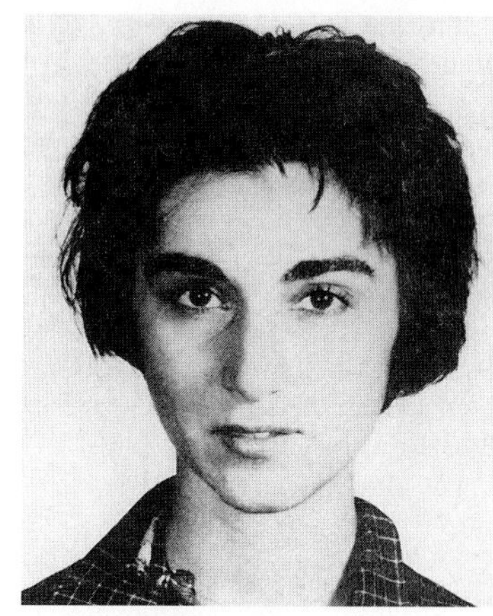

● Kitty Genovese was murdered in her neighborhood while 38 of her neighbors watched. Why didn't somebody help? The answer is not what most people think.

Harm doesn't always come from a hurtful act. It can also come from *inaction* when someone needs help. We can illustrate this fact with a news event that stunned the nation and then inspired some vital psychological research. In Queens, New York, 38 ordinary citizens watched for more than half an hour as a man with a knife stalked and killed Kitty Genovese in three separate attacks. Twice the sound of the bystanders' voices and the sudden glow of their bedroom lights interrupted the assailant and frightened him. Each time, however, he returned and stabbed her again. Not a single person telephoned the police during the assault! Only one witness called the police—after the woman was finally raped and murdered (*New York Times,* March 13, 1964, as cited in Darley & Latané, 1968). The newspaper and TV accounts of this gruesome story played up the angle of bystander "apathy," the callous indifference of New Yorkers, and a bewildered nation.

Why didn't bystanders help? Was it something in the *person* (again the dispositional analysis: New Yorkers being "callous" types), or was it something in the *situation* (something outside of any of the individuals)? Come let us see again how social psychology is done.

Contrived Emergencies Soon after hearing of Kitty Genovese's murder and the analysis in the press, social psychologists Bibb Latané and John Darley began a series of studies on the bystander intervention problem. These studies all ingeniously created laboratory analogues of the difficulties faced by bystanders in real emergency situations. In one such experiment, a college student, placed alone in a room with an intercom, was led to believe that he was communicating with one or more students in adjacent rooms. During a discussion about personal problems, this individual heard what sounded like another student having a seizure and gasping for help. During the "seizure" the bystander couldn't talk to the other students or find out what, if anything, they were doing about the emergency. The dependent variable was the speed with which he reported the emergency to the experimenter. The independent variable was the number of people he believed were in the discussion group with him.

CONNECTION: CHAPTER 2
The *independent variable* refers to the various stimulus conditions for different groups in an experiment.

It turned out that the speed of response by those in this situation depended on the number of bystanders they thought were present. The more other people they believed to be listening in on the situation in other rooms, the *slower* they were to report the seizure, if they did so at all. As you can see in Figure 14.3, all those in a two-person situation intervened within 160 seconds, but only 60% of those who believed they were part of a large group ever informed the experimenter that another student was seriously ill (Latané & Darley, 1968).

Was it the person or the situation? Personality tests showed no significant relationship between particular personality characteristics of the participants and their speed or likelihood of intervening. The best predictor of bystander intervention was the situational variable of *group size.* By way of explanation, Darley and Latané proposed that the likelihood of intervention *decreases* as the group *increases* in size, because each person assumes that others will help, so he or she does not have to make that commitment. Individuals who perceive themselves as part of a large group of potential interveners experience a **diffusion of responsibility:** a dilution or weakening of each group member's obligation to help, to become personally involved. You may have experienced moments of diffused responsibility if you have driven past a disabled car beside a busy highway because "surely someone else" would stop and help.

■ **Diffusion of responsibility** Dilution or weakening of each group member's obligation to act when responsibility is perceived to be shared with all group members.

Another factor was undoubtedly also at work: conformity. As you will remember from our Core Concept and from Asch's studies of conformity, when people don't know what to do, they take their cues from others. The same thing

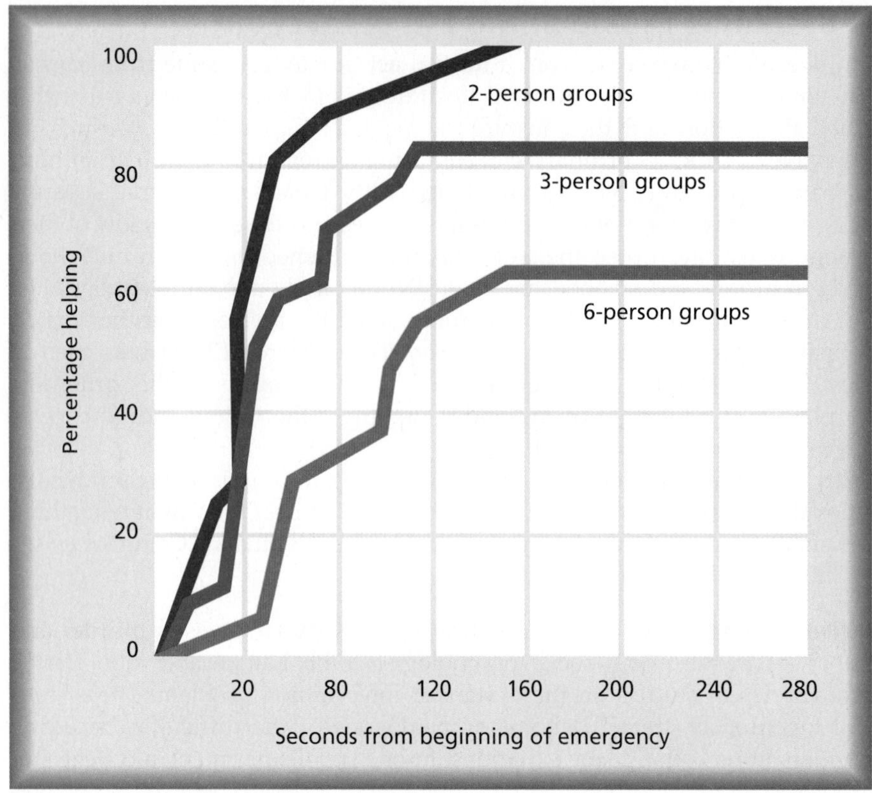
100
80
60
40
20
0
Percentage helping
2-person groups
3-person groups
6-person groups
20
80
120
160
200
240
280
Seconds from beginning of emergency

FIGURE 14.3 Bystander Intervention in an Emergency

The more people present in a crisis, the less likely it is that any one bystander will intervene. As this summary of research findings shows, bystanders act most quickly in two-person groupings. (*Source:* From "Bystander Intervention in Emergencies: Diffusion of Responsibilities," by S. M. Darley and B. Latané, *Journal of Personality & Social Psychology,* 1968, Vol. 8, No. 4, pp. 377–384. Copyright © 1968 by the American Psychological Association. Reprinted by permission of the American Psychological Association.)

occurred in the bystander studies, where subjects who failed to intervene were observing and conforming to the behavior of other people who were doing nothing.

Does Training Encourage Helping? Two studies suggest that the bystander problem can be countered with appropriate training. Ted Huston and his colleagues (1981) found no personality traits that distinguished people who had helped in actual emergency situations from those who had not. But they did find that helpers more often had had some medical, police, first-aid, or CPR training in dealing with emergency situations. And another study shows that even a psychology class lecture on the bystander problem can help (Beaman et al., 1978). Students had an opportunity to help a "victim" slumped in a doorway while walking by with a nonresponsive confederate of the experimenter. Those who had attended a lecture on bystander intervention were twice as likely to stop and attempt to help as those who had not received the lecture on helping. Education apparently makes some difference.

Need help? Ask for it! To demonstrate the positive effects of situational power, social psychologist Tom Moriarity (1975) arranged two fascinating experiments. In the first study, New Yorkers watched as a thief snatched a woman's suitcase in a restaurant when she left her table. In the second, they watched a thief grab a portable radio from a beach blanket when the owner left it for a few minutes. What did these onlookers do? Some did nothing, letting the thief go on his merry way. But others did intervene. What were the conditions under which some helped and others did not?

In each experiment, the would-be theft victim (the experimenter's accomplice) had first asked the soon-to-be observer of the crime either "Do you have the time?" or "Will you please keep an eye on my bag (radio) while I'm gone?"

DO IT YOURSELF! What Makes a Samaritan Good or Bad?

Now that you know something about bystander intervention, let's see how good you are at picking the crucial variable out of a bystander situation inspired by the biblical tale of the Good Samaritan (see Luke 10:30–37). In the biblical account, several important people are too busy to help a stranger in distress. He is finally assisted by an outsider, a Samaritan, who takes the time to offer aid. Could the failure of the distressed individual's countrymen to help be due to character flaws or personal dispositions? Or was it determined by the situation?

Social psychologists decided to put students at the Princeton Theological Seminary into a similar situation. It was made all the more ironic because they thought that they were being evaluated on the quality of the sermons they were about to deliver on the parable of the Good Samaritan. Let's see what happened when these seminarians were given an opportunity to help someone in distress.

With sermon in hand, each was directed to a nearby building where the sermon was to be recorded. But as the student walked down an alley between the two buildings, he came upon a man slumped in a doorway, in obvious need of help. The student now had the chance to practice what he was about to preach. What would you guess was the crucial variable that predicted how likely a seminarian—ready to preach about the Good Samaritan—was to help a person in distress? Choose one:

a. How religious the seminarian was (as rated by his classmates)
b. How "neurotic" the seminarian was (as rated on the "Big Five" personality traits)
c. How much of a hurry the seminarian was in
d. How old the seminarian was

All of the dispositional variables (personal characteristics) of the seminarians were controlled by random assignment of subjects to three different conditions. Thus, we know that personality was not the determining factor. Rather, it was a situational variable: time. Before the seminarians left the briefing room to have their sermons recorded in a nearby building, each was told how much time he had to get to the studio. Some were assigned to a late condition, in which they had to hurry to make the next session; others to an on-time condition, in which they would make the next session just on time; and a third group to an early condition, in which they had a few spare minutes before they would be recorded.

What were the results? Of those who were in a hurry, only 10% helped. Ninety percent failed to act as Good Samaritans! If they were on time, 45% helped the stranger. The greatest bystander intervention came from 63% of those who were not in any time bind.

Remarkably, the manipulation of time urgency made those in the "late" condition six times less likely to help than those in the "early" condition. While fulfilling their obligation to hurry, these individuals appeared to have a single-minded purpose that blinded them to other events around them. Again, it was the power of the situation.

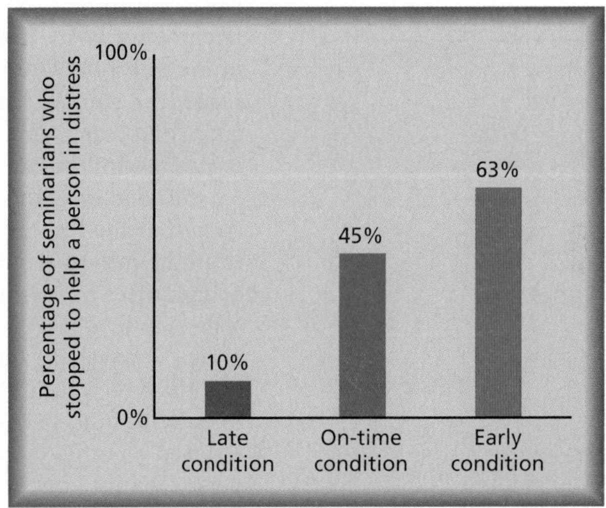
Percentage of seminarians who stopped to help a person in distress
100%
0%
10%
45%
63%
Late condition
On-time condition
Early condition

Results of the "Good Samaritan" Study

Even with a sermon on the Good Samaritan in hand, seminary students who were in a hurry didn't usually stop to help (Darley & Batson, 1973).

The first interaction elicited no personal responsibility, and almost all of the bystanders stood by idly as the theft unfolded. However, of those who had agreed to watch the victim's property, almost every bystander intervened. They called for help, and some even tackled the runaway thief on the beach.

The encouraging message is that we can often convert apathy to action and transform callousness to kindness just by asking for it. The mere act of requesting a favor forges a special human bond that involves other people in ways that materially change the situation. It makes them feel responsible to you, and thereby responsible for what happens in your shared social world. You can use this knowledge to increase your chances of getting aid from would-be helpers in several ways (Schroeder et al., 1995):

- *Ask for help.* Let others know you need it rather than assuming they realize your need or know what is required.
- *Reduce the ambiguity* of the situation by clearly explaining the problem and what should be done: "She's fainted! Call an ambulance right away," or "Someone broke into my house—call the police and give them this address!"

- *Identify specific individuals* so they do not diffuse responsibility with others present: "You, in the red shirt: Call 911!" or "Will the person in the blue Toyota please call for a tow truck right away?"

None of these tactics guarantees the safety of your person or possessions, of course. (Kitty Genovese did call for help.) Nevertheless they probably represent your best hope if you find yourself, alone in a crowd, facing a real emergency.

PSYCHOLOGY IN YOUR LIFE: ON BEING "SHOE" AT YALE[1]

When I (PGZ) arrived at Yale University to start my graduate career in the mid-1950s, I was dressed in all my south Bronx splendor—blue suede shoes, peg pants, big rolled collar (Billy Eckstein model), and other cool clothes. A month or two later, I was wearing chino pants, button-down shirt, and loafers. I was not fully aware of the subtle social pressures to change my "taste" in apparel but knew that I felt more "in" in those weird Yalie clothes than I had in my good old Bronx duds. But as a budding psychologist, I used my personal case study to motivate me to find out more about that unwritten dress code, one that everyone around the campus at that time was following as if a Marine drill instructor were ordering our total mindless compliance.

Interviews with seniors revealed that indeed there was a powerful dress code that the "in group" formulated regularly in order to distinguish them from the mass of "out group" pretenders. Every single item of clothing could be identified by those in the know as socially appropriate at that time for real Yale men to wear (it was all male at that time). I was informed that the underlying concept was being "shoe." (Yale men of that era and earlier could be identified as wearing white buck shoes.) To be "shoe" was to be in, to be cool, to be with it, to be right on, and so forth. Not only was every bit of clothing indexed as to its degree of shoeness, but so was everything else in that universe. Tennis, golf, and crew were shoe, basketball was not. Asking questions in lecture classes was not shoe; tailgating before football games was shoe, but only if done with the right style, or panache. Of equal interest to me was the fact that shoe ratings changed periodically to keep outsiders from being mistaken as really true blue shoe. One year the Yale Senior ring was shoe to wear, the next year it might be un-shoe; or handmade bow ties would become unshoe and clip-on bow ties would vault from low-shoe to high-shoe rating.

My team of informants helped me to form an index of the shoe strengths of every conceivable item of clothing that a Yale student might wear that year. With the help of my introductory psychology students, we went into the dormitories and found out what students from each college class actually had in their wardrobes. We then multiplied each of those items of clothing by their Shoe Index and averaged those ratings across each class from frosh to senior. Next, we separated out students' shoe scores by whether they had come from prep schools or public high schools.

Three major significant results were obvious from our graphs of the quantification of Shoeness at Yale:

1. Student wardrobes become ever more shoe as they progress from lowly frosh up to high-powered seniors.
2. Preppy frosh were much more shoe than their classmates from public high schools.

[1]Zimbardo, P. G. (2004a). *On being "shoe" at Yale: A study in institutional conformity.* In preparation, Stanford University.

3. Over the four years, the gap between prep schoolers and high schoolers diminished, so that by senior year they were almost equally shoe.

When Yale became co-ed in the next decade, this kind of shoeness became less apparent, went undergound, and now may exist only in very modified forms. But let this be a lesson to you whatever school you are in: Much of what you think is the You in Your Taste, is really the Them in social conformity pressures subtly imposed on you to be like Them and liked by Them.

CHECK YOUR UNDERSTANDING

1. **RECALL:** The Stanford prison experiment illustrates the power of ______ to influence people's behavior.
   a. personality
   b. heredity
   c. childhood experiences
   d. the situation
   e. habituation

2. **RECALL:** Which of the following would be a social role?
   a. prisoner
   b. student
   c. professor
   d. all of the above
   e. none of the above

3. **RECALL:** In the Asch studies, which of the following produced a decrease in conformity?
   a. The task was seen as difficult or ambiguous.
   b. The subject had to respond publicly, rather than privately.
   c. The majority was not unanimous in its judgment.
   d. The group was very large.
   e. The group was very small.

4. **RECALL:** In Milgram's original study, about what proportion of the teachers gave the maximum shock?
   a. about two-thirds
   b. about 10%
   c. about 3%
   d. nearly all
   e. about 50%

5. **APPLICATION:** In an emergency situation, you would have the best chance of getting help from a
   a. lone bystander.
   b. large group of people.
   c. group of people who are friends of each other.
   d. group of six people.
   e. group of strangers.

6. **UNDERSTANDING THE CORE CONCEPT:** Which of the following best illustrates people in ambiguous situations taking their cues from others?
   a. those who obeyed Milgram
   b. those who disobeyed Milgram
   c. helpers who have had CPR training
   d. the experimenter in the Latané & Darley study of bystander intervention
   e. the majority of participants who expressed false judgments in the Asch experiments

ANSWERS: 1. d 2. d 3. c 4. a 5. a 6. e

KEY QUESTION

CONSTRUCTING SOCIAL REALITY: WHAT INFLUENCES OUR JUDGMENTS OF OTHERS?

Powerful as a social situation is, it doesn't account for everything that people do. For example, it does not account for the individual differences we see in people's choices of friends and romantic partners, nor does it account for their prejudices. To explain the patterns we find in social interaction, we must also look at cognitive processes. In the language of social psychology, we need to understand how we construct our **social reality**—our subjective interpretations of other people and of our relationships. Thus, the social reality that we construct determines whom we find attractive, whom we find threatening, whom we seek out, and whom we avoid. This, then, leads us to the second lesson of social psychology, captured in our next Core Concept:

■ **Social reality** An individual's subjective interpretation of other people and of relationships with them.

CORE CONCEPT

The judgments we make about others depend not only on their behavior but also on our interpretation of their actions within a social context.

We will illustrate how these cognitive factors operate by analyzing how they affect our attitudes toward other people. Let's start out on the positive end of the scale by asking a simple question: What makes people like each other? That is, what produces *interpersonal attraction?* Then we will move to the opposite end of the scale with a look at the negative feelings that often underlie *prejudice.*

Interpersonal Attraction

It is no surprise that we are attracted to people who have something to offer us (Brehm et al., 2002; Simpson & Harris, 1994). We tend to like those who give us gifts, agree with us, act friendly toward us, share our interests, entertain us, and help us in times of need—unless, of course, we suspect that their behavior is self-serving. Although we don't necessarily mind giving something back in the form of a social exchange, we shrink from relationships that merely take from us and offer nothing in return. In the best of relationships, as in a friendship, partnership, marriage, or business relationship, both parties receive rewards. You might consider whether this is true in your own relationships as we look at the *reward theory of attraction* next.

Reward Theory: We (Usually) Prefer Rewarding Relationships Most good relationships can be seen as an exchange of benefits (Batson, 1987; Clark et al., 1989). The benefits could be some combination of money and material possessions. Or the exchange might involve something intangible like praise, status, information, sex, or emotional support.

CONNECTION: CHAPTER 6
Social learning involves expectations of rewards and punishments learned through social interaction and the observation of others.

Social psychologist Elliot Aronson (2004) summarizes this in a **reward theory of attraction,** which says that attraction is a form of social learning. By looking at the social costs and benefits, claims Aronson, we can usually understand why people are attracted to each other. In brief, reward theory says that we like best those who give us maximum rewards at minimum cost. After we look at the evidence, we think you will agree that this theory explains (almost) everything about interpersonal attraction.

Social psychologists have found four especially powerful sources of reward that predict interpersonal attraction: *proximity, similarity, self-disclosure,* and *physical attractiveness.* Most of us choose our friends, associates, and lovers because they offer some combination of these factors at a relatively low social cost.

Proximity An old saying advises, "Absence makes the heart grow fonder." Another contradicts with "Out of sight, out of mind." Which one is correct? Studies show that frequent sightings best predict our closest relationships and the people we see most often are the people who live and work nearest us (Simpson & Harris, 1994). In college dormitories, residents more often become close friends with the person who lives in the next room than they do with the person who lives two doors down (Priest & Sawyer, 1967). Residents of apartments make more friendships among people who live on the same floor than among those who live on other floors (Nahemow & Lawton, 1975). Those who live in neighborhoods more often become friends with the occupants of the house next door than with people living two houses away (Festinger et al., 1950). This **principle of proximity** (nearness) also accounts for the fact that many people end up married to the boy or girl next door (Ineichen, 1979). And it correctly predicts that people at work will make more friends among those with whom they have the most contact (Segal, 1974).

Although you don't have to like your neighbors, the proximity rule says that when two individuals are equally attractive, you are more likely to make friends with the nearest one: The rewards are equal, but the cost is less in time and inconvenience (Gilbertson et al., 1998). Apparently, another old saying,

■ **Reward theory of attraction** A social-learning view that says we like best those who give us maximum rewards at minimum cost.

■ **Principle of proximity** The notion that people at work will make more friends among those who are nearby–with whom they have the most contact. Proximity means "nearness."

that familiarity breeds contempt, should be revised in light of social psychological research: In fact, familiarity more often breeds friendship. Increased contact, itself, often increases peoples' liking for each other (Bornstein, 1989).

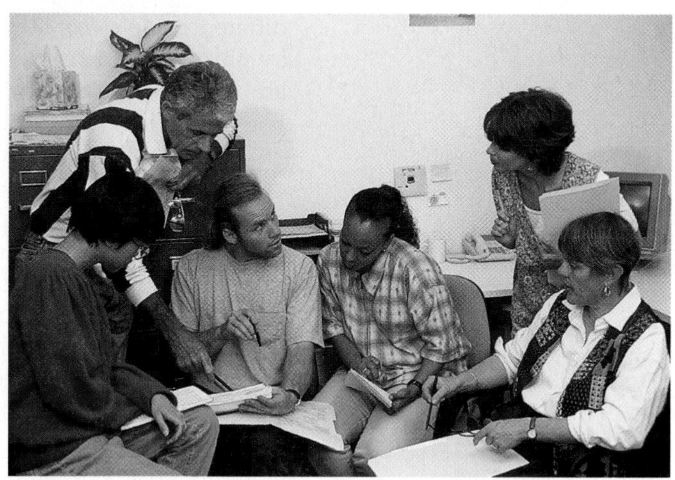

The principle of proximity predicts that coworkers are likely to become friends.

Similarity People usually find it more rewarding to strike up a friendship with someone who shares their attitudes, interests, values, and experiences than to bother with people who are disagreeable or merely different (Hatfield & Rapson, 1993; Hendrick & Hendrick, 1992; Kelley et al., 1983; Simpson & Harris, 1994). If two people have just discovered that they share tastes in music, politics, and attitudes toward education, they will probably hit it off because they have, in effect, exchanged compliments that reward each other for their tastes and attitudes (Byrne, 1969). The **similarity principle** also explains why teenagers are most likely to make friends among those who share their political and religious views, educational aspirations, and attitudes toward music, alcohol, and drugs (Kandel, 1978). Likewise, similarity accounts for the fact that most people find marriage partners of the same age, race, social status, attitudes, and values (Brehm, 1992; Hendrick & Hendrick, 1992). In general, similarity, like proximity, makes the heart grow fonder.

CONNECTION: CHAPTER 4

The Gestalt principle of *similarity* refers to perceptual grouping of objects that share common features.

Self-Disclosure Good friends and lovers share intimate details about themselves (Sternberg, 1998). This practice not only allows people to know each other more deeply but also sends signals of trust. It is as if I say, "Here is a piece of information that I want you to know about me, and I trust you not to hurt me with it." Friends and lovers usually find such exchanges highly rewarding. When you observe people exchanging confidences and details about their lives, you can predict that they are becoming more and more attracted to each other. Given that sharing personal disclosures comes after a sense of trust has been created in a relationship, it both takes time to reach this level of intimacy and is an index of the trust that the disclosing person has in the other.

Physical Attractiveness Yet another old saying tells us that beauty is only skin deep. Nevertheless, people usually find it more rewarding to associate with people they consider physically attractive than with those they consider plain or homely (Patzer, 1985). Fair or not, good looks are a real social asset. Potential employers, for example, prefer good-looking job candidates to plainer applicants (Cash & Janda, 1984). Looks also affect people's judgments of children. Attractive children are judged as happier and more competent than their peers (Dion, 1986; Eagly et al., 1991; Hatfield & Sprecher, 1986). Even babies judge people by their appearances. We know this because babies gaze longer at pictures of normal faces than at those of distorted faces (Langlois et al., 1987).

Most people are repelled by the idea that they might make judgments based only on looks. Indeed, when asked what they look for in a dating partner, college students rank physical attractiveness last. But what people *say* does not match what they *do*—at least as far as their first impressions go. Across many studies, involving a variety of characteristics, including intelligence, sincerity, masculinity, femininity, and independence, physical attractiveness overwhelmed everything else as the best predictor of how well a person would be liked after a first meeting (Aronson, 1999; Feingold, 1990; Langlois et al., 1998; Tesser & Brodie, 1971).

■ **Similarity principle** The notion that people are attracted to those who are most similar to themselves.

Other research shows that the principle of attractiveness applies equally to same-sex and opposite-sex relationships (Maruyama & Miller, 1975). Gender differences do exist, however. Both males and females are strongly influenced by physical attractiveness, but men seem to be more influenced by looks than are women (Cash & Killcullen, 1985; Feingold, 1990; Folkes, 1982; Hatfield & Sprecher, 1986).

These findings may come as bad news for the majority of us, who consider ourselves rather average-looking at best. But we can take some comfort in a study that suggests that people actually consider a composite of "average" features to be the most attractive. Investigators fed images of many students' faces into a computer program that manipulated the facial features to be more or less of an average combination of all features from the many different student portraits. Surprisingly, they found that people usually liked best the images having features closest to the average size and shape (Langlois & Roggman, 1990; Langlois et al., 1994; Rhodes et al., 1999).

Now some bad news for exceptionally attractive readers: While we usually associate positive qualities with attractive individuals (Calvert, 1988), extreme attractiveness can also be a liability. Although physically attractive people are seen as more poised, interesting, sociable, independent, exciting, sexual, intelligent, well-adjusted, and successful, they are also perceived as more vain and materialistic (Brigham, 1980; Cash & Duncan, 1984; Hassebrauck, 1988; Moore et al., 1987). A "double standard" also comes into play. For example, the public favors good-looking male politicians but disparages their attractive female counterparts (Sigelman et al., 1986). It is also double trouble to be shy and handsome or beautiful because others mistakenly interpret such people's reserved demeanor as signaling that they are cold and indifferent or feel superior.

These effects of physical attractiveness hint that reward, as powerful as it is, does not account for everything. We will see this more clearly below, as we explore some important exceptions to the reward theory of attraction.

Exceptions to the Reward Theory of Attraction Although the rules of proximity, similarity, self-disclosure, and physical attractiveness may explain a great deal about interpersonal attraction, a casual look around reveals lots of relationships that don't seem especially rewarding. Why, for example, might a woman be attracted to a man who abuses her? Why would a person want to join an organization that requires a difficult or degrading initiation ritual? Such relationships pose most interesting puzzles (Aronson, 2004). Could some people actually feel *more* attraction when they find that another person has *less* to offer them? Let's try to uncover the principles of social cognition operating behind some interesting exceptions to a reward theory of attraction.

Expectations and the Influence of Self-Esteem We have seen that reward theory predicts our attraction to smart, good-looking, nearby, self-disclosing, like-minded, and powerful people. Yet you have probably observed that most people end up with friends and mates whom you would judge to be of about their same level of attractiveness—the so-called **matching hypothesis** (Feingold, 1988; Harvey & Pauwels, 1999). How does this happen? Is our selection of associates the result of a sort of bargaining for the best we can get in the interpersonal marketplace?

Yes, says **expectancy-value theory.** People usually decide whether to pursue a relationship by weighing the value they see in another person (including such qualities as physical attractiveness, wit, interests, and intelligence) against their expectation of success in the relationship (Will the other person be attracted to me?). Most of us don't waste too much time on interpersonal causes we think are lost. Rather, we initiate relationships with the most attractive people we think will probably like us in return. In this sense, expectancy-value theory is not so much a competitor of reward theory as a refinement of it.

■ **Matching hypothesis** The prediction that most people will find friends and mates that are perceived to be of about their same level of attractiveness.

■ **Expectancy-value theory** A theory in social psychology that people decide whether to pursue a relationship by weighing the potential value of the relationship against their expectation of success in establishing the relationship.

One noteworthy exception to this argument involves people who suffer from low self-esteem. Sadly, people with low opinions of themselves tend to establish relationships with people who share their views, often with people who devalue them. Such individuals generally feel a stronger commitment to a relationship when their partner thinks poorly of them than when the partner thinks well of them (Swann et al., 1992).

Cognitive dissonance theory predicts that these recruits will increase their loyalty to the Marine Corps as a result of their basic training ordeal.

Those individuals who appear to be extremely competent can also be losers in the expectancy-value game. Why? Most of us keep such people at a distance, probably because we fear that they will be quick to reject our approaches. But if you happen to be one of these stunningly superior people, do not despair: Social psychologists have found hope! When highly competent individuals commit minor blunders—spilling a drink or dropping a sheaf of papers—other people actually like them better, probably because blunders bring them down to everyone else's level and "normalize" them (Aronson et al., 1966, 1970). Don't count on this, however, unless you are so awesomely competent as to be unapproachable. The latté-in-the-lap trick only makes most of us look like klutzes whom people like less.

Attraction and Self-Justification *Semper fidelis,* says the Marine Corps motto: "Always faithful." Considering the discomforting experiences that people must go through to become Marines (grueling physical conditioning, loss of sleep, lack of privacy, being yelled at, suffering punishment for small infractions of rules), it may seem remarkable that recruits routinely develop so much loyalty to their organization. Obviously, some powerfully attractive and interesting forces are at work.

Cognitive dissonance theory offers a compelling explanation for the mental adjustments that occur in people who voluntarily undergo unpleasant experiences (Festinger, 1957). The theory says that when people voluntarily act in ways that produce discomfort or otherwise clash with their attitudes and values, they develop a highly motivating mental state called **cognitive dissonance.** A Republican politician who makes a public statement agreeing with a Democratic opponent is likely to feel cognitive dissonance. The same holds true for people who find themselves acting in ways that cause them to experience physical discomfort. Thus, our Marine recruits may feel cognitive dissonance when they find that they have volunteered for an experience that is far more punishing than they had imagined. And what is the psychological result?

CONNECTION: CHAPTER 8

Social psychologists view *cognitive dissonance* as a powerful psychological motive.

According to cognitive dissonance theory, people are motivated to avoid the uncomfortable state of dissonance. If they find themselves experiencing cognitive dissonance, they attempt to reduce it in ways that are predictable, even if not always entirely logical. The two main ways of reducing dissonance are to change either one's behavior or one's cognitions. So, in civilian life, if the boss is abusive, you might avoid dissonance by simply finding another job. But in the case of a Marine recruit, changing jobs is not an option: It is too late to turn back once basic training has started. A recruit experiencing cognitive dissonance therefore is motivated to adjust his or her thinking. Most likely the recruit will resolve the dissonance by rationalizing the experience ("It's tough, but it builds character!") and by developing a stronger loyalty to the organization ("Being a member of such an elite group is worth all the suffering!").

Cognitive dissonance A highly motivating state in which people have conflicting cognitions, especially when their voluntary actions conflict with their attitudes.

In general, cognitive dissonance theory says that *when people's cognitions and actions are in conflict (a state of dissonance) they often reduce the conflict by changing their thinking to fit their behavior.* Why? People don't like to see themselves as being foolish or inconsistent. So, to explain their own behavior to themselves, people are motivated to change their attitudes. Otherwise, it would threaten their self-esteem.

One qualification on this theory has recently come to light. Studies show that in Japan, and perhaps in other parts of Asia, people have a lesser need to maintain high self-esteem than do North Americans (Bower, 1997a; Heine et al., 1999). As a result, cognitive dissonance was found to have less power to change attitudes among Japanese. Apparently, cognitive dissonance is yet another psychological process that operates differently in collectivist and individualistic cultures.

CONNECTION: CHAPTER 9

Collectivist cultures socialize people to put the needs of the group before the desires of the individual.

The Explanatory Power of Dissonance Despite cultural variations, cognitive dissonance theory explains many things that people do to justify their behavior and thereby avoid dissonance. For example, it explains why smokers so often rationalize their habit. It explains why people who have put their efforts into a project, whether it be volunteering for the Red Cross or writing a letter of recommendation, become more committed to the cause as time goes on—in order to justify their effort. It also explains why, if you have just decided to buy a Chevrolet, you will attend to new information supporting your choice (such as Chevrolet commercials on TV), but you will tend to ignore dissonance-producing information (such as a Chevy broken down alongside the freeway).

Cognitive dissonance theory also helps us understand certain puzzling social relationships, such as a woman who is attracted to a man who abuses her. Her dissonance might be summed up in this thought: "Why am I staying with someone who hurts me?" Her powerful drive for self-justification may make her reduce the dissonance by focusing on his good points and minimizing the abuse. And, if she has low self-esteem, she may also tell herself that she deserved his abuse. To put the matter in more general terms: *Cognitive dissonance theory predicts that people are attracted to those for whom they have agreed to suffer.* A general reward theory, by contrast, would never have predicted that outcome.

To sum up our discussion on interpersonal attraction: You usually will not go far wrong if you use a reward theory to understand why people are attracted to each other. People initiate social relationships because they expect some sort of benefit. It may be an outright reward, such as money or status or sex, or it may be an avoidance of some feared consequence, such as pain. But social psychology also shows that a simple reward theory cannot, by itself, account for all the subtlety of human social interaction. A more sophisticated and useful understanding of attraction must take into account such cognitive factors as expectations, self-esteem, and cognitive dissonance. That is, a complete theory must take into account the ways that we *interpret* our social environment. This notion of interpretation also underlies other judgments that we make about people, as we shall see next in our discussion of *attributions.*

Making Cognitive Attributions

We are always trying to explain to ourselves why people do what they do. Suppose you are riding on a bus when a middle-aged woman with an armload of packages gets on. In the process of finding a seat, she drops everything on the floor as the bus starts up. How do you explain her behavior? Do you think of her as the victim of circumstances, or is she a klutz, or is she eliciting sympathy so someone will give up a seat to her?

Social psychologists have found that we tend to attribute other people's actions and misfortunes to their personal traits, rather than to situational forces, such as the unpredictable lurching of the bus. This helps explain why we often hear attributions of laziness or low intelligence to the poor or homeless, rather than an externally imposed lack of opportunity (Furnham, 1982; Pandey et al., 1982; Zucker & Weiner, 1993). It also helps us understand why most commentators on the Kitty Genovese murder attributed the inaction of the bystanders to defects in character of those who did not help, rather than to social influences on them.

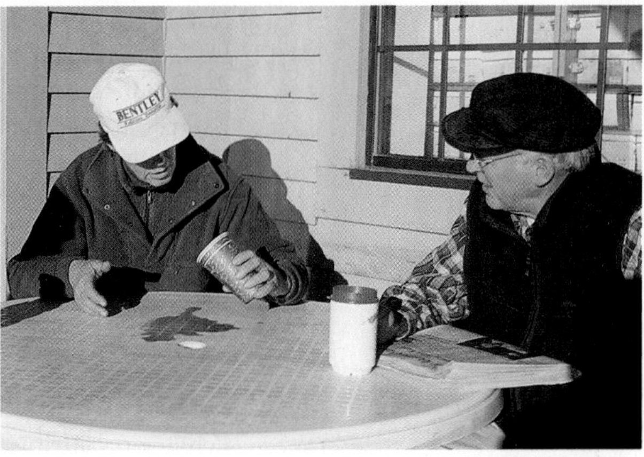
BENTLEY

● If this observer attributes the other man's blunder to clumsiness or carelessness, he commits the fundamental attribution error. This is more likely in Western cultures, such as those of Canada and the United States, than in Eastern cultures, such as those of China and Japan.

On the other side of the attributional coin, we find that people use the same process to explain each other's successes. Thus we may ascribe the success of a favorite singer, athlete, or family member to personal traits, such as exceptional talent or intense motivation. In doing so, we tend to ignore the effects of situational forces, such as the influence of family, coaches, a marketing blitz, long practice, sacrifices, or just a "lucky break."

The Fundamental Attribution Error Psychologists refer to the **fundamental attribution error (FAE)** as the dual tendency to overemphasize personal traits (the rush to the dispositional) while minimizing situational influences. Despite its name, however, the fundamental attribution error is not as fundamental as psychologists at first thought. Cross-cultural research has suggested that it is more pervasive in individualistic cultures, as found in the United States or Canada, than in collectivist cultures, as found in Japan or China (Fletcher & Ward, 1988; Miller, 1984; Norenzayan & Nisbett, 2000; Triandis, 1996). Even within the United States, urban children are more susceptible to the fundamental attribution error than their country cousins (Lillard, 1999).

The FAE is not always an "error," of course. If the causes really are dispositional, the observer's guess is correct. So the FAE is best thought of as a *bias* rather than a mistake. However, the FAE is an error in the sense that an observer may overlook legitimate, situational explanations for another's actions. For example, if the car in front of you brakes suddenly so that you almost collide, your first impression may be that the other driver is at fault, a dispositional judgment. But what if the driver slowed down in order to avoid hitting a dog that ran into the road? Then the explanation for the near-accident would be situational, not dispositional. By reminding ourselves that circumstances may account for seemingly inexplicable actions, we are less likely to commit the FAE. As a general principle, your authors encourage you to practice *"attributional charity,"* which involves always trying to find a situational explanation for strange or unusual behavior of others before blaming them with dispositional explanations.

Biased Thinking About Yourself Oddly, you probably judge yourself by two different standards depending on whether you experience success or failure. When things go well, most people attribute their own success to internal factors, such as motivation, talent, or skill ("I am good at taking multiple-choice tests."). But when things go poorly, they attribute failure to external factors beyond their control ("The professor asked trick questions.") (Smith & Ellsworth, 1987). Psychologists have dubbed this tendency the **self-serving bias** (Bradley, 1978; Fletcher & Ward, 1988). Self-serving biases are probably rooted in the need for self-esteem, a preference for interpretations that save face and cast our actions in the best possible light (Epstein & Feist, 1988; Ickes

■ **Fundamental attribution error (FAE)** The tendency to emphasize internal causes and ignore external pressures. The FAE is more common in individualistic cultures than in collectivistic cultures.

■ **Self-serving bias** An attributional pattern in which one takes credit for success but denies responsibility for failure. (Compare with the *fundamental attribution error.*)

& Layden, 1978; Schlenker et al., 1990). Social pressures to excel as an individual make the self-serving bias, like the fundamental attribution error, more common in individualist cultures than in collectivist cultures (Markus & Kitayama, 1994). In addition, we noted earlier that when trying to understand the behavior of others, we tend often to use dispositional explanations, finding things "in them" that might explain why they did this or that. However, when we are trying to figure out the reasons for *our own actions,* we tend to look to the situational factors acting on us, because we are more aware of them than in our judgments of others.

Prejudice and Discrimination

While our attributions can be positive or negative, prejudice, as social psychologists use the term, is always a negative judgment. Prejudice can make an employer discriminate against women (or men) for a management job. It can make a teacher expect poor work from a minority student. And in some places in the world, it can still lead to *genocide,* the systematic extermination of a group of people because of their racial or ethnic origins. We will define **prejudice** as negative attitudes, beliefs, and feelings toward an individual based solely on his or her membership in a particular group. Prejudice may be expressed as negative emotions (such as dislike or fear), negative attributions or stereotypes that justify the attitude, and/or the attempt to avoid, control, dominate, or eliminate those in the target group. Prejudiced attitudes serve as extreme biasing filters that influence the way others are perceived and treated. Thus, prejudice exerts a powerful force for selectively processing, organizing, and remembering pertinent information about particular people.

We should distinguish prejudice from discrimination, a related concept. While prejudice is an *attitude,* discrimination is a *behavior.* We will define **discrimination,** then, as a negative action taken against an individual as a result of his or her group membership. Racial profiling, for example, is often considered a discriminatory procedure because it singles out people based solely on racial features. But, while discrimination can arise from prejudice, we will see that this is not always the case.

Causes of Prejudice Prejudice can grow from many sources (Allport, 1954; Aronson, 2004). Some prejudices we acquire at an early age. Some are defensive reactions when we feel threatened. Some are the result of conformity to social customs. And some help us distinguish strangers (and possible foes) from friends (Whitley, 1999). An understanding of these sources of prejudice will provide us with the foundation necessary for thinking about possible "cures," ways to combat these antisocial reactions. Here, then, are five causes of prejudice that have been studied by social psychologists.

Dissimilarity and Social Distance If similarity breeds liking, then dissimilarity can breed disdain—and prejudice. If you wear baggy shorts, a baseball cap backwards, and a nose ring, it's a good bet that some middle-aged people from a traditional background will feel uncomfortable around you. They are likely to perceive you as a part of a social group that flaunts values and behaviors quite distinct from those of their own group. This perceived difference in appearance can easily become fertile ground for the growth of prejudice.

What psychological principles are at work? When you perceive someone to be unlike the people in your **in-group,** you mentally place that person at a greater **social distance** than members of your own group. You are then less likely to view that individual as a social equal (Turner & Oakes, 1989). This inequality easily translates into inferiority, making it easier for you to treat

■ **Prejudice** A negative attitude toward an individual based solely on his or her membership in a particular group.
■ **Discrimination** A negative action taken against an individual as a result of his or her group membership.
■ **In-group** The group with which an individual identifies.
■ **Social distance** The perceived difference or similarity between oneself and another person.

members of an **out-group** with contempt. Historically, more powerful groups have discriminated against out-groups by withholding privileges; sending members of out-groups to different schools; making them sit in the back of the bus; forcing them into low-wage jobs, jail, and ghettos; and otherwise treating them punitively.

SCHULE

● Schoolchildren in Nazi Germany (1930s and 1940s) read textbooks describing Jews as inferior to the "Aryan race." Illustrations in those books also depicted Jewish children excluded from schools.

Economic Competition A second cause of prejudice occurs in highly competitive situations, where one group wins economic benefits or jobs at the other group's expense, can easily fan the flames of prejudice. For example, in the Pacific Northwest, where competition over old-growth forests threatens jobs and wildlife habitat, prejudice sets timber workers and environmentalists against each other. Likewise, surveys have found, for example, prejudice against black Americans to be greatest among white groups poised at an economic level just above the black American average—precisely the ones who would feel their jobs most threatened by black Americans (Greeley & Sheatsley, 1971). It is often true that much prejudice exists not only down from those in privileged positions to those in minority positions but across minority groups, between recent immigrants from different countries, or when new immigrants threaten the financial security of established minorities.

Scapegoating To understand a third cause of prejudice, consider how the Hebrew priests of old performed a ritual that symbolically transferred the sins of the people to a goat—the scapegoat. The animal was then driven into the desert to carry its burden of guilt away from the community. The term *scapegoat* has been applied in modern times to an innocent person or group who receives blame when others feel threatened. On a large and horrifying scale, German Jews served as scapegoats for the Nazis in World War II. Hitler's propaganda program encouraged this by creating images of German Jews as totally different from the rest of the German population; such terrible images set them apart as the "faces of the enemy" (Keen, 1991). **Scapegoating** may also explain why the number of lynchings in the southern United States between 1882 and 1930 was related to the price of cotton. When cotton prices dropped, the number of lynchings increased, and when cotton prices rallied, the number of lynchings fell (Hovland & Sears, 1940). Scapegoating is most effective when the object of scorn is readily identifiable by skin color or some distinctive physical features, or propaganda can create such differences in the minds of the dominant group.

Conformity to Social Norms The source of discrimination and prejudice that is perhaps the most pervasive is an unthinking tendency to maintain conditions the way they are, even when those conditions involve unfair assumptions, prejudices, and customs (see Aronson, 2004). For example, in many offices it is the norm for secretaries to be female and executives to be male. Because of this norm, it may be difficult for a woman to break into the executive ranks. We may find the same process where the norm says that nurses and lab technicians should be females and that engineers and mathematicians should be males. When we see that most people in a given profession are of a particular gender or race, we assume that is the way of the world, the way the social order meant it to be, rather than considering the social and economic conditions that have made it that way. So when women note that most computer workers are males, they are likely to avoid taking computer science courses or going into such careers, which then become for "men only."

So we see, then, that discrimination itself can cause prejudice. To reinforce the point, imagine that you were the male executive who discriminated against

■ **Out-group** Those outside the group with which an individual identifies.

■ **Scapegoating** Blaming an innocent person or a group for one's own troubles.

a woman applying for an executive position. Or imagine that you were the white bus driver in the mid-20th-century South who routinely sent black passengers to a special section in the back of the bus. In either case, you would have had to justify your own behavior to yourself. And if you have just treated people as second-class citizens because of their gender or ethnicity, it will be difficult, perhaps impossible, for you to think of them as anything other than inferior beings (without having a severe attack of cognitive dissonance). In this way, your discriminatory behavior can cause or strengthen prejudices. Because we are rationalizing creatures as much as rational ones, we endlessly justify our decisions and behavior to make them appear reasonable by generating "good reasons" for our bad behaviors.

Media Stereotypes Our fifth cause of prejudice occurs when stereotyped images used to depict groups of people in film, in print, and on television reinforce prejudicial social norms. Such images are far from harmless, because people have learned many of their prejudices from the stereotypes they saw on TV and in books, movies, and magazines (Greenberg, 1986). On the other hand, images in the media can also change those norms. Until the Black Power movement gained media attention, Africans and African Americans were most often portrayed in movies and on TV as simple, slow, comic characters, perpetuating the "Sambo" image that many whites held. Fortunately, the most blatant racial stereotypes have disappeared from the national media in the past few decades. Media distortions still occur, of course, but they are more subtle. Prime time features three times as many male as female characters (Aronson, 1999). Most are shown in professional and managerial positions, even though two-thirds of the U.S. workforce is employed in blue-collar and service jobs. The proportion of nonwhites and older persons who appear on TV is also much smaller than in the general population. For viewers, the result is a biased picture of the world. This is where it becomes critical to have a variety of role models in the media that portray positions of influence and credibility to young people from those subgroups, such as woman and ethnic/racial minority members as TV news anchors.

Combating Prejudice During the civil rights struggles of the 1950s and 1960s, educators believed that prejudice could be overcome through a gradual process of information campaigns and education. But experience provided no encouragement for this hope. In fact, these informational approaches are among the least effective tools for combating prejudice. The reason? Prejudiced people (like everyone else) usually avoid information that conflicts with their view of the world, so they never watched or listened to those messages. Even for those who want to change their prejudiced attitudes, erasing the strong emotions and motivational foundations associated with long-standing prejudices is difficult (Devine & Zuwerink, 1994). The process is even more difficult for those who cherish their prejudices because their sense of self-worth is based on perceiving others as less worthy.

So how can one attack the prejudices of people who do not want to listen to another viewpoint? Research in social psychology suggests several possibilities. Among them are the use of new role models, equal status contact, and (surprisingly) new legislation.

New Role Models Golfer Tiger Woods, Secretary of State Condaleeza Rice, and many others serve as role models in prestigious jobs and leadership positions where few of their race or gender have appeared before. These role models encourage people in these groups who might never have considered such careers. What we do not know much about, however, is the ability of role models to change the minds of people who are already prejudiced. Role models may serve better to prevent prejudice than to cure it.

Equal Status Contact Slave owners had always had plenty of contact with their slaves, but they always managed to hang on to their prejudices. Obviously, mere contact with people from an out-group is not enough to erase prejudices against them. Evidence, however, from integrated public housing (where the economic threat of lowered property values is not an issue) suggests that when people are placed together under conditions of equal status, where neither wields power over the other, the chances of developing understanding increase (Deutsch & Collins, 1951; Wilner et al., 1955). In an extensive review of all available literature, Tom Pettigrew (1998) found strong support for the power of equal-status contact to prevent and reduce prejudice among many different kinds of groups.

● Golfer Tiger Woods is a role model in a sport that has traditionally had few representatives of minority groups.

Legislation You can't legislate morality. Right? The evidence of several studies suggests, however, that the old cliché may be wrong. One of the most convincing of these studies was an experiment, done in the late 1940s, comparing the attitudes of white tenants toward black tenants in public housing projects. In one project, white and black occupants were assigned to different buildings; that is, the project was racially segregated. A second project mixed or integrated the two racial groups by assigning housing in the same buildings. Only in the racially integrated project did prejudicial attitudes sharply decrease (Deutsch & Collins, 1951). This result strongly suggests that rules requiring equal-status contact can diminish prejudice.

This notion is reinforced by a larger social "experiment" that was done under far less controlled conditions. During the past half-century, the United States has adopted laws abolishing racial discrimination. The consequences were sometimes violent, but prejudice and discrimination have gradually diminished. Evidence for this shift comes from polls showing that in the 1940s, fewer than 30% of white Americans favored desegregation. That percentage has steadily climbed to well above 90% today (Aronson, 2004).

Because these changes in public opinion were not part of a carefully controlled experiment, we cannot say that the data prove that legislation has caused people's prejudices to diminish. Nevertheless, we can argue that the increased number of white Americans favoring desegregation is exactly what one might predict from cognitive dissonance theory: When the law requires people to act in a less discriminatory fashion, people have to justify their new behavior by softening their prejudiced attitudes. From this vantage point, it appears that legislation can affect prejudiced attitudes, after all.

Other Topics in Social Psychology

One of the most interesting components of social psychology involves group dynamics—the study of how groups form and interact. One of the ways in which we look at how groups work is by examining a phenomenon known as social facilitation.

Social facilitation occurs when an individual's performance improves because of being in a group. For example, research has shown that people who work in small groups in class learn more and are more productive than people who work alone. As part of a group, individuals can compare their thoughts and ideas with others in the group and those comparisons can be used to make improvements. Another component of group dynamics is **social loafing,** where one's productivity and learning decrease because one is in a group. This can occur because the group is too large and/or because people do not think that their contributions to the group will be valued.

Another negative aspect of group dynamics is **deindividuation,** the individual's loss of a sense of personal responsibility, as the group "assumes" responsibility for the behavior. This is seen, for example, in situations where

■ **Social facilitation** An increase in an individual's performance because of being in a group.

■ **Social loafing** A decrease in performance because of being in a group.

■ **Deindividuation** Occurs when group members lose their sense of personal identity and responsibility and the group "assumes" responsibility for their behavior.

fans storm the field at soccer games or loot and riot to protest or cheer victories. Actually, of course, each person in the group is fully responsible for her or his own behavior; the concept of deindividuation is simply a social psychology construct.

Given all that we have seen above (good and bad), why do people join groups? Our main reasons for joining a group involve accomplishing goals, enhancing self-esteem, developing social identity, and expanding our social network. Groups are generally characterized by three features: roles, norms, and cohesiveness. Roles are an expected set of behaviors for members of the group, norms are the rules of conduct within the group, and cohesiveness is the force that pulls group members together and forms bonds that last.

Even in the most cohesive of groups there can be differences of opinion. This is where **group polarization** comes into play. When members of a group have similar, though not identical, views about a particular subject, and discuss them, their opinions become more extreme and pronounced.

Groupthink occurs when members of the group are highly cohesive and strive for concurrence among the members. A number of factors can contribute to groupthink, including a highly controlling leader, stressful situations, and the need for decisions to be unanimous. The atrocities at Abu Ghraib prison in Iraq are an example. To counteract groupthink, groups can consult outsiders (or bring in a new member), encourage the leader to be less controlling, encourage constructive criticism and research, and/or have one member take on the roll of being the "devil's advocate" and question consensus when it is reached.

Each person is unique and brings different experiences and ideas to each situation and to each group they participate in. When we talk about all of the good (and bad) aspects of group dynamics and social psychology, we have to look at the impact that group dynamics has on the individual.

PSYCHOLOGY IN YOUR LIFE: LOVING RELATIONSHIPS

We end this section on a more positive note. Although people often do terrible things to one another, the complexity and beauty of the human mind also enable people to be caring and loving. Liking and loving are essential for happiness (Kim & Hatfield, 2004). Further, the pleasure of attraction and love appear to be part of the very circuitry and chemistry of our brains (Bartels & Zeki, 2004).

How do we know when attraction becomes love? To a large extent, our culture tells us how. Each culture has certain common themes defining love—such as sexual arousal, attachment, concern for the other's welfare, and a willingness to make a commitment. But the idea of "love" can vary greatly from culture to culture (Aron & Aron, 1994; Beall & Sternberg, 1995; Berscheid, 1988; Fehr, 1988; Hatfield, 1988; Sprecher & McKinney, 1994; Sternberg, 1998).

There are also many kinds of love. The love that a parent has for a child differs from the love that longtime friends have for each other. Both differ from the commitment found, say, in a loving couple who have been married for 40 years. Yet, for many Americans, the term *love* brings to mind yet another form of attraction based on infatuation and sexual desire: **romantic love,** a temporary and highly emotional condition that generally fades after a few months (Hatfield et al., 1995; Hatfield & Rapson, 1993, 1998). But the American assumption that romantic love is the basis for a long-term intimate commitment is not universal. In many other cultures, marriage is seen as an economic bond or, perhaps, as a political relationship linking families.

■ **Group polarization** When individuals in a group have similar, though not identical, views, their opinions become more extreme.

■ **Groupthink** An excessive tendency to seek concurrence among group members.

■ **Romantic love** A temporary and highly emotional condition based on infatuation and sexual desire.

Psychologist Robert Sternberg (1998) has proposed an interesting view in his **triangular theory of love.** He says that love can have three components: passion (erotic attraction), intimacy (sharing feelings and confidences), and commitment (dedication to putting this relationship first in one's life). Various forms of love can be understood in terms of different combinations of these three components. Thus, Sternberg suggests that

- *Romantic love* is high on passion and intimacy but low on commitment.
- Liking and friendship are characterized by intimacy but not by passion and commitment.
- *Infatuation* has a high level of passion, but it has not developed into intimacy or a committed relationship.
- *Complete love* (consummate love) involves all three: passion, intimacy, and commitment.

● Is it love? Social psychologists have been exploring the psychology of the human heart, collecting and interpreting data about how people fall in love and strengthen their bonds of intimacy. Most recently the emphasis has shifted to the factors that keep relationships together.

The need to understand what strengthens and weakens loving relationships in our own culture has acquired some urgency because of the "divorce epidemic" in the United States (Brehm, 1992; Harvey & Pauwels, 1999). If current rates hold, approximately half of all today's first marriages—and up to 60% of second marriages—will end in divorce. Much research stimulated by concern about high divorce rates has focused on the effects of divorce on children (Ahrons, 1994; Edwards, 1995).

In the past decade or so, however, research emphasis has shifted to the processes by which couples maintain loving relationships and the environments that challenge relationships (Berscheid, 1999; Brehm, 1992; Duck, 1992; Hatfield & Rapson, 1993). We now know, for example, that for a relationship to stay healthy and thrive, both partners must see it as rewarding and equitable. As we saw in our discussion of reward theory, both must, over the long run, feel that they are getting something out of the relationship, not just giving. What they get—the rewards of the relationship—can involve many things, including adventure, status, laughter, mental stimulation, and material goods, as well as nurturance, love, and social support.

In addition, for a relationship to thrive, communication between partners must be open, ongoing, and mutually validating (Gottman et al., 1998; Gottman & Silver, 1994; Harvey & Omarzu, 1997; Monaghan, 1999). Research shows that couples in lasting relationships have five times more positive interactions than negative ones—including exchanges of smiles, loving touches, laughter, and compliments (Gottman, 1994). Yet, because every relationship experiences an occasional communication breakdown, the partners must know how to deal with conflicts effectively. Conflicts must be faced early and resolved fairly and effectively. Ultimately, each partner must take responsibility for his or her own identity, self-esteem, and commitment to the relationship—rather than expecting the partner to engage in mind reading or self-sacrifice.

This has been the briefest sampling from the growing social psychology of relationships. Such research has practical applications. Teachers familiar with research findings can now inform their students about the basic principles of healthy relationships. Therapists apply these principles in advising clients on how to communicate with partners, negotiate the terms of their relationships, and resolve inevitable conflicts. More immediately, as you yourself learn about the factors that influence how you perceive and relate to others, you should gain a greater sense of self-control and well-being in your own intimate connections with others (Harvey, 1996; Harvey et al., 1990).

■ **Triangular theory of love** A theory that describes various kinds of love in terms of three components: passion (erotic attraction), intimacy (sharing feelings and confidences), and commitment (dedication to putting this relationship first in one's life).

CHECK YOUR UNDERSTANDING

1. **RECALL:** According to Aronson, we can explain almost everything about interpersonal attraction with a theory of
   a. love.
   b. rewards.
   c. genetics.
   d. gender.
   e. environmental influences.

2. **RECALL:** Which of the following does the research say is most important in predicting initial attraction?
   a. physical attractiveness
   b. money
   c. personality
   d. nurturing qualities
   e. sense of humor

3. **RECALL:** Which theory of attraction best explains why people who are considered extremely competent are often not the people we are most attracted to?
   a. reward theory
   b. expectancy-value theory
   c. cognitive dissonance theory
   d. psychoanalytic theory
   e. conformity theory

4. **APPLICATION:** According to cognitive dissonance theory, which of the following would be the best strategy for getting people to like you?
   a. Give them presents.
   b. Show interest in their interests.
   c. Tell them that you like them.
   d. Reward them for good behavior.
   e. Persuade them to perform a difficult or unpleasant task for you.

5. **RECALL:** Prejudice is a(n) ______, while discrimination is a(n) ______.
   a. behavior/attitude
   b. instinct/choice
   c. attitude/behavior
   d. stimulus/response
   e. choice/ethic

6. **RECALL:** The evidence suggests that one of the most effective techniques for eliminating racial prejudice has been
   a. education.
   b. threat and force.
   c. legislation.
   d. tax incentives.
   e. choice.

7. **UNDERSTANDING THE CORE CONCEPT:** Reward theory, expectancy-value theory, cognitive dissonance theory, and attribution theory all tell us that we respond not just to situations but also to
   a. our cognitive interpretations of them.
   b. our social instincts.
   c. the intensity of the stimuli.
   d. our biological needs and drives.
   e. our unconscious needs.

ANSWERS: 1. b 2. a 3. b 4. e 5. c 6. c 7. a

KEY QUESTION

WHAT ARE THE ROOTS OF VIOLENCE AND TERRORISM?

The terrorist attacks of September 11, 2001, raise questions for which there are no easy answers. In this section, however, we will see that social psychology's findings on the *power of the situation* offer a useful starting point for understanding why people commit violent acts. But, your authors will argue, putting together a complete picture of violence and terrorism requires the combined insights of many perspectives—and not just those from psychology. Issues of money, power, resources, and ancient grudges must be considered as well. Our Core Concept says:

CORE CONCEPT

The power of the situation can help us understand violence and terrorism, but a broader understanding requires multiple perspectives that go beyond the boundaries of traditional psychology.

CONNECTION: CHAPTER 6
Aggression often results from *punishment* or the threat of punishment.

■ **Violence and aggression** Terms that refer to behavior that is intended to cause harm.

Before we plunge into these chilling waters, however, let us clarify two basic terms, **violence** and **aggression,** that have overlapping definitions. In the following discussion, we will use these terms interchangeably for any behavior that is intended to cause harm to others (whether or not harm actually results). A key component of this definition is *intent,* but it is also important to note that violence and aggression are social—or, perhaps more aptly, antisocial—phenomena.

The Social Psychology of Aggression and Violence

In this chapter we have seen repeatedly that the pressures of a social situation can make ordinary people commit horrible acts (Zimbardo, 2003). Social influence was at work in Milgram's obedience studies, where subjects obeyed orders to deliver apparently lethal shocks to a stranger. Likewise, the social situation provoked aggression in the Stanford prison study, where ordinary students acting as guards behaved with brutality toward fellow students in the role of prisoners. Still other research has shown that aggressive behavior can be induced by situations that create prejudice, conformity, frustration, threat, or wounded pride (Aronson, 2004; Baumeister et al., 1996). Now, let us take a detailed look at another important study that showed how aggression could arise out of intergroup conflict—again caused by the power of the situation.

The Robbers Cave: An Experiment in Conflict

The setting was a Boy Scout Camp known as the "Robbers Cave." There, the experimenters, Muzafer Sherif and his colleagues (1961) randomly assigned 11- and 12-year-old boys to two groups, dubbed the Eagles and the Rattlers. The experiment called for conditions similar to those at many other summer camps for boys: days filled with competitive games and activities. Competition, the experimenters hoped, would create conflict between the two groups.

● Competition can promote aggressive behavior.

Initially, the Eagles and Rattlers were kept apart, allowing within-group activities to build group **cohesiveness** (solidarity, loyalty, and a sense of group membership). Later the experimenters brought the two groups together for competitions, such as tug-of-war and football. Prizes for the winners heightened the competitive atmosphere. The final straw was a "party" at which the experimenters arranged to have the Eagles arrive an hour early. Half the food was mouth-watering, and half was deliberately unappealing. As you might expect, when the Rattlers arrived they found that the Eagles had devoured the more desirable food. This led to name-calling and scuffling, which culminated in a food fight.

With a rancorous atmosphere well established, Sherif and his colleagues tried various tactics for promoting cooperation between the groups. Their initial attempts were, however, complete failures. In particular, it did not help merely to bring the Eagles and Rattlers together for social events, such as movies or eating in the same dining room. Such occasions just offered opportunities for more hostility.

What *did* help was to contrive situations in which the groups had to cooperate in order to serve their mutual interests. First, however, the experimenters called a halt to the competitive games. Then, they assembled the boys to inform them of a "problem" that had developed with the camp's vital water line. Both groups agreed to search the line for the trouble spot, which they did together—harmoniously. On another day, the experimenters arranged for the camp's truck to break down—which meant that it could not go to town for food. To get the truck running, the two groups had to work cooperatively by pulling it with the same rope previously used for the divisive tug-of-war game.

To serve its own needs, each group had to cooperate with the "enemy." And, as dissonance theory would predict, hostility changed to friendliness. The change in behavior led directly to a change in attitude. That is, the attitude change resulted from a need to justify the altered behavior.

It took several such crises to break down the hostile barriers between the two groups and to build a sense of **mutual interdependence,** a working

■ **Cohesiveness** Solidarity, loyalty, and a sense of group membership.

■ **Mutual interdependence** A shared sense that individuals or groups need each other in order to achieve common goals relationship based on shared goals. But in the end, the groups actively sought opportunities to mingle with each other, and friendships developed between members of the Eagles and Rattlers. One group even used its own money to buy treats for members of the other group. (Do you see a parallel between this study and the ethnic conflicts in the Middle East?)

Fuel for Terrorism

The flammable combination of poverty, powerlessness, and hopelessness is the tinder that the September 11 attacks were intended to ignite, says Jonathan Lash, president of the World Resources Institute in Washington, D.C. (2001). Much of the world lives in poverty and hunger and sees no way out. Ethnic hatred and wars aggravate their plight. Moreover, the number of people living in these miserable conditions is increasing, as most of the world's population explosion is occurring in poorer countries. And to make matters more volatile, says Lash, a large proportion of these desperate people depend directly on resources that are rapidly being depleted: fisheries, forests, soils, and water resources. As a result, every day thousands flee their traditional homelands and stream into the largest and poorest cities. Most are young—a result of the high birth rates in the Third World. Lash warns that urban slums, filled with restless, jobless young men, are "tinderboxes of anger and despair; easy recruiting grounds for bin Laden or those who may come after him" (p. 1789). Consider this warning in light of Milgram's obedience studies: If ordinary, well-fed people can be induced to deliver apparently lethal shocks, how much easier it would be to persuade angry, hopeless young men and women to commit violent acts.

Thus, says Lash, removing the flint that sets off the spark is not sufficient; the Western world must also deal with the tinder. In other words, even if the terrorists' leaders are struck down and their resources captured, the anger and despair of the world's poor and desperate people will continue to pose a threat to the United States and other wealthy nations. As psychologists, we can understand this threat as a political restatement of the pain–aggression relationship that we saw in Chapter 6.

Understanding the tinderbox conditions that arise from poverty and despair and the tension between rich and poor nations, then, requires that we take economic and political perspectives. In addition, we must see that many of the conflicts that breed terrorism have historical roots. We cannot understand, for example, the tensions between Christianity and Islam without knowing about the 200-year-war that the Western world calls the Crusades (1095–1291) or the fall of the six-centuries-old Ottoman empire (1300–1922) at the end of World War I. Although such events may seem remote, they changed the trajectory of history, and their religious significance continues to fuel conflict in the Middle East today.

What We Can Do About Terrorism **Terrorism** is really about psychology. It typically involves a relatively small group of people who take dramatic, violent actions against a larger group with the intention of spreading fear among them and inducing anxiety and uncertainty about their government's ability to protect them. Terrorists do not want to conquer other nations' land, as in traditional wars, but to conquer the minds of their enemies by making them feel victimized and fearful. Your authors believe that taking multiple perspectives can provide important insights into the problems of aggression, violence, and terrorism. In this vein, please consider the following suggestions.

As citizens and critical thinkers, we need to call for better information from our politicians, educators, journalists, and others who may try to assign easy answers to complex problems. Meeting aggression with aggression may be necessary, but it is never sufficient. We should encourage our political repre-

■ **Terrorism** The use of violent, unpredictable acts by a small group against a larger group for political, economic, or religious goals.

sentatives to consider responses based on multiple perspectives. More specifically, we can support efforts to find common goals—in much the same way that Sherif and his colleagues reduced conflict among the Eagles and Rattlers.

Unfortunately, the easiest and most simplistic response is to demonize those who perpetrate evil deeds—but that is merely name-calling, and we should resist it. This tactic blinds us to the power of the situation to create aggression in ordinary people. More important, it prevents us from dealing with the situations that nurture violence. Labeling others as "evil," or "pathological" usually prevents any attempt to understand the reasons for their actions, instead making them into objects of scorn or disdain.

A related mistake is to think of violence and terrorism as "senseless." On the contrary, destructive deeds always make sense from the perpetrator's frame of reference. As Shakespeare's Hamlet said, there is "method" in madness: We must understand the method in the minds of potential terrorists, if we are to deter them.

Finally, as individuals and as a society, we must refuse to adopt the terrorists' devaluing of human life. If we act on the desire to destroy our enemy at any cost, we will have succumbed to the power of the situation. Moreover, we will have played into the hands of the ones we would destroy.

Kelman's Conflict Resolution Approach The hope that the psychology of cooperation and conflict reduction might ease international tensions lies behind a quiet program currently operating in Israel. There, social psychologist Herbert Kelman applies the lessons of the Eagles and Rattlers to the long-standing hostilities and prejudices between the Israelis and the Palestinians (Kelman, 1997, 1999; Rouhana & Kelman, 1994). His approach involves bringing community leaders from both sides together for small-group discussions of mutual problems. Not just anyone could have started such a program: Kelman's credibility with both sides is a product of his stature as a scholar and the prestige of his affiliation with Harvard University.

Kelman's approach was carefully planned to encourage cooperation and minimize the rewards for hostile behaviors. Representatives of both groups are invited to attend a series of meetings. These are not the usual, high-profile public negotiation sessions, however. Kelman has found that the process works best when the participants are mid-level community leaders who have some power and status but who are in close touch with ordinary, grassroots citizens. Also important is the fact that meetings are held in private to avoid competitive posturing for the press. Removed from the public spotlight, tensions between the two factions have eased, and earnest communication has developed.

Proof that this approach works is difficult to come by, especially in these times of political crisis and upheaval, although Kelman can recite case studies in which old hatreds have been soothed. In fact, several participants in these workshops have later become involved in other peace efforts in their communities. Although the method is inspired by solid science, Kelman is performing no laboratory experiment. Rather, he is applying principles of social psychology to the world beyond the laboratory, where most of the variables remain uncontrolled.

PSYCHOLOGY IN YOUR LIFE: MULTIPLE PERSPECTIVES ON TERRORISM

How does the Robbers Cave experiment apply to our understanding of the terrorist attacks of September 11? Admittedly, it is a stretch between experiments in the laboratory and conflicts on the international stage. Nevertheless, please consider the following ideas.

First, understanding terrorism does not mean condoning or accepting it—any more than understanding prejudice means approving of it. There can be no moral justification for the vicious attacks on the United States—or any other terrorist attacks. But—like it or not—many people in the world perceive the United States as the enemy. Understanding this perception—and dealing constructively with it—demands that Americans see the conflict from someone else's point of view: those who consider the United States to be the enemy. Doing so involves a cultural perspective.

Second, the Eagles and Rattlers study suggests that effective conflict resolution can come from identifying goals of mutual benefit and persuading the antagonistic groups to pursue these shared goals. This task requires leadership of exceptional vision and skill. It will take this same level of leadership to resolve the conflict resulting from the terrorist attacks on the United States.

Third, we must realize that terrorism does not always involve international conflict. The shootings at Columbine High School were terrorist acts, as was the bombing of the Federal Building in Oklahoma City, along with thousands of racial/ethnic hate crimes, attacks against gays, and violence directed at abortion providers that have made news in recent years (Doyle, 2001). It would be a mistake to believe that terrorism is always an outside threat from foreigners: Even though some cultures are more violent than others, every culture can breed violent people who terrorize others (Moghaddam et al., 1993; Shiraev & Levy, 2001).

Fourth, as in other areas of psychology, understanding the problem of violence and terrorism requires application of multiple perspectives—perhaps the most profound and far-reaching idea in psychology. In an earlier chapter, for example, we viewed aggression from a biological perspective, noting its association with testosterone and with certain parts of the brain (Davidson et al., 2000; Enserink, 2000; Holden, 2000b). From a behavioral perspective, we saw how aggression often results from pain or punishment (Shiraev & Levy, 2001). From an evolutionary perspective, we can see that aggression involves an impulse built into our genetic makeup and triggered by fear, threat, scarce resources, and sexual rivalry. Experiments in social learning have also shown how role models can stimulate aggression. And, in this chapter, we have seen how other forms of social influence can lead to aggression and violence.

CONNECTION: CHAPTER 6

Through social learning we acquire behaviors observed in our role models.

A complete picture, however, necessitates taking perspectives that extend beyond psychology (Segall et al., 1999). When we expand our view of terrorism, we can see that long-standing hostilities arise from religious, ethnic, and racial prejudices and from poverty, powerlessness, and hopelessness. To arrive at this understanding, however, we must view terrorism from historical, economic, and political perspectives—again, not to excuse violent acts but to understand their origins.

CHECK YOUR UNDERSTANDING

1. **RECALL:** Conflict between the groups in the Robbers Cave experiment was encouraged by
   a. punishing nonaggressive boys.
   b. showing movies featuring hostile role models.
   c. competitive games.
   d. putting a particularly aggressive boy in charge of each group.
   e. encouraging cooperation.

2. **RECALL:** In Kelman's work in the Middle East, he removed much of the incentive for competitive responses by
   a. punishing those who responded competitively.
   b. holding the meetings in private.
   c. taking hostages from both sides.
   d. publicly denouncing those who responded competitively.
   e. encouraging cooperation.
3. **UNDERSTANDING THE CORE CONCEPT:** In both the Robbers Cave experiment and Kelman's work in the Middle East, helping people to build a sense of mutual interdependence encouraged them to
   a. become more aggressive.
   b. punish those who had encouraged hostilities.
   c. become more creative.
   d. adopt new personality traits.
   e. alter their perceptions of each other.

ANSWERS: 1. c 2. b 3. e

SOCIAL PSYCHOLOGY: THE STATE OF THE ART

More than anything else, social psychology has demonstrated the *power of the situation* to shape people's behavior. Depending on how it is structured, the situation can make people conform, obey, act aggressively, develop prejudices, and even commit terrorist acts. On the other hand, the power of the situation can induce cooperation, liking, and loving. The most recent research has focused not only on the conditions but also on the *social processes* that shape these attitudes and behaviors. And, despite the complexity of their subject matter, social psychologists have been exemplars in the use of the experimental method in studying social processes.

In our opinion, the social psychology of the future lies in two domains: (a) work on validating (or invalidating) our knowledge across cultures and (b) the application of basic principles, theories, and methods to political and social problems at home and abroad—to situations as diverse as discrimination, poverty, crime, prisoner abuse, terrorism, ethnic conflict, and war.

USING PSYCHOLOGY TO LEARN PSYCHOLOGY

Persuasion in the Classroom

You may associate persuasion with advertising and politics, but persuasion does not stop there. It is woven into all human interaction—including the exchanges of ideas that occur in the classroom. There, your teachers and fellow students will attempt to persuade you with reasoned arguments, and they will expect you to set out your points of view in the same fashion. But aside from the open exchange of ideas and opinions, there are other, more subtle persuasive pressures of which you should be aware, says social psychologist Robert Cialdini (2001a, b). If you don't know about these, you run the risk of letting other people make up your mind for you. We will discuss three such subtle forms of influence that you will encounter in your college or university experience.

Social Validation

Although you may see a popular movie because your friends like it, going along with the crowd is a poor basis for judging the theories you encounter in your classes. Many of the world's discarded ideas were once accepted by nearly everyone. In psychology, these include the false notions that we use only 10% of our brain, that personality is determined by the first two years of life, and that IQ tests are a good measure of innate abilities. So, rather than accepting what you hear and read, questioning even the most widely held concepts is a good habit. In fact, most famous scientists have built their careers on challenging ideas that everyone else accepted.

Authority

The lectures you hear and the textbooks you read are full of authority figures. Every parenthetical reference in this book, for example, cites an authority. Most are given, in part, to persuade you that the argument being offered is credible. The problem, of course, is that ideas are not true merely because some authority says so. For example, just a few years ago, every introductory psychology text in print taught that no new neurons were created in the brain after birth. Now we know that the textbooks and the experts they cited were wrong. Real proof of such assertions, however, requires more objective evidence obtained by the scientific method—not just the declaration of an authority.

The Poison Parasite Argument

In advertising, a good way to undermine a competitor, says Cialdini, is with a message that calls into question the opponent's credibility. Then, to get people to remember what you have said, you can infect your opponent with a "parasite"—a mnemonic link that reminds people of your message every time they hear your opponent's pitch (Brookhart, 2001). A classic example involved antismoking ads that looked like Marlboro commercials, except that they featured a coughing, sickly "Marlboro Man." You may encounter the same sort of poison parasite argument in a lecture or a textbook that attempts to hold someone's ideas up to ridicule. That's not necessarily bad: In the academic world, weak ideas should perish. The sneaky, dishonest form of this technique, however, involves a misrepresentation or oversimplification of the opponent's arguments. The antidote is to be alert for ridicule and to check out the other side of the argument yourself.

The social psychology of persuasion, of course, involves much more than we have discussed here. A good place to look for more information is Cialdini's book *Influence: Science and Practice* (2001a). Perhaps the most important idea is that some knowledge of persuasion can forearm you against the persuasive techniques you will encounter, both in and out of the classroom. When you know how effective persuaders operate, you are less likely to donate money to causes you don't care about, buy a car you don't really like, or accept a theory without examining the evidence critically.

A PERSONAL ENDNOTE

And so we come to the end of our journey together through psychology. If you are a curious people-watcher, perhaps you will continue on to the next phase of the journey into more advanced psychology and social science courses and into the books and films we have suggested at the end of each chapter. If you scan back through the Core Concepts in this book, you will realize that you have learned much already. Yet, because people are so complex, we have scarcely scratched the surface of the excitement and challenges that the field of psychology has to offer you.

One day you may be among those who contribute to this dynamic enterprise as a scientific researcher. (Wouldn't it be great if your name could appear in a future edition of this book? Please send us word of your discoveries!) Or perhaps you will decide to be a practitioner who applies what is known in psychology to the solution of personal and social problems. (Again, we would like to know if your career in psychology began with our journey together.) But even if you don't become a professional psychologist, your authors hope that this introduction to psychology has sparked a lasting interest in mind and behavior because you cannot help but be an intuitive psychologist—psychology is all around you, and in you.

Playwright Tom Stoppard reminds us that "Every exit is an entry somewhere else." We would like to believe that the entry into the next phase of your life will be facilitated by what you have learned from *Psychology: Core Concepts,* and from your introductory psychology course. In that next journey, may you infuse new life into the study of human nature, while strengthening the human connections among all people you encounter. Here's to a long, mindful, and wonderful journey through life.

CHAPTER SUMMARY

KEY QUESTION

CORE CONCEPT

● HOW DOES THE SOCIAL SITUATION AFFECT OUR BEHAVIOR?

The Stanford prison experiment demonstrated how norms and social roles can be major sources of situational influence. The Asch studies demonstrated the powerful effect of the group to produce conformity, even when the group is clearly wrong. Another shocking demonstration of situational power came from Stanley Milgram's controversial experiments on obedience to authority. Situational influence can also lead to inaction: The bystander studies showed that individuals are inhibited by the number of bystanders, the ambiguity of the situation, and their resultant perception of their social role and responsibility.

● **We usually adapt our behavior to the demands of the social situation, and in ambiguous situations we take our cues from the behavior of others.**

● CONSTRUCTING SOCIAL REALITY: WHAT INFLUENCES OUR JUDGMENTS OF OTHERS

The situation, by itself, does not determine behavior. Rather, it is our interpretation of the situation—our constructed social reality—that regulates behavior, including our social interactions. Usually we are attracted to relationships that we find rewarding, although there are exceptions, predicted by expectancy-value theory and cognitive dissonance theory. Attribution theory predicts that we will attribute other people's blunders to their traits or character (the fundamental attribution error) and our own to the situation (the self-serving bias), although this tendency depends on one's culture. Prejudice and discrimination also demonstrate how we construct our own social reality through such cognitive processes as the perception of social distance and threats, the influence of media stereotypes, scapegoating, and self-justification. Group dynamics, the study of how groups form and interact, helps us to explain our behavior and choices in specific situations. Healthy, loving relationships also demonstrate the social construction of reality, because there are many kinds of love and many cultural variations in the understanding of love.

● **The judgments we make about others depend not only on their behavior but also on our interpretation of their actions within a social context.**

● WHAT ARE THE ROOTS OF VIOLENCE AND TERRORISM?

Many studies in social psychology—particularly those dealing with obedience and conformity—show that the power of the situation can pressure ordinary people to commit horrible acts. In the Robbers Cave experiment, conflict between groups arose from an intensely competitive situation. Cooperation, however, replaced conflict when the experimenters contrived situations that fostered mutual interdependence and common goals for the groups.

The Robbers Cave experiment may hold a valuable lesson about dealing with violence and terrorism: the need for leadership that will find common goals for groups in conflict. A fuller understanding of violence and terrorism, however, requires taking multiple perspectives—including those that go beyond the boundaries of psychology to include the historical, economic, and political roots. Unfortunately, the easiest responses involve demonizing those who commit violent acts or labeling such acts as "senseless"—responses that interfere with our understanding them and dealing with them effectively.

A constructive approach, based on understanding conflict from multiple perspectives, is now under way in the Middle East. There, social psychologist Herbert Kelman has created noncompetitive situations in which Israeli and Palestinian community leaders are seeking solutions that benefit all sides.

● **The power of the situation can help us understand violence and terrorism, but a broader understanding requires multiple perspectives that go beyond the boundaries of psychology.**

REVIEW TEST

For each of the following items, choose the single correct or best answer. The answer key appears at the end.

1. Which of the following is the social psychological principle illustrated by the Stanford prison experiment and its findings about participants' behavior?
   a. Social situations have powerful influences on human behavior.
   b. An experience is socially real only when the group is unanimous about interpreting it.
   c. Because everyone is basically different, no two people will respond to the same circumstances in the same way.
   d. Even in healthy circumstances, disturbed people will behave in unhealthy ways.
   e. Participants felt positive about their participation.

2. Theodore Newcomb's study of the attitudes of Bennington College students showed that, 20 years after they were first studied,
   a. many of the women had gradually shifted to more conservative attitudes.
   b. many of the women had gradually shifted to more liberal attitudes.
   c. the liberals were still liberal, and the conservatives were still conservative.
   d. None of the above.
   e. All of the above.

3. According to research on the Asch effect, which of the following is not a condition that encourages greater conformity?
   a. The task being judged is difficult.
   b. Each group member responds privately and anonymously.
   c. The group is extremely cohesive.
   d. The group members perceive each other to be highly competent.
   e. The task being judged is ambiguous.
4. Which of the following statements about Milgram's obedience experiments is true?
   a. All participants were unable to resist the authority figure's orders, no matter how high the level of shock they believed they were administering.
   b. The majority of subjects delivered increasingly intense shocks until the learner complained of a heart condition, at which point most subjects refused to go on.
   c. Although most subjects verbally dissented and complained, most obeyed.
   d. Despite predictions by human nature experts that no one would comply, subjects enjoyed the experiment and had no trouble obeying the authority figure's commands.
   e. The experiments were never completed.
5. Research on the factors that influence helping behavior suggests that the best predictor of bystander intervention is
   a. each individual's measurable level of personal altruism.
   b. the appearance or attractiveness of the victim.
   c. an individual's degree of religiousness or agreement with conventional religious values.
   d. the size of the group of bystanders to the emergency.
   e. the age of the victim.
6. According to research on interpersonal attraction and close relationships, which of the following is *false?*
   a. The more you interact with someone, the more likely you are to like him or her.
   b. We form friendships on the basis of our similarity of backgrounds and attitudes.
   c. As far as first impressions go, a pleasing personality counts more than good looks.
   d. If you voluntarily undergo a hardship or suffering at someone's request, you will probably like that person more than you did before.
   e. Humor is the most telling factor in long-term relationships.
7. Which of the following situations would be likely to create a feeling of cognitive dissonance in the mind of the individual described?
   a. A woman who has said she is on a diet declines the offer of dessert.
   b. A young man who says he loves his girlfriend spends a great deal of time choosing just the right valentine card to send her.
   c. When a man finds out the car he wants costs more than he can afford, he decides not to buy it and looks instead for a less expensive vehicle.
   d. A person must choose between two colleges.
   e. A woman with a prejudice against Jews finds herself agreeing to do a favor for a Jewish neighbor.
8. Which of the following illustrates the effects of the fundamental attribution error?
   a. Explaining why he is turning his paper in late, a student tells the professor that he had car trouble on the way to campus.
   b. Watching an acquaintance hurry from the overcrowded dining hall, a woman remarks, "Amy's in such a hurry—she must be a pretty impatient person."
   c. After waiting an unusually long time to be waited on in a restaurant, a customer thinks there must be something wrong in the kitchen that is interfering with the waitress's ability to work as quickly as usual.
   d. All of the above.
   e. None of the above.
9. In the Robbers Cave experiment, hostility between the groups was reduced by
   a. having the groups engage in social activities with each other.
   b. creating crisis situations that the groups had to work on cooperatively.
   c. punishing aggressive behavior.
   d. allowing the groups to take out their hostilities in competitive sports.
   e. All of the above.
10. In an application of social psychological findings on promoting cooperation between hostile groups, Herbert Kelman has
   a. used the power of conformity (the Asch effect) to reduce hostilities.
   b. advocated the use of rewards for peaceful actions and punishments for hostile actions.
   c. brought community officials on both sides together for private discussions of mutual problems.
   d. promoted "friendly" athletic competition as a means of displacing harmful aggressions and "burning off" energy that could explode into violence.
   e. demonstrated the effectiveness of negative reinforcement on group interactions.

ANSWERS: 1.a 2.c 3.b 4.c 5.d 6.c 7.e 8.b 9.b 10.c

KEY TERMS

Social psychology (p. 567)
Social context (p. 567)
Situationism (p. 568)
Social role (p. 569)
Script (p. 569)
Social norms (p. 569)
Asch effect (p. 571)
Conformity (p. 571)
Diffusion of responsibility (p. 579)
Social reality (p. 583)
Reward theory of attraction (p. 584)
Principle of proximity (p. 584)
Similarity principle (p. 585)
Matching hypothesis (p. 586)
Expectancy-value theory (p. 586)
Cognitive dissonance (p. 587)
Fundamental attribution error (FAE) (p. 589)
Self-serving bias (p. 589)
Prejudice (p. 590)
Discrimination (p. 590)
In-group (p. 590)
Social distance (p. 590)
Out-group (p. 591)
Scapegoating (p. 591)
Social facilitation (p. 593)
Social loafing (p. 593)
Deindividuation (p. 593)
Group polarization (p. 594)
Groupthink (p. 594)
Romantic love (p. 594)
Triangular theory of love (p. 595)
Violence and aggression (p. 596)
Cohesiveness (p. 597)
Mutual interdependence (p. 597)
Terrorism (p. 598)

AP* REVIEW: VOCABULARY

Match each of the following vocabulary terms to its definition.

1. Script
2. Cognitive dissonance
3. Prejudice
4. Scapegoating
5. Social facilitation
6. Social loafing
7. Deindividuation
8. Norms
9. Group polarization
10. Groupthink

_____ **a.** A negative attitude toward an individual based solely on her or his group membership.

_____ **b.** A decrease in an individual's performance because of being in a group.

_____ **c.** Knowledge about the sequence of events and actions that is expected in a particular setting.

_____ **d.** An increase in an individual's performance because of being in a group.

_____ **e.** A person's loss of personal identity and responsibility as the group "assumes" the responsibility for behavior.

_____ **f.** An excessive tendency to seek concurrence among group members.

_____ **g.** Blaming an innocent person or a group for one's own troubles.

_____ **h.** When individuals in a group have similar, though not identical, views, their opinions become more extreme.

_____ **i.** A highly motivating state in which people have conflicting thoughts, especially when their voluntary actions conflict with their attitudes.

_____ **j.** The rules of conduct for a group.

AP* REVIEW: ESSAY

Use your knowledge of the chapter concepts to answer the following essay question.

Define each of the following concepts and explain how each contributes to the phenomenon of prejudice.

a. Stereotyping

b. Self-fulfilling prophecy

c. Fundamental attribution error

d. Schema

OUR RECOMMENDED BOOKS AND VIDEOS

BOOKS

Aronson, E. (2000). *Nobody left to hate: Teaching compassion after Columbine.* New York: W. H. Freeman. Renowned social psychologist Elliot Aronson argues that violent shootings by young students are in part fostered by the pressures and negativity in the schools themselves, including bullying, taunting, and exclusion. To end such tragedies, he offers strategies by which students, teachers, and communities might work to make schools humane, compassionate, and respectful.

Cialdini, R. B. (2001). *Influence: Science and Practice.* Boston: Allyn & Bacon. Noted social psychologist Robert Cialdini summarizes the key principles of social influence, by which you get others to do what you want—or they get you to obey, agree, or buy. Whether you're selling, buying, or trying not to buy, this review arms you with the principles and research explaining how ideas and relationships alter behavior.

Coplin, W. D. (2000). *How you can help: An easy guide to doing good deeds in your everyday life.* New York: Routledge. Since September 11, 2001, many citizens want to "do good" but aren't sure how to start. This guide lists needy groups and worthwhile causes, strategies and principles for efficient helping, and brief, inspiring case histories of people who have made a difference in ways both large and small.

Davis, J. M. (2003). *Martyrs: Innocence, vengeance, and despair in the Middle East*. New York: Macmillan. What are the origins of the hatred and fanaticism that turn people into terrorists? Journalist Joyce Davis interviews people on both sides of the Israeli–Palestinian conflict to uncover the conditions and motives that turn young men, mothers, and children into warriors and suicide bombers.

Friday, N. (1996). *The power of beauty.* New York: HarperCollins. Bestselling author Nancy Friday takes a careful, critical look at life in the "age of the empty package," when looks take precedence over personal qualities and everyone lusts for beauty.

Kohn, A. (1990). *The brighter side of human nature: Altruism and empathy in everyday life.* New York: Basic Books. Kohn provides an uplifting review of the many ways in which people help and cooperate with each other and the challenge this poses for more cynical views of human nature as "naturally" warlike and selfish.

Stern, J. (2003). *Terror in the name of God: Why religious militants kill.* New York: Ecco. Jessica Stern, former fellow on terrorism at the Council of Foreign Relations, traveled the world to study the people and issues behind "religious" murders, ranging from Muslim jihadists in Indonesia to Americans who murder abortion providers in the name of Christianity. Religious militancy, she notes, is maintained by religious groups' support and the façade of normality and can be countered only with effective nonviolent strategies.

VIDEOS

Ghosts of Mississippi. (1996, color, 130 min.). Directed by Rob Reiner; starring Alec Baldwin, Whoopi Goldberg, James Woods. This is the involving drama of the murder of civil rights leader Medgar Evers, the campaign by his widow to arrest and convict Byron De La Beckwith (the admitted but not confessed killer), and the attorney who finally agreed to prosecute the case at great cost to his own life. It is a portrait of a culture's doomed efforts to protect their prejudices and resist change. (*Rating PG-13*)

Pay It Forward. (2001, color, 123 min.). Directed by Mimi Leder; starring Kevin Spacey, Helen Hunt, Haley Joel Osment. Challenged by a talented but afflicted new teacher, a young boy initiates a program of helping others in threes, with each recipient obligated to do the same for others in need. The engaging plot about the personalities and relationships of the principal characters also shows how such a plan might work and suggests that altruism might yet prevail. (*Rating PG-13*)

Separate but Equal. (1991, color, 193 min.). Directed by John Stevens, Jr., starring Sidney Poitier, Richard Kiley, Burt Lancaster. Originally a two-part TV movie, this docudrama tells the story of a young Thurgood Marshall's 1954 argument of *Brown v. Board of Education* before the Supreme Court, of which he was later to become the first black justice. Includes depiction of classic research by black psychologists Kenneth and Mamie Clark, who discovered that segregated children's self-concepts had been harmed, even to the point of preferring white dolls to black ones. (*Rating PG*)

To Kill a Mockingbird. (1962, b&w, 129 min.). Directed by Robert Mulligan; starring Gregory Peck, Mary Badham, Philip Alford, Brock Peters, Robert Duvall. This dramatization of Harper Lee's novel about a small-town Southern lawyer defending a black man falsely accused of rape shows the impact of his unpopular efforts on his young children and his community. (*Not rated*)

12 Angry Men. (1957, b&w, 95 min.). Directed by Sidney Lumet; starring Henry Fonda, Lee J. Cobb, E. G. Marshall, Ed Begley, Jack Klugman, Jack Warden, Robert Webber. In this absorbing drama of 12 jurors' deliberation over a verdict in a murder trial, their own prejudices, eyewitness memory, and group influence all play a part. (*Rating PG-13*)

Preparing for the AP* Psychology Exam

WHAT IS THE AP* PSYCHOLOGY EXAM?

The AP* Psychology exam consists of 100 multiple-choice questions and two essays on the 14 topics covered in the text. The multiple-choice questions have five possible responses, just like the questions at the end of each section of this text, at the end of each chapter, and in the testbank. The multiple-choice questions are arranged in sequence from easiest to hardest, and you have 70 minutes to answer all of them. Although this may not seem like a lot of time, past history has shown that the test is not "timed"—that is, the majority of test takers finish all 100 questions within the time allowed. The essays test your ability to synthesize information from two or more chapters; you have 50 minutes to complete both essays.

The AP* exam is designed to assess how much you know about the entire discipline of psychology, not just one or two favorite topics. Although you may find the information on psychological disorders and treatment fascinating, just as many questions will be asked about research methods and personality. *In general,* the number of multiple-choice questions on a particular subject will equal the percentage listed on the course outline. Therefore, the percentage assignments will prove to be very useful information as you prepare for the exam. For example, if you didn't have time to study every section as well as you should have, you might focus more attention on the biological bases of behavior (8–10%) than on states of consciousness (2–4%).

The following sections describe various studying methods as well as some approaches that we specifically recommend for preparing for the AP* Psychology Exam.

STUDYING FOR THE AP* EXAM

As you review and prepare for the AP* Psychology Exam (or for any exam), there are a number of strategies you can use to ensure that you do your best. As we have noted often throughout this book, there are a lot of different ways to study and learn. Each of you will have a different "best" way of studying.

SQ4R

Perhaps the most well-known studying method is the SQ4R (Survey, Question, Read, Recite, Relate, Review). *Survey* means to preview the chapter. Look at the chapter and section headings. These will give you an idea what is going to be covered in the chapter. In addition, you should read the captions under the pictures, as well as the graphs, charts, and tables. By surveying before you read and study the chapter, you will get a preview of the topics and their relationship to each other.

After you survey the material, the next step is the *Question* component. First, look at all of the subject and chapter headings and turn them into questions. This method will help you use each section's content to answer these questions. Second, look at the questions at the end of each section and those at the end of the chapter. These questions are designed to test your knowledge of what you have read and learned. Reviewing these questions before reading the chapter helps you to identify the key ideas and components of each chapter. At the beginning of each chapter of this text is an outline which reflects the chapter organization and connections between topics. The "Key Questions" and "Core Concepts" target the main ideas and unifying threads that run throughout each chapter. Knowing them is essential to your success.

Next comes the *Read* element of the SQ4R study method. This is what most students think of when they think of studying. (*Note:* Students who begin their studying with reading have skipped the first two steps!) Reading does not mean simply plowing though the text, but rather thinking about the questions you asked during the Question phase. Also, reread the captions of pictures and graphs. What do they tell you now that they did not tell you earlier? When you get to a passage in the text that is difficult, read more slowly; furthermore, read only one section at a time. Make a note of any of the terms that are printed in boldface or italic type. They are important. You must know them to speak and understand the language of psychology.

The next step is *Recite.* After reading you should go over each individual section that you have read, one at a time. Ask yourself questions about what you have read and either underline key concepts or take written notes on concepts that are interesting or difficult to understand. When you write down the questions and answers from the text, do so in your own words. Even though the words in the text may make sense to you, explaining them in your own words ensures that you really know and understand the information being presented.

The penultimate step is *Relate.* Throughout this book, your authors have given you examples to help make the information more meaningful. You can also do this for yourself by relating the information and anecdotes to events in your own life or, even more effectively, by relating the information you are learning to your understanding of other areas of knowledge. Ideas and concepts that have a special meaning for you, or perhaps are humorous, will be easier to remember than others.

The last step is *Review.* In order to really learn and understand psychology you must continually review the information. When you've finished a chapter, go back and reread your notes and all the section headings. Quiz yourself using the questions you generated in the Survey and Question stages, as well as the questions in each section and at the end of the chapter.

As you progress through the book, spend a little time reviewing each of the chapters you have already studied. This continual review will make studying for the AP* Psychology Exam in spring much less of a chore.

Vocabulary

Apart from the SQ4R, there are other study skills you can use to help you retain the information you will need to succeed. For example, one of the most vital and difficult aspects of learning psychology is learning the language of psychology. The best way to do that is to learn its vocabulary.

There are 643 vocabulary terms in this book. That number may seem daunting, but we have identified all the terms in the chapter where they are first introduced, in the margins of the chapters, at the end of each chapter, and at the end of the text glossary to continually reinforce your comprehension. A vocabulary quiz at the end of each chapter gives you another way to check your understanding. For some students, a good way to study is to use the terms listed at the end of each chapter as a kind of quiz. Write out your own list of the terms and then define as many of them as you can. Often the terms you cannot define are clustered around specific concepts and topics—a clear indication of where you need to concentrate your review efforts.

For those trouble areas go back and reread that section (or sections), paying particular attention to the vocabulary. This is important for many reasons, the most practical of which is that in the multiple-choice questions, all five of the possible answer options consist of real psychological terms. Nothing is made up, so if you know the vocabulary or *language* of psychology, you won't be misled by an answer option that seems correct but is, in fact, a distracter.

Outlines

Another effective studying technique is the use of outlines. For some students, using the chapter and section headings to create a detailed chapter outline is ideal. This method enables you to get an overview of the organization of the chapter, as well as placing the information in context. It is in the proper context of information that is required to synthesize the information you will need to present in your essays.

Creating chapter outlines as you read each chapter also makes the review process in April/May much easier. Once you have created outlines, execute the SQ4R to help ensure that you remember and can retrieve the information needed for the AP* exam.

Practice Tests

One of the most effective studying methods involves obtaining practice test resources from your teacher. The College Board has released three full-length exams, those from 1994, 1999, and 2004. These practice exams can be of great use. Taking a released exam can give you a good general idea of how you would score on the actual exam. (There are a few caveats, however; for example, the 1994 exam is now out of date.) One of the primary benefits of taking the released exams is what we refer to as the *practice effect*. The more practice you have on a particular task, the easier it will be. Therefore, the more practice tests you take, the less stressful the exam will be. In addition, the results on the practice exams can give you and your teacher an idea how well prepared you are.

Some teachers give the released exam at the beginning of the review time to help you determine in what topics you are weakest so that you can focus on reviewing those areas. Other teachers use the tests, and questions from them, to assess what you and your classmates already know. This benchmark enables these teachers to tailor their instruction to the relative strengths and weaknesses of each class.

What is most important is that any practice test mirrors what will take place on the AP* exam. All of the review questions at the end of each chapter in this book have five options, as will every multiple-choice question on the exam. A number of teachers also structure their practice tests to reflect the structure of the AP* exam. For example, in a 50-minute class period, a chapter or unit test would have between 40 and 44 multiple-choice questions and one essay question. This arrangement would approximate the time constraints of the actual AP* exam. Students who are accustomed to this pattern will not feel rushed when they take the AP* Psychology Exam.

Of course, not all courses lend themselves to this type of continual pretesting. It is incumbent upon you, the student, to ensure that you are ready.

Managing Exam Stress

In the Motivation and Emotion chapter of this text, we discussed arousal theory, and now is the time for a practical application of it. Based on your performance on tests throughout the text, your teachers' tests, practice exams, and your notes and reviewing, you should have a general idea how well you will do on the AP* exam. If you are happy with your predicted level of performance, then review just a little before the exam. If not, focus your review on the three main areas in which you are weakest.

The most important factor in this equation for success is you. Mihaly Csikszentmihalyi (1990) equation for success describes two main ways of coping with stress; he calls one of them the "mature defense" and the other "regressive coping." In regressive coping, you might see the exam as a highly stressful event that may be overwhelming, even though your performance and preparations indicate that you should score a 3 or higher (on a scale of 1–5). Behaviors associated with regressive coping include withdrawing in class, sleeping late, and avoiding thinking about class and the exam. In contrast, to mount a "mature defense" is to recognize that the AP* exam may be difficult, suppress your feelings of anxiety, analyze what you need to do to be successful (what you need to study), and move forward.

Of course, in all likelihood, you will rely a little on both methods of coping. Csikszentmihalyi reminds us that "no trait is more useful, more essential for survival, and more likely to improve the quality of life than the ability to transform adversity into an enjoyable challenge" (1990). We are not suggesting that the AP* exam and studying for it will be fun all the time, but acquiring and applying psychology knowledge is!

We also discussed the inverted-U theory in the motivation chapter. Taking the AP* exam is a great way to see that theory in action. It is essential that you match your level of arousal to the difficulty level of the exam. If you are very well prepared, then a low level of arousal will suffice, but if you haven't studied as much as you should have or haven't been reviewing or paying attention in class, then you will benefit from a higher level of arousal.

Perhaps the most important thing to remember is not to panic. If you have studied, you should do just fine.

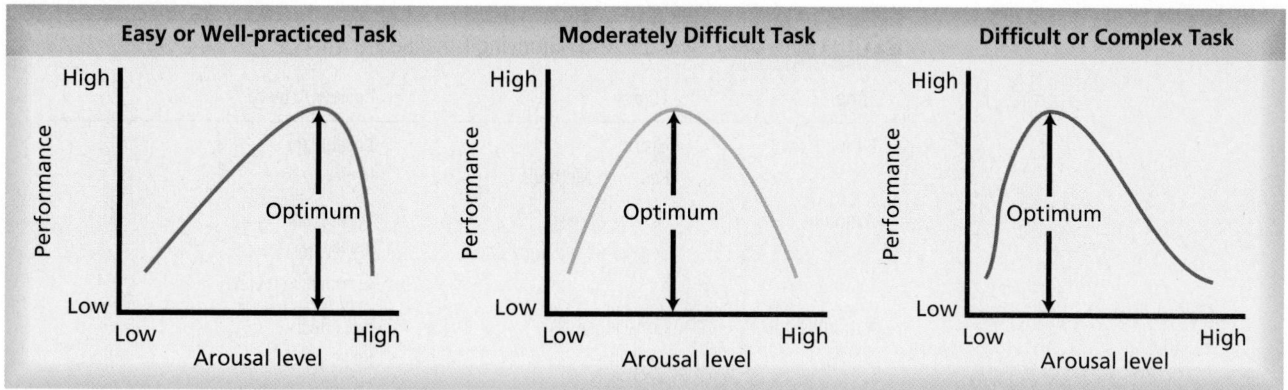
Easy or Well-practiced Task
High
Performance
Optimum
Low
Low
High
Arousal level
Moderately Difficult Task
High
Performance
Optimum
Low
Low
High
Arousal level
Difficult or Complex Task
High
Performance
Optimum
Low
Low
High
Arousal level

The Inverted U

Performance varies with arousal level and task difficulty. For easy or well-practiced tasks, a higher level of arousal increases performance effectiveness. However, for difficult or complex tasks, a lower level of arousal is optimal. A moderate level of arousal is generally best for tasks of moderate difficulty. These inverted U-shaped functions show that performance is worst at both low and high extremes.

Timing

Whether you are taking a one-semester course or a full-year course in AP* psychology, you should be successful. Obviously a year-long course allows for more in-depth examination of the material, but there are lots of very comprehensive semester courses being taught, and yours is probably one of them. Table A.1 shows a suggested timeline for studying in a one-semester course. The timing is tight, but it will ensure that you have covered all the topics addressed in the exam. Table A.2 is a suggested timeline for a year-long course.

TABLE A.1 One-Semester AP* Exam Studying Timeline

Time	Topics	Review activity
4 months out	History Research Methods	Vocabulary Review tests
3 months out	Biological Bases Sensation and Perception Consciousness Learning	Vocabulary Review tests Cumulative review
2 months out	Cognition Motivation and Emotion Developmental Personality	Vocabulary Review tests Cumulative review Practice essay questions
1 month out	Testing Abnormal Treatment Social	Vocabulary Review tests Cumulative review Practice essay questions
2 weeks out	REVIEW	Practice test (released exam) Targeted review (three areas of weakness)
1 week out	REVIEW	Question and Answer Study groups Practice test (released exam) Targeted review (three areas of weakness)

TABLE A.2 Two-Semester Studying Timeline

Time	Topics	Review Activity
6 months out	History Research Methods	Vocabulary Review tests
5 months out	Biological Bases Sensation and Perception	Vocabulary Review tests Cumulative review
4 months out	Consciousness Learning Cognition	Vocabulary Review tests Cumulative review Practice essay questions
3 months out	Motivation and Emotion Developmental Personality	Vocabulary Review tests Cumulative review Practice essay questions
2 months out	Testing Abnormal	Vocabulary Review tests Cumulative review Practice essay questions
1 month out	Treatment Social	Vocabulary Review tests Cumulative review Practice essay questions
2 weeks out	REVIEW	Practice test (released exam) Targeted review (three areas of weakness)
1 week out	REVIEW	Question and Answer Study groups Practice test (released exam) Targeted review (three areas of weakness)

*When possible, the mid-term exam should be 2 hours long, with 100 multiple-choice and two essay questions.

Final Thoughts

Spread out your review for the exam over the entire course. For each successive chapter, review any concepts in the previous chapter that eluded you. As you progress through the course (and text), keep adding concepts to your review, and as you gain mastery, move on. Then, roughly every three or four chapters, retake the review test and vocabulary quiz in each chapter, just to make sure you are still current, and review the topics and ideas you may have forgotten.

Most of all, have fun. Psychology is the most fun subject you can study (at least that's what we—Phil, Ann, Bob, and Craig—think). So enjoy it!

Discovering Psychology Viewing Guide

Chapter 1: Introduction and History of Psychology

Watch the following video by logging onto MyPsychLab (www.mypsychlab.com). After you have watched the video, complete the activities that follow.

PROGRAM 1: PAST, PRESENT, AND FUTURE

Program 1 introduces psychology as the scientific study of behavior and mental processes. It looks at how psychologists work from a variety of theoretical models and traditions, record and analyze their observations, and attempt to unravel the mysteries of the mind.

KEY TERMS AND PEOPLE

As you watch the program, pay particular attention to these terms and people in addition to those covered in this textbook.

ERP (Event-Related Potentials)—variations in brain waves as recorded by the electroencephalograph (EEG) that are triggered by specific internal or external events.

Heisenberg indeterminacy principle—principle stating that our impressions of other people are distorted by how we observe and assess them.

Mahzarin Banaji—uses indirect measures of reaction time and brain activity to study prejudice.

Emanuel Donchin—discovered that brains measure surprise before we are aware of it.

G. Stanley Hall—founded the first American psychology lab in 1883.

Liz Phelps—collaborates with M. Banaji in conducting brain-based studies of prejudice.

Robert Rosenthal—showed that body language can reflect what we think and feel.

PROGRAM REVIEW

1. What is the best definition of *psychology?*
   a. the scientific study of how people interact in social groups
   b. the philosophy explaining the relation between brain and mind
   c. the scientific study of the behavior of individuals and of their mental processes
   d. the knowledge used to predict how virtually any organism will behave under specified conditions

2. As scientists, psychologists do which of the following?
   a. develop methods of inquiry that are fundamentally at odds with those of physics and chemistry
   b. test their theories under carefully controlled experimental circumstances
   c. ignore their own observational biases when collecting data
   d. rely completely on introspective techniques

3. What is the main focus of Donchin's research involving the P-300 wave?
   a. the relation between brain and mind
   b. the role of heredity in shaping personality
   c. the development of mental illness
   d. the role of situational factors in perception

4. What is the main goal of psychological research?
   a. to cure mental illness
   b. to find the biological bases of the behavior of organisms
   c. to predict and, in some cases, control behavior
   d. to provide valid legal testimony

5. The reactions of the boys and the girls to the teacher in the *Candid Camera* episode were essentially similar. Professor Zimbardo attributes this reaction to
   a. how easily adolescents become embarrassed.
   b. how an attractive teacher violates expectations.
   c. the way sexual titillation makes people act.
   d. the need people have to hide their real reactions.

6. What do EEGs measure?
   a. heart rate
   b. changes in hormone levels in the body
   c. energy expended in overcoming gravity
   d. brain activity

7. According to Robert Rosenthal's research, you are most likely to detect a liar by
   a. observing eye movements.
   b. listening to tone of voice.
   c. considering sociocultural factors.
   d. looking at body language.

8. Which cluster of topics did William James consider the main concerns of psychology?
   a. reaction times, sensory stimuli, word associations
   b. consciousness, self, emotions
   c. conditioned responses, psychophysics
   d. experimental design, computer models

9. What do we learn from our misreading of the "Paris in the spring" sign?
   a. We are accustomed to an artist's use of perspective.
   b. Experience disposes us to respond in a particular way.
   c. Unexpected events trigger P-300 waves in the brain.
   d. We laugh at those things that violate our expectations.

10. The amygdala is an area of the brain that processes
   a. sound.
   b. social status.
   c. faces.
   d. emotion.

11. According to Mahzarin Banaji, the IAT could potentially be used for what practical application?
   a. studying latent prejudice in police officers
   b. assessing relationships among family members
   c. evaluating intellectual ability
   d. determining when someone is lying during negotiation

12. Who founded the first psychology laboratory in the United States?
   a. Wilhelm Wundt
   b. William James
   c. G. Stanley Hall
   d. Sigmund Freud

13. How did Wundtian psychologists, such as Hall, react to William James's concept of psychology?
   a. They accepted it with minor reservations.
   b. They expanded it to include consciousness and the self.
   c. They rejected it as unscientific.
   d. They revised it to include the thinking of Sigmund Freud.

14. Which level of analysis concerns a person's behavior within a complex situation?
   a. cosmological level
   b. molar level
   c. molecular level
   d. micro level

15. Which of the following, according to Robert Rosenthal, predicts success in getting alcoholics into treatment?
   a. their income
   b. the number of years they'd been drinking
   c. the physical appearance of the doctor recommending treatment
   d. the doctor's tone of voice

16. Which of the following psychologists was the first to study people's sensory processing, judgment, attention, and word associations?
   a. G. Stanley Hall
   b. William James
   c. Wilhelm Wundt
   d. Sigmund Freud

17. Most psychologists study human behavior at which level of analysis?
   a. molecular
   b. macro
   c. micro
   d. molar

18. Who wrote *Principles of Psychology* and thereby became arguably the most influential psychologist of the last century?
   a. G. Stanley Hall
   b. Wilhelm Wundt

c. William James
d. Sigmund Freud

19. What assumption underlies the use of reaction times to study prejudice indirectly?
   a. People of different ethnic backgrounds are quicker intellectually than people of other ethnicities.
   b. Concepts that are associated more strongly in memory are verified more quickly.
   c. Prejudice can't be studied in any other way.
   d. People respond to emotional memories more slowly than emotionless memories.

20. Prejudice can be studied at
   a. the micro level.
   b. the molecular level.
   c. the molar level.
   d. all of the above.

QUESTIONS TO CONSIDER

1. Although psychologists are involved in many different kinds of research and professional activities, there are certain fundamental issues that form the basic foundation of psychology. What are they?

2. Why would the study of normal behavior be more important to the science of psychology than an understanding of abnormal behavior?

3. List as many reasons as you can think of for why people who would benefit from seeing a therapist might not do it.

4. How do your culture, age, gender, education level, and past experience bias your observations about events, your own actions, and the behavior of others?

5. Is thinking a behavior? How can it be studied?

6. Imagine the year 2500. How do you think the boundaries of psychological and biological research might have become redefined by then? Do you think the two fields will have become more integrated or more distinct?

ACTIVITIES

1. Start a personal journal or a log. Make a daily practice of recording events, thoughts, feelings, observations, and questions that catch your attention each day. Include the ordinary and the unusual. Then speculate on the possible forces causing your behavior. As you progress through the course, review your notes and see how your observations and questions reflect what you have learned.

2. Look ahead to one or two psychological principles described in the book. After describing the experimental situation to your friends, ask them to introspect about what their own data would have shown if they had participated. How closely do their introspections match the actual results of the study? What factors might lead their introspections to be more or less accurate?

3. As you go through your day-to-day life, watching the news, battling traffic, and making decisions about how to spend your time and money, consider all the ways that psychologists might be interested in studying, facilitating, or intervening in human behavior.

Discovering Psychology Viewing Guide

Chapter 2: Research Methods

Watch the following video by logging onto MyPsychLab (www.mypsychlab.com). After you have watched the video, complete the activities that follow.

PROGRAM 2: UNDERSTANDING RESEARCH

Program 2 demonstrates the how's and why's of psychological research. By showing how psychologists rely on systematic observation, data collection, and analysis to find out the answers to their questions, this program reveals why the scientific method is used in all areas of empirical investigation.

KEY TERMS AND PEOPLE

As you watch the program, pay particular attention to these terms and people in addition to those covered in this textbook.

burnout—a work-related condition in which stress, lack of support, and negative self-evaluation disrupt performance and well-being.

field study—research carried on outside the laboratory where naturally occurring, ongoing behavior can be observed.

random sample—an unbiased population selected at random.

subjective reality—the perceptions and beliefs that we accept without question.

Daryl Bem—psychologist who illustrated the importance of critical thinking in scientific experiments.

Jerome Frank—psychiatrist who studies the common features of miracle cures and healings, political and religious conversions and psychotherapy.

Christina Maslach—uses psychometric research to study job burnout.

Leonard Saxe—studies the use and misuse of polygraphs to detect lying.

PROGRAM REVIEW

1. Which of the following describes a field study?
   a. observing a natural, ongoing situation
   b. randomly assigning participants to treatment groups
   c. randomly assigning participants to a control group
   d. distributing a questionnaire to a large group

2. Which of the following is desirable in research?
   a. having the control and experimental conditions differ on several variables
   b. interpreting correlation as implying causality
   c. systematic manipulation of the variable(s) of interest
   d. using samples of participants who are more capable than the population you want to draw conclusions about

3. What is the main reason that the results of research studies are published?
   a. so researchers can prove they earned their money
   b. so other researchers can try to replicate the work
   c. so the general public can understand the importance of spending money on research
   d. so attempts at fraud and trickery are detected

4. Why does the placebo effect work?
   a. because researchers believe it does
   b. because participants believe in the power of the placebo
   c. because human beings prefer feeling they are in control
   d. because it is part of the scientific method

5. What is the purpose of a double-blind procedure?
   a. to test more than one variable at a time
   b. to repeat the results of previously published work
   c. to define a hypothesis clearly before it is tested
   d. to eliminate experimenter bias

6. If you had been one of the participants in the lie detector study, what information would have helped you earn some money?
   a. The results depend on the skill of the person administering the lie detector test.
   b. Lie detectors only measure arousal level, not lying.
   c. The polygraph is used to make millions of decisions each year.
   d. The placebo effect works with lie detectors.

7. According to Jerome Frank, placebos work through
   a. emotional arousal.
   b. brainwashing.
   c. chemical alteration of neural transmission.
   d. cognitive reassessment of the illness.

8. A report on children's television watching found that children who watch more TV have lower grades. What cause-effect conclusion are we justified in making on the basis of this study?
   a. TV watching causes low grades.
   b. Poor school performance causes children to watch more TV.
   c. Cause-effect conclusions can never be based on one study.
   d. None; cause-effect conclusions cannot be based on correlation.

9. What was the major weakness of the Hite report on women's attitudes toward sex and marriage?
   a. The sample was not representative.
   b. Hypotheses were not clearly stated beforehand.
   c. Experimenter bias arose because the double-blind procedure was not used.
   d. No control group was used.

10. A prediction of how two or more variables are likely to be related is called a
   a. theory.
   b. conclusion.
   c. hypothesis.
   d. correlation.

11. Imagine a friend tells you that she has been doing better in school since she started taking vitamin pills. When you express disbelief, she urges you to take vitamins too. Why might the pills "work" for her but not necessarily for you?
   a. Healthy people don't need vitamins.
   b. A belief in the power of the vitamins is necessary for any effect to occur.
   c. She is lying.
   d. They would work for her and not for you if she was a poor student and you were a straight-A student.

12. In which experiment would a double-blind test be most appropriate?
   a. a lab experiment by a technician who does not understand the theory under scrutiny
   b. a study designed to test the researcher's own controversial theory
   c. a survey asking subjects how many siblings they have
   d. an experiment on the effect of a drug on maze running ability in rats

13. The "card trick" in the program demonstrates what about good science?
   a. Predictions should be made explicitly before data collection.
   b. Chance must be ruled out as an explanation.
   c. The experimenter's effect on the subject must be ruled out as an explanation.
   d. All of the above.

14. When long-term stress and lack of support on the job lead to chronic deficits in a worker's productivity and health, the worker is likely to be suffering from
   a. generalized anxiety disorder.
   b. post-traumatic stress.
   c. job burnout.
   d. insomnia.

15. Christina Maslach uses all of the following to study job burnout *except*
   a. interviews.
   b. hospitalization records.
   c. surveys.
   d. psychometric scales.

16. How could you improve on Shere Hite's survey techniques?
   a. Redo her study using her methods, but send the survey to ten times as many recipients.
   b. Hire one subject, pay her for a full day's work, and spend eight hours interviewing her thoroughly.
   c. Redo her study, using her methods, but send the survey to an equal number of men.
   d. Redo her study, but ensure that the percentage of respondents was much higher and much more representative of the population of interest.

17. Why would other scientists want to replicate an experiment that has already been done?
    a. to have their names associated with a well-known phenomenon
    b. to gain a high-odds, low-risk publication
    c. to ensure that the phenomenon under study is real and reliable
    d. to calibrate their equipment with those of another laboratory

18. Because experiments involve careful manipulation of all factors of interest and careful control of all others, which experiment would not be ethically allowable?
    a. the effect of classical music on the ability to solve crossword puzzles
    b. the effect of room lighting on color preference
    c. the effect of supplementary vitamins on retirement age
    d. the effect of prolonged solitary confinement of toddlers on language development

19. Because of what it actually does measure, under what circumstances would an innocent person likely fail a polygraph test?
    a. if she is extremely worried about the possibility of being found guilty
    b. if she is drunk
    c. if she is acquainted with the actual guilty party
    d. if she is confident in the validity of the polygraph test

QUESTIONS TO CONSIDER

1. If some people really get healed by faith healers, why condemn the practice of faith healing?

2. If there is value in running studies with within-subjects designs, why would an experimenter ever use a between-subjects design?

3. What are some of the practical objections to studying mental processes?

4. What is your reaction to the guidelines prohibiting research if it would require deception and if distress is a likely result? Are there studies you think would be valuable to perform but that could not be? Could the same research questions be answered in some other way?

5. Are animals adequately protected by the APA's guidelines? Why or why not?

6. How could a study be biased simply because it uses volunteer participants?

7. Can the results of experiments conducted mostly on college students, who are among the more highly educated members of our society, really be extended to the rest of society? Which sorts of psychological phenomena would be more likely or less likely to generalize to people of other age groups, socio-economic status, and education levels?

ACTIVITIES

1. Write operational definitions of the following:

green	thirst	wealth
warm	anger	learning
cleverness	intelligence	jealousy
suffering	comprehension	

2. Design a study that would test whether children come to learn self-control better if they are physically punished vs. receive time-outs for bad behavior. What features of the problem determine whether you can run an experiment to test this? What confounding variables might be present in a study like this? How would you eliminate them as possible alternative explanations?

3. Design an experiment that would allow you to show whether a two-week-old child knows who her mother is. Be sure that your experimental design can eliminate alternative explanations for your data.

Discovering Psychology Viewing Guide

Chapter 3: Biopsychology and the Foundations of Neuroscience

Watch the following videos by logging onto MyPsychLab (www.mypsychlab.com). After you have watched the videos, complete the activities that follow.

PROGRAM 3: THE BEHAVING BRAIN

Psychologists who study the structure and composition of the brain believe that all our thoughts, feelings, and actions have a biological and chemical basis. Program 3 explains the nervous system and the methods scientists use to explore the link between physiological processes in the brain and psychological experience and behavior.

PROGRAM 4: THE RESPONSIVE BRAIN

Program 4 takes a closer look at the dynamic relationship between the brain and behavior. We'll see how the brain controls behavior and, conversely, how behavior and environment can cause changes in the structure and the functioning of the brain.

KEY TERMS AND PEOPLE

As you watch the programs, pay particular attention to these terms and people in addition to those covered in this textbook.

Program 3

agonist–a chemical or drug that mimics the action of a neurotransmitter.

amnesia–a type of profound and generalized forgetting, generally affecting factual information, and involving the inability to learn new information and/or to retrieve important old information.

antagonist–a chemical or drug that blocks the action of a neurotransmitter.

physostigmine–enhances the effect of acetylcholine in the brain by inhibiting the enzyme that breaks it down.

scopolamine–depletes the availability of acetylcholine in the brain by blocking the receptors for acetylcholine.

Emanuel Donchin–studies the manner in which the mind is implemented by the brain using psychophysiological measures.

John Gabrieli–studies amnesic patients to determine how different types of memory are physically stored in and retrieved from the brain.

E. Roy John–studies neurometrics and uses precise electrophysiological measures to determine neural functioning.

Joseph Martinez–studies how brain chemicals affect learning and memory.

Mieke Verfaellie–studies the effects of amnesia on memory and cognition.

Program 4

enzymes–protein molecules that act as catalysts in body chemistry by facilitating chemical reactions.

glucocorticoid–substances produced by the adrenal cortex that act on the hippocampus to alter the stress response.

maternal deprivation–the lack of adequate affection and stimulation from the mother or mother substitute.

Russell Fernald–neuroethologist who studies how brain, behaviors and the environment interact in animals in their natural habitat.

Tiffany Field–studies the effect of infant massage on the cognitive and motor development of infants.

Michael Meaney–developmental psychologist who studies how early experiences can change the brains and behavior of animals, especially under stress.

Robert Sapolsky–neurobiologist who studies the social structure of baboon communities. Argues that dominance affects physiological functioning, with higher ranks being associated with greater control, predictability, and better physiological functioning.

Saul Schanberg–works with infant rats to demonstrate how touch is a brain-based requirement for normal growth and development. Argues that a mother's touch has real biological value to offspring and is required to maintain normal growth and development.

PROGRAM REVIEW

Programs 3 and 4

1. What section of a nerve cell receives incoming information?
   a. the axon
   b. the terminal button
   c. the synapse
   d. the dendrite

2. In general, neuroscientists are interested in the
   a. brain mechanisms underlying normal and abnormal behavior.
   b. biological consequences of stress on the body.
   c. comparison of neurons with other types of cells.
   d. computer simulation of intelligence.

3. Which section of the brain coordinates body movement and maintains equilibrium?
   a. the brain stem
   b. the cerebellum
   c. the hippocampus
   d. the cerebrum

4. Which brain structure is most closely involved with emotion?
   a. the cortex
   b. the brain stem
   c. the limbic system
   d. the cerebellum

5. Which method of probing the brain produces actual pictures of the brain's inner working?
   a. autopsies
   b. lesioning
   c. brain imaging
   d. electroencephalograms

6. E. Roy John cites the example of the staff member responding to a personal question to show how imaging can detect
   a. abnormal structure in the brain.
   b. abnormal personality.
   c. abnormal but transient states.
   d. pathological states, such as alcoholism.

7. If a scientist was studying the effects of endorphins on the body, the scientist would be likely to look at a participant's
   a. memory.
   b. mood.
   c. ability to learn new material.
   d. motivation to compete in sports.

8. Joseph Martinez taught rats a maze task and then gave them scopolamine. What effect did the drug have on brain functioning?
   a. It enhanced the rats' memory.
   b. It made the rats forget what they had learned.
   c. It enabled the rats to learn a similar task more quickly.
   d. It had no effect.

9. Research related to acetylcholine may someday help people who
   a. have Alzheimer's disease.
   b. have Parkinson's disease.
   c. suffer spinal cord trauma.
   d. suffer from depression.

10. A scientist who uses the methodologies of brain science to examine animal behavior in natural habitats is a
    a. naturalist.
    b. bioecologist.
    c. neuroethologist.
    d. cerebroetymologist.

11. When we say the relationship between the brain and behavior is reciprocal, we mean that
    a. the brain controls behavior, but behavior can modify the brain.
    b. behavior determines what the brain will think about.
    c. the brain and behavior operate as separate systems with no interconnection.
    d. the brain alters behavior as it learns more about the world.

12. Before an operation, men and women were gently touched by a nurse. What effect did this touch have on the patients' anxiety levels?
    a. It decreased anxiety in both men and women.
    b. It increased anxiety in both men and women.
    c. It decreased anxiety in men, but increased it in women.
    d. It increased anxiety in men, but decreased it in women.

13. A group of people comfortable with touching others is compared with a group uncomfortable with touching others. Those comfortable with touch were generally higher in
    a. self-esteem.
    b. social withdrawal.
    c. conformity.
    d. suspicion of others.

14. What long-term effect did Tiffany Field find massage had on premature infants?
    a. Massaged infants had better social relationships.
    b. Massaged infants were physically and cognitively more developed.
    c. Massaged infants slept and ate better.
    d. There were no long-term effects noted.

15. What is the relationship between the results of Saul Schanberg's research and that of Tiffany Field?
    a. Their results are contradictory.
    b. The results of Schanberg's research led to Field's research.
    c. Their results show similar phenomena in different species.
    d. Their results are essentially unrelated.

16. What area of the brain seems to be affected in psychosocial dwarfism?
    a. the hippocampus
    b. the cerebellum
    c. the brain stem
    d. the hypothalamus

17. What physical change did Mark Rosenzweig's team note when they studied rats raised in an enriched environment?
    a. a thicker cortex
    b. more neurons
    c. fewer neurotransmitters
    d. no physical changes were noted, only functional changes

18. In Michael Meaney's research on aged rats' performance in a swimming maze, the rats that performed best were those that
    a. had received doses of glucocorticoid.
    b. had been subjected to less stress in their lives.
    c. had been handled early in life.
    d. could use spatial clues for orientation.

19. Repeated exposure to stress hormones
    a. increases the number of glucocorticoid neurons.
    b. has its greatest effect on the brain stem.
    c. affects learning and memory.
    d. makes brain cells live longer.

20. In his study of Cichlid fish, Russell Fernald found that there was growth in a specific area of the brain following
    a. improved diet.
    b. social success.
    c. gentle handling.
    d. loss of territory.

21. In Robert Sapolsky's study of stress physiology among baboons, what is the relationship between high status and "good" physiology?
    a. Animals attain high status because they have good physiology.
    b. Attaining high status leads to good physiology.
    c. Lowering one's status leads to improved physiology.
    d. Animals with high status produce high levels of stress hormone, which break down the immune system.

22. Which of the following is true about how neurons communicate with each other?
    a. All neuronal communication is excitatory.
    b. Neurons communicate with each other by sending electrical discharges across the connecting synapse.
    c. Neurons of any given type can communicate only with other neurons of the same type.
    d. The sum of excitatory and inhibitory signals to a neuron determines whether and how strongly it will respond.

23. Which part of the brain controls breathing?
    a. cerebellum
    b. brain stem
    c. hypothalamus
    d. limbic system

24. The cerebrum
    a. consists of two hemispheres connected by the corpus callosum.
    b. relays sensory impulses to the higher perceptual centers.
    c. releases seven different hormones to the pituitary gland.
    d. controls temperature and blood pressure.

25. With respect to the neurochemistry of the brain, all of these are true, *except* that
    a. scopolamine blocks the establishment of long-term memories.
    b. opioid peptides are naturally occurring chemicals in the brain.
    c. physostigmine is responsible for information transmission in the perceptual pathways.
    d. endorphins play a major role in pleasure and pain experiences.

26. What did Robert Sapolsky discover is the optimal style of behavior for dominant baboons?
    a. unpredictable aggression
    b. social style
    c. active curiosity
    d. frequent vocalizing

QUESTIONS TO CONSIDER

Program 3

1. What is the advantage of knowing that mental illness is caused by neurochemical problems if we don't know how to correct them?

2. There are millions of people who will try just about anything to control their weight. They buy diet pills and nutritional supplements that claim to alter the chemistry of their appetite. Some are so desperate that they have their mouths wired shut. Why don't doctors treat people with eating disorders by placing electrodes in their brains?

3. Different technologies for measuring brain activity help psychologists view structures and functioning of the brain. What advantages do these advanced techniques offer?

4. Imagine that you were a relative of Phineas Gage. How do you think you would have reacted to the changes in his behavior in the years following his accident at the railroad construction site? Would you have been willing to believe that the changes were permanent, or that they weren't under Gage's control?

Program 4

5. Many different factors influence your performance on a test: your study habits, recollection of the material, familiarity with the test format, and confidence. Given the choice, would you take a drug that might improve your performance? Would you take a beta-blocker that interferes with the effects of adrenaline (used by some actors and musicians to reduce stage fright) or a drug that enhances retention and recall of information? Would taking a drug give you an unfair advantage over other test takers? Is there any danger in taking drugs for this purpose?

6. Program 4 suggests that children raised with significantly different patterns of physical contact and touching will develop different behavioral, social, and personality characteristics. What do you imagine might happen as the Internet age progresses and people become used to spending less and less time around other people? Will this significantly affect our experience with physical contact?

7. Considering what is known about the damaging effects of poor nutrition, drugs, cigarettes, and alcohol on the fetus, what can be done to protect a baby from the effects of its mother's activities? Should any legal action be taken?

8. Given the advances being made in the imaging of brain activity, will it ever be possible for scientists to "read someone's mind" or to control someone's thoughts?

9. The socialization process in our culture relies heavily on both rewards (for example, praise in school or promotions at work) and punishments of various kinds. Given what we know about the influence of social standing on health, should we restructure our culture to rely more heavily on rewards and gains in status? Do Robert Sapolsky's findings from his work on baboons extend to human social status and health?

10. Speculate on why music, having no survival benefit or pharmacological properties, would have the strong effect on people's emotions and brains that it seems to have.

11. Imagine that you were designing an animal brain. Why would you want to design neurons to have an all-or-none response rather than a graded potential? Why would you want to create a brain that responded to several different neurotransmitters rather than creating one all-purpose neurotransmitter that affected all cells equally?

ACTIVITIES

Program 3

1. Can you feel the effects of your hormones? Try this: Imagine yourself falling down the stairs, stubbing your toe, or suddenly losing control of your car on a busy highway. Did your heart skip a beat? Did you catch your breath or feel a tingle up your back? Did the hair on your neck stiffen? Your imagination has caused a biochemical reaction in your brain, and you are feeling the effect of the hormones it produces. Can you name the hormones involved?

Program 4

2. Interview a few parents from different generations and from different cultures about the infancy of their children. Did they read books on child development or follow an expert's advice? Did they sleep with their babies? How did they comfort them? Which early experiences do they believe were most influential in their children's future development?

3. As science enters an era of being able to study the brain's activities, our imaginations about what is possible run much faster than the development of neuroimaging and simulation techniques. Watch films like *The Cell, The Matrix*, and *AI*, and identify several ways in which the "science" they portray is impossible given the current state of the field. Think about which aspects will likely remain impossible even hundreds of years from now.

Discovering Psychology Viewing Guide

Chapter 4: Sensation and Perception

Watch the following video by logging onto MyPsychLab (www.mypsychlab.com). After you have watched the video, complete the activities that follow.

PROGRAM 7: SENSATION AND PERCEPTION

Program 7 explores how we make contact with the world outside our brain and body. We'll see how biological, cognitive, social, and environmental influences shape our personal sense of reality, and we'll gain an understanding of how psychologists use our perceptual errors to study how the constructive process of perception works.

KEY TERMS AND PEOPLE

As you watch the program, pay particular attention to these terms and people in addition to those covered in this textbook.

receptor—a specialized nerve cell sensitive to particular kinds of stimulus energy.

Misha Pavel—studies the successive stages of information processing that take place as we continually perceive the world.

PROGRAM REVIEW

1. Imagine that a teaspoon of sugar is dissolved in two gallons of water. Rita can detect this level of sweetness at least half the time. This level is called the
   a. distal stimulus.
   b. perceptual constant.
   c. response bias.
   d. absolute threshold.

2. What is the job of a receptor?
   a. to transmit a neural impulse
   b. to connect new information with old information
   c. to detect a type of physical energy
   d. to receive an impulse from the brain

3. In what area of the brain is the visual cortex located?
   a. in the front
   b. in the middle
   c. in the back
   d. under the brain stem

4. What is the function of the thalamus in visual processing?
   a. It relays information to the cortex.
   b. It rotates the retinal image.
   c. It converts light energy to a neural impulse.
   d. It makes sense of the proximal stimulus.

5. David Hubel discusses the visual pathway and the response to a line. The program shows an experiment in which the response to a moving line changed dramatically with changes in the line's
   a. thickness.
   b. color.
   c. speed.
   d. orientation.

6. Misha Pavel used computer graphics to study how
   a. we process visual information.
   b. rods differ from cones in function.
   c. we combine information from different senses.
   d. physical energy is transduced in the visual system.

7. Imagine that a baseball player puts on special glasses that shift his visual field up ten degrees. When he wears these glasses, the player sees everything higher than it actually is. After some practice, the player can hit with the glasses on. What will happen when the player first tries to hit with the glasses off?
   a. He will think that the ball is lower than it is.
   b. He will think that the ball is higher than it is.
   c. He will accurately perceive the ball's position.
   d. It is impossible to predict an individual's reaction in this situation.

8. Imagine that a dog is walking toward you. As the dog gets closer, the image it casts on your retina
   a. gets larger.
   b. gets darker.
   c. gets smaller.
   d. stays exactly the same size.

9. You want to paint your room yellow, so you get some samples at the paint store. When you hold the sample against your white wall, it looks different from the way it looks against the green curtain. A psychologist would attribute this to
   a. perceptual constancy.
   b. visual paradoxes.
   c. contrast effects.
   d. threshold differences.

10. Which of the following phenomena best illustrates that perception is an active process?
   a. bottom-up processing
   b. motion parallax
   c. top-down processing
   d. parietal senses

11. The program shows a drawing that can be seen as a rat or as a man. People were more likely to identify the drawing as a man if they
   a. were men themselves.
   b. had just seen pictures of people.
   c. were afraid of rats.
   d. looked at the picture holistically rather than analytically.

12. Where is the proximal stimulus to be found?
   a. in the outside world
   b. on the retina
   c. in the occipital lobe
   d. in the thalamus

13. How is visual information processed by the brain?
   a. It's processed by the parietal lobe, which relays the information to the temporal lobe.
   b. It's processed entirely within the frontal lobe.
   c. It's processed by the occipital lobe, which projects to the thalamus, which projects to a succession of areas in the cortex.
   d. If the information is abstract, it's processed by the cortex; if it's concrete, it's processed by the thalamus.

14. Which of the following is true about the proximal stimulus in visual perception?
   a. It's identical to the distal stimulus because the retina produces a faithful reproduction of the perceptual world.
   b. It's upside-down, flat, distorted, and obscured by blood vessels.
   c. It's black-and-white and consists of very sparse information about horizontal and vertical edges.
   d. It contains information about the degree of convergence of the two eyes.

15. Which of the following is an example of pure top-down processing?
   a. hallucinating
   b. understanding someone else's speech when honking horns are obscuring individual sounds
   c. perceiving a circular color patch that has been painted onto a canvas
   d. enjoying a melody

16. Which sensory information is *not* paired with the cortical lobe that is primarily responsible for processing it?
   a. visual information, occipital lobe
   b. speech, frontal lobe
   c. body senses, parietal lobe
   d. hearing, central sulcus lobe

17. When your eyes are shut, you cannot
   a. hallucinate.
   b. use contextual information from other senses to make inferences about what's there.
   c. transform a distal visual stimulus into a proximal stimulus.
   d. experience perceptual constancy.

18. The researcher David Hubel is best known for
   a. mapping visual receptor cells.
   b. discovering subjective contours.
   c. identifying the neural pathways by which body sensations occur.
   d. realizing that hearing and smell originate from the same brain area.

19. The primary reason why psychologists study illusions is because
    a. they help to identify areas of the cortex that have been damaged.
    b. they serve as good "public relations" material for curious novices.
    c. they help us to categorize people into good and bad perceivers.
    d. they help us to understand how perception normally works.

20. The shrinking-square illusion demonstrated by Misha Pavel relies on processing of which kinds of feature?
    a. edges and corners
    b. color and texture
    c. torque and angular momentum
    d. density gradients and motion

QUESTIONS TO CONSIDER

1. Why do psychologists identify sensation and perception as two different fields of study? Does this reflect the relative youth of psychology as a science, or does it represent a scientific distinction that will still be favored in fifty years?

2. As the population ages, adapting the environment for people with a range of sensory abilities and deficits will become increasingly important. Architects will need to improve access to and safety of buildings, taking into account that older people need about three times as much light as young people in order to distinguish objects. They also need higher visual contrasts to detect potential hazards, such as curbs or steps. How might you identify some changes you could make in and around your home to create a safer, more comfortable environment for a disabled or visually- or hearing-impaired person?

3. Investigations of people who claim to have extrasensory perception reveal that the better controlled the study, the less likely it is to support claims of ESP. Does it do any harm to believe in ESP? Why do most psychologists suggest that we should be skeptical of people who claim to have extrasensory perception?

4. Choose a familiar context, like a grocery store, and describe how the Gestalt principles of perceptual organization are used to help people perceive objects and group them.

5. Describe how film and television directors use sight and sound techniques to create meaning and feeling. As you watch a television commercial, program, or film, notice the way the camera frames the image and how angle and motion create a mood or point of view. Notice the use of sound. Consider how these elements shape viewers' desires, expectations, and feelings.

6. Although the neural pathways serving perception are similar in all of us, our internal perceptual experience could theoretically differ. What sorts of differences in our experiences can you imagine as being possible? What sorts of differences would you think would be unlikely?

7. Absolute thresholds seem to differ across species. For example, you are much better at detecting degraded visual stimuli than animals of some other species would be, but at the same time you may be much worse than them at smelling faint odors. Why do you think that humans evolved to favor the visual sense?

ACTIVITIES

1. Closure and continuity of line are organizing principles that we use to make sense out of stimuli. Make line drawings of familiar objects by tracing pictures from comics, children's coloring books, or magazines. Leave out sections of the drawing, and ask family members or friends to identify the objects. See how incomplete the line drawing can be and still be identified.

2. Blindfold yourself. (Have someone standing by to prevent injury or damage.) Contrast the experience of moving about in a familiar room, such as your bedroom or kitchen, with the experience of moving about a room in which you spend little time. Note the expectations and significant sensory cues you depend on to avoid tripping and bumping into things. How relaxed or tense were you in each room?

3. Listen to a conversation, trying hard to (a) notice all of the other noise going on around you and (b) notice all the instances of imperfect transmission of speech sounds. For example, the speaker might mispronounce something or say it with his or her mouth full, or an outside noise may obscure the sound coming from the speaker. Is it hard for you to snap out of top-down mode to do this exercise?

4. If you have access to a virtual reality game, try playing it while also monitoring what is going on in the room around you. While interacting with the virtual objects in the game, think about how you must look to passersby, and think about the layout of the objects in the space that physically surrounds you. How good are you at immersing yourself in two worlds at once? Do you find that you have to switch back and forth, or are you able to consider yourself as being in two very different realities simultaneously?

DISCOVERING PSYCHOLOGY VIEWING GUIDE

Chapter 5: States of Consciousness

Watch the following videos by logging onto MyPsychLab (www.mypsychlab.com). After you have watched the videos, complete the activities that follow.

PROGRAM 13: THE MIND AWAKE AND ASLEEP

Program 13 describes how psychologists investigate the nature of sleeping, dreaming, and altered states of conscious awareness. It also explores the ways we use consciousness to interpret, analyze, and even change our behavior.

PROGRAM 14: THE MIND HIDDEN AND DIVIDED

Program 14 considers the evidence that our moods, behavior, and even our health are largely the result of multiple mental processes, many of which are out of conscious awareness. It also looks at some of the most dramatic phenomena in psychology, such as hypnosis and the division of human consciousness into "two minds" when the brain is split in half by surgical intervention.

KEY TERMS AND PEOPLE

As you watch the programs, pay particular attention to these terms and people in addition to those covered in this textbook.

Program 13

hypnagogic state—a period of reverie at the onset of the sleeping state.

Ernest Hartmann—an expert on sleep who believes that it serves a restorative function.

Program 14

posthypnotic amnesia—forgetting selected events by suggestion.

Michael Gazzaniga—conducts research on the psychological study of split brain phenomena.

Jonathan Schooler—studies discovered memories in people who had previously had no memory of major, traumatic events in their lives.

PROGRAM REVIEW

Programs 13 and 14

1. Which of the following is an example of a circadian rhythm?
   a. eating three meals a day at approximately the same time
   b. experiencing alternate periods of REM and non-REM sleep
   c. having systematic changes in hormone levels during twenty-four hours
   d. having changes in fertility levels during a month

2. How normal is it to experience alternate states of consciousness?
   a. It happens to most people, mainly in times of stress.
   b. It is something we all experience every day.
   c. It is rare and generally indicates a mental disorder.
   d. It is common in childhood and becomes rarer with age.

3. In the program, the part of the brain that is identified as the "interior decorator" imposing order on experience is the
   a. pons.
   b. hippocampus.
   c. limbic system.
   d. cerebral cortex.

4. Which of the following is an example of the lower-level processing of sensory input that is nonconscious?
   a. recognizing a friend's face
   b. detecting edges
   c. working on an assembly line
   d. noticing something tastes good

5. Edward Titchener was the leader of structuralism in the United States. What aspect of the concept of consciousness interested him?
   a. the contents of consciousness
   b. the material repressed from conscious awareness
   c. the uniqueness of consciousness
   d. He viewed consciousness as a scientifically worthless concept.

6. In Donald Broadbent's research, what happened when people heard two stories but were asked to attend to only one?
   a. They comprehended both stories.
   b. They comprehended only the attended story.
   c. They wove bits of the unattended story into the attended story.
   d. They were not able to follow either story.

7. What is a positive function of daydreaming?
   a. It focuses attention on a task.
   b. It reduces demands made on the brain.
   c. It enables us to be mentally active when we are bored.
   d. It provides delta wave activity normally received only in sleep.

8. Ernest Hartmann points out the logic behind Shakespeare's description of sleep. According to Hartmann, a major function of sleep is that it allows the brain to
   a. process material too threatening to be dealt with consciously.
   b. integrate the day's events with previously learned material.
   c. make plans for the day ahead.
   d. discharge a buildup of electrical activity.

9. According to Freud, dreams are significant because they
   a. permit neurotransmitters to be regenerated.
   b. reveal unconscious fears and desires.
   c. forecast the future.
   d. supply a story line to patterns of electrical charges.

10. According to McCarley and Hobson's activation synthesis theory of dreams, what activates dreams?
    a. the needs of the dreamer's unconscious
    b. the sending of electrical charges to the forebrain
    c. the memories contained in the cerebral cortex
    d. the synthesis of chemicals needed for brain function

11. According to McCarley and Hobson, what is true about REM sleep?
    a. Adults spend more time in REM sleep than infants.
    b. REM sleep is an unnecessary physiological function.
    c. The random burst of brain activity occurs first, followed by the dreamer's attempt to make sense of it.
    d. The subconscious expresses its deepest desires during REM sleep.

12. In his work on lucid dreaming, why does LaBerge use a flashing light?
    a. so participants are consciously aware of their dream and can control it
    b. so participants can incorporate the light itself into their dream narrative
    c. so participants get feedback about where they are in the REM sleep cycle
    d. so measurements can be made of physiological response

13. In the experiment described in the program, patients under anesthesia were exposed to a positive or negative message. What effect did getting a positive message have?
    a. It meant less anesthesia was needed.
    b. It shortened patients' hospital stays.
    c. It created more positive attitudes toward surgery.
    d. Positive messages had no effect because patients were unaware of them.

14. Which part of the brain is responsible for conscious awareness?
    a. cerebral cortex
    b. brain stem
    c. limbic system
    d. hypothalamus

15. When societies around the world were studied, what proportion of them practiced some culturally patterned form of altering consciousness?
    a. practically none
    b. about a third
    c. about half
    d. the vast majority

16. Edward Tichener is to structuralism as William James is to
   a. introspection.
   b. functionalism.
   c. lucid dreaming.
   d. discovered memories.

17. According to Freud, how do we feel when painful memories or unacceptable urges threaten to break into consciousness?
   a. relieved
   b. guilty
   c. sad
   d. anxious

18. What are Freudian slips thought to reveal?
   a. what we have dreamed about
   b. how we really feel
   c. who we would like to be transformed into
   d. why we make certain choices

19. What happens if a hypnotized person who expects to smell cologne actually smells ammonia?
   a. The ammonia smell wakes him from the trance.
   b. He recognizes the ammonia smell, but he remains hypnotized.
   c. He interprets the ammonia smell as a musky cologne.
   d. He overgeneralizes and finds the cologne smells like ammonia.

20. All of the following appear to fluctuate based on circadian rhythm, *except*
   a. intelligence.
   b. hormone levels.
   c. blood pressure.
   d. body temperature.

21. Michael Gazzaniga has worked with split-brain, or "broken-brain," patients. What has this led him to believe about our individuality?
   a. It comes from an interpreter in the left hemisphere.
   b. It is an illusion based on our emotional needs.
   c. It derives from our unique set of independent mind-modules.
   d. It is located in the corpus callosum.

22. Consciousness performs all of the following functions, *except*
   a. filtering sensory data.
   b. enabling us to respond flexibly.
   c. allowing us to have a sense of our own mortality.
   d. guiding performance of highly routinized actions.

23. Which of the following people would have the strongest objection to the concept of consciousness?
   a. William James
   b. John Watson
   c. Edward Titchener
   d. Wilhelm Wundt

24. Instances in which people believe they have remembered long-forgotten traumatic events are known as
   a. repression.
   b. suppression.
   c. recovered memories.
   d. fugue states.

25. One of the most important techniques that psychologists commonly use to confirm the validity of a recovered memory is to
   a. have the subject recount the memory under hypnosis.
   b. subject the rememberer to a lie-detector test.
   c. count the number of details in the rememberer's story.
   d. collect confirming evidence from other people who knew about the event.

26. Sigmund Freud is to the unconscious as ________ is to discovered memories.
   a. B. F. Skinner
   b. Jonathan Schooler
   c. Michael Gazzaniga
   d. Stephen LaBerge

27. According to Freud, normal people banish undesirable memories from their conscious minds through
   a. repression.
   b. projection.
   c. anterograde amnesia.
   d. hysteria.

28. According to Freud, the "alarm" that signals that unconscious thoughts or memories are about to break loose to consciousness is
   a. sexual desire.
   b. lethargy.
   c. confusion.
   d. anxiety.

29. Which topic related to human consciousness is conveyed by the story of Dr. Jekyll and Mr. Hyde?
   a. witchcraft
   b. hypnosis
   c. identity transformation
   d. sleep disorders

30. Communication between the two hemispheres of the brain is disrupted when
    a. a person is in deep meditation.
    b. a person is in deep Freudian denial.
    c. a person has just recovered an early memory.
    d. the corpus callosum is severed.

31. What occurs about every ninety minutes throughout sleep?
    a. rapid eye movement
    b. rapid irregular changes in brain activity
    c. dreaming
    d. more than one of the above

QUESTIONS TO CONSIDER

Program 13

1. Donald Broadbent conceived of attention as a selective filter that acts like a tuner on a radio, selecting one message from all the others. According to Broadbent, the unattended sensory information is sent to a buffer, where it either receives attention and gets processed or is ignored and lost. How is this buffer similar to the concept of the sensory memory? What role might it play in subliminal perception?

2. What are the benefits and drawbacks of mindlessness?

3. Consider the role of culture and language in structuring consciousness or focused perception. In what ways is awareness culturally determined?

4. How do you experience REM rebound effects when you have been deprived of sleep? Do you begin dreaming soon after falling asleep? Do you experience vivid visual imagery when you are awake?

Program 14

5. Changes in perceptions, time sense, memory, feelings of self-control, and suggestibility are aspects of an altered state of consciousness. Would you consider illness, love, or grief to be altered states of consciousness?

6. Psychoactive drugs are only partially responsible for the changes in the drug taker's consciousness. Mental sets, expectations, and the context in which the drugs are taken can also have significant influences. What are the implications for alcohol and drug education and treatment?

7. Do you consider television or other electronic media to have mind-altering influence? What do they have in common with other mind-altering substances or experiences? Are children more susceptible to these effects than adults?

8. Do you think you could benefit from hypnosis or meditation? Do you believe you could easily enter these states? If someone finds it difficult to become hypnotized or to meditate, would you advise him or her that it is worth the effort of learning? And how would you suggest he or she learns?

ACTIVITIES

Program 13

1. Keep a pad and pencil by your bed and start a dream journal. Just before you fall asleep, remind yourself to remember your dreams. Immediately upon awakening, record what you remember: images, actions, characters, emotions, events, and settings. Does your ability to recall your dreams improve over time? Does this change if you set your alarm for different times during the sleep cycle? Does your recall become more vivid or more organized? Can you shape your dreams by telling yourself at bedtime what you want to dream about?

2. Make a list of common examples of dissociation and divided consciousness. Do these examples support the concept of mini-minds or different areas of the brain operating independently? What other explanations might account for your ability to divide your consciousness?

Program 14

3. Use this visualization technique to achieve a state of relaxation and, perhaps, alter your consciousness. Select a quiet place where you won't be interrupted. Choose a scene in which you have been very relaxed. To help you create a good mental picture, recall all the sensations that enhance in you a feeling of deep calm. Focus on the scene for fifteen to thirty minutes. Practice this visualization exercise several times over a period of a few weeks. With practice, calling up the visual image may trigger a sensation of calm whenever you want it to.

4. Try to think of a time when you surprised yourself by having a very strong feeling in response to an incident that didn't seem to warrant such a strong response. Could nonconscious factors have played a role in your response? What did you think about your response at the time? What did you think about it later?

5. Go on the Internet and look up various cultures, religions, and communities that practice altered states of consciousness. See if you can develop any insights into what aspects of their art, social interaction, and values appear to be influenced by such practices.

Discovering Psychology Viewing Guide

Chapter 6: Learning

Watch the following video by logging onto MyPsychLab (www.mypsychlab.com). After you have watched the video, complete the activities that follow.

PROGRAM 8: LEARNING

Learning is the process that enables humans and other animals to profit from experience, anticipate events, and adapt to changing conditions. Program 8 explains the basic learning principles and the methods psychologists use to study and modify behavior. It also demonstrates how cognitive processes, such as insight and observation, influence learning.

KEY TERMS AND PEOPLE

As you watch the program, pay particular attention to these terms and people in addition to those covered in this textbook.

Howard Rachlin—studies how operant principles can be used to train self-control.

PROGRAM REVIEW

1. Which of the following is an example of a fixed-action pattern?
   a. a fish leaping at bait that looks like a fly
   b. a flock of birds migrating in winter
   c. a person blinking when something gets in her eye
   d. a chimpanzee solving a problem using insight

2. What is the basic purpose of learning?
   a. to improve one's genes
   b. to understand the world one lives in
   c. to find food more successfully
   d. to adapt to changing circumstances

3. How have psychologists traditionally studied learning?
   a. in classrooms with children as participants
   b. in classrooms with college students as participants
   c. in laboratories with humans as participants
   d. in laboratories with nonhuman animals as participants

4. In his work, Pavlov found that a metronome could produce salivation in dogs because
   a. it signaled that food would arrive.
   b. it was the dogs' normal reaction to a metronome.
   c. it was on while the dogs ate.
   d. it extinguished the dogs' original response.

5. What is learned in classical conditioning?
   a. a relationship between an action and its consequence
   b. a relationship between two stimulus events
   c. a relationship between two response events
   d. classical conditioning does not involve learning

6. What point is Professor Zimbardo making when he says, "Relax," while firing a pistol?
   a. There are fixed reactions to verbal stimuli.
   b. The acquisition process is reversed during extinction.
   c. Any stimulus can come to elicit any reaction.
   d. Unconditioned stimuli are frequently negative.

7. What point does Ader and Cohen's research on taste aversion in rats make about classical conditioning?
   a. It can be extinguished easily.
   b. It takes many conditioning trials to be effective.
   c. It is powerful enough to suppress the immune system.
   d. It tends to be more effective than instrumental conditioning.

8. What is Thorndike's law of effect?
   a. Learning is controlled by its consequences.
   b. Every action has an equal and opposite reaction.
   c. Effects are more easily changed than causes.
   d. A conditioned stimulus comes to have the same effect as an unconditioned stimulus.

9. According to John B. Watson, any behavior, even strong emotion, could be explained by the power of
   a. instinct.
   b. inherited traits.
   c. innate ideas.
   d. conditioning.

10. In Watson's work with Little Albert, why was Albert afraid of the Santa Claus mask?
    a. He had been classically conditioned with the mask.
    b. The mask was an unconditioned stimulus creating fear.
    c. He generalized his learned fear of the rat.
    d. Instrumental conditioning created a fear of strangers.

11. What was the point of the Skinner box?
    a. It kept animals safe.
    b. It provided a simple, highly controlled environment.
    c. It set up a classical conditioning situation.
    d. It allowed psychologists to use computers for research.

12. Skinner found that the rate at which a pigeon pecked at a target varied directly with
    a. the conditioned stimulus.
    b. the conditioned response.
    c. the operant antecedents.
    d. the reinforcing consequences.

13. Imagine a behavior therapist is treating a person who fears going out into public places. What would the therapist be likely to focus on?
    a. the conditioning experience that created the fear
    b. the deeper problems that the fear is a symptom of
    c. providing positive consequences for going out
    d. reinforcing the patient's desire to overcome the fear

14. When should the conditioned stimulus be presented in order to optimally produce classical conditioning?
    a. just before the unconditioned stimulus
    b. simultaneously with the unconditioned response
    c. just after the unconditioned stimulus
    d. just after the conditioned response

15. Operant conditioning can be used to achieve all of the following, *except*
    a. teaching dogs to assist the handicapped.
    b. teaching infants English grammar.
    c. teaching self-control to someone who is trying to quit smoking.
    d. increasing productivity among factory workers.

16. Which psychologist has argued that in order to understand and control behavior, one has to consider both the reinforcements acting on the selected behavior and the reinforcements on the reinforcements acting an the alternatives?
    a. E. Thorndike
    b. J. Watson
    c. B. F. Skinner
    d. H. Rachlin

17. If given a choice between an immediate small reinforcer and a delayed larger reinforcer, an untrained pigeon will
    a. select the immediate small one.
    b. select the delayed larger one.
    c. experiment and alternate across trials.
    d. not show any signs of perceiving the difference.

18. In order to produce extinction of a classically conditioned behavior, an experimenter would
    a. reward the behavior.
    b. pair the behavior with negative reinforcement.
    c. present the conditioned stimulus in the absence of the unconditioned stimulus.
    d. model the behavior for the organism.

19. In Pavlov's early work, bell is to food as
    a. unconditioned response is to conditioned response.
    b. conditioned stimulus is to unconditioned stimulus.
    c. unconditioned is to conditioned stimulus.
    d. conditioned stimulus is to conditioned response.

20. Howard Rachlin has discovered that animals can be taught self-control through
    a. reinforcement.
    b. operant conditioning.
    c. instrumental conditioning.
    d. all of the above.

QUESTIONS TO CONSIDER

1. Approximately 2 percent of Americans are hooked on gambling, which experts claim can be just as addictive as drugs. Is compulsive gambling a disease or a learned behavior? Consider the kind of reinforcement gamblers get. Using the terms you learned in this program, how would you characterize the nature of the reinforcement and the reinforcement schedule? What techniques do you predict would work best to help compulsive gamblers change their behavior?

2. You are a school principal, and you are trying to get your students to help clean up the school. Given what you now know about the control of behavior, what sorts of techniques would you use in order to get students to comply?

3. What role does intention to learn play in classical and operant conditioning? Would these techniques work on people who do not know they are being used? Would they work on people who oppose their use?

4. Is it possible that children learn their native language through operant conditioning? When parents and young children interact, do the parents reinforce the use of some grammar and punish others? Are some aspects of language, such as the rules of politeness, more likely to be taught through conditioning than other aspects?

ACTIVITIES

1. Design your own behavior change program based on the learning principles described in Program 8. First, identify a specific behavior. Instead of setting a broad goal, such as becoming more fit, design a strategy to reinforce a desired behavior—going for jogs, cutting out midnight snacks, or taking the stairs rather than the elevator. Analyze the specific behavior you would like to change in terms of antecedents-behavior-consequences. Then get a baseline measurement of the target behavior, try out your plan for a predetermined amount of time, and evaluate the results.

2. Have someone teach you something new, such as how to juggle, play basic guitar chords, or serve a tennis ball. Analyze the teacher's method. How does it apply principles of theories of learning? How would you change the teacher's method to be more effective?

3. Choose a member of your family and some trivial behavioral detail, such as standing still. See if you can train the person to reliably perform the behavior without having them catch on to what you're doing.

Discovering Psychology Viewing Guide

Chapter 7: Cognition

Watch the following videos by logging onto MyPsychLab (www.mypsychlab.com). After you have watched the videos, complete the activities that follow.

PROGRAM 9: REMEMBERING AND FORGETTING

Program 9 explores memory, the complex mental process that allows us to store and recall our previous experiences. It looks at the ways cognitive psychologists investigate memory as an information-processing task and at the ways neuroscientists study how the structure and functioning of the brain affect how we remember and why we forget.

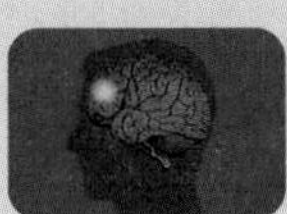

PROGRAM 10: COGNITIVE PROCESSES

The study of mental processes and structures—perceiving, reasoning, imagining, anticipating, and problem solving—is known as cognition. Program 10 explores these higher mental processes, offering insight into how the field has evolved and why more psychologists than ever are investigating the way we absorb, transform, and manipulate knowledge.

PROGRAM 11: JUDGMENT AND DECISION MAKING

Program 11 explores the decision-making process and the psychology of risk taking, revealing how people arrive at good and bad decisions. It also looks at the reasons people lapse into irrationality and how personal biases can affect judgment.

KEY TERMS AND PEOPLE

As you watch the program, pay particular attention to these terms and people in addition to those covered in this textbook.

Program 9

Gordon Bower—studies how mnemonic techniques can enhance learning and retrieval.

Richard Thompson—studies the brain mechanisms underlying classical conditioning.

Diana Woodruff-Pak—uses eyeblink classical conditioning to detect early-onset dementia.

Program 10

Robert Glaser—studies learning.

Michael Posner—uses brain imaging techniques to explore what parts of the brain are used in accomplishing specific cognitive tasks.

Program 11

dread factor—the fear of unfamiliar or potentially catastrophic events that make us judge these to be riskier than familiar events.

framing—the way information is presented, which tends to bias how it is interpreted.

invariance—the principle stating that preferences between options should be independent of different representations.

similarity heuristic—an error based on the tendency to see a connection between belonging to a certain category and having the characteristics considered typical of members of that category.

Max Bazerman—discusses the five most common cognitive mistakes that negotiators make.

Leon Festinger—developed cognitive dissonance theory.

Irving Janis—studied the Cuban Missile Crisis and looked at distorted "groupthink" reasoning.

PROGRAM REVIEW

Program 9

1. What pattern of remembering emerged in Hermann Ebbinghaus's research?
   a. Loss occurred at a steady rate.
   b. A small initial loss was followed by no further loss.
   c. There was no initial loss, but then there was a gradual decline.
   d. A sharp initial loss was followed by a gradual decline.

2. The way psychologists thought about and studied memory was changed by the invention of
   a. television.
   b. electroconvulsive shock therapy.
   c. the computer.
   d. the electron microscope.

3. What do we mean when we say that memories must be encoded?
   a. They must be taken from storage to be used.
   b. They must be put in a form the brain can register.
   c. They must be transferred from one network to another.
   d. They must be put in a passive storehouse.

4. About how many items can be held in short-term memory?
   a. three
   b. seven
   c. eleven
   d. an unlimited number

5. Imagine you had a string of twenty one-digit numbers to remember. The best way to accomplish the task, which requires increasing the capacity of short-term memory, is through the technique of
   a. selective attention.
   b. peg words.
   c. rehearsing.
   d. chunking.

6. According to Gordon Bower, what is an important feature of good mnemonic systems?
   a. There is a dovetailing between storage and retrieval.
   b. The acoustic element is more important than the visual.
   c. The learner is strongly motivated to remember.
   d. Short-term memory is bypassed in favor of long-term memory.

7. According to Freud, what is the purpose of repression?
   a. to protect the memory from encoding too much material
   b. to preserve the individual's self-esteem
   c. to activate networks of associations
   d. to fit new information into existing schemas

8. In an experiment, people spent a few minutes in an office. They were then asked to recall what they had seen. They were most likely to recall objects that
   a. fit into their existing schema of an office.
   b. carried little emotional content.
   c. were unusual within that particular context.
   d. related to objects they owned themselves.

9. The paintings Franco Magnani made of an Italian town were distorted mainly by
   a. repression, causing some features to be left out.
   b. a child's perspective.
   c. sensory gating, changing colors.
   d. false memories of items that were not really there.

10. What was Karl Lashley's goal in teaching rats mazes and then removing part of their cortexes?
    a. finding out how much tissue was necessary for learning to occur
    b. determining whether memory was localized in one area of the brain
    c. discovering how much tissue loss led to memory loss
    d. finding out whether conditioned responses could be eradicated

11. What has Richard Thompson found in his work with rabbits conditioned to a tone before an air puff?
    a. Rabbits learn the response more slowly after lesioning.
    b. Eyelid conditioning involves several brain areas.
    c. The memory of the response can be removed by lesioning.
    d. Once the response is learned, the memory is permanent, despite lesioning.

12. What is the chief cause of functional amnesia?
    a. Alzheimer's disease
    b. substance abuse
    c. traumatic injury to the brain
    d. severe anxiety

13. The best way to keep items in short-term memory for an indefinite length of time is to
    a. chunk.
    b. create context dependence.
    c. use the peg-word system.
    d. rehearse.

14. Long-term memory is organized as
    a. a complex network of associations.
    b. a serial list.
    c. a set of visual images.
    d. a jumble of individual memories with no clear organizational scheme.

15. You remember a list of unrelated words by associating them, one at a time, with images of a bun, a shoe, a tree, a door, a hive, sticks, Heaven, a gate, a line, and a hen. What mnemonic technique are you using?
    a. method of loci
    b. peg-word
    c. link
    d. digit conversion

16. What did Karl Lashley conclude about the engram?
    a. It is localized in the brain stem.
    b. It is localized in the right hemisphere only.
    c. It is localized in the left hemisphere only.
    d. Complex memories cannot be pinpointed within the brain.

17. Long-term memories appear to be stored in the
    a. cortex.
    b. occipital lobe.
    c. hippocampus.
    d. parietal lobe.

18. How has Diana Woodruff-Pak utilized Richard Thompson's work on eye blink conditioning?
    a. as a precursor to early-onset dementia
    b. as a predictor of musical genius
    c. as a mechanism for growing brain cells in intact animals
    d. as a tool for training long-term visual memories

19. Which neurotransmitter(s) is/are disrupted in Alzheimer's patients?
    a. scopolamine
    b. acetylcholine
    c. both of the above
    d. none of the above

20. Alzheimer's disease is associated with the loss of
    a. memory.
    b. personality.
    c. life itself.
    d. all of the above.

Programs 10 and 11

21. Michael Posner's work on brain imaging showed
    a. major differences between the brains of young and old adults, with cognitive processes more localized in brains of the elderly.
    b. that blood flow decreases in the brain as thinking becomes more efficient.
    c. that electrical stimulation of the brain can enhance performance on logic puzzles reliably.
    d. that patterns of brain activity differ in predictable ways when people see words, vs. read them aloud, vs. name the function of the objects to which they refer.

22. The movement in psychology known as cognitive psychology developed primarily
    a. at the turn of the nineteenth to twentieth century.
    b. in the 1920s.
    c. after World War II.
    d. during the last five years.

23. What analytic tool did Donald Broadbent use to model the process by which information is perceived and stored in memory?
    a. statistical analysis on a computer
    b. a flow chart
    c. a set of categories
    d. an analogy to a steam engine

24. A cognitive psychologist would be most interested in which one of the following issues?
    a. how you decide which answer is correct for this question
    b. how pain stimuli are processed
    c. maturation of the efferent system
    d. how to distinguish mania from schizophrenia

25. When we distinguish between groups of letters on the basis of the kinds of lines that form them, we are performing the mental process of
    a. relating.
    b. categorizing.
    c. creating prototypes.
    d. activating schema.

26. Concepts are mental representations. Which is a concept of an attribute?
    a. bed
    b. jumping
    c. slow
    d. courage

27. What is our prototype of a tree most likely to be similar to?
   a. a maple tree
   b. a palm tree
   c. a Christmas tree
   d. a dead tree

28. According to the program, why do we assume that Montreal is farther north than Seattle?
   a. because we have learned it
   b. because we are less familiar with Montreal than with Seattle
   c. because Canada is north of the United States in our mental maps
   d. because we are not good at making such judgments

29. When Steve Kosslyn asked people about the picture of a motorboat, he was primarily interested in
   a. how they scanned a mental image.
   b. how much detail they noted.
   c. how they compared a new picture with a prototype.
   d. how sure they felt about what they had seen.

30. What is one way in which human problem solving appears to be quite different from the way computers solve problems?
   a. Humans can solve problems that don't involve numbers.
   b. Humans are more logical in their approach to problems.
   c. Humans have trouble when content is unfamiliar.
   d. Humans are less likely to be misled by bias.

31. What did Michael Posner find when he conducted PET scans of people reading a word and associating it with a function?
   a. Localized activity occurred, but the location varied widely.
   b. Similar localized activity was seen in all the participants.
   c. Brain activity was general, rather than localized.
   d. No general pattern of activity was observed.

32. According to Robert Glaser, what is the general purpose of the research at the University of Pittsburgh's Learning and Research Development Center?
   a. to create new types of computers
   b. to model the organic functions of the brain
   c. to classify errors and mistakes
   d. to improve the way people use their intelligence

33. What is a cognitive illusion?
   a. a mental map that we can scan for information
   b. a biased mental strategy
   c. a concept formed on the basis of a perceptual illusion
   d. a decision motivated by emotion

34. How did Freud explain the fact that human beings sometimes make irrational decisions?
   a. They are driven by primitive needs.
   b. They are influenced by the emotions of the crowd.
   c. They are basing their decisions on availability.
   d. They are using standard human mental processes.

35. Why did the people questioned assume that there were more words beginning with "k" than with "k" as the third letter?
   a. There is a general tendency to favor the initial position.
   b. The anchoring effect biased their answers.
   c. It's easier to find examples of words beginning with "k."
   d. It seems less risky as an answer.

36. A heuristic is a kind of
   a. mistake.
   b. meaning.
   c. mathematical model.
   d. shortcut.

37. A researcher asks two groups of students to estimate the average price of a new car. One group is asked if the price is more or less than $9,000. The other group is asked if the price is more or less than $18,000. Each group is asked to estimate the actual average price. How will the two averages compare?
   a. The first group will take longer to answer.
   b. The second group will take longer to answer.
   c. The first group will have a higher average.
   d. The second group will have a higher average.

38. When people were confronted with a choice of a sure loss of $85 or an eighty-five percent chance of losing $100, how did most people react?
   a. They chose the loss.
   b. They chose the chance.
   c. They pointed out the statistical equivalence of the alternatives.
   d. They revised to make the choice.

39. Why would smokers be likely to underestimate the chance of developing lung cancer?
   a. They do not dread the disease.
   b. It is an unfamiliar risk.
   c. It is not representative.
   d. It represents a delayed consequence.

40. Irving Janis studied how the decision to invade Cuba was made during the Kennedy administration. What advice does Janis offer to promote better decision making?
    a. Encourage groupthink by team-building exercises.
    b. Appoint one group member to play devil's advocate.
    c. Restrict the size of the group.
    d. Assume that silence means consent on the part of all group members.

41. Imagine that you are a business leader who has been to a negotiating workshop led by Max Bazerman and Lawrence Susskind. Which statement shows something you should have learned from the experience?
    a. "I will escalate conflict."
    b. "I know this is a zero-sum game."
    c. "I will enlarge my frame of reference."
    d. "I am confident that I am right and will prevail."

42. How does cognitive dissonance make us feel?
    a. We are so uncomfortable that we try to reduce the dissonance.
    b. We enjoy it so much that we actively seek dissonance.
    c. Our reaction to dissonance depends largely on personality.
    d. It creates boredom, which we try to overcome.

43. In Festinger's experiment, which students felt dissonance?
    a. both the students who got $20 and those who got $1
    b. the students who got $20 but not those who got $1
    c. the students who got $1 but not those who got $20
    d. neither the students who got $1 nor those who got $20

44. You read the following sentences: "Mary heard the ice cream truck. She remembered her birthday money and ran into the house." What allowed you to understand how these sentences are related?
    a. a cognitive illusion
    b. reasoning by analogy
    c. a schema
    d. the anchoring heuristic

45. When people believe that Linda is more likely to be a bank teller and active in the feminist movement than she is likely to be a bank teller, their error is due to
    a. the availability heuristic.
    b. the representativeness heuristic.
    c. the anchoring heuristic.
    d. groupthink.

46. Which of the following is true of groupthink?
    a. Groupthink is characterized by people's strong motivation to provide their colleagues with information that will change their minds.
    b. To avoid groupthink, a company should hire people who were all trained in the same business philosophy.
    c. Groupthink occurs only in the political world, but not in other domains.
    d. Groupthink is characterized by a self-censorship of one's doubts.

47. According to Howard Gardner, which popular approach to psychology did the field of cognitive science overthrow?
    a. functionalism
    b. structuralism
    c. behaviorism
    d. evolutionism

48. All of the following are true about our representation of schema, *except* that
    a. memory errors can stem from activating inappropriate schema.
    b. schema are complex concepts.
    c. they can be used to understand language.
    d. their use is limited to decision making.

49. According to Robert Glaser, intelligence
    a. is a skill and can be developed.
    b. is genetically determined.
    c. is a myth.
    d. is no higher in humans than it is in chimpanzees and bonobos.

50. Greg is visiting a foreign country that is known for its current political unrest, and he has seen news reports over the past week about tourists being kidnapped. Although his chances of being killed in a car accident during his vacation are higher than his chances of being killed by terrorists, he believes the opposite. What cognitive process is behind his error?
    a. representativeness heuristic
    b. availability heuristic
    c. anchoring and adjustment heuristic
    d. framing heuristic

51. Jim has greater dread of the possible consequences for him of a small meteorite impact on the earth than of the consequences of jaywalking across a busy street. According to the program, this difference is likely because
    a. the consequences of the meteorite impact are less familiar.
    b. the consequences of the meteorite impact are less immediate.
    c. the consequences of jaywalking are smaller for him than of a meteorite impact somewhere on Earth.
    d. the anchoring heuristic leads to greater attention for perceptual events.

52. According to Max Bazerman, all of the following are mistakes commonly made during negotiation, *except*
  a. being willing to compromise on points of lesser importance.
  b. failure to consider the judgments made by one's counterpart.
  c. limiting one's thinking to the specific points of conflict.
  d. assuming that whenever one side wins, the other must lose.

53. Which of these is a likely consequence of cognitive dissonance?
  a. becoming more entrenched in one's beliefs
  b. increasing the behavior that is causing dissonance
  c. becoming more sociable
  d. changing an attitude

54. Al's parents are paying for his college tuition. Joe is working two jobs to put himself through college. Both are taking a fairly dry chemistry course together. Who is more likely to say he likes the course, and why?
  a. Al, because of cognitive dissonance
  b. Joe, because of cognitive dissonance
  c. Al, because of the availability heuristic
  d. Joe, because of the availability heuristic

55. Why is the normative approach to decision making different from the descriptive approach?
  a. because people are not rational
  b. because the normative approach is interested in cross-cultural effects, while the descriptive approach is not
  c. because the normative approach studies framing effects, while the descriptive approach does not
  d. because the descriptive approach is a less scientifically rigorous study of human cognition than the normative approach

QUESTIONS TO CONSIDER

Program 9

1. What memory strategies can you apply to help you better retain the information in this course? Why is rote rehearsal not the optimal strategy?

2. What is your earliest memory? How accurate do you think it is? Can you recall an experience that happened before you could talk? If not, why not? How does language influence what we remember? How do photographs and other mementos aid memory?

3. Most American kids learn their ABCs by singing them. Why does singing the ABCs make it easier to remember them?

4. Many quiz shows and board games, like Trivial Pursuit, are based on recalling items of general knowledge that we do not use every day. Why is it so much fun to recall such trivia?

5. As a member of a jury, you are aware of the tendency to reconstruct memories. How much weight do you give to eyewitness testimony? Is it possible ever to get "the whole truth and nothing but the truth" from an eyewitness? Do you think memory distortions (for details of what was said during a trial) occur in jurors as well?

6. Why might metamemory, one's knowledge of the capabilities of and principles governing one's memory, be an important skill when one is studying for a test?

Program 10

7. Where does the poem "Jabberwocky," by Lewis Carroll, get its meaning? Read the excerpt below and consider the concepts and rules of language and underlying structure that help you make sense of it. Can you paraphrase it?

   'Twas brillig, and the slithy toves
   Did gyre and gimble in the wabe;
   All mimsy were the borogoves,
   And the mome raths outgrabe.

   Beware the Jabberwock, my son!
   The jaws that bite, the claws that catch!
   Beware the Jubjub bird, and shun
   The frumious Bandersnatch!

8. Think of all the ways you can categorize people (e.g., by their gender, their age, their ethnicity, their intelligence, their taste in music). Do you have different schemas for people who belong to these various groups? How does your schema influence your behavior toward people?

9. Can language and knowledge be separated? How do children acquire knowledge before they are able to use verbal labels?

10. Where does "meaning" come from? How much of the meaning that we draw from objects and events is actually generated from our own inferences and expectations?

11. Why can you be so confident that when you say something sarcastically, the person you're talking to will understand your meaning? Under what circumstances are you less sure?

Program 11

12. According to the *Journal of the American Medical Association*, strep throat is one of the most common reasons that children and young adults visit the doctor. It is difficult to diagnose by history or examination only. Ten doctors working in a university health center overestimated the incidence of strep throat by 81 percent. Of the 308 patients in the study, only 15—about 5 percent—actually had strep throat. What might explain the doctors' overestimation?

13. Knowing about problem-solving strategies and using them are two different things. Based on the information in the program and in your text, what are some of the pitfalls you need to avoid in both day-to-day problem solving and decision making about major life changes? How optimistic are you that you can really learn to consistently avoid these pitfalls?

14. Creative people often have such qualities as nonconformity, curiosity, a high degree of verbal fluency, flexibility with numbers and concepts, a sense of humor, a high energy level, impatience with routine tasks, and a vivid imagination that may take the form of wild stories or fibs. What would be the implications for this type of child in the typical school classroom?

15. How does the framing effect, which shows how the description of a situation can heavily influence decision making, jibe with the evidence encountered in the previous chapter that the limitations inherent in one's native language only weakly limits one's thinking?

16. How might cognitive heuristics, like representativeness and availability, perpetuate ethnic stereotypes?

Program 9

1. Do you have an official family historian? In individual interviews, ask family members to recall and describe their memories of a shared past event, such as a wedding or holiday celebration. Perhaps a photograph or memento will trigger a story. Compare how different people construct the event and what kind of details are recalled. What are different people revealing about their personal interests, needs, and values when they describe the experience?

2. Try to recall an experience from your childhood that at least one friend or family member would also have a memory of. Have each person write down details of his or her memories, and then compare notes. Are there any details you hadn't remembered that you now do, based on other people's mention of them? Are there any details that you have contradictory memories for? How do you resolve the disagreement?

3. Make up a list of ten unrelated words. Have five friends study the list for one minute with only the instruction to "remember as many of them as you can." After one minute, have them write down as many as they can remember. Have another five friends learn the list for one minute after you teach them the peg-word mnemonic. Do they outperform the control group? What sort of strategies, if any, did the control group tend to use?

Program 10

4. There are many variations on the game "Ghost." This version challenges players to manipulate concepts by using words in different contexts. Players may find it easier to think up new word pairs as time goes on. What might explain the change? How would you measure it?

5. To play "Ghost": The first player starts off by offering a pair of words that are commonly used together. They may be compounded, hyphenated, or entirely separate. The next player must come up with another pair of words using the last word of the previous pair as the first word of the new pair. (Example: Baseball, ball game, game show, show girl, girlfriend, friendship.) Players keep the chain going until someone cannot come up with a word pair. He or she gets the letter "g." The game resumes. A player is out of the game when he or she gets all the letters of the word "ghost."

6. All of us tend to categorize the world into convenient units and to use common labels for our categories. Often those labels become permanent, and we tend to view our world in a rigid or stereotypical way. When this stops us from producing new ideas, it is called functional fixedness. Can you overcome it?

7. Try this: How many uses can you think of for an empty milk carton, a brick, a sock with a hole in it, a paper clip, a bandanna, or another ordinary household object? After you feel you've exhausted all possibilities, list as many attributes of the object as possible. Draw a picture of the object from various points of view. Then see if you can generate any new uses.

8. Draw a map of the United States from memory, in as much detail as possible. Then compare it to a real map of the U.S. Where is your map systematically distorted or simplified?

Program 11

9. Go to a busy intersection and observe pedestrian street-crossing behavior. Observe the kinds of risks people take crossing the street. What do you consider risky behavior? Who is most likely to engage in it? Why do you suppose certain people take more risks than others?

10. Interview people of different economic statuses and ages about their approaches to the stock market. How do their approaches differ with respect to the assessment of risk and their willingness to accept various forms of risk? Find out how much of their behavior is determined by memories, heuristics, and decision aversion.

Discovering Psychology Viewing Guide

Chapter 8: Emotion and Motivation

Watch the following video by logging onto MyPsychLab (www.mypsychlab.com). After you have watched the video, complete the activities that follow.

PROGRAM 12: MOTIVATION AND EMOTION

What moves us to act? Why do we feel the way we do? Program 12 shows how psychologists study the continuous interactions of mind and body in an effort to explain the enormous variety and complexities of human behavior.

KEY TERMS AND PEOPLE

As you watch the programs, pay particular attention to these terms and people in addition to those covered in this textbook.

arousal—a heightened level of excitation or activation.

optimism—the tendency to attribute failure to external, unstable, or changeable factors and to attribute success to stable factors.

pessimism—the tendency to attribute failure to stable or internal factors and to attribute success to global variables.

Norman Adler—studies the physiological and behavioral mechanisms of sexual behavior.

PROGRAM REVIEW

1. What is the general term for all the physical and psychological processes that start behavior, maintain it, and stop it?
   a. explanatory style
   b. repression
   c. addiction
   d. motivation

2. Phoebe has a phobia regarding cats. What is her motivation?
   a. environmental arousal
   b. overwhelming fear
   c. repressed sexual satisfaction
   d. a need for attachment to others

3. What is the role of the pleasure-pain principle in motivation?
   a. We repress our pleasure in others' pain.
   b. We seek pleasure and avoid pain.
   c. We persist in doing things, even when they are painful.
   d. We are more intensely motivated by pain than by pleasure.

4. Which activity most clearly involves a "reframing" of the tension between desire and restraint?
   a. eating before you feel hungry
   b. seeking pleasurable physical contact with others
   c. working long hours for an eventual goal
   d. getting angry at someone who interferes with your plans

5. Freud thought there were two primary motivations. One of these is
   a. expressing aggression.
   b. seeking transcendence.
   c. fulfilling creativity.
   d. feeling secure.

6. Compared with Freud's view of human motivation, that of Abraham Maslow could be characterized as being more
   a. negative.
   b. hormonally based.
   c. optimistic.
   d. pathologically based.

7. Behaviors, such as male peacocks displaying their feathers or male rams fighting, are related to which part of sexual reproduction?
   a. providing a safe place for mating
   b. focusing the male's attention on mating
   c. selecting a partner with good genes
   d. mating at the correct time of year

8. In Norman Adler's research on mating behavior in rats, what is the function of the ten or so mountings?
   a. to trigger hormone production
   b. to prepare the male for ejaculation
   c. to cause fertilization
   d. to impress the female

9. What kinds of emotions tend to be involved in romantic love?
   a. mainly intense, positive emotions
   b. mainly intense, negative emotions
   c. a mixture of intense and weak emotions that are mainly positive
   d. a mixture of positive and negative emotions that are intense

10. Darwin cited the similarity of certain expressions of emotions as evidence that
    a. all species learn emotions.
    b. emotions are innate.
    c. emotions promote survival of the fittest.
    d. genetic variability is advantageous.

11. Pictures of happy and sad American workers are shown to American college students and to Italian workers. Based on your knowledge of Paul Ekman's research, what would you predict about how well the groups would identify the emotions?
    a. Both groups will identify the emotions correctly.
    b. Only the Americans will identify the emotions correctly.
    c. Only the Italians will identify the emotions correctly.
    d. Neither group will identify the emotions correctly.

12. Theodore has an explanatory style that emphasizes the external, the unstable, and the specific. He makes a mistake at work that causes his boss to become very angry. Which statement is Theodore most likely to make to himself?
    a. "I always make such stupid mistakes."
    b. "I was just distracted by the noise outside."
    c. "All my life, people have always gotten so mad at me."
    d. "If I were a better person, this wouldn't have happened."

13. Why does Martin Seligman believe that it might be appropriate to help children who develop a pessimistic explanatory style?
    a. These children are unpleasant to be around.
    b. These children lack contact with reality.
    c. These children are at risk for depression.
    d. Other children who live with these children are likely to develop the same style.

14. What other outcome will a pessimistic explanatory style likely affect, according to Seligman?
    a. health
    b. artistic ability
    c. reasoning skills
    d. language competence

15. All of the following are possible origins of a pessimistic explanatory style, *except*
    a. assessments by important adults in our lives.
    b. the reality of our first major negative life event.
    c. our mother's pessimism level.
    d. our level of introversion/extraversion.

16. Which theorist is best known for positing a hierarchy of needs that humans strive to meet?
    a. Freud
    b. Rogers
    c. Maslow
    d. Seligman

17. Although motivation can lead to unpleasant states (e.g., hunger, frustration), it seems to have evolved because of its benefits to
    a. survival.
    b. propagation of the species.
    c. health.
    d. all of the above.

18. What has Robert Plutchik argued about emotions?
    a. There are three basic types of emotions: happiness, sadness, and anger.
    b. There are eight basic emotions, consisting of four pairs of opposites.
    c. Love is not a universal emotion; some cultures do not show signs of having it.
    d. Emotional experience is determined by physiology alone.

19. Four people have been obese for as long as they can remember. Their doctors tell all of them that their obesity is putting them at risk for several illnesses. Who is most likely to join a gym, go on a diet, and get in shape?
    a. Al, whose explanatory style includes an internal locus of control
    b. Bob, who has a pessimistic explanatory style
    c. Chuck, whose explanatory style includes an unstable locus of control
    d. Dwayne, who is depressed about his obesity

20. Wolves and squirrels are most likely to show which of the following in their mating patterns?
    a. romantic love
    b. competition by females for males
    c. competition by males for females
    d. a preference for mating in the autumn so that the offspring will be born during the winter

QUESTIONS TO CONSIDER

1. Human sexual motivation expresses itself in sexual scripts that include attitudes, values, social norms, and expectations about patterns of behavior. Consider how males and females might develop different sexual scripts. How might lack of synchronization affect a couple? How might sexual scripts change as the bad news about sexually transmitted diseases and AIDS increases?

2. Do you consider yourself an optimist or a pessimist? Pick a recent success and a recent failure or disappointment and consider how an optimist and a pessimist would explain each experience. How did you handle each situation?

3. If degree of self-restraint and stress determine how likely it is that people will "cheat" on their diets, what sorts of psychological supports would you build into a diet plan?

4. Consider how eating disorders, such as anorexia and bulimia, contradict the pain-pleasure principle.

5. If you could choose between taking this course pass/fail (credit only) or getting a letter grade, which would you choose? How would your decision affect your study time, motivation, and test-taking behavior?

6. How do the relative priorities of motivators change for you when you are hungry or sick?

7. Imagine you were to move to a country whose culture you aren't familiar with. Describe some of the social problems you might encounter because you don't know the cultural norms regarding expression of emotion.

ACTIVITIES

1. Are we sad because we cry, or do we cry because we are sad? Can making a sad face make us feel sad? Does going through the motions trigger the emotion?

   Try this: Set aside from ten to fifteen minutes for this experiment. Write down the words *happy, sad, angry*, and *fearful* on slips of paper. In front of a mirror, select one of the slips, and watch yourself as you create the facial expression for it. Hold the expression for at least a minute. Note the thoughts and physical reactions that seem to accompany your facial expression. Then relax your face and repeat the exercise with another slip of paper. Which theories does your experience support or challenge?

2. Observe the activities on which you need to concentrate when your hunger has been satisfied, compared with when you are very hungry. How well can you focus on more abstract motivations when your biological motivations have been left unmet?

Discovering Psychology Viewing Guide

Chapter 9: Psychological Development

Watch the following videos by logging onto MyPsychLab (www.mypsychlab.com). After you have watched the videos, complete the activities that follow.

PROGRAM 5: THE DEVELOPING CHILD

Program 5 looks at how advances in technology and methodology have revealed the abilities of newborn infants, giving researchers a better understanding of the role infants play in shaping their environment. In contrast to the nature-versus-nurture debates of the past, today's researchers concentrate on how heredity and environment interact to contribute to the developmental process.

PROGRAM 17: SEX AND GENDER

Program 17 looks at the similarities and differences between the sexes resulting from the complex interaction of biological and social factors. It contrasts the universal differences in anatomy and physiology with those learned and culturally acquired, and it reveals how roles are changing to reflect new values and psychological knowledge.

PROGRAM 18: MATURING AND AGING

Thanks to growing scientific interest in the elderly, research on aging has replaced many myths and fears with facts. Program 18 focuses on what scientists are learning about life cycle development as they look at how aging is affected by biology, environment, and lifestyle.

KEY TERMS AND PEOPLE

As you watch the program, pay particular attention to these terms and people in addition to those covered in this textbook.

Program 5

stage theory—a theory that describes development as a fixed sequence of distinct periods of life.

Judy DeLoache—studies cognitive development in older children and how they come to understand symbols.

Jerome Kagan—studies inherited behavioral differences between bold and timid children.

Steven Suomi—studies the behavior of genetically shy monkeys. Argues that at least some shyness is an inherited tendency.

Program 17

androgynous—having both masculine and feminine traits.

cognitive developmental theory—the theory stating that children use male and female as fundamental categories and actively sex-type themselves to achieve cognitive consistency.

developmental strategies—behaviors that have evolved to conform to the sex roles typical of the adult members of a species.

sex typing—the psychological process by which boys and girls become masculine or feminine.

social learning theory—the theory stating that children are socialized by observing role models and are rewarded or punished for behaving appropriately.

stereotype—the belief that all members of a group share common traits.

Michael Meaney—developmental neuroscientist who studies the interaction of biology and psychology in the development of sex differences.

Program 18

senile dementia—biochemical and neuronal changes in the brain that lead to a gradual reduction in mental efficiency.

Daniel Levinson—studies the life course as a sequence of developmental experiences.

Pat Moore—reporter who disguised herself as an 85-year-old woman to find out more about the experience of being old in America.

Werner Schaie—studies long-term effects of aging.

Sherry Willis—uses new educational training methods to help the elderly function more effectively.

PROGRAM REVIEW QUESTIONS

Program 5

1. Imagine that someone familiar with the last twenty years of research on babies was able to converse with William James. What would this time traveler probably say to James?
   a. "You were ahead of your time in understanding babies."
   b. "Babies are more competent than you thought."
   c. "Babies' senses are less sophisticated than you said."
   d. "Babies' perceptions actually depend on their cultures."

2. Which smell do newborns like?
   a. the smell of a banana
   b. the smell of shrimp
   c. newborns can't smell anything.
   d. newborns can smell, but we have no way of knowing what smells they prefer.

3. What task of infancy is aided by a baby's ability to recognize its mother's voice?
   a. avoiding danger
   b. seeking sustenance
   c. forming social relationships
   d. learning to speak

4. A toy company wants to use Robert Fantz's research to design a new mobile for babies to look at in their cribs. The research suggests that the mobile should
   a. be as simple as possible.
   b. use soft colors such as pink.
   c. be made of a shiny material.
   d. have a complex design.

5. Which of a baby's senses is least developed at birth?
   a. hearing
   b. taste
   c. sight
   d. touch

6. Jean Piaget has studied how children think. According to Piaget, at what age does a child typically master the idea that the amount of a liquid remains the same when it is poured from one container to another container with a different shape?
   a. two years old
   b. four years old
   c. six years old
   d. eight years old

7. A baby is shown an orange ball a dozen times in a row. How would you predict the baby would respond?
   a. The baby will make the same interested response each time.
   b. The baby will respond with less and less interest each time.
   c. The baby will respond with more and more interest each time.
   d. The baby will not be interested at any time.

8. Renée Baillargeon and other researchers have investigated object permanence in babies. How do their results compare with Piaget's views?
   a. They show Piaget's age estimates for achieving object permanence were too high.
   b. They contradict Piaget's concept of what object permanence consists of.
   c. They support Piaget's timetable.
   d. They indicate that babies show more variation than Piaget found.

9. When Judy DeLoache hid the small and large toy dogs, what was she investigating?
   a. stranger anxiety
   b. activity level
   c. conservation of volume
   d. symbolic representation

10. In a discussion of the nature-nurture controversy, who would be most likely to cite Steven Suomi's research on shyness in monkeys to support his or her point of view?
    a. someone arguing that nature is the only factor determining shyness or boldness
    b. someone arguing that nurture is the only factor determining shyness or boldness
    c. someone arguing that nature can be modified by nurture
    d. the research does not support any of these viewpoints

11. At what stage in their development do babies refuse to cross the visual cliff?
    a. as soon as their eyes can focus on it
    b. when they develop conditioned fears
    c. just before they are ready to walk
    d. about a month after they learn to crawl

12. What conclusion has Jerome Kagan come to about shyness in young children?
    a. It is inherent but can be modified by experience.
    b. It is created by parents who misunderstand their child's temperament.
    c. It is an inherited trait that cannot be changed.
    d. It is normal for all children to be shy at certain stages.

13. How does Steven Suomi modify shyness reactions in young monkeys?
    a. by putting them in an enriched environment
    b. by providing highly supportive foster mothers
    c. by placing a shy monkey with other shy monkeys
    d. by administering drugs that reduce the level of social anxiety

14. Which of the following do newborns appear not to already be equipped with?
    a. a temperament
    b. a preference for novelty
    c. a preference for complexity
    d. the ability to understand reversibility in conservation

15. The Wild Boy of Aveyron represents which important issue in developmental psychology?
    a. ethics in experimentation
    b. the relation of physical development to social development
    c. nature vs. nurture
    d. interpretation of experimental data

16. At one month of age, babies
    a. are best described as "a blooming, buzzing confusion."
    b. prefer stimuli that are constant and don't vary.
    c. have not yet opened their eyes.
    d. prefer human faces over other visual stimuli.

17. Which of the following is *not* a method that measures what a two-month-old is interested in?
    a. asking questions in very short, simple sentences
    b. measuring looking time
    c. examining dishabituation
    d. recording heart rate

18. Which of the following developmental psychologists made the mistake of confusing children's physical ability with their cognitive ability and thus believed children were cognitively less capable than they actually are?
    a. Robert Fantz
    b. Jean Piaget
    c. Renée Baillargeon
    d. Eleanor Gibson

19. Which of the following is last to emerge in children?
    a. fear of heights
    b. preference for mother's voice over other people's voices
    c. temperament
    d. ability to see analogies between a real situation and a scale model of it

20. Which of the following psychological characteristics appear(s) to have a genetic component?
    a. activity level
    b. tendency to be outgoing
    c. risk for some psychopathologies
    d. all of the above

Program 17

21. According to research by Zella Lurin and Jeffrey Rubin, the difference in the language parents use to describe their newborn sons or daughters is primarily a reflection of
    a. actual physical differences in the newborns.
    b. differences in the way the newborns behave.
    c. the way the hospital staff responds to the babies.
    d. the parents' expectations coloring their perceptions.

22. Which set of adjectives best characterizes the feminine gender role in the United States?
    a. gentle, emotional, dependent
    b. creative, intelligent, attractive

c. aggressive, independent, dominant
d. industrious, nurturing, ambitious

23. Which difference between the ways in which boys and girls play seems linked to sex hormones?
    a. Girls play with dolls.
    b. Boys engage in rough and tumble play.
    c. Boys play in larger groups than girls do.
    d. Girls build rooms, and boys build towers.

24. Michael Meaney attributes the differences in the behavior of male and female rats to the fact that these behaviors "feel good" to the animals. The reason for this is that the behaviors
    a. increase hormone production.
    b. prepare the organism for its life tasks.
    c. stimulate certain brain regions.
    d. fit the preferred pattern of motor activity.

25. How does the health of men compare with the health of women throughout the life cycle?
    a. Men are more vulnerable throughout the life cycle.
    b. Women are more vulnerable throughout the life cycle.
    c. Women are more vulnerable only during their childbearing years.
    d. There is no consistent sex difference in health.

26. Which learned behavior associated with the masculine gender role poses a health risk?
    a. having recessive genes
    b. relying on social networks
    c. being assertive
    d. drinking alcohol

27. What is the likeliest source of the behavioral difference between the sexes regarding crying?
    a. It is an innate difference.
    b. Initial innate differences are reinforced by parents.
    c. It is learned during the socialization process.
    d. We do not know the source.

28. What typically happens when a girl behaves in gender-inappropriate ways?
    a. She feels uncomfortable.
    b. She is praised.
    c. She is scolded.
    d. The behavior is not noticed.

29. According to Jeanne Block, the sociopsychological contexts for boys and girls tend to be different. One such difference is that the context for girls tends to be more
    a. home-centered.
    b. achievement-oriented.
    c. filled with risk.
    d. involved with same-sex peers.

30. According to Jeanne Block, the sociopsychological context typically provided to boys is
    a. less protective than for girls.
    b. more supervised than for girls.
    c. less likely to provide opportunities for inventing and discovering than for girls.
    d. more restricted in the network of friends they come into contact with.

31. What is one of the negative consequences of the masculine gender role?
    a. It makes men more vulnerable to depression.
    b. It imposes limits on intellectual development.
    c. It provides little sense of belonging.
    d. It encourages risk-taking behaviors.

32. According to Eleanor Maccoby, at about what age do children begin to prefer same-sex playmates?
    a. two years old
    b. three years old
    c. four years old
    d. five years old

33. Which statement about sex differences in psychological traits and abilities is best supported by research?
    a. There are no identifiable differences.
    b. The differences that exist are more a matter of degree than a difference in kind.
    c. The differences are the result of differences in brain chemistry and organization.
    d. The differences are arbitrary, because they are the result of social learning.

34. Which is true about gender roles in children?
    a. Girls tend to be the first to segregate themselves and play among members of their own gender.
    b. Girls are more aggressive in their physical behavior.
    c. Boys and girls will develop strong gender role stereotypes and will segregate themselves based on gender only if adults strongly encourage that.
    d. None of the above.

35. The term *androgynous* would best apply to which of the following people?
    a. a macho man who participates in body-building competitions
    b. a dainty woman who belongs to a sewing club
    c. a young boy who never talks in class because he feels shy
    d. a male rock star who wears heavy make-up, long hair, and feminine clothing.

36. According to the film, boys' greater propensity for rough-and-tumble play is likely the result of
   a. biological differences between boys and girls.
   b. different cultural treatment of boys and girls.
   c. both of the above.
   d. none of the above.

37. Boys tend to have ______ friends than girls and tend to be ______ intimate with their friends than girls are.
   a. more; more
   b. more; less
   c. less; more
   d. less; less

38. Because of the way we socialize our children, men tend to experience more freedom to _______, while women tend to experience more freedom to ______.
   a. explore; criticize
   b. withdraw; invent
   c. discover; express themselves
   d. express themselves; explore

39. Which of the following appears in children by six years of age?
   a. gender role-related depression
   b. sexual desire
   c. secondary sexual characteristics
   d. extreme gender-based segregation

40. Imagine that a set of parents avoids using gender role stereotypes in the house and that they encourage their son to play with other neighborhood children of both genders. What can we expect will happen?
   a. The boy will show no signs of gender role stereotypes and will be happy playing with both trucks and dolls.
   b. The boy will develop cooperative play patterns that are typical of little girls.
   c. Through social pressure, the boy will develop male gender role-stereotypic behavior.
   d. The boy will be about 10 percent less competent in physical tasks than his male peers.

Program 18

41. How has research on life-span development changed our idea of human nature?
   a. We see development as a growth process of early life.
   b. We see that a longer life span creates problems for society.
   c. We view people as continuing to develop throughout life.
   d. We regard development as a hormonally based process.

42. What does the term *psychological adolescing* mean?
   a. coming into conflict with parents
   b. entering into a senile state
   c. being swept up by emotional conflicts
   d. developing to our full potential

43. What personal experience does Erik Erikson cite as leading to his redefinition of himself?
   a. having a religious conversion
   b. being an immigrant
   c. surviving a major illness
   d. getting married

44. According to Erikson, the young adult faces a conflict between
   a. isolation and intimacy.
   b. heterosexuality and homosexuality.
   c. autonomy and shame.
   d. wholeness and futility.

45. Which statement sounds most typical of someone in the throes of a midlife crisis?
   a. "I enjoy my connections with other people."
   b. "I'd like to run off to a desert island."
   c. "My work is my greatest source of satisfaction."
   d. "I accept the fact that I've made some bad decisions."

46. During which period of life does Erikson argue that people face the issue of wholeness vs. futility?
   a. old age
   b. middle adulthood
   c. adolescence
   d. toddlerhood

47. Daniel Levinson divides the life cycle into a series of eras. For which era is a major problem the hazard of being irrelevant?
   a. childhood
   b. early adulthood
   c. middle adulthood
   d. late adulthood

48. What has happened to the life expectancy of the average American over the past fifty years?
   a. It has lessened.
   b. It has remained stable.
   c. It has risen very slowly.
   d. It has nearly doubled.

49. When Pat Moore transformed herself into an 85-year-old woman, she was surprised by the
   a. compassion with which others treated her.
   b. lack of facilities designed to accommodate the aged.
   c. extent of ageism in our society.
   d. poverty faced by many older people.

50. How do psychosomatic symptoms tend to change with age?
   a. People develop more of them.
   b. The ones people develop are more severe.
   c. They tend to be more related to sleeping and less related to eating.
   d. They are less common.

51. What has Sherry Willis found about the abilities of older people with regard to spatial orientation tasks?
   a. Irreversible decline is inevitable.
   b. Training programs yield improved skills.
   c. Skills can be maintained but not improved.
   d. If memory loss occurs, other skills deteriorate.

52. About what percent of people over age 65 suffer from senile dementia?
   a. 5 percent
   b. 15 percent
   c. 25 percent
   d. 40 percent

53. There is a(n) ________ in paranoid disorders with age largely because _____.
   a. decrease; people have become more at peace with their lives.
   b. decrease; life becomes more sheltered and more predictable during retirement.
   c. increase; life becomes more chaotic during retirement.
   d. increase; of hearing and vision losses that make the world harder to process.

54. Assuming that a person remains healthy, what happens to the ability to derive sexual pleasure as one ages?
   a. It does not change.
   b. It gradually diminishes.
   c. It abruptly ceases.
   d. It depends on the availability of a suitable partner.

55. In general, how does the view of the elderly among the population at large compare with the actuality?
   a. It is more negative.
   b. It is more positive.
   c. It is generally accurate.
   d. It is more accurate for men than for women.

56. The results of the long-term study by Werner Schaie suggest that the people who do best in the later stages of life are people with
   a. high incomes.
   b. advanced degrees.
   c. flexible attitudes.
   d. large, close-knit families.

57. In nursing homes, the staff often behave in ways that treat the elderly like children. What is the effect of this treatment on most older people?
   a. It makes them feel more secure.
   b. It makes them behave in dependent, childlike ways.
   c. It increases their sense of autonomy and control.
   d. It improves their health by reducing their stress levels.

58. In which of the following areas do the elderly typically have an advantage over college students?
   a. The elderly are better able to climb stairs.
   b. The elderly generally have higher short-term memory capacity.
   c. The elderly are less lonely.
   d. The elderly have a more developed sense of humor.

59. Cognitive agility in the elderly
   a. is considered to have completely disappeared in the average 85-year-old person.
   b. tends to improve radically in the years just before death.
   c. is one of the most predictable outcomes of the aging process.
   d. does not necessarily decline.

60. The elderly are particularly adept at processing information with
   a. emotional content.
   b. spatial content.
   c. mathematical content.
   d. folkloric content.

QUESTIONS TO CONSIDER

Program 5

1. Consider different theories of infant abilities, and contrast the influence of both Gesell and Watson on developmental psychology and child-rearing practices.

2. How might the knowledge of developmental norms affect a parent's response to a child? How might advanced techniques to detect prenatal perception and cognition inform parents? Speculate on what would happen if parents raised their children following inaccurate or out-of-date theories of child development.

3. Is it easier or harder to tell what a child is thinking than to tell what an adult is thinking? How can some of the measures used to detect an infant's interest or learning be used to measure adult cognitive functioning?

4. Can some of the measures used to determine the cognitive capabilities of pre-verbal infants be applied to non-human animals? What would we be able to conclude from patterns of results that are similar to or different from those found in human infants?

5. Besides a predisposition to be interested in humans and to be interested in novelty, what other interests might an infant benefit from being predisposed toward?

6. As people age and restructure their lives based on gains and losses in what they are capable of doing, do you think their values change to fit their capabilities? For example, do you think they come to value physical activity less as they become physically more restricted?

Program 17

7. People organize their perceptions, expectations, and judgments around social schema and scripts. How are sexual scripts related to gender roles?

8. How does gender-typing influence perceptions?

9. How do young children show that they are aware of their gender identity?

10. Research suggests that androgynous people are better adjusted than those who are traditionally sex-role stereotyped. But critics contend that the masculine traits lead to higher self-esteem and better adjustment than a combination of masculine and feminine traits. How can having masculine traits enhance a woman's self-esteem?

11. Many women writers, including J. K. Rowling, have published under masculine-sounding or gender-ambiguous names. Does the sex of the writer make a difference? Should it?

12. If you tried to raise a child without exposing him or her to any gender-typing biases, how extensively would you need to change the social and physical environments that the child would normally encounter? How big of a job would this be? Could you ultimately be successful?

Program 18

13. Define normal aging. How has science helped to differentiate between the normal processes of aging and the effects of illness?

14. What are the psychological themes unique to the middle years, sometimes called the midlife crisis?

15. How does cognitive capability change in the later adult years?

16. Is the increased divorce rate over the last few decades related to patterns of attachment and parent-child relationships developed early in life? How could such a hypothesis be tested?

17. How do social conditions help create the characteristics of adolescence and adulthood in the human life cycle?

18. How does becoming a parent help define the developmental stages of adulthood? What other sorts of roles might accomplish a similar end?

ACTIVITIES

Program 5

1. Recall your earliest memory. Speculate as to why you recall it, what you might have distorted in your memory, and what effects the event has had on your development.

2. Can you remember ever having thought in a qualitatively different way from the way you think now? How well do you think you can really take the perspective of a 4-year-old who is forming a conceptualization of the world? Do you think there are any barriers to your ability to do that, and how do you think they might affect your ability to interact with the child?

3. Compare yourself to your siblings. What traits, abilities, and interests do you share? Speculate on the roles of genetics and environment in the development of your similarities and differences.

4. Go to a grocery store or mall and observe the children there. At approximately what age does it appear that children engage in cooperative play? Can cooperative play be taught?

5. Interview an elderly person to find out what their experiences have been of the costs and benefits, both cognitively and socially, of aging in this country. Do they ever find that they are discriminated against? Do they find that people are more generous with them than with other people?

Program 17

6. Pick three close relatives or friends. How would your relationship with them be different if you were of the opposite sex? Which aspects of your personal identity and behavior would change? Which would stay the same?

Program 18

7. At what age will you consider yourself to be "old"? Define your personal concept of old age, and describe what you expect your life to be like. Describe the health status, activities, satisfactions, and concerns you anticipate in your late adult years.

8. Keep track of the images of people over 60, over 70, and over 80 that you encounter during an average day. Notice how older adults are depicted in television programs and advertisements. What stereotypes persist? Is there evidence that images are changing?

9. Make a list of the labels used to describe people at various stages of life from infancy to old age. Which age group has the most labels? Compare the synonyms and modifiers for childhood to the words that help define adulthood. What might explain the difference?

10. Take a close look at your own generation. Identify ways in which that generation has attempted to distinguish itself as a subculture. Does the "retro" style serve to create any links to previous generations?

DISCOVERING PSYCHOLOGY VIEWING GUIDE

Chapter 10: Personality

Watch the following video by logging onto MyPsychLab (www.mypsychlab.com). After you have watched the video, complete the activities that follow.

PROGRAM 15: THE SELF

What makes each of us unique? What traits and experiences make you? Program 15 describes how psychologists systematically study the origins and development of self-identity, self-esteem, and other aspects of our thoughts, feelings, and behaviors that make up our personalities.

KEY TERMS AND PEOPLE

As you watch the program, pay particular attention to these terms and people in addition to those covered in this textbook.

reference standard—a norm or model of behavior that we use to decide how to behave in a situation.

status transaction—a form of interpersonal communication in which we establish relative degrees of social status and power.

Teresa Amabile—studies the psychology of creativity.

Mark Snyder—studies strategic self-presentation and behavioral confirmation

PROGRAM REVIEW

1. What name did William James give to the part of the self that focuses on the images we create in the mind of others?
   a. the material self
   b. the spiritual self
   c. the social self
   d. the outer self

2. Gail is a toddler who is gradually separating from her mother. This process is called
   a. identification.
   b. individuation.
   c. self-presentation.
   d. self-consciousness.

3. In Freudian theory, the part of the person that acts as a police officer restraining drives and passions is called the
   a. superego.
   b. ego.
   c. id.
   d. libido.

4. Which statement reflects the humanistic view of the self, according to Carl Rogers?
   a. Our impulses are in constant conflict with society's demands.
   b. We have a capacity for self-direction and self-understanding.
   c. We form an image of ourselves that determines what we can do.
   d. Our views of ourselves are created by how people react to us.

5. When we characterize self-image as a schema, we mean that
   a. we use it to organize information about ourselves.
   b. other people see us in terms of the image we project.

c. it is a good predictor of performance in specific situations.
d. we rationalize our behavior to fit into an image.

6. In Albert Bandura's research, people were given the task of improving production at a model furniture factory. They performed best when they believed that performance
   a. depended on their intelligence.
   b. related mainly to how confident they felt.
   c. would be given a material reward.
   d. was based on learning an acquirable skill.

7. Which of the following behaviors signals low status in a status transaction?
   a. maintaining eye contact
   b. using complete sentences
   c. moving in a slow, smooth way
   d. touching one's face or hair

8. According to the principles of behavioral confirmation, what reaction do people generally have to a person who is depressed?
   a. People sympathetically offer help to the person.
   b. People regard the person as inadequate.
   c. People act falsely cheerful to make the person happy.
   d. People treat a depressed person the same as anybody else.

9. What was referred to in the film as a type of psychological genocide?
   a. drugs
   b. falling emphasis on education
   c. prejudice
   d. immigration

10. What is the relevance of schemas to the self?
    a. We try to avoid schemas in constructing our sense of self.
    b. We organize our beliefs about ourselves in terms of schemas.
    c. Schemas are what makes us individuals.
    d. Schemas are always negative, since they underlie prejudice.

11. In Teresa Amabile's work on creativity, how did being in a competitive situation affect creativity?
    a. It reduced creativity.
    b. It increased creativity.
    c. Its effects varied depending on the person's innate creativity.
    d. There was no effect.

12. According to Hazel Markus, culture is what you
    a. think.
    b. see.
    c. do.
    d. hate.

13. "Mutual constitution" refers to which two components, according to Hazel Markus?
    a. parent and child
    b. art and scholarship
    c. religion and society
    d. self and culture

14. In which culture are you most likely to find a definition of the person as a part of the group?
    a. Japanese
    b. American
    c. Portuguese
    d. Russian

15. The high rate of alcoholism among Native Americans was cited as an example of
    a. individualism.
    b. social handicapping.
    c. mutual constitution.
    d. striving for superiority.

16. According to William James, which part of the self serves as our inner witness to outside events?
    a. the material self
    b. the spiritual self
    c. the social self
    d. the outer self

17. Of the following psychologists, who is considered to be the least optimistic about the human condition?
    a. Freud
    b. Adler
    c. Rogers
    d. Maslow

18. Which of the following refers to how capable we believe we are of mastering challenges?
    a. self-efficacy
    b. self-handicapping
    c. confirmatory behavior
    d. status transaction

19. Amabile is to creativity as ________ is to behavioral confirmation.
    a. Alfred Adler
    b. Patricia Ryan
    c. Mark Snyder
    d. Albert Bandura

20. Who is credited as being responsible for psychology's return to the self?
    a. William James
    b. B. F. Skinner
    c. Patricia Ryan
    d. Carl Rogers

QUESTIONS TO CONSIDER

1. Different kinds of standardized tests have been criticized over the years because they may not apply equally well to people of different genders, socioeconomic status, or cultural backgrounds. Speculate on what sorts of problems might arise when standardized personality tests (such as the MMPI-2) are used. Think about what sorts of items might lead to problems, and think about what sorts of consequences might arise from the use of a biased instrument.

2. How is Seligman's concept of pessimism related to shyness?

3. What are some of the positive and negative aspects of the id, according to Freud?

4. Do you have higher self-esteem in some situations than in others? How do different environments and conditions affect you? Do you think that self-esteem is constant or variable?

5. Compare the social skills of your friends and yourself to people who did not grow up with computers and the Internet playing a central role in their lives. Do you see systematic differences in sociability, shyness, and apparent self-concept?

ACTIVITIES

1. How do you recognize extroverts and introverts? Observe people on television, in a public place, or at home. Rate their behavior on a continuum between the opposites of extrovert and introvert. How helpful is the distinction? Do these qualities seem to be a primary dimension of personality?

2. Describe yourself by highlighting your special abilities, admirable qualities, and accomplishments. Write a brief description of your parents, spouse, children, or a close friend. Consider how often you appreciate the positive aspects of your own or another's personality and how often you focus on the negatives. How does your focus affect your own self-esteem and your relationships?

3. Take some characteristic about yourself that you have never liked (e.g., the tendency to interrupt, or the tendency to become tongue-tied around people of higher status than you). Spend the next month seeing if you can completely rid yourself of that characteristic. If you are successful, how would you describe the shift? Was it a change in your personality, or was it a change in behavior despite the underlying traits that used to produce it?

4. Interview a new parent and find out how his or her attitudes and behavior toward small children have changed.

Discovering Psychology Viewing Guide

Chapter 11: Testing and Individual Differences

Watch the following video by logging onto MyPsychLab (www.mypsychlab.com). After you have watched the video, complete the activities that follow.

PROGRAM 16: TESTING AND INTELLIGENCE

Just as no two fingerprints are alike, no two people have the same set of abilities, aptitudes, interests, and talents. Program 16 explains the tools psychologists use to measure these differences. It also describes the long-standing controversy over how to define intelligence and how IQ tests have been misused and misapplied. Is it wise, accurate, or fair to reduce intelligence to a number? Researchers are currently debating the value of intelligence and personality tests.

KEY TERMS AND PEOPLE

As you watch the program, pay particular attention to these terms and people in addition to those covered in this textbook.

W. Curtis Banks—an expert on psychological testing.

PROGRAM REVIEW

1. What is the goal of psychological assessment?
   a. to derive a theory of human cognition
   b. to see how people vary in ability, behavior, and personality
   c. to measure the stages of growth in intellectual abilities
   d. to diagnose psychological problems

2. You are taking a test in which you are asked to agree or disagree with statements, such as "I give up too easily when discussing things with others." Which test would this be?
   a. the Scholastic Aptitude Test
   b. the Rorschach test
   c. the Strong Interest Inventory
   d. the Minnesota Multiphasic Personality Inventory

3. What was Binet's aim in developing a measure of intelligence?
   a. to identify children in need of special help
   b. to show that intelligence was innate
   c. to weed out inferior children
   d. to provide an empirical basis for a theory of intelligence

4. How were the results of Binet's test expressed?
   a. in terms of general and specific factors
   b. as an intelligence quotient
   c. as a mental age related to a norm
   d. as a percentile score

5. What formula did Terman create to express intelligence?
   a. MA/CA = IQ
   b. MA × CA = IQ
   c. CA/MA × 100 = IQ
   d. MA/CA × 100 = IQ

6. In 1939, David Wechsler designed a new intelligence test. What problem of its predecessors was the test designed to overcome?
   a. bias in favor of minority groups
   b. unreliable scores
   c. dependence on language
   d. norms based on a restricted population

7. A test for prospective firefighters has been shown to predict success on the job. Which statement about the test is true?
   a. The test is reliable.
   b. The test is valid.
   c. The test is standardized.
   d. The test is unbiased.

8. Cultural biases in tests can lead to the overvaluing of some attributes and the undervaluing of others. Which of the following is likely to be overvalued in the United States?
   a. common sense
   b. motivation
   c. creativity
   d. verbal ability

9. Imagine that anyone who wants a job as a hospital orderly has to take a test. The test is valid for its norm group, white men. Imagine a black woman is taking the test. Which statement about the woman's score is most likely to be accurate?
   a. It will accurately predict her job performance.
   b. It will be lower than that of white men.
   c. It may indicate she is not capable when she in fact is capable.
   d. It cannot indicate anything about her because there were no blacks or women in the norm group.

10. What new perspective did Howard Gardner introduce to the study of intelligence?
   a. He redefined intelligence as "practical intelligence."
   b. He expanded intelligence to include other types.
   c. He argued for a biological basis for describing intelligence in terms of brain waves.
   d. He argued that the term *intelligence* should be abolished.

11. Robert Sternberg has devised a test for managers. How does its prediction of success compare with predictions from a standard IQ test?
   a. They predict equally well and are not correlated.
   b. They predict equally well, probably because they are measuring the same thing.
   c. Sternberg's test predicts twice as well as IQ and is not correlated with IQ.
   d. Sternberg's test predicts twice as well as IQ and is moderately correlated with IQ.

12. The attempt by neuroscientists to find biologically based measures of intelligence rests on the assumption that intelligence involves
   a. multiple factors.
   b. cultural learning.
   c. speed of adaptation.
   d. high excitability.

13. Standardized intelligence tests typically
   a. overvalue verbal ability.
   b. give too much value to creative problem solving.
   c. are biased to give exceptionally high scores to people from other cultures.
   d. are the best available predictors of life success.

14. Which of these is a self-fulfilling prophesy that can be based on age, race, or gender?
   a. test-retest reliability
   b. stereotype threat
   c. crystallized intelligence
   d. criterion validity

15. The growing practice of "teaching for tests" creates the possibility of
   a. lessened ecological validity.
   b. eliminating stereotype threat.
   c. lowered reliability.
   d. eliminating genetic influences on intelligence.

16. Which of the following is an innovation in intelligence assessment that David Wechsler introduced?
   a. displaying physical coordination
   b. demonstrating social sensitivity
   c. producing appropriate verbal metaphors
   d. putting pictures in a logical sequence

17. William Curtis Banks argued for the importance of all of the following, *except*
   a. correlating intelligence measures with vocational success.
   b. ensuring validity of intelligence tests.
   c. being confident that our assessment measures are reliable.
   d. standardizing assessment measures with respect to the larger population.

18. Which is the most effective way to break the influence of stereotype threat?
    a. Assure the test-taker that the test cannot discriminate between members of their own group and members of other groups.
    b. Provide the test-taker with a visualization exercise ahead of time to enhance his or her self-esteem.
    c. Provide the test-taker with a very simple task beforehand in order to boost confidence.
    d. Suggest that the test-taker should try to make his or her minority group proud.

19. Stereotype threat requires that the test-taker
    a. believe in the stereotype.
    b. be of relatively high intelligence.
    c. know that others believe in the stereotype.
    d. be of relatively low intelligence.

20. What we have learned about intelligence over the years is that it is *not*
    a. complex.
    b. influenced by environment.
    c. a singular process.
    d. culturally defined.

QUESTIONS TO CONSIDER

1. Does evidence of a genetic basis for intelligence mean that intelligence is unchangeable?

2. What would happen if everyone knew everyone else's IQ scores? How might it affect decisions about whom to marry or hire?

3. Would you rather score high on a standardized test of intelligence or a test of creativity?

4. What are some of the ethical questions related to intelligence testing and psychological assessment?

5. Does it seem reasonable that you can score very high on one type of intelligence and very low on others? Does that change your view of what it means to be "intelligent"?

ACTIVITIES

1. Pick a special interest of yours, such as cooking, baseball, woodworking, dancing, or traveling. Design a test that includes both questions and tasks that would measure knowledge and ability in that area. How would you ensure the test's validity?

2. Consider the possibility that intelligence could be improved. Design a one-year plan to improve your intelligence. What would be the most important components of your plan? Would the plan you devised work equally well for someone else?

3. Talk to an elementary school teacher about his or her experience with children's intellectual development under different kinds of teaching conditions. In his or her view, is it a good idea to "teach to the test," knowing that his or her students will be given standardized tests later on that will determine whether they are "advanced," "average," or "below average?" In his or her experience, what happens to students with respect to educational opportunities and attention after they are categorized in these different ways?

DISCOVERING PSYCHOLOGY VIEWING GUIDE

Chapter 12: Psychological Disorders

Watch the following video by logging onto MyPsychLab (www.mypsychlab.com). After you have watched the video, complete the activities that follow.

PROGRAM 21: PSYCHOPATHOLOGY

Program 21 describes the major types of mental illnesses and some of the factors that influence them—both biological and psychological. It also reports on several approaches to classifying and treating mental illness and explains the difficulties of defining abnormal behavior.

KEY TERMS AND PEOPLE

As you watch the program, pay particular attention to these terms and people in addition to those covered in this textbook.

Hans Strupp—argues that psychological factors are of primary importance in the origin of schizophrenia.

Fuller Torrey—studies the psychology and biology of schizophrenia.

PROGRAM REVIEW

1. Psychopathology is defined as the study of
   a. organic brain disease.
   b. perceptual and cognitive illusions.
   c. clinical measures of abnormal functioning.
   d. mental disorders.

2. What is the key criterion for identifying a person as having a mental disorder?
   a. The person has problems.
   b. The person's functioning is clearly abnormal.
   c. The person's ideas challenge the status quo.
   d. The person makes other people feel uncomfortable.

3. Which is true about mental disorders?
   a. They are extremely rare, with less than one-tenth of 1 percent of Americans suffering from any form of mental illness.
   b. They are not that uncommon, with about one-fifth of Americans suffering from some form of recently diagnosed mental disorder.
   c. The number of Americans with psychotic disorders fluctuates with the calendar, with more cases of psychosis during the weekends than during weekdays.
   d. The actions of people with mental disorders are unpredictable.

4. Fran is a mental health specialist who has a Ph.D. in psychology. She would be classified as a
   a. psychiatrist.
   b. clinical psychologist.
   c. social psychologist.
   d. psychoanalyst.

5. What happened after David Rosenhan and his colleagues were admitted to mental hospitals by pretending to have hallucinations and then behaved normally?
   a. Their sanity was quickly observed by the staff.
   b. It took several days for their deception to be realized.
   c. In most cases, the staff disagreed with each other about these "patients."
   d. Nobody ever detected their sanity.

6. Olivia is experiencing dizziness, muscle tightness, shaking, and tremors. She is feeling apprehensive. These symptoms most resemble those found in cases of
   a. anxiety disorders.
   b. affective disorders.
   c. psychoses.
   d. schizophrenia.

7. Agoraphobia is one of the most common phobias. What does a person with this condition fear?
   a. being at the top of a tall building
   b. going out in public
   c. being violently attacked
   d. having experiences

8. When Freud studied patients with anxiety, he determined that their symptoms were caused by
   a. actual childhood abuse, both physical and sexual.
   b. imbalances in body chemistry.
   c. childhood conflicts that had been repressed.
   d. cognitive errors in the way patients viewed the world.

9. What happens to most people who are suffering from serious clinical depression?
   a. They commit suicide.
   b. They are hospitalized.
   c. They receive treatment outside a hospital.
   d. They receive no treatment at all.

10. People lose touch with reality in cases of
    a. neurosis but not psychosis.
    b. psychosis but not neurosis.
    c. both psychosis and neurosis.
    d. all psychoses and some neuroses.

11. When Hans Strupp speaks of the importance of psychological factors in schizophrenia, he specifically cites the role of
    a. feelings of inadequacy.
    b. antisocial personality.
    c. delayed development.
    d. early childhood experiences.

12. Irving Gottesman and Fuller Torrey have been studying twins to learn more about schizophrenia. If the brain of a twin with schizophrenia is compared with the brain of a normal twin, the former has
    a. less cerebrospinal fluid.
    b. larger ventricles.
    c. a larger left hemisphere.
    d. exactly the same configuration as the latter.

13. For Teresa LaFromboise, the major issue in the treatment of mental disorders among Native Americans is
    a. the prevalence of genetic disorders.
    b. alcohol's impact on family structure.
    c. the effect of imposing white American culture.
    d. isolation due to rural settings.

14. According to experts, what proportion of Americans suffer from some form of mental illness?
    a. about one-fifth
    b. less than one in ten thousand
    c. about two-thirds
    d. about one in a thousand

15. Which of the following people would argue that psychopathology is a myth?
    a. Philippe Pinel
    b. Thomas Szasz
    c. Teresa LaFromboise
    d. Sigmund Freud

16. What might a severe viral infection do to a woman who has a genetic predisposition toward schizophrenia?
    a. make her schizophrenic
    b. destroy the genetic marker and make her mentally more stable
    c. redirect the predisposition toward a different class of mental illness
    d. kill her with greater likelihood than if she did not have a predisposition toward mental illness

17. Which of the following has been nicknamed "the common cold of psychopathology" because of its frequency?
    a. phobia
    b. personality disorder
    c. schizophrenia
    d. depression

18. All of the following are typically true about schizophrenia, *except* that
    a. less than one-third improve with treatment.
    b. the people who have it are aware that they are mentally ill.
    c. about 1 percent of the world's total population is schizophrenic.
    d. it is associated with impaired thinking, emotion, and perception.

19. Who is credited as being the first to introduce the idea that insane people are ill?
    a. Sigmund Freud
    b. Jean Charcot
    c. Emil Kraepelin
    d. Philippe Pinel

20. Which of the following is characterized by boundless energy, optimism, and risk-taking behavior?
    a. a manic episode
    b. paranoid schizophrenia
    c. anxiety disorders
    d. depression

QUESTIONS TO CONSIDER

1. If a person is mentally ill and has violated the law, under what circumstances should he or she be considered responsible for the criminal actions? Under what circumstances should we consider the person to be rehabilitatable?

2. Why has the *DSM* been criticized?

3. Is homosexuality a deviant behavior?

4. Are standards for psychological health the same for men and women? Why are most patients women?

5. How can you tell whether your own behavior, anxieties, and moods are within normal limits or whether they signal mental illness?

ACTIVITIES

1. Collect the advice columns in the daily papers for a week or two (such as "Ann Landers" or "Dear Abby"). What kinds of problems do people write about? How often does the columnist refer people to a psychologist, psychiatrist, or other professional for counseling? Why do people write to an anonymous person for advice about their problems?

2. Ask several people (who are not psychology professionals) to define the terms *emotionally ill, mentally ill,* and *insane*. Ask them to describe behaviors that characterize each term. Do some terms indicate more extreme behavior than others? How do their definitions compare with the ones in your text? What can you conclude about the attitudes and understanding of mental illness shown by the people you interviewed?

3. Read through the *DSM-IV-TR* with an eye toward seeing that it is a statistically based manual. The behaviors that define mental illness fall on the same continuum as those that define mental health. Notice whether there are any classifications within the *DSM-IV-TR* for which some of the criteria are a partial match to you.

Discovering Psychology Viewing Guide

Chapter 13: Therapies for Psychological Disorders

Watch the following video by logging onto MyPsychLab (www.mypsychlab.com). After you have watched the video, complete the activities that follow.

PROGRAM 22: PSYCHOTHERAPY

Program 22 looks at psychotherapy and therapists, the professionals trained to help us solve some of our most critical problems. You will learn about different approaches to the treatment of mental, emotional, and behavioral disorders and the kind of helping relationships that therapists provide.

KEY TERMS AND PEOPLE

As you watch the program, pay particular attention to these terms and people in addition to those covered in this textbook.

biological biasing—a genetic predisposition that increases the likelihood of getting a disorder with exposure to prolonged or intense stress.

genetic counseling—counseling that advises a person about the probability of passing on defective genes to offspring.

time-limited dynamic psychotherapy—a form of short-term therapy.

Enrico Jones—investigates which type of treatment is best for which type of problem.

Hans Strupp—psychodynamic therapist.

PROGRAM REVIEW

1. What are the two main approaches to therapies for mental disorders?
   a. the Freudian and the behavioral
   b. the client-centered and the patient-centered
   c. the biomedical and the psychological
   d. the chemical and the psychosomatic

2. The prefrontal lobotomy is a form of psychosurgery. Though no longer widely used, it was at one time used in cases in which a patient
   a. was an agitated schizophrenic.
   b. had committed a violent crime.
   c. showed little emotional response.
   d. had a disease of the thalamus.

3. Leti had electroconvulsive shock therapy a number of years ago. She is now suffering a side effect of that therapy. What is she most likely to be suffering from?
   a. tardive dyskinesia
   b. the loss of her ability to plan ahead
   c. depression
   d. memory loss

4. Vinnie suffers from manic-depressive disorder, but his mood swings are kept under control because he takes the drug
   a. chlorpromazine.
   b. lithium.
   c. Valium.
   d. tetracycline.

5. The Silverman family is receiving genetic counseling because a particular kind of mental retardation runs in their family. What is the purpose of such counseling?
   a. to explain the probability of passing on defective genes
   b. to help eliminate the attitudes of biological biasing

c. to repair specific chromosomes
d. to prescribe drugs that will keep problems from developing

6. In psychodynamic theory, what is the source of mental disorders?
   a. biochemical imbalances in the brain
   b. unresolved conflicts in childhood experiences
   c. the learning and reinforcement of nonproductive behaviors
   d. unreasonable attitudes, false beliefs, and unrealistic expectations

7. Imagine you are observing a therapy session in which a patient is lying on a couch, talking. The therapist is listening and asking occasional questions. What is most likely to be the therapist's goal?
   a. to determine which drug the patient should be given
   b. to change the symptoms that cause distress
   c. to explain how to change false ideas
   d. to help the patient develop insight

8. Rinaldo is a patient in psychotherapy. The therapist asks him to free associate. What would Rinaldo do?
   a. describe a dream
   b. release his feelings
   c. talk about anything that comes to mind
   d. understand the origin of his present guilt feelings

9. According to Hans Strupp, in what major way have psychodynamic therapies changed?
   a. Less emphasis is now placed on the ego.
   b. Patients no longer need to develop a relationship with the therapist.
   c. Shorter courses of treatment can be used.
   d. The concept of aggression has become more important.

10. In the program, a therapist helped a girl learn to control her epileptic seizures. What use did the therapist make of the pen?
    a. to record data
    b. to signal the onset of an attack
    c. to reduce the girl's fear
    d. to reinforce the correct reaction

11. When Albert Ellis discusses with the young woman her fear of hurting others, what point is he making?
    a. It is the belief system that creates the "hurt."
    b. Every normal person strives to achieve fulfillment.
    c. Developing a fear-reduction strategy will reduce the problem.
    d. It is the use of self-fulfilling prophecies that cause others to be hurt.

12. What point does Enrico Jones make about investigating the effectiveness of different therapies in treating depression?
    a. All therapies are equally effective.
    b. It is impossible to assess how effective any one therapy is.
    c. The job is complicated by the different types of depression.
    d. The most important variable is individual versus group therapy.

13. What is the most powerful anti-depressant available for patients who cannot tolerate drugs?
    a. genetic counseling
    b. electro-convulsive therapy
    c. psychoanalysis
    d. family therapy

14. All of the following appear to be true about the relation between depression and genetics, *except* that
    a. depression has been linked to a defect in chromosome #11.
    b. depression appears to cause genetic mutation.
    c. most people who show the genetic marker for depression do not exhibit depressive symptoms.
    d. genetic counseling allows families to plan and make choices based on their risk of mental illness.

15. For which class of mental illness would Chlorpromazine be prescribed?
    a. mood disorder
    b. psychosis
    c. personality disorder
    d. anxiety disorder

16. Which approach to psychotherapy emphasizes developing the ego?
    a. behavioral
    b. desensitization
    c. humanistic
    d. psychodynamic

17. In behavior modification therapies, the goal is to
    a. understand unconscious motivations.
    b. learn to love oneself unconditionally.
    c. change the symptoms of mental illness through reinforcement.
    d. modify the interpretations that one gives to life's events.

18. Which style of therapy has as its primary goal to make the client feel as fulfilled as possible?
    a. humanistic
    b. cognitive-behavioral
    c. Freudian
    d. social learning

19. Which psychologist introduced rational-emotive therapy?
    a. Carl Rogers
    b. Hans Strupp
    c. Albert Ellis
    d. Rollo May

20. Which type of client would be ideal for modern psychoanalytic therapy?
    a. someone who is smart, wealthy, and highly verbal
    b. someone who is reserved and violent
    c. someone who has a good sense of humor but takes herself seriously
    d. someone who grew up under stressful and economically deprived conditions

QUESTIONS TO CONSIDER

1. How do the placebo effect and the spontaneous remission effect make evaluating the success of therapy difficult?

2. Why might it be that behavioral and medical approaches to the same psychological problem can result in similar effects on the brain? Does this imply that in the future, effective behavioral treatments can be developed for cases that had been successful only through medical intervention?

3. How does someone decide on an appropriate therapy?

4. Can everyone benefit from psychotherapy, or do you think it is only for people with serious problems?

5. Why is there a stigma sometimes associated with seeking professional help for psychological problems? What might be some effective ways to change that?

6. Should we have any concerns about an overreliance on or abuse of drug therapies?

7. If you found that you had a specific phobia, would you be willing to undergo exposure therapy?

ACTIVITIES

1. Identify the services and resources available in your community in case you ever need emotional support in a crisis, want to seek therapy, or know someone who needs this information. How much do these services cost? Look for names of accredited professional therapists and counselors, support groups, hotlines, medical and educational services, and in church and community programs. Is it difficult to find information?

2. Do you have any self-defeating expectations? Do you feel that you might benefit from cognitive therapy? Write out statements of positive self-expectations. Then try to use them in situations in which you feel anxious or insecure. Do they have any effect?

3. Run an Internet search with the goal of finding social support groups for various psychological disorders. In what ways do they serve a therapeutic role? How are they helpful, and how might they potentially be counterproductive?

Discovering Psychology Viewing Guide

Chapter 14: Social Psychology

Watch the following videos by logging onto MyPsychLab (www.mypsychlab.com). After you have watched the videos, complete the activities that follow.

PROGRAM 19: THE POWER OF THE SITUATION

Program 19 investigates the social and situational forces that influence our individual and group behavior and how our beliefs can be manipulated by other people.

PROGRAM 20: CONSTRUCTING SOCIAL REALITY

Program 20 explores our subjective view of reality and how it influences social behavior. It reveals how your perceptions and reasoning ability can be influenced in positive and negative ways, and it increases our understanding of how psychological processes govern interpretation of reality.

KEY TERMS AND PEOPLE

As you watch the program, pay particular attention to these terms and people in addition to those covered in this textbook.

Program 19

autocratic—governed by one person with unlimited power.

democratic—practicing social equality.

laissez-faire—allowing complete freedom, with little or no interference or guidance.

legitimate authority—a form of power exercised by someone in a superior role such as a teacher or president.

Program 20

cognitive control—the power of beliefs to give meaning to a situation.

Pygmalion effect—the effect of positive and negative expectations on behavior.

thought-stopping—a technique employed by cults to suppress critical thinking by its members.

Elliot Aronson—helped change the way students saw themselves and others in terms of cooperation and not competition through creating the "Jigsaw classroom" with Alex Gonzalez.

Jane Elliot—conducted an experiment where she induced prejudice in third-graders based on blue-eyed versus brown-eyed children.

Steven Hassan—once a high-ranking member of the Sun Myung Moon Unification Church, he has devoted twenty-five years to understanding and counseling people on the manipulative techniques used by cults to recruit and retain their members.

PROGRAM REVIEW

1. What do social psychologists study?
   a. how people are influenced by other people
   b. how people act in different societies
   c. why some people are more socially successful than others
   d. what happens to isolated individuals

2. What precipitated Kurt Lewin's interest in leadership roles?
   a. the rise of social psychology
   b. the trial of Adolf Eichmann
   c. Hitler's ascent to power
   d. the creation of the United Nations after World War II

3. In Lewin's study, how did the boys behave when they had autocratic leaders?
   a. They had fun but got little accomplished.
   b. They were playful and did motivated, original work.
   c. They were hostile toward each other and got nothing done.
   d. They worked hard but acted aggressively toward each other.

4. In Solomon Asch's experiments, about what percent of participants went along with the group's obviously mistaken judgment at least once?
   a. 70 percent
   b. 50 percent
   c. 30 percent
   d. 90 percent

5. Before Stanley Milgram did his experiments on obedience, experts were asked to predict the results. The experts
   a. overestimated people's willingness to administer shocks.
   b. underestimated people's willingness to administer shocks.
   c. gave accurate estimates of people's behavior.
   d. believed most people would refuse to continue with the experiment.

6. Which light did Milgram's experiment shed on the behavior of citizens in Nazi Germany?
   a. Situational forces can bring about blind obedience.
   b. Personal traits of individuals are most important in determining behavior.
   c. Cultural factors unique to Germany account for the rise of the Nazis.
   d. Human beings enjoy being cruel when they have the opportunity.

7. Which statement most clearly reflects the fundamental attribution error?
   a. Everyone is entitled to good medical care.
   b. Ethical guidelines are essential to conducting responsible research.
   c. People who are unemployed are too lazy to work.
   d. Everyone who reads about the Milgram experiment is shocked by the results.

8. Why did the prison study conducted by Philip Zimbardo and his colleagues have to be called off?
   a. A review committee felt that it violated ethical guidelines.
   b. It consumed too much of the students' time.
   c. The main hypothesis was supported, so there was no need to continue.
   d. The situation that had been created was too dangerous to maintain.

9. How did Tom Moriarity get people on a beach to intervene during a robbery?
   a. by creating a human bond through a simple request
   b. by reminding people of their civic duty to turn in criminals
   c. by making the thief look less threatening
   d. by providing a model of responsible behavior

10. Which leadership style tends to produce hard work when the leader is watching but much less cooperation when the leader is absent?
    a. authoritative
    b. autocratic
    c. democratic
    d. laissez-faire

11. Typically, people who participated in Milgram's study
    a. appeared to relish the opportunity to hurt someone else.
    b. objected but still obeyed.
    c. refused to continue and successfully stopped the experiment.
    d. came to recruit others into shocking the learner.

12. Psychologists refer to the power to create subjective realities as the power of
    a. social reinforcement.
    b. prejudice.
    c. cognitive control.
    d. the Pygmalion effect.

13. When Jane Elliot divided her classroom of third-graders into the inferior brown-eyed people and the superior blue-eyed students, what did she observe?
    a. The students were too young to understand what was expected.
    b. The students refused to behave badly toward their friends and classmates.
    c. The boys tended to go along with the categorization, but the girls did not.
    d. The blue-eyed students acted superior and were cruel to the brown-eyed students, who acted inferior.

14. In the research carried out by Robert Rosenthal and Lenore Jacobson, what caused the performance of some students to improve dramatically?
    a. Teachers were led to expect such improvement and so changed the way they treated these students.
    b. These students performed exceptionally well on a special test designed to predict improved performance.
    c. Teachers gave these students higher grades, because they knew the researchers were expecting the improvement.
    d. The students felt honored to be included in the experiment and so were motivated to improve.

15. Robert Rosenthal demonstrated the Pygmalion effect in the classroom by showing that teachers behave differently toward students for whom they have high expectations in all of the following ways, *except*
    a. by punishing them more for goofing off.
    b. by providing them with a warmer learning climate.
    c. by teaching more to them than to the other students.
    d. by providing more specific feedback when the student gives a wrong answer.

16. What happens to low-achieving students in the Jigsaw Classroom?
    a. They tend to fall further behind.
    b. They are given an opportunity to work at a lower level, thus increasing the chance of success.
    c. By becoming "experts," they improve their performance and their self-respect.
    d. By learning to compete more aggressively, they become more actively involved in their own learning.

17. When Robert Cialdini cites the example of the Hare Krishnas' behavior in giving people at airports a flower or other small gift, he is illustrating the principle of
    a. commitment.
    b. reciprocity.
    c. scarcity.
    d. consensus.

18. Salesmen might make use of the principle of scarcity by
    a. filling shelves up with a product and encouraging consumers to stock up.
    b. claiming they have a hard time ordering the product.
    c. imposing a deadline by which the consumer must make a decision.
    d. being difficult to get in touch with over the phone.

19. Nancy is participating in a bike-a-thon next month and is having a large group of friends over to her house in order to drum up sponsorships for the event. She is capitalizing on the principle of
    a. liking.
    b. consensus.
    c. commitment.
    d. authority.

20. An appropriate motto for the principle of consensus would be
    a. "I've reasoned it through."
    b. "I am doing it of my own free will."
    c. "It will be over quickly."
    d. "Everyone else is doing it."

21. All of the following manipulation techniques were described as being used by cults to maintain control over their members, *except*
    a. sleep deprivation.
    b. suggestive questioning.
    c. thought-stopping.
    d. bribery.

22. Which of the following people would be most likely to advise that you try to understand a cult member by adopting his or her perspective?
    a. Hassan
    b. Festinger
    c. Aronson
    d. Cialdini

QUESTIONS TO CONSIDER

Program 19

1. Some psychologists have suggested that participants in Milgram's research must have suffered guilt and loss of dignity and self-esteem, although they were told later that they hadn't actually harmed the learner. Follow-up studies to the prison experiment revealed that the participants had not suffered long-term ill effects. What psychological principle might explain these outcomes? Did the value of the research outweigh the risks for participants? Was Milgram in a position to weigh the relative value and risks ahead of time? Would you participate in such experiments?

2. In emerging democracies like Iraq, people are faced with freedoms that they previously had not known. When the situation shifts so dramatically and being in a position of submission to power is suddenly removed, what sorts of new risks also emerge?

3. In Zimbardo's prison experiment, students were randomly assigned the role of guard or prisoner. All participants in the study were surprised when the true identities of the guards and prisoners were erased during the course of the experiment. Each of us plays many roles: child, spouse, friend, student, parent, boss, employee, citizen, consumer, sibling. Do you feel that any of the roles you play conflict with your "true identity"? How do you know what your true identity is?

4. Think about your own experiences in school, at work, and in group situations. Consider which factors bring out the best and worst in you. Recall and compare examples of how teachers, bosses, or leaders brought out positive and negative aspects of your personality.

5. What is the difference between respect for authority and blind obedience? How do you tell the difference? How would you explain the difference to a child?

6. Imagine that you are on vacation in New York City and that you have dropped your keys in the pond in Central Park. What could you do to counteract people's tendency toward diffusion of responsibility? Using what you know about social psychology, how might you increase the odds of actually getting people to help you?

Program 20

7. How can personal factors interact with social influences to affect behavior?

8. How is nationalism used to structure social reality? Does this become a more powerful force for people's attitudes and interaction during times of actual war or cold war than it is during times of peace? How might it be affected by phenomena like globalized economics and common languages across borders?

9. What do dissonance reduction, the self-serving bias, and the defense mechanism of rationalization all have in common?

10. How do programs on television construct a distorted reality for children? Has this problem gotten better or worse with the introduction of "reality TV"?

11. Many of the socially undesirable aspects of human behavior (e.g., violent crime, rudeness, apathy) seem to be more likely in urban than in suburban or rural environments. How can social psychology help to explain this phenomenon?

ACTIVITIES

Program 19

1. Architects and interior designers use specific elements—furnishings, lighting, color, seating arrangements—to encourage certain behaviors and to discourage others. Compare the comfort level of chairs in various public places. Which chairs are designed to encourage lingering or to discourage loitering? What types of people use the spaces? What physical changes would influence who uses the space and how they behave there?

2. Norms of social behavior include "social distances" that we place between ourselves and friends, acquaintances, and strangers. Observe and compare the social distance you maintain between yourself and family members, friends, and strangers. Purposely change how close to them you would normally stand. Observe their responses. Does anyone mention it? Do others adjust their positions to achieve normal distances?

3. Observe the interactions of several different kinds of pairs of people: for example, a boss speaking with an employee, a minister speaking with a church member, a customer speaking with a clerk, or two close friends speaking with each other. Compare how those conversations differ (e.g., in terms of how often each has the floor, how often polite requests vs. direct requests are made, and how often each looks the other directly in the eye or physically touches the other person). If you can, observe the same person in many different kinds of situations in which he or she does nor does not have the more powerful position. How does the person's behavior differ?

Program 20

4. Look for editorials, news stories, or political cartoons that portray an international situation. Which words, labels, and images promote "us versus them" thinking? How might someone with opposite views have written the articles or drawn the cartoons differently? Do you find that the tendency to present an "us versus them" view changes over time or that it differs across cultures?

5. Think of norms of proper dress or social behavior that you can violate. For example, what would happen if you wore shorts to a formal gathering? Or asked a stranger an extremely personal question? Or arrived at work in your bedroom slippers? Pay attention to your feelings as you think about carrying out these activities. What fears or inhibitions do you have? How likely is it that you could actually carry out these activities?

6. How are more modern attitudes toward education, such as Montessori-style education, similar to Lewin's democratic leaders? What sorts of outcomes, in school, in the home, and in the children's future social interactions, would you expect from such a teaching style?

Glossary

Absent-mindedness Forgetting caused by lapses in attention.

Absolute threshold The amount of stimulation necessary for a stimulus to be detected. In practice, this means that the presence or absence of a stimulus is detected correctly half the time over many trials.

Acceptance Patient realized death is inevitable and accepts fate.

Accommodation A mental process that restructures existing schemes so that new information is better understood.

Acoustic encoding The conversion of information, especially semantic information, to sound patterns in working memory.

Acquisition The initial learning stage in classical conditioning, during which the conditioned response comes to be elicited by the conditioned stimulus.

Action potential The nerve impulse caused by a change in the electrical charge across the cell membrane of the axon. When the neuron "fires," this charge travels down the axon and causes neurotransmitters to be released by the terminal buttons.

Activation-synthesis theory The theory that dreams begin with random electrical *activation* coming from the brain stem. Dreams, then, are the brain's attempt to make sense of—to *synthesize*—this random activity.

Active listener A person who gives the speaker feedback in such forms as nodding, paraphrasing, maintaining an expression that shows interest, and asking questions for clarification.

Acute stress A temporary pattern of stressor-activated arousal with a distinct onset and limited duration.

Addiction A condition in which a person continues to use a drug despite its adverse effects—often despite repeated attempts to discontinue using the drug. Addiction may be based on physical or psychological dependence.

Adolescence In industrial societies, a developmental period beginning at puberty and ending (less clearly) at adulthood.

Affect A term referring to emotion or mood.

Afterimages Sensations that linger after the stimulus is removed. Most visual afterimages are *negative afterimages,* which appear in reversed colors.

Agonist Drug or other chemical that enhances or mimics the effects of neurotransmitters.

Agoraphobia A fear of public places and open spaces, commonly accompanying panic disorder.

Alarm reaction First stage of the GAS, during which the body mobilizes its resources to cope with a stressor.

Algorithms Problem-solving procedures or formulas that guarantee a correct outcome, if correctly applied.

All-or-none principle Refers to the fact that the action potential in the axon occurs either full-blown or not at all.

Alzheimer's disease A degenerative brain disease usually noticed first by its debilitating effects on memory.

Ambiguous figures Images that are capable of more than one interpretation. There is no "right" way to see an ambiguous figure.

Amplitude The physical strength of a wave. This is usually measured from peak (top) to valley (bottom) on a graph of the wave.

Amygdala A limbic system structure involved in memory and emotion, particularly fear and aggression. Pronounced *a-MIG-da-la.*

Analysis of transference The Freudian technique of analyzing and interpreting the patient's relationship with the therapist, based on the assumption that this relationship mirrors unresolved conflicts in the patient's past.

Analytical intelligence According to Sternberg, the ability measured by most IQ tests; includes the ability to analyze problems and find correct answers.

Anchoring bias A faulty heuristic caused by basing (anchoring) an estimate on a completely unrelated quantity.

Anger Patient displays anger that they are sick, "why me!"

Animistic thinking A preoperational mode of thought in which inanimate objects are imagined to have life and mental processes.

Anorexia nervosa An eating disorder that involves persistent loss of appetite that endangers an individual's health and stems from emotional or psychological reasons rather than from organic causes.

Antagonist Drug or other chemical that inhibits the effects of neurotransmitters.

Anterograde amnesia The inability to form memories for new information (as opposed to retrograde amnesia, which involves the inability to remember information previously stored in memory).

Antianxiety drugs A category of drugs that includes the barbiturates and benzodiazepines, drugs that diminish feelings of anxiety.

Antidepressant drugs Medicines that affect depression, usually by their effect on the serotonin and/or norepinephrine pathways in the brain.

Antipsychotic drugs Medicines that diminish psychotic symptoms, usually by their effect on the dopamine pathways in the brain.
Antisocial personality disorder Characterized by a long-standing pattern of irresponsible behavior indicating a lack of conscience and a diminished sense of responsibility to others.
Anxiety disorders Mental problems characterized mainly by anxiety. Anxiety disorders include panic disorder, specific phobias, and obsessive–compulsive disorder.
Applied psychologists Psychologists who use the knowledge developed by experimental psychologists to solve human problems.
Approach–approach conflict A conflict in which one must choose between two equally attractive options.
Approach–avoidance conflict A conflict in which there are both appealing and negative aspects to a possible course of action.
Aptitudes Innate potentialities (as contrasted with abilities acquired by learning).
Archetypes The ancient memory images in the collective unconscious. Archetypes appear and reappear in art, literature, and folktales around the world.
Artificial concepts Concepts defined by rules, such as word definitions and mathematical formulas.
Asch effect A form of conformity in which a group majority influences individual judgments.
Assimilation A mental process that modifies new information to fit it into existing schemes.
Association cortex Cortical regions throughout the brain that combine information from various other parts of the brain.
Attachment The enduring social-emotional relationship between a child and a parent or other regular caregiver.
Attention-deficit hyperactivity disorder (ADHD) A developmental disability involving short attention span, distractibility, and extreme difficulty in remaining inactive for any period; a common problem in children who have difficulty controlling their behavior and focusing their attention.
Autism A developmental disorder marked by disabilities in language, social interaction, and the ability to understand another person's state of mind.
Autonomic nervous system The portion of the peripheral nervous system that sends communications between the central nervous system and the internal organs and glands.
Availability bias A faulty heuristic strategy that estimates probabilities based on information that can be recalled (made available) from personal experience.
Aversion therapy As a classical conditioning procedure, aversive counterconditioning involves presenting individuals with an attractive stimulus paired with unpleasant (aversive) stimulation in order to condition revulsion.
Avoidance–avoidance conflict A conflict in which one must choose between options that have both many attractive and many negative aspects.
Axon In a nerve cell, an extended fiber that conducts information from the *soma* to the *terminal buttons.* Information travels along the axon in the form of an electric charge, called the *action potential.*
Bargaining Making a deal, in return for a cure, they will fulfill promises.
Basic anxiety An emotion, proposed by Karen Horney, that gives a sense of uncertainty and loneliness in a hostile world and can lead to maladjustment.
Basilar membrane A thin strip of tissue sensitive to vibrations in the cochlea. The basilar membrane contains hair cells connected to neurons. When a sound wave causes the hair cells to vibrate, the associated neurons become excited. As a result, the sound waves are converted (transduced) into nerve activity.
Behavior modification Another term for behavior therapy.
Behavior therapy Any form of psychotherapy based on the principles of behavioral learning, especially operant conditioning and classical conditioning.
Behavioral learning Forms of learning, such as classical conditioning and operant conditioning, that can be described in terms of stimuli and responses.
Behavioral view A psychological perspective that finds the source of our actions in environmental stimuli, rather than in inner mental processes.
Behaviorism A historical school (as well as a modern perspective) that has sought to make psychology an objective science that focused only on behavior—to the exclusion of mental processes.
Binding problem Refers to the process used by the brain to combine (or "bind") the results of many sensory operations into a single percept. This occurs, for example, when sensations of color, shape, boundary, and texture are combined to produce the percept of a person's face. No one knows exactly how the brain does this. Thus the binding problem is one of the major unsolved mysteries in psychology.
Binocular cues Information taken in by both eyes that aids in depth perception, including binocular convergence and retinal disparity.
Biological view The psychological perspective that searches for the causes of behavior in the functioning of genes, the brain and nervous system, and the endocrine (hormone) system.
Biomedical therapies Treatments that focus on altering the brain, especially with drugs, psychosurgery, or electroconvulsive therapy.
Biopsychology The specialty in psychology that studies the interaction of biology, behavior, and mental processes.
Bipolar disorder A mental abnormality involving swings of mood from mania to depression.
Blind spot The point where the optic nerve exits the eye and where there are no photoreceptors. Any stimulus that falls on this area cannot be seen.
Blocking Forgetting that occurs when an item in memory cannot be accessed or retrieved. Blocking is caused by *interference.*
Borderline personality disorder An unstable personality given to impulsive behavior.
Bottom-up processing Perceptual analysis that emphasizes characteristics of the stimulus, rather than our concepts and expectations. "Bottom" refers to the stimulus, which occurs at the first step of perceptual processing.
Brain stem The most primitive of the brain's three major layers. It includes the medulla, pons, and the reticular formation.
Brightness A psychological sensation caused by the intensity of light waves.
Bulimia nervosa An eating disorder characterized by eating binges followed by "purges" induced by vomiting or laxatives; typically initiated as a weight-control measure.
Cannon–Bard theory The counterproposal that an emotional feeling and an internal physiological response occur at the same time: One is not the cause of the other. Both were believed to be the result of cognitive appraisal of the situation.
Cardinal traits personality components that define people's lives; very few individuals have cardinal traits.
Cataplexy Sudden loss of muscle control.
Central nervous system The brain and the spinal cord.
Central traits According to trait theory, traits that form the basis of personality.
Centration A preoperational thought pattern involving the inability to take into account more than one factor at a time.
Cerebellum The "little brain" attached to the brain stem. The cerebellum is responsible for coordinated movements.
Cerebral cortex The thin gray-matter covering of the cerebral hemispheres, consisting of a 1⁄4-inch layer dense with cell bodies of neurons. The cerebral cortex carries on the major portion of our "higher" mental processing, including thinking and perceiving.
Cerebral dominance The tendency of each brain hemisphere to exert control over different functions, such as language or perception of spatial relationships.
Chromosome Tightly coiled threadlike structure along which the genes are organized, like beads on a necklace. Chromosomes consist primarily of DNA.
Chronic stress Continuous stressful arousal persisting over time.
Chronological age (CA) The number of years since the individual's birth.
Chunking Organizing pieces of information into a smaller number of meaningful units (or chunks)—a process that frees up space in working memory.
Circadian rhythms Physiological patterns that repeat approximately every 24 hours, such as the sleep–wakefulness cycle.

Classical conditioning A form of behavioral learning in which a previously neutral stimulus acquires the power to elicit the same innate reflex produced by another stimulus.

Client-centered therapy A humanistic approach to treatment developed by Carl Rogers, emphasizing an individual's tendency for healthy psychological growth through self-actualization.

Clinical view The psychological perspective emphasizing mental health and mental illness. Psychodynamic and humanistic psychology are variations on the clinical view.

Closure The Gestalt principle that identifies the tendency to fill in gaps in figures and to see incomplete figures as complete.

Cochlea The primary organ of hearing; a coiled tube in the inner ear, where sound waves are transduced into nerve messages.

Cognitions Mental processes, such as thinking, memory, sensation, and perception.

Cognitive appraisal theory An individual makes a conscious decision as to how one should feel about an event after it has occurred.

Cognitive–behavioral therapy A newer form of psychotherapy that combines the techniques of cognitive therapy with those of behavior therapy.

Cognitive dissonance A highly motivating state in which people have conflicting cognitions, especially when their voluntary actions conflict with their attitudes.

Cognitive map A mental representation of physical space.

Cognitive neuroscience An interdisciplinary field emphasizing brain activity as information processing; involves cognitive psychology, neurology, biology, computer science, linguistics, and specialists from other fields who are interested in the connection between mental processes and the brain.

Cognitive therapy Emphasizes rational thinking (as opposed to subjective emotion, motivation, or repressed conflicts) as the key to treating mental disorder.

Cognitive view The psychological perspective emphasizing mental processes, such as learning, memory, perception, and thinking, as forms of information processing.

Cohesiveness The force that pulls group members together and keeps them as a unit.

Cohort-sequential study A research method in which a cross section of the population is chosen and then each cohort is followed for a short period of time.

Collective unconscious Jung's addition to the unconscious, involving a reservoir for instinctive "memories," including the archetypes, which exist in all people.

Collectivism The view, common in Asia, Africa, Latin America, and the Middle East, that values group loyalty and pride over individual distinction.

Color Also called *hue.* Color is *not* a property of things in the external world. Rather, it is a *psychological sensation* created in the brain from information obtained by the eyes from the wavelengths of visible light.

Color blindness Typically a genetic disorder (although sometimes the result of trauma, as in the case of Jonathan) that prevents an individual from discriminating certain colors. The most common form is red–green color blindness.

Community mental health movement An effort to deinstitutionalize mental patients and to provide therapy from outpatient clinics. Proponents of community mental health envisioned that recovering patients could live with their families, in foster homes, or in group homes.

Compensation Making up for one's real or imagined deficiencies.

Computer metaphor The idea that the brain is an information-processing organ that operates in some ways, like a computer.

Concept hierarchies Levels of concepts, from most general to most specific, in which a more general level includes more specific concepts—as the concept of "animal" includes "dog," "giraffe," and "butterfly."

Concepts Mental representations of categories of items or ideas, based on experience.

Concrete operational stage The third of Piaget's stages, when a child understands conservation but still is incapable of abstract thought.

Conditioned reinforcers or **secondary reinforcers** Stimuli, such as money or tokens, that acquire their reinforcing power by a learned association with primary reinforcers.

Conditioned response (CR) In classical conditioning, a response elicited by a previously neutral stimulus that has become associated with the unconditioned stimulus.

Conditioned stimulus (CS) In classical conditioning, a previously neutral stimulus that comes to elicit the conditioned response. Customarily, in a conditioning experiment, the neutral stimulus is called a conditioned stimulus when it is first paired with an unconditioned stimulus (UCS).

Conduction deafness An inability to hear resulting from damage to structures of the middle or inner ear.

Cones Photoreceptors in the retina that are especially sensitive to colors but not to dim light. You may have guessed that the cones are cone-shaped.

Confirmation bias The tendency to attend to evidence that complements and confirms our beliefs or expectations, while ignoring evidence that does not.

Conformity The tendency for people to adopt the behaviors, attitudes, and opinions of other members of a group.

Confounding or **extraneous variables** Variables that have an unwanted influence on the outcome of an experiment.

Conscious motivation Having the desire to engage in an activity and being aware of the desire.

Consciousness The process by which the brain creates a model of internal and external experience.

Conservation The understanding that the physical properties of an object or substance do not change when appearances change but nothing is added or taken away.

Consolidation The process by which short-term memories are changed to long-term memories over a period of time.

Contact comfort Stimulation and reassurance derived from the physical touch of a caregiver.

Content validity A property exhibited by a test in which each item is representative of the larger body of knowledge about the subject that the test covers.

Contingency management An operant conditioning approach to changing behavior by altering the consequences, especially rewards and punishments, of behavior.

Continuity view The perspective that development is gradual and continuous—as opposed to the discontinuity (stage) view.

Continuous reinforcement A type of reinforcement schedule by which all correct responses are reinforced.

Controls Constraints that the experimenter places on the experiment to ensure that each subject has the exact same conditions.

Conversion disorder A type of somatoform disorder, marked by paralysis, weakness, or loss of sensation but with no discernible physical cause.

Corpus callosum The band of nerve cells that connects the two cerebral hemispheres.

Correlation A relationship between variables, in which changes in one variable are reflected in changes in the other variable—as in the correlation between a child's age and height.

Correlation coefficient A number between –1 and +1 expressing the degree of relationship between two variables.

Correlational study A type of research that is mainly statistical in nature. Correlational studies determine the relationship (or correlation) between two variables.

Creative intelligence According to Sternberg, the form of intelligence that helps people see new relationships among concepts; involves insight and creativity.

Creativity A mental process that produces novel responses that contribute to the solutions of problems.

Criterion validity A property exhibited by a test that accurately measures performance of the test taker against a specific learning goal.

Cross-sectional study A study in which a representative cross section of the population is tested or surveyed at one specific time.

Crystallized intelligence The knowledge a person has acquired, plus the ability to access that knowledge.

CT scanning or **computerized tomography** A computerized imaging technique that uses X rays passed through the brain at various angles and then combined into an image.

Culture A complex blend of language, beliefs, customs, values, and traditions developed by a group of people and shared with others in the same environment.

Cytokines Hormonelike chemicals facilitating communication between brain and immune system.

Data Pieces of information, especially information gathered by a researcher to be used in testing a hypothesis. (Singular: *datum*.)

Daydreaming A common (and quite normal) variation of consciousness in which attention shifts to memories, expectations, desires, or fantasies and away from the immediate situation.

Declarative memory A division of LTM that stores explicit information; also known as fact memory. Declarative memory has two subdivisions: episodic memory and semantic memory.

Deindividuation Occurs when group members lose their sense of personal identity and responsibility and the group "assumes" responsibility for their behavior.

Deinstitutionalization The policy of removing patients, whenever possible, from mental hospitals.

Delusions Extreme disorders of thinking, involving persistent false beliefs. Delusions are the hallmark of paranoid disorders.

Dendrite A branched fiber that extends outward from the main cell body and carries information into the neuron.

Denial Refusing to believe the individual is sick.

Dependent variable (DV) The measured outcome of a study; the responses of the subjects in a study.

Depersonalization disorder An abnormality involving the sensation that mind and body have separated, as in an "out-of-body" experience.

Depressants Drugs that slow down mental and physical activity by inhibiting transmission of nerve impulses in the central nervous system.

Depression Generally depressed affect includes sleep, loss of appetite, etc.

Descriptive statistics Statistical procedures used to describe characteristics and responses of groups of subjects.

Developmental psychology The psychological specialty that studies how organisms change over time as the result of biological and environmental influences.

Developmental stages Periods of life initiated by significant transitions or changes in physical or psychological functioning.

Developmental view The psychological perspective emphasizing changes that occur across the lifespan.

Diathesis–stress hypothesis In reference to schizophrenia, the proposal that says that genetic factors place the individual at risk while environmental stress factors transform this potential into an actual schizophrenic disorder.

Difference threshold The smallest amount by which a stimulus can be changed and the difference be detected half the time.

Diffusion of responsibility Dilution or weakening of each group member's obligation to act when responsibility is perceived to be shared with all group members.

Discontinuity view The perspective that development proceeds in an uneven (discontinuous) fashion—as opposed to the continuity view.

Discrimination A negative action taken against an individual as a result of his or her group membership.

Display rules The permissible ways of displaying emotions in a particular society.

Dissociative amnesia A psychologically induced loss of memory for personal information, such as one's identity or residence.

Dissociative disorders A group of pathologies involving "fragmentation" of the personality, in which some parts of the personality have become detached, or dissociated, from other parts.

Dissociative fugue Essentially the same as dissociative amnesia, but with the addition of flight from one's home, family, and job. *Fugue* (pronounced *FEWG*) means "flight."

Dissociative identity disorder A condition in which an individual displays multiple identities, or personalities; formerly called "multiple personality disorder."

Distributed learning A technique whereby the learner spaces learning sessions over time, rather than trying to learn the material all in one study period.

DNA A long, complex molecule that encodes genetic characteristics. DNA is an abbreviation for deoxyribonucleic acid.

Double-blind study An experimental procedure in which both researchers and participants are uninformed about the nature of the independent variable being administered.

Drive Biologically instigated motivation.

DSM-IV The fourth edition of the *Diagnostic and Statistical Manual of Mental Disorders,* published by the American Psychiatric Association; the most widely accepted psychiatric classification system in the United States.

Dyslexia A reading disability, thought by some experts to involve a brain disorder.

Eclectic Either switching theories to explain different situations or building one's own theory of personality from pieces borrowed from many perspectives.

Ego The conscious, rational part of the personality, charged with keeping peace between the superego and the id.

Ego defense mechanisms Largely unconscious mental strategies employed to reduce the experience of conflict or anxiety.

Egocentrism In Piaget's theory, the self-centered inability to realize that there are other viewpoints beside one's own.

Eidetic imagery An especially clear and persistent form of memory that is quite rare; sometimes known as "photographic memory."

Elaborative rehearsal A working-memory process in which information is actively reviewed and related to information already in LTM.

Electroconvulsive therapy (ECT) A treatment used primarily for depression and involving the application of an electric current to the head, producing a generalized seizure. Sometimes called "shock treatment."

Electroencephalograph or **EEG** A device for recording brain waves, typically by electrodes placed on the scalp. The record produced is known as an electroencephalogram (also called an EEG).

Electromagnetic spectrum The entire range of electromagnetic energy, including radio waves, X rays, microwaves, and visible light.

Embryo In humans, the name for the developing organism during the first eight weeks after conception.

Emotion A four-part process that involves physiological arousal, subjective feelings, cognitive interpretation, and behavioral expression—all of which *interact,* rather than occurring in a linear sequence. Emotions help organisms deal with important events.

Emotional intelligence The ability to understand and control emotional responses.

Empirical approach A study conducted via careful observations and scientifically based research.

Empirical investigation An approach to research that relies on sensory experience and observation as research data.

Encoding One of the three basic tasks of memory, involving the modification of information to fit the preferred format for the memory system.

Encoding specificity principle The doctrine that memory is encoded and stored with specific cues related to the context in which it was formed. The more closely the retrieval cues match the form in which the information was encoded, the better it will be remembered.

Endocrine system The hormone system—the body's chemical messenger system, including the endocrine glands: pituitary, thyroid, parathyroid, adrenals, pancreas, ovaries, and testes.

Engram The physical changes in the brain associated with a memory. It is also known as the *memory trace.*

Episodic memory A subdivision of declarative memory that stores memory for personal events, or "episodes."

Eugenics A philosophy and a political movement that encouraged biologically superior people to interbreed and sought to discourage biologically inferior people from having offspring.

Event-related potentials Brain waves shown on the EEG in response to stimulation.

Evolution The gradual process of biological change that occurs in a species as it adapts to its environment.

Evolutionary psychology A relatively new specialty in psychology that sees behavior and mental processes in terms of their genetic adaptations for survival and reproduction.
Expectancy bias The researcher allowing his or her expectations to affect the outcome of a study; or, in memory, a tendency to distort recalled events to make them fit one's expectations.
Expectancy-value theory A theory in social psychology that people decide whether to pursue a relationship by weighing the potential value of the relationship against their expectation of success in establishing the relationship.
Experiment A kind of research in which the researcher controls all the conditions and directly manipulates the conditions, including the independent variable.
Experimental neurosis A pattern of erratic behavior resulting from a demanding discrimination learning task, typically one that involves aversive stimuli.
Experimental psychologists Psychologists who do research on basic psychological processes—as contrasted with applied psychologists; also called *research psychologists.*
Explicit memory Memory that has been processed with attention and can be consciously recalled.
Ex post facto Research in which we choose subjects based on a pre-existing condition.
Exposure therapy A form of desensitization therapy in which the patient directly confronts the anxiety-provoking stimulus (as opposed to imagining the stimulus).
Extinction (in classical conditioning) The weakening of a conditioned response in the absence of an unconditioned stimulus.
Extinction (in operant conditioning) A process by which a response that has been learned is weakened by the absence or removal of reinforcement. (Compare with *extinction in classical conditioning.*)
Extraversion The Jungian personality dimension involving turning one's attention outward, toward others; a personality descriptor indicating the "outgoing" nature of some individuals.
Extrinsic motivation The desire to engage in an activity to achieve an external consequence, such as a reward.
Face validity Measures whether a test looks like it tests what it is supposed to test.
Feature detectors Cells in the cortex that specialize in extracting certain features of a stimulus.
Fechner's Law The magnitude of a stimulus can be estimated by the formula $S = k \log R$, where S = sensation, R = stimulus, and k = a constant that differs for each sensory modality (sight, touch, temperature, etc.).
Fetus In humans, the term for the developing organism between the embryonic stage and birth.
Fight-or-flight response Sequence of internal processes preparing an organism for struggle or escape.
Figure The part of a pattern that commands attention. The figure stands out against the ground.
Five-factor theory A trait perspective suggesting that personality is composed of five fundamental personality dimensions: openness to experience, conscientiousness, extraversion, agreeableness, and neuroticism.
Fixation Occurs when psychosexual development is arrested at an immature stage.
Fixed-action patterns Genetically based behaviors, seen across a species, that can be set off by a specific stimulus. The concept of fixed-action patterns has replaced the older notion of instinct.
Fixed interval (FI) schedules Programs by which reinforcement is contingent on a certain, fixed time period.
Fixed ratio (FR) schedules Programs by which reinforcement is contingent on a certain, unvarying number of responses.
Flashbulb memory A clear and vivid long-term memory of an especially meaningful and emotional event.
Fluid intelligence The ability to see complex relationships and solve problems.
fMRI or **functional magnetic resonance imaging** fMRI enables us to see the brain actually working, or *in vivo* (Parry & Matthews, 2002).
Forgetting curve A graph plotting the amount of retention and forgetting over time for a certain batch of material, such as a list of nonsense syllables. The typical forgetting curve is steep at first, becoming flatter as time goes on.
Formal operational stage The last of Piaget's stages, during which abstract thought appears.
Fovea The tiny area of sharpest vision in the retina.
Fraternal twins A pair who started life as two separate fertilized eggs that happened to share the same womb. Fraternal twins, on the average, have about 50% of their genetic material in common.
Frequency The number of cycles completed by a wave in a given amount of time, usually a second.
Frequency distribution A summary chart, showing how frequently each of the scores in a set of data occurs.
Frontal lobes Cortical regions at the front of the brain that are especially involved in movement and in thinking.
Fully functioning person Carl Rogers's term for a healthy, self-actualizing individual, who has a self-concept that is both positive and congruent with reality.
Functional fixedness The inability to perceive a new use for an object associated with a different purpose; a form of mental set.
Functionalism A historical school of psychology that believed mental processes could best be understood in terms of their adaptive purpose and function.
Fundamental attribution error (FAE) The assumption that another person's behavior, especially clumsy, inappropriate, or otherwise undesirable behavior, is the result of a flaw in the personality, rather than in the situation; the tendency to emphasize internal causes and ignore external pressures. The FAE is more common in individualistic cultures than in collectivistic cultures.
***g* factor** A general ability, proposed by Spearman as the main factor underlying all intelligent mental activity.
Gate-control theory An explanation for pain control that proposes we have a neural "gate" that can, under some circumstances, block incoming pain signals.
Gene Segment of a chromosome that encodes the directions for the inherited physical and mental characteristics of an organism. Genes are the functional units of a chromosome.
General adaptation syndrome (GAS) Pattern of general physical responses that take essentially the same form in responding to any serious chronic stressor.
Generalized anxiety disorder A psychological problem characterized by persistent and pervasive feelings of anxiety, without any external cause.
Generativity In Erikson's theory, a process of making a commitment beyond oneself to family, work, society, or future generations.
Genotype An organism's genetic makeup.
Gestalt psychology A historical school of psychology that sought to understand how the brain works by studying perception and perceptual learning. Gestalt psychologists believed that percepts consist of meaningful wholes (in German, *Gestalts*).
Gestalt psychology From a German word (pronounced *gush-TAWLT*) that means "whole" or "form" or "configuration." (A Gestalt is also a *percept.*) The Gestalt psychologists believed that much of perception is shaped by innate factors built into the brain.
Giftedness Often conceived as representing the upper 2% of the IQ range, commencing about 30 points above average (at about 130 IQ points).
Glial cells Cells that bind the neurons together. Glial cells also provide an insulating covering (the myelin sheath) of the axon for some neurons, which facilitates the electrical impulse.
Grammar The rules of a language, specifying how to use words, morphemes, and syntax to produce understandable sentences.
Ground The part of a pattern that does not command attention; the background.
Group polarization When individuals in a group have similar, though not identical, views, their opinions become more extreme.
Group therapy Any form of psychotherapy done with more than one client/patient at a time. Group therapy is often done from a humanistic perspective.
Groupthink An excessive tendency to seek concurrence among group members.
Gustation The sense of taste—from the same word root as "gusto"—also called the *gustatory sense.*

Habituation Learning not to respond to the repeated presentation of a stimulus.

Hallucinations False sensory experiences that may suggest mental disorder. Hallucinations can have other causes, such as drugs or sensory isolation.

Hallucinogens Drugs that create hallucinations or alter perceptions of the external environment and inner awareness.

Heritability The amount of trait variation within a group, raised under the same conditions, that can be attributed to genetic differences. Heritability tells us nothing about between-group differences.

Heuristics Cognitive strategies or "rules of thumb" used as shortcuts to solve complex mental tasks. Unlike algorithms, heuristics do not guarantee a correct solution.

Hierarchy of needs In Maslow's theory, the notion that needs occur in priority order, with the biological needs as the most basic.

Hindsight bias The tendency, after learning about an event, to "second guess" or believe that one could have predicted the event in advance.

Hippocampus A component of the limbic system, involved in establishing long-term memories.

Histogram A bar graph depicting a frequency distribution. The height of the bars indicates the frequency of a group of scores.

Homeostasis The body's tendency to maintain a biologically balanced condition, especially with regard to nutrients, water, and temperature.

Hormone A chemical messenger used by the endocrine system. Many hormones also serve as neurotransmitters.

Humanistic psychology A clinical viewpoint emphasizing human ability, growth, potential, and free will.

Humanistic therapies Treatment techniques based on the assumption that people have a tendency for positive growth and self-actualization, which may be blocked by an unhealthy environment that can include negative self-evaluation and criticism from others.

Humors Four body fluids—blood, phlegm, black bile, and yellow bile—that, according to an ancient theory, control personality by their relative abundance.

Hypnosis An induced state of awareness, usually characterized by heightened suggestibility, deep relaxation, and highly focused attention.

Hypochondriasis A somatoform disorder involving excessive concern about health and disease; also called *hypochondria*.

Hypothalamus A limbic structure that serves as the brain's blood-testing laboratory, constantly monitoring the blood to determine the condition of the body.

Hypothesis A statement predicting the outcome of a scientific study; a statement describing the relationship among variables in a study.

Id The primitive, unconscious portion of the personality that houses the most basic drives and stores repressed memories.

Identical twins A pair who started life as a single fertilized egg, which later split into two distinct individuals. Identical twins have exactly the same genes.

Identification The mental process by which an individual tries to become like another person, especially the same-sex parent.

Illusion You have experienced an illusion when you have a demonstrably incorrect perception of a stimulus pattern, especially one that also fools others who are observing the same stimulus. (If no one else sees it the way you do, you could be having a *delusion* or a *hallucination*. We'll take those terms up in a later chapter on mental disorder.)

Immune system Bodily organs and responses that protect the body from foreign substances and threats.

Implicit memory A memory that was not deliberately learned or of which you have no conscious awareness.

Implicit personality theory Assumptions about personality that are held by people (especially nonpsychologists) to simplify the task of understanding others.

Imprinting A primitive form of learning in which some young animals follow and form an attachment to the first moving object they see and hear.

In-group The group with which an individual identifies.

Independent variable (IV) A stimulus condition so named because the experimenter changes it independently of all the other carefully controlled experimental conditions.

Individualism The view, common in the Euro-American world, that places a high value on individual achievement and distinction.

Infancy In humans, infancy spans the time between the end of the neonatal period and the establishment of language—usually at about 18 months to 2 years.

Inferential statistics Statistical techniques (based on probability theory) used to assess whether the results of a study are reliable or whether they might be simply the result of chance. Inferential statistics are often used to determine whether two or more groups are essentially the same or different.

Inferiority complex A feeling of inferiority that is largely unconscious, with its roots in childhood.

Information-processing model A cognitive understanding of memory, emphasizing how information is changed when it is encoded, stored, and retrieved.

Insanity A legal term, not a psychological or psychiatric one, referring to a person who is unable, because of a mental disorder or defect, to conform his or her behavior to the law.

Insight learning A form of cognitive learning, originally described by the Gestalt psychologists, in which problem solving occurs by means of a sudden reorganization of perceptions.

Insight therapies Psychotherapies in which the therapist helps patients/clients understand (gain insight into) their problems.

Insomnia The most common of sleep disorders—involving insufficient sleep, the inability to fall asleep quickly, frequent arousals, or early awakenings.

Instinct theory The now-outmoded view that certain behaviors are completely determined by innate factors. The instinct theory was flawed because it overlooked the effects of learning and because it employed instincts merely as labels, rather than as explanations for behavior.

Institutional Animal Care and Use Committee (IACUC) A committee at each institution where research is conducted to review every experiment *involving animals* for ethics and methodology.

Institutional Review Board (IRB) A committee at each institution where research is conducted to review every experiment for ethics and methodology.

Intelligence quotient (IQ) A numerical score on an intelligence test, originally computed by dividing the person's mental age by chronological age and multiplying by 100.

Interaction A process by which forces work together or influence each other—as in the interaction between the forces of heredity and environment.

Intermittent reinforcement A type of reinforcement schedule by which some, but not all, correct responses are reinforced; also called *partial reinforcement*.

Interneuron A nerve cell that relays messages between nerve cells, especially in the brain and spinal cord.

Inter-rater reliability A measure of how similarly two different test scorers would score a test.

Interval schedule A program by which reinforcement depends on the time interval elapsed since the last reinforcement.

Intrinsic motivation The desire to engage in an activity for its own sake, rather than for some external consequence, such as a reward.

Introspection The process of reporting on one's own conscious mental experiences.

Introversion The Jungian dimension that focuses on inner experience—one's own thoughts and feelings—making the introvert less outgoing and sociable than the extravert; a personality descriptor indicating the quiet and reserved nature of some individuals.

Inverted U function Describes the relationship between arousal and performance. Both low and high levels of arousal produce lower performance than a moderate level of arousal.

Irreversibility The inability, in the preoperational child, to think through a series of events or mental operations and then mentally reverse the steps.

Item analysis The process of examining each question on a test to see how it is related to the objectives being tested.

James–Lange theory The proposal that an emotion-provoking stimulus produces a physical response that, in turn, produces an emotion.

Just noticeable difference (JND) Same as the difference threshold.

Kinesthetic sense The sense of body position and movement of body parts relative to each other (also called *kinesthesis*).

Language acquisition device or LAD A biologically organized mental structure in the brain that facilitates the learning of language because (according to Chomsky) it is innately programmed with some of the fundamental rules of grammar.

Latent content The symbolic meaning of objects and events in a dream. Latent content is usually an interpretation based on Freud's psychoanalytic theory or one of its variants. The latent content of a dream involving clocks might involve fear of the menstrual cycle and, hence, of one's sexuality.

Lateralization of emotion Different influences of the two brain hemispheres on various emotions. The left hemisphere apparently influences positive emotions (for example, happiness), and the right hemisphere influences negative emotions (anger, for example).

Law of common fate The Gestalt principle that we tend to group similar objects together that share a common motion or destination.

Law of continuity The Gestalt principle that we prefer perceptions of connected and continuous figures to disconnected and disjointed ones.

Law of effect The idea that responses that produced desirable results would be learned, or "stamped" into the organism.

Law of Prägnanz The most general Gestalt principle, which states that the simplest organization, requiring the least cognitive effort, will emerge as the figure. *Prägnanz* shares a common root with *pregnant,* and so it carries the idea of a "fully developed figure." That is, our perceptual system prefers to see a fully developed Gestalt, such as a complete circle—as opposed to a broken circle.

Law of proximity The Gestalt principle that we tend to group objects together when they are near each other. *Proximity* means "nearness."

Law of similarity The Gestalt principle that we tend to group similar objects together in our perceptions.

Laws of perceptual grouping The Gestalt principles of similarity, proximity, continuity, and common fate. These "laws" suggest how our brains prefer to group stimulus elements together to form a percept (Gestalt).

Learned helplessness Pattern of failure to respond to noxious stimuli after an organism learns its responses are ineffective.

Learning A lasting change in behavior or mental processes that results from experience.

Learning-based inference The view that perception is primarily shaped by learning (or experience), rather than by innate factors.

Levels-of-processing theory The explanation for the fact that information that is more thoroughly connected to meaningful items in long-term memory (more "deeply" processed) will be remembered better.

Libido The Freudian concept of psychic energy that drives individuals to experience sensual pleasure.

Limbic system The middle layer of the brain, involved in emotion and memory. The limbic system includes the hippocampus, amygdala, hypothalamus, and other structures.

Lithium carbonate A simple chemical compound that is highly effective in dampening the extreme mood swings of bipolar disorder.

Locus of control An individual's sense of where his or her life influences originate—internally or externally.

Longitudinal study A type of study in which one group of subjects is followed and observed (or examined, surveyed etc.) for an extended period of time (years).

Long-term memory (LTM) The third of three memory stages, with the largest capacity and longest duration; LTM stores material organized according to meaning.

Long-term potentiation A biological process, involving physical changes that strengthen the synapses in groups of nerve cells, which is believed to be the neural basis of learning.

Loudness A sensory characteristic of sound produced by the *amplitude* (intensity) of the sound wave.

Maintenance rehearsal A working-memory process in which information is merely repeated or reviewed to keep it from fading while in working memory. Maintenance rehearsal involves no active elaboration.

Major depression A form of depression that does not alternate with mania.

Manifest content The story line of a dream, taken at face value without interpretation.

Matching hypothesis The prediction that most people will find friends and mates that are perceived to be of about their same level of attractiveness.

Maturation The process by which the genetic program manifests itself over time.

Mean The measure of central tendency most often used to describe a set of data—calculated by adding all the scores and dividing by the number of scores.

Median A measure of central tendency for a distribution, represented by the score that separates the upper half of the scores in a distribution from the lower half.

Medical model The view that mental disorders are diseases that, like ordinary physical diseases, have objective physical causes and require specific treatments.

Meditation A state of consciousness often induced by focusing on a repetitive behavior, assuming certain body positions, and minimizing external stimulation. Meditation may be intended to enhance self-knowledge, well-being, and spirituality.

Medulla A brain-stem structure that controls breathing and heart rate. The sensory and motor pathways connecting the brain to the body cross in the medulla.

Memory Any system—human, animal, or machine—that encodes, stores, and retrieves information.

Mental age (MA) The average age at which normal (average) individuals achieve a particular score.

Mental operations Solving problems by manipulating images in one's mind.

Mental representation The ability to form internal images of objects and events.

Mental retardation Often conceived as representing the lower 2% of the IQ range, commencing about 30 points below average (below about 70 points). More sophisticated definitions also take into account an individual's level of social functioning and other abilities.

Mental set The tendency to respond to a new problem in the manner used for a previous problem.

Mere exposure effect A learned preference for stimuli to which we have been previously exposed.

Method of loci A mnemonic technique that involves associating items on a list with a sequence of familiar physical locations.

Misattribution A memory fault that occurs when memories are retrieved but are associated with the wrong time, place, or person.

Misinformation effect The distortion of memory by suggestion or misinformation.

MMPI-2 A widely used personality assessment instrument that gives scores on ten important clinical traits. Also called the Minnesota Multiphasic Personality Inventory.

Mnemonics Techniques for improving memory, especially by making connections between new material and information already in long-term memory.

Mode A measure of central tendency for a distribution, represented by the score that separates the upper half of the scores in a distribution from the lower half.

Monocular cues Information about depth that relies on the input of just one eye—includes relative size, light and shadow, interposition, relative motion, and atmospheric perspective.

Mood-congruent memory A memory process that selectively retrieves memories that match (are congruent with) one's mood.

Mood disorders Abnormal disturbances in emotion or mood, including bipolar disorder and unipolar disorder. Mood disorders are also called *affective disorders.*

Morphemes The meaningful units of language that make up words. Some whole words are morphemes (example: *word*); other morphemes include grammatical components that alter a word's meaning (examples: *-ed, -ing,* and *un-*).

Motivation Refers to all the processes involved in starting, directing, and maintaining physical and psychological activities.

Motive An internal mechanism that selects and directs behavior. The term *motive* is often used in the narrower sense of a motivational process that is learned, rather than biologically based (as are drives).

Motor cortex A narrow vertical strip of cortex in the frontal lobes, lying just in front of the central fissure; controls voluntary movement.

Motor neuron Nerve cell that carries messages away from the central nervous system toward the muscles and glands. Also called an *efferent neuron.*

MRI or **magnetic resonance imaging** An imaging technique that relies on cells' responses in a high-intensity magnetic field.

Multiple approach–avoidance conflict A conflict in which one must choose between options that have both many attractive and many negative aspects.

Multiple intelligences A term used to refer to Gardner's theory, which proposes that there are seven (or more) forms of intelligence.

Mutual interdependence A shared sense that individuals or groups need each other in order to achieve common goals

Myers–Briggs Type Indicator (MBTI) A widely used personality test based on Jungian types.

Narcissistic personality disorder Characterized by a grandiose sense of self-importance, a preoccupation with fantasies of success or power, and a need for constant attention or admiration.

Narcolepsy A disorder of REM sleep, involving sleep-onset REM periods and sudden daytime REM-sleep attacks usually accompanied by cataplexy.

Natural concepts Mental representations of objects and events drawn from our direct experience.

Natural language mediators Words associated with new information to be remembered.

Natural selection The driving force behind evolution, by which the environment "selects" the fittest organisms.

Naturalistic observation A research method in which subjects are observed in their natural environment.

Nature–nurture issue The long-standing discussion over the relative importance of nature (heredity) and nurture (environment) in their influence on behavior and mental processes.

Need for achievement *(n Ach)* In Murray and McClelland's theory, a mental state that produces a psychological motive to excel or to reach some goal.

Need In drive theory, a need is a biological imbalance (such as dehydration) that threatens survival, if the need is left unmet. Biological needs are believed to produce drives.

Negative reinforcement The removal of an unpleasant or aversive stimulus, contingent on a particular behavior. Compare with *punishment.*

Neo-Freudian psychodynamic therapies Therapies for mental disorder that were developed by psychodynamic theorists who embraced some of Freud's ideas but disagreed with others.

Neo-Freudians Literally "new Freudians"; refers to theorists who broke with Freud but whose theories retain a psychodynamic aspect, especially a focus on motivation as the source of energy for the personality.

Neonatal period In humans, the neonatal (newborn) period extends through the first month after birth.

Nerve deafness An inability to hear that is linked to a deficit in the body's ability to transmit impulses from the cochlea to the brain, usually involving the auditory nerve or higher auditory processing centers.

Nervous system The entire network of neurons in the body, including the central nervous system, the peripheral nervous system, and their subdivisions.

Neural pathway Bundle of nerve cells that follow generally the same route and employ the same neurotransmitter.

Neuron Cell specialized to receive and transmit information to other cells in the body—also called a *nerve cell.* Bundles of many neurons are called *nerves.*

Neuroscience A relatively new interdisciplinary field devoted to understanding how the brain creates thoughts, feelings, motives, consciousness, memories, and other mental processes.

Neurosis Before the *DSM-IV*, this term was used as a label for subjective distress or self-defeating behavior that did not show signs of brain abnormalities or grossly irrational thinking.

Neurotic needs Signs of neurosis in Horney's theory, these 10 needs are normal desires carried to a neurotic extreme.

Neuroticism Susceptibility to neurotic problems.

Neurotransmitters Chemical messengers that relay neural messages across the synapse. Many neurotransmitters are also hormones.

Neutral stimulus Any stimulus that produces no conditioned response prior to learning. When it is brought into a conditioning experiment, the researcher will call it a conditioned stimulus (CS). The assumption is that some conditioning occurs after even one pairing of the CS and UCS.

Night terrors Deep sleep episodes that seem to produce terror, although any terrifying mental experience (such as a dream) is usually forgotten upon awakening. Night terrors occur mainly in children.

Nonconscious processes Any brain process that does not involve conscious processing, including both preconscious memories and unconscious processes.

Non-REM (NREM) sleep The recurring periods, mainly associated with the deeper stages of sleep, when a sleeper is not showing rapid eye movements.

Normal distribution A bell-shaped curve, describing the spread of a characteristic throughout a population.

Normal range Scores falling near the middle of a normal distribution.

Object permanence The knowledge that objects exist independently of one's own actions or awareness.

Objective tests Tests that can be scored easily by machine, such as multiple-choice tests and selected-reponse tests.

Observational learning A form of cognitive learning in which new responses are acquired after watching others' behavior and the consequences of their behavior.

Obsessive–compulsive disorder A condition characterized by patterns of persistent, unwanted thoughts and behaviors.

Occipital lobes The cortical regions at the back of the brain, housing the visual cortex.

Oedipus complex According to Freud, a largely unconscious process whereby boys displace an erotic attraction toward their mother to females of their own age and, at the same time, identify with their fathers.

Olfaction The sense of smell.

Omission training (negative punishment) The removal of an appetitive stimulus after a response, leading to a decrease in behavior.

Operant An observable, voluntary behavior that an organism emits to "operate" on, or have an effect on, the environment.

Operant chamber A boxlike apparatus that can be programmed to deliver reinforcers and punishers contingent on an animal's behavior. The operant chamber is often called a "Skinner box."

Operant conditioning A form of behavioral learning in which the probability of a response is changed by its consequences—that is, by the stimuli that *follow* the response.

Operational definitions Specific descriptions of concepts involving the conditions of a scientific study. Operational definitions are stated in terms of how the concepts are to be measured or what operations are being employed to produce them.

Opiates Highly addictive drugs, derived from opium, that can produce a profound sense of well-being and have strong pain-relieving properties.

Opponent-process theory The idea that cells in the visual system process colors in complementary pairs, such as red or green or as yellow or blue. The opponent-process theory explains color sensation from the bipolar cells onward in the visual system.

Opponent-process theory Theory of emotion which theorizes that emotions have pairs. When one is triggered, the other is suppressed (for example, when we feel happy, sad is the suppressed emotion).

Optic nerve The bundle of neurons that carries visual information from the retina to the brain.

Osmotic thirst A drop in intracellular fluid levels.

Out-group Those outside the group with which an individual identifies.
Overjustification The process by which extrinsic (external) rewards can sometimes displace internal motivation, as when a child receives money for playing video games.
Overlearning A strategy whereby the learner continues to study and rehearse the material after it has been initially brought to mastery.
Overregularization Applying a grammatical rule too widely and creating incorrect forms.
Panic disorder A disturbance marked by panic attacks that have no obvious connection with events in the person's present experience. Unlike generalized anxiety disorder, the victim is usually free of anxiety between panic attacks.
Parasympathetic division The part of the autonomic nervous system that monitors the routine operations of the internal organs and returns the body to calmer functioning after arousal by the sympathetic division.
Parietal lobes Cortical areas lying toward the back and top of the brain; involved in touch sensation and in perceiving spatial relationships (the relationships of objects in space).
Participant modeling A social learning technique in which a therapist demonstrates and encourages a client to imitate a desired behavior.
Penis envy According to Freud, the female desire to have a penis—a condition that usually results in their attraction to males.
Percept The meaningful product of perception—often an image that has been associated with concepts, memories of events, emotions, and motives.
Perception A process that makes sensory patterns meaningful. It is perception that makes these words meaningful, rather than just a string of visual patterns. To make this happen, perception draws heavily on memory, motivation, emotion, and other psychological processes.
Perceptual constancy The ability to recognize the same object as remaining "constant" under different conditions, such as changes in illumination, distance, or location.
Perceptual set Readiness to detect a particular stimulus in a given context—as when a person who is afraid interprets an unfamiliar sound in the night as a threat.
Peripheral nervous system All parts of the nervous system lying outside the central nervous system. The peripheral nervous system includes the autonomic and somatic nervous systems.
Persistence A memory problem in which unwanted memories cannot be put out of mind.
Personal bias The researcher allowing personal beliefs to affect the outcome of a study.
Personal unconscious Jung's term for that portion of the unconscious corresponding roughly to the Freudian id.
Personality disorders Conditions involving a chronic, pervasive, inflexible, and maladaptive pattern of thinking, emotion, social relationships, or impulse control.
Personality The psychological qualities that bring continuity to an individual's behavior in different situations and at different times.
Person–situation controversy A theoretical dispute concerning the relative contribution of personality factors and situational factors in controlling behavior.
PET scanning or **positron emission tomography** An imaging technique that relies on the detection of radioactive sugar consumed by active brain cells.
Phenomenal field Our psychological reality, composed of one's perceptions and feelings.
Phenotype An organism's observable physical characteristics.
Pheromones Chemical signals released by organisms to communicate with other members of their species. Pheromones are often used by animals as sexual attractants. It is unclear whether or not humans employ pheromones.
Phobias A group of anxiety disorders involving a pathological fear of a specific object or situation.
Photoreceptors Light-sensitive cells (neurons) in the retina that convert light energy to neural impulses. The photoreceptors are as far as light gets into the visual system.
Physical dependence A process by which the body adjusts to, and comes to need, a drug for its everyday functioning.
Pitch A sensory characteristic of sound produced by the *frequency* of the sound wave.
Pituitary gland The "master gland" that produces hormones influencing the secretions of all other endocrine glands, as well as a hormone that influences growth. The pituitary is attached to the brain's hypothalamus, from which it takes its orders.
Placebo effect A response to a placebo (a fake drug), caused by subjects' belief that they are taking real drugs.
Placenta The organ interface between the embryo or fetus and the mother. The placenta separates the bloodstreams, but it allows the exchange of nutrients and waste products.
Plasticity The nervous system's ability to adapt or change as the result of experience. Plasticity may also help the nervous system adapt to physical damage.
Polygraph A device that records or graphs many ("poly") measures of physical arousal, such as heart rate, breathing, perspiration, and blood pressure. A polygraph is often called a "lie detector," even though it is really an arousal detector.
Pons A brain-stem structure that regulates brain activity during sleep and dreaming. The name *pons* derives from the Latin word for "bridge."
Positive psychology A recent movement within psychology, focusing on desirable aspects of human functioning, as opposed to an emphasis on psychopathology.
Positive punishment The application of an aversive stimulus after a response.
Positive reinforcement A stimulus presented after a response and increasing the probability of that response happening again.
Posttraumatic stress disorder (PTSD) Delayed stress reaction in which an individual involuntarily reexperiences emotional, cognitive, and behavioral aspects of past trauma.
Practical intelligence According to Sternberg, the ability to cope with the environment; sometimes called "street smarts."
Preconscious memories Information that is not currently in consciousness but can be recalled to consciousness voluntarily or after something calls attention to them.
Prejudice A negative attitude toward an individual based solely on his or her membership in a particular group.
Premack principle The concept, developed by David Premack, that a more-preferred activity can be used to reinforce a less-preferred activity.
Prenatal period The developmental period before birth.
Preoperational stage The second stage in Piaget's theory, marked by well-developed mental representation and the use of language.
Preparedness hypothesis The notion that we have an innate tendency, acquired through natural selection, to respond quickly and automatically to stimuli that posed a survival threat to our ancestors.
Primary reinforcers Reinforcers, such as food and sex, that have an innate basis because of their biological value to an organism.
Primary sex characteristics The sex organs and genitals.
Priming A technique for cuing implicit memories by providing cues that stimulate a memory without awareness of the connection between the cue and the retrieved memory.
Principle of proximity The notion that people at work will make more friends among those who are nearby—with whom they have the most contact. Proximity means "nearness."
Proactive interference A cause of forgetting by which previously stored information prevents learning and remembering new information.
Procedural memory A division of LTM that stores memories for how things are done.
Projective tests Personality assessment instruments, such as the Rorschach and TAT, which are based on Freud's ego defense mechanism of projection.
Prototype An ideal or most representative example of a conceptual category.
Pseudopsychology Erroneous assertions or practices set forth as being scientific psychology.
Psychiatry A medical specialty dealing with the diagnosis and treatment of mental disorders.

Psychic determinism Freud's assumption that all our mental and behavioral responses are caused by unconscious traumas, desires, or conflicts.

Psychoactive drugs Chemicals that affect mental processes and behavior by their effects on the brain.

Psychoanalysis An approach to psychology based on Sigmund Freud's assertions, which emphasize unconscious processes. The goal of psychoanalysis is to release conflicts and memories from the unconscious. The term is used to refer broadly both to Freud's psychoanalytic theory and to his psychoanalytic treatment method.

Psychoanalytic theory Freud's theory of personality.

Psychodynamic psychology A clinical viewpoint emphasizing the understanding of mental disorders in terms of unconscious needs, desires, memories, and conflicts.

Psychological dependence A desire to obtain or use a drug, even though there is no physical dependence.

Psychological therapies Therapies based on psychological principles (rather than on the biomedical approach); often called "psychotherapy."

Psychology The scientific study of behavior and mental processes.

Psychoneuroimmunology Multidisciplinary field that studies the influence of mental states on the immune system.

Psychopathology Any pattern of emotions, behaviors, or thoughts inappropriate to the situation and leading to personal distress or the inability to achieve important goals. Other terms having essentially the same meaning include *mental illness, mental disorder,* and *psychological disorder.*

Psychopharmacology The prescribed use of drugs to help treat symptoms of mental illness so that individuals are more receptive to talk therapies.

Psychosexual stages Successive, instinctive patterns of associating pleasure with stimulation of specific bodily areas at different times of life.

Psychosis A disorder involving profound disturbances in perception, rational thinking, or affect.

Psychosocial stages In Erikson's theory, the developmental stages are defined by eight major challenges that appear successively across the lifespan, which require an individual to rethink his or her goals, and relationships with others.

Psychosurgery The general term for surgical intervention in the brain to treat psychological disorders.

Puberty The onset of sexual maturity.

Punishment An aversive stimulus that, occurring after a response, diminishes the strength of that response. (Compare with *negative reinforcement.*)

Random assignment Each subject of the sample has an equal likelihood of being chosen for the experimental group of an experiment.

Random presentation A process by which chance alone determines the order in which the stimulus is presented.

Random sample A sample group of subjects selected by chance (without biased selection techniques).

Range The simplest measure of variability, represented by the difference between the highest and the lowest values in a frequency distribution.

Ratio schedule A program by which reinforcement depends on the number of correct responses.

Rational–emotive behavior therapy (REBT) Albert Ellis's brand of cognitive therapy, based on the idea that irrational thoughts and behaviors are the cause of mental disorders.

Recall A retrieval method in which one must reproduce previously presented information.

Reciprocal determinism The process in which cognitions, behavior, and the environment mutually influence each other.

Recognition A retrieval method in which one must identify present stimuli as having been previously presented.

Reflection of feeling Carl Rogers's technique of paraphrasing the clients' words, attempting to capture the emotional tone expressed.

Reflex A simple, unlearned response triggered by stimuli—such as the knee-jerk reflex set off by tapping the tendon just below your kneecap.

Reinforcement contingencies Relationships between a response and the changes in stimulation that follow the response.

Reinforcer A condition (involving either the presentation or removal of a stimulus) that occurs after a response and strengthens that response.

Reliability An attribute of a psychological test that gives consistent results; a property exhibited by a test that yields the same results over time.

REM rebound A condition of increased REM sleep caused by REM-sleep deprivation.

REM sleep A stage of sleep that occurs approximately every 90 minutes, marked by bursts of rapid eye movements occurring under closed eyelids. REM sleep periods are associated with dreaming.

Replicate In research this refers to doing a study over to see whether the same results are obtained. As a control for bias, replication is often done by someone other than the researcher who performed the original study.

Representative sample A sample obtained in such a way that it reflects the distribution of important variables in the larger population in which the researchers are interested—variables such as age, income level, ethnicity, and geographic distribution.

Representativeness bias A faulty heuristic strategy based on the presumption that once people or events are categorized, they share all the features of other members in that category.

Repression An unconscious process that excludes unacceptable thoughts and feelings from awareness and memory.

Resting potential The electrical charge of the axon in its inactive state, when the neuron is ready to "fire."

Reticular formation A pencil-shaped structure forming the core of the brain stem. The reticular formation arouses the cortex to keep the brain alert and attentive to new stimulation.

Retina The thin, light-sensitive layer at the back of the eyeball. The retina contains millions of photoreceptors and other nerve cells.

Retrieval The third basic task of memory, involving the location and recovery of information from memory.

Retrieval cues Stimuli that are used to bring a memory to consciousness or into behavior.

Retroactive interference A cause of forgetting by which newly learned information prevents retrieval of previously stored material.

Retrograde amnesia The inability to remember information previously stored in memory. (Compare with anterograde amnesia.)

Reward theory of attraction A social-learning view that says we like best those who give us maximum rewards at minimum cost.

Rites of passage Social rituals that mark the transition between developmental stages, especially between childhood and adulthood.

Rods Photoreceptors in the retina that are especially sensitive to dim light but not to colors. Strange as it may seem, they are rod-shaped.

Romantic love A temporary and highly emotional condition based on infatuation and sexual desire.

Rorschach inkblot technique A projective test requiring subjects to describe what they see in a series of ten inkblots.

Savant syndrome Found in individuals who have a remarkable talent (such as the ability to determine the day of the week for any given date) even though they are mentally slow in other domains.

Scapegoating Blaming an innocent person or a group for one's own troubles.

Schedules of reinforcement Programs specifying the frequency and timing of reinforcements.

Schema A knowledge cluster or general conceptual framework that provides expectations about topics, events, objects, people, and situations in one's life; in Piaget's theory, mental structures or programs that guide a developing child's thoughts.

Schemas In Piaget's theory, mental structures of programs that guide a developing child's thoughts.

Schizophrenia (pronounced *skits-o-FRENNY-a*) A psychotic disorder involving distortions in thoughts, perceptions, and/or emotions.

Scientific method A five-step process for empirical investigation of a hypothesis under conditions designed to control biases and subjective judgments.

Script A cluster of knowledge about sequences of events and actions expected to occur in particular settings.

Seasonal affective disorder (SAD) Technically *Seasonal pattern specifier*, this DSM-IV course specifier for mood disorders is believed to be a form of depression caused by deprivation of sunlight.

Secondary sex characteristics Gender-related physical features that develop during puberty, including facial hair and deepening voice in males, widened hips and enlarged breasts in females, and the development of pubic hair in both sexes.

Secondary traits In trait theory, preferences and attitudes.

Selective social interaction Choosing to restrict the number of one's social contacts to those who are the most gratifying.

Self-actualizing personalities Healthy individuals who have met their basic needs and are free to be creative and fulfill their potentialities.

Self-consistency bias The commonly held idea that we are more consistent in our attitudes, opinions, and beliefs than we actually are.

Self-fulfilling prophecy Observations or behaviors that result primarily from expectations.

Self-help support groups Groups, such as Alcoholics Anonymous, that provide social support and an opportunity for sharing ideas about dealing with common problems. Such groups are typically organized and run by laypersons, rather than professional therapists.

Self-serving bias An attributional pattern in which one takes credit for success but denies responsibility for failure. (Compare with the *fundamental attribution error.*)

Semantic memory A subdivision of declarative memory that stores general knowledge, including the meanings of words and concepts.

Sensation The process by which stimulation of a sensory receptor produces neural impulses that the brain interprets as a sound, a visual image, an odor, a taste, a pain, or other sensory image. Sensation represents the first series of steps in processing of incoming information.

Sensation seekers In Zuckerman's theory, individuals who have a biological need for higher levels of stimulation than do other people.

Sensorimotor stage The first stage in Piaget's theory, during which the child relies heavily on innate motor responses to stimuli.

Sensory adaptation Loss of responsiveness in receptor cells after stimulation has remained unchanged for a while, as when a swimmer becomes adapted to the temperature of the water.

Sensory memory The first of three memory stages, preserving brief sensory impressions of stimuli.

Sensory neuron Nerve cell that carries messages from sense receptors toward the central nervous system. Also called an *afferent neuron.*

Serial position effect A form of interference related to the sequence in which information is presented. Generally, items in the middle of the sequence are less well remembered than items presented first or last.

Set point Refers to the tendency of the body to maintain a certain level of body fat and body weight.

Sex chromosomes The X and Y chromosomes that determine our physical sex characteristics.

Sexual orientation One's erotic attraction toward members of the same sex (a homosexual orientation), the opposite sex (heterosexual orientation), or both sexes (a bisexual orientation).

Sexual response cycle The four-stage sequence of arousal, plateau, orgasm, and resolution occurring in both men and women.

Sexual scripts Socially learned ways of responding in sexual situations.

Shaping An operant learning technique in which a new behavior is produced by reinforcing responses that are similar to the desired response.

Signal detection theory Explains how we detect "signals," consisting of stimulation affecting our eyes, ears, nose, skin, and other sense organs. Signal detection theory says that sensation is a judgment the sensory system makes about incoming stimulation. Often, it occurs outside of consciousness. In contrast to older theories from psychophysics, signal detection theory takes observer characteristics into account.

Significant difference Psychologists accept a difference between the groups as "real," or significant, when the probability that it might be due to an atypical sample drawn by chance is less than 5 in 100 (indicated by the notation $p < .05$).

Similarity principle The notion that people are attracted to those who are most similar to themselves.

Situationism The view that environmental conditions influence people's behavior as much or more than their personal dispositions do.

Skin senses Sensory systems for processing touch, warmth, cold, texture, and pain.

Sleep apnea A respiratory disorder in which the person intermittently stops breathing many times while asleep.

Sleep debt A sleep deficiency caused by not getting the amount of sleep that one requires for optimal functioning.

Sleep paralysis A condition in which a sleeper is unable to move any of the voluntary muscles, except those controlling the eyes. Sleep paralysis normally occurs during REM sleep.

Social–cognitive–behavioral approach A psychological alternative to the medical model that views psychological disorder through a combination of the social, cognitive, and behavioral perspectives.

Social context The combination of (a) people, (b) the activities and interactions among people, (c) the setting in which behavior occurs, and (d) the expectations and social norms governing behavior in that setting.

Social distance The perceived difference or similarity between oneself and another person.

Social facilitation An increase in an individual's performance because of being in a group.

Social loafing A decrease in performance because of being in a group.

Social norms A group's expectations regarding what is appropriate and acceptable for its members' attitudes and behaviors.

Social psychology The branch of psychology that studies the effects of social variables and cognitions on individual behavior and social interactions.

Social reality An individual's subjective interpretation of other people and of relationships with them.

Social role One of several socially defined patterns of behavior that are expected of persons in a given setting or group.

Sociocultural view A psychological perspective emphasizing the importance of social interaction, social learning, and a cultural perspective.

Soma The part of a cell (such as a neuron) containing the nucleus, which includes the chromosomes. Also called the *cell body.*

Somatic nervous system A division of the peripheral nervous system that carries sensory information to the central nervous system and also sends voluntary messages to the body's skeletal muscles.

Somatoform disorders Psychological problems appearing in the form of bodily symptoms or physical complaints, such as weakness or excessive worry about disease. The somatoform disorders include conversion disorder and hypochondriasis.

Somatosensory cortex A strip of the parietal lobe lying just behind the central fissure. The somatosensory cortex is involved with sensations of touch.

Split-half reliability A measure of reliability in which a test is split into two parts and an individual's scores on both halves are compared.

Spontaneous recovery The reappearance of an extinguished conditioned response after a time delay.

Stage of exhaustion Third stage of the GAS, during which the body depletes its resources in responding to an ongoing stressor.

Stage of resistance Second stage of the GAS, during which the body adapts to and uses resources to cope with a stressor.

Standard deviation (SD) A measure of variability that indicates the average difference between the scores and their mean.

Steven's power law A law of magnitude estimation that is more accurate than Fechner's law and covers a wider variety of stimuli. It is represented by the formula $S = kI^a$, where S = sensation, k = *constant,* I = stimulus intensity, and a = a power exponent that depends on the sense being measured.

Stimulants Drugs that arouse the central nervous system, speeding up mental and physical responses and increasing activity level by encouraging communication among neurons in the brain. Stimulants, however, have been found to suppress activity level in persons with attention-deficit/hyperactivity disorder.

Stimulus discrimination Learning to respond to one stimulus but not to stimuli that are similar.

Stimulus generalization The extension of a learned response to stimuli that are similar to the conditioned stimulus.

Storage One of the three basic tasks of memory, involving the retention of encoded material over time.

Stress A physical and mental response to a challenging or threatening situation.

Stressor A stressful stimulus, a condition demanding adaptation.

Structuralism A historical school of psychology devoted to uncovering the basic structures that make up mind and thought. Structuralists sought the "elements" of conscious experience.

Subjective tests Tests in which individuals are given an ambiguous figure or an open-ended situation and asked to describe what they see or finish a story.

Suggestibility The process of memory distortion as the result of deliberate or inadvertent suggestion.

Superego The mind's storehouse of values, including moral attitudes learned from parents and from society; roughly the same as the common notion of the conscience.

Survey A quasi-experimental method in which questions are asked to subjects. When designing a survey, the researcher has to be careful that the questions are not skewed or biased toward a particular answer.

Sympathetic division The part of the autonomic nervous system that sends messages to internal organs and glands that help us respond to stressful and emergency situations.

Synapse The microscopic gap that serves as a communications link between neurons. Synapses also occur between neurons and the muscles or glands they serve.

Synaptic transmission The relaying of information across the synapse by means of chemical neurotransmitters.

Synaptic vesicle A small "container" holding neurotransmitter molecules that then connects to the presynaptic membrane, releasing the neurotransmitter into the synapse.

Systematic desensitization A behavioral therapy technique in which anxiety is extinguished by exposing the patient to an anxiety-provoking stimulus.

Talk therapies Psychotherapies that focus on communicating and verbalizing emotions and motives to understand their problems.

Tardive dyskinesia An incurable disorder of motor control, especially involving muscles of the face and head, resulting from long-term use of antipsychotic drugs.

Taste-aversion learning A biological tendency in which an organism learns, after a single experience, to avoid a food with a certain taste, if eating it is followed by illness.

Teachers of psychology Psychologists whose primary job is teaching, typically in high schools, colleges, and universities.

Temperament An individual's characteristic manner of behavior or reaction—assumed to have a strong genetic basis; the basic and pervasive personality dispositions that are apparent in early childhood and that establish the tempo and mood of the individual's behaviors.

Temporal lobes Cortical lobes that process sounds, including speech. The temporal lobes are probably involved in storing long-term memories.

Tend-and-befriend model Stress response model proposing that females are biologically predisposed to respond to threat by nurturing and protecting offspring and seeking social support.

Teratogens Substances from the environment, including viruses, drugs, and other chemicals, that can damage the developing organism during the prenatal period.

Terminal buttons Tiny bulblike structures at the end of the axon, which contain neurotransmitters that carry the neuron's message into the synapse.

Terrorism The use of violent, unpredictable acts by a small group against a larger group for political, economic, or religious goals.

Test–retest reliability A property exhibited by a test on which people get about the same scores when they take the test more than once.

Thalamus The brain's central "relay station," situated just atop the brain stem. Nearly all the messages going into or out of the brain go through the thalamus.

Thematic Apperception Test (TAT) A projective test requiring subjects to make up stories that explain ambiguous pictures.

Theory A testable explanation for a set of facts or observations. In science, a theory is *not* just speculation or a guess.

Theory of mind An awareness that other people's behavior may be influenced by beliefs, desires, and emotions that differ from one's own.

Therapeutic community Jones's term for a program of treating mental disorder by making the institutional environment supportive and humane for patients.

Therapy A general term for any treatment process; in psychology and psychiatry, therapy refers to a variety of psychological and biomedical techniques aimed at dealing with mental disorders or coping with problems of living.

Timbre The quality of a sound wave that derives from the wave's complexity (combination of pure tones). *Timbre* comes from the Greek word for "drum," as does the term *tympanic membrane,* or eardrum.

Token economy An operant technique applied to groups, such as classrooms or mental hospital wards, involving the distribution of "tokens" or other indicators of reinforcement contingent on desired behaviors. The tokens can later be exchanged for privileges, food, or other reinforcers; a therapeutic method, based on operant conditioning, by which individuals are rewarded with tokens, which act as secondary reinforcers. The tokens can be redeemed for a variety of rewards and privileges.

Tolerance The reduced effectiveness a drug has after repeated use.

Top-down processing Perceptual analysis that emphasizes the perceiver's expectations, concept memories, and other cognitive factors, rather than being driven by the characteristics of the stimulus. "Top" refers to a mental set in the brain—which stands at the "top" of the perceptual processing system.

TOT phenomenon The inability to recall a word, while knowing that it is in memory. People often describe this frustrating experience as having the word "on the tip of the tongue."

Trait view A psychological perspective that views behavior and personality as the products of enduring psychological characteristics.

Traits Stable personality characteristics that are presumed to exist within the individual and guide his or her thoughts and actions under various conditions.

Transcranial magnetic stimulation (TMS) A treatment that involves magnetic stimulation of specific regions of the brain. Unlike ECT, TMS does not produce a seizure.

Transduction Transformation of one form of energy into another—especially the transformation of stimulus information into nerve signals by the sense organs. Without transduction, ripe tomatoes would not appear red (or pinkish-gray, in the case of tomatoes purchased in many grocery stores).

Transience The impermanence of a long-term memory. Transience is based on the idea that long-term memories gradually fade over time.

Traumatic stressor A situation that threatens one's physical safety, arousing feelings of fear, horror, or helplessness.

Triangular theory of love A theory that describes various kinds of love in terms of three components: passion (erotic attraction), intimacy (sharing feelings and confidences), and commitment (dedication to putting this relationship first in one's life).

Triarchic theory The term for Sternberg's theory of intelligence; so called because it combines three ("tri-") main forms of intelligence.

Trichromatic theory The idea that colors are sensed by three different types of cones sensitive to light in the red, blue, and green wavelengths. The trichromatic theory explains the earliest stage of color sensation.

Two-factor theory The proposal claiming that emotion results from the cognitive appraisal of both physical arousal (Factor #1) and an emotion-provoking stimulus (Factor #2).

Tympanic membrane The eardrum.

Type Refers to especially important dimensions or clusters of traits that are not only central to a person's personality but are found with essentially the same pattern in many people.

Type A Behavior pattern characterized intense, angry, competitive, or perfectionistic responses to challenging situations.

Type B Behavior pattern characterized by relaxed, unstressed approach to life.

Unconditioned response (UCR) In classical conditioning, the response elicited by an unconditioned stimulus without prior learning.

Unconditioned stimulus (UCS) In classical conditioning, the stimulus that elicits an unconditioned response.

Unconscious In classic Freudian theory, the psychic domain of which the individual is not aware but that houses memories, desires, and feelings that would be threatening if brought to consciousness. Many modern cognitive psychologists view the unconscious in less sinister terms, merely as a collection of mental processes that operate outside of awareness—but not typically suppressing information or working at odds with consciousness.

Unconscious motivation Having a desire to engage in an activity but being consciously unaware of the desire. Freud's psychoanalytic theory emphasized unconscious motivation.

Validity An attribute of a psychological test that actually measures what it is being used to measure; a property exhibited by a test that measures what it purports to measure.

Variable interval (VI) schedules Programs by which the time period between reinforcements varies from trial to trial.

Variable ratio (VR) schedules Reinforcement programs by which the number of responses required for a reinforcement varies from trial to trial.

Vestibular sense The sense of body orientation with respect to gravity. The vestibular sense is closely associated with the inner ear and, in fact, is carried to the brain on a branch of the auditory nerve.

Violence and aggression Terms that refer to behavior that is intended to cause harm.

Visible spectrum The tiny part of the electromagnetic spectrum to which our eyes are sensitive. The visible spectrum of other creatures may be slightly different from our own.

Visual cortex The visual processing areas of cortex in the occipital and temporal lobes.

Volumetric thirst A drop in extracellular fluid levels.

Weber's law This concept says that the size of a JND is proportional to the intensity of the stimulus; the JND is large when the stimulus intensity is high and is small when the stimulus intensity is low. (This concept has *no* connection with Ann Weber, one of your authors.)

Whole method The mnemonic strategy of first approaching the material to be learned "as a whole," forming an impression of the overall meaning of the material. The details are later associated with this overall impression.

Withdrawal A pattern of uncomfortable or painful physical symptoms and cravings experienced by the user when the level of drug is decreased or the drug is eliminated.

Working memory The second of three memory stages, and the most limited in capacity. It preserves recently perceived events or experiences for less than a minute without rehearsal.

Zone of proximal development The difference between what a child can do with help and what the child can do without any help or guidance.

Zygote A fertilized egg.

References

ABC News. (1995). "My Family, Forgive Me." *20/20*, Transcript #1526, June 30, pp. 6–10. New York: American Broadcasting Companies, Inc.

Abelson, P., & Kennedy, D. (2004, June 4). Editorial: The obesity epidemic. *Science, 304,* 1413.

Abelson, R. P. (1981). Psychological status of the script concept. *American Psychologist, 36,* 715–729.

Abrams, A. R. (1992). *Electroconvulsive therapy.* New York: Oxford University Press.

Abramson, L. Y., Metalsky, G. I., & Alloy, L. B. (1989). Hopelessness depression: A theory-based subtype. *Psychological Review, 96,* 358–372.

Ackerman, S. J., Benjamin, L. S., Beutler, L. E., Gelso, C. J., Goldfried, M. R., Hill, C., Lambert, M. J., Norcross, J. C., Orlinsky, D. E., & Rainer, J. (2001). Empirically supported therapy relationships: Conclusions and recommendations of the Division 29 task force. *Psychotherapy, 38,* 495–497.

Adams, J. (1979). Mutual-help groups: Enhancing the coping ability of oncology clients. *Cancer Nursing, 2,* 95–98.

Ader, R., & Cohen, N. (1993). Psychoneuroimmunology: Conditioning and stress. *Annual Review of Psychology, 44,* 53–85.

Adolphs, R., Jansari, A., & Tranel, D. (2001). Hemispheric perception of emotional valence from facial expressions. *Neuropsychology, 15,* 516–524.

Adorno, T. W., Frenkel-Brunswick, E., Levinson, D. J., & Sanford, R. N. (1950). *The authoritarian personality.* New York: Harper.

Aftergood, S. (2000, November 3). Polygraph testing and the DOE National Laboratories. *Science, 290,* 939–940.

Agras, W. S., Brandt, H. A., Bulik, C. M., Dolan-Sewell, R., Fairburn, C. G., Halmi, K. A., Herzog, D. B., Jimerson, D. C., Kaplan, A. S., Kaye, W. H., le Grange, D., Lock, J., Mitchell, J., Rudorfer, M. V., Street, L. L., Striegel-Moore, R., Vitousek, K. M., Walsh, B. T., & Wilfley, D. E. (2004). Report of the National Institutes of Health workshop on overcoming barriers to treatment research in anorexia nervosa. *International Journal of Eating Disorders, 35,* 509–521.

Ahern, G. L., & Schwartz, G. E. (1985). Differential lateralization for positive and negative emotion in the human brain: EEG spectral analysis. *Neuropsychologia, 23,* 744–755.

Ahrons, C. R. (1994). *The good divorce: Keeping your family together when your marriage comes apart.* New York: HarperCollins.

Ainsworth, M. D. S. (1973). The development of infant–mother attachment. In B. M. Caldwell & H. N. Ricciuti (Eds.), *Review of child development research* (Vol. 3). Chicago: University of Chicago Press.

Ainsworth, M. D. S. (1989). Attachments beyond infancy. *American Psychologist, 44,* 709–716.

Ainsworth, M. D. S., Blehar, M., Water, E., & Wall, S. (1978). *Patterns of attachment.* Hillsdale, NJ: Erlbaum.

Ainsworth, M. D. S., & Wittig, B. A. (1969). Attachment and exploratory behavior of one-year-olds in a strange situation. In B. M. Foss (Ed.), *Determinants of infant behavior* (Vol. 4). London, U.K.: Methuen.

Allen, M. G. (1976). Twin studies of affective illness. *Archives of General Psychiatry, 33,* 1476–1478.

Allen, V. S., & Levine, J. M. (1969). Consensus and conformity. *Journal of Experimental Social Psychology, 5,* 389–399.

Allport, G. W. (1954). *The nature of prejudice.* Cambridge, MA: Addison-Wesley.

Allport, G. W., & Odbert, H. S. (1936). Trait-names, a psycho-lexical study. *Psychological Monographs, 47*(1, Whole No. 211).

Alper, J. (1985, March). The roots of morality. *Science 85,* 70–76.

Alper, J. (1993). Echo-planar MRI: Learning to read minds. *Science, 261,* 556.

Amabile, T. M. (1983). *The social psychology of creativity.* New York: Springer-Verlag.

Amabile, T. M. (1987). The motivation to be creative. In S. Isaksen (Ed.), *Frontiers in creativity: Beyond the basics.* Buffalo, NY: Bearly Limited.

Amabile, T. M. (2001). Beyond talent: John Irving and the passionate craft of creativity. *American Psychologist, 56,* 333–336.

Amabile, T. M., Hadley, C. N., & Kramer, S. J. (2002, August). Creativity under the gun, *Harvard Business Review, 80*(8), 52–60.

American Academy of Pediatrics, Subcommittee on Attention Deficit Hyperactivity Disorder, Committee on Quality Improvement. (2001). Clinical practice guideline: Treatment of the school-aged child with attention-deficit/hyperactivity disorder. *Pediatrics, 108,* 1033–1044.

American Psychiatric Association. (1994). *Diagnostic and statistical manual of mental disorders* (4th ed.). Washington, DC: American Psychiatric Association.

American Psychiatric Association. (2000). *Diagnostic and statistical manual of mental disorders, 4th edition, text revision.* Washington, DC: American Psychiatric Association.

American Psychological Association. (2002). Ethical principles of psychologists and code of conduct. *American Psychologist, 57,* 1060–1073.

American Psychological Association. (2003a). Careers in psychology for the twenty-first century. Retrieved on October 14, 2004, from http://www.apa.org/students/brochure/brochurenew.pdf

American Psychological Association. (2003b). Council policy manual. Retrieved on October 14, 2004, from http://www.apa.org/about/division/cpmscientific.html

American Psychological Association. (2003c). Degree Fields of Psychology PhDs Awarded in 1981–2001. Retrieved on October 14, 2004, from http://research.apa.org/doctoraled05.html

American Psychological Association. (2004). *About APA.* Retrieved on October 14, 2004, from http://www.apa.org/about/

Anand, K. J. S., & Scalzo, F. M. (2000). Can adverse neonatal experiences alter brain development and subsequent behavior? *Biology of the Neonate, 77,* 69–82.

Anastasi, A. (1988). *Psychological testing* (6th ed.). New York: Macmillan.

Anch, A. M., Browman, C. P., Mitler, M. M., & Walsh, J. K. (1988). *Sleep: A scientific perspective.* Englewood Cliffs, NJ: Prentice Hall.

Anderson, A. E., & DiDomenico, L. (1992). Diet vs. shape content of popular male and female magazines: A dose-response relationship to the incidence of eating disorders? *International Journal of Eating Disorders, 11,* 283–287.

Anderson, C. A., & Bushman, B. J. (2002). Media violence and the American public revisited. *American Psychologist, 57,* 448–450.

Anderson, J. R. (1982). Acquisition of cognitive skill. *Psychological Review, 89,* 369–406.

Andreasen, N. C., Arndt, S., Alliger, R., Miller, D., et al. (1995). Symptoms of schizophrenia: Methods, meanings, and mechanisms. *Archives of General Psychiatry, 52,* 341–351.

Andreasen, N. C., Rice, J., Endicott, J., Coryell, W., Grove, W. W., & Reich, T. (1987). Familial rates of affective disorder. *Archives of General Psychiatry, 44,* 461–472.

Andrews, J. D. W. (1967). The achievement motive and advancement in two types of organization. *Journal of Personality and Social Psychology, 6,* 163–168.

Anglin, J. M. (1993). Vocabulary development: A morphological analysis. *Monographs of the Society for Research in Child Development, 58*(Serial No. 238).

Anglin, J. M. (1995, March). *Word learning and the growth of potentially knowable vocabulary.* Paper presented at the biennial meetings of the Society for Research in Child Development, Indianapolis, IN.

Angold, A., Erkanli, A., Egger, H. L., & Costello, E. J. (2000). Stimulant treatment for children: a community perspective. *Journal of the American Academy of Child and Adolescent Psychiatry, 39,* 975–984.

Ansbacher, H., & Ansbacher, R. R. (eds.) (1964). *The Individual Psychology of Alfred Adler,* New York: Harper Torchbook.

Antonova, I., Arancio, O., Trillat, A-C., Hong-Gang W., Zablow, L., Udo, H., Kandel, E. R., & Hawkins, R. D. (2001, November 16). Rapid increase in clusters of presynaptic proteins at onset of long-lasting potentiation, *Science, 294,* 1547–1550.

Antonuccio, D. (1995). Psychotherapy for depression: No stronger medicine. *American Psychologist, 50,* 450–452.

Antony, M. M., Brown, T. A., & Barlow, D. H. (1992). Current perspectives on panic and panic disorder. *Current Directions in Psychological Science, 1,* 79–82.

APA Online. (2004). *Empirical studies on lesbian and gay parenting.* Retrieved on November 8, 2004, from http://www.apa.org/pi/l&gbib.html

Archer, J. (1996). Sex differences in social behavior: Are the social role and evolutionary explanations compatible? *American Psychologist, 51,* 909–917.

Aristotle, *de Anima,* Books 1 and 3, in J. S. Smith (Trans.), *Introduction to Aristotle.* Chicago: University of Chicago Press, 1973.

Arnett, J. J. (1999). Adolescent storm and stress, reconsidered. *American Psychologist, 54,* 317–326.

Arnhoff, F. N. (1975). Social consequences of policy toward mental illness. *Science, 188,* 1277–1281.

Arnsten, A. F. T. (1998, June 12). The biology of being frazzled. *Science, 280,* 1711–1712.

Aron, A., & Aron, E. (1994). Love. In A. L. Weber & J. H. Harvey (Eds.), *Perspectives on close relationships* (Chapter 7, pp. 131–152). Boston: Allyn & Bacon.

Aronson, E. (2004). *The social animal* (9th ed.). New York: Worth.

Aronson, E. (2000). *Nobody left to hate: Teaching compassion after Columbine.* New York: W. H. Freeman & Company.

Aronson, E. (1999). *The Social Animal* (8th ed.). New York. W. H. Freeman.

Aronson, E., Helmreich, R., & LeFan, J. (1970). To err is humanizing—sometimes: Effects of self-esteem, competence, and a pratfall on interpersonal attraction. *Journal of Personality and Social Psychology, 16,* 259–264.

Aronson, E., Willerman, B., & Floyd, J. (1966). The effect of a pratfall on increasing interpersonal attractiveness. *Psychonomic Science, 4,* 227–228.

Asarnow, J., Glynn, S., Pynoos, R. S., Nahum, J., Guthrie, D., Cantwell, D. P., & Franklin, B. (1999). When the earth stops shaking: Earthquake sequelae among children diagnosed for pre-earthquake psychopathology. *Journal of the American Academy of Child and Adolescent Psychiatry, 38,* 1016–1025.

Asbell, B. (1995). *The Pill: A biography of the drug that changed the world.* New York: Random House.

Asch, S. E. (1940). Studies in the principles of judgments and attitudes: 11. Determination of judgments by group and by ego standards. *Journal of Social Psychology, 12,* 433–465.

Asch, S. E. (1956). Studies of independence and conformity: A minority of one against a unanimous majority. *Psychological Monographs, 70*(9, Whole No. 416).

Aserinsky, E., & Kleitman, N. (1953). Regularly occurring periods of eye mobility and concomitant phenomena during sleep. *Science, 118,* 273–274.

Ashby, F. G., & Waldron, E. M. (2000). The neurpsychological bases of category learning. *Current Directions in Psychological Science, 9,* 10–14.

Atkinson, R. C., & Schiffrin, R. M. (1968). Human memory: A control system and its control processes. In K. Spence (Ed.), *The psychology of learning and motivation* (Vol. 2). New York: Academic Press.

Austin, J. H. (1998). *Zen and the brain: Toward an understanding of meditation and consciousness.* Cambridge, MA: MIT Press.

Averill, J. A. (1980). A constructivist view of emotion. In R. Plutchik & H. Kellerman (Eds.), *Emotion: Theory, research, and experience: Vol. 1. Theories of emotion.* New York: Academic Press.

Axel, R. (1995, October). The molecular logic of smell. *Scientific American, 273,* 154–159.

Ayllon, T., & Azrin, N. H. (1965). The measurement and reinforcement of behavior of psychotics. *Journal of Experimental Analysis of Behavior, 8,* 357–383.

Ayllon, T., & Azrin, N. H. (1968). *The token economy: A motivational system for therapy and rehabilitation.* New York: Appleton-Century-Crofts.

Azar, B. (1994, October). Seligman recommends a depression "vaccine." *APA Monitor,* 4.

Azar, B. (1995, June). New cognitive research makes waves. *APA Monitor,* 16.

Azar, B. (1996, November). Some forms of memory improve as people age. *APA Monitor,* 27.

Azar, B. (1998a, January). Certain smells evoke stronger memories. *APA Monitor,* 10.

Azar, B. (1998b, January). Communicating through pheromones. *APA Monitor,* 1, 12.

Azar, B. (2002, September). Searching for genes that explain our personalities. *Monitor on Psychology, 33*(8), 44–45.

Baddeley, A. (1998). *Human memory: Theory and practice.* Boston: Allyn & Bacon.

Baddeley, A., Gathercole, S., & Papagno, C. (1998). The phonological loop as a language learning device. *Psychological Review, 105,* 158–173.

Baddeley, A. D. (2001). Is working memory still working? *American Psychologist, 56,* 851–864.

Baell, W. K., & Wertheim, E. H. (1992). Predictors of outcome in the treatment of bulimia nervosa. *British Journal of Clinical Psychology, 31*(3), 330–332.

Bahrick, H. P., Bahrick, L. E., Bahrick, A. S., & Bahrick, P. E. (1993). Maintenance of foreign language vocabulary and the spacing effect. *Psychology Science, 4,* 316–321.

Bailey, J. M., Bobrow, D., Wolfe, M., & Mikach, S. (1995). Sexual orientation of adult sons of gay fathers. *Developmental Psychology, 31,* 124–129.

Balch, P., & Ross, A. W. (1975). Predicting success in weight reduction as a function of locus of control: A uni-dimensional and multi-dimensional approach. *Journal of Consulting and Clinical Psychology, 43,* 119.

Baldwin, D. A. (2000). Interpersonal understanding fuels knowledge acquisition. *Current Directions in Psychological Science, 9,* 40–45.

Baldwin, M. W. (1992). Relational schemas

and the processing of social information. *Psychological Bulleting, 112,* 461–484.

Balter, M. (2000, October 20). Celebrating the synapse. *Science, 290,* 424.

Baltes, M. M. (1995). Dependency in old age: Gains and losses. *Current Directions in Psychological Science, 4,* 14–19.

Baltes, P. B. (1987). Theoretical propositions on life-span developmental psychology: On the dynamics between growth and decline. *Developmental Psychology, 23,* 611–626.

Baltes, P. B. (1990, November). *Toward a psychology of wisdom.* Invited address presented at the annual convention of the Gerontological Society of America, Boston, MA.

Baltes, P. B. (1993). The aging mind: Potential and limits. *The Gerontologist, 33,* 580–594.

Baltes, P. B., & Kliegl, R. (1992). Further testing of limits of cognitive plasticity: Negative age differences in a mnemonic skill are robust. *Developmental Psychology, 28,* 121–125.

Bamshad, M. J., & Olson, S. E. (2003, December). Does race exist? *Scientific American, 289*(6), 78–85.

Bandura, A. (1970). Modeling therapy. In W. S. Sahakian (Ed.), *Psychopathology today: Experimentation, theory and research.* Itasca, IL: Peacock.

Bandura, A. (1981). In search of pure unidirectional determinants. *Behavior Therapy, 12,* 30–40.

Bandura, A. (1986). *Social foundations of thought and action: A social cognitive theory.* Englewood Cliffs, NJ: Prentice-Hall.

Bandura, A. (1992). Exercise of personal agency through the self-efficacy mechanism. In R. Schwarzer (Ed.), *Self-efficacy: Thought control of action* (pp. 3–38). Washington, DC: Hemisphere.

Bandura, A. (1999). Social cognitive theory of personality. In L. A. Pervin & O. P. John (Eds.), *Handbook of personality: Theory and research* (2nd ed., pp. 154–196). New York: Guilford Press.

Bandura, A., Ross, D., & Ross, S. A. (1963). Imitation of film-mediated aggressive models. *Journal of Abnormal and Social Psychology, 66,* 3–11.

Banich, M. T. (1998). Integration of information between the cerebral hemispheres. *Current Directions in Psychological Science, 7,* 32–37.

Banks, M. S., & Bennet, P. J. (1988). Optical and photoreceptor immaturities limit the spatial and chromatic vision of human neonates. *Journal of the Optical Society of America, 5,* 2059–2079.

Barab, S. A., & Plucker, J. A. (2002). Smart people or smart contexts? Cognition, ability, and talent development in an age of situated approaches to knowing and learning. *Educational Psychologist, 37,* 165–182.

Barber, T. X. (1976). *Hypnosis: A scientific approach.* New York: Psychological Dimensions.

Barber, T. X. (1979). Suggested ("hypnotic") behavior: The trance paradigm versus an alternative paradigm. In E. Fromm & R. E. Shor (Eds.), *Hypnosis: Developments in research and new perspectives.* New York: Aldine.

Barber, T. X. (1986). Realities of stage hypnosis. In B. Zilbergeld, M. G. Edelstein, & D. L. Araoz (Eds.), *Hypnosis: Questions and answers.* New York: Norton.

Barinaga, M. (1994, July 29). To sleep, perchance to . . . learn? New studies say yes. *Science, 265,* 603–604.

Barinaga, M. (1995, December 1). Brain researchers speak a common language. *Science, 270,* 1437–1438.

Barinaga, M. (1996, January 19). Social status sculpts activity of crayfish neurons. *Science, 271,* 290–291.

Barinaga, M. (1997a, July 25). How jet-lag hormone does double duty in the brain. *Science, 277,* 480.

Barinaga, M. (1997b, June 27). New imaging methods provide a better view into the brain. *Science, 276,* 1974–1976.

Barinaga, M. (1998a, April 17). Listening in on the brain. *Science, 280,* 376–377.

Barinaga, M. (1998b, July 24). How the brain sees in three dimensions. *Science, 281,* 500–501.

Barinaga, M. (1999, July 9). The mapmaking mind. *Science, 285,* 189, 191–192.

Barinaga, M. (2000, October 27). Synapses call the shots. *Science, 290,* 736–738.

Barinaga, M. (2002, February 8). How the brain's clock gets daily enlightenment. *Science, 295,* 955–957.

Barinaga, M. (2003a, January 3). Newborn neurons search for meaning. *Science, 299,* 32–34.

Barinaga, M. (2003b, October 3). Studying the well-trained mind. *Science, 302,* 44–46.

Barker, L. M., Best, M. R., & Domjan, M. (Eds.). (1978). *Learning mechanisms in food selection.* Houston: Baylor University Press.

Barker, S. L., Funk, S. C., & Houston, B. K. (1988). Psychological treatment versus nonspecific factors: A meta-analysis of conditions that engender comparable expectations for improvement. *Clinical Psychology Review, 8,* 579–594.

Barkley, R. A. (1998, September). Attention-deficit hyperactivity disorder. *Scientific American, 279*(9), 66–71.

Barlow, D. H. (1996). Health care policy, psychotherapy research, and the future of psychotherapy. *American Psychologist, 51,* 1050–1058.

Barlow, D. H. (2000). Unraveling the mysteries of anxiety and its disorders from the perspective of emotion theory. *American Psychologist, 55,* 1247–1263.

Barlow, D. H. (2001). A modern learning theory perspective on the etiology of panic disorder. *Psychological Review, 108,* 4–32.

Barlow, D. H., & Durand, V. M. (2005). *Abnormal psychology: An integrative approach.* Belmont, CA: Wadsworth.

Barnes, D. M. (1987). Biological issues in schizophrenia. *Science, 235,* 430–433.

Barnett, R. C., & Hyde, J. S. (2001). Women, men, work, and family: An expansionist theory. *American Psychologist, 56,* 781–796.

Barnier, A. J., & McConkey, K. M. (1998). Posthypnotic responding away from the hypnotic setting. *Psychological Science, 9,* 256–262.

Barnouw, V. (1963). *Culture and personality.* Homewood, IL: Dorsey Press.

Baron, L., & Straus, M. A. (1985). *Four theories of rape in American society: A state-level analysis.* New Haven, CT: Yale University Press.

Barron, F., & Harrington, D. M. (1981). Creativity, intelligence and personality. *Annual Review of Psychology, 32,* 439–476.

Bartels, A., & Zeki, S. (2004). The neural correlates of maternal and romantic love. *NeuroImage, 22,* 419–433.

Bartoshuk, L. M. (1990, August–September). Psychophysiological insights on taste. *Science Agenda,* 12–13.

Bartoshuk, L. M. (1993). The biological basis of food perception and acceptance. *Food Quality and Preference, 4,* 21–32.

Bartoshuk, L. M., Duffy, V. B., & Miller, I. J. (1994). PCT/PROP tasting: Anatomy, psychophysics and sex effects. *Physiology and Behavior, 56,* 1165–1171.

Basbaum, A. I., Clanton, C. H., & Fields, H. L. (1976). Opiate and stimulus-produced analgesia: Functional anatomy of a medullospinal pathway. *Proceedings of the National Academy of Sciences, 73,* 4685–4688.

Basbaum, A. I., & Fields, H. L. (1984). Endogenous pain control systems: Brainstem spinal pathways and endorphin circuitry. *Annual Review of Neuroscience, 7,* 309–338.

Basic Behavioral Science Task Force of the National Advisory Mental Health Council. (1996). Basic behavioral science research for mental health: Family processes and social networks. *American Psychologist, 51,* 622–630.

Bass, E., & Davis, L. (1988). *The courage to heal.* New York: Harper-Collins.

Batista, A. P., Buneo, C. A., Snyder, L. H., & Andersen, R. A. (1999, July 9). Reach plans in eye-centered coordinates. *Science, 285,* 257–260.

Batson, C. D. (1987). Prosocial motivation: Is it ever truly altruistic? In L. Berkowitz (Ed.), *Advances in experimental social psychology* (Vol. 20). Orlando, FL: Academic Press.

Bauer, P. J. (2002). Long-term recall memory: Behavioral and neuro-developmental changes in the first 2 years of life. *Current Directions in Psychological Science, 11,* 137–141.

Baum, A. (1990). Stress, intrusive imagery, and chronic distress. *Health Psychology, 9,* 653–675.

Baum, D. (2004, July 12, 19). The price of valor. *The New Yorker, 80,* 44–52.

Baum, W. M. (1994). *Understanding behaviorism: Science, behavior, and culture.* New York: HarperCollins.

Baumeister, A. A. (1987). Mental retardation: Some conceptions and dilemmas. *American Psychologist, 42,* 796–800.

Baumeister, R. F. (Ed.). (1993). *Self-esteem: The puzzle of low self-regard.* New York: Plenum.

Baumeister, R. F., Campbell, J. D., Krueger, J. I., & Vohs, K. D. (2003). Does high self-esteem cause better performance, interpersonal success, happiness, or healthier lifestyles? *Psychological Science in the Public Interest, 4,* 1–44.

Baumeister, R. F., & Leary, M. R. (1995). The need to belong: Desire for interpersonal attachments as a fundamental human motivation. *Psychological Bulletin, 117,* 427–529.

Baumeister, R. F., Smart, L., & Boden, J. M. (1996). Relation of threatened egotism to violence and aggression: The dark side of high self-esteem. *Psychological Review, 103,* 5–33.

Baumeister, R. F., Stillwell, A. M., & Wotman, S. R. (1990). Victim and perpetrator accounts of interpersonal conflict: Autobiographical narratives about anger. *Journal of Personality and Social Psychology, 59,* 994–1005.

Baumrind, D. (1967). Child care practices anteceding three patterns of preschool behavior. *Genetic Psychology Monographs, 75,* 43–88.

Baumrind, D. (1971). Current patterns of parental authority. *Developmental Psychology Monograph, 4*(1, Part 2).

Baumrind, D. (1985). Research using intentional deception: Ethical issues revisited. *American Psychologist, 40,* 165–174.

Baynes, K., Eliassen, J. C., Lutsep, H. L., & Gazzaniga, M. S. (1998). Modular organization of cognitive systems masked by interhemispheric integration. *Science, 280,* 902–905.

Beall, A. E., & Sternberg, R. J. (1995). The social construction of love. *Journal of Social and Personal Relationships, 12*(3), 417–438.

Beaman, A. L., Barnes, P. J., Klentz, B., & McQuirk, B. (1978). Increasing helping rates through information dissemination: Teaching pays. *Personality and Social Psychology Bulletin, 4,* 406–411.

Beardsley, T. (1996, July). Waking up. *Scientific American,* 14, 18.

Beardsley, T. (1997a, August). The machinery of thought. *Scientific American, 277,* 78–83.

Beardsley, T. (1997b, March). Memories are made of . . . *Scientific American,* 32–33.

Bechara, A., Damasio, H., Tranel, D., & Damasio, A. R. (1997, February 28). Deciding advantageously before knowing the advantageous strategy. *Science, 275,* 1293–1295.

Bechara, A., Tranel, D., Damasio, H., Adolphs, R., Rockland, C., & Damasio, A. R. (1995, August 25). Double dissociation of conditioning and declarative knowledge relative to the amygdala and hippocampus in humans. *Science, 269,* 1115–1118.

Beck, A., Kline, S., & Greenfeld, L. (1988). *Survey of youth in custody, 1987.* Washington, DC: Bureau of Justice Statistics.

Beck, A. T. (1976). *Cognitive therapy and emotional disorders.* New York: International Universities Press.

Beck, A. T., Rush, A. J., Shaw, B. F., & Emery, G. (1979). *Cognitive therapy of depression.* New York: Guilford Press.

Bédard, J., & Chi, M. T. H. (1992). Expertise. *Current Directions in Psychological Science, 1,* 135–139.

Bee, H. (1994). *Lifespan development.* New York: HarperCollins.

Beeman, M. J., & Chiarello, C. (1998). Complementary right- and left-hemisphere language comprehension. *Current Directions in Psychological Science, 7,* 2–8.

Behrmann, M. (2000). The mind's eye mapped onto the brain's matter. *Current Directions in Psychological Science, 9,* 50–54.

Beigel, A., & Berren, M. R. (1985). Human-induced disasters. *Psychiatric Annals, 15,* 143–150.

Beilin, H. (1992). Piaget's enduring contribution to developmental psychology. *Developmental Psychology, 28,* 191–204.

Bell, A. P., Weinberg, M. S., & Hammersmith, S. K. (1981). *Sexual preference.* Bloomington: Indiana University Press.

Bem, D. J. (1996). Exotic becomes erotic: A developmental theory of sexual orientation. *Psychological Review, 103,* 320–335.

Bem, D. J. (2001). *Interplay of theory and politics in explaining the enigma of sexual orientation.* Address given at the annual convention of the American Psychological Association in San Francisco, CA.

Bem, D. J., & Allen, A. (1974). On predicting some of the people some of the time: The search for cross-situational consistencies in behavior. *Psychological Review, 81*(6), 506–520.

Benassi, V. A., Sweeney, P. D., & Dufour, C. L. (1988). Is there a relation between locus of control orientation and depression? *Journal of Abnormal Psychology, 97,* 357–367.

Benedict, R. (1934). *Patterns of culture.* Boston: Houghton Mifflin.

Benjamin, L. T., Jr., & Nielsen-Gammon, E. (1999). B. F. Skinner and psychotechnology: The case of the heir conditioner. *Review of General Psychology, 3,* 155–167.

Benson, H. (1975). *The relaxation response.* New York: Morrow.

Berk, L. E. (2004). *Development through the lifespan.* Boston: Allyn & Bacon.

Berlyne, D. E. (1960). *Conflict, arousal, and curiosity.* New York: McGraw-Hill.

Berman, J. S., & Norton, N. C. (1985). Does professional training make a therapist more effective? *Psychological Bulletin, 98,* 401–407.

Berndt, T. J. (1992). Friendship and friends' influence in adolescence. *Current Directions in Psychological Science, 1,* 156–159.

Bernstein, I. L. (1988). *What does learning have to do with weight loss and cancer?* Proceedings of the Science and Public Policy Seminar of the Federation of Behavioral, Psychological and Cognitive Sciences. Washington, DC.

Bernstein, I. L. (1990). Salt preference and development. *Developmental Psychology, 26,* 552– 554.

Bernstein, I. L. (1991). Aversion conditioning in response to cancer and cancer treatment. *Clinical Psychology Review, 11,* 185–191.

Berry, J. (1992). Cree conceptions of cognitive competence. *International Journal of Psychology, 27,* 73–88.

Berry, J. W., Poortinga, Y. H., Segall, M. H., & Dasen, P. R. (1992). *Cross-cultural psychology: Research and applications.* New York: Cambridge University Press.

Berscheid, E. (1988). Some comments on love's anatomy: or, Whatever happened to old-fashioned lust? In R. J. Sternberg & M. L. Barnes (Eds.), *The psychology of love.* New Haven, CT: Yale University Press.

Berscheid, E. (1999). The greening of relationship science. *American Psychologist, 54,* 260–266.

Beutler, L. E., Brown, M. T., Crothers, L., Booker, K., & Seabrook, M. K. (1996). The dilemma of factitious demographic distinctions in psychological research. *Journal of Consulting and Clinical Psychology, 64,* 892–902.

Beutler, L. E., & Machado, P. P. (1992). Research on psychotherapy. In M. R. Rosenzweig (Ed.), *International psychological science: Progress, problems, and prospects* (pp. 227–252). Washington, DC: American Psychological Association.

Bevins, R. A. (2001). Novelty seeking and reward: Implications for the study of high-risk behaviors. *Current Directions in Psychological Science, 10,* 189–193.

Bicklen, D. (1990). Communication unbound: Autism and praxis. *Harvard Educational Review, 60*(3), 291–314.

Biederman, I. (1989). Higher-level vision. In D. N. Osherson, H. Sasnik, S. Kosslyn, K. Hollerbach, E. Smith, & N. Block (Eds.), *An invitation to cognitive science.* Cambridge, MA: MIT Press.

Biehl, M., Matsumoto, D., Ekman, P., Hearn, V., Heider, K., Kudoh, T., & Ton, V. (1997). Matsumoto and Ekman's Japanese and Caucasian facial expressions of emotion (JACFEE): Reliability data and cross-national differences. *Journal of Nonverbal Behavior, 21,* 3–21.

Bilkey, D. (2004, August 27). In the Place Space. *Science, 305,* 1245–1246.

Binet, A. (1911). *Les idées modernes sur les enfants.* Paris: Flammarion.

Binitie, A. (1975). A factor-analytical study of depression across cultures (African and European). *British Journal of Psychiatry, 127,* 559–563.

Bink, M. L., & Marsh, R. L. (2000). Cognitive regularities in creative activity. *Review of General Psychology, 4,* 59–78.

Birenbaum, M., & Montag, I. (1986). On the location of the sensation seeking construct in the personality domain. *Multivariate Behavioral Research, 21,* 357–373.

Bjork, R. (1991, November). How do you improve human performance? *APS Observer,* 13–15.

Bjork, R. A. (2000). *Creating desirable difficulties for the learner. Implications for theory and practice.* Address given at the American Psychological Society's annual convention, Miami Beach, FL.

Bjork, R. A., & Richardson-Klarehn, A. (1989). On the puzzling relationship between environmental context and human memory. In C. Izawa (Ed.), *Current issues in cognitive processes: The Tulane-Floweree symposium on cognition.* Hillsdale, NJ: Erlbaum.

Bjorklund, D. F., & Shackelford, T. K. (1999). Differences in parental investment contribute to important differences between men and women. *Current Directions in Psychological Science, 8,* 86–89.

Blass, E. M. (1990). Suckling: Determinants, changes, mechanisms, and lasting impressions. *Developmental Psychology, 26,* 520–533.

Blass, T. (1996). Experimental invention and controversy: The life and work of Stanley Milgram. *The General Psychologist, 32,* 47–55.

Blatt, S. J., Sanislow III, C. A., & Pilkonis, P. A. (1996). Characteristics of effective therapists: Further analyses of data from the National Institute of Mental Health treatment of depression collaborative research program. *Journal of Consulting and Clinical Psychology, 64,* 1276–1284

Bloom, R. W. (2002). On media violence: Whose facts? Whose misinformation? *American Psychologist, 57,* 447–448.

Blum, D. (2002). *Love at Goon Park: Harry Harlow and the science of affection.* New York: Perseus Publishing.

Bodmer, W. F., & Cavalli-Sforza, L. L. (1970, October). Intelligence and race. *Scientific American,* 19–29.

Bond, M. H., Nakazato, H. S., & Shiraishi, D. (1975). Universality and distinctiveness in dimensions of Japanese person perception. *Journal of Cross-Cultural Psychology, 6,* 346–355.

Boomsma, D., Anokhin, A., & de Geus, E. (1997, August). Genetics of electrophysiology: Linking genes, brain, and behavior. *Current Directions in Psychological Science, 6,* 106–110.

Booth, A., Johnson, D. R., Granger, D. A., Crouter, A. C., & McHale, S. (2003). Testosterone and child and adolescent adjustment: The moderating role of parent–child relationships. *Developmental Psychology, 39,* 85–98.

Bornstein, R. F. (1989). Exposure and affect: Overview and meta-analysis of research, 1968– 1987. *Psychological Bulletin, 106,* 265–289.

Borod, C., Koff, E., Lorch, M. P., Nicholas, M., & Welkowitz, J. (1988). Emotional and non-emotional facial behavior in patients with unilateral brain damage. *Journal of Neurological and Neurosurgical Psychiatry, 5,* 826–832.

Bostwick, J. M., & Pankratz, V. S. (2000). Affective disorders and suicide risk: A reexamination. *American Journal of Psychiatry, 157,* 1925–1932.

Bouchard, T. J., Jr. (1994, June 17). Genes, environment, and personality. *Science, 264,* 1700–1701.

Bouchard, T. J., Lykken, D. T., McGue, M., Segal, N. L., & Tellegen, A. (1990). Sources of human psychological differences: The Minnesota study of twins reared apart. *Science, 250,* 223–228.

Bourguignon, E. (1979). *Psychological anthropology: An introduction to human nature and cultural differences.* New York: Holt, Rinehart and Winston.

Bowden, C. L., Calabrese, J. R., McElroy, S. L., Gyulai, L., Wassef, A., Petty, F., Pope, H. G. Jr., Chou, J. C., Keck, P. E. Jr., Rhodes, L. J., Swann, A. C., Hirschfeld, R. M., & Wozniak, P. J. (2000). A randomized, placebo-controlled 12-month trial of divalproex and lithium in treatment of outpatients with bipolar I disorder. Divalproex Maintenance Study Group. *Archives of General Psychiatry, 57,* 481–489.

Bower, B. (1992, August 22). Genetic clues to female homosexuality. *Science News, 142,* 117.

Bower, B. (1995b, March 4). Virus may trigger some mood disorders. *Science News, 147,* 132.

Bower, B. (1996, April 27). Mom–child relations withstand day care. *Science News, 149,* 261.

Bower, B. (1997a, October 18). My culture, my self: Western notions of the mind may not translate to other cultures. *Science news, 152,* 248–249.

Bower, B. (1997b). Preschoolers get grip on hidden emotions. *Science News, 152,* 70.

Bower, B. (1998a, February 21). All fired up: Perception may dance to the beat of collective neuronal rhythms. *Science News, 153,* 120–121.

Bower, B. (1998b). Dr. Freud goes to Washington. *Science News, 154,* 347–349.

Bower, B. (1998c, April 25). The name game: Young kids grasp new words with intriguing dexterity. *Science News, 153,* 268–269.

Bower, B. (1998d, June 20). Psychology's tangled web. *Science News, 153,* 394–395.

Bower, B. (2000a, January 22). Cultures of reason: Thinking styles may take Eastern and Western routes. *Science News, 157,* 56–58.

Bower, B. (2000b, September, 30). Memory echoes in brain's sensory terrain. *Science News, 158,* 213.

Bower, B. (2004, July 24). Suicide watch: Antidepressants get large-scale inspection. *Science News, 166,* 51.

Bower, G. H. (1972). A selective review of organizational factors in memory. In E. Tulving & W. Donaldson (Eds.), *Organization of memory.* New York: Academic Press.

Bower, G. H. (1981). Mood and memory. *American Psychologist, 36,* 129–148.

Bower, J. M., & Parsons, L. M. (2003, August). Rethinking the "lesser brain." *Scientific American,* 50–57.

Bower, T. G. R. (1971, October). The object in the world of the infant. *Scientific American, 225*(4), 30–39.

Bowers, K. S. (1983). *Hypnosis for the seriously curious* (2nd ed.) New York: Norton.

Bowlby, J. (1969). *Attachment and loss: Vol. 1. Attachment.* New York: Basic Books.

Bowlby, J. (1973). *Attachment and loss: Vol. 2. Separation, anxiety and anger.* London: Hogarth.

Bradbury, J. (2001, May 19). Teasing out the genetics of bipolar disorder. *Lancet, 357,* 1596.

Bradley, G. W. (1978). Self-serving biases in the attribution process: A re-examination of the fact or fiction question. *Journal of Personality and Social Psychology, 35,* 56–71.

Bradshaw, G. (1992). The airplane and the logic of invention. In R. N. Giere (Ed.). *Minnesota studies in the philosophy of science* (pp. 2239–2250). Minneapolis: University of Minnesota Press.

Braine, M. D. S. (1976). Children's first word combinations. *Monographs of the Society for Research in Child Development, 41* (Serial No. 164).

Bransford, J., Sherwood, R., Vye, N., & Rieser, J. (1986). Teaching thinking and problem solving: Research foundations. *American Psychologist, 41,* 1078–1089.

Bransford, J. D., & Franks, J. J. (1971). The abstraction of linguistic ideas. *Cognitive Psychology, 2,* 331–350.

Braun, K. A., Ellis, R., & Loftus, E. F. (2002). Make my memory: How advertising can change our memories of the past. *Psychology and Marketing, 19,* 1–23.

Breggin, P. R. (1979). *Electroshock: Its brain disabling effects.* New York: Springer.

Breggin, P. R. (1991). *Toxic psychiatry.* New York: St. Martin's Press.

Breggin, P. R., & Breggin, G. R. (1994). *Talking back to Prozac.* New York: St. Martin's Press.

Brehm, S. S. (1992). *Intimate relationships* (2nd ed.). Boston: McGraw-Hill.

Brehm, S. S., Miller, R., Perlman, D., & Campbell, S. M. (2002). *Intimate relationships* (3rd ed). New York: McGraw-Hill.

Breier, J. I., Simos, P. G., Fletcher, J. M., Castillo, E. M., Zhang, W., & Papanicolaou, A. C. (2003). Abnormal activation of temporoparietal language areas during phonetic analysis in children with dyslexia. *Neuropsychology, 17,* 610–621.

Brett, A. S., Phillips, M., & Beary, J. F., III. (1986, March 8). Predictive power of the polygraph: Can the "lie detector" really detect liars? *Lancet, 1*(8480), 544–547.

Brewer, C. L. (1991). Perspectives on John B. Watson. In G. A. Kimble, M. Wertheimer, & C. L. White (Eds.), *Portraits of pioneers in psychology* (pp. 170–186). Washington, DC: American Psychological Association.

Brewer, M. B., Dull, V., and Lui, L. (1981). Perceptions of the elderly: Stereotypes and prototypes. *Journal of Personality and Social Psychology, 41,* 656–670.

Brigham, J. C. (1980). Limiting conditions of the "physical attractiveness stereotype": Attributions about divorce. *Journal of Research in Personality, 14,* 365–375.

Brislin, R. (1974). The Ponzo illusion: Additional cues, age, orientation, and culture. *Journal of Cross-Cultural Psychology, 5,* 139–161.

Brislin, R. (1993). *Understanding culture's influence on behavior.* Fort Worth, TX: Harcourt Brace Jovanovich.

Brislin, R. W. (1981). *Cross-cultural encounters: Face-to-face interaction.* Boston: Allyn & Bacon.

Broman, S. H., Nichols, P. I., & Kennedy, W. A. (1975). *Preschool IQ: Prenatal and early developmental correlates.* Hillsdale, NJ: Erlbaum.

Bronfenbrenner, U., & Ceci, S. J. (1994). Nature–nurture reconceptualized in developmental perspective: A bioecological model. *Psychological Review, 101,* 568–586.

Bronheim, S. (2000, January/February). The impact of the Human Genome Project on the science and practice of psychology. *Psychological Science Agenda, 13*(1), 12.

Brookhart, S. (2001). Persuasion and the "poison parasite." *APS Observer, 14*(8), 7.

Brooks, R., & Goldstein, S. (2004). *The power of resilience: Achieving balance, confidence, and personal strength in your life.* New York: Contemporary Books.

Brown, A. L., & Campione, J. C. (1986). Psychological theory and the study of learning disabilities. *American Psychologist,* 41, 1059–1068.

Brown, A. M. (1990). *Human universals.* Unpublished manuscript, University of California, Santa Barbara.

Brown, B. (1999). Optimizing expression of the common human genome for child development. *Current Directions in Psychological Science, 8,* 37–41.

Brown, C. (2003, October). The stubborn scientist who unraveled a mystery of the night. *Smithsonian,* 92–99.

Brown, J. D. (1991). Accuracy and bias in self-knowledge. In C. R. Snyder & D. F. Forsyth (Eds.), *Handbook of social and clinical psychology: The health perspective.* New York: Pergamon.

Brown, J. L., & Pollitt, E. (1996, February). Malnutrition, poverty and intellectual development. *Scientific American, 274*(2), 38–43.

Brown, K. (2003a, March 14). The medication merry-go-round. *Science, 299,* 1646–1649.

Brown, K. (2003b, July 11). New attention to ADHD genes. *Science, 301,* 160–161.

Brown, R., & Kulik, J. (1977). Flashbulb memories. *Cognition, 5,* 73–99.

Brown, R., & McNeill, D. (1966). The "tip of the tongue" phenomenon. *Journal of Verbal Learning and Verbal Behavior, 5,* 325–337.

Brown, S. L., Nesse, R. M., Vinokur, A. D., & Smith, D. M. (2003). Providing social support may be more beneficial than receiving it: Results from a prospective study of mortality. *Psychological Science, 14,* 320–327.

Brown, W. A. (1998, January). The placebo effect. *Scientific American,* 90–95.

Bruce, D. (1991). Integrations of Lashley. In G. A. Kimble, M. Wertheimer, & C. L. White (Eds.), *Portraits of pioneers in psychology* (pp. 306–323). Washington, DC: American Psychological Association.

Bruch, H. (1978). *The golden cage: The enigma of anorexia nervosa.* Cambridge, MA: Harvard University Press.

Bruck, M., & Ceci, S. (1997). The suggestibility of young children. *Current Directions in Psychological Science, 6,* 75– 79.

Bruner, J. (1992). Another look at new look 1. *American Psychologist, 47,* 780–783.

Bruner, J. S., Olver, R. R., & Greenfield, P. M. (1966). *Studies in cognitive growth.* New York: Wiley.

Brunner, H. G., Nelen, M., Breakefield, X. O., Ropers, H. H., & van Oost, B. A. (1993). Abnormal behavior associated with a point mutation in the structural gene for monoamine oxidase A. *Science, 262,* 578.

Buck, L., & Axel, R. (1991). A novel multigene family may encode odorant receptors: A molecular basis for odor recognition. *Cell, 65,* 175–187.

Buhrmester, D. (1996). Need fulfillment, interpersonal competence, and the developmental contexts of early adolescent friendship. In W. M. Bukowski, A. F. Newcomb, & W. W. Hartup (Eds.), *The company they keep: Friendship during childhood and adolescence* (pp. 158–185). New York: Cambridge University Press.

Buie, J. (1988, July). "Control" studies bode better health in aging. *APA Monitor,* 20.

Bushman, B. J., & Anderson, C. A. (2001). Media violence and the American public: Scientific facts versus media misinformation. *American Psychologist, 56,* 477–489.

Buss, D. M. (1999). *Evolutionary psychology: The new science of the mind.* Boston: Allyn and Bacon.

Buss, D. M. (2000). The evolution of happiness. *American Psychologist, 55,* 15–23.

Buss, D. M. (2001). *Human mating strategies and human nature.* Address given at the annual convention of the American Psychological Association, San Francisco, CA.

Buss, D. M. (2004). *Evolutionary psychology: The new science of the mind* (2nd ed.). Boston: Allyn & Bacon.

Buss, D. M., Haselton, M. G., Shackelford, T. K., Bleske, A. L., & Wakefield, J. C. (1998). Adaptations, exaptations, and spandrels. *American Psychologist, 53,* 533–548.

Buss, D. M., & Schmitt, D. P. (1993). Sexual strategies theory: An evolutionary perspective on human mating. *Psychological Review, 100,* 204–232.

Bussey, K., & Bandura, A. (1999). Social cognitive theory of gender development and differentiation. *Psychological Review, 106,* 676–713.

Butcher, J. N., Graham, J. R., Williams, C. L., & Ben-Porath, Y. (1989). *Development and use of the MMPI-2 content scales.* Minneapolis: University of Minnesota Press.

Butcher, J. N., & Williams, C. L. (1992). *Essentials of MMPI-2 and MMPI-A interpretation.* Minneapolis: University of Minnesota Press.

Byne, W. (1995). The biological evidence challenged. *Scientific American, 270*(5), 50–55.

Byrne, D. (1969). Attitudes and attraction. In L. Berkowitz (Ed.), *Advances in experimental social psychology* (Vol. 4). New York: Academic Press.

Cabay, M. (1994). A controlled evaluation of facilitated communication using open-ended and fill-in questions. *Journal of Autism and Developmental Disorders, 24*(4), 517–527.

Cabeza, R. (2002). Hemispheric asymmetry reduction in older adults: The HAROLD model. *Psychology & Aging, 17*(1), 85–100.

Cahill, L., Prins, B., Weber, M., & McGaugh, J. L. (1994). *b*-Adrenergic activation and memory for emotional events. *Nature, 371,* 702–704.

Caldwell, M. (1995, June). Kernel of fear. *Discover, 16,* 96–102.

Calev, A., Nigal, D., Shapira, B., Tubi, N., Chazan, S., Ben-Yehuda, Y., Kugelmass, S., & Lerer, B. (1991). Early and long-term effects of electroconvulsive therapy and depression on memory and other cognitive functions. *Journal of Nervous and Mental Disorders, 179,* 526–533.

Callahan, J. (1997, May/June). Hypnosis: Trick or treatment? *Health, 11*(1), 52–55.

Callaway, C. W. (1987). Obesity. *Public Health Reports Supplement, 102,* 26–29.

Calvert, J. D. (1988). Physical attractiveness: A review and reevaluation of its role in social skill research. *Behavioral Assessment, 10,* 29–42.

Camara, W. J., & Schneider, D. L. (1994). Integrity tests: Facts and unresolved issues. *American Psychologist, 49,* 112–119.

Campbell, S. S., & Murphy, P. J. (1998, January 16). Extraocular circadian phototransduction in humans. *Science, 279,* 396–399.

Campfield, L. A., Smith, F. J., & Burn, P. (1998, May 29). Strategies and potential molecular targets for obesity treatment. *Science, 280,* 1383–1387.

Campos, J. J., Barrett, K. C., Lamb, M. E., Goldsmith, H. H., & Stenberg, C. (1983). *Socioemotional development* (Vol. 2). New York: Wiley.

Canli, T., Sivers, H., Whitfield, S. L., Gotlib, I. H., & Gabreli, J. D. E. (2002, June 21). Amygdala response to happy faces as a function of extraversion. *Science, 296,* 2191.

Cann, A., Calhoun, L. G., Selby, J. W., & Kin, H. E. (Eds.). (1981). Rape. *Journal of Social Issues, 37* (Whole No. 4).

Cannon, W. B. (1914). The interrelations of emotions as suggested by recent physiological researchers. *American Journal of Psychology, 25,* 256.

Cannon, W. (1936). The interrelations of emotions as suggested by recent physiological researches. *American Journal of Psychology, 25,* 256.

Caplow, T. (1982). *Middletown families: Fifty years of change and continuity.* Minneapolis: University of Minnesota Press.

Caporeal, L. R. (1976). Ergotism: The Satan loosed in Salem? *Science, 192,* 21–26.

Caprara, G. V., Barbaranelli, C., Borgoni, L., & Perugini, M. (1993). The Big Five Questionnaire: A new questionnaire for the measurement of the five-factor model. *Personality and Individual Differences, 15,* 281–288.

Carey, S. (1978). The child as word learner. In M. Halle, J. Bresnan, & G. A. Miller (Eds.), *Linguistic theory and psychological reality* (pp. 265–293). Cambridge, MA: MIT Press.

Carlson, N. R. (2004). *Physiology of behavior* (8th ed.). Boston: Allyn & Bacon.

Carlsson, A. (1978). Antipsychotic drugs, neurotransmitters, and schizophrenia. *American Journal of Psychiatry, 135,* 164–173.

Carmichael, L. (1970). The onset and early development of behavior. In P. H. Mussen (Ed.), *Carmichael's manual of child psychology* (3rd ed., Vol. 1). New York: Wiley.

Carpenter, G. C. (1973). Differential response to mother and stranger within the first month of life. *Bulletin of the British Psychological Society, 16,* 138.

Carpenter, S. (1999, August 14). A new look at recognizing what people see. *Science News, 156,* 102.

Carpenter, S. (2001a, February). Different

dispositions, different brains. *Monitor on Psychology, 32(2),* 66–68.

Carpenter, S. (2001b, January). When at last you don't succeed . . . *Monitor on Psychology, 32*(1), 70–71.

Carson, R. C., Butcher, J. N., & Mineka, S. (1996). *Abnormal psychology and modern life.* 10th ed. New York: HarperCollins.

Carson, R. C., Butcher, J. N., & Mineka, S. (2000). *Abnormal psychology and modern life* (11th ed.). Boston: Allyn & Bacon.

Carstensen, L. L. (1987). Age-related changes in social activity. In L. L. Carstensen & B. A. Edelstein (Eds.), *Handbook of clinical gerontology* (pp. 222–237). New York: Pergamon Press.

Carstensen, L. L. (1991). Selectivity theory: Social activity in life-span context. In K. W. Schaie (Ed.), *Annual Review of Geriatrics and Gerontology* (Vol. 11). New York: Springer.

Carstensen, L. L., and Freund, A. M. (1994). Commentary: The resilience of the aging self. *Developmental Review, 14,* 81–92.

Cartwright, R. D. (1977). *Night life: Explorations in dreaming.* Englewood Cliffs, NJ: Prentice Hall.

Cartwright, R. D. (1978). *A primer on sleep and dreaming.* Reading, MA: Addison-Wesley.

Cartwright, R. D. (1984). Broken dreams: A study of the effects of divorce and depression on dream content. *Psychiatry, 47,* 251–259.

Carver, C. S., & Scheier, M. F. (1992). *Perspectives on personality,* 2nd ed. Boston: Allyn and Bacon.

Carver, C. S., & Scheier, M. F. (2000). *Perspectives on personality* (4th ed.). Boston: Allyn & Bacon.

Casey, J. F., & Wilson, L. (1991). *The flock.* New York: Fawcett Columbine.

Cash, T. F., & Duncan, N. C. (1984). Physical attractiveness stereotyping among black American college students. *Journal of Social Psychology, 122,* 71–77.

Cash, T. F., & Janda, L. H. (1984, December). The eye of the beholder. *Psychology Today,* 18, 46–52.

Cash, T. F., & Kilcullen, R. N. (1985). The aye of the beholder: Susceptibility to sexism and beautyism in the evaluation of managerial applicants. *Journal of Applied Social Psychology, 15,* 591–605.

Caspi, A., McClay, J., Moffitt, T. E., Mill, J., Martin, J., Craig, I. W., Taylor, A., & Poulton, R. (2002, August 2). Role of genotype in the cycle of violence in maltreated children. *Science, 297,* 851–852.

Cattaneo, E., Rigamonti, D., & Zuccato, C. (2002, December). The enigma of Huntington's disease. *Scientific American,* 92–97.

Cattell, R. B. (1963). Theory of fluid and crystallized intelligence: A critical experiment. *Journal of Educational Psychology, 54,* 1–22.

Cattell, R. B. (1950). *Personality: A systemic, theoretical, and factual study.* New York: McGraw Hill.

Ceci, S. J., & Bruck, M. (1993). Suggestibility of the child witness: A historical review and synthesis. *Psychological Bulletin, 113,* 403–439.

Ceci, S. J., & Liker, J. K. (1986). A day at the races: A study of IQ, expertise, and cognitive complexity. *Journal of Experimental Psychology: General, 115,* 255–266.

Ceci, S. J., & Williams, W. M. (1997). Schooling, intelligence, and income. *American Psychologist, 52,* 1051–1058.

Centers for Disease Control and Prevention. (2000). *Health, United States, 2000: Adolescent Health Chartbook.* Retrieved on November 8, 2004, from http://www.cdc.gov/nchs/hus.htm

Cervone, D. (2004). The architecture of personality. *Psychological Review, 111,* 183–204.

Cervone, D., & Shoda, Y. (1999). Beyond traits in the study of personality coherence. Current *Directions in Psychological Science, 8,* 27–32.

Chalmers, D. J. (1995, December). The puzzle of conscious experience. *Scientific American, 273*(6), 80–86.

Chambless, D. L., Sanderson, W. C., Shoham, V., Johnson, S. B., Pope, K. S., Crits-Christoph, P., Baker, M., Johnson, B., Woody, S. R., Sue, S., Beutler, L., Williams, D. A., & McCurry, S. (1996). An update on empirically validated therapies. *The Clinical Psychologist, 49,* 5–18.

Chapman, P. D. (1988). *Schools as sorters: Lewis M. Terman, applied psychology, and the intelligence testing movement, 1890–1930.* New York: New York University Press.

Chartrand, T. L., & Bargh, J. A. (1999). The chameleon effect: The perception–behavior link and social interaction. *Journal of Personality & Social Psychology, 76,* 893–910.

Chaudhari, N., Landin, A. M., & Roper, S. D. (2000). A metabotropic glutamate receptor variant functions as a taste receptor. *Nature Neuroscience, 3,* 113–119.

Chi, M., Glaser, R., & Rees, E. (1982). Expertise in problem solving. In R. Sternberg (Ed.)., *Advances in the psychology of human intelligence* (Vol. 1). Hillsdale, NJ: Erlbaum.

Chilman, C. S. (1983). *Adolescent sexuality in a changing American society* (2nd ed.). New York: Wiley.

Chomsky, N. (1965). *Aspects of a theory of syntax.* Cambridge, MA: MIT Press.

Chomsky, N. (1975). *Reflections on language.* New York: Pantheon Books.

Chorney, M. J., Chorney, N. S., Owen, M. J., Daniels, J., McGuffin, P., Thompson, L. A., Detterman, D. K., Benbow, C., Lubinski, D., Eley, T., & Plomin, R. (1998). A quantitative trait locus associated with cognitive ability in children. *Psychological Science, 9,* 159–166.

Christensen, A., & Jacobson, N. S. (1994). Who (or what) can do psychotherapy: The status and challenge of nonprofessional therapies. *Psychological Science, 5,* 8–14.

The Chronicle of Higher Education. (2004, August 27). *2001–2002 Almanac, 51*(1), 19.

Church, R. M. (2001). A turning test for computational and associative theories of learning. *Current Directions in Psychological Science, 10,* 132–136.

Churchland, P. M. (1995). *The engine of reason, the seat of the soul: A philosophical journey into the brain.* Cambridge, MA: MIT Press.

Cialdini, R. B. (2001a). *Influence: Science and practice* (4th ed.). Boston: Allyn & Bacon.

Cialdini, R. B. (2001b, February). The science of persuasion. *Scientific American, 284,* 76–81.

Clark, H. H., & Clark, E. V. (1977). *Psychology and language: An introduction to psycholinguistics.* New York: Harcourt Brace Jovanovich.

Clark, M. S., Mills, J. R., & Corcoran, D. M. (1989). Keeping track of needs and inputs of friends and strangers. *Personality and Social Psychology Bulletin, 15,* 533–542.

Clark, R. E., & Squire, L. R. (1998, April 3). Classical conditioning and brain systems: The role of awareness. *Science, 280,* 77–81.

Clarke-Stewart, K. A. (1989). Infant day care: Maligned or malignant? *American Psychologist, 44,* 266–273.

Clay, R. (2003a, April). An empty nest can promote freedom, improved relationships. *Monitor on Psychology,* 40–41.

Clay, R. (2003b, April). Researchers replace midlife myths with facts. *Monitor on Psychology,* 38–39.

Clay, R. A. (1998, November). Preparing for the future: Practitioners seek training for prescribing medication. *APA Monitor,* 22–23.

Clay, R. A. (2000, January). Psychotherapy is cost-effective. *Monitor on Psychology, 31*(1) 40–41.

Clay, R. A. (2001, January). Research to the heart of the matter. *Monitor on Psychology, 32*(1), 42–49.

Cleek, M. B., & Pearson, T. A. (1985). Perceived causes of divorce: An analysis of interrelationships. *Journal of Marriage and the Family, 47,* 179–191.

Cochran, S. D., Sullivan, J. G., & Mays, V. M. (2003). Prevalence of mental disorders, psychological distress, and mental health services use among lesbian, gay, and bisexual adults in the United States. *Journal of Consulting and Clinical Psychology, 71,* 53–61.

Coghill, R. C., McHaffie, J. G., & Yen, Y. (2003, July 8). Neural correlates of interindividual differences in the subjective experience of pain. *Proceedings of the National Academy of Sciences, 14,* 8538–8542.

Cognitive–behavior therapy effective for panic disorder. (1991, November). APS Observer, 8.

Cohen, D., & Gunz, A. (2002). As seen by the other . . . : Perspectives on the self in the memories and emotional perceptions of Easterners and Westerners. *Psychological Science,* 55–59.

Cohen, J. (2002, February 8). The confusing mix of hype and hope. *Science, 295,* 1026.

Cohen, J. D., & Tong, F. (2001, 28 September). The face of controversy. *Science, 293,* 2405–2407.

Cohen, M. N. (1998). *Culture of intolerance: Chauvinism, class, and racism in the United States.* New Haven, CT: Yale University Press.

Cohen, R. E., & Ahearn, F. L., Jr. (1980). *Handbook for mental health care of disaster victims.* Baltimore: Johns Hopkins University Press.

Cohen, S., & Syme, S. L. (Eds.). (1985). *Social support and health.* Orlando, FL: Academic Press.

Colby, A., Kohlberg, L., Gibbs, J., & Lieberman, M. (1983). A longitudinal study of moral judgment. *Monographs of the Society for Research in Child Development, 481*(1–2, Serial No. 200).

Colcombe, S. J., Kramer, A. F., Erickson, K. I., Scalf, P., McAuley, E., Cohen, N. J., Webb, A., Jerome, G. J., Marquez, D. X., & Elavsky, S. (2004). Cardiovascular fitness, cortical plasticity, and aging. *Proceedings of the National Academy of Sciences, 101,* 3316–3321.

Collins, A. W., Maccoby, E. E., Steinberg, L., Hetherington, E. M., & Bornstein, M. H. (2000). Contemporary research on parenting: The case for nature *and* nurture. *American Psychologist, 55,* 218–232.

Collins, G. P. (2001, October). Magnetic revelations: Functional MRI highlights neurons receiving signals. *Scientific American,* 21.

Committee on Substance Abuse and Committee on Children with Disabilities (2000). Fetal alcohol syndrome and alcohol-related neurodevelopmental disorders. *Pediatrics, 106,* 358–361.

Comuzzie, A. G., & Allison, D. B. (1998, May 29). The search for human obesity genes. *Science, 280,* 1374–1377.

Conger, J. J., & Peterson, A. C. (1984). *Adolescence and youth* (3rd ed.) New York: Harper & Row.

Conrad, R. (1964). Acoustic confusions in immediate memory. *British Journal of Psychology, 55,* 75–84.

Consumer Reports. (1995, November). Mental health: Does therapy help? 734–739.

Conway, J. K. (1992). *Written by herself: Autobiographies of American women: An anthology.* New York: Vintage.

Cook, M., Mineka, S., Wolkenstein, B. & Laitsch, K. (1985). Observational conditioning of snake fear in unrelated rhesus monkeys. *Journal of Abnormal Psychology, 94,* 591–610.

Coon, D. J. (1992). Testing the limits of sense and science: American experimental psychologists combat spiritualism, 1880–1920. *American Psychologist, 47,* 143–151.

Cooper, W. H. (1983). An achievement motivation normological network. *Journal of Personality and Social Psychology, 44,* 841–861.

Coren, S., & Girgus, J. S. (1978). *Visual illusions.* In *Handbook of Sensory Physiology; Volume VIII.* In Held, R., Liebowitz, H., & Teuber, H. L. (Eds.). New York: Springer-Verlag Incorporated, 1978, 549–568.

Costa, P. T., Jr., & McCrae, R. R. (1992a). Four ways five factors are basic. *Personality and Individual Differences, 13,* 653–665.

Costa, P. T., Jr., & McCrae, R. R. (1992b). *Revised NEO Personality Inventory (NEO-PI-R) and NEO Five-Factor Inventory (NEO-FFI) professional manual.* Odessa, FL: Psychological Assessment Resources.

Coughlin, E. K. (1994, October 26). Class, IQ, and heredity. *The Chronicle of Higher Education,* A12, A20.

Covington, M. V. (2000). Intrinsic versus extrinsic motivation in schools: A reconciliation. *Current Direction in Psychology Science, 9,* 22–25.

Coyne, J. C., Burchill, S. A. L., & Stiles, W. B. (1991). An interactional perspective on depression. In C. R. Snyder & D. O. Forsyth (Eds.), *Handbook of social and clinical psychology: The health perspective* (pp. 327–349). New York: Pergamon Press.

Coyne, K. J. C. (2001, February). Depression in primary care: Depressing news, exciting research opportunities. *APS Observer, 14*(2), 1, 18.

Craig, A. D., & Reiman, E. M. (1996, November 21). Functional imaging of an illusion of pain. *Nature, 384,* 258–260.

Craik, F. I. M. (1979). Human memory. *Annual Review of Psychology, 30,* 63–102.

Craik, F. I. M., & Lockhart, R. S. (1972). Levels of processing: A framework for memory research. *Journal of Verbal Learning and Verbal Behavior, 11,* 671–684.

Craik, F. I. M., Moroz, T. M., Moscovitch, M., Stuss, D. T., Winocur, G., Tulving, E., & Shitij, K. (1999). In search of the self: A positron emission tomography study. *Psychological Science, 10,* 26–34.

Craik, F. I. M., & Tulving, E. (1975). Depth of processing and the retention of words in episodic memory. *Journal of Experimental Psychology: General, 104,* 268–294.

Cramer, P. (2000). Defense mechanisms in psychology today. *American Psychologist, 55,* 637–646.

Craske, M. G., Brown, T. A., & Barlow, D. H. (1991). Behavioral treatment of panic disorder: A two year follow-up. *Behavior Therapy, 19,* 577–592.

Cree, G. S., & McRae, K. (2003). Analyzing the factors underlying the structure and computation of the meaning of chipmunk, cherry, cheese, and cello (and many other such concrete nouns). *Journal of Experimental Psychology: General, 132,* 163–201.

Crick, F. (1994). *The astonishing hypothesis: The scientific search for the soul.* New York: Charles Scribner's Sons.

Crick, F., & Mitchison, G. (1983). The function of dream sleep. *Nature, 304,* 111–114.

Cromwell, R. L. (1993). Searching for the origins of schizophrenia. *Psychological Science, 4,* 276–279.

Crowder, R. G. (1992). Eidetic images. In L. R. Squire (Ed.), *The encyclopedia of learning and memory* (pp. 154–156). New York: MacMillan.

Crowell, T. A. (2002). Neuropsychological findings in combat-related posttraumatic stress disorder. *Clinical Neuropsychologist, 16,* 310–321.

Csikszentmihalyi, M. (1990). *Flow: The psychology of optimal experience.* New York: Harper & Row.

Csikszentmihalyi, M. (1996, July/August). The creative personality. *Psychology Today, 29*(4), 34–40.

Csikszentmihalyi, M. (1998). *Finding flow.* New York: Basic Books.

Csikszentmihalyi, M., Larson, R., & Prescott, S. (1977). The ecology of adolescent activity and experience. *Journal of Youth and Adolescence, 6,* 281–294.

Csikszentmihalyi, M., Rathunde, K. R., Whalen, S., & Wong, M. (1993). *Talented teenagers: The roots of success and failure.* New York: Cambridge University Press.

Cushman, P. (1990). Why the self is empty: Toward a historically situated psychology. *American Psychologist, 45,* 599–611.

Dabbs, J. M. (2000). *Heroes, rogues, and lovers: Testosterone and behavior.* New York: McGraw-Hill.

Dackman, L. (1986). Everyday illusions. *Exploratorium Quarterly, 10,* 5–7.

Daily, D. K., Ardinger, H. H., & Holmes, G. E. (2000). Identification and evaluation of mental retardation. *American Family Physician, 61,* 1059–1067.

Daley, K. C. (2004). Update on attention-deficit/hyperactivity disorder. *Current Opinion in Pediatrics, 16,* 217–226.

Daly, R. C., Su, T.-P., Schmidt, P. J., Pagliaro, M., Pickar, D., & Rubinow, D. R. (2003). Neuroendocrine and behavioral effects of high-dose anabolic steroid administration in male normal volunteers. *Psychoneuroendocrinology, 28,* 317–331.

Damasio, A. (2003). *Looking for Spinoza: Joy, sorrow, and the feeling brain.* Orlando, FL: Harcourt.

Damasio, A. B. (1994). *Descartes' error: Emotion, reason, and the human brain.* New York: Avon Books.

Damasio, A. R. (1999, December). How the brain creates the mind. *Scientific American,* 112–117.

Damasio, A. R. (2000). *The feeling of what happens: Body and emotion in the making of consciousness.* New York: Harcourt Brace.

Danion, J., Rizzo, L., & Bruant, A. (1999). Functional mechanisms underlying impaired recognition memory and conscious awareness in patients with schizophrenia. *Archives of General Psychiatry, 56,* 639–644.

Dannefer, D., & Perlmutter, M. (1990). Developmental as a multidimensional process: Individual and social constituents. *Human Development, 33,* 108–137.

Darley, J. M., & Batson, C. D. (1973). From Jerusalem to Jericho: A study of situational and dispositional variables in helping behavior. *Journal of Personality and Social Psychology, 27,* 100–108.

Darley, J. M., & Latané, B. (1968) Bystander intervention in emergencies: Diffusion of responsibility. *Journal of Personality and Social Psychology, 8,* 377–383.

Darling, N., & Steinberg, L. (1993). Parenting style as context: An integrative model. *Psychological Bulletin, 113,* 487–496.

Darwin, C. (1963). *On the origin of species.* London: Oxford University Press. (Original work published in 1859.)

Darwin, C. (1998). *The expression of the emotions in man and animals* (3rd ed., with Introduction, Afterword, and Commentaries by P. Ekman). New York: Oxford University Press. (Original work published in 1862.)

Darwin, C. J., Turvey, M. T., & Crowder, R. G. (1972). The auditory analogue of the Sperling partial report procedure: Evidence for brief auditory stage. *Cognitive Psychology, 3,* 255–267.

Dattilio, F. M., & Padesky, C. A. (1990). *Cognitive therapy with couples.* Sarasota, FL: Professional Resource Exchange.

Davidson, R. J. (1992a). Anterior cerebral asymmetry and the nature of emotion. *Brain and Cognition, 20,* 125–151.

Davidson, R. J. (1992b). Emotion and affective style: Hemispheric substrates. *Psychological Science, 3,* 39–43.

Davidson, R. J. (2000a). *Affective neuroscience.* Address given at the American Psychological Association's annual convention, Washington, DC.

Davidson, R. J. (2000b). Affective style, psychopathology, and resilience: Brain mechanisms and plasticity. *American Psychologist, 55,* 1196–1214.

Davidson, R. J. (2002, April). Synaptic substrates of the implicit and explicit self. *Science, 296,* 268.

Davidson, R. J., Kabat-Zinn, J., Schumacher, J., Rosenkranz, M., Muller, D., Santorelli, S. F., Urbanowski, F., Harrington, A., Bonus, K., & Sheridan, J. F. (2003). Alternations in brain and immune function produced by mindfulness meditation. *Psychosomatic Medicine, 65,* 564–570.

Davidson, R. J., Putnam, K. M., & Larson, C. L. (2000, July 28). Dysfunction in the neural circuitry of emotion regulation—a possible prelude to violence. *Science, 289,* 591–594.

Davison, K. P., Pennebaker, J. W., & Dickerson, S. S. (2000). Who talks? The social psychology of illness support groups. *American Psychologist, 55,* 205–217.

Daw, J. (2001, June). The Ritalin debate. *Monitor on Psychology, 32*(6), 64–65.

Daw, J. (2002, November). Why and how normal people go mad. *Monitor on Psychology,* 20–21.

Dawkins, K., Lieberman, J. A., Lebowitz, B. D., & Hsiao, J. K. (1999). Antipsychotics: Past and future. *Schizophrenia Bulletin, 25,* 395–405.

Deadwyler, S. A., & Hampson, R. E. (1995, November 24). Ensemble activity and behavior: What's the code? *Science, 270,* 1316–1318.

DeAngelis, T. (1997, January). Chromosomes contain clues on schizophrenia. *APA Monitor,* 26.

DeAngelis, T. (2002a, June). A bright future for PNI. *Monitor on Psychology,* 46–50.

DeAngelis, T. (2002b, July–August). If you do just on thing, make it exercise. *Monitor on Psychology,* 4–51.

DeAngelis, T. (2003, March). When anger's a plus. *Monitor on Psychology, 34,* 44–45.

DeCasper, A. J., & Fifer, W. P. (1980). Of human bonding: Newborns prefer their mothers' voices. *Science, 208,* 1174–1176.

DeCasper, A. J., & Spence, M. J. (1986). Prenatal maternal speech influences newborns' perception of speech sounds. *Infant Behavior and Development, 9,* 133–150.

Deckers, L. (2001). *Motivation: Biological, psychological, and environmental.* Boston: Allyn & Bacon.

de Gelder, B. (2000, August 18). More to seeing than meets the eye. *Science, 289,* 1148–1149.

DeGrandpre, R. J. (2000). A science of meaning: Can behaviorism bring meaning to psychological science? *American Psychologist, 55,* 721–739.

de Groot, A. D. (1965). *Thought and choice in chess.* The Hague: Mouton.

Delgado, J. M. R. (1969). *Physical control of the mind: Toward a psychocivilized society.* New York: Harper & Row.

Dembroski, T. M., & Costa, P. T., Jr. (1987). Coronary prone behavior: Components of the Type A pattern and hostility. *Journal of Personality, 55,* 211–235.

Dembroski, T. M., Weiss, S. M., Shields, J. L., et al. (1978). *Coronary-prone behavior.* New York: Springer-Verlag.

Dement, W. C. (1980). *Some watch while some must sleep.* San Francisco: San Francisco Book Company.

Dement, W. C. (2000, September 25). *Sleep debt.* Retrieved March 9, 2004, from Sleep-Quest website: http://www.sleepquest.com/d_column_archive6.html

Dement, W. C., & Kleitman, N. (1957). Cyclic variations in EEG during sleep and their relations to eye movement, body mobility and dreaming. *Electroencephalography and Clinical Neurophysiology, 9,* 673–690.

Dement, W. C., & Vaughan, C. (1999). *The promise of sleep.* New York: Delacorte Press.

Dennis, W. (1960). Causes of retardation among institutionalized children: Iran. *Journal of Genetic Psychology, 96,* 47–59.

Dennis, W., & Dennis, M. G. (1940). The effect of cradling practices upon the onset of walking in Hopi children. *Journal of Genetic Psychology, 56,* 77–86.

DePaulo, B. M., Lindsay, J. J., Malone, B. E., Muhlenbruck, L., Charlton, K., & Cooper, H. (2003). Cues to deception. *Psychological Bulletin, 129,* 74–118.

Deregowski, J. B. (1980). *Illusions, patterns and pictures: A cross-cultural perspective* (pp. 966–977). London, U.K.: Academic Press.

DeSalvo, L. (2000). *Writing as a way of healing: How telling our stories transforms our lives.* Boston: Beacon Press.

Dess, N. K., and Foltin, R. W. (2005). In Akins, C. K., Panicker, S., & Cunningham, C. L. (Eds.), *Laboratory animals in research and teaching: Ethics, care and methods.* Washington, DC: American Psychological Association.

Detterman, D. K. (1999). The psychology of mental retardation. *International Review of Psychiatry, 11,* 26–33.

Deutsch, M., & Collins, M. E. (1951). *Interracial housing: A psychological evaluation of a social experiment.* Minneapolis: University of Minnesota Press.

Deutsch, M., & Gerard, H. B. (1955). A study of normative and informational social influence upon individual judgment. *Journal of Abnormal and Social Psychology, 51,* 629–636.

Devereux, G. (1981). *Mohave ethnopsychiatry and suicide: The psychiatric knowledge and psychic disturbances of an Indian tribe. Bureau of American Ethology Bulletin 175.* Washington, DC: Smithsonian Institution.

Devine, P. G., & Zuwerink, J. R. (1994). Prejudice and guilt: The internal struggle to overcome prejudice. In W. J. Lonner & R. Malpass (Eds.), *Psychology and culture* (pp. 203–207). Boston: Allyn & Bacon.

de Waal, F. B. M. (1999, December). The end of nature versus nurture. *Scientific American,* 94–99.

Dewsbury, D. A. (1990). Early interactions between animal psychologists and animal activists and the founding of the APA Committee on Precautions in Animal Experimentation. *American Psychologist, 45,* 315–327.

Dewsbury, D. A. (1997). In celebration of the centennial of Ivan P. Pavlov's (1897/1902) *The work of the digestive glands. American Psychologist, 52,* 933–935.

Dickens, W. T., & Flynn, J. R. (2001). Heritability estimates versus large environmental effects: The IQ paradox resolved. *Psychological Review, 108,* 346–369.

Dickinson, A. (2001). Causal learning: Association versus computation. *Current Directions in Psychological Science, 10,* 127–132.

Diener, E. (1984). Subjective well-being. *Psychological Bulletin, 95,* 542–575.

Diener, E. (2000). Subjective well-being: The science of happiness and a proposal for a national index. *American Psychologist, 55,* 34–43.

Digman, J. M. (1990). Personality structure: Emergence of the five-factor model. *Annual Review of Psychology, 41,* 417–440.

Dillbeck, M. C., & Orme-Johnson, D. W. (1987). Physiological differences between transcendental meditation and rest. *American Psychologist, 42*(9), 879–881.

Dion, K. K. (1986). Stereotyping based on physical attractiveness: Issues and conceptual perspectives. In C. P. Herman, M. P. Zanna, & E. T. Higgins (Eds.), *Physical appearance, stigma, and social behavior: The Ontario symposium on personality and social psychology* (Vol. 3). Hillsdale, NJ: Erlbaum.

Dittmann, M. (2003). Psychology's first prescribers. *Monitor on Psychology, 34*(2), 36.

Dittmann, M. (2004). Prescriptive authority. *Monitor on Psychology, 35*(5), 34–35.

Dixon, R. A., Kramer, D. A., & Baltes, P. B. (1985). Intelligence: A life-span developmental perspective. In B. B. Wolman (Ed.), *Handbook of intelligence* (pp. 301–352). New York: Wiley.

Dobbins, A. C., Jeo, R. M., Fiser, J., & Allman, J. M. (1998, July 24). Distance modulation of neural activity in the visual cortex. *Science, 281,* 552–555.

Dobelle, W. (1977). Current status of research on providing sight to the blind by electrical stimulation of the brain. *Journal of Visual Impairment and Blindness, 71,* 290–297.

Doetsch, F. (2002). Genetics of childhood disorders: XXXVIII. Stem cell research, part 2: Reconstructing the brain. *Journal of the American Academy of Child & Adolescent Psychiatry, 41,* 622–624.

Dolan, R. J. (2002). Emotion, cognition, and behavior. *Science, 298,* 1191–1194.

Domhoff, G. W. (1996). *Finding meaning in dreams: A quantitative approach.* New York: Plenum Press.

Doob, L. W. (1964). Eidetic images among the Ibo. *Ethnology, 3,* 357–363.

Dowling, J. E. (1992). *Neurons and networks: An introduction to neuroscience.* Cambridge, MA: Harvard University Press.

Downing, P. E., Jiang, Y., Shuman, M., &

Kanwisher, N. (2001, 28 September). A cortical area selective for visual processing of the human body. *Science, 293,* 2470–2473.

Doyle, R. (2001, June). The American terrorist. *Scientific American, 285*(6), 28.

Doyle, R. (2002a). Deinstitutionalization: Why a much maligned program still has life. *Scientific American, 287,* 38.

Doyle, R. (2002b, January). Going solo: Unwed motherhood in industrial nations rises. *Scientific American,* 24.

Dracheva, S., Marras, S. A. E., Elhakem, S. L., Kramer, F. R., Davis, K. L., & Haroutunian, V. (2001). N-methyl-d-aspartic acid receptor expression in the dorsolateral prefrontal cortex of elderly patients with schizophrenia. *American Journal of Psychiatry, 158,* 1400–1410.

Draguns, J. (1980). Psychological disorders of clinical severity. In H. Triandis & J. Draguns (Eds.), *Handbook of cross-cultural psychology, Vol. 6: Psychopathology* (pp. 99–174). Boston: Allyn & Bacon.

Draguns, J. G. (1979). Culture and personality. In A. J. Marsella, R. G. Tharp, & T. J. Ciborowski (Eds.), *Perspectives on cross-cultural psychology* (pp. 179–207). New York: Academic Press.

Drake, R. E., Osher, F. C., & Wallach, M. A. (1991). Homelessness and dual diagnosis. *American Psychologist, 46,* 1149–1158.

Druckman, D., & Bjork, R. A. (1991). *In the mind's eye: Enhancing human performance.* Washington, DC: National Academy Press.

Duck, S. (1992). *Human relationships* (2nd ed.). Newbury Park, CA: Sage.

Duncan, J., Seitz, R. J., Kolodny, J., Bor, D., Herzog, H., Ahmed, A., Newell, F. N., & Emslie, H. (2000, July 21). A neural basis for general intelligence. *Science, 289,* 457–460.

Dutton, D. G., & Aron, A. P. (1974). Some evidence for heightened sexual attraction under conditions of high anxiety. *Journal of Personality and Social Psychology, 30,* 510–517.

Eagly, A. H., Ashmore, R. D., Makhijani, M. G., & Kennedy, L. C. (1991). What is beautiful is good, but. . . : A meta-analytic review of the social psychological literature. *Psychological Bulletin, 100,* 283–308.

Eagly, A. H., & Wood, W. (1999). The origins of sex differences in human behavior: Evolved dispositions versus social roles. *American Psychologist, 54,* 408–423.

Eccles, J. S., Midgley, C., Wigfield, A., Buchanan, C. M., Reuman, D., Flanagan, C., & Mac Iver, D. (1993). Development during adolescence: The impact of stage-environment fit on young adolescents' experiences in schools and in families. *American Psychologist, 48,* 90–101.

Eckensberger, L. H. (1994). Moral development and its measurement across cultures. In W. J. Lonner & R. Malpass (Eds.), *Psychology and culture* (pp. 71–78). Boston, MA: Allyn & Bacon.

Edwards, A. E., & Acker, L. E. (1962). A demonstration of the long-term retention of a conditioned galvanic skin response. *Psychosomatic Medicine, 24,* 459–463.

Edwards, K. J., Hershberger, P. J., Russell, R. K., & Markert, R. J. (2001). Stress, negative social exchange, and health symptoms in university students. *Journal of American College Health, 50,* 75–86.

Edwards, S. R. (1995, February). Healthy divorces can lead to well-adjusted children. APA Monitor, p. 7.

Ehrlich, P. R. (2000a). *Genes, cultures and the human prospect.* Washington, DC: Island Press.

Ehrlich, P. R. (2000b, September 22). The tangled skeins of nature and nurture in human evolution. *The Chronicle of Higher Education,* B7–B11.

Eich, E., Macaulay, D., Loewenstein, R. J., & Dihle, P. H. (1997). Memory, amnesia, and dissociative identity disorder. *Psychological Science, 8,* 417–422.

Eichenbaum, H. (1997, July 18). How does the brain organize memories? *Science, 277,* 330–332.

Eichorn, D. H., & VandenBos, G. R. (1985). Dissemination of scientific and professional knowledge: Journal publication within the APA. *American Psychologist, 40,* 1309–1316.

Eisenberger, R., & Cameron, J. (1996). Detrimental effects of reward: Reality or myth? *American Psychologist, 51,* 1153–1166.

Eisler, R., & Levine, D. S. (2002). Nurture, nature, and caring: We are not prisoners of our genes. *Brain and Mind, 3,* 9–52.

Ekman, P. (1984). Expression and the nature of emotion. In K. R. Scherer & P. Ekman (Eds.), *Approaches to emotion.* Hillsdale, NJ: Erlbaum.

Ekman, P. (1992). Facial expressions of emotion: New findings, new questions. *Psychological Science, 3,* 34–38.

Ekman, P. (1993). Facial expression and emotion. *American Psychologist, 48,* 384–392.

Ekman, P. (1994). Strong evidence for universals in facial expressions: A reply to Russell's mistaken critique. *Psychological Bulletin, 115,* 268–287.

Ekman, P. (2003). *Emotions revealed: Recognizing faces and feelings to improve communication and emotional life.* New York: Times Books, Henry Holt and Company.

Ekman, P., & Friesen, W. V. (1971). Constants across cultures in the face and emotion. *Journal of Personality and Social Psychology, 17,* 124–129.

Ekman, P., & Friesen, W. V. (1986). A new pan-cultural facial expression of emotion. *Motivation and Emotion, 10,* 159–168.

Ekman, P., Friesen, W. V., O'Sullivan, M., Chan, A., Diacoyanni-Tarlatzis, I., Heider, K., Krause, R., LeCompte, W. A., Pitcairn, T., Ricci-Bitti, P. E., Scherer, K., Tomita, M., & Tzavaras, A. (1987). Universal and cultural differences in the judgments of facial expressions of emotion. *Journal of Personality and Social Psychology, 53,* 712–717.

Ekman, P., & Rosenberg, E. (1997). *What the face reveals.* New York: Oxford University Press.

Ekman, P., Sorenson, E. R., & Friesen, W. V. (1969). Pan-cultural elements in facial displays in emotion. *Science, 764,* 86–88.

Elbert, T., Pantev, C., Wienbruch, C., Rockstroh, B., & Taub, E. (1995, October 13). Increased cortical representation of the fingers of the left hand in string players. *Science, 270,* 305–307.

Eley, T. C. (1997). General genes: A new theme in developmental psychopathology. *Current Directions in Psychological Science, 6,* 90–95.

El-Hai, J. (1999). Uniquely twins. *Minnesota Medicine.* Retrieved on November 8, 2004, from http://www.mnmed.org/Protected/99MNMED/9903/El-Hai.html

Ellis, A. (1987). *The practice of rational emotive therapy (RET).* New York: Springer.

Ellis A. (1990). *The essential Albert Ellis: Seminal writings on psychotherapy.* New York: Springer.

Ellis, A. (1996). *Better, deeper, and more enduring brief therapy: The rational emotive behavior therapy approach.* New York: Brunner/Mazel Publishers.

Ellison, J. (1984, June). The seven frames of mind. *Psychology Today, 18,* 21–24, 26.

Ellsworth, P. C. (1994). William James and emotion: Is a century of fame worth a century of misunderstanding? *Psychological Review, 101,* 222–229.

Engle, R. W. (2002). Working memory capacity as executive attention. *Current Directions in Psychological Science, 11,* 19–23.

Ennis, M., Kelly, K. S., & Lambert, P. L. (2001). Sex differences in cortisol excretion during anticipation of a psychological stressor: Possible support for the tend-and-befriend hypothesis. *Stress and Health, 17,* 253–261.

Enserink, M. (2000, July 28). Searching for the mark of Cain. *Science, 289,* 575–579.

Epstein, S. (1980). The stability of confusion: A reply to Mischel and Peake. *Psychological Review, 90,* 179–184.

Epstein, S., & Feist, G. J. (1988). Relation between self- and other-acceptance and its moderation by identification. *Journal of Personality and Social Psychology, 54,* 309–315.

Erdberg, P. (1990). Rorschach assessment. In G. Goldstein & M. Hersen (Eds.), *Psychological assessment* (2nd ed.). New York: Pergamon.

Erdelyi, M. H. (1992). Psychodymanics and the unconscious. *American Psychologist, 47,* 784–787.

Ericsson, K. A., & Charness, N. (1994). Expert performance: Its structure and acquisition. *American Psychologist, 49,* 725–747.

Ericsson, K. A., Krampe, R. T., & Tesch-Römer, C. (1993). The role of deliberate practice in the acquisition of expert performance. *Psychological Review, 100,* 363–406.

Erikson, E. H. (1963). *Childhood and society* (2nd ed.). New York: Norton.

Exner, J. E., Jr. (1974). *The Rorschach: A comprehensive system: Vol. 1.* New York: Wiley.

Exner, J. E., Jr. (1978). *The Rorschach: A comprehensive system: Vol. 2: Current research and interpretation.* New York: Wiley.

Exner, J. E., Jr., & Weiner, I. B. (1982). *The Rorschach: A comprehensive system: Vol. 3: Assessment of children and adolescents.* New York: Wiley.

Ezzell, C. (2003, February). Why??? The neuroscience of suicide. *Scientific American, 288,* 45–51.

Fackelmann, K. (1998, November 28). It's a girl! Is sex selection the first step to designer children? *Science News, 154,* 350–351.

Fadiman, J., & Frager, R. (2001). *Personality and personal growth.* Upper Saddle River, NJ: Prentice-Hall.

Fajans, J. (1985). The person in social context: The social character of Baining "psychology." In G. M. White & J. Kirkpatrick (Eds.), *Person, self, and experience* (pp. 367–400). Berkeley: University of California Press.

Fallon, A., & Rozin, P. (1985). Sex differences in perceptions of desirable body states. *Journal of Abnormal Psychology, 94,* 102–105.

Fancher, R. E. (1979). *Pioneers of psychology.* New York: W. W. Norton.

Fantz, R. L. (1963). Pattern vision in newborn infants. *Science, 140,* 296–297.

Farina, A., Fischer, E. H., Boudreau, L. A., & Belt, W. E. (1996). Mode of target presentation in measuring the stigma of mental disorder. *Journal of Applied Social Psychology, 26,* 2147–2156.

Faulkner, M. (2001). The onset and alleviation of learned helplessness in older hospitalized people. *Aging and Mental Health, 5* (379–386).

Fehr, B. (1988). How do I love thee? Let me consult my prototype. *Journal of Personality and Social Psychology, 55*(4), 557–579.

Fein, M. L. (1993). *I.A.M.: A common sense guide to coping with anger.* Westport, CT: Praeger/Greenwood.

Feingold, A. (1988). Matching for attractiveness in romantic partners and same-sex friends: A meta-analysis and theoretical critique. *Psychological Bulletin, 104,* 226–235.

Feingold, A. (1990). Gender differences in effects of physical attractiveness on romantic attraction: A comparison across five research paradigms. *Journal of Personality and Social Psychology, 59,* 981–993.

Ferguson, C. J. (2002). Media violence: Miscast causality. *American Psychologist, 57,* 446–447.

Fernandez, A., & Glenberg, A. M. (1985). Changing environmental context does not reliably affect memory. *Memory and Cognition, 13,* 333–345.

Ferster. D., & Spruston, N. (1995, November 3). Cracking the neuronal code. *Science, 270,* 756–757.

Festinger, L. (1957). *A theory of cognitive dissonance.* Stanford, CA: Stanford University Press.

Festinger, L., Schachter, S., & Back, K. (1950). *Social pressures in informal groups: A study of a housing community.* New York: Harper & Row.

Field, T. F., & Schanberg, S. M. (1990). Massage alters growth and catecholamine production in preterm newborns. In N. Gunzenhauser (Ed.), *Advances in touch* (pp. 96–104). Skillman, NJ: Johnson & Johnson Co.

Fields, H. L. (1978, November). Secrets of the placebo. *Psychology Today,* 172.

Fields, H. L., & Levine, J. D. (1984). Placebo analgesia: A role for endorphins. *Trends in Neuroscience, 7,* 271–273.

Fields, R. D. (2004, April). The other half of the brain. *Scientific American, 290*(4), 54–61.

Figley, C. R. (2002). *Treating compassion fatigue.* New York: Brunner-Routledge.

Filsinger, E. E., & Fabes, R. A. (1985). Odor communication, pheromones, and human families. *Journal of Marriage and the Family, 47,* 349–359.

Finamore, D. C. (2000). *The relationship of learned helplessness, hardiness, and depression in married, abused women.* Doctoral dissertation, University of Sarasota.

Findley, M. J., & Cooper, H. M. (1983). Locus of control and academic achievement: A literature review. *Journal of Personality and Social Psychology, 44,* 419–427.

Finer, B. (1980). Hypnosis and anaesthesia. In G. D. Burrows & L. Donnerstein (Eds.), *Handbook of hypnosis and psychosomatic medicine.* Amsterdam: Elsevier/North Holland Biomedical Press.

Fiorillo, C. D., Tobler, P. N., & Schultz, W. (2003, March 21). Discrete coding of reward probability and uncertainty by dopamine neurons. *Science, 299,* 1898–1902.

Fiorito, G., & Scotto, P. (1992). Observational learning in Octopus vulgaris. *Science, 256,* 545–547.

Fischer, A. H. (1993). Sex differences in emotionality: Fact or stereotype? *Feminism & Psychology, 3,* 303–318.

Fischer, A. H., Rodriguez Mosquera, P. M., van Vianen, A. E. M., & Manstead, A. S. R. (2004). Gender and culture differences in emotion. *Emotion, 4,* 87–94.

Fischer, P. J., & Breakey, W. R. (1991). The epidemiology of alcohol, drug, and mental disorders among homeless persons. *American Psychologist, 46,* 1115–1128.

Fischhoff, B. (1975). Hindsight ≠ foresight: The effect of outcome knowledge on judgment under uncertainty. *Journal of Experimental Psychology: Human Perception and Performance, 1,* 288–299.

Fisher, H. E. (1992). *Anatomy of love: The natural history of monogamy, adultery, and divorce.* New York: W. W. Norton and Company.

Fisher, S., & Greenberg, R. P. (1985). *The scientific credibility of Freud's theories and therapy.* New York: Columbia University Press.

Fishman, H. C. (1993). *Intensive structural therapy: Treating families in their social context.* New York: Basic Books.

Fiske, D. W., & Fogg, L. (1990). But the reviewers are making different criticisms of my paper! Diversity and uniqueness in reviewer comments. *American Psychologist, 45,* 591–598.

Fiske, S. T., & Neuberg, S. L. (1990). A continuum of impression formation, from category-based to individuating processes: Influences of information and motivation on attention and interpretation. In M. P. Zanna (Ed.), *Advances in experimental social psychology* (Vol. 23). San Diego, CA: Academic Press.

Flavell, J. H. (1985). *Cognitive development* (2nd ed.). Englewood Cliffs, NJ: Prentice-Hall.

Flavell, J. H. (1996). Piaget's legacy. *Psychological Science, 7,* 200–203.

Fleischman, J. (2002). *Phineas Gage: A gruesome but true story about brain science.* Boston: Houghton Mifflin.

Fletcher, A., Lamond, N., van den Heuvel, C. J., & Dawson, D. (2003). Prediction of performance during sleep deprivation and alcohol intoxication using a quantitative model of work-related fatigue. *SleepResearch Online, 5,* 67–75. Retrieved on November 6, 2004, from http://www.sro.org/2003/Fletcher/67/

Fletcher, G. J. O., & Ward, C. (1988). Attribution theory and processes: A cross-cultural perspective. In M. H. Bond (Ed.), *The cross-cultural challenge to social psychology* (pp. 230–244). Newbury Park, CA: Sage.

Fogel, A. (1991). Movement and communication in human infancy: The social dynamics of development. *Human Movement Science, 11,* 387–423.

Foley, V. D. (1979). Family therapy. In R. J. Corsini (Ed.), *Current psychotherapies* (2nd ed., pp. 460–469). Itasca, IL: Peacock.

Folkes, V. S. (1982). Forming relationships and the matching hypothesis. *Journal of Personality and Social Psychology, 8,* 631–636.

Ford, C. S., & Beach, F. A. (1951). *Patterns of sexual behavior.* New York: Harper & Row.

Forgatch, M. S., Patterson, G. R., & Ray, J. A. (1994). Divorce and boys' adjustment problems: Two paths with a single model. In E. M. Hetherington, D. Reiss, & R. Plomin (Eds.), *Stress, coping, and resiliency in children and the family* (pp. 96–110). Hillsdale, NJ: Erlbaum.

Fowers, B. J., & Richardson, F. C. (1996). Why is multiculturalism good? *American Psychologist, 31,* 609–621.

Fowler, H. (1965). *Curiosity and exploratory behavior.* New York: Macmillan.

Fraser, S. (Ed.). (1995). *The bell curve wars: Race, intelligence, and the future of America.* New York: Basic Books.

Freedman, D. J., Riesenhuber, M., Poggio, T., & Miller, E. K. (2001, January 12). Categorical representation of visual stimuli in the primate prefrontal cortex. *Science, 291,* 312–316.

Freedman, J. L. (1984) Effect of television violence on aggression. *Psychological Bulletin, 96,* 227–246.

Freedman, J. L. (1996, May). Violence in the mass media and violence in society: The link is unproven. *Harvard Mental Health Letter, 12*(11), 4–6.

French, E. G. & Thomas, F. H. (1958). The relation of achievement motivation to problem-solving effectiveness. Journal of Abnormal and Social Psychology, 56, 46–48.

Freud, S. (1925). The unconscious. In S. Freud, *The collected papers* (Vol. 4). London: Hogarth.

Freud, S. (1953). *The interpretation of dreams.* New York: Basic Books. (Original edition published in 1900).

Fridlund, A. J. (1990). Evolution and facial action in reflex, social motive, and paralanguage. In P. K. Ackles, J. R. Jennings, & M. G. H. Coles (Eds.), *Advances in psychophysiology*. Greenwich, CT: JAI Press.

Friedman, H. S., & Booth-Kewley, S. (1988). Validity of the Type A construct: A reprise. *Psychological Bulletin, 104,* 381–384.

Friedman, H. S., Hawley, P. H., & Tucker, J. S. (1994). Personality, health, and longevity. *Current Directions in Psychological Science, 3,* 37–41.

Friedman, J. M. (2003, February 7). A war on obesity, not the obese. *Science, 299,* 856–858.

Friedman, M., & Rosenman, R. F. (1974). *Type A behavior and your heart.* New York: Knopf.

Friedman, M., & Ulmer, D. (1984). *Treating Type A behavior—and your heart.* New York: Knopf.

Friedman, M. J. (2004). Acknowledging the psychiatric cost of war. *New England Journal of Medicine, 351,* 75–77.

Friend, R., Rafferty, Y., & Bramel, D. (1990). A puzzling misinterpretation of the Asch "conformity" study. *European Journal of Social Psychology, 20,* 29–44.

Frijda, N. (1986). *The Emotions.* Cambridge University Press.

Fringke, J. L., & Pate, W. E., II (2004). Yesterday, today, and tomorrow. Careers in psychology: 2004. What students need to know. Retrieved on October 14, 2004, from http://research.apa.org

Frith, C. D., & Frith, U. (1999, November 26). Interacting minds—A biological basis. *Science, 286,* 1692–1695.

Frith, U. (1993, June). Autism. *Scientific American, 268,* 108–114.

Frith, U. (1997). Autism. *Scientific American (Special Issue: The Mind), 7*(1), 92–98.

Fromm, E., & Shor, R. E. (Eds.). (1979). *Hypnosis: Developments in research and new perspectives* (2nd ed.). Hawthorne, NY: Aldine.

Funder, D. C. (1983a). Three issues in predicting more of the people: A reply to Mischel & Peake. *Psychological Review, 90,* 283–289.

Funder, D. C. (1983b). The "consistency" controversy and the accuracy of personality judgments. *Journal of Personality, 51,* 346–359.

Funder, D. C., & Ozer, D. J. (1983). Behavior as a function of the situation. *Journal of Personality and Social Psychology, 44,* 107–112.

Furnham, A. (1982). Explanations for unemployment in Britain. *European Journal of Social Psychology, 12,* 335–352.

Furumoto, L. (1991). From "paired associates" to a psychology of self: The intellectual odyssey of Mary Whiton Calkins. In G. A. Kimble, M. Wertheimer, & C. White (Eds.), *Portraits of pioneers in psychology* (pp. 57–72). Washington, DC: American Psychological Association; and Hillsdale, NJ: Erlbaum.

Furumoto, L., & Scarborough, E. (1986). Placing women in the history of psychology: The first American women psychologists. *American Psychologist, 41,* 35–42.

Fyhn, M., et al., (2004, August 27). Spatial representation in the entorhinal cortex. *Science, 305,* 1258–1264.

Gabbay, F. H. (January, 1992). Behavior-genetic strategies in the study of emotion. *Psychological Science, 3*(1), 50–54.

Gadsby, P. (2000, July). Tourist in a taste lab. *Discover, 21,* 70–75.

Gage, F. H. (2003, September). Brain, repair yourself. *Scientific American, 289*(3), 46–53.

Gahlinger, P. M. (2004). Club drugs: MDMA, gamma-hydroxybutyrate (GHB), rohypnol, and ketamine. *American Family Physician, 69,* 2619–2626.

Gainetdinov, R. R., Wetsel, W. C., Jones, S. R., Levin, E. D., Jaber, M., & Caron, M. G. (1999). Role of serotonin in the paradoxical calming effect of psychostimulants on hyperactivity. *Science, 283,* 397–401.

Galambos, N. L. (1992). Parent–adolescent relations. *Current Directions in Psychological Science, 1,* 146–149.

Gallagher, W. (1994, September). How we become what we are. *The Atlantic Monthly,* 39–55.

Gallo, P. S., & McClintock, C. G. (1965). Cooperative and competitive behavior in mixed-motive games. *Journal of Conflict Resolution, 9,* 68–78.

Gallo, V., & Chittajallu, R. (2001, May 4). Unwrapping glial cells from the synapse: What lies inside? *Science, 292,* 872–873.

Ganchrow, J. R., Steiner, J. E., & Daher, M. (1983). Neonatal facial expressions in response to different qualities and intensities of gustatory stimuli. *Infant Behavior and Development, 6,* 189–200.

Garcia, J. (1981). The logic and limits of mental aptitude testing. *American Psychologist, 36,* 1172–1180.

Garcia, J. (1990). Learning without memory. *Journal of Cognitive Neuroscience, 2,* 287–305.

Garcia, J. (1993). Misrepresentations of my criticisms of Skinner. *American Psychologist, 48,* 1158.

Garcia, J., & Koelling, R. A. (1966). The relation of cue to consequence in avoidance learning. *Psychonomic Science, 4,* 123–124.

Gardiner, H. W., Mutter, J. D., & Kosmitzki, C. (1998). *Lives across cultures: Cross-cultural human development.* Boston: Allyn & Bacon.

Gardner, H. (1983). *Frames of mind.* New York: Basic Books.

Gardner, H. (1985). *The mind's new science: A history of the cognitive revolution.* New York: Basic Books.

Gardner, H. (1993). *Creating minds: An anatomy of creativity seen through the lives of Freud, Einstein, Picasso, Stravinsky, Eliot, Graham, and Gandhi.* New York: Basic Books.

Gardner, H. (1999a). *Intelligence reframed.* New York: Basic Books.

Gardner, H. (1999b, February). Who owns intelligence? *The Atlantic Monthly,* 67–76

Gardyn, R., & Wellner, A. S. (2001, February). Blowin' smoke. *American Demographics, 23*(2), 20–22.

Garland, A., & Zigler, E. (1993). Adolescent suicide prevention: Current research and social policy implications. *American Psychologist, 48,* 169–182.

Garnsey, S. M. (1993). Event-related brain potentials in the study of language: An introduction. *Language and Cognitive Processes, 8,* 337–356.

Gazzaniga, M. (1970). *The bisected brain.* New York: Appleton-Century-Crofts.

Gazzaniga, M. S. (1998a). *The mind's past.* Berkeley: University of California Press.

Gazzaniga, M. S. (1998b, July). The split brain revisited. *Scientific American, 279,* 50–55.

Gehring, W. J., & Willoughby, A. R. (2002, March 22). The medial frontal cortex and the rapid processing of monetary gains and losses. *Science, 295,* 2279–2282.

Gelernter, J. (1994, June 17). Behavioral genetics in transition. *Science, 264,* 1684–1689.

Gelman, S. A., & Wellman, H. M. (1991). Insides and essences: Early understandings of the non-obvious. *Cognition, 38,* 213–244.

Gentner, D., & Stevens, A. L. (1983). *Mental models.* Hillsdale, NJ: Erlbaum.

George, M. S. (2003, September). Stimulating the brain. *Scientific American, 289*(3), 67–73.

George, M. S., Nahas, Z., Kozel, F. A., Goldman, J., Molloy, M., & Oliver, N. (1999). Improvement of depression following transcranial magnetic stimulation. *Current Psychiatry Reports, 1,* 114–124.

Gergen, K. J., Gulerce, A., Lock, A., & Misra, G. (1996). Psychological science in cultural context. *American Psychologist, 51,* 496–503.

Getzels, J. W., & Csikszentmihalyi, M. (1976). *The creative vision.* New York: Wiley.

Gibbons, A. (1998, September 4). Which of our genes make us human? *Science, 281,* 1432–1434.

Gibbs, W. W. (1995, March). Seeking the criminal element. *Scientific American,* 100–107.

Gibbs, W. W. (1996, August). Gaining on fat. *Scientific American, 275*(2), 88–94.

Gibbs, W. W. (2001). Side splitting. *Scientific American, 284,* 24–25.

Gibbs, W. W. (2003, December). The unseen genome: Beyond DNA. *Scientific American, 289*(6), 106–113.

Gibson, E. J., & Walk, R. D. (1960, April). The "visual cliff." *Scientific American,* 64–71.

Gilbert, P., & Gilbert, J. (2003). Entrapment and arrested fight and flight in depression: An exploration using focus groups. *Psychology and Psychotherapy: Theory, research, and practice.* 76, 173–188.

Gilbert, R. M. (1992). *Extraordinary relationships: A new way of thinking about human interactions.* New York: Wiley.

Gilbertson, J., Dindia, K., & Allen, M. (1998). Relational continuity, constructional units, and the maintenance of relationships. *Journal of Social and Personal Relationships, 15,* 774–790.

Gilligan, C. (1982). *In a different voice: Psychological theory and women's development.* Cambridge, MA: Harvard University Press.

Gilligan, S. G., & Bower, G. H. (1984). Cognitive consequences of emotional arousal.

In C. Izard, J. Kagan, & R. Zajonc (Eds.), *Emotions, cognitions and behavior.* New York: Cambridge University Press.

Gitlin, M. J. (1990). *The psychotherapist's guide to psychopharmacology.* New York: The Free Press.

Glanz, J. (1998, April 3). Magnetic brain imaging traces a stairway to memory. *Science, 280,* 37.

Glaser, R. (1984). Education and thinking: The role of knowledge. *American Psychologist, 39,* 93–104.

Glaser, R. (1990). The reemergence of learning theory within instructional research. *American Psychologist, 45,* 29–39.

Glass, R. M. (2001, March). Electroconvulsive therapy: Time to bring it out of the shadows. *JAMA: Journal of the American Medical Association. 285,* 1346–1348.

Gleitman, H. (1991). Edward Chace Tolman: A life of scientific and social purpose. In G. A. Kimble, M. Wertheimer, & C. L. White (Eds.), *Portraits of pioneers in psychology* (pp. 226–241). Washington, DC: American Psychological Association.

Glenn, D. (2003, October 24). Nightmare scenarios. *The Chronicle of Higher Education,* A-14–A-16.

Goel, V., & Dolan, R. J. (2001). The functional anatomy of humor: Segregating cognitive and affective components. *Nature Neuroscience, 4,* 237–238.

Goldberg, L. R. (1981). Language and individual differences: The search for universals in personality lexicons. In L. Wheeler (Ed.), *Review of personality and social psychology* (Vol. 2, pp. 141–165). Beverly Hills, CA: Sage.

Goldberg, L. R. (1993). The structure of phenotypic personality traits. *American Psychologist, 48,* 26–34.

Golden, O. (2000). The federal response to child abuse and neglect. *American Psychologist, 55,* 1050–1053.

Goldin-Meadow, S., & Mylander, C. (1990). Beyond the input given: The child's role in the acquisition of language. *Language, 66,* 323–355.

Goldman-Rakic, P. S. (1992, September). Working memory and the mind. *Scientific American, 267,* 110–117.

Goleman, D. (1980, February). 1528 little geniuses and how they grew. *Psychology Today, 14,* 28–53.

Goleman, D. (1995). *Emotional intelligence.* New York: Bantam Books.

Golombok, S., & Tasker, F. (1996). Do parents influence the sexual orientation of their children? Findings from a longitudinal study of lesbian families. *Developmental Psychology, 32,* 3–11.

Gonzalvo, P., Cañas, J. J., & Bajo, M. (1994). Structural representations in knowledge acquisition. *Journal of Educational Psychology, 86,* 601–616.

Gorman, J. (1999, January). The 11-year-old debunker. *Discover, 20*(1), 62–63.

Gottesman, I. I. (1991). *Schizophrenia genesis: The origins of madness.* New York: Freeman.

Gottesman, I. I. (1997, June 6). Twins: En route to QTLs for cognition. *Science, 276,* 1522–1523.

Gottesman, I. I. (2001). Psychopathology through a life span–genetic prism. *American Psychologist, 56,* 867–878.

Gottman, J., & Silver, N. (1994). *Why marriages succeed or fail.* New York: Simon and Schuster.

Gottman, J., Coan, J., Carrere, S., & Swanson, C. (1998). Predicting marital happiness and stability from newlywed interactions. *Journal of Marriage and the Family, 60,* 5–22.

Gottman, J. M. (1994). *What predicts divorce?* Hillsdale, NJ: Erlbaum.

Gottman, J. M. (1999). *Seven principles for making marriages work.* New York: Crown.

Gottman, J. M., & Krokoff, L. J. (1989). Marital interaction and satisfaction: A longitudinal view. *Journal of Consulting & Clinical Psychology, 57,* 47–52.

Gottman, J. M., & Levenson, R. W. (1986). Assessing the role of emotion in marriage. *Behavioral Assessment, 8,* 31–48.

Gould, E., Tanapat, P., McEwen, B. S., Flüge, G., & Fuchs, E. (1998). Proliferation of granule cell precursors in the dentate gyrus of adult monkeys is diminished by stress. *Proceedings of the National Academy of Science, 99,* 3168–3171.

Gould, S. J. (1996). *The mismeasure of man* (2nd ed.). New York: Norton.

Graham, J. R. (1990). *MMPI-2: Assessing personality and psychopathology.* New York: Oxford University Press.

Gray, C. R., & Gummerman, K. (1975). The enigmatic eidetic image: A critical examination of methods, data, and theories. *Psychological Bulletin, 82,* 383–407.

Gray, P. (1993, November 29). The assault on Freud. *Time, 142*(23), 46–51.

Graziano, M. S. A., Cooke, D. F., & Taylor, C. S. R. (2000, December 1). Coding the location of the arm by sight. *Science, 290,* 1782–1786.

Greeley, A., & Sheatsley, P. (1971). The acceptance of desegregation continues to advance. *Scientific American, 225*(6), 13–19.

Green, D. M. & Swets, J. A. (1966). *Signal detection theory and psychophysics.* New York: Wiley.

Greenberg, B. S. (1986). Minorities and the mass media. In J. Bryant & D. Zillman (Eds.), *Perspectives in media effects* (pp. 17–40). Hillsdale, NJ: Erlbaum.

Greenberg, L. S., & Johnson, S. (1988). *Emotionally focused therapy for couples.* New York: Guilford.

Greene, R. L. (1991). *The MMPI-2/MMPI: An interpretive manual.* Boston: Allyn & Bacon.

Greeno, J. G. (1989). A perspective on thinking. *American Psychologist, 44,* 134–141.

Greenspan, S. (1999, February). What is meant by mental retardation? *International Review of Psychiatry, 11,* 6–18.

Greenwald, A. G. (1992). New Look 3: Unconscious cognition reclaimed. *American Psychologist, 47*(6), 766–779.

Greenwald, A. G., Draine, S. C., & Abrams, R. L. (1996, September 20). Three cognitive markers of unconscious semantic activation. *Science, 273,* 1699–1702.

Gregory, R. (1997). *Mirrors in mind.* New York: W. H. Freeman.

Gregory, R. L. (1977). *Eye and brain: The psychology of seeing,* 3rd ed. New York: World University Library.

Grevert, P., & Goldstein, A. (1985). Placebo analgesia, naloxone, and the role of endogenous opioids. In L. White, B. Turks, & G. E. Schwartz (Eds.), *Placebo* (pp. 332–351). New York: Guilford.

Grice, D. E., Halmi, K. A., Fichter, M. M., Strober, M., Woodside, D. B., Treasure, J. T., Kaplan, A. S., Magistretti, P. J., Goldman, D., Bulik, C. M., Kaye, W. H., & Berrettini, W. H. (2002). Evidence for a susceptibility gene for anorexia nervosa on chromosome 1. *American Journal of Human Genetics, 70,* 787–792.

Grinspoon, L., Bakalar, J. B., Zimmer, L., & Morgan, J. P. (1997, August 8). Marijuana addiction. *Science, 752,* 748.

Gross, J. J. (1998). The emerging field of emotion regulation: An integrative review. *Review of General Psychology, 2,* 271–299.

Grossman, D. (1996). *On killing: The psychological cost of learning to kill in war and society.* New York: Brown & Co.

Gruber, C. W. (2005). In Akins, C. K., Panicker, S., & Cunningham, C. L. (Eds.), *Laboratory animals in research and teaching: Ethics, care and methods.* Washington, DC: American Psychological Association.

Guisinger, S. (2003). Adapted to flee famine: Adding an evolutionary perspective on anorexia nervosa. *Psychological Review, 110,* 745–761.

Guisinger, S., & Blatt, S. J. (1994). Individuality and relatedness: Evolution of a fundamental dialectic. *American Psychologist, 49,* 104–111.

Gulya, M., Rovee-Collier, C., Galluccio, L., & Wilk, A. (1998). Memory processing of a serial list by young infants. *Psychological Science, 9,* 303–307.

Gur, R. E., & Maany, V. (1998). Subcortical MRI volumes in neuroleptic-naive and treated patients with schizophrenia. *American Journal of Psychiatry, 155,* 1711–1718.

Gura, T. (1998, May 29). Uncoupling proteins provide new clue to obesity's causes. *Science, 280,* 1369–1370.

Gura, T. (2003, February 7). Obesity drug pipeline not so fat. *Science, 299,* 849–852.

Guthrie, G. M., & Bennett, A. B. (1970). Cultural differences in implicit personality theory. *International Journal of Psychology, 6,* 305–312.

Guthrie, R. V. (1998). *Even the rat was white.* Boston: Allyn & Bacon.

Haber, R. N. (1969, April). Eidetic images. *Scientific American,* 36–44.

Haber, R. N. (1970, May). How we remember what we see. *Scientific American,* 104–112.

Haber, R. N. (1980, November). Eidetic images are not just imaginary. *Psychology Today, 14,* 72–82.

Haberlandt, K. (1999). *Human memory: Exploration and application.* Boston: Allyn & Bacon.

Haidt, J. (2001). The emotional dog and its rational tail: A social intuitionist approach to moral judgment. *Psychological Review, 108,* 814–834.

Haimov, I., & Lavie, P. (1996). Melatonin—A soporific hormone. *Current Directions in Psychological Science, 5,* 106–111.

Halberstam, D. (2002). *Firehouse.* New York: Hyperion.

Hall, C., (1951). What people dream about. *Scientific American, 184,* 60–63.

Hall, C. (1953/1966). *The meaning of dreams.* New York: Harper & Row/McGraw-Hill.

Hall, C. S. (1984). "A ubiquitous sex difference in dreams" revisited. *Journal of Personality and Social Psychology, 46,* 1109–1117.

Hall, M. J., Norwood, A. E., Ursano, R. J., Fullerton, C. S., & Levinson, C. J. (2002). Psychological and behavioral impacts of bioterrorism. *PTSD Research Quarterly, 13,* 1–2.

Haller, E. (1992). Eating disorders: A review and update. *Western Journal of Medicine, 157,* 658–662.

Halpern, D. F. (2002). *Thought & knowledge: An introduction to critical thinking.* Mahwah, NJ: Erlbaum.

Hamann, S. B., Ely, T. D., Hoffman, J. M., & Clinton, D. K. (2002). Ecstasy and agony: Activation of the human amygdala in positive and negative emotion. *Psychological Science, 13,* 135–141.

Hamer, D. (1997). The search for personality genes: Adventures of a molecular biologist. *Current Directions in Psychological Science, 6,* 111–112.

Hamer, D. (2002, October 4). Rethinking behavior genetics. *Science, 298,* 71–72.

Hamer, D. H., Hu, S., Magnuson, V. L., Hu, N., & Pattatucci, A. M. L. (1993, December 24). Male sexual orientation and genetic evidence. *Science, 261,* 2863–2865.

Hamilton, L. (1989). Fight, flight or freeze: Implications of the passive fear response for anxiety and depression. *Phobia Practice and Research Journal, 2,* 17–27.

Haney, C., Banks, W. C., & Zimbardo, P. G. (1973). Interpersonal dynamics in a simulated prison. *International Journal of Criminology and Penology, 1,* 69–97.

Haney, C., & Zimbardo, P. (1998). The past and future of U.S. prison policy: Twenty-five years after the Stanford prison experiment. *American Psychologist, 53,* 709–727.

Harder, B. (2004, June 19). Narcolepsy science reawakens. *Science News, 165,* 394–396.

Hariri, A. R., Mattay, V. S., Tessitore, A., Kolachana, B., Fera, F., Goldman, D., Egan, M. F., & Weinberger, D. R. (2002, July 19). Serotonin transporter genetic variation and the response of the human amygdala. *Science, 297,* 400–403.

Harlow, H. F. (1965). Sexual behavior in the rhesus monkey. In F. Beach (Ed.), *Sex and behavior.* New York: Wiley.

Harlow, H. F., & Harlow, M. K. (1966). Learning to love. *American Scientist, 54,* 244–272.

Harris, B. (1979). Whatever happened to Little Albert? *American Psychologist, 34,* 151–160.

Harris, G., Thomas, A., & Booth, D. A. (1990). Development of salt taste in infancy. *Developmental Psychology, 26,* 534–538.

Harris, J. A. (2004). Measured intelligence, achievement, openness to experience, and creativity. *Personality & Individual Differences, 36,* 913–929.

Harris, J. R. (1995). Where is the child's environment? A group socialization theory of development. *Psychological Review, 102,* 458–489.

Harrist, S. (2003). Recognition for marginalized losses. *Death Studies, 27,* 560–565.

Hart, R. A., & Moore, G. I. (1973). The development of spatial cognition: A review. In R. M. Downs & D. Stea (Eds.), *Image and environment.* Chicago: Aldine.

Harvey, J. H. (1996). *Embracing their memory: Loss and the social psychology of storytelling.* Boston: Allyn & Bacon.

Harvey, J. H. (2000). *Give sorrow words: Perspectives on loss and trauma.* New York: Taylor and Francis.

Harvey, J. H., & Hofmann, W. J. (2001). Teaching about loss. *Journal of Loss and Trauma, 6,* 263–268.

Harvey, J. H., & Omarzu, J. (1997). Minding the close relationship. *Personality and Social Psychology Review, 1,* 224–240.

Harvey, J. H., & Pauwels, B. G. (1999). Recent developments in close-relationships theory. *Current Directions in Psychological Science, 8,* 93–95.

Harvey, J. H., Weber, A. L., & Orbuch, T. L. (1990). *Interpersonal accounts: A social psychological perspective.* Cambridge, MA: Basil Blackwell.

Harvey, S. M., & Spigner, C. (1995). Factors associated with sexual behavior among adolescents: A multivariate analysis. *Adolescence, 30,* 253–264.

Hassebrauck, M. (1988). Beauty is more than "name" deep: The effect of women's first names on ratings of physical attractiveness and personality attributes. *Journal of Applied Social Psychology, 18,* 721–726.

Hatfield, E. (1988). Passionate and compassionate love. In R. J. Sternberg & M. L. Barnes (Eds.), *The psychology of love.* New Haven, CT: Yale University Press.

Hatfield, E., & Rapson, R. (1993). *Love, sex, and intimacy: Their psychology, biology, and history.* New York: HarperCollins.

Hatfield, E., & Rapson, R. (1998). On love and sex in the 21st century. *The General Psychologist, 33*(2), 45–54.

Hatfield, E., Rapson, R. L., & Rapson, R. (1995). *Love and sex: Cross-cultural perspectives.* Boston: Allyn & Bacon.

Hatfield, E., & Sprecher, S. (1986). *Mirror, mirror: The importance of looks in everyday life.* New York: State University of New York Press.

Hauser, M. D., Chomsky, N., & Fitch, W. T. (2002, November 22). The faculty of language: What is it, who has it, and how did it evolve? *Science, 298,* 1569–1579.

Hawkins, S. A., & Hastie, R. (1990). Hindsight: Biased judgments of past events after the outcomes are known. *Psychological Bulletin, 108,* 311–327.

Hayes, S. C., & Heiby, E. (1996). Psychology's drug problem: Do we need a fix or should we just say no? *American Psychologist, 51,* 198–206.

Haynes, S. G., & Feinleib, M. (1980). Women, work, and coronary heart disease: Prospective findings from the Framingham Heart Study. *American Journal of Public Health, 70,* 133–141.

Hazan, C., & Diamond, L. M. (2000). The place of attachment in human mating. *Review of General Psychology, 4,* 186–204.

Hazeltine, E., & Ivry, R. B. (2002, June 14). Can we teach the cerebellum new tricks? *Science, 296,* 1979–1980.

Hecht, A. (1986, April). A guide to the proper use of tranquilizers. *Healthline Newsletter,* 5–6.

Heckler, S. (1994). Facilitated communication: A response by Child Protection. *Child Abuse and Neglect: The International Journal, 18*(6), 495–503.

Heeger, D. J. (1994). The representation of visual stimuli in primary visual cortex. *Current Directions in Psychological Science, 3,* 159–163.

Heine, S. J., Lehman, D. R., Markus, H. R., & Kitayama, S. (1999). Is there a universal need for positive self-regard? *Psychological Review, 106,* 766–794.

Heinrichs, R. W. (1993). Schizophrenia and the brain: Conditions for a neuropsychology of madness. *American Psychologist, 48,* 221–233.

Heller, W., Nitschke, J. B., & Miller, G. A. (1998). Lateralization in emotion and emotional disorders. *Current Directions in Psychological Science, 7,* 26–32.

Helmes, E., & Reddon, J. R. (1993). A perspective on developments in assessing psychopathology: A critical review of the MMPI and MMPI-2. *Psychological Bulletin, 113,* 453–471.

Helms, J. E. (1992). Why is there no study of cultural equivalence in standardized cognitive ability testing? *American Psychologist, 47,* 1083–1101.

Helmuth, L. (2000, December 1). Where the brain monitors the body. *Science. 290.* 1668.

Helmuth, L. (2001a, November 2). Beyond the pleasure principle. *Science, 294,* 983–984.

Helmuth, L. (2001b, May 18). Boosting brain activity from the outside in. *Science, 292,* 1284–1286.

Helmuth, L. (2001c, March 16). Dyslexia: Same brains, different languages. *Science, 291,* 2064–2065.

Helmuth, L. (2002, June 21). A generation gap in brain activity. *Science, 296,* 2131, 2133.

Helmuth, L. (2003a, November 14). Brain model puts most sophisticated regions front and center. *Science, 302,* 1133.

Helmuth, L. (2003b, April 25). Fear and trembling in the amygdala. *Science, 300,* 568–569.

Helmuth, L. (2003c, February 28). The wisdom of the wizened. *Science, 299,* 1300–1302.

Hendrick, S. S., & Hendrick, C. (1992). *Liking, loving, and relating* (2nd ed.) Pacific Grove, CA: Brooks/Cole.

Henig, R. M. (1998, May). Tempting fates. *Discover,* 58.

Henker, B., & Whalen, C. K. (1989). Hyperactivity and attention deficits. *American Psychologist, 44,* 216–223.

Herek, G. M. (2000). The psychology of sexual prejudice. *Current Directions in Psychological Science, 9,* 19–22.

Herrnstein, R. J., & Murray, C. (1994). *The bell curve.* New York: Free Press.

Heston, L. L. (1970). The genetics of schizophrenic and schizoid disease. *Science, 167,* 249–256.

Hetherington, E. M., & Parke, R. D. (1975). *Child psychology: A contemporary viewpoint.* New York: McGraw-Hill.

Hetherington, M. M., Spalter, A. R., Bernat, A. S., Nelson, M. L. et al. (1993). Eating pathology in bulimia nervosa. *International Journal of Eating Disorders, 13*(1), 13–24.

Hibbard, S. (2003). A critique of Lilienfeld et al.'s (2000) "The scientific status of projective techniques." *Journal of Personality Assessment. 80,* 260–271.

Hicks, R. A. (1990). *The costs and benefits of normal insomnia.* Paper presented to the annual meeting of the Western Psychological Association, Los Angeles, CA.

Hilgard, E. R. (1968). *The experience of hypnosis.* New York: Harcourt Brace Jovanovich.

Hilgard, E. R. (1973). The domain of hypnosis with some comments on alternative paradigms. *American Psychologist, 28,* 972–982.

Hilgard, E. R. (1992). Dissociation and theories of hypnosis. In E. Fromm & M. R. Nash (Eds.), *Contemporary hypnosis research.* New York: Guilford.

Hill, J. O., & Peters, J. C. (1998, May 29). Environmental contributions to the obesity epidemic. *Science, 280,* 1371–1374.

Hilts, P. J. (1995). *Memory's ghost: The strange tale of Mr. M. and the nature of memory.* New York: Simon & Schuster.

Hiroto, D. S. (1974). Locus of control and learned helplessness. *Journal of Experimental Psychology, 102,* 187–193.

Hirsch, J., Harrington, G., & Mehler, B. (1990). An irresponsible farewell gloss. *Educational Theory, 40,* 501–508.

Hirschfeld, R. M. A. (1999). Efficacy of SSRIs and newer antidepressants in severe depression: Comparison with TCAs. *Journal of Clinical Psychiatry, 60,* 326–335.

Hirschfeld, R. M. A., & Goodwin, F. K. (1988). Mood disorders. In J. A. Talbott, R. E. Hales, & S. C. Yudofsky (Eds.), *The American Psychiatric Press textbook of psychiatry.* Washington, DC: American Psychiatric Press.

Hobson, J. A. (1988). *The dreaming brain.* New York: Basic Books.

Hobson, J. A. (2002). *Dreaming: An introduction to the science of sleep.* New York: Oxford University Press.

Hobson, J. A., & McCarley, R. W. (1977). The brain as a dream state generator: An activation-synthesis hypothesis of the dream process. *American Journal of Psychiatry, 134,* 1335–1348.

Hobson, J. A., Pace-Schott, E., & Stickgold, R. (2000) Dreaming and the brain: Towards a cognitive neuroscience of conscious states. *Behavioral and Brain Sciences* (special issue). Retrieved on November 6, 2004, from Behavioral and Brain Sciences Web site: http://www.bbsonline.org/documents/a/00/00/05/44/index.html

Hochwalder, J. (1995). On stability of the structure of implicit personality theory over situations. *Scandinavian Journal of Psychology, 36,* 386–398.

Hoffman, H. G. (2004, August). Virtual-reality therapy. *Scientific American, 291,* 58–65.

Hogan, R., Curphy, G. J., & Hogan, J. (1994). What we know about leadership: Effectiveness and personality. *American Psychologist, 49,* 493–504.

Hogan, R., Hogan, J., & Roberts, B. W. (1996). Personality measurement and employment decisions: Questions and answers. *American Psychologist, 51,* 469–477.

Hogarty, G. E., Kornblith, S. J., Greenwald, D., DiBarry, A. L., Cooley, S., Ulrich, R. F., Carter, M., & Flesher, S. (1997). Three-year trials of personal therapy among schizophrenic patients living with or independent of family, I: Description of study and effects on relapse rates. *American Journal of Psychiatry, 154,* 1504–1513.

Hoge, C. W., Castro, C. A., Messer, S. C., McGurk, D., Cotting, D. I., & Koffman, R. L. (2004). Combat duty in Iraq and Afghanistan, mental health problems, and barriers to care. *New England Journal of Medicine, 351,* 13–22.

Holden, C. (1978). Patuxent: Controversial prison clings to belief in rehabilitation. *Science, 199,* 665–668.

Holden, C. (1980a). Identical twins reared apart. *Science, 207,* 1323–1325.

Holden, C. (1980b, November). Twins reunited. *Science, 80,* 55–59.

Holden, C. (1996a, July 5). New populations of old add to poor nations' burdens. *Science, 273,* 46–48.

Holden, C. (1996b, July 19). Sex and olfaction. *Science, 273,* 313.

Holden, C. (1997, October 3). A special place for faces in the brain. *Science, 278,* 41.

Holden, C. (2000a, April 7). Global survey examines impact of depression. *Science, 288,* 39–40.

Holden, C. (2000b, July 28). The violence of the lambs. *Science, 289,* 580–581.

Holden, C. (2001a, April 27). How the brain understands music. *Science News, 292,* 623.

Holden, C. (2001b, February 9). Panel seeks truth in lie detector debate. *Science, 291,* 967.

Holden, C. (2003a, January 17). Deconstructing schizophrenia. *Science, 299,* 333–335.

Holden, C. (2003b, October 31). Future brightening for depression treatments. *Science, 302,* 810–813.

Hollis, K. L. (1997). Contemporary research on Pavlovian conditioning. *American Psychologist, 52,* 956–965.

Hollon, S. D. (1996). The efficacy and effectiveness of psychotherapy relative to medications. *American Psychologist, 51,* 1025–1030.

Hollon, S. D., Thase, M. E., & Markowitz, J. C. (2002, November). Treatment and prevention of depression. *Psychological Science in the Public Interest, 3,* 39–77.

Holloway, J. D. (2003a, March). Advances in anger management. *Monitor on Psychology, 34,* 54–55.

Holloway, J. D. (2003b, December). Snapshot from the therapy room. *Monitor on Psychology, 34*(11), 31.

Holloway, M. (1999, November). The ascent of scent. *Scientific American, 281,* 42, 44.

Holloway, M. (2003, September). The mutable brain. *Scientific American, 289*(3), 78–85.

Holmes, D. S. (1984). Meditation and somatic arousal: A review of the experimental evidence. *American Psychologist, 39,* 1–10.

Holmes, D. S. (2001). *Abnormal psychology* (4th ed.). Boston: Allyn & Bacon.

Holtzworth-Munroe, A., & Jacobson, N. S. (1985). Causal attributions of marital couples: When do they search for causes? What do they conclude when they do? *Journal of Personality and Social Psychology, 48,* 1398–1412.

Homme, L. E., de Baca, P. C., Devine, J. V., Steinhorst, R., & Rickert, E. J. (1963). Use of the Premack principle in controlling the behavior of nursery school children. *Journal of the Experimental Analysis of Behavior, 6,* 544.

Hopkins, B., & Westra, T. (1988). Maternal handling and motor development: An intracultural study. *Genetic, Social and General Psychology Monographs, 14,* 377–420.

Horgan, J. (1993, June). Eugenics revisited. *Scientific American, 268,* 122–131.

Horgan, J. (1996, November). Multicultural studies: Rates of depression vary widely throughout the world. *Scientific American, 275*(6), 24–25.

Horne, J. A. (1988). *Why we sleep: The functions of sleep in humans and other mammals.* Oxford U.K.: Oxford University Press.

Horney, K. (1939). *New ways in psychoanalysis.* New York: Norton.

Horney, K. (1942). *Self-analysis.* New York: Norton.

Horney, K. (1967). *Feminine psychology.* New York: W. W. Norton.

Horowitz, M. J. (1997). *Stress response syndromes: PTSD, grief, and adjustment disorders* (3rd ed.). Northvale, NJ: Jason Aronson.

Horvath, A. O., & Luborsky, L. (1993). The role of the therapeutic alliance in psychotherapy. *Journal of Consulting and Clinical Psychology, 61,* 561–573.

Hovland, C. I., & Sears, R. (1940). Minor studies of aggression: Correlation of lynchings with economic indices. *Journal of Psychology, 9,* 301–310.

Howe, M. L., & Courage, M. L. (1993). On resolving the enigma of infantile amnesia. *Psychological Bulletin, 113,* 305–326.

Howes, C., Rodning, C., Galluzzo, D. C., & Myers, L. (1988). Attachment and child care: Relationships with mother and caregiver. *Early Childhood Research Quarterly, 3,* 403–416.

Hubel, D. H., & Wiesel, T. N. (1979, September). Brain mechanisms of vision. *Scientific American, 241,* 150–162.

Huesmann, L. R., & Moise, J. (1996, June). Media violence: A demonstrated public health threat to children. *Harvard Mental Health Letter, 12*(12), 5–7.

Huesmann, L. R., Moise-Titus, J., Podolski, C-L., & Eron, L. D. (2003). Longitudinal relations between children's exposure to TV violence and their aggressive and violent behavior in young adulthood:

1977–1992. *Developmental Psychology, 39,* 201–221.
Hughes, G. H., Pearson, M. A., & Reinhart, G. R. (1984). Stress: Sources, effects, and management. *Family and Community Health, 7,* 47–58.
Hull, C. L. (1943). *Principles of behavior: An introduction to behavior theory.* New York: Appleton-Century-Crofts.
Hull, C. L. (1952). *A behavior system: An introduction to behavior theory concerning the individual organism.* New Haven, CT: Yale University Press.
Humphrey, T. (1970). The development of human fetal activity and its relation to postnatal behavior. In H. W. Reese & L. P. Lipsitt (Eds.), *Advances in child development and behavior* (Vol. 5). New York: Academic Press.
Hunt, E. (1989). Cognitive science: Definition, status, and questions. *Annual Review of Psychology, 40,* 603–629.
Hunter, I. (1964). *Memory.* Baltimore: Penguin.
Huston, A. C., Watkins, B. A., & Kunkel, D. (1989). Public policy and children's television. *American Psychologist, 44,* 424–433.
Huston, T. L., Ruggiero, M., Conner, R., & Geis, G. (1981). Bystander intervention into crime: A study based on naturally-occurring episodes. *Social Psychology Quarterly, 44,* 14–23.
Huttenlocher, J., Haight, W., Bryk, A., Seltzer, M., & Lyons, T. (1991). Early vocabulary growth: relation to language input and gender. *Developmental Psychology, 27,* 236–248.
Hyman, I. A. (1996). Using research to change public policy: Reflections on 20 years of effort to eliminate corporal punishment in schools. *Pediatrics, 98,* 818–821.
Hyman, I. A., McDowell, E., & Raines, B. (1977). Corporal punishment and alternatives in the schools: An overview of theoretical and practical issues. In J. H. Wise (Ed.), *Proceedings: Conference on corporal punishment in the schools* (pp. 1–18). Washington, DC: National Institutes of Education.
Hyman, I. E., Jr., Husband, T. H., & Billings, F. J. (1995). False memories of childhood experiences. *Applied Cognitive Psychology, 9,* 181–197.
Hyman, R. (1989). The psychology of deception. *Annual Review of Psychology, 40,* 133–154.
Iacono, W. G., & Grove, W. M. (1993). Schizophrenia reviewed: Toward an integrative genetic model. *Science, 4,* 273–276.
Ickes, W., & Layden, M. A. (1978). Attributional styles. In J. H. Harvey, W. Ickes, & R. F. Kidd (Eds.), *New directions in attributional research* (Vol. 2). Hillsdale, NJ: Erlbaum.
Ineichen, B. (1979). The social geography of marriage. In M. Cook & G. Wilson (Eds.), *Love and attraction.* New York: Pergamon Press.
Institute of Medicine. (2002). *Dietary reference intakes for energy, carbohydrate, fiber, fat, fatty acids, cholesterol, protein, and amino acids.* Washington, DC: National Institutes of Health.
Isay, R. A. (1990). Psychoanalytic theory and the therapy of gay men. In D. P. McWhirter, S. A. Sanders, & J. M. Reinisch (Eds.), *Homosexuality/heterosexuality: Concepts of sexual orientation* (pp. 283–303). New York: Oxford University Press.
Ishai, A., & Sagi, D. (1995). Common mechanisms of visual imagery and perception. *Science, 268,* 1772–1774.
Ishai, A., & Sagi, D. (1997). Visual imagery: Effects of short- and long-term memory. *Journal of Cognitive Neuroscience, 9,* 734–742.
Iverson, P., Kuhl, P. K., Akahane-Yamada, R., Diesch, E., Tohkura, Y., Kettermann, A., & Siebert, C. (2003). A perceptual interference account of acquisition difficulties for non-native phonemes. *Cognition, 87,* B47–B57.
Izard, C. E. (1989). The structure and functions of emotions: Implications for cognition, motivation, and personality. In I. S. Cohen (Ed.), *The G. Stanley Hall lecture series* (Vol. 9, pp. 39–73). Washington, DC: American Psychological Association.
Izard, C. E. (1993). Four systems for emotion activation: Cognitive and noncognitive processes. *Psychological Review, 100,* 68–90.
Izard, C. E. (1994). Innate and universal facial expressions: Evidence from developmental and cross-cultural research. *Psychological Bulletin, 115,* 288–299.
Jackson, D. D. (1980, October). Reunion of identical twins, raised apart, reveals some astonishing similarities. *Smithsonian,* 48–57.
Jacobs, B. L. (1987). How hallucinogenic drugs work. *American Scientist, 75,* 386–392.
Jacobs, L. F., & Schenk, F. (2003). Unpacking the cognitive map: The parallel map theory of hippocampal function. *Psychological Review, 110,* 285–315.
Jacobs, M. K., & Goodman, G. (1989). Psychology and self-help groups: Predictions on a partnership. *American Psychologist, 44,* 536–545.
Jacobson, N. S., & Christensen, A. (1996). Studying the effectiveness of psychotherapy: How well can clinical trials do the job? *American Psychologist, 51,* 1031–1039.
Jacoby, L. L., Lindsay, D. S., & Toth, J. P. (1992). Unconscious influences revealed: Attention, awareness, and control. *American Psychologist, 47,* 802–809.
Jacowitz, K. E., Kahneman, D. (1995). Measures of anchoring in estimation tasks. *Personality & Social Psychology Bulletin, 21,* 1161–1166.
Jaffe, J., Beebe, B., Feldsein, S., Crown, C. L., & Jasnow, M. D. (2001). Rhythms of dialogue in infancy: Coordinated timing in development. *Monographs of Society for Research in Child Development, 66,* vii, 1–132.
James, W. (1950). *The principles of psychology* (2 vols.). New York: Holt, Rinehart & Winston. (Original work published 1890).
Janata, P., Birk, J. L., Van Horn, J. D., Leman, M., Tillmann, B., & Bharucha, J. J. (2002, December 13). The cortical topography of tonal structures underlying western music. *Science, 298,* 2167–2170.
Janis, I. (1972). *Victims of groupthink: A psychological study of foreign-policy decisions and fiascoes.* Boston: Houghton Mifflin.
Janis, I., & Mann, L. (1977). *Decision making: A psychological analysis of conflict, choice and commitment.* New York: The Free Press.
Jansen, A. S. P., Nguyen, X. V., Karpitskiy, V., Mettenleiter, T. C., & Loewy, A. D. (1995, October 27). Central command neurons of the sympathetic nervous system: Basis of the fight-or-flight response. *Science, 270,* 644–646.
Janus, S. S., & Janus, C. L. (1993). *The Janus Report on sexual behavior.* New York: Wiley.
Javitt, D. C., & Coyle, J. T. (2004). Decoding schizophrenia. *Scientific American, 290,* 48–55.
Jeffery, R. W. (1987). Behavioral treatment of obesity. *Annals of Behavioral Medicine, 9,* 20–24.
Jenkins, C. D. (1976). Recent evidence supporting psychologic and social risk factors for coronary disease. *New England Journal of Medicine, 294,* 987–994, 1033–1038.
Jenkins, J. H. (1994). Culture, emotion, and psychopathology. In S. Kitayama & H. R. Markus (Eds.), *Emotion and culture: Empirical studies of mutual influence.* Washington, DC: American Psychological Association.
Jensen, A. R. (1969). How much can we boost IQ and scholastic achievement? *Harvard Educational Review, 39,* 1–123.
Jensen, A. R. (1980). *Bias in mental testing.* New York: Free Press.
Jensen, A. R. (1985). Methodological and statistical techniques for the chronometric study of mental abilities. In C. R. Reynolds & V. L. Wilson (Eds.), *Methodological and statistical advances in the study of individual difference* (pp. 51–116). New York: Plenum.
Jensen, A. R. (1998). The g factor and the design of education. In R. J. Sternberg & W. M. Williams (Eds.), *Intelligence, instruction, and assessment: Theory into practice.* Mahwah, NJ: Lawrence Erlbaum Associates.
Jensen, A. R. (2000). Testing: The dilemma of group differences. *Psychology, Public Policy, and Law, 6,* 121–127.
Jensen, A. R., & Figueroa, R. A. (1975). Forward and backward digit-span interaction with race and IQ: Predictions from Jensen's theory. *Journal of Educational Psychology, 67,* 882–893.
Jick, H., Kaye, J. A., & Jick, S. S. (2004, July 21). Antidepressants and the risk of suicidal behaviors. *JAMA: Journal of the American Medical Association, 292,* 338–343.
Jog, M. S., Kubota, Y., Connolly, C. I., Hillegaart, V., & Grabiel, A. M. (1999, November 26). Building neural representations of habits. *Science, 286,* 1745–1749.
Johnson, D. L. (1989). Schizophrenia as a brain disease: Implications for psychologists and families. *American Psychologist, 44,* 553–555.
Johnson, J. G., Cohen, P., Smailes, E. M., Kasen, S., & Brook, J. S. (2001, March 29). Television viewing and aggressive behavior during adolescence and adulthood. *Science, 295,* 2468–2471.
Johnson, M. (1991). Selye's stress and the body in the mind. *Advances in Nursing Science, 7,* 38–44.

Johnson, M. H. (1998). The neural basis of cognitive development. In D. Kuhn & R. S. Siegler (Eds.), *Handbook of child psychology: Vol. 2. Cognition, perception, and language* (5th ed.), pp. 1–49. New York: Wiley.

Johnson, R. L., & Rudmann, J. L. (2004). Psychology at community colleges: A survey. *Teaching of Psychology, 31,* 183–185.

Johnson, S. (2003, March). Fear. *Discover, 24,* 32–39.

Johnston, L. D., O'Malley, P. M., & Bachman, J. G. (1989). *Drug use, drinking, and smoking: National survey results from high school, college, and young adult populations, 1975–1988.* Rockville, MD: U.S. Department of Health and Human Services.

Joiner, T. E., Jr., & Schmidt, N. B. (1995). Dimensions of perfectionism, life stress, and depressed and anxious symptoms: Prospective support for diathesis-stress but not specific vulnerability among male undergraduates. *Journal of Social and Clinical Psychology, 14,* 165–183.

Jones, E. E., Cumming, J. D., & Horowitz, M. J. (1988). Another look at the nonspecific hypothesis of therapeutic effectiveness. *Journal of Consulting and Clinical Psychology, 56,* 48–55.

Jones, M. (1953). *The therapeutic community.* New York: Basic Books.

Jones, M. C. (1924). A laboratory study of fear: The case of Peter. *Pedagogical Seminary, 31,* 308–315.

Jones, M. C. (1991). A laboratory study of fear: The case of Peter. 1924. *Journal of Genetic Psychology 152*(4): 462–469.

Juliano, S. L. (1998, March 13). Mapping the sensory mosaic. *Science, 279,* 1653–1654.

Julien, R. M. (2001). *A primer of drug action* (9th ed.). New York: W. H. Freeman.

Jung, C. G. (1959). The concept of the collective unconscious. In *The archetypes and the collective unconscious, collected works* (Vol. 9, Part 1, pp. 54–77). Princeton, NJ: Princeton University Press. (Original work published 1936)

Kabot, S., Masi, W., & Segal, M. (2003). Advances in the diagnosis and treatment of autism spectrum disorders. *Professional Psychology: Research and Practice, 34,* 26–33.

Kagan, J. (1994a). *Galen's prophecy: Temperament in human nature.* New York: Basic Books.

Kagan, J. (1996). Three pleasing ideas. *American Psychologist, 51,* 901–908.

Kagan, J. (1998). *Three seductive ideas.* Cambridge, MA: Harvard University Press.

Kagan, J. (2001). Temperamental contributions to affective and behavioral profiles in childhood. In S. G. Hofmann & P. M. DiBartolo (Eds.), *From social anxiety to social phobia: Multiple perspectives.* (pp. 216–234). Boston: Allyn & Bacon.

Kagan, J., Reznick, J. S., & Snidman, N. (1986). Temperamental inhibition in early childhood. In R. Plomin & J. Dunn (Eds.), *The study of temperament: Changes, continuities, and challenges.* Hillsdale, NJ: Erlbaum.

Kagan, J., Reznick, J. S., & Snidman, N. (1988). Biological basis of childhood shyness. *Science, 20,* 167–171.

Kagan, J., & Snidman, N. (1991). Infant predictors of inhibited and uninhibited profiles. *Psychological Science, 2,* 40–44.

Kagan, J., & Snidman, N. (1998). Childhood derivatives of high and low reactivity in infancy. *Child Development, 69,* 1483–1493.

Kagan, J., Snidman, N., Arcus, D., & Reznick, J. S. (1994). *Galen's prophecy: Temperament in human nature.* New York: Basic Books.

Kahneman, D., & Tversky, A. (2000). *Choice, values, and frames.* New York: Cambridge University Press.

Kallman, M., & Rydlun, Y. (2002). Japan versus America: Differences in health and body image, *Whitman Journal of Psychology, 10*(2), 35–38.

Kamil, A. C., Krebs, J., & Pulliam, H. R. (1987). *Foraging behavior.* New York: Plenum.

Kamin, L. (1994, November 23). Intelligence, IQ tests, and race. *Chronicle of Higher Education,* B5.

Kamin, L. J. (1969). Predictability, surprise, attention, and conditioning. In B. A. Campbell & R. M. Church (Eds.), *Classical conditioning: A symposium.* New York: Appleton-Century-Crofts.

Kamin, L. J. (1974). *The science and politics of IQ.* Potomac, MD: Erlbaum.

Kamin, L. J. (1995, February). Book review: Behind the curve. *Scientific American, 272,* 99–103.

Kandel, D. B. (1978). Similarity in real-life adolescent friendship pairs. *Journal of Personality and Social Psychology, 36,* 306–312.

Kandel, E. (2000, November 10). Neuroscience: Breaking down scientific barriers to the study of brain and mind. *Science, 290,* 1113–1120.

Kandel, E. R. (2001, November 2). The molecular biology of memory storage: A dialogue between genes and synapses. *Science, 294,* 1030–1038.

Kandel, E. R., & Hawkins, R. D. (1992, September). The biological basis of learning and individuality. *Scientific American, 267,* 79–86

Kandel, E. R., & Squire, L. R. (2000, November 10). Neuroscience: Breaking down scientific barriers to the study of brain and mind. *Science, 290,* 1113–1120.

Kane, J. M., & Marder, S. R. (1993). Psychopharmacologic treatment of schizophrenia. *Schizophrenia Bulletin, 19,* 287–302.

Kantrowitz, B. (1992, January 27). A Head Start does not last. *Newsweek, 119,* 44–45.

Karlsen, C. F. (1998). *The devil in the shape of a woman: Witchcraft in colonial New England.* New York: W. W. Norton & Company.

Karni, A., Tanne, D., Rubenstein, B. S., Askenasy, J. J. M., & Sagi, D. (1994, July 29). Dependence on REM sleep of overnight improvement in perceptual skill. *Science, 265,* 679–682.

Kasamatsu, A., & Hirai, T. (1966). An electroencephalographic study on the Zen meditation (Zazen). *Folia Psychiatrica et Neurological Japonica, 20,* 315–336.

Kassinove, H., Sukhodolsky, D. G., Tsytsarev, S. V., & Solovyova, S. (1997). Self-reported anger episodes in Russia and America. *Journal of Social Behavior & Personality, 12,* 301–324.

Kaye, W. H., Devlin, B., Barbarich, N., Bulik, C. M., Thornton, L., Bacanu, S-A, Fichter, M. M., Halmi, K. A., Kaplan, A. S., Strober, M., Woodside, D. B., Bergen, A. W., Crow, S., Mitchell, J., Rotondo, A., Mauri, M., Cassano, G., Keel, P., Plotnicov, K., Pollice, C., Klump, K. L., Lilenfeld, L. R., Ganjei, J. K., Quadflieg, N., & Berrettini, W. H. (2004). Genetic analysis of bulimia nervosa: Methods and sample description. *International Journal of Eating Disorders, 35,* 556–570.

Kazdin, A. E. (1986). Comparative outcome studies of psychotherapy: Methodological issues and strategies. *Journal of Consulting and Clinical Psychology, 54,* 95–105.

Kazdin, A. E. (1994). *Behavior modification in applied settings* (5th ed.). Pacific Grove, CA: Brooks/Cole.

Kazdin, A. E., & Wilcoxin, L. A. (1976). Systematic desensitization and nonspecific treatment effects: A methodological evaluation. *Psychological Bulletin, 83,* 729–758.

Keating, C. F. (1994). World without words: Messages from face and body. In W. J. Lonner & R. Malpass (Eds.), *Psychology and culture* (pp. 175–182). Boston: Allyn & Bacon.

Keel, P. K., & Klump, K. L. (2003). Are eating disorders culture-bound syndromes? Implications for conceptualizing their etiology. *Psychological Bulletin, 129,* 747–769.

Keen, S. (1991). *Faces of the enemy: reflections of the hostile imagination.* San Francisco: Harper.

Keesey, R. E., & Powley, T. L. (1975). Hypothalamic regulation of body weight. *American Scientist, 63,* 558–565.

Keller, M. B., McCullough, J. P., Klein, D. N., Arnow, B., Dunner, D. L., Gelenberg, A. J., Markowitz, J. C., Nemeroff, C. B., Russell, J. M., Thase, M. E., Trivedi, M. H., & Zajecka, J. (2000, May 18). A comparison of nefazodone, the cognitive behavioral-analysis system of psychotherapy, and their combination for the treatment of chronic depression. *New England Journal of Medicine, 342,* 1462–1461.

Kelley, H. H., Berscheid, E., Christensen, A., Harvey, J., Huston, T., Levinger, G., McClintock, E., Peplau, A., & Peterson, D. (1983). *Close relationships.* San Francisco, CA: Freeman.

Kelley, J. E., Lumley, M. A., & Leisen, J. C. C. (1997). Health effects of emotional disclosure in rheumatoid arthritis patients. *Health Psychology, 16,* 331–340.

Kelman, H. C. (1997). Group processes in the resolution of international conflicts: Experiences from the Israeli–Palestinian case. *American Psychologist, 52,* 212–220.

Kelman, H. C. (1999). Interactive problem solving as a metaphor for international conflict resolution: Lessons for the policy process. *Peace & Conflict: Journal of Peace Psychology, 5,* 201–218.

Kempermann, G., & Gage, F. H. (1999, May). New nerve cells for the adult brain. *Scientific American, 280,* 48–53.

Kendler, K. S., & Gardner, C. O., Jr. (1998). Boundaries of major depression: An evaluation of DSM-IV criteria. *American Journal of Psychiatry, 155,* 172–177.

Kennedy, D. M. (1970). *Birth control in America: The career of Margaret Sanger.* New Haven, CT: Yale University Press.

Kennedy, M. B. (2000, October 27). Signal-processing machines at the postsynaptic density. *Science, 290,* 750–754.

Kenrick, D. T., & Funder, D. C. (1988). Profiting from controversy: Lessons from the person–situation debate. *American Psychologist, 43,* 23–34.

Kenrick, D. T., & Stringfield, D. O. (1980). Personality traits and the eye of the beholder: Crossing some traditional philosophical boundaries in the search for consistency in all of the people. *Psychological Review, 87,* 88–104.

Kerlinger, F. N. (1985). *Foundations of behavioral research* (3rd ed.). New York: Holt, Rinehart & Winston.

Kershner, J. R., & Ledger, G. (1985). Effect of sex, intelligence, and style of thinking on creativity: A comparison of gifted and average IQ children. *Journal of Personality and Social Psychology, 48,* 1033–1040.

Kesner, R., & Olton, D. S. (1990). *The neurobiology of comparative cognition.* Hillsdale, NJ: Erlbaum.

Kessler, R. C., Berglund, P., Demler, O., Jin, R., Koretz, D., Merikangas, K. R., Rush, A. J., Walters, E. E., & Wang, P. S. (2003, June). The epidemiology of major depressive disorder: Results from the National Comorbidity Survey Replication (NCS-R). *Journal of the American Medical Association, 289,* 3095–3105.

Keynes, R. (2002). *Darwin, his daughter, and human evolution.* New York: Penguin Putnam.

Kiecolt-Glaser, J. K., & Glaser, R. (1987). Psychosocial moderators of immune function. *Annals of Behavioral Medicine, 9,* 16–20.

Kiecolt-Glaser, J. K., & Glaser, R. (2001). Stress and immunity: Age enhances the risks. *Current Directions in Psychological Science, 10,* 18–21.

Kiesler, C. A. (1982a). Mental hospitals and alternative care: Noninstitutionalization as potential public policy for mental patients. *American Psychologist, 37,* 349–360.

Kiesler, C. A. (1993). Mental health policy and mental hospitalization. *Current Directions in Psychological Science, 2,* 93–95.

Kiester, E. (1980, May/June). Images of the night. *Science, 80,* 36–42.

Kihlstrom, J. F. (1985). Hypnosis. *Annual Review of Psychology, 36,* 385–418.

Kihlstrom, J. F. (1987). The cognitive unconscious. *Science, 237,* 1445–1452.

Kihlstrom, J. F. (1990). The psychological unconscious. In L. Pervin (Ed.), *Handbook of personality: Theory and research* (pp. 445–464). New York: Guilford Press.

Kihlstrom, J. F. (1998). Dissociations and dissociation theory in hypnosis: Comment on Kirsch and Lynn (1998). *Psychological Bulletin, 123,* 186–191.

Kihlstrom, J. F., Barnhardt, T. M., & Tartaryn, D. J. (1992). The psychological unconscious: Found, lost, and regained. *American Psychologist, 47,* 788–791.

Kim, J. E., & Moen, P. (2001). Is retirement good or bad for subjective well-being? *Current Directions in Psychological Science, 10,* 83–86.

Kimble, G. A. (1991). The spirit of Ivan Petrovich Pavlov. In G. A. Kimble, M. Wertheimer, & C. L. White (Eds.), *Portraits of pioneers in psychology* (pp. 26–40). Washington, DC: American Psychological Association.

Kinoshita, J. (1992, July). Dreams of a rat. *Discover, 13,* 34–41.

Kinsey, A. C., Pomeroy, W. B., & Martin, C. E. (1948). *Sexual behavior in the human male.* Philadelphia: Saunders.

Kinsey, A. C., Pomeroy, W. B., Martin, C. E., & Gebhard, P. H. (1953). *Sexual behavior in the human female.* Philadelphia: Saunders.

Kintsch, W. (1981). Semantic memory: A tutorial. In R. S. Nickerson (Ed.), *Attention and performance* (Vol. 8). Hillsdale, NJ: Erlbaum.

Kirsch, I., & Braffman, W. (2001). Imaginative suggestibility and hypnotizability. *Current Directions in Psychological Science, 10,* 57–61.

Kirsch, I., & Lynn, S. J. (1995). Altered state of hypnosis: Changes in the theoretical landscape. *American Psychologist, 50,* 846–858.

Kirsch, I., & Lynn, S. J. (1998). Dissociation theories of hypnosis. *Psychological Bulletin, 123,* 100–115.

Kitayama, S., Duffy, S., Kawamura, T., & Larsen, J. T. (2003). Perceiving an object and its context in different cultures: A cultural look at new look. *Psychological Science, 14,* 201–206.

Klagsbrun, F. (1985). *Married people: Staying together in the age of divorce.* New York: Bantam Books.

Klahr, D., & Simon, H. A. (2001). What have psychologists (and others) discovered about the process of scientific discovery? *Current Directions in Psychological Science, 10,* 75–79.

Kleinfeld, J. (1994). Learning styles and culture. In W. J. Lonner & R. Malpass, *Psychology and culture* (pp. 151–156). Boston: Allyn & Bacon.

Kleinke, C. (1975). *First impressions: The psychology of encountering others.* Englewood Cliffs, NJ: Prentice Hall.

Kleinman, A., & Cohen, A. (1997). Psychiatry's global challenge. *Scientific American, 276*(3), 86–89.

Kleinmuntz, B., & Szucko, J. J. (1984). Lie detection in ancient and modern times: A call for contemporary scientific study. *American Psychologist, 39,* 766–776.

Klinger, E. (1987, May). The power of daydreams. *Psychology Today,* 37–44.

Klüver, H., & Bucy, P. C. (1939). Preliminary analysis of temporal lobes in monkeys. *Archives of Neurology and Psychiatry, 42,* 979–1000.

Knecht, S., Flöel, A., Dräger, B., Breitenstein, C., Sommer, J. Henningsen, H., Ringelstein, E. B., & Pascual-Leone, A. (2002, July 1). Degree of language lateralization determines susceptibility to unilateral brain lesions *Nature Neuroscience, 5,* 695–699.

Koechlin, E., Ody, C., & Kouneiher, F. (2003, November 14). The architecture of cognitive control in the human prefrontal cortex. *Science, 302,* 1181–1185.

Kohlberg, L. (1964). Development of moral character and moral ideology. In M. L. Hoffman & L. W. Hoffman (Eds.), *Review of child development research* (Vol. 1). New York: Russell Sage Foundation.

Kohlberg, L. (1968, April). The child as a moral philosopher. *Psychology Today, 2*(4), 25–30.

Kohlberg, L. (1981). *The philosophy of moral development.* New York: Harper & Row.

Köhler, W. (1925). *The mentality of apes.* New York: Harcourt Brace Jovanovich.

Kohout, J. (2000, January). A look at recent baccalaureates in psychology. *Monitor on Psychology,* p. 13.

Kohout, J. (2001, February). Facts and figures: Who's earning those psychology degrees? *Monitor on Psychology, 32*(2). Retrieved on October 14, 2004, from http://www.apa.org/monitor/feb01/facts.html

Kohout, J., & Wicherski, M. (2000, December). Where are the new psychologists working? *Monitor on Psychology,* p. 13.

Kolb, B. (1989). Development, plasticity, and behavior. *American Psychologist, 44,* 1203–1212.

Koob, G. F., & Le Moal, M. (1997, October 3). Drug abuse: Hedonic homeostatic dysregulation. *Science, 278,* 52–58.

Kopta, S. M., Lueger, R. J., Saunders, S. M., & Howard, K. I. (1999). Individual psychotherapy outcome and process research: Challenges leading to greater turmoil or a positive transition? *Annual Review of Psychology,* 30, 441–469.

Kosko, B., & Isaka, S. (1993, July). Fuzzy logic. *Scientific American, 269,* 76–81.

Kosslyn, S., Thompson, W., Kim, I., & Alpert, N. (1995). Topographical representations of mental images in primary visual cortex. *Nature, 378,* 496–498.

Kosslyn, S. M. (1976). Can imagery be distinguished from other forms of internal representation? Evidence from studies of information retrieval times. *Memory and Cognition, 4,* 291–297.

Kosslyn, S. M. (1983). *Ghosts in the mind's machine: Creating and using images in the brain.* New York: Norton.

Kosslyn, S. M., Cacioppo, J. T., Davidson, R. J., Hugdahl, K., Lovallo, W. R., Speigel, D., & Rose, R. (2002). Bridging psychology and biology: The analysis of individuals in groups. *American Psychologist, 57,* 341–351.

Kotchoubey, B. (2002). Do event-related brain potentials reflect mental (cognitive) operations? *Journal of Psychophysiology, 16,* 129–149.

Kramer, A. F., & Willis, S. L. (2002). Enhancing the cognitive vitality of older adults. *Current Directions in Psychological Science, 11,* 173–177.

Kramer, P. D. (1993). *Listening to Prozac: A psychiatrist explores antidepressant drugs and the remaking of the self.* New York: Viking.

Krampe, R. T., & Ericsson, K. A. (1996). Maintaining excellence: Deliberate practice and elite performance in young and older pianists. *Journal of Experimental Psychology: General, 125,* 331–359.

Krantz, D. S., Grunberg, N. E., & Baum, A.

(1985). Health psychology. *Annual Review of Psychology, 36,* 349–383.

Kristol, I. (1994, November 3). Children need their fathers. *The New York Times,* A15.

Kubler-Ross, E. (1969). *On Death and Dying.* New York: MacMillan Publishing Co.

Kukla, A. (1989). Nonempirical issues in psychology. *American Psychologist, 44,* 785–794.

Lai, C. S. L., Fisher, S. E., Hurst, J. A., Vargha-Khadem, F., & Monaco, A. P. (2001, October 4). A forkhead-domain gene is mutated in a severe speech and language disorder. *Nature, 413,* 519–523.

Lakoff, R. T. (1990). *Talking power.* New York: Basic Books.

Lamb, H. R. (1998). Deinstitutionalization at the beginning of the new millennium. *Harvard Review of Psychiatry, 6,* 1–10.

Lamb, M. E. (1999, May/June). Mary D. Salter Ainsworth 1913–1999 attachment theorist. *APS Observer, 32,* 34–35.

Lambo, T. A. (1978). Psychotherapy in Africa. *Human Nature, 1*(3), 32–39.

Lampl, M., Veldhuis, J. D., & Johnson, M. L. (1992). Saltation and stasis: A model of human growth. *Science, 258,* 801–803.

Landesman, S., & Butterfield, E. C. (1987). Normalization and deinstitutionalization of mentally retarded individuals: Controversy and facts. *American Psychologist, 42,* 809–816.

Landry, D. W. (1997, February). Immunotherapy for cocaine addiction. *Scientific American,* 42–45.

Lang, F. R., & Carstensen, L. L. (1994). Close emotional relationships in late life: Further support for proactive aging in the social domain. *Psychology and Aging, 9,* 315–324.

Lang, P. J., & Lazovik, D. A. (1963). The experimental desensitization of a phobia. *Journal of Abnormal and Social Psychology, 66,* 519–525.

Langleben, D. D., Schroeder, L., Maldjian, J. A., Gur, R. C., McDonald, S., Ragland, J. D., O'Brien, C. P., & Childress, A. R. (2002). Brain activity during simulated deception: An event-related functional magnetic resonance study. *NeuroImage, 15,* 727–732.

Langlois, J. H., & Roggman, L. A. (1990). Attractive faces are only average. *Psychological Science, 1,* 115–121.

Langlois, J. H., Roggman, L. A., Casey, R. J., Ritter, J. M., Rieser-Danner, L. A., & Jenkins, V. Y. (1987). Infant preferences for attractive faces: Rudiments of a stereotype. *Developmental Psychology, 23,* 363–369.

Langlois, J. H., Roggman, L. A., & Musselman, L. (1994). What is average and what is not average about attractive faces? *Psychological Science, 5,* 214–220.

Larson, R. W. (2000). Toward a psychology of positive youth development. *American Psychologist, 55,* 170–183.

Larson, R. W. (2001). How U.S. children and adolescents spend time: What it does (and doesn't) tell us about their development. *Current Directions in Psychological Science, 10,* 160–164.

Lash, J. (2001). Dealing with the tinder as well as the flint. *Science, 294, 1789,* November 30, 2001.

Lashley, K. S. (1950). In search of the engram. In *Physiological mechanisms in animal behavior: Symposium of the Society for Experimental Biology* (Vol. 4). New York: Academic Press.

Latané, B., & Darley, J. M. (1968). Group inhibition of bystander intervention in emergencies. *Journal of Personality and Social Psychology, 10,* 215–221.

Laumann, E. O., Gagnon, J. H., Michael, R. T., & Michaels, S. (1994). *The social organization of sexuality: Sexual practices in the United States.* Chicago: University of Chicago Press.

Lawton, M. P. (2001). Emotion in later life. *Current Directions in Psychological Science, 10,* 120–123.

Lazar, I., & Darlington, R. (1982). Lasting effects of early education: A report from the Consortium for Longitudinal Studies. *Monographs of the Society for Research in Child Development, 47*(2–3, Serial No. 195).

Lazarus, R. S. (1984). On the primacy of cognition. *American Psychologist, 39,* 124–129.

Lazarus, R. S. (1991a). Cognition and motivation in emotion. *American Psychologist, 46,* 352–367.

Lazarus, R. S. (1991b). Progress on a cognitive-motivational-relational theory of emotion. *American Psychologist, 46,* 819–834.

Lazarus, R. S. (1991c). *Emotions and adaptations.* New York, NY: Oxford University Press.

Lazarus, R. S., DeLongis, A., Folkman, S., & Gruen, R. (1985). Stress and adaptational outcomes: The problem of confounded measures. *American Psychologist, 40,* 770–779.

LeDoux, J. (2002). *Synaptic self: How our brains become who we are.* New York: Viking.

LeDoux, J. E. (1994). Emotion, memory and the brain. *Scientific American, 270*(6), 50–57.

LeDoux, J. E. (1996). *The emotional brain: The mysterious underpinnings of emotional life.* New York: Simon & Schuster.

LeDoux, J. E. (2000). Emotion circuits in the brain. *Annual Review of Neuroscience, 23,* 155–184.

Lee, V. E., Brooks-Gunn, J., & Schnur, E. (1988). Does Head Start work? A 1-year follow-up of disadvantaged children attending Head Start, no preschool. *Developmental Psychology, 24,* 210–222.

Leeper, R. W., & Madison, P. (1959). *Toward understanding human personalities.* New York: Appleton-Century-Crofts.

Leerhsen, C. (1990, February 5). Unite and conquer: America's crazy for support groups. *Newsweek,* 50–55.

Lencer, R., Malchow, C. P., Trillenberg-Krecker, K., Schwinger, E., & Arolt, V. (2000). Eye-tracking dysfunction (ETD) in families with sporadic and familial schizophrenia. *Biological Psychiatry, 47,* 391–401.

Lennenberg, E. H. (1967). *Biological Foundations of Language.* New York: Wiley.

Leonard, J. (1998, May–June). Dream-catchers: Understanding the biological basis of things that go bump in the night. *Harvard Magazine, 100,* 58–68.

Lepper, M. R., Greene, D., & Nisbett, R. E. (1973). Undermining children's intrinsic interest with extrinsic reward: A test of the over-justification hypothesis. *Journal of Personality and Social Psychology, 28*(1), 129–137.

Lerner, R. M., Orlos, J. R., & Knapp, J. (1976). Physical attractiveness, physical effectiveness and self-concept in adolescents. *Adolescence, 11,* 313–326.

Leshner, A. I. (1997, October 3). Addiction is a brain disease, and it matters. *Science, 278,* 45–47.

Leslie, A. M. (2001). Learning: Association or computation? Introduction to a special section. *Current Directions in Psychological Science, 10,* 124–127.

Leslie, M. (2000, July/August). The vexing legacy of Lewis Terman. *Stanford, 28*(4), 44–51.

Lesperance, F., & Frasure-Smith, N. (1996, February 17). Negative emotions and coronary heart disease: Getting to the heart of the matter. *Lancet, 347,* 414–415.

Lettvin, J. Y., Maturana, H. R., McCulloch, W. S., & Pitts, W. H. (1959). What the frog's eye tells the frog's brain. *Proceedings of the Institute of Radio Engineers, 47,* 1940–1951.

Leutgeb, S., Leutgeb, J. K., Treves, A., Moser, M-B., & Moser, E. I. (2004, August 27). Distinct ensemble codes in hippocampal areas ca3 and ca1. *Science, 305,* 1295–1298.

Leutwyler, K. (1994, March). Prosthetic vision: Workers resume the quest for a seeing-eye device. *Scientific American, 270,* 108.

Leutwyler, K. (1995, June). Depression's double standard. *Scientific American, 272,* 23–24.

LeVay, S. (1991). A difference in hypothalamic structure between heterosexual and homosexual men. *Science, 253,* 1034–1037.

LeVay, S., & Hamer, D. (1995). Evidence for a biological influence in male homosexuality. *Scientific American, 270*(5), 44–49.

Levenson, R. W. (1992). Autonomic nervous system differences among emotions. *Psychological Science, 3,* 23–27.

Leventhal, H., & Tomarken, A. J. (1986). Emotion: Today's problems. *Annual Review of Psychology, 37,* 565–610.

Levine, J. A., Eberhardt, N. L., & Jensen, M. D. (1999, January 8). Role of nonexercise activity thermogenesis in resistance to fat gain in humans. *Science, 283,* 212–214.

Levine, K., Shane, H. C., & Wharton, R. H. (1994). What if . . . : A plea to professionals to consider the risk–benefit ratio of facilitated communication. *Mental Retardation, 32*(4), 300–304.

Levine, L. J. (1997). Reconstructing memory for emotions. *Journal of Experimental Psychology: General, 126,* 165–177.

Levine, L. J., & Safer, M. A. (2002). Sources of bias in memory for emotions. *Current Directions in Psychological Science, 11,* 169–173.

Levine, M., & Perkins, D. V. (1987). *Principles of community psychology: Perspectives and applications.* New York: Oxford University Press.

Lewinsohn, P. M., Clarke, G. N., Hops, H., & Andrews, J. A. (1990). Cognitive-behavioral treatment for depressed adolescents. *Behavior Therapy, 21,* 385–401.

Lewinsohn, P. M., & Gotlib, I. H. (1995). Behavioral theory and treatment of depression. In E. E. Beckham, & W. R. Leber (Eds.), *Handbook of depression* (2nd ed., pp. 352–375). New York: Guilford Press.

Lewinsohn, P. M., & Rosenbaum, M. (1987). Recall of parental behavior by acute depressives, remitted depressives, and nondepressives. *Journal of Personality and Social Psychology, 52,* 611–619.

Lewinsohn, P. M., Sullivan, J. M., & Grosscup, S. J. (1980). Changing reinforcing events: An approach to the treatment of depression. *Psychotherapy: Theory, Research and Practice, 17,* 322–334.

Lewis, D. A., Cruz, D. A., Melchitzky, D. S., & Pierri, J. N. (2001). Lamina-specific deficits in parvalbumin-immunoreactive varicosities in the prefrontal cortex of subjects with schizophrenia: Evidence for fewer projections from the thalamus. *American Journal of Psychiatry, 158,* 1411–1422.

Lewy, A. J., Sack, R. L., Miller, S., & Hoban, T. M. (1987). Antidepressant and circadian phase-shifting effect of light. *Science, 235,* 352–354.

Liegeois, F., Baldeweg, T., Connelly, A., Gadian, D. G., Mishkin, M., & Vargha-Khadem, F. (2001). Language fMRI abnormalities associated with FOXP2 gene mutation. *Nature Neuroscience 11,* 1230–1237.

Lilienfeld, S. O., Wood, J. M., & Garb, H. N. (2000a). The scientific status of projective techniques. *Psychological Science in the Public Interest, 1,* 27–66.

Lilienfeld, S. O., Wood, J. M., & Garb, H. N. (2000b). What's wrong with this picture? *Scientific American, 284*(5), 80–87.

Lillard, A. (1999). Developing a cultural theory of mind: The CIAO approach. *Current Directions in Psychological Science, 8,* 57–61.

Lillard, A. S. (1997). Other folks' theories of mind and behavior. *Psychological Science, 8,* 268–274.

Lindsay, D. S. (1990). Misleading suggestions can impair eyewitnesses' ability to remember event details. *Journal of Experimental Psychology: Learning, Memory, and Cognition, 16*(6), 1077–1083.

Lindsay, D. S. (1993). Eyewitness suggestibility. *Current Directions in Psychological Science, 2,* 86–89.

Linsheid, T. R., Iwata, B. A., Ricketts, R. W., Williams, D. E., & Griffin, J. C. (1990). Clinical evaluation of the self-injurious behavior inhibiting system (SIBIS). *Journal of Applied Behavior Analysis, 23,* 53–78.

Lipsey, M. W., & Wilson, D. B. (1993). The efficacy of psychological, educational, and behavioral treatment: Confirmation from meta-analysis. *American Psychologist, 48,* 1181–1209.

Lipsitt, L. P., Reilly, B., Butcher, M. G., & Greenwood, M. M. (1976). The stability and interrelationships of newborn sucking and heart rate. *Developmental Psychobiology, 9,* 305–310.

Liu, W., Vichienchom, K., Clements, M., DeMarco, S. C., Hughes, C., McGucken, E., Humayun, M.S., De Juan, E., Weiland, J. D., & Greenberg, R. (2000, October). A neuro-stimulus chip with telemetry unit for retinal prosthetic device. *IEEE Journal of Solid-State Circuits, 35,* 1487–1497.

Loftus, E. F. (1979). *Eyewitness testimony.* Cambridge, MA: Harvard University Press.

Loftus, E. F. (1984). The eyewitness on trial. In B. D. Sales & A. Alwork (Eds.), *With liberty and justice for all.* Englewood Cliffs, NJ: Prentice Hall.

Loftus, E. F. (1992). When a lie becomes memory's truth: Memory distortion after exposure to misinformation. *Current Directions in Psychological Science, 1,* 121–123.

Loftus, E. F. (1993). The reality of repressed memories. *American Psychologist, 48,* 518–537.

Loftus, E. F. (1997a, September). Creating false memories. *Scientific American, 227,* 70–75.

Loftus, E. F. (1997b). Memory for a past that never was. *Current Directions in Psychological Science, 6,* 60–65.

Loftus, E. F. (2003a). Make-believe memories. *American Psychologist, 58,* 867–873.

Loftus, E. F. (2003b). Our changeable memories: Legal and practical implications. *Nature Reviews: Neuroscience, 4,* 231–234.

Loftus, E. F., & Ketcham, K. (1991). *Witness for the defense: The accused, the eyewitness, and the expert who puts memory on trial.* New York: St. Martin's Press.

Loftus, E. F., & Ketcham, K. (1994). *The myth of repressed memory: False memories and allegations of sexual abuse.* New York: St. Martin's Griffin.

Loftus, E. F., & Klinger, M. R. (1992). Is the unconscious smart or dumb? *American Psychologist, 47,* 761–765.

Loftus, E. F., & Palmer, J. C. (1973). Reconstruction of automobile destruction: An example of the interaction between language and memory. *Journal of Verbal Learning and Verbal Behavior, 13,* 585–589.

Loftus, G. R., Duncan, J., & Gehrig, P. (1992). On the time course of perceptual information that results from a brief visual presentation. *Journal of Experimental Psychology: Human Perception and Performance, 18*(2), 530–549.

London, K. A., Mosher, W. D., Pratt, W. F., & Williams, L. B. (1989, March). *Preliminary findings from the National Survey of Family Growth, Cycle IV.* Paper presented at the annual meeting of the Population Association of America, Baltimore, MD.

Lonner, W. J., & Malpass, R. (1994). *Psychology and culture.* Boston: Allyn & Bacon.

Lonner, W. J. (1990). An overview of cross-cultural testing and assessment. In R. W. Brislin (Ed.), *Applied cross-cultural psychology.* Newbury Park, CA: Sage.

Lott, A. J., & Lott, B. E. (1961). Group cohesiveness, communication level, and conformity. *Journal of Abnormal and Social Psychology, 62,* 408–412.

Lourenço, O., & Machado, A. (1996). In defense of Piaget's theory: A reply to 10 common criticisms. *Psychological Review, 103,* 143–164.

Lovaas, O. I. (1977). *The autistic child: Language development through behavior modification.* New York: Halstead Press.

Lovaas, O. I. (1993). The development of a treatment-research project for developmentally disabled and autistic children. *Journal of Applied Behavior Analysis, 26,* 617–630.

Lovaas, O. I., Schreibman, L., & Koegel, R. L. (1974). A behavior modification approach to the treatment of autistic children. *Journal of Autism and Childhood Schizophrenia, 4,* 111–129.

Lovibond, S. H., Adams, M., & Adams, W. G. (1979). The effects of three experimental prison environments on the behavior of nonconflict volunteer subjects. *Australian Psychologist, 14,* 273–285.

Luborsky, L., Singer, B., & Luborsky, L. (1975). Comparative studies of psychotherapies: Is it true that everyone has won and all must have prizes? *Archives of General Psychiatry, 32,* 995–1008.

Lutz, C. (1988). *Unnatural emotions.* Chicago: University of Chicago Press.

Lykken, D., & Tellegen, A. (1996). Happiness is a stochastic phenomenon. *Psychological Science, 7,* 186–189.

Lykken, D. T. (2001). Parental licensure. *American Psychologist, 56,* 885–894.

Lykken, D. T., McGue, M., Tellegen, A., & Bouchard, T. J. (1992). Emergenesis: Genetic traits that may not run in families. *American Psychologist, 47,* 1565–1577.

Lynch, G., & Staubli, U. (1991). Possible contributions of long-term potentiation to the encoding and organization of memory. *Brain Research Reviews, 16,* 204–206.

Maas, J. B. (1999). *Power sleep: The revolutionary program that prepares your mind for peak performance.* New York: HarperPerennial.

Maccoby, E. (1998). *The two sexes: Growing up apart, coming together.* Cambridge, MA: Belknap Press.

Maccoby, E. (2000). *Gender differentiation in childhood: Broad patterns and their implications.* Address given at the American Psychological Association annual convention, Washington, DC.

Maccoby, E. E., & Martin, J. A. (1983). Socialization in the context of the family: Parent–child interaction. In E. M. Hetherington (Ed.), *Handbook of child psychology: Vol. 4, Socialization, personality, and social development* (4th ed., pp. 1–101). New York: Wiley.

Maccoby, N., Farquhar, J. W., Wood, P. D., & Alexander, J. K. (1977). Reducing the risk of cardiovascular disease: Effects of a community-based campaign on knowledge and behavior. *Journal of Community Health, 3,* 100–114.

MacCoun, R. J. (1998). Toward a psychology of harm reduction. *American Psychologist, 53,* 1199–1208.

MacLeod, C., & Campbell, L. (1992). Memory accessibility and probability judgments: An experimental evaluation of the availability heuristic. *Journal of Personality and Social Psychology, 63,* 890–902.

Macmillan, J. C. (2000). *An odd kind of fame: Stories of Phineas Gage.* Cambridge, MA: MIT Press.

MacNair, R. M. (1999). *Symptom pattern differences for perpetration-induced traumatic stress in veterans: Probing the National Vietnam Veterans Readjustment Study.* Doctoral dissertation, University of Kansas City, Missouri.

MacNair, R. M. (2002). *Perpetration-induced traumatic stress: The psychological consequences of killing.* Westport, CT: Praeger.

Macrae, C. N., Milne, A. B., & Bodenhausen, G. V. (1994). Stereotypes as energy-saving devices: A peek inside the cognitive toolbox. *Journal of Personality and Social Psychology, 66,* 37–47.

Magee, W. J., Eaton, W. W., Wittchen, H.-U., McGonagle, K. A., & Kessler, R. C. (1996). Agoraphobia, simple phobia, and social phobia in the national comorbidity survey. *Archives of General Psychiatry, 53,* 159–168.

Maher, B. A., & Maher, W. B. (1985). Psychopathology: II. From the eighteenth century to modern times. In G. A. Kimble & K. Schlesinger (Eds.), *Topics in the history of psychology* (Vol. 2, pp. 295–329). Hillsdale, NJ: Erlbaum.

Maher, B. A., & Ross, J. S. (1984). Delusions. In H. E. Adams & P. B. Sutker (Eds.), *Comprehensive handbook of psychopathology* (pp. 383–987). New York: Plenum.

Maier, S. F., & Watkins, L. R. (1999). Bidirectional communication between the brain and the immune system: Implications for behaviour. *Animal Behaviour, 57,* 741–751.

Maier, S. F., & Watkins, L. R. (2000). The immune system as a sensory system: Implications for psychology. *Current Directions in Psychological Science, 9,* 98–102.

Maier, S. F., Watkins, L. R., & Fleshner, M. (1994). Psychoneuroimmunology: The interface between behavior, brain, and immunity. *American Psychologist, 49,* 1004–1017.

Maisto, S. A., Galizio, M., & Connors, G. J. (1995). *Drug use and abuse* (2nd ed). Fort Worth, TX: Harcourt Brace.

Majewska, M. D., Harrison, N. L., Schwartz, R. D., Barker, J. L., & Paul, S. M. (1986). Steroid hormone metabolites are barbiturate-like modulators of the GABA receptor. *Science, 232,* 1004–1007.

Malinowski, B. (1927). *Sex and repression in savage society.* London, U.K.: Humanities Press.

Malitz, S., & Sackheim, H. A. (1984). Low dosage ECT: Electrode placement and acute physiological and cognitive effects. *American Journal of Social Psychiatry, 4,* 47–53.

Manderscheid, R. W., Witkin, M. J., Rosenstein, M. J., Milazzo-Sayre, L. J., Bethel, H. E., & MacAskill, R. L. (1985). In C. A. Taube & S. A. Barrett (Eds.), *Mental Health, United States, 1985.* Washington, DC: National Institute of Mental Health.

Manfredi, M., Bini, G., Cruccu, G., Accornero, N., Beradelli, A., & Medolago, L. (1981). Congenital absence of pain. *Archives of Neurology, 38,* 507–511.

Mann, C. C. (1994, June 17). Behavioral genetics in transition. *Science, 264,* 1686–1689.

Manschreck, T. C. (1989). Delusional (paranoid) disorders. In H. I. Kaplan & B. J. Sadock (Eds.), *Comprehensive textbook of psychiatry* (pp. 816– 829). Baltimore: Williams & Wilkins.

Manson, S. M. (1994). Culture and depression: Discovering variations in the experience of illness. In W. J. Lonner & R. Malpass (Eds.), *Psychology and culture* (pp. 285–290). Boston: Allyn & Bacon.

Maquet, P. (2001, November 2). The role of sleep in learning and memory. *Science, 294,* 1048–1052.

Marcus, G. B. (1986). Stability and change in political attitudes: Observe, recall, and "explain." *Political Behavior, 8,* 21–44.

Marcus, G. F. (1996). Why do children say "breaked"? *Current Directions in Psychological Science, 3,* 81–85.

Markman, H. J., & Notarius, C. I. (1993). *We can work it out.* Berkeley, CA: Berkeley Publishing Group.

Markus, H. R., & Kitayama, S. (1994). The cultural construction of self and emotion: Implications for social behavior. In H. R. Markus & S. Kitayama (Eds.), *Emotion and culture: Empirical studies of mutual influence* (pp. 89–130). Washington, DC: American Psychological Association.

Marsh, P. (1988). Detecting insincerity. In P. Marsh (Ed.), *Eye to eye: How people interact.* (Ch. 14, pp. 116–119). Oxford, U.K.: Oxford Andromeda.

Marshall, E. (2000, August 4). Duke study faults overuse of stimulants for children. *Science, 289,* 721.

Martin, A., Haxby, J. V., Lalonde, F. M., Wiggs, C. L., & Ungerleider, L. G. (1995). Discrete cortical regions associated with knowledge of color and knowledge of action. *Science, 270,* 102–105.

Martin, G., & Pear, J. (1999). *Behavior modification: What it is and how to do it* (6th ed.). Upper Saddle River, NJ: Prentice-Hall.

Martin, J. A. (1981). A longitudinal study of the consequences of early mother–infant interaction: A microanalytic approach. *Monographs of the Society for Research in Child Development, 46* (203, Serial No. 190).

Maruyama, G., & Miller, N. (1975). *Physical attractiveness and classroom acceptance* (Research Report 75–2). Los Angeles: University of Southern California, Social Science Research Institute.

Marx, J. (2003, February 7). Cellular warriors at the battle of the bulge. *Science, 299,* 846–849.

Maslow, A. H. (1968). *Toward a psychology of being* (2nd ed.). New York: Van Nostrand.

Maslow, A. H. (1970). *Motivation and personality* (rev. ed.). New York: Harper & Row.

Maslow, A. H. (1971). *Farther reaches of human nature.* New York: Viking Penguin.

Masters, W. H., & Johnson, V. E. (1966). *Human sexual response.* Boston: Little, Brown.

Masters, W. H., & Johnson, V. E. (1970). *Human sexual inadequacy.* Boston: Little, Brown.

Masters, W. H., & Johnson, V. E. (1979). *Homosexuality in perspective.* Boston: Little, Brown.

Matossian, M. K. (1982). Ergot and the Salem witchcraft affair. *American Scientist, 70,* 355–357.

Matossian, M. K. (1989). *Poisons of the past: Molds, epidemics, and history.* New Haven, CT: Yale University Press.

Matsumoto, D. (1994). *People: Psychology from a cultural perspective.* Pacific Grove, CA: Brooks/Cole.

Matsumoto, D. (1996). *Culture and psychology.* Pacific Grove, CA: Brooks/Cole.

Matthews, K. A. (1982). Psychological perspectives on the Type-A behavior pattern. *Psychological Bulletin, 91,* 293–323.

Matus, A. (2000, October 27). Actin-based plasticity in dendritic spines. *Science, 290,* 754–758.

Maunsell, J. H. R. (1995, November 3). The brain's visual world: Representation of visual targets in cerebral cortex. *Science, 270,* 764–769.

Mauron, A. (2001, February 2). Is the genome the secular equivalent of the soul? *Science, 291,* 831–833.

Mayer, D. J. (1979). Endogenous analgesia systems: Neural and behavioral mechanisms. In Bonica, J. J. (Ed.), *Advances in pain research and therapy* (Vol. 3). New York: Raven Press.

Mayer, J. D. (1999, September). Emotional intelligence: Popular or scientific psychology? *American Psychological Association Monitor,* 50.

Mayer, J. D., & Salovey, P. (1997). What is emotional intelligence? In P. Salovey & D. J. Sluyter (Eds.), *Emotional development and emotional intelligence: Educational implications.* New York: Basic Books.

Mayer, R. E. (1983). *Thinking, problem solving, and cognition.* San Francisco: W. H. Freeman.

Mayr, E. (2000, July). Darwin's influence on modern thought. *Scientific American,* pp. 79–83.

McAdams, D. P. (1992). The five-factor model in personality: A critical appraisal. *Journal of Personality, 60,* 239–361.

McAdams, D. P., de St. Aubin, E., & Logan, R. L. (1993). Generativity among young, midlife, and older adults. *Psychology and Aging, 8,* 221–230.

McAnulty, R. D., & Burnette, M. M. (2004). *Exploring human sexuality: Making healthy decisions* (2nd ed.). Boston: Allyn & Bacon.

McArdle, J. J., Ferrer-Caja, E. Hamagami, F., & Woodcock, R. W. (2002). Comparative longitudinal structural analyses of the growth and decline of multiple intellectual abilities over the life span. *Developmental Psychology, 38,* 115–142.

McCarley, N., & Carskadon, T. G. (1983). Test–retest reliabilities of scales and subscales of the Myers–Briggs Type Indicator and of criteria for clinical interpretive hypotheses involving them. *Research in Psychological Type, 6,* 24–36.

McCarthy, K. (1991, August). Moods—good and bad—color all aspects of life. *APA Monitor,* 13.

McCartney, K., Harris, M. J., & Bernieri, F.

(1990). Growing up and growing apart: A developmental meta-analysis of twin studies. *Psychological Bulletin, 107,* 226–237.

McClearn, G. E., Johansson, B., Berg, S., Pedersen, N. L., Ahern, F., Petrill, S. A., & Plomin, R. (1997, June 6). Substantial genetic influence on cognitive abilities in twins 80 or more years old. *Science, 276,* 1560–1563.

McClelland, D. C. (1965). Achievement and entrepreneurship: A longitudinal study. *Journal of Personality and Social Psychology, 1,* 389–392.

McClelland, D. C. (1975). *Power: The inner experience.* New York: Irvington.

McClelland, D. C. (1985). *Human motivation.* New York: Scott Foresman.

McClelland, D. C. (1987a). Characteristics of successful entrepreneurs. *The Journal of Creative Behavior, 21,* 219–233.

McClelland, D. C. (1987b). *Human motivation.* New York: Cambridge University Press.

McClelland, D. C. (1993). Intelligence is not the best predictor of job performance. *Current Directions in Psychological Science, 2,* 5–6.

McClelland, D. C., & Boyatzis, R. E. (1982). Leadership motive pattern and long-term success in management. *Journal of Applied Psychology, 67,* 737–743.

McClelland, J. L., McNaughton, B. L., & O'Reilly, R. C. (1995). Why there are complementary learning systems in the hippocampus and neocortex: Insights from the successes and failures of connectionist models of learning and memory. *Psychological Review, 102,* 419–457.

McCrae, R. R., & Costa, P. T., Jr. (1997). Personality trait structure as a human universal. *American Psychologist, 52,* 509–516.

McCullough, M. L. (2001). Freud's seduction theory and its rehabilitation: A saga of one mistake after another. *Review of General Psychology, 5,* 3–22.

McGaugh, J. L. (2000, January 14). Memory—A century of consolidation. *Science, 287,* 248–251.

McGuire, P. A. (2000, February). New hope for people with schizophrenia. *Monitor on Psychology, 31*(2), 24–28.

McIntosh, A. R., & Lobaugh, N. J. (2003, July 18). When is a word not a word? *Science, 301,* 322–323.

McKeachie, W. J. (1990). Research on college teaching: The historical background. *Journal of Educational Psychology, 82,* 189–200.

McKeachie, W. J. (1997). Good teaching makes a difference—and we know what it is. In R. B. Perry & J. C. Smart (Eds.), *Effective teaching in higher education: Research and practice* (pp. 396–408). New York: Agathon Press.

McKeachie, W. J. (1999). *McKeachie's teaching tips: Strategies, research, and theory for college and university teachers* (10th ed.). Boston: Houghton Mifflin.

McNally, R. J. (1994, August). Cognitive bias in panic disorder. *Current Directions in Psychological Science, 3,* 129–132.

McNally, R. J., Bryant, R. A., & Ehlers, A. (2003). Does early psychological intervention promote recovery from posttraumatic stress. *Psychology Science in the Public Interest, 4,* 45–79

Medin, C., Lynch, J., & Solomon, H. (2000). Are there kinds of concepts? *Annual Review of Psychology, 52,* 121–147.

Medin, D. L. (1989). Concepts and conceptual structure. *American Psychologist, 44,* 1469–1481.

Medin, D. L., & Ross, B. H. (1992). *Cognitive psychology.* Fort Worth, TX: Harcourt Brace Jovanovich.

Meier, R. P. (1991). Language acquisition by deaf children. *American Scientist, 79,* 60–70.

Meltzoff, A. N. (1998). *The nature of the preverbal mind: Towards a developmental cognitive science.* Paper presented at the Western Psychological Association/ Rocky Mountain Psychological Association joint convention, Albuquerque, NM.

Meltzoff, A. N., & Prinz, W. (2002). *The imitative mind.* New York: Cambridge University Press.

Meltzoff, J., & Kornreich, M. (1970). *Research in psychotherapy.* New York: Atherton.

Melzack, R. (1990, February). The tragedy of needless pain. *Scientific American, 262,* 27–33.

Melzack, R., & Wall, P. D. (1965). Pain mechanisms: A new theory. *Science, 150,* 971–979.

Melzack, R., & Wall, P. D. (1983). *The challenge of pain.* New York: Basic Books.

Menzel, E. M. (1978). Cognitive mapping in chimpanzees. In S. H. Hulse, H. Fowler, & W. K. Honzig (Eds.), *Cognitive processes in animal behavior* (pp. 375–422). Hillsdale, NJ: Erlbaum.

Meredith, N. (1986, June). Testing the talking cure. *Science 86, 7,* 30–37.

Merikle, P. M., & Reingold, E. M. (1990). Recognition and lexical decision without detection: Unconscious perception? *Journal of Experimental Psychology: Human Perception & Performance, 16,* 574–583.

Mervis, C. B., & Rosch, E. (1981). Categorization of natural objects. *Annual Review of Psychology, 32,* 89–115.

Mesulam, M. M. (1990). Schizophrenia and the brain. *New England Journal of Medicine, 322,* 842–845.

Meyer, I. H. (2003). Prejudice, social stress, and mental health in lesbian, gay, and bisexual populations: Conceptual issues and research evidence. *Psychological Bulletin, 129,* 674–697.

Michael, R. T., Gagnon, J. H., Laumann, E. O., & Kolata, G. (1994). *Sex in America: A definitive survey.* New York: Little, Brown.

Milgram, S. (1965). Some conditions of obedience and disobedience to authority. *Human Relations, 18,* 56–76.

Milgram, S. (1974). *Obedience to authority.* New York: Harper & Row.

Miller, A. G. (1986). *The obedience paradigm: A case study in controversy in social science.* New York: Praeger.

Miller, G. A. (1956). The magic number seven plus or minus two: Some limits in our capacity for processing information. *Psychological Review, 63,* 81–97.

Miller, J. (1984). Culture and the development of everyday social explanation. *Journal of Personality and Social Psychology, 46,* 961–978.

Miller, K. E., Barnes, G. M., Sabo, D. F., Melnick, M. J., & Farrell, M. P. (2002). Anabolic-androgenic steroid use and other adolescent problem behaviors: Rethinking the male athlete assumption. *Sociological Perspectives, 45,* 467–489.

Miller, M. E., & Bowers, K. S. (1993). Hypnotic analgesia: Dissociated experience of dissociated control? *Journal of Abnormal Psychology, 102,* 29–38.

Miller, M. W. (1993, December 2). Dark days: The staggering cost of depression. *The Wall Street Journal,* B1.

Miller, N. (1959). *Liberalization of basic S-R concepts: Extensions to conflict behavior, motivation, and social learning.* In Sigmund Koch (Ed.), Psychology: A Study of Science (Study I, Vol. 2). New York: McGraw-Hill.

Miller, P. Y., & Simon, W. (1980). The development of sexuality in adolescence. In J. Adelson (Ed.), *Handbook of adolescent psychology.* New York: Wiley.

Miller, W. R., & Brown, S. A. (1997). Why psychologists should treat alcohol and drug problems. *American Psychologist, 52,* 1269–1279.

Miller-Jones, D. (1989). Culture and testing. *American Psychologist, 44,* 360–366.

Milner, B., Corkin, S., & Teuber, H. H. (1968) Further analysis of the hippocampal amnesic syndrome: 14-year follow-up study of H. M. *Neuropsychologia, 6,* 215–234.

Mineka, S., Davidson, M., Cook, M., & Keir, R. (1984). Observational conditioning of snake fear in rhesus monkeys. *Journal of Abnormal Psychology, 93,* 355–372.

Mintz, L. B., & Betz, N. E. (1986). Sex differences in the nature, realism, and correlates of body image. *Sex Roles, 15,* 185–195.

Mischel, W. (1968). *Personality and assessment.* New York: Wiley.

Mischel, W. (1973). Toward a cognitive social learning conceptualization of personality. *Psychological Review, 80,* 252–283.

Mischel, W. (1990). Personality dispositions revisited and revised: A view after three decades. In L. A. Pervin (Ed.), *Handbook of personality: Theory and research.* New York: Guilford Press.

Mischel, W. (1993). *Introduction to personality* (5th ed.). Fort Worth, TX: Harcourt Brace Jovanovich College Publishers.

Mischel, W., & Shoda, Y. (1995). A cognitive-affective system theory of personality: Reconceptualizing situations, dispositions, dynamics, and invariance in personality structure. *Psychological Review, 102,* 246–268.

Miyashita, Y. (1995). How the brain creates imagery: Projection to primary visual cortex. *Science, 268,* 1719–1720.

Mizukami, K., Kobayashi, N., Ishii, T., & Iwata, H. (1990). First selective attachment begins in early infancy: A study using telethermography. *Infant Behavior and Development, 13,* 257–271.

Moar, I. (1980). The nature and acquisition of cognitive maps. In D. Cantor & T. Lee (Eds.), *Proceedings of the international con-*

ference on environmental psychology. London, U.K.: Architectural Press.

Moghaddam, F. M., Taylor, D. M., & Wright, S. C. (1993). *Social psychology in cross-cultural perspective.* New York: W. H. Freeman.

Mogilner, A., Grossman, J. A. I., & Ribary, W. (1993). Somatosensory cortical plasticity in adult humans revealed by magnetoencephalography. *Proceedings of the National Academy of Sciences, 90*(8), 3593–3597.

Mombaerts, P. (1999, October 22). Seven-transmembrane proteins as odorant and chemosensory receptors. *Science, 286,* 707–711.

Monaghan, P. (1999, February 26). Lessons from the "marriage lab." *The Chronicle of Higher Education,* A9.

Moncrieff, R. W. (1951). *The chemical senses.* London, U.K.: Leonard Hill.

Money, J. (1987). Sin, sickness, or status? Homosexual gender identity and psychoneuroendocrinology. *American Psychologist, 42,* 384–399.

Monte, C. F. (1980). *Beneath the mask: An introduction to theories of personality* (2nd ed.). New York: Holt, Rinehart and Winston.

Moore, J. S., Graziano, W. G., & Millar, M. G. (1987). Physical attractiveness, sex role orientation, and the evaluation of adults and children. *Personality and Social Psychology Bulletin, 13,* 95–102.

Moore-Ede, M. (1993). *The twenty-four-hour society: Understanding human limits in a world that never stops.* Reading, MA: Addison-Wesley.

Morgan, A. H., Hilgard, E. R., & Davert, E. C. (1970). The heritability of hypnotic susceptibility of twins: A preliminary report. *Behavior Genetics, 1,* 213–224.

Mori, K., Nagao, H., & Yoshihara, Y. (1999). The olfactory bulb: Coding and processing of odor molecule information. *Science, 286,* 711–715.

Moriarity, T. (1975). Crime, commitment and the responsive bystander: Two field experiments. *Journal of Personality and Social Psychology, 31,* 370–376.

Morrell, E. M. (1986). Meditation and somatic arousal. *American Psychologist, 41*(6), 712–713.

Morris, M. W., & Peng, K. (1994). Culture and cause: American and Chinese attributions for social and physical events. *Journal of Personality & Social Psychology, 8,* 949–971.

Morris, W. N., & Miller, R. S. (1975). The effects of consensus-breaking and consensus-preempting partners on reduction of conformity. *Journal of Experimental Social Psychology, 11,* 215–223.

Morrison-Bogorad, M., & Phelps, C. (1997, March 12). Alzheimer disease research comes of age. *JAMA: Journal of the American Medical Association, 277,* 837–840.

Moskowitz, H. (1985). Marihuana and driving. *Accident Analysis & Prevention, 17,* 323–345.

Mowrer, O. (1960). *Learning theory and symbolic processes.* New York: Wiley.

Mowrer, O. H., & Mowrer, W. M. (1938). Enuresis—a method for its study and treatment. *American Journal of Orthopsychiatry, 8,* 436–459.

Mroczek, D. K. (2001). Age and emotion in adulthood. *Current Directions in Psychological Science, 10,* 87–90.

MTA Cooperative Treatment Group. (2004). National Institute of Mental Health Multimodal Treatment Study of ADHD Follow-up: 24-Month Outcomes of Treatment Strategies for Attention-Deficit/Hyperactivity Disorder. *Pediatrics, 113,* 754–761.

Mukerjee, M. (1995, October). Hidden scars: Sexual and other abuse may alter a brain region. *Scientific American, 273*(4), 14, 20.

Munakata, Y., McClelland, J. L., Johnson, M. H., & Siegler, R. S. (1997). Rethinking infant knowledge: Toward an adaptive process account of successes and failures in object permanence tasks. *Psychological Review, 104,* 686–713.

Munroe, R. L. (1955). *Schools of psychoanalytic thought.* New York: Dryden.

Murnen, S. K., & Stockton, M. (1997). Gender and self-reported sexual arousal in response to sexual stimuli: A meta-analytic review. *Sex Roles, 37,* 135–153.

Murphy, G., & Murphy, L. B. (Eds.). (1968). *Asian psychology.* New York: Basic Books.

Murphy, J. M. (1976, March 12). Psychiatric labeling in cross-cultural perspective. *Science, 191,* 1019–1028.

Murray, B. (1995, October). Americans dream about food, Brazilians dream about sex. *APA Monitor,* 30.

Murray, B. (1997, September). Why aren't antidrug programs working? *APA Monitor,* 30.

Murray, B. (2002, June). Writing to heal. *APA Monitor,* 54–55.

Murray, D. J., Kilgour, A. R., & Wasylkiw, L. (2000). Conflicts and missed signals in psychoanalysis, behaviorism, and Gestalt psychology. *American Psychologist, 55,* 422–426.

Murray, J. P., & Kippax, S. (1979). Children's social behavior in three towns with differing television experience. *Journal of Communication, 28,* 19–29.

Myers, D. G. (2000). The funds, friends, and faith of happy people. *American Psychologist, 55,* 56–67.

Myers, D. G. (2002). *Intuition: Its powers and perils.* New Haven, CT: Yale University Press.

Myers, D. G., & Diener, E. (1995). Who is happy? *Psychological Science, 6,* 10–19.

Myers, I. B. (1962). *The Myers–Briggs type indicator.* Palo Alto, CA: Consulting Psychologists Press.

Myers, I. B. (1976). *Introduction to type* (2nd ed.). Gainesville, FL: Center for Applications of Psychological Type.

Myers, I. B. (1987). *Introduction to type: A description of the theory and applications of the Myers–Briggs Type Indicator.* Palo Alto, CA: Consulting Psychologists Press.

Myers, I. B., & Myers, P. B. (1995). *Gifts differing: Understanding personality type.* Palo Alto, CA: Consulting Psychologists Press.

The mysteries of twins. (1998, January 11). *The Washington Post.* Retrieved on November 8, 2004, from http://www.washingtonpost.com/wp-srv/national/longterm/twins/twins2.htm

Nahemow, L., & Lawton, M. P. (1975). Similarity and propinquity in friendship formation. *Journal of Personality and Social Psychology, 32,* 205–213.

Naigles, L. (1990). Children use syntax to learn verb meanings. *Child language, 17,* 357–374.

Naigles, L. G., & Kako, E. T. (1993). First contact in verb acquisition: Defining a role for syntax. *Child Development, 64,* 1665–1687.

Napier, A. Y. (2000). Making a marriage. In W. C. Nichols, M. A. Pace-Nichols, D. S. Becvar, & A. Y. Napier (Eds.), *Handbook of family development and intervention* (pp. 145–170). New York: Wiley.

Nash, M. R. (2001, July). The truth and the hype of hypnosis. *Scientific American, 285,* 46–49, 52–55.

Nathan, P. E. (1998). Practice guidelines: Not yet ideal. *American Psychologist, 53,* 290–299.

National Academies of Science. (2003). *The polygraph and lie detection.* Washington, DC: National Academies Press.

National Institute of Mental Health (NIMH). (2000). *Depression.* Retrieved on August 20, 2004, from http://www.nimh.nih.gov/publicat/depression.cfm#ptdep1

National Institute of Mental Health, Electroconvulsive Therapy. NIH Consens Statement Online 1985. June 10–12; 5(11): 1–23.

National Institute of Mental Health (NIMH). (2003). *Childhood-onset schizophrenia: An update from the NIMH.* Retrieved August 19, 2004, from http://www.nimh.nih.gov/publicat/schizkids.cfm

National Institute on Aging (2004). *Alzheimer's Disease Education & Referral Center.* Retrieved on November 8, 2004, from http://www.alzheimers.org/generalinfo.htm

National Press Club. (1999, Summer). Seligman on positive psychology: A session at the National Press Club. *The General Psychologist, 34*(2), 37–45.

National Public Radio. (2004, March 17). Analysis: New research may dispute theory that source of depression is in the brain. *Morning Edition.*

Needleman, H., Schell, A., Belinger, D., Leviton, A., & Allred, E. (1990). The long-term effects of exposure to low doses of lead in childhood: An 11-year follow-up report. *New England Journal of Medicine, 322,* 83–88.

Neimark, J. (2004, August). Are Recovered Memories Real? *Discover,* 25, 8.

Neisser, U. (1967). *Cognitive psychology.* New York: Appleton-Century-Crofts.

Neisser, U. (1991). A case of misplaced nostalgia. *American Psychologist, 46,* 34–36.

Neisser, U. (1997). Never a dull moment. *American Psychologist, 52,* 79–81.

Neisser, U., Boodoo, B., Bouchard, T. J., Jr., Boyukin, A. W., Brody, N., Ceci, S. J., Halpern, D. F., Loehlin, J. C., Perloff, R., Sternberg, R. J., & Urbina, S. (1996). Intelligence: Knowns and unknowns. *American Psychologist, 51,* 77–101.

Nelson, C. A. (1987). The recognition of facial expressions in the first two years of life: Mechanisms of development. *Child Development, 58,* 889–909.

Nelson, T. D. (1993). The hierarchical organization of behavior: A useful feedback model of self-regulation. *Current Directions in Psychological Science, 2,* 121–126.

Nemacek, S. (1999, January). Unequal health. *Scientific American, 280*(1), 40–41.

Nemeroff, C. B. (1998, June). The neurobiology of depression. *Scientific American, 278,* 42–49.

Nesse, R. M., & Berridge, K. C. (1997, October 3). Psychoactive drug use in evolutionary perspective. *Science, 278,* 63–66.

Nestler, E. J. (2001, June 22). Total recall—the memory of addiction. *Science, 292,* 2266–2267.

Netting, J., & Wang, L. (2001, February 17). The newly sequenced genome bares all. *Science News, 159.* 100–101.

Newcomb, T. M. (1943). *Personality and social change.* New York: Holt.

Newcomb, T. M., Koenig, D. E., Flacks, R., & Warwick, D. P. (1967). *Persistence and change: Bennington College and its students after twenty-five years.* New York: Wiley.

Newman, B. S., & Muzzonigro, P. G. (1993). The effects of traditional family values on the coming out process of gay male adolescents. *Adolescence, 28,* 213–226.

Newman, C. (2004, August). Why are we so fat? *National Geographic, 206,* 46–61.

Newman, R., Phelps, R., Sammons, M. T., Dunivin, D. L., & Cullen, E. A. (2000). Evaluation of the psychopharmacology demonstration project: A retrospective analysis. *Professional Psychology: Research and Practice, 31,* 598–603.

NICHD Early Child Care Research Network. (2000). The relation of child care to cognitive and language development. *Child Development, 71,* 960–980.

NICHD Early Child Care Research Network. (2003). Does quality of child care affect child outcomes at age 41/2? *Developmental Psychology, 39,* 451–469.

Nickerson, R. S. (1998). Confirmation bias: A ubiquitous phenomenon in many guises. *Review of General Psychology, 2,* 175–220.

Nicol, S. E., & Gottesman, I. I. (1983). Clues to the genetics and neurobiology of schizophrenia. *American Scientist, 71,* 398–404.

Niederhoffer, & Pennebaker, J. W. (2002). Sharing one's story: On the benefits of writing or talking about one's experience. In C. R. Snyder & S. J. Lopez (Eds.), *Handbook of positive psychology.* London, U.K.: Oxford University Press

Nietzel, M. T., Speltz, M. L., McCauley, E. A., & Bernstein, D. A. (1998). *Abnormal psychology.* Boston, MA: Allyn & Bacon.

NIMH, MTA Cooperative Group. (2004). National Institute of Mental Health multimodal treatment study of ADHD follow-up: Changes in effectiveness and growth after the end of treatment. *Pediatrics, 113,* 762–769.

Nisbett, R. E. (1972). Hunger, obesity, and the ventromedial hypothalamus. *Psychological Review, 79,* 433–453.

Nisbett, R. E. (2000). *Culture and systems of thought: Holistic versus analytic cognition in East and West.* Master Lecture presented at the annual convention of the American Psychological Association, Washington, DC.

Nisbett, R. E., Peng, K., Choi, I., & Norenzayan, A. (2001). Culture and systems of thought: Holistic versus analytic cognition. *Psychological Review, 108,* 291–310.

Nobel Committee (1981). The Nobel Prize in Physiology or Medicine 1981. Press Release.

Nobles, W. W. (1976). Black people in white insanity: An issue for black community mental health. *Journal of Afro-American Issues, 4,* 21–27.

Nolen-Hoeksema, S. (1987). Sex differences in unipolar depression: Evidence and theory. *Psychological Bulletin, 101,* 259–282.

Nolen-Hoeksema, S. (1990). *Sex differences in depression.* Stanford, CA: Stanford University Press.

Nolen-Hoeksema, S. (2001). Gender differences in depression. *Current Directions in Psychological Science, 10,* 173–176.

Norenzayan, A., & Nisbett, R. E. (2000). Culture and causal cognition. *Current Directions in Psychological Science, 9,* 132–135.

Norman, D. A., & Rumelhart, D. E. (1975). *Explorations in cognition.* San Francisco: Freeman.

Notarius, C., & Markman, H. (1993). *We can work it out: Making sense of marital conflict.* New York: G. P. Putnam's Sons.

Notarius, C. I. (1996). Marriage: Will I be happy or sad? In N. Vanzetti and S. Duck, *A lifetime of relationships.* Pacific Grove, CA: Brooks/Cole Publishing Company.

Novak, M. A., & Suomi, S. J. (1988). Psychological well-being of primates in captivity. *American Psychologist, 43,* 765–773.

Nungesser, L. G. (1990). *Axioms for survivors: How to live until you say goodbye.* Santa Monica, CA: IBS Press.

Oakland, T., & Glutting, J. J. (1990). Examiner observations of children's WISC-R test-related behaviors: Possible socioeconomic status, race, and gender effects. *Psychological Assessment, 2,* 86–90.

Oatley, K., & Duncan, E. (1994). The experience of emotions in everyday life. *Cognition and Emotion, 8,* 369–381.

O'Connor, E. M. (2001, December). Medicating ADHD: Too much? Too soon? *Monitor on Psychology, 32*(11), 50–51.

Oden, G. C. (1968). The fulfillment of promise: 40-year follow-up of the Terman gifted group. *Genetic Psychology Monographs, 77,* 3–93.

Oden, G. C. (1987). Concept, knowledge, and thought. *Annual Review of Psychology, 38,* 203–227.

Offer, D., Ostrov, E., & Howard, K. I. (1981). *The adolescent: A psychological self-portrait.* New York: Basic Books.

Offer, D., Ostrov, E., Howard, K. I., & Atkinson, R. (1988). *The teenage world: Adolescents' self-image in ten countries.* New York: Plenum Medical.

Ofshe, R., & Watters, E. (1994). *Making monsters: False memories, psychotherapy, and sexual hysteria.* New York: Charles Scribner's Sons.

Ohlsson, S. (1996). Learning from performance errors. *Psychological Review, 103,* 241–262.

Öhman, A., & Mineka, S. (2001). Fears, phobias, and preparedness: Toward an evolved module of fear and fear learning. *Psychological Review, 108,* 483–522.

Olds, M. E., & Fobes, J. L. (1981). The central basis of motivation: Intracranial self-stimulation studies. *Annual Review of Psychology, 32,* 523–574.

O'Leary, K. D. (Ed.). (1987). *Assessment of marital discord: An integration for research and clinical practice.* Hillsdale, NJ: Erlbaum.

Olton, D. S. (1979). Mazes, maxes, and memory. *American Psychologist, 34,* 583–596.

Olton, D. S. (1992). Tolman's cognitive analyses: Predecessors of current approaches in psychology. *Journal of Experimental Psychology: General, 121,* 427–428.

Oren, D. A., & Terman, M. (1998, January 16). Tweaking the human circadian clock with light. *Science, 279,* 333–334.

Orne, M. T. (1980). Hypnotic control of pain: Toward a clarification of the different psychological processes involved. In J. J. Bonica (Ed.), *Pain* (pp. 155–172). New York: Raven Press.

Ornstein, R., & Sobel, D. (1989). *Healthy pleasures.* Reading, MA: Addison-Wesley.

Osterhout, L., & Holcomb, P. J. (1992). Event-related brain potentials elicited by syntactic anomaly. *Journal of Memory and Language, 31,* 785–806.

Overmier, J., & Seligman, M. (1967). Effects of inescapable shock upon subsequent escape and avoidance learning. *Journal of Comparative and Physiological Psychology, 63,* 23–33.

Overmier, J. B. (2002). On learned helplessness. *Integrative Behavioral and Physiological Science, 37,* 4–8.

Paikoff, R. L., & Brooks-Gunn, J. (1991). Do parent-child relationships change during puberty? *Psychological Bulletin, 110,* 47–66.

Paivio, A. (1983). The empirical case for dual coding. In J. C. Yuille (Ed.), *Imagery, memory and cognition* (pp. 307–332). Hillsdale, NJ: Erlbaum.

Paivio, A. (1986). *Mental representations: A dual coding approach.* New York: Oxford University Press.

Palmer, S. E. (2002). Perceptual grouping: It's later than you think. *Current Directions in Psychological Science, 11,* 101–106.

Pandey, J., Sinha, Y., Prakash, A., & Tripathi, R. C. (1982). Right–left political ideologies and attribution of the causes of poverty. *European Journal of Social Psychology, 12,* 327–331.

Panksepp, J. (2000). The riddle of laughter: Neural and psychoevolutionary underpinnings of joy. *Current Directions in Psychological Science, 9,* 183–186.

Parr, W. V., and Siegert, R. (1993). Adults' conceptions of everyday memory failures in others: Factors that mediate the effects of target age. *Psychology and Aging, 8,* 599–605.

Parry, A., & Matthews, P. M. (2002). A "window" into the brain. Centre for Functional Magnetic Resonance Imaging of the Brain, Department of Clinical Neurology, University of Oxford, The John Radcliffe Hospital, Headley Way, Headington, Oxford OX3 9DU UK.

Patenaude, A. F., Guttmacher, A. E., & Collins, F. S. (2002). Genetic testing and psychology: New roles, new responsibilities. *American Psychologist, 57,* 271–282.

Patrick, C. J., & Iacono, W. G. (1991). Validity of the control question polygraph test: The problem of sampling bias. *Journal of Applied Psychology, 76,* 229–238.

Patzer, G. L. (1985). *The physical attractiveness phenomena.* New York: Plenum Press.

Paulesu, E. D., Démonet, J.-F., Fazio, F., McCrory, E., Chanoine, V., Brunswick, N. Cappa, S. F., Cossu, G., Habib, M., Frith, C. D., & Frith, U. (2001, March 16). Dyslexia: Cultural diversity and biological utility. *Science, 291,* 2165–2167.

Paunonen, S. P., Jackson, D. N., Trzebinski, J., & Fosterling, F. (1992). Personality structure across cultures: A multimethod evaluation. *Journal of Personality and Social Psychology, 62,* 447–456.

Pavlov, I. P. (1928). *Lectures on conditioned reflexes: Twenty-five years of objective study of higher nervous activity (behavior of animals)* (Vol. 1, W. H. Gantt, Trans.). New York: International Publishers.

Pawlik, K., & d'Ydewalle, G. (1996). Psychology and the global commons: Perspectives of international psychology. *American Psychologist, 51,* 488–495.

Pearman, R. R. (1991, November 13). Disputing a report on "Myers–Briggs" test. *Chronicle of Higher Education,* B7.

Pedersen, P. (1979). Non-Western psychology: The search for alternatives. In A. J. Marsella, R. G. Tharp, & T. J. Ciborowski (Eds.), *Perspectives on cross-cultural psychology* (pp. 77–98). New York: Academic Press.

Penfield, W. (1975). *The mystery of the mind.* Princeton, NJ: Princeton University Press.

Penfield, W., & Baldwin, M. (1952). Temporal lobe seizures and the technique of subtotal lobectomy. *Annals of Surgery, 136,* 625–634.

Penfield, W., & Jasper, H. (1954). *Epilepsy and the functional anatomy of the human brain.* Boston: Little, Brown & Co.

Penfield, W., & Rasmussen, T. (1950). *The cerebral cortex of man: A clinical study of the localization of function.* New York: Macmillan.

Penfield, W., & Roberts, L. (1959). *Speech and brain mechanisms.* Princeton, NJ: Princeton University Press.

Peng, K., & Nisbett, R. E. (1999). Culture, dialectics, and reasoning about contradiction. *American Psychologist, 54,* 741–754.

Pennebaker, J. W. (1990). *Opening up: The healing power of confiding in others.* New York: William Morrow.

Pennebaker, J. W. (1997). Writing about emotional experiences as a therapeutic process. *Psychological Science, 8,* 162–166.

Pennebaker, J. W., Barger, S. D., & Tiebout, J. (1989). Disclosure of traumas and health among Holocaust survivors. *Psychosomatic Medicine, 51,* 577–589.

Pennebaker, J. W., & Harber, K. D. (1991, April). *Coping after the Loma Prieta earthquake: A preliminary report.* Paper presented at the Western Psychological Association Convention, San Francisco, CA.

Pennebaker, J. W., Kiecolt-Glaser, J., & Glaser, R. (1988). Disclosure of traumas and immune function: Health implications for psychotherapy. *Journal of Consulting and Clinical Psychology, 56,* 239–245.

Pennisi, E. (2001, February 16). The human genome. *Science, 291,* 1177–1180.

Pennisi, E. (2002, October 25). Jumbled DNA separates chimps and humans. *Science, 298,* 719–720.

Pennisi, E. (2003, August 22). Gene counters struggle to get the right answer. *Science, 301,* 1040–1041.

Peplau, L. A., Garnets, L. D., Spalding, L. R., Conley, T. D., & Veniegas, R. C. (1998). Critique of Bem's "Exotic becomes erotic" theory of sexual orientation. *Psychological Review, 105,* 387–394.

Perkins, D. F., & Lerner, R. M. (1995). Single and multiple indicators of physical attractiveness and psychosocial behaviors among young adolescents. *Journal of Early Adolescence, 15,* 268–297.

Perry, W. G., Jr. (1970). *Forms of intellectual and ethical development in the college years: A scheme.* New York: Holt, Rinehart and Winston.

Perry, W. J., Jr. (1994). Forms of intellectual and ethical development in the college years: A scheme. In B. Puka (Ed.), *Defining perspectives in moral development: Vol. 1. Moral development: A compendium* (pp. 231–248). New York: Garland Publishing.

Pert, C. (1997). *Molecules of emotion.* New York: Scribner.

Pervin, L. A. (1985). Personality: Current controversies, issues, and directions. *Annual Review of Psychology, 36,* 83–114.

Peterson, C. (2000). The future of optimism. *American Psychologist, 55,* 44–55.

Petrill, S. A., Plomin, R., Berg, S., Johansson, B., Pedersen, N. L., Ahern, F., & McClearn, G. E. (1998). Specific cognitive abilities in twins age 80 and older. *Psychological Science, 9,* 183–195.

Petrovic, P., Kalso, E., Petersson, K. M., & Ingvan, M. (2002, March 1). Placebo and opioid analgesia—Imaging a shared neuronal network. *Science, 295,* 1737–1740.

Phelps, J. A., Davis, J. O., & Schartz, K. M. (1997). Nature, nurture, and twin research strategies. *Current Directions in Psychological Science, 6,* 117–121.

Physician's desk reference (58th ed.). (2004). Montvale, NJ: Medical Economics Company.

Pifer, A., & Bronte L. (Eds.). (1986). *Our aging society: Paradox and promise.* New York: Norton.

Pilcher, J. J., & Walters, A. S. (1997). How sleep deprivation affects psychological variables related to college students' cognitive performance. *Journal of American College Health, 46,* 121–126.

Pillard, R., & Bailey, M. (1991). A genetic study of male sexual orientation. *Archives of General Psychiatry, 48,* 1089–1096.

Pillemer, D. B. (1984). Flashbulb memories of the assassination attempt on President Reagan. *Cognition, 16,* 63–80.

Pinel, J. P. J. (2003). *Biopsychology* (5th ed.). Boston: Allyn & Bacon.

Pinel, J. P. J., Assanand, S., & Lehman, D. R. (2000). Hunger, eating, and ill health. *American Psychologist, 55,* 1105–1116.

Pinker, S. (1994). *The language instinct: How the mind creates language.* New York: Morrow.

Pinker, S. (2002). *The blank slate: The modern denial of human nature.* New York: Viking.

Piper, A., Jr. (1998, May/June). Multiple personality disorder: Witchcraft survives in the twentieth century. *Skeptical Inquirer, 22*(3), 44–50.

Pitman, G. E. (2003). Evolution, but no revolution: The "tend-and-befriend" theory of stress and coping. *Psychology of Women Quarterly, 27,* 194–195.

Pittenger, D. J. (1993). The utility of the Myers–Briggs Type Indicator. *Review of Educational Research, 63,* 467–488.

Plato, "Book VII, The Story of the Cave." In B. Jowett (Trans.), *The Republic of Plato.* New York: Colonial Press, 1901. Original work written in 380 B.C.

Plomin, R. (1989). Environment and genes: Determinants of behavior. *American Psychologist, 44,* 105–111.

Plomin, R. (1997, August). Current directions in behavioral genetics: Moving into the mainstream. *Current Directions in Psychological Science, 6,* 85.

Plomin, R. (2000, September). Psychology in a post-genomics world: It will be more important than ever. *American Psychological Society Observer, 3,* 27.

Plomin, R. (2003). 50 years of DNA: What it has meant to psychological science. *Observer, 16*(4), 7–8.

Plomin, R., & DeFries, J. C. (1998). The genetics of cognitive abilities and disabilities. *Scientific American, 278*(5), 62–69.

Plomin, R., & McClearn, G. E. (Eds.). (1993). *Nature, nurture, and psychology.* Washington, DC: American Psychological Association.

Plomin, R., Owen, M. J., & McGuffin, P. (1994). The genetic basis of complex human behaviors. *Science, 264,* 1733–1739.

Plomin, R., & Rende, R. (1991). Human behavioral genetics. *Annual Review of Psychology, 42,* 161–190.

Plutchik, R. (1980). *Emotion: A psychoevolutionary synthesis.* New York: Harper & Row.

Plutchik, R. (1984). Emotions: A general psychoevolutionary theory. In K. Scherer & P. Ekman (Eds.), *Approaches to emotion.* Hillsdale, NJ: Erlbaum.

Polefrone, J. M., & Manuck, S. B. (1987). Gender differences in cardiovascular and neuroendocrine response to stressors. In R. C. Barnett, L. Biener, & G. K. Baruch (Eds.), *Gender and stress.* New York: Free Press.

Poling, A., Gadow, K. D., & Cleary, J. (1991). *Drug therapy for behavior disorders: An introduction.* New York: Pergamon Press.

Polivy, J., & Herman, C. P. (1993). Etiology of binge eating: Psychological mechanisms. In C. G. Fairburn & G. T. Wilson (Eds.), *Binge eating: Nature, assessment, and treatment* (pp. 173–205). New York: Guilford Press.

Pool, R. (1997, October). Portrait of a gene guy. *Discover,* 51–55.

Pool, R. (1998). Saviours: Someday the transplant you need may be growing on the hoof—or in a lab. *Discover, 19*(5), 52–57.

Poole, D. A., Lindsay, D. S., Memon, A., & Bull, R. (1995). Psychotherapy and the recovery of memories of childhood sexual abuse: U.S. and British practitioners' opinions, practices, and experiences. *Journal of Consulting and Clinical Psychology, 63,* 426–437.

Poon, L. W. (1985). Differences in human memory with aging: Nature, causes, and clinical implications. In J. E. Birren & W. K. Schaie (Eds.), *Handbook of the psychology of aging* (pp. 427–462). New York: Van Nostrand Reinhold.

Posner, M. I., & McCandliss, B. D. (1993). Converging methods for investigating lexical access. *Science, 4,* 305–309.

Posner, M. I., & Raichle, M. E. (1994). *Images of mind.* New York: W. H. Freeman.

Premack, D. (1965). Reinforcement theory. In D. Levine (Ed.), *Nebraska Symposium on Motivation (pp. 128–180).* Lincoln: University of Nebraska Press.

Prentice, D. A., & Miller, D. T. (1993). Pluralistic ignorance and alcohol use on campus: Some consequences on misperceiving the social norm. *Journal of Personality and Social Psychology, 64,* 243–256.

Price, D. D., Rafii, A., Watkins, L. R., & Buckingham, B. (1984). A psychophysical analysis of acupuncture analgesia. *Pain, 19,* 27–42.

Priest, R. F., & Sawyer, J. (1967). Proximity and peership: Bases of balance in interpersonal attraction. *American Journal of Sociology, 72,* 633–649.

Primavera, L. H., & Herron, W. G. (1996). The effect of viewing television violence on aggression. *International Journal of Instructional Media, 23,* 91–104.

Prinzmetal, W. (1995). Visual feature integration in a world of objects. *Current Directions in Psychological Science, 5,* 90–94.

Putnam, F. W., Guroff, J. J., Silberman, E. K., Barban, L., & Post, R. M. (1986). The clinical phenomenology of multiple personality disorder: Review of 100 recent cases. *Journal of Clinical Psychiatry, 47,* 285–293.

Qualls, S. H., & Abeles, N. (2000). *Psychology and the aging revolution: How we adapt to longer life.* Washington, DC: American Psychological Association.

Quiñones-Vidal, E., López-García, J. J., Peñaranda-Ortega, M., & Tortosa-Gil, F. (2004). The nature of social and personality psychology as reflected in JPSP, 1965–2000. *Journal of Personality and Social Psychology, 86,* 435–452.

Rabasca, L. (1999, September). High marks for psychologists who prescribe. *APA Monitor, 30*(8), 21.

Rachman, S. (1966). Sexual fetishism: An experimental analogue. *Psychological Record, 6,* 293–296.

Rachman, S. (2000). Joseph Wolpe (1915–1997). *American Psychologist, 55,* 431–432.

Raichle, M. E. (1994). Visualizing the mind. *Scientific American, 270*(4), 58–64.

Rakic, P. (1985). Limits of neurogenesis in primates. *Science, 227,* 1054–1057.

Ramachandran, V. S. (1992). Filling in gaps in perception: Part 1. *Current Directions in Psychological Science, 1,* 199–205.

Ramachandran, V. S., & Blakeslee, S. (1998). *Phantoms in the brain.* New York: William Morrow.

Ramey, C. T., & Ramey, S. L. (1998a). Early intervention and early experience. *American Psychologist, 53,* 109–120.

Ramey, C. T., & Ramey, S. L. (1998b). In defense of special education. *American Psychologist, 53,* 1159–1160.

Ramsey, J. L., Langlois, J. H., Hoss, R. A., Rubenstein, A. J., & Griffin, A. (2004). Origins of a Stereotype: Categorization of Facial Attractiveness by 6-Month-old Infants. *Developmental Science,* 7, 201–211. PDF Version (116K) © Blackwell Publishing.

Rand, C. S., & Kuldau, J. M. (1992). Epidemiology of bulimia and symptoms in a general population: Sex, age, race, and socioeconomic status. *International Journal of Eating Disorders, 11,* 37–44.

Rapoport, J. L. (1989, March). The biology of obsessions and compulsions. *Scientific American, 263,* 83–89.

Rathus, S. A., Nevid, J. S., & Fichner-Rathus, L. (2000). *Human sexuality in a world of diversity* (4th ed.). Boston: Allyn & Bacon.

Ravussin, E., & Danforth, E., Jr. (1999, January 8). Beyond sloth—physical activity and weight gain. *Science, 283,* 184–185.

Raymond, C. (1989, September 20). Scientists examining behavior of a man who lost his memory gain new insights into the workings of the human mind. *The Chronicle of Higher Education,* A4, A6.

Raymond, J. L., Lisberger, S. G., & Mauk, M. D. (1996, May 24). The cerebellum: A neuronal learning machine? *Science, 272,* 1126–1131.

Raynor, J. O. (1970). Relationships between achievement-related motives, future orientation, and academic performance. *Journal of Personality and Social Psychology, 15,* 28–33.

Raz, S., & Raz, N. (1990). Structural brain abnormalities in the major psychoses: A quantitative review of the evidence from computerized imaging. *Psychological Bulletin, 16,* 491–402.

Reber, A. S. (1993). *Implicit learning and tacit knowledge: An essay on the cognitive unconscious. (Oxford Psychology Series No. 19).* Oxford, U.K.: Oxford University Press.

Rechtschaffen, A. (1998). Current perspectives on the function of sleep. *Perspectives in Biology and Medicine, 41,* 359–390.

Redding, R. E. (2001). Sociopolitical diversity in psychology: The case for pluralism. *American Psychologist, 56,* 205–215.

Redding, R. E. (2002). Grappling with diverse conceptions of diversity. *American Psychologist, 57,* 300–301.

Regier, D. A., Boyd, J. H., Burke, J. D., Rae, D. S., Myers, J. K., Kramer, M., Robins, L. N., George, L. K., Karno, M., & Locke, B. Z. (1988). One-month prevalence of mental disorders in the United States. *Archives of General Psychiatry, 45,* 977–986.

Regier, D. A., Narrow, W. E., Rae, D. S., Manderscheid, R. W., Locke, B. Z., & Goodwin, F. K. (1993). The de facto U.S. mental and addictive disorders service system: Epidemiologic Catchment Area prospective 1-year-prevalence rates of disorders and services. *Archives of General Psychiatry, 50,* 85–94.

Reinisch, J. M. (1990). *The Kinsey Institute new report on sex: What you must know to be sexually literate.* New York: St. Martin's Press.

Reis, B., & Saewyc, E. (1999). *Eighty-three thousand youth: selected findings of eight population-based studies as they pertain to anti-gay harassment and the safety and well-being of sexual minority students.* Seattle, WA: Safe Schools Coalition of Washington. Document also retrieved online November 8, 2004, from http://www.safeschools-wa.org/83000youth.pdf

Rescorla, R. A. (1972). Information variables in Pavlovian conditioning. In G. Bower (Ed.), *The psychology of learning and motivation* (Vol. 6). New York: Academic Press.

Rescorla, R. A. (1988). Pavlovian conditioning: It's not what you think it is. *American Psychologist, 43,* 151–160.

Rescorla, R. A., & Wagner, A. R. (1972). A theory of Pavlovian conditioning: Variations in the effectiveness of reinforcement and nonreinforcement. In A. H. Black & W. F. Prokasy (Eds.), *Classical conditioning, II: Current research and theory* (pp. 64–94). New York: Appleton-Century-Crofts.

Resnick, S. M. (1992). Positron emission tomography in psychiatric illness. *Current Directions in Psychological Science, 1,* 92–98.

Rest, J. R., & Thoma, S. J. (1976). Relation of moral judgment development to formal education. *Developmental Psychology, 21,* 709–714.

Reuter-Lorenz, P. A., & Miller, A. C. (1998). The cognitive neuroscience of human laterality: Lessons from the bisected brain. *Current Directions in Psychological Science, 7,* 15–20.

Reynolds, C. R. (2000). Why is psychometric research on bias in mental testing so often ignored? *Psychology, Public Policy, and Law, 6,* 144–150.

Rhodes, G., Sumich, A., & Byatt, G. (1999). Are average facial configurations attractive only because of their symmetry? *Psychological Science, 10,* 52–58.

Ripple, C. H., Gilliam, W. S., Chanana, N., & Zigler, E. (1999). Will fifty cooks spoil the broth? The debate over entrusting Head Start to the states. *American Psychologist, 54,* 327–343.

Ripple, C. H., & Zigler, E. (2003). Research, policy, and the Federal role in prevention initiatives for children. *American Psychologist, 58,* 482–490.

Robbins, D. (1971). Partial reinforcement: A selective review of the alleyway literature since 1960. *Psychological Bulletin, 76,* 415–431.

Robbins, J. (2000, April). Wired for sadness. *Discover, 21*(4), 77–81.

Robins, C. J. (1988). Attributions and depression: Why is the literature so inconsistent? *Journal of Personality and Social Psychology, 54,* 880–889.

Robins, L. N., Locke, B. Z., & Regier, D. A. (1991). An overview of psychiatric disorders in America. In L. N. Robins & D. A. Regier (Eds.), *Psychiatric disorders in America: The epidemiologic catchment area study.* New York: Free Press.

Robinson, N. M., Zigler, E., & Gallagher, J. J. (2000). Two tails of the normal curve: Similarities and differences in the study of mental retardation and giftedness. *American Psychologist, 55,* 1413–1424.

Roche, S. M., & McConkey, K. M. (1990) Absorption: Nature, assessment, and correlates. *Journal of Personality & Social Psychology, 59,* 91–101.

Rock, I., & Palmer, S. (1990, December). The legacy of Gestalt psychology. *Scientific American, 263,* 84–90.

Rodin, J. (1986). Aging and health: Effects of the sense of control. *Science, 233,* 1271–1276.

Rodin, J., Striegel-Moore, R. H., & Silberstein, L. R. (1985, July). *A prospective study of bulimia among college students on three U. S. campuses.* Unpublished manuscript. New Haven: Yale University.

Roediger, H. L., III. (1990). Implicit memory: Retention without remembering. *American Psychologist, 45,* 1043–1056.

Roediger, H. L., III, & McDermott, K. B. (1995). Creating false memories: Remembering words not presented in lists. *Journal of Experimental Psychology: Learning, Memory, and Cognition, 21,* 803–814.

Roediger, H. L., III, & McDermott, K. B. (2000, January/February). *Psychological Science Agenda,* 8–9.

Rogers, C. R. (1951). *Client-centered therapy: Its current practice, implications and theory.* Boston: Houghton Mifflin.

Rogers, C. R. (1961). *On becoming a person: A therapist's view of psychotherapy.* Boston: Houghton Mifflin.

Rogers, C. R. (1977). *On personal power: Inner strength and its revolutionary impact.* New York: Delacorte.

Rogers, C. R. (1980). *A way of being.* Boston: Houghton Mifflin.

Rogers, C. R. (1982, July/August) Roots of madness. In T. H. Carr & H. E. Fitzgerald (Eds.), *Psychology 83/84* (pp. 263–267). Guilford, CT: Dushkin. (Originally published in *Science 82,* July/August, 1982).

Rogoff, B. (1990). *Apprenticeship in thinking: Cognitive development in social context.* New York: Oxford University Press.

Roll, S., Hinton, R., & Glazer, M. (1974). Dreams and death: Mexican Americans vs. Anglo-American. *Interamerican Journal of Psychology, 8,* 111–115.

Rollman, G. B., & Harris, G. (1987). The detectability, discriminability, and perceived magnitude of painful electrical shock. *Perception & Psychophysics, 42,* 257–268.

Rolls, B. J., Federoff, I. C., & Guthrie, J. F. (1991). Gender differences in eating behavior and body weight regulation. *Health Psychology, 10,* 133–142.

Rolnick, J. (1998, December 4). Treating mental disorders: A neuroscientist says no to drugs. *The Chronicle of Higher Education,* A10.

Rooney, S. C. (2002). Examining Redding's (2001) claims about lesbian and gay parenting. *American Psychologist, 57,* 298–299.

Rorschach, H. (1942). *Psychodiagnostics: A diagnostic test based on perception.* New York: Grune & Stratton.

Rosa, L., Rosa, E., Sarner, L., & Barrett, S. (1998). A close look at therapeutic touch. *Journal of the American Medical Association, 279,* 1005–1010.

Rosch, E. (1999). Is wisdom in the brain? *Psychological Science, 10,* 222–224.

Rosch, E., & Mervis, C. B. (1975). Family resemblances: Studies in the internal structure of categories. *Cognitive Psychology, 7,* 573–605.

Rosch, E. H., Mervis, C. B., Gray, W. D., Johnson, D. M., & Boyes-Braem, P. (1976). Basic objects in natural categories. *Cognitive Psychology, 8,* 382–439.

Rosen, J. B., & Schulkin, J. (1998). From normal fear to pathological anxiety. *Psychological Review, 105,* 325–350.

Rosenblatt, P. C. (1966). A cross-cultural study of child-rearing and romantic love. *Journal of Personality and Social Psychology, 4,* 336–338.

Rosenhan, D. L. (1969). Some origins of concern for others. In P. Mussen, J. Langer, & M. Covington (Eds.), *Trends and issues in developmental psychology.* New York: Holt, Rinehart & Winston.

Rosenhan, D. L. (1973). On being sane in insane places. *Science, 179,* 250–258.

Rosenhan, D. L. (1983). Psychological abnormality and law. In C. J. Scheirer & B. C. Hammonds (Eds.)., *The master lecture series: Vol. 2. Psychology and the law.* Washington, DC: American Psychological Association.

Rosenhan, D. L., & Seligman, M. E. P. (1995). *Abnormal psychology* (3rd ed.). New York: Norton.

Rosenthal, R. & Jacobson, L. F. (1968a). *Pygmalion in the classroom: Teacher expectations and intellectual development.* New York: Holt.

Rosenthal, R., & Jacobson, L. F. (1968b). Teacher expectations for the disadvantaged. *Scientific American, 218*(4), 19–23.

Rosenzweig, M. R. (1992). Psychological science around the world. *American Psychologist, 47,* 718–722.

Rosenzweig, M. R. (1999). Continuity and change in the development of psychology around the world. *American Psychologist, 54,* 252–259.

Ross, B. (1991). William James: Spoiled child of American psychology. In G. A. Kimble, M. Wertheimer, & C. L. White (Eds.), *Portraits of pioneers in psychology* (pp. 13–25). Washington, DC: American Psychological Association.

Ross, C. A., Miller, S. D., Reagor, P., Bjornson, L., Fraser, G. A., & Anderson, G. (1990). Structured interview data on 102 cases of multiple personality disorder from four centers. *American Journal of Psychiatry, 147,* 596–601.

Ross, C. A., Norton, G. R., & Wozney, K. (1989). Multiple personality disorder: An analysis of 236 cases. *Canadian Journal of Psychiatry, 34,* 413–418.

Ross, L., & Nisbett, R. E. (1991). *The person and the situation: Perspectives of social psychology.* New York: McGraw-Hill.

Ross, P. (2003, September). Mind readers. *Scientific American, 289,* 74–77.

Ross, P. E. (1992, July). Compulsive canines. *Scientific American, 266*(5), 24–25.

Rothbaum, B. O., & Hodges, L. F. (1999). The use of virtual reality exposure in the treatment of anxiety disorders. *Behavior Modification, 23,* 507–525.

Rothbaum, B. O., Hodges, L. Smith, S., Lee, J. H., & Price, L. (2000a). A controlled study of virtual reality exposure therapy for the fear of flying. *Journal of Consulting & Clinical Psychology, 68,* 1020–1026.

Rothbaum, F., Weisz, J., Pott, M., Miyake, K., Morelli, G. (2000b). Attachment and culture: Security in the United States and Japan. *American Psychologist, 55,* 1093–1104.

Rotter, J. B. (1954). *Social learning and clinical psychology.* Englewood Cliffs, NJ: Prentice-Hall.

Rotter, J. B. (1966). Generalized expectancies for internal versus external control of reinforcement. *Psychological Monographs, 80* (Whole no. 609).

Rotter, J. B. (1971, June). External control and internal control. *Psychology Today, 4,* 37–42, 58–59.

Rotter, J. B. (1990). Internal versus external control of reinforcement: A case history of a variable. *American Psychologist, 45,* 489–493.

Rouhana, N. N., & Kelman, H. C. (1994). Promoting joint thinking in international conflicts: An Israeli-Palestinian continuing workshop. *Journal of Social Issues, 50,* 157–168.

Roush, W. (1996, July 5). Live long and prosper? *Science, 273,* 42–46.

Rozin, P. (1976). The evolution of intelligence and access to the cognitive unconscious. In J. M. Sprague & A. A. Epstein (Eds.), *Progress in psychobiology and physiological psychology* (pp. 245–280). New York: Academic Press.

Rozin, P. (1996). Towards a psychology of food and eating: From motivation to module to model to marker, morality, meaning, and metaphor. *Current Directions in Psychological Science, 5,* 18–24.

Rubinstein, J. S., Meyer, D. E., & Evans. J. E. (2001). Executive control of cognitive processes in task switching. *Journal of Experimental Psychology: Human Perception and Performance, 27,* 763–797.

Russell, A., Mize, J., & Bissaker, K. (2002). Parent-child relationships. In P. K. Smith & C. H. Hart (Eds.), *Handbook of childhood social development.* Oxford, U.K.: Blackwell.

Rusting, C. L., & Nolen-Hoeksema, S. (1998). Regulating responses to anger: Effects of rumination and distraction on angry mood. *Journal of Personality and Social Psychology, 74,* 790–803.

Ryff, C. D. (1989). In the eye of the beholder: Views of psychological well-being among middle-aged and older adults. *Psychology and Aging, 4,* 195–210.

Saarinen, T. F. (1987). *Centering of mental maps of the world: Discussion paper.* Tucson:

University of Arizona, Department of Geography and Regional Development.

Sackett, P. R. (1994). Integrity testing for personnel selection. *Current Directions in Psychological Science, 3,* 73–76.

Sackheim, H. A., Prudic, J., Devanand, D. P., Nobler, M. S., Lisanby, S. H., Peyser, S., Fitzsimons, L., Moody, B. J., & Clark, J. (2000). A prospective, randomized, double-blind comparison of bilateral and right unilateral electroconvulsive therapy at different stimulus intensities. *Archives of General Psychiatry, 57,* 425–434.

Sacks, O. (1995). *An anthropologist on Mars.* New York: Random House.

Salovey, P., & Mayer, J. D. (1990). Emotional intelligence. *Imagination, Cognition, and Personality, 9,* 185–211.

Salovey, P., Rothman, A. J., Detweiler, J. B., & Steward, W. T. (2000). Emotional states and physical health. *American Psychologist, 55,* 110–121.

Saltzstein, H. D., & Sandberg, L. (1979). Indirect social influence: Change in judgmental processor anticipatory conformity. *Journal of Experimental Social Psychology, 15,* 209–216.

Sanger, M. (1971). *Margaret Sanger: An autobiography.* New York: W. W. Norton/ Dover Publications. (Original work published in 1938).

Sapolsky, R. M. (1998). Why zebras don't get ulcers: An updated guide to stress, stress-related disease, and coping. New York: Freedman.

Sapolsky, R. (2002, November). The loveless man . . . who invented the science of love. *Scientific American,* 95–96.

Sapolsky, R. M. (1990). Adrenocortical function, social rank, and personality among wild baboons. *Biological Psychiatry, 28,* 1–17.

Sapolsky, R. M. (1992). *Stress: The aging brain and the mechanisms of neuron death.* Cambridge, MA: MIT Press.

Sarbin, T. R., & Coe, W. C. (1972). *Hypnosis: A social psychological analysis of influence communication.* New York: Holt, Rinehart & Winston.

Satir, V. (1983). *Conjoint family therapy* (3rd ed.). Palo Alto, CA: Science & Behavior Books.

Satir, V., Banmen, J., Gerber, J., & Gomori, M. (1991). *Satir model: Family therapy and beyond.* Palo Alto, CA: Science & Behavior Books.

Sattler, J. M. (1970). Racial "experimenter effects" in experimentation, testing, interviewing, and psychotherapy. *Psychological Bulletin, 73,* 137–160.

Saudino, K. J. (1997, August). Moving beyond the heritability question: New directions in behavioral genetic studies of personality. *Current Directions in Psychological Science, 6,* 86–90.

Saufley, W. H., Otaka, S. R., & Bavaresco, J. L. (1985). *Context independence. Memory and Cognition, 13,* 522–528.

Savitsky, J. C., & Lindblom, W. D. (1986). The impact of the guilty but mentally ill verdict on juror decisions: An empirical analysis. *Journal of Applied Social Psychology, 16,* 686–701.

Sawa, A., & Snyder, S. H. (2002, April 26). Schizophrenia: Diverse approaches to a complex disease. *Science, 296,* 692–695.

Sax, L., & Kautz, K. J. (2003). Who first suggests the diagnosis of attention-deficit/hyperactivity disorder? *Annals of Family Medicine, 1,* 171–174.

Saxe, L. (1991). Lying: Thoughts of an applied social psychologist. *American Psychologist, 46,* 409–415.

Saxe, L. (1994). Detection of deception: Polygraph and integrity tests. *Current Directions in Psychological Science, 3,* 69–73.

Saxe, L., Dougherty, D., & Cross, T. (1985). The validity of polygraph testing: Scientific analysis and public controversy. *American Psychologist, 40,* 355–366.

Scarr, S. (1997). Why child care has little impact on most children's development. *Current Directions in Psychological Science, 6,* 143–148.

Scarr, S. (1998). American child care today. *American Psychologist, 53,* 95–108.

Scarr, S., & Weinberg, R. (1976). IQ test performance of black children adopted by white families. *American Psychologist, 31,* 726–739.

Scarr, S., & Weinberg, R. A. (1978, April). Attitudes, interests, and IQ. *Human Nature,* 29–36.

Schachter, S. (1971). *Emotion, obesity and crime.* New York: Academic Press.

Schachter, S. (1977). Nicotine regulation in heavy and light smokers. *Journal of Experimental Psychology: General, 106,* 5–12.

Schacter, D. L. (1992). Understanding implicit memory: A cognitive neuroscience approach. *American Psychologist, 47,* 559–569.

Schacter, D. L. (1996). *Searching for memory: The brain, the mind, and the past.* New York: Basic Books.

Schacter, D. L. (1999). The seven sins of memory: Insights from psychology and cognitive neuroscience. *American Psychologist, 54,* 182–203.

Schacter, D. L. (2001). *The Seven Sins of Memory: How the Mind Forgets and Remembers.* Boston: Houghton Mifflin.

Schaefer, H. H., & Martin, P. L. (1966). Behavioral therapy for "apathy" of hospitalized patients. *Psychological Reports, 19,* 1147–1158.

Schank, R. C., & Abelson, R. (1977). *Scripts, plans, goals and understanding: An inquiry into human knowledge and structures.* Hillsdale, NJ: Erlbaum.

Scharfe, E., & Bartholomew, K. (1998). Do you remember? Recollections of adult attachment patterns. *Personal Relationships, 5,* 219–234.

Schatzberg, A. F. (1991). Overview of anxiety disorders: Prevalence, biology, course, and treatment. *Journal of Clinical Psychiatry, 42,* 5–9.

Schechter, B. (1996, October 18). How the brain gets rhythm. *Science, 274,* 339–340.

Schick, T., Jr., & Vaughn, L. (2001). *How to think about weird things: Critical thinking for a new age* (3rd ed.). New York: McGraw-Hill.

Schiff, M., & Bargal, D. (2000). Helping characteristics of self-help and support groups: Their contribution to participants' subjective well-being. *Small Group Research, 31,* 275–304.

Schill, R. A., & Marcus, D. K. (1998). Incarceration and learned helplessness. *International Journal of Offender Therapy and Comparative Criminology, 42,* 224–232.

Schlenker, B. R., Weingold, M. F., Hallam, J. R. (1990). Self-serving attributions in social context: Effects of self-esteem and social pressure. *Journal of Personality and Social Psychology, 58,* 855–863.

Schmidt, R. A., & Bjork, R. A. (1992). New conceptualizations of practice: Common principles in three paradigms suggest new concepts for training. *Psychological Science, 3,* 207–217.

Schmolck, H., Buffalo, E. A., & Squire, L. R. (2000). Memory distortions develop over time: Recollections of the O. J. Simpson trial verdict after 15 and 32 months. *Psychological Science, 11,* 39–45.

Schneider, K., & May, R. (1995). *The psychology of existence: An integrative, clinical perspective.* New York: McGraw-Hill.

Schou, M. (1997). Forty years of lithium treatment. Archives of General Psychiatry, 54, 9–13.

Schreiber, F. R. (1973). *Sybil.* New York: Warner Books.

Schroeder, D. A., Penner, L. A., Dovidio, J. F., & Piliavin, J. A. (1995). *The psychology of helping and altruism.* New York: McGraw-Hill.

Schroeder, D. A., & Prentice, D. A. (1995). *Pluralistic ignorance and alcohol use on campus II: Correcting misperceptions of the social norm.* Unpublished manuscript, Princeton University.

Schroeder, S. R., Schroeder, C. S., & Landesman, S. (1987). Psychological services in educational settings to persons with mental retardation. *American Psychologist, 42,* 805–808.

Schulkin, J. (1994). Melancholic depression and the hormones of adversity: A role for the amygdala. *Current Directions in Psychological Science, 3,* 41–44.

Schulz, R., & Heckhausen, J. (1996). A life span model of successful aging. *American Psychologist, 51,* 702–714.

Schwartz, B. (1997). Psychology, idea technology, and ideology. *Psychological Science, 8,* 21–27.

Schwartz, J., & Wald, M. L. (2003, March 9). Smart people working collectively can be dumber than the sum of their brains: "Groupthink" is 30 years old, and still going strong. *New York Times.* Retrieved on December 15, 2004, from http://www.mindfully.org/Reform/2003/Smart-People-Dumber9mar03.htm

Schwartz, J. M., Stoessel, P. W., Baxter, L. R., Martin, K. M., & Phelps, M. E. (1996). Systematic changes in cerebral glucose metabolic rate after successful behavior modification treatment of obsessive–compulsive disorder. *Archives of General Psychiatry, 53,* 109–116.

Schwartz, P. (1994). *Peer marriage: How love between equals really works.* New York: The Free Press.

Schwarzer, R. (Ed.). (1992). *Self-efficacy:*

Thought control of action. Washington, DC: Hemisphere.

Schwebel, A. I., & Fine, M. A. (1994). *Understanding and helping families: A cognitive behavioral approach.* Hillsdale, NJ: Erlbaum.

Schweinhart, L. J., & Weikart, D. P. (1986, January). What do we know so far? A review of the Head Start Synthesis Project. *Young Children, 41*(2), 49–55.

Scott, K. G., & Carran, D. T. (1987). The epidemiology and prevention of mental retardation. *American Psychologist, 42,* 801–804.

Scovern, A. W., & Kilmann, P. R. (1980). Status of electro-convulsive therapy: Review of outcome literature. *Psychological Bulletin, 87,* 260–303.

Seeman, T. E., Dubin, L. F., & Seeman, M. (2003). Religiosity/spirituality and health: A critical review of the evidence for biological pathways. *American Psychologist, 58,* 53–63.

Segal, M. W. (1974). Alphabet and attraction: An unobtrusive measure of the effect of propinquity in a field setting. *Journal of Personality and Social Psychology, 30,* 654–657.

Segall, M. H. (1994). A cross-cultural research contribution to unraveling the nativist/empiricist controversy. In W. J. Lonner & R. Malpass, *Psychology and culture* (pp. 135–138). Boston: Allyn & Bacon.

Segall, M. H., Dasen, P. R., Berry, J. W., & Poortinga, Y. H. (1990). *Human behavior in global perspective: An introduction to cross-cultural psychology.* Boston: Allyn & Bacon.

Segall, M. H., Dasen, P. R., Berry, J. W., & Poortinga, Y. H. (1999). *Human behavior in global perspective: An introduction to cross-cultural psychology* (2nd ed.). Boston: Allyn & Bacon.

Segall, M. H., Lonner, W. J., & Berry, J. W. (1998). Cross-cultural psychology as a scholarly discipline: On the flowering of culture in behavioral research. *American Psychologist, 53,* 1101–1110.

Segall, M. N., Campbell, D. T., & Herskovits, M. J. (1966). *The influence of culture on visual perception.* Indianapolis: Bobbs-Merrill.

Segerstrom, S. C., & Miller, G. E. (2004). Psychological stress and the human immune system: A meta-analytic study of 30 years of inquiry. *Psychological Bulletin, 130,* 601–630.

Seidler, R. D., Purushotham, A., Kim, S. G., Urbil, K., Willingham, D., & Ashe, J. (2002, June 14). Cerebellum activation associated with performance change but not motor learning. *Science, 296,* 2043–2046.

Selfridge, O. G. (1955). Pattern recognition and modern computers. In *Proceedings of the Western Joint Computer Conference.* New York: Institute of Electrical and Electronics Engineers.

Seligman, M. E. P. (1971). Preparedness and phobias. *Behavior Therapy, 2,* 307–320.

Seligman, M. E. P. (1973, June). Fall into helplessness. *Psychology Today, 7,* 43–48.

Seligman, M. E. P. (1975). *Helplessness: On depression, development and death.* San Francisco: Freeman.

Seligman, M. E. P. (1991). *Learned optimism.* New York: Knopf.

Seligman, M. E. P. (1995). The effectiveness of psychotherapy: The *Consumer Reports* study. *American Psychologist, 50,* 965–974.

Seligman, M. E. P. (1998). *Learned optimism: How to change your mind and your life.* New York: Free Press.

Seligman, M. E. P., Abramson, L. Y., Semmel, A., & von Baeyer, C. (1979). Depressive attributional style. *Journal of Abnormal Psychology, 88,* 242–247.

Seligman, M. E. P., & Csikszentmihalyi, M. (2000). Positive psychology: An introduction. *American Psychologist, 55,* 5–14.

Seligman, M. E. P., & Maier, S. F. (1967). Failure to escape traumatic shock. *Journal of Experimental Psychology, 74,* 1–9.

Seligson, S. V. (1994, November/December). Say good night to snoring. *Health, 8*(7), 89–93.

Selye, H. (1956). *The stress of life.* New York: McGraw-Hill.

Selye, H. (1991). *Stress without distress.* New York: Signet Books.

Serpell, R. (1994). The cultural construction of intelligence. In W. J. Lonner & R. Malpass, *Psychology and culture* (pp. 157–163). Boston: Allyn & Bacon.

Service, R. F. (1999, April 23). Bypassing nervous system damage with electronics. *Science, 284,* 579.

Shadish, W. R., Matt, G. E., Navarro, A. M., & Phillips, G. (2000). The effects of psychological therapies under clinically representative conditions: A meta-analysis. *Psychological Bulletin, 126,* 512–529.

Shapiro, D. H. (1985). Clinical use of meditation as a self-regulation strategy: Comments on Holmes's conclusions and implications. *American Psychologist, 40,* 719–722.

Shapiro, F. (1995). *Desensitization and reprocessing: Basic principles, protocols, and procedures.* New York: Guilford.

Sharps, M. J., & Wertheimer, M. (2000). Gestalt perspectives on cognitive science and on experimental psychology. *Review of General Psychology, 4,* 315–336.

Shatz, M., Wellman, H. M., & Silber, S. (1983). The acquisition of mental verbs: A systematic investigation of the first reference to mental state. *Cognition, 14,* 301–321.

Shaver, P., & Hazan, C. (1987). Romantic love conceptualized as an attachment process. *Journal of Personality and Social Psychology, 52,* 511–524.

Shaver, P. R., & Hazan, C. (1994). Attachment. In A. L. Weber & J. H. Harvey (Eds.), *Perspectives on close relationships* (Chapter 6, 110–130). Boston: Allyn & Bacon.

Shaywitz, S. E. (1996, November). Dyslexia. *Scientific American,* 98–104.

Shaywitz, S. E., Shaywitz, B. A., Fletcher, J. M., & Escobar, M. D. (1990). Prevalence of reading disability in boys and girls: Results of the Connecticut Longitudinal Study. *Journal of the American Medical Association, 264,* 998–1002.

Shea, C. (1998, January 30). Why depression strikes more women than men: "Ruminative coping" may provide answers. *The Chronicle of Higher Education,* 14.

Shepard, R. N., & Metzler, J. (1971). Mental rotation of three-dimensional objects. *Science, 171,* 701–703.

Sherif, C. W. (1981, August). *Social and psychological bases of social psychology.* The G. Stanley Hall Lecture on social psychology, presented at the annual convention of the American Psychological Association, Los Angeles, CA.

Sherif, M., Harvey, O. J., White, B. J., Hood, W., & Sherif, C. (1961). *Intergroup conflict and cooperation: The Robbers Cave experiment.* Norman: University of Oklahoma Institute of Intergroup Relations.

Sherrill, R., Jr. (1991). Natural wholes: Wolfgang Köhler and Gestalt theory. In G. A. Kimble, M. Wertheimer, & C. L. White (Eds.), *Portraits of pioneers in psychology* (pp. 256–273). Washington, DC: American Psychological Association.

Shields, S. A. (1991). Gender in the psychology of emotion: A selective research review. In K. T. Strongman (Ed.), *International review of studies on emotion* (Vol. 1). New York: Wiley.

Shiffrin, R. M. (1993). Short-term memory: A brief commentary. *Memory and Cognition, 21*(2), 193–197.

Shimamura, A. P. (1996, September/October). Unraveling the mystery of the frontal lobes: Explorations in cognitive neuroscience. *Psychological Science Agenda,* 8– 9.

Shiraev, E., & Levy, D. (2004). *Introduction cross-cultural: Critical thinking and contemporary applications.* Boston: Allyn & Bacon.

Shizgal, P., & Arvanitogiannis, A. (2003, March 21). Gambling on dopamine. *Science, 299,* 1856–1858.

Shneidman, E. (1987, March). At the point of no return. *Psychology Today,* 54–58.

Shobe, K. K., & Kihlstrom, J. F. (1997). Is traumatic memory special? *Current Directions in Psychological Science, 6,* 70–74.

Siegel, J. M. (1990). Stressful life events and use of physician services among the elderly: The moderating role of pet ownership. *Journal of Personality and Social Psychology, 58,* 1081–1086.

Siegel, J. M. (2001). The REM sleep–memory consolidation hypothesis. *Science, 294,* 1058–1063.

Siegel, J. M. (2003, November). Why we sleep. *Scientific American, 289,* 92–97.

Siegel, R. K. (1980). The psychology of life after death. *American Psychologist, 35,* 911–931.

Siegler, R. S. (1994). Cognitive variability: A key to understanding cognitive development. *Current Directions in Psychological Science, 3,* 1–5.

Sigelman, C. K., Thomas, D. B., Sigelman, L., & Robich, F. D. (1986). Gender, physical attractiveness, and electability: An experimental investigation of voter biases. *Journal of Applied Social Psychology, 16,* 229–248.

Simeon, D., Gross, S., Guralnik, O., Stein, D. J., et al. (1997). Feeling unreal: 30 cases of *DSM-III-R* depersonalization disorder. *American Journal of Psychiatry, 154,* 1107–1113.

Simon, H. A. (1992). What is an "explanation" of behavior? *Psychological Science, 3,* 150–161.

Simons, D. J., & Levin, D. T. (1998). Failure to detect changes to people during a real-world interaction. *Psychonomic Bulletin & Review, 4,* 644–649.

Simonton, D. K. (2001). Talent development as a multidimensional, multiplicative, and dynamic process. *Current Directions in Psychological Science, 10,* 39–43.

Simpson, J. A., & Harris, B. A. (1994). Interpersonal attraction. In A. L. Weber & J. H. Harvey (Eds.), *Perspectives on close relationships* (pp. 45–66). Boston: Allyn & Bacon.

Sinclair, R. C., Hoffman, C., Mark, M. M., Martin L. L., & Pickering, T. L. (1994). Construct accessibility and the misattribution of arousal: Schacter and Singer revisited. *Psychological Sciences, 5,* 15–18.

Singer, J. L. (1966). *Daydreaming: An introduction to the experimental study of inner experience.* New York: Random House.

Singer, J. L. (1975). Navigating the stream of consciousness: Research in daydreaming and related inner experience. *American Psychologist, 30,* 727–739.

Singer, J. L., & McCraven, V. J. (1961). Some characteristics of adult daydreaming. *Journal of Psychology, 51,* 151–164.

Singer, J. L., Singer, D. G., & Rapaczynski, W. S. (1984). Family patterns and television viewing as predictors of children's beliefs and aggression. *Journal of Communication, 34,* 73–89.

Singer, W. (1995, November 3). Development and plasticity of cortical processing architectures. *Science, 270,* 758–763.

Skinner, B. F. (1953). *Science and human behavior.* New York: Macmillan.

Skinner, B. F. (1987). Whatever happened to psychology as the science of behavior? *American Psychologist, 42,* 780–786.

Skinner, B. F. (1989). The origins of cognitive thought. *American Psychologist, 44,* 13–18.

Skinner, B. F. (1990). Can psychology be a science of mind? *American Psychologist, 45,* 1206–1210.

Skoog, I., Nilsson, L., Palmertz, B., Andreasson, L. A., & Svanborg, A. (1993). A population-based study of dementia in 85-year-olds. *New England Journal of Medicine, 328,* 153.

Sleek, S. (1994, April). Could Prozac replace demand for therapy? *APA Monitor,* 28.

Sleek, S. (1996, May). Shifting the paradigm for prescribing drugs. *APA Monitor,* 1, 29.

Slobin, D. I. (1985a). Introduction: Why study acquisition crosslinguistically? In D. I. Slobin (Ed.), *The crosslinguistic study of language acquisition. Vol. 1: The data* (pp. 3–24). Hillsdale, NJ: Erlbaum.

Slobin, D. I. (1985b). Cross-linguistic evidence of the language making capacity. In D. I. Slobin (Ed.), *The crosslinguistic study of language acquisition. Vol. 2: Theoretical issues* (pp. 1157–1256). Hillsdale, NJ: Erlbaum.

Small, D. M., Zatorre, R. J., Dagher, A., Evans, A. C., & Jones-Gotman, M. (2001). Changes in brain activity related to eating chocolate. *Brain, 124,* 1720–1733.

Smith, C. A., & Ellsworth, P. C. (1987). Patterns of appraisal and emotion related to taking an exam. *Journal of Personality and Social Psychology, 52,* 475–488.

Smith, D. (2001, October). Sleep psychologists in demand. *Monitor on Psychology,* 36–39.

Smith, D. (2002, January). Guidance in treating ADHD. *Monitor on Psychology, 33*(1), 34–35.

Smith, E. E. (2000). Neural bases of human working memory. *Current Directions in Psychological Science, 9,* 45–49.

Smith, E. E., & Jonides, J. (1999, March 12). Storage and executive processes in the frontal lobes. *Science, 283,* 1657–1661.

Smith, E. E., & Medin, D. L. (1981). *Cognitive Science Series: 4. Categories and concepts.* Cambridge, MA: Harvard University Press.

Smith, G. B., Schwebel, A. I., Dunn, R. L., & McIver, S. D. (1993). The role of psychologists in the treatment, management, and prevention of chronic mental illness. *American Psychologist, 48,* 966–971.

Smith, M. L., & Glass, G. V. (1977). Meta-analysis of psychotherapy outcome studies. *American Psychologist, 32,* 752–760.

Smith, R. E., Haroutunian, V., Davis, K. L., & Meador-Woodruff, J. H. (2001). Expression of excitatory amino acid transporter transcripts in the thalamus of subjects with schizophrenia. *American Journal of Psychiatry, 158,* 1393–1399.

Smith, S. (1991, Spring). Two-generation program models: A new intervention strategy. *Social Policy Report of the Society for Research in Child Development, 5* (No. 1).

Smythe, J. (1998). Written emotional expression: Effect sizes, outcome types, and moderator variables. *Journal of Consulting and Clinical Psychology, 66,* 174–184.

Snyder, H. N., & Sickmund, M. (1995). *Juvenile offenses and victims: A national report.* Washington, DC: Office of Juvenile Justice and Delinquency Prevention.

Snyder, S. H. (1986). *Drugs and the brain.* New York: Scientific American Books.

Solso, R. L. (2001). *Cognitive psychology* (6th ed.). Boston: Allyn & Bacon.

Solvason, H. B., Ghanta, V. K., & Hiramoto, R. N. (1988). Conditioned augmentation of natural killer cell activity: Independence from nociceptive effects and dependence on interferon-beta. *Journal of Immunology, 140,* 661–665.

Sommer, D. H. (2000). *Relationships between sexual abuse, cognitive style, and depression among adolescent psychiatric inpatients.* Doctoral dissertation, University of Texas at Austin.

Sow, I. (1977). *Psychiatrie dynamique africaine.* Paris, France: Payot.

Spear, L. P. (2000). Neurobehavioral changes in adolescence. *Current Directions in Psychological Science, 9,* 111–114.

Spearman, C. (1927). *The abilities of man.* New York: Macmillan.

Spelke, E. S. (2000). Core knowledge. *American Psychologist, 55,* 1233–1243.

Spelke, E. S., & Owsley, C. J. (1979). Intermodal exploration and knowledge in infancy. *Infant Behavior and Development, 2,* 13–27.

Spencer, R. M. C., Zelaznik, H. N., Diedrichsen, J., & Ivry, R. B. (2003, May 30). Disrupted timing of discontinuous but not continuous movements by cerebellar lesions. *Science, 300,* 1437–1439.

Sperling, G. (1960). The information available in brief visual presentations. *Psychological Monographs, 74,* 1–29.

Sperling, G. (1963). A model for visual memory tasks. *Human Factors, 5,* 19–31.

Sperry, R. W. (1964). The great cerebral commissure. *Scientific American, 210,* 42–52.

Sperry, R. W. (1968). *Mental unity following surgical disconnection of the cerebral hemispheres. The Harvey Lectures, Series 62.* New York: Academic Press.

Sperry, R. W. (1982). Some effects of disconnecting the cerebral hemispheres. *Science, 217,* 1223–1226.

Sperry, R. W. (1988). Psychology's mentalist paradigm and the religion/science tension. *American Psychologist, 43,* 607–613.

Spiegel, D., & Cardeña, E. (1991). Disintegrated experience: The dissociate disorders revisited. *Psychological Bulletin, 100,* 366–378.

Spinweber, C. (1990). *Insomnias and parasomnias in young adults.* Paper presented to the annual meeting of the Western Psychological Association, Los Angeles, CA.

Spiro, R. J. (1980). Constructive processes in prose comprehension and recall. In R. J. Spiro, B. C. Bruce, & W. F. Brewer (Eds.), *Theoretical issues in reading comprehension* (pp. 245–278). Hillsdale, NJ: Lawrence Erlbaum Associates.

Spitz, R. A. (1946). Hospitalism: A follow-up report on investigation described in Volume I, 1945. *The Psychoanalytic Study of the Child, 2,* 113–117.

Spitzer, R. L., Gibbon, M., Skodol, A. E., Williams, J. B. W., & First, M. B. (1989). *DSM-III-R casebook.* Washington, DC: American Psychiatric Press.

Sprang, G. (1999). Post-disaster stress following the Oklahoma City bombing: An examination of three community groups. *Journal of Interpersonal Violence, 14,* 169.

Sprecher, S., Barbee, A., & Schwartz, P. (1995). "Was it good for you, too?": Gender differences in first sexual intercourse experiences. *Journal of Sex Research, 32,* 3–15.

Sprecher, S., & McKinney, K. (1994). Sexuality in close relationships. In A. L. Weber & J. H. Harvey (Eds.), *Perspectives on close relationships* (pp. 193–216). Boston: Allyn & Bacon.

Springer, S. P., & Deutsch, G. (1993). *Left brain, right brain* (4th ed.). New York: W. H. Freeman.

Sprock, J., & Blashfield, R. K. (1991). Classification and nosology. In M. Hersen, A. E. Kazdin, & A. S. Bellack (Eds.), *The clinical psychology handbook* (2nd ed., pp. 329–344). New York: Pergamon Press.

Squier, L. H., & Domhoff, G. W. (1998). The presentation of dreaming and dreams in introductory psychology textbooks: A critical examination with suggestions for textbook authors and course instructors. *Dreaming: Journal of the Association for the Study of Dreams, 8,* 149–168.

Squire, S. (1983). *The slender balance: Causes and cures for bulimia, anorexia, and the weight loss/weight gain seesaw.* New York: Putnam.

St. George-Hyslop, P. H. (2000). Piecing together Alzheimer's. *Scientific American, 283*(6), 76–83.

Stapley, J. C., & Haviland, J. M. (1989). Beyond depression: Gender differences in normal adolescents' emotional experiences. *Sex Roles, 20,* 295–308.

Stapp, J., Tucker, A. M., & VandenBos, G. R. (1985). Census of psychological personnel: 1983. *American Psychologist, 40,* 1317–1351.

Statistics Canada. (2002). *Family studies kit.* Retrieved on November 8, 2004, from http://www.statcan.ca/english/kits/Family/pdf/ch3_3e.pdf

Stavish, S. (1994b, Fall). Breathing room. *Stanford Medicine, 12*(1), 18–23.

Steele, C. M. (1997). A threat in the air: How stereotypes shape intellectual identity and performance. *American Psychologist, 52,* 613–629.

Stein, M. B., Walker, J. R., & Forde, D. R. (1996). Public-speaking fears in a community sample: Prevalence, impact on functioning, and diagnostic classification. *Archives of General Psychiatry, 53,* 169–174.

Sternberg, R. J. (1994). A triarchic model for teaching and assessing students in general psychology. *The General Psychologist, 30,* 42–48.

Sternberg, R. J. (1998). *Cupid's arrow: The course of love through time.* New York: Cambridge University Press.

Sternberg, R. J. (1999). The theory of successful intelligence. *Review of General Psychology, 3,* 292–316.

Sternberg, R. J. (2000b). Implicit theories of intelligence as exemplar stories of success: Why intelligence test validity is in the eye of the beholder. *Psychology, Public Policy, and Law, 6,* 159–167.

Sternberg, R. J. (2003). It's time for prescription privileges. *Monitor on Psychology, 34*(6), 5.

Sternberg, R. J., & Grigorenko, E. L. (1997). Are cognitive styles still in style? *American Psychologist, 52,* 700–712.

Sternberg, R. J., & Lubart, T. I. (1991). An investment theory of creativity and its development. *Human Development, 34,* 1–31.

Sternberg, R. J., & Lubart, T. I. (1992). Buy low and sell high: An investment approach to creativity. *Current Directions in Psychological Science, 1,* 1–5.

Sternberg, R. J., Wagner, R. K., Williams, W. M., & Horvath, J. A. (1995). Testing common sense. *American Psychologist, 50,* 912–927.

Stevenson, H. W., Chen, C., & Lee, S. Y. (1993). Mathematics achievement of Chinese, Japanese, and American children: Ten years later. *Science, 259,* 53–58.

Stevenson, J., Graham, P., Fredman, G., & McLoughlin, V. A. (1987). Twin study of genetic influences on reading and spelling ability and disability. *Journal of Child Psychiatry, 28,* 229–247.

Stewart, V. M. (1973). Tests of the "carpentered world" hypothesis by race and environment in America and Zambia. *International Journal of Psychology, 8,* 83–94.

Stickgold, R., Hobson, J. A., Fosse, R., & Fosse, M. (2001). Sleep, learning, and dreams: Off-line memory processing. *Science, 294,* 1052–1057.

Storms, M. D. (1980). Theories of sexual orientation. *Journal of Personality and Social Psychology, 38,* 783–792.

Storms, M. D. (1981). A theory of erotic orientation development. *Psychological Review, 88,* 340–353.

Strasburger, V. C. (1995). *Adolescents and the media.* Thousand Oaks, CA: Sage.

Strauss, E. (1998). Writing, speech separated in split brain. *Science, 280,* 827.

Strayer, D. L., Drews, F. A., & Johnston, W. A. (2003). Cell phone-induced failures of visual attention during simulated driving. *Journal of Experimental Psychology: Applied, 9,* 23–32.

Strickland, B. R. (1992). Women and depression. *Current Directions in Psychological Science, 1,* 132–135.

Strickland, B. R. (2000). Misassumptions, misadventures, and the misuse of psychology. *American Psychologist, 55,* 331–338.

Striegel-Moore, R. H., Silberstein, L. R., & Rodin, J. (1993). The social self in bulimia nervosa: Public self-consciousness, social anxiety, and perceived fraudulence. *Journal of Abnormal Psychology, 102,* 297–303.

Stromeyer, C. F., & Psotka, J. (1970). The detailed texture of eidetic images. *Nature, 225,* 346–349.

Styron, W. (1990). *Darkness visible: A memoir of madness.* New York: Random House.

Suddath, R. L., Christison, G. W., Torrey, E. F., Casanova, M. F., & Weinberger, D. R. (1990). Anatomical abnormalities in the brains of nonpsychotic twins discordant for schizophrenia. *New England Journal of Medicine, 322,* 789–794.

Sue, S. (1991). Ethnicity and culture in psychological research and practice. In J. D. Goodchilds (Ed.), *Psychological perspectives on human diversity in America* (pp. 47–86). Washington, DC: American Psychological Association.

Sulloway, F. J. (1992). *Freud, biologist of the mind: Beyond the psychoanalytic legend.* Cambridge, MA: Harvard University Press.

Suls, J., & Marco, C. A. (1990). Relationship between JAS- and FTAS-Type A behavior and non-CHD illness: A prospective study controlling for negative affectivity. *Health Psychology, 9,* 479–492.

Suls, J., & Sanders, G. S. (1988). Type A behavior as a general risk factor for physical disorder. *Journal of Behavioral Medicine, 11,* 201–226.

Swann, W. B., Jr., Hixon, J. G., & De La Ronde, C. (1992). Embracing the bitter "truth": Negative self-concepts and marital commitment. *Psychological Science, 3,* 118–121.

Sweeney, P. D., Anderson, K., & Bailey, S. (1986). Attributional style in depression: A meta-analytic review. *Journal of Personality and Social Psychology, 50,* 974–991.

Szasz, T. S. (1961). *The myth of mental illness.* New York: Harper & Row.

Szasz, T. S. (1977). *The manufacture of models.* New York: Dell.

Tafrate, R. C., Kassinove, H., & Dundin, L. (2002). Anger episodes in high and low trait anger community adults. *Journal of Clinical Psychology, 58*(12), 1573–1590.

Taubes, G. (1998, May 29). As obesity rates rise, experts struggle to explain why. *Science, 280,* 1367–1368.

Tavris, C. (1989). *Anger: The misunderstood emotion.* New York: Touchstone.

Tavris, C. (1991). The mismeasure of woman: Paradoxes and perspectives in the study of gender. In J. D. Goodchilds (Ed.), *Psychological perspectives on human diversity in America* (pp. 87–136). Washington, DC: American Psychological Association.

Tavris, C. (1995). From excessive rage to useful anger. *Contemporary Psychology, 40*(11), 1101–1102.

Tavris, C. (2000). *Psychobabble and biobunk: Using psychology to think critically about issues in the news.* Upper Saddle River, NJ: Prentice Hall.

Taylor, S. E. (2003). *The tending instinct: Women, men, and the biology of relationships.* New York: Owl Books/Henry Holt.

Taylor, S. E., Klein, L., Lewis, B. P., Gruenewald, T. L., Gurung, R. A. R., & Updegraff, J. A. (2000). Biobehavioral responses to stress in females: Tend-and-befriend, not fight-or-flight. *Psychological Review, 107,* 411–429.

Teicher, M. H. (2002, March). Scars that won't heal: The neurobiology of child abuse. *Scientific American, 286*(3), 68–75.

Tellegen, A., Lykken, D. T., Bouchard, T. J., Wilcox, K. J., Segal, N. L., & Rich, S. (1988). Personality similarity in twins reared apart and together. *Journal of Personality and Social Psychology, 54,* 1031–1039.

Teller, D. Y. (1998). Spatial and temporal aspects of infant color vision. *Vision Research, 38,* 3275–3282.

Terman, L. M. (1916). *The measurement of intelligence.* Boston: Houghton Mifflin.

Terman, L., & Oden, M. H. (1959). *Genetic studies of genius: Vol 4. The gifted group at midlife.* Stanford, CA: Stanford University Press.

Terry, W. S. (2000). *Learning and memory: Basic principles, processes, and procedures.* Boston: Allyn & Bacon.

Tesser, A., & Brodie, M. (1971). A note on the evaluation of a "computer date." *Psychonomic Science, 23,* 300.

Thio, A. (1995). *Deviant behavior.* New York: HarperCollins.

Thomas, F. F. (1991). *Impact on teaching: Research with culturally diverse populations.* Symposium conducted at the Western Psychological Association Convention, San Francisco.

Thompson, D. M. (1988). Context and false recognition. In G. M. Davies & D. M. Thompson (Eds.), *Memory in context: Context in memory* (pp. 285–304). New York: Wiley.

Thorpe, S. J., & Fabre-Thorpe, M. (2001, January 12). Seeking categories in the brain. *Science, 291,* 260–263.

Tienari, P., Sorri, A., Lahti, I., Naarala, M., Wahlberg, K.-E., Moring, J., Pohjola, J., & Wynne, L. C. (1987). Genetic and psychosocial factors in schizophrenia: The Finnish adoptive family study. *Schizophrenia Bulletin, 13,* 476–483.

Tirozzi, G. N., & Uro, G. (1997). Education reform in the United States: National policy in support of local efforts for school improvement. *American Psychologist, 52,* 241–249.

Todes, D. P. (1997). From the machine to the ghost within: Pavlov's transition from digestive physiology to conditional reflexes. *American Psychologist, 52,* 947–955.

Tolman, E. C. (1932). *Purposive behavior in animals and men.* New York: Appleton.

Tolman, E. C. (1948). Cognitive maps in rats and men. *Psychological Review, 55,* 189–208.

Tolman, E. C., & Honzik, C. H. (1930). "Insight" in rats. *University of California Publications in Psychology, 4,* 215–232.

Tolman, E. C., Ritchie, B. G., & Kalish, D. (1946). Studies in spatial learning: I. Orientation and the short-cut. *Journal of Experimental Psychology, 36,* 13–24.

Tomasello, M. (2000). Culture and cognitive development. *Current Directions in Psychological Science, 9,* 37–40.

Tononi, G., & Edelman, G. M. (1998, December 4). Consciousness and complexity. *Science, 282,* 1846–1850.

Torrey, E. F. (1996). *Out of the shadows: Confronting America's mental illness crisis.* New York: Wiley.

Torrey, E. F. (1997). The release of the mentally ill from institutions: A well-intentioned disaster. *The Chronicle of Higher Education,* B4–B5.

Totterdell, P. (2000). Catching moods and hitting runs: Mood linkage and subjective performance in professional sport. *Journal of Applied Psychology, 85,* 848–859.

Totterdell, P., Kellett, S., Briner, R. B., & Teuchmann, K. (1998). Evidence of mood linkage in work groups. *Journal of Personality and Social Psychology, 74,* 1504–1515.

Travis, J. (2000a, October 14). Pioneers of brain-cell signaling earn Nobel. *Science News, 158,* 247.

Travis, J. (2000b, September 23). Snap, crackle, and feel good? Magnetic fields that map the brain may also treat its disorders. *Science News, 158,* 204–206.

Treffert, D. A., & Wallace, G. L. (2002, June). Islands of genius. *Scientific American,* 76–85.

Triandis, H. (1989). The self and social behavior in differing cultural contexts. *Psychological Review, 96,* 506–520.

Triandis, H. (1990). Cross-cultural studies of individualism and collectivism. In J. Berman (Ed.), *Nebraska Symposium on Motivation, 1989* (pp. 42–133). Lincoln: University of Nebraska Press.

Triandis, H. C. (1994). *Culture and social behavior.* New York: McGraw-Hill.

Triandis, H. C. (1995). *Individualism & collectivism.* Boulder, CO: Westview Press.

Triandis, H. C. (1996). The psychological measurement of cultural syndromes. *American Psychologist, 51,* 407–415.

Triandis, H. C., & Gelfand, M. J. (1998). Converging measurement of horizontal and vertical individualism and collectivism. *Journal of Personality and Social Psychology, 74,* 118–128.

Tronick, E., Als, H., & Brazelton, T. B. (1980). Moradic phases: A structural description analysis of infant-mother face to face interaction. *Merrill-Palmer Quarterly, 26,* 3–24.

Trope, I., Rozin, P., Nelson, D. K., & Gur, R. C. (1992). Information processing in separated hemispheres of the callosotomy patients: Does the analytic–holistic dichotomy hold? *Brain and Cognition, 19,* 123–147.

Tsai, M., & Uemura, A. (1988). Asian Americans: The struggles, the conflicts, and the successes. In P. Bronstein & K. Quina (Eds.), *Teaching a psychology of people: Resources for gender and sociocultural awareness.* Washington, DC: American Psychological Association.

Tsuang, M. T., & Faraone, S. V. (1990). *The genetics of mood disorders.* Baltimore, MD: Johns Hopkins University Press.

Tulving, E. (1983). *Elements of episodic memory.* Oxford, U.K.: Clarendon Press.

Turk, D. C. (1994). Perspectives on chronic pain: The role of psychological factors. *Current Directions in Psychological Science, 3,* 45–48.

Turk, D. J., Heatherton, T. F., Kelly, W. M., Funnell, M. G., Gazzaniga, M. S., & Macrae, C. N. (2002, September 1). Mike or me? Self-recognition in a split-brain patient. *Nature Neuroscience, 5,* 841–842.

Turkington, C. (1993, January). New definition of retardation includes the need for support. *APA Monitor,* pp. 26–27.

Turner, J. C., & Oakes, P. J. (1989). Self-categorization theory and social influence. In P. B. Paulus (Ed.), *Psychology of group influence* (2nd ed.). Hillsdale, NJ: Erlbaum.

Turvey, M. T. (1996). Dynamic touch. *American Psychologist, 51,* 1134–1152.

Tversky, A., & Kahneman, D. (1973). Availability: A heuristic for judging frequency and probability. *Cognitive Psychology, 5,* 207–232.

Tversky, A., & Kahneman, D. (1974). Judgment under uncertainty: Heuristics and biases. *Science, 185,* 1124–1131.

Tyler, L. (1988). Mental testing. In E. R. Hilgard (Ed.), *Fifty years of psychology* (pp. 127–138). Glenview, IL: Scott, Foresman.

Ulrich, R. E., & Azrin, N. H. (1962). Reflexive fighting in response to aversive stimulation. *Journal of the Experimental Analysis of Behavior, 5,* 511–520.

U.S. Bureau of the Census. (2002). *Statistical abstract of the United States* (122nd ed.). Washington, DC: U.S. Government Printing Office.

U.S. Merit Systems Protection Board. (1995). *Sexual harassment in the federal workplace: Trends, progress, continuing challenges.* Washington, DC: U.S. Government Printing Office.

U.S. Senate Select Committee on Intelligence. (2004). *Report on the U.S. Intelligence Community's Prewar Intelligence Assessments on Iraq: Conclusions.* Retrieved on November 23, 2004, from http://intelligence.senate.gov/conclusions.pdf

Valenstein, E. S. (1973). *Brain control.* New York: John Wiley & Sons.

Valenstein, E. S. (Ed.). (1980). *The psychosurgery debate.* New York: Freeman.

Valenstein, E. S. (1998). *Blaming the brain: The truth about drugs and mental health.* New York: The Free Press.

Vallee, B. L. (1998, June). Alcohol in the Western world. *Scientific American, 278*(6), 80–85.

van Dam, L. (1996, October 1). Mindful healing: An interview with Herbert Benson. *Technology Review, 99*(7), 31–38.

Van de Castle, R. L. (1983). Animal figures in fantasy and dreams. In A. Katcher & A. Beck (Eds.), *New perspectives on our lives with companion animals.* Philadelphia: University of Pennsylvania Press.

Van de Castle, R. L. (1994). *Our dreaming mind.* New York: Ballantine Books.

VandenBos, G. R. (1986). Psychotherapy research: A special issue. *American Psychologist, 41,* 111–112.

Van Dongen, H. P. A., Maislin, G., Mullington, J. M., & Dinges, D. F. (2003). The cumulative cost of additional wakefulness: Dose-response effects on neurobehavioral functions and sleep physiology from chronic sleep restriction and total sleep deprivation. *Journal Sleep, 26,* 117–126.

Verbaten, M. N. (2003). Specific memory deficits in ecstasy users? The results of a meta-analysis. *Human Psychopharmacology: Clinical and Experimental, 18,* 281–290.

Vernon, P. E. (1969). *Intelligence and cultural environment.* London: Methuen.

Vernon, P. E. (1987). The demise of the Stanford-Binet Scale. *Canadian Psychology, 28,* 251–258.

Viken, R. J., & McFall, R. M. (1994). Paradox lost: Implications of contemporary reinforcement theory for behavior therapy. *Current Directions in Psychological Science, 3,* 121–125.

Vincent, K. R. (1991). Black/white IQ differences: Does age make a difference? *Journal of Clinical Psychology, 47,* 266–270.

Vincent, M., & Pickering, M. R. (1988). Multiple personality disorder in childhood. *Canadian Journal of Psychiatry, 33,* 524–529.

Vingerhoets, G., Berckmoes, C., & Stroobant, N. (2003). Cerebral hemodynamics during discrimination of prosodic and semantic emotion in speech studied by transcranial doppler ultrasonography. *Neuropsychology, 17,* 93–99.

Vogel, G. (1996, November 22). Illusion reveals pain locus in brain. *Science, 274,* 1301.

Vogel, G. (1997, February 28). Scientists probe feelings behind decision-making. *Science, 275,* 1269.

Volpe, K. (2004). Taylor takes on "fight-or-flight." *Psychological Science, 17,* 391.

Volz, J. (2000, February). In search of the good life. *Monitor on Psychology, 31*(2), 68–69.

von Hofsten, C., & Lindhagen, K. (1979). Observations on the development of reaching for moving objects. *Journal of Child Psychology, 28,* 158–173.

Vygotsky, L. S. (1978). *Mind in society: The development of higher psychological processes.* Cambridge, MA: Harvard University Press.

Wade, T. J. (1991). Race and sex differences in adolescent self-perceptions of physical attractiveness and level of self-esteem during early and late adolescence. *Journal of Personality and Individual Differences, 12,* 1319–1324.

Wagner, U., Gais, S., Haider, H., Verleger, R., & Born, J. (2004, January 22). Sleep inspires insight. *Nature, 427,* 352–355.

Walden, J., Normann, C., Langosch, J.,

Berger, M., & Grunze, H. (1998). Differential treatment of bipolar disorder with old and new antiepileptic drugs. *Neuropsychobiology, 38,* 181–184.

Walker, E. F., & Diforio, D. (1997). Schizophrenia: A neural diathesis-stress model. *Psychological Review, 104,* 667–685.

Walker, L. J. (1989). A longitudinal study of moral reasoning. *Child Development, 60,* 157–166.

Walker, L. J. (1991). Sex differences in moral reasoning. In W. M. Kurtines & J. L. Gewirtz (Eds.), *Handbook of moral behavior and development: Research* (Vol. 2, pp. 333–364). Hillsdale, NJ: Erlbaum.

Walker, L. J., & de Vries, B. (1985). *Moral stages/moral orientations: Do the sexes really differ?* Paper presented at the annual meeting of the American Psychological Association, Los Angeles.

Walker, L. J., de Vries, B., & Trevethan, S. D. (1987). Moral stages and moral orientations in real-life and hypothetical dilemmas. *Child Development, 58,* 842–858.

Wallace, A. F. C. (1959). Cultural determinants of response to hallucinatory experience. *Archives of General Psychiatry, 1,* 58–69.

Wallace, B., & Fisher, L. E. (1999). *Consciousness and behavior.* Boston: Allyn & Bacon.

Wallis, C. (1984, June 11). Unlocking pain's secrets. *Time,* 58–66.

Walsh, R. (1984). Asian psychologies. In R. Corsini (Ed.), *Encyclopedia of psychology* (pp. 90–94). New York: Wiley.

Walters, E. E., Neale, M. C., Eaves, L. J., Heath, A. C., Kessler, R. C., & Kendler, K. S. (1992). Bulimia nervosa and major depression: A study of common genetic and environmental factors. *Psychological Medicine, 22*(3), 617–622.

Wassermann, E. M., & Lisanby, S. H. (2001). Therapeutic application of repetitive transcranial magnetic stimulation: A review. *Clinical Neurophysiology, 112,* 1367– 377.

Watkins, L. R., & Mayer, D. J. (1982). Organization of the endogenous opiate and nonopiate pain control systems. *Science, 216,* 1185–1193.

Watson, J. B., & Rayner, R. (2000). Conditioned emotional reactions. *American Psychologist, 55,* 313–317. (Original work published by J. B. Watson and R. Rayner, 1920, *Journal of Experimental Psychology, 3,* 1–14.)

Watson, J. D. (1968). *The double helix.* New York: The New American Library (Signet).

Weber, A. L., & Harvey, J. H. (1994a). Accounts in coping with relationship loss. In A. L. Weber & J. H. Harvey (Eds.), *Perspectives on close relationships* (pp. 285–306). Boston, MA: Allyn & Bacon.

Weber, A. L., & Harvey, J. H. (Eds.). (1994b). *Perspectives on close relationships.* Boston, MA: Allyn & Bacon.

Wegner, D. M. (1989). *White bears and other unwanted thoughts.* New York: Guilford.

Wegner, D. M., Schneider, D. J., Carter, S., III, & White, T. (1987). Paradoxical effects of thought suppression. *Journal of Personality and Social Psychology, 53,* 5–13.

Wehr, T. A., & Rosenthal, N. E. (1989). Seasonality and affective illness. *American Journal of Psychiatry, 146,* 829–839.

Weil, A. T. (1977). The marriage of the sun and the moon. In N. E. Zinberg (Ed.), *Alternate states of consciousness* (pp. 37–52). New York: Free Press.

Weiner, J. (1994). *The beak of the finch.* New York: Vintage Books.

Weingardt, K. R., Loftus, E. F., & Lindsay, D. S. (1995). Misinformation revisited: New evidence on the suggestibility of memory. *Memory and Cognition, 23,* 72–82.

Weisberg, R. (1986). *Creativity, genius, and other myths.* New York: Freeman.

Weissman, M. M., Bland, R. C., Canino, G. J., Faravelli, C., Greenwald, S., Hwu, H. G., Joyce, P. R., Karam, E. G., Lee, C. K., Lellouch, J., Lepine, J. P., Newman, S. C., Rubio-Stipec, M., Wells, J. E., Wickramaratne, P. J., Wittchen, H., & Yeh, E. K. (1996, July 24–31). Cross-national epidemiology of major depression and bipolar disorder. *Journal of the American Medical Association, 276,* 293–299.

Weissman, M. M., Merikangas, K. R., Wickramaratne, P., Kidd, K. K., Prusoff, B. A., Leckman, J. F., & Pauls, D. L. (1986). Understanding the clinical heterogeneity of major depression using family data. *Archives of General Psychiatry, 43,* 430–434.

Wellman, H. M., & Estes, D. (1986). Early understanding of mental entities: A reexamination of childhood realism. *Child Development, 57,* 910–923.

Welsh, E. J., Gullotta, C., & Rapoport, J. (1993). Classroom academic performance: Improvement with both methylphenidate and dextroamphetamine in ADHD boys. *Journal of Child Psychology and Psychiatry and Allied Disciplines, 34,* 785–804.

Wertheimer, M. (1923). Untersuchungen zur Lehre von der Gestalt, II. *Psychologische Forschung, 4,* 301–350.

Wesson, D. R., Smith, D. E., & Seymour, R. B. (1992). Sedative-hypnotics and tricyclics. In J. H. Lowinson, P. Ruiz, R. B. Millman, & J. G. Langrod (Eds.), *Substance abuse: A comprehensive textbook* (2nd ed.) (pp. 271–279). Baltimore: Williams & Wilkins.

Whalen, P. J. (1998). Fear, vigilance, and ambiguity: Initial neuroimaging studies of the human amygdala. *Current Directions in Psychological Science, 7,* 177–188.

What we learn from twins. The mirror of your soul. (1998, January 3). *The Economist.* Retrieved November 8, 2004, from http://search.epnet.com/direct.asp?an=35349&db=aph

Wheeler, D. L. (1999, January 22). Prospect of fetal-gene therapy stimulates high hopes and deep fears. *The Chronicle of Higher Education,* A13.

Wheeler, D. L., Jacobson, J. W., Paglieri, R. A., and Schwartz, A. A. (1993). An experimental assessment of facilitated communication. *Mental Retardation, 31,* 49–60.

Wheeler, M. E., Petersen, S. E., & Buckner, R. L. (2000). Memory's echo: Vivid remembering reactivates sensory-specific cortex. *Proceedings of the National Academy of Sciences, 97,* 11125–11129.

Whiteman, M. C., & Fowkes, F. G. R. (1997, August 16). Hostility and the heart. *British Medical Journal, 7105,* 379–380.

Whitley, B. E., Jr. (1999). Right-wing authoritarianism, social dominance orientation, and prejudice. *Journal of Personality and Social Psychology, 7,* 126–134.

Whyte, W. F. (1972, April). Skinnerian theory in organizations. *Psychology Today,* 67–68, 96, 98, 100.

Wickelgren, I. (1997, June 27). Marijuana: Harder than thought? *Science, 276,* 1967–1968.

Wickelgren, I. (1998b, May 29). Obesity: How big a problem? *Science, 280,* 1364–1367.

Wickelgren, I. (1998c, June 26). Teaching the brain to take drugs. *Science, 280,* 2045–2047.

Wickelgren, I. (1999, March 19). Nurture helps mold able minds. *Science, 283,* 1832–1834.

Wickelgren, I. (2001, March 2). Working memory helps the mind focus. *Science, 291,* 1684–1685.

Wickelgren, W. (1974). *How to solve problems: Elements of a theory of problems and problem solving.* San Francisco: W. H. Freeman.

Wiggins, J. S. (1973). *Personality and prediction: Principles of personality assessment.* Reading, MA: Addison-Wesley.

Wills, T. A., & DePaulo, B. M. (1991). Interpersonal analysis of the help-seeking process. In C. R. Snyder & D. R. Forsyth (Eds.), *Handbook of social and clinical psychology: The health perspective* (pp. 350–375). New York: Pergamon Press.

Wilner, D., Walkley, R., & Cook, S. (1955). *Human relations in interracial housing.* Minneapolis: University of Minnesota Press.

Wilson, E. D., Reeves, A., & Culver, C. (1977). Cerebral commissurotomy for control of intractable seizures. *Neurology, 27,* 708–715.

Wilson, R. I., & Nicoll, R. A. (2002, April 26). Endocannabinoid signaling in the brain. *Science, 296,* 678–682.

Wilson, S. M., & Medora, N. P. (1990). Gender comparisons of college students' attitudes toward sexual behavior. *Adolescence, 25,* 615–627.

Windholz, G. (1997). Ivan P. Pavlov: An overview of his life and psychological work. *American Psychologist, 52,* 941–946.

Winner, E. (2000). The origins and ends of giftedness. *American Psychologist, 55,* 159–169.

Winograd, E., & Neisser, U. (Eds.). (1992). *Affect and accuracy in recall: Studies of "flashbulb" memories.* New York: Cambridge University Press.

Winson, J. (1990, November). The meaning of dreams. *Scientific American, 263,* 86–96.

Winter, D. G., John, O. P., Stewart, A. J., & Klohnen, E. C. (1998). Traits and motives: Toward an integration of two traditions in personality research. *Psychological Review, 105,* 230–250.

Winters, J. (2002, January). Hey birder, this phone's for you. *Discover,* 75.

Wirth, S., Yanike, M., Frank, L. M., Smith, A. C., Brown, E. N., & Suzuki, W. A. (2003, June 6). Single neurons in the monkey hippocampus and learning of new associations. *Science, 300,* 1578–1581.

Wolpe, J. (1958). *Psychotherapy by reciprocal inhibition.* Stanford, CA: Stanford University Press.

Wolpe, J. (1973). *The practice of behavior therapy* (2nd ed.). New York: Pergamon.

Wolpe, J. (1985). Existential problems and behavior therapy. *The Behavior Therapist, 8,* 126–127.

Wolpe, J., & Plaud, J. J. (1997). Pavlov's contributions to behavior therapy: The obvious and the not so obvious. *American Psychologist, 52,* 966–972.

Wolraich, M. L., Wilson, D. B., & White, J. W. (1995, November 22/29). The effect of sugar on behavior or cognition in children: A meta-analysis. *Journal of the American Medical Association, 274,* 1617–1621.

Wong, M. M., & Csikszentmihalyi, M. (1991). Motivation and academic achievement: The effects of personality traits and the quality of experience. *Journal of Personality, 59,* 539–574.

Wood, J. M., Nezworski, M. T., & Stejskal, W. J. (1996). The comprehensive system for the Rorschach: A critical examination. *Psychological Science, 7,* 3–10.

Wood, J. V., Saltzberg, J. A., & Goldsamt, L. A. (1990a). Does affect induce self-focused attention? *Journal of Personality and Social Psychology, 58,* 899–908.

Wood, J. V., Saltzberg, J. A., Neale, J. M., Stone, A. A., & Rachmiel, T. B. (1990b). Self-focused attention, coping responses, and distressed mood in everyday life. *Journal of Personality and Social Psychology, 58,* 1027–1036.

Woods, S. C., Seeley, R. J., Porte, Jr., D., Schwartz, M. W. (1998, May 29). Signals that regulate food intake and energy homeostasis. *Science, 280,* 1378–1383.

Woodworth, R. S. (1918). *Dynamic psychology.* New York: Columbia University Press.

Woody, E., & Sadler, P. (1998). On reintegrating dissociated theories: Comment on Kirsch and Lynn (1998). *Psychological Bulletin, 123*(2), 192–197.

World Health Organization. (1973). *Report of the International Pilot Study of Schizophrenia* (Vol. 1). Geneva, Switzerland: Author.

World Health Organization. (1979). *Schizophrenia: An international follow-up study.* New York: Wiley.

Wright, E. R., Gronfein, W. P., & Owens, T. J. (2000). Deinstitutionalization, social rejection, and self-esteem of former mental patients. *Journal of Health and Social Behavior, 41,* 68–90.

Wright, K., & Mahurin, M. (1997, October). Babies, bonds, and brains. *Discover,* 74–78.

Wright, L. (1988). The Type A behavior pattern and coronary artery disease: Quest for the active ingredients and the elusive mechanism. *American Psychologist, 43,* 2–14.

Wu, C. (1998, April 4). Ritalin may work better as a purer compound. *Science News, 153,* 213.

Wynn, K. (1992). Addition and subtraction by human infants. *Nature, 358,* 749–759.

Wynn, K. (1995). Infants possess a system of numerical knowledge. *Current Directions in Psychological Science, 4,* 172–177.

Yacoubian, G. S. Jr., Deutsch, J. K., & Schumacher, E. J. (2004). Estimating the prevalence of ecstasy use among club rave attendees. *Contemporary Drug Problems, 31,* 163–177.

Yalom, I. D., & Greaves, C. (1977). Group therapy with the terminally ill. *American Journal of Psychiatry, 134,* 396–400.

Yee, A. H., Fairchild, H. H., Weizmann, F., & Wyatt, G. E. (1993). Addressing psychology's problems with race. *American Psychologist, 48,* 1132–1140.

Yee, P. L., Pierce, G. R., Ptacek, J. R., & Modzelesky, K. L. (2003). Learned helplessness, attributional style, and examination performance: Enhancement effects are not necessarily moderated by prior failure. *Anxiety, Stress & Coping, 16,* 359–373.

Yerkes, R. M. (1921). Psychological examining in the United States Army. In R. M. Yerkes (Ed.), *Memoirs of the National Academy of Sciences: Vol. 15.* Washington, DC: U.S. Government Printing Office.

Young, J. R. (2003, February 14). Prozac campus. *The chronicle of Higher Education,* A-37–A-38.

Zajonc, R. B. (1968). Attitudinal effects of mere exposure. *Journal of Personality and Social Psychology. Monograph Supplement, 9*(2, Part 2), 1–27.

Zajonc, R. B. (1980). Feeling and thinking: Preferences need no inferences. *American Psychologist, 35,* 151–175.

Zajonc, R. B. (1984). On the primacy of affect. *American Psychologist, 39,* 117–123.

Zajonc, R. B. (2001). *Mere exposure effects explained . . . finally!* Address given to the Western Psychological Association annual convention in Lahaina (Maui), Hawaii.

Zaman, R. M. (1992). Psychotherapy in the third world: Some impressions from Pakistan. In U. P. Gielen, L. L. Adler, & N. A. Milgram (Eds.), *Psychology in international perspective* (pp. 314–321). Amsterdam: Swets & Zeitlinger.

Zarit, S. H., & Pearlin, L. I. (Eds.). (2003). *Personal control in social and life course contexts: Societal impact on aging* (pp. 127–164). New York: Springer Publishing.

Zatorre, R. J., & Krumhansl, C. L. (2002, December 13). Mental models and musical minds. *Science, 298,* 2138–2139.

Zeki, S. (1992, September). The visual image in mind and brain. *Scientific American, 267,* 68–76.

Zeman, N. (1990, Summer/Fall). The new rules of courtship (Special Edition). *Newsweek,* 24–27.

Zigler, E., & Muenchow, S. (1992). *Head Start: The inside story of America's most successful educational experiment.* New York: Basic Books.

Zigler, E., & Styfco, S. J. (1994). Head Start: Criticisms in a constructive context. *American Psychologist, 49,* 127–132.

Zilbergeld, B. (1986, June). Psychabuse. *Science 86, 7,* 48.

Zimbardo, P. G. (1973). On the ethics of investigation in human psychological research: With special reference to the Stanford Prison Experiment. *Cognition, 2,* 243–256.

Zimbardo, P. G. (1975). On transforming experimental research into advocacy for social change. In M. Deutsch & H. Hornstein (Eds.), *Applying social psychology: Implications for research, practice, and training* (pp. 33–66). Hillsdale, NJ: Erlbaum.

Zimbardo, P. G. (1990). *Shyness: What it is, what to do about it* (Rev. ed.). Reading, MA: Perseus Books. (Original work published 1977).

Zimbardo, P. G. (2004a). *On being shoe at Yale: A study in institutional conformity.* In preparation, Stanford University.

Zimbardo, P. G. (2004c, May 9). Power turns good soldiers into "bad apples." *Boston Globe,* D11.

Zimbardo, P. G. (2004d). A situationist perspective on the psychology of evil: Understanding how good people are transformed into perpetrators. In A. G. Miller (Ed.), *The Social Psychology of Good and Evil* (pp. 21–50). New York: Guilford Press.

Zimbardo, P. G., Andersen, S. M., & Kabat, L. (1981). Induced hearing deficit generates experimental paranoia. *Science, 212,* 1529–1531.

Zimbardo, P. G., Maslach, C., & Haney, C. (1999). Reflections on the Stanford prison Experiment: Genesis, transformations, consequences. In T. Blass (Ed.), *Obedience to authority: Current perspectives on the Milgram paradigm* (pp. 193–237). Mahwah, NJ: Erlbaum.

Zimbardo, P. G., & Montgomery, K. D. (1957). The relative strengths of consummatory responses in hunger, thirst, and exploratory drive. *Journal of Comparative and Physiological Psychology, 50,* 504–508.

Zimmerman, S. (2002). *Writing to heal the soul: Transforming grief and loss through writing.* New York: Three Rivers Press/Crown Publishing.

Zucker, G. S., & Weiner, B. (1993). Conservatism and perceptions of poverty: An attributional analysis. *Journal of Applied Social Psychology, 23,* 925–943.

Zuckerman, M. (1978, February). The search for high sensation. *Psychology Today, 12,* 38–46.

Zuckerman, M. (1990). Some dubious premises in research and theory on racial differences: Scientific, social, and ethical issues. *American Psychologist, 45,* 1297–1303.

Zuckerman, M. (1995). Good and bad humors: Biochemical bases of personality and its disorders. *Psychological Science, 6,* 325–332.

Zuckerman, M. (2004). The shaping of personality: Genes, environments, and chance encounters. *Journal of Personality Assessment, 82,* 11–22.

Zuckerman, M., Buchsbaum, M. S., & Murphy, D. L. (1980). Sensation seeking and its biological correlates. *Psychological Bulletin, 88,* 187–214.

Zuckerman, M., Depaulo, B. M., & Rosenthal, R. (1981). Verbal and nonverbal communication of deception. *Advances in Experimental Social Psychology, 14,* 1–59.

Zuckerman, M., Kuhlman, D. M., Joireman, J., Teta, P., & Kraft, M. (1993). A comparison of three structural models for personality: The Big Three, the Big Five, and the Alternative Five. *Journal of Personality and Social Psychology, 65,* 575–768.

Photo Credits

Chapter 5: page 157, Henri Rousseau, "The Sleeping Gypsy." 1897. Oil on Canvas. 51″ × 6′ 7″ (129.5 × 200.7 cm). Gift of Mrs. Simon Guggenheim. 646.39. © The Museum of Modern Art/Scala/Art Resource, NY; page 158, © 2004 Gala-Salvador Dali Foundation, Figueres, Spain, © Salvador Dali Museum, Inc. St. Petersburg, Florida, USA/Bridgeman Art Library; page 159, © Volker Steger/Peter Arnold, Inc.; page 160, Courtesy of Marcus E. Raichle, M.D. Washington University School of Medicine; page 166, © Rhoda Signey/The Image Works; page 172, © Paul Conklin/PhotoEdit; page 175, Henri Rousseau, "The Sleeping Gypsy." 1897. Oil on Canvas. 51″ × 6′ 7″ (129.5 × 200.7 cm). Gift of Mrs. Simon Guggenheim. 646.39. © The Museum of Modern Art/Scala/Art Resource, NY; page 176, © Ogust/The Image Works; page 177, © Louis Psihoyos; page 178, (top), © Chad Slattery/Getty Images/Stone; page 178 (bottom), © Amy Etra/PhotoEdit; page 181, PhotoDisk, Inc.; page 182 (left), © Richard Heinzen/Superstock, Inc.; page 182 (right), © Michael Newman/PhotoEdit; page 185, © Jeff Greenberg/PhotoEdit; page 186, Images in Neuroscience, Carol A. Timminga, M.D., Editor, Neuroimaging, XIII, SPECT Imaging of Synaptic Dopamine, Photographs courtesy of Dr. Innis from the Yale Neurochemical Brain Imaging Program, Am J Psychiatry 153:10, October 1996; page 188 (top), © Thinkstock/Getty Images (Royalty-free); page 188 (bottom), © Ghislain & Marie David de Lossy/Getty Images/The Image Bank.

Chapter 6: page 195, © Jeff Greenberg/PhotoEdit; page 197, © John Chaisson/Getty Images; page 198, © Bettmann/CORBIS; page 203, Archives of the History of American Psychology, University of Akron; page 204, Courtesy of Dr. Stuart R. Ellins, California State University, San Bernadino; page 205, © David Young-Wolff/PhotoEdit; page 206, © Esbin-Anderson/The Image Works; page 207, © Time Life Pictures/Getty Images; page 208 (top), Yerkes Regional Primate Research Center, Emory University; page 208 (bottom), © Cindy Charles/PhotoEdit; page 209 (top), © Jeff Greenberg/PhotoEdit; page 209 (bottom), AP/Wide World Photos; page 211, © Peter Menzel/Stock Boston, LLC; page 212, Calvin & Hobbes by Bill Watterson/Universal Press Syndicate; page 213, © Bettmann/CORBIS; page 215, © Steve Azzara/CORBIS SYGMA; page 219 (left, middle, right), © Superstock, Inc.; page 220, © The New Yorker Collection 1994, Sam Gross from cartoonbank.com. All Rights Reserved; page 222, from A. Bandura and R. Walters/Photos Courtesy of Dr. Albert Bandura; page 225, © LWA-JDC/CORBIS.

Chapter 7: page 233, © Patrick Batchelder; page 241, © Catherine Karnow/Woodfin Camp & Associates; page 247, AP/Wide World Photos; page 248, © Courtesy Everett Collection; page 249, © Custom Medical Stock; page 250, AP/Wide World Photos; page 251, AP/Wide World Photos; page 255, © Craig Aurness/CORBIS; page 258, © Susan Van Etten/PhotoEdit; page 261 (left), © Bettmann/CORBIS; page 261 (right), © Bettmann/CORBIS; page 265, © Will Hart/PhotoEdit; page 271, © Bonnie Kamin/PhotoEdit; page 278 (top), © L. Kolvoord/The Image Works, page 278 (middle), © Richard Lord/The Image Works; page 281 (left), © Ken Eward/Photo Researchers, Inc.; page 281 (right), © Jan Butchofskyk-Houser/CORBIS; page 287, © Bettmann/CORBIS.

Chapter 8: page 297, © Digital Vision/Getty Images; page 299, © Larry Williams/CORBIS; pages 300 and 301, Dr. Paul Ekman/Human Interaction Laboratory/University of California/San Francisco; page 308, Courtesy of Bob Johnson; page 309, © Lauren Goodsmith/The Image Works; page 310, © Giraudon/Art Resource, NY: page 315 (bottom), Meet the Parents, Robert DeNiro, Ben Stiller, 2000 © The Everett Collection; page 315 (top), © Dachner Keltner; page 319, © Bob Daemmrich/Stock Boston, LLC; page 324, © David Young-Wolff/PhotoEdit; page 326, © Ariel Skelley/CORBIS; page 330, © Joel Gordon 1988; page 335, © Mark Richards/PhotoEdit.

Chapter 9: page 359, © Bob Daemmrich/Stock Boston, LLC; page 361, © T. K. Wanstal/The Image Works; page 364 (bottom left), Mauritshuis, The Hague, The Netherlands Dutch, out of copyright/Bridgeman Art Library; page 364 (top right), Staatliche Kunstsammlungen, Kassel, Germany/Bridgeman Art Library Lauros/Giraudon; page 364 (bottom right), Galleria degli Uffizi, Florence Italy Dutch, out of copyright/Bridgeman Art Library; page 364 (top left), Rijksmuseum Amsterdam, Holland/Bridgeman Art Library; page 365, © Chemical Design Ltd/Science Photo Library/Photo Researchers, Inc.; page 367, © Lennart Nilsson, A Child Is Born/Bonnier-Forlagen AB; page 371 (top), © Nina Leen/Time Life Pictures/Getty Images; page 371 (bottom), © 1996 Thomas Hoepker/Magnum Photos; page 373, © Martin Roger/Stock Boston, LLC; page 377 (top), © Daniel Giry/CORBIS SYGMA; page 377 (middle), © Michelle D. Bridwell/PhotoEdit; page 378 (top), Lew Merrim/Photo Researchers, Inc.; page 378 (bottom), Lew Merrim/Photo Researchers, Inc.; page 379, © Marcia Weinstein; page 384, © Bob Daemmrich/Stock Boston, LLC; page 389, © Bob Daemmrich/Stock Boston, LLC; page 390, © Grantpix/Stock Boston, LLC; page 399, © Bob Daemmrich/The Image Works.

Chapter 10: page 409, © Mark Adams/Getty Images/Taxi; page 410 (left and right), © Frank Siteman/Index Stock Photography; page 412, Photograph by Max Halberstadt/Courtesy of W. E. Freud, Sigmund Freud Copyrights. Mary Evans Picture Library; page 415, © Mark Adams/Getty Images/Taxi; page 416, © Punch/Rothco; page 417, Reprinted by permission of the publishers from Thematic Appreciation Test, by Henry A. Murray, Cambridge, MA: Harvard University Press, © 1943 by the President and Fellows of Harvard College: © 1971 by Henry A. Murray; page 420, Lord of the Rings; The Fellowship of the Rings, Ian McKellen, 2001 © Everett Collection; page 422, © Bettmann/CORBIS; page 423, Franklin D. Roosevelt Library, Hyde Park, New York; page 426, © Richard T. Nowitz/CORBIS; page 429, © Bruno Vincent/Getty Images for MTV; page 431, © David Young-Wolff/PhotoEdit; page 435, The Far Side® by Gary Larson © 1990 FarWorks, Inc. All rights reserved. Used with permission; page 436, © D. Wells. The Image Works; page 437, © J. Greenberg/The Image Works; page 440, © Michael Newman/PhotoEdit; page 442, © Mario Tama/Getty Images.

Chapter 11: page 451, © CORBIS/Bettmann, page 456, © Gary Conner/PhotoEdit; page 459 (right), © Bob Daemmrich/Stock Boston, LLC; page 459 (left), Copyright © 1986 by The Riverside Publishing Company. All rights reserved; page 461, © Richard Hutchings/PhotoEdit; page 466, © Patrick Ward/Stock Boston, LLC; page 467, © Lawrence Migdale; page 470, © Aaron Haupt/Stock Boston, LLC; page 471, © Joan Clifford/Index Stock Imagery; page 476, © Ed Clark/Time Life Pictures/Getty Images.

Chapter 12: page 483, © Paul Seheult; Eye Ubiquitous/CORBIS; page 484, Courtesy of the National Mental Health Association; page 488, Courtesy Peabody Essex Museum, Salem, MA; page 489, © Jean-Loup Charmet/CORBIS; page 490, © Paul Seheult; Eye Ubiquitous/CORBIS; page 491, © L. Fernandez/The Image Works; page 493, © Burstein Collection/CORBIS; page 499, © Sky Bonillo/PhotoEdit; page 501, © 1996 Margaret Ross/Stock Boston, LLC; page 504, Courtesy of Dr. Cornelia Wilbur; page 505, © Alessandro Bianchi/Reuters/CORBIS; page 508, Daniel Weinberger, M.D., Clinical Brain Disorders Branch, Division of Intramural Research Programs, NIMH, 1990; page 510, Hannibal, Anthony Hopkins, Julianne Moore, 2001 © The Everett Collection; page 513 (top) © The New Yorker Collection 1995. Bruce Eric Kaplan from cartoonbank.com. All Rights Reserved; page 513 (bottom), © Bob Daemmrich/Stock Boston, LLC; page 517, © A. Ramey/PhotoEdit.

Chapter 13: page 523, © The New Yorker Collection 1995. Mick Stevens from cartoonbank.com. All Rights Reserved; page 524, © Phanie/Photo Researchers, Inc.; page 525, © The New Yorker Collection 1995. Mick Stevens from cartoonbank.com. All Rights Reserved; page 526, Cathy by Cathy Guisewite/Universal Press Syndicate; page 529, Courtesy of Sir John Soane's Museum; page 530 (top), © Peter Tumley/CORBIS; page 530 (bottom), © Zigy Kaluzny/Getty Images/Stone; page 533, Courtesy of the Freud Museum, London; page 534, © Time Life Pictures/Getty Images; page 536, © David Young-Wolff/PhotoEdit; page 539, The Far Side® by Gary Larson © 1986 FarWorks, Inc. All rights reserved. Used with permission; page 540, Courtesy of Virtually Better, Inc.; page 541, © Lester Sloan/Woodfin Camp & Associates; page 543, Courtesy of Philip G. Zimbardo; page 550, © Will & Deni McIntyre/Photo Researchers, Inc.; page 554, © Najlah Feanny/Stock Boston, LLC; page 556, © Michael Newman/PhotoEdit.

Chapter 14: page 565, © Myrleen F. Cate/PhotoEdit; page 566 (top, middle, bottom), Courtesy of Philip G. Zimbardo; page 567, AP/Wide World Photos; page 569 (middle), © Ted Goffl; page 569 (bottom), © Bob Daemmrich/Stock Boston, LLC; page 572, William Vandivert/Scientific American; page 573, © Isaac Menashe/CORBIS; page 576 (top and bottom), From the film Obedience copyright 1965 by Stanley Milgram and distributed by Penn State Media Sales; page 577, AP/Wide World Photos; page 579, © New York Times Pictures; page 585, © Myrleen F. Cate/PhotoEdit; page 587, © D. Wells/The Image Works; page 589, © Scott Goodwin Photography, Inc.; page 591 (top and bottom), Courtesy of Philip G. Zimbardo; page 593, AP/Wide World Photos; page 595, © Michael Newman/PhotoEdit; page 597, Dr. J. O. Harvey, co-author Robbers Cave Experiment.

Answers to AP* Review: Vocabulary

Chapter 1

1. c 2. g 3. i 4. a 5. j 6. h 7. b 8. e 9. f 10. d

Chapter 2

1. b 2. j 3. i 4. c 5. h 6. a 7. d 8. g 9. f 10. e

Chapter 3

1. d 2. j 3. a 4. i 5. b 6. h 7. e 8. g 9. f 10. c

Chapter 4

1. f 2. j 3. a 4. h 5. b 6. i 7. e 8. g 9. d 10. c

Chapter 5

1. c 2. j 3. h 4. a 5. b 6. g 7. f 8. e 9. d 10. i

Chapter 6

1. j 2. d 3. a 4. g 5. i 6. c 7. e 8. b 9. h 10. f

Chapter 7

1. c 2. g 3. i 4. h 5. a 6. j 7. d 8. b 9. f 10. e

Chapter 8

1. a 2. c 3. h 4. g 5. i 6. b 7. d 8. f 9. j 10. e

Chapter 9

1. i 2. d 3. j 4. h 5. a 6. f 7. c 8. e 9. g 10. b

Chapter 10

1. b 2. g 3. h 4. a 5. j 6. c 7. f 8. i 9. d 10. e

Chapter 11

1. b 2. d 3. j 4. a 5. h 6. c 7. g 8. f 9. i 10. e

Chapter 12

1. h 2. a 3. i 4. c 5. d 6. g 7. f 8. j 9. e 10. b

Chapter 13

1. f 2. c 3. j 4. a 5. g 6. b 7. e 8. i 9. d 10. h

Chapter 14

1. c 2. i 3. a 4. g 5. d 6. b 7. e 8. j 9. h 10. f

Name Index

C

G

H

Subject Index

D

N

O